KODANSHA
ENCYCLOPEDIA OF
JAPAN

Distributors
JAPAN: KODANSHA LTD., Tokyo.
OVERSEAS: KODANSHA INTERNATIONAL LTD., Tokyo.
  U.S.A., Mexico, Central America, and South America: KODANSHA INTERNATIONAL/USA LTD.
    through HARPER & ROW, PUBLISHERS, INC., New York.
  Canada: FITZHENRY & WHITESIDE LTD., Ontario.
  U.K., Europe, the Middle East, and Africa: INTERNATIONAL BOOK DISTRIBUTORS LTD.,
    Hemel Hempstead, Herts., England.
  Australia and New Zealand: HARPER & ROW (AUSTRALASIA) PTY. LTD., Artarmon, N.S.W.
  Asia: TOPPAN COMPANY (S) PTE. LTD., Singapore.

Published by Kodansha Ltd., 12-21, Otowa 2-chome, Bunkyo-ku, Tokyo 112 and Kodansha
International/USA Ltd., 10 East 53rd Street, New York, New York 10022.

LCC 83-80778
ISBN 0-87011-624-x (Volume 4)
ISBN 0-87011-620-7 (Set)
ISBN 4-06-144534-0 (0) (in Japan)

Library of Congress Cataloging in Publication Data
Main entry under title:

Kodansha encyclopedia of Japan.

  Includes index.
  1. Japan—Dictionaries and encyclopedias. I. Title:
Encyclopedia of Japan.
DS805.K633 1983   952′.003′21   83-80778
ISBN 0-87011-620-7 (U.S.)

KODANSHA
ENCYCLOPEDIA OF
JAPAN

4

KODANSHA

J

Jagatara-bumi

(letters from Jakarta). Letters sent to Japan in the 17th century by persons of Japanese descent who found themselves exiled in the Dutch colony on Java by the Tokugawa shogunate's policy of NATIONAL SECLUSION. Many of these people were the wives and offspring of Dutch traders, who in 1639 had been forbidden by the shogunate "to have children in Japan." The most famous of these letters, that of Oharu (Jeronima Simonsen; d 1694), with its poetic allusions and the phrase "How I miss Japan!" was a fabrication of the Nagasaki savant NISHIKAWA JOKEN; others are authentic.

George ELISON

Jahana Noboru (1865–1908)

Pioneer leader in the movement for popular rights in Okinawa. Born to a middle-class farming family, he went to Tōkyō as one of the first government scholarship students from Okinawa and graduated from the agriculture division of Tōkyō University in 1891. In the same year he returned home to become an agriculture specialist for the prefectural government and two years later became the first Okinawan to enter Japan's higher civil service. He soon came into conflict with the prefectural governor, Narahara Shigeru (1834–1918), over the latter's decision to sell forest land that had been used as commonage by local farmers. Dismissed from office in 1898, he assembled sympathizers to form the Okinawa Kurabu (Okinawa Club), which criticized prefectural policies. He was also active in the movement to secure Okinawan representation in the national government, but the movement collapsed under fierce opposition from Narahara. In 1901, while on his way to take up a new post in Yamaguchi Prefecture, he went insane and remained incapacitated until his death. See also OKINAWA. *TANAKA Akira*

Jakkōin

Convent in Ōhara, Sakyō Ward, Kyōto, belonging to the TENDAI SECT of Buddhism. Although the temple records variously attribute the origins of the Jakkōin to Prince SHŌTOKU (574–622), the monk KŪKAI (774–835), or the monk RYŌNIN (1073–1132), there is little reliable information about Jakkōin until the famous Kenrei Mon'in (1155–1213) took up residence there.

Kenrei Mon'in was the daughter of TAIRA NO KIYOMORI, the head of the Taira family; she was adopted at the age of 16 by the retired emperor Go-Shirakawa (r 1155–58). In 1172 she was married to Emperor Takakura (r 1168–80) and two years later gave birth to his son, the boy emperor Antoku (r 1180–85). She accompanied the Taira (Heike) forces after their flight from Kyōto in 1183 and when, in 1185, they were utterly defeated in the naval engagement at Dannoura, she threw herself into the sea, holding the boy emperor in her arms. Although the child was lost, Kenrei Mon'in was rescued and brought back to Kyōto. Grief-stricken, she became a nun at Jakkōin, where she spent the remainder of her life praying for the souls of her deceased father, husband, and son, as well as for the slain Taira people. The convent, which figures in the HEIKE MONOGATARI (13th century; tr *Tale of the Heike,* 1975) and the NŌ drama *Ōhara gokō* (The Imperial Visit to Ōhara), contains many relics of the Taira family. After a period of decline, the temple was refurbished by YODOGIMI (1567?–1615), concubine of Toyotomi Hideyoshi. The central image of worship is the bodhisattva JIZŌ (Skt: Kṣitigarbha).

Stanley WEINSTEIN

Jakuchū → Itō Jakuchū

Jakugon (1702–1771)

Monk, Sanskrit expert, and outstanding calligrapher of the Edo period (1600–1868). Born in Asaguchi, Bitchū Province (now part of Okayama Prefecture), Jakugon became a monk at the age of eight. At first he studied Buddhism, but later concentrated on Sanskrit textual studies. After visiting the temple Tōji in Kyōto in 1736 for further study, he published several books on this subject. He served in Hōtōji in Bitchū until 1767, when he retired to Gyokusenji in Kurashiki. Jakugon wrote primarily in running script, but also occasionally used cursive, regular, clerical, *kana,* and even Sanskrit scripts. His calligraphy has an unusual, almost awkward combination of power and rhythmic fluctuation that marks him as one of the most original calligraphers of his period. He displays a penchant for rough, swirling brush strokes contrasted with occasional blunt, angular thrusts; his character structures are reshaped, almost distorted, and the ink tonality is often dry. Along with JIUN ONKŌ, RYŌKAN, and Meigetsu (1726–97), Jakugon is known as one of the Four Monk-Writers. *Stephen* ADDISS

Jakuren (ca 1139–1202)

Classical (WAKA) poet, Buddhist priest, and one of the six compilers of the eighth imperial anthology, SHIN KOKINSHŪ (1205). Jakuren's lay name was Fujiwara no Sadanaga. His father Shunkai was a younger brother of the great poet FUJIWARA NO TOSHINARI (Shunzei). When Shunkai took holy orders in 1150, the young Sadanaga was adopted by his famous uncle, who for a time apparently intended him as his heir. However, Shunzei later sired two male children—the untalented Nariie and the gifted FUJIWARA NO SADAIE—and when the latter was nine years old Sadanaga resigned his position as Shunzei's adoptive son and took holy orders and the priestly name by which he is known to posterity. Throughout his life Jakuren was active in court poetry gatherings, contests, and the like, but especially during the five or six years before his death. After becoming a priest he also traveled rather extensively around the country as his older contemporary SAIGYŌ had done, composing poems on his travels. As one of the participants in the famous Poetry Contest in 600 Rounds (*Roppyakuban uta-awase*) of 1193, Jakuren is said to have vigorously defended the interests of the pupils and adherents of Shunzei against the conservative Rokujō poets, their archrivals; his sharp encounters with his priestly counterpart KENSHŌ (ca 1130–ca 1210) of the Rokujō side are famous in the annals of poetic lore.

In 1201 Jakuren was appointed fellow in the Bureau of Poetry (Wakadokoro) established by ex-Emperor Go-Toba, and with five others he was designated compiler of the *Shin kokinshū.* He died, however, in the summer of the following year. Jakuren's close association with the poetic school of Shunzei and Sadaie was fundamental in developing his individual style. Accepting Shunzei's neoclassical dictum of "old diction, new treatment," and aesthetic ideal of mystery and depth (YŪGEN), Jakuren composed some of the most memorable lines of the age. His best poems create the atmosphere of SABI, or loneliness, with a traditional diction rich in overtones and evocative power. Some 117 of Jakuren's poems are included in various imperial anthologies beginning with the SENZAI WAKASHŪ (ca 1188, Collection of a Thousand Years).

🔲——Robert H. Brower and Earl Miner, *Japanese Court Poetry* (1961). *Robert H.* BROWER

Jakushitsu Genkō (1290–1367)

Also known as Ennō Zenji and Shōtō Kokushi. Zen monk of the RINZAI SECT and founder of its Eigenji subsect. Born in Mimasaka (now Okayama Prefecture), he became a monk at the age of 13 under Mui Shōgen of the temple Sanshōji in Kyōto. Later he entered Zenkōji in Kamakura to study with Yakuō Tokken, an eminent disciple of RANKEI DŌRYŪ. Accompanying his master, he moved successively to KENNINJI, KENCHŌJI, and NANZENJI. In 1320, he traveled to Ming China with Kaō Sonen and others, where he visited

Zhongfeng Mingben (Chung-feng Ming-pen) at Mt. Tianmu (T'ienmu), and received the name Jakushitsu. He also received instructions from Wujian Xiandu (Wu-chien Hsien-tu) and Duanai Liaoyi (Tuan-ai Liao-i) and returned to Japan in 1326. Thereupon he took up residence in Eitokuji in Bingo (now Hiroshima Prefecture), and Fukugonji in Settsu (now Ōsaka Prefecture). In 1359 he became abbot of Seiunji in Kai (now Yamanashi Prefecture). In 1360, under the patronage of the warrior Sasaki family, based in Ōmi (now Shiga Prefecture), he founded Eigenji in that province and became heir to the teachings of Yakuō Tokken. Although he was invited to head Tenryūji and Kenchōji by the Muromachi shogunate, he refused, preferring the seclusion of Eigenji. The records of his sayings, *Eigen Jakushitsu wajō goroku* in two fascicles, as well as his last testament in his own hand, are extant.　　　　　Murakami Shigeyoshi

Janes, Leroy Lansing (1838–1909)

American educator who taught in Japan early in the Meiji period (1868-1912). A graduate of the United States Military Academy, Janes served in the American Civil War. In 1871, on the recommendation of Guido VERBECK, a missionary in Japan, Janes accepted an invitation to teach at the KUMAMOTO YŌGAKKŌ, the Kumamoto domainal school for Western studies. Although Janes knew no Japanese and had no intention of learning it, he was given full authority over the program of studies. His classes in mathematics, history, and natural sciences were given in English; the first year of instruction, however, was confined to reading and writing. Janes also acted as a moral guide. For the first three years he refrained from discussing Christianity, choosing to wait until he thought his students had learned enough English to understand the relation between Christianity and Western learning. Under his influence 35 students were converted, the so-called Kumamoto Band. Many of its members, among them EBINA DANJŌ and UKITA KAZUTAMI, eventually became Christian leaders in education and politics. Persecution by conservative elements in Kumamoto forced the school to close in August 1876, and members of the Kumamoto Band moved to the Dōshisha school in Kyōto. Janes taught briefly at the Ōsaka Eigakkō and returned to the United States in 1877. He was invited in 1893 to teach at the Third Higher School in Kyōto, where he remained for two years. He died in California.

Jan Joosten, Lodenstijn (1556?–1623)

One of the first Dutchmen in Japan. Born in Delft in the Netherlands. In 1600 Jan Joosten was second mate on the Dutch trading vessel LIEFDE, which was disabled while crossing the Pacific and landed in Kyūshū. Jan Joosten, the English pilot William ADAMS, and other survivors were received by the future shōgun TOKUGAWA IEYASU; Jan Joosten and Adams later became his advisers and confidants. Jan Joosten was given a residence in Edo (now Tōkyō) — the place name Yaesu near Tōkyō Station is thought to be a corruption of his name — and married a Japanese woman. He received official permission to engage in overseas trade and, after the establishment of the DUTCH FACTORY at Hirado, became a middleman between Dutch traders and the shogunate. Later, hoping to return to the Netherlands, he sailed as far as Batavia (now Djakarta) in Java but was refused permission by the Dutch authorities to proceed. On his way back to Japan, Jan Joosten drowned when his ship foundered off the Paracel Islands in the South China Sea.

janken → ken

Janome Sewing Machine Co, Ltd

(Janome Mishin Kōgyō). Sewing machine manufacturing company; second to BROTHER INDUSTRIES, LTD, in the production of home sewing machines. It was founded in 1921 and succeeded in establishing the domestic production of sewing machines. After World War II it grew steadily by adopting a direct sales system. It purchased the New Home Sewing Machine Co of the United States in 1960 and expanded overseas production by establishing the Dorina Nähmaschinen GmbH in West Germany in 1968. It has recently developed a sewing machine with a built-in microcomputer. Sales for the fiscal year ending March 1982 totaled ¥71.8 billion (US $298.3 million), the export ratio was 18 percent, and capitalization stood at ¥7.6 billion (US $31.6 million). Corporate headquarters are located in Tōkyō.

Japan

territory and administrative divisions
natural features of Japan
geological structure

TERRITORY AND ADMINISTRATIVE DIVISIONS

Japan (Nippon or Nihon) consists of an archipelago extending approximately from northeast to southwest. It lies off the east coast of the Asian continent. The latitudes and longitudes of the four extremities are as follows:

north	Bentenjima, an island, administratively a part of the city of Wakkanai, Hokkaidō 45° 31' north
east	Minami Torishima, one of the Ogasawara Islands, administratively a part of Tōkyō Prefecture 153° 58' east
south	Okinotorishima, one of the Ogasawara Islands, administratively a part of Tōkyō Prefecture 20° 25' north
west	Yonagunijima, an island, administratively a part of Okinawa Prefecture 122° 55' east

The total land area as of October 1980 was 377,708 square kilometers (145,800 sq mi), only slightly larger than that of Finland or Italy and approximately 1/25 that of the United States; it is about the same size as the state of Montana. It consists of the four major islands of HOKKAIDŌ, HONSHŪ, Shikoku (see SHIKOKU REGION), and Kyūshū (see KYŪSHŪ REGION). The northernmost islands of Kunashiri (Kunashir), Etorofu (Iturup), the Habomai Islands, and Shikotan, claimed by the Japanese, have been under occupation by the Soviet Union since the end of World War II (see TERRITORY OF JAPAN). The OGASAWARA ISLANDS and OKINAWA ISLANDS, under American rule since the end of World War II, were returned to Japan in 1968 and 1972, respectively. The areas of the main islands (including offshore islands under their administrative control) are as follows:

Hokkaidō	83,517 sq km
Honshū	231,012
Shikoku	18,800
Kyūshū	42,129
Okinawa Islands	2,250
Total	377,708 sq km

Honshū is larger than Great Britain, and Hokkaidō is a little smaller than Ireland. Kyūshū is a little larger than Taiwan, and Shikoku is a little smaller than Sardinia. Following the recent tendency among countries to enlarge TERRITORIAL WATERS, Japan also set the limit of 12 nautical miles from the coast in 1977.

Population —— At the time of the Meiji Restoration (1868) Japan's population was about 33 million. In 1980 it was 117 million. In terms of population Japan ranks seventh in the world, following China, India, the Soviet Union, the United States, Indonesia, and Brazil. The density per square kilometer (0.386 sq mi), which was an average of 147 persons according to the first precise census in 1920, was 314 persons in 1980. Though this figure is comparable to 346 persons in the Netherlands and 323 in Belgium, the density of the Japanese population per unit area under cultivation is the highest in the world because over two-thirds of Japan is occupied by mountainous terrain, and alluvial plains occupy only 13 percent. Among the main islands the density is highest in Honshū, followed by Kyūshū and Shikoku.

Density of population per square kilometer:

Honshū	404
Kyūshū	308
Shikoku	221
Hokkaidō	71
Okinawa Islands	492

The population was distributed comparatively equally all over the country about a century ago, when Japan was still predominantly agricultural. With industrialization, however, there was a strong

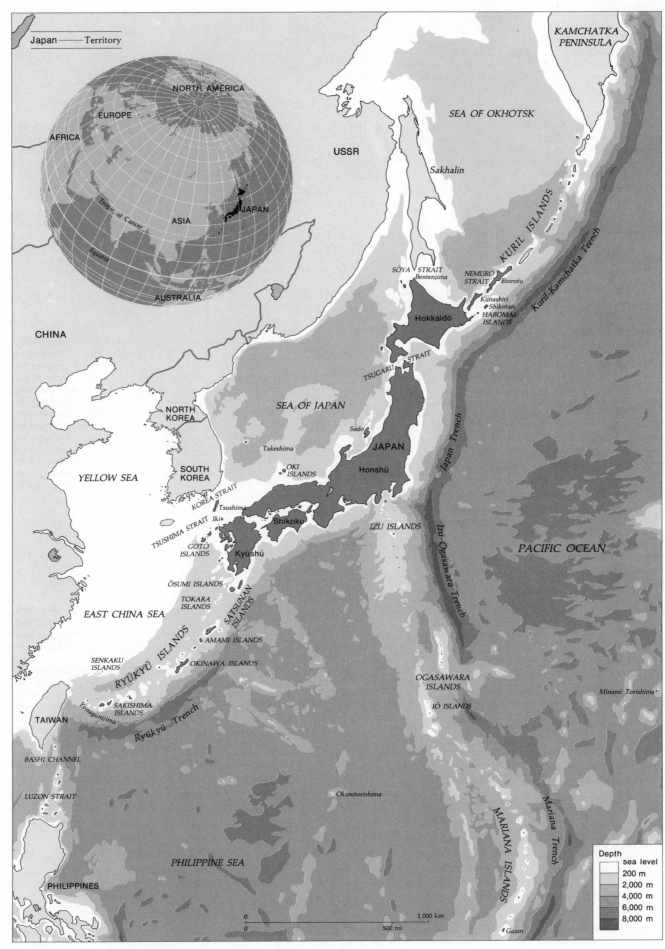

Japan —— Territory

NORTH AMERICA

EUROPE

AFRICA

Tropic of Cancer

ASIA

JAPAN

Equator

AUSTRALIA

CHINA

KAMCHATKA PENINSULA

SEA OF OKHOTSK

USSR

Sakhalin

KURIL ISLANDS

Kuril-Kamchatka Trench

SŌYA STRAIT
Bentenjima

NEMURO STRAIT — *Etorofu*

Kunashiri
Shikotan
HABOMAI ISLANDS

Hokkaidō

TSUGARU STRAIT

Japan Trench

SEA OF JAPAN

Sado

Takeshima

JAPAN

Honshū

OKI ISLANDS

KOREA STRAIT

Tsushima
Iki

TSUSHIMA STRAIT

Shikoku

IZU ISLANDS

Izu-Ogasawara Trench

PACIFIC OCEAN

NORTH KOREA

SOUTH KOREA

YELLOW SEA

GOTO ISLANDS

Kyūshū

ŌSUMI ISLANDS

TOKARA ISLANDS

SATSUNAN ISLANDS

AMAMI ISLANDS

EAST CHINA SEA

SENKAKU ISLANDS

RYŪKYŪ ISLANDS

OKINAWA ISLANDS

OGASAWARA ISLANDS

IŌ ISLANDS

Minami Torishima

SAKISHIMA ISLANDS
Yonagunijima

Ryūkyū Trench

TAIWAN

BASHI CHANNEL

LUZON STRAIT

Okinotorishima

MARIANA ISLANDS

Mariana Trench

PHILIPPINE SEA

PHILIPPINES

Guam

Depth	
	sea level
	200 m
	2,000 m
	4,000 m
	6,000 m
	8,000 m

0   1,000 km

0   500 mi

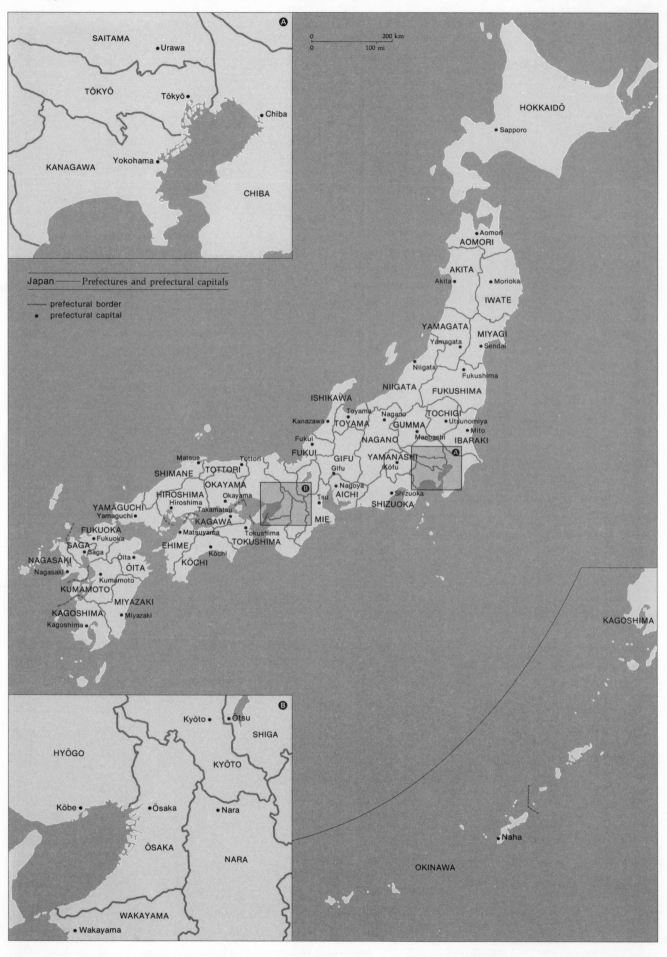

Japan ——— Prefectures and prefectural capitals

——— prefectural border
● prefectural capital

Inset A

SAITAMA
●Urawa
TŌKYŌ
Tōkyō ●
●Chiba
KANAGAWA
Yokohama ●
CHIBA

0 ———— 200 km
0 ———— 100 mi

Main map

HOKKAIDŌ
●Sapporo

●Aomori
AOMORI
AKITA
Akita ●
●Morioka
IWATE
YAMAGATA
MIYAGI
Yamagata ●
●Sendai
●Niigata
●Fukushima
ISHIKAWA
NIIGATA
FUKUSHIMA
Toyama ●
Nagano ●
TOCHIGI
Kanazawa ●
TOYAMA
GUMMA
●Utsunomiya
●Mito
Fukui ●
NAGANO
Maebashi ●
IBARAKI
Matsue ●
Tottori ●
FUKUI
GIFU
YAMANASHI
Ⓐ
SHIMANE
TOTTORI
Gifu ●
Kōfu ●
OKAYAMA
●Nagoya
HIROSHIMA
Okayama ●
AICHI
●Shizuoka
YAMAGUCHI
Hiroshima ●
Takamatsu ●
SHIZUOKA
Yamaguchi ●
KAGAWA
Ⓑ
FUKUOKA
Matsuyama ●
Tsu ●
SAGA
EHIME
Tokushima ●
MIE
●Fukuoka
Ōita ●
TOKUSHIMA
NAGASAKI
Saga ●
Kōchi ●
Nagasaki ●
ŌITA
KŌCHI
Kumamoto ●
KUMAMOTO
MIYAZAKI
KAGOSHIMA
●Miyazaki
Kagoshima ●

KAGOSHIMA

Inset B

Kyōto ● ●Otsu
SHIGA
HYŌGO
KYŌTO
Kōbe ●
●Ōsaka
●Nara
ŌSAKA
NARA
WAKAYAMA
●Wakayama

OKINAWA
●Naha

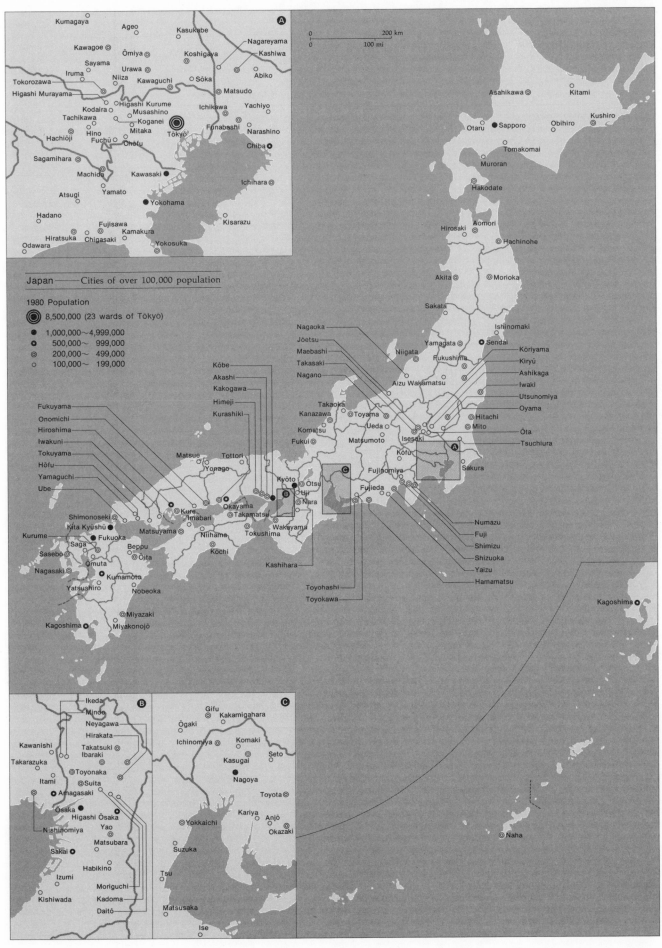

0   200 km
0   100 mi

Japan——Cities of over 100,000 population

1980 Population

◎ 8,500,000 (23 wards of Tōkyō)

● 1,000,000～4,999,000
● 500,000～ 999,000
◎ 200,000～ 499,000
○ 100,000～ 199,000

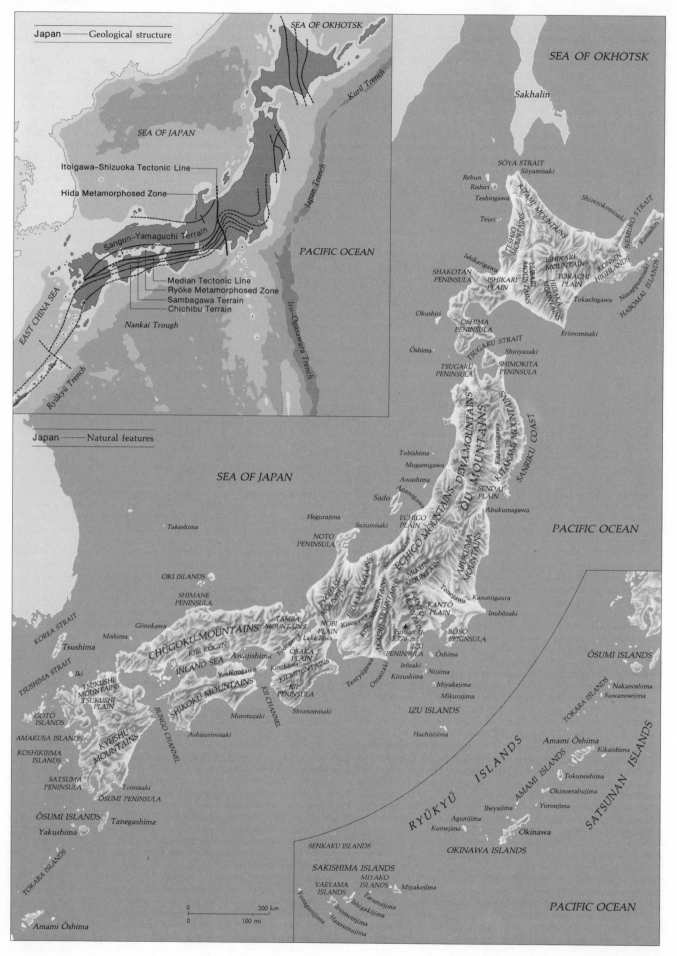

Japan——Geological structure

SEA OF OKHOTSK

SEA OF JAPAN

Itoigawa–Shizuoka Tectonic Line

Hida Metamorphosed Zone

Kuril Trench

Sangun–Yamaguchi Terrain

PACIFIC OCEAN

Japan Trench

Median Tectonic Line
Ryōke Metamorphosed Zone
Sambagawa Terrain
Chichibu Terrain

EAST CHINA SEA

Nankai Trough

Izu-Ogasawara Trench

Ryūkyū Trench

Japan——Natural features

SEA OF JAPAN

SEA OF OKHOTSK

Sakhalin

SŌYA STRAIT
Sōyamisaki
Rebun
Rishiri
Teshiogawa
KITAMI MOUNTAINS
Shiretokomisaki
NEMURO STRAIT
Teuri
TESHIO MOUNTAINS
ISHIKARI MOUNTAINS
KONSEN HIGHLANDS
Kunashiri
Ishikarigawa
SHAKOTAN PENINSULA
YŪBARI MOUNTAINS
HIDAKA MOUNTAINS
TOKACHI PLAIN
Nosappumisaki
HABOMAI ISLANDS
Okushiri
ISHIKARI PLAIN
Tokachigawa
OSHIMA PENINSULA
Erimomisaki
Ōshima
TSUGARU STRAIT
Shiriyazaki
TSUGARU PENINSULA
SHIMOKITA PENINSULA

Takeshima

Tobishima
Mogamigawa
DEWA MOUNTAINS
ŌU MOUNTAINS
KITAKAMI MOUNTAINS
SANRIKU COAST
Awashima
Kitakamigawa
Sado
Aganogawa
SENDAI PLAIN
Hegurajima
ECHIGO PLAIN
Abukumagawa
Suzumisaki
ECHIGO MOUNTAINS
PACIFIC OCEAN
NOTO PENINSULA
ABUKUMA MOUNTAINS

OKI ISLANDS
RYŌHAKU MOUNTAINS
MIKUNI MOUNTAINS
SHIMANE PENINSULA
Shinanogawa
Tonegawa
Kasumigaura
HIDA MOUNTAINS
KAN-Ō MOUNTAINS
KANTŌ PLAIN
TAMBA MOUNTAINS
KISO MOUNTAINS
Inubōzaki
Gōnokawa
KIBI KŌGEN
NOBI PLAIN
AKAISHI MOUNTAINS
Kisogawa
ŌSUMI ISLANDS
CHŪGOKU MOUNTAINS
Fujisan
3,776 m
BŌSŌ PENINSULA
Mishima
INLAND SEA
Awajishima
Yodogawa
Lake Biwa
IZU PENINSULA
KOREA STRAIT
OSAKA PLAIN
Ōshima
Tsushima
Yoshinogawa
Kinokawa
Irōzaki
Niijima
Iki
SHIKOKU MOUNTAINS
KII MOUNTAINS
Tenryūgawa
Kōzushima
TSUSHIMA STRAIT
KII PENINSULA
Ōmaezaki
Miyakejima
TSUKUSHI MOUNTAINS
Murotozaki
KII CHANNEL
Mikurajima
TOKARA ISLANDS
Nakanoshima
Suwanosejima
TSUKUSHI PLAIN
Shionomisaki
IZU ISLANDS
GOTŌ ISLANDS
Ashizurimisaki
BUNGO CHANNEL
AMAKUSA ISLANDS
KYŪSHŪ MOUNTAINS
Hachijōjima
KOSHIKIJIMA ISLANDS
Amami Ōshima
Kikaishima
SATSUMA PENINSULA
Toimisaki
AMAMI ISLANDS
Tokunoshima
ŌSUMI PENINSULA
RYŪKYŪ ISLANDS
SATSUNAN ISLANDS
ŌSUMI ISLANDS
Tanegashima
Okinoerabujima
Yakushima
Yoronjima
Iheyajima
TOKARA ISLANDS
Agunijima
Okinawa
Kumejima
SENKAKU ISLANDS
OKINAWA ISLANDS
PACIFIC OCEAN
Amami Ōshima
SAKISHIMA ISLANDS
YAEYAMA ISLANDS
MIYAKO ISLANDS
Miyakojima
Yonagunijima
Taramajima
Iriomotejima
Ishigakijima
Haterumajima

0   200 km
0   100 mi

tendency toward regional concentration. This became even more pronounced in the postwar years, and as a result, 42.4 percent of Japanese live in the three major urban areas of Tōkyō, Ōsaka, and Nagoya. The Tōkyō Metropolitan Area in particular, though less than 2.0 percent in terms of area, has a concentration of 22.5 percent of the national population. The Ōsaka area has a concentration of 13.2 percent of the national population within an area of only 2.0 percent.

The phenomenon of urbanization is especially pronounced in the so-called Pacific-belt zone, composed of the southern coast of Honshū, the Inland Sea coast, and northern Kyūshū, where nine out of the ten cities with a population over one million (Tōkyō, Yokohama, Kawasaki, Nagoya, Kyōto, Ōsaka, Kōbe, Kita Kyūshū, and Fukuoka) are located. In contrast, Hokkaidō, northern Honshū, the mountainous area of central Honshū, and the southern parts of Shikoku and Kyūshū are relatively sparsely populated. See also POPULATION.

Formation of the Country —— Among the various theories on the formation of Japan as a nation state, one school holds that because of its proximity to the continent, northern Kyūshū was the site of the first political center. The leaders are believed to have moved gradually to the east along the Inland Sea and to have finally settled in the Yamato region (now the Nara area) in central Japan. By the 4th century a sovereign court had emerged, which by conquest and alliance eventually unified the country. The YAMATO COURT repeatedly dispatched expeditionary forces to northeastern Honshū and succeeded in subduing it in the 7th century. From the end of the 4th century to the latter half of the 6th century, it is believed that Japan maintained a colony in the southern part of the Korean peninsula (see KAYA). Thus by around the 7th century the prototype of a unified Japan, consisting of Honshū, Shikoku, and Kyūshū, had been established. Under the TAIKA REFORM of 645, the KOKUGUN SYSTEM of administration was instituted, and the country was divided into 58 (later 66) provinces (kuni), with subunits called gun. This division remained in effect nominally until the Meiji Restoration of 1868. However, under the BAKUHAN SYSTEM of the Tokugawa shogunate (1603–1867), there was superimposed on it a system of feudal daimyō domains (han), whose boundaries did not necessarily coincide with those of the ancient provinces. It was also soon after the Taika Reform that the name Nippon was used in diplomatic documents. The name Japan is said to be a corruption of Marco Polo's "Jipang," which in turn was based on the southern Chinese pronunciation of the Chinese characters for Nippon. The present official name of the nation is Nippon Koku or Nihon Koku.

Changes in Territory —— The territory of Japan remained essentially the same from the 7th century, but in 1609 the daimyō of the Satsuma domain (now Kagoshima Prefecture) established control over the Ryūkyū Kingdom (see OKINAWA). The Ogasawara Islands (also known as the Bonin Islands) were discovered by the Japanese in 1593 and were officially incorporated into Japan in 1876. Hokkaidō, once called EZO, was settled by the Japanese in the Edo period (1600–1868). As trade with the AINU in the interior developed, the Japanese gradually made their way into the southern part of SAKHALIN (J: Karafuto) and the Kuril Islands, where they came into conflict with the Russians. In 1875 Japan concluded the treaty of ST. PETERSBURG with Russia and gave up the southern part of Sakhalin in exchange for the Kuril Islands. Hokkaidō became a new frontier in the late 19th century, and many emigrants moved there from the main islands. After the SINO-JAPANESE WAR OF 1894–1895 Japan acquired TAIWAN, and after the RUSSO-JAPANESE WAR (1904–05) it acquired the southern half of Sakhalin and leased the southern part of the Liaodong (Liaotung) Peninsula. It annexed Korea in 1910 (see KOREA, ANNEXATION OF) and secured the mandate over former German territories in the South Sea Islands after World War I (see VERSAILLES, TREATY OF). Thus at the time of the outbreak of World War II the total land area was 680,729 square kilometers (262,761 sq mi), but after defeat, Japan was stripped of all territories acquired during its period of COLONIALISM, and until the restoration of Okinawa in 1972 was left with essentially the four main islands.

Modern Administrative System —— After the Meiji Restoration the country was administratively reorganized into the prefectural system (see PREFECTURAL SYSTEM, ESTABLISHMENT OF). Tōkyō, Ōsaka, and Kyōto were made fu (urban prefectures) in 1871, and the rest of the country was divided into 302 ken (prefectures). By 1888 this system had been integrated into a system of 3 fu and 43 ken. Hokkaidō was administered directly by the central government in the beginning but later came to be treated on an equal footing with other prefectures, though it was called a dō (circuit) rather than a ken. In 1943 Tōkyō Fu was designated as a special administrative area and named Tōkyō To (Tōkyō Metropolitan Prefecture). At present Japan is administratively divided into 1 to (Tōkyō To), 1 dō (Hokkaidō), 2 fu (Ōsaka Fu and Kyōto Fu), and 43 ken.

Cities, towns, and villages were also reorganized: under the city-town-village system instituted in 1889, 39 towns were designated cities, and 70,000 villages (mura) were reorganized into some 13,300 towns and villages. Another large-scale reorganization was carried out under the 1953 Towns and Villages Annexation Promotion Law (Chōson Gappei Sokushin Hō). Towns and villages with a population under 8,000 were merged with larger cities in order to improve administrative efficiency. At the same time, towns and villages with a population over 50,000 and where 60 percent or more of the workers engaged in commerce, industry, and urban business were designated cities. As of 1980 there were 646 cities. As a part of regional development programs promoted by the government, merging of suburban areas with neighboring cities has further accelerated. See also LOCAL GOVERNMENT.

BEKKI Atsuhiko

NATURAL FEATURES OF JAPAN

Topography —— The physical character of the Japanese archipelago was determined by its original formation as an arc-shaped mountain range in the circum-Pacific mountain belt at the eastern rim of the Asian continent. The chief feature of the Japanese archipelago is the instability of its ground, with a great amount of volcanic activity and many EARTHQUAKES. This cannot be understood to mean simply that earthquakes are numerous and that volcanic activity is severe; it also demonstrates that the rise and fall of the land and the amount of horizontal migration through minute leveling is also extensive. Another distinctive characteristic of the topography is the fact that the Japanese archipelago is made up almost entirely of steep mountain districts (over two-thirds of the total land surface) with very few plains. The swiftly flowing short rivers that traverse these regions of sharp mountains give variation to the topography by carving out deep valleys and creating small plains at the foot of the mountains.

High, precipitous mountains of about 1,500–3,000 meters (5,000–10,000 ft) run along the Pacific Ocean side of Southwest Japan (i.e., the western half of the country). Deep, V-shaped valleys are cut into these mountain districts. The mountain ranges and mountainous districts of Akaishi, Kii, Shikoku, Kyūshū are representative of this zone. In contrast, on the Sea of Japan side of southwestern Japan are groupings of plateaus and low mountain districts with a height of about 500–1,500 meters (1,600–5,000 feet) such as the Hida, Tamba, and Chūgoku mountain districts, the Kibi plateau, and the Tsukushi Mountains. Thus the mountain districts in the outer zone (the Pacific Ocean side) and the inner zone (the Sea of Japan side) differ, and this configuration dominates the overall structure of the Japanese archipelago; in northeastern Japan also, high steep mountains are found in the outer zone.

The representative mountain districts of Japan are steep and rugged, with high peaks, deep valleys, and spectacular gorges similar to those seen in the outer zone mountain districts. Mountain districts with rounded mountaintops and gentle slopes, such as those found in the Abukuma, Kitakami, Teshio, and Kitami mountain districts, are quite rare.

The large number and variety of VOLCANOES found throughout the Japanese archipelago constitute another remarkable feature. One hundred eighty-eight volcanoes have been active at some time or another since the Quaternary geological period and more than 40 of these remain active today. Among these are volcanoes which have had numerous violent eruptions like Asamayama and Bandaisan. Further, a special characteristic of Japan's volcano zone is the development of large craters or calderas such as those at Akan, Daisetsu, Tōya, Towada, Inawashiro, Hakone, Aso, and Aira. The caldera at Aso, which has remained in its original form, is on a scale unrivaled anywhere else in the world.

The area of the Japanese archipelago occupied by plains does not exceed 13 percent and the percentage of plateau land is only 12 percent. The plains are distributed in small bits at the edges of mountain districts and between mountains. Most of them are small, made by swift rivers—the alluvial fans. Only a small number of large rivers such as the Ishikarigawa, Shinanogawa, Tonegawa, Kisogawa, Yodogawa, and Chikugogawa have a fair-sized delta plain at their mouths. Diluvial uplands and river and marine terraces have developed in many coastal areas of Japan and these are utilized along with the plains for agriculture and for habitation.

Climate —— The most notable features of the climate of the Japanese archipelago, located in the monsoon zone of the eastern coast of the Asian continent, are the large yearly temperature change and the large amount of rainfall. However, because of the complexity of the land configuration, there are numerous regional differences throughout the seasons.

Spring. When low pressure areas pass over the Pacific coast of Japan in March, the temperature rises with each rainfall and the zone of plum and cherry blossoms moves gradually from south to north. When low pressure areas start to develop over the Sea of Japan, the strong wind from the south called *haru ichiban,* or the first tidings of spring, blows over Japan. This wind is the cause of both flood waters from suddenly melting mountain snow, and the foehn phenomenon, which sometimes results in great fires on the Sea of Japan side. Migratory high pressure areas develop from the end of April to the first part of May and these sometimes cause frost damage. The coming rainy season *(baiu)* can already be felt in the middle of May.

Summer. The setting-in of the rainy season takes place around 7 June. The rainy season, a truly gloomy time of year, starts from the southern part of Japan and moves northward. The position of the *baiu* front varies each year; when it leans to the south, northeastern Japan suffers damage from cold summers, and when it leans to the north, southwestern Japan suffers drought. During the close of the season there are frequent severe and localized downpours but the season ends around 20 July. With its passing, the Ogasawara air masses blanket Japan and the weather takes on a summer pattern. The peak of summer is at the end of July but the summer heat lingers on into mid-August. Temperatures begin to fall from the end of August.

Fall. September is the typhoon season. Weather resembling that of the rainy season also occurs because of the autumnal rainfronts. The weather clears in mid-October, and the winter seasonal winds start to blow. Around this time migratory high pressure areas appear and the weather stabilizes. The atmospheric pressure configuration gradually changes to the winter pattern, and snow begins to fall in the northern part of the country.

Winter. In December, when the atmospheric pressure configuration has completely changed to the winter pattern, northwest winds bring snow to the mountains and to the plains on the Sea of Japan side, and a dry wind blows on the Pacific Ocean side. The peak of winter comes around 25 January, and after that warm and cold spells alternate as the weather gradually turns toward spring. See also CLIMATE.

Life and Nature —— The land area of Japan is on a small scale but its configuration is complex, so that the climate and the flora and fauna vary regionally, extending from the subarctic zone in the north to the subtropical zone in the south (see PLANTS), and there is also much seasonal change. There is an abundance of HOT SPRINGS accompanying the many volcanoes, and these are popular as health resorts. Since there is a large annual rainfall and plentiful ground and river water, favorable conditions exist for both agricultural and hydroelectric use of water (see ELECTRIC POWER).

The beautiful natural setting with its many seasonal changes also brings many natural disasters. The heavy rains due to the *baiu* front and the autumn typhoons bring about flood and wind damage. The heavy snows of winter cause snow damage and also flooding and cold damage because of the unusually low temperature of the rivers when the snows melt. The heavy rains often lead to landslides. The Green Tuff zone, the mountain districts of the Tertiary formation, and the shear zone of the Paleozoic strata, are areas particularly prone to frequent landslides. In addition, earthquakes on the scale of the TŌKYŌ EARTHQUAKE OF 1923 strike somewhere in Japan every several decades. The tidal waves accompanying earthquakes and typhoons also inflict damage on the heavily populated low-lying coastal areas.

There are also disasters caused by advances in human technology. For example, the building up of river beds and the reclamation of land by draining or filling (see LAND RECLAMATION) has sometimes brought about flood damage, and excess pumping of the groundwater from the low-lying coastal areas has caused land subsidence. Thus Japan suffers from the combined problem of a large population concentration on a land particularly vulnerable to disaster. *Masatoshi M. YOSHINO*

GEOLOGICAL STRUCTURE

(chishitsu kōzō). The Japanese archipelago is a part of the island arc that borders the eastern edge of the Asian continent and corresponds to the edge of the continental crust that forms the Asian continent. The eastern side of the Japanese islands touches the oceanic crust of the Pacific Ocean directly. The fact that the islands are located near the border of the two crusts has much to do with their geological characteristics.

Topography —— Topographically, the Kuril Arc; the Sakhalin-Hokkaidō Arc; the Honshū Arc, connecting Kyūshū, Shikoku, Honshū, and the western part of Hokkaidō; and the Ryūkyū and Izu-Ogasawara arcs make up the Japanese islands, with each arc assuming a form projecting toward the Pacific Ocean.

The Kuril Trench, the Japan Trench, and the Izu-Ogasawara Trench are one continuous trench, which assumes the form of an arc projecting toward the west. This continuous trench is a narrow submarine channel with a depth of 9,000 meters (about 30,000 ft) in some areas. The Japan Trench is not connected to the Nankai Trough in the offing of Shikoku and Kyūshū. The Nankai Trough is separate from the Ryūkyū Trench and is not as deep as the Japan Trench. The Philippine Basin is separated from the Pacific Ocean by the Izu-Ogasawara Arc, and the Nankai Trough and the Ryūkyū Trench together correspond to the northern edge of the Philippine Basin.

The Sea of Okhotsk, the Sea of Japan, and the East China Sea separate Japan topographically from the Asian continent. They are of the kind called marginal seas, which are generally shallow, though some basins are 3,000–4,000 meters deep (9,800–13,000 ft) in the Sea of Okhotsk and the Sea of Japan.

The geological structure of Japan is reflected in the fact that the Japan Trench is not connected to the Nankai Trough, and that the Kuril Arc, the northeastern part of the Honshū Arc, and the Izu-Ogasawara Arc are one continuous island arc. The southwestern part of the Honshū Arc and the Ryūkyū Islands are a separate arc formed in a comparatively older period. Geologically the former is called northeastern Japan and the latter southwestern Japan.

The border of northeastern Japan and southwestern Japan is a great fault called the Itoigawa-Shizuoka Tectonic Line. The beltlike area east of this fault and running from the western part of Niigata Prefecture to the central part of Nagano Prefecture and from Yamanashi Prefecture to the eastern part of Shizuoka Prefecture, forms a single valley crossing Honshū that is called the FOSSA MAGNA. The mountain ranges and volcanic zones that form northeastern Japan turn south-southeast at the Fossa Magna and are connected to the Izu Islands; southwestern Japan is cut off diagonally at the Itoigawa-Shizuoka Tectonic Line. The Fossa Magna, now buried by sediments of the Neocene period and volcanoes of the Quaternary period, was originally formed as a depressed area in the shape of a trench.

Southwestern Japan is divided into an inner belt (the side facing the Sea of Japan) and an outer belt (the side facing the Pacific Ocean) by the great fault called the Median Tectonic Line, which runs lengthwise along the axis of southwestern Japan from the Ina Mountains to Ōita Prefecture. Both the inner and outer belts are also divided into lesser belts parallel to the Median Tectonic Line. Each belt has its own unique rocks, the stratum of a particular age, and a singular structure. These belts can be traced as far as the Ryūkyū Islands, and the entirety of southwestern Japan is characterized by a considerably regular beltlike structure. The greater part of these rocks and strata were formed either in the Paleozoic era or the Mesozoic era. In southwestern Japan there are fewer volcanoes than in northeastern Japan, and they are concentrated in the area facing the Sea of Japan and Kyūshū.

The stratum of the Neocene period extends over wide areas throughout northeastern Japan, and the rocks of the Paleozoic and Mesozoic eras that form the greater part of the rocks in southwestern Japan are revealed only here and there in the mountain ranges of Kitakami, Abukuma, Ashio, and in the mountains of the Kantō region. These fractures form a continuation from southwestern Japan, but they are broken into fragments by the deforming motions of the Cenozoic era. When the structures of the Mesozoic and Paleozoic groups are traced from southwestern Japan, they are found to be curved in the shape of a reverse S, which is also considered to be the result of deformation motions. Volcanic activity is vigorous in northeastern Japan, and two volcanic zones are present, one running along the Ōu Mountains and the other along the coast of the Sea of Japan. They change direction at the Fossa Magna and are connected to the Izu-Ogasawara Arc. Plains of the Quaternary period that have formed in these mountainous areas and on the seashore have step-like terraces.

Crustal Movement —— The Japanese islands have severe crustal movements, which are still progressing. Crustal movements include movements of short duration, such as seismic activity (see EARTHQUAKES), and also slow movements of long duration. Volcanic activity, gravity anomaly, and crustal heat flow are also directly caused by the crustal deformation. When the locations and scales of these various phenomena are classified and plotted on a map, it is clear that the mode of distribution agrees well with the shape of the northeastern part of the Honshū Arc, providing a basis for the theory that the topographical structure, geological structure, and crustal deformations are all caused by common crust motions.

The hypocenters of earthquakes in northeastern Japan tend to concentrate on a plane on the west side of the Japan Trench tilted 45° from the horizontal. When the pattern of distribution of hypocenters of equal depth is plotted, they form an arc which parallels the northeastern part of the Honshū Arc. In the southwestern part of the Honshū Arc, there is no such regularity, and the frequency of earthquakes is low. The energy released by the earthquakes occurring in and around Japan amounts to an average of 2×10^{23} ergs per year.

Volcanoes have been particularly active in northeastern Japan since the Quaternary period. The mode of distribution is in parallel with the topography. There is a narrow nonvolcanic zone along the Pacific coast, the rest of the region being volcanic. Further, the chemical components of the rocks forming a volcano vary gradually from the inside of the arc to the outside. There is no clear regularity observed in southwestern Japan as in northeastern Japan.

At the eastern edge of the volcanic zone in the northeastern part of the Honshū Arc, the crustal heat flow increases in volume suddenly to over 2.0 HFU from the average of 1.0 HFU (unit of heat flow $= 10^{-6}$ cal/cm²·s) in the Pacific Ocean. A similar value is observed on the continental side, in the Sea of Japan and the Sea of Okhotsk. The isopleth of heat flow also runs in parallel with the northeastern part of the Honshū Arc and agrees with the volcanic zone. Heat flow is almost uniformly low in the southwestern part of the Honshū Arc.

There is a strong negative anomaly in the balance of gravity amounting to −100 milligals along the line from the Japan Trench to the Izu–Ogasawara Trench and there is a positive anomaly in the balance of gravity amounting to +100 milligals in the nonvolcanic zone of northeastern Japan. This pattern is also nearly in parallel with the northeastern part of the Honshū Arc. There is no conspicuous anomaly in the balance of gravity in southwestern Japan.

The crust is 7–10 kilometers (23,000–33,000 ft) thick in the bottom of the Pacific Ocean and the Japan Trench. Granitic crust begins to appear from the western side of the Japan Trench, and the crust suddenly becomes approximately 30 kilometers (98,000 ft) thick. It is about 36 kilometers (118,000 ft) thick in the mountains of the Chūbu district. In northeastern Japan variations in the thickness of the crust correspond to the island arc, but in southwestern Japan the geological structure is not directly related to the thickness of the crust.

History of the Japanese Islands—— The Japanese islands were formed as the result of several orogenic movements and are not the product of a single crustal movement. Their history goes back at least to the Silurian period in the Paleozoic era (about 400 million years ago), and the crustal movement still continues.

There is evidence of metamorphism in the Precambrian age (about 1.6 billion years ago) in the gneiss of the Hida Mountains, and gravels of the Precambrian age are contained in the conglomerate of the Mesozoic and Paleozoic groups in the Mino district. There is granite of the Ordovician period (430 million years ago) in the eastern part of Shikoku, which implies that there existed a granite crust forming the basement when the principal part of the Japanese islands became geosynclinal after the Silurian period.

The oldest stratum, as shown by fossil evidence, is that of the mid-Silurian period. The principal part of the Japanese islands had been under the surface of the sea from this period through the end of the Paleozoic era or through the beginning of the Mesozoic era. Although they continued to be filled with sediments such as sandstone, mudstone, limestone, and chert, the islands were in the so-called geosynclinal condition, in which ejecta from volcanoes, including submarine volcanoes, accumulated. The geosyncline in question was not a simple hollow; there occurred an upheaval along the central axis after the late Carboniferous period, and it was divided into three belts. The belt nearest the Asian continent is known as the Sangun-Yamaguchi Terrain, the middle belt as the Sambagawa Terrain, and the belt on the Pacific Ocean side as the Chichibu Terrain. This geosyncline is called the Chichibu Geosyncline (Honshū Geosyncline). The outer shape is considered to have been a simple arc with no geological flections. In the volcanic activities in the geosyncline, an active period and an inactive period seem to have occurred at each location, as is known from mainly acidic rocks

belonging to the Silurian period and Devonian period and basic rocks belonging to the Carboniferous and Permian periods.

With the arrival of the Triassic period, the condition of the geosyncline approached the last stage, and in the late Triassic period the geosyncline began to form land by means of the folding movement, starting at the innermost part, as thick postorogenic sediments accumulated in the hollow of the new land. At this time regional metamorphism took place in the zone deep under the ground, creating the metamorphic rocks of the Hida and Sangun metamorphosed zones. The folding moved to the outer side, and the whole area of the Chichibu Geosyncline was subjected to folding and fault movement until the end of the Cretaceous period, and thus land was formed. By the end of the Cretaceous period, the Ryōke metamorphic rocks and Sambagawa metamorphic rocks had been created, and a large granite basement (the Hiroshima Granite) had been created inside the Ryōke Metamorphosed Zone.

The Hidaka Mountains in Hokkaidō have been in a geosynclinal condition since the Permian period, and sediments of the Mesozoic era and volcanic ejecta have been deposited. Although the Chichibu Geosyncline was subjected to orogenic movements, the Shimanto Geosyncline was produced outside it. Sediments of the Cretaceous through the Paleocene periods (flysch type) and volcanic products were deposited in the Shimanto Geosyncline. These two geosynclines began orogenic movements in the late Cretaceous period through the early Cenozoic era and formed early mountain ranges.

The greater part of the Japanese islands became land in the Paleocene period. It was only after the Neocene period that the sea again began to invade the land. The present northeastern part of the Honshū Arc originated after the Cretaceous period. As the newly produced orogenic zone intersected obliquely with the island arc that had already existed, the northeastern extension of southwestern Japan was curved like a reverse S, forming a block. The sea moved into the hollow created behind it, and volcanic activities began. This is the Green Tuff zone.

Sedimentation took place gradually from east to west in the Green Tuff zone, and foldings occurred. This crustal movement still continues, and volcanic and seismic activities are regarded as representing this movement. Thus the shape of the present Japanese islands had nearly been formed by the Quaternary period, and the sedimentation of the Quaternary period took place in the lowlands scattered all over the Japanese islands and created plains.

SATŌ Tadashi

📖——Yoshikawa Torao, ed, *Shimpen Nihon chikeiron* (1973). Ichikawa Kōichirō, ed, *Nihon rettō chishitsu kōzō hattatsushi* (1970). Minamoto Masao, ed, *The Geologic Development of the Japanese Islands* (1965). Saitō Ren'ichi, ed, *Nihon no kikō* (1958).

Japan Academy

(Nihon Gakushiin). The preeminent learned society of Japan, established in 1879 to honor scholars who have made outstanding contributions to their fields of study. Election to the academy is considered the highest distinction a Japanese scholar can receive. Of the 150 members, 70 represent the humanities and social sciences and 80 the natural sciences. Academicians enjoy life tenure and a yearly stipend. The academy awards two annual prizes—the Academy Prize (Gakushiin Shō) and the Imperial Prize (Gakushiin Onshi Shō)—for important scholarly work and publishes the *Proceedings of the Japan Academy* or *Gakushiin kiyō*. WATANABE Tadashi

Japan Advertisers Association

(Nihon Kōkokunushi Kyōkai). An organization of approximately 180 major advertisers in such media as newspapers, magazines, radio, and television. It was organized in 1956 to take effective countermeasures against the rising costs of advertising. Afterward the organization came to promote a wide range of activities such as education for member advertisers, research and publication of improved advertising techniques, studies in overseas marketing and advertising business, and information gathering.

KAWAKAMI Hiroshi

Japan Advertising Review Organization

(Nihon Kōkoku Shinsa Kikō). An organization established in 1974 for the self-regulation of the advertising industry. Its members include all major advertisers, the media, advertising agencies, and producers of television commercials. It accepts complaints about advertisements from consumers and reviews them in a seven-man committee comprised of specialists in various fields such as economics, history, medicine, and law. When the committee determines an advertisement to be improper, it notifies all affiliated members and requests the suspension of publication or broadcast of the advertisement by the media. In addition to screening operations, it carries on a wide range of undertakings in order to ensure social responsibility in advertising. See also ADVERTISING; ADVERTISING AGENCIES.

KAWAKAMI Hiroshi

Japan Air Lines Co, Ltd

(Nihon Kōkū; often called JAL). Air transport company. With flights to 49 cities in 29 countries of the world, in 1982 this airline ranked third in the volume of transport among International Air Transport Association (IATA) members. It also operated domestic trunk routes. The company was founded in 1951 as a joint-stock company and reorganized in 1953 as a semigovernmental enterprise under the provisions of the Japan Air Lines Law, with exclusive rights to operate international routes. It first crossed the Pacific in 1954, and in 1967 it became the third airline to establish a round-the-world flight. In 1970 it was the first non-Soviet airline to establish a regular route over Siberia.

In 1982 the JAL fleet comprised a total of 82 aircraft, including 41 Boeing 747s, 17 McDonnell–Douglas DC–10s, 22 DC–8s, and 2 Boeing 727s. The airline has an excellent safety record: as of September 1979 JAL pilots had logged a total of 480,000 flight hours without an accident. The company also operates hotels and other businesses through affiliated firms. The Japan Air Lines Development Co operates hotels in Paris and at the NEW TŌKYŌ INTERNATIONAL AIRPORT at Narita and also has chain contracts with a total of 58 hotels around the world, forming JAL Hotel System International. The Japan Creative Tours Co sells package tours under the brand names JALPAK and ZERO. A terminal at Narita equipped with an automatic freight handling system is operated for freight transport under the name of JALTOS. The company is planning to expand this system in the future. Over 110 flights are operated every day on JAL's domestic trunk lines, accounting for about 60 percent of the total passenger volume on these routes. Annual revenue totaled ¥723.6 billion (US $30 billion) in the fiscal year ending March 1982, of which passenger fares accounted for 74 percent, cargo 18 percent, mail freight 2 percent, and others 6 percent. In the same year the company's capitalization stood at ¥63.8 billion (US $265 million), of which 37.7 percent was held by the Ministry of Transport. Corporate headquarters are located in Tōkyō.

Japan Amateur Sports Association

(Nihon Taiiku Kyōkai). National organization for the regulation as well as the promotion of amateur sports and recreation in Japan. Originally founded in 1911 by representatives from several Tōkyō universities in order to prepare Japan for participation in its first Olympics, the association quickly broadened its role in amateur sports and became the governing body for such sports as track and field, swimming, *karate*, and *jūdō*. It sponsors national competitions such as the National Sports Festival and supervises participation in international events such as the Olympics, the Asian Games, and the Universiade Games. It also promotes physical education in schools and raises funds for sports facilities and competitions. Present membership includes 39 amateur athletic organizations and 47 prefectural sports associations. The first chairman was KANŌ JIGORŌ. See also SPORTS.

TAKEDA Fumio

Japan-American Student Conference

(Nichibei Gakusei Kaigi). A conference planned and administered by students from Japan and the United States to promote Japanese-American understanding and cooperation. The conference, roughly one month long, is held each year alternately in Japan or the United States.

The conference was first proposed by Japanese students after the MANCHURIAN INCIDENT of 1931, when relations between the two countries began to worsen. The first meeting was held at Aoyama Gakuin University in 1934; the second was held the following year at Reed College in Portland, Oregon. The conference was held several more times until its suspension at the outbreak of World War II. It resumed with the 8th conference in 1947. It is still in operation at the present time; the 33rd conference was held in Tōkyō in 1981 with 90 participants.

The conference is chiefly conducted in English, with discussions covering a broad range of topics, such as politics, economics, social problems, education, and culture. Lecturers are also invited to take part.

Japan Art Academy

(Nihon Geijutsuin). Established in its present form in 1947 and placed under the control of the Ministry of Education in 1949, it deliberates on important issues related to art, promotes art, and advises the minister of education on issues concerning art. It is composed of no more than 120 members who belong to one of the three departments: fine arts; literature; and music, drama, and dance. The history of the academy can be traced back to the Bijutsu Shinsa Iinkai (Fine Art Screening Committee) of 1907, which in 1919 became the Teikoku Bijutsuin (Imperial Fine Arts Academy), headed by MORI ŌGAI. The name was changed to Teikoku Geijutsuin (Imperial Art Academy) in 1937, and at that time the scope was expanded to include literature and music. The academy annually gives Japan Art Academy Awards to people who have made important contributions in the fields of fine arts, literature, music, drama, and dance. See also BUNTEN.

James R. MORITA

Japan Association of National Universities

(Kokuritsu Daigaku Kyōkai). An association established in 1950 to promote cooperation among four-year national universities. General meetings and committee meetings of the association are presided over by the presidents of the member universities; executives of the association are presidents and professors of universities that have doctoral degree programs. The association influences the formation of government policies on higher education. Among its opinion papers, "Positions on Standards for Establishment of Graduate Schools" (1967), "Survey and Research on University Reforms" (1971), and "Survey and Research on the Improvement of Entrance Examinations to National Universities" (1974–78) have exerted considerable influence.

NAKAJIMA Naotada

Japan Atomic Power Company

(Nihon Genshiryoku Hatsuden). Manufacturer and operator of nuclear power plants and supplier of electrical power. Capitalized by nine major electric power companies and related firms, it was founded in 1957 with the aim of commercializing the nuclear generation of power. In 1966 Japan's first commercial nuclear power plant began operations in Tōkai Mura, Ibaraki Prefecture. Subsequently two more nuclear power plants were constructed by Japan Atomic Power, one in Tsuruga, Fukui Prefecture, and an additional plant in Tōkai Mura. The company continues to play a pioneering role in the introduction and improvement of technology and equipment for the nuclear generation of power and in the training of technicians. In 1978 electric power generation capacity was 16,230,000 kilowatts. In the same year total sales were ¥22.3 billion (US $106 million) and capitalization stood at ¥62 billion (US $29 million). The corporate headquarters are located in Tōkyō.

Japan Book Publishers Association

(Nihon Shoseki Shuppan Kyōkai). Organization of leading publishing companies formed in 1957. As of January 1982 it had 418 member companies. It was founded to ensure the continuing growth of the publishing industry and to raise the general cultural level of the reading public. The Publishers Association and the JAPAN MAGAZINE PUBLISHERS ASSOCIATION (Nihon Zasshi Kyōkai) cooperate to formulate ethical guidelines for publishers. In 1968 it published the *Nihon shuppan hyakunen shi nempyō*, a detailed chronology of Japanese publications of the last 100 years, and since 1977 it has published the *Nihon shoseki sōmokuroku*, a general catalog of books in print in Japan.

SHIMIZU Hideo

Japan Braille Library

(Nihon Tenji Toshokan). A social welfare institution for the visually handicapped, located in Shinjuku Ward, Tōkyō. It opened in 1940 with a small collection of braille books owned by Homma Kazuo (b 1915), who is himself blind, and it was established as a social welfare corporation in 1952. The library publishes braille books, tape-recorded books, and newsletters; its holdings of some 91,000 books and 105,000 reels of tape are available to borrowers. The library provides braille instruction and also designs and distributes games, tape recorders, small household appliances, and other items for the use of the blind. *TAKAKUWA Yasuo*

Japan Broadcasting Corporation → NHK

Japan Buddhist Federation → Zen Nihon Bukkyō Kai

Japan Chamber of Commerce and Industry

(Nihon Shōkō Kaigisho; commonly abbreviated Nisshō). Central organ of regional chambers of commerce situated in 478 Japanese cities. In 1878 the first chambers of commerce and industry were established in Tōkyō, Ōsaka, and several other cities. Nisshō was created in 1922 to represent the views of member organizations in various domestic and overseas commercial activities. It is especially concerned with international commerce, and business offices of such economic organizations as the Pacific Economic Committee, the Japan–Australia–New Zealand Economic Committee, and the Federation of Asian Chambers of Commerce and Industry have been set up within Nisshō (see KEIDANREN). *HIRATA Masami*

Japan Committee for Economic Development

(Keizai Dōyū Kai). Organization made up of business managers and executives of various corporations. The committee's purpose is to promote progress and stability in the Japanese economy by making proposals aimed at benefiting the national economy as a whole and it avoids taking stands on political issues.

At the time of its establishment in 1946, the committee was composed of progressive business leaders and industrialists concerned with the problem of reconstructing and democratizing the Japanese economy. It was intended to provide an informal forum for developing and advancing new ideas. Membership has grown to some 1,000 businessmen. Various subcommittees exist, which conduct research and issue recommendations under the guidance of a board of 200 trustees. The committee has stressed the social responsibility of business and promoted the cooperation of business and academia, resulting in the formation of organizations such as the Japan Center for Area Research and Development which works on problems of urban areas and of regional development, the Japan Research Council on Economics Education which tries to improve education about economics in the secondary schools, and the Japan Greening Center which works to increase green areas in cities. It also cooperates with similar organizations in other countries and is particularly concerned with promoting the economic development of Southeast Asia.

Japan Communist Party

(JCP; Nihon Kyōsantō). Political party. A leading opposition party of the post–World War II era. Founded on 15 July 1922 as a branch of the Comintern by a group of socialist activists including YAMAKAWA HITOSHI, ARAHATA KANSON, SAKAI TOSHIHIKO, and TOKUDA KYŪICHI. The party initially attracted socialists such as NOSAKA SANZŌ, younger intellectuals such as SANO MANABU, ICHIKAWA SHŌICHI, and SHIGA YOSHIO, and workers such as WATANABE MASANOSUKE.

History through 1945—— Until it was legalized after World War II, the party remained a small secretive organization subject to frequent suppression by government authorities opposed to its aim of creating a workers' state free of monarchy. In the 1920s and 1930s the party, usually in vain, sought to extend its influence through publications like its newspaper *Sekki* (Red Flag; see AKAHATA) and through various political activities. In the early years it won a following in the SHINJINKAI and other student associations. It tried to infiltrate the SŌDŌMEI (Japan Federation of Labor), but right-wing members of the federation forced a split that led to the creation of the left-wing Hyōgikai (Council of Japanese Labor Unions). It attempted to enter politics legally through the ranks of the RŌDŌ NŌMINTŌ (Labor-Farmer Party), a left-wing party formed in 1926, and succeeded in getting two communist-backed candidates of this party elected to the Diet in 1928. The government responded by arresting

many of the JCP leaders in the MARCH 15TH INCIDENT of 1928 and the APRIL 16TH INCIDENT of 1929 and by dissolving the Rōdō Nōmintō, the Hyōgikai, and other supporting organizations. A public trial of top JCP leaders ended in 1932 with convictions for all. The following year saw recantations (TENKŌ) by Sano and some other eminent party leaders, and with the arrest of party chairman Hakamada Satomi (b 1904) in early 1935, party activity in effect ceased. Marxism, nonetheless, gained increasing support from academics, drawing such personages as KAWAKAMI HAJIME. A major intellectual event of this era was the heated debate over the development of modern Japanese capitalism. See NIHON SHIHON SHUGI RONSŌ.

Prewar basic party programs reflected leadership changes and world events. In the beginning, the party was dominated intellectually by Yamakawa Hitoshi, who emphasized the need to "go to the masses." Ironically, his logic led him to call for the dissolution of the JCP to lead the way for the formation of a legal united-front mass party. The JCP was dissolved in effect in 1923 and formally in 1924. In 1924 a young communist, FUKUMOTO KAZUO, returned from two years of intensive study of Marxism in Germany and France and strongly criticized Yamakawa's ideas. Fukumoto argued in favor of the theoretical need for a vanguard party on the basis of "division before unity." He took part in the reestablishment of the party at the end of 1926.

In July 1927 the Comintern issued a thesis to direct the activities and ideology of the burgeoning Japanese communist movement (see COMINTERN 1927 THESIS). It attacked the ideas of Yamakawa as "opportunist" and those of Fukumoto as "sectarian" and called for a two-stage revolution: bourgeois-democratic and socialist. As a result of greater domestic oppression by Japanese government authorities and the Great Depression, which began in 1929, the party drafted a new thesis in 1931 that urged moving directly into a socialist revolution. The radical approach embodied by this thesis led to factionalism and blistering attacks against social democrats, but it did not receive Comintern approval. However, the 1932 COMMINTERN THESIS also called for a two-stage revolution and claimed that the emperor system fostered "military feudal imperialism."

Postwar History—— The JCP was legally constituted on 4 October 1945 by veteran communists released from prison the preceding month. They were later joined by members who returned from China, notably Nosaka Sanzō. Portraying themselves as peace-loving moderates free of any outside influence, they captured 5 seats in the House of Representatives and 2.1 million votes in the 1946 election. In a whirl of feverish activity, party membership and influence on organized labor grew rapidly until General Douglas MacArthur banned the GENERAL STRIKE OF 1947. This event signaled the displeasure of the OCCUPATION authorities (SCAP) with the JCP and caused a split within the ranks of labor. Nonetheless, the communists at first increased their influence, winning 35 seats and almost 3 million votes in the 1949 election as voters critical of the Occupation's "reverse course" shifted their support from the socialists to the communists after the fall of the socialist-led cabinet of KATAYAMA TETSU (1947–48).

However, this success evaporated quickly in the heightened cold war atmosphere of the early 1950s. In January 1950 the Cominform criticized the JCP for not opposing the Occupation sufficiently, and Nosaka accepted the criticism. SCAP responded on 6-7 June 1950 by ordering the purge from politics of the top JCP leadership, which, it said, was endangering the Occupation. After the outbreak of the Korean War on 25 June 1950, the RED PURGE was extended to suspected communist sympathizers in government and private industry. This move hastened the development of anticommunist "democratization leagues" in labor, resulting in the creation of the General Council of Trade Unions of Japan (SŌHYŌ) and the collapse of JCP influence in organized labor.

The JCP leaders reacted by adopting a policy of violent revolution to achieve its aims. Some of them went underground, leaving the party to contend with great internal dissension. The terrorist acts committed by JCP members at the time of the Korean War resulted in the loss of whatever public support the party had enjoyed, and the government listed it as a subversive group under the SUBVERSIVE ACTIVITIES PREVENTION LAW. In the 1952 election the party lost all of its 35 seats in the House of Representatives.

In the mid-1950s the party gradually moderated its policies and activities, and party leaders began to reappear. This trend was reflected in a new basic program that was drafted in 1957, approved in 1961, and remained in force in 1982. The new program stresses the possibility of a peaceful transition to socialism after the achievement of a "bourgeois-democratic revolution." It bears the stamp of MIYA-

MOTO KENJI, the party's leader throughout most of the postwar period.

In 1976 the JCP added a "Manifesto of Freedom and Democracy" to its 1961 party program. It advocates parliamentary democracy and denies the need for "dictatorship" as practiced in the Soviet Union. Although the JCP has opposed the United States–Japan Security Treaty (see UNITED STATES–JAPAN SECURITY TREATIES), and took part in the two biggest campaigns against its renewal, in 1960 and 1970, it was criticized by leftist student groups for not being militant enough. In the early 1980s it had modified its opposition to the existence of the SELF DEFENSE FORCES and, with the end of the Vietnam War, has become less critical of the United States. It was calling for the nationalization of certain big businesses only, the promotion of voluntary cooperatives, and comprehensive social welfare.

Party Strength —— After its debacle in the 1952 elections, the JCP gradually recovered and consistently held a handful of seats in the lower house of the Diet. Its most dramatic gains came in the 1969 elections, when it won over three million votes for the first time and increased its membership in the lower house from 5 to 14. It won just over 10 percent of the vote in the 1972, 1976, and 1979 elections and dropped only slightly, to 9.8 percent in 1980, but the number of its Diet members varied tremendously. It won 40 seats in the 1972 lower house election, 19 in 1976, 41 in 1979, and 29 in 1980.

Until the LIBERAL DEMOCRATIC PARTY's (LDP) whirlwind membership registration campaign in 1977–78, the JCP had the largest membership of any postwar Japanese party. In 1978 its membership reached 370,000, one-third of which was female. Its newspaper, *Akahata,* has attained a circulation of over three million. This and other publications provide over 70 percent of the party's finances. The JCP does not rely on labor federations for funds and election campaign workers as do the two socialist parties. Its auxiliary organizations have also attracted wide support. Among student movements its main support comes from the MINSEI (Democratic Youth League of Japan), which has about 200,000 members, 70 percent of whom are working youths rather than students. It is considered the most moderate of the leftist STUDENT MOVEMENTS. Some JCP members are active in organizations such as the Zen Nihon Minshu Iryō Kikan Rengōkai (Min'iren; All Japan Leagues of Democratic Medical Institutes), which consists of clinical and volunteer doctors and nurses who help people unlikely to receive medical assistance elsewhere, and in associations of merchants and small manufacturers that advise small businessmen on tax problems.

The turnover in party membership has apparently been high, but the leadership has so far been stable and not suffered major splits, unlike the JAPAN SOCIALIST PARTY. After the party's break with the Russian Communist Party in 1963–64, one of the earliest and most prominent JCP leaders, Shiga Yoshio, was expelled in 1964 because of his support of the Nuclear Test Ban Treaty. Other leaders left or were expelled when the JCP broke ranks with the Chinese Communist Party in 1966–67.

The JCP has adopted an independent and nationalist stance that has increased its popularity and respectability at home. Its nationalism is expressed in various ways; it emphasizes traditional Japanese folk culture and has been outspoken in its demands for the return to Japan of the Soviet-occupied islands north of Hokkaidō. Because of China's antipathy toward it, the JCP was the only party that played no role in the normalization of relations (1972) and the signing of the CHINA–JAPAN PEACE AND FRIENDSHIP TREATY (1978). The party now appears to have the closest relations with the communist parties of Italy, France, and other Western states.

Despite recent electoral reverses, it seems unlikely that popular support for the JCP has reached a permanent plateau. However, its prospects of becoming part of a ruling party coalition seem dim. In the eyes of many voters the JCP appears not to have completely disassociated itself from the unpopular policies and acts of the Soviet Union. Others, however, feel that the party has become so "respectable" that a more radical party might develop in its place. ◼ ——Hans H. Baerwald, "The Japanese Communist Party: Yoyogi and Its Rivals," in Robert A. Scalapino, ed, *The Communist Revolution in Asia* (1965). George M. Beckman and Genji Ōkubo, *The Japanese Communist Party, 1922–1945* (1969). Allan B. Cole, George O. Totten, and Cecil H. Uyehara, *Socialist Parties in Postwar Japan* (1966). Paul F. Langer, *Communism in Japan: A Case Study of Political Naturalization* (1972). Robert A. Scalapino, *The Japanese Communist Movement, 1920–1966* (1967). George Oakley Totten III, *The Social Democratic Movement in Prewar Japan* (1966).

George Oakley TOTTEN III

Japanese Alps

Yarigatake, the fourth highest mountain in Japan, with other peaks of the Hida Mountains (the Northern Alps) in the distance.

Japan Current → Kuroshio

Japan Development Bank

(Nihon Kaihatsu Ginkō). Government financial institution. Established 20 April 1951 pursuant to the Japan Development Bank Law "to supplement and encourage the credit operation of ordinary financial institutions by supplying long-term funds in order to promote industrial development and economic and social progress." The bank is capitalized solely by the Japanese government, and its operations are controlled and supervised by the government. Lending activities are carried out in accordance with an annual policy determined by the cabinet. Operations are divided into seven categories: urban development, regional development, improvement of the quality of life, resources and energy, ocean shipping, development of technology, and miscellaneous. Domestic sources of funds for lending operations come from the government, loan repayments, and reserves. Outstanding borrowings from the government amounted to ¥5.1 trillion (US $21.2 billion) at the end of March 1982. The bank's sources of international funds are external loan bonds and note issues, all of which are guaranteed by the government. New loans extended in fiscal 1981 amounted to ¥1.1 trillion (US $4.6 billion), and outstanding loans totaled ¥5.9 trillion (US $24.5 billion) at the end of the same year. The bank's headquarters are in Tōkyō.

Japanese Alps

(Nihon Arupusu). Three mountain ranges extending north to south in central Honshū, consisting of the HIDA MOUNTAINS (also called the Northern Alps), the KISO MOUNTAINS (Central Alps), and the AKAISHI MOUNTAINS (Southern Alps). The highest peak is KITADAKE (3,192 m; 10,470 ft). The term Japanese Alps was used by various English visitors to Japan in the late 19th century and was made popular by Walter WESTON in *Mountaineering and Exploration in the Japanese Alps* (1896). The Chūbu Sangaku and Southern Alps national parks are situated in the Japanese Alps.

Japanese American Citizens League

(JACL). Political and civil rights organization of the Japanese American community, corresponding roughly to the National Association for the Advancement of Colored People for American blacks or the Anti-Defamation League of the B'nai Br'ith for American Jews. At its founding in 1930 it was an organization exclusively for *nisei* (second generation JAPANESE AMERICANS). Limiting its membership to citizens only, it in effect barred *issei* (first generation Japanese Americans). Although JACL attempted to influence US government policy from its very inception—the first convention called for the granting of the rights of citizenship to Asian aliens who had served in the US armed forces during World War I—its major influence was felt after Pearl Harbor, when, almost by default, it became the sole organized voice of the Japanese American community.

The JACL not only supported, unambiguously, the US war effort against Japan, but it also chose an accommodationist stance when in early 1942 the US government decided to relocate and incarcerate the Japanese American population of the West Coast, citizens as well as aliens (see JAPANESE AMERICANS, WARTIME RELOCATION OF). Although this stance was unpopular with many—JACL leaders inside the concentration camps were often denounced as *inu* (dogs) and in some instances physically assaulted—it ensured that the organization's views were listened to by at least some key federal officials. The JACL's major objectives during the war were to have *nisei* reaccepted fully into American military service and to allow *nisei* whose loyalty had been proven beyond doubt to return to their homes.

In the postwar era the JACL campaigned with a great deal of success for a Japanese American Claims Act, for a revision of the naturalization laws so that Asians could be naturalized under the same terms as Europeans and Africans, and for an equitable immigration system that no longer discriminated against Asians (see UNITED STATES IMMIGRATION ACTS OF 1924, 1952, AND 1965). In the early 1980s it was engaged in a campaign for some kind of redress for Japanese Americans who were incarcerated during World War II.

Although many now see it as a functionless organization, since the overt statutory discrimination against Japanese Americans is a thing of the past, the JACL has never enjoyed more influence or prestige outside of the ethnic community than at present. Like the organizations of other ethnic groups on which it modeled itself, it has never attracted more than a tiny fraction of the Japanese American population into formal membership. At the end of the 1970s, however, it had some 32,000 members.

📖 —— Bill Hosokawa, *Nisei: The Quiet Americans* (1969). Roger Daniels, "The Japanese," in John Higham, ed, *Ethnic Leadership in America* (1978). Roger DANIELS

Japanese Americans

A racial minority group in the United States consisting of immigrants from Japan and their descendants. According to the 1980 US census, there were 700,747 Japanese Americans, with the largest concentrations in California (261,817), Hawaii (239,618), Washington (26,369), New York (24,524), and Illinois (18,550). Japanese Americans have been victims of extreme racial prejudice and discrimination, the most tragic episode being their incarceration during World War II. They have nonetheless made important contributions to American society in agriculture, the arts, military service, science, business, and other fields. Their significance in the annals of American race relations stems from their real or presumed affiliations with Japan as their homeland.

In recent years, a somewhat heroic mythology has developed about Japanese Americans in the popular press and to a certain extent in race relations research. Japanese Americans have been depicted as a "model minority" group, which, having faced seemingly insurmountable racial and economic barriers, has finally risen to prominent socioeconomic status. Although this view can be buttressed with demographic data on educational and income levels, it also disguises a wide range of unresolved social issues and problems facing Japanese Americans, as well as the extreme diversity of the group.

The Japanese American experience in the United States, which spans more than a century, can be analyzed as follows: (1) 1868–1924, the major period of Japanese immigration to Hawaii and the United States, as well as the first major phase of organized anti-Japanese agitation, culminating with the Immigration Act of 1924, which in effect barred further immigration from Japan (see UNITED STATES IMMIGRATION ACTS OF 1924, 1952, AND 1965). During this period, approximately 270,000 Japanese migrated to the United States, of which over 125,000 came during the peak years 1901–08. (2) 1924–41, the major period of Japanese settlement and community development in the United States and the emergence of American-born Japanese Americans. (3) 1941–45, the years of wartime incarceration, when 120,000 Japanese Americans from the Pacific Coast were placed in American concentration camps called relocation centers. (4) 1945 to the present, the postwar recovery period, when Japanese Americans rebuilt their lives and communities. It also was during this period that the third generation emerged.

Some scholars have analyzed Japanese American history according to successive generations of Japanese Americans: *issei, nisei, sansei,* and *yonsei,* Japanese terms referring to first, second, third, and fourth generations of Japanese Americans. These terms are often used to categorize Japanese Americans in terms of age cohorts, which exhibit somewhat different American and Japanese behavioral, cultural, and attitudinal traits. For instance, the *issei* usually read, write, and speak Japanese with greater fluency than their *nisei* offspring or *sansei* grandchildren. Social groupings by generation tend to share and be affected by common historical experiences and circumstances. Thus, one can speak of the *issei* experience and the *nisei* experience, as well as other generational experiences that correspond to particular times and specific episodes in Japanese American history. The *nisei* experience, for example, begins in the 1920s and 1930s and encompasses events such as the American Depression, Japan's invasion of China, their own relocation during World War II, and the postwar era. Although the *nisei* experience overlaps with that of the *issei* and *sansei* generations, many special concerns arose from the unique sociohistorical position of the *nisei.* For instance, many *nisei* reached adulthood in the 1930s and found that severe economic conditions and continued racial discrimination prevented them from getting jobs commensurate with their education. The "vocational problem," as the *nisei* labeled it, usually meant that college graduates had to accept low-paying jobs. During this period many college-educated *nisei,* including some who became prominent during the postwar era, went to Japan to seek greater economic and social opportunities.

Immigration Background —— Japanese immigration to the United States began in the late 1860s. In 1868 a shipload of 148 contract laborers arrived in Honolulu to work on Hawaii's flourishing sugar plantations. These laborers, known as *gannen-mono* or "first-year men," because they came in the first year of Emperor Meiji's reign, were recruited from the Tōkyō and Yokohama areas by Eugene Van Reed. Reed was an American citizen commissioned by King Kamehameha IV as Hawaii's consul general in Kanagawa. Within a month after their arrival, there were numerous complaints from laborers and from plantation owners. Japanese government officials were aware of the harsh treatment accorded to Chinese laborers in America and the demeaning perception of China as a storehouse for cheap labor and did not want the same fate for Japan and its people. They subsequently stopped immigration to Hawaii until 1885.

In an unrelated and unsanctioned venture, Japanese immigration to the mainland had its symbolic beginning in 1869 with the arrival of the so-called Wakamatsu colony, whose twenty-odd members came from the Aizu Wakamatsu area of Japan. The group was led by John Henry Schnell, a European military adviser to Matsudaira Katamori, the feudal lord of the Aizu Wakamatsu domain, who had supported the Tokugawa shogunate at the time of the Meiji Restoration (1868). The Wakamatsu colony was an advance party of farmers and *samurai,* sent to determine whether the United States could serve as a place of political refuge. The group arrived in San Francisco and made its way to Gold Hill near Sacramento. They planted mulberries, tangerines, Kōshū grapes, and tea. However, the group soon disbanded after a severe drought destroyed its crops. A grave marker near Gold Hill remains as evidence of their presence.

The origins of Japanese immigration can be traced to these and other isolated travelers, but large-scale immigration to Hawaii and the United States mainland did not begin until 1885–86, when the Japanese government relaxed restrictions against emigration. It also signed a treaty with Hawaii, the Irwin Convention, named after Robert Walker IRWIN, an American businessman and the Hawaiian Board of Immigration representative in Japan, who subsequently played a major role in recruiting Japanese laborers. The treaty required that each laborer sign a three-year contract with the Hawaiian government, which guaranteed free travel, employment, housing, food, and other services. Although there were many abuses of these conditions, vigorous promotional campaigns, coupled with glamorized accounts of individual successes, motivated large numbers of Japanese to migrate to Hawaii, the United States, Canada, and various Latin American countries, especially Brazil (see JAPANESE AMERICANS IN HAWAII; CANADA, JAPANESE IMMIGRANTS IN; BRAZIL, JAPANESE IMMIGRANTS IN).

Japanese immigrants to the United States were far from homogeneous, but they shared some common features. In early years, they tended to be young, single men with the equivalent of an eighth-grade education, who came from farming backgrounds in the southern and western prefectures of Hiroshima, Yamaguchi, Wakayama, Kumamoto, and Fukuoka. Most viewed themselves as sojourners, seeking to make enough money abroad to live comfortably in Japan when they returned. Those who went to Hawaii usually worked on sugar plantations, and those who came to the mainland (directly from Japan or through Hawaii) served as laborers in agricultural, railroad, mining, and lumber industries. Before 1908, when the GENTLEMEN'S AGREEMENT between the United States and Japan went into effect and placed restrictions on the types of individual who could emigrate, the ratio of men to women was 7 to 1. However, for the remaining years of large-scale immigration to the United States, more women than men migrated, and most came as so-called PICTURE BRIDES of immigrant men. The picture-bride practice, which was consistent with the prevailing Japanese custom of using go-betweens and viewing marriage as a collective decision by families rather than individuals, was promoted by immigrant leaders, who believed that a viable and prosperous immigrant society could not be developed until the immigrants viewed themselves as permanent settlers. Permanent residency in the United States gradually replaced the dream of returning to Japan for many immigrant laborers who saved enough money to start small businesses and farms. Marriage and the creation of families further reinforced permanent settlement in America.

Individual motivation was instrumental in immigration, but large-scale immigration was due to major economic and political developments in the United States and Japan. In the United States, decades of organized anti-Chinese agitation and violence culminated with the enactment of the 1882 Chinese Exclusion Act, the first restrictive federal immigration law based solely on race. As a result, there developed a severe shortage of cheap and reliable labor, which was needed for the further development of agricultural, mining, and railroad industries in California and other western states. Likewise, Hawaiian plantations were confronted with a diminishing labor pool as many Chinese laborers fulfilled their contractual obligations and returned to China or began their own businesses.

The Meiji government's ambitious drive for industrialization and international parity generated internal political conflicts and severe economic dislocations, which had an unusually adverse impact on the agricultural sector. Emigration was viewed as a safety valve by the Japanese government and as one means of coping with difficult economic conditions by those who went abroad. A major distinguishing feature of Japanese immigration was the active role of the Japanese government in monitoring and controlling the immigration process. Government officials took numerous measures, which included the creation of a special government bureau and government-sponsored emigration companies to ensure that immigrants would be treated fairly and that they would not undermine Japan's rising international status or its relations with the United States. The close attention Japanese government officials paid to the immigration process, coupled with the American government's view of Japan as an emerging major power, elevated many regionally based controversies and issues, such as the San Francisco school board's 1906 decision to segregate Japanese schoolchildren, to major areas of negotiation and contention between the two countries (see SEGREGATION OF JAPANESE SCHOOLCHILDREN IN THE UNITED STATES).

The Evacuation during World War II —— The World War II incarceration of 120,000 Japanese Americans from the Pacific Coast to American concentration camps (see JAPANESE AMERICANS, WARTIME RELOCATION OF) is the most tragic event in Japanese American history. The roots of what has been called "America's worst wartime mistake" reach back to decades of anti-Japanese hatred and agitation in the western states and most profoundly to the bombing of Pearl Harbor. Numerous works have been written about its causes, chronological sequence, and broader societal consequences, but there has been less research on its immediate and enduring impact on Japanese Americans. It is evident that the evacuation had profound effects on Japanese Americans as a group and as individuals.

Existing research, for example, indicates that the evacuation had an all-encompassing economic impact on Japanese Americans involving not only personal loss of property, income, and savings, but also the destruction of a viable ethnically based economy. In recent years, scholars have challenged the US Federal Reserve Bank's oft-cited figure of $400 million in property losses as being a misleading underestimate and have argued that total economic losses were at least 3 or 4 times greater. Other studies have shown that the evacuation served to disperse a sizable proportion of the Japanese American population to cities in the Midwest and East Coast, where few Japanese Americans had resided before the war; destroy a number

of previously existing Japanese American communities such as the fishing village on Terminal Island in Southern California; and cause various forms of social disorganization for the Japanese American family unit in adapting to the abnormal situation of life in concentration camps. Other writers have argued that the wartime incarceration permanently altered the structure and goals of Japanese American organizational life and leadership by hastening the generational transition of community leadership from the *issei* to the *nisei*. And finally, many scholars have argued that the incarceration had immediate and enduring psychological consequences for Japanese Americans, which parallel those observed among survivors of other major tragedies and disasters.

In 1980 a US presidential fact-finding commission finally was established to investigate the causes and consequences of the wartime incarceration on Japanese Americans and to recommend appropriate remedies and compensation.

Japanese American Organizations —— Japanese Americans have had many and diverse organizations during their history in the United States. Beginning with the founding in 1877 of the Japanese Gospel Society of San Francisco, an *issei* Christian and English-language study group, Japanese Americans have formed an extensive network of organizations to advance their economic, social, religious, cultural, and political goals. These organizations have varied in terms of their exclusiveness of membership and specificity of goals to particular generations and social classes of the Japanese American community and in terms of their importance at specific times. *Kenjinkai,* for instance, were founded by *issei* from a particular *ken* or prefecture in Japan and provided many social services for the early immigrants. Although *kenjinkai* still exist, their members are largely elder *issei, kibei* (*nisei* who have returned to the United States after a period of residence and sometimes education in Japan), and recent immigrants. Japanese American religious institutions, Protestant, Buddhist, Shintō, or Catholic, have members from all generations and social classes and have been the most long-standing organized units in the community.

Most Japanese American organizations are rarely visible to outside observers because their activities and memberships are largely confined to the ethnic community. It is only on rare occasions, such as during Los Angeles' annual Nisei Week festival, that some groups engage in outside promotion. Other organizations, such as the JAPANESE AMERICAN CITIZENS LEAGUE (JACL) and the Japanese American Bar Association, actively participate in issues external to the community. Like other American immigrant groups, Japanese American organizations reflect an ever-changing diversity of orientations and relationships with institutions of American society as well as of Japanese society. Although greatly misunderstood and under attack during periods of intense anti-Japanese activity, there have been and continue to be many groups like the prewar Japanese Associations, Buddhist Churches of America, as well as cultural, martial arts, and fine arts organizations which have had ties with affiliates in Japan. There have been numerous chapters of major American organizations such as the American Legion, Democratic and Republican parties, and Optimists which are predominantly Japanese American and participate in the affairs of their parent groups. Finally, since the late 1960s, a number of organizations with many Japanese American members have been founded on the concept of Asian American, reflecting the commonality of experiences, concerns, and goals of all Asian ethnic minorities in America and the desire to seek collective remedies. The Asian American concept has its roots in the Asian American student movement of the late 1960s and 1970s, which featured substantial participation by college-age *sansei* and is now embraced by other sectors of the Japanese American community.

Although diversity characterizes Japanese American organizational life, there are two groups which deserve special attention because of their significance during crucial periods in Japanese American history. During the pre–World War II era, the JAPANESE ASSOCIATIONS OF AMERICA were clearly the most important and multifunctional group in the Japanese American community. Founded beginning at the end of the 19th century, they "assisted new arrivals through immigration stations, fought the exclusion movement, promoted social and educational programs, and depending on the locale, even promoted economic functions" (Ichioka, see Bibliography). Local associations were established at all major Japanese immigrant settlements, and these locals were formally linked to larger coordinating bodies like the Japanese Association of America, which encompassed chapters in California, Nevada, Utah, Colorado, and Arizona. Attacked as a "government within a government," the associations maintained varying degrees of relationship with local Japanese consulates and the Japanese government during their existence. In 1909–26, for instance, they were delegated the "endorsement right" of certifying that an immigrant was a bona-fide resident of the United States in accordance with the Gentlemen's Agreement and various Japanese laws. These associations were not controlled by the Japanese government. The other group, the Japanese American Citizens League, was founded in 1930 by *nisei* along the Pacific Coast, and came to prominence during and after World War II. Its initial goals were to represent the special interests of American-born Japanese Americans, and to expand the participation and acceptance of Japanese Americans in American life. Although the accommodationist orientation of its leadership has been continuously criticized, especially in relation to the wartime incarceration, the organization has had a number of legislative successes during its existence. During the postwar period, for example, it played a major role in overturning prewar, anti-Japanese laws and statutes. In 1982 the organization had over 30,000 members and local chapters in all parts of the mainland. In recent years, *sansei* have begun to occupy leadership positions in the group.

Military Service——The involvement of Japanese Americans, especially *nisei*, in America's military ventures during the 20th century has received wide notoriety. This is due, in large part, to the exploits of the 442ND REGIMENTAL COMBAT TEAM and the 100th Battalion, all-*nisei* fighting units formed during World War II. Guided by their motto, "Go for Broke," they became America's most decorated military units during the war and gained substantial recognition and publicity for their heroics. Like other racially segregated American combat teams during the war, they sought to demonstrate their loyalty and patriotism to America and to gain the equality of opportunity and treatment that had been denied to their groups. During World War II, close to 30,000 Japanese Americans served in the American armed forces. Over 6,000 were trained in Japanese and other Asian languages at the Military Intelligence Service Language School in Minnesota, and served as translators, interpreters, and interrogators in the Pacific War.

Japanese Americans in Japan——There are an estimated 10,000 Japanese Americans, primarily *nisei*, who reside and work in Japan. Many are involved in some area of United States–Japan relations—trade activities, defense and intelligence work, or journalism—and use their bilingual and bicultural backgrounds and skills to sustain ties between the two countries. Although most remain anonymous, some, like interpreter Sen Nishiyama, former baseball great Wally Yonamine, and diplomat Henry Shimanouchi (an *issei* raised and educated in California), have become prominent in Japanese society. They reside in all parts of Tōkyō and throughout Japan and hardly constitute a visible community in Japan, but they maintain informal networks of communication through various social gatherings and organizations.

Japanese Americans in Japan are products of several major waves of migration from the United States. The largest group is composed of *nisei* who returned with or were sent by their *issei* parents during the 1920s and 1930s to receive a Japanese education. Most left the United States at an early age and returned to their parents' native villages. Many returned to Hiroshima and became victims of the atomic bombing. Although the number of *nisei* killed is not known, over 500 *nisei hibakusha* (survivors) returned to the United States after the war. A second wave of *nisei* went to Japan during the 1930s after receiving an American education and, in many cases, a college degree. Most went to Japan to seek greater opportunities than could be found in the racially discriminatory climate of the Pacific Coast. Iva Toguri D'Aquino, who was later singled out and wrongfully tried as TŌKYŌ ROSE, was one of the *nisei* who went to Japan during this period. During the war, these *nisei* were closely watched by local Japanese police and were compelled in some cases to perform translating and interpreting tasks for the Japanese military. The final major wave of migration occurred during the Allied Occupation. An estimated 10,000 Japanese American military and civilian personnel went to Japan to aid in the reconstruction. Most were graduates of the Military Intelligence Service Language School and served as interpreters and intermediaries between American and Japanese officials. A small group of *nisei* entrepeneurs also went to Japan and started businesses such as Tōkyō's American Pharmacy and the American Potato Chip Company. At the same time, there were an estimated 5,000 *issei* and *nisei* repatriates from the TULE LAKE RELOCATION CENTER who decided to return to Japan. In recent years, many *sansei* have traveled to Japan to receive language training as

well as to work with American corporations in Japan.

Political Involvement——Japanese Americans have been greatly affected by American domestic politics, as well as the bilateral relations between Japan and the United States. Indeed, much has been written about the effects of external political decisions, groups, and individuals on Japanese Americans. However, Japanese Americans of various ideological persuasions have participated in a variety of political issues and activities throughout their history. What is commonplace in Hawaii, namely the election of Japanese Americans to public office, has become less than a surprising novelty in the mainland states with the election and appointment of many Japanese Americans to federal, state, and local positions. In 1980, for example, California had one US senator, two US congressmen, two state assemblymen, over 30 elected city officials, and close to 20 judges who were Japanese Americans.

The political history of Japanese Americans differs from that of other American immigrant groups because of *issei* disenfranchisement. Since *issei* were ineligible for citizenship, they could not vote and therefore could not use electoral politics for advancing their goals like other immigrant groups. Instead, they had to resort to alternative strategies such as legal advocacy, public relations, and appeals to the Japanese government to seek remedies for their situation. During the prewar period, the JACL and other Japanese American groups launched voter registration drives aimed at increasing the political awareness and participation of American-born Japanese Americans in American electoral politics. Clarence Arai, a major JACL leader in Seattle, and Karl Yoneda, a leading San Francisco communist, both ran for local offices in the early 1930s, and were the first Japanese Americans along the Pacific Coast to seek elected positions. However, it was not until the late 1960s that Japanese Americans in the mainland states won elected offices, and began to organize a number of Democratic and Republican party organizations.

Cultural Change and Adaptation——The migration of Japanese to the United States has involved more than a movement of people. Like other American immigrant groups, Japanese immigrants carried with them a unique set of cultural baggage, which contained values, beliefs, traditions, behavioral practices, culinary arts, and other elements of the homeland they left. Although a good deal of serious, as well as jingoistic, commentary has attempted to demonstrate the maintenance of these cultural characteristics, especially those of the Meiji period (1868–1912), there is also much research which has tried to show that Japanese Americans have forsaken their Japanese heritage and have become fully acculturated to American lifestyles and values. Often these two perspectives are combined in a broadly longitudinal analysis, in which each succeeding generation of Japanese Americans is viewed as becoming less Japanese and more American. At the same time, there is much evidence to suggest that Japanese Americans, like other American immigrant groups, have developed a unique ethnic culture and social system, which shares ingredients from both their American and Japanese heritages and experiences, and yet is different from both.

Current Issues of Japanese Americans——In recent years Japanese Americans have been described as a "model minority" that other disadvantaged American racial groups ought to emulate to gain parity and equity in American society. Although this designation is laudatory, it is misleading and unwarranted. It masks the persistence of racial discrimination and prejudice faced by Japanese Americans, especially in employment, and overlooks many unresolved social issues facing the group. On the average, Japanese Americans still make less money than white Americans with the same educational background, and there is still a significant paucity of Japanese Americans who have attained major managerial and decision-making positions in American business and political circles.

Many major social issues confront Japanese Americans in the 1980s. The most controversial one deals with whether Japanese Americans should gain redress and reparations for their World War II incarceration. Other issues include providing adequate housing and social services for an increasingly large elderly population consisting of *issei* and *nisei;* planning redevelopment projects in traditional Japanese American communities, and determining the role of Japanese multinational corporations in those projects; providing for the special needs of a growing postwar immigrant sector among the Japanese American population; and increasing the political representation of Japanese Americans in local and national governments.

📖——Roger Daniels, *The Politics of Prejudice* (1968). Audrie Girdner and Anne Loftis, *The Great Betrayal* (1969). Yamato Ichihashi, *The Japanese in the United States* (1932). Yuji Ichioka, "Japanese Associations and the Japanese Government: A Special Relationship, 1909–1926," *Pacific Historical Review* (1977). Yuji Ichioka, "The Early Japanese Immigrant Quest for Citizenship: The Background of the 1922 Ozawa Case," *Amerasia Journal* (1977). Yuji Ichioka, *"Amerika Nadeshiko:* Japanese Immigrant Women in the United States, 1900–1924," *Pacific Historical Review* (1980). Itō Kazuo, *Hokubei hyakunen-zakura* (1972; tr *Issei*, 1973). Harry Kitano, *Japanese Americans* (1976). Toshio Mori, *The Chauvinist* (1979). Jacobus ten Broek et al, *Prejudice, War and the Constitution* (1954). Michi Weglyn, *Years of Infamy* (1976).

Don T. NAKANISHI

Japanese Americans in Hawaii

Japanese immigrants to Hawaii and their American descendants. In 1970 the 217,000 residents of Japanese ancestry made up 28 percent of Hawaii's total population and 37 percent of the Japanese American population of the entire United States. Japanese immigrants *(issei)* came to Hawaii in the Meiji (1868–1912) and Taishō (1912–26) periods, primarily to work on Hawaii's sugar plantations. Their American-born children *(nisei),* grandchildren *(sansei),* and great-grandchildren (*yonsei,* or fourth generation) now form the great majority, over 90 percent, of Hawaii's Japanese American population, and are widely distributed in the state's occupational structure and body politic. Like JAPANESE AMERICANS on the West Coast, Hawaii's Japanese experienced, although less traumatically, the difficulties of World War II, but are now an integral part of Hawaii's multiracial society.

History of Japanese Immigration—— The first Japanese to reach Hawaiian shores were a few migrants, shipwrecked fishermen picked up by American whalers or other foreign vessels. The first sponsored immigrants were 148 laborers who responded in 1868 to a work offer by American and European sugar planters and the Hawaiian government. It was not until 1885, however, that sustained immigration began with a formal immigration agreement between Japan and the Kingdom of Hawaii. Over 85,000 Japanese, most of them men, arrived in Hawaii in the following 15 years and, although some returned to Japan after expiration of their three-year indenture contracts, many remained. In 1900 the remaining 61,000 Japanese constituted 40 percent of the total population of Hawaii, by then an annexed territory of the United States. They were not only the numerical mainstay of the plantation labor forces, which also included other groups like the Chinese and the Portuguese, but had also become the single largest ethnic group in the islands.

Plantation agriculture continued to expand, and Japanese workers came to Hawaii freely as immigrants until 1907; some 71,000 had come by that year, including workers from Okinawa as well as from the earlier major sources of Hiroshima, Yamaguchi, and Kumamoto prefectures. A sizable proportion of these newcomers, however, moved on to California and other areas of the West Coast. A congressional act in 1907 prohibited Japanese aliens from entering the continental United States from Hawaii, and the GENTLEMEN'S AGREEMENT of 1907–08 between Japan and the United States effectively cut off new laborer immigration to the United States, including Hawaii.

Between 1908 and 1924, the year of the immigration act that virtually ended all immigration to the United States from Japan, about 61,000 Japanese disembarked in Hawaii (see UNITED STATES IMMIGRATION ACTS OF 1924, 1952, AND 1965). During this period only former residents and parents, wives, and children of residents were permitted to immigrate to the United States. For the first time since the beginning of migration to Hawaii, the newcomers included as many females as males. Among the incoming women were about 15,000 PICTURE BRIDES, women affianced through the mail, and, from about 1910 on, the population increase among the Japanese was mainly a result of high birth and low mortality rates rather than an excess of new arrivals over departures. By 1924 nearly 220,000 Japanese in all had arrived in Hawaii and about 150,000 had left, either to return to Japan or to move on to the continental United States.

By 1940, a year before war broke out between Japan and the United States, there were nearly equal numbers of males and females in the Japanese American population, and there were already more than three times as many Japanese American citizens born in Hawaii as there were immigrant Japanese, although the average age of the former group was only 16. The 1940 Japanese-ancestry population of 185,000 made up 37 percent of Hawaii's people. They were low in social status but continued to have the largest population of any single ethnic group in the islands.

Occupational Trends and Economic Standing—— The occupational experience of the Japanese has closely paralleled that of most immigrant groups that settled in Hawaii in the period of economic predominance of plantation agriculture. For 20 or 30 years the Japanese, primarily laborers, provided the majority of the work force for sugarcane cultivation. Only a limited degree of occupational mobility was possible on the plantations for these immigrants, but there were opportunities outside the plantation for the more enterprising in small-scale businesses, farming, fishing, and the skilled and semiskilled trades.

With the coming of age of the *nisei* and *sansei* citizens, the Japanese began entering professional fields and were able to enjoy a higher standard of living. In the 1970s the average family income of the Japanese American households was roughly equal to that of Chinese, Korean, and nonmilitary Caucasian households. Relative to their labor force, the proportion of Japanese in the prestigious professions of medicine and law was almost equal to or slightly less than that of the Chinese, Koreans, and Caucasians. In general, their relatively large numbers and high level of educational attainment have permitted them wider-ranging activity in the white-collar, technical, and professional fields. The category of "laborer" has virtually disappeared from the list of occupations for the Japanese Americans but they are still heavily represented among skilled craftsmen such as masons, mechanics, machinists, and carpenters.

Political Participation—— The native Hawaiian government in the 1880s, heavily influenced by American residents, excluded Japanese as well as Chinese settlers from obtaining citizenship and thus from direct participation in political affairs and government employment. Disenfranchisement continued for these Asian-born people after Hawaii became a part of the United States, with the American legal definition of Asian immigrants as persons ineligible for citizenship remaining in effect until after World War II. Their Hawaiian-born children, however, were citizens by birth and in time were to participate in voting, running for public office, and seeking government employment. In the period just before World War II, there was only a handful of Japanese in the local legislature or in positions of responsibility in local governments. But in 1978, about half of the elected legislators were *nisei* and *sansei;* the governor was a *nisei,* and two of Hawaii's four members of Congress were *nisei.* Increasing numbers of local government positions in the executive and judiciary branches occupied by Japanese Americans also reflected this electoral strength and greater participation in public affairs.

Full participation in the community for Japanese Americans came less easily than for any of the other major ethnic groups in Hawaii. When the Japanese sugar-plantation workers struck for higher pay in 1909, 1920, and again in 1924, they were considered threats to management labor-control policies. Attempts by important elements of the dominant English-speaking Caucasian community to regulate and eventually eliminate the Japanese language schools of Hawaii in the 1920s culminated in a United States Supreme Court decision declaring such restrictions unconstitutional. The successful resistance of a vociferous segment of the Japanese community leadership during this incident widened the breach between the Japanese and dominant Caucasian communities in particular. The unusual and sensational kidnap-murder in 1928 of the young son of a prominent Caucasian family by a disturbed young *nisei* further aggravated the relationship between the Japanese and the Caucasians. The dual citizenship status of *nisei* born before 1924 raised the question of their political loyalty in the event of a crisis.

A further problem was posed by deteriorating relations between the United States and Japan in the 1920s and the 1930s, a situation that brought attention to the existence of a large Japanese population in a vital outpost of the American military. Nevertheless, despite Hawaii's strategic importance, only about a thousand Japanese, nearly all *issei,* were shipped to mainland internment centers in contrast to the wholesale relocation of Japanese and Japanese Americans from the West Coast. The status of the *nisei* as Americans of Japanese parentage prevented them from being conscripted or permitted to join the armed services until 1943, when they were permitted to volunteer for a special segregated combat team. This unit subsequently fought with great distinction in Europe (see 442ND REGIMENTAL COMBAT TEAM). Others served primarily in the Pacific as military interpreters.

Cultural Continuity and Change—— Some of the cultural traits that the immigrants brought to Hawaii have retained their vitality, while others have faded or lost their original functional and emotional meanings. Arranged marriages are things of the past, while funerals, for those other than Christians, still generally call for Buddhist rites. Elaborate New Year celebrations are definitely on the wane, but BON FESTIVALS appear to be as popular as ever.

At the time of large-scale Japanese immigration, mainly from rural areas, traditional arts such as flower arrangement and the tea ceremony were not very evident in Hawaii, but along with the martial arts, these skills have come to draw a considerable number of students, including non-Japanese, especially since World War II. Both the Japanese-language schools and the Japanese press, immigrant-established institutions of great importance up until the war, have survived, but with a decreasing sense of need. With a more tolerant, and even encouraging, attitude in the wider community, Japanese is now taught in many public and private high schools as well as at the University of Hawaii.

Traditional religion is now taken rather lightly by most Japanese Americans in Hawaii. There is no denying the comforting and educating role that Buddhist sects and, to a lesser extent, Shintō representatives have played in Hawaii, but the traditional Japanese sects did not so much cater to spiritual needs as to secular needs. The most vigorous religious movements involving Japanese followers appear to be the so-called NEW RELIGIONS, although the number of adherents is limited.

Thanks to the larger number of families in the immigrant generation after 1900, the Japanese community not only grew rapidly but also exercised effective social control over its members. Juvenile delinquency, adult crime rates, and other indices of social breakdown were usually lower than the community average. The second generation studied diligently in the public schools and continued their schooling after hours by learning Japanese, not always wholeheartedly, in language schools. They absorbed the strictures of parental emphasis on family cohesion and honor, married overwhelmingly within their own group (more recent figures indicate that about a third of the *sansei* marry non-Japanese), and in general strove to do well in Hawaii's occupational and social worlds.

It appears that groups with different ancestral backgrounds retain their ethnic identities and at the same time increasingly become "Hawaii's people." The one-third of Hawaii's civilian population who are Japanese American, whose adults are now mainly two and even three generations removed from their immigrant forebears, readily acknowledge their ancestry, although they are keenly aware of how much they are part of the American middle class or aspire to be a part of it. Among the Japanese in Hawaii today, relatively few speak Japanese or have been to Japan. Most Japanese Americans probably still have close-knit family ties, but not because, as may have previously been the case, they are constantly reminded that good Japanese respect their parents and do not bring shame to their families. They are proud of the aesthetic traditions of Japan and of the contributions of their immigrant ancestors in Hawaii. But like others in the islands, their identification with Hawaii as their home is foremost. See also JAPANESE AMERICANS, WARTIME RELOCATION OF.

📖 ——Hilary Conroy, *The Japanese Frontier in Hawaii, 1868–1898* (1953). Louise Hunter, *Buddhism in Hawaii, Its Impact on a Yankee Community* (1971). Andrew W. Lind, *Hawaii's Japanese, An Experiment in Democracy* (1946). Mitsugu Matsuda, *The Japanese in Hawaii: An Annotated Bibliography* (1975). Dennis M. Ogawa, *Kodomo no tame ni: For the Sake of the Children* (1978). William Petersen, *Japanese Americans* (1971).   *George K.* YAMAMOTO

Japanese Americans, wartime relocation of

The incarceration and relocation of the entire Japanese American population of the Pacific coastal area of the United States in 1942; now widely decried as the grossest domestic violation of civil liberties by the American government during World War II. More than two-thirds of the approximately 112,000 persons imprisoned were native-born citizens of the United States. This massive evacuation program should not be confused with the selective internment of several thousand *issei* (first generation JAPANESE AMERICANS) who, as community leaders and enemy aliens, were presumed to be dangerous.

Genesis of the Evacuation —— It is clear that the root cause of the evacuation, in addition to the fact that Japan and the United States were at war, was racial prejudice. Japanese immigrants to the United States, like other Asians who preceded and followed them, had been discriminated against by federal, state and local laws, and by custom as well. The most basic discrimination stemmed from the inequitable federal immigration and naturalization statutes, which made immigrants from Asia "aliens ineligible to citizenship." From this stemmed many other discriminations, including the infamous ALIEN LAND ACTS. *Nisei,* American-born children of Japanese immigrants, however, were citizens of the United States. Another reason for the evacuation was that, like so many of the immigrant groups in the United States, Japanese tended to cluster. By 1940, 112,353 or 88.5 percent of the Japanese population of the continental United States resided on the Pacific Coast where they comprised 1.2 percent of the population. The 157,905 Japanese residents of the Territory of Hawaii were not generally affected by the relocation process.

Apart from the aforementioned roundup of community leaders by the Federal Bureau of Investigation, the US government had contingency plans for mass incarceration of Japanese aliens or citizens. But immediately after the attack on Pearl Harbor on 7 December 1941, a public hue and cry began for some kind of confinement for all persons of Japanese ancestry. Quickly espoused by journalists, politicians, and other public figures and, fatefully, by some officials of the US Army and Navy, the growing demand that something be done about the Japanese became very insistent by early 1942. Most of the political leaders of the West Coast, including the entire congressional delegation from California, Oregon, and Washington, led the way and had the vocal support of Lieutenant General John L. De Witt, commander of the Western Defense Command. Behind-the-scenes maneuvering by Major General Allen W. Gullion, the army's provost marshal general, helped to gain the support of Secretary of War Henry L. Stimson and his deputy, John J. McCloy, who asked for and received from President Franklin Delano Roosevelt "carte blanche" to do whatever they wished with the West Coast Japanese, despite protests from Attorney General Francis Biddle, who opposed interfering with the liberties of citizens. On 19 February 1942 Roosevelt signed Executive Order 9066, which delegated authority to the secretary of war "to prescribe military areas . . . from which any or all persons may be excluded." The military authorities designated most of the Pacific Coast as such an area. The only persons actually excluded were those of Japanese birth or descent, although General De Witt had wanted to eventually evacuate German and Italian aliens as well. This latter project was aborted by presidential mandate: no white persons were made to suffer guilt by nativity. Congress, without a dissenting vote, passed legislation supporting the evacuation.

Evacuation and Relocation —— The actual rounding up of the West Coast Japanese was a model of bureaucratic order. The army set up a Wartime Civil Control Administration headed by Colonel Karl R. Bendetsen, Gullion's deputy, which divided the entire Pacific slope into 108 areas of unequal size but containing about 1,000 Japanese each. Beginning with Civilian Exclusion Order No. 1, dated 24 March 1942, which affected Japanese living on Bainbridge Island, Washington, near Seattle, Japanese were collected and taken to assembly centers set up in places like the fairgrounds at Puyallup, Washington, or racetracks like Tanforan outside San Francisco and Santa Anita outside Los Angeles. In many cases the evacuees were domiciled in quarters intended for livestock. Almost the entire Japanese American population complied with these orders without overt resistance. They were allowed to take with them into exile "only that which can be carried"; unlike most prisoners, they were ordered to furnish their own bed linen and eating utensils. Apart from untold psychic damage, the property losses of the West Coast Japanese were staggering for a recently established immigrant community. A conservative contemporary estimate by the Federal Reserve Bank of San Francisco put Japanese American property losses due to the evacuation at US $400 million. Between 1948 and 1965 some $38 million in compensation was paid under terms of the Japanese American Claims Act of 1948. This was less than 10 cents on the dollar without allowing for interest or the tremendous subsequent inflation.

The assembly centers were only a temporary stop for the evacuees; their ultimate destinations were relocation centers. These camps were run by a newly established civilian agency, the WAR RELOCATION AUTHORITY. Located in desolate parts of the United States, where no one has lived before or since, they were surrounded by barbed wire and guarded by troops. Terrible and desolate as they were, they must not be likened to either the extermination camps of the Nazis or the "Gulag Archipelago" of the Soviets. Treatment was generally humane, diet more than sufficient; births outnumbered deaths. And, almost from the start, there were ways to gain release from camp. Young citizens could leave to attend college. Individuals and families could at first receive furloughs to harvest sugar beets and other crops and later obtain leave clearance to resettle in the midwestern or eastern parts of the United States. In addition, Japanese American citizens of military age could enter the armed forces. At first this was done by enlistment, but eventually the draft was extended to those in relocation centers. It was in relation to the draft that the major "resistance" of the relocation occurred. About 10 percent of those ordered to report for induction into the armed forces refused and were tried, convicted, and sent to federal penitentiaries. Including some 1,200 young men who had been accepted as volunteers from various camps, about 10,000 Japanese Americans served in the military during World War II.

A few Japanese Americans challenged the evacuation process in a traditional American way by instituting legal proceedings contesting its constitutionality. Three of these suits eventually figured in major decisions of the Supreme Court of the United States. In *Hirabayashi* v. *US* (320 US 81), decided in 1943, the court unanimously upheld General De Witt's various preevacuation orders affecting the rights of Japanese American citizens. In *Korematsu* v. *US* (323 US 214), decided in December 1944, a court split 6-3 upheld the legality of the evacuation of US citizens of Japanese ancestry. (The government's right to move aliens had never been in dispute.) On the same day the court also ruled in *Ex parte Endo* (323 US 283) that once loyal Japanese American citizens had been evacuated, it was illegal for the War Relocation Authority to keep them imprisoned. Despite this, some Japanese remained in relocation centers until March 1946. Many citizens were minors who stayed with alien parents; others, though adult, remained with aged parents to whom the Caucasian world seemed threatening. As the camps closed, some inmates actually had to be forced to leave.

Aftermath —— The relocation remains one of the central facts of Japanese American life. For those who lived in Hawaii or outside the Pacific Coast, it was something that happened to someone else. For most of those who went to camp, it was an experience never to be forgotten, but one from which they made a successful readjustment. For a sizable minority, however, faith in the United States was destroyed by the experience and continued residence in the United States became intolerable. Shortly after the war 4,724 Japanese Americans were transported to Japan under government auspices as either repatriates or expatriates. Of these, 1,659 were aliens, 1,949 were American citizens accompanying repatriating parents, and 1,116 were adult *nisei*. Some in the last category were from the much larger number of *nisei*—5,766—who had formally renounced their American citizenship during incarceration. Most of these never emigrated to Japan, and federal courts eventually ruled that their renunciations had been made behind barbed wire under duress and hence were null and void.

During the war and immediately after, the official policy of the United States had been to encourage the Japanese Americans who remained in the United States to resettle permanently outside the Pacific Coast area and thus break up the typical immigrant cluster pattern and thereby lessen tensions. While Japanese Americans are now more dispersed than before the war, the 1970 census showed that 69 percent of the Japanese in the continental United States still lived on the Pacific Coast, where they comprised nine-tenths of one percent of the population.

In the postwar era legal discriminations against Japanese and other Asians quickly disappeared from the statute books, culminating in the Immigration Act of 1952, which established immigration quotas for Asian immigrants and made Asians eligible for naturalization on the same basis as other aliens (see UNITED STATES IMMIGRATION ACTS OF 1924, 1952, AND 1965). Finally, on 19 February 1976, on the 34th anniversary of Roosevelt's order which made the evacuation possible, President Gerald R. Ford formally declared: "We know now what we should have known then—not only was the evacuation wrong, but Japanese Americans were and are loyal Americans." See also articles on individual relocation centers: AMACHE; GILA RIVER; HEART MOUNTAIN; JEROME; MANZANAR; MINIDOKA; POSTON; ROHWER; TOPAZ; TULE LAKE.

📖 ——Roger Daniels, *Concentration Camps, USA: Japanese Americans and World War II* (1971). Roger Daniels, *The Decision to Relocate the Japanese Americans* (1975). Morton Grodzins, *Americans Betrayed: Politics and the Japanese Evacuation* (1949). Dillon S. Myer, *Uprooted Americans: Japanese Americans and the War Relocation Authority during World War II* (1971). Edward H. Spicer et al, *Impounded People* (1969). Jacobus ten Broek et al, *War, Prejudice and the Constitution* (1954). Dorothy S. Thomas, *The Salvage* (1952). Dorothy S. Thomas and Richard S. Nishimoto, *The Spoilage* (1946). *Roger DANIELS*

Japanese and the Altaic languages

Altaic is the designation for a large and important family of genetically related languages. Its principal subbranches consist of Turkic, Mongolian, and Tungusic, each of these divisions in turn embracing many different but related languages. The Altaic elements that may be traced in Japanese show important isoglosses (clusters of similar linguistic features) that are respectively shared with both the Turkic and Tungusic languages. Features relating Japanese to Mongolian are less evident, though present. In particular, elements of Japanese that may be shown to be of Altaic origin are the number system, the pronouns and interrogatives, and a major portion of the verb and adjective morphology, especially the Japanese verb stem suffixes.

The distinction of first having undertaken to demonstrate the genetic relationship of Japanese to the Altaic languages belongs to the Viennese scholar Anton Boller. His 1857 monograph treated the question in terms of a relationship to Ural-Altaic, a broader grouping of languages than Altaic proper as recognized today, but his pioneering treatment of the question nevertheless remains a milestone in Japanese historical linguistics. Progress in refining Boller's thesis has been intermittent, but from the late 1950s on, thanks largely to the work of N. N. Poppe in reconstructing the prehistory of the Altaic languages, Altaic linguistic studies began to enjoy something of a revival. As a result the relationship of Japanese to Altaic has become increasingly clear, especially from the mid-1970s on.

Virtually all new research on Altaic-Japanese relations has been done by non-Japanese scholars working in Europe and America. Two exceptions are Murayama Shichirō and Ozawa Shigeo, both of whom have made important contributions. Apart from the work of these men, Japanese scholarship has generally maintained a rigidly negative approach to this problem, taking positions that range from nihilism ("nothing is known about this") to defeatism ("nothing can ever be learned about this").

There are no written records of the original linguistic medium used by the Altaic peoples in their Central Asian homeland around the first or second millennium BC. However, this ancient protolanguage, which we call proto-Altaic, has been painstakingly reconstructed in many of its important details by several scholars. Earlier written records for the Altaic languages include the Old Turkish of the Orxon inscriptions of about 720, the Middle Mongolian of the *Secret History of the Mongols*, and the early records of the Manchu founders of the Qing (Ch'ing) dynasty (1644–1912) in China.

The original homeland of the Altaic speakers was most likely located somewhere in the Trans-Caspian steppes. Sometime in the first half of the second millennium BC they began to migrate eastward, still maintaining a unified linguistic group *(Spracheinheit),* and eventually reached a site on the Central Asiatic steppes. From this second or Central Asiatic Altaic homeland, the Altaic linguistic community subsequently split up with various subgroups of the original community moving away from the main body. Ancestors of the Tungusic speakers appear to have been the first of the subgroups to break away, migrating into northeast Asia, where they brought the Altaic languages into geographical proximity with the Korean peninsula and Japanese islands. Turkic migrations away from the homeland took place later, probably not before the Chinese destroyed the empire of the Huns in the Han dynasty (206 BC–AD 220).

The presence in Japanese of important isoglosses with both Turkic and Tungusic, therefore, suggests the existence of proto-Japanese elements in the Altaic linguistic unity in the second Altaic homeland before the earliest movements away from this community by the proto-Tungusic speakers. The many points of formal and semantic detail by means of which the Japanese verb corresponds to the formation of the verb in the Tungusic languages provide especially striking evidence for proto-Japanese membership in that part of the second Altaic homeland where these proto-Tungusic elements were located, prior to their early severance from the bulk of the original Altaic community.

As is the case in all language families, the internal history of the Altaic languages and their intrafamily relationships to one another are extensively complicated by the existence of many historical levels of linguistic loans, which resulted when words were "borrowed," or imitated back and forth, as a result of early contacts among these various languages. These borrowed forms must be distinguished from genetically related words, which are not imitated from one language to another but are instead later, changed forms of earlier common terms and inherited from the original linguistic unity, in this case from proto-Altaic. But such discrimination, particularly in the absence of early written records, is not always easy. Still, there is little question but that Japanese has its full share of such early loans from Altaic, some of them entering the language as late as the Kofun period (ca AD 300–710); but these forms are over and above the Japanese inherited stock of words (lexicon), word formations (morphology), and syntactic patterns that are genetically inherited from proto-Altaic.

Comparative Method—— At the heart of the comparative method lies the technique of establishing regular phonological correspondences between words of identical or closely related meanings in the different languages studied; each such correspondence ("sound law," *Lautgesetz*) provides evidence for an original phoneme (distinctive sound) in the earlier proto-language to which all the languages being studied are related by reason of being later, changed forms of that original proto-language (in this case, proto-Altaic, or PA). Each of these sound laws also permits the "reconstruction" or recovery of a phoneme in the proto-language; in this way the historical linguist is able to reconstruct forms and even words from the now lost proto-language, even though it has no written records. (These reconstructed items the linguist indicates with the symbol *, in order to distinguish them from data actually attested in written records.) Application of this technique of linguistic comparison and reconstruction based upon it to Japanese and the other Altaic languages has now made it possible to establish an impressive number of rigorous correspondences between Japanese and the other Altaic languages; it also shows us, at least in broad outline, just what the phonological entities were that Japanese inherited from its Altaic original, despite the enormous distances of time and space that separate the two.

In some words, comparative work shows that certain original Altaic phonemes have come down to Japanese with relatively little change, while others were much altered in the process. But this is hardly surprising, since the time span between proto-Altaic and Japanese must be measured in millennia. In a word like the Japanese verb *kir-u* "cut," for example, neither the form as we have it today, nor even the form that we find in written records for Old Japanese *(kĭr-)* are very different from what we can reconstruct as the original Altaic form for this word, PA *kir-*, which also meant "cut." The same Altaic verb also appears, with only minor changes, in such other languages as Turkic *qïr-q-* "scrape," Mongolian *kirga-* "clip, shear," and Manchu *giri-* "cut." Similarly closely resembling its proto-Altaic original is Japanese *shiri* "buttocks, rear end," only slightly changed from PA *sili* "rear, behind," which also may be traced in the historically related (cognate) words Mongolian *šili* "nape, back of the neck," and Evenki *sil* "back of the head." PA *sïgür* "snowstorm or rain in cold season of year" changed only slightly to give Japanese *shigure* "intermittent drizzle in autumn or winter," as well as Mongolian *šiyurgan* "snowstorm," and Evenki *sigir* "rain with wind, a storm." But in a word like PA *bēl* "midsection of the human body" we see more complicated changes: its initial *b-* eventually changed into modern Japanese *h-*, its vowel to *-a-*, and its final *-l* to *-r-*, to which Japanese then added another, final *-a* (since no Japanese word ended in a consonant like *r*), eventually to result in modern Japanese *hara* "stomach, womb." Meanwhile, other changes in other parts of the original Altaic linguistic unity brought into being such cognate words as Korean *pä* "stomach," Old Turkish *bäl* "waist," and Mongolian *bel* "waist," each slightly different in form and meaning, but each nevertheless going back to the same original. Sometimes the changes between PA and Japanese are so great that they almost obscure the relationship of the words involved; this is particularly true when one or more original Altaic phoneme has changed by completely dropping out (shift to zero). This is what happened in the word PA *pūtü* "hole, opening," which became Old Japanese *Fotö* "vulva," as well as Ryūkyū *hoo* and Korean *pōci*, which mean the same thing, while in Uighur Turkish, where the *p-* changed to zero, the word became *üt* "opening, passage through something," as also in Mongolian *ütügün*, where the meaning is again "vulva." Proto-Altaic *d-* originally changed to *y-* in Japanese (a similar change also took place in Turkic); but in Japanese words with the vowel *-i-*, this secondary *y-* then disappeared, leaving only the vowel. These changes help explain the relationship between words that otherwise might appear to be so very different in form that we might not even suspect that they are related to one another, as for example Old Japanese *irö* "color, facial appearance," which may be demonstrated to be cognate with Old Turkish *jüz* "face," Mongolian *düri* "appearance, form" and Manchu *durun* "form, shape, figure"; the original word of which all these are later, changed forms was PA *dür₂i* "face, appearance."

The last reconstruction cited above contains an Altaic phoneme written *r₂*, which was one of a set of four original proto-Altaic sounds of particularly great importance not only for the history of the Altaic languages in general, but also for tracing the Altaic relationship to Japanese. This is because the developments of these four phonemes, generally written *r₂*, *l₂*, *r*, and *l*, in the various Altaic languages involve complicated sound changes of a type that cannot possibly have resulted from borrowing, and are most unlikely to have come about simply through coincidence. The first two of these phonemes were special kinds of *l*- and *r*-like sounds in the original Altaic language, where however they were significantly different from the last two, which remain unchanged as *r* and *l* in the later languages (except in Japanese and Korean, where both appear as a single phoneme, Japanese *r*, Korean *l*). We do not know just how *r₂* and *l₂* were pronounced in the Altaic homeland, or just how they were different from *r* and *l*; but we do know that the original phoneme that we write *l₂* changed to become *l* in most of the Altaic languages, including Mongolian and Tungusic, but at the same time changed differently, to become *š* in the Turkic languages, except for the Turkic language known as Chuvash (still spoken in the USSR); in Chuvash, this sound also became *l*. Furthermore, we now understand that this same Altaic *l₂* also became Japanese *s*, in a historical development that closely paralleled its course of change in the Turkic languages apart from Chuvash. This important discovery has clarified, for example, the historical relationship (etymology) of such a word as Japanese *ishi* "stone," which goes back to Old Japanese *isi*, itself a slightly changed form of a still earlier *yisi*. These Japanese forms may now be directly related to PA *tʲāl₂* "stone," which also changed into such other words as Old Turkish *taš*, Chuvash *čul*, and Korean *tol*, all of which mean "stone." Thus, the comparative method not only supplies us with convincing evidence for the genetic relationship of Japanese to the other Altaic languages, but it also provides us with etymologies for many Japanese words for the first time.

Working along parallel lines, it has been established that Altaic *r₂*, which became *r* in most languages, including Chuvash, but appears as Turkic *z*, had two developments in Japanese, one as *r*, as in Japanese *iro* from *dür₂i* cited above, the other as *t*, illustrated by PA *ñār₂* "warm season of the year," which changed into Old Turkish *jaz* "spring," Chuvash *śur* "summer," Mongolian *nirai* "new-born," and Manchu *niyarhun* "fresh," but gave Japanese *natsu* and Korean *yölüm*, both meaning "summer." These two different Japanese developments for Altaic *r₂* are regular and predictable depending upon the syllabic environment of the phoneme in the original Altaic forms. Again, the order and regularity of such examples enhance the overall value, as historical evidence, of the words in which these critical phonemes appear.

Once the comparative phonology that relates Japanese to the other Altaic languages has been established in this fashion, it is relatively simple to demonstrate the Altaic origin of much of Japanese morphology, vocabulary, and syntax; unfortunately the space available does not permit many specific examples, and we can only note in passing the major grammatical categories involved.

Unlike Indo-European, the Altaic languages did not generally inherit most of their numbers from the original language; nevertheless, Altaic etymologies have been established for all the Japanese numbers except "three" and "six." A characteristic of the Altaic pronouns and interrogatives was the existence of distinct stem-forms for nominatives as against the oblique cases; this formal dichotomy has inherited parallels in Japanese and was still important in the earliest Old Japanese texts.

But it is in the morphology of the Japanese verb and adjective that the most important of the inherited Altaic grammatical elements in the language are to be found. Japanese transitive and intransitive verb pairs such as *tar-u* "be sufficient" and *tas-u* "fill up" have precise parallels, in both forms and meanings, in such Altaic sets as Old Turkish *tol-* and *toš-*, which has led to the discovery of the Altaic origin of such morphological distinctions in the Japanese verb. Most important of all are probably the suffixes used in Japanese to form secondary verb stems from noun and adjective roots. These are elements such as the *+k-* meaning "become" in *shirak-* "to become white," formed from the adjective base *shira* "white," or another suffix *+k-* meaning "do," as in *wanak-* "throttle," from the noun *wana* "a collar," or the *+g-* in *shirag-* "make something white," or the *+r-* in *takar-* "become high" from *taka* "high, height," or *kumor-* "cloud up," from *kumo* "cloud." All these and many other examples that might be cited of similar verb stem suffixes in Japanese have been inherited directly from proto-Altaic (e.g., with the first +k- suffix cited above, cf. PA *+k-, which also appears as +q- in Old Turkish *qaryq-* "become dark," from *qara* "dark, black").

Conclusions —— In view of the quantity and nature of the evidence, the persistent reluctance of most contemporary Japanese scholarship to recognize the importance of the relationship of Japanese to the other Altaic languages poses a curious problem; but essentially it is a nonlinguistic issue, in the sense that none of the reasons behind this continued reluctance relates directly either to the nature or to the substance of the Japanese language. As causes for this reluctance, one may identify several inhibiting factors that continue to limit much contemporary Japanese scholarship in this and related fields. The most serious of these is probably the continued unfamiliarity of Japanese academic circles with the techniques and implications of the comparative method of historical linguistics; apparently not enough time has passed since this method was first introduced into Japan for most Japanese scholars to have become at home in its principles. There is also the apparent difficulty in obtaining foreign books and other scientific publications, which has led to continued neglect, by Japanese scholars, of the bulk of the non-Japanese literature on this question. Until these two major limiting factors can be overcome, the study of the genetic relationship of Japanese to other languages, and in particular the study of the Altaic relationship of Japanese, must apparently continue to be one of the few areas in Japanese studies where the major contributions will be made outside Japan.

■ ——Anton Boller, "Nachweis, dass das Japanische zum uralaltaischen Stamme gehört," *Sitzungsberichte der philos.-histor. Classe der kais. Akademie der Wissenschaften, Wien* 23 (1857). Karl H. Menges, *Altajische Studien,* vol 2, *Japanisch und Altajisch* (Abhandlungen für die Kunde des Morgenlandes, 41.3; 1975). Roy Andrew Miller, *Japanese and the Other Altaic Languages* (1971). Roy Andrew Miller, "The Relevance of Historical Linguistics for Japanese Studies," *Journal of Japanese Studies* 2 (1976). Roy Andrew Miller, *Origins of the Japanese Language* (1980). Murayama Shichirō, "Nihongo no seiritsu," in Matsumura Akira, ed, *Kōza kokugoshi,* vol 1, *Kokugoshi sōron* (1977). Ozawa Shigeo, "Nihongo no keitō," in Kindaichi Haruhiko, ed, *Nihongo kōza,* vol 1, *Nihongo no sugata* (1976). Nikolaus Poppe, *Vergleichende Grammatik der altaischen Sprachen,* Teil 1, *Vergleichende Lautlehre* (Porta Linguarum Orientalium, ns, 4; 1960). G. J. Ramstedt and Pentti Aalto, ed, *Einführung in die altaische Sprachwissenschaft,* 3 vols (Suomalais-ugrilaisen Seuran Toimituksia, 104:1–3; 1952, 1957, 1966).

Roy Andrew Miller

Japanese and the Malayo-Polynesian languages

Malayo-Polynesian is a name used by linguists to identify a proto-language for which we have no written records and which has been reconstructed from contemporary languages that are historically ("genetically") related to it. This same language family has also often been called Austronesian. A surprisingly large number of languages, covering an enormous geographical expanse, has survived from this original Malayo-Polynesian linguistic unity. Today they extend from Taiwan to Easter Island and are found in such diverse places as Madagascar, the Philippines, and New Zealand. They include such languages as Indonesian, Tagalog, Hawaiian, and Tahitian. The major work in reconstructing proto-Malayo-Polynesian was originally done by the German linguist Otto Dempwolff. Later additions and revisions to the reconstruction have been made by Isidore Dyen (US) and Otto Christian Dahl (Norway). At present, comparative data from an impressive total of nearly 200 different but genetically related languages have been accounted for in these reconstructions.

In view of the pan-Pacific distribution of the surviving Malayo-Polynesian languages, it is hardly surprising that attempts should have been made to establish some kind of historical connection between this language family and Japanese. Matsumoto Nobuhiro in 1928 published an important study on the possibility of a Japanese relationship with Malayo-Polynesian. However, subsequent Japanese scholarship did not prove eager to follow up the promising leads that his pioneering work provided; Izui Hisanosuke, who worked on this question in the early 1950s, was for many years virtually the only Japanese scholar to take a serious interest in the problem.

Even earlier, the Soviet scholar E. D. Polivanov, in a series of papers published between 1918 and 1938, had begun to evolve the thesis that Japanese was a variety of "mixed language" and that it combined both Altaic and Malayo-Polynesian elements. Polivanov's suggestions were largely ignored for many years, until they were revived by Murayama Shichirō, who in 1968 began publishing important studies along these same directions.

Murayama has subsequently refined and elaborated the Polivanov hypothesis in an attempt to support it with more lexical evidence than Polivanov had at his command, both from Japanese and from a large number of the Malayo-Polynesian languages, including several languages from Taiwan that in Polivanov's day had not yet been identified as belonging to the Malayo-Polynesian family. Murayama's present view is that Japanese is, in the literal sense of the term, a "mixed language," formed both of Malayo-Polynesian and Altaic elements. The Japanese lexical stock, in his opinion, is particularly in debt to Malayo-Polynesian, while the major grammatical elements of the language (the verb morphology, in particular) he holds to be almost entirely Altaic.

Murayama's "mixed language" hypothesis has been criticized on theoretical grounds; one may very well argue that all languages are mixed (particularly because of the phenomenon of loanwords), while at the same time, linguistic science has yet to document any other true example of a "mixed language" in the precise sense in which Murayama is using the term. Probably the most satisfactory evaluation of the Murayama hypothesis at present is to recognize the presence of important Malayo-Polynesian elements in the pre-Japanese lexical stock and to interpret their role in the historical formation of the Japanese language as having been somehow analogous to the process generally known to linguists as creolization, if indeed those elements are more than simply an early stratum of loanwords resulting from ancient landings of Malayo-Polynesian-speaking wanderers in the Japanese archipelago.

Certainly there are elements in the Japanese vocabulary stock that cannot be explained historically by comparison with the other Altaic languages, and a few of these words may very well have originated through some variety of extremely remote historical contact with Malayo-Polynesian speakers. It would certainly be more satisfactory to explain, in this way, the sometimes striking similarities observed in forms and meanings between such words as proto-Malayo-Polynesian (PMP) *mata* "eye" and Old Japanese (OJ) ma-~mĕ, PMP *kaji* "tree, wood," and OJ kï, PMP *t'ut'u* "breasts" and OJ titi and PMP *i(m)pi* "to dream" and OJ imĕ, modern Japanese yume, rather than simply to ascribe these and other lexical parallels to chance.

In certain specialized areas of the vocabulary, particularly for words that have to do with marine life and types of flora for which the Altaic peoples were, by reason of their original geographical setting, most unlikely to have had specific terms, the discovery of likely Malayo-Polynesian etymologies for Japanese words occasions little surprise. In this category may be mentioned Japanese *ika* "cuttlefish," surely to be compared with PMP *ikan* "fish," or *hana* "flower," which has been compared with PMP *buŋa,* meaning the same thing. It has also been suggested that a number of isolated Old Japanese terms found in the early Fudoki texts and fragments, where they are identified as "popular" or "vulgar" words, may have resulted from ancient Malayo-Polynesian lexical contacts: notably OJ Fisi "sandbar," from PMP *pat'iy* "seashore," and OJ isa "whale," from PMP *it'i* "flesh, meat."

But whatever position historical linguistics eventually reaches on this question—and at present the issue is still open to much discussion and disagreement—there is no denying that Murayama's revival and reinvestigation of the fuller implications of the Polivanov hypothesis has brought a much needed impetus to this hitherto largely neglected aspect of Japanese historical linguistics and enhanced our present understanding of the genetic relationships of the Japanese language. See also JAPANESE LANGUAGE; JAPANESE AND THE ALTAIC LANGUAGES.

■ ——Otto Christian Dahl, *Proto-Austronesian* (2nd rev ed, 1976). Otto Dempwolff, *Vergleichende Lautlehre des austronesischen Wortschatzes* (Beiheft zur Zeitschrift für Eingeborenen-Sprachen, 15, 17, 19; 1934–38). Izui Hisanosuke, "Nihongo to nantō shogo," *Minzokugaku kenkyū* 17.2 (1952). N. Matsumoto, *Le japonais et les langues austro-asiatiques* (1928). Murayama Shichirō, "About the Origins of the Japanese Language," *Proceedings, VIIIth International Congress of Anthropological and Ethnological Sciences,* 3 (1968). Murayama Shichirō, *Nihongo no kigen* (1973). Murayama Shichirō, *Nihongo no gogen* (1974). Murayama Shichirō, *Nihongo no kenkyū hōhō* (1974). Murayama Shichirō, "The Malayo-Polynesian Component in the Japanese Language," *Journal of Japanese Studies* 2 (1976). Murayama Shichirō, *Nihongo kenkyū* (1976), which translates into Japanese the articles relating to Japanese in E. D. Polivanov, *Stati po obščemu jazykoznaniju* (1968).   *Roy Andrew* MILLER

Japanese as a foreign language

The study of Japanese as a foreign language is a subject of increasing interest around the world. The expansion of programs has been especially marked since the 1970s, as Japan emerged as one of the world's major economic powers. Japanese language study programs are now to be found in virtually every country of the world.

The Pre–World War II Period——Prior to World War II, the study of Japanese as a foreign language outside Japan was almost unknown. A few major universities around the world offered limited opportunities that focused on the reading of Japanese—for the most part the translation of literary works and historical documents—but such study was regarded as esoteric in the extreme. Diplomats and missionaries with a work-related interest in learning Japanese usually satisfied this need by studying in Japan. Even there, programs for teaching Japanese as a foreign language were extremely limited.

The World War II Period——With the outbreak of World War II, foreign language study in the United States took a tremendous leap. Huge language programs were organized by the military, enrolling thousands of military personnel. But more than size was involved in these new programs: under the auspices of the military establishment and with the cooperation of several American learned societies, a whole new approach to language study was launched, utilizing new analyses of hitherto uncommonly taught languages, based on the principles of modern linguistics and new pedagogical approaches. Instruction involved team teaching by native speakers of the target language along with trained linguists who were native speakers of the students' native language. New teaching materials were prepared, and full-time intensive programs were inaugurated as the quickest and most efficient way of beginning the study of a foreign language.

Japanese was one of the most important languages affected by this new approach. While some wartime programs followed a more traditional format, using prewar instructional materials and concentrating heavily on the written language, many others were launched under the new format, and for the first time, the study of modern spoken Japanese became the subject of scientific analysis and pedagogical concern. These programs included in their curricula the teaching of the four skills—speaking, listening, reading, and writing—but initial emphasis was placed on the oral skills.

An interesting phenomenon of this wartime Japanese language training in the United States was that the development and rapid expansion of the teaching of Japanese occurred at the very time when the study and use of English were being curtailed in Japan. Many individuals introduced to the language under military auspices became interested in Japan as a field of study, with the result that a high percentage of the next generation of recognized foreign scholars on Japan were graduates of intensive wartime programs.

The Post–World War II Period——The increase in the study of Japanese as a foreign language since World War II has reflected a number of different world developments. As Japan has emerged as a major economic power, the importance of the study of the language has become increasingly evident. Nowhere has this been more dramatically demonstrated than in Australia, where trade with Japan is of crucial economic importance. There the Japanese language is widely taught not only in universities and technical schools, but in high schools as well. In the late 1970s, Australia had the highest percentage of its population studying elementary Japanese of any nation in the world.

There has also been a tremendous increase in interest in Japanese literature, art, and philosophy throughout the world, and this, too, has been reflected in increased language study. Translations of Japanese literary works by foreign scholars are being published in steadily increasing numbers. Travel to Japan has also been responsible for encouraging a number of students to study Japanese, and the growing interest in national and racial heritage has also encouraged those whose ethnic background is Japanese to study the language. As interest has increased, programs have been inaugurated at an ever increasing number of universities around the world. It is now rare to find a nation where Japanese is not taught in at least one of its academic institutions. The methodologies employed in these world-wide programs are extremely varied, and predictably the quality also reflects a considerable range.

Through sheer number of programs, the United States probably reflects the greatest range, from the most traditional grammar-translation courses to programs experimenting with new techniques of foreign language instruction; from programs using untrained native speakers as instructors to those using Japanese and non-Japanese specialists in foreign language pedagogy, linguistics, and literature; from traditional three-hour a week courses to full-time intensive programs modeled after the wartime programs, at least in terms of maximally rapid language acquisition as the goal.

There have been a number of specific developments and trends in the teaching of Japanese since World War II that warrant special mention.

1. The field has expanded to the point where associations of Japanese language teachers have been formed in various countries around the world, including Japan. They hold annual meetings and publish professional journals. The United States-based Association of Teachers of Japanese alone had almost 500 members in 1980.

2. Developments in the field of linguistics have been reflected in the linguistic research into the Japanese language. Along with descriptivist studies that started in the World War II period, various new analyses that are based on new approaches in theoretical linguistics have appeared. Unfortunately, the results of such analyses reach the language classroom only in those cases in which the theoretical analyst is also involved in language pedagogy, or the instructor conscientiously avails himself of the results of such analyses.

3. There has been a marked increase in the number of native Japanese becoming language teachers after taking advanced degrees in Japanese linguistics and literature in universities outside Japan. These teachers constitute a sizable group of Japanese expatriates who return to Japan for visits but reside permanently abroad. At the same time there continues to be a significant number of non-Japanese, also holders of advanced degrees, who teach Japanese language, linguistics, and literature in educational institutions around the world.

4. With the increase in the worldwide interest in Japanese language studies, a number of native Japanese have been sent out from Japan as instructors, on temporary assignment, by agencies of the Japanese government. They are usually individuals who have previously taught Japanese as a foreign language in Japan or have taken training courses in Japan based on the methodologies most commonly used within Japan.

5. Among the less commonly taught foreign languages, Japanese ranks high as a language for which a wide variety of pedagogical materials has been prepared, for both the written and spoken language. These materials reflect a broad spectrum of approaches, innovativeness, and pedagogical sophistication. Many are accompanied by tape recordings, with newer formats experimenting with videotapes.

6. As communication between Japan and the outside world has increased, the motivation for study of the language has become markedly more diversified. Traditional courses that assumed primary interest in literary Japanese are no longer valid for all students. Diversified motivation is gradually being met at some institutions through the introduction of such courses as Japanese for business purposes and for lawyers, advanced courses in the spoken language, and courses in communicative competence.

7. With few exceptions, Japanese as a foreign language has traditionally been a subject found in colleges and universities. One notable exception has been the after-school private schools, offering Japanese principally to children of Japanese descent, in areas where there was a concentration of such residents. In these areas, Japanese was sometimes also offered within the high school foreign-language curriculum.

8. The surge of interest in bilingualism in the United States has had its effect on Japanese instruction. Programs at the elementary school level have been introduced at a few institutions.

9. A number of colleges and universities which do not offer Japanese on a regular basis have instituted programs in a self-instructional mode. Students in these programs study elementary Japanese through the use of textbooks and tape recordings, supplemented by several hours of drill each week with a native speaker resident in the area, who is not a trained teacher. Students' progress is checked periodically by professional Japanese language professors invited in as visiting examiners. Those students who are interested in pursuing their language study beyond the introductory level are

encouraged to enroll in intensive summer programs or transfer to institutions offering advanced courses within regular programs.

10. Japanese is the first Asian language for which an objective proficiency test was prepared by the Educational Testing Service in Princeton, New Jersey. The initial format, covering oral comprehension and reading, was first administered in 1979 to a sampling of 885 students throughout the United States.

Until recently, the foreigner in Japan who had competence in the language was regarded with amazement by the Japanese. Perhaps the clearest indication that significant progress is being made in the field of Japanese as a foreign language comes through the gradually but steadily decreasing reaction of surprise to foreigners' use of the Japanese language. However, further progress is sorely needed, particularly among the business community where foreign language competence has traditionally lagged. See also JAPANESE LANGUAGE.

Eleanor H. JORDEN

Japanese Associations of America

A general term for the major organizations of *issei*, first-generation JAPANESE AMERICANS, in the United States; a similar organization, the Canadian Japanese Association, existed in Canada. Starting in 1891, Japanese consular officials in San Francisco created a series of ephemeral organizations, the first of which was called the Greater Japanese Association; the last, dissolved in 1908, was called the Japanese Deliberative Council of America. In assuming special responsibilities for Japanese residents in the United States under the terms of the GENTLEMEN'S AGREEMENT of 1907–08, the Japanese government felt that it needed a more effective vehicle for social control. In February 1908 the Japanese Consulate General in San Francisco created the Japanese Association of America. This central body or "umbrella group" took directions from the Japanese Consul General and was run by well-to-do Japanese American businessmen. Its president from 1908 until his death in 1926 was George Shima (Ushijima Kinji), the "Potato King" of California. Below the central body were regional or local Japanese associations, for example, the Sacramento Valley Japanese Association and the Japanese Association of Berkeley. In theory all Japanese residents in the United States belonged to one of these lesser bodies, paying membership dues ranging from $1 to $3 per year. In practice, many Japanese residents never joined.

Both for its own bureaucratic convenience and to apply pressure on individual Japanese to join, the Japanese government gave the associations an official role and made them the intermediaries through which *issei* had to pass if they were to maintain official connections with the Japanese government. The Gentlemen's Agreement required *issei* to obtain certificates if they wished to leave the United States temporarily or if they wished to have wives, parents, children or other family members join them. Japanese law required that men of military age who had not discharged their military obligations register annually, and the government was willing to register marriages, divorces, births, and other vital statistics. Requisite documents were obtained through the associations, which charged fees for their services. These fees provided much if not most of the association revenue. The organizations also acted as spokesmen for the Japanese American community and had social functions as well. The abrogation of the Gentlemen's Agreement in 1924 lessened the importance of the associations, and in the late 1920s, their semiofficial functions were reassumed by the consulates. Although their importance was diminished, the associations continued to play important community roles until shortly after Pearl Harbor, when, with their leaders interned as enemy aliens and their funds frozen, they simply ceased to function. See JAPANESE AMERICANS, WARTIME RELOCATION OF.

The role of the Japanese associations has been misunderstood. Japanophobes insisted that they were a sinister "invisible government," part of the Mikado's plan to take over America; Japanese apologists insisted that they were simply immigrant self-help organizations. As semiofficial organs of the Japanese government, the associations were bureaucratic, not sinister. Their functions were dictated not by imperial ambition but rather by attempts to comply with an executive agreement between Japan and the United States. Nothing shows more clearly the nature of the associations than their support in 1919 and 1920 of the Japanese government's decision to stop issuing passports to PICTURE BRIDES, despite the wishes of most of the Japanese American community. As the historian Hilary Conroy pointed out in a different context, Japan's activities on behalf of its citizens abroad were motivated chiefly by the desire to protect its own "prestige as a nation"; the history of the Japanese associations is another demonstration of that perception. See also JAPANESE AMERICAN CITIZENS LEAGUE.

—— Roger Daniels, "The Japanese," in John Higham, ed, *Ethnic Leadership in America* (1978). Roger Daniels, ed, *Valentine Stuart McClatchy, Four Anti-Japanese Pamphlets* (1979). M. Fujita, "The Japanese Associations of America," *Sociology and Social Research* 14 (1929). Yamato Ichihashi, *Japanese in the United States* (1932). Yuji Ichioka, "Japanese Associations and the Japanese Government: A Special Relationship, 1909–1926," *Pacific Historical Review* (1977).

Roger DANIELS

Japanese beetle

(*manekogane*). *Popillia japonica*. A beetle of the order Coleoptera, f. Scarabaeidae. It measures 9 to 12 millimeters (0.4–0.5 in) in length. The body is oval and black tinged with a glossy copper green; the wings are brown with green edges. The adult beetle appears in late spring and feeds on the leaves of various plants such as soybean, *kunugi* (a kind of oak), roses, and grapes; the larva damages lawns and sapling roots. It takes from one to two years for an egg to develop into an adult. The beetle is indigenous to Japan, but its larvae apparently entered the United States in 1911 in the soil around bulbs of *hanashōbu* (a kind of iris). Several larvae were found in New Jersey in 1916 and they spread rapidly, feeding on soybeans and white potatoes (which they seldom damage in Japan) and becoming a major pest in some areas. In 1920 an American research station was established in Yokohama to discover a natural enemy for the beetle, but it was closed with the coming of World War II.

NAKANE Takehiko

Japanese business in America

The establishment of ongoing business operations through direct investment in the United States by firms having their headquarters in Japan.

Japanese companies have maintained active operations in the United States since at least 1879, when the trader Mitsui & Co opened its New York office. Following the break in activity during World War II, an ever-increasing number of large and small Japanese firms have established themselves in the United States to take advantage of a wide variety of perceived opportunities. Principal centers of Japanese business are New York, Los Angeles, San Francisco, Chicago, and Houston. The four basic categories of Japanese direct investment in the United States are service industries, basic resources, sales and distribution organizations, and manufacturing.

Service Industries —— Japan's largest trading and financial firms, inherently international in nature, were among the first to become active in the United States, both before and after World War II. Firms of the type known as *sōgō shōsha* (GENERAL TRADING COMPANIES) and city banks have often acted as scouts or agents for other Japanese firms, bringing to their attention opportunities for competitive developments in the US environment. *Sōgō shōsha* became involved in many types of joint ventures with client Japanese firms, particularly in the 1960s. At that stage, many Japanese firms possessed a competitive advantage, but were disinclined to start their own US operations because of their unfamiliarity with the American environment.

Japanese banks, as active participants in world financial markets, were naturally drawn to wholesale banking operations in New York and other major US centers of business. Agencies, branches, and subsidiaries were established. A number of Japanese banks were also attracted to retail banking in California, where statewide branch banking presented many opportunities. From a base of serving Japanese-American residents in California, some of these banks have grown to substantial size in retail banking through expansion and merger.

Other Japanese service-industry investments include real estate development and the operation of hotels, restaurants, shipping, warehousing, and similar businesses. Some of these activities can be considered as auxiliary to the flow of trade and tourism between the two countries.

Basic Resources —— Japanese firms have been drawn to the United States for many of the raw materials which Japan lacks. Especially prominent have been investments in agribusiness, lumber, aluminum, and coal. In the 1970s a trend developed toward the processing of raw materials in the United States for export to Japan in finished or semifinished form. Traditional Japanese products such as soy sauce and *sake* are now made from American raw materials and exported.

Sales and Distribution —— The number of sales and distribution subsidiaries of Japanese firms in the United States is greater than that in all other categories combined, a statistic that reflects the importance of exports of Japanese manufactured goods to the United States. Whether selling industrial or consumer goods, Japanese firms whose products are not commodity items have found it advantageous to keep close track of developments in the US market through their own organizations rather than relying on agents. The large investment in building an American organization has been justified by the size of the market and by its sophistication, which enables firms to spot market and technological developments that could have an impact on their business elsewhere.

Manufacturing —— Manufacturing investments in the United States have become especially marked in the 1970s, as changes in currency values, increase in the relative technological sophistication of Japanese manufacturers, difficulty in obtaining plant sites in Japan, American protectionism, and other factors have made such ventures more advantageous. Once Japanese firms had already invested in marketing organizations, investments in manufacturing capacity to fill those channels seemed more attractive.

Many Japanese manufacturing investments in the United States start as assembly or finishing operations, putting together Japanese-made components or finishing goods to specifications of the American market. A good example is the color television industry, in which all of the major Japanese manufacturers assemble imported parts into finished products. This industry also illustrates several other key tendencies. One is competitive matching: once a major Japanese firm establishes itself in the United States, other firms in the industry, fearing a loss of competitiveness, rush to follow. Another is a gradual trend toward substitution of American-made parts for Japanese parts as volume grows, as sources for domestic parts are uncovered, and as currency values continue to change. Japanese color television firms had by the late 1970s begun to produce or procure parts and other items in the United States.

The color television manufacturers also illustrate another characteristic of Japanese manufacturing investment: a combination of building new factories and purchasing older American firms. In the late 1970s Japanese firms began actively buying up American manufacturers whose brand names, technology, expertise, physical plant, or skilled labor attracted them. By 1979 a Japanese firm, DAI NIPPON INK & CHEMICALS, INC, had even outbid a French multinational enterprise, Rhône–Poulenc, in a competitive takeover bid for an American firm, Polychrome Corporation. This kind of corporate behavior is virtually unknown in Japan.

Conclusions —— The well-developed markets for commodities, labor, professional services, and even companies have enabled Japanese businesses to establish themselves in the United States readily by purchasing these resources. By contrast, markets for these things in Japan are relatively closed to both foreigners and other Japanese, so time and personal relationships must come first. In this sense, for Japanese firms, expansion can be considered easier in the United States than in Japan. Japanese managers' increased knowledge of the United States and the availability of financial resources for international expansion have thus given rise to a tremendous growth of Japanese business in America.

The magnitude of Japanese investment in the United States is still not large compared to the magnitude of overseas investments by US firms, but it is growing. It has been estimated that in 1975 Japanese direct investment in the United States was $1 billion. By 1979 that total had grown, perhaps doubled. The fastest growth had been in the manufacturing sector, which probably equaled ¥220 billion (US $1 billion) by 1979.

This kind of cross-cultural contact produces problems along with opportunities. While Japanese management of American factories, applying modified Japanese-style paternalism, is reported to be successful in many instances, American managers have expressed frustration at working within a Japanese-style system. That most Japanese firms dispatch a large number of Japanese managers both to manage American subsidiaries and learn from the American environment has sometimes been perceived as a barrier to promotion for Americans. But unless the world economic situation is drastically altered in the 1980s, it is likely that Japanese business in America will continue to be a growing force.

■ ——Yoshi Tsurumi, *The Japanese Are Coming* (1976). M. Y. Yoshino, *Japan's Multinational Enterprises* (1976).

Thomas B. LIFSON

Japanese Cities, A Geographical Approach

A series of English monographs published by the ASSOCIATION OF JAPANESE GEOGRAPHERS in 1970 (Special Publication No. 2). The chief editor is Kiuchi Shinzō. These monographs cover the results of various projects and research undertaken since 1958 by the association's Study Group on Urbanization, and its successor, the Study Group on Urban Geography. *NISHIKAWA Osamu*

Japanese Exclusion Act

Although such phrases as "the Japanese Exclusion Act" or "the Exclusion Act of 1924" are often encountered, there never was a Japanese Exclusion Act in United States law. Exclusion of Japanese from the United States was effected by the Immigration Act of 1924, which did not actually name the Japanese. See UNITED STATES IMMIGRATION ACTS OF 1924, 1952, AND 1965. *Roger DANIELS*

Japanese language

The native language of the overwhelming majority of the over 100 million inhabitants of the Japanese archipelago, including the Ryūkyū Islands, and significant numbers of Japanese immigrants in other countries, especially in North and South America. Japanese is spoken as a second language by many Chinese and Korean residents of Japan and by older residents of areas once dominated by the Japanese such as Korea and Taiwan. Comparative figures are difficult to assess because of inconsistency in the types of speakers included, but by any account Japanese is one of the major languages of the world.

The only other indigenous language of the Japanese islands is the apparently unrelated AINU LANGUAGE. This was, during historic times, gradually confined to the northern island of Hokkaidō and then overwhelmed by Japanese, and it is now close to extinction. The RYŪKYŪ DIALECTS are closely related to Japanese, though mutually unintelligible.

Although the Japanese and Chinese languages are entirely unrelated genetically, the Japanese writing system derives from that of Chinese. Chinese characters were introduced sometime in the 6th century, if not before, and the modern writing system is a complex one in which they are used in conjunction with two separate phonetic scripts developed in Japan from the characters. Japanese has also absorbed LOANWORDS freely from other languages, especially Chinese and English, the former chiefly from the 8th to the 19th century and the latter in the 20th.

Genetic Relationships —— The genetic relationship of Japanese to other languages remains a subject of scholarly controversy. Some scholars have maintained that no relationship to any known language can be demonstrated. However, the syntactic similarity of Japanese to Korean is widely acknowledged, and its resemblance in certain respects to the Altaic languages in general has also been pointed out. The situation is complicated by similarities in vocabulary between Japanese and the Malayo-Polynesian languages, and theories of a genetic relationship to various other Asian languages have also been advanced. There seems to be a growing consensus among Japanese scholars that syntactically Japanese shows an Altaic affinity, but that at some time in its prehistory it received an influence in vocabulary and morphology from the Malayo-Polynesian languages to the south. See JAPANESE AND THE ALTAIC LANGUAGES; JAPANESE AND THE MALAYO-POLYNESIAN LANGUAGES; KOREAN LANGUAGE.

The Japanese Dialects and the Speech of Tōkyō —— The modern Japanese language is marked by the persistence of a large number of local dialects existing alongside, but gradually being overwhelmed by, the officially sponsored standard language *(hyōjungo)*, which is based on the speech of the capital, Tōkyō. The Japanese dialects, however, show less variety in syntax and morphology than do the strong regional languages of Italy, for example, or Austria. Although it is true that a speaker of the Kagoshima dialect in the southwest of Kyūshū and a speaker of the Aomori dialect in the northeast of Honshū will be unable to understand each other, the distance by train separating these two dialects is 1,300 kilometers (about 800 mi), whereas in some of the smaller countries of Europe in which dialects persist a distance of 50 kilometers (about 30 mi) is sufficient for them to be mutually unintelligible. Japan has differences of this magnitude only among the dialects of the Ryūkyū Islands, and there, too, the pressure of the standard language is considerable.

Two other urban dialects, which have maintained their vitality despite the encroachments of the standard language, are those of the cities of Kyōto and Ōsaka. Kyōto was the imperial capital for over a thousand years, from 794 to 1868, and, though it was not always the seat of real political or economic power, it remained a center of traditional literature, art, and learning, and both it and its language continued to have the highest prestige. The language of its court nobility during the Heian period (794–1185) as preserved in the literary works of that period became the basis of CLASSICAL JAPANESE, which remained the standard for the written language until the beginning of the 20th century. During the Edo period (1600–1868) the castle town of Edo (now Tōkyō), which had been made the seat of the TOKUGAWA SHOGUNATE (by then the actual government of Japan), grew into an important commercial and administrative city. Both it and the older commercial city of Ōsaka became thriving centers of the culture and language of the merchant classes (CHŌ-NIN), and the language of Edo in particular—the locus of political power and the home of the increasingly educated samurai bureaucracy—gradually developed a prestige of its own. When Edo, renamed Tōkyō, was made the new imperial capital shortly after the Meiji Restoration of 1868, the language of its educated elite was gradually systematized and transformed into what is now the standard language. Incorporated into this language were a number of expressions from the language of the nobility who accompanied Emperor Meiji on his move from Kyōto. The resulting mixture became what is now the standard language. During the 20th century the standard language has been spread throughout Japan, first by means of centralized compulsory education and later even more effectively by radio and television. It is probably safe to say that 99 percent of the population now understand the standard language, even if they may speak it with a strong touch of some local dialect.

The standard language (also called the Tōkyō language or Tōkyō Standard) is sometimes loosely referred to as "the Tōkyō dialect," whereas it is actually only the most prestigious of a number of dialects in the Tōkyō dialect group. The others, which are now classed by definition as nonstandard, include most notably the speech of the traditional merchant and artisan classes of the inner city (shitamachi). The modern standard language, then, is the speech of the educated elite of Tōkyō, which has been influenced by the speech of Kyōto, enriched by the large number of Chinese loanwords that the Japanese language as a whole has accumulated over the centuries, and encumbered by a more recent influx of borrowings from English and other European languages.

The Phonology of the Standard Language —— The short or unit vowels of standard Japanese, a, i, u, e, and o, are pronounced more or less as in Spanish or Italian. (In this description the phonemes of Japanese will be written in the standard Hepburn romanization used throughout this encyclopedia, phonetic symbols being added only when necessary for clarity.) The long vowels, ā, ii, ū, ei, and ō, are pronounced double the length of the short vowels ([aː], [iː], [uː], [eː], and [oː]), except that ei is often pronounced as a sequence of two vowels. (When transcribing the Japanese pronunciation of loanwords from Western languages, in this encyclopedia ii and ei are written ī and ē, respectively.) The distinction between long and short vowels is essential for meaning. Aside from ei, sequences of vowels such as ai, au, ae, oi, ue, and so forth are so pronounced that the individual vowels retain their identity, although a glide often occurs; they are treated as separate syllables.

The consonants are k, s, sh, t, ch, ts, n, h, f, m, y, r, w, g, j, z, d, b, and p. The fricative sh ([ʃ] as in English "shoe") and the affricates ch, ts, and j ([tʃ] as in English "church," [ts] as in German zu or English "patsy," and [dʒ] as in English "judge," respectively) are treated as single consonants. G is always pronounced as in English "good" (never as in "genetics"); however, it is often nasalized as [ŋ]. The rest are pronounced more or less as in English except that f is a bilabial rather than labio-dental fricative, r is flapped, and t, d, and n are dental. When n is used at the end of a syllable as opposed to the beginning, it expresses a uvular syllabic nasal [N]; this changes to one of three different types of nasals when followed by certain consonants: n (dental) before t, d, or n; [ŋ] (velar, as in English "thank") before k or g; and m (bilabial) before p, b, or m. The older Hepburn spelling used in this encyclopedia reflects the last named of these pronunciations by changing n to m before p, b, or m as in san (three) versus sammai (three sheets); however, the modified Hepburn romanization used in many recent publications retains the n in all cases (sanmai). When followed by a vowel or y, this syllable-final n must be distinguished from syllable-initial n. In this encyclopedia an apostrophe is used after the former for this purpose (e.g., jin'in "personnel" as opposed to jinin "resignation"). In the double conso-

nants, -kk-, -pp-, -tt-, and -ss-, and in the combinations -ssh- [ʃʃ] and -tch- (all of which are always medial) both of the two consonants are pronounced—without release but with, in effect, a short interval of silence—much as in the English "bookcase," "shirttail," and "hatcheck."

The basic pattern of the Japanese syllable as traditionally analyzed and as reflected in the scansion of classical Japanese poetry is either a single short vowel or a combination of consonant followed by short vowel, counting in the latter category certain combinations in which there is a y glide between the consonant and vowel. This includes, in other words, any syllable in the traditional syllable chart known as the GOJŪON ZU (a, i, u, e, o, ka, ki, ku, ke, ko, etc), the variants of these in which the consonant is voiced (ga, gi, gu, ge, go, za, ji, zu, ze, zo, etc), and certain combinations involving a y glide (kya, kyu, kyo, nya, nyu, nyo, etc). (The combinations romanized as sha, shu, sho, cha, chu, cho, ja, ju, jo, etc fall into the last named category.) Syllables of this basic open syllabic pattern are often closed by one of two types of syllable-final consonants, one being the syllabic nasal [N] or any of its variants and the other being the first consonant in any of the medial double consonants or consonant combinations described above. These syllable-final consonants are themselves traditionally counted as syllables; however, it would be more precise to describe them as moras of the syllables they end and the syllables themselves as long syllables as distinguished from short open (one-mora) syllables consisting of consonant plus short vowel or short vowel alone. In the traditional analysis, which is heavily influenced by the use of the Japanese phonetic syllabary (KANA), long vowels are counted as two syllables each (they are each written with two characters from the syllabary). In summary, hon (book) would be two syllables (ho-n), hattatsu (development) would be four (ha-t-ta-tsu), and ōkii (big) would be four (o-o-ki-i). An analysis more appropriate to the structure of the words, which is preferred by linguists, classifies both the syllable-final consonants and the elements of the long vowels as moras of the (long) syllables to which they belong, giving for the above examples a syllabification of hon, hat-ta-tsu, and ō-kii, a count of one, three, and two syllables, respectively. However, by this analysis students of classical Japanese poetry with its "syllable-count" meter would have to be careful to count moras rather than syllables or their verses would not scan.

Japanese has no stress accent like that of English. Each syllable is given equal stress, successions of syllables being pronounced with a metronomic quality. Standard Japanese and a number of the dialects do have, however, a high-low pitch accent system, accent in a word or sequence of words being marked by the syllable after which the pitch drops. The way in which the same word (or the same set of contrasting homophones) is accented can differ significantly among those dialects that have pitch accents. (See ACCENT IN THE JAPANESE LANGUAGE.)

Another characteristic of standard Japanese is the strong tendency to devoice the vowels i and u when they fall between two voiceless consonants, so that shitakusa (undergrowth) becomes sh'tak'sa [ʃtaksa]. The vowels are not always dropped entirely, however: often they are sounded faintly, or at least their metronomic beat preserved. The vowel u at the end of a word after a voiceless consonant is also often devoiced or dropped, most notably in desu, the polite form of the copula, and in the polite verb ending -masu, which are often pronounced des' and mas', respectively.

The Grammar of Modern Japanese —— Nouns. Japanese nouns are uninflected words which have neither number nor gender and do not influence the inflection of the adjectives modifying them. There do exist a number of pluralizing suffixes that can be attached to nouns referring to human beings, and a few nouns can be pluralized by reduplication, as in hitobito (people) from hito (person); however, such devices are not used as a matter of course, and in most cases there is no explicit indication of plurality. Whether a noun is singular or plural in meaning is usually made clear by the context or by the addition of some modifier or appositive that conveys such ideas as "various," "successive," or "many."

One device for making singularity or plurality clear is the statement of actual number, as "one man" or "five men," for example. The set of number words most commonly used in Japanese is of Chinese origin; when stating the number of something, these are used with special words called counters, which indicate the quality or nature of the thing being enumerated (these counters are analogous to the English "sheets" as of paper and "head" as of cattle but are much more numerous). For numbers up to ten there is also a set of native number words, which can be used with or without counters (see COUNTERS).

In Japanese the grammatical function of nouns within a sentence is not indicated by word order as in English; neither are nouns inflected for grammatical case as in some languages. Instead grammatical function is indicated by grammatical particles (sometimes called postpositions) which follow the noun. Among the more important of these are *ga, o, ni,* and *no,* which function as case markers, *ga* indicating subject of verb, *o* direct object of verb, *ni* dative or indirect object, and *no* genitive. For example, in *kaze ga fuku* (the wind blows/will blow), *ga* marks *kaze* as the subject of the verb *fuku;* in *kodomo ga tomodachi no inu ni mizu o yaru* (the child gives/will give water to his/her friend's dog), *ga* marks *kodomo* (child) as the subject of the verb *yaru, no* marks *tomodachi* (friend) as possessor of *inu* (dog), *ni* marks *inu* as indirect object, and *o* marks *mizu* (water) as direct object of the verb. A particularly important particle is *wa.* This is not a case marker but rather marks the topic or theme of the sentence. In *zō wa hana ga nagai* (elephants have long noses; literally, "as for elephants, the nose is long"), *wa* marks *zō* (elephant/elephants) as the topic of the sentence and *ga* marks *hana* (nose/noses) as the subject of the adjective *nagai* (is long). (In Japanese, adjectives are inflected for tense and can function as the predicate of a sentence; see the section on adjectives below.) All of these particles also have various other functions and meanings depending on grammatical structure and context. There are a number of other postpositions that function much as prepositions do in English.

Japanese lacks the definite and indefinite articles of English and some other languages. Some of the distinctions in reference conveyed by these can in certain contexts be indicated by distinctions in the use of the subject marker *ga* and the topic marker *wa.* For example, *tegami ga kuru,* in which *tegami* is merely marked as the subject of the verb *kuru* (comes/will come), could mean either "a letter will come" or "the letter will come"; however, *tegami wa kuru* (literally, "as for the letter, it will come") could only mean the latter. Similar types of nuances are sometimes conveyed by the demonstratives *kono, sono,* and *ano,* which are placed before the nouns they govern. As opposed to the two-way distinction of the English "this" and "that," these mark a three-way distinction, *kono* referring to something near the speaker, *sono* referring to something near or connected with the hearer, and *ano* referring to something distant from both in place and time. For example, *kono empitsu* would mean "this pencil near me"; *sono empitsu* would mean "that pencil near you," "the pencil you have in mind," "the pencil I just mentioned to you," etc; and *ano empitsu* would mean "that pencil over there," "the pencil we talked of the other day," etc.

Japanese makes a distinction between nouns referring to animate and nouns referring to inanimate things as subjects of the verb meaning "to be, exist," there being two verbs of that meaning: *iru* and *aru,* respectively. For example, *kodomo no mae ni neko ga iru* (there is a cat in front of the child) as opposed to *kodomo no mae ni empitsu ga aru* (there is a pencil in front of the child).

Verbs. Japanese verbal inflections do not indicate person or number. The dictionary form of all verbs in the modern language ends in the vowel *-u.* When citing the dictionary form of Japanese verbs in English, it is conventional to refer to them by the English infinitive; thus *kaku* is often cited as "to write," although this form is actually the "present" (more precisely "nonpast") tense, which means "write/writes" or "will write."

Verb conjugations are classified in two main types. One of these, consonant-stem verbs (verbs whose stem ends in a consonant), includes verbs such as *kaku* (write), *hanasu* (talk), and *utsu* (hit), whose stems are *kak-, hanas-,* and *uts-,* respectively (as mentioned above, *ts* is treated as a single consonant). The other type, vowel-stem verbs, are themselves of two types, with stems ending in either the vowel *i* or the vowel *e,* e.g., *miru* (see) and *taberu* (eat), whose stems are *mi-* and *tabe-,* respectively. (The dictionary forms of vowel-stem verbs all end in *-iru* or *-eru;* however, not all verbs so ending are vowel-stem verbs; some are consonant-stem verbs with stems ending in *r,* e.g., *kiru* "cut.") In modern Japanese there are two fully conjugated irregular verbs, *kuru* (come) and *suru* (do), and a few other irregular verbs which are used in only some part of their theoretical conjugation.

The inflectional forms of the traditional grammar. In the traditional Japanese grammar developed in the 18th century and still in use in school grammar in Japan today, verb conjugations are analyzed as consisting of six forms or bases, which either have various inflectional suffixes added to them or function by themselves in various ways in the sentence. These all have names suggestive of the types of suffixes added or functions performed. They are, with some of the differing English equivalents commonly used for them: (1)

mizenkei (indefinite or negative form), (2) *ren'yōkei* (continuative or conjunctional form), (3) *shūshikei* (conclusive or final form), (4) *rentaikei* (attributive form), (5) *kateikei* (conditional form), and (6) *meireikei* (imperative form). (In speaking of classical Japanese the fifth of these is called *izenkei* or indefinite form.) To cite two examples, the forms for the modern consonant-stem verb *kaku* (write) are (1) *kaka,* (2) *kaki,* (3) *kaku,* (4) *kaku,* (5) *kake,* and (6) *kake,* and those for the vowel-stem verb *taberu* (eat) are (1) *tabe,* (2) *tabe,* (3) *taberu,* (4) *taberu,* (5) *tabere,* and (6) *tabeyo* (or *tabero*).

This traditional analysis, which is affected by the Japanese syllabic *kana* script (in which consonants are inseparable from some following vowel), tends to obscure the actual structure of these verbs, especially the consonant-stem verb (the stem of the one cited is really *kak-*). It further tends to mix grammatical categories, some of the forms being bases to which inflectional endings must be added and others fully inflected forms that are used by themselves, as can be seen from the examples that follow. Nevertheless, it is a very workable system when the verbs are considered as written in Japanese, as they normally are.

Some uses of these forms. (1) takes negative suffixes, e.g., *-nai,* as in *kakanai/tabenai* (does not write/eat); other suffixes include the passive *-reru/-rareru,* as in *kakareru/taberareru* (is written/eaten). These passive forms are themselves verbs of the vowel-stem type, which are further inflected.

(2) takes the past-tense suffix *-ta,* as in *kaita/tabeta* (wrote/ate), and the suffix *-te,* which resembles the English "-ing," as in *kaite/tabete* (writing/eating). (In taking these suffixes, *kaku* undergoes the sound change known as OMBIN, as do most consonant-stem verbs, the form differing according to the consonant of the stem.) This form (2) has many other uses: for example, it is used as the first part of compound verbs, in a conjunctive sense as the main verb in a coordinate clause, and by itself as a verbal noun.

(3) is the dictionary form or nonpast tense, a fully inflected form; its name (final or conclusive) refers to its use as a sentence-ending form (Japanese main verbs come at the end of the sentence); e.g., *kodomo ga kaku/taberu* (the child writes/eats).

(4) is a form used to modify nouns, being placed before them; e.g., *kaku/taberu hito* (the person who writes/eats). In modern Japanese this form is identical to (3); in classical Japanese, however, (3) and (4) have distinctive forms in vowel-stem verbs.

(5) takes the suffix *-ba* to form an adverbial known as the conditional or provisional, as in *kodomo ga kakeba/tabereba* (if the child writes/eats). (6) is itself the abrupt (nonpolite) imperative: *kake* (write!); *tabeyo* or *tabero* (eat!).

The traditional names of the conjugations. The traditional order of these verb forms or bases follows that of the horizontal rows *(dan)* (*a, i, u, e,* and *o*) in the traditional chart of syllables *(gojūon zu).* The traditional names of the conjugations also derive from this arrangement. Consonant-stem verbs are called *yodan* (four-row) verbs because the final vowels of the six forms *(kaka, kaki, kaku, kaku, kake, kake)* involve four of the five vowels. The vowel-stem verbs *miru* and *taberu* are called *kamiichidan* (upper one-row) and *shimoichidan* (lower one-row) verbs because their stems (removing the final *-ru*) involve one each of the vowel rows, *i* being the upper (in the vertical arrangement of rows) and *e* the lower. The irregular verbs *kuru* and *suru* are called *kagyō henkaku* (*ka*-column irregular) and *sagyō henkaku* (*sa*-column irregular) verbs (abbreviated *kahen* and *sahen,* respectively) because their stem consonants fall in the *k (ka)* and *s (sa)* consonant columns of the chart, respectively. In contemporary school grammar, consonant-stem verbs are often referred to as *godan* (five-row) rather than *yodan* because in the contemporary orthography (see KANA) the writing of one inflection of these verbs involves the vowel row in the chart *(o).* The form in question is the "tentative" or "hortatory" as in *kakō* (I may write/let's write/etc) and *tabeyō* (I may eat/let's eat/etc). Under the older orthography this was analyzed as derived from the *mizenkei* (negative or indefinite form or base) as in *tabe + yo* and *kaka + u (a + u* spelling *ō*). In the new orthography this *ō* is written *o + u,* as in *kako + u = kakō,* thus involving a different initial short vowel. This fifth vowel is usually classified as an alternate form of the *mizenkei.*

The most common inflected forms. The inflected forms that result from this system of conjugation are much more numerous than those of the English verb. However, they are few enough that the more common of them for the verb *kaku* can be summarized briefly. These include some that have already been mentioned: (1) *kaku* (nonpast: "write/will write"); (2) *kaita* (past: "wrote"); both of these are sentence-ending forms, but they can also be used attributively before a noun as in *kaku hito* (the person who writes) or *kaita hito* (the person who wrote); (3) *kaite* ("writing"; this form is sometimes misleadingly called a gerund; its typical use is adverbial or conjunctive); (4) *kakeba* (provisional or conditional: "if [someone] writes"); (5) *kaitara* (conditional: "if [someone] writes"); in some contexts, (4) and (5) are interchangeable; (6) *kakō* (tentative or hortatory: "[someone] may write"; "let's write"); (7) *kaitari* (sometimes called "frequentive": "writing [from time to time]"; "writing [among other things]"); (8) *kakareru* (passive: "is written"); this form, which has various other uses and meanings, is itself conjugated as a vowel-stem verb; (9) *kakaseru* (causative: "make/let [someone] write"); conjugates as a vowel-stem verb; (10) *kakaserareru* (causative-passive: "[someone] is made to write"); conjugates as a vowel-stem verb; (11) *kakeru* (potential: "can write"); conjugates as a vowel-stem verb; (12) *kakitai* (often called "desiderative": "want to write"); (13) *kakanai* (negative: "does not/will not write"). Both -*tai* and -*nai*, the suffixes of (12) and (13), respectively, are adjectives in form, and both (12) and (13) are themselves inflected as adjectives (for adjective inflections, see below); thus *kakitai* becomes *kakitakatta* (wanted to write), *kakitakute* (wanting to write), and so forth; *kakanai* becomes *kakanakatta* (did not write), *kakanakereba* (if [someone] does not write), *kakanakattara* (similar to the preceding), and *kakanakute* (not writing). *Kakitai* also has a negative form, *kakitakunai* (not want to write), which itself undergoes similar inflection.

The verb forms cited so far have all been in what is called the plain or informal style, which is used in speaking among intimates or equals or to children and in certain types of writing. When speaking to superiors or when the situation requires politeness, the final verbs of sentences would be put in what is called the polite style. This is formed by the addition of some form of the polite suffix -*masu* or the use of *desu*, the polite form of the copula (discussed below). Some examples, again involving the verb *kaku*, are *kakimasu* (write/will write), *kakimashita* (wrote), *kakimasen* (does not/will not write), *kakimasen deshita* (did not write), and *kakitai desu* (want to write). There are a number of alternative polite forms of the imperative, one of which is *kaite kudasai* (please write), using the imperative of the polite verb *kudasaru* (give). There are also more elaborate forms of politeness which are discussed in the section on levels of speech below.

The copula. The Japanese copula or linking verb (plain form *da*; polite form *desu*) is used to link two nouns (or nominal phrases) in the pattern *A wa B da* or *A wa B desu* (A is B). The literal meaning of this pattern is "as for A, it is B" or "as for A, it is in the category of B," e.g., *neko wa dōbutsu da* (cats are animals or, literally, "as for cats, they are animals." For this reason the Japanese copula cannot always be translated by the English "to be." For example, *watakushi wa bīru desu* does not mean "I am beer" but "I am having beer" (literally, "as for me, [it] is beer"). The more important inflections of the plain copula are *da* (nonpast sentence-ending form: "is"), *datta* (past: "was"), *de* ("being"), *na* (nonpast attributive form; used before nouns), and *darō* (tentative: "will probably be"). The forms of the polite copula are *desu* (nonpast sentence-ending form), *deshita* (past), *deshite* or *de* ("-ing" form), and *deshō* (tentative). Used as negative forms for the copula are the phrases *de wa nai* or *ja nai* (plain) and *de wa arimasen* or *ja arimasen* (polite). The tentative forms of the copula are often used after verbs to indicate probability, as in *kaku darō/deshō* (will probably write) and *kaita darō/deshō* (probably wrote).

Adjectives. Japanese adjectives are inflected in some ways like verbs (e.g., for tense) and like verbs they can function either attributively, coming before the nouns they modify, or as the predicates of sentences or clauses, in the latter case appearing at the end of the sentence or clause. The dictionary form of all adjectives ends in one of four vowels (*a, i, u,* or *o*) followed by a final *i*. The stem of the adjective is obtained by dropping the final *i*; e.g., *takai* (high; stem *taka*), *utsukushii* (beautiful; stem *utsukushi*), *samui* (cold; stem *samu*), and *shiroi* (white; stem *shiro*).

In the traditional school grammar, adjectives are analyzed as having the same kind of conjugational forms or bases as verbs (some of them being fully inflected forms and others bases to which inflectional suffixes are added), and these are given the same names (*mizenkei, ren'yōkei,* etc). However, their application to modern adjectives seems somewhat forced, and they will be omitted here. The more important forms of the modern adjective (using *shiroi,* "white," as an example) are (1) *shiroi* (the dictionary form; present tense); this form is used either attributively as in *shiroi hana* (a white flower) or as a predicate as in *hana wa shiroi* (the flower is white); in classical Japanese the attributive and sentence final forms of adjectives differed as did those of verbs; (2) *shiroku* (an adverbial form: "whitely"); (3) *shirokatta* (past tense: "was white"); (4) *shirokute* ("-ing" form: "being white"); (5) *shirokereba* (provisional or condi-

tional: "if [something] is white"); (6) *shirokattara* (conditional; similar to the preceding); (7) *shirokunai* (negative: "is not white"); the negative suffix is itself an adjective which has further inflections, e.g., *shirokunakatta* (was not white). As adjectives themselves function as verbs, the copula is never used with them as a linking verb (it would be wrong to say **hana wa shiroi da*). However, the polite form of the copula, *desu*, is often added to the plain present or past tense forms of adjectives to change them to polite style, as in *shiroi desu* (is white) or *shirokatta desu* (was white). Also, the tentative forms of the plain or polite copula are often added to adjectives to convey the idea of probability, as in *shiroi darō/deshō* (is probably white) and *shirokatta darō/deshō* (was probably white). The polite negative form of adjectives uses the polite negative of the verb *aru* (be, exist), as in *shiroku arimasen* (is not white); an alternative form adds the polite copula to the plain negative adjective, as in *shirokunai desu.*

Copular nouns (or nominal adjectives). Japanese has a large class of words that are always followed by some form of the copula, functioning together with it as a unit that can be used either as a modifier or as a predicate. These units behave like adjectives, and the word before the copula can often be translated into English only as an adjective; however, the words are morphologically nouns, which with the copula form a verbal phrase. This class of words is called copular nouns or nominal adjectives in English, and in Japanese usually *keiyō dōshi* (adjectival verbs). One such word is *kirei* (beautiful, pretty, clean), as in *hana wa kirei da/desu* (the flower is pretty); *kirei na hana* (a pretty flower), using the attributive form of the copula; *kirei ni kaku* (write beautifully), *ni* being analyzed as an adverbializing form of the copula; and so forth. Copular nouns are often cited in the attributive form: *kirei na.* Most of them are, like *kirei na,* of Chinese origin; however, there are also many of native origin such as *shizuka na* (quiet). There are many Western loanwords such as *shikku na* (chic).

Levels of speech. In addition to the distinction between plain and polite styles in verbs and adjectives, there is a complex system of levels of speech that expresses a consciousness of social relationships. What is involved with the plain versus polite verb forms is essentially a distinction between easy informality and abruptness on the one hand and a correct, neutral politeness on the other. In the system of levels known as honorific or respect language *(keigo),* the speaker chooses among a number of alternative ways of saying the same thing (this including not only verbs, but also other parts of speech), the choice being determined by such factors as relative age, sex, and social status. Briefly stated, one uses respectful or exalting forms with reference to an addressee or third person of higher status and humble terms with reference to oneself or a third person who falls into the same category as oneself. This system not only reflects the vertical relationships of traditional Japanese society; it is an integral part of the structure of the Japanese language.

Some actions often referred to in social situations, such as "go", "come," "be," "say," "look," "eat," "give," and "receive," are represented by sets of three completely different verbs, one neutral, one humble, and one exalting; for example *yū* (neutral), *mōsu* (humble), and *ossharu* (exalting) all mean "to say." There are also sets of humble and exalting nouns for common kinship terms, and so forth. Ordinary verbs also have humble and exalting forms which are derived from the neutral ones; for example, *kaku* (write), of which the polite neutral form is *kakimasu*, has *okaki ni narimasu* (write) for use in referring to writing done by the exalted person and *okaki shimasu* to refer to writing done by the humble subject to or for the exalted person. The passive forms of verbs are also often used as honorific verbs (with active meaning) when referring to actions of the exalted. Japanese also has a large range of different words for the first and second pronouns, each expressing a degree of respect or intimacy; however, the tendency of Japanese to omit subject and object is particularly strong in the case of pronouns, and in fact one of the features of the honorific system is that the exalted or humble verbs usually make it quite clear whether speaker or hearer is the subject. See HONORIFIC LANGUAGE; FEMININE LANGUAGE; MASCULINE LANGUAGE.

The sentence. The typical Japanese sentence is built on the pattern of subject-object-verb (SOV) as in *neko ga nezumi o tsukamaeta* (the cat caught the mouse). However, since the particle *ga* marks *neko* (cat) as the subject, and the particle *o* marks *nezumi* (mouse) as the object of the verb *tsukamaeta,* a certain amount of inversion, as for stylistic purposes, is possible; *nezumi o neko ga tsukamaeta* (OSV) would have virtually the same meaning as the SOV sentence, whereas in English such inversion of subject and object would change the meaning entirely. To return to the basic

SOV sentence, if an adverbial modifier, for instance, *subayaku* (swiftly), is inserted, it may come before the subject, the object, or the verb, with slight differences of emphasis. As noted before, adjectival modifiers always precede the nouns they modify. There is a strong tendency in Japanese to omit the subject or the object or even both if the speaker or writer feels that it is clear from the context what they would be, so that, depending on the situation, this sentence might be stated *nezumi o tsukamaeta* (it caught the mouse), *neko ga tsukamaeta* (the cat caught it), or simply *tsukamaeta* (it caught it).

There are no relative pronouns in Japanese as in the English "the cat that caught the mouse died." In Japanese the entire subordinate clause is placed directly in front of the noun as a modifier: *nezumi o tsukamaeta neko ga shinda* (literally, "the caught-the-mouse cat died"). A sentence can also be made into a subordinate clause in another sentence by inserting either the nominalizing particle *no* (not to be confused with the genitive particle *no* mentioned earlier) or the function word *koto* (thing; matter) after the final verb of the sentence, which then modifies the particle, forming a noun clause. For example, in the sentence *kodomo ga tabako o nomu* (the child smokes cigarettes) is in this way used as the object of the main verb in the sentence *hahaoya wa kodomo ga tabako o nomu no* [or *koto*] *o shiranai* (the mother does not know that her child smokes cigarettes). The elements in this sentence are *hahaoya* (mother), *wa* (the topic marker), *kodomo* (child), *ga* (the subject particle), *tabako* (cigarettes), *o* (the object particle), *nomu* (smoke [literally, "drink"]: the verb in the subordinate clause), *no* or *koto* (the nominalizer), *o* (the object particle), *shiranai* ("does-not-know": the main verb of the sentence). A fairly literal rendering of the whole would be "as for the mother, (she) does not know the child-smokes-cigarettes matter."

A series of coordinate clauses or verb phrases is often strung together by means of the form of the verb that ends in the suffix *-te* ("-ing"), as in *uchi e kaette, gohan o tabete, hon o yonda* (I went home, ate supper, and read a book). In this sentence the elements are *uchi* (house/home), *e* (directional particle), *kaette* (returning), *gohan* (rice/meal), *o* (accusative particle), *tabete* (eating), *hon* (book), *o* (accusative particle), and *yonda* ("read"; past tense), and the subject of all three verbs is understood to be the speaker. Thus a literal rendering would be "returning home, eating meal, read book"; however, in such sentences the coordinate verbs are understood to take on the tense of the final verb, and this is reflected in the idiomatic translation.

Vocabulary. Japanese has an extremely rich and varied vocabulary, not only its large stock of native words, which are felt to be particularly expressive and sonorous, but also a great quantity of words of Chinese origin. To these are added the many loanwords from English and other European languages that have come into Japanese, especially during the 20th century. Many of the loanwords from Chinese, some of which date from the 6th century, have been so thoroughly absorbed into the daily vocabulary that their foreign origin is no longer felt, while others are felt to be scholarly or difficult words. The situation is roughly analogous to that of English, with its large vocabulary of French, Latin, and Greek loanwords superimposed on an Anglo-Saxon base. As in the case of English, the basic function words that hold a sentence together are native, and words fundamental to daily life tend to be also; however Chinese has made inroads here, too. For example, such a fundamental item as the set of number words is, as was mentioned earlier, of Chinese origin, though some native number words continue to be used as alternates for some of the lower numbers. As might be expected, much of the intellectual and philosophical vocabulary is of Chinese origin, but not all of this is due entirely to Chinese cultural influence: an important part of the modern intellectual vocabulary consists of words coined in Japan in the late 19th and early 20th century by devising new combinations of Chinese characters as translations of concepts then being introduced from the West for the first time. This process of coinage still continues, but there is a growing tendency, particularly in the sciences, to use the Western words intact. Aside from the sciences, words are often used in meanings quite different from those of their original languages, and new Japanese words are sometimes coined by combining parts of Western-language words in startling ways (for examples, see LOANWORDS). One particularly interesting feature of the native Japanese vocabulary is the large number of established onomatopoetic words it contains. These include not only words imitating sounds but also words expressing abstract qualities or subjective feelings. These words add a great liveliness to the daily language, roughly corresponding to the role of gestures in Italian social life (for examples, see ONOMATO-POEIA).

Writing System——The Japanese writing system uses Chinese characters (KANJI) in combination with two separate forms of the phonetic syllabic script known as KANA; the names of the latter are *hiragana* and *katakana*. Some words are written entirely in *kana*, others entirely in Chinese characters, and others in a combination of the two. In the latter case the stem of the word is written with a Chinese character, or characters, and inflectional endings or other suffixes with *kana* (the final syllable of the stem is often expressed in *kana* for the sake of clarity). Grammatical particles and function words (such as demonstratives and auxiliary verbs) are written in *kana*. The resulting text is often sprinkled with roman letters (e.g., acronyms such as PTA, model numbers, and occasionally entire foreign words), so that the number of scripts needed to write modern Japanese actually comes to four.

Of the two *kana* scripts or syllabaries, *hiragana* is a cursive script and *katakana* an angular one. Both were derived from Chinese characters used phonetically, the present forms being either stylized or abbreviated versions of the original characters. Although in a few cases their symbols for a particular sound resemble each other, they are in essence entirely separate scripts for producing the same set of sounds. Each script contains 48 symbols, each symbol representing the sound of one Japanese syllable (to be precise, short syllable or mora). For example, the syllables *a, ka, sa, ta,* and *na* are written あ , か , さ , た , and な in *hiragana* and ア , カ , サ , タ , and ナ in *katakana*. The syllable-final *n* ([N]) is written ん in *hiragana* and ン in *katakana*. By using diacritical marks to indicate the voiced consonants in such syllables as *ga, za,* and *da,* and by using combinations of *kana* symbols to represent the postconsonantal *y* glides of some syllables (e.g., *kya, myo*), all of the possible syllables of Japanese can be written with either script (see table in KANA). It is therefore possible to write Japanese entirely in *kana,* and although that is not normally done, there is a fair amount of individual discretion in writing particular words with *kana* instead of Chinese characters in the mixed writing system described above, some people tending to use a higher proportion of Chinese characters than others. The *hiragana* script is the one that is normally used together with the Chinese characters for writing Japanese, including any words of Chinese origin that may happen to be written in *kana. Katakana* is used to write the numerous loanwords from Western languages as well as onomatopoetic words, and Japanese words are occasionally written in *katakana* for emphasis or some other technical reason. The *hiragana* used to write the inflectional endings of a word written in characters are called *okurigana.* Another special term is *furigana,* which refers to the small *hiragana* that are sometimes placed alongside a Chinese character to indicate its pronunciation.

The most formidable element in the Japanese writing system is obviously the Chinese characters. There are 1,945 of them in the JŌYŌ KANJI, the list officially approved by the Japanese government for use in publications intended for the general public and for writing personal names, and it is these that are taught in the nation's schools. (Since the 1,945 characters do not suffice for writing all common personal names, there are an additional 166 characters approved for writing names alone.) The *jōyō kanji* are supposed to be learned (or at least "taught") by the end of the 9th grade. Thus the standard for a middle-school education and for the ability to read newspapers and popular magazines and books is a command of around 2,000 Chinese characters. Learned and literary publications are free to exceed the government guidelines and many scholarly or literary people know an additional one or two thousand characters. This may seem far short of the tens of thousands contained in large dictionaries; however, it has been estimated that even before the post-World War II language reforms that led to adoption of the government-approved list, the number of characters in actual use probably did not exceed five or six thousand.

What makes the Chinese characters such a formidable burden, however, in reading and writing Japanese, is less their sheer numbers than the complex and cumbersome way that they are used. Most characters have more than one pronunciation that can be given them, depending on what word they are used to write. These pronunciations, called "readings," are classified in two types: ON READINGS and KUN READINGS. The former are the pronunciations that result when characters are used to write Chinese loanwords. They reflect an original Chinese pronunciation of the character, but as pronounced in Japan. Some characters have two or three possible *on* readings, reflecting loanwords brought in from different parts of China or in different periods. *Kun* readings are native Japanese words that have the same meaning as the character (or more precisely, the Chinese morpheme the character represents); they are in effect the Japanese words that the character stands for. Often several Japanese words of similar meaning have become associated with a particular character, with the result that it may have several *kun* readings. It is not unusual for commonly used characters to have two or more readings of each type, and in extreme cases a single character may have a total of ten or more possible pronunciations (for some examples, see the section on *on* and *kun* readings in KANJI).

Under these circumstances reading correctly—that is, apprehending what word a character or group of characters is being used to write—depends largely on rote memorization of the way particular words are written and ability to recognize context, though the grammatical particles and inflectional endings written in *kana* often provide important clues.

There is considerable variety in the way in which reading matter is arranged for the reader in Japan. Japanese is normally written or printed in vertical lines reading from top to bottom, with the lines starting at the right-hand side of the page and proceeding across from right to left. For this reason most ordinary books open from what would be the back of an English book, and most ordinary newspapers and magazines are arranged in the same way. However, books and periodicals on certain special subjects—including scientific and technical matter—are usually printed in horizontal lines reading from left to right as in English, and these also open in the Western manner. The same is often true of reference works. (Also some individuals prefer to write in horizontal lines when writing by hand.) The vertical lines of type in newspapers and magazines are printed in horizontal columns, and this is also often done in books. Newspapers have both vertical and horizontal headlines. The latter usually read from left to right—in the opposite direction from the progress of the columns. However, it is not at all unusual to find Japanese headings printed horizontally from right to left, particularly the titles and other headings of older books. In public places one still sometimes encounters signboards written in this manner.

When writing Chinese characters or Japanese *kana* by hand, the order of strokes proceeds in a general direction of left to right and top to bottom. When written in vertical lines by someone with a flowing cursive hand, the natural order of strokes is such that characters, and particularly *kana*, are often connected by vertical joins.

The Alleged Difficulty of Japanese —— Japan's long period of NATIONAL SECLUSION from the 17th to the mid-19th century, and the absence of readily apparent genetic relationships with neighboring languages, have resulted in a broadly accepted myth in Japan proclaiming the "uniqueness" of the Japanese language. This myth, which has not yet been completely dispelled by the evidence that scholars have gathered of the relationship of Japanese to certain other languages, is no doubt itself related to the widely held belief that Japanese is a very "difficult" language for foreigners to learn (many Japanese believe firmly that not only their language but also many aspects of their culture are somehow "unique" and can never be fully understood by anyone who is not Japanese). However, it is not easy to measure the relative inherent difficulty of language with any degree of scientific objectivity, and any such sweeping statements are probably essentially meaningless. Actually, Japanese, with its relatively small number of phonemes and its paucity of irregular verbs, is an easy language in which to acquire at least a superficial daily conversational ability. Although its verbal inflections are complex compared with English, they are regular and easy to remember, especially as compared with some other, highly inflected, European languages. On the other hand, the Japanese language does undeniably have some features that make extra effort necessary (and even a certain amount of familiarity with Japanese social customs and interpersonal psychology) if one is to attain a command of it beyond the superficial level. These include, for example, the existence of levels of speech in terms of politeness or deference among which the speaker must choose according to social situation or attitude. Another example is the degree to which parts of a statement are customarily left unspoken or unwritten, to be inferred by the hearer or reader. Even in formal expository writing this reliance on implication is practiced to a degree that would be intolerable in English. However, the one aspect of Japanese that has contributed most to its reputation for difficulty is its extremely complex and cumbersome writing system, which requires years of study for the foreign student to master and even imposes a severe mental burden on the Japanese themselves. And it must be remembered that this writing system is not an inherent part of Japanese, but something imposed on it from the outside when, through an acci-

dent of geography and history, the Japanese imported from China and adapted to their language a script to which it was totally unsuited, both in terms of phonology and morphology.

History —— The oldest recorded hints as to the nature of the early Japanese language are found in a description of Japan in the WEI ZHI *(Wei chih)*, a Chinese historical work of the 3rd century. The 40-odd words appearing there are transcribed into Chinese characters and are mainly names of persons and places and official titles. The question of how they were actually pronounced is a controversial one that has not yet been satisfactorily solved. However, there is evidence that the system of transcription found in the *Wei zhi* corresponds with that used in the 8th century to record the eight vowels of 8th-century Japanese, and it is therefore believed that these transcriptions provided some kind of basis for the subsequent development of a method of writing the Japanese language.

Old Japanese (Jōko Nihongo): the Nara period (710–794). The Chinese writing system is known to have been introduced into Japan by at least the early 6th century—in all likelihood a century or so before. However, the earliest surviving Japanese writing of any substantial length—in Chinese or Japanese—dates from the 8th century in the form of the chronicles KOJIKI (712) and NIHON SHOKI (720) and the poetry anthology MAN'YŌSHŪ (ca 759). Thus the 8th century constitutes the first of the standard periods of Japanese linguistic history.

The Chinese writing system was probably first used in Japan for the writing of official records in classical Chinese. For this, and for the study of the literary works of China, a method was devised of reading Chinese texts directly into Japanese by changing the word order during the reading and adding the inflectional endings needed to make sense in Japanese. A system of notation was developed to aid in this (see KAMBUN; POETRY AND PROSE IN CHINESE). Of the three works mentioned, the *Nihon shoki* is written in Chinese. The *Man'yōshū* is written in Japanese by means of Chinese characters used in the system of writing known as *man'yōgana*. This system, in which Chinese characters are used phonetically to write Japanese, eventually developed into the later phonetic *kana* script. Not all the words in the *Man'yōshū* are written phonetically; some are represented by characters used to convey their meaning (as in *kun* readings), and others written in various ingenious ways (see the section on the *man'yō* writing system in MAN'YŌSHŪ). The *Kojiki* is written chiefly in a heavily Japanized hybrid form of Chinese similar to HENTAI KAMBUN. Studies of the phonetic characters used in the *man'yōgana* writing system have demonstrated that the Japanese language of this period had eight vowels as opposed to the five of modern standard Japanese.

Late Old Japanese (Chūko Nihongo): the Heian period (794–1185). Both the *kana* scripts had been developed by the early 10th century. The cursive script, *hiragana*, developed from a cursive form of *man'yōgana* and the angular script, *katakana*, from a square form. The latter developed among priests as an aid to reading Chinese Buddhist texts. The former became the customary medium for the writing of personal correspondence and classical Japanese poetry (WAKA). Also known as *onnade* or "women's hand," it flourished among the court ladies who wrote most of the period's great works of prose literature such as the TALE OF GENJI and the *Pillow Book* (see SEI SHŌNAGON). Although the tradition of writing in Chinese continued in the form of official documents and courtiers' diaries, it was the works of these women and the male and female poets of the period—works written in a relatively "pure" Japanese with few Chinese characters—that made this the golden age of classical Japanese literature. It is these works that established the standards for classical Japanese, the formal written language of subsequent periods.

The classical language compared to the modern. By the Heian period the eight vowels of Old Japanese had diminished to something like the five vowels of modern Japanese. The great changes were thus phonological and orthographic (the Heian people could no longer read the cumbersome *man'yōgana*) rather than grammatical, although some Nara-period suffixes and other forms had become archaic. Whereas Nara-period Japanese had had eight verb conjugations, Heian Japanese had nine: a consonant-stem conjugation, four vowel-stem conjugations, and four irregular conjugations. The terminology used in describing these is that of the traditional school grammar already used above in speaking of the modern verbs, except that the fifth of the six forms or bases in classical Japanese is called *izenkei* (indefinite form) instead of *kateikei* (conditional) as in modern Japanese. The forms or bases of the consonant-stem (*yodan* or four-row) are the same as those of modern Japanese. Of the vowel-stem verbs, the *kamiichidan* (upper one-row) and *shimoichidan* (lower one-row) conjugations also have the same six bases as those of their modern counterparts. The two vowel-stem conjugations that are lacking in modern Japanese are called *kaminidan* (upper two-row) and *shimonidan* (lower two-row) verbs because the final vowels of their bases involve two rows of the *gojūon* syllable chart: both verbs have bases ending in *u* in addition to the ones ending in *i* of the former (upper) and *e* of the latter (lower). Their bases also differ in other ways from their modern "one-row" counterparts.

To give one example, *tabu* (eat), the classical *shimonidan* equivalent of the modern *shimoichidan* verb *taberu* that was described above, has the following bases (giving them in the same order as in the case of the modern verbs): (1) *tabe,* (2) *tabe,* (3) *tabu,* (4) *taburu,* (5) *tabure,* (6) *tabeyo* (cf *tabe, tabe, taberu, taberu, tabere, tabeyo* for the modern verb). The significant difference, aside from the changing stem vowel, is the presence of different forms for the *shūshikei* (sentence-ending) and *rentaikei* (attributive) bases. Of the irregular conjugations, two, the *kahen* (*k* column irregular) and *sahen* (*s* column irregular) conjugations involve the same verbs as in modern Japanese (*kuru* "come" and *suru* "be"), but the classical verbs (*ku* and *su,* respectively) have different forms. The other two classical irregular verbs are called *rahen* and *nahen;* they are *ari* (be/exist; cf modern *aru*) and *shinu* (die) both regular consonant verbs in modern Japanese. The one new conjugation added to the Nara-period eight was the *shimoichidan* verb *keru* (kick); in modern Japanese this has become a consonant verb, and the classical *shimonidan* verbs have entered the *shimoichidan* class.

Other differences between the classical language and modern Japanese include the following. Classical consonant verbs lack the sound change *(ombin)* that occurs in their modern Japanese equivalents when certain suffixes are added to their bases; e.g., modern *kaita* versus classical *kakitari* (both past-tense forms of "write"). Classical verbs have a large number of suffixes that themselves inflect as verbs, and there is a tendency for several of these to attach successively to the verb in a chain. Classical adjectives have, as mentioned above, separate sentence ending and attributive forms. For the classical equivalent of *shiroi* (white), for example, these are *shiroshi* and *shiroki,* respectively. The *kana* spelling of classical Japanese, which was itself not standardized until a much later period, was quite different from that of modern Japanese, reflecting phonological differences not discussed here. (For this see KANA; CLASSICAL JAPANESE.)

Middle Japanese (Chūsei Nihongo). Middle Japanese corresponds to the Kamakura (1185–1333), Muromachi (1333–1568), and Azuchi-Momoyama (1568–1600) periods. In contrast to the clear line between Japanese and Chinese during the Heian period, considerable Chinese influence on the native language (the wholesale incorporation of Chinese words and phrases and an increased use of Chinese characters) becomes apparent in such Kamakura-period martial tales (GUNKI MONOGATARI) as the *Tale of the Heike* (HEIKE MONOGATARI). This period also saw the development of the epistolary style known as SŌRŌBUN. Other important texts are the NŌ and KYŌGEN theatrical works of the Muromachi period. The latter provide valuable evidence of changes in the spoken language. Also particularly valuable as records of actual contemporary pronunciation are works produced in the late 16th and early 17th centuries by the JESUIT MISSION PRESS such as the *Arte da Lingoa de Iapam* (a grammar by João RODRIGUES) and the dictionary *Vocabulario da Lingoa de Iapam* (NIPPO JISHO).

Early Modern Japanese (Kinsei Nihongo). Early Modern Japanese is the language of the Edo period (1600–1868). The colorful colloquial language of the merchant classes of Edo and Ōsaka is preserved in the theatrical works of the KABUKI drama and the puppet theater (BUNRAKU) as well as in the various genres of Edo popular fiction (GESAKU). This was also the age of the great premodern Japanese scholars of the language (see JAPANESE LANGUAGE STUDIES, HISTORY OF).

By the beginning of the Meiji period (1868–1912) the divergence between the spoken and the classical written languages had become pronounced. In the spirit of modernization and Westernization that characterized the period, a movement arose to develop a literary form of the spoken language, a thing for which no model existed in Japan. The first success in spoken-language novels came at the end of the 19th century, and by the early 20th the new medium had become established (see GEMBUN ITCHI). There were also movements for language reform in general, especially directed at the writing system. The existing *kana* spelling did not at all represent the actual pronunciations of words, and a need was also felt to rationalize the use of Chinese characters and reduce their number. However, these reform movements did not really bear fruit until after

World War II, when the modern *kana* spelling and the reduced list of characters were officially adopted. See JAPANESE LANGUAGE REFORMS.

▬——General: Kindaichi Haruhiko, *Nihongo* (1957), tr Umeo Hirano as *The Japanese Language* (1978). Kokugo Gakkai, ed, *Kokugogaku jiten* (Tōkyōdō, 1974); revised edition, *Kokugogaku daijiten* (1980). Susumu Kuno, *The Structure of the Japanese Language* (1972). S. Y. Kuroda, *Generative Grammatical Studies in the Japanese Language* (1965). Bruno Lewin, *Abriss der japanischen Grammatik, auf der Grundlage der klassischen Schriftsprache* (1959). Samuel E. Martin, *Reference Grammar of Japanese* (1975). Roy Andrew Miller, *The Japanese Language* (1967). Roy Andrew Miller, *Bernard Bloch on Japanese* (1969). Roy Andrew Miller, *The Japanese Language in Contemporary Japan* (1977). Roy Andrew Miller, *Japan's Modern Myth: The Language and Beyond* (1982). Mizutani Osamu, *Nihongo no seitai* (1979), tr Janet Ashby as *Japanese: The Spoken Language in Japanese Life* (1981). Ōno Susumu, *Nihongo no kigen* (1957), tr as Susumu Ohno, *The Origin of the Japanese Language* (1970).

Textbooks and dictionaries: Anthony Alfonso, *Japanese Language Patterns* (1971). C. G. Dunn and S. Yanada, *Teach Yourself Books: Japanese* (1958). Howard Hibbett and Gen Itasaka, *Modern Japanese: A Basic Reader,* 2 vols (1965). Tadashi Ikeda, *Classical Japanese Grammar Illustrated with Texts* (1975). Japanese Language Promotion Center, *Intensive Course in Japanese, Elementary,* Parts I, II (1970). Eleanor H. Jorden and H. I. Chaplain, *Beginning Japanese,* Parts I, II (1962–63). Fumiko Koide, *Modern Japanese for University Students* (1963–68). Bruno Lewin, *Japanische Chrestomathie von der Nara-Zeit bis zur Edo-Zeit,* 2 vols (1965). Samuel E. Martin, *Essential Japanese: An Introduction to the Standard Colloquial Language* (1954). Koh Masuda, *Kenkyusha's New Japanese-English Dictionary* (rev ed, 1974). P. G. O'Neill, *A Programmed Course on Respect Language in Modern Japanese* (1966). Andrew Nelson, *The Modern Reader's Japanese-English Character Dictionary* (2nd rev ed, 1974). Florence Sakade, *Reading and Writing Japanese* (1959).

Willem A. GROOTAERS

Japanese language reforms

The term language reform refers to extensive and radical changes in linguistic usage as a conscious response to the existence of language problems. Language reforms are usually widely discussed in the community by individuals, groups, or associations formed for that purpose and are designed as well as implemented by the government or its specialized agencies. Together with less extensive or radical measures directed toward language, language reforms constitute the system of "language treatment" within the community. Although much of the development of modern Japanese proceeded by spontaneous uncontrolled changes, the role of planned development was considerable. Modern Japan belongs to those nations of the world which have developed a most vigorous and interesting system of relatively systematic treatment of language problems.

The overall communication problem of post-Meiji Japan was the modernization of the language. In particular, the following four interrelated types of problems called for action.

National language. The language inherited from the feudal society consisted of a surprisingly large number of styles and dialects, ranging from the language of classical Chinese texts to a dialect spoken in a single village of northeastern Japan. There was no style or dialect which could be widely used as the tool of both written and oral communication throughout the new nation.

Development. Apart from the problem of selecting one variety of Japanese as the national language, there was the subsequent problem of developing this variety of language to serve as a reliable tool of modern communication. It was necessary to create an extensive modern vocabulary and to codify the unstable grammatical and stylistic usage.

Accessibility. There were problems in the accessibility of the written language. In the Edo period (1600–1868) the rate of literacy was relatively high within the urban population, but the creation of a modern nation required a radically increased competence in reading and writing. Most of the written styles of the premodern period were too difficult to be mastered by the masses.

Westernization. Finally, the written language had to liberate itself from its dependence on classical Chinese. The only way to modernize was in affiliation with the modern languages of the developed West.

The post-Meiji history of language treatment in Japan can be divided into three major periods. The first two are reformist and partly overlap with regard to their aims. The third period, which commences in the 1960s, follows the completion of the modernization process, and is distinctly antireformist.

First Period, 1868–1900 —— At the outset of the Meiji period (1868–1912) the communication problems of the nation were so serious that in 1872 MORI ARINORI contemplated giving up Japanese and adopting English as the national language of Japan. However, within the next three decades most of the problems were basically solved. Though admittedly many issues still remained, there was no question of a radical change of course in 1900.

The first period is characterized by considerable activity in the language treatment networks, but no major language reforms emerged. The changes that did occur during this period were largely spontaneous.

The fact that the development of a national language was an uncontrolled process can be seen from the fact that two separate varieties of Japanese emerged to fill the role: the Classical Standard, based on the written styles of pre-Meiji Japanese (*bungo*) and only used in writing, and the Colloquial Standard, based on the spoken language (*kōgo*) and basically identical with present-day Standard Japanese. The process of the creation of these standards was little affected by discussions initiated either by individuals or by a number of language treatment associations. On the other hand the undesirability of this "diglottic" situation and the need to remove the difficult Classical Standard was extensively discussed during the GEMBUN ITCHI movement. However, the removal was a gradual process and the discussions did not result in any radical decision to change usage during this period.

In connection with the problem of the national language the issue of the most suitable system of writing for the language appeared at the very beginning of the first period. MAEJIMA HISOKA became famous for his early plea (1866) to abandon Chinese characters in favor of the KANA syllabary. In 1869 Nambu Yoshikazu suggested the use of romanization. Associations were formed to promote both ideas, and attempts were made to put them into practice. However, these radical ideas lacked sufficient support to influence the strong spontaneous language development. This development led to changes in the character of the writing system, but the characters and *kana* were retained as the most basic components.

An amazingly fast development of the Japanese vocabulary occurred in this period so that in this respect Japanese caught up with other developed languages of the world by the end of the century. The modern vocabulary used elements of Chinese origin but its conceptual structure was either purely Japanese or identical with that of the Western languages which served as models. All this was achieved without much intervention from the language treatment system. Similarly, the radical extension of literacy was achieved through the introduction of general and compulsory education, not through special literacy programs.

Second Period, 1900–1960 —— On the whole it can be said that the first period of language treatment in Japan was a time when basic issues were discussed. The second period concentrated more on adjustments which aimed at increasing the efficiency of the standard language as well as completing the process of modernization and spreading the modern changes throughout the community.

The individual, private groups as well as language associations (with some new additions) remained active in this period, but the Ministry of Education now created its own specialized language treatment agencies. After multiple transformations this process resulted in the creation in 1934 of the COUNCIL ON THE NATIONAL LANGUAGE (Kokugo Shingikai).

The second period was a period of unceasing attempts at partial reforms of the language and of the writing system in particular. One of the early reforms which met with success was the unification of the shapes of *kana* (1900). However, most such moves remained unsuccessful. This is true of the repeated attempts at the removal of the difficult, historically motivated, *kana* spelling, as well as of the attempts to restrict the number of characters used. Especially important was the proposal of 1923 which listed 1,962 characters to be used and which was accepted and partly implemented in 1925 by the large newspapers. The era before World War II was characterized by a struggle between the utilitarian reformists and the nationalists. The former group approved of reforms because they aimed at efficiency. With the colonial expansion of the Shōwa period (1926–) the difficulty of teaching Japanese to people in the colonies contributed to the arguments of the reformists, and it is interesting that both the army and navy, at least initially, were supporters of the reforms. It was, however, the nationalists who won in each case.

The defeat of Japan in 1945 created excellent conditions for the reformists to push through the long-prepared reforms. They had the welcome support of the Allied OCCUPATION as well as of the progressive forces within the country, which aimed at a real democratization of Japan. The Classical Standard was now removed from its last stronghold, the area of administration and law, and the style of the language of Japanese officialdom was thoroughly modernized. A series of writing reforms was begun in 1946 by "phoneticizing" the historical *kana* spelling and restricting the number of characters used in public life to 1,850. These characters were called TŌYŌ KANJI (Chinese characters for daily use). A strongly restrictive list of approved readings of the *tōyō kanji* appeared in 1948 and the shapes of the characters were standardized in 1949. It was decided that 881 characters out of the *tōyō kanji* list should be required for writing as well as reading during the nine years of compulsory school education (it was later decided that these 881 characters would be taught during the six years of elementary school). Some additional characters were approved for use in newly registered given names, but many formerly used characters could now not be used. The last reform in this first postwar series, promulgated in 1959, concerned the spelling of words which consist of a character and affixed *kana* (*okurigana*).

These reforms were not revolutionary but they were radical. They exerted a marked influence not merely on the writing system but also on the Japanese vocabulary and contributed toward further reduction of the distance between the style of language used in speaking and in writing. However, the restrictions imposed by the reforms did not necessarily apply in journals, books, or in the usage of individuals, such as in private correspondence. As a result of this the actual social usage of the 1960s and 1970s still included a certain number of features of the writing system, especially of characters, of the prereform period.

Third Period, 1960–Present —— Many reformists and progressivists of the postwar period believed that the reforms of the late 1940s represented only the beginning of a final attack on the characters. This, however, proved to be a false assumption. However difficult the present-day writing system may be, it became obvious that it is not incompatible with the functioning of a modern society. At the same time it became clear that within contemporary Japan a radical social reform of any kind was a politically unfeasible procedure.

The great change in the balance of power within the Council on National Language came in 1960. Toward the end of the decade the council began launching a series of recommendations, subsequently implemented, which softened the restrictions imposed on public usage by the postwar reforms. The number of characters to be taught during compulsory school education was raised from 881 to 996 (1968), the number of approved readings for the *tōyō kanji* was increased (1973), and the list of *tōyō kanji* was revised. The new JŌYŌ KANJI list of 1981 includes 1,945 characters, an increase of 95.

Apart from individual inconsistencies the new language treatment measures seem to command the support not merely of the Old Right, which interprets them as a sign of commencing revival, but of the public in general. In fact they do not mean anything beyond the acknowledgment of present-day middle-class usage. There is little chance that they will lead to a radical increase in the number of characters within the community. There is also no doubt that they take no regard of the language problems of those classes of the Japanese society which do not possess the advantage of higher education.

The Future of Language Reforms in Japan —— Language reforms of the past, together with the spontaneous development of the Japanese language, have resulted in the creation of the contemporary Japanese standard language. This language is modern and serves adequately the needs of modern Japanese society. No doubt, many problems exist, and new problems are emerging. However, within the present-day climate of language treatment in Japan there is no reason to expect that a radical reform of the writing system or of any other aspect of the language will take place in the coming decades.

■ —— F. J. Daniels, "Japanese Officialdom and the Language," *Journal of the Association of Teachers of Japanese* 13.1 (1978). Hirai Masao, *Kokugo kokuji mondai no rekishi* (1948). J. V. Neustupný, *Post-Structural Approaches to Language: Language Theory in a Japanese Context* (1978). Suzuki Yasuyuki, ed, *Kokugo kokuji mondai no riron* (1977). J. V. NEUSTUPNÝ

Japanese language studies, history of

Japanese language studies may be defined in a narrow sense as attempts to describe or explain the Japanese language and its various properties. By this definition, with few significant exceptions, Japanese language studies began in the Edo period (1600–1868). The principal reason for this relatively late beginning was the prestige of Chinese; there is some parallel here to the position of Western European vernacular languages vis-à-vis Latin. For present purposes, the history of Japanese language studies may be divided into three major periods: the seminal period, up to 1600; the formative period, coinciding with the Edo period; and the modern period, after 1868.

The history of Japanese language studies (kokugogaku shi) is a recognized subdiscipline of linguistics in Japan, and possesses a substantial literature. It tends to define Japanese language studies more broadly than above, including those portions of Japanese literature which bear on linguistic questions in whatever context. On the other hand, it tends to overlook both the study of foreign languages in Japan and the study of Japanese by foreigners. While the latter has had relatively little influence in Japan, the mainstream of Japanese language study hardly makes sense in isolation from Japanese efforts to master other languages.

The seminal period. The decisive external stimuli to the development of Japanese civilization came principally via Chinese. This applies both to Buddhist religious thought as well as to Chinese sociopolitical thought. Japanese was used for poetry and other creative or popular literature, but Chinese remained the language of scholarship into the Edo period. However, Chinese was read or written by means of an elaborate annotation system called *kambun kundoku* (interpretive reading of Chinese), which provided simultaneous translation into or from Japanese. The adoption of Chinese by the Japanese thus follows the pattern evident in other areas of influence: extensive assimilation and adaptation to Japanese needs and capacities.

The construction of a workable writing system for Japanese took place within this context. Chinese characters (KANJI) were employed, either on the basis of phonetic similarity (ON READINGS) or semantic similarity (KUN READINGS). These usages developed into KANA with standardized Japanese readings. Dictionaries such as SHINSEN JIKYŌ (ca 900), WAMYŌ RUIJU SHŌ (ca 934), RUIJŪ MYŌGI SHŌ (ca 1100), or SETSUYŌSHŪ (ca 1450) record the process. They are more accurately classified as studies of Chinese than of Japanese. More appropriate examples of Japanese language study are the *kana* spelling manuals associated with the poet Fujiwara no Teika (FUJI-WARA NO SADAIE; 1162–1241).

Phonetic descriptions of both Chinese and Sanskrit were known in Japan from the 9th century. The latter apparently influenced, for example, the GOJŪON ZU (50-sound table) inventory of *kana*. Like the dictionaries, however, Japanese works in these areas were not studies of Japanese as such, regardless of their later value as sources of information about it. Grammatical descriptions of Japanese began to appear in the 14th century in works devoted to poetic theory. The Chinese had not developed grammar independently, nor absorbed Indian grammar, but they did pay some attention to poetic form. In Japanese, the appropriate usage of grammatical particles and inflected forms was an important aspect of poetic style.

The formative period. The development of Japanese language studies in the Edo period was closely associated with the KOKUGAKU (National Learning) movement. The ideological component of the movement, which devalued both Buddhism and Confucianism as foreign contamination in favor of native Japanese culture and religion, brought the Japanese language into a position of value and prestige in competition with Chinese. At the same time, this development was no more than an aspect of the remarkable explosion which affected Japanese intellectual life at that time and cut across almost every ideological and disciplinary boundary. The rise of Japanese philology paralleled scholarly activity in Chinese philology, Buddhism, political science, agriculture, technology, mathematics, and so on.

A case in point is the work of KEICHŪ (1640–1701). In his philological studies of the 8th-century poetry anthology MAN'YŌSHŪ, he noted many discrepancies in *kana* spelling between this ancient monument of Japanese literature and his contemporary usage. Keichū's WAJI SHŌRAN SHŌ (1695) showed that the Fujiwara no Teika system of spelling was historically arbitrary and offered a new system based on the usages of the *Man'yōshū*. This achievement occasioned great controversy, but it became a paradigm for the Kokugaku movement, and in time was generally adopted. Japanese phonological studies in the formative period proceeded within the context of orthography. MOTOORI NORINAGA (1730–1801), ISHI-ZUKA TATSUMARO (1764–1823) and TŌJŌ GIMON (1786–1843) corrected and extended Keichū's results, often in the light of Chinese phonology.

The formative period also witnessed the emergence of large comprehensive dictionaries based on philological investigation of Japanese literature. The WAKUN NO SHIORI, compiled by TANI-GAWA KOTOSUGA (1709–76), the GAGEN SHŪRAN, compiled by ISHI-KAWA MASAMOCHI (1753–1830), and the RIGEN SHŪRAN, probably compiled by Ōta Zensai (1759–1829), are notable examples; none was published in its entirety during the Edo period. The last of the three, together with the BUTSURUI SHŌKO compiled by Aida Gozan (1717–87) represent the beginnings of the systematic study of Japanese dialects.

Japanese grammar was established in the work of Motoori Norinaga and FUJITANI NARIAKIRA (1738–79). The concern with grammatical particles in Norinaga's *Kotoba no tama no o* (1785) and Nariakira's *Ayuishō* (1778) grew out of a desire to appreciate and revive the classical WAKA poetic form. Nariakira set up a consistent part-of-speech system for Japanese, which was developed by students of Norinaga, in particular his son MOTOORI HARUNIWA (1763–1828) and SUZUKI AKIRA (1764–1837). Haruniwa's study of Japanese inflection, *Kotoba no yachimata* (1806–08), and Akira's treatise on grammatical categories, *Gengyo shishu ron* (1824), represent the culmination of this work. It was systematized as the received traditional grammar of Japanese by Tōjō Gimon.

The modern period. By the end of the Edo period, Japanese-language studies were flourishing on a solid basis in a variety of directions. The political and other changes which centered on 1868 affected their subsequent development in two significant ways: the Japanese began to look to the West for guidance, and they intended to apply what they received toward resolving practical social problems. The Kokugo Chōsa Iinkai (Commission to Investigate the National Language) between 1903 and 1928 provided the basis for defining and promulgating a Standard Japanese language. Its tradition has been carried on in the postwar period by the Kokugo Shingikai (COUNCIL ON THE NATIONAL LANGUAGE) and the Kokuritsu Kokugo Kenkyūjo (NATIONAL JAPANESE LANGUAGE RESEARCH INSTITUTE).

Reflecting European priorities of the period, the first wave of Western influence in Japanese language studies stressed the historical study of Japanese and the question of its relationship to other languages in East Asia. UEDA KAZUTOSHI (1867–1937), the first Japanese trained in European linguistics, and SHIMMURA IZURU (1876–1967) pursued historical and comparative research, while YA-NAGITA KUNIO (1875–1962) and TŌJŌ MISAO (1884–1966) were particularly involved in the growth of Japanese dialectology. The already well-developed lexicographical tradition was much enriched in the process: examples are Ueda's *Daijiten* (1917), Shimmura's *Kō-jien* (1955) and Tōjō's *Zenkoku hōgen jiten* (1951).

Phonology was similarly reshaped by Western influences. Phonetic investigations of Japanese were carried out by Jimbō Kaku (1883–1965) and SAKUMA KANAE (1888–1970), with serious attention being paid to the phenomenon of accent, and a permanent experimental tradition established. In the area of historical phonology, HASHIMOTO SHINKICHI (1882–1945) and ARISAKA HIDEYO (1908–1952) followed the Edo-period beginnings with fully modern accounts based on historical and comparative methods. Ōno Susumu (b 1919) and Mabuchi Kazuo (b 1918) have pursued related philological approaches in the postwar years. Hirayama Teruo (b 1909) and Kindaichi Haruhiko (b 1913) have combined dialectological perspectives with the phonological tradition.

The development of grammar in the modern period has been affected by the shift from classical to modern colloquial style, which took place over a period of time. The major early grammars of scholars like YAMADA YOSHIO (1873–1958) or MATSUSHITA DAIZA-BURŌ (1878–1935) dealt primarily with the literary language and included the colloquial (if at all) in a derivative way. In the subsequent work of scholars like Hashimoto Shinkichi and TOKIEDA MOTOKI (1900–1967), the priority is in effect reversed. The variety of approaches to Japanese grammar in the postwar period is as great and as rich as for English or French and is an active focus of popular concern.

Modern Western linguistics has also had an impact on Japanese-language studies. The structuralist approach is best represented in the work of HATTORI SHIRŌ (b 1908), who has contributed to both phonology and grammar in addition to historical and comparative studies. The transformational or generative approach is represented in the work of Inoue Kazuko (b 1919), Kuno Susumu (b 1933), and Kuroda Shigeyuki (b 1934). The increasing prominence of Japan in the international community in recent years has brought official support for developing programs to teach Japanese as a foreign language, as well as the materials and personnel necessary for this purpose.

Japanese language studies by non-Japanese. Aside from the mainstream just surveyed, there is a body of studies of Japanese language which bear no relation to, and have not had major influence on, the progress made within the Japanese world. There were studies of Japanese of a practical nature (largely vocabularies or phrase books) done by Chinese or Koreans in premodern times. More significant were the grammars, dictionaries, and religious materials prepared by the Jesuit mission to Japan in the 16th and 17th centuries, before its expulsion by the Tokugawa government. The *Arte da Lingoa de Iapam* (1608) by the Portuguese João RODRIGUES (1561?–1633) is representative of this work.

With the onset of the modern period, many missionaries and diplomats attempted to meet the needs of their fellow foreigners for access to the Japanese language via dictionaries and grammars. The Dutch first opened this field, but the English eventually took the lead. Perhaps the work of Basil Hall CHAMBERLAIN (1850–1935) is representative of this phase. Many foreign scholars with a professional interest in Japanese have added to the corpus over the intervening years. Notable examples are the Russian Evgenij POLIVANOV (1891–1938), the Frenchman Charles Haguenauer (1896–1976), the American Bernard BLOCH (1907–65), and the German Günther Wenck (b 1916). See also DICTIONARIES; JAPANESE AS A FOREIGN LANGUAGE.

📖 ——Furuta Tōsaku and Tsukishima Hiroshi, *Kokugogaku shi* (1972). Susumu Kuno, *The Structure of the Japanese Language* (1972). Miki Kōshin and Fukunaga Seiya, *Kokugogaku shi* (1966). Roy Andrew Miller, *The Japanese Language* (1967). Satō Kiyoji, ed, *Kokugogaku kenkyū jiten* (1977).   *George* BEDELL

Japanese literature and Christianity

The history of Christianity in Japan can be divided into two periods: the mid-16th to mid-17th centuries, when the Jesuits and Franciscans propagated Roman Catholicism, and the period from the mid-19th century to the present, during which both Protestants and Catholics have been active. However, because Christianity was virtually extinguished under the ruthless shogunate policy, Christianity exerted very little influence on Japanese literature. This article, therefore, will deal exclusively with the relation between Christianity and Japanese literature in the modern period.

Toward the end of the Edo period (1600–1868), the Tokugawa shogunate began to relax its NATIONAL SECLUSION laws. A Protestant missionary, B. J. Bettelheim, opened a mission in the Ryūkyū Islands (now Okinawa Prefecture) in 1846. Catholic missionary activity began in 1859, when P. S. B. Girard of the Foreign Missionary Society of Paris arrived. Many Christian converts of the Meiji (1868–1912) and Taishō (1912–26) periods came from the educated segment, and Protestantism, with its emphasis on the individual conscience, particularly appealed to younger intellectuals.

The writers KITAMURA TŌKOKU, SHIMAZAKI TŌSON, and KUNIKIDA DOPPO, all of whom were baptized as young men, were drawn to Christianity's emphasis on nature as God's handiwork, the inner life, and the dignity of the common man. In these writers we find a romanticized Christianity. TOKUTOMI ROKA, KINOSHITA NAOE, and KAGAWA TOYOHIKO were drawn to its message of love and service to mankind. MUSHANOKŌJI SANEATSU, a leader of the SHIRAKABA SCHOOL, believed in "letting oneself live meaningfully" *(jiko o ikasu)*. Through his study of Christ and the Bible, he came to regard Christ as a genius of the highest order and as the "greatest brother," but in so doing, he completely humanized Christianity. SHIGA NAOYA, another writer of the Shirakaba school, followed a similar route, as did ARISHIMA TAKEO. Many of these writers were eventually to abandon Christianity for a secularized humanism.

The early twenties saw a renewed interest in Christianity. Writers like AKUTAGAWA RYŪNOSUKE, NAKAHARA CHŪYA, and DAZAI OSAMU were fascinated by Christian symbolism and the existential aspects of the religion.

After Japan's total defeat in World War II, Christianity came to be recognized as a legitimate literary theme. The writers who contributed most to this new trend were SHIINA RINZŌ, a Protestant, and ENDŌ SHŪSAKU, a Catholic. Shiina discovered in Christ the basis of human freedom, and Endō explored the relationship between a religion of foreign origin and the Japanese cultural climate. Other writers (some of them converts) who deal with Christian themes are TANAKA CHIKAO, TANAKA SUMIE, MIURA SHUMON, SONO AYAKO, ARIYOSHI SAWAKO, and SHIMAO TOSHIO.

📖 ——Sasabuchi Tomoichi, "Meiji Taishō ki no kirisutokyō bungaku to Arishima Takeo," *Bungaku* 3–4 (1954). Takeda Tomoju, "Seitō to itan ni kansuru bungaku nōtō," *Seiki* (March 1954–August 1955).   SASABUCHI Tomoichi

Japanese National Commission for UNESCO → UNESCO activities in Japan

Japanese nationality

Legal status denoting membership in, allegiance to, and protection by the Japanese state. Article 18 of the Meiji CONSTITUTION of 1889 provided that the conditions of Japanese nationality be stipulated by law. Accordingly, in 1899 the Nationality Law (Kokuseki Hō) of Japan (Law No. 66) was promulgated. The statutory provisions contained therein set the criteria for determining who shall be Japanese nationals. This law was amended twice, in 1916 and 1924, in order to provide for the renunciation of Japanese citizenship by those persons born in countries that adhered to the principle of *jus soli* whereby nationality is determined according to place of birth.

Under the provisions set forth in article 10 of the new 1947 Constitution, a new Nationality Law (Law No. 147) was enacted on 4 May 1950. It introduced some important changes to the old law concerning the acquisition and loss of nationality, recognizing the individual's right of choice and the equality of the sexes in such matters. The proviso of the old law based upon the Japanese traditional family system (IE) was abolished, and people were given the freedom to renounce their Japanese nationality. The new law, like the old, adopted the rule of *jus sanguinis* ("right of blood," whereby one acquires nationality by virtue of one's descent or parentage) through the father only. It abolished, however, the acquisition or loss of nationality based upon a change in an individual's status, for example, through marriage, acknowledgment of parentage, adoption, and so forth.

The acquisition of nationality is permitted only by naturalization, which includes the recovery of nationality. The restrictions preventing naturalized persons from assuming some important offices, such as that of state minister, were nullified under the principle of equality of persons under the law stated in the 1947 Constitution.

The granting of naturalization has been considered a discretionary power of the minister of justice. However, a decision was recently delivered affirming that an unfair denial of naturalization could be the subject of administrative litigation.

Since Japanese nationality by birth is acquired by *jus sanguinis* only through the father, there have been lawsuits raised in Japan demanding Japanese nationality by *jus sanguinis* through the mother on the grounds that since the constitution provides for equality of the sexes, denial of *jus sanguinis* through the mother is unconstitutional. These lawsuits were denied by the courts of first and second instances and appeals had been taken to the Supreme Court in June 1982. Accusations of sex discrimination have been made because of the obviously more difficult conditions required for the naturalization of husbands than for wives of Japanese nationals. In the meantime, Japan signed the United Nations Convention on the Elimination of All Forms of Discrimination against Women (1979) and began to adapt its internal laws to comply with the convention. In December 1981 a special commission was appointed by the minister of justice to study the matter and to develop proposals. It was expected that the Nationality Law would be revised in the near future to incorporate the principle of equality of sexes in the acquisition of nationality *jus sanguinis* and in granting naturalization.

Acquisition of Nationality —— Nationality can be acquired by birth or by naturalization. In the first instance, covered under article 2 of the Nationality Law, a child shall be a Japanese national in any of the following cases: (1) the father is a Japanese national at the time of the child's birth; (2) the father died prior to the birth and was a Japanese national at the time of his death; (3) the father is unknown or has no nationality, but the mother is a Japanese national; (4) the child is born in Japan, and both parents are unknown or have no nationality.

Nationality acquired through naturalization is covered under articles 3–7 of the Nationality Law. It falls into three categories.

Ordinary naturalization. The following are the conditions for ordinary naturalization (art. 4): the applicant (1) has had his domicile in Japan consecutively for five years or more; (2) is 20 years of age or older and is a person of mental competency under the law of the

Japanese National Railways

| JNR Traffic Volume | | | | |
| | Freight metric ton-km (billions) | Passenger-km (billions) | Percentage of total domestic transport | |
			Freight	Passenger
1950	33	69	51.4	58.9
1955	43	91	52.0	55.0
1960	54	124	38.6	51.0
1965	56	174	30.3	45.5
1970	62	190	17.8	32.3
1975	47	215	12.9	30.3
1980	37	193	8.4	24.7

SOURCE: Un'yushō (Ministry of Transport), *Un'yu keizai tōkei yōran* (annual): 1982.

country of his nationality; (3) is a person of upright conduct; (4) has property or ability permitting him to maintain an independent livelihood; (5) has no nationality, or has one that acquisition of Japanese nationality will cause him to lose; (6) since the promulgation of the Japanese constitution, has never plotted or advocated, organized, or belonged to a political party or other organization that has plotted or advocated the forceful overthrow of the Japanese constitution or the government.

Special naturalization. Any alien who comes under one of the following classifications may be permitted naturalization even though he does not meet conditions for ordinary naturalization. The applicant: (1) is the husband of a Japanese national and has had his domicile or residence in Japan consecutively for three years or more; (2) is the child of a former Japanese national (excluding an adopted child), and has had his domicile or residence in Japan consecutively for three years or more; (3) was born in Japan and has had his domicile or residence in Japan consecutively for three years or more, or his father or mother (excluding a father or mother by adoption) was born in Japan; (4) has resided in Japan consecutively for 10 years or more.

Any alien who falls under one of the following classifications may be permitted naturalization even though he does not meet the first, second, and fourth conditions for ordinary naturalization: (1) the wife of a Japanese national; (2) the child (excluding an adopted child) of a Japanese national who has his domicile in Japan; (3) the adopted child of a Japanese national who has had his domicile in Japan consecutively for one year or more and was a minor under the law of the country of his nationality at the time of his adoption; (4) one who has lost his Japanese nationality (excluding one who has lost his nationality after his naturalization in Japan) and has his domicile in Japan.

Grand naturalization. An alien who has rendered especially meritorious service to Japan may be permitted naturalization with the approval of the Diet, waiving the conditions for ordinary naturalization. Nevertheless, no such case of naturalization has been registered.

Under the old law, a foreign woman who married a Japanese acquired Japanese nationality according to the principle of unity of nationality of spouses, but the new law has adopted the principle of independence of nationality of spouses.

Loss of Nationality (Articles 8 to 10 of the Nationality Law)
A Japanese national who voluntarily acquires a foreign nationality, or who acquires a foreign nationality by reason of his birth in a foreign country shall lose his Japanese nationality retroactively unless within 14 days after birth he (or his parents) manifests his intention to preserve his Japanese nationality according to the provisions of the Family Registration Law (Law No. 224 of 1947). Furthermore, a Japanese national having a foreign nationality may renounce and lose his Japanese nationality by notifying the minister of justice.

Under the old law, conditions for the loss of Japanese nationality were narrower. There were provisions forbidding loss of nationality by a Japanese male who had not completed or had an obligation to serve in the armed forces, and people who occupied an official post, civil or military, had to renounce the post. On the other hand, there was involuntary loss of nationality, for example, a Japanese woman losing her Japanese nationality when she acquired the nationality of her husband. NINOMIYA Masato

Japanese National Railways

(Nihon Kokuyū Tetsudō; commonly abbreviated Kokutetsu). Public corporation (see PUBLIC CORPORATIONS), founded in 1949, which operates the national railway, ferry, and bus services as well as various subsidiary concerns. Japan's largest enterprise, with assets totaling ¥11 trillion (US $48.5 billion) in 1980, the JNR forms the mainstay of the nation's railway network.

Background——In 1869 the Japanese government decided to embark upon railway construction as a public undertaking, completing in 1872 the nation's first railway line, which linked Shimbashi and Yokohama. Owing to its strained finances, however, the government also permitted private construction, which began in 1881. Private railways soon outstripped the state lines in extent and by 1905 accounted for just over two-thirds of the entire network. Under the Railway Nationalization Law of 1906, the major private lines were purchased by the government in 1906 and 1907. This action left only small, local lines in private hands; thereafter, private initiative centered on the development of electric commuter lines and light railways. Meanwhile, between 1917 and 1945, the government extended its ownership and control by buying up 69 private local railways. In 1949, with the aim of rationalizing the enterprise and increasing its efficiency, the state railways were reorganized under the Japanese National Railways Law as a public corporation, independent of the Ministry of Transport. The government, however, provided all of the capital and retained powers of supervision.

Organization and Scale of Operation——The officers of the JNR consist of a president appointed by the cabinet, a vice-president, a chief engineer, and several directors and auditors. With some 414,000 employees, the corporation operated just over 21,300 kilometers (13,200 mi) of railway line in 1980, having increased in length from 29 kilometers (18 mi) in 1872 to 10,000 kilometers (6,210 mi) in 1920 and to 20,000 kilometers (12,430 mi) in 1953. In 1980, the volume of traffic on the JNR amounted to 193 billion passenger-kilometers, or 24.7 percent of domestic passenger traffic, and 37 billion (metric) ton-kilometers of freight, or 8.4 percent of domestic freight traffic.

Problems and Plans——The national railways have been hard hit by competition from private automotive transport, which began to grow in the late 1950s and rose rapidly in the 1960s. Between 1960 and 1970 the corporation's share of domestic passenger traffic declined from 51 percent to 32 percent and its share of domestic freight traffic from 38 to 18 percent, while that of private motor vehicles increased from 23 to 49 percent for passenger traffic and from 15 to 40 percent for freight traffic. These trends, however, have slowed sharply during the last decade.

Added to the problem of competition from automotive transport has been the financial burden of maintaining nonpaying local lines, which make up some 40 percent of the total state network. These lines accounted for more than a fourth of the corporation's annual deficit of over ¥800 billion (US $3 billion) in the late 1970s. Devising measures for financial rehabilitation, therefore, has been a pressing concern. One recent proposal would bring the national railways full circle by having the majority of local lines transferred to private railway or bus companies.

The JNR has been a world leader in railway technology, a position confirmed by the development of the high-speed "bullet train" line (the SHINKANSEN), the first section of which was opened in 1964. In 1980, plans called for completion of the northern extension of this line to connect Hokkaidō with the main island via the Aomori-Hakodate tunnel. The corporation was also moving ahead with the development of a linear-motor car, the post-Shinkansen superspeed train, capable of linking Tōkyō and Ōsaka in one hour and scheduled for introduction in the mid-1980s. See also RAILWAYS; TRANSPORTATION. *Steven J. ERICSON*

Japanese people, origin of

Time Depth and Early Man——The formation of the Japanese people has been markedly influenced by geography and climate. In glacial periods the central mountain range was capped with ice, but the coastal zone and mountain slopes were habitable and lowered sea levels exposed three major migration routes: from Sakhalin and Siberia in the north; from China and Korea to the west; and from Okinawa and the Ryūkyūs in the south. During interglacial periods the islands were isolated, but navigation had replaced the land corridors by the time the sea level had risen at the end of the last glacial period, about 10,000 BC. Oriental flora and fauna assured an abundant food supply in the warm interglacial periods and in glacial

Origin of the Japanese people

Cranial and Facial Dimensions of Japanese from Jōmon to Early Historic Times Compared with Recent Japanese, Ainu, Korean, and N. Chinese Populations

	Cranial length	Cranial breadth	Cranial height[1]	Facial breadth	Facial height	Cranial index	Cranio-facial index
	(in millimeters)						
Jōmon	186	144	134	143	116	77	81
Yayoi	185	146	134	142	125	79	88
Kofun	182	141	133	135	118	77	87
Early historic	178	142	140	134	122	80	91
Recent	179	141	139	135	122	80	95
Ainu	185	141	140	137	118	77	86
Korean	175	142	140	136	123	82	90
N. Chinese	179	140	139	134	125	78	93

[1] Basion-bregma.

SOURCE: W. W. Howells, *The Jōmon Population of Japan*, Peabody Museum Papers, vol 57 (Harvard University, 1966). M. G. Levin, "Ethnic Origins of the Peoples of Northeastern Asia," Arctic Institute of North America, Russian Translation Series, no. 3 (1963). Hisashi Suzuki, "Racial History of the Japanese," in *Rassengeschichte der Menscheit* (8 Lieferung, Asien I: Japan, Indonesien, Ozeanien; 1981).

periods mammoths, deer, and other continental megafauna roamed the grassy plains.

Thousands of artifacts and caches of broken animal bones have been recovered from rock shelters, limestone fissures, and glacial loam sites, some dating from as early as the end of the second glacial period a half million years or more ago. A few associated hominid bone fragments have been found but are identifiable only as belonging to the genus Homo. Part of an ilium recovered from a mid-Pleistocene site at Akashi (Hyōgo Prefecture) falls into the same category. Elsewhere, a broken humerus from a quarry near Ushikawa in Aichi Prefecture, thought at first to be hominid, has since been identified as probably that of a hominoid ape. In Shizuoka Prefecture some broken leg bones associated with a late Pleistocene dwarf elephant tusk from Mikkabi, and part of a skull from Hamakita, remain inconclusively identified. It has been conjectured that some of the sites are probably those of a pithecanthropine *(Homo erectus)*, but no finds have yet been made which are comparable with those of Peking or Java Man (see PALEOLITHIC CULTURE).

Modern Man—— The oldest definitely identified human *(Homo sapiens)* remains, though incomplete, date from upper paleolithic times of the last glacial period, about 30,000 BC. The oldest remains satisfactory for comparative analysis are from the early part of the Jōmon period (ca 10,000 BC–ca 300 BC), but Jōmon skeletal assemblages satisfactory for statistical analysis date from about 5000 BC after the seafaring population of that period had begun spreading in increasing numbers along the coastal shores—first from the south and west and later from the north.

Because of marked differences in economies and rates of population growth the genetic impact of the surviving pre-Jōmon cold fauna hunters on the immigrant Jōmon population was probably marginal. The former lived mainly in small scattered groups away from coastal shores near water holes and stream beds which attracted game and where inland plant foods were available. The neolithic Jōmon population, on the other hand, exploited the rich coastal and estuarine fish, shellfish, waterfowl, and marine plant resources. They had the advantage of a relatively advanced technology: pottery, traps, weirs, wood-cutting tools, navigation, and by late Jōmon, the beginnings of garden agriculture. Living in clusters of semipermanent shelters in shell mound settlements, they shifted from site to site either seasonally or on a rotational basis as local food supplies became depleted.

The population growth differential was even more significant. Based on comparable mainland sites, existence was precarious for the pre-Jōmon inland hunters with life expectancy less than 20 years and the total population probably never exceeding 20,000. Based on skeletal remains, average life expectancy in the early Jōmon population may still have been less than 20 years, but for those who survived past adolescence it had increased to 25 by middle Jōmon and to 31 by the beginning of the Yayoi period (ca 300 BC–ca AD 300). There was also a constant influx of migrants and population estimates for the end of Jōmon range from 100,000 to 300,000.

Jōmon Hunters and Yayoi Cultivators—— Over a thousand Jōmon skeletons dating from 5000 BC to 500 BC have been recovered of which approximately half are useful for comparative purposes. In spite of superior technology and agriculture, the total for Yayoi is

probably no greater. Burials were mainly in areas of subsequent intensive farming and subject to destruction. For obvious reasons, remains from the Tomb Culture or KOFUN PERIOD (ca 300–710) are better preserved but confined mainly to the military aristocracy. In spite of these limitations, the collective remains of each period are statistically distinctive and follow a generally unilinear sequence of morphological transitions from Jōmon to modern times. Scholars are not agreed on interpretations: some favor minimal immigration with rapid microevolution attributable to environmental selective pressures, changing economies, and minor mutations; others favor continuing migration and admixture from south coastal China and Korea during Yayoi and assimilation of the horse riders from Korea and North China in the succeeding period (see HORSE-RIDER THEORY). Generally neglected in most studies, however, are factors of differential demographic fertility and social stratification.

Shortness of time would militate against a rapid change thesis, whereas intensive rice and taro production by settled Yayoi agriculturists would favor their increase at the expense of shoreline Jōmon hunters and gatherers. There is archaeological evidence that the Yayoi cultivators spread rapidly throughout the southern islands and along both sides of the Inland Sea to the Yamato plain by the early Kofun period.

The Jōmon population was generally short-statured with heavy skeletal structure; leg bones were laterally flattened (platymeria and platycnemia), a condition reminiscent of other prehistoric and existing hunting and gathering isolates; skulls were longheaded (dolichocephalic), faces short and broad with markedly concave nasal profiles; supraorbital ridges were massive with marked medial depressions. There was considerable alveolar prognathism, the teeth were large and the bite mainly edge-to-edge. Multivariate discriminant analyses place Jōmon skulls between those of the native AINU and modern Japanese, but closer to the Ainu and more variable.

Formation of the Yamato—— Crania of the early historic period Japanese are shorter and slightly narrower than those of Jōmon times and there are marked increases in cranial height and both cranial and facial indices (see table). The Yamato of history are probably mainly descendants of the Yayoi cultivators with regionally varying admixtures of the earlier Jōmon population and a continuing addition of immigrants from the insular south, but more especially from Korea and China. Complete assimilation and genetic balance (homeostatis) have not yet been achieved. Some marginal local populations approximate the Jōmon population more closely than the majority population while traits associated with the horse-riding invaders are more characteristic of the *bushi* or warrior class. See also JAPANESE PEOPLE, PHYSICAL CHARACTERISTICS OF; ARCHAEOLOGY.

▪ —— W. W. Howells, *The Jōmon Population of Japan* (1966). Takeo Kanaseki et al, *Craniological Studies of the Yayoi Period Ancients* (1960). Kiyono Kenji, *Kodai jinkotsu no kenkyū ni motozuku Nippon jinshu ron* (1949). Motoji Kohama, *An Anthropometrical Study of the Japanese: On the Local Differences and the Origins of the Japanese* (1960). Komatsu Isao, *The Japanese People: Origins of the People and the Language* (1962). M. G. Levin, "Ethnic Origins of the Peoples of Northeastern Asia," Arctic Institute of North America, Russian Translation Series, no. 3 (1963). Naotune Watanabe,

Chronological Background for Studies on Microevolution and Population History in Japan (1969). H. Suzuki, "Racial History of the Japanese," in *Rassengeschichte der Menschheit* (8 Lieferung, Asien I: Japan, Indonesien, Ozeanien; 1981).   *Gordon T. Bowles*

Japanese people, physical characteristics of

The Japanese people, the Yamato or Wa people of history, have a reputation for homogeneity, but this seems to be more a cultural than a biologically demonstrable reality. There exists a strong sense of ethnicity and common cultural heritage which transcends local cultural differences in spite of some marked individual and significant regional evidences of past racial mixtures. By definition, the term Japanese as applied to the present population excludes all resident Koreans, Chinese, wartime spouses from Southeast Asia and the postwar legacy of about 20,000 mixed children (KONKETSUJI). Included, however, are the numerous mixed descendants of several thousand Korean and Chinese craftsmen and scholars who were induced to come to Japan between the 5th and 12th centuries (see KIKAJIN). All the latter have long since been assimilated, leaving only a few traceable mainland names and family traditions.

Apart from the AINU, who fall into a special category as the sole surviving non-Japanese native minority, the most distinguishable regional populations are the Okinawans and Tsu Islanders of Tsushima. Excluding recent Japanese migrants from the main islands, the Okinawans are statistically intermediate in physical characteristics between some of the coastal populations of China and those of Kyūshū. Similarly, the Tsu Islanders reflect a strong population influx from the fishing and diving communities of southern Korea.

Descriptive Traits—— Generally considered as part of the Mongoloid division of mankind, the Japanese are described as having relatively broad heads, prominent cheekbones, dark eyes, abundant straight black head hair, scanty body hair and beard; light yellowish to tan skin color; large teeth and a marked overbite with the medial incisors scalloped or "shovel-shaped" on the inner surfaces; and inner epicanthic eyefolds. Such a stereotype ignores the wide range that actually exists not only in these traits but also in nose form, facial prognathism and general body build. Traces of reddish tint in the hair are commonly observed and from 5 to 10 percent of many local populations, especially in the urban centers of Kyūshū, the Inland Sea, and central Japan, have lightish skin color, mixed greyish-brown eyes and straight to lightly convex noses and absence of the inner eyefold. Hair form also varies in texture and tendency toward waviness. These latter variables are generally attributed to the horse riders who may have entered Japan in the proto-historic period (AD 300–AD 500; see HORSE-RIDER THEORY). Some scholars suggest that the invaders represented a mixed population stemming in part from the eastward thrust of early Indo-European speaking Scytho-Sarmatians and early Altaic speakers who swept across the steppeland zone of Inner Asia into northern China sometime during the second millennium BC. Historical evidence for direct ties is lacking, but the occurrence of Europoid traits in North China, Korea, and Japan lends partial credence to the argument.

Morphological Types—— Differences in facial features and bodily form, both masculine and feminine, were a recognized means of depicting social class distinctions in the canons of traditional art, especially in the Edo period (1600–1868). The short-faced, stockily built peasantry were contrasted with the longer, narrower-faced, more aquiline-nosed and gracile elite military aristocracy (*bushi*, see SAMURAI). While not specifically localized or described in Japanese literature, the contrasting canons were first distinguished to European readers by Erwin von BÄLZ as the "coarse" Satsuma and "fine" Chōshū types. Such a clear-cut distinction was never emphasized by Japanese scholars, but there has been a recognition of regional differences. The "coarse" type, which was described as short-statured, brachycephalic (broad-headed), and darker-skinned, was thought to be mainly of southern origin; the longer-headed, longer-faced and lighter skinned "fine" type was identified with the later more northerly migrants and invaders.

Following Bälz were a number of attempts at classification by Japanese scholars. The best known are probably those of Matsumura Akira and HASEBE KOTONDO, both of whom recognized four types among the Japanese: the Okayama type, concentrated ostensibly in south central Honshū and described as relatively short-statured, long-faced and brachycephalic; the Ishikawa type of northeastern Honshū, also relatively short but mesocephalic (intermediate in head breadth) and short-faced; the Chikuzen type of Shikoku and northern Kyūshū, described as tall, mesocephalic, and short-faced; and the Satsuma type of southern Kyūshū: short, brachycephalic,

and short-faced. Such attempts at typological classification have generally been abandoned, but national, regional, and local variability have become subjects of intensive scientific analysis.

Regional Variability—— Japanese scholars have noted that the inhabitants of northern Honshū approximate the Ainu more closely in facial features and body hairiness than do those of other regions. Similarly, southerners approximate Southeast Asians more closely, and coastal villagers around the Inland Sea and offshore islanders of southern Honshū and northern Kyūshū are closer to Koreans. Statistical validations for such conclusions are determined, however, on a collective basis and individuals with Europoid, Ainu, Indonesian, and Korean, as well as Mongol, Tungus, and even Eskimo and American Indian traits appear randomly throughout the total population. (With respect to the former outcaste groups, there appear to be no distinguishing characteristics which set them apart biologically. The discrimination against them is thought to have resulted from the fact that many among them were flesh eaters, slaughterers, leather workers and those who handle corpses—all of which were considered polluting occupations or activities by some of the stricter Buddhist sects.)

While variability is relatively high in such externally visible features as nose, chin or lip form, pigment factors, and hair texture, such traits appear to be genetically so complex both individually and regionally that they tend to assume more significance as familial than as racially determinable characteristics. Other traits such as fingerprints or the number of hair follicles can be more accurately determined regardless of genetic complexity.

Fingerprints (Dermatoglyphs), Hair Follicles, and Earwax

Dermatoglyphic studies show the percentages of digital ridge counts of Chinese, Koreans, and Japanese are approximately the same: whorls 47 percent, loops 52 percent, and arches 3 percent. In Southeast Asia the percentage of whorls is lower and loops higher. As a temperate to cold climatic adaptation, peoples with straight coarse hair, including the Japanese, have relatively fewer hair follicles per square centimeter than those in the tropics. Even more distinctive is the distribution of dry versus moist earwax (cerumen). The percentages of dry earwax of East Asians (Japanese 96 percent, Koreans and North Chinese 98 percent) are among the highest in the world. Southward they drop to 52 percent in Thailand and 40 percent in southern India. The Ainu figure of 37 percent matches that of North Europeans and many Tungus (native Siberian) populations.

Serological Gene Markers—— While not minimizing the importance of externally visible polygenic (multiple gene) traits, various monogenic polymorphic (alternate form or allelic) traits such as blood group antigens (blood group types), serum proteins, and glandular secretions have proven useful for comparative studies, although the significances of the differences are often unclear and the results sometimes contradictory. All gene markers are in varying degrees adaptive or subject to the processes of natural selection, gene flow (mixture) mutation and the chance effect of sampling or drift, especially in small highly inbred populations. For example, most of the various blood group antigen systems are linked and related to disease immunity and hemolytic compatability and are not directly concerned with growth or ultimate shape and form. People with A type blood are generally more susceptible to a variety of cancers and it has been demonstrated in India that A type individuals are more susceptible to smallpox. Thus it follows that B type percentages are automatically increased in former smallpox endemic areas.

Blood Group Antigens—— Virtually all large-scale Japanese blood group antigen studies approximate closely to Hardy–Weinberg Law expectations, which indicates considerable genetic stability and normal random mating. The gene frequency distributions in the ABO, MNS and Rh systems are generally closer to those of the Chinese and Koreans than to Southeast Asians, Ainu, Mongols, or Eskimos.

In the ABO group the prefectural range for A(p) shows a slight clinal rise from .25 in northern Honshū to .29 in southern Kyūshū. Conversely, B(q) decreases from .19 in the north to .16 in the south, while O(r) fluctuates between .53 and .59. The overall frequencies are closest to the Ainu and next to the Chinese and Koreans. Among A type individuals the proportion of those with subtype A_2 (versus A_1) varies up to .03, or 3 percent.

In the MNS blood group there is a prefectural range in M from .52 to .59 and in N from .48 to .41, whereas in Southeast Asia the frequency of M rises varyingly up to .68 with a corresponding drop to .32 in N. The Ainu figures are reversed: M = .46 and N = .54; but both Japanese and Ainu figures are close to Korean, North Chinese, and various Siberian populations. The frequencies of S (MS and

Physical characteristics of the Japanese people——Table 1

Blood Group Antigens of East Asian Populations (frequencies follow standard biological notation: 1.00 = 100%)														
	ABO			MNS				Rh (Rhesus)					
	A	B	O	MS	Ms	NS	Ns	CDE	CDe	cDE	cDe	Cde	cde
	(p)	(q)	(r)										
Vietnamese	.19	.13	.68	.61[1]		.39[2]		.05	.76	.17	—	—	.02
Korean	.22	.21	.57	.49[1]		.51[2]		.01	.62	.31	.06	—	—
Chinese	.20	.24	.56	.04	.57	.01	.38	—	.71	.18	.03	—	.08
Japanese	.30	.16	.54	.04	.49	.02	.46	.003	.65	.26	.02	.01	.03
Ainu	.25	.16	.59	.06	.40	.10	.44	.003	.58	.36	.06	—	—
Mongol	.22	.31	.41	.61[1]		.39[2]		.05	.51	.25	.03	—	.016
Eskimo	.25	.02	.73	.19	.62	—	.19	.03	.73	.22	.02	—	—

[1] Frequencies for M only.
[2] Frequencies for N only.
SOURCE: Adapted from Mourant et al, *The Distribution of Human Blood Groups and Other Polymorphisms* (1976).

NS) in both the Ainu and the Japanese range from .02 to .10, a favorable comparison with those of Koreans and Chinese and markedly below the European figures which range up to .30.

More instructive is the Rh (Rhesus) system which may cause hemolysis in the newborn if the mother is Rh negative (cde) and the father positive (CDE, CDe). Among the Japanese the Rh positive CDe gene ranges from .58 to .65 which is higher than the Ainu figure but lower than that of the Chinese (.71–.74) or Vietnamese (.76). Rh negative (cde) ranges between .03 and .08 in Japanese and Chinese but is virtually absent among Koreans.

In other blood group antigens, the Chinese, Koreans, and Japanese follow a similar pattern. The Lu^a (Lutheran) and K^a (Kell) genes are both absent and Lu^b and K^b follow the general "Mongoloid" frequency of 1.00 (100 percent). In the P group, P_1 drops to .17. The Le^a (Lewis) positive gene at .76 is within the European range but the JK^a (Kidd) range is only .37–.47. The Duffy gene Fy^b is virtually absent in Japan and the neighboring mainland but reaches .10 in Southeast Asia with Fy^a at .90. The Di^a (Diego) gene frequencies also fall within the general East Asian range (.01–.05).

Red Cell Enzymes——Among the scores of red-cell enzyme genes acid phosphatase (AcP), Glucose 6-phosphate dehydrogenase (G6PD), 6 Phosphogluconate dehydrogenase (PGD), Phosphoglucomutase (PGM), Adenylate kinase (AK) and Adenosine deaminase (ADA) have been most extensively studied in East Asia. The G6P deficiency gene is absent among Japanese and there are no abnormal variants of AK. Furthermore, the ranges of the four red-cell enzyme genes shown in Table 2 indicate no collective clinal gradients and the frequencies for PGD, PGM, and ADA are highly irregular in distribution.

Among the rarer enzymes which occur significantly (.01–.02) in the Japanese, Chinese, and Koreans are the alpha-2 polymorphisms Cp^A, Cp^6 and Bg^N. The Pi^F and Pi^S alleles are entirely absent.

Serum Proteins——Among the numerous blood serum proteins are various albumins, globulins, and globins which synthesize other proteins through catalytic action. These in turn complement the protective immunizing role of the red-cell antigens. Identified by electrophoretic patterning resulting from differential migration in an electrical field, the globulins have proven highly distinctive as gene markers, especially the alpha-2 chain haptoglobins which bind hemoglobin in the red cells, the beta chain transferrins which have iron-binding properties, and the slow-fractioning gamma globulins.

The Hp^1 haptoglobin gene frequency range (.23–.24) among Japanese rises to an average of .34 among the Chinese and drops to .10–.20 in Southeast Asia and among the Ainu.

The transferrin TfC exceeds .85 throughout most of Eurasia but its allele TfD_1 is found in .03 of Thai and Japanese and .04 of Chinese. In South Asia it rises in places to .08 but is entirely absent in Europe. The most distinctive is the Dchi gene which reaches .02 among Japanese, Okinawans, and Ainu and rises to .06 in the Chinese.

Gamma Globulins——As indicated in Table 3, the gamma globulins fall into three clinally distributed groups: the Japanese, Ainu, Okinawans, Koreans, and North Chinese forming a northern group; the Taiwan aborigines and Indonesians a central group; and the Thai

Physical characteristics of the Japanese people——Table 2

Red Cell Enzyme Frequencies in East Asian Populations				
	AcP (p^a)	PGD (PGD^A)	PGM ($PGM+$)	ADA (ADA^1)
Japanese	.17–.25	.90–1.00	.68–.80	.97–.99
Okinawan	.23–.27	.92	.72	.98
Ainu	.22–.32	.93	.82–.90	.98
Chinese	.22–.23	.92	.79	.93
Taiwan aborigines	.38–.51	.85–.92	.70–.82	.93–.98

NOTE: Alleles given in parentheses.
SOURCE: Adapted from tables compiled by G. Ishimoto in S. Watanabe, S. Kondō, and W. Matsunaga, ed, *Anthropological and Genetic Studies on the Japanese* (1975).

representing populations extending into Burma and parts of India.

The northern group range is high in Gm^{ag}, Gm^{axg}, and Gm^{abst}, but low in Gm^{afb} whereas the Thai reverse the frequencies and the Taiwan aborigines and Indonesians are intermediate.

Abnormal Hemoglobins——The sickle-cell gene (HbS) so prevalent in malarially infested regions of Mediterranean countries, tropical Africa and Southeast Asia is not found among the Japanese, North Chinese, or Koreans. Similarly the thalassemia gene (ThT), which is associated in Southeast Asia with other hemoglobin anomalies such as HbE, is likewise absent in Japan and the adjacent mainland except where introduced by recent immigrants from tropical areas. Some 20 thalassemia-syndrome-related cases have been recorded, however, as well as a number of rare HbG variants.

Virus Studies——Recent World Health Organization viral studies have added a new field of comparative research. Roughly 3 percent of Japanese carry one of three types (ayw, adr, adw) of the HB virus group. The adw type, so prevalent in Southeast Asia, reaches over 80 percent in Okinawa. In Kyūshū the proportion drops sharply but rises to 40 percent in northern Honshū. The adr type on the other hand is concentrated mainly in the central prefectures, while the adw type is fairly evenly distributed in all prefectures. An interpretation for the irregularity is that the adw is the older type which was partially displaced by a later intrusive adr type.

Color Blindness——As determined by the Ishihara test among children, color blindness is relatively prevalent in Japan: boys 3.93 percent (100 A/N) and girls 0.61 percent. Other frequencies for East Asia are Chinese 0.16–0.41 percent, Koreans up to 0.38 percent, and Taiwan aborigines up to 0.60 percent. It is totally absent among the Ainu.

Glandular Secretions——The ability to taste phenylthiocarbamide (PTC) has been considered a useful gene marker although distribution is rather erratic. The Japanese range (80–95 percent) matches that of the Chinese and European figures, but in intermediate populations the percentages decline sharply: Inner Asia (60–70 percent), Siberian Mongoloids (50–60 percent). Southward in India and western Asia there is a fairly wide range (40–70 percent).

Physical characteristics of the Japanese people —— Table 3

	Gm^{ag}	Gm^{axg}	Gm^{abst}	Gm^{afb}	Gm^{xg}	INV
			Gamma Globulin Frequencies in East Asian Populations			
Japanese	.45	.16	.26	.13	—	.31
Ainu	.56	.09	.25	.04	.05	.22
Okinawan	.43	.22	.26	.08	—	.28
Korean	.48	.20	.23	.09	—	.30
North Chinese	.55	.10	.12	.22	—	.34
Taiwan Chinese	.23	.08	.05	.64	—	.20
Taiwan aborigines	.19	.04	—	.76	—	.20
Indonesian	.13	.12	—	.75	—	.15
Thai	.02	.02	.02	.94	—	.20

SOURCE: Compiled from tables in M. S. Schanfield, *Population Studies on the Gm and Inv Antigens in Asia and Oceania,* PhD dissertation, University of Michigan (1971).

The Se (secretor) gene, controlling the ability to secrete ABH substances in the saliva, is 66 percent among Japanese, again within the European range of 60–75 percent, whereas the percentages drop to 20–60 percent in South Asia.

Japanese figures are high for the amino acid BAIB (B-aminoisobutyric acid) which is excreted in the urine, and similar to those of Chinese and Koreans; South Asians are intermediate and west Asians and Europeans lower. Tests have shown, however, that in immigrant colonies of East Asians in North and South America the percentages gradually adjust to approximate the local populations, a factor which calls into question the reliability of BAIB as a gene marker.

Adaptation —— Studies of growth, aerobic (lung) capacity, thermal tolerance, work capacity, response to stress, and maturation have been conducted on local and migrant adult Japanese as well as racially mixed children of both sexes. Wherever statistically significant differences have been noted between Japanese and non-Japanese populations they appear to be attributable to earlier selective processes and their value seems to lie, therefore, mainly in indicating time depth of spread or mutation under given environmental pressures.

Scientists have recently demonstrated the importance of the changing diet of Japanese in relation to their natural environment. It has been demonstrated that, where there is seasonal variation in climate, the basal metabolism (BM) rate increases in winter and decreases in summer and that undue increase in the BM rate may alter unfavorably the internal acclimatizational mechanisms, including thyroid activity. It has also been proven that a heavy carbohydrate diet increases the BM rate, so it follows that a shift in diet from heavy rice consumption to increased protein intake—the current Japanese trend—lowers BM variation and is therefore a desirable health measure. At the same time the changing diet has also had the effect of increasing body size, especially stature (see secular trend below) with consequent increase in the skin surface ratio to body mass and concurrent loss of body heat, a trend which has caused considerable debate among Japanese scientists.

By way of contrast, the physique of the Indonesians is well adapted to their tropical environment. They are proportionally taller and slenderer than Japanese and, because of greater skin surface and thinner skin tissue, heat loss is greater; their diet, which is rich in rice but minimal in lipid and protein, is also well adjusted to reduction of sensitivity to heat.

Japanese and North Europeans demonstrate comparable responses to changing work loads and local environments. In Japan, mountain hunters and sea divers develop high aerobic capacities whereas sedentarization induces the opposite effect. Centuries of selective adaptation by the AMA pearl and abalone divers to the seasonally variable coastal waters of Korea and Japan have also shown that females have greater cold tolerance than males and are more efficient in conserving heat through the seasonal acquisition of more adequate subcutaneous fatty tissue insulation. Unlike divers, whose physiological specializations and social institutions are the result of centuries of adaptation, specializations of SUMŌ wrestlers are acquired during their lifetimes. Professional *sumō* schools are constantly on the lookout for prospective candidates who are drawn from the general public regardless of family occupation or regional distribution. Strict dietary and training regulations are imposed no later than early adolescence and few family lines have acquired reputations for producing more than one or two candidates.

Secular Trend Increases —— Less spectacular than the development of highly selected and trained occupational groups is the present general trend in Japan toward increased body size. Usually referred to as secular trend, the increases reflect adaptive pressures resulting mainly from improved nutrition and exercise during the period of ontogenetic growth—pressures which have become so markedly apparent since the turn of the century and especially during the postwar period.

The mean stature of male conscripts aged 18 rose from approximately 158.5 centimeters in 1900 to 161 centimeters in 1940. During the five-year wartime period statistics are inadequate, but mainly because of malnutrition there was a drop of more than a centimeter among 18-year-olds. Studies by the Atomic Bomb Casualty Commission (ABCC) also show that, apart from genetic dislocations, radiation victims under the age of 15 suffered decelerations in growth and retardation of menarche closely correlated with distance from impact epicenters in both Hiroshima and Nagasaki.

Statistics published by the ministries of education and of health and welfare indicate that by 1950 the people of Japan as a whole had recovered from the impact of the war years (malnutrition, stress, genetic dislocations, etc) with figures for stature, weight, and general fitness roughly equaling those of 1940. During the next two decades there was a steady increase in stature among general population 20-year-old males from 162 to 168 centimeters, but after that the rate of increase slackened and in 1980 mean stature was slightly less than 170 centimeters. Among students over the same 30-year period there was a steady rise from 164 to slightly over 170 centimeters. Correlated with these increases was a rise in the cephalic index from 80 to 82 percent. Figures for 20-year-old females during the same postwar decades in the general population and student categories registered comparable gains: 151 to 155 centimeters and 154 to 157 centimeters respectively.

Weight increases, however, have not kept pace with stature in either sex. The increase in the three postwar decades was just over 5 kilograms in males and about 2.5 kilograms in females. The result has been the development of a slenderer, longer-legged and longer-armed population.

While stature increase in both sexes has been impressive, the figures are somewhat deceptive. In 1980 the mean stature figures for 20-year-olds, for example, were based upon those born in 1960 when acceleration in growth rate was gaining momentum. Among 14-year-olds, in 1980 males were approximately 7 centimeters taller than those measured in 1960, and among females the difference was about 5 centimeters. By extrapolation, therefore, it might be expected that, in spite of the slackening in growth velocity in the later 1970s, general population stature for males should reach 172 centimeters, and for females about 160 centimeters, by 1990.

Reflecting the accelerated growth velocity among females has been a drop in age at menarche averaging 3.6 months per decade between 1950 and 1980, whereas the average drop per decade was slightly over 2 months between the turn of the century and the outbreak of the war. There is agreement that size increase and proportional changes in body segments and cranial and facial indices are attributable in large measure to better nutrition, health care, urbanization, living habits, and social mobility, collectively referred to in Japan as "modernization." There is also the factor of outbreeding, concerning which there is considerable disagreement. The argument is advanced that the tremendous influx of rural youth to the cities has drastically altered mate selection patterns and that much of the secular trend change can be attributed to hybrid vigor or "heterosis," but the claim has not been adequately substantiated.

Mate Selection and Inbreeding —— Traditional mate selection patterns have varied regionally in accordance with differing social structures and economies, but customarily lineage and family status, occupation, seniority among siblings and hereditary obligations were major considerations.

Postwar changes in inheritance laws and other aspects of the Civil Code have generally encouraged more individual freedom of choice and lessened the feeling of necessity to adopt heirs, especially males. Among rural migrants to urban areas, however, traditional patterns tend to prevail and mates from home villages are still generally preferred. Such mates are not infrequently relatives: those who are best known, most likely to be companionable, and acceptable to their families.

Sociological studies in half a dozen major cities, including Tōkyō and Nagoya, show continuing high rates of consanguineous marriages with correspondingly high coefficients of inbreeding—up to .063. Because of the possibility of hereditary ill effects of close inbreeding, efforts have been made to discourage marriages between near relatives, but nationwide studies as late as 1965 showed that as many as 4–5 percent of all marriages in Japan were still between first cousins. While there has been a drop of nearly 1 percent in the decade and a half up to 1980, figures still run as high as 10 percent in some isolated mountain and fishing communities.

Among families resident in urban communities for several generations mate selection has been strongly influenced by professional considerations and consanguineous marriages are inclined to be less frequent. Only in the past two decades, however, has there been a genuine shift toward individual as opposed to collective mate selection throughout the nation. Influenced also by more opportunities for social contacts, urban dwellers have taken the lead and those in rural areas should not be far behind.

■ ——Kunihiko Kimura and S. Kitano, *Growth of the Japanese Physique in Four Successive Decades before World War II* (1959). W. J. Schull, *The Effects of Inbreeding on Japanese Children* (1965). S. Watanabe, S. Kondō, and W. Matsunaga, ed, *Anthropological and Genetic Studies on the Japanese* (1975). Werner Klenke, *Rassengeographische Betrachtungen über die Bevölkerung Japans* (1959). Schanfield, M. S., "Population Studies on the GM and Inv Antigens in Asia and Oceania," PhD dissertation, University of Michigan (1971). H. Yoshimura and S. Kobayashi, ed, *Physiological Adaptability and Nutritional Status of the Japanese* (1975).

Gordon T. BOWLES

Japanese people, psychology of

The psychology of the Japanese people has yet to be adequately studied. Only a few psychological characteristics, such as the dependency need, sensitivity to others, conformity, the achievement drive, and the self-effacing tendency, have been empirically identified in relatively small-size samples. Most of what has been, and still often is, discussed as Japanese psychology or mentality, and frequently as the "national character," is largely the product of impressionistic descriptions, stereotyping, or methodologically inadequate approaches.

Early National Character Studies —— In contrast to descriptions of the Japanese by early travelers, visitors, and missionaries, Ruth BENEDICT's *The Chrysanthemum and the Sword* (1946) is widely known as the first "scientific" study of Japanese national character. For reasons to be stated later, however, it is clearly a study of cultural patterns, rather than of national character. Benedict mistakenly believed that these two concepts were identical. Other than Benedict, those who claim to have studied Japanese national character include Geoffrey Gorer, Weston LaBarre, H. M. Spitzer, and James Clark Molony.

Geoffrey Gorer believed that the most consistent and severe aspect of the life of Japanese children was training in cleanliness and control of the sphincter, and that this "drastic toilet training" lay at the bottom of the value system of Japanese society. Consequently, in his opinion, the Japanese had no absolutes, no "right" or "wrong"; they had instead a very strong emphasis on "doing the right thing at the right time," the minute following of ritual, and physical and ceremonial cleanliness, that is, "correct" or "suitable" behavior

which would be defined by the context in which the behavior took place. He saw these characteristics in tea ceremony, flower arrangement, court rituals, gardens, and so forth. Gorer believed that underneath an emphasis on tidiness, ritualism, and politeness was a deeply hidden, unconscious, and extremely strong desire to be aggressive. Outwardly, however, the Japanese do not show aggression because they are conditioned not to do so by early childhood training which restricts their movements (by being tied to the mother's back and being taught to sit properly). These rituals are psychological protections against the indulgence of dangerous urges and emotions. Gorer's description of this aspect of Japanese character is almost identical to the Freudian discussion of "anal" character traits or "obsessive-compulsive" neurosis of an individual.

Weston LaBarre was less restrained than Gorer in his diagnosis. He concluded that the Japanese "are probably the most compulsive people in the world's ethnological museum." LaBarre went over the list of the personality traits of a compulsive individual and looked for them in Japanese social institutions and group behavior. Besides listing the same tendencies Gorer had found, he noted that the Japanese "carry through to the finish" any undertaking once begun and that such perseverence is one of the fundamental compulsive characteristics. They also display self-righteousness, which springs from the ego's obedience to a tyrannical superego. Japanese "fanaticism" is explained as the compulsive individual's selfless devotion in order to drown the ego's doubt about superego. Japanese "arrogance" and "touchiness" are explained as the reaction formation against, or as a sign of, a feeling of inferiority or a weak and insecure ego. As Gorer also pointed out, LaBarre said that the precision and perfectionism of a compulsive individual are reflected in the Japanese emphasis on neatness and ritualistic cleanliness. A sadistic tendency is reflected in male dominance and terrorism, and masochistic behavior is displayed in the high suicide rate and hypochondriasis in Japanese society.

Thinking along the same lines as Gorer and LaBarre, H. M. Spitzer stated that Japanese culture as a whole indicates the symptoms of obsessive-compulsive neurosis. The importance of rituals, detailed rules about behavior, fear of uncleanliness, identification of sin with pollution, and general compulsiveness are all the result of a reaction formation against repressed hostility. Even ancestor worship indicated to Spitzer repressed aggression toward ancestors.

It is possible that all these psychologists used as their source of information regarding toilet training an ethnographic report by John F. EMBREE from the late 1930s, whose observations might very well have been inaccurate. While talking to a field anthropologist, people generally tend to mix, unwittingly, what they think they should do with what they actually do. Fred Kerlinger, who made field observations in the village of Niiike in Okayama Prefecture, did not find evidence of early severe toilet training and other alleged frustrating aspects of Japanese child-training practices.

Douglas Haring did not refute the "compulsive personality theory" of the above-mentioned authors. Nevertheless, pointing to the noncompulsive behavior patterns among the people of the islands of Amami Ōshima, who had never experienced the ruthlessly suppressive rule of the Tokugawa shogunate, he suggested that the features of the alleged "compulsive personality" are the logical consequences of a police state. He criticized the "diaperism" of Gorer and others who had neglected to take into account three centuries of fear-inspired discipline in their preoccupation with toilet training.

Perhaps the most imaginative of all the researchers on Japanese national character has been James Clark Molony, who believed that Japanese society and family are potential incubators of paranoid schizophrenia. According to Molony, self-determination is repressed in the Japanese mind. The rage consequent to the repression of self is not permitted spontaneous expression, and this results in a high frequency of apoplexy, allergy, and suicide. In a patriarchal family system, love and emotion are suppressed and depreciated, and power and authoritarianism exalted. Under such conditions one usually encounters a high incidence of paranoid mental disorder. The Japanese are "rigid," and where there is rigidity there is always an underlying resentment, bitterness, or hatred. Why then are the Japanese not psychotic? Why does the "power-mad Japanese nation" not abound in paranoid schizophrenia? Molony decided that consistently good physical relations between Japanese babies and their mothers reduced to a minimum the danger of the child developing a psychosis.

Francis L. K. Hsu differentiated between cultures that employ relatively more suppression (restraint from certain actions because of external circumstances) and those that use more repression (the exclusion of socially unacceptable materials from consciousness and motor expression) as a mechanism of socialization. In the former cultures, external controls are more important to the individual and the basic patterns of life tend to be situation-centered; in the latter cultures internal controls are more important and the basic pattern of life tends to be individual-centered. Hsu selected Japan and China as examples of cultures primarily utilizing suppression, and contrasted them with the United States and Germany, whose cultures primarily use repression. In a culture such as Japan, the regulations are external and therefore less omnipresent and all-pervasive than in a culture like that of the United States. The sex urge tends to be completely absent in some areas, while it is channeled into socially permissible areas where it can be expressed directly. In Japanese art and literature, sex is compartmentalized; it is almost completely lacking in respectable paintings and literature, while explicitly portrayed or dramatized in pornography, which is enjoyed in the privacy of the bedroom. The Japanese personality-culture pattern, developed out of suppressive mechanisms, emphasizes the external relationships of the individual who in turn looks for satisfactory adjustments from a number of gods, each for a specific purpose. Japan's religion is tolerant and concerns itself with group responsibility and individual salvation within the group; the search for suitable rapport with the spiritual world is primary.

Both suppression and repression are functions of the ego in the Freudian sense, and thus Hsu was discussing the "psychologies" of the four countries. The distinction between suppression (or perhaps compartmentalization, which can occur unconsciously) and repression may be helpful in understanding the Japanese distinction between principle and real intent (see TATEMAE AND HONNE) that puzzles many Westerners. However, Hsu, like other early researchers, linked individual psychology directly with social institutions and cultural products such as sanctions on sexual anomaly, religion, art, and literature.

Psychological Reductionism——There is a temptation to explain the similar behavior of a group of people as the expression of a common personality structure. But similar behavior patterns can be, and very often are, the result of conformity to social norms. Sharing social norms may very well produce certain psychological tendencies, strong in some individuals and weak in others. However, it does not mean that people become psychologically alike, because some internalize the norms while others do not. Individual members of a group are often psychologically variant. In most cases they behave similarly because they act, willingly or unwillingly, in accordance with the social norms. Furthermore, what looks like similar behavior can very well be motivated by variant needs among individuals. Japanese individuals may exhibit "group-oriented behavior" for a variety of reasons: conformity to norms, a sense of security, convenience, practicality, expediency, and also dependency need. If one forgets this reality and tries to attribute group behavior to a single motivational factor or a "national character," one falls into the pitfall of psychological reductionism. This is what is involved in most descriptions of the psychology of the Japanese people.

Modal Personality: Conceptual Problems——A pioneer in the field of culture and personality, Ruth Benedict had a strong influence upon the field of national character studies. In her *Patterns of Culture* (1934) she went beyond the mere behavioral description of the individual as a product of his culture to the characterization of the essential psychological coherence of the "ethos" of the culture as a whole. However, she did not have a well-rounded and integrated conception of individual psychology and was neglectful of the developmental aspects of personality. Her emphasis was on "the psychological coherence of the varied institutions which make up a society." This indicates that she did not make a clear conceptual distinction between the sociocultural system of role patterns, norms, and values, and the personality as a system of needs, attitudes, defense mechanisms, and so forth. Apparently, she assumed that the psychological coherence of the individual personality was isomorphic with the psychological coherence of the culture. Such conceptual weakness is clear in her statement that "to the anthropologist the study of national character is the study of learned cultural behavior," and the same confusion of sociocultural system and personality system runs through her study of the Japanese. Frederick S. Hulse criticized *The Chrysanthemum and the Sword*, pointing out the necessity to differentiate between norms and normative behavior (which he calls "convention") and actual behavior and motivational patterns underlying behavior (which he calls "reality") that may be discrepant with normative patterns. Benedict's book deals with those actions which the Japanese think they ought to do rather than with those which they frequently do in fact. The two basic problems of the book are that Benedict confused "convention" with the "reality" of Japanese behavior patterns, and "behavior patterns" with "national character."

National character should be equated with modal personality structure; it should refer to a mode or modes of the distribution of personality variants within a given society. It requires the psychological investigation of adequately large and representative samples of persons, studied individually, rather than guesses from group behavior patterns, child-rearing practices, or cultural products. Until such an investigation is made, whether or not and how many modal personality characteristics exist within a group will remain unanswered questions. Given the limits of our knowledge and present research techniques, it cannot be an a priori assumption that any nation "has" a national character. Particularly in the case of a complex industrial nation, a multimodal conception of national character would seem to be theoretically the most meaningful as well as empirically the most realistic. Some scholars have estimated that any specific personality characteristic or any character type is not likely to be found in as much as 60–70 percent of any modern national population. They consider as a reasonable hypothesis that a nation may be characterized in terms of a limited number of modes, five or six, some of which apply to perhaps 10–15 percent, others to perhaps 30 percent of the total population. Also important is the fact that modal personality or personalities is one of several sets of factors that determine actions, and therefore group behavior and social institutions should not be reduced to "psychology" alone. There have been few empirical studies of a large sample of individuals in Japan. Questionnaires and opinion surveys are commonly used for a large sample, but they usually reveal only the surface of the individual psyche. Projective tests, such as TAT and Rorschach, often allow researchers to look into the psychodynamics at a deeper level, but their time-consuming administration tends to limit the sample size.

Using TAT and Rorschach, William Caudill and George DeVos saw a strong achievement orientation among the Japanese and Japanese Americans. Undoubtedly, achievement in various areas has been one of the Japanese characteristics since the beginning of Japan's industrialization in the 19th century. However, to acknowledge that achievement is desirable ("achievement value") is one thing, and to be actually driven by such a desire ("achievement motivation") is another. The value of achievement is widely accepted in Japanese society, but it remains a question as to how many of the individual members of the society are spontaneously motivated toward achievement and how many go along in compliance with the prevalent value.

In another study using TAT results from a small sample of villagers, DeVos and Wagatsuma found a strong concern with death and illness among women. On the basis of TAT responses from an equally small sample, DeVos discussed the feeling of guilt among the Japanese about having hurt their parents, especially mothers, in the course of growing up. They offer an interesting insight into Japanese psychology, but again, it remains an empirical question how common these traits actually are.

Doi Takeo, through clinical experience and self-analysis, concluded that the dependency need (AMAE) is an important feature of the Japanese personality. Doi's observation has been corroborated by Caudill and Weinstein's systematic study of mother-child closeness (see CHILDHOOD AND CHILD REARING). However, the recent overuse of the concept of *amae* in discussions of the Japanese national character has created another instance of psychological reductionism. On the basis of his observation of close interaction between an infant and its mother, Caudill suggested a lesser degree of psychological differentiation of the child's self from that of its mother. Further empirical research is needed on the developmental phase of the ego boundaries among the Japanese.

Surveys have yielded some clues to the Japanese psychology, although they cannot be reliable descriptions of behavior. Mary Ellen Goodman analyzed the essays entitled "What I want to be when I grow up and why," written by 1,250 Japanese and 3,750 American school children, and found that the Japanese child did not think of himself as autonomous; that he stressed his duties and obligations rather than his rights; and that his attention was deflected away from self and toward family, community, and the wider society.

F. K. Berrien, using questionnaires, compared value attitudes among Japanese and American college students and found that the

Japanese, when compared with the Americans, were "more deferent, more respectful of and dependent upon high status persons, more self-abasing and more willing to work long hours, and individual aspiration was less important than the achievement of the work group."

Large-scale opinion surveys, with a stratified nationwide sample of over 4,500 individuals, have been conducted every fifth year since 1953 under the somewhat misleading project name, "Study of National Character." Many identical questions have been repeated in every survey, enabling one to see whether Japanese opinions have remained constant over the past 20 years. It is interesting that the opinions that can be considered "typical" of the Japanese are very few; only four questions elicited the same answer from more than two-thirds (71–90 percent) of both sexes, of all age groups, at every socioeconomic and educational level, throughout 20 years. These "majority answers" indicate that (1) a Japanese would hire, if in the position of a company president, not his or her relative who ranks second in the examination but anybody who ranks at the top; (2) a Japanese would like to work under the section chief in a company who makes his subordinates work overtime, even departing from rules at times, but also looks after his subordinates outside work and would not like to work under the section chief who neither makes his subordinates work overtime nor looks after them outside work; (3) a Japanese would like the garden of the Katsura Palace in Kyōto better than that of the Versailles Palace; and (4) a Japanese thinks that he or she has faith in a religion or thinks that belief and piety are important.

It should also be noted that few Japanese individuals are "typical" in the sense of having given these answers to all four questions. In other words, we can speak of "majority opinions," but few Japanese share all of their opinions in common.

According to the results of the 1973 survey, a majority of the respondents (68 percent) preferred to live their lives as they chose, rather than try to become wealthy, famous, or to contribute to society, or live righteously or irresponsibly. Seventy percent said they intended to continue working even after they had saved enough money to spend the rest of their lives in leisure. Eighty-seven percent said they would teach their school-age children that there are things in this world more valuable than money, and 70 percent that they should not be concerned with "saving face." Seventy-two percent thought discipline was very important (among freedom, piety, patriotism, ancestor worship, filial piety, repayment, and money). Sixty-seven percent thought that people should not spend large sums of money on wedding ceremonies, and that it is good to pay respect to one's ancestors. Seventy-six percent thought that filial piety was very important, and 72 percent that it was good to associate themselves with their superiors even outside work. Seventy-five percent responded that people should give advice to each other to make social life smooth, rather than refrain from doing so. Seventy-four percent preferred to work for a company that had a familial atmosphere and provided group recreation activities. Seventy-three percent preferred to have a friend who would listen to them sympathetically when confided in, rather than a friend who would give them unsolicited advice.

There are matters about which the Japanese have greatly changed their opinions over the past 20 years: (1) In 1953, 73 percent said that if childless, they would adopt even a totally unrelated child to continue their family line, but such an opinion was held by only 36 percent of the respondents in 1973. (2) In 1953, 65 percent stated that they would teach their children the value of money; only 44 percent said so in 1973. (3) In 1973, 70 percent felt that children should be taught not to be concerned with "saving face," but only 43 percent agreed with this in 1953. (4) Women who wished to be reborn as men constituted 64 percent in 1953 but decreased to 43 percent in 1973, and those who wished to be reborn as women increased from 27 to 50 percent. These responses would seem to indicate that the traditional Japanese family system has declined and that the position of women has been much improved.

In responding to a questionnaire, people tend to say what they think they should say, expressing their *tatemae* instead of *honne*. This is particularly true of the Japanese. Many more empirical studies of individual Japanese are needed before we can speak of the psychology of the Japanese with any degree of confidence.

◾ ——Richard K. Beardsley, "Personality Psychology," in John W. Hall and Richard K. Beardsley, *Twelve Doors to Japan* (1965). Ruth Benedict, *The Chrysanthemum and the Sword* (1946). Ruth Benedict, *Patterns of Culture* (1934). Ruth Benedict, "The Study of Cultural Patterns in European Nations," *Transactions of the New York Academy of Sciences* (1946). F. K. Berrien, "Japanese vs American Values," *Journal of Social Psychology* 65 (1965). William Caudill, "Child Behavior and Child Rearing in Japan and the U.S.," *Journal of Nervous and Mental Disease* 157 (1973). William Caudill, "Patterns of Emotion in Modern Japan," in R. J. Smith and R. K. Beardsley, ed, *Japanese Culture—Its Development and Characteristics* (1962). William Caudill and H. A. Scarr, "Japanese Value Orientation and Culture Change," *Ethnology* 1 (1962). William Caudill and George DeVos, "Achievement, Culture and Personality—The Case of the Japanese Americans," *American Anthropologist* 58 (1956). George DeVos and Hiroshi Wagatsuma, "Psychocultural Significance of Concern over Death and Illness Among Rural Japanese," *The International Journal of Social Psychiatry* 5 (1959). George DeVos, "Relation of Guilt toward Parents to Achievement and Arranged Marriage among the Japanese," *Psychiatry* 23 (1960). Doi Takeo, *Amae no kōzo* (1971) tr John Bester as *The Anatomy of Dependence* (1973). John L. Fischer and Teigo Yoshida, "Some Issues in the Study of Japanese Modal Personality," in E. Norbeck and S. Parman, ed, *The Study of Japan in the Behavioral Sciences* 56 (1970). Mary Ellen Goodman, "Values, Attitudes and Social Concepts of Japanese and American Children," *American Anthropologist* 59 (1957). Geoffrey Gorer, "Themes in Japanese Culture," *Transactions of the New York Academy of Sciences* 2.5 (1943). Douglas Haring, "Japanese National Character: Cultural Anthropology, Psychoanalysis and History," *Yale Review* 42 (1953). Francis L. K. Hsu, "Suppression vs. Repression—A Limited Psychological Interpretation of Four Cultures," *Psychiatry* 12 (1949). Frederick S. Hulse, "Convention and Reality in Japanese Culture," *Southwestern Journal of Anthropology* 4.4 (1948). Fred Kerlinger, "Behavior and Personality in Japan: A Critique of Three Studies of Japanese Personality," *Social Forces* 31 (1953). Weston LaBarre, "Some Observations on Character Structure in the Orient: The Japanese," *Psychiatry* 8 (1945). James Clark Molony, *Understanding the Japanese Mind* (1954). Nihonjin Kenkyūkai, *Nihonjin no kokoro wa kawatta*, vol 1 of *Nihonjin kenkyū* (1974). H. M. Spitzer, "Psychoanalytic Approaches to the Japanese Character," in Geza Roheim, ed, *Psychoanalysis and the Social Sciences*, 1 (1947). Hiroshi Wagatsuma, "Ishiwara Shintaro's Early Novels and Japanese Male Psychology," *Journal of Nervous and Mental Disease* 157 (1973). Hiroshi Wagatsuma, "Pencil Making in a Tokyo Ward," in Gianni Fedella, ed, *Social Structure and Economic Dynamics in Japan up to 1980* (1975). Hiroshi Wagatsuma, "Some Aspects of Changing Family in Contemporary Japan—Once Confucian, Now Fatherless?" *Daedalus* 106.2 (1977).

Hiroshi WAGATSUMA

Japanese Red Cross Society

(Nihon Sekijūjisha). Affiliate of the International Red Cross. Its predecessor was the Hakuaisha, a relief organization established by SANO TSUNETAMI in 1877 for those wounded in the SATSUMA REBELLION, an uprising of former *samurai*. The Hakuaisha joined the International Red Cross in 1887 and changed its name to the Japanese Red Cross Society. The object of the society is to further the ideals of the Red Cross as embodied in its conventions and to implement the principles drawn up at Red Cross international conferences. In 1952 it was given legal status as a special nonprofit corporation. Its activities include training nurses, managing medical institutions, and setting up blood banks. In 1957, the Japanese Red Cross was elected to serve on the executive committee of the League of Red Cross Societies.

SŌDA Hajime

Japanese spaniel

(chin). Also called Japanese chin in English. A small pet dog breed. It is generally thought that the etymology of *chin* is *chi-inu* or *chinu*, "small dog." It resembles the Pekingese breed in general body conformation but has a somewhat more delicate build and longer and more slender legs. Its weight is about 2.5–4 kilograms (5.5–8.8 lb); height about 22–30 centimeters (8.7–11.8 in). Breed standards emphasize smallness. The head is brachycephalic, that is, a high domed head, with snub nose and large, round eyes. The hair is long, silky, and straight. The ears are V-shaped and pendulous, and the tail curls over the back and is covered with tufty hair. The coat is usually black and white in color, but red and white is also seen.

There have been occasional references in historical texts to small pet dogs brought from China or elsewhere, and even a dwarf variety of the native dog in the Satsuma (now Kagoshima Prefecture) area. In its present form, however, the Japanese chin seems to have developed from around the beginning of the Edo period (1600–1868), based on a Pekingese-like toy breed imported from China. It soon became popular as a woman's pet as Tokugawa culture flourished. Several books about the care of pet dogs were published during that time, and there were even doctors who specialized in the care of these small dogs.

The breed first became known in the West after Commodore Perry's expedition to Japan in 1853, when he was presented with some of these dogs as a gift from the Japanese government and brought them back to the United States. A pair of them was sent to Queen Victoria of England. Many specimens have been imported into Europe and America since. The breed was officially recognized first in Britain in 1895 as the Japanese spaniel and was recognized a little later in the United States and in other Western countries. Since then, the breed has steadily gained in popularity as a pet dog in the West.

◼ ▬▬Edward Ash, *The Pekingese* (1936). B. H. Chamberlain, *Things Japanese* (1904), reprinted as *Japanese Things* (1971). V. W. F. Collier, *Dogs of China and Japan* (1921). Nagakura Yoshio et al, *Chin* (1965). Uchida Tōru, *Inu* (1948).　*Hiroshi* SAKAMOTO

Japanese studies abroad

The birth of Western interest in Japan owes much to Catholic missionaries, like Francis XAVIER and Luis FROIS, from Portugal and Spain, the countries which first came into direct contact with Japan in the 16th century. Through their travel accounts, diaries, and letters they introduced contemporary Japanese customs, history, geography, and flora and fauna to Europeans.

Under the Tokugawa shogunate's (1603–1867) policy of NATIONAL SECLUSION beginning in the 1630s, all official contact with the outside world was broken off with the exception of the Dutch and the Chinese, who were allowed to come to the island of DEJIMA at Nagasaki. Europeans at Dejima who wrote about Japan included Engelbert KAEMPFER, Philipp Franz von SIEBOLD, and Carl Peter THUNBERG.

From about the 18th century on, there was awakened interest in East Asia, especially China. The European interest in Japanese literature, woodblock prints, and ceramics was part of this larger interest in things oriental. Research on Japanese language and literature at European universities and academies began early in the 19th century, for example at the University of Paris and the University of Leyden. After the opening of Japan in the 1860s, many Englishmen, usually diplomats stationed in Japan, took up the study of the country. Among the more prominent were Ernest SATOW, William ASTON, and Basil CHAMBERLAIN.

After World War I the Harvard-Yenching Institute was founded at Harvard University in 1928 and in 1932 Serge ELISSÉEFF, a Russian-born scholar who had studied in Japan, was invited to Harvard from France. In due course the first generation of American Japanologists, including Edwin REISCHAUER and Hugh Borton, appeared. Until World War II, Japanese studies in both the United States and Europe tended to be in humanistic studies such as classical literature, history, folklore, and language. Often scholars worked alone in isolation from other Japanologists. Institutions active in promoting Japanese studies in the period between the wars included the INSTITUTE OF PACIFIC RELATIONS, founded in Hawaii in 1925, and the Kokusai Bunka Shinkōkai (Japan Culture Society), founded in Japan in 1934, to work for international understanding of Japan. The Kokusai Bunka Shinkōkai was absorbed into the JAPAN FOUNDATION when the latter was founded in 1972.

After World War II, the "area studies" approach spread, especially in the United States, and there was a trend toward specialization and interdisciplinary work. Although the study of Japanese culture, literature, and history remains strong, more work is being done in the social sciences as well. With the emergence of Japan as an economic and technological power, there has also been an increase in programs with a more utilitarian cast, often stressing a practical command of the Japanese language for trade or industry, especially in Australia, New Zealand, and Southeast Asia. Japan has also been taking a more active role in promoting Japanese studies abroad, primarily through the Japan Foundation.

Another trend has been increased contact between foreign Japanologists and Japanese scholars, as aided by the programs of the Fulbright Commission, the Japanese Ministry of Education, and the Japan Foundation, and among Japanologists themselves. Many national associations of specialists have been founded, and the European Association for Japanese Studies was established in 1973.

The United States. Japanese studies in the United States date back to the early 20th century. A report issued by the American Council of the Institute of Pacific Relations in 1935 (*Japanese Studies in the Universities and Colleges of the United States*) found that 25 institutions of higher education offered courses related to Japan and 8 offered some Japanese-language instruction. Of these, Harvard had 10 faculty members teaching Japanese subjects, Columbia University 7, and the University of Michigan 7; other universities offering courses in this field included the University of California at Berkeley, Chicago, Hawaii, Stanford, Washington, and Yale.

However, the majority of courses related to Japan were taught by generalists who also taught Chinese subjects. These were often part-time amateurs who had lived in Japan as missionaries, professionals involved in international relations, or the like. Only 13 of the persons engaged in Japanese studies in 1934 were proficient enough in Japanese to do research using Japanese materials, and in 1941 the academic experts on Japan could still be counted on two hands. In fact, American graduate students in Japanese studies in the prewar period often studied abroad: Edwin Reischauer and C. Burton Fahs at the Sorbonne and in Japan and Hugh Borton at the University of Leyden and in Japan. Influential teachers at this time included, in addition to Eliséeff at Harvard, ASAKAWA KAN'ICHI at Yale and TSUNODA RYŪSAKU at Columbia.

World War II provided the impetus for the wide-scale growth of Japanese studies in the United States. The American military embarked on the training of language officers; some of those who studied Japanese in this training program were Marius Jansen, James Morley, Donald Keene, Robert Ward, Edward Seidensticker, Howard Hibbett, Solomon Levine, William McCullough, and Robert Scalapino. A younger group of scholars was brought into the field by service in the Occupation of Japan or the Korean War. One should also mention those who, like Edwin Reischauer, were born in Japan as the children of missionaries: John Hall, Roger Hackett, and Donald Shively. It was this second generation of Japanologists who brought the insights of other disciplines to work related to Japan and established Japanese studies as a separate area of specialization.

With the Korean War and "Sputnik shock" of the 1950s, government and private funds became readily available for area studies, including Asian studies. Under the influence of the cultural anthropological methods used by Ruth BENEDICT in *The Chrysanthemum and the Sword* (1946), scholars tried to understand Japan in all its aspects. The multidisciplinary approach was perhaps best exemplified by the University of Michigan research group led by Richard Beardsley, John Hall, and Robert Ward, which published its findings in *Village Japan* (1969). From the early 1960s Japan began to attract world interest as it achieved rapid economic growth, and American scholars focused on Japan's modernization as a key to understanding this phenomenon.

According to a 1970 report prepared under the chairmanship of John Hall (*Japanese Studies in the United States*; also known as the Hall report), the number of Japan scholars in the United States in 1968 exceeded 400, of whom half were under 40 years of age. These figures showed that a third, postwar generation of Japanologists had come into existence. It also reported that full graduate programs in Japanese studies were available at 11 institutions: the University of California (Berkeley), the University of California (Los Angeles), Chicago University, Columbia University, Harvard University, the University of Hawaii, the University of Michigan, Princeton University, Stanford University, the University of Washington, and Yale University.

By 1974 there were some 840 Japan scholars and over 200 universities offering courses in Japanese studies in the United States, according to a 1977 report prepared for the Subcommittee on Japanese Studies of the American Panel of the United States–Japan Conference of Cultural and Educational Interchange (Elizabeth and Joseph Massey, *Japanese Studies at Colleges and Universities in the United States in the Mid-1970's*; also called the Massey report or the CULCON report). The number of Japanese language students was reported to be approximately 9,600 in 1976. A report by a Japanese government mission, *Beikoku ni okeru Nihon kenkyū* (1977, Japanese Studies in the United States), also provides detailed information about the state of Japanese studies in the United States.

There is no doubt that the sudden growth in the postwar period leading to some program in Japanese studies in almost every state was largely owing to the generous financial assistance of the US government in such forms as the National Defense Education Act (NDEA) and the Fulbright-Hayes Act (see JAPAN–UNITED STATES EDUCATIONAL COMMISSION), and of other institutions such as the

Ford, Rockefeller, Carnegie, and Asia foundations. When these sources began to dry up in the 1970s, aid came from the Japan Foundation, founded in 1972; the Japan–United States Friendship Commission, founded in 1977; the JAPAN SOCIETY FOR THE PROMOTION OF SCIENCE (JSPS); and from Japanese business. American organizations involved with Japanese studies include the Japan Society and the Association for Asian Studies; the latter publishes the *Journal of Asian Studies*. The Association of Teachers of Japanese, created in 1962 by American and Canadian teachers of the language, publishes its own journal.

Canada. Canada's contacts with Japan began with an adventurer, Ranald MACDONALD, who visited Japan in the mid-19th century. A Canadian legation was opened in Tōkyō in 1929, and such diplomats as Hugh L. Keenleyside and Russell P. Kirkwood did work on Japan. Another notable figure was E. H. NORMAN, a Canadian diplomat born to a missionary family in Japan who was active in the field of Japanese history in the years immediately before and after World War II.

However, Japanese studies in Canada may be said to have begun in 1956 when, partially in recognition of the injustice of the wartime internment of Japanese-Canadians, the University of British Columbia invited Ronald Dore from England to establish a program of Asian studies. Since then centers for Japanese studies have been created at the University of Toronto and York University (the Joint Center on Modern East Asia) and at the University of British Columbia, and courses related to Japan have been begun at 16 more colleges and universities. Seven Canadian universities offer regular Japanese language instruction—Toronto, York, McGill, Montreal, British Columbia, Alberta, and Victoria; in 1978 there were 24 faculty members teaching Japanese and 432 students.

United Kingdom. As mentioned earlier, the first generation of British scholars on Japan mainly consisted of men who had served in Japan in the diplomatic service in the late 19th century. This generation included such figures as Ernest Satow, William Aston, Basil Chamberlain, Rutherford ALCOCK, Frank BRINKLEY, Sir Charles ELIOT, and James MURDOCH. Many scholars from this generation taught at British universities after their return to Britain, but the second generation in the 1930s, which included Sir George SANSOM, also a diplomat, and Arthur WALEY, known for his translation of the TALE OF GENJI, worked in isolation.

The third generation of Japanologists in Britain came into the field under the impetus of World War II. Frank Daniels was in charge of the wartime training program at the School of Oriental and African Studies at the University of London; students trained in Japanese here included Charles Dunn, Patrick O'Neill, Ronald Dore, and Douglas Mills. After the war, Japanese studies continued at the School of Oriental and African Studies under Patrick O'Neill, Charles Dunn, and Kenneth Strong in the Japanese department and W. G. Beasley in the history department. A program of Japanese studies began at Cambridge University soon after the war and was developed by Douglas Mills, Carmen Blacker, and Charles Sheldon. Oxford University also instituted Japanese studies in this period, in the Oriental Institute and in the Far East Center at St. Anthony's College, directed from 1970 by the late Richard Storry. Study at these three universities tends to center on history and literature.

The Hayter Committee report on Oriental Studies in 1961 recommended more stress on the modern, nonlinguistic, and nonliterary aspects of Japanese studies, and the Center of Japanese Studies founded at Sheffield University in 1963 has focused on multidisciplinary research on contemporary Japan in the social sciences under the directorship of Geoffrey Bownas. Work on Japan is also being done at the London School of Economics and Political Science under such figures as Ian Nish and MORISHIMA MICHIO and by isolated scholars outside of Japanese departments at various universities throughout the United Kingdom. Japanese-language instruction has long been offered at the Polytechnic of Central London, and Japanese studies courses are also available at the Huddersfield Polytechnic.

The growth of Japanese studies in Britain from the 1960s owed much to aid from the British government and from Japanese sources, especially the Japan Foundation from the 1970s. The Japan Library Group was founded in 1966 to pool experience and resources, and the British Association for Japanese Studies was established in 1974. This trend toward the coming together of British scholars on Japan and toward cooperative ventures can be expected to continue in the future.

France. Study of Japan began in France in the late 19th century under such figures as Léon de ROSNY and Léon PAGÈS in language, Maurice Courant in Chinese studies, Henri Cordier in diplomatic history, George Appert in law, and Michel Revon in law and literature, but the first great French Japanologists were Nöel Peri, known for his work on Buddhism and Nō, and Claude Maître in the first quarter of the 20th century. The next major figure was Charles Haguenauer, who revived French Japanology through his work in history and linguistics and became the leader of several generations of teachers and researchers. The Russian-born Serge Elisséeff also did important work in Japanese art history in Paris before assuming the directorship of the Yenching Institute at Harvard in 1934.

In contrast to the situation in the United States and the United Kingdom, World War II brought a break in Japanese studies in France. After the war, courses on Japan began again at the Ecole des Langues Orientales and in the Religious Sciences Section at the Ecole pratique des Hautes Etudes. Elisséeff returned to France in 1957 and taught modern Japanese history in a newly created post at the Ecole pratiques des Hautes Etudes, Section VI (Economics and Social Sciences); he was succeeded in this post by Paul Akamatsu. In 1959 a major center for research and documentation, the Institut des Hautes Etudes japonaises de l'Université de Paris, was created (attached administratively to the Collège de France since 1973). In 1965 a chair of Japanese history and philology, first filled by Bernard Frank, was created at the Ecole pratique des Hautes Etudes, IV (Historical and Philological Sciences); Hartmut O. Rotermund succeeded Haguenauer at the Ecole pratique des Hautes Etudes, V (Religious Sciences) in 1967.

After the university upheavals of 1968, extensive reorganization took place. A new university, Université de Paris VII (UER: Langues et Civilisations de l'Asie Orientale), was formed in 1970 with Hubert Maës as the head of the Japanese section, and the Institut National des Langues et Civilisations Orientales attached to the University of Paris III and headed by René Sieffert was formed the following year. Japanese is also taught at the University of Paris VI, devoted to scientific studies, as well as at the University of Lyon III, Bordeaux III, and the University of Provence (Aix-Marseille).

An important role has also been played by the Maison franco-japonaise. Founded in Tōkyō in 1924, it has brought numerous French scholars to Japan and published much significant work. One of its major publications is the multivolume *Dictionnaire historique du Japon* (1963–).

Germany. Japanese studies in Germany were largely founded by the German scholars and professional experts who aided the new Meiji government in its modernization efforts at the end of the 19th century (see FOREIGN EMPLOYEES OF THE MEIJI PERIOD). These included the geographer Johann Justus Rein, the physician Erwin von BÄLZ, the jurist Hermann ROESLER, the economist Adolph von Wenckstern, the mining expert Curt Netto, the philosopher Raphael von Koeber, the engineer Rudolf Lehmann, and the philologists Rudolf Lange and Karl Florenz.

Karl Florenz in particular developed Japanology in Germany after his return in 1914 from 25 years of teaching at the University of Tōkyō. Before World War II, Japanese studies programs had been developed in Hamburg, Berlin, and Leipzig, and the Japanese language was also taught in Frankfurt and Bonn. In addition, the Japaninstitut was established in Berlin in 1926 and the Japanisch-Deutsches Kulturinstitut in Kyōto in 1927.

Japanese studies in Germany suffered a setback when the German-Japanese military alliance ended, with the Japaninstitut and various German-Japanese societies disbanding after 1945. The field slowly developed once again with the chair of Japanology at the University of Hamburg being filled by Oscar Benl and a new one established at the University of Munich in 1957. New programs were created at the universities of Bonn (Otto Karow, Herbert Zachert), Münster (Otto Karow, Bruno Lewin), Marburg (Wolf Haenisch), and Frankfurt a.M. (Otto Karow). A Japanese department was founded in the Ostasiatisches Seminar of the Free University of West Berlin (Hans Eckardt), and a new Japanese studies center was established at the University of Ruhr at Bochum in 1964 with a chair for Japanese language and literature (Bruno Lewin) and for Japanese history and history of thought (Horst Hammitzsch). Japanese studies are now available at the universities of Bochum, Bonn, Cologne, Frankfurt, Freiburg, Hamburg, Marburg, Munich, Tübingen, and West Berlin. Japanese language courses are also available at Erlangen, Göttingen, Heidelberg, Münster, and Würzburg.

Although work tends to be centered on Japanese culture, history, and literature, at Bochum, Munich, and West Berlin, area studies are branching into economics, geography, political science, and sociology, and a tendency can be seen in German Japanology toward specialization, area studies, and interdisciplinary studies. Numerous Japanological organizations are also active, including the Deutsche

Gesellschaft für Natur- und Völkerkunde Ostasiens (OAG), founded in Tōkyō in 1873 and now having a branch in Hamburg as well; the Deutsch-Japanische Gesellschaften, established in Berlin in 1928; and the Japanisches Kulturinstitut (Nippon Bunka Kaikan), founded at Cologne in 1966.

Italy. Japanese studies began in Italy at the end of the 19th and beginning of the 20th century, with courses in the Japanese language available in Florence, Venice, Rome, and Naples. Italians who had lived and worked in Japan, such as the artist and copperplate engraver Edoardo CHIOSSONE, the painter Antonio FONTANESI, and the sculptor Vincenzo RAGUSA, played an important role in introducing Japan in Italy. The teaching of Japanese started at the University Oriental Institute in Naples in 1903, and the Italian Institute for the Middle and Far East (IsMEO) was established in Rome in 1933. Numerous individuals outside such specialized institutions were also involved in Japanese studies and the popularization of Japanese culture in Italy in the decades before and after World War II. Two important figures in the prewar period were Pietro Silvio Rivetta and Bartolomeo Balbi.

Activities in Italian Japanology intensified during the 1960s, which witnessed the opening of the Instituto Giapponese di Cultura (Nihon Bunka Kaikan) in Rome in 1962 and the development of a new center of Japanology in Milan. The Institute of Economic and Social Studies for East Asia was established under the chairmanship of Innocenzo Gasparini there at the Luigi Bocconi Commercial University in 1973, and a general reorganization of the state universities resulted in more extensive programs in East Asian studies, especially at Naples, where Adolfo Tamburello became a professor of the History and Civilization of the Far East, and Venice, where Paolo Beonio-Brocchieri became a professor of Religions and Philosophies of East Asia.

Japanese language studies are now available at the universities of Bologna, Florence, Naples, Rome, Turin, Urbin, and Venice. The widest range of degrees is granted by the University Oriental Institute of Naples and postgraduate studies are offered only at the University of Rome. The Italian Association for Japanese Studies was established in 1974 with Fosco Maraini acting as general secretary.

Switzerland. Japanese studies in Switzerland are limited to the University of Zurich, where the Japanese department of the Ostasiatisches Seminar was added to the Chinese department in 1968. In 1975–76 the Japanese department had a teaching staff of 5 and an enrollment of about 40 students and auditors, some 10 of whom had chosen Japanology as their main discipline. The Japanology program is mainly devoted to literature (especially modern literature), social sciences (focusing on Japanese folk culture), and religion (concentrating on Shintō and folk religion). The journal of the Swiss Society for Asian Studies, *Asiatische Studien—Études Asiatiques,* regularly publishes articles and reviews in the field of Japanese studies.

Austria. Although individual Austrian scholars such as August Pfizmaier and Anton Boller did work in Japanese language and literature from the mid-19th century, systematic Japanese studies did not begin in Austria until after World War I. Japanese language education started at the University of Vienna in the 1920s, and the Japan-Institut was founded there in 1938 with the aid of Baron Mitsui of the MITSUI financial combine. Concentrating on the anthropological study of Japanese culture, this institute was absorbed into the Institute for Oriental Studies and then the Institute of Ethnology, becoming independent once again in 1965 as the Institut für Japanologie at the University of Vienna through the efforts of the anthropologist Alexander Slawik.

The basic orientation of Japanese studies at the University of Vienna is still strongly anthropological, and some team studies have been done, for example, the Aso project in which Slawik, Josef Kreiner, Erich Pauer, and Sepp Linhart conducted interdisciplinary research in the Aso county of Kumamoto Prefecture in central Kyūshū in 1968–69. Research into Japanese theater and music is also being done at the University of Vienna. Other Japanese studies in Austria include the training of translators in the Japanese section of the Institute for Education of Translators and Interpreters and sociological work at the University for Social and Economic Sciences at Linz. The Institut für Japanologie publishes a journal, *Beiträge zur Japanologie,* and there are many Japanese holdings at the Museum of Ethnology and the Museum for Applied Arts in Vienna.

The Netherlands and Belgium. Japanese studies have a long history in the Netherlands, as the Dutch were the only Westerners allowed to trade with Japan from 1639 to 1854. Early works on Japan were written in the 17th and 18th centuries by Francois Caron,

Engelbert Kaempfer, and Izaak TITSINGH, and a Dutch-Japanese dictionary, the *Dōyaku Haruma,* was completed in 1815 under the supervision of Hendrik DOEFF. Johann Joseph HOFFMANN, who became the first professor of Japanese at the State University of Leyden, assisted Philipp Franz von Siebold in editing his book about his experiences in Japan, and he himself wrote an important work on Japanese grammar, *Japanese Spraakleer,* in 1867.

Japanese studies continued at the University of Leyden under Marinus W. de Visser, Johannes Rahder, and Frits Vos, and from the early 1930s through the mid-1950s the Japanese language was also taught at the University of Utrecht. In 1969 the Japanologisch Studiecentrum was established at Leyden. As of the mid-1970s more than 30 students were majoring in Japanese and slightly more than that number were studying it as a side-subject. In addition, the Japan–Nederland Instituut (Nichi-Ran Gakkai) was founded in Tōkyō in 1975 for the study of historical relations between the Netherlands and Japan and Japanese studies in general.

In Belgium, courses related to Japan are offered both at the Université Catholique de Louvain and at Katholieke Universiteit Leuven.

Scandinavia. Japanese studies started in Sweden with the appointment of the Sinologist Bernard KARLGREN to the chair of Far Eastern Linguistics and Culture at the University of Göteborg in 1918. He taught Japanese as well as Chinese at Göteborg and later at the University of Stockholm. The teaching of Japanese at the University of Uppsala was begun by Seung-bog Cho in the mid-1950s. In accordance with the recommendations of the Nordic Cultural Commission in the mid-1960s, Japanese studies are now concentrated at the University of Stockholm with Japanese-language instruction also available at the universities of Uppsala and Göteborg. The emphasis at the University of Stockholm is on language and linguistic studies, and the Sweden–Japan Foundation for Research and Development, founded in 1971, promotes scientific and technological cooperation between the two nations and assists Swedish scholars working in this area.

Japanese studies at the university level started in Denmark in 1961 with the establishment of Japanese-language teaching at the East Asian Institute of the University of Copenhagen. Graduate degrees are now available, although the Japanese studies program is relatively small due to the limited resources available. Japanese studies are also offered at the University of Århus.

In Norway, the East Asian Institute founded at the University of Oslo in 1966 offers courses in modern Japanese language and literature, and elementary Japanese language courses are available at Helsinki University in Finland.

Israel. Israel is a relative newcomer to Japanese studies; formal state relations between Israel and Japan were not established until 1952. The main center of Japanese studies in Israel is the Hebrew University of Jerusalem. The Japanese Studies Section of the Department of East Asian Studies offers courses in Japanese language, political science, history, and economics. Several courses on Japan are also offered at Tel-Aviv University and Haifa University. In addition, the Museum of Japanese Art is found in Haifa.

Eastern Europe. Japanese studies have a long history in Prague, and the two major centers for Japanese studies in Czechoslovakia today, the Oriental Institute of the Czechoslovak Academy of Sciences and Charles University, are both located in this city. Work is particularly strong in Japanese literature, although many Czech Japanologists have emigrated since 1968. One major figure known for his translations and other work in Japanese literature is Miroslav Novák.

Another major center for Japanese studies in Eastern Europe is the Japanese Studies Division of the Far East Department of the University of Warsaw. Japanese culture has been the subject of university study in Poland for more than 50 years, but the Japanese Studies Division was not established as a separate unit until 1956. Headed by Wieslaw Kotanski and having a teaching staff of 8, the division regularly receives about 50 applications a year but only admits about 15 students to its 5-year program.

In East Germany work is strong in economics; Japanese studies are taught at Humboldt-Universität zu Berlin. In Yugoslavia and Bulgaria most of the information about Japan has been from translations, principally from German, French, and Russian. In Yugoslavia Japanese-language instruction and courses on Japanese literature, history, economics, politics, and sociology are offered at Belgrade University, but no degree program is available. There is no center for Japanese studies in Bulgaria, but Japanese language courses have been offered at Sofia University since the mid-1960s. Courses related to Japan are also offered in Hungary at Eötvös Loránd University in Budapest and Attila József University in Szeged.

Soviet Union. Interest in Japan in the Soviet Union dates back to the 17th century, a time when territory in Siberia and along the Pacific coast was added to Russia and contacts with neighboring countries in East Asia were established. Japanese sailors shipwrecked on Kamchatka in the 18th century were a major source of information about Japan and served as language instructors in the School of Japanese attached to the Academy of Sciences opened in St. Petersburg in 1736 and transferred to Irkutsk in 1754.

Interest in Japan continued to grow in the 19th century, and books about Japan by Russians who had travelled there, such as those by the naval officer Vasilii GOLOVNIN and the novelist Ivan GONCHAROV, were influential. After the opening of Russian-Japanese relations in 1855, the Russian Foreign Office needed Japan specialists, and the teaching of Japanese began at the Oriental Languages Faculty of St. Petersburg University in 1870; a chair of Japanese philology was created here in 1898 and one at the Oriental Institute in Vladivostok in 1900.

In the early 20th century many outstanding Japanologists emerged at St. Petersburg University, including O. Rosenberg, Nikolai KONRAD, Evgenij POLIVANOV, Serge Elisséeff, and Nikolai NEVSKII. Another Japanologist from St. Petersburg University, Dmitrii POZDNEEV, was the director of the Oriental Institute at Vladivostok in 1910–17. After the Russian Revolution new centers for Japanese studies were founded in Petrograd (the former St. Petersburg) and Moscow.

Before World War II oriental studies were centered in Leningrad (the former Petrograd). The Institute of Oriental Studies of the USSR Academy of Sciences was organized here in 1930 and the Association for Japanese Studies was founded here in 1933. Prewar research concentrated on either the study of contemporary Japanese language, literature, history, economics, internal and external policy, and ideology or the study of classical literature, ethnography, ancient beliefs, and problems of class-society-formation in precapitalist Japan.

Research and teaching were disrupted by World War II, and after the war Moscow became the major center for Japanese studies in the Soviet Union. By the mid-1970s some 70 specialists in 11 institutions were located in Moscow. The Institute of Oriental Studies of the USSR Academy of Sciences, reorganized in Moscow in 1950 and estimated to have approximately 33 Japan specialists in 1975, is the largest institution for Japanese studies, but Japanologists are also present in other institutes of the Academy of Sciences such as the Institute of World Economy and International Relations, the Institute of the Far East, the Institute of World Literature, and the Institute of Ethnography, as well as the Institute of International Relations of the Ministry of Foreign Affairs. Japanologists are trained in a six-year program at the Institute of the Countries of Asia and Africa at Moscow University. Applicants outnumber vacancies 20 to 1, and the annual number of graduates reportedly averaged 15–20 in the 1970s.

After the postwar reorganization of the Institute of Oriental Studies, only the Manuscript Sector was left in Leningrad. The Leningrad Branch of the Institute uses these resources for the study of premodern topics, specializing in the cultural history of the peoples of the Orient and oriental linguistics. Japanese studies are taught in a five-year program at Leningrad University and also at the Far Eastern State University in Vladivostok, the third center of Japanese studies in the Soviet Union.

The shift of oriental studies to Moscow resulted in the growth of modern studies, and an increase in specialization is also evident. In recent years many reference works on Japan have been published, such as *Contemporary Japan* in 1968 and the *Japan Yearbook* (edited by Ivan Kovalenko and others) from the Academy of Sciences since 1973. Another major trend is the effort to write comprehensive general works.

Australia and New Zealand. James Murdoch and then A. L. Sadler served as professor of oriental studies at the University of Sydney from soon after World War I to 1947, but the major growth in Japanese studies in Australia has occurred since World War II as part of a general interest in Asia leading to the growth of Chinese, Indian, and Indonesian studies as well.

At the Australian National University in Canberra an extensive program in Japanese studies has been developed under John Caiger and Richard Mason in the Department of Asian Civilizations, Anthony Alfonso and Roger Pulvers in the Department of Japanese,

J.A.A. Stockwin in the Department of Political Science, and E.S. Crawcour, Andrew Fraser, and David Sissons at the Research School of Pacific Studies. Comprehensive programs are also available at the University of Queensland in Brisbane, Monash University in Melbourne, the University of Sydney, and the University of Western Australia in Perth. The latter program emphasizes economics, reflecting the growth of the mining industry with its sales to Japan in the state of Western Australia.

Japanese studies are also taught at the Western Australian Institute of Technology, the University of Melbourne, and, more recently, La Trobe University in Melbourne, the University of Adelaide, the University of Tasmania, and Griffith University in Brisbane. The Canberra College of Advanced Education has a strong Japanese studies program, and courses on Japan are also offered in New South Wales at the University of New South Wales, MacQuarie University, and the University of Newcastle.

Study of the Japanese language has spread, with 1,960 students in Australian primary schools and 6,242 secondary school students studying Japanese in 1975. However, the priority is now consolidation rather than expansion of Japanese studies in Australia. Two problems facing the field are funding and the vast physical distances between both Japanologists and library resources, and it is hoped that the Australia–Japan Foundation and the Asian Studies Association of Australia, both founded in 1976, will help alleviate these difficulties.

In New Zealand, Japanese studies first developed in the mid-1960s when its traditional trading relationship with Britain was threatened by the latter's decision to enter the European Common Market. Since the formation of close economic ties with Japan then became more important, New Zealand Japanese studies have stressed developing competency in the Japanese language. All six universities in New Zealand—the University of Auckland, the University of Waikato, Massey University, Victoria University of Wellington, the University of Canterbury, and the University of Otago—offer some work in Japanese studies, and all but Victoria and Otago have some Japanese-language instruction. Japanese is also taught at three polytechnic institutes and numerous secondary schools throughout New Zealand (1,640 students in the third through seventh forms in 1976).

Funds for Japanese studies have become scarce in recent years, and an interuniversity conference held in 1976 recommended that full-scale development of the Japanese-language program to the MA level be limited to Auckland, Massey, and Canterbury universities. Thus the outlook for Japanese studies for the immediate future in New Zealand, as in Australia, is for consolidation rather than future growth.

Asia. The development of Japanese studies in Asia has been hampered by the traditional orientation of the higher educational systems in many of the countries toward the West and resentment stemming from Japanese occupation during World War II. In recent years, however, interest in Japan is increasing through its role as a trading partner, source of technical information and training, and possible model for modernization.

The Japanese government decided in the 1960s to assist in the establishment of Japanese studies in five Asian cities—Manila, Djakarta, Kuala Lumpur, Bangkok, and Hong Kong—and has played an active role through the dispatch of teachers from Japan and the provision of financial assistance for study in Japan. Asian universities offering Japanese studies now include the University of Indonesia in Djakarta, Thammasat and Chulalongkorn universities in Thailand, Nanyang University in Singapore, the Chinese University of Hong Kong, and Jawaharlal Nehru University and the University of Delhi in India. As of 1980, centers for Japanese studies were also being established at the University of the Philippines in Quezon City and the University of Malaya in Kuala Lumpur.

The study of Japan and the Japanese language in South Korea largely recommenced after the normalization of Japanese-Korean diplomatic relations in 1965. Colleges and universities that have opened Japanese departments include Kun Kuk University, Soong Jun University, Won Kwang University, Kyung Nam College, Kyung Sang National College, Kook Je College, Han Kuk University of Foreign Studies, Sung Shin Women's Teachers College, Sang Myung Women's Teachers College, Soo Do Women's Teachers College, Kwan Dong College, Chung-ju College, Kye Myung College, Busan Women's College, and Je-ju National College. The teaching of the Japanese language has also begun at the high school level. Research institutes include the Korea-Japan Relations Research Center and the

Language Research Institute at Seoul National University. The Korean Society of Japanology was established in 1973.

With the normalization of relations between China and Japan in 1972, Japanese studies, particularly Japanese-language study, have also been growing in China. Programs have been created to train Chinese teachers of Japanese and to prepare students for study at Japanese universities. The Institute for Japanese Studies of the Chinese Academy of Social Sciences was established in 1980 in Beijing (Peking).

Central and South America. The MA program of the Center of Asian and North African Studies at El Colegio de México has trained many Latin American Japanologists since 1964. Of the 200 Latin American Orientalists in the late 1970s, 42 percent came out of the center program; there were no more than 8 specialists in Japanese studies in 1960, but by 1978 some 30 such specialists had graduated from the Center. It has also been active in organizing conferences and has published *Estudios de Asia* since 1966.

Courses in Japanese studies or the Japanese language are also available at the Universidad del Salvador in Argentina, the Universidade Federal da Bahia and Universidade de São Paulo in Brazil, and the National University of Trujillo in Peru.

Japan. Mention should also be made of study and research facilities available for foreigners in Japan. Institutions offering Japanese studies courses in English include Aoyama Gakuin University, International Christian University, Sophia University, and Waseda University in Tōkyō, as well as Kansai University of Foreign Studies in Ōsaka, Kōnan University in Kōbe, Nanzan University in Nagoya, and Seinan Gakuin University in Fukuoka. The Inter-University Center for Japanese Language Studies (the former Stanford Center), which is sponsored by a consortium of American and Canadian universities, offers Japanese-language instruction for foreigners.

Many English-language periodicals relating to Japan are also published in Japan, including *Monumenta Nipponica, Transactions of the Asiatic Society of Japan, Acta Asiatica,* the *Japan Quarterly,* and the *Japan Interpreter* (formerly the *Journal of Social and Political Ideas in Japan*). See also JAPANESE AS A FOREIGN LANGUAGE.

📖——Fukuoka UNESCO Association, ed, *Overseas Japanese Studies, Institutions and Students* (1976). Fukuoka UNESCO Association, ed, *Overseas Japanese Studies, Institutions and Specialists* (1980). Japan Foundation, ed, *An Introductory Bibliography for Japanese Studies* (1974–). Japan Foundation, ed, *Conference of European Japanologists* (1975). Japan Foundation, ed, *Japanese Studies in the United States* (1977). Japan Foundation, ed, *Directory of Japan Specialists in Australia and New Zealand* (1981). Japan Foundation, ed, *Directory of Japan Specialists in the United Kingdom* (1981). Japan Foundation, ed, *Directory of Japan Specialists in Canada* (1981). Frank H. H. King, ed, *The Development of Japanese Studies in Southeast Asia; Proceedings of the Fourth Leverhulme Conference* (1969). E. Stuart Kirby, *Russian Studies of Japan; An Exploratory Survey* (1981). Josef Kreiner et al, *Japanforschung in Österreich* (1976). Maison Franco-Japonaise, ed, *Le Japon Vu Depuis la France; Les Études Japonaises en France* (1981). Frank J. Shulman, ed, *Japan and Korea: An Annotated Bibliography of Doctoral Dissertations in Western Languages, 1877–1969* (1970). Frank J. Shulman, ed, *Supplement, 1969–1974* (1976).　　　　MURATA Hiroshi

Japanese terrier

(Nippon *teriya*). A breed of dog developed from small foreign toy terriers during the Taishō (1912–26) and Shōwa (1926–) periods. Small, slender pet dogs with smooth short hair similar to European toy terriers are described in books of the Edo period (1600–1868). They were supposedly of foreign origin and were called *shika-bane* or *shika-bone* (deer skeleton). Today's breed was probably bred from newly imported foreign terriers, possibly the black-and-tan terrier and the toy smooth fox terrier brought to Japan in the middle of the Meiji period (1868–1912). Through a few fanciers' efforts, the breed gradually formed from the end of Taishō through the beginning of the Shōwa period.

The Japanese terrier has exceptionally fine, velvety short hair. The coat coloring is white with small black markings, and there is often a trace of tan on the face. The breed was very popular between World War I and World War II but is rarely seen today.

📖——Takahisa H. et al, *Nihonken no kenkyū* (1938). Uchida Tōru, *Inu* (1948).　　　　Hiroshi SAKAMOTO

Japan External Trade Organization → JETRO

Japan Federation of Bar Associations

(Nihon Bengoshi Rengōkai; abbreviated Nichibenren; JFBA). The statutorily created national association of private attorneys (exclusive of judges and prosecutors). The Lawyers' Law (Bengoshi Hō) of 1949 requires every lawyer to register as a member of one of the 52 local bar associations and of the Japan Federation of Bar Associations. The JFBA, although subject to judicial review and potentially to the rulemaking powers of the Supreme Court, has practically complete autonomy in the governance of the private legal profession, including the legal responsibility to screen entrants and to discipline members.

The present independence of the JFBA and the private bar contrasts sharply with pre-World War II practice when the discipline of private attorneys was under the control of the Ministry of Justice and bar associations were relatively powerless. The prewar government frequently used its disciplinary power to punish lawyers involved in the defense of political defendants. Disciplinary cases handled by the JFBA since 1949, on the other hand, have almost always involved pecuniary or fiduciary indiscretions rather than political activities.

The JFBA and the local bar associations are involved in various other activities aside from the self-governance of the profession. The JFBA has over 39 committees (including the Qualification Screening Committee and the Disciplinary Committee), which are mandated by the Lawyers' Law, and is engaged in areas such as the defense of human rights, research and recommendations for law reform, the representation of the interests of private attorneys in relation to the other branches of the legal profession, and the overseeing of the bar associations' role in the training of new attorneys. Local bar associations are frequently involved in continuing legal education and sponsor research and publications in various fields of law. The Ōsaka Bar Association, for example, is particularly active in environmental law and sociology of law, sponsoring research and publications in both areas.

📖——Kenzō Ōtsubo, *Japan Federation of Bar Associations* (1978).
Frank K. UPHAM

Japan Federation of Employers' Associations → Nikkeiren

Japan Federation of Religions

(Nihon Shūkyō Remmei). A loosely affiliated council of religious groups organized in 1946. It is composed of five federations of religious groups: the Association of Shintō Shrines (Jinja Honchō; see SHINTŌ SHRINES, ASSOCIATION OF), the Association of Sect Shintō (Kyōha Shintō Rengōkai; see SECT SHINTŌ, ASSOCIATION OF), the Japan Federation of Buddhists (ZEN NIHON BUKKYŌ KAI), the Japan Association of Christian Churches (Nihon Kirisutokyō Rengōkai; see CHRISTIAN CHURCHES, JAPAN ASSOCIATION OF), and the Union of New Religious Organizations of Japan (Shin Nihon Shūkyō Dantai Rengōkai). Its purpose is to promote fellowship among religious organizations, especially for the sake of maintaining freedom of religion under the Japanese constitution and to ensure the separation of church and state so that a society based on moral principles may develop freely.　　　　Kenneth J. DALE

Japan Fine Arts Academy

(Nihon Bijutsuin). An association of artists in the NIHONGA (Japanese-style painting) tradition; formed in Tōkyō for the purpose of fostering the study of Japanese art and for holding exhibitions. Founded in 1898 by OKAKURA KAKUZŌ and a group of artists including HASHIMOTO GAHŌ, YOKOYAMA TAIKAN, SHIMOMURA KANZAN, and HISHIDA SHUNSŌ. In 1906, after some internal dispute and acrimonious censure by conservative art circles, the academy moved to Izura, Ibaraki Prefecture. Many artists worked and even lived at the academy. In 1913 Okakura died and the academy almost dissolved. But in 1914, Yokoyama Taikan took over and reorganized the academy, after which it was often referred to as the Saikō Nihon Bijutsuin or Reorganized Japan Fine Arts Academy. The academy included a section for Western-style painting (YŌGA) until 1920, and for sculpture until 1961. The most notable later painters fostered by the academy include YASUDA YUKIHIKO, MAEDA SEISON, Katayama Nampū (1887–1980), and, more recently, Hirayama Ikuo (b 1930). The academy continues to hold its exhibition of Japanese-style paintings, the Inten, twice a year. *Joseph* SEUBERT

Japan Folk-Craft Museum

(Nihon Mingeikan). The first and most important folk-craft museum in Japan; located in Komaba, Meguro Ward, Tōkyō. Founded in 1936 by YANAGI MUNEYOSHI, the leader of the folk-craft movement, and others with financial assistance provided by ŌHARA MAGOSABURŌ. Yanagi served as the first curator of the museum. The collection includes paintings, pottery, porcelain, prints, textiles, lacquer, masks, toys, furniture, metalwork, and costumes from various regions of Japan. All are either examples of ancient folk craft or objects made by contemporary artists working in the folk tradition. Approximately 13,000 items are housed in the museum. Aside from its exhibitions, the museum conducts research on folk craft and encourages interest in contemporary folk arts and crafts. It publishes the monthly magazine *Mingei*.

Japan Foundation

(Kokusai Kōryū Kikin). A public corporation under the jurisdiction of the Ministry of Foreign Affairs, specially commissioned to administer programs for INTERNATIONAL CULTURAL EXCHANGE. It was established in 1972 through the reorganization of an existing organization, the Kokusai Bunka Shinkōkai (Japan Cultural Society; KBS), founded in 1934. The foundation undertakes exchange programs for scholars, artists, and specialists; provides financial support for research on Japan and the promotion of Japanese language teaching abroad; participates in the presentation of cultural events; produces and distributes printed and audiovisual materials on Japanese culture; and performs the necessary surveys and research in order to administer international cultural exchange programs. Headquarters are located in Tōkyō, with a branch office in Kyōto. The foundation maintains cultural centers in Cologne, Djakarta, and Rome, and liaison offices in Bangkok, Canberra, London, Los Angeles, Paris, São Paulo, and Washington, DC. It operates its programs on a budget of about ¥5.7 billion (US $26 million)—as of 1982—which comes from the proceeds on an endowment from the government, amounting to about ¥48.5 billion (US $200 million). *SUGIYAMA Yasushi*

Japan Foundation Library

(Kokusai Kōryū Kikin Toshoshitsu). Collection of books and journals about Japan; started in the early 1930s by the Kokusai Bunka Shinkōkai (KBS; Japan Cultural Society) and transferred to the JAPAN FOUNDATION in 1972. The approximately 15,000 volumes that make up the small but historically important collection are primarily in European languages, mostly in English. Focusing on the humanistic and social sciences, the strength of the library lies in its holdings on pre-1945 literature, history, politics, and sociology. Some 1,000 volumes are added to the collection annually, including, in recent years, Japanese-language material. Landmark studies of Japan by Lafcadio HEARN, Philipp Franz von SIEBOLD, and Engelbert KAEMPFER are among the library's most notable holdings. The library publishes guides to its collection, continuing the work started by KBS, as well as *Current Contents of Academic Journals,* an English-language annual that analyzes selected scholarly journals in the humanistic and social sciences. The library also publishes a series of special bibliographies on history, literature, foreign relations, and other subjects. *Theodore F. WELCH*

Japan Herald

Influential English language newspaper whose existence spanned the Meiji period (1868–1912); launched as a weekly in Yokohama in November 1861 by Albert W. Hansard. Its motto was "The Most Thorough Independence." It expanded to become a daily, the *Daily Japan Herald,* in October 1863 under the capable editorship of John Reddie BLACK. An evening edition was added later. The paper was sold to a German syndicate in 1902 and ceased publication in 1914. *HARUHARA Akihiko*

Japan Highway Public Corporation

(Nihon Dōro Kōdan). A public corporation which constructs and administers the nation's major toll roads and related facilities. Cap-

italized wholly by the government, it was established in 1956. At the time of its establishment, the corporation took over all the toll roads belonging to the national and prefectural governments and at the same time concentrated its efforts on the construction of EXPRESSWAYS. In July 1963, the corporation's Meishin Expressway between Nagoya and Kōbe, the first road of its kind in Japan, was partially opened to traffic. The corporation is currently engaged in the construction of 32 expressways which will run through the entire Japanese archipelago with a combined length of 5,700 kilometers (3,540 mi); the project is expected to be completed by 1990. By February 1980, the corporation was operating a total of 19 expressways throughout the country, including the Tōmei, Meishin, Chūō, Tōhoku, Hokuriku, Chūgoku, and Kyūshū expressways, with a total length of approximately 2,500 kilometers (1,550 mi). The corporation also manages other general toll roads with a total length of 743 kilometers (461.4 mi) and two ferry routes. An average of 1,150,000 automobiles utilize the corporation's toll roads each day. Because this heavy traffic affects the inhabitants of the districts through which the roads pass, the corporation takes great pains with environmental and safety measures. See also METROPOLITAN EXPRESSWAY PUBLIC CORPORATION. *HIRATA Masami*

Japan Housewives Association → Shufuren

Japan Housing Corporation → Housing and Urban Development Corporation

Japan Incorporated

A term coined in the late 1960s suggesting that Japan's economic success was in its unique government-business relationship. A central feature of this concept is the notion that government and business work closely together to achieve common ends, usually defined in terms of economic growth, or success in commercial rivalry with foreign competitors.

"Japan Inc" has enjoyed widespread currency among journalists, businessmen, and government officials outside Japan, particularly in the United States, and was decidedly in vogue during the early 1970s. Secretaries of commerce Maurice Stans and Peter Peterson of the Nixon administration, together with James Abegglen of the Boston Consulting Group (a private firm of business consultants based in Boston) were among those who made the term popular.

Of the many formulations of the concept, one common feature is the assertion of a close correspondence between the structure of the Japanese econopolitical system and that of a giant, multidivisional, conglomerate corporation. According to this analogy, the role of the government in the Japanese economy is like that of a corporate headquarters responsible for planning and coordination, for formulation of long-term policies, and for major investment decisions. Large corporations in Japan are viewed as akin to corporate divisions, possessing considerable operating autonomy and free to compete with one another within broad limits, but nevertheless subject to the ultimate control of central authority.

Japan Inc theorists rarely specify which parts of the Japanese government are central in decision making. But the Ministry of International Trade and Industry, the Bank of Japan, and the Economic Planning Agency are most frequently mentioned as centers of coordination and control. Compared with other industrialized nations, particularly the United States, the pattern of government-business collaboration in Japan is considered to be far more pronounced, with government controlled capabilities vis-à-vis the private sector unusually strong.

However, since the mid-1970s, the popularity of the concept outside Japan (within Japan it has never been widely accepted) has declined. A major criticism directed against the concept has been its failure to identify variations by sector in Japanese government-business relations. While public-private sector collaboration has been relatively widespread and continuous, for instance, in steel and, to a lesser degree, in other basic industries, it has been much less pronounced in consumer goods industries, such as consumer electronics and food products. Failure to take account of increasing pluralism in the Japanese political economy, particularly since the early 1970s, has also been pointed out. As one American observed, the Japan Inc model may have been relevant to the Japan of 1970, but it was distinctly less so in the following decade.

The concept hardly recognized the role of politics—both bureaucratic and party politics—in undermining the coherence of policy, particularly in long-established, inefficient sectors such as agriculture, coal mining, and shipping. Furthermore, there is insufficient emphasis on the competitive dimensions of Japanese economic life, for example, oligopolistic rivalry among major *keiretsu*, or industrial groups, that could, as in the petrochemical industry, force modification of government plans. And lastly, in its claims to uniqueness in the pattern of government-business collaboration in Japan, the Japan Inc paradigm overlooks analogous patterns of collaboration in the United States (within the national security-related sector, for example) and, particularly, in Europe.

■——James C. Abegglen, *Business Strategies for Japan* (1970). James C. Abegglen, "The Sources of Japanese Economic Growth," *Scientific American* 222.3 (March 1970). Chalmers Johnson, *MITI and the Japanese Miracle* (1982). Eugene J. Kaplan, *Japan: The Government-Business Relationship* (1972). Miyazaki Yoshikazu, *Sengo Nihon no keizai kikō* (1966). Morikawa Hidemasa, *Nihon no kigyō to kokka* (1976). Kent E. CALDER

Japan International Cooperation Agency

(Kokusai Kyōryoku Jigyōdan). A special public corporation established in August 1974 to provide technological assistance to developing countries and to aid Japanese emigrants. Fully funded by the Japanese government, the agency is authorized to extend loans and issue bonds. The agency's activities include accepting trainee technicians from, and supplying specialists and equipment to, developing countries; providing research and advice on development programs; recruiting, selecting, and training Japanese youth for international cooperation programs overseas; and extending and guaranteeing loans for investment in agricultural and industrial development in developing countries. See also OVERSEAS ECONOMIC COOPERATION FUND. Suzuki Kōichi

Japan Labor-Farmer Party → Nihon Rōnōtō

Japan Line, Ltd

Leading Japanese shipping firm, operating regularly scheduled and tramp ships. Established in 1964 through the merger of Nittō Shōsen and Daidō Kaiun. During the Japanese economy's period of rapid growth in the 1960s the company constructed a number of supertankers to handle the increase in crude oil imports and became for a period the foremost operator of Japanese tankers. It also entered the field of third-nation transport and in 1973, including both owned and chartered vessels, controlled the world's largest fleet. However, with the instability of the shipping industry brought on by the oil crisis of the 1970s, it required financial aid from the Industrial Bank of Japan, Ltd, and other institutions. It has established subsidiary corporations in New York, Hong Kong, Panama, and various islands in the Caribbean Sea. In 1981 the firm owned 29 ships, with an aggregate of 3,552,088 deadweight tons. Sales for the fiscal year ending March 1982 totaled ¥269.1 billion (US $1.1 billion) and capitalization stood at ¥34.5 billion (US $143.3 million). The corporate headquarters are located in Tōkyō.

Japan Magazine Publishers Association

(JMPA; Nihon Zasshi Kyōkai). Association established in 1956 with a membership of 30 representative magazine publishers, increasing to 62 members by 1982. Its objective is to ensure the ethics of the magazine publishing industry. In October 1963 it established a set of general principles of ethical magazine editing, and in 1966 it joined the International Federation of the Periodical Press. Shimizu Hideo

Japan Medical Association

(Nihon Ishikai). Organization of physicians. In 1906 voluntary medical associations were formed in various parts of Japan. In 1919 the Japan Medical Association was legally established with the inauguration of the health insurance system. During World War II it was made a part of the government and charged with national medical policy. In 1948 it was reorganized completely, and membership was put on a voluntary basis. In the same year it was legally recognized as a nonprofit corporation with the aim of enhancing profes-

sional ethics, developing and spreading medical science and art, improving public health, and promoting social welfare. In 1950 the association absorbed the Japanese Association of Medical Sciences and organized sectional meetings of medical specialists. With 98,400 members (1980), most of whom are practicing doctors, the association exerts great influence on government medical policies. Takemi Tarō (b 1904) served as president of the association for several terms after 1957. SŌDA Hajime

Japan Metals & Chemicals Co, Ltd

(Nihon Jūkagaku Kōgyō). Steel company. Japan's largest producer of ferroalloys, the company also manufactures fertilizers and constructs geothermal electrical power plants. It is affiliated with the NIPPON STEEL CORPORATION. It was established in 1917 as a carbide manufacturer and later converted to the production of ferroalloys. During the depression in sales of specialized steel in the 1970s, the company absorbed numerous steel firms to expand its scale of operations. It is also working on the development of new energy sources; it began a geothermal project in 1957 and in 1966 constructed Japan's first geothermal electric plant. Annual sales totaled ¥91.7 billion (US $419 million) in 1980; capitalization stood at ¥6.8 billion (US $31 million) in the same year. Corporate headquarters are located in Tōkyō.

Japan Newspaper Publishers and Editors Association

(Nihon Shimbun Kyōkai; NSK). A cooperative organization founded on 23 July 1956, whose membership is composed of major daily newspaper publishers, news agencies, and broadcasting companies. The association is not affiliated with any political party or special interest group. Its activities include: research on newspapers, communication, and broadcasting; the encouragement of high journalistic standards; the inspection of news articles by member news publishers according to accepted guidelines of journalism; and the collection, cataloging, and microfilming of the newspapers of member publishers. The association publishes a regular bulletin, yearbook, and other collected data. It also publishes an English edition of its NSK newsletter and a yearbook, *The Japanese Press*. HARUHARA Akihiko

Japan Overseas Cooperation Volunteers

(Nihon Seinen Kaigai Kyōryoku Tai). Often called the Japanese Peace Corps. A program founded by the Japanese government in 1965 to provide technical services and instruction to developing countries. Originally under the Overseas Technical Cooperation Agency (absorbed by the new Japan International Cooperation Agency in 1974) and financed exclusively by the Japanese government, the Japan Overseas Cooperation Volunteers (JOCV) sent out 3,582 volunteers between 1965 and 1981.

The volunteers, all young people, serve a term of two years and receive a monthly living allowance of not less than US $250; their housing is provided by the host country and they work as a member of that country's government. The JOCV places strong emphasis on technical qualifications and experience, and nearly half of its volunteers have been in agriculture, fishing, and other areas of primary industry.

Recruitment of volunteers takes place twice a year, in April and October, with volunteers being given a roughly four-month training program before being sent overseas. The de facto lifetime employment system in Japan, and the resulting problems of reentry for returning volunteers, constitutes a serious obstacle in recruitment. Janet ASHBY

Japan P.E.N. Club

(Nihon Pen Kurabu). Japanese branch of the International Association of Poets, Playwrights, Editors, Essayists, and Novelists. Founded in 1935, its first president was SHIMAZAKI TŌSON. The following year Shimazaki and Arishima Ikuma, the vice-president, attended the International P.E.N. Conference in Argentina. In 1942 P.E.N.'s activities ceased because of the war, but the club was reestablished nationally in 1947, and then rejoined the International P.E.N. Club in 1948. The new president was KAWABATA YASUNARI. In 1957 the club hosted the 29th International P.E.N. Conference held in Tōkyō. In 1972 the P.E.N. club organized an International

Conference on Japanese Studies, with 199 Japanologists from 39 countries invited. The club publishes *Japanese Literature Today*.

Japan Productivity Center

(Nihon Seisansei Hombu). Headquarters of the Japanese movement to increase industrial productivity—part of a worldwide movement that began in the late 1940s. The center was established in 1955 as a result of an agreement between the governments of the United States and Japan. Funds were provided by business and financial circles as well as by the two governments. The center's staff represented the labor and management sectors and included neutral members as well. At the time Japan was plagued by low productivity and high material costs. Both exports and national income were declining. The center began its activities in the belief that workers and consumers would benefit from increased productivity. Since its establishment, the center has dispatched a total of 1,420 study teams (22,100 individuals) abroad. Starting in the late 1970s the center began to set an example for the United States, where productivity was deteriorating. The center is also active in providing advice to the Chinese government.   HIRATA Masami

Japan Proletarian Party → Nihon Musantō

Japan Pulp & Paper Co, Ltd

(Nihon Kami Parupu Shōji). Firm engaged in the export, import, and domestic sale of paper, paperboard, pulp, and wrapping machines. Established in 1845, it is the industry leader in the domestic sale and export of paper products. Japan Pulp and Paper is the chief distributor for major paper manufacturers such as ŌJI PAPER CO, LTD; JŪJŌ PAPER CO, LTD; and HONSHŪ PAPER CO, LTD. The firm has numerous overseas offices, including several in Southeast Asia, one in New York, and another in Düsseldorf, and plans to continue development of overseas markets. Sales for the fiscal year ending March 1982 totaled ¥372.2 billion (US $1.5 billion) and capitalization stood at ¥3.5 billion (US $14.5 million). Corporate headquarters are located in Tōkyō.

Japan Securities Finance Co, Ltd

(Nihon Shōken Kin'yū). Japan's largest securities financing company. The company was established in 1927 to act as an agency for short-term futures transactions on behalf of the Tōkyō Stock Exchange (then called the Tōkyō Kabushiki Torihikijo; see STOCK EXCHANGES). With the reorganization of the Tōkyō Stock Exchange after World War II, it assumed its present name in 1949 and initiated securities financing. In 1951 it began making loans to securities companies in the form of stocks and settlement funds for margin transactions. The operations of the company are strictly controlled by the Ministry of Finance and the Bank of Japan. At the end of March 1982, annual revenue totaled ¥49.3 billion (US $204.8 million) and the company was capitalized at ¥3 billion (US $12.5 million). The head office is in Tōkyō.

Japan Socialist League → Nihon Shakai Shugi Dōmei

Japan Socialist Party

(JSP; Nihon Shakaitō). Also referred to in English as the Socialist Party of Japan. Political party. The short-lived pre–World War II Japan Socialist Party was founded on 28 January 1906 by a coalition of radical socialists such as SAKAI TOSHIHIKO and moderates such as NISHIKAWA MITSUJIRŌ, KATAYAMA SEN, and TAZOE TETSUJI. The party was forced by the government to disband on 22 February 1907 after radical members such as KŌTOKU SHŪSUI had begun to call for "direct action." The radical-moderate coalition dissolved along with the party; both factions going on to found a succession of other short-lived socialist parties and to engage in underground activities.

The postwar Japan Socialist Party was founded in November 1945. Since then it has been the major political opponent of conservative, principally LIBERAL DEMOCRATIC PARTY (LDP), rule. Its sole experience running the government lasted only 15 months (1947–48), when it participated in a three-party coalition government

headed first by its chairman KATAYAMA TETSU and later by ASHIDA HITOSHI of the MINSHUTŌ. However, the JSP suffered a great loss in the 1949 election of the House of Representatives, where its number of seats fell from 143 to 48. By the late 1950s the JSP had managed to gain a third of the seats in the House of Representatives and was thus assured of enough votes to veto a constitutional amendment. Since 1960, in contrast to the opposition parties as a whole, it has suffered a gradual decline in electoral support. In the June 1980 general election its Diet membership fell from 52 to 47 seats in the upper house and remained unchanged at 107 seats in the lower house. Like many other left-wing parties, it is riven with ideological disagreements, particularly regarding the UNITED STATES–JAPAN SECURITY TREATIES. Whereas its left wing retains the party's traditional opposition to this pact, the right wing, encouraged by the Chinese government, has muted its hostility since the mid-1970s. The party has often cosponsored regional electoral candidates with the JAPAN COMMUNIST PARTY, particularly in gubernatorial elections. But in recent years disagreements over the issue concerning the BURAKUMIN (Japan's largest minority group) and greater rivalry for electoral funding from the same limited circle of sources have driven the two parties farther apart. The JSP remains the major opposition party in the Diet.

The JSP was founded by socialists of various ideological positions who had been active in parties of the Left before World War II. In the April 1947 election of the House of Representatives, the JSP emerged with a small plurality (30.7 percent) of seats over other parties. This enabled it to form a coalition government, led by Katayama Tetsu, which also included the Minshutō and the KOKUMIN KYŌDŌTŌ. The coalition government took office in extremely difficult political and economic circumstances, and strains were soon apparent. Because of policy differences, Katayama dismissed his agriculture minister, Hirano Rikizō (b 1898) in November 1947, and Hirano took a number of his followers out of the party. The Katayama government fell in February 1948 (its rule continued until 10 March), when the JSP left-wing faction under SUZUKI MOSABURŌ, whose members had been excluded from the cabinet by agreement with the other coalition partners, played a key role in having the government's budget rejected by the Diet. The Ashida cabinet, which followed, contained two members of the JSP left-wing faction, and this in turn precipitated a further split in that party between those left wingers prepared to serve in the coalition cabinet and those who refused on ideological grounds. In July 1948 this last group, led by KURODA HISAO, voted against the government's budget and was expelled from the JSP. A little later NISHIO SUEHIRO, leader of the JSP right-wing faction and a powerful figure in the coalition cabinets, was expelled from the party and later arrested for alleged involvement in the SHŌWA DENKŌ SCANDAL. The Ashida government fell in October 1948.

This turbulent period in office was followed by catastrophic defeat in the 1949 general elections. The defeat precipitated a determined bid by the party's left-wing faction (whose ideology was based on Marxism of the RŌNŌHA tradition) to seize control from the right wing, which had dominated the JSP during the Katayama and Ashida cabinets. A crucial but inconclusive debate, known as the Inamura–Morito dispute (after its chief proponents Inamura Junzō [1900–1955] and MORITO TATSUO), took place over whether the party should be narrowly based on the working class, or whether it should be a broader "mass" party. Strategies of revolution were also at issue. Relations between the contending factions so deteriorated that the party split into left, center, and right factions in January 1950; however, the division was patched up in April.

An even more serious split developed over the postwar peace settlement in October 1951, when the party was divided into two factions, each claiming the name Nihon Shakaitō. This division, which was to last for four years, was precipitated by a foreign policy debate over the prospective peace settlement. In essence the Left opposed both the SAN FRANCISCO PEACE TREATY and the United States–Japan Security Treaty, advocated neutralism, and opposed rearmament; whereas the Right was much more positive toward the peace settlement in general. During the period in which the JSP was split into two separate parties, the socialist movement as a whole gained ground electorally, and the left-wing socialists, whose ties with the SŌHYŌ group of labor unions were being consolidated, made particularly rapid progress.

In October 1955, after some two years of complex negotiations, the left and right socialist parties were reunited, and the party soon rose to the height of its influence and popularity. In the 1955 election of the House of Representatives the socialists were able to muster the one-third of the total seats necessary to block revision of the constitution (see CONSTITUTION, DISPUTE OVER REVISION OF), which was one of the principal party platforms. Their best result ever was in the lower house election of 1958, when they gained 166 seats. During the late 1950s, however, the party was gradually moving toward the Left on a number of issues, and in 1959 Nishio Suehiro, protesting the party's increasing "pro-communist" tendency, led his right-wing faction, plus some members of the centrist KAWAKAMI JŌTARŌ faction, out of the JSP. In 1960 this group formed the DEMOCRATIC SOCIALIST PARTY.

The JSP was heavily involved in the security treaty revision crisis of May and June 1960, when it led the attack on the policies of Prime Minister KISHI NOBUSUKE, both within and outside the Diet. After the crisis the JSP chairman, ASANUMA INEJIRŌ, was assassinated by a rightist fanatic during an election speech in October 1960.

Subsequently, EDA SABURŌ rose rapidly to prominence within the party and, along with NARITA TOMOMI, propounded policies of "structural reform" (derived in part from the Italian communist leader Palmiro Togliatti, 1893–1964) designed to give the party a more positive and relevant approach to rapid economic growth under capitalism. The proposed structural reform was, however, firmly resisted by the party's powerful left wing, and Eda's influence after 1962 started to decline. In May 1965 his left-wing rival, SASAKI KŌZŌ, was elected chairman.

During the late 1960s the JSP was in considerable disarray, and in a political atmosphere charged by the Vietnam War and related issues, the leadership engaged in extreme left-wing rhetoric. The party suffered a serious reverse in the 1969 lower-house general election, when its number of seats fell from 140 to 90. A stabilization, and even some improvement, of the party's electoral fortunes soon occurred under the durable (1970–77) leadership of Narita and Ishibashi Masashi (b 1924). The party remained badly divided, however, between the left-wing Shakai Shugi Kyōkai (Socialist League) of SAKISAKA ITSURŌ and more moderate elements, the former being entrenched among rank-and-file members who were able to bind the party through resolutions at national party congresses but had little support among JSP Diet members. Early in 1977 Eda defected from the party after losing his seat in the December 1976 lower-house general election and founded the Shakai Shimin Rengō (Socialist Citizens' League), only to die shortly thereafter. A number of prominent figures on the Right of the party were expelled in the latter half of 1977. In December 1977, after a long period of factional strife and indecision, Narita was replaced as chairman by the popular mayor of Yokohama, ASUKATA ICHIO.

Under Asukata's leadership, the temperature of intraparty feuding was somewhat lowered, and the Shakai Shugi Kyōkai was ordered to moderate its activities. Nevertheless, significant innovations in policy or organization did not seem to be forthcoming. The JSP remained closely dependent on the Sōhyō unions for electoral backing (see also PRESSURE GROUPS), and in the decentralized nature of its electoral organization was closer to the LDP than to the smaller parties such as the KŌMEITŌ and the Japan Communist Party. Whereas in the late 1950s the main base of support for the JSP was located in the cities, it subsequently lost ground in urban areas. In rural and semirural areas, where the minor parties made less electoral headway, support for the JSP held up rather well, based in most cases on branches of the public-sector unions which, because of the nature of their work, tended to be well represented even in the most remote rural constituency. At the beginning of the 1980s, however, any prospect of the JSP emerging once more as a creative and dynamic force in Japanese politics seemed remote. See also UNITED SOCIAL DEMOCRATIC PARTY.

■——Allan B. Cole, George O. Totten, and Cecil H. Uyehara, *Socialist Parties in Postwar Japan* (1966). Nihon Shakaitō Gekkan Shakaitō Henshūbu, ed, *Nihon Shakaitō no sanjūnen* (1976). Nihon Shakaitō Kettō Nijusshūnen Kinen Jigyō Jikkō Iinkai, ed, *Nihon Shakaitō nijusshūnen no kiroku* (1965). Ōta Kaoru and Okuda Hachiji, *Shakaitō: sono byōkon to katsuro* (1974). Sasada Shigeru, *Nihon Shakaitō*, 2 vols (1960). J. A. A. Stockwin, *The Japanese Socialist Party and Neutralism* (1968). Cecil H. Uyehara, *Leftwing Social Movements in Japan, an Annotated Bibliography* (1959).

J. A. A. STOCKWIN

Japan Society for the Promotion of Science

(Nihon Gakujutsu Shinkōkai). A semiofficial organization that helps implement Japanese government policies pertaining to the development of the sciences. Established in 1967; a predecessor with the same name (sometimes romanized as Nippon Gakujutsu Shinkōkai) had been established in 1932. The society provides assistance to researchers in such forms as visiting professorships and postdoctoral fellowships; it carries on international scientific cooperation in accordance with such formal agreements as the Japanese-American and the Japanese-French agreements for scientific cooperation; it arranges for exchange of scholars with other nations; and it publishes scholarly books in Japanese and English on the sciences and on Japanese culture. WATANABE Tadashi

Japan Steel Works, Ltd

(Nihon Seikōsho). General manufacturer of steel and machinery, established in 1907 by the Hokkaidō Colliery & Steamship Co, Ltd, in a joint venture with Sir W. G. Armstrong, Whitworth & Co, Ltd, and Vickers Sons and Maxim, Ltd, both of the United Kingdom. A member of the MITSUI group, the company produces large steel forgings and castings, high-quality steel plates, and industrial machinery. It plays a vital role in the development of many industries, from shipbuilding, power generation, steel manufacturing, construction, and petrochemicals to food and medicine. A fully integrated manufacturing system from steel production to completed machinery, unique to the company, has earned it worldwide recognition. Development efforts have combined advanced engineering techniques with large-scale manufacturing facilities to produce new composite machinery and equipment, leading to the construction of plants. Future plans will emphasize the fields of nuclear power, ocean development, and medical electronic technology.

Sales for the fiscal year ending March 1982 totaled ¥137.6 billion (US $571.6 million), distributed as follows: machinery, including plant engineering and construction 51 percent; steel forgings and castings 21 percent; heavy machinery and structures 16 percent; and others 12 percent. In the same year the export ratio was 43 percent and capitalization stood at ¥16.9 billion (US $70.2 million) in the same year. Corporate headquarters are located in Tōkyō.

Japan Synthetic Rubber Co, Ltd

(Nippon Gōsei Gomu). The leading manufacturer of synthetic rubber in Japan; its products, including rubber and plastics, are marketed under the brand name "JSR." The company was established in 1957 with 40 percent capital investment by the Japanese government. It became totally independent in 1968. It is the third largest synthetic rubber maker in the world and is quite active in technology development. Exports accounted for 7 percent of its total output in 1981, primarily destined for the United States, Western Europe, and Southeast Asia; overseas offices are maintained in London and New York. Japan Synthetic Rubber has benefited from the surge of sales of Japanese automobiles and auto tires since the mid-1970s. Future plans call for an increased emphasis on marketing fine chemicals for use in the electronics and computer industries. Sales for the fiscal year ending March 1982 totaled ¥163.9 billion (US $680.1 million), of which synthetic rubber accounted for 61 percent, synthetic resins 20 percent, and emulsion 19 percent. Capitalization stood at ¥9.1 billion ($37.8 million) in 1982. Corporate headquarters are in Tōkyō.

Japan Teachers' Union → Nikkyōso

Japan Times

The first English-language newspaper in Japan to be put out by Japanese publishers; started in 1897 by Zumoto Motosada (1862–1943) and Yamada Sueji (1848–1916) with the backing of government leader ITŌ HIROBUMI. An earlier, but separate, paper with the same name had been published by the Englishman Charles Rickerby in Yokohama for resident foreigners from 1865 to 1870, when it merged with the *Japan Mail*. The *Japan Times* absorbed the *Japan Mail* in 1918 and then in 1940 consolidated two other English-language papers being published by foreigners, the *Japan Chronicle* and the *Japan Advertiser*. It was for many years the sole foreign-language news publication in Japan. The paper's news format was patterned on that of *The Times* of London and aimed at explaining Japan's position on international affairs and at fostering mutual understanding between the Japanese and foreigners living in Japan. Dating back to the years before World War II the *Japan Times* had close ties with the Ministry of Foreign Affairs, from whom it received financial support during the war. Between the years 1943 and 1956 the name was changed to *Nippon Times*. It continues to publish actively and in addition to a daily edition, puts out the *Japan Times Weekly,* the *Student Times,* and various books and dictionaries, all in English. Circulation: 54,000 (1979).

Japan Tobacco and Salt Public Corporation

(Nihon Sembai Kōsha). One of three major PUBLIC CORPORATIONS *(kōsha);* it monopolizes the production and sale of tobacco and salt in Japan. These activities were the responsibility of the Monopoly Bureau of the MINISTRY OF FINANCE until 1949, when the corporation was established under the Monopoly Corporation Law (Sembai Kōsha Hō). Until 1962 camphor products were also included in the monopoly's business. The corporation is currently engaged in the purchase and processing of raw tobacco and salt, and the import, export, distribution, and sale of tobacco and salt products. Sales for fiscal 1978 totaled ¥2 trillion (US $9.4 billion); tobacco sales accounted for approximately 97 percent of the total, with salt providing the remainder. The corporation returns to the government a portion of its annual income less operational expenses. In fiscal 1978 the returns to the government amounted to ¥566 billion (US $2.7 billion). This revenue has been decreasing due to a rapid rise in costs coupled with a relatively small increase in sales.

HIRATA Masami

Japan Travel Bureau, Inc

(Nihon Kōtsū Kōsha; commonly known as JTB). Japan's largest travel agency. Founded in 1912 as the Japan Tourist Bureau for the purpose of attracting foreign tourists, it was incorporated in 1945 as a nonprofit foundation *(zaidan hōjin),* changing its name to the Japan Travel Bureau. In 1963 the foundation's business department was reorganized as an independent private corporation, Japan Travel Bureau, Inc. Aside from the sale of tour packages to both foreign and domestic travelers, Japan Travel Bureau also sponsors other business undertakings, such as ticket sales for JAPANESE NATIONAL RAILWAYS and other transport organizations, sale of accommodation coupons for hotels and inns, development of tourist resorts, and publication of travel literature and maps. The firm has about 331 branch offices in Japan and 11 offices overseas. Future plans call for expansion of its overseas travel department and, through its approximately 40 affiliated firms, for the increase of its operations in the recreational field. Sales for the fiscal year ending March 1982 totaled ¥835 billion (US $3.5 billion), of which 79 percent came from the sale of domestic tours to Japanese travelers, 18 percent from Japanese traveling abroad, 2 percent from foreign tourists traveling in Japan, and 1 percent from publications. In the same year capitalization stood at ¥1.6 billion (US $6.6 million). Corporate headquarters are in Tōkyō.

Japan–United States Educational Commission

(Nichibei Kyōiku Iinkai). Often referred to as the (Japan) Fulbright Commission. Based on the exchange program introduced by former US Senator J. William Fulbright in 1946 to facilitate educational interchange between the United States and foreign countries, the commission was established to administer educational and cultural activities between Japan and the United States. Its governing board is composed of 10 members, 5 each from Japan and the United States. The commission was established in 1952; until 1981 it was called the United States Educational (Fulbright) Commission in Japan, with the United States providing all operational funds. Since December 1979, however, the governments of the two countries have financed the commission on an equal basis ($1 million each for fiscal year 1980), and as a result, the name of the commission was changed to its present one.

From the commission's inception in 1952 until 1978, Fulbright grants have been awarded to approximately 5,800 Japanese and 1,200 Americans who studied or taught in Japan and the United States as lecturers, researchers, graduate students, language instructors, and journalists. These Fulbright scholars received all-expense grants or travel-only grants, depending on the nature of their teaching or research. Grants are also provided by the commission under the Visiting American Lecturer Program to Americans who wish to teach or lecture in Japan. In addition, the commission acts as an information service for persons who wish to study in the United States and serves as the Japan Office of the Center for Cultural and Technical Interchange between East and West (the East-West Center), providing information about this US-government educational organ, which was established at the University of Hawaii in 1960. See also STUDY ABROAD.

KATŌ Kōji

Japan Women's University

(Nihon Joshi Daigaku). A private, women's university located in Mejirodai, in Bunkyō Ward, Tōkyō. Founded in 1901 by NARUSE JINZŌ as the first liberal arts college for women. Under such educational principles as "true conviction," "creativity," and "service," the aim of the university is to educate its students as human beings, as women, and as Japanese citizens. In 1948 the school was given university status. Faculties are home economics and letters. Its Institute for Child Study and the Rural Research Institute are well known. The university has its own kindergarten, elementary school, and junior and senior high schools. See also WOMEN'S EDUCATION.

Japan Wool Textile Co, Ltd

(Nippon Keori). Manufacturer of wool textiles. Established in 1896, the firm initially concentrated on the development of the indigenous wool industry and improvement in the quality of Japanese woolen cloth for Western-style clothing. The company later became a major supplier of the cloth required by the Japanese government for the uniforms of civil servants. In the 1960s the company began production of carpets. Sales for the fiscal year ending November 1981 totaled ¥61 billion (US $272.6 million) and capitalization stood at ¥4.1 billion (US $18.3 million). The main office is in Kōbe.

JAS

(Japanese Agricultural Standard; Nihon Nōrin Kikaku). The official standard set by the Ministry of Agriculture, Forestry, and Fisheries for agricultural, forestry, and marine products based on the 1950 law for standardization of these products (Nōrin Busshi Kikaku Hō). It aims to improve the quality of agricultural, forestry, and marine products; to standardize product descriptions in order to maintain fair transactions; and to protect consumers' rights. The stamp "JAS" is attached to those items that meet the standards.

KATŌ Masashi

jellyfish

(kurage). Floating animals belonging to classes Hydrozoa and Scyphomedusae of phylum Coelenterata and to phylum Ctenophora. The most common species in Japan is the *mizukurage (Aurelia aurita),* which has a translucent, whitish color and is found in bays. It occasionally forms large colonies which cause damage to fisheries and the water intake apparatus of thermoelectric power plants. The *akakurage (Dactylometra pacifica)* has nematocysts (stinging cells) in its tentacles and may harm ocean bathers. The *katsuo no eboshi (Physalia physalis utriculus)* has strong poison in its nematocysts. The *bizenkurage (Rhopilema esculenta)* lacks tentacles with nematocysts and grows to 40 centimeters (about 16 in) across; it is salted for use in Chinese cooking. The *mamizukurage (Craspedacusta sowerbyi)* is a freshwater species said to have originated in the Yangzi (Yangtze) River of China; it is now extensively distributed in Japan.

HABE Tadashige

The jellyfish appears as a symbol of chaos in the opening section of cosmogony in the KOJIKI (completed in 712). It is also mentioned in *Honzō wamyō* (completed in 918), the oldest dictionary of natural history in Japan, and WAMYŌ RUIJU SHŌ (completed in about 934), the oldest classified encyclopedia in Japan, both of which contain descriptions based on the Chinese classics. The Chinese have favored cooked dried jellyfish since ancient times, and its popularity at the imperial court in early Japan is thought to have been an imitation of the Chinese practice. Later, jellyfish dishes were served at the coming-of-age and marriage ceremonies of nobles.

SAITŌ Shōji

Jerome Relocation Center

A wartime relocation facility for Japanese Americans located near the town of Jerome, in Chicot and Drew counties, Arkansas; in operation from 6 October 1942 until 30 June 1944. It held a maximum of 8,497 persons at any one time; a total of 10,241 persons were

Extant Publications of the Jesuit Mission Press

(J = Japanese script, R = romanized Japanese, L = Latin, P = Portuguese)

Short title	Author	Place of publication	Date	Remarks
1. *Oratio habita a Fara D. Martino Iaponio*	Martin Hara	Goa	1588	Address given in Goa on 4 June 1587; probably printed by Mission Press. L
2. *Christiani Pueri Institutio*	João Bonifacio	Macao	1588	Adapted version of a work on Christian education; first published at Salamanca in 1575. First European book printed on Chinese soil. L
3. *De Missione Legatorum*	Alessandro Valignano	Macao	1590	Dialogue of Japanese youths who visited Europe. Often attributed to Duarte de Sande, who translated Valignano's Spanish text. L
4. *Dochirina Kirishitan*		Kazusa	1591?	Catechism. J
5. *Sanctos no Gosagueo no Uchi Nuqigaqi*		Kazusa	1591	Biographies of Christian saints. R
6. *Doctrina Christan*		Amakusa	1592	Manual of Christian doctrine. R
7. *Fides no Dŏxi*	Luis de Granada	Amakusa	1592	Abridged version of *Introduction del Symbolo de la Fe*, Salamanca, 1588. R
8. *Bauchizumo no sazukeyŏ*		Amakusa	1593	Pamphlet on baptism. J
9. *Feiqe no Monogatari, Esopo no Fabulas, Xixo Xixxo*		Amakusa	1592–93	Abridged, simplified versions of *Heike monogatari*, *Aesop's Fables*, *Shisho*, *Shissho*, and *Kinkushū*. All bound together in the only known extant copy. R
10. *De Institutione Grammatica*	Manuel Alvarez	Amakusa	1594	Adaptation of Latin grammar first published in Lisbon in 1572. L
11. *Dictionarium Latino Lusitanicum, ac Iaponicum*	Ambrosio Calepino	Amakusa	1595	Three-language dictionary based on Calepino's well-known work.
12. *Contemptus Mundi*	Thomas à Kempis	Amakusa	1596	Partial translation of spiritual classic. R
13. *Exercitia Spiritualia*	Ignatius Loyola	Amakusa	1596	Text of *Spiritual Exercises*. L
14. *Compendium Spiritualis Doctrinae*	Bartholomeu de Martyribus	Amakusa	1596	Ascetical work, first published at Lisbon in 1582. L
15. *Salvator Mundi*		Nagasaki	1598	Manual on sacrament of confession. J
16. *Racuyoxu*		Nagasaki	1598	Three-part dictionary of *kanji*, official titles, and provinces. J
17. *Guia do Pecador*	Luis de Granada	Nagasaki	1599	Abridged translation of famous spiritual work. J
18. *Doctrina Christan*		Nagasaki	1600	Enlarged edition of no. 6. R
19. *Doctrina Christam*		Nagasaki	1600	Another edition of no. 18, but J.
20. *Orashio no honyaku*		Nagasaki	1600	Prayer book. J
21. *Royei. Zafit.*		Nagasaki	1600	Collection of poems and songs from *Wakan rōeishū*, *Zahitsushō*, and other sources. J
22. *Aphorisimi Confessariorum*	Manuel Sa	Nagasaki	1603	Textbook of moral theology; first published at Venice in 1595. L
23. *Vocabulario da Lingoa de Iapam*		Nagasaki	1603–04	Japanese-Portuguese dictionary with 32,000 entries; title page, 1603, but supplement, 1604. P
24. *Arte da Lingoa de Iapam*	João Rodrigues	Nagasaki	1604–08	Japanese grammar; title page, 1604, but last page, 1608. P
25. *Manuale ad Sacramenta Ecclesiae Ministranda*	Luis de Cerqueira	Nagasaki	1605	Liturgical manual, printed in black and red. L
26. *Spiritual Xuguio*		Nagasaki	1607	Manual of spiritual meditations. R
27. *Flosculi*	Manuel Barreto	Nagasaki	1610	Anthology of spiritual writings. L
28. *Contemptus Mundi*	Thomas à Kempis	Kyōto	1610	Similar to the 1596 version (no. 12) but printed by the layman Antonio Harada in Kyōto. Possibly a woodblock print. J
29. *Fides no Quio*	Luis de Granada	Nagasaki	1611	Abridged translation of *Introduction del Symbolo de la Fe* (see no. 7). J
30. *Taiheiki nukigaki*		?	?	Adapted abridgement of *Taiheiki*. J
31. *Arte Breve da Lingoa Iapoa*	João Rodrigues	Macao	1620	Shorter, revised edition of no. 24. P

NOTE: Includes all known extant publications, most of which are held by major libraries in various countries. All are extremely rare and in some cases only one copy is known to exist. Recently, however, a number of titles have been published in facsimile form by publishers in Japan and other countries.

SOURCE: Based on Johannes Laures, *Kirishitan Bunkō: A Manual of Books and Documents on the Early Christian Mission in Japan* (1940; rev ed 1941, 1957).

confined there. Internees came from central and southern California. See JAPANESE AMERICANS, WARTIME RELOCATION OF; WAR RELOCATION AUTHORITY.

◼——William C. Anderson, "Early Reaction to the Relocation of Japanese in the State," *Arkansas Historical Quarterly*, 23 (1964).
Roger DANIELS

Jesuit mission press

The term Jesuit mission press refers to the printing and publishing activities of the Jesuit missionaries in the late 16th and early 17th centuries, or, more strictly, the European printing press they imported into Japan.

The introduction of a European printing press to Japan was due to the initiative of the Italian Jesuit Alessandro VALIGNANO, who realized that the printed word would be an effective means of propagating the Christian message among literate Japanese; a local press could also produce works specifically intended for Japanese readership and would reduce the missionaries' dependence on the tenuous supply of books from Europe.

Accordingly, in 1590 the Jesuits imported a European press. Owing to the unsettled situation of the Christian mission during the next decade (see CHRISTIANITY), the press was first operated in Japan in the remote areas of Kazusa in Hizen Province (now Nagasaki Prefecture) and Amakusa in Higo Province (now Kumamoto Prefecture). It was later transferred to the city of Nagasaki, where printing was begun in 1598. With the expulsion of the missionaries from Japan in 1614, the press was sent back to Macao, where it was used to print at least one more book. The subsequent fate of the machinery is not known.

The press was the first in Japan to use movable metal type. During its 25 years of activity in Japan it produced books and pamphlets (known collectively as *kirishitan-ban*) which were, in view of the difficult circumstances under which the European and Japanese printers worked, remarkable for their quantity, quality, and variety. Not surprisingly, religious works made up the largest category; these included liturgical manuals, prayer books, catechisms, and spiritual classics translated into Japanese and printed in either *rōmaji* (romanized Japanese) or Japanese script. A second category, language books, included dictionaries and grammars of the Japanese language for the use of European missionaries and also Latin textbooks for the students of Jesuit schools. Of the former, the two grammars by João RODRIGUES and the *Vocabulario* dictionary provide valuable information about spoken Japanese in the early 17th century and are often cited in historical studies of the Japanese language. A miscellaneous literary category included anthologies of Japanese and Chinese poetry, a translation of *Aesop's Fables,* and abridged versions of *Heike monogatari* and *Taiheiki.*

As a result of the limited printing runs and the subsequent anti-Christian persecution, relatively few copies of the original editions have survived to the present; these have become collectors' items of great value. Copies of about 30 different titles are extant and are preserved in institutions such as the Vatican Library, the Roman Archives of the Society of Jesus, the British Library, the Bodleian Library at Oxford, TENRI CENTRAL LIBRARY, and the TŌYŌ BUNKO in Tōkyō. Of some works, like *Feiqe no Monogatari,* only one copy is known to exist, while other works, such as various stories in Japanese and Cicero's speeches in Latin, have not survived and are known only through references in contemporary writings. The increasing interest of Japanese and Western scholars in the works brought out by the mission press has led to the recent publication of most of the surviving books in facsimile form. The table on page 51 sets out the principal books and pamphlets extant today.

◼——Johannes Laures, *Kirishitan Bunko: A Manual of Books and Documents on the Early Christian Mission in Japan* (1940; rev ed 1941, 1957). Ernest Mason Satow, *The Jesuit Mission Press in Japan, 1591–1610* (1888).
Michael COOPER

Jesuits

(Iezusukai, or Society of Jesus). A Catholic religious order for men founded by Ignatius of Loyola in Paris in 1534; it received official canonical recognition in 1540. One of its founder members, Francis XAVIER, reached Kagoshima in 1549 and thus began the Christian mission in Japan. The Jesuits labored in Japan for the best part of a century until the Tokugawa persecution finally put an end to its activities there. Numerous members of the order, both Japanese and

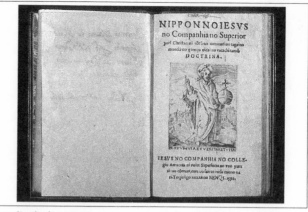

Jesuit mission press

Doctrina Christan, a manual of Christian doctrine published in romanized Japanese in Amakusa in 1592. Tōyō Bunko, Tōkyō.

foreign, were martyred during this period. The Jesuits returned to Japan at the beginning of the 20th century and established Sophia University (Jōchi Daigaku) in Tōkyō in 1913. The order also runs Elizabeth University of Music in Hiroshima (Erizabēto Ongaku Daigaku), three high schools, and various parishes. As of 1981, there were 375 Jesuits in Japan. See also CHRISTIANITY; CATHOLIC MISSIONARIES.
Michael COOPER

JETRO

(Japan External Trade Organization; Nihon Bōeki Shinkōkai; former English name Japan Export Trade Research Association). Japan's official trade promotion association, supervised by the Ministry of International Trade and Industry. The chief function of JETRO, prior to the early 1970s, was to provide information to help Japanese companies, both large and small, expand exports. JETRO offices were set up in chief overseas business centers to collect market information and to provide services to companies interested in expanding exports. These services included performing and commissioning market research and helping to plan marketing.

JETRO's role changed as Japan's export competitiveness increased, and as the balance of payments surpluses became too large. In the early 1970s, JETRO began promoting imports to Japan. Import activities included the preparation of publications on the Japanese market in English and other languages to assist present and potential exporters to Japan. JETRO also began sponsoring trade exhibitions for the products of various nations and played an active role in establishing the World Trade Mart in Tōkyō, where products of all nations can be shown regularly to potential purchasers. Through overseas offices, JETRO also provides information to persons interested in the Japanese market, and sponsors lectures, missions, and other activities to promote foreign goods in Japan.
C. Tait RATCLIFFE

JGC Corporation

(Japan Gasoline Company; Nikki). General engineering firm. One of Japan's three largest engineering companies. Established in 1928, the firm developed as an engineering company chiefly concerned with oil refining and the design and construction of petrochemical plants. In recent years JGC has entered a wide range of industrial fields, including nuclear power, food and pharmaceutical products, environmental protection, natural gas, and the development of city gas systems. Since 1965 the company has erected plants in 40 countries. It controls a network of overseas offices and subsidiary firms and has concluded agreements for technology exchange with a number of foreign engineering companies, including UOP, Inc, of the United States and Uhde GmbH of West Germany. The company's policy for the future is to develop further its technology related to natural gas and nuclear power and to develop technology for the utilization of coal and geothermal and solar energy. Sales for the fiscal year ending March 1982 totaled ¥308.9 billion (US $1.3 billion), of which overseas projects contributed 70 percent. In 1982 the firm was capitalized at ¥2.8 billion (US $11.6 million). The corporate headquarters are located in Tōkyō.

Jiaozhou (Kiaochow) concession

(Kōshūwan *soshakuchi*). A former Japanese territory in present-day Jiao County, along the southern shore of the Shandong (Shantung) Peninsula in China. Originally wrested from China by Germany in 1898, it was seized by Japan in November 1914, less than three months after Japan had declared war on Germany upon the outbreak of World War I. The concession included the city of QINGDAO (Tsingtao), a surrounding leasehold between the Yellow Sea and Jiaozhou Bay, several offshore islands, railway rights to the provincial capital Jinan (Tsinan), and, most important, Jiaozhou Bay, wellsheltered and deep enough to accommodate a modern naval base. An adjoining neutral zone stretching 50 kilometers (31 mi) inland, which the Germans had set up as a buffer zone from Chinese attack, was also maintained. In 1915 Japan forced the Chinese government to accept in secret its acquisition of Germany's former rights to the Jiaozhou concession (see TWENTY-ONE DEMANDS). Japan's refusal to return these holdings after World War I led to widespread Chinese demonstrations and eventually, the MAY FOURTH MOVEMENT. Only at the WASHINGTON CONFERENCE in 1922 did Japan, under American and British pressure, agree to return the concession to China, upon receiving compensation for improvements it had made to the territory.

Ji-Cha (Chi-Ch'a) Autonomous Political Council

(J: Kisatsu Seimu Iinkai). Council established in December 1935 to take over administrative functions in the two North China provinces Hebei (Hopeh) and Chahar, also known as Ji and Cha, respectively. Following the HE–UMEZU (HO–UMEZU) AGREEMENT and DOIHARA–QIN (DOIHARA–CH'IN) AGREEMENT, both of June 1935, the Guomindang (Kuomintang; Nationalist Party) agreed to withdraw, militarily and politically, from Hebei and Chahar. Chinese warlords there formed a council that would be independent of the Guomindang government in Nanjing (Nanking) and act as a pro-Japanese buffer for the puppet state of MANCHUKUO. The two provinces, however, remained formally a part of Nationalist China, and the head of the council, General SONG ZHEYUAN (Sung Che-yüan), while not a Guomindang official, refused to act as a puppet of the Japanese. The council lasted for two years until the outbreak of fullscale war between China and Japan and Japan's establishment of the PROVISIONAL GOVERNMENT OF THE REPUBLIC OF CHINA in Beiping (Peiping), as Beijing (Peking) was then called, in December 1937.

Jichirō

(abbreviation of Zen Nihon Jichi Dantai Rōdō Kumiai; All Japan Prefectural and Municipal Workers' Union). The largest labor organization in Japan, with a membership of over 1.2 million in 1978. The union's membership comprises employees of local governments and public entities but does not include teachers, who are members of a separate union, the Japan Teachers' Union (see NIKKYŌSO). Organized in 1954, Jichirō is affiliated with the General Council of Trade Unions of Japan (SŌHYŌ). Under the Local Civil Service Law (Chihō Kōmuin Hō), the union members do not have the right to bargain collectively or to strike. Attainment of these rights has been a primary goal of Jichirō, and the union has gone so far as to organize illegal strikes (see PUBLIC EMPLOYEES). The union also takes great interest in local municipal elections, seeking to strengthen ties with citizens' organizations on local issues. *Kurita Ken*

Jichishō → Ministry of Home Affairs

Jidai Festival

(Jidai Matsuri; "Festival of the Ages"). A festival of the HEIAN SHRINE in Kyōto. Held annually on 22 October, it is one of the major festivals and tourist attractions of the city. It was begun in 1895 when the shrine was built to commemorate the 1,100th anniversary of the founding of the city, originally known as the capital HEIANKYŌ. The main event of the festival is a procession of people dressed in costumes representing various periods of Japanese history and famous historical personages. The procession now starts from the old Imperial Palace grounds (Gosho), circles the downtown area, and ends at the Heian Shrine. *Inokuchi Shōji*

jidan

(settlement). A contract to resolve a civil dispute through discussion and mutual compromise between parties rather than through litigation. In Japan most legal disputes are resolved by such settlement. In recent years there have been many negotiations involving groups of people adversely affected by pollution, by the unwanted side effects of drugs, or by a new building which blocks sunlight. In such cases issues of criminal law sometimes complicate the matter, and settlement is often used as a supralegal means to resolve the conflict. Settlements, though they often entail less time and expense than a court procedure, can work to the disadvantage of inexperienced parties who are not represented by an attorney. See also WAKAI.
Kojima Takeshi

Jidōsha Sōren

(abbreviation of Zen Nihon Jidōsha Sangyō Rōdō Kumiai Sōrengōkai; Japan Confederation of Automobile Workers' Unions). Nationwide organization of unions of automobile workers. Jidōsha Sōren was established in 1972 as the result of the reorganization of Zenkoku Jidōsha Rōkyō (Japan Council of Automobile Workers' Unions). It includes the workers' unions of TOYOTA MOTOR CORPORATION, ISUZU MOTORS, LTD, and others, and Jidōsha Rōren, composed of the workers' unions of NISSAN MOTOR CO, LTD, and its affiliated companies. Immediately after its formation, the organization became a member of IMF-JC. Politically moderate, Jidōsha Sōren emphasizes labor-management communication. In 1978 it had 561,000 members. *Kurita Ken*

Jieitai → Self Defense Forces

Jien (1155–1225)

Buddhist prelate; poet; historian. A member of the most noble branch of the FUJIWARA FAMILY, Jien was the sixth son of the imperial regent Tadamichi, and thus the younger brother of Motofusa and Kanezane and the uncle of FUJIWARA NO YOSHITSUNE. On the 13th anniversary of his death, the court honored him with the posthumous name Jichin, by which he is also commonly known.

Jien became a Buddhist novice at the age of 10, and took orders at 14 at ENRYAKUJI, headquarters of the Tendai sect, where he received the priestly name Dōkai. Thenceforward he rose rapidly through the ecclesiastical ranks, as his birth entitled him, becoming abbot of the Hosshōji in 1178 and receiving the highest Buddhist rank bestowed by the court (Hōin; literally, "Seal of the Law") in 1181. At this time he changed his name to Jien. He was appointed palace chaplain to Emperor GO-TOBA (1180–1239; r 1183–98), who placed great confidence in him, as did the whole court, and he was accorded unprecedented special privileges. His great intelligence, many accomplishments, and wide learning earned him the respect of the Tendai monks of Mt. Hiei (Hieizan) as well, and he became the foremost Buddhist prelate of the age, providing a link between the religious communities and the court. In 1192 he was named acting bishop *(gon sōjō)* and abbot of Enryakuji, a post he resigned and resumed no fewer than four times as a result of the very unsettled political conditions of the day. In 1203 he was appointed archbishop *(daisōjō)* and intendant *(bettō)* of the temple Shitennōji, a post he retained together with his palace chaplaincy after his resignation as abbot of Enryakuji in 1214.

Over the years Jien exerted considerable political influence as a kind of gray eminence, assisting the proshogunate policy of his brother Kanezane and the SAIONJI FAMILY and attempting to dissuade Go-Toba from his design to overthrow the shogunate. To this end he wrote his famous GUKANSHŌ, the first historical work in Japan which attempted to deal critically and morally with the record of human events. From the time of the JŌKYŪ DISTURBANCE, Go-Toba's abortive uprising of 1221, Jien was beset by frequent illness, and he finally died at a hermitage that he kept at the eastern foot of Mt. Hiei.

As a poet Jien was one of the most eminent men of a very gifted age and also one of the most influential. He showed an interest and aptitude for poetry when very young, and he transcended the role of talented amateur and patron, to which his high rank might otherwise have assigned him, understanding and agreeing with the view of the great poets Fujiwara no Shunzei (FUJIWARA NO TOSHINARI) and Fujiwara no Teika (FUJIWARA NO SADAIE) that poetry was a way of life (michi), an art that could lead to enlightenment as surely as Buddhist meditation and discipline. In seeing poetry as more than an elegant accomplishment and pastime, he differed from the most exalted patron of the age, ex-Emperor Go-Toba, on whom he exerted a gentle but beneficial influence, encouraging the former sovereign's interest in poetry and his plans for commissioning an imperial anthology. When Go-Toba established his Bureau of Poetry (Wakadokoro) for this purpose in 1201, he appointed Jien as one of 11 fellows (yoriudo) and nearly always included him among the participants in the many poetry parties and contests that he sponsored during the early 1200s. Indeed, Jien's poetic activity and production was astonishing. Gifted with a quick wit and intelligence, he was especially good in impromptu and "speed" composition, at which he challenged and defeated Teika on at least two occasions. He was master of all the accepted poetic styles of the age but on the whole steered a middle course between the conventional wit and elegant conceits of the conservatives and the poetry of evocation and tonal depth of the innovators. Thus, with Go-Toba (though excelling him in the art), he may be classed as one of the rhetoricians of the age. Ninety-two of his poems—second only in number to SAIGYŌ's 94—were included in the Shin kokinshū, and some 225 in other imperial anthologies. His personal collection, Shūgyokushū (Collection of Gathered Gems), contains the unusually high total of some 4,000 poems, including a large number of the 100-poem sequences so popular in his day.

Jien not only played a role in the age of the Shin kokinshū, but also in the following period. He was particularly respected by Teika's son and heir Tameie, whom he encouraged in his youth and dissuaded from abandoning the hereditary poetic calling of his family. In this respect Jien exerted a decisive influence upon the subsequent history of classical poetry.

In exile after 1221, Go-Toba showed his appreciation of Jien's many-sided talent by writing of him that he was "inferior to no other accomplished poet in his finest poems. He used to be particularly fond of a style emphasizing ingenuity of conception . . . Notwithstanding, some of his finest poems are in a more ordinary style of elegant beauty."

◼——Robert H. Brower and Earl Miner, Japanese Court Poetry (1961). Delmer H. Brown and Ichirō Ishida, The Future and the Past: A Translation and Study of the Gukanshō (1979).

Robert H. BROWER

jige

(literally, "below, on the ground"). Also called jigenin ("people on the ground"). Low-ranking court officials of the Heian period (794–1185) who were not allowed to enter the Seiryōden, the emperor's personal quarters in the palace. An alternate term was shimobito (people below) in contrast to the uebito (people above) or TENJŌBITO, officials who did enjoy such access to the emperor. The term jige normally referred to officials of the lower (sixth through ninth) ranks of the civil service (see COURT RANKS); but since access to the Seiryōden was granted in accordance with an official's actual functions and his enjoyment of imperial favor, not simply his rank, higher-ranking officials too were sometimes classified as jige. The term was also used more broadly throughout Japanese history to refer to all those without official rank, that is, the common people.

jigoku → hell

Jigoku-zōshi

(Scrolls of Hells). A group of late-12th-century handscrolls (EMAKIMONO) alternating textual descriptions and paintings of the torments encountered by sinners in the Buddhist hells. In all, 23 sections of text and 24 illustrations survive from the Jigoku-zōshi. In addition, there are two later copies of hell scrolls in the Tōkyō National Museum, and these augment our knowledge of the possible content of lost scenes. The surviving scrolls and detached segments from the original Jigoku-zōshi belong to several collections. A scroll of six text sections and seven paintings 26.5 centimeters (10.4 in) wide and 434.05 centimeters (147.3 in) long formerly in the Hara Collection is now in the Nara National Museum; a scroll of four sections of text and corresponding paintings 26.1 centimeters (10.3 in) wide and 242.7 centimeters (95.5 in) long formerly in the Anjūin Collection is now in the Tōkyō National Museum. Two additional scrolls having seven and five sections, respectively, of text and corresponding paintings (one, 26.1 centimeters [10.3 in] wide and 568.2 centimeters

[223.7 in] long; the other, 26.0 centimeters [10.2 in] wide and 308.1 centimeters [121.3 in] long) formerly in the Masuda Collection were broken up and are now in several collections. One section of text and painting from the Masuda scrolls is in the Seattle Art Museum. In addition, the Museum of Fine Arts, Boston, has since 1911 possessed a segment of text and painting that is stylistically consistent with the Nara National Museum scroll.

The short sections of text describing the hells come from Buddhist sutras such as the Kisekyō, the Shōbōnenjokyō, and the Butsumyō-kyō. In Buddhist belief, 8 great hells and 16 lesser hells are included among the so-called Six Realms of Existence (Rokudō), into which a person could be reborn repeatedly until attaining release from the cycle. The Gaki-zōshi (Scrolls of Hungry Ghosts) and the Yamai no sōshi (Scroll of Diseases), two works closely related to the Jigoku-zōshi in period and manner of execution, also treat themes related to the concept of the Six Realms.

Although once regarded as part of a common effort by different artists, the Jigoku-zōshi scrolls manifest noticeable differences in style and artistic quality. The most remarkable calligraphy and paintings are found in the scroll now in the Nara National Museum and the single section in the Boston Museum of Fine Arts. Although all of the Jigoku-zōshi scrolls have traditionally been regarded as works of the early part of the Kamakura period (1185–1333), some scholars today consider the Nara and Boston works to date back to the end of the Heian period (794–1185). It has recently been suggested that the Masuda scrolls may be of slightly later date, circa 1200.

The Jigoku-zōshi segments are among the most important of the surviving early Japanese narrative paintings. It is thought that the artists were highly trained professional Buddhist painters (EBUSSHI), who created vivid and realistic images based on descriptions in Buddhist literature.

◼——Ienaga Saburō, ed, Jigoku-zōshi, Gaki-zōshi, Yamai no sōshi, vol 7 of Shinshū Nihon emakimono zenshū (Kadokawa Shoten, 1976).

Ann YONEMURA

Jiji Press

(Jiji Tsūshinsha). Important Japanese news agency. Established in 1945 upon the demise of the Dōmei News Agency (DŌMEI TSŪSHINSHA). In its early years the firm concentrated on providing specialized news and information for use by companies, organizations, and government offices. After 1959 it expanded into a general news service for newspapers and broadcasting stations. ARAI Naoyuki

Jiji shimpō

An influential newspaper started by the well-known educator and thinker FUKUZAWA YUKICHI in Tōkyō in 1882. Fukuzawa's editorial policy was politically nonpartisan; he stressed news stories and feature articles on economics. After the Tōkyō Earthquake of 1923, financial management deteriorated, and the paper was absorbed in 1936 by the Tōkyō nichinichi shimbun (now the MAINICHI SHIMBUN). It was revived in 1946 and published for nine years before being absorbed in 1955 by the Sangyō keizai shimbun (now the SANKEI SHIMBUN).

jikata

Term referring to local administration that was used during the Muromachi (1333–1568) and Edo (1600–1868) periods. During the former it referred to urban administration; during the latter, when it was in much wider use, it referred to rural administration.

Muromachi period. During the Muromachi period those shogunate officials who handled questions involving residences, estates, and legal disputes within Kyōto were designated jikata. The jikata office included a chief jikata (tōnin) and his subordinates. By 1379 the authority of the chief included the supervision of residences, estates, shops, and roads within the larger Kyōto metropolitan district. From about 1400 the position became hereditary in the Settsu family.

Edo period. Whereas the Muromachi shogunate had been based on Kyōto, its environs, and the considerable income it generated, the Tokugawa shogunate attempted to base itself on rural tax sources. Accordingly, Tokugawa leaders used the term jikata to mean rural administration rather than urban and to embrace a broader conception of civil governance. Jikata involved supervision of agriculture;

encouragement of sound agronomics; management of mountains, streams, and tilled lands; resolution of peasant disputes; and most important, operation of the complex land-tax system. Proper local administration was intended to sustain rural productivity and foster rural tranquillity in order to assure tax income and social stability.

Administrative arrangements differed somewhat from jurisdiction to jurisdiction within the Tokugawa political system (see BAKU-HAN SYSTEM). In general, however, daimyō adhered to procedures utilized by the shogunate. On shogunal lands (TENRYŌ) rural administration was carried out by officials who were designated intendants (DAIKAN or GUNDAI) and stationed at district offices known as jin'ya or daikansho. They were subordinate to the commissioners of finance (KANJŌ BUGYŌ) in Edo (now Tōkyō) and performed their duties in accordance with a vast body of accumulated administrative regulations, of which the jikata sanchō or "three codices on rural administration" came to be considered the fundamental codes.

The jikata sanchō date from the 1640s and the rule of TOKU-GAWA IEMITSU, the third Tokugawa shōgun. Effective territorial administration had been crucial to the 16th-century process of reunification, and administrative regulations had developed in conjunction with that reunification. During the early 17th century, however, shogunal intendants had acquired great autonomy. To strengthen his control over the daikan and their resources, Iemitsu ordered them to organize and standardize their administrative procedures, notably those relating to taxation. The resulting "codices," which spelled out in elaborate detail the complex procedures for tax assessment, payment, and adjustment, were the jikata sanchō.

Officials at the daikansho were expected to enforce the regulations of the jikata sanchō. However, their areas of jurisdiction were large, embracing populations of as many as 100,000 people, and their staffs were small, and so they were not able to execute the required procedures directly. Accordingly, actual implementation was delegated to local notables called jikata san'yaku or "three offices of rural administration" (also known as murakata san'yaku). In essence that title identified the most influential members of local society, namely the MYŌSHU (or SHŌYA; taxpaying landholders), kumigashira (village elders), and hyakushōdai (peasant spokesmen). It was their task to ensure that villages adhered to governing regulations, settled problems promptly, and paid their taxes properly.

Jikata literature. The prominent role of jikata in Tokugawa government and society was reflected in a flourishing agronomic literature called jikatasho. These were privately written treatises on techniques of horticulture and husbandry, land and resource usage, family, farm, and village management, and related legal and fiscal matters. They varied greatly in scope, size, and scientific quality, but in toto they constituted a substantial body of practical agricultural wisdom that circulated widely throughout rural Japan. Some of the more prominent of these works were Jikata kikigaki (Notes on Rural Management) in 2 fascicles, dating from 1668, NŌGYŌ ZENSHO (Agricultural Encyclopedia) in 10 fascicles, dating from 1697, Jikata ochiboshū (Gleanings on Rural Management) in 14 fascicles, dating from about 1763, and JIKATA HANREI ROKU (Principles of Rural Management) in 11 fascicles, dating from about 1791.

The term jikata was also used to distinguish those samurai (jikatatori) who held assigned fiefs from those (kuramaitori or kirimaitori; see KURAMAI and KIRIMAI) who received stipends from their lord's warehouse. Such landholding vassals were also known as jitō or chigyōtori. The term jikatatori reflected the fact that such landholders were responsible for administering the lands assigned them and were supported by taxes they collected directly from the producers. Most samurai were supported by stipends, however, and only a small minority held fiefs. Thus, of the shogunate's approximately 22,500 direct vassals (jikisan or HATAMOTO and GOKENIN), some 2,500 held fiefs (the jikata jikisan) while 20,000 received stipends (the kuramaitori). Nonetheless, in the cases of both shogunate and domains, it was the greater vassals who were jikatatori, while the stipendiaries tended to be minor vassals; and so the political role of jikatatori in the Tokugawa polity was appreciably greater than their relative numbers suggest.

▬▬——Andō Hiroshi, Tokugawa bakufu kenchi yōryaku (1915, repr 1966). Murakami Tadashi, Tenryō (1965). Conrad Totman, Politics in the Tokugawa Bakufu (1967).　　Conrad TOTMAN

Jikata hanrei roku

(Principles of Rural Management). Eleven-volume work on local administration (JIKATA) by Ōishi Hisataka, an official of the Takasaki domain (now part of Gumma Prefecture). It was begun in 1791

by order of the domainal authorities; the original plan for 16 volumes was cut short by the author's death in 1794. Citing precedents from history and local custom, the work systematically discusses land surveys (KENCHI), land and miscellaneous taxes (NENGU; KOMONONARI) and their methods of assessment (JŌMEN; KEMI), corvée labor services (SUKEGŌ), coinage, weights and measures, rules of behavior for village officials (MURA YAKUNIN), and other fiscal and legal aspects of rural administration.

jikifu

(sustenance allotments). A part of the stipendiary system from the 7th century onward. Imperial kinsmen, high-ranking nobles, and temples and shrines were assigned a certain number of "vested households" (FUKO) and received half of the rice tax and all of the other taxes paid by those households for their support. The assignees did not exercise control over the households, however, and the taxes were collected for them by local government officials. These allotments were originally instituted as compensation for powerful local chieftains who had been dispossessed by the TAIKA REFORM of 645, but they soon became an important source of income for the central ruling class under the RITSURYŌ SYSTEM of government. From the middle of the Heian period (794–1185), the importance of such allotments diminished considerably as many of the vested households were absorbed into privately held estates (SHŌEN).

G. Cameron HURST III

jikiso

Direct appeal to high authorities, bypassing official channels; a form of OSSO. The term was used in the Edo period (1600–1868) to refer especially to petitions for the redress of grievances addressed to the shōgun or daimyō. Jikiso took various forms, including peasant uprisings (HYAKUSHŌ IKKI), written appeals presented directly to the ruler as he passed through the streets in his palanquin (kagoso), and pleas written and placed in an "appeals" box (MEYASUBAKO) to be read by the shōgun. Only the last form of jikiso, instituted in 1721, was sanctioned; others were punishable by death. After the Meiji Restoration of 1868, jikiso meant a direct appeal to the emperor. The Meiji government enacted ordinances strictly prohibiting this form of protest but could not prevent it entirely. The most famous modern incident of jikiso occurred in 1901, when TANAKA SHŌZŌ presented a petition concerning pollution from the Ashio Copper Mines to Emperor Meiji (see ASHIO COPPER MINE INCIDENT). After World War II, when the doctrine of imperial sovereignty was abandoned, jikiso lost all meaning.

jikkan jūnishi

(literally, "10 stems and 12 branches"). Usually referred to in English as the sexagenary cycle or "Chinese zodiacal symbols"; also called eto in Japanese. An ancient system, originally Chinese, for counting days, months, and years; also used to indicate directions and the divisions of the day. The system consists of two ordered sets of symbols (Chinese characters), one of 10 units, called the 10 stems or trunks (J: jikkan; Ch: shi gan or shih kan) and the other of 12 units called the 12 branches (J: jūnishi; Ch: shier zhi or shih-erh chih). The two sets were used together in 2-symbol combinations, 1 from each set, to create a cycle of 60, the total number of possible combinations. In counting years the cycle was repeated ad infinitum. See table for the names of the stems and branches and the total cycle of 60 combinations.

Symbols representing these units are incised on tortoise shells uncovered at Chinese Yin-dynasty (before 1100 BC) archaeological sites, and it is thought that the 10 stems were first used to count days of the month (in three groups of 10) and the 12 branches to count months of the year. The two series were subsequently combined into the cycle of 60, and by the earlier part of the Later Han dynasty (AD 25–220) had been regularized as a system for counting days, months, and years, and for indicating directions. The 12 branches were employed to mark the time of day in combination with the concepts of yin-yang (see OMMYŌDŌ) and the five elements (wood, fire, earth, metal, and water), and the two series were used to determine auspicious and inauspicious days and directions. From the time of the Later Han it also became the custom to refer to the 12 branches as animals (perhaps attributable to Hellenic astrological influence by way of India); this contributed to the increasing use of the system as a means of divination analogous to astrology.

Jikkan jūnishi

The 10 stems or trunks (jikkan)

Chinese character	甲	乙	丙	丁	戊	己	庚	辛	壬	癸
On reading	*kō*	*otsu*	*hei*	*tei*	*bo*	*ki*	*kō*	*shin*	*jin*	*ki*

How the five elements are combined with yin and yang to give alternate names to the 10 stems

Five elements	木 *ki* (wood)		火 *hi* (fire)		土 *tsuchi* (earth)		金 *kane* (metal)		水 *mizu* (water)	
E and *to* (*yang* and *yin*)	*e* (elder)	*to* (younger)	*e*	*to*	*e*	*to*	*e*	*to*	*e*	*to*
Name	*kinoe*	*kinoto*	*hinoe*	*hinoto*	*tsuchinoe*	*tsuchinoto*	*kanoe*	*kanoto*	*mizunoe*	*mizunoto*

NOTE: The *"no"* of these combinations is the genitive particle. *"Kane"* becomes *"ka"* in its two combinations.

The 12 branches (jūnishi)

Chinese character	子	丑	寅	卯	辰	巳	午	未	申	酉	戌	亥
On reading	*shi*	*chū*	*in*	*bō*	*shin*	*shi*	*go*	*bi*	*shin*	*yū*	*jutsu*	*gai*
Animal name	*ne*	*ushi*	*tora*	*u*	*tatsu*	*mi*	*uma*	*hitsuji*	*saru*	*tori*	*inu*	*i*
English	rat	ox	tiger	hare or rabbit	dragon	snake	horse	ram or sheep	monkey	rooster	dog	boar

The stems and branches combined to form the cycle of 60

① 甲子 *kōshi (kasshi)* *kinoe ne*	⑪ 甲戌 *kōjutsu* *kinoe inu*	㉑ 甲申 *kōshin* *kinoe saru*	㉛ 甲午 *kōgo* *kinoe uma*	㊶ 甲辰 *kōshin* *kinoe tatsu*	(51) 甲寅 *kōin* *kinoe tora*
② 乙丑 *itchū* *kinoto ushi*	⑫ 乙亥 *itsugai* *kinoto i*	㉒ 乙酉 *itsuyū* *kinoto tori*	㉜ 乙未 *itsubi* *kinoto hitsuji*	㊷ 乙巳 *isshi* *kinoto mi*	(52) 乙卯 *itsubō* *kinoto u*
③ 丙寅 *heiin* *hinoe tora*	⑬ 丙子 *heishi* *hinoe ne*	㉓ 丙戌 *heijutsu* *hinoe inu*	㉝ 丙申 *heishin* *hinoe saru*	㊸ 丙午 *heigo* *hinoe uma*	(53) 丙辰 *heishin* *hinoe tatsu*
④ 丁卯 *teibō* *hinoto u*	⑭ 丁丑 *teichū* *hinoto ushi*	㉔ 丁亥 *teigai* *hinoto i*	㉞ 丁酉 *teiyū* *hinoto tori*	㊹ 丁未 *teibi* *hinoto hitsuji*	(54) 丁巳 *teishi* *hinoto mi*
⑤ 戊辰 *boshin* *tsuchinoe tatsu*	⑮ 戊寅 *boin* *tsuchinoe tora*	㉕ 戊子 *boshi* *tsuchinoe ne*	㉟ 戊戌 *bojutsu* *tsuchinoe inu*	㊺ 戊申 *boshin* *tsuchinoe saru*	(55) 戊午 *bogo* *tsuchinoe uma*
⑥ 己巳 *kishi* *tsuchinoto mi*	⑯ 己卯 *kibō* *tsuchinoto u*	㉖ 己丑 *kichū* *tsuchinoto ushi*	㊱ 己亥 *kigai* *tsuchinoto i*	㊻ 己酉 *kiyū* *tsuchinoto tori*	(56) 己未 *kibi* *tsuchinoto hitsuji*
⑦ 庚午 *kōgo* *kanoe uma*	⑰ 庚辰 *kōshin* *kanoe tatsu*	㉗ 庚寅 *kōin* *kanoe tora*	㊲ 庚子 *kōshi* *kanoe ne*	㊼ 庚戌 *kōjutsu* *kanoe inu*	(57) 庚申 *kōshin* *kanoe saru*
⑧ 辛未 *shimbi* *kanoto hitsuji*	⑱ 辛巳 *shinshi* *kanoto mi*	㉘ 辛卯 *shimbō* *kanoto u*	㊳ 辛丑 *shinchū* *kanoto ushi*	㊽ 辛亥 *shingai* *kanoto i*	(58) 辛酉 *shin' yū* *kanoto tori*
⑨ 壬申 *jinshin* *mizunoe saru*	⑲ 壬午 *jingo* *mizunoe uma*	㉙ 壬辰 *jinshin* *mizunoe tatsu*	㊴ 壬寅 *jin' in* *mizunoe tora*	㊾ 壬子 *jinshi* *mizunoe ne*	(59) 壬戌 *jinjutsu* *mizunoe inu*
⑩ 癸酉 *kiyū* *mizunoto tori*	⑳ 癸未 *kibi* *mizunoto hitsuji*	㉚ 癸巳 *kishi* *mizunoto mi*	㊵ 癸卯 *kibō* *mizunoto u*	㊿ 癸丑 *kichū* *mizunoto ushi*	(60) 癸亥 *kigai* *mizunoto i*

NOTE: The first of the two names for each of the combinations is a combination of the *on* readings of the two symbols. Note that the combination of *kō* and *shi* (number 1) can be pronounced *kasshi* and that *otsu* becomes *itsu* in combination and undergoes other sound changes. The second of the two names combines an alternate name of the stem with the animal name for the branch.

This calendric and geomantic complex is said to have been first implemented in Japan by the empress SUIKO (r 593–628) in 604. In Japan there developed two ways of naming the combinations of the cycle of 60. The simpler method was to use the *on* readings of the symbols (the Japanese pronunciation of their original Chinese sounds). These names are the first of the two names below each combination of symbols in the table. In the other, more complex method, each of the 12 branches was given, after the Chinese fashion, the name of an animal (the names were Japanese): *ne* (rat), *ushi* (ox), *tora* (tiger), *u* (hare or rabbit), *tatsu* (dragon), *mi* (snake), *uma* (horse), *hitsuji* (ram or sheep), *saru* (monkey), *tori* (rooster), *inu* (dog), and *i* (boar). The 10 stems were given names based on yin-yang concepts, i.e., by expressing each of the five elements (wood, fire, earth, metal, and water) as either *yang* (*e* or elder brother) or *yin* (*to* or younger brother), as in *kinoe* (wood-yang) and *kinoto* (wood-yin). These names were combined with the animal names of the 12 branches to form names for the 2-symbol combinations of the cycle. These names are the second of the two names below each combination of symbols in the table. Thus the first unit in the cycle, the *on* reading of which is *kasshi*, becomes *kinoe ne* (wood-yang rat), the second, *itchū, kinoto ushi* (wood-yin ox), and so on.

Among divinatory methods introduced with the 10 stems and 12 branches was *shier zhi* (*shih-erh chih*; J: *jūnichoku*, the 12 watches), which was in use from the Asuka period (latter part of the 6th century to 710). The 12 watches were a series of values, such as "fulfillment," "failure," "control," and "disorder," which were applied to consecutive days beginning with the first day of the rat in the 11th month (there were two or sometimes three, given the repetition of the symbol in the cycle of combination), the first day of the ox in the 12th month, and so forth through the first day of the boar in the 10th month of the succeeding calendar year. The casting of fortunes by this or similar means was often resorted to when planning some endeavor, and there developed numerous indigenous superstitions surrounding the practice, which flourished among townsmen of the Edo period (1600–1868), and persists in some measure today. Like the Chinese the Japanese believed that one took on the character of the animal of one's birth year: those born in the year of the rat (i.e., any year for which *ne*, or the symbol for rat, appeared in the combination) were restless, while those born in the year of the ox were patient. In Japan women born in the year *hinoe uma* (fire-yang horse), the 43rd year of the 60-year cycle, were thought to be particularly headstrong and inclined to kill their husbands. The year was also thought to bring a rash of fires. Similarly, it was once a widely observed practice for pregnant women to begin wearing a band to help support their bellies on a day of the dog *(inu)*, an animal thought to protect infants and children (see INU HARIKO).

The 12 branches were long used to mark time and indicate directions. When they were written out clockwise about a circle, the symbol for rat indicated a two-hour interval surrounding midnight or pointed north, and the horse indicated a two-hour interval at midday or pointed south. See also CALENDAR, DATES, AND TIME; PERIODIZATION; KANREKI; KŌSHIN. *Fujita Tomio*

Jikkoku Pass

(Jikkoku Tōge). Also called Higaneyama. Located in the western part of the city of Atami, eastern Shizuoka Prefecture, central Honshū. Situated within the Fuji–Hakone–Izu National Park, it offers a panoramic view of 10 former provinces from Hitachi Province (now Ibaraki Prefecture) in the east to Tōtōmi Province (now part of Shizuoka Prefecture) in the west. A road connecting Hakone Pass and Atami Pass runs on its western side. Altitude: 766 m (2,512 ft).

Jikkunshō

Also known as *Jikkinshō*. Collection of tales with moral lessons for the young, compiled in the Kamakura period (1185–1333). Published in 1252; authorship uncertain. The 280 stories, divided into 10 categories, are gathered from various Heian period (794–1185) works as well as from China and India. The stories, full of commonsense teachings and anecdotes, are humorous and often tend toward the bizarre.

Jimmin Sensen Jiken → Popular Front Incident

Jimmu, Emperor

The legendary first sovereign *(tennō)* of Japan according to the ancient chronicles KOJIKI (712) and NIHON SHOKI (720). According to the latter he reigned from 660 BC to 585 BC; however, these are impossibly early dates, and there is some doubt that he actually existed (see below). The name Jimmu is a posthumous title given him in the late 8th century; the chronicles refer to him as Kamu Yamato Iware Hiko no Mikoto and several other names. According to these accounts, Jimmu's father was Hiko Nagisatake Ugaya Fukiaezu no Mikoto, great-grandson of the sun goddess AMATERASU ŌMIKAMI, and his mother was Tamayorihime, daughter of the god of the sea. After growing up in the Takachiho Palace in Hyūga (thought by most historians to be what is now Miyazaki Prefecture in Kyūshū) Jimmu, at the age of 45, resolved to conquer the YAMATO region to the east in the Nara Basin. In an expedition that lasted several years, he made his way along the Inland Sea, subjugating various regions on his route, and landed his forces at the site of modern Ōsaka, northwest of Yamato. Meeting fierce resistance from local chieftains, he was at first defeated and so decided to enter Yamato from the south, through Kii (now Wakayama Prefecture). He ultimately subdued the area with the aid of a golden bird and was enthroned at the "Kashihara Palace" (said to have been in what is now the Unebi district of the city of Kashihara, Nara Prefecture) as Japan's first emperor.

The accounts in the two chronicles differ in many respects. First of all the route of Jimmu's conquest and the length of his stay in each area vary in the two records. The subjugation of Kawachi (now Ōsaka Prefecture), Kii, and Yamato is also described in more detail in the *Nihon shoki,* which in particular gives much information about the tribal chieftains fighting Jimmu and his forces. The conclusion of the account of the conquest of Yamato also differs in the two chronicles. In the *Kojiki* this ends with the submission of Nigihayahi no Mikoto, who is said to have descended to Yamato from heaven at the time of its conquest by Jimmu. In the *Nihon shoki,* on the other hand, Nigihayahi no Mikoto had come to Yamato before the conquests by Jimmu, made an alliance with the local chieftain Nagasunehiko, killed him, and then submitted to Jimmu. This narrative is then followed by the story of the subjugation of a large number of fierce chieftains together referred to as the Yasotakeru.

The *Nihon shoki* also contains an account of Jimmu's attempt to enter Yamato from Kawachi along the Tatsutamichi, a road joining what are now the cities of Kashiwara and Habikino in Ōsaka Prefecture to Tatsuta in what is now the town of Ōji in Nara Prefecture. This episode is not found in the *Kojiki,* and some scholars believe it was added to the *Nihon shoki* after the capital was moved to Nara in 710 and the Tatsutamichi became a widely travelled route.

The central question, however, is whether such a person as Jimmu ever existed. The story of the conquest of Yamato is full of mythic and legendary elements. Various theories have been advanced about the myth surrounding Jimmu: that it reflects the spread of the rice-growing, metal-using YAYOI CULTURE from Kyūshū to the Kinai region; that it explains the origins of Japan's imperial line in terms of the conquest of that region by a horse-riding people from the Asian continent who had first established themselves in northern Kyūshū (see HORSE-RIDER THEORY); and that the figure of Jimmu is a composite of several others including the legendary nation-building emperor SUJIN, whose legend resembles Jimmu's in several respects, and Emperor KEITAI (first half of the 6th century), who supposedly entered Yamato from the Ōsaka area and was enthroned at the Iware Palace (near what is now the city of Sakurai, Nara Prefecture). Whatever the case, it seems clear that the ancestors of the present imperial house originally came to Yamato from Kyūshū in western Japan.

Although the *Nihon shoki* places Jimmu's accession on the first day of the first lunar month of 660 BC, the date was arrived at arbitrarily by computations based on the ancient Chinese belief that 660 BC, the year of *kanoto tori* in the sexagenary cycle (see JIKKAN JŪNISHI), was highly auspicious for reform (see KIGEN). The historicity of Jimmu's enthronement and its bearing on the founding of the Japanese nation have long been issues of lively debate among historians.

▬——Nihonshi Kenkyūkai, ed, *Nihon no kenkoku* (1966). Uemura Seiji, *Jimmu tennō* (1957). *Ueda Masaaki*

jimoku

Court ceremonies for the appointment of all but the most senior officials in the Heian period (794–1185). The two principal *jimoku* ceremonies were that for appointment to offices in the capital, the so-called Tsukasameshi no Jimoku in the 11th or 12th month, and that for appointing provincial officials, the Agatameshi no Jimoku in the 1st month. There were others for the appointment of officials to serve newly named empresses or crown princes, for the appointment of female officials, and the like. These ceremonies began to lose their importance in medieval times.　　　*G. Cameron* HURST *III*

Jimpūren Rebellion

(Jimpūren no Ran). Rebellion in 1876 by former *samurai* (see SHI-ZOKU) in Kumamoto Prefecture. Since the restoration of imperial rule in 1868, discontent among the warrior class had mounted as they were gradually stripped of their privileges by the new government. In the former Kumamoto domain, where opposition to the government's Westernization policies was particularly strong, dissident former samurai in 1872 organized themselves as the Jimpūren or League of the Divine Wind. The ordinance forbidding the wearing of swords (HAITŌREI) of March 1876 seemed to them the final indignity. On 24 October, about 170 members led by Ōtaguro Tomoo (1835–76) attacked the Kumamoto garrison and killed the commander and several other officials. They were subdued the following day. Many were killed, among them Ōtaguro, and most of those who escaped were eventually captured. Their action inspired the HAGI REBELLION, the AKIZUKI REBELLION OF 1876, and other uprisings in southwestern Japan.

jinaichō

(literally, "town within the precincts of a temple"). Also called *jinaimachi.* A form of walled, fortified town that grew up around temples in the Muromachi period (1333–1568); particularly associated with the JŌDO SHIN SECT, whose adherents were deeply involved in the military struggles of the late 15th and 16th centuries (see IKKŌ IKKI). As the sect's power grew and its followers became more numerous, the various *jinaichō* became major commercial centers that attracted nonsectarian as well as Jōdo Shin artisans and merchants. The *jinaichō* may thus be considered halfway between temple towns (MONZEN MACHI) and CASTLE TOWNS. The modern city of Ōsaka originated as the *jinaichō* for ISHIYAMA HONGANJI, one of the main religious centers. Other notable examples include Inami in Etchū Province (now Toyama Prefecture) and Kaizuka in Izumi Province (now part of Ōsaka Prefecture).

━━Akamatsu Toshihide and Kasahara Kazuo, ed, *Shinshūshi gaisetsu* (1966). Fujiki Hisashi, *Oda Toyotomi seiken,* in *Nihon no rekishi,* vol 15 (Shōgakukan, 1975).　　　*Michael* SOLOMON

Jindaiji

Temple in the city of Chōfu, Tōkyō Prefecture, belonging to the TENDAI SECT of Buddhism. According to tradition, Jindaiji was built in 733 as a temple of the HOSSŌ SECT but changed its affiliation to Tendai during the Jōgan era (859–877). Under the patronage of the MINAMOTO FAMILY Jindaiji became a major center in eastern Honshū for the practice of ESOTERIC BUDDHISM. The temple was also patronized by the TOKUGAWA FAMILY. Among the temple treasures is a gilded image of Shaka (Śākyamuni) Buddha dating from the latter half of the 7th century. Of the many festivals associated with Jindaiji, the most popular is the Darumaichi (see DARUMA FAIRS), celebrated on 3–4 March, which is believed to bring prosperity and good fortune to participants.　　　*Stanley* WEINSTEIN

jindai moji

(literally, "characters of the mythological age"). Letters or characters once claimed to have been used in Japan before the introduction of Chinese characters (KANJI) in the 5th or 6th century. The claim that such characters existed was made from about the Kamakura period (1185–1333), mainly by Shintoists, and was strongly held by KOKU-GAKU (National Learning) scholars during the Edo period (1600–1868). Although there was no general agreement as to what exactly the individual *jindai moji* were, HIRATA ATSUTANE actually gave a list of *jindai moji* in his *Kanna hifumi no tsutae* (1819). These characters, which bear a close resemblance to the Korean HAN'GŬL script, have since been proven to be latter-day forgeries.
　　　Yamazaki Yukio

jingi

(Ch: *renyi* or *jen-i*). A moral concept formulated by the Chinese Confucian philosopher Mencius (ca 371 BC–ca 289 BC), who integrated what had been two separate virtues in the philosophy of Con-

fucius: *ren* (*jen;* J: *jin;* benevolence or brotherly love) and *yi* (*i;* J: *gi;* righteousness or proper conduct). In contrast to Mo Di (Mo Ti; late 5th century BC to early 4th century BC; also known as Motsu) and his followers, who insisted on universal, indiscriminate love, Mencius contended that love must be in conformity with social distinctions and degrees of intimacy and that love and righteousness must work together in harmony. *Renyi* was the objective of the Kingly Way or ideal government; at the same time it is found potentially in everyone in the form of feelings of compassion and shame. In the Edo period (1600–1868) in Japan, the Japanese Confucian scholar Itō Jinsai maintained that *jingi* (*renyi*) was the most basic tenet of orthodox Confucianism. In a corrupted usage the word *jingi* in modern Japan refers to the code of conduct or formal greetings among gangsters (*yakuza*).　　　*Miyake Masahiko*

Jingikan → Dajōkan

Jingō, Empress → Jingū, Empress

Jingoji

A temple-monastery of the esoteric SHINGON SECT of Buddhism; founded in the 9th century on the mountain Takaosan, just west of the river Kiyotakigawa, in the northwest sector of Kyōto.

A temple complex called Takaosanji had been built on the same site by at least the end of the 8th century. WAKE NO KIYOMARO (733–799), the most important early patron of the Takaosanji, founded another temple, Jinganji, in Kawachi Province (now part of Ōsaka Prefecture) between 782 and 805, and in 824 his son Wake no Matsuna moved Jinganji and its treasures, some of which survive today, to the present Jingoji site. The already existing Takaosanji and Jinganji merged to form an imperial temple, Jingo Kokuso Shingonji, commonly called Jingoji from then on.

Meanwhile, KŪKAI, the founder of Shingon esoteric Buddhism in Japan, had returned from China, and shortly afterward, in 809, proceeded to the Mt. Takao monastery by imperial request and began giving instruction in Shingon Buddhism. A temple document written in Kūkai's own hand, known as the *Kanjō rekimei,* records his arrival, and tells of the 812 ceremony in which he conducted formal initiation rites, or *kanjō* (Skt: *abhiṣeka*), for SAICHŌ, transmitter of TENDAI SECT Buddhism, and numerous other disciples.

Kūkai was eventually succeeded as temple curate by his disciple Shinzei, who strongly supported building projects. Two disastrous fires, one in 994 and the other in 1149, later destroyed most of the monastery. Around 1168 the monk MONGAKU came to Jingoji. He eventually carried out extensive repairs with funds supplied by the retired emperor GO-SHIRAKAWA. The rebuilding was completed in 1182. In 1199 Mongaku was banished to the island of Sado and Jingoji then became attached to the temple TŌJI in Kyōto, eventually coming under its jurisdiction. The temple's fortunes declined again during the ŌNIN WAR (1467–77). There were two late phases of repair and rebuilding, the first in about 1623 by order of the Tokugawa shogunate, when some of the meditation and lecture halls were restored, and the second in this century.

Since the majority of its buildings were repaired or rebuilt in the Edo period (1600–1868) or later, the importance of the monastery to art historians lies not in its architecture but in its sculpture and other treasures. Eight of its holdings have been declared National Treasures, including the image of Yakushi (Skt: Bhaiṣajyaguru), the Buddha of Healing, probably the best surviving example of Jōgan sculpture (late 9th century); the Takao mandala, dated 824–834, the oldest surviving painted mandala in Japan; the *Kanjō rekimei,* Kūkai's record of the initiation mentioned above; five bodhisattva statues made just after 845; probably the oldest Japanese screens depicting landscape, signed 1182; and portraits of TAIRA NO SHIGE-MORI, MINAMOTO NO YORITOMO, and Fujiwara no Mitsuyoshi, said to have been painted in about 1173 by FUJIWARA NO TAKA-NOBU. In addition, more than 20 Important Cultural Properties are housed at Jingoji, including Kamakura-period (1185–1333) sculpture, illustrated sutras, and maps.　　　*Nancy* SHATZMAN STEINHARDT

Jingōki → Yoshida Mitsuyoshi

Jingū Bunko

(Shrine Library). Library known for its unequaled holdings on Japan's native Shintō religion. It contains the collections formerly held by the Inner and Outer Shrines (Naikū and Gekū) of the ancient ISE SHRINE at Uji-Yamada (now the city of Ise, Mie Prefecture) and is now housed in its own building in the suburbs of the city. The Outer Shrine Library, called the Toyomiyazaki Bunko, was built in 1648; its collection was assembled largely by the Shintō scholar Deguchi Nobuyoshi (1615–90). The Inner Shrine Library, called the Hayashizaki Bunko, was built in 1687. Originally intended for the use of Shintō priests and novices, the collections contain ancient records pertaining to Shintō deities and to the emperors from the 8th century onward. The Inner Shrine collections were consolidated in 1873, and the library was placed under the Ministry of Shintō Religion (Jingishō). In 1906 a new building was erected and officially named the Jingū Bunko; the Outer Shrine collection was added to it in 1911. In 1914 the editorial office of the KOJI RUIEN transferred its holdings to the library, and the collection has since grown to nearly 250,000 volumes. Many of the Jingū Bunko's holdings have been received through a depository program in which authors send copies of their works on Shintō and other topics to the library "for the pleasure of the gods." It now contains books on all subjects and is open to the public. *Theodore F.* WELCH

Jingū, Empress

Also known as Empress Jingō. Legendary nonreigning empress (*kōgō*). According to the chronicle NIHON SHOKI (720), she ruled as regent during a period between the reigns of the legendary emperor Chūai and the emperor ŌJIN (late 4th to early 5th century) when there was no official sovereign. (According to the *Nihon shoki*, the period was 69 years.) Jingū is described as the daughter of Okinaga no Sukune and Princess Katsuragi no Takanuka and the consort of Chūai. The traditional account is that after her husband's death in a campaign against the KUMASO people of Kyūshū, Jingū completed their subjugation and then sailed to Korea to defeat the forces of the state of SILLA. Shortly after her return to Japan she gave birth to the future emperor Ōjin but did not permit him to ascend the throne in her lifetime. Modern scholars believe that the legend of her military exploits grew out of Japanese campaigns in Korea late in the 4th century and that the figure of Jingū herself is a composite of several ancient shaman-rulers. See also HIMIKO.

jinin → jinnin

jinja → shrines

Jinja Honchō → Shintō Shrines, Association of

Jinjiin → National Personnel Authority

Jinkaishū

(Dust and Ashes). A domainal law code (BUNKOKUHŌ) of the Sengoku (Warring States) period (1467–1568); enacted by Date Tanemune (1488–1565; see DATE FAMILY), the lord of an extensive region in the provinces of Mutsu and Dewa, the northeastern region of Honshū, on 4 May 1536 (Tembun 5.4.14). The title may be a reference to the minute particulate matter of the text, or merely the artfully self-depreciative turn of a current literary phrase. The most complete extant version comprises 171 articles, making the Jinkaishū the most detailed code of its type. A major part of the text (arts 16–75) is devoted to criminal law; other articles deal with such matters as the relations between the domain's military gentry and the farmers working their lands (76–83), the regulation of trade in the domain (93–120), and marital problems (162–167). The underlying purpose is to establish the *daimyō* as the public authority in the domain; accordingly, the absolute supremacy of his law is stressed, and private acts of the redress of grievances are prohibited (art 39). The code itself, however, offers ample evidence that the Date daimyō had not yet managed to monopolize the exercise of justice in the face of the entrenched power of his realm's petty barons, who retained the right to punish their peasantry. A related document in 13 articles, called Kurakata no Okite (Regulations for Pawnbrokers) and dated 7 April 1533 (Tembun 2.3.13), is attached to the Jinkaishū. *George* ELISON

jinnin

Also known as *jinin*. Dependents of Shintō shrines (*jinja*); one of several similar groups originating in the Heian period (794–1185) among persons who sought to escape the exactions of agricultural labor and public duties by subordinating themselves to powerful institutions or individuals and providing various types of service in exchange for their protection. Analogous service groups include *kugonin*, YORYŪDO, and SANJO, attached respectively to the imperial household, Buddhist temples, and aristocratic families.

Religious functions were only a part of the relationship between the *jinnin* and their shrines. Through the intercession of their patrons, *jinnin* who engaged in trade obtained exemptions from dues as well as other advantages. In 1111, for instance, the Gion Shrine in Kyōto even threatened the cancellation of the GION FESTIVAL to enforce certain demands of usurers affiliated with it as *jinnin*. By the Kamakura period (1185–1333), most of the usurers (KASHIAGE) of Kyōto were *jinnin* of the HIE SHRINE or priests of the ENRYAKUJI, who on occasion, for example in 1213, called on the WARRIOR-MONKS of their parent institution on Mt. Hiei (Hieizan) to protect their interests by intimidating the authorities (see GŌSO). In the Muromachi period (1333–1568), some guilds (ZA) organized by *jinnin* gained monopolistic rights in their manufacturing and trading specialties; the best-known examples are the rice-maltsters' guild (*kōji za*) of the KITANO SHRINE in Kyōto and the oil-traders' guild (*abura za*) of the Rikyū Hachiman Shrine in Ōyamazaki. Along with tradesmen and artisans, from whose commercial activities the shrines profited financially, *jinnin* groups included theatrical performers, needed in shrine rituals, who eventually formed professional troupes. Farmers such as those of Sugaura in Ōmi Province (now Shiga Prefecture), who affiliated themselves with the Hie Shrine in 1305, became *jinnin* as a device for maintaining their community against encroaching neighbors.

Some *jinnin* were used in menial tasks and enjoyed at best a lowly status. The duties of the *inu jinin* ("dog" *jinin*) of the Gion Shrine, for instance, included the policing of the shrine grounds, demolition of squatters' huts, and disposal of corpses; in 1371 they fought a group of KAWARAMONO (riverbed dwellers) over the right to strip corpses abandoned beside the river Kamogawa in Kyōto. Evidently, their social standing was not much higher than that of their *kawaramono* rivals (who were regarded as outcastes), especially since their trade in items made of gut or leather, which gave the *inu jinin* their alternative name *tsurumeso* ("bowstrings for sale"), was considered defiling and base. With the transformation of Japanese society at the end of the 16th century, the specialized functions of the *jinnin* disappeared, but the term continued to be applied to certain low-ranking shrine personnel in the Edo period (1600–1868). *George* ELISON

Jinnō shōtō ki

(Chronicle of the Direct Descent of Divine Sovereigns). A history of Japan from the mythical founding of the country by the gods (*kami*) until the mid-14th century. It was written between 1339 and 1343 by KITABATAKE CHIKAFUSA (1293–1354)—a high-ranking courtier who was a member of a family descended from the Murakami Genji branch of the Minamoto family and a leader of the Southern Court at Yoshino after the failure of the KEMMU RESTORATION in 1336 and the commencement of a half-century (1336–92) of dynastic schism between it and the Northern Court at Kyōto (see NORTHERN AND SOUTHERN COURTS).

Jinnō shōtō ki begins with the famous pronouncement that "Great Japan is a divine land (*shinkoku*)." To many Japanese of the early medieval age (late 12th through early 14th centuries), the idea of *shinkoku* meant that Japan was divinely protected by the gods, a fact dramatically demonstrated in 1274 and 1281 by the *kamikaze* or "divine winds" that thwarted the two MONGOL INVASIONS OF JAPAN. But to Chikafusa the most important reason why Japan was a *shinkoku*, and thus superior to other countries, was that it had "ever been ruled by the line of the Sun Goddess, AMATERASU ŌMIKAMI." Whereas countries like India and China had often undergone dynastic change and had even suffered periods of anarchic disruption, Japan had been benevolently governed by an unbroken succession of sovereigns descended directly from Amaterasu.

The title *Jinnō shōtō ki* is often translated as "Chronicle of the Legitimate Descent of Divine Sovereigns," but Chikafusa accepted the legitimacy of the imperial succession as an article of faith and directed his attention more to what he identified as a special "direct line" *(shōtō)* of generational descent within the legitimate succession. Behind his theory of a direct line of generational descent—that is, one sovereign per generation—there lay a desire to equate hereditary emperorship in Japan with ethical rule. Thus he attempted to show that, although sovereigns who were unfit or bad might legitimately accede to the throne, their reigns would be brief and time would reveal that they were aberrations from the direct and true line. A corollary to Chikafusa's theory of direct descent was the belief that the repository of imperial virtue was the IMPERIAL REGALIA (mirror, sword, and jewels), and that virtue would therefore adhere to the throne even during the reigns of sovereigns who personally lacked it.

Chikafusa also argued in *Jinnō shōtō ki* that when Amaterasu mandated the imperial family to reign over Japan eternally, she also granted certain other families, led by the Nakatomi (later called the FUJIWARA FAMILY), an equally sacred right to assist the throne. And indeed the ideal form of government to Chikafusa was one in which the emperor's principal function was to legitimize actual rule by others—namely, by an oligarchic group of senior ministers at court headed by the Fujiwara but including also members of Chikafusa's own Murakami Genji family. Of course, real power in Japan had historically been assumed by the military houses from the time of the founding of the Kamakura shogunate in 1192. But Chikafusa believed that, despite the failure of Emperor Go-Daigo's Kemmu Restoration, it would be possible for the courtier class, under the emperor, to restore its governance of the country once again by combining the civil *(bun)* and military *(bu)* aspects of rule. As effective leader of the Southern Court after Go-Daigo's death in 1339, Chikafusa himself became a model of the courtier turned military commander.

Jinnō shōtō ki is probably best known as a historical tract designed to support the Southern Court's claim to legitimacy over the Northern Court in Chikafusa's own time. But, in fact, Chikafusa did not devote very much space in the book to arguing the cause of the Southern Court, quite likely because most of his contemporaries already believed that it was legitimate. Justifying the southern claim to legitimacy by the simple fact that Go-Daigo never willingly relinquished the regalia or symbols of emperorship, Chikafusa addressed himself primarily to the task of persuading leading warrior chieftains, especially in the Kantō region, to join the Yoshino side. Yet so reactionary were Chikafusa's own political views in favor of courtier supremacy that he probably alienated more chieftains than he persuaded. Nevertheless his work was received by succeeding generations of Japanese as a classical study of imperial loyalism and was even elevated to the status of a canonical text by nationalist scholars from the Edo period (1600–1868) on (see NAMBOKUCHŌ SEIJUN RON).

━━ Iwasa Tadashi et al, ed, *Jinnō shōtō ki, Masukagami,* in *Nihon koten bungaku taikei,* vol 87 (Iwanami Shoten, 1965). H. Paul Varley, *Imperial Restoration in Medieval Japan* (1971). H. Paul Varley, *A Chronicle of Gods and Sovereigns: Jinno Shōtōki of Kitabatake Chikafusa* (1980).   H. Paul VARLEY

jinrikisha → rickshaw

Jinshin Disturbance

(Jinshin no Ran; Civil War of 672). War of succession, following the death of Emperor TENJI (r 661–672), in which Prince Ōama, Tenji's younger brother, succeeded in deposing Prince Ōtomo, Tenji's son and designated heir. The insurrection is named for the sexagenary cyclical designation, *jinshin,* of the year corresponding to AD 672.

At that time there was no fixed rule of succession, an emperor's brother or son being equally eligible. Shortly before his death, Tenji had expressed his preference for his son Ōtomo by appointing him grand minister of state *(dajō daijin)* and establishing him in charge of the court, which was then located at Ōtsu on the shore of Lake Biwa in Ōmi Province (now Shiga Prefecture). Prince Ōama, who had long chafed under his brother's rule, thereupon withdrew from the court to the Yoshino Mountains in Yamato Province (now Nara Prefecture), ostensibly entered holy orders, and awaited his chance to strike.

After Tenji's death early in 672, Prince Ōtomo attempted to secure his position by strengthening his provincial military alliances. The local rulers and magnates, however, especially in eastern Japan, gave their support to Prince Ōama, who, within two months of the outbreak of hostilities in mid-672, isolated and defeated the forces of the Ōmi court. Prince Ōtomo committed suicide during one of the last battles of the conflict; 12 centuries later, in 1870, he was designated Emperor KŌBUN. Late in 672 Prince Ōama ascended the throne as Emperor TEMMU (r 672–686).

Ōama's skill as a military leader and strategist would have been unavailing without the allegiance of the local rulers. This he secured by appealing to their distrust of the court. Emperor Tenji, one of the architects of the TAIKA REFORM of 645, had devoted his reign to implementing its provisions, most notably the concentration of land ownership and provincial administration in the hands of the central government. This policy of centralization, which Ōtomo seemed likely to continue, had deeply antagonized the local magnates, whose position it directly threatened. Thus they were easily persuaded that support of Ōama would serve their own interests.

Ironically, Ōama's decisive victory left him a strong ruler and led to even greater centralization in the last quarter of the 7th century. As Emperor Temmu, he worked vigorously to carry out the reforms prescribed in the Taika edicts. His reign and that of his widow, Empress JITŌ (r 686–697), saw the promulgation of the ASUKA KIYOMIHARA CODE beginning in 681 and the completion of the nationwide census of 690. The trend toward a centralized state proved irreversible despite the resurgence of local power during the Jinshin Disturbance.

━━ Hoshino Ryōsaku, *Kenkyūshi: Jinshin no ran* (1973). Cornelius J. Kiley, "State and Dynasty in Archaic Yamato," *Journal of Asian Studies* 23.1 (1973).   Wayne FARRIS

Jinshin Koseki

Census registration carried out pursuant to the Family Registration Law (Kosekihō) of 4 April 1871; begun in 1872, it was named *jinshin* after the sexagenary designation of that year. Completed in 1873, it was the Meiji government's first attempt to carry out a nationwide census. The last census registration carried out under this law was in 1886.

The Jinshin Koseki took as its model the Kyōto Fu Tojaku Shihō of 1868, a set of registration rules drawn up for Kyōto Prefecture that was itself modeled on the Tojakuchō Shihōsho (1825) of the Chōshū domain (now Yamaguchi Prefecture). The 1872–73 census took the domicile or household as its basic unit. The head *(koshu)* of each household *(ie)* was designated as its representative, holding full authority over and responsibility for all its members. The *koshu* was required to list the name, age, relationship, occupation, and temple or shrine affiliation of each household member, beginning with himself. He was also obliged to record marriages, adoptions, the establishment of branch families (see HONKE AND BUNKE), and any other changes in the composition of the household. Such acts and transactions were not legal until the *koshu* had formally registered them at a prefectural office. Thus it was through the household head that the Meiji government chose to control the lives of the populace.

There were significant differences between the Jinshin Koseki and the SHŪMON ARATAME registration carried out by the Tokugawa shogunate (1603–1867). In the older system, families had been classified according to their status as *samurai,* farmers, artisans, or merchants (SHI-NŌ-KŌ-SHŌ). In contrast, the Meiji census in theory treated everyone uniformly as "his majesty's subjects" and was classified only geographically. This reflected the government's avowed policy of equalizing the four traditional social classes (shimin byōdō). In practice, however, distinctions between the nobility (kazoku; see PEERAGE), former samurai (SHIZOKU), commoners (HEIMIN), and former outcastes *(shin heimin)* were duly recorded, and the registers thereby perpetuated these class distinctions until the end of World War II. For that reason, free access to these family registers is no longer permitted.

The second difference was the Jinshin Koseki's emphasis on the Confucian ideal of the family. Although there were regional differences, in the *shūmon aratame* aged parents who had retired from active participation in family and worldly affairs had normally been listed after their daughter-in-law and grandchildren. The 1872 census stressed seniority, direct kinship, and patrilineal descent. Grandparents and parents were listed immediately after the *koshu,* preceding the *koshu*'s wife, children, grandchildren, brothers, and sisters.

A third difference was that, while the Tokugawa registers had been kept by local village officials and temples, the Jinshin registers were administered in theory by the central government. The home minister delegated his authority to the prefectural governors, who in turn delegated their authority downward to the district heads, ward heads, heads of towns and villages (kochō), and eventually to the koshu. The kochō made official copies of the registers and forwarded them to the Shihaisho, an agency of the prefectural government. The prefectural office abstracted statistical information (on occupation, age, sex, status, etc) from the registers and submitted it to the central government every six years. In this manner the government was able to collect vital statistics for use in formulating policies on conscription, taxation, education, the police system, and other matters.

Jinshin Koseki also refers to a census registration carried out in Awa Province (now Tokushima Prefecture) in the year 902; the accuracy and even the historical authenticity of the document are, however, widely doubted. See also HOUSEHOLD REGISTERS.

TANAKA Akira

Jinshin no Ran → Jinshin Disturbance

Jinzūgawa

River in Gifu and Toyama prefectures, central Honshū, flowing north from northern Gifu Prefecture into Toyama Prefecture and emptying into Toyama Bay. The upper reaches, sometimes called the Miyagawa, converge with the Takaharagawa to form the Jinzūgawa. Numerous electric power plants are located along the river, and the port of Toyama forms a part of its mouth. In the 1960s the waters, contaminated with cadmium from Mitsui Mining and Smelting Company's plant on the upper reaches, caused an outbreak of itai itai disease among inhabitants along the lower reaches (see POLLUTION-RELATED DISEASES). Mountainous regions along the river are noted for heavy snowfall. Length: 120 km (75 mi); area of drainage basin: 2,720 sq km (1,050 sq mi).

Jippensha Ikku (1765–1831)

GESAKU fiction writer; playwright; artist. Born the son of a low-ranking samurai official in the province of Suruga (now Shizuoka Prefecture), Jippensha Ikku was one of the most popular and prolific writers of the early 19th century, best known for his comic novel series Tōkaidōchū hizakurige (1802–22; also known as Dōchū hizakurige; tr Shank's Mare, 2nd ed 1960). Ikku's real name was Shigeta Sadakazu. After some years' service in Edo (now Tōkyō), he accompanied his lord to Ōsaka where, renouncing his official employment and samurai status, he began a new career around 1790 as a JŌRURI playwright. In 1794 he returned to Edo and became a protégé of the publisher Tsutaya Jūzaburō. His first work of fiction, a KIBYŌSHI ("yellow cover"), a variety of late-18th-century popular illustrated fiction, entitled Shingaku tokeigusa, was published the following year, and thereafter Ikku published at a furious pace, producing as many as 20 kibyōshi in a single year.

Like many authors of his period, Ikku's talents extended in many directions. In a career spanning four decades he produced not only his Hizakurige series but also a staggering total of about 320 kibyōshi and GŌKAN ("bound volumes"), another form of lavishly illustrated fiction popular from the early 19th century onward. He wrote in addition a large number of SHAREBON and NINJŌBON, two genres of gesaku fiction that deal rather exclusively with the pleasure quarters; many YOMIHON ("reading books"), gesaku fiction written in a serious tone; as well as occasional nonfiction works, among them a commentary on the famous puppet play Kanadehon chūshingura (1748, The Treasury of Loyal Retainers) entitled Chūshingura okame hyōban (1803), which is a useful historical source. He was active in the field of comic verse (KYŌKA) and senryū (see ZAPPAI AND SENRYŪ) poetry as well and was an accomplished artist, illustrating many of his own works (including Hizakurige).

What little is known of Ikku's private life suggests that it was full of crisis and instability. While his first two marriages (one in Ōsaka, the other in Edo) ended in divorce, his third marriage seems to have been a happy one; however, his home was twice destroyed by fire. In spite of his reputation as a humorist, the most reliable accounts describe him as having been not very jolly in person, and at his worst surly and sometimes even violent. Whether in order to collect materials for his Hizakurige series or simply out of wanderlust, Ikku traveled extensively in his middle years, but ill health attributed to heavy drinking and irregular habits later confined him to Edo. According to his contemporary, yomihon writer Takizawa BAKIN, Ikku was the first fiction writer in Japan able to earn a living solely from the proceeds of his books, but in spite of his immense popularity he

seems to have spent his final years in straitened circumstances, attended only by his daughter. Most authorities doubt the truth of the tale, but Ikku is said to have ordered on his deathbed that fireworks be secretly placed with his body on the funeral pyre as a final practical joke to entertain his friends.

Tōkaidōchū hizakurige is indisputably Ikku's masterpiece. The work depicts the comic adventures of Yajirobei and Kitahachi, a footloose pair of bankrupt commoners from Edo, as they travel along the highway Tōkaidō from Edo to Kyōto and Ōsaka. Ikku, who at the time was known as a kibyōshi author of only middling talent, had trouble finding a publisher for Hizakurige, his first kokkeibon ("funny book"), a variety of humorous gesaku fiction, but its first book was an instant success when it appeared in 1802, and Ikku soon abandoned his plan to conclude the work with its second book, expanding it finally to eight books, the last published in 1809. The immensely popular series immediately began to be reprinted, and capitalizing on its success, Ikku began to publish a sequel, Zoku hizakurige, in 1810. This second series, which had ultimately grown to 12 books by the time Ikku called a halt in 1822, took Yaji and Kita on a number of shorter trips to popular shrines and along other major highways. In the meantime, Ikku added to the original series a new introductory volume describing his heroes' lives in Edo before they took to the road to escape the consequences of a series of domestic disasters.

The humor of Hizakurige is in large part that of situation comedy. As they move from town to town on their journey, Yaji and Kita, through ignorance of local custom, practical jokes that backfire, greed, or simple high spirits, find themselves in embarrassing, dangerous, or comical circumstances from which they invariably escape by the exercise of wit or sheer, brazen gall. They are eternally on the lookout for something for nothing, be it food, drink, money, or sex, no matter that a moment's reflection should remind them that they have never yet paid anything but dearly for their schemes.

The sustaining appeal of Hizakurige lies not so much in its individual, disconnected comic scenes as in the characters of Yajirobei and Kitahachi. While in the description of their lives in Edo that he appended to the first volume of Hizakurige Ikku describes Yaji as considerably older than Kita—who was originally his boy lover—throughout their adventures their behavior and personalities are virtually interchangeable. Between them they portray a composite ideal of the edokko, the spirited "child of Edo" who is absurdly free with whatever money comes his way, never planning a day ahead, never admitting that life is anything but a succession of pleasures and triumphs in spite of all evidence to the contrary. The Yaji–Kita character is distinguished by an eternal resiliency: whether scalded in an unfamiliar kind of bathtub, robbed blind, or tricked into bed with an old crone, he never really suffers. Every injury, humiliation, or comeuppance can be overcome by a snappy bit of punning repartee, self-deluding rationalization, or flight disguised as a simple change in itinerary. Yaji and Kita pepper their conversation with puns, comic doggerel, and scatology; the pages are filled with this endless, chaffing banter beloved of the Edo townsman. Though much of the verbal humor of Hizakurige has lost its sparkle for the more sophisticated readers of a later time, Yaji and Kita themselves have lost little of their charm.

Hizakurige draws upon many sources. With travel and pilgrimage its basic premise, its inclusion of geographical detail and local color, and its doggerel alluding to place names and local custom, it is a burlesque addition to the long tradition of travel diaries and guides. Yaji and Kita themselves, and many of the comic situations in which they are placed, are drawn from the KYŌGEN repertoire, while other scenes seem borrowed from RAKUGO and other comic storytelling forms. The format in which the story is presented, with its emphasis on realistic dialogue, comes from the sharebon, and the word play and comic verse show the influence of the kyōka movement. Ikku's successful mingling of these disparate forms of entertainment and his gift for characterization made Hizakurige, even as it was being written, more a monument of popular culture than simply a piece of comic literature.

■ ——Jippensha Ikku, Tōkaidōchū hizakurige, tr Thomas Satchell as Shank's Mare (1929, rev ed 1960).   Robert W. LEUTNER

jiriki → tariki

JIS

(Japanese Industrial Standard; Nihon Kōgyō Kikaku). The official standard for mining and industrial products set by the Industrial

Standardization Law (Kōgyō Hyōjunka Hō) of 1949. This law aims to rationalize production and consumption patterns, improve product quality, and help increase productivity. More than 7,000 specifications have been set by the Ministry of International Trade and Industry, which supervises the standards program. Areas covered include technical terminology, symbols, and signs; quality and performance of products; and testing and measuring methods. Products that meet official standards are marked with the label JIS.

Katō Masashi

Ji sect

(Jishū). Originally a mendicant order of Pure Land (Jōdo) Buddhists (see PURE LAND BUDDHISM), prominent from the 13th through the 15th centuries, which was transformed into a sect in the Edo period (1600–1868) and continues to the present day. The Jishū was founded by IPPEN (1239–89), a wayfaring holy man (HIJIRI) trained in the Seizan school of the Jōdo sect. Ippen emphasized that the name of the Buddha AMIDA contained within it both Amida's attainment of Buddhahood and the salvation of all beings, united as a single, timeless event. Accordingly, he distributed paper talismans *(fuda)* inscribed with this name and the curious phrase "The Established Rebirth of 600,000 people," by which he probably signified all Japanese. His distribution of these talismans was justified by an oracle from a god of Kumano, himself a manifestation of Amida, who stressed that this name alone, and not the piety of the recipient of the talisman, effected salvation. With this mission, Ippen traveled throughout Japan distributing his talismans. He also practiced the *nembutsu* dance *(odori nembutsu;* see NEMBUTSU ODORI), originally an ecstatic dance celebrating the immediacy of salvation available in the name of Amida Buddha.

In his travels Ippen acquired many disciples, whom he organized into the Jishū. The name Jishū translates literally as "hourly group," but means "twenty-four-hours-a-day group," referring to its incessant devotion to the name. Male members were even given names which contained the words Amida Buddha (Amida Butsu), and women's names contained the phrase *ichibō,* signifying the one Buddha. Both showed the unity of humans and Buddha in Amida's name. The ideal Jishū life was one of impoverished, mendicant wayfaring, distributing the paper talismans with Amida's name and thus saving all who received them.

After Ippen's death, the Jishū grew in two ways. The first was by eliciting the allegiance of similar mendicant orders based at established temples, as well as perhaps independent orders similar to itself. The second was by establishing its own permanent institutions *(dōjō).* Chief among these was Shōjōkoji, also called YUGYŌJI, in Fujisawa (Kanagawa Prefecture), which was founded by the fourth head of the sect, who belonged to one of several groups in the line of Shinkyō Taamidabutsu (1237–1319), Ippen's leading disciple. Other Jishū branches, however, grew independently in other areas of the country. By the Edo period, 12 were recognized.

The Jishū found its support largely among the warrior class, for whom it provided both ordinary funerals and services for battlefield deaths. Among Pure Land Buddhist groups, the Jishū alone strongly advocated the worship of native deities, since it regarded them as ultimately manifestations of Amida. Thus the Pure Land Buddhism of the Jishū was compatible with the local and clan religious requirements of the warriors. Because of their status as social outsiders, the Jishū retinues of leading warriors evolved into, or more probably became the models for, guilds of artists and aesthetes known as *dōbōshū.* The *dōbōshū* of the eighth Ashikaga shōgun, Yoshimasa (1436–90), is particularly famous. This social convention may account for the abbreviation of Amida's name, *ami,* appearing in the names of many of the artists of the period (eg, Sōami, Zeami). Many Jishū members, too, were prominent in literature and the arts.

The Jishū might well have been the leading Pure Land Buddhist group in the 14th and 15th centuries, but it was too closely tied to a social order that would crumble in the Sengoku (Warring States) period (1467–1568). Many of its local devotional groups undoubtedly shifted allegiance to the rising Jōdo Shin sect. In the Edo period, the Jishū was made to conform to a sectarian mold imposed by the government. Today, it is so minor that many Japanese have not heard of it. Although the abbot of Shōjōkoji is still called the "wayfaring saint" *(yugyō shōnin),* in fact Jishū temples now function in ways indistinguishable from those of other Buddhist sects.

■——Kanai Kiyomitsu, *Ippen to jishū kyōdan* (1975). Ōhashi Toshio, *Jishū no seiritsu to tenkai* (1973).   *James H. FOARD*

jisha bugyō

(commissioners of temples and shrines). An office of the Tokugawa shogunate (1603–1867). It had antecedents dating from the Kamakura period (1185–1333), when commissioners (BUGYŌ) were appointed by the shogunate to supervise the affairs of major Shintō shrines and Buddhist temples. The Muromachi shogunate (1338–1573) also assigned commissioners to oversee principal shrines and temples. In 1635 the shōgun TOKUGAWA IEMITSU formalized the office of *jisha bugyō,* appointing four FUDAI *bugyō* who served in rotation at monthly intervals *(tsukibansei).* They performed their duties in their own mansions *(yashiki),* largely with the assistance of their own vassals. In addition to supervising the affairs of temples and shrines throughout the country, they oversaw judicial matters in HATAMOTO lands outside the Kantō region and supervised the activities of various professionals, such as musicians, linked-verse *(renga)* poets, and *go* players, as well as numerous service personnel in the shōgun's household.   *Conrad TOTMAN*

jishi

Land rent, a term variously used from the 7th century, when the RITSURYŌ SYSTEM of administration was established; also called *chishi.* It originally referred to the annual rent from the state-owned rice lands *(kōden)* that remained after the cultivators had received their prescribed shares under the field-allotment system (see HANDEN SHŪJU SYSTEM.) These lands were rented on a year-to-year basis, and the *jishi,* which was set at one-fifth of the crop, was collected by the central government. From the middle of the Heian period (794–1185), with the development of private landed estates (SHŌEN), the rent charged by the estate proprietor for rice land was known as *jishi,* the rent for other productive fields as *hatajishi,* and that for land occupied by dwellings as *yajishi.* From late in the Muromachi period (1333–1568), land rent paid in rice was called *jishimai,* while that paid in cash was called *jishisen.* During the Edo period (1600–1868), *jishi* became the general term for taxes on urban residential land, and it was paid in silver or in copper coins. In some areas, however, it referred to rent paid by tenant farmers.

jishimban and tsujiban

Two major organs of neighborhood civil patrol during the Edo period (1600–1868). Established in large cities, they were an important supplement to the inadequate forces available to the city commissioners (MACHI BUGYŌ).

Jishimban were officially approved patrol groups manned and supported by neighborhoods of commoners. Those in Edo (now Tōkyō) were formed during the latter 1600s, and by the mid-19th century there were some 990 *jishimban* posts located throughout commoners' sections of the city at busy intersections and other strategic spots. Each *jishimban* post consisted of a small building that provided duty space for a squad of three to five men, a fire-watch platform, storage space for firefighting buckets and ladders, and a site for neighborhood gatherings. *Jishimban* members patrolled at night, served as fire lookouts *(hinoban),* apprehended and escorted suspicious persons to the city commissioners' offices, and helped the commissioners' patrols to detain and interrogate suspects. They also arranged neighborhood conferences, resolved disputes, and performed various local tasks. Initially these units were staffed on a rotating basis by neighborhood residents, but later the posts were often filled by hire, and some *jishimban* units became nearly useless, the job simply providing income for old and infirm people who devoted their patrols to such ventures as selling sweets or making loans.

Tsujiban were similar to *jishimban* except that they were manned and supported through regular levies imposed on *daimyō,* HATAMOTO, and GOKENIN. First established in Edo in 1629 to prevent murders and other street violence (see TSUJIGIRI), some 890 *tsujiban* were situated at strategic points in *samurai* residential areas. They were composed of men aged 20 to 60, who performed functions similar to those of *jishimban* in other sections of the city.   *Conrad TOTMAN*

Jishōji → Ginkakuji

jitō

(estate stewards). The office of *jitō* or *jitō shiki;* usually understood to mean the elite estate stewardships distributed by the KAMAKURA

SHOGUNATE to its warrior vassals. Along with the office of SHUGO (constable or military governor), it has come to be recognized as distinctive of the Kamakura period (1185–1333). The term emerged during the middle part of the Heian period (794–1185), though, significantly, the office did not evolve into a regular post until the early 12th century. There is controversy regarding why it came into existence at that time and whether it was in use within private estates (SHŌEN) or provincial lands (kokugaryō). There is also debate as to whether jitō shiki were awarded in large numbers by TAIRA NO KIYOMORI after 1160. There is little actual proof that they were, which could mean that jitō were still relatively uncommon at the start of the TAIRA–MINAMOTO WAR 20 years later.

During the course of the fighting between the Taira and the Minamoto, however, something altogether revolutionary occurred. In scattered parts of the country local warriors began to style themselves as jitō (and also as gesu, a comparable but much more common title) and to use this to justify seizures of administrative control over estates. The Kyōto-based landowners (see HONKE AND RYŌKE) who were adversely affected by this turned to the retired emperor's headquarters (In no Chō; see INSEI) for redress and, when this failed, to the emerging Minamoto bloc in Kamakura. This had the effect of associating Kamakura with the control of jitō, which in turn paved the way for a dramatic development late in 1185. The Minamoto chieftain, MINAMOTO NO YORITOMO, had been casting about for a reward system that would be acceptable to his followers but not grant them complete autonomy. He ultimately hit upon a disbursement scheme using the newly current title jitō. Recipients of that title would be guaranteed tenure in the office but would also be obliged to owe regular estate services to traditional proprietors.

At the end of 1185 the emerging Kamakura shogunate secured an authorization from the court to appoint jitō selectively around the country. It is noteworthy that for generations of historians this development marked the establishment of "feudalism" in Japan, a formal joining of systems of vassalage and benefice under a supreme warrior-chieftain. In fact, though, this exaggerates what happened. Jitō were given the rights confiscated from warriors associated with the Taira. This meant two things: that true fiefs were not involved, since actual title to the land did not change hands; and that the range of jitō appointments remained strictly limited. Indeed, large sections of the country, including the entire possessions of some proprietors, had no jitō at all. Beyond that, the Kamakura chieftain adopted a strict policy against appointees who abused their office, as is evidenced by the numerous cancellations of jitō shiki in the period after 1185.

Thus, the network of jitō was spread unevenly across the country, and the shogunate's involvement in local areas was correspondingly defined. The converse of this was that estate and provincial administration of the traditional type came largely to be restored. Thus Japan can hardly be said to have been feudalized. Nevertheless, in those land units to which jitō had been appointed, the potential for aggrandizement was considerable. Jitō were the country's first land stewards who stood outside the estate system's regular chain of command. From early on, therefore, estate proprietors began directing their complaints of jitō lawlessness to the shogunate, and it was from this practice that the warrior regime's remarkably precocious system of justice evolved. Throughout the period, the reconciling of antagonisms between jitō and proprietors was to be the shogunate's principal governmental concern.

After the Taira–Minamoto War (1180–85), the next occasion on which large numbers of new jitō came to be appointed was the JŌKYŪ DISTURBANCE of 1221. An army of the imperial court was defeated by a shogunate army, which meant that the land rights of the losers could now be redistributed as new jitō shiki. As a result, the shogunate enlarged its influence in central and western Japan, where most of the new jitō shiki were located. From this point forward the jitō shiki was truly a national institution. Still, it cannot be said that these stewardships became ubiquitous. Neither then nor later were estates with jitō ever more than a minority.

It was the shogunate's clear objective to ensure continuity in its appointments wherever possible. This meant that, ideally, the set of rights acquired by the jitō would be identical with the authority and perquisites of the particular warrior he replaced. In cases where jitō titles were to a vassal's own homelands, all that estate owners lost, in effect, was their power to dismiss the jitō. It is clear, at any rate, that the prerogatives and privileges of jitō were potentially different. By and large, however, most holders of a stewardship controlled a substantial portion of a domain's affairs.

Jitō were especially prominent as local policemen and tax collectors, with the precise extent of authority determined by precedent. Whether these rights coincided with a domain's boundaries or were limited in some other way would thus vary widely. The same held true with regard to control of estate officials. Sometimes a jitō enjoyed the right of appointment over various lower functionaries, while in other cases this power was exercised by the proprietor. Finally, the jitō's authority to oversee the agricultural cycle gave him access to peasant labor, domain storage facilities, and specialty products.

It was Kamakura's clear intention that most jitō shiki be hereditary, the shogunate merely reserving to itself the right to renew investitures with each generation. It also served as arbitrator in the event of family disputes over an inheritance. On this point, it is noteworthy that ranking vassal houses might hold multiple jitō rights scattered across the country. Such families were invariably from the Kantō area, which meant that deputies (jitōdai) had to be appointed to administer far-flung territories. These jitōdai tended to be younger sons or brothers, though non-kin vassals were sometimes assigned, either from the local areas in question or from the jitō's home region. Theoretically, jitōdai were not subject to shogunate authority, though in practice Kamakura did often communicate with them directly. Ultimate disciplinary rights, at any rate, lay with the jitō. Toward the end of the Kamakura period, jitō who retained their eastern bases found it increasingly difficult to exercise control over widely dispersed deputies.

The historical importance of jitō lies principally in the progress they represented in the warrior class's struggle against absentee proprietors based in Kyōto. In other words, jitō gained control largely in proportion to their infringement of older privileges. The basis for this was their unique status: estate owners bearing grievances against them had to lodge formal complaints with the shogunate; whereas Kamakura, for its part, could not afford to move too harshly against too many of its own men. Injunctions were therefore much more common than outright dismissals. As a result, jitō were able to advance their interests by seeking areas of vulnerability within estates and by applying measured—rather than overwhelming—pressure. The control gained by jitō was gradual rather than sudden.

The most common abuses concerned taxes, either short delivery or unauthorized levies. The jitō could also exploit his police powers: extortion became a way of life, and the residents of an estate were often gradually reduced to subject status. A direct outgrowth of this was a decline in the proprietors' own powers of enforcement, which in turn led them to seek new solutions to their problem. One device, called ukesho, involved the surrendering of full control over an estate in return for the jitō's promise, confirmed by the shogunate, to deliver a fixed annual tax. A second device, SHITAJI CHŪBUN, involved the physical partitioning of a domain between a rival jitō and proprietor. Both of these bore witness to the increasing plight of estate owners. Concessions yielded under duress usually further whetted jitō appetites.

By the final generation of Kamakura rule, jitō were being joined by other types of warrior who were beginning to make similar inroads. Consequently, by the period of the Northern and Southern Courts (1336–92) jitō came to be subsumed under a more generalized category of local magnates—the "provincial men" (KOKUJIN). The title itself survived, and it is likely that many daimyō of the Sengoku (Warring States) period (1467–1568) could trace their roots back to a status as Kamakura jitō. This is significant because it suggests a direct connection between these two figures of authority. The assault against civilian supremacy was begun by jitō during the 13th century and reached final completion in the 15th and 16th at the hands of Japan's new class of warrior lords (SENGOKU DAIMYŌ).
——Jeffrey P. Mass, *Warrior Government in Early Medieval Japan* (1974).　　　　　*Jeffrey* MASS

Jitō, Empress (645–703)

The 41st sovereign (tennō) in the traditional count (which includes several nonhistorical emperors); reigned 686–697. Second daughter of Emperor TENJI; wife of Prince Ōama (Tenji's younger brother), who later became Emperor TEMMU. After Temmu's death in 686, she gained control of state affairs and, following the death of the crown prince, formally ascended the throne as reigning empress in 690. During her reign she was responsible for completing and enacting the ASUKA KIYOMIHARA CODE, Japan's first set of administrative and penal laws. In 697 she relinquished the throne to her grandson Prince Karu (later Emperor MOMMU) and became the first to assume the official title of *dajō tennō* (retired sovereign). She is known to have been a devout Buddhist as well as a talented *waka* poet; her works are included in the 8th-century poetry anthology MAN'YŌ-SHŪ.

Jitsugyō Dōshikai

(Businessmen's Association). Small political party founded in 1923 by MUTŌ SANJI, the president of Kanegafuchi Bōseki (Kanegafuchi Spinning Company). Although its call for business tax cuts and further industrialization initially won some support among financial circles in the Kansai region, its laissez-faire economic policy did not sit well with many of its supposed supporters, small- and middle-sized companies that preferred to rely on government protection and financial aid. Its electoral support was also weak, never giving it more than 10 Diet seats. Aligned often with the RIKKEN SEIYŪKAI, it participated in the TANAKA GIICHI cabinet of 1927 to assure passage of some of its bills, such as relief to the poor. Reorganized under the name Kokumin Dōshikai in April 1929, it disbanded in January 1932 immediately after the dissolution of the 60th Diet.

jitsurokumono

Documentary stories of the latter part of the Edo period (1600–1868). They were popular chronicles of historical events and the lives of folk heroes, often dealing with such themes as vendettas, succession disputes in the houses of feudal lords, shogunal tribunals, valiant warriors, brigands, or the tragic fate of star-crossed lovers. In 1722 the Tokugawa shogunate proscribed the publication of all literary works based on contemporary social issues and historical events; nevertheless, handwritten transcriptions of oral narratives (KŌDAN) were available through commercial lending libraries and circulated throughout the country. Subsequently, the *jitsurokumono*, which borrowed from KABUKI plays and YOMIHON ("reading books," a genre of Edo prose fiction derived in part from the tradition of the Chinese vernacular novel) the practice of embellishing historical fact, developed into a distinct genre of historical fiction by the beginning of the Kansei era (1789–1801). SAN'YŪTEI ENCHŌ, a Meiji-period (1868–1912) professional storyteller, entertained his audiences with narratives drawn from *jitsurokumono*. Taken down in shorthand and published, they attracted the notice of writer-critic TSUBOUCHI SHŌYŌ, who advised the novelist FUTABATEI SHIMEI to adopt Enchō's conversational style. The last popular edition of *jitsurokumono* appeared in *Teikoku bunko* (1893–97), a Meiji-period anthology of Edo literature.

jitte

Iron weapon with a shaft about 46 centimeters (1.5 ft) long and an L-shaped hook attached parallel to the shaft just below the hilt. It was used to catch an opponent's sword blade and twist it from his grasp. Introduced from China, the use of this weapon developed as one of the martial arts during the Sengoku period (1467–1568). In the Edo period (1600–1868) it was used by shogunal constables (YORIKI AND DŌSHIN), who hung red tassels from the hilts of their *jitte* as a symbol of their office.   *INAGAKI Shisei*

Jiun Onkō (1718–1804)

(also known as Jiun Sonja). Monk of the Shingon sect, outstanding calligrapher, and Japan's greatest Sanskrit scholar. He was born in Harima near Ōsaka and received a Confucian education in his youth. When his father, a *samurai* official, died, the young Jiun entered a Shingon temple in Ōsaka. He was then sent by the abbot to Kyōto to study Shingon doctrine and also to pursue an understanding of the Chinese classics under ITŌ TŌGAI. Jiun also studied Shintō, Zen, and Sanskrit at this time. He spent most of the rest of his life in Shingon temples as an adherent of the Shingon Ritsu sect, founding both Shingon Shōbōritsu, a Shingon subsect, and Unden Shintō, a union of Buddhism with Shintō.

Jiun was an outstanding scholar. His works were reprinted in 1926 by Hase Tamahide under the title *Jiun Sonja zenshū*. This collection, however, contains only the table of contents of Jiun's greatest work, the thousand-volume Sanskrit study *Bongaku shinryō*. This opus exists only in manuscript form; it consists of literary references to Sanskrit in China and Japan with commentaries, as well as the first thorough study of Sanskrit grammar to appear in East Asia. Many confusions in Mantrayanic texts are clarified in this major work.

Although Jiun occasionally wrote his calligraphy in Japanese or in the Sanskrit script known as SIDDHAM, he wrote most often in Chinese. He favored brushing large-size characters in bold compositions, often using a split-bamboo brush that imparts a rough and powerful effect. In his paintings Jiun chose simple subjects such as a bowl, a staff, or a one-stroke Daruma (Skt: Bodhidharma). He practiced Zen meditation, and his works have the direct and spontaneous strength that is typical of Edo-period (1600–1868) ZENGA.
                                                Stephen ADDISS

Jiun Sonja → Jiun Onkō

jiuta

A genre of traditional Japanese music. The literal meaning of the term *jiuta* is "local songs." In its most common usage, it refers to the songs of the Kyōto-Ōsaka region, as distinguished from those of Edo (now Tōkyō). These songs, an introverted music of quiet elegance, originated in the 17th century. They were composed for voice with SHAMISEN accompaniment, but in the case of *hauta*, *tegoto-mono*, and NAGAUTA, parts for the KOTO and *shakuhachi* were added to create the standard *sankyoku* ensemble.

The varieties of *jiuta* pieces include, in the order of their introduction, *shamisen kumiuta*, *nagauta*, *hauta*, *tegoto-mono*, *jōruri-mono*, *sakumono* and others. The most characteristic form is the song in two or three parts. In the two-part song, there is a *maeuta* or fore song, sometimes preceded by an instrumental introduction; the *tegoto* or instrumental passage, itself subdivided into several sections; and finally the *atouta* or after song. The three-part song consists of instrumental introduction, *maeuta*, first *tegoto*, *nakauta* or middle song, a second *tegoto*, and the *atouta*. The distinctions between the various types of *jiuta* are based on the relative importance of the instrumental and vocal passages, the content, the strictness of form, and the sources of the songs.

Although the *shamisen* is the characteristic instrument, it is the two major schools of *koto* music that are the present guardians of the *jiuta* tradition. The *shamisen* of the Ikuta school is large and heavy, exceeded in size only by the Gidayū *shamisen* of the puppet theater. The *shamisen* of the Yamada school, which originated in Edo, is a lighter instrument that is essentially identical to the Edo *nagauta shamisen*. Both are played with a plectrum made of buffalo horn, the flexibility of which is enhanced by an extremely thin playing edge. This gives the *jiuta shamisen* a less percussive, more singing tone than the other versions of the instrument, while decreasing its power and brilliance.

The earliest known *shamisen* music is the *kumiuta*. Like the *koto* pieces of the same name, these were sequences of popular verses sung to instrumental accompaniment. The first composer of *shamisen kumiuta* seems to have been a certain Yanagawa with the title of *kengyō* or master, who was active in the second quarter of the 17th century. The titles *kengyō* and *kōtō* were inherited from the blind musicians of the earlier *heikyoku* tradition of lute music, and blind musicians bearing these titles dominated *koto* and *shamisen* music throughout the Edo period (1600–1868). The next part of the repertoire to be developed was the *nagauta* or long song. These pieces, which were also the forerunners of Edo *nagauta*, were based each on a single long verse, making possible a coherence of theme and mood that was lacking in the *kumiuta*. The *nagauta* was followed by the *hauta*, or "convention breaking song," so called because it dealt with topical themes and was less strict in form. By the late 18th century, the *tegoto-mono* were introduced, giving the instrumentalists new freedom and importance.

In the late 17th century, Ikuta Kengyō began to use the *koto* as a second accompanying instrument, although the *shamisen* continued to dominate in this school until very recently. At the beginning of the 19th century, the contrasting timbre and phrasing of the *koto* and the *shamisen* were more fully exploited with the introduction of the *kaede* or counter melody for the *koto*. The SHAKUHACHI began to be used in *jiuta* performances at about the same time. The *shakuhachi* was replaced for a time by the KOKYŪ, a bowed instrument shaped like a small *shamisen*. This fashion soon passed and the *kokyū* is now rarely heard. The *sankyoku* ensemble of *koto*, *shamisen*, and *shakuhachi* serves as the point of departure for larger chamber groups, usually formed by doubling or tripling in the *koto* parts.

With the appearance of instrumental virtuosi in the latter part of the 17th century, the *jiuta* played an important role in theatrical music. Sayama Kengyō (d 1694) moved to Edo where he founded Edo *nagauta*. This school eventually broke with the *jiuta* tradition to become the primary music of the KABUKI theater. In the main *jiuta* tradition, association with the theater was a passing phase, resistance being due in part to the loss of prestige inherent in association with theatrical people. The *kengyō* enjoyed the honorary status of a middling feudal lord; actors were nominal outcasts.

The current repertoire includes both traditional and modern pieces. Many of the contemporary compositions show Western influences, although more frequently in an increased formal freedom than in details of content. In recent times *koto* players far outnumber performers on the more demanding *shamisen*, and *jiuta* pieces are now usually heard in public as supplements to *koto* and *shakuhachi* recitals.

There are several schools of elegant and austere dance which use *jiuta* for their accompaniment. These dances are known as *jiutamai*. They were originally intended to be performed before small audiences but they too are now undergoing marked changes to adapt to new tastes and to new performing conditions. *William E. NAFF*

Jiyū Minken Undō → Freedom and People's Rights Movement

Jiyū Minshutō → Liberal Democratic Party

Jiyūtō

(Liberal Party). 1. In 1880 the LEAGUE FOR ESTABLISHING A NATIONAL ASSEMBLY collected almost 250,000 signatures for a petition to create a national assembly (authorities differ on the number of signatures; the figure 96,900 is often given). Even earlier, ITAGAKI TAISUKE and other leaders of the FREEDOM AND PEOPLE'S RIGHTS MOVEMENT had advocated the formation of a political party in preparation for parliamentary government, and in December 1880 steps were taken to convert the league into such a party. On 29 October 1881, only days after an imperial rescript announced that a parliamentary form of government would be established by 1890, the Jiyūtō, Japan's first national political party, was founded. Other political parties, such as the Kaishintō (see RIKKEN KAISHINTŌ) and the progovernment RIKKEN TEISEITŌ, were founded soon after, but only the Jiyūtō could claim to be a direct outgrowth of the people's rights movement. Itagaki assumed the position of party president, NAKAJIMA NOBUYUKI was appointed vice-president, and the standing committee included GOTŌ SHŌJIRŌ, BABA TATSUI, SUEHIRO TETCHŌ, and other prominent political leaders. UEKI EMORI and NAKAE CHŌMIN, both influenced by French political liberalism, served as intellectual spokesmen for the new party.

The Jiyūtō set forth its program in three brief articles. The first read, "The Jiyūtō will work for the expansion of liberty, the preservation of people's rights, the increase of happiness, and the progress of society." The second promised to work for a constitutional system, and the third to cooperate with fellow Japanese who were working for the same goals. The party later issued a prospectus criticizing the government for suppressing human liberty.

Both the Jiyūtō and the Kaishintō stood for reduction of the land tax, expansion of civil and political freedoms, and revision of the so-called Unequal Treaties (see UNEQUAL TREATIES, REVISION OF). But on the whole the Jiyūtō took a more radical position. Its members were largely former *samurai* and large landholders, in contrast to the bureaucrats, intellectuals, and entrepreneurs who composed the bulk of the Kaishintō. At the end of 1881 Jiyūtō membership stood at 101 people; by 1884, when the party was dissolved, nearly 2,500 had joined its ranks. These numbers do not, however, give an accurate picture of the party's influence, for there were many sympathizers who did not formally join. Moreover, there were many who belonged to local affiliates of the Jiyūtō, such as the Fukushima Jiyūtō and the Saitama Jiyūtō.

The activities of the Jiyūtō consisted largely in propagating its political philosophy and lobbying on behalf of a liberal constitution. To this end the party began publication of a newspaper, the *Jiyū shimbun* on 24 June 1882, and many of the local parties did likewise. Rallies were held in urban and rural areas to urge the people to unite in order to preserve and expand their rights. At the prefectural level, Jiyūtō politicians and members of other political parties campaigned for prefectural assemblies along party lines and whenever possible followed party parliamentary practice when the assemblies were in session. In this way they gained valuable training for the national parliamentary system.

The Meiji government did not view the activities of the new parties sympathetically. It issued new press laws (PRESS ORDINANCE OF 1875) and restrictions on assembly (SHŪKAI JŌREI) and in other ways attempted to obstruct their growth. The Jiyūtō was unable to withstand these attacks, for its leadership was weak and divided. In November 1882 Itagaki and Gotō accepted a government grant for a tour of Europe, thereby causing a scandal and alienating many party members. The party was divided also in its response to the FUKUSHIMA INCIDENT and other violent uprisings instigated by local Jiyūtō politicians. An extremist group, led by ŌI KENTARŌ, concluded that only "direct action" would serve to check despotic government; a more conservative group, comprising the majority of the leaders and supported by large landholders, called for a more gradual approach but proved unable to halt the terrorism that was taking place in the name of the Jiyūtō. On 29 October 1884, just before the largest of these violent popular uprisings, the CHICHIBU INCIDENT, a party convention voted to dissolve the Jiyūtō. On that occasion Itagaki voiced the hope that under more favorable conditions the Jiyūtō would rise again.

2. In October 1887 Gotō Shōjirō began to regroup the former members of the Jiyūtō to prepare for the 1890 elections for the new Diet. He called on all politically concerned people to forget petty differences and unite behind the larger common cause (see DAIDŌ DANKETSU MOVEMENT), the struggle against despotic government. He undertook several speaking tours of Japan to reunite the Jiyūtō. But petty differences proved difficult to overcome, and by 1890 three competing parties had emerged as successors to the former Jiyūtō: the Daidō Kurabu led by KŌNO HIRONAKA, the Daidō Kyōwakai led by Ōi Kentarō, and Itagaki's middle-of-the-road party, the AIKOKU KŌTŌ. Itagaki spent much effort to unite the three factions, and finally in September 1890 he succeeded in establishing the Rikken Jiyūtō (renamed Jiyūtō in March 1891). The new covenant stated that the Jiyūtō would seek to preserve the glory of the imperial institution while expanding the rights of the people. To do so it would be necessary to negotiate equal treaties with the Western powers and establish a parliamentary system with responsible party cabinets. In the first election the Jiyūtō won 130 of the 296 seats in the lower house. Itagaki Taisuke again served as head of the party.

The Jiyūtō and the Kaishintō, which won 40 seats, attempted to use their majority in the lower house to reduce the budget, but both parties (the Jiyūtō especially) continued to be hampered by internal division and government interference. Nevertheless, they won concessions from the government. In 1896 Itagaki was appointed home minister. In 1898 Itagaki and ŌKUMA SHIGENOBU, head of the SHIMPOTŌ (formerly the Kaishintō), decided to form a united front by combining their two parties into the KENSEITŌ. The Meiji oligarchs then turned over the reins of government, hoping to embarrass the opposition. Divided from the start over cabinet appointments, Japan's first party cabinet (see ŌKUMA CABINET) quickly disintegrated; but it was clear that the government could no longer ignore the political parties. One of the oligarchs in particular, ITŌ HIROBUMI, argued that the government must compromise with the parties. Thus, after the Kenseitō split in 1898, former Jiyūtō members rallied around Itō when he formed a new political party, the RIKKEN SEIYŪKAI, in 1900. The politics of compromise had finally given political parties an effective voice in government, but it marked a clear departure from the idealism of the early Jiyūtō.

3. Post–World War II party formed in 1945 by HATOYAMA ICHIRŌ; more properly called the Nihon Jiyūtō. It won the election of 1946, but because Hatoyama had been barred from public office by the OCCUPATION PURGE, YOSHIDA SHIGERU assumed the premiership. In 1948 the Jiyūtō merged with dissidents from the MINSHUTŌ to form the Minshu Jiyūtō (Democratic Liberal Party), but two years later it reorganized as the Jiyūtō (LIBERAL PARTY) after it accepted some of the remnants of the newly dissolved Minshutō. Under Yoshida's leadership it remained the majority party throughout the Occupation years. In 1955 it merged with the NIHON MINSHUTŌ to form the Jiyū Minshutō (LIBERAL DEMOCRATIC PARTY). See also POLITICAL PARTIES.

—— George Akita, *Foundations of Constitutional Government in Modern Japan, 1868–1900* (1967). Itagaki Taisuke, ed, *Jiyūtō shi* (1910). *M. William STEELE*

Jiyūtō shi

(History of the Liberal Party). Two-volume official history of the JIYŪTŌ (Liberal Party); published in 1910. In 1900 a general meeting of the KENSEITŌ (Constitutional Party) decided that a history of its predecessor, the Jiyūtō, should be compiled by a committee headed by Uda Tomoi. A draft was completed the following year and given for further editing to ITAGAKI TAISUKE, the first president of the Jiyūtō and leader of the FREEDOM AND PEOPLE'S RIGHTS MOVEMENT. The narrative, which emphasizes the role of Itagaki and other men from Kōchi Prefecture, ends with the promulgation of the Meiji Constitution in 1889.

jizaikagi

An apparatus for suspending cooking pots or kettles over a traditional Japanese hearth, allowing for rotation of the pot and adjustment of the distance between pot and fire. It usually consisted of a vertically hung bamboo tube through which an iron rod, bent into the shape of a hook at the bottom end, was passed. The hooked end of the iron rod was fed through a hole in a horizontal crosspiece whose pressure against the rod held it at the adjusted height. The horizontal piece was often carved in the decorative shape of a fish, fan, or so-called good luck mallet *(uchide no kozuchi)*. Traditionally there were many taboos associated with the *jizaikagi,* which was considered the lodging place of the hearth god.

MIYAMOTO Mizuo

jizamurai

Medieval yeoman warriors *(bushi)* who instead of serving in or for the shogunate remained in their villages and retained power as local magnates there. The decline of shogunate power late in the Kamakura period (1185–1333) generally allowed powerful landholders (MYŌSHU) to seize actual ruling power in the villages; those who became militarized were known as *jizamurai*. In the Nambokuchō (Northern and Southern Courts) period (1336–92), their power over the alignment of their villages and manors could greatly affect the fate of battles and peasant insurrections. During this time and into the Sengoku (Warring States) period (1467–1568), *jizamurai* gradually became local military rulers (SENGOKU DAIMYŌ), their retainers, or simply rural warriors (GŌSHI). Their on-the-spot village control played a leading role in the formation and establishment of the *daimyō*. See also SAMURAI.

Jizō

One of the most popular BODHISATTVAS in Japanese Buddhism. Jizō (Skt: Kṣitigarbha; "womb of the earth") is usually represented as a monk with a jewel in one hand and a staff in the other. Jizō's vow to aid and benefit all suffering beings has made him an object of popular veneration, often syncretized with native deities, from the Heian period (794–1185) onward. He is in particular regarded as the savior of children and those beings suffering in hell. See also DŌSOJIN.

Robert RHODES

Jōban Coalfield

(Jōban Tanden). Located in southeastern Fukushima and northeastern Ibaraki prefectures, northern Honshū. Situated along the coast of the Pacific Ocean. It produced about 10 percent of the national coal yield at its peak, but numerous mines were almost entirely closed down by the early 1970s.

Jōchō (?–1057)

The most eminent Buddhist sculptor in the Kyōto area during the middle of the Heian period (794–1185). Credited with creating an elegant Japanese style of sculpture *(wayō)*, perfecting the assembled woodblock sculptural technique called *yosegi-zukuri*, and instituting the workshop system (BUSSHO) for the production of Buddhist sculpture. Jōchō received unprecedented recognition: in 1022, in recognition for his work at the temple Hōjōji, he was given the rank of *hokkyō* by FUJIWARA NO MICHINAGA; in 1048, for his sculpture and restoration work at the temple Kōfukuji, he was elevated by the court to the rank of *hōgen*. Jōchō was the first Buddhist sculptor to be honored with these titles, formerly reserved for the highest-ranking members of the Buddhist clergy. This not only contributed to raising the social status of the professional Buddhist sculptor in Jōchō's time, but became an important precedent in later periods for the imperial court's conferring of similar awards on professional artists in all disciplines. Jōchō's single surviving work is the image of

Jizaikagi

A *jizaikagi* with a fish-shaped crosspiece (used to adjust the height). It is suspended from a ceiling beam (not visible) and holds an iron kettle over the embers of a typical open hearth *(irori)*. The surrounding floor is covered with *tatami* mats, on which are placed cushions *(zabuton)* for seating.

Jizō

Statues of Jizō within a temple compound. Such images are often placed along roadsides and dressed, as here, in bibs by worshipers.

Amida, carved in 1053 as the main icon of the Hōōdō (Phoenix Hall) of the temple BYŌDŌIN at Uji.

jōdai

Castellan or keeper of the castle. From the 16th century onward, it was customary for warrior lords to place trusted vassals called *jōdai* in charge of their castles during their absence. During the Edo period (1600–1868) the title was used to designate those officials commanding certain castles on behalf of the Tokugawa shōgun. Initially these officials included the *jōdai* of NIJŌ CASTLE in Kyōto, Sumpu Castle (see SUMPU), ŌSAKA CASTLE, and FUSHIMI CASTLE, but after 1699 only two remained, the Sumpu *jōdai* as a post for a high-ranking bannerman (HATAMOTO) and Ōsaka *jōdai* as a major post for middle-ranking hereditary (FUDAI) *daimyō*. Of the two, the Ōsaka post was by far the more important, being responsible not only for that mighty bastion but also for the behavior of daimyō in western Japan. Holders of the Ōsaka *jōdai* post frequently were promoted to the posts of Kyōto deputy (KYŌTO SHOSHIDAI) and senior councillor (RŌJŪ).

Conrad TOTMAN

Jōdogahama

Coastal area, east of the city of Miyako, Iwate Prefecture, northern Honshū. Faces the Pacific Ocean. Oddly shaped white dolerite rocks contrast with green pine trees. Part of Rikuchū Coast National Park, it is noted as a swimming resort.

Jōdo sect

(Jōdoshū). The school of PURE LAND BUDDHISM founded by HŌNEN (1133–1212), known for its advocacy of NEMBUTSU, the practice of chanting the phrase *Namu Amida Butsu* (I take my refuge in Amida Buddha), for the purpose of *ōjō*, rebirth in AMIDA Buddha's Pure Land in the West. The first of the new Buddhist sects to emerge in the latter part of the Heian period (794–1185), it remains the second largest after its independent subsect, the JŌDO SHIN SECT.

Doctrinal Basis——The Pure Land faith is based on the early Māhāyana corpus of Pure Land *(Sukhāvatīvyūha)* sutras: the *Larger* and *Smaller Pure Land Sutra* and the *Meditation Sutra,* called by Hōnen the "Threefold Pure Land sutras."

Pure Lands *(jōdo)* are realms of purity, the residence of Buddhas and bodhisattvas, in contradistinction to the impure and polluted human realm. Whereas our world has been without a reigning Buddha since the departure of the historical Buddha Śākyamuni, the Pure Land of Amida promises both the illuminating wisdom and eternal presence of its resident Buddha, known according to these attributes as Amitābha (Eternal Light) or Amitāyus (Eternal Life). Amida is also characterized as a Buddha of compassion: formerly the bodhisattva Dharmākara (J: Hōzō), he created his Pure Land through an aeons-long accumulation of merit and power and a series of 48 vows. Among the 48 vows, the 12th and 13th secured the aspects of eternal life and eternal light; these pertain to the absolute or Dharmakāya character of Amida. The 18th vow, the most important, promises rebirth in this realm to all who call on Amida's name 10 times at death; this exemplifies Amida's compassionate response to sinful worldlings. These three vows were regarded by Hōnen as the most central.

Lineage——Among the various lineages of Pure Land teaching in China, Hōnen selected that of Tanluan (T'an-luan; J: Donran), Daochuo (Tao-ch'o; J: Dōshaku), and Shandao (Shan-tao; J: Zendō) as his own patriarchal line. The evolution of Jōdo doctrine is primarily a matter of creative, selective reading of scriptures pointing toward a radical reliance on Amida. Tanluan borrowed the distinction between the Hard Path and the Easy Path made by Nāgārjuna (Indian Māhāyana philosopher, ca AD 150–ca AD 250) in his commentary on a work by Vasubandhu and identified the Easy Path with the Pure Land teachings. Daochuo further differentiated the Pure Land path from that of the sage, ruling out the latter as impossible in this age of *mappō* (the end of the law; see ESCHATOLOGY), dated then to commence in 552. Both Tanluan and Daochuo drew on the distinction between enlightenment through self-power *(jiriki)* and other-power (TARIKI). Finally, Shandao designated vocalization of the *nembutsu* (Ch: *nianfo* or *nien-fo,* literally and originally, "contemplation of the Buddha") as the major and superior means excelling all other spiritual paths. Shandao also defended the thesis that rebirth in the Pure Land *(ōjō)*, hitherto believed to be reserved for deserving bodhisattvas only, was attainable by ordinary men.

Development of Pure Land Faith in Japan——Pure Land piety existed in Japan prior to the emergence of the Jōdo sect. In the Heian period the TENDAI SECT cultivated an Amida-related meditation *(samādhi)* based on "perpetual walking or circumambulation" of the Buddha image and designated special halls for this practice. The SHINGON SECT also venerated Amida as one of the five Wisdom Buddhas *(dhyani-Buddhas)* and enshrined Amida as the chief object of worship in many of the older monasteries at Mt. Kōya (KŌYA-SAN). KŪYA (903–972) chanted the *nembutsu* in marketplaces to the accompaniment of song and dance, and GENSHIN (942–1017) advocated the popular practice of the *nembutsu* and founded fellowships which brought together monks and the laity, nobles and commoners. RYŌNIN (1073–1132) founded the YŪZŪ NEMBUTSU SECT, which taught that the merits of reciting the *nembutsu* accrued both to oneself and others. The Heian nobility often took refuge in Amida and sought to reproduce the serenity and beauty of the Pure Land in their retreats such as the BYŌDŌIN. By late Heian, itinerant monks or HIJIRI were popularizing the *nembutsu,* and the later *Ōjōden* (Legends of Birth in the Pure Land) included commoners and sinful persons as those who could attain the Pure Land through chanting the *nembutsu.*

These Pure Land cults, however, never claimed exclusive status and always remained adjuncts to the larger Tendai and Shingon traditions, in which the easy path of faith was judged expedient but ultimately inferior to the path of meditation. Nor had consciousness of sin become so radical as to encourage doubts concerning the efficacy or presumptuousness of good works. Not even Genshin doubted the necessity of *bodhicitta,* the aspiration for enlightenment. Hōnen broke with this tradition when he discovered Shandao's *Guanjing xuanyi (Kuan-ching hsüan-i;* J: *Kangyō gengi;* On the Hidden Meaning of the Meditation Sutra). Instead of interpreting this work as a justification of the meditative visualization of the Pure Land, Hōnen saw Shandao as ultimately endorsing the vocalization of the *nembutsu* as a superior path grounded in Amida's vows. Reliance upon faith was thereby elevated above mystical contemplation, and faith in Amida's vow superseded *bodhicitta* as the basis for rebirth in the Pure Land. Though himself a scholarly monk who wrote in Chinese, Hōnen repudiated pride in learning and mere preceptual purity, justifying the *nembutsu* as the universal path because all other means—scholarship, observances of the monastic precepts, temple building, and so on—would always exclude some people who cannot pursue them from salvation, whereas everyone can practice the *nembutsu.*

Foundation of the Jōdo Sect in Japan——The founding of the Jōdo sect is traditionally dated to 1175, the year Hōnen left his mountain hermitage and descended to the capital of HEIANKYŌ (now Kyōto) to preach the selective or exclusive practice of *nembutsu.* It is now thought by some that Hōnen no more anticipated founding a new sect than Luther intended to split his church. It is likely that as he offered his interpretation of the Threefold Pure Land sutras in an exegesis of 1190, his departure from tradition was such that his pioneering and definitive personal statement of 1198, the *Senchaku hongan nembutsu shū* (also known as the SENCHAKUSHŪ), became inevitable. By then, Hōnen's doctrinal independence was firmly established as he professed to "rely solely on Shandao." In a trance *(samādhi)* Hōnen had a vision of Shandao with a half-golden body, a completely golden body being one of the conventional extraordinary attributes of a Buddha's body. (In China Shandao had already come to be regarded as a manifestation of Amida.) This mystical experience, reported in 1198 in the privately circulated editions of Hōnen's *Senchakushū,* legitimized a divinely instituted beginning for the Jōdo sect: Hōnen had received the true understanding from Shandao; henceforth Hōnen and Shandao were regarded by Pure Land adherents as manifestations of the two attendant bodhisattvas of Amida Buddha. An independent sect was proclaimed.

No school could be established without the permission of the state and the recognition of the RITSU SECT in Nara, charged with the supervision of ordination platforms (required of any lineage). Hōnen's willingness to forego this world for the Pure Land and his renunciation of the monastic precepts as a criterion for salvation enabled him to challenge both state and church officialdom.

In turning his back on the elite path of the sage or *arhat,* Hōnen undermined the heart of Tendai Buddhism: *ichinen sanzen,* meditative realization of the absolute nature of the universe ("the three thousand worlds") as immanent in the here-and-now ("in one instant of thought"). Moreover, in his reverence for the Pure Land, Hōnen forsook this world and the Shingon practice of sanctifying it with magic, spells, and an immanentalist philosophy based on the notion of a priori enlightenment (HONGAKU). In rejecting the temporal and ecclesiastical authorities, Hōnen injected the element of spiritual independence—what the scholar Ienaga Saburō (b 1913) termed the logic of negation *(hitei no ronri)*—which was to characterize Kamakura Buddhism. Because of that, he was banned and exiled. Hōnen was subsequently criticized by the Kegon sect master MYŌE (1173–1232) for eliminating the *arhat* path and the ideal of *bodhicitta;* and by NICHIREN (1222–82), who, above all others, assailed the schism created by the "evil" Hōnen, whom he charged with betrayal of this world, its Buddha (Śākyamuni), and the holism of Ekayāna (One Vehicle) doctrine, which had been maintained by the Tendai sect.

Hōnen did not advocate an abstract faith *(shinjin,* more the province of SHINRAN) but favored a simple means—the "10 recitations" of the *nembutsu*—for achieving *ōjō.* Rebirth in the Pure Land at the moment of death remained central to the Jōdo sect, although in the Edo period (1600–1868) the two Pure Land sects became somewhat homogenized, and the influence of Shinran's understanding of the Pure Land as an ever-present state of grace came to be felt. Yet the Jōdo sect largely retained its original abhorrence of the world and desire for the pure beyond and did not as readily resanctify the world or secularize the vocation by reintroducing the ideal of original enlightenment *(hongaku)* as did the Jōdo Shin sect. See also RAIGŌZU.

▪ ——Bukkyō Daigaku, ed, *Hōnen shōnin kenkyū* (1975). Ishii Kyōdō, *Senchakushū no kenkyū* (1951). Katsuki Jōkō, ed, *Jōdoshū kaisōki no kenkyū* (1957). Koten Isan no Kai, ed, *Ōjōden no kenkyū* (1968). Shigematsu Akihisa, *Nihon Jōdokyō seiritsu katei no kenkyū* (1964).   Whalen LAI

Jōdo Shin sect

(Jōdo Shinshū; often called the True Pure Land sect in English). One of the traditional 13 schools of Japanese sect Buddhism and a major form of PURE LAND BUDDHISM. Its founder, SHINRAN (1173–1263), had no intention of establishing an independent movement and used the term Jōdo Shinshū to denote the "true essence" *(shinshū)* of Pure Land teaching as expounded by his teacher HŌNEN, but the term later came to designate the sect *(shū)* that evolved around Shinran's teachings. The year 1224, one of the dates suggested for the compilation of his major work, the KYŌGYŌSHINSHŌ, is considered to be the year of the founding of the sect. It was not until 1872, however, that Jōdo Shinshū became the generally accepted name of the sect, which until then was called Ikkōshū, Montoshū, or HONGANJI. Today it is frequently referred to simply as Shinshū, and sometimes in the West as Shin Buddhism. Jōdo Shinshū, consisting of 10 branches, claims the largest following among the Buddhist sects in Japan.

According to Shinran, the Pure Land tradition originated beyond history in the Primal Vow of the Buddha AMIDA to save all mankind, the profound import of the Primal Vow becoming progressively clarified as human degradation becomes manifest in ineffectual religious practices, spiritual bankruptcy, brutish egoism, and social chaos. Historically, such an age was called *mappō* (literally, the end-time of the Buddhist Law; see ESCHATOLOGY). It was in the midst of *mappō* that Hōnen founded an independent JŌDO SECT in 1175. Hōnen stressed the singular power of the Primal Vow, and, rejecting all existing forms of Buddhism, proclaimed the recitation of the name of Amida Buddha (NEMBUTSU) to be the sole practice suited for the age and relevant to human needs. Among the many disciples who gathered around this revolutionary figure was Shinran.

When the emerging *nembutsu* movement, centered in Kyōto, was persecuted in 1207 for both real and imagined social abuses, Hōnen was exiled to Tosa Province (now Kōchi Prefecture), several of his disciples were executed, and Shinran was banished to Echigo Province (now part of Niigata Prefecture) facing the Sea of Japan. Though subsequently pardoned, Hōnen died in the spring of 1212 shortly after his return to Kyōto. Shinran was pardoned in 1211, but he chose to remain in Echigo and a few years later moved with his family to the Kantō area. When he eventually returned to Kyōto around the year 1235, he found several of Hōnen's disciples preaching the *nembutsu* path, each according to his own interpretation. Shinran, attempting to transmit his master's true teaching, poured his creative energies into composing religious poetry, writing commentaries, copying texts, sending countless letters to his followers in Kantō, and rewriting and revising his major work, *Kyōgyōshinshō*. The *nembutsu* path taught by Hōnen's disciples eventually developed into the five branches of the Jōdo sect, and Shinran's teaching led to the formation of the Jōdo Shin sect.

The fortunes of Shinran's sect remained at low ebb following his death in 1262. His disciples and his youngest daughter Kakushin Ni (1224–83) erected a monument in his memory at Yoshimizu, Kyōto, transferring his ashes from nearby Ōtani. Kakushin Ni and her descendants became caretakers of the place, and her grandson Kakunyo (1270–1351), attempting to unify all the followers of Shinran into a single sect, named the mausoleum Honganji, Temple of the Primal Vow. With the appearance of the energetic RENNYO (1415–99), the 8th head abbot of Honganji, the sect showed a sudden, dramatic growth both in the number of followers and in social impact. The Jōdo Shin sect became one of the most influential Buddhist movements, especially among the masses. Later, because of a succession struggle following the death of the 11th abbot Kennyo (1543–92), the Honganji split into two factions, the Honganji branch (Nishi or West Honganji) and the Ōtani branch (Higashi or East Honganji). In addition, there developed eight other rather small branches of the Jōdo Shin sect, such as the Takada, Bukkōji, and the Kōshō. Some of these branches were directly descended from Shinran, whereas others were descended from Shinran's disciples. Dur-

ing the Edo period (1600–1868), the Jōdo Shin sect secured a permanent place in society.

At the time of the Meiji Restoration (1868), the government tried to unite the nation by means of Shintoism and suppressed Buddhism (see HAIBUTSU KISHAKU), and it was the Jōdo Shin sect which led the Buddhist world in opposing this imperial policy. During this time, the thinker and reformer KIYOZAWA MANSHI (1863–1903), among others, introduced Shinran's thought to a wide audience of non-Shinshū readers and intellectuals, resulting in a renewed appreciation of Shinran's position in Japanese history.

The doctrines of the Jōdo Shin sect are based on the three central sutras of the Pure Land tradition: the Larger *Sukhāvatī-vyūha*, the Smaller *Sukhāvatī-vyūha*, and the *Amitāyurdhyāna-sūtra*, as well as on the writings of the seven patriarchs: Nāgārjuna (ca AD 150–ca AD 250) and Vasubandhu (5th century) of India; Tanluan (T'an-luan; 476–542), Daochuo (Tao-cho'o; 562–645), and Shandao (Shan-tao; 613–681) of China; and Genshin (942–1017) and Hōnen of Japan; and on the writings of Shinran and the abbots who succeeded him.

The basic goal of Shin Buddhism coincides with that of Mahāyāna Buddhism: realizing the wisdom to see things, including the self, as they truly are; this in turn inspires the life of true compassion. In this tradition, however, such a wisdom is brought forth from within each person by the transforming powers of Amida's Primal Vow and not through calculative thinking or self-generated effort. Since the working of the Primal Vow is fundamental, the task of the Shin practitioner is to comprehend fully the origin, content, and aim of the Primal Vow through constant hearing, so that he is made to realize, together with Shinran, that "When I ponder on the compassionate vow of Amida, established through five *kalpas* of profound meditation, it is for myself, Shinran, alone. So I feel even more deeply grateful to the Primal Vow which is designed to save me for I am a being bound by so much karmic evil." (TANNISHŌ, Epilogue.)

Karmic evil, or the source of suffering rooted in the very nature of human existence, prevents man from manifesting true wisdom and true compassion. All forms of self-generated religious endeavor, whether the practice of meditation, or the upholding of precepts and good works, are neither satisfying nor productive. The only meaningful act, according to the Pure Land teaching, is the *nembutsu*, the invocation of the name of Amida Buddha, because it is not the act of man but of Amida, containing both his call from and our response to true and real life. Thus, it is called the great practice that comes from the vow of true compassion.

The urge to recite the *nembutsu*, then, comes from the fathomless depth of true compassion awakening man to the depth of karmic evil. These two, true compassion and karmic evil, form the twofold structure of *shinjin* or faith which is neither belief in a higher power nor hope for miraculous redemption. *Shinjin*, according to Shinran, is the true and real mind of Amida which enters the defiled mind of man, making it possible for him to entrust himself completely to the true and real life that is Amida. The dynamic quality of *shinjin*, although unknown to the person, comes from *dharmakāya* or the body of reality itself. When this occurs in the depth of self, one is said to be born in the Pure Land and to attain the stage of nonretrogression here and now. This goes against the traditional view of the Pure Land as the place to be born after death, attain the stage of nonretrogression, and realize enlightenment. Shinran's radical view is based upon the concept of twofold *dharmakāya*: *dharmakāya* of suchness, which is nameless and formless, and *dharmakāya* of compassionate means, manifested in the name and form of Amida. The *dharmakāya* of suchness *(hosshō-hosshin)*, being of uncreated, timeless nature, permeates all of existence, including the hearts and minds of people, forming the basis for *shinjin*. Nevertheless, it is only through the *dharmakāya* of compassionate means *(hōben-hosshin)* that such an awakening is made possible. The manifestation of *dharmakāya* enables Shinran to assert that birth in the Pure Land and attainment of nonretrogression take place here and now in this life.

The immediacy of birth in the Pure Land, found in *shinjin*, did not eliminate the idea of birth in such a land after death, but here again Shinran's view differs somewhat from that of earlier Pure Land teachers. The traditional view was that birth in the Pure Land meant entry into an ideal environment for Buddhist practice. For Shinran, however, the moment of death, when one sheds all karmic limitations, is at the same time the moment of supreme enlightenment when *dharmakāya* becomes completely manifest. But this moment of unexcelled enlightenment does not mean stasis and quiescence, for it is the beginning of the work of true compassion to save all beings in the ocean of suffering. Nothing remains static in the world of enlightenment, and one now becomes an active participant in the working of the Primal Vow. See also SHINRAN   *Taitetsu* UNNO

Jōei Shikimoku → Goseibai Shikimoku

Jōetsu

City in southwestern Niigata Prefecture, central Honshū, on the Sea of Japan. Formed by the merger of the cities of Takada and Naoetsu in 1971, it is the political, cultural, and industrial center of the region. Naoetsu was designated a provincial capital in the 8th century and prospered as a POST-STATION TOWN and port from the 14th century. Takada developed as a castle town under the UESUGI FAMILY and later under the Matsudaira. At present, heavy and chemical industries predominate in the Naoetsu district, and light industries (foodstuffs, skiing equipment) are being developed in the Takada district. Of interest are the remains of the fortress built by UESUGI KENSHIN and the temple Gochi Kokubunji, associated with SHINRAN. Jōetsu is also known as the birthplace of skiing in Japan (it was introduced by the Austrian military officer Theodore von LERCH in 1911); a ski festival is held at the mountain Kanayasan every winter. Pop: 127,843.

Jogaku zasshi

(Magazine of Women's Learning). First major women's magazine in Japan, with 526 published issues between 1885 and 1904. Originally called *Jogaku shinshi* in 1884, it was founded by Kondō Kenzō, IWA-MOTO YOSHIHARU, and Ōba Sōkichi. Iwamoto became its chief editor after Kondō's death in 1886. Starting as a Christian ethics magazine devoted to enlightening Japanese women about education, foreign affairs, and culture, it later focused more on literature and published works by such women writers as KISHIDA TOSHIKO (under the pen name Shōen), WAKAMATSU SHIZUKO, KOZAI SHIKIN, and MIYAKE KAHO. Its special literary issues, *Jogaku zasshi bunga-kukai,* led to the independent launching in 1893 of the important literary journal *Bungakukai* (Literary World) by KITAMURA TŌ-KOKU, SHIMAZAKI TŌSON, and other young writers.

Jōganjigawa

River in eastern Toyama Prefecture, central Honshū, originating in the Hida Mountains and flowing into Toyama Bay. It forms an alluvial fan at the entry into the Toyama Plain. The lower reaches are a raised-bed river *(tenjōgawa).* The Shōmyō Falls of the Shōmyō-gawa, a tributary, are the highest falls in Japan with a head of 350 m (1,148 ft). Water is used for irrigation and for generating electric power. Length: 56 km (35 mi).

Jōgashima

Island off the tip of the Miura Peninsula, Kanagawa Prefecture, central Honshū. It is connected with the Miura Peninsula by a bridge, 575 m (1,886 ft) long, completed in 1960. The island is famous because of KITAHARA HAKUSHŪ's poem "Jōgashima no ame" (The Rain of Jōgashima). A tourist area, the island makes up the Jōga-shima Prefectural Park. Area: 0.7 sq km (0.3 sq mi).

Jōgū Shōtoku Hōōtei setsu

(Traditions concerning His Holiness, Prince Shōtoku). Title of a small corpus of documents concerning Prince SHŌTOKU, one of the most influential political leaders of the 7th century. The original book is said to have been stored at the temple HŌRYŪJI in Nara. The only extant copy is a manuscript preserved at the temple CHION'IN in Kyōto that is believed to have been copied from the original by a priest of the Hōryūji some time during the Heian period (794–1185). The records include genealogical information on Shōtoku, a transcription of the text of the *Tenjukoku shūchō*—an embroidered mandala dedicated to the prince's memory by his widow—and a statement regarding the date of the introduction of Buddhism to Japan. The documents are valuable in that they supplement the information given in the KOJIKI (712) and the NIHON SHOKI (720), Japan's earliest chronicles.   *Michiko Y.* AOKI

Jōhei and Tengyō Rebellions → Fujiwara no Sumitomo; Taira no Masakado

jōheisō

(literally, "ever-normal granary"). Government granaries established in ancient Japan to stabilize the price of rice. In years of abundant harvest the government bought rice cheaply and stored it; in years of famine or drought the government sold the stored rice to lower the price. The idea was originally developed under the Former Han dynasty (206 BC–AD 8) of China and was first introduced to the provinces of Japan in 759, during the reign of Emperor Junnin (733–765; r 758–764), at the suggestion of FUJIWARA NO NAKA-MARO. The intent of the *jōheisō* was soon lost sight of, however, and the granaries were only occasionally effective during the Heian period (794–1185) before being abolished during the Kamakura period (1185–1333). The idea was revived by several *daimyō* domains after the TEMPŌ FAMINE in the 1830s.   *G. Cameron* HURST III

Johnston Report

Also known as the Draper–Johnston Report. Report of a 15-member committee sent to Japan in March 1948 by the secretary of the US Army to evaluate political and economic conditions in Japan and Korea. The group was led by Percy H. Johnston, chairman of the board of directors, Chemical Bank of New York, and William H. Draper, assistant secretary of the army. They presented their report on 18 May 1948. Aside from discussion of currency exchange rates and foreign investment, the report recommended a lenient reparations settlement and other measures to accelerate Japan's economic recovery. It reflected the shift in emphasis in the policy of the American OCCUPATION authorities in the years 1947 to 1950 from political and social reform to economic stability and rehabilitation. See also DODGE LINE; SHOUP MISSION.

jōin

(surplus employees). Workers who must leave their jobs because management has no further need of them. To avoid having to let surplus workers go, Japanese enterprises take such steps as stopping further hiring of middle-aged workers, limiting overtime, discontinuing the contracts of or firing temporary workers, or instituting temporary lay-offs. They may also take such steps as job rotation, transferring workers to other departments, or transferring employees from the parent company to a subsidiary (see SHUKKŌ). Only when these above steps cannot improve the situation would a regular employee be dismissed.

In 1975, when employment declined more drastically than in any other recent year, 45 percent of the enterprises that made adjustments put limits on overtime, 45 percent limited their hiring of new employees, 19 percent fired temporary workers, 17 percent made temporary lay-offs, and only 6 percent dismissed regular employees.

Generally, when an enterprise dismisses a regular employee, the employee receives a pension and special retirement benefits which would not normally be due him until regular retirement for reasons of age. In addition, help is provided through unemployment insurance benefits distributed by the government. Individual enterprises are also responsible for providing half pay for 75 days to workers on temporary lay-off (two-thirds pay for 75 days to workers of minor enterprises). See EMPLOYMENT, FORMS OF.   KURITA Ken

Joint Staff College

(Tōgō Bakuryō Gakkō). Educational institution for field grade officers in the SELF DEFENSE FORCES. It specializes in teaching and research in the field of military operations and administration. The college is supervised by the JOINT STAFF COUNCIL and headed by the principal executive officer of the Council's Secretariat. The school is located at the Ichigaya post of the Self Defense Forces in Tōkyō.   ICHIKI Toshio

Joint Staff Council

(Tōgō Bakuryō Kaigi). The advisory organization for the director-general of the DEFENSE AGENCY. It consists of the chairman, who is the highest ranking officer of the SELF DEFENSE FORCES, and the chiefs of staff of the Ground, Maritime, and Air Self Defense Forces. The council's principal function is to assist the director-general of the Defense Agency in drawing up an overall defense plan and in coordinating joint military operations. There is a Secretariat with five sections in charge of general affairs and personnel, information, strategy, logistics, and planning. The council also supervises the JOINT STAFF COLLEGE. *Ichiki Toshio*

joint-stock company

(*kabushiki kaisha*, also pronounced *kabushiki-gaisha;* abbreviated as KK). The *kabushiki kaisha* is the Japanese equivalent of the joint-stock company or limited liability public company and the most common form of business entity in Japan. In 1975 business entities that had adopted this organizational form accounted for some 840,000 business establishments, employing over 18 million workers, and were capitalized at over ¥17 trillion (US $57 billion). Most *kabushiki kaisha* are small by American standards; the overwhelming majority are capitalized at less than $230,000, and only some 460 companies, operating about 37,000 establishments and employing 3.5 million people, have a capital fund in excess of $25 million. By 1978 this number had increased to 533 companies.

Any business enterprise, large or small, is free to incorporate as a *kabushiki kaisha*. Virtually all such business entities are domestically run; the number of foreign-controlled *kabushiki kaisha* is small, as there are probably fewer than 1,500 foreign-affiliated corporations in Japan.

Governing law. The *kabushiki kaisha* is a juristic entity created by the COMMERCIAL CODE. The parts of the code dealing with companies were first put into force in 1893, prior to the enactment of the code in 1899. The company provisions were revised in important respects in 1951 under the influence of the Occupation authorities and subsequent revisions occurred in 1955, 1966, 1974, and most recently in June 1981, taking effect on 1 October 1982.

Formation. The *kabushiki kaisha* must be formed by at least seven promoters, who must prepare, subscribe to, and register articles of incorporation in the prescribed form. A heavy onus is placed on the promoters, or incorporators, who among other things are personally liable for all acts performed in establishing the company. They owe a fiduciary duty to the company in relation to those acts and must personally take up shares in the company. The promoters must also appoint directors and auditors at the time of formation, and these appointees are immediately required to petition the courts for the appointment of an inspector who must examine the promoters' activities. The promoters meanwhile call for subscriptions to the share capital of the company, and when the shares have been fully paid for and allotted they must call a STOCKHOLDERS' GENERAL MEETING which receives reports from the inspector and the promoters and appoints directors and auditors.

Capital. The authorized capital of the company and the number of units into which the capital is to be divided must be specified in the articles together with the total number of shares to be issued at the time of formation. Shares may be par value or no-par-value, but the actual division of authorized capital into these two kinds of shares must be stated in the articles at the time of registration. From 1 October 1982 the minimum value of a share was raised to ¥50,000, and a par-value share may not be issued for less than its par value. If no-par-value shares are issued on formation, the minimum price must also be stated in the articles. Companies whose shares were listed on a Stock Exchange were required to consolidate their existing, issued shares into ¥50,000 units on 1 October 1982.

In contrast to most Anglo-American corporation laws, the Commercial Code specifies that at least one-quarter of the total authorized number of shares must be issued on formation, and so the actual paid-up capital of the company bears some relationship to the potential capital fund. The promoters therefore must be more realistic in arriving at a figure for authorized capital. The liability of the shareholder is limited to the par value of the share, or the amount that he has agreed to pay if he holds no-par-value shares. The capital structure of the *kabushiki kaisha* therefore resembles the American joint-stock or British public company.

Shares in the *kabushiki kaisha* are transferable, although it is permissible for the articles to provide that the prior approval of the directors is necessary. The Japanese corporation may acquire its own shares when it wishes to reduce its capital, when it takes over a company that is in fact one of its own shareholders, or when it is required by the Commercial Code to purchase shares from disgruntled shareholders or when required to purchase fractional holdings as a consequence of the unit system of shareholdings introduced in

October 1982. Different classes of shares may be issued, and par-value shares may be converted into no-par-value shares, thereby giving the company flexibility in its capital raisings.

The *kabushiki kaisha* may raise new capital by issuing new shares after incorporation or by issuing DEBENTURES. The authorized share capital may be raised to a higher amount by a special resolution, while new shares may be subject to preemptive rights vested in existing shareholders. A right of preemption is not automatically required by law but may be included in the articles or granted by the directors. The company may not invite subscriptions for debentures in excess of the total amount of the stated capital and reserves as shown in the accounts of the company. No new debentures may be issued until all previous debentures have been fully paid up by the existing debenture holders, and each debenture must be at least ¥20 in value. A system of convertible debentures was incorporated into the Commercial Code in 1982. On the other hand, the company may by special resolution decrease the capital of the company, subject to any objections from debenture holders, without obtaining a court order.

Management. The management of the company is divided between the stockholders' general meeting, the board of directors, and the statutory auditors. The first two organs play roles similar to those of their Anglo-American counterparts, but the auditors potentially may play a more significant part in the management of the affairs of the company, particularly since the 1974 and 1981 reforms of the auditing provisions of the Commercial Code. The reforms of the Occupation (1945–52) significantly altered the balance of power among these three organs of management. Prior to 1949 the general meeting was the supreme authority in all matters, and a resolution of the general meeting could bind the company on any issue or in any transaction. The Commercial Code, in article 230–2, now adopts what is generally thought to be the Anglo-American approach, and the general meeting has power only to pass resolutions on matters prescribed in the Commercial Code or in the articles of incorporation. There must be an annual general meeting, and other meetings may be held at such times as the board or 3 percent of the shareholders determine. For a quorum to be established, the members present and voting at a meeting must represent one-half of the total issued capital of the company, and ordinary resolutions can be carried only if they are supported by half of those members. In general each share carries one vote, although the company may not vote its own shares, and preference shareholders may be denied a vote.

The concept of a board of directors was also introduced in 1949. Prior to that date each director possessed a general agency authority and could bind the company subject to any limitations in the articles. The board is now elected solely by the general meeting, and the articles of incorporation may not require that the directors be shareholders. There must be at least three directors, each of whom may be appointed for a term of up to two years subject to reappointment. The general meeting may also remove a director at any time by special resolution. The corporation's affairs are now entrusted to the board, whose decisions are arrived at by a simple majority vote at a board meeting. Reforms in 1981 disqualify certain people from board membership (art. 259–2) and require that specified decisions must be taken by the board (art. 260–2). The directors are individually required to observe the provisions of the Civil Code relating to mandates and to fulfill a general duty to act in good faith in the interests of the corporation.

The 1974 reform of the auditing system effectively divided *kabushiki kaisha* into three groups and established three different auditing procedures. The 1981 reforms significantly refined these procedures. All companies with capital in excess of $2.5 million are now classified as large corporations; their accounts must be audited by a certified public accountant, and they must have two statutory auditors whose role has been increased. The statutory auditor is under a duty to be a guardian of the corporate interest vis-à-vis the directors, a position not unlike the prewar role of the auditor in Japan. The auditor must supervise the directors in the performance of all their duties and has significant powers to assist him in discharging his responsibilities, including the right to attend board meetings which was added in 1981. Medium-sized enterprises, whose paid-up capital fund falls in the range $500,000 to $2.5 million, are not required to have their accounts audited by chartered public accountants, but the provisions governing the role of the statutory auditor are exactly the same as those for large enterprises. The position of the statutory auditor in small corporations, whose paid-up capital fund is less than $500,000, continues as before the 1974 reforms. Significantly, the auditor of a small enterprise is not subject to the same onerous standard of care in the performance of his duties as is imposed on the auditor in larger enterprises by the 1974 provisions.

Rights of minority shareholders. The minority shareholder in Japan is subject to the same sorts of disincentives to challenge the decisions of the board of directors that confront his counterpart in other corporate systems. The situation is complicated in Japan because of the relatively high level of debt financing, which tends to diminish the importance of the shareholder. Although minority shareholders have a specific right under article 267 of the Commercial Code to bring an action against directors, the imposition in most cases of a sizable advance payment as a security against the costs of a successful defense by the directors operates as a significant deterrent to this form of private action. The 1981 reforms do give the holder of 1 percent of the issued stock or 300 shares the right to submit proposals to the general meeting of shareholders, to demand explanations from directors and statutory auditors, and to ask a court to appoint an inspector to investigate the conduct of a meeting.

The *kabushiki kaisha* is very similar to the joint-stock or limited liability public company form and fulfills a corresponding role in the Japanese economy. Overseas lawyers have had little difficulty in adjusting to the minor differences in relation to incorporation, capital structure, and management rules. The *kabushiki kaisha* is the most important of the corporate forms available under Japanese law for commercial enterprise, both national and international. See also UNLIMITED PARTNERSHIP COMPANY; LIMITED PARTNERSHIP COMPANY; and LIMITED LIABILITY COMPANY.

■——Dan Fenno Henderson, *Foreign Enterprise in Japan* (1973). Shin'ichirō Michida, "The Legal Structure for Economic Enterprise: Some Aspects of Japanese Commercial Law," in Arthur Taylor von Mehren, ed, *Law in Japan: The Legal Order in a Changing Society* (1963). Shin Motoki, Takeo Kosugi, and William D. Johnson, "Explanation of the Amended Stock Corporation Law," *The Japan Business Law Review* (1981). Ōmori Tadao and Yazawa Makoto, *Chūshaku kaisha hō*, 10 vols (1967–). M. Smith, "Comment; The 1974 Revisions to the Commercial Code," *Law in Japan: An Annual* (1975). Makoto Yazawa, "The Legal Structure for Corporate Enterprise: Shareholder-Management Relations under Japanese Law," in Arthur Taylor von Mehren, ed, *Law in Japan: The Legal Order in a Changing Society* (1963). Malcolm D. SMITH

joint ventures

(*gōben kaisha*). Companies jointly owned by Japanese and foreign interests. Japan has more joint ventures between domestic and foreign interests than the United States or Europe, for a number of reasons. First, Japan restricted entry of foreign capital during the 1950s, 1960s, and early 1970s, so non-Japanese companies found it impossible to set up wholly owned business ventures in significant industries. In response, foreign firms usually sought a Japanese partner to work out a joint investment. Second, Japanese strongly resist takeovers and acquisitions, even by other Japanese, except in dire circumstances. A joint venture allows a foreign firm access to Japanese staff and expertise, which the foreign firm would otherwise have to build, at great expense of time and money, on its own.

Success for joint ventures of Japanese and foreign companies has varied. In some cases, the Japanese side has devoted some of its best talent and resources to the venture, while the foreign company has provided technology, capital, or other resources. The result has been development of successful companies. In other cases, the Japanese partner has used the joint venture to tie down a potential competitor. (Most joint venture partners are in the same or closely related industries.) This has led to serious management problems or abandonment of the venture by the foreign or the Japanese company. The joint venture has advantages, but most business analysts think greater variety in forms of participation by foreigners in the Japanese market, including wholly owned ventures and acquisitions, might be in Japan's long-term interest. Since the 1970s there have also been increasing numbers of joint ventures involving Japanese firms in foreign countries. See also MULTINATIONAL ENTERPRISES.

C. Tait RATCLIFFE

Jōjitsu school

Buddhist school centered on the study of the *Jōjitsuron* (Skt: *Satyasiddhi-śāstra* or "Treatise on Establishing Reality") written by the Indian Buddhist scholar Harivarman (ca 250–350), of which the Sanskrit original has been lost. Kumārajīva (344–413), the Central-

Asian translator of Buddhist philosophical works, translated the text into Chinese, and his disciples, such as Sengdao (Seng-tao, 362–457), founded a tradition based on this treatise. It was studied intensively in the 5th and 6th centuries but lost popularity thereafter. The treatise emphasizes *śūnyatā* (J: *kū*; see EMPTINESS) as the middle way, negating the dichotomy between the all-things-non-existent and all-things-existent theories. It draws upon central teachings of Mahāyāna Buddhism to interpret critically the Hīnayāna Sarvastivādin school and appears as a bridge between the two Buddhist traditions. It arrived in Japan via Korea with the SANRON SCHOOL and was counted among the six Buddhist schools of Nara (see NARA BUDDHISM). It was not popular enough to form a sect and was treated later as a part of the Sanron school. MATSUNAMI Yoshihiro

jōka machi → castle towns

jōkō

Abbreviation of *dajō tennō* (retired sovereign), the character for *nō* being also read as *kō*. A formal title given to sovereigns upon abdication, although from the middle of the Heian period (794–1185) onward they were more commonly known as *in* ("cloistered" sovereigns). A retired emperor who took formal Buddhist vows was called *dajō hōō* or simply HŌŌ (priestly retired sovereign). The title *jōkō* was first assumed by Empress JITŌ at her abdication in 697 and became standard thereafter. In the period 1087–1192, when retired emperors dominated the government (see INSEI), there were often several retired emperors at a given time, designated as senior retired emperor (*hon'in* or *ichiin*), newly retired emperor (*shin'in*), and the like. G. Cameron HURST III

Jokō aishi

(Tragic History of Women Workers). Book about women textile workers by Hosoi Wakizō (1897–1925); published in 1925. With the writings of YOKOYAMA GENNOSUKE and the 1903 government report SHOKKŌ JIJŌ, it is one of the best-known books on workers during Japan's earlier stages of industrialization. *Jokō aishi* gives a comprehensive description of the poor working conditions in textile mills; it was based on the personal experience of Hosoi and his wife Toshio (b 1902) as textile workers and labor activists (both had participated in the KAMEIDO INCIDENT).

In the 1920s textile mills employed nearly 40 percent of the industrial work force, and over 80 percent of the textile workers were women. Mostly young farm girls, they provided a generally cheap, docile, and efficient work force. Harsh working conditions and long hours in factories were of course common throughout the world, but Hosoi contended that Japan's situation was unique because Japanese companies justified their exploitation by claiming that they had assumed the role of surrogate parents, teaching young women the traditional virtues of discipline and obedience while closely supervising them in the crowded company dormitories. However, many such women tried to escape, and others frequently fell ill and died.

Hosoi's book, appearing only one month before his death, was widely read but failed to produce any substantial changes in policy or practice. With the arrival of the SHŌWA DEPRESSION in 1930 and Japan's militarism in the 1930s and 1940s, labor and social reform movements lost support. Thus it was only after World War II that working conditions in factories substantially improved. See also WOMEN IN THE LABOR FORCE. Masako M. ŌSAKO

jokotoba

(preface). Also called *joshi* or *jo*. A phrase of variable length preceding the main statement of a poem and joined to it by an implied metaphorical relationship, similarity of sound, or wordplay. In the following poem by Taira no Sadabumi (also called Taira no Sadafun; d 923) from the KOKINSHŪ (no. 823), the first imperially commissioned collection of WAKA poetry compiled about 905, the first three lines are a preface linked to the statement of the poem by a pun on the word *uramite* ("to feel bitter" or "to see the underside"):

Akikaze no	A teasing glance is all,
Fukiuragaesu	White underleaves of arrowroot
Kuzu no ha no	Tossed by the autumn wind—
Uramite mo nao	Though bitter thoughts find vent,
Urameshiki kana	Unspoken depths of bitterness remain.

When the relationship between the *jokotoba* and the main statement is weak, the effect of the preface is largely decorative; where the metaphorical connection is close, however, the preface functions like a simile. The preface resembles the MAKURA KOTOBA ("pillow word" or conventional epithet) in that it modifies the main statement of the poem. The *makura kotoba*, however, usually occupied only one line and modified a single word, while the *jokotoba* could extend over as many as three or four lines and modify a phrase of some length. Both the *jokotoba* and *makura kotoba* show the tendency of early Japanese poets to use preposited figurative elements.

Susan Downing VIDEEN

Jōkyū Disturbance

(Jōkyū no Ran). Attempt by the retired emperor GO-TOBA in 1221 (Jōkyū 3) to overthrow the KAMAKURA SHOGUNATE. The establishment of a military government in Kamakura had been a considerable blow to the imperial court in Kyōto, and the court nobility was looking for a chance to regain power. The death in 1199 of the shogunate's founder, MINAMOTO NO YORITOMO, sowed seeds of unrest among the vassals (gokenin) of the shogunate, and the murder in 1219 of the third shōgun, MINAMOTO NO SANETOMO, brought further internal strife. The court nobles were quick to seize the opportunity. Rallying around Go-Toba, they issued a decree in 1221 calling for chastisement of the shogunal regent (shikken) HŌJŌ YO-SHITOKI and formed a punitive expedition. In response, Yoshitoki and HŌJŌ MASAKO, Yoritomo's widow, rallied the shogunate's forces. A large army under HŌJŌ YASUTOKI marched on Kyōto and defeated the supporters of the court. The shogunate then deposed Emperor Chūkyō (1218–34), who had reigned for barely two months, and placed Emperor Go-Horikawa (1212–34; r 1221–32) on the throne; it also exiled the retired emperors Go-Toba and JUN-TOKU. The shogunate further confiscated the lands of the nobles and warriors who had sided with the retired emperors and assigned them to vassals who were designated *shimpo* or "newly appointed" JITŌ (estate stewards); in Kyōto it established special shogunal deputies (ROKUHARA TANDAI) to keep the court under strict surveillance and to administer the western provinces. As a result of the Jōkyū Disturbance not only was it made clear who ruled Japan, but the Kamakura shogunate further consolidated its position by handsomely rewarding its vassals.

jōmen

Method used during the Edo period (1600–1868) to assess the annual land tax (NENGU). In contrast to the earlier KEMI, which assessed taxes according to the actual yield and differed from year to year, the *jōmen* method was determined by averaging the harvest over a span of time, commonly 5, 10, or 20 years, and remained fixed thereafter. Adjustments were made only in times of exceptionally poor harvests. The method was introduced by the Tokugawa shogunate in 1721 as part of the KYŌHŌ REFORMS in order to ensure a steady income, and it was subsequently adopted by many domainal governments. Although it caused hardship initially, productivity increased while the tax did not, and it worked to the advantage of the farmers.

Conrad TOTMAN

Jōmon culture

The Jōmon period (ca 10,000 BC–ca 300 BC) was the chief food-gathering stage of Japanese prehistory, following the paleolithic and mesolithic periods and preceding the rice-cultivating stage of the Yayoi period (ca 300 BC–ca AD 300). It received its name from the cord-marked (jōmon) pottery that is present in most sites. It is now known to have had a duration of more than 8,000 years, with a slow development in part attributable to limited outside contacts. The Jōmon embodies some neolithic characteristics in the sense that it was nonmetal-using and was probably not exclusively a hunting and gathering economy. There are, however, wide differences of opinion as to whether some form of simple agriculture existed and, if so, what role it played in the economy of the later millennia of the period.

The Jōmon period witnessed early contributions to such elements in Japanese culture as shamanistic practices, views of nature and higher life, and fishing and shellfish gathering techniques. Certain features of the language may be traceable to Jōmon times.

While some archaeologists include Incipient or Subearliest Jōmon (ca 10,000 BC–ca 7500 BC)—marked by the first appearance of pottery—as the threshold stage of the Jōmon culture, others regard it as a Japanese mesolithic and begin Jōmon with the earliest shellfish gatherers of the east coast, who left their remains at the Natsushima shell mound in the city of Yokosuka. These were the Earliest or Initial Jōmon people (ca 7500 BC–ca 5000 BC), who built simple surface shelters supported by thin poles and used bullet-shaped pots covered with a primitive cord-marking.

A gradually warming climate increased the food supply, and Early Jōmon (ca 5000 BC–ca 3500 BC) people developed small villages consisting of several PIT HOUSES of square shape. They cooked and stored food in cord-marked, flat-bottomed pots and wicker baskets, and used stone awls, all-purpose tanged scrapers, and chipped and occasionally polished axes (see STONE TOOLS). Bone needles and thimbles have been recovered in sites. Mulberry bark was probably woven into loose hanging clothes. By the middle of the period, many pits for storing foodstuffs were being dug inside and outside the houses.

Middle Jōmon (ca 3500 BC–ca 2500 BC; also dated as ca 3500 BC–ca 2000 BC) —— The Middle Jōmon period is unique in several respects. One theory holds that it was stimulated from outside Japan and that the yam and taro were introduced from South China at this time; another that there is some connection with the painted pottery culture of China. But how it rose first in the central mountains and then diffused toward the coasts is still a major point of discussion.

Many large sites in the Kantō and Chūbu regions consist of numerous house pits yielding vast quantities of pottery and other remains indicating that much time was devoted to handicrafts. Such conditions suggest considerable economic stability. These communities, ranging in altitude between 800 and 1,200 meters (2,600 and 3,900 ft), rose rapidly along the southern slopes of the Shinshū Mountains. They were usually located 2 or more kilometers (1.2 mi) apart and always close to substantial springs. An invigorating life encouraged a sharp population increase. Archaeologists disagree on whether there was actual cultivation of plants, or only manipulation, or whether it was simply a matter of situating the houses suitably close to the food sources.

Food sources and preparation. Nuts were the chief source of food in the fall, especially walnuts and chestnuts. Horse chestnuts were collected in September and acorns in October and November. Fruit included wild grapes, "mountain peaches," and *akebi,* a vine with a pomegranatelike fruit. Berries, mushrooms, parsley, and bracken were gathered. Butterbur provided a condiment. The SHELL MOUNDS or middens yield bones of deer, wild bear, rabbits, flying squirrels, raccoons, pheasants, and ducks, all of which were caught with the aid of traps and snares, together with various fish remains.

Pebbles and cobbles clustered in Middle Jōmon sites are heat-blackened, reddened, and cracked from their use in cooking. Starches were steamed on wicker trays held in the cup-shaped rims of pots. The starch had been leached out of lily bulbs and tubers in springs, ground in stone mortars of scoria, and made up into cakes like lumps of bread. Charred oval pieces of "bread" about 10 centimeters (3.9 in) in length have been found at Idojiri in Nagano Prefecture (see IDOJIRI ARCHAEOLOGICAL HALL); at Okinohara in Niigata Prefecture, they are the size of a small cookie.

Despite the large scale of these sites, not many houses were in use at a given time. Skeletons found in 1927 in a house pit at the Ubayama shell mound in Chiba Prefecture suggest an average of five occupants to a house, and pottery typology indicates that a village usually consisted of five or six houses. The ideal pit house evolved with a superstructure supported by five or six posts over an open center for the fireplace, in a plan perhaps devised for the cooler temperature of mountains and later adopted at lower altitudes. The hard labor of digging the soil, cutting trees for building materials, and extracting roots, combined with other activities, took its toll. Skeletons from Middle Jōmon shell mounds show that people suffered many broken arms, especially fractures of the right arm, which occur in five times as many men as women. In some mountain sites they built platforms on one side on which upright stones were placed, possibly for ceremonial use. Storage pits were common and were supplemented by large storage vessels, often heavily encrusted with decoration.

Pottery vessels in mountain sites were shaped for specific uses, and the use of various symbolic motifs reflected the feeling of closer contact with the supernatural. Female figurines increased in number and stone phalli appeared. Lamps or "incense burners" were made, and clay drum bodies were the trappings for ceremonies.

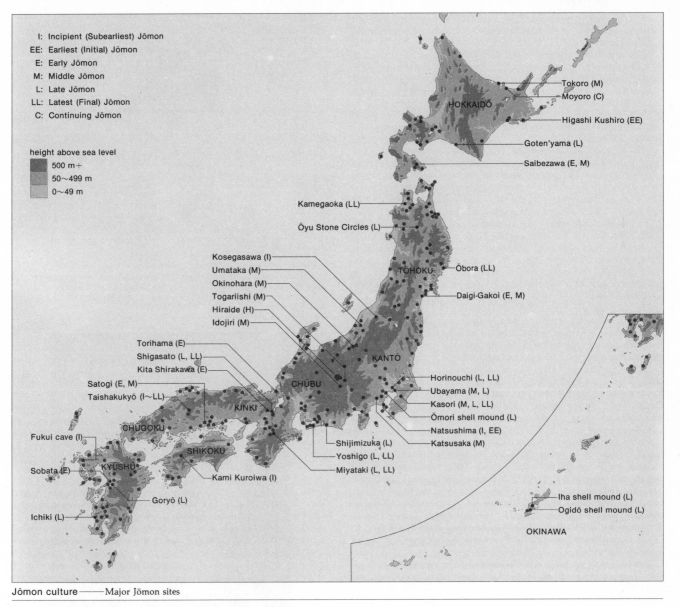

I: Incipient (Subearliest) Jōmon
EE: Earliest (Initial) Jōmon
E: Early Jōmon
M: Middle Jōmon
L: Late Jōmon
LL: Latest (Final) Jōmon
C: Continuing Jōmon

height above sea level
500 m+
50~499 m
0~49 m

Tokoro (M)
Moyoro (C)
Higashi Kushiro (EE)
Goten'yama (L)
Saibezawa (E, M)
HOKKAIDŌ

Kamegaoka (LL)
Ōyu Stone Circles (L)

Kosegasawa (I)
Umataka (M)
Okinohara (M)
Togariishi (M)
Hiraide (H)
Idojiri (M)

TŌHOKU
Ōbora (LL)
Daigi-Gakoi (E, M)

Torihama (E)
Shigasato (L, LL)
Kita Shirakawa (E)
Satogi (E, M)
Taishakukyō (I~LL)

CHŪBU
KANTŌ

Horinouchi (L, LL)
Ubayama (M, L)
Kasori (M, L, LL)
Ōmori shell mound (L)
Natsushima (I, EE)
Katsusaka (M)

KINKI
CHŪGOKU
Fukui cave (I)
SHIKOKU

Shijimizuka (L)
Yoshigo (L, LL)
Miyataki (L, LL)

Sobata (E)
KYŪSHŪ
Kami Kuroiwa (I)

Goryō (L)
Ichiki (L)

Iha shell mound (L)
Ogidō shell mound (L)

OKINAWA

Jōmon culture——Major Jōmon sites

Late Jōmon (ca 2500 BC–ca 1000 BC or ca 2000 BC–ca 1000 BC)

The Chūbu climate became too damp by around 2400 BC, and the population dispersed to the foothills and elsewhere. Late Jōmon people settled in rather large groups along the east coast and used the same sites for long periods, their debris forming immense shell middens. Concentrations of fishers led to technical improvements such as the toggle harpoon, which was employed extensively in the Tōhoku maritime zone by the end of this stage. Despite its usefulness, other regions failed to adopt it, perhaps because exhaustion was slowly overtaking the culture in its last millennia. The Kantō rivers and bays could support fewer people, and the northern population hoped to ensure its survival by elaborating its ceremonies. In Late Jōmon, independent ceremonial sites consisting of stone circles came into existence; they functioned as centers for burials and fertility rites. Many are recorded in northern Japan, the most notable at Ōyu in Akita Prefecture, where thousands of stones constitute two large pairs of concentric circles (see ŌYU STONE CIRCLES).

These stone circles are the strongest evidence for community ceremonies and illustrate the "cemetery" principle of burial. Starting with Middle Jōmon, the placing of the dead together in the middle of the shell mound became a progressively more consistent feature and one that may be regarded as reflecting a fear of the dead and their spirits.

Late Jōmon represents the country's first plateau of cultural uniformity. Artifact characteristics transcended regional boundaries, as deteriorating conditions at the end of Middle Jōmon drove most of the population out of the mountains, sending people north and south in search of adequate subsistence sources. The consistent use of zoned cord-marking on the pottery, polished stone axes, and tanged arrowheads suggests an increasing systematization of life and somewhat more specialized workmanship.

Repeated patterns on the pottery, coordinated with rim projections and ornaments, for the first time produced a predictable decorative system. Smaller vessels had simple, trim shapes. Clay figurines simulating pregnant women with heart-shaped or triangular faces exist in large enough numbers in many sites for every household to have had at least one of its own (see JŌMON FIGURINES).

Latest or Final Jōmon (ca 1000 BC–ca 300 BC)——In all but northern Japan, Latest (Final) Jōmon seems to have been a period of coalescing groups, smaller offshoots, and a notable population reduction. It also marked a return to strong regionalism. The cultural differences are most striking between northern and southern Japan, the former becoming a more ritualized and tightly organized society, the latter fragmenting into more mobile and informal groups.

Many large Middle and Late Jōmon shell mounds have only a small number of Latest (Final) Jōmon remains, reflecting the dwindling population. Exceptions do occur, as in Yoshigo in Aichi Prefecture, where a midden of considerable dimensions has yielded 344 human skeletons.

The Jōmon physical types lack regional homogeneity, because the early people who had entered from widely separated points rarely mixed with one another, a factor that can be recognized in the great number of pottery types. They were small in stature and short in life span, but physical improvements such as increased bone dimensions occurred during Middle Jōmon as a result of better conditions and diet.

The prehistoric material in the Tōhoku region goes by the name of Kamegaoka after a peat-bog site in Aomori Prefecture where large quantities of cultural remains have been found since it was first recorded in 1623 (see KAMEGAOKA SITE). More recently the pottery sequence in the north has been based on excavations carried out in 1925 by YAMANOUCHI SUGAO (1902–70) and HASEBE KOTONDO (1882–1969) at the Ōbora shell mounds on the coast of Ōfunato Bay in Iwate Prefecture.

The Kamegaoka and related Tōhoku sites have yielded many small pottery vessels, clay figurines, plaques, and bone, horn, and wooden objects. The pottery tends to be separated into modestly decorated utilitarian ware and strikingly decorated ceremonial ware. There are so many pieces of the latter and other ritual objects that one has the impression of a ritual-bound society.

In the far north, where rice cultivation was not introduced until much later, the surviving Jōmon-like stage is usually termed Zoku Jōmon, that is, Continuing Jōmon or Post-Jōmon. Subsequently, there were metal-using cultures in the northern islands, the SATSU-MON CULTURE in Hokkaidō of the 8th and later centuries and the OKHOTSK CULTURE along the northern littoral, in Sakhalin and the southern Kurils.

To sum up the Jōmon period, following the discovery of the value of the coastal resources, and as the climate warmed steadily and the water level rose, stimulating the growth of more varied flora and introducing marine life deep into inland areas, the population increased accordingly. The average temperature reached well above today's level during Early Jōmon. Kyūshū and Shikoku became separated from Honshū, and regional differences in tools, pottery, house construction, and ways of acquiring food took on rather sharp distinctions. During Middle Jōmon the temperature stabilized. Abundant nut crops in the mixed forests of central Honshū provided a millennium of stability, the invigorating mountain life leaving its mark in the extensive remains found in the Chūbu and western Kantō regions. But climate deterioration eventually forced the people to disperse toward the coastal areas. They settled in the Kantō region and especially in the Tōhoku region, depending heavily on shellfish-gathering, fishing, and probably cultivating some vegetables. The regional differences became less conspicuous. Throughout Late and Latest (Final) Jōmon, the population declined at an alarming rate, to less than half the peak reached in Middle Jōmon, as if the environment was unable to sustain it anywhere but in the Tōhoku region.

Latest (Final) Jōmon in Kyūshū witnessed the introduction of rice cultivation to Japan. It was first raised in dry beds or swamps and later, when the Yayoi pattern of agriculture took hold, by transplanting seedlings into paddies. But it seems to have taken several centuries before society was sufficiently organized to form agricultural villages, water management systems, and community ceremonies. The introduction of new burial methods, weaving techniques, and metallurgy combined in the last centuries of the era before Christ to shape the social habits usually associated with the Yayoi culture. See also the section on the Jōmon period in HISTORY OF JAPAN: prehistory; JŌMON POTTERY.

—— Esaka Teruya et al, *Jōmon doki to kaizuka*, in *Kodaishi hakkutsu*, vol 2 (Kōdansha, 1974). Kamaki Yoshimasa, *Jōmon jidai*, in *Nihon no kōkogaku*, vol 2 (Kawade Shobō, 1965). Ōba Iwao, Naitō Masatsune, and Yawata Ichirō, ed, *Shimpan kōkogaku kōza*, vol 3 (Yūzankaku, 1969). Serizawa Chōsuke, *Sekki jidai no Nihon* (1960). Takeuchi Rizō et al, ed, *Kodai no Nihon*, vols 3–8 (Kadokawa Shoten, 1970–71). *J. Edward* KIDDER, *Jr.*

Jōmon figurines

(*dogū*). Clay images of humans and animals between 3 to 30 centimeters (1.2 to 12 in) high made by the hunters and gatherers of the Jōmon period (ca 10,000 BC–ca 300 BC). Figurines were already being made in eastern Japan as early as the Initial Jōmon period (ca 7500 BC–ca 5000 BC) and had become quite numerous by Middle Jōmon times (ca 3500 BC–ca 2000 BC). First crafted as flat, two-dimensional images, they were given three-dimensional volume in the Late Jōmon period (ca 2000 BC–ca 1000 BC); the figurines discovered in Late Jōmon sites throughout Japan belong to the second group. In the Final Jōmon period (ca 1000 BC–ca 300 BC), large figu-

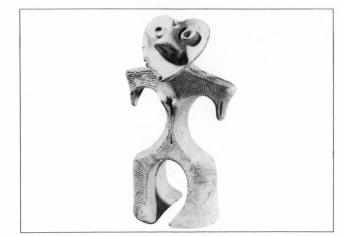

Jōmon figurines

Unearthed at Gōhara in Gumma Prefecture, this figurine shows the exaggerated facial features, rudimentary arms and legs, and pronounced body decoration typical of *dogū*. The heart-shaped face and tattoo-like coil and spiral motifs are regional features. Clay. Height 30.5 cm. Final Jōmon period.

Jōmon pottery

Example of a Middle Jōmon pot from the Chūbu region. The sculptured rim zone and elaborate decoration are characteristic features of Middle Jōmon pottery. Umataka type; excavated from the Tokushōji site, Niigata Prefecture. Earthenware. Height 29 cm. Yoitachō Kyōdo Shiryōkan, Niigata Prefecture.

rines with distinctive faces were common. Some clay images continued to be made into the Yayoi period (ca 300 BC–ca AD 300), but these are not to be confused with the HANIWA funerary sculptures of the ensuing Kofun period (ca 300–710). Most of the figurines represent human females, and that the majority of these have large breasts and stomachs may indicate that they symbolize pregnancy or fertility, much like the mother-goddess figures of Egypt, Mesopotamia, and Europe. Because the figurines are seldom found unbroken, it is thought that they were meant to be broken, possibly as substitutes for actual persons, intended to receive in their stead the effects of wounds, illness, or disaster. See also JŌMON CULTURE.

—— Esaka Teruya and Noguchi Yoshimaro, ed, *Dogū geijutsu to shinkō*, in *Kodaishi hakkutsu*, vol 3 (Kōdansha, 1974).

UENO Yoshiya

Jōmon period

(Jōmon *jidai*). A prehistoric period, dated from about 10,000 BC to about 300 BC, during which the peoples of Japan followed a hunting and gathering way of life. It was preceded by the PALEOLITHIC PERIOD (pre-10,000 BC), from which it is distinguished by the presence of pottery impressed with cord patterns *(jōmon)*, and was followed by the YAYOI PERIOD (ca 300 BC–ca AD 300), when agriculture and metals first appeared. See also HISTORY OF JAPAN: prehistory; JŌMON CULTURE. *Gina Lee BARNES*

Jōmon pottery

Earthenware made during the Jōmon period (ca 10,000 BC–ca 300 BC; see HISTORY OF JAPAN: prehistory). Jōmon ceramics are distributed throughout Japan, from the Kuril Islands in the north to the Ryūkyū Islands in the south. Shapes vary depending upon the time and locality. They are brown to reddish in color and are characterized by a cord-marked surface. First called "shell mound pottery" and "Ainu pottery," it was eventually called Jōmon ("cord-marked"), a direct translation of the English term used in the ŌMORI SHELL MOUNDS excavation report by Edward S. MORSE in 1879. Nevertheless, not all pottery of the Jōmon period is decorated with cord-marking.

Site names began to be applied to pottery types in the 1930s, and in 1937 YAMANOUCHI SUGAO employed the pottery typology of the Tōhoku and Kantō regions to subdivide the Jōmon period into five stages: Earliest (Initial), Early, Middle, Late, and Latest (Final). This chronology has since been extended to other regions, and a sixth stage has been added as Subearliest (Incipient) Jōmon at the beginning. However, the Incipient Jōmon stage (ca 10,000 BC–ca 7,500 BC) is not accepted by all archaeologists as being part of the Jōmon period, since they do not regard it as instrumental in changing the character of the PALEOLITHIC CULTURE. This stage is best described as mesolithic in nature.

The oldest pottery belonging to Incipient Jōmon or earlier, discovered in FUKUI CAVE in Nagasaki Prefecture, has a coarse, linear-relief decoration *(ryūsemmon)*. This decorative technique may have diffused from there, becoming more refined in the process. It is found as far north as Yamagata Prefecture. Linear relief is followed by nail-marking decoration *(tsumegatamon;* "fingernail impression") in the succeeding layer at Fukui Cave.

Widely used techniques of decoration in the Earliest (ca 7500 BC–ca 5000 BC) and Early (ca 5000 BC–ca 3500 BC) Jōmon periods include marking by a rolled carved stick *(oshigatamon;* rouletting) in the south and indenting and scraping with a shell in the north. Nail-marking of the sort that characterized Early Jōmon in the Kantō, Chūbu, and Kansai regions was done with a split bamboo stick. The earliest forms of cord-marking, not appearing until about 7500 BC, were done with simple strands of plant fibers. In Early Jōmon there was much twisting and knotting of multiple strands, and by the latter part of Middle Jōmon (ca 3500 BC–ca 2000 BC) considerable uniformity had been achieved. Application of cord-marking within incised zones of decoration during Late Jōmon (ca 2000 BC–ca 1000 BC)—chiefly among the Horinouchi and Kasori B types—was the only decorative technique to penetrate the entire country; this tradition survived into Latest Jōmon (ca 1000 BC–ca 300 BC) in the Kantō and Tōhoku regions.

Throughout Earliest and Early Jōmon, pots were designed for boiling foods. Any other use was incidental. They were first given pointed bases; conversion to flat bases in Early Jōmon coincided with improved house construction and more indoor living. Greater economic stability in the early part of Middle Jōmon stimulated a strong sense of style and imaginative uses of pottery. Enormous quantities were produced in the Chūbu and Kantō regions. Bottomless bowls were used to line fireplaces, and lamps or incense burners were hung from the rafters of PIT HOUSES, while steamers were made for cooking starches, and large pots served for storage of nuts and root vegetables.

Ceramic decoration at Middle Jōmon mountain sites such as the TOGARIISHI SITE became strikingly plastic, sometimes to an excessive degree. Pots of the Katsusaka and related types occasionally bear snake motifs, and others have animal heads worked into the decoration of the rim. In the latter half of Middle Jōmon, the Kasori E (see KASORI SHELL MOUNDS) and Daigi 8 types dominate the lowland eastern regions. These vessels carry dense, oblique cord-marking and carved spiral patterns in the rim zone. Large jars were

occasionally used for burials, deposited upside down after the bases had been removed or perforated (see PREHISTORIC BURIALS).

Middle Jōmon pots used in food preparation are estimated to have lost about 10 percent of their liquid contents overnight. Consequently, efforts were made to reduce the porosity by painting the surface with red ocher or by polishing and burnishing. Thinner walls and improved firing techniques were also tried.

Kamegaoka-type pottery (see KAMEGAOKA SITE) marked a cultural florescence in the Latest Jōmon period of northern Japan. The chronological sequence of this northern pottery has been based on excavations of the Ōbora shell mounds in Ōfunato Bay in Iwate Prefecture. Pottery recovered from three connected middens designated A, B, and C was placed in the complicated typological sequence of B, C, and A and then intricately subdivided. Kamegaoka pottery consists of both simple vessels for domestic use and ornate vessels of a ritual nature. Shapes include many small, finely made cups, bowls, plates, pots, vases, ewers, and incense burners. Most are meticulously carved and sometimes cord-marked and smoothed or painted.

Eclectic styles with much less variety typified southwest Japan, except for Goryō, a black, polished type centered in Kumamoto Prefecture. Beginning in ca 300 BC, YAYOI POTTERY was made in western Japan, gradually replacing Jōmon techniques eastward, but Kamegaoka pottery and its successors endured for several centuries in the north, eventually being transformed into the pottery of the SATSUMON CULTURE. See also JŌMON CULTURE; CERAMICS.

📖 ——J. Edward Kidder, Jr, *Prehistoric Japanese Arts: Jōmon Pottery* (1968). *J. Edward KIDDER, Jr.*

jōri

(natural reason). A Japanese legal term which essentially means "the nature of things" or "the right way of being." It is a translation of the German phrase "Natur der Sache." It has importance in the following two respects.

First, *jōri* is important because of proclamation 103 of the Great Council of State (DAJŌKAN; 1875) which states that "civil courts of law shall base their judgments with reference to custom when statutory law is lacking and upon natural reason *(jōri)* when applicable custom is not to be found." As this statement is not negated by the present CONSTITUTION, it should be understood as still being valid today. However, there are many who do not regard *jōri* as a source of law as it is an abstract concept that does not have the form of a legal standard (i.e., a societal standard that can be enforced by physical power). In other words, they believe that judges apply *jōri* even though it is not law. Regardless of whether *jōri* is interpreted to be a source of law or not, its application is limited to those situations where statutory law or custom is not to be found. It is possible to understand the role of *jōri* as the same as the principle found in article 1, paragraph 2 of the Swiss Civil Code which says that where there is no statutory law or custom, the judge shall proceed according to the rule that he himself would establish if he were a legislator.

Second, *jōri* is important because it functions as a standard of interpretation. As the substance of laws or legal acts must not be contrary to natural reason *(jōri)*, the ultimate standard for the interpretation of laws and legal acts is *jōri*. This is also made clear in court decisions. *ENDŌ Hiroshi*

jōri system

System of land division in use in the 7th and 8th centuries. Under the TAIKA REFORM of 645, tracts of land were divided into squares measuring 6 *chō* to a side (1 *chō* = 109 m or 358 ft). Counting from north to south, these units were designated *jō* 1, *jō* 2, etc; from east to west, the same units were called *ri* 1, *ri* 2, etc. Each of these units was further divided into 36 equal and numbered squares, called *tsubo*, each having an area of 1 square *chō*. Thus it was possible to indicate any parcel of land by specifying in which *tsubo, ri, jō, gun* (district), and *kuni* (province) it lay. The field divisions were demarcated by foot paths and irrigation ditches.

Each *tsubo* was subdivided into 10 strips, called *tan,* according to one of two methods. Under the *nagachigata* method, the *tsubo* was divided into 10 equal strips running from north to south or into 10 equal strips running east to west; under the *haorigata* method, the *tsubo* was divided into 5 north-south strips and once again at midpoint, from east to west, also producing 10 *tan*. (One *tan* theoretically produced enough rice to feed a man for a year.) The *haorigata*

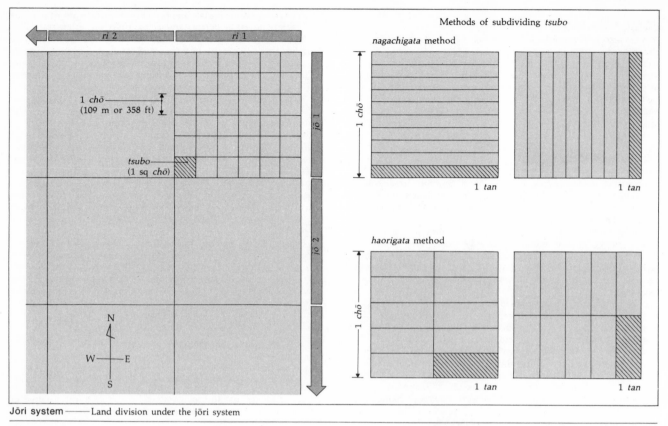

Jōri system——Land division under the jōri system

Under the *jōri* system of land division, large, square tracts of land were divided into 36 smaller squares called *tsubo*. *Tsubo* were subdivided into 10 strips (*tan*) using either the *nagachigata* ("long land style") or *haorigata* ("half fold style") method of division.

method corresponds to the land divisions prescribed in the Taika edicts and is thought to have been the one put into effect at that time. It is, however, believed to antedate the Taika Reform.

Because the lines of field division at the TORO SITE in Shizuoka Prefecture resemble those of the *jōri* system, some have sought its origins there. The *jōri* system was also referred to by the Chinese term *qian mo* (*ch'ien mo;* J: *sempaku*), however, and there is good reason to believe that it was based on the ancient Chinese system of dividing land with paths running from north to south and east to west. It is further believed that the basic outlines of the system were introduced to Japan from Korea sometime during the 4th or 5th century.

The new system made it possible for the government to allocate land smoothly to individual cultivators (see HANDEN SHŪJU SYSTEM), and the rationalization of field boundaries also encouraged cultivation of new lands. Scholars disagree as to who opened up lands under the *jōri* system—whether the Yamato court, local chieftain families, or both in concert. In any case, land development under the *jōri* system was discontinued at the beginning of the Heian period (794–1185), although early in the 9th century the system was extended to cover uncultivated areas as a means of bringing more territory under central control. Even after the *handen shūju* system was abandoned, the divisions of the *jōri* system remained in use. The designations went out of existence only with Toyotomi Hideyoshi's nationwide cadastral survey (KENCHI) of 1582. To this day, fields in the Kyōto–Nara–Ōsaka region retain the dimensions and contours of the ancient *jōri* system. Traces have been found as far north as Akita Prefecture and as far south as Kagoshima Prefecture, as well as in remote mountain areas.   *OCHIAI Shigenobu*

jōruri

A form of dramatic narrative chanting to SHAMISEN accompaniment which is commonly associated with the BUNRAKU puppet theater and which flourished during the Edo period (1600–1868). As applied to the puppet theater, it refers to the part of the performance that does not involve the puppets, their manipulation, or the staging. Thus the texts of the puppet plays are in effect *jōruri*.

Origin——Of the several combinations of Chinese characters, with or without the Japanese syllabary, with which the term *jōruri* has been written in the last four centuries, the authentic version has the meaning "pure *ruri,*" *ruri* in modern Japanese being lapis lazuli, but in Buddhist scriptures probably rock crystal. According to legend, Jōruri was the name given to the daughter of a rich man of Yahagi, a town near what is now Nagoya, who had a one-night love affair with the warrior hero MINAMOTO NO YOSHITSUNE and later rescued him when he fell ill and was abandoned. This apocryphal addition to the more authentic Yoshitsune legend was recited to the accompaniment of a BIWA (lute) by blind minstrels known as BIWA HŌSHI. References to the story occur from the late 15th century. During the 16th century the *shamisen* was introduced into Japan from Okinawa and was adopted by some of these chanters for popular pieces like this tale, which came to be known as the *Jōruri hime monogatari* (Tale of the Lady Jōruri) or *Jūnidan sōshi* (Story in 12 Parts). This branch of HEIKYOKU (Heike music) came to be called *jōruri*. Another account, which makes an otherwise unknown story called *Yasuda monogatari* the original version of this tale, is now discounted, as is the role of a probably imaginary lady-in-waiting to Oda Nobunaga, Ono no Otsū, credited by some with the version of the story performed about 1600.

Development——*Jōruri* reached early maturity when the chanter Menukiya Chōzaburō collaborated with the puppeteer Hikita (both late 16th to early 17th centuries), who later received the title Awaji no Jō, to present dramatic performances in Kyōto. The early repertory included some adaptations of KŌWAKA tales, some Yoshitsune stories, probably including the *Jūnidan,* and some Buddhist tales like *Amida no munewari* (1614, tr *Amida's Riven Breast,* 1966).

The period 1600–86 is known as that of old *jōruri,* with separate developments in Edo (now Tōkyō) and the Kamigata or Kyōto–Ōsaka region. Works of this period are always recorded with the name of the chanter. His playbooks are called *shōhon* (certified texts), and the text is extremely important. A chanter, even when blind, always sits in front of a stand on which the playbook is placed, with the *shamisen* accompanist to his left. The puppets enact the story of the text and are under the ultimate control of the chanter's words. The earliest *jōruri* playbook extant is *Takadachi* (1625), probably belonging to Satsuma Tayū (later called Jōun), a reciter who typified the violent Edo style of theater. From about 1615 the main progress in *jōruri* was in Edo, with Jōun and his successors chanting rough, active pieces. In 1657 a great fire in Edo brought a halt to theater activity, and some Edo chanters moved to Kyōto. They took with them Kimpira *jōruri*, tales of the fictional hero Kimpira, which were in great vogue in Edo and dealt with feats of phenomenal strength and violence. These were chanted mainly by a pupil of Jōun, Sakurai Tamba no Shōjō, and his son Izumi-Dayū. The violence of the plays was reflected in the roughness of the chanting (Tamba no Shōjō beat the rhythm with a six-foot iron rod, and is known to have broken puppets and fittings) and the bulging-eyed sensational illustrations in the playbooks. This was also the age of the first ICHIKAWA DANJŪRŌ's *aragoto* (rough business) in KABUKI, which with Kimpira *jōruri* was highly appreciated by the audiences of low-ranking, underemployed Edo *samurai*.

It seems that Edo *jōruri* remained static until the end of the 17th century but, in Ōsaka, Inoue Harima no Jō combined the violence of the Kimpira tales with elements of the traditional "soft" style of Kyōto and developed a more advanced style, known as the Harima school, in the 1670s. Another contribution was made in Kyōto by Uji Kadayū (later known as Kaga no Jō). He had been early trained in NŌ and helped to change *jōruri* from a simple narrative to a more structured dramatic form, often in five acts.

Gidayū-bushi—— From the Harima school in Ōsaka emerged the greatest chanter of all, Takemoto Gidayū (1651–1714), the founder of the style that still bears his name and prevails in the modern puppet theater. Gidayū engaged in a rivalry with Kaga no Jō until the latter's death in 1711, but he had the great CHIKAMATSU MON-ZAEMON as his playwright and Kaga, after chanting an unsuccessful play by Ihara SAIKAKU, *Koyomi* (1685, The Calendar), remained in Kyōto. Although *Shusse Kagekiyo* (1686, Kagekiyo Victorious) is usually designated the first of Chikamatsu's new *jōruri*, perhaps the greatest step forward was in 1703 with his *Sonezaki shinjū* (tr *The Love Suicides at Sonezaki*, 1961), the first puppet drama of contemporary life (*sewamono*), dramatizing an actual suicide pact. From this time on, even though a rival emerged in Toyotake Wakatayū (1681–1764), with KI NO KAION as his writer, the chanting to accompany the puppets has remained in *gidayū-bushi* style; and the present bunraku theater of Ōsaka is a successor to the Takemoto and Toyotake theaters. The title *tayū* (-*dayū*, as in Gidayū), by which chanters are known is an old term of respect for performers in Japan. It was replaced as a name when a court title such as Kaga no Jō was conferred as a sign of recognition. After the Meiji period (1868–1912) this custom lapsed until 1947, when Toyotake Yamashiro no Shōjō (1878–1967) received his title. See also GIDAYŪ-BUSHI.

Other Jōruri and Fushi—— Although *gidayū-bushi* is the most significant style of *jōruri* chanting, the word *jōruri* is used in other contexts: *ayatsuri jōruri* and *ningyō jōruri* both mean puppets accompanied by chanting, and Kimpira *jōruri* has been mentioned. *Sekkyō jōruri* is a style of performance which developed from the early 17th century with plays on Buddhist themes performed with string puppets; the still-existing Yūki Magosaburō school also dates from that time. The different styles of *jōruri* chanting are known as *fushi* (-*bushi*). Most of the early chanters had *fushi* named after them (*satsuma-bushi*, *harima-bushi*, etc), but since the introduction of *gidayū-bushi* no other school of chanting has been successful. However, other *jōruri fushi* are still in existence, some performed with puppets and some without. Often these survive in amateur performances, notably in the form of *dan-mono shū*, collections of "high points" with notation to facilitate performance created by chanters like Kaga no Jō. *Itchū-bushi*, *shinnai-bushi*, and *sonohachi-bushi* are three of many of these. *Sekkyō-bushi* still exists on the island of Sado (Niigata Prefecture), as does *bun'ya-bushi* (fl in Ōsaka 1670–80), as an accompaniment to early-type puppets. The live kabuki theater, apart from the *gidayū-bushi* that serves mainly as a chorus in plays borrowed from the puppets, uses other styles of *jōruri* chanting called TOKIWAZU-BUSHI (founded in Edo ca 1750) and KIYOMOTO-BUSHI (Edo, 1814). NAGAUTA, also used in kabuki, is not normally considered a type of *jōruri* but rather as a derivative of Nō, while *ōzatsuma-bushi*, a particularly bravura style now part of *nagauta*, is said to date back to Jōun in the 17th century.

Extant *fushi* vary in their chanting character and the equipment used for their performance (e.g., the shape of the playbook stand and the size of the *shamisen*). *Gidayū-bushi* utilizes the largest instrument, in order to be heard throughout a large theater. *Bun'ya-bushi* was called the weeping style, while *kiyomoto-bushi* and *tokiwazu-bushi* specialize in delicate, sometimes eerie, high-pitched

singing. *Gidayū-bushi* often incorporated the best elements of other *fushi* and of popular songs. The subject is often a tragic conflict between duty and sentiment, chanted with variety and realism. It requires great artistry, and is still popularly performed without puppets, by women as well as men.

■ ——C. J. Dunn, *The Early Japanese Puppet Drama* (1966). Donald Keene, *Major Plays of Chikamatsu* (1961). Donald Keene, *Bunraku* (1965). Koyama Tadashi, *Jōkyoku no shin kenkyū* (1962). William P. Malm, *Japanese Music and Musical Instruments* (1959). Yokoyama Tadashi, *Jōruri ayatsuri shibai no kenkyū* (1963).

Charles DUNN

Jōruriji

Also known as Kutaiji. A temple of the Shingon Ritsu sect of Buddhism (see EIZON). Located in Kamo Chō, Kyōto Prefecture. Noted for the 12th-century architecture of its main hall and pagoda, its statuary, and the charm of its remote setting.

According to unconfirmed legends, the temple was founded either in 739 or 982, but more likely accurate is a 14th-century manuscript that describes the building by the monk Gimyō in 1047 of the main hall housing the image of Yakushi (the healing Buddha; Skt: Bhaiṣajyaguru). The main hall was reconstructed in 1108 to house nine images of AMIDA (Skt: Amitābha). The name Jōruriji, literally "clear lapis lazuli temple," is thought to derive from the association of this jewel with the land of the Buddha Yakushi, formerly the main image enshrined there.

The main hall (*hondō*), moved to its present site in 1157, is the only surviving example of a style of temple structure of the Heian period (794–1185) known as "hall of the nine Amida Buddhas" (*kutai amidadō*). It is 11 bays (*ken*; 1 *ken* = about 6 ft or 1.8 m) long and 4 bays deep, the oblong shape allowing the housing of nine gilded images of Amida, symbolizing the nine levels of the Western Paradise. These statues are arranged in the central nine bays. There is no ceiling, and the rafters on the underside of the inner roof are exposed, as are the transverse beams running from front to back over the heads of the statues. The inner roof over the central figure is recessed to accommodate its greater height; the central figure, slightly larger than the others, is in the style of JŌCHŌ.

Also in the main hall are a set of Shitennō or Four Heavenly Kings (see TEMBU), from the late Heian period. Carved in cypress, highly painted and decorated with thin strips of gold foil glued on the base material, they are examples of the revived high Tang (T'ang) style. Much more famous, however, is the statue of Kichijōten (Skt: Śrīmahadevī) dating from 1212, now one of the most popular statues in Japan. The figure's elaborately colored and ornate clothing, covered with complicated carved jewelry, reflects more of the atmosphere of the court than of the Buddhist pantheon.

The three-storied pagoda on the far side of the pond was moved to Jōruriji in 1178 from Ichijō Ōmiya in Kyōto. It contains an image of Yakushi and the interior is painted with esoteric motifs. Although it has had some later alterations, the cypress bark roof with the gently curving rafters and inset eaves retains much of the feeling of the late Heian period when it was built.

Josetsu (early 15th century)

Buddhist monk-painter of the temple SHŌKOKUJI in Kyōto; an early master of INK PAINTING (*suibokuga*). The earliest reference to Josetsu is found in the diary of Zuikei Shūhō (1391–1473), a scholar-monk of the Shōkokuji, which mentions Josetsu as the stonecutter commissioned by the shōgun Ashikaga Yoshimochi in 1405 to carve a stone inscription honoring the memory of the great Zen master MUSŌ SOSEKI.

Although several paintings are attributed to Josetsu, only two are firmly accepted as his: *Catching a Catfish with a Gourd* (*Hyōnenzu*, ca 1413; Myōshinji, Kyōto) and *Wang Xizhi (Wang Hsi-chih) Writing on Fans* (*Ō Gishi shosen zu*; Agency for Cultural Affairs, Tōkyō). The former is a figure painting within a landscape setting and illustrates a paradoxical Zen riddle, or KŌAN, about catching a catfish with a gourd. It was originally commissioned by the Ashikaga shōgun and pasted on the back of a low partition screen (*zahei*); on a separate sheet of paper on the front of the screen (now mounted above the painting) are poems by 31 contemporary Zen monks on the subject of the riddle. The second painting was originally on a fan and bears an inscription by the monk Taigaku Shūsō (1345–1423); it was later mounted as a hanging scroll with a long inscription dated 1430 by the scholar-monk Ishō Tokugan (d 1439).

The figure style reflected in both paintings is that of the Chinese Southern Song (Sung; 1127–1279) painter Liang Kai (Liang K'ai; active mid-13th century), whose works were admired and collected by the Ashikaga shōguns. The *Hyōnenzu* has special importance as one of the earliest examples of Japanese ink landscape painting. The evocative range of hills in the distance, rendered in filmy ink washes, reveals Josetsu's interest in spatial tonality. It is this new aesthetic element that was to be more fully developed by his followers beginning with SHŪBUN and culminating with SESSHŪ TŌYŌ.

📖 ——Matsushita Takaaki and Tamamura Takeji, *Josetsu, Shūbun, San'ami*, vol 6 of *Suiboku bijutsu taikei* (Kōdansha, 1974).

Yoshiaki SHIMIZU

Jōshin'etsu Kōgen National Park

(Jōshin'etsu Kōgen Kokuritsu Kōen). Situated in central Honshū, in Niigata, Gumma, and Nagano prefectures. Comprises two separate mountainous regions (the Jōshin'etsu and the Myōkō–Togakushi regions), and has active volcanoes over 2,000 m (6,560 ft) high, an extensive plateau, lakes, and hot spring resorts. It is also a popular mountain-climbing and skiing area.

In the Jōshin'etsu region lie the volcanoes TANIGAWADAKE (1,963 m or 6,439 ft) and NAEBASAN (2,145 m or 7,036 ft), the latter of which slopes southwest to SHIGA KŌGEN, an extensive highland over 1,600 m (5,248 ft) high, with marshland, numerous small lakes, and forests of silver birch. South of the highland are two active volcanoes: SHIRANESAN (2,176 m or 7,137 ft), on whose slopes are MANZA HOT SPRING and Kusatsu Hot Spring; and ASAMAYAMA (2,542 m or 8,338 ft), at whose foot lies the fashionable summer resort town of KARUIZAWA (not included in the park).

Myōkō–Togakushi, the smaller region, to the northwest, contains the three peaks of MYŌKŌSAN (2,446 m or 8,023 ft), KUROHIME-YAMA (2,053 m or 6,734 ft), and TOGAKUSHIYAMA (1,911 m or 6,268 ft), and has extensive forests of Japanese beech *(buna)* and many alpine plants. Area: 1,889.2 sq km (729.2 sq mi).

Jōtō Mon'in (988–1074)

The "palace name" *(ingō)* of Fujiwara no Shōshi, daughter of FUJIWARA NO MICHINAGA and Minamoto no Rinshi. Shōshi entered the women's quarters of Emperor ICHIJŌ in 999, and through her father's influence became CHŪGŪ (empress) the next year when the former *chūgū,* FUJIWARA NO TEISHI, was appointed KŌGŌ. (The latter title also means empress, and this case established the precedent of two empresses in one reign.) Shōshi bore sons who became the emperors GO-ICHIJŌ and Go-Suzaku (1009–45, r 1036–45); she became empress dowager *(kōtaigō)* in 1012 and then grand empress dowager *(tai kōtaigō)* in 1018. In 1026 she became a nun and was thereafter known by the name of the palace to which she retired, Jōtō Mon'in. Among the ladies in her service were the writers MURASAKI SHIKIBU, IZUMI SHIKIBU, and probably AKAZOME EMON. There are detailed references to Jōtō Mon'in in both the EIGA MONOGATARI and the *Murasaki Shikibu nikki* (the diary of Murasaki Shikibu).

G. Cameron HURST III

Jōwa Conspiracy

A political plot of 842 (Jōwa 9) believed to have been fabricated by FUJIWARA NO YOSHIFUSA, the powerful head of the Fujiwara family, to effect the downfall of the Tomo family and other rivals in the court. After the deaths of the retired emperor Junna (r 823–833) in 840 and the retired emperor SAGA (r 809–823) in 842, the officials Tomo no Kowamine and TACHIBANA NO HAYANARI were accused by Yoshifusa, apparently unjustly, of plotting a rebellion to enthrone Prince Tsunesada (825–884), a son of Junna and grandson of Saga who had been designated heir apparent to the reigning emperor, Nimmyō (r 833–850). Kowamine and Hayanari were exiled, and the crown prince was deposed. He was replaced by Prince Michiyasu, Yoshifusa's nephew and son of Nimmyō. Michiyasu later reigned as Emperor Montoku (r 850–858), and his son by a daughter of Yoshifusa was named crown prince. The crown prince became Emperor Seiwa in 858, and Yoshifusa eventually served as his regent *(sesshō),* paving the way for a permanent Fujiwara REGENCY GOVERNMENT.

G. Cameron HURST III

Josetsu

Detail of *Catching a Catfish with a Gourd,* a painting illustrating a Zen *kōan* in which attaining enlightenment is likened to trying to catch a catfish with a gourd. Ink and pale colors on paper. 111.5 × 75.8 cm. Ca 1413. Myōshinji, Kyōto. National Treasure.

jōyaku kaisei → Unequal Treaties, revision of

Jōyō

City in southern Kyōto Prefecture, central Honshū, some 19 km (12 mi) south of Kyōto. Farm products include rice, pears, sweet potatoes, and tea. With convenient transportation, Jōyō has become a suburb of Kyōto in recent years. The gold and silver thread used in Nishijin fabrics (see NISHIJIN-ORI) is manufactured in Jōyō. Pop: 74,350.

jōyō kanji

(Chinese characters for common use). A list of 1,945 Chinese characters (KANJI) officially designated by the Japanese government on 1 October 1981 for common use in writing Japanese. The list supersedes the 1,850-character TŌYŌ KANJI (Chinese characters for daily use), a similar list that had been officially adopted in November 1946. The *tōyō kanji,* along with a reform of the spelling rules for the native phonetic syllabary (KANA) that was also announced in 1946, simplified what had been an extremely complex writing system, in which several thousand Chinese characters were used, and made the written Japanese language easier both to learn and to use. They thus had a great impact on both Japanese education and daily life; however, the *tōyō kanji* were criticized as placing undue restrictions on the number of characters that could be used and on the ways that those characters could be used to write words (for more information on the *tōyō kanji* and a discussion of the criticism, see TŌYŌ KANJI). Consequently, in June 1966 the minister of education requested the Council on National Language to draft recommendations for further language reforms. The council's first recommendations concerned changes in the ways that the characters on the *tōyō kanji* list could be pronounced and changes in the ways that the *kana* syllabary could be used, together with the characters, to express the inflectional endings of such words as verbs and adjectives. These recommendations were adopted in June 1973. Finally the council took up the question of changes in the characters themselves (their number and physical form). Its new recommendations were adopted in October 1981 under the title *Jōyō kanji hyō* (Table of Chinese Characters for Common Use).

The *Jōyō kanji hyō* is a comprehensive table, which includes not only the designated characters in their designated physical form, but also their designated pronunciations and examples of their use in writing words. It increases the number of Chinese characters officially designated for general use by 95. With regard to the forms of characters and their pronunciations, it adopts the basic principles of the *tōyō kanji* table and its later modifications. The issuance of the new table, however, makes one important change in language policy. Whereas the *tōyō kanji* were understood as restricting the use, in publications intended for the general public, of characters not on the table, the *jōyō kanji* are understood as a guideline. They present a standard for the use of Chinese characters in daily life, but the necessity of additional characters in specialized areas is recognized. Indeed, the Japanese Newspaper Association decided to remove 11 characters from the list and add 6, and this modified list has been adopted by the newspapers and broadcast media in Japan. Along with the announcement of the *jōyō kanji* table, the list of 881 characters that had been designated to be learned within the first six years at school (the so-called KYŌIKU KANJI) was formally replaced by a list of 996 characters that had already been in use in the official course outlines for elementary schools. The number of characters in the supplementary list (to the *tōyō kanji*) of characters approved for use only in personal names was increased to 166. Since the 1,945 characters of the *jōyō kanji* can also be used for personal names, the number of characters available for naming newborn infants was thus brought up to a total of 2,111. *TAKEBE Yoshiaki*

Jōzankei Hot Spring

(Jōzankei Onsen). Located in the southwest part of the city of Sapporo, northern Hokkaidō. A weak saline hot spring; maximum water temperature 94°C (201°F). Situated on the upper reaches of the river Toyohiragawa, a tributary of the Ishikarigawa, it is located within Shikotsu–Tōya National Park. The name "Jōzan" is taken from the Zen priest Jōzan, who is said to have opened the spa in 1866. This area, within the Hōhei Gorge, is noted for its abundant scenic spots and crimson autumn foliage. The surrounding mountains provide good skiing grounds.

jūbako

(literally, "stacked-up boxes"). Small lacquered wood boxes, stacked on top of each other in groups of two, three, or five, and used for storing, carrying, or serving food. They are most commonly lacquered black on the outside and red on the inside, but some are elaborately decorated with gold lacquer (MAKI-E). *Jūbako* became very popular in the Edo period (1600–1868), when they were used as picnic boxes at the theater or on flower-viewing (HANAMI) excursions; for giving *sekihan* (a dish of *azuki* beans and rice cooked on auspicious occasions) or rice cakes to friends and neighbors; or for storing and presenting precooked food for the many guests at wedding or New Year's festivities. It is still customary at New Year's time to serve *jūbako* filled with special seasonal foods.

judges

(saibankan). As of the mid-1970s there were 15 Supreme Court justices, 278 high court judges, 805 judges and 399 assistant judges of the district courts, 193 judges and 148 assistant judges of the family courts, and 767 summary court judges in Japan. The judicial function is to resolve conflicting interests between two litigants, and, at 41,500 persons per judge, there is a relatively small number of judges in Japan. Judges are guaranteed independence in the exercise of their conscience, and no competent judge can be removed except by public impeachment. A judge's salary cannot be decreased during his term of office.

Post-university legal training is given to those who pass the national LAW EXAMINATION at the LEGAL TRAINING AND RESEARCH INSTITUTE. A trainee chooses one of three legal careers, that of judge, PUBLIC PROSECUTOR, or lawyer in private practice, during the two years at the institute. Judges' salaries are fixed higher than those of prosecutors, but there has been little switchover to judgeships because of the heavy workload.

All judges, except for the emperor-appointed Supreme Court chief justice, are appointed by the cabinet. A new judge is normally appointed for 10 years to the post of assistant judge, and then he is up for reappointment and promotion to a full judge. An assistant judge after the initial five years is expected to function as a full judge, and in another five years he is made a full judge. Then he is appointed acting high court judge, and after another five years he is promoted to regular high court judge. After the first 20 years, the seniority system is replaced by a merit system under which young and able judges pass over less competent older judges. The compulsory retirement age is 70 for Supreme Court justices and summary court judges and 65 for career judges of high courts and district courts. An analysis of 66 Supreme Court justices who served on the bench from the inception of the postwar Supreme Court in 1947 to mid-1977 indicates that the average age at the time of their appointments was 62 with an average of 6.2 years service; breakdowns of

their prior occupations showed 25 judges, 6 prosecutors, 22 attorneys, and 13 scholars. Supreme Court justices are subject to popular review and dismissal by voters at the first general election after their initial appointment and every 10 years thereafter. See also JUDICIAL SYSTEM; LEGAL SYSTEM: history of Japanese law. *Hiroshi ITOH*

judicial precedents

(hanrei). Precedents established by previous court decisions. In Japan, judicial precedents are recognized as having binding force, but whether or not they should be considered a source of law is currently a matter of debate among scholars of jurisprudence. Judicial precedents are considered binding for the following reasons: since the SUPREME COURT has the final power of decision in litigation, lower courts tend to follow its lead in handing down decisions; modification of a previous position held by the Supreme Court can be made only by the Grand Bench of the Supreme Court (Court Law, art. 10, item 9); and decisions rendered by lower courts contrary to judicial precedents set by the Supreme Court become grounds for appeal (Code of Civil Procedure, art. 48; Code of Criminal Procedure, art. 405). Judicial precedents have considerable significance; they play a major role in determining legal questions in such matters as common-law marriage and the transfer of securities, which have not yet become subject to legislation. *ENDŌ Hiroshi*

judicial review

(iken rippō shinsa ken; also referred to as *hōrei shinsa ken*). The power of the courts to determine the constitutionality of legislative and administrative acts. The 1947 CONSTITUTION is characterized by a strong emphasis on fundamental human rights. Under the old system, the courts had no power to protect these rights from infringement by the legislature or the executive. In applying the principles of separation of powers and checks and balances, the new charter freed the judiciary from ministerial tutelage, established it as a truly independent third branch of the government, and entrusted it with the power of judicial review under the following provisions: "The SUPREME COURT is the court of last resort with power to determine the constitutionality of any law, order, regulation or official act" (art. 81). It further provides that "This Constitution shall be the supreme law of the nation and no law, ordinance, imperial rescript or other act of government, or part thereof, contrary to the provisions hereof, shall have legal force or validity" (art. 98, para. 1). Japanese legal scholars were initially divided as to the meaning of these provisions of the constitution. According to the predominant school of thought, these articles provided an American-style system of judicial review, where ordinary courts exercise the power of judicial review in connection with specific cases or controversies. Another interpretation of the articles maintained that such power should be vested exclusively in the Supreme Court, which, like the German Constitutional Court, would perform that sole function for general and abstract, as well as specific questions. The former view has been adopted by the Supreme Court of Japan (see SUZUKI DECISION) and, in their actual operation of judicial review, Japanese courts tend to give weight to the example of American courts.

Japanese courts are reluctant to deal with constitutional issues related to political questions, party standing, or similar matters. In the ENIWA CASE (*Japan v. Nozaki*, Sapporo District Court, 29 March 1967), which involved a violation of the Self Defense Forces (SDF) Law, the defense argued that the law was unconstitutional because it violated the so-called pacifist provision of the constitution (art. 9). The Sapporo District Court disposed of the case on technicalities without dealing with the issue of constitutionality.

Justiciability of so-called political questions (tōchi kōi) that involve legislative internal matters, legislative reapportionment, and foreign affairs is a subject of some discussion. In the Tomabechi case (*Tomabechi v. Japan*, Supreme Court, GB, 8 June 1960, 14 Minshū 1206), for example, the plaintiff challenged the constitutionality of a dissolution of the House of Representatives. The Japanese Supreme Court refused to deal with the constitutionality issue on the ground that the dispute was a political question and therefore not subject to judicial review.

Another issue of justiciability of legislative internal matters is the question whether an expelled member of a legislature may seek redress and reinstatement through the courts. The courts and legal scholars generally regard this affirmatively where members of local assemblies are concerned and negatively where members of the Diet are concerned, because of the doctrine of separation of powers. In

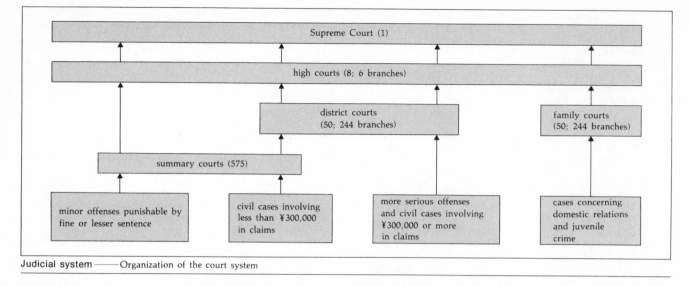

Judicial system——Organization of the court system

the second case, to give the court judicial review power over the Diet would make the court superior to the legislature.

Initially, Japanese courts took the position that the question of legislative reapportionment was essentially political and therefore not justiciable. In 1976, however, the Japanese Supreme Court for the first time dealt directly with the question and declared misapportionment of an electoral district unconstitutional, on the ground that it violated the equal protection clause (art. 14) of the constitution (*Kurokawa* v. *Chiba Prefectural Election Administration Commission*, Supreme Court Judgment, 14 April 1976, 30 Minshū 223). This decision was apparently influenced by a similar decision in 1962 by the United States Supreme Court (*Baker* v. *Carr*, 369 US 186 [1962]).

The views of Japanese jurists are split in cases involving justiciability of treaties. One view denies the courts' power to review the constitutionality of treaties, based on the language of article 81 of the constitution, which does not specifically enumerate the word "treaty" and on article 98, paragraph 2: "The treaties concluded by Japan and established laws of nations shall be faithfully observed." Another view regards treaties as being included within the words "regulation" or "official act" in article 81. Decisions of courts vary. In the SUNAGAWA CASE (*Japan* v. *Sakata*, Tōkyō District Court, 30 March 1959), the Tōkyō District Court reviewed the validity of the United States–Japan Security Treaty (see UNITED STATES–JAPAN SECURITY TREATIES) and found a violation of the "pacifist provision" of the constitution (1 Kakyū Keishū 776). However, on appeal, the Supreme Court unanimously reversed the decision of the Tōkyō District Court on the ground that the issue was highly political in nature and outside the purview of judicial review (Supreme Court, GB, 16 December 1959, 13 Keishū 3225). In the United States, by contrast, it seems to be established that treaties are subject to judicial review in order to secure the supremacy of the constitution.

The justiciability of cases involving the declaration of war has never been presented to the courts because the "pacifist provision" of the constitution has precluded raising such an issue. This will most likely remain a problem for as long as the SDF exists.

Certain procedural barriers interfere with judicial review, such as the standing to sue doctrine. An increasing number of class actions is an indication of the gradual liberalization of this doctrine.

Up to now, the lower courts have shown a greater inclination to declare governmental acts unconstitutional, particularly when a violation of civil rights is claimed. The Supreme Court, on the other hand, has exercised more restraint in the review of legislation than in the review of administrative acts. It has frequently and, some critics maintain, excessively balanced the rights and freedoms of the individual with considerations of public welfare on the basis of article 12 of the constitution, which directs the people to refrain from any abuse of these freedoms and to utilize them for the public welfare. On the whole, it may be recognized that Japanese courts make strenuous efforts to live up to their role as the guardians of the constitution. See also TŌKYŌ ORDINANCE DECISION.

ISHIMINE Keitetsu

judicial scrivener

(*shihō shoshi*). A legal functionary who can be engaged by the public to act as an agent in matters relating to the registration of trans-

fers of title to land or the making of deposits at a public deposit office, and for drafting documents to be filed in a court of law (Hōmukyoku), public prosecutor's office, or one of the eight regional Legal Affairs Bureaus. This status is granted to persons who have passed the judicial scriveners' examination or who have been recognized by the minister of justice as having the necessary qualifications to perform such duties (in actual practice the Ministry of Justice usually only recognizes experienced persons such as those who have previously served as administrative officers of courts, procurators' offices, or one of the Legal Affairs Bureaus), and their names are enrolled on a judicial scriveners' list maintained by each Legal Affairs Bureau. There are currently about 15,000 persons who have qualified as judicial scriveners. Under Japanese law, attorneys are generally charged with the handling of legal affairs and thus the scope of the practice of judicial scriveners is narrow. However, since in Japan attorneys are few in number and concentrated in metropolitan areas, judicial scriveners in rural localities often play a large role in the legal affairs of their clients.

KOJIMA Takeshi

judicial system

The unified national structure of courts for the administration of justice. The 1947 CONSTITUTION (art. 76) provides that "the whole judicial power is vested in a Supreme Court and in such inferior courts as are established by law." All courts on all levels are parts of a single system under the sole and complete administration of the Supreme Court; there are no separate municipal, county, state, and federal systems as in the United States.

The structure of the judicial system is as follows: the SUPREME COURT (Saikō Saibansho); high courts (*kōtō saibansho*), eight, with six branches located in the eight principal geographical subdivisions of the country; district courts (*chihō saibansho*), 50, in the principal administrative units, with 244 branches; FAMILY COURTS (*katei saibansho*), the same number as the district courts and their branches; and summary courts (*kan'i saibansho*), 575, located throughout the country. The DIET as the sole law-making organ of the state can change the organization of the courts by passing the necessary legislation, but the administration of the court system remains constitutionally vested in the Supreme Court.

The Supreme Court is headed by the chief justice, who is appointed by the emperor after designation by the cabinet. The other 14 justices (the number being determined by law) are appointed by the cabinet. The court is organized into a grand bench consisting of all 15 justices and three petty benches of five justices each. Cases are initially referred to the petty benches, which decide whether they should be heard by the grand bench or one of the petty benches. Constitutional cases for which there are no precedents, cases deemed by a petty bench to be of outstanding importance, and cases involving tie votes or the overruling of a grand bench precedent by a petty bench on a nonconstitutional issue must be heard by the grand bench. When the full court considers administrative matters of the judiciary, it sits as the judicial assembly. All cases before the Supreme Court are appeals; it possesses original jurisdiction over no cases.

The Court Organization Law (Saibansho Kōsei Hō) provides that Supreme Court justices must be at least 40 years old and possess broad vision and extensive knowledge of the law, gained through between 10 and 20 years experience as judges, prosecutors, lawyers, or professors of law at leading universities. The constitution provides that appointments of Supreme Court justices must be reviewed by the people in the first general election for the House of Representatives following appointment and every 10 years thereafter. No justice has ever failed to receive popular approval, the favorable vote being typically 90 percent or better. Justices, as is true of all judges, can be removed from office only by impeachment or by being judicially declared mentally or physically incompetent to discharge their duties.

In addition to its power to administer the entire judicial system, the Supreme Court constitutionally possesses the rule-making power under which it determines the rules of litigation and those concerning matters relating to attorneys, the discipline of the courts, and the administration of judicial affairs. The constitution also provides that public prosecutors are subject to the court's rule-making power. The rule-making power is circumscribed to some extent by the codes of CRIMINAL PROCEDURE of 506 articles and of CIVIL PROCEDURE of 805 articles, both of which have been enacted and can be amended by the Diet. The Supreme Court's rules of criminal and civil procedure are supplementary to the codes and focus on the conduct of trials and litigation. See also CRIMINAL LAW.

The constitution also provides that the Supreme Court is the court of last resort "with power to determine the constitutionality of any law, order, regulation or official act." This power resembles that of the US Supreme Court. However, the court in several decisions has established the view that it will exercise this power only in cases where there is clearly obvious constitutionality or invalidity. The court bases this position on the explicit statement in the constitution that the Diet is "the highest organ of state power," deriving its position from the sovereignty of the people. Under this view, constitutional ambiguity can be removed by amendment by the legislative branch or, ultimately perhaps, by the sovereign people, who can vote out of office legislators responsible for constitutionally questionable laws. The court has also ruled that it does not possess the character of a constitutional court, that is, one that can rule abstractly in the absence of concrete legal disputes on constitutional questions. Because of this position and its acceptance of legislative supremacy, the court has found unconstitutionality in only a handful of cases.

Although the court accepts the doctrine of legislative supremacy, it has also defended its constitutionally bestowed monopoly of judicial power. In 1948 the Judicial Committee of the House of Councillors issued a report strongly critical of a court decision in a controversial criminal case. The Supreme Court then issued a strong attack on the report as being a legislative infringement on the judicial power. Since then there has not been an attempt at legislative interference with the courts.

The Supreme Court, under law, operates three training institutes: one for court clerks, one for family court probation officers, and finally and most important, the LEGAL TRAINING AND RESEARCH INSTITUTE. The last is responsible for research, for training judges and other court officials, and for the education of judicial apprentices. All who enter the legal profession—as judges, prosecutors, or lawyers—are trained in the institute as legal apprentices. Universities have faculties (or schools) of law, but students acquire only a general knowledge of law. University graduates wishing to enter the Legal Training and Research Institute and subsequently the legal profession must pass a highly competitive entrance examination. The two-year course is divided into one-third classroom work and two-thirds field training in the civil and criminal divisions of district courts, district prosecutors' offices, and prefectural attorneys' associations. Entering classes average under 400 students and almost no one fails to complete the course. A majority become attorneys, with judges and prosecutors following in that order. The number in the last two categories is fixed.

The high courts are essentially appellate courts. They are courts of first instance for the crimes of insurrection, preparation for or plotting of insurrection, and of assistance in the acts enumerated. High courts may also be granted jurisdiction over other types of case by special provisions in duly enacted laws. High courts are collegiate courts, that is, the number of judges is three, except in cases involving insurrection when the number is five. One of the judges acts as presiding judge.

District courts have original jurisdiction over most cases with the exception of offenses carrying minor punishment and a few others reserved for other courts. In addition, they are courts of appeal for actions taken by the summary courts. District court trials are conducted by a single judge, except for those which must be heard by a

three-member collegiate court. The exceptions are: cases in which a collegiate court has ruled that hearings will be held and judgments rendered by a collegiate court; cases involving the death penalty, life imprisonment, or imprisonment of more than one year; and appeals of judgments, rulings, or orders of summary courts. Assistant judges may sit in district courts, but they cannot render independent decisions (unless empowered to do so by a specific law), nor can they constitute a majority of a collegiate court or serve as a presiding judge of a collegiate court.

Family courts came into existence under the Allied Occupation (1945–52). Family courts have jurisdiction over such matters as juvenile crime (the age of majority being 20), problems of minors, divorce, and disputes over family property. Most formal proceedings are handled by a single judge. However, the emphasis in these courts is on CONCILIATION, not on formal trial. Conciliation is handled by a three-member committee, consisting of a judge and two commissioners who, in most instances, are not lawyers. Conciliation is reached when both parties agree to a proposed settlement. Cases come to trial only when conciliation fails.

Summary courts have jurisdiction over minor cases involving less than ¥300,000 (about US $1,500) in claims or fines or lighter punishment in offenses. With certain exceptions summary courts cannot impose imprisonment or graver sentences. If a summary court believes that an offense should be punished by a sentence heavier than it is empowered to impose, it must transfer the case to a district court. A single judge presides over a summary court.

There is no jury system in Japan. A jury system did exist between 1923 and 1943, but it differed significantly from the American system, for example. The jury was used only in cases involving serious crime. The accused could request a jury in some cases, and in others the right to a jury trial could be waived. Some types of crime were excluded from trial by jury. Even when used, juries had only a minor role in trials, being limited to answering questions submitted by the judge on the existence or nonexistence of facts. Juries were very little used, both because of their limited powers and because the Japanese preferred trial by judge.

Because the old system of criminal justice was conspicuously lacking in guarantees of the rights of the accused in court, the 1947 constitution contains a number of such guarantees. In addition to the principle that all are equal under the law, the constitution provides for: no deprivation of life or liberty or imposition of any criminal penalty except under legally established procedures; no denial of access to the courts; no arrest except under warrant; no arrest or detention without immediate notification of charges, without adequate cause or without the privilege of counsel; the right to a speedy and public trial; freedom from double jeopardy; and so on. The courts are bound by all these provisions. Some conservative critics have argued that to have such guarantees in the constitution goes too far in the defense of the rights of alleged criminals and that they really belong in the Code of Criminal Procedure.

The Japanese people as a whole reveal far less inclination to go to court to decide disputes than many other peoples. It has been estimated, for example, that the number of civil suits per capita in Japanese courts is between one-tenth and one-twentieth of the number in common-law countries. This lack of litigiousness is reflected in the fact that in 1982 there were only about 12,000 lawyers in Japan, almost half of whom were concentrated in Tōkyō. Not only are the Japanese reluctant to go to court, but many choose not to be represented by an attorney.

The common explanation of the Japanese attitude toward litigation is that traditionally the society has placed a very high value on the maintenance of harmony in social relations. By definition the adversary relationship inherent in litigation is disruptive of harmonious relationships. Furthermore, the normal outcome of litigation is the determination of a winner and a loser which results in a further impairment of harmony. See also LAW, ATTITUDES TOWARD; LAWYERS. Conciliation, either informal or formal as expressed through the legally recognized device of conciliation commissions, is regarded as an acceptable alternative to litigation. Conciliation ideally does not result in clear winners and losers as in litigation, but in an adjustment of positions in which each side gains on some points and yields on others. See also DISPUTE RESOLUTION SYSTEMS OTHER THAN LITIGATION.

━━Hiroshi Itoh and Lawrence Beer, ed, *The Constitutional Case Law of Japan: Selected Supreme Court Decisions, 1961–70* (1978). John M. Maki, *Court and Constitution in Japan: Selected Supreme Court Decisions, 1948–60* (1964). Arthur von Mehren, ed, *Law in Japan: The Legal Order in a Changing Society* (1963). Hideo Tanaka, *The Japanese Legal System* (1976).   John M. MAKI

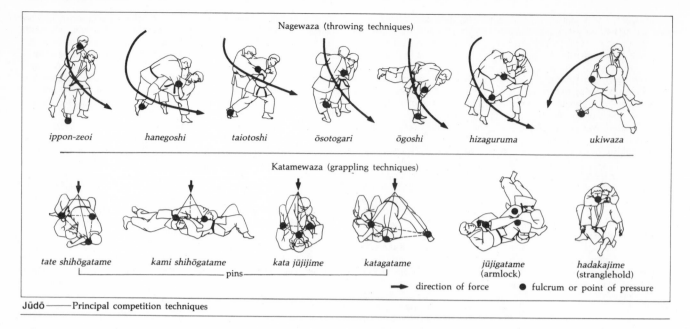

Nagewaza (throwing techniques)

ippon-zeoi hanegoshi taiotoshi ōsotogari ōgoshi hizaguruma ukiwaza

Katamewaza (grappling techniques)

tate shihōgatame kami shihōgatame kata jūjijime katagatame jūjigatame (armlock) hadakajime (stranglehold)

————— pins —————

→ direction of force ● fulcrum or point of pressure

Jūdō——Principal competition techniques

jūdō

(literally, "the Way of softness"). A form of unarmed combat that stresses agile motions, astute mental judgment, and rigorous form, rather than sheer physical strength. Techniques include throwing, grappling, and attacking vital points. It was developed as a sport by KANŌ JIGORŌ (1860–1938) from jūjutsu, which had been transmitted to Japan from the Asian continent in ancient times. It has been valued as a method of exercise, moral training, and self-defense.

History and Development——Jūjutsu was one of the MARTIAL ARTS used for subduing an armed opponent without the use of weapons. Although known by various names throughout history, after the middle of the Edo period (1600–1868) this technique was called jūjutsu. The Chinese character for jū derives from a passage in the ancient Chinese military treatise, the Sanlüe (San-lüeh), that states, "Softness (jū; Ch: rou or jou) controls hardness well." In order for a weaker force to defeat a stronger, the weaker force must submit to being pushed or pulled, without opposing the attacker's established power, thus nullifying the striking force. Before being touched by an opponent, the position of one's body should be changed; it is then necessary to be quick to attack and topple the opponent when he or she is off balance. The ability to move quickly and with agility is essential, and this is the reason why the basic posture of jūdō is a loose and natural stance.

Jūjutsu began with sechie-zumō (court banquet wrestling), a court event popular in the Nara (710–794) and Heian (794–1185) periods. Beginning in the Kamakura period (1185–1333), samurai SUMŌ wrestling was encouraged, since warriors practiced yoroi kumiuchi (grappling while suited in armor) on the battlefield. After 1543, when firearms were introduced, warriors on the battlefield changed to lighter dress. During the sustained peace of the Edo period, jūjutsu developed as a self-defense martial art and was used in making arrests. It was then called heifuku kumiuchi (grappling in ordinary clothes). Throwing and holding-down techniques were especially emphasized as a means of controlling opponents without shedding blood. The mental attitude that makes no distinction between emergencies and normal situations gave rise to such delicate moves as suwariwaza (the squatting technique).

In the Edo period, many schools arose that developed new features derived from the basic jūjutsu. These new forms were guarded as secret methods by each school; at least 179 schools are recorded. The main schools were the Takenouchi school founded by Takenouchi Hisamori (1503–95), the Sekiguchi school founded by Sekiguchi Ujimune (1597–1670), the Kitō school founded by Terada Masashige (1618–74), the Shibukawa school founded by Shibukawa Yoshikata (1652–1704), and the Tenjin Shin'yō school founded by Iso Masatari (1786–1863).

These jūjutsu schools declined with the collapse of the samurai class after the Meiji Restoration of 1868. Kanō Jigorō, who was a student at that time, studied the methods of the Tenjin Shin'yō and Kitō schools. He modernized these techniques and in 1882 orga-

nized the KŌDŌKAN jūdō school at Eishōji, a temple in the Shitaya section of Tōkyō. The school moved five times before finally settling at the Shintomizaka gymnasium in 1906. During that time, Kanō arranged a system of training in the techniques and fostered a great number of accomplished disciples. He also established freestyle exercise (randori), based on throwing and grappling techniques. He was the first to organize jūdō matches.

Expansion——The Peers' School (see GAKUSHŪIN UNIVERSITY), recognizing the educational value of jūdō, was the first to include it in a school curriculum, in 1883. In 1911, in accordance with a directive of the Ministry of Education, jūdō became a requirement in middle school physical education programs. After 1939, jūdō became a required subject for all male primary school pupils above the fifth grade. Immediately after World War II, school jūdō was prohibited by the Allied Occupation. In 1949, however, the All-Japan Jūdō Federation (Zen Nihon Jūdō Remmei) was organized with support from the Japan Amateur Sports Association (Nihon Taiiku Kyōkai). In 1951, school jūdō was revived, and leagues were established at the various levels. Jūdō clubs were also set up in various large companies. In 1952 the International Jūdō Federation was established with 17 participating countries; and in 1956 the first world jūdō championships were held in Tōkyō. Jūdō was made a formal entry in the Olympics for the first time in 1964 at the Tōkyō games. At present, about 107 countries belong to the International Jūdō Federation.

Competition Techniques——Techniques (waza) are divided into three categories: throwing (nagewaza), grappling (katamewaza), and attacking vital points (atemiwaza). The first two are used in competition, but the atemiwaza is used only in practice. Nagewaza comprises hand, hip, foot, head-on sacrificing, and side-sacrificing techniques. Katamewaza (grappling) is made up of holding, strangling, and armlocks.

The Kōdōkan Jūdō Umpirage Regulations require one main referee and two assistant referees. International competitions take place according to the rules of the International Jūdō Federation. Tournament divisions are either unrestricted, or limited by weight, rank, and age.

The floor space for the contest is, by rule, 14.55 square meters (47.74 sq ft) with an inner area 9.1 square meters (29.84 sq ft) covered by 50 tatami mats. A 2.73 meter (8.95 ft) border of tatami mats surrounds the inner area. A 7 cm (2.75 in) warning strip is laid out in order to divide the inner area clearly from the outer. The tournament time is decided in advance and ranges from 3 to 20 minutes.

After the contestants bow to each other, they begin the match on command from the main judge. The bout commences in the standing position. Floor techniques are used only after some throwing or grappling in the standing position has been fairly effective. A full point (ippon) is awarded for a throwing, holding, strangling, or joint-lock (e.g., armlock) technique; the match ends when one contestant receives ippon. If time runs out, the judges can award victory based on partial points or call a draw.

Jūdō

A *jūdō* match being won by the *ōsotogari* throw, the initial movement of which is shown in the accompanying drawing.

A contestant scores a full point for a throwing technique when he has thrown his opponent with considerable force and has made him fall on his back or when he has evaded his opponent's throwing technique. For a grappling technique, *ippon* is awarded when the opponent declares "I'm beaten" *(maitta)* or signals this by tapping the opponent, the *tatami*, or himself two or more times with hand or foot. With grappling techniques, *ippon* is gained for holding down the opponent for 30 seconds, or through strangling or joint-lock techniques that are judged to be sufficient.

Partial points *(waza ari)* are awarded when the throwing technique is close to being perfect and when the hold was maintained for 25 or 30 seconds. Thus a victory may be narrowly awarded through accumulation of partial points; or one may lose through accumulated warnings (i.e., demerits). When a decision is not awarded within the set time, a draw is declared.

The System of Ranks——Kanō Jigorō set up a system of ranks *(dan)* and classes *(kyū)* as an encouragement for his disciples. These ranks have been recognized internationally. There are ranks from 1 to 10, with 10 the highest. Those in ranks 1 to 5 wear a black belt, ranks 6 to 8 have a scarlet and white striped belt, and those in ranks 9 to 10 have a scarlet belt. The classes are below the ranks and range from the fifth class to the first and highest class. Adults in the first to third class wear a brown belt; boys in the first to third class wear a purple belt. Those in the fourth and fifth class wear a white belt. Women have a white stripe inserted in the middle of the belt to indicate the particular rank and class. *Tomiki Kenji*

Jūgatsu Jiken → October Incident

Jūhachi Daitsū

("The 18 Connoisseurs"). A group of wealthy men who dominated the *beau monde* of Edo (now Tōkyō) during the An'ei (1772–81) and Temmei (1781–89) eras. The group was not necessarily limited to 18, the number being chosen as auspicious. Since the mid-18th century the townspeople (CHŌNIN) of Edo had channeled much of their energy and rapidly increasing wealth into a distinctive and extravagant world of entertainment and pleasure. The recognized leaders of this sophisticated, style-conscious society proclaimed themselves *tsū* ("discerning ones"), and prominent among them were the *daitsū* ("great *tsū*"; connoisseurs), whose aesthetic of elegance and refinement set the standard for the rest. Most of the Jūhachi Daitsū were wealthy merchants such as rice brokers (FUDASASHI) and money changers (RYŌGAESHŌ), but some were also high-ranking *samurai*, one indication of the pervading attraction of urban merchant culture and the breakdown of traditional Confucian discipline among the warrior class. See also IKI AND SUI.

Jūichigatsu Jiken → November Incident

Jūjō Paper Co, Ltd

(Jūjō Seishi). A manufacturer of paper and pulp, the Jūjō Paper Co was established in 1949 when the ŌJI PAPER CO, LTD, was divided

into three companies. It controls a large share of Japan's newsprint and uncoated printing-paper markets. The firm began export of its noncarbon paper to Europe in the 1960s. The North Pacific Paper Corporation, a joint company established by Jūjō with the Weyerhaeuser Co of the United States, began production of newsprint in 1979, stabilizing the supply of the product in Japan. The company is also participating in joint enterprises for pulp production in Brazil and Canada. It has seven paper manufacturing plants and two carbon plants. Sales for the fiscal year ending March 1982 totaled ￥311 billion (US $1.3 billion), with paper and pulp making up 88 percent of the sales. The company was capitalized at ￥12.8 billion (US $53.2 million). Corporate headquarters are located in Tōkyō. See also HONSHŪ PAPER CO, LTD.

Jūjūshin ron

(Treatise on the Ten Stages of the Development of Mind). Full title, *Himitsu mandara jūjūshin ron*. A work in 10 volumes by KŪKAI, the founder of the SHINGON SECT of Japanese Buddhism. It was most probably written in 830. When in 829 Emperor Junna (r 823–833) requested the abbots of the six Buddhist sects to present in writing the main points of their sects' doctrines, Kūkai wrote this treatise to explain the Shingon philosophy. Using a scheme of 10 stages to rank the profundity of various Buddhist and non-Buddhist doctrines, he places Shingon at the highest stage and each of the other doctrines at one of the lower nine stages. The 10 stages also describe the spiritual ascent of a Shingon monk. The more popular *Hizōhōyaku* (The Precious Key to the Secret Treasure) is a condensed edition of this work. *Robert Rhodes*

jūjutsu → jūdō

juka bijin

(literally, "beauty under a tree"). A pictorial motif of Indian origin that is the subject of a famous folding screen in the SHŌSŌIN repository in Nara. Each of the six extant panels depicts a single lady standing or seated on a rock beneath a tree. Originally their hair and garments glistened with colorful pheasant feathers, but now only the ink underdrawing and the flesh tones on faces and hands remain. With arched eyebrows and bowed lips on pear-shaped faces framed by ballooning masses of hair, these plump ladies embody the Chinese ideal of feminine beauty prevailing in Tang (T'ang) dynasty (618–907) court circles. Besides being an important dated example of 8th-century pictorial style, this work documents the eastern terminus of a motif that can be traced from its appearance in India (ca 100 BC) across Central Asia, through China, to Japan. *Carolyn Wheelwright*

juku

(private tutoring school). In the Edo period (1600–1868) the term *juku* referred to small schools founded by individual scholars or educators specifically for the teaching of martial arts, some other special skill, or the doctrines of a particular philosophical school. Other types of schools were *hankō* (domain schools) for *samurai* youth and TERAKOYA for the children of commoners (see EDUCATION: Edo-period education). After a system of universal elementary education was implemented in the early part of the Meiji period (1868–1912) *juku* came to mean privately run tutoring establishments, often specializing in a particular subject such as English, the abacus, or piano, as opposed to ordinary public or private schools.

Modern *juku* may offer lessons in nonacademic subjects such as arts and sports or in the academic subjects that are important in school ENTRANCE EXAMINATIONS, primarily English, mathematics, and Japanese. *Juku* range from home establishments to large national chains. *Juku* for high school students must compete for enrollments with *yobikō* (CRAM SCHOOLS), which are solely geared to helping students pass university entrance examinations. The more rigorous *juku* require harder work, longer hours, and greater competitive spirit than the ordinary public or private school.

According to a Ministry of Education survey conducted in 1976, 20 percent of all Japanese elementary school students and 38 percent of all middle school students were attending *juku*; the percentages were much higher in large cities. At that time approximately 22,000 *juku* were in operation, with an average of five teachers and 137 students per school. More than half of these *juku* were founded after 1966. Most of the instructors were university students, followed by retired schoolteachers and schoolteachers willing to take on a second job. The annual expenditure for *juku* lessons was an estimated ¥200 billion (approximately US $800 million).

🔲————Mombushō, Daijin Kambō Chōsa Tōkeika, *Jidō seito no gakkōgai gakushū katsudō ni kansuru jittai chōsa hōkokusho* (1978). Thomas P. Rohlen, "The *Juku* Phenomenon: An Exploratory Essay," *Journal of Japanese Studies* 6.2 (1980).

jūmin soshō

(resident's lawsuit). A legal action by a resident of a locality to seek rectification of an illegality in the financial administration of local government; such suits are authorized by article 242 of the Local Autonomy Law (Chihō Jichi Hō, 1947).

This system was patterned after the American system of taxpayer's suits and was instituted after World War II. These suits are brought by residents for the sake of the public good, not for the purpose of seeking relief from the direct infringement of individual rights by local government. In the event of an illegal act or forbearance in financial accounting by an executive organ or official of a local government, a resident may first file a demand for an audit with a member of the auditing commission of the local government. If this does not suffice to achieve the purpose, the resident may then file a *jūmin soshō* in court.

In such a suit, a resident may seek an injunction against the unlawful act of the executive organ or official, a cancellation or a judgment of the invalidity of an administrative disposition, or a judgment of the illegality of a forbearance, or the resident may subrogate himself into the position of the local government and seek compensation for damages or demand the return of unjust enrichment.   *KOTANI Kōzō*

jumpō tōsō

(work-to-rule struggle). A form of labor dispute activity that falls short of a strike, a *jumpō tōsō* is conducted through the strict observance of work regulations with the purpose of disrupting the normal operations of an enterprise in order to press union demands. The tactic takes a number of forms, including strict enforcement of safety and sanitation regulations, refusal to work overtime, and simultaneous exercise of personal holiday privileges by a large number of workers.

In 1972 the Japanese National Railways Labor Union engaged in a "safe operation struggle" *(anzen unten tōsō)* in the Tōkyō metropolitan area, during which train speeds were lowered and trains were stopped whenever the automatic train stop buzzer sounded. By following operation regulations to the letter, the union was able to paralyze tightly scheduled railway traffic and disrupt the transportation of hundreds of thousands of commuters. The tactic was repeated the following year and led to widespread rioting by commuters on 13 March at Ageo station in Saitama Prefecture and on 24 April at 38 stations in Tōkyō.

The work-to-rule tactic originated with public employees, who are prohibited by law from striking, in an effort to avoid responsibility and criticism for engaging in illegal acts. Despite the "work-to-rule" tag, however, the courts have generally found these actions to be prohibited dispute activities. Private sector workers have on occasion employed these tactics, in which case they have been protected by the law. See also LABOR DISPUTES; LABOR LAWS; STRIKES AND OTHER FORMS OF LABOR DISPUTE.   *SUGENO Kazuo*

junior colleges

(tanki daigaku). Two- or three-year colleges designated in 1950, as part of the post–World War II educational reforms, to provide both general education and specialized training. Initially, the Ministry of Education considered that junior colleges would train middle-grade technicians in response to strong demand from Japanese industry, but this function was taken over by various specialized technical schools and company training programs. Now junior colleges are associated mainly with WOMEN'S EDUCATION, since they accommodate around two-thirds of the women who continue their schooling after high school.

As of 1978 there were 519 junior colleges in Japan with about 380,000 students. Of these the majority were private colleges (436 schools with 347,000 students). Approximately 30 percent of the Japanese who continue their education after high school attend junior colleges; of these, 90 percent are women. The subjects most studied there by women are home economics, education, and the humanities, since the majority of women still seek employment as teachers or office workers before marriage.   *AMANO Ikuo*

junshi

Self-immolation of a nobleman's retainer following the death of his lord. Historically derived from *junsō* (Ch: *xunzang* or *hsun-tsang*), the ancient Chinese custom of burying attendants alive with the lord's body. The annotation to the *Book of Rites* (Ch: *Li ji* or *Li chi*) defines *xun* (J: *jun*) as "the killing of a person or persons to guard a dead man." Thus the practice did not originally mean suicide. Some of the imperial graves of the Shang dynasty (?–BC 1027) reveal that the emperor's attendants were killed and buried with the emperor's body in order to attend to the latter's needs in the other world.

It is not certain whether or not this custom was practiced in ancient Japan. The NIHON SHOKI (720) records that in the 28th year of the reign of Emperor Suinin, when the emperor's younger brother Yamatohiko no Mikoto passed away, the prince's closest attendants were buried alive with the body. They were found to be alive several days after the burial, however, and the emperor prohibited the custom. The chronicle further states that upon the death of Suinin's consort in the 32nd year of his rule, the emperor adopted the recommendation of Nomi no Sukune to place clay figures of men and horses (HANIWA) around the grave. The account is generally considered a later fabrication to explain the origins of *haniwa*. The account of Japan in the 3rd-century Chinese chronicle WEI ZHI *(Wei chih)* states that more than 100 slaves were killed and buried with the body of HIMIKO, queen of Yamatai. In spite of these references to the custom in ancient records, there is little archaeological evidence to support them.

Historically speaking, in Japan the term *junshi* is applied to the suicide of a *samurai* for the purpose of following his lord in death. In most cases, this took the form of disembowelment (HARAKIRI), which was in the case of *junshi* variously called *oibara* ("disembowelment to follow") or *tomobara* ("disembowelment to accompany"). With the emergence of the warrior class in the 10th century, it was not uncommon for retainers to perish with their lord in battle or to commit suicide immediately afterward if their lord was killed. A retainer did not in those days commit *junshi* if his lord died a natural death, although the *Meitokuki* (compiled ca 1400) mentions an unprecedented case in which a certain Mishima Geki committed *harakiri* following the natural death of his lord, the shogunal deputy *(kanrei)* Hosokawa Yoriyuki, in the year 1392.

It was not until the 17th century, when peace was established by the Tokugawa shogunate, that many retainers took to committing *junshi* on the death of their lord through illness or natural causes. These acts were considered ultimate expressions of loyalty and gratitude for favors received. The first recorded case is in 1607, when two retainers committed *junshi* after the death by natural causes of Matsudaira Tadayoshi, the fourth son of TOKUGAWA IEYASU and lord of the Kiyosu domain (in what is now Aichi Prefecture). When Yūki Hideyasu, Ieyasu's second son and lord of the Fukui domain (now Fukui Prefecture), died of illness the same year, two of his retainers committed *junshi*. The suicide of Hideyasu's chief retainer *(karō)*, Honda Tomimasa, was only prevented by the shōgun TOKUGAWA HIDETADA and the retired shōgun Ieyasu, who were both opposed to the custom. Tomimasa subsequently took Buddhist orders.

Although Ieyasu viewed the custom with distaste (which is perhaps the reason why his own death was not followed by any such acts), *junshi* was generally considered an act of virtue, and retainers who committed suicide were honored by being buried beside their lord and having their families well provided for. These factors accounted for a growing increase in the number of *junshi*. In fact it came to be expected of retainers who had been given special favors such as high stipends and high posts or had been specially pardoned for certain crimes, and to shirk it was considered cowardly and disloyal. Moreover, some *daimyō* came to regard the number of self-immolating retainers as a mark of prestige. When DATE MASAMUNE, daimyō of the Sendai domain, died in 1636, 15 of his men committed suicide. These men were followed by 5 of their own retainers. In 1641 when the daimyō of the Kumamoto domain, Hosokawa Tadatoshi, died 18 of his retainers committed suicide.

Despite Ieyasu's censure of *junshi*, the custom of *junshi* following the deaths of shōguns persisted. Notable instances are the suicide in 1632 of the *rōjū* (senior councillor) Morikawa Shigetoshi following the death of the second shōgun Hidetada and the suicide in 1651 of the *rōjū* Hotta Masamori and Abe Shigetsugu following the death from illness of the third shōgun Iemitsu.

The growing number of deaths by *junshi* laid bare its negative aspects—the loss of men of ability and the formalization of a custom that was observed not out of loyalty but to save face. A contemporary document, the *Meiryō kōhan*, lists three types of *junshi*: *gibara*, performed from the depths of the heart according to the moral ties between lord and retainer; *rombara*, performed upon the reasoning that, since others committed suicide, one had no choice but to die; and *shōbara*, committed for mercenary purposes to benefit one's descendants.

Criticism of the custom arose from several quarters, and in 1663 shōgun TOKUGAWA IETSUNA orally forbade *junshi* and added that the successors of daimyō would be made responsible for any *junshi* that might ensue upon their deaths. Thus in 1668, when Sugiura Saemon no Hyōe committed suicide following the death of Okudaira Tadamasa, daimyō of the Utsunomiya domain, Tadamasa's successor Masayoshi was punished by having his domain reduced by 20,000 *koku* (1 *koku* = about 180 liters or 5 US bushels), and the two sons of Sugiura were beheaded. The prohibition against *junshi* was formally added to the BUKE SHOHATTO (Laws for Military Houses) during the rule of the fifth shōgun, TOKUGAWA TSUNAYOSHI.

Although the custom of *junshi* was a phenomenon peculiar to the transition years from the Sengoku period (1467–1568) to the early part of the Edo period (1600–1868), its motivating force was derived from the Way of the warrior (BUSHIDŌ), a long-revered code that demanded unconditional loyalty, even unto death. As long as the motive was pure, *junshi* could be a virtuous act. In time, however, loyalty and obligation came to be seen in terms of exchange of services for favors granted, and duty, too, came to be interpreted as living up to one's social station. Thus, what had been an act of self-effacement became an act of saving face.

During the Tokugawa rule, the prohibition of *junshi* was violated only once more—in the celebrated FORTY-SEVEN RŌNIN INCIDENT. In 1701 Asano Naganori, the lord of the Akō domain, was ordered to commit *harakiri* after inflicting a wound on KIRA YOSHINAKA at Edo Castle. A band of his retainers killed Kira early in 1703. They were ordered to commit suicide by the shōgun, but since they had acted in full awareness of their inevitable punishment, their deaths were regarded as a form of *junshi*.

In Japan's modern period there has been one isolated case of *junshi*—the suicide of General NOGI MARESUKE on the day of Emperor Meiji's funeral. His act drew criticism from several young intellectuals at the time, but the majority of people were deeply moved. The novelist MORI ŌGAI was impelled by the incident to write *Okitsu Yagoemon no isho* (1913; The Last Will of Okitsu Yagoemon) and *Abe ichizoku* (1913; tr *The Abe Family*, 1977), the latter a historical novel centering on the *junshi* of retainers of Hosokawa Tadatoshi. Nogi's death plays an important part in NATSUME SŌSEKI's novel *Kokoro* (1914; tr *Kokoro*, 1957). It should be noted that Nogi was subsequently enshrined by the government and held up as a shining example of loyalty to the emperor.

Bitō Masahide

Juntoku, Emperor (1197–1242)

The 84th sovereign *(tennō)* in the traditional count (which includes several nonhistorical emperors); reigned 1210–21. Third son of Emperor GO-TOBA, who ruled from retirement throughout Juntoku's reign. With his father, Juntoku formed a plot to overthrow the Kamakura shogunate (1192–1333) and reassert the authority of the court. In 1221 he abdicated in favor of his son Emperor Chūkyō (1218–34; r 1221) and mobilized his forces, which were quickly defeated by those of the shogunate. For his part in the uprising, known as the JŌKYŪ DISTURBANCE, Juntoku was exiled to the island of Sado (now part of Niigata Prefecture), where he died 21 years later. Juntoku was the author of a book of poetry criticism and of KIMPISHŌ, a work on court ceremonial. *G. Cameron Hurst III*

jurisprudence

(hōtetsugaku). Study of the nature and the origin and development of law. The term jurisprudence has been used in England (since the 1830s) and the United States to denote theoretical studies of law, as distinguished from legal learning from a purely practical point of view. In continental Europe, especially in the German-speaking countries, the term *Rechtsphilosophie* (philosophy of law) has been widely used. This difference in nomenclature reflected an actual difference between the Anglo-Saxon and the Continental traditions regarding the scope and methods of approach in theoretical studies of law and legal phenomena. After World War II, however, as a result of the increasing rapprochement between the common law and the civil law traditions, international cooperation has reached a stage in which there is now a fairly broad area of consensus among scholars of many civilized countries as to the general scope and subdivisions of this branch of learning. This field may be divided into three problem areas: definition and analysis; legal reasoning; and the criticism of law.

In Japan, jurisprudence in the modern sense came into being only after the "reception" of Western legal systems and legal learning in the Meiji period (1868–1912). If one includes, however, what have been commonly known as "natural law doctrines," one cannot overlook the fact that during the Edo period (1600–1868) there had been Confucian (Jugaku) schools of thought having some affinity with natural law doctrines.

Modern jurisprudence in Japan began in the 1880s with HOZUMI NOBUSHIGE, a gifted and original thinker who played a leading role in drafting the Civil Code. When Hozumi began to give lectures at Tōkyō University, he deliberately chose the word *hōrigaku* in preference to *hōritsu tetsugaku*, on the ground that the latter would have the strong metaphysical implications that characterized philosophy of law in the tradition of German idealism.

After Hozumi, however, the Anglo-Saxon tradition of empirically oriented jurisprudence receded to the background, giving way to metaphysical philosophy in the grand tradition of German idealism, which was often mingled with strains of nationalism. From the early 1920s, there emerged a marked tendency—as in other fields of social sciences and the humanities—toward eclecticism and pluralism. Among the various trends, Neo-Kantian schools of philosophy of law, represented by men like Gustav Radbruch, Emil Lask, and others, played a leading role.

After 1945 there came a remarkable burst of research and literature in the field of philosophy of law. As a result of extensive personnel exchanges under various projects, there has been a remarkable fusion of the Continental (and above all German) tradition of legal learning (including the field of jurisprudence) with the Anglo-Saxon tradition. During the first decade after World War II, a number of leading scholars, who had already been active in the pre-World War II period, published important new works and trained the younger generation. The tendency toward eclecticism and pluralism continued into the postwar period. During the first two decades of this period, the most important schools of thought were Marxism (partly because it had been suppressed for almost 20 years up to 1945); Neo-Thomism; and some of the new trends in German philosophy of law (new schools of implicit natural law doctrine represented by Hans Welzel, Arthur Kaufmann, and others).

After the mid-1960s, however, some new trends emerged, including the influence of the so-called Oxford school in philosophy, represented by H. L. A. Hart in jurisprudence; the influence of analytic philosophy (in the tradition of the Vienna Circle and "logical empiricism"); the influence of Karl Popper's critical rationalism, and so on. On the organizational level, it is noteworthy that since the early 1960s, the Japan Association for Legal Philosophy has been actively cooperating with the IVR (International Vereinigung für Rechts- und Sozialphilosophie), which currently has its headquarters in Basel, Switzerland. At present there is an IVR national section in Japan consisting of about 90 members, one of the largest national sections in the world.

At present, a broad consensus seems to prevail among the leading specialists in the field of jurisprudence in Japan regarding, at least, the major areas for research. These are the methodology of legal studies in the broader sense of the word, including studies of legal reasoning and of the judicial process; the history of social and political thought, with special emphasis on theories of law and the state (including studies of doctrines of dictatorship, democracy, world organization, etc.); "theories of justice" (or of "the just law"), including both what is called "normative" evaluation and criticism of existing legal institutions and "meta-ethical theories of justice."

📖——Jun'ichi Aomi, "Trends in Legal Learning: Japan," *International Social Science Journal* 22.3 (1970). *Aomi Jun'ichi*

juristic act

(hōritsu kōi). Action, regarding which the actor's intended effect is accorded recognition by law. The concept of the juristic act is illustrated with reference to a contract for the sale of immovable property as follows. The intent of parties to a sale, in particular, the intent of the seller, is to effect, using the device of a contract, the transfer of ownership of an immovable property from the seller to the buyer in exchange for a purchase price. The statement that this intended effect is recognized by law means that the law will assist the accomplishment of that intended effect. That is, either party may demand performance of the contract and where necessary, by resort to the courts, receive legal redress, such as compulsory execution of judgment (KYŌSEI SHIKKŌ).

Juristic acts are classified according to the nature of the intent expressed. The juristic act embodied in a sales contract is established by the concurrence of the parties' mutual expressions of intent, one to buy, the other to sell. This bilateral concurrence of mutual and interdependent expressions of intent is called a contract (keiyaku).

A juristic act which can be established by a unilateral expression of intent is called an independent act (tandoku kōi). Independent acts are divided into those that involve another party, such as avoidance, cancellation, and set-off, and those that do not involve another party, such as the making of a will. Juristic acts established by the concurrence of a multiplicity of mutual expressions of intent, such as the establishment of a company, are called joint acts (gōdō kōi).

Conditions for validity. In order for a juristic act to be valid, the content of the juristic act must be clearly determinable, and its object must be realizable. It must not be contrary to the public order or good morals. It must be free from false expressions of intent and mistakes of fact. The act must also be free from defects, such as the use of fraud or coercion to induce the other party's expression of intent.

The principle of freedom to perform juristic acts. Under the CIVIL CODE legal relationships among private persons are freely conducted pursuant to the intent of the individuals, and to the extent possible, intervention by the state is to be avoided. This is called either the principle of individual autonomy (shiteki jichi no gensoku) or the principle of freedom in juristic acts (hōritsu kōi no jiyū) or the principle of freedom of contract (keiyaku jiyū no gensoku).

The Japanese concept of the juristic act is derived from the German civil code. Both the German and Japanese systems attempt to explain all private legal relationships on the basis of the intent of the parties involved. By contrast, in Anglo-American law, which views rights and duties stemming from legal relationships as incidental to those relationships, the juristic act does not exist.　　　OKA Takashi

juristic person → hōjin

jūroku musashi

Children's game using a board with 1 master piece and 16 secondary pieces. Dating from the middle of the 17th century, jūroku musashi was originally a gambling game but later became popular as a family pastime. The master piece, named after the legendary warrior-monk Musashibō BENKEI, can take subordinate pieces when they fall on both sides of it in a straight line. The person wins who drives Benkei into a corner so that he cannot move.　　　SAITŌ Ryōsuke

Jūsan, Lake

(Jūsanko). Lagoon on the western coast of the Tsugaru Peninsula, northwestern Aomori Prefecture, northern Honshū. Connected by a canal to the Sea of Japan. Corbicula is the principal catch. From the Kamakura period (1185–1333) through the Edo period (1600–1868), the port town of Tosaminato flourished at the mouth of the lake. Land reclamation has been underway since 1948. Area: 20.6 sq km (8.0 sq mi); circumference: 25 km (16 mi); depth: 3 m (9.8 ft).

Jusco Co, Ltd

(Jasuko). Major chain store selling foodstuffs, clothing, and household goods. Jusco is an acronym for Japan United Stores Company. The company was established in 1969 with the merger of three chain stores; the nucleus of the present company was formed by one of them, the Okadaya chain, which had been established in 1926. Dur-ing the 1970s Jusco expanded its network of chain stores by absorbing small and medium supermarkets and small department stores; by the end of the decade it had a total of 30 of these stores as part of its chain. In the fiscal year ending February 1982 its 141 chain stores generated annual sales of ¥609.4 billion (US $2.6 billion), making it fourth among chain stores in the country, and the company was capitalized at ¥7.3 billion (US $31 million). Corporate headquarters are in Ōsaka.

Jūshichijō no Kempō → Seventeen-Article Constitution

jūshin

A group of senior statesmen, often retired prime ministers, who acted as unofficial advisers to the emperor in the selection of prime ministers from the early 1930s until the end of world War II. Since the middle of the Meiji period (1868–1912), the elder statesmen (GENRŌ) had performed that function, and with the death of YAMAGATA ARITOMO in 1922 and MATSUKATA MASAYOSHI in 1924, the responsibility fell to SAIONJI KIMMOCHI, the last surviving genrō. But in the 1930s his own advancing age and the growing military inference in politics made him increasingly reluctant to recommend prime ministers. Consequently a new advisory group, the jūshin, was formed to replace the genrō. They included the lord keeper of the privy seal (naidaijin), the president of the Privy Council (Sūmitsuin), and former prime ministers. In 1940 KIDO KŌICHI became lord keeper of the privy seal and in his capacity as jūshin nominated the bellicose TŌJŌ HIDEKI for the prime ministership in 1941. Jūshin were also summoned by the emperor on extraordinary occasions, for example, when declaring war against the Allies in December 1941 and accepting defeat in August 1945.

juvenile crime

Illegal acts committed by a person under 20 years of age fall under the jurisdiction of the JUVENILE LAW in Japan. Persons under 14 years of age are not subject to the Penal Code, and acts committed by them in violation of criminal laws and ordinances are not called crimes. The CHILD WELFARE LAW is sometimes applied to a person under the age of 18 when he or she commits a crime; especially in the case of a person under 14 years of age, the Child Welfare Law is first considered, and the Juvenile Law is applied only when the case cannot be resolved under the Child Welfare Law.

In 1978 a total of 136,801 juveniles between the ages of 14 and 19 were arrested for criminal offenses, excluding motor vehicle violations. This represented 35.8 percent of the total number of arrests, the largest percentage of all age groups. In contrast, the age group of 20–29 accounted for 23.7 percent of the arrests. Juvenile arrests have been increasing steadily since 1973, with an exceptional increase witnessed in 1978. Since the end of World War II, Japan has experienced two other waves of juvenile crime, with peaks in 1951 and 1964. The number of such arrests passed the postwar high in 1979. Because the crime rate for the over-20 age group has fallen since 1951, the target of countermeasures has shifted to juveniles. The highest crime rate and the highest rate of increase was for 15-year-olds, followed by 14- and 16-year-olds. The crime rate for 18- and 19-year-olds has fallen over the past decade and registered a small increase in 1978.

Shoplifting accounted for 31.3 percent of juvenile crime in 1978, followed by motorcycle theft (11.8 percent) and bicycle theft (11 percent). High school students (37.3 percent) and middle school students (31.1 percent) account for a growing proportion of the number of arrests. There were five arrests of boys to every girl arrested, but the ratio was ten to one a decade before.

Most cases of DRUG ABUSE among juveniles have involved the sniffing of organic solvents such as paint thinner that contain toluene. In 1978, 76 cases of death from drug abuse were recorded, the highest level in five years. The number of motorcycle gangs has been decreasing under strict surveillance by the police, but 307 groups with 22,442 members were entered on official lists in 1978; it is estimated that 70 percent of the members were under 20 years of age.

The number of juveniles arrested for the use of violence has been decreasing, but the incidence of such crime is still not negligible. In 1978 there were 1,292 reported cases of violence in the schools, with 6,763 students placed under guidance; 66 percent of these incidents took place in middle school. The number of cases of violence in the home is difficult to determine, since many of the cases are not reported, but magazines often publish letters from parents seeking advice, and the police and psychiatric clinics encounter the problem with some regularity. The use of violence by juveniles in the home sometimes leads to homicide or collective family SUICIDE, making this a serious social problem even though the cases are not numerous.

Juveniles arrested for criminal acts are turned over to the juvenile department of the FAMILY COURT, unless it is a serious offense, in which instance the case is turned over to the PUBLIC PROSECUTOR for an opinion on criminal prosecution. Juveniles under 14 years of age are turned over to a child consultation center, a social welfare office, or in some cases to the juvenile department of the family court. Nearly 95 percent of the juveniles who are arrested for a criminal offense are turned over to their guardian after interrogation by the police; they are then examined by the prosecutor or investigated by the family court without being placed in confinement. More than 70 percent of juveniles under 14 are returned to their guardians and are not committed to the consultation center.

The juvenile departments of the family courts receive reports on about 500,000 juveniles a year, of which nearly 60 percent are traffic offenses. Pretrial probation is ordered in about 10 percent of the cases heard by the family courts. The probation is supervised by an officer of the family court; in about 70 percent of the cases, the actual guidance and counseling is handled by a volunteer who reports to the officer. Another 10 percent of the juveniles arrested are given a careful medical and psychiatric examination at a juvenile diagnostic center; about one-fifth of these examinations result in the ordering of pretrial probation.

More than 45 percent of the arrested juveniles are released without punishment on the grounds of probable rehabilitation, and another 30 percent are released on the grounds of low criminality. About 8 percent are punished with post-trial probation under the supervision of the Ministry of Justice. Thus, over 80 percent of all arrested juveniles are returned to their guardians. Juveniles on probation are counselled by probation officers or volunteers (usually teachers, priests, or other community leaders) who are designated by the Ministry of Justice. In most cases, however, specialists play little role in the rehabilitation process, which is entrusted to the guardian instead. See also YOUTH; CRIME; PENAL SYSTEM; SOCIAL PROBLEMS.

Hemmi Takemitsu

juvenile labor

(nenshō rōdō). The Ministry of Labor's Women's and Minors' Bureau—which handles young workers' legal problems—defines juveniles (seishōnen) as persons between 15 and 24 years old. In 1979 the juvenile work force, of which 96.5 percent was employed, totaled 7,060,000. This constituted 44.0 percent of the total population of juveniles and 12.6 percent of the entire labor force. Because of changes in the age categories of the population and the increasing percentage of people entering institutions of higher learning in recent years, the youth labor force has been decreasing in relative terms.

The Labor Standards Law (see LABOR LAWS) of 1947 prohibits employment of children under 15 years old except in certain types of light labor. The law also has special protective provisions for workers under 18 years of age. According to the Ministry of Labor, youth labor in 1979 was primarily employed in commerce and finance (33.5 percent), manufacturing (22.3 percent), and the service industries (22.2 percent). In that same year, jobs in which the youth labor force was employed were mostly blue-collar (30.7 percent), followed by clerical work (29.7 percent). Labor law administrators investigate violations of the law and offer guidance and leisure-hour activities through the operation of Youth Labor Homes (Kinrō Seishōnen Hōmu); there are 456 such homes established by the national and regional governments. See also YOUTH. *Kurita Ken*

Juvenile Law

(Shōnen Hō). The present Juvenile Law went into effect in 1949; it differs fundamentally from the former pre–World War II law, both in ideas and in actual application, by placing greater emphasis on rehabilitation. Article 1 of the law aims at "the healthy rearing of juveniles and, in conjunction with rehabilitative measures for reforming the character of juvenile delinquents and the improvement of their environment, has as its objective the devising of special measures concerning criminal activities of minors and criminal ac-

tivities of adults that injure the welfare of juveniles." The prewar law applied to persons under 18, but the present law defines a juvenile as a person under 20 years of age.

In accordance with this objective, the law transferred jurisdiction over the misdeeds of juveniles to the FAMILY COURT, a judicial institution that replaced the Juvenile Court, a prewar administrative institution. Juvenile crimes are all sent to the family court for examination and adjudication. Juveniles under 14 years of age who commit acts that would constitute a criminal offense and some minors who commit acts that give rise to concern about their committing crimes are sent to a consultation office for children (jidō sōdansho). At the family court a trained examiner conducts an investigation of the character and environment of the juveniles sent there. One of the methods of investigation is a trial probation where the juvenile is placed in the custody of a volunteer family while the case is pending. A decision on punishment is made by the judge after examining the report of the investigation.

When a judge decides on punishment, the law requires that preference be given to probation, of which there are three kinds: rehabilitative supervision, dispatch to a reformatory, and dispatch to a correctional school or a children's home. The cases of juveniles 16 years or older who commit a crime can also be referred to a prosecutor for disposition in criminal court. In 1977, 51.5 percent of juvenile cases were dismissed without a hearing, and 32.8 percent of the cases were dismissed after a hearing. Thus, the vast majority of misbehaving minors were returned to their homes without punishment. Only 4 percent of the juveniles were subjected to criminal penalties; an exceedingly low 0.7 percent of the juveniles were sent to reformatories, and 8.8 percent were subjected to supervised probation. *Sawanobori Toshio*

juvenile reformatories and classification centers

(shōnen'in; shōnen kambetsusho). Government institutions for internment of juvenile delinquents who are subject to a FAMILY COURT order of dispatch to a reformatory (shōnen'in); these institutions are under the jurisdiction of the Ministry of Justice. There are four types of juvenile reformatory: (1) reformatories for the internment of 14- and 15-year-olds who do not have any serious physical or emotional disabilities; (2) reformatories for the internment of 16- to 19-year-olds who are free from serious disabilities; (3) special juvenile reformatories for 16- to 22-year-olds who, though free from serious physical and emotional disabilities, have displayed advanced criminal tendencies; and (4) reformatories for the internment of 14- to 25-year-olds who have serious physical or emotional disabilities.

At juvenile reformatories, in addition to academic and social guidance, vocational training is stressed. Recently, many institutions have taken positive steps to implement short but concentrated guidance programs.

In cases where the juvenile has already been interned and the family court recognizes that examination and judgment are necessary, the court may order custodial observation (kango sochi) and intern the person in a juvenile classification center. At the juvenile classification center, various medical and psychological tests are made, and the juvenile's problems are diagnosed in order to assist the court in its evaluation, judgment, and sentencing. The initial period of internment in a juvenile classification center prescribed by law is two weeks and is extendable to four weeks.

The family court counselor (chōsakan) completes a composite report of the juvenile's character and environment, based upon the results of his own evaluation and those physical and emotional evaluations performed at the juvenile classification center. Then, a memorandum based on the composite report is prepared, recommending measures for treatment, and presented to a judge. The judge examines the composite report and the family court counselor's memorandum and determines the appropriate measures to be taken. *Sawanobori Toshio*

juvenile workers, protective legislation for

(nenshōsha no rōdō hō jō no hogo). Special protection extended to juvenile workers, because they are physically and psychologically not yet fully developed as adults. The Labor Standards Law (Rōdō Kijun Hō) divides juveniles into three categories: those under 15, those between 15 and 18, and those under 20. Each is given corresponding protection. Prohibitions on the employment of children are based on article 27, section 3 of the constitution (prohibition of exploitation of children). Children over 12 can be employed in non-manufacturing industries where their health or welfare is not in danger, and children under 12 years of age may be employed in theatrical or motion picture productions. In order to employ a juvenile, the employer must have at the place of employment an age certificate, a certificate from the school principal, and written permission from a parent or guardian. As a rule, late night work, work on holidays, and extension of the 8-hour work day and 48-hour work week are prohibited. Employment in dangerous industries and coal mines is also prohibited.

Parents and guardians cannot conclude employment contracts for minors in a representative capacity, but government authorities and legal representatives have the right to authorize such contracts in special cases where they will be advantageous to the minor. Persons with parental authority cannot receive the earnings of minors in their place. Under the EMPLOYMENT SECURITY LAW OF 1947, PUBLIC EMPLOYMENT SECURITY OFFICES must cooperate with schools in extending their employment services to middle and high school students and graduates. Under the VOCATIONAL TRAINING LAW, vocational training is to be given to young people in accordance with their aptitude. See also LABOR LAWS. *Katō Shunpei*

Jūyō Sangyō Tōsei Hō → Law concerning the Control of Important Industries

juzu → Buddhist rosary

K

kabane

A hereditary title indicating the social rank and specific duty of the *uji no kami*, the chieftain of a lineage group (UJI) who served the YAMATO COURT during the latter half of the 5th through the late 7th centuries. *Kabane* were also borne by the *uji no kami*'s close kin as well, and with the passage of time came to form a sociopolitical hierarchy. These titles are said to have originated in the terms of deference with which the *uji-bito* (the constituent members of *uji*) addressed their chieftain. The titles *omi, muraji,* or *miyatsuko* were traditionally conferred on chieftains in service at the court and the titles of *kimi, atae,* or *obito* on regional chieftains. The title of *imiki* or *fuhito* was often conferred on lineage groups of continental origin (KIKAJIN). In 684 the traditional *kabane* system was reorganized into a new YAKUSA NO KABANE system but did not die out completely until the 10th century. See also UJI-KABANE SYSTEM.

Hirano Kunio

Kabasan Incident

(Kabasan Jiken). Revolutionary plot by radical members of the JI-YŪTŌ (Liberal Party) to assassinate leaders of the Meiji government. The plot reached its climax on 23 September 1884 when 16 of the rebels issued a revolutionary manifesto to the residents of the Mt. Kaba (Kabasan) region, Makabe district, Ibaraki Prefecture. Local policemen and troops sent from Tōkyō engaged the rebels in combat on 24 September, resulting in the death of one policeman and one rebel. By February 1885 the remaining 15 rebels had been apprehended and in July 1886 seven were sentenced to hang and the others to terms in prison.

The Kabasan Incident was one of a dozen so-called *gekika jiken* (incidents of intensified violence) occurring in the early 1880s. Most of these incidents took place in the Kantō region of eastern Japan. In general the incidents shared two characteristics: ties with the FREE-DOM AND PEOPLE'S RIGHTS MOVEMENT (Jiyū Minken Undō) and largely economic demands aimed at alleviating the plight of indebted farmers whose fortunes had declined after the deflation policy (1881) of MATSUKATA MASAYOSHI began taking its toll on the rural markets. Both these characteristics applied to some extent to the Kabasan Incident, but in addition this incident was a reaction to the government's violent suppression of participants involved in another *gekika jiken*, the FUKUSHIMA INCIDENT of 1882. In fact, several of the leading Kabasan rebels had been prosecuted two years earlier for their involvement in the Fukushima Incident, and one of their assassination targets was MISHIMA MICHITSUNE, former governor of Fukushima Prefecture who had been responsible for the suppression of that incident.

Prominent among the Kabasan rebels was Kōno Hiromi, the young nephew of KŌNO HIRONAKA, a Jiyūtō leader. Both men had been arrested during the Fukushima affair, though Hiroshi, unlike his uncle, had escaped conviction for treason. Also freed were two other young activists, Monna Shigejirō and Yokoyama Shinroku. During the winter of 1883–84 these three youths plotted the assassination of Governor Mishima. Through their contacts with young popular rights activists they discovered that there were other young radicals who were independently plotting the assassinations of different high-ranking government officials such as YAMAGATA ARITOMO. In the course of 1884 several of these small groups united under the leadership of Koinuma Kuhachirō, a Jiyūtō activist from Tochigi Prefecture. He instructed his young liberal comrades in the techniques of manufacturing bombs, which, it was unanimously agreed, would be the ideal weapon for assassination. Their source of inspiration for using bombs was foreign—the killing by bomb of the Russian tsar in 1881 by members of the Narodnaya Volya, a populist organization subscribing to the notion that assassination of government officials would induce revolution.

On 20 August 1884 the newspapers reported that on 15 September ber many of Japan's highest-ranking government leaders would be assembling for an official ceremony in the town of Utsunomiya, Tochigi Prefecture, not far from Mt. Kaba. Though the Kabasan rebels regarded this opportunity as "one chance in a thousand," several problems interfered. As the date for their assassination attempt drew near, disagreement among the rebels over the question of the proper strategy resulted in the defection of several comrades. On 10 September four of the rebels bungled an attempt to rob a Tōkyō pawnshop for money to buy weapons. During the robbery attempt, one of the rebels exploded his home-made bomb, causing injury to several people one of whom was a comrade; the others escaped but the injured rebel fell into the hands of the police.

A Tōkyō-wide manhunt ensued; the police failed to capture the other rebels, and the authorities cancelled the Utsunomiya ceremony a day before it was to take place. Finally, on 12 September Koinuma lost his right arm when a bomb that was being assembled accidentally exploded. With Koinuma hospitalized and their ranks now reduced to 15 members, the remaining diehards made their way to the town of Shimodate in Ibaraki to seek help from the well-known popular rights activist Tomimatsu Masayasu. Tomimatsu agreed to assist them in their plans. The rebels waited for news of the rescheduling of the Utsunomiya ceremony. On 22 September, however, all 16 rebels fled to nearby Mt. Kaba upon learning that the authorities were approaching with warrants for arrest. They distributed about 50 copies of their manifesto to peasants in the area. Their battle with the authorities and their capture soon followed.

Though the immediate goal of the rebels was to assassinate high-ranking government leaders, their ultimate aim was "to establish a constitutional system based on the rights of the people" (Kōno Hiromi). To create a democratic system of government, they reasoned, it would first be necessary "to overthrow the despotic government that has made itself the enemy of freedom" (Kabasan manifesto, 23 September 1884). Once accomplished, according to their early leader Koinuma, a new democratic system of government would "aid the people in accordance with Jiyūtō ideas."

The Kabasan rebels can clearly be placed among the radical wing of the popular rights movement, and of the Jiyūtō in particular. These early Japanese liberals were guided by, and justified their acts in terms of, a more democratic conception of government than was commonly accepted either by most moderate Jiyūtō leaders or, certainly, by the conservative ruling oligarchy of the early Meiji period. Ironically, the Kabasan incident, along with similar attempts at revolution during this period, served to discredit the Jiyūtō and, most likely, helped strengthen the hand of the oligarchic government.

📖——Aoki Keiichirō, *Nihon nōmin undō shi* II (1958). Roger W. Bowen, *Rebellion and Democracy in Meiji Japan: A Study of Commoners in the Popular Rights Movement* (1979). Endō Shizuo, *Kabasan jiken* (1971). Inaba Seitarō, ed, *Kabasan jiken kankei shiryō shū* (1970). Nojima Ikutarō, *Kabasan jiken* (1900). Takahashi Tetsuo, *Fukushima jiken* (1970). Taoka Reiun, *Meiji hanshin den* (1909).

Roger W. Bowen

Kabayama Sukenori (1837–1922)

Admiral and politician from the Satsuma domain (now Kagoshima Prefecture). His original family name was Hashiguchi. He took an active role on the imperial side in the BOSHIN CIVIL WAR and on the government side in the SATSUMA REBELLION, distinguishing himself in the latter by his defense of Kumamoto Castle. After promotion to rear admiral he became navy minister in the first YAMAGATA ARI-TOMA cabinet (1889) and remained in that post in the first MATSU-KATA MASAYOSHI cabinet (1891). He returned to active duty during the SINO-JAPANESE WAR OF 1894–1895, after which he was appointed admiral and first governor-general of the newly acquired colony of Taiwan. Kabayama served as home minister in the second Matsukata cabinet (1896) and as education minister in the second Yamagata cabinet (1898). He was named a field marshal in 1903.

Identified throughout his career with the Satsuma clique, which together with the Chōshū-domain (now Yamaguchi Prefecture) clique dominated politics (see HAMBATSU), he once aroused a controversy by saying, "What Japan is today owes everything to the government of men from Satsuma and Chōshū."

kabegaki

(also pronounced *hekisho;* literally, "wall writings"). Placards posted on walls or written on notice boards in public places; a medieval method of promulgating laws, decrees, and regulations. The term occurs in *Ruijū fusen shō,* a collection of official documents from the years 737–1093, as a notation to a decree dated Daidō 2 (807) and governing certain officials' attendance at court; it is defined in SATA MIRENSHO, an early 14th century manual of legal terms, as a letter by which a judge announces the interruption of a litigation process when one of the parties is forced by a taboo, such as mourning, into abstinence from action; but it assumed a wider meaning in the Muromachi period (1333–1568), when it was applied to public notices issued by various offices of the Muromachi shogunate and incorporated into the body of shogunal law.

Kemmu irai tsuika hō, the supplementary articles to the shogunate's fundamental constitution (the KEMMU SHIKIMOKU), contain a good number of items identified as *kanrei kabegaki* and Mandokoro *kabegaki,* that is, proclamations issued by the shogunate's chief executive officer (KANREI) and its central Administrative Board (MANDOKORO) and determining matters within their respective jurisdictions. In particular, such public notices regulated the legal status of loans, debts, and the exchange of real property; hence the term *kabegaki* was repeatedly applied to TOKUSEI edicts canceling debts and dues, whether they were "posted at the office of the *kanrei* and the Mandokoro" and "proclaimed on notice boards *(seisatsu)* erected at the seven entrances to Kyōto" (Kakitsu 1 or 1441) or "posted on two boards, one for the Upper and one for the Lower Capital" (Eishō 17 or 1520), as is recorded in contemporary sources. In the main, shogunal *kabegaki* were confined to the area of Kyōto; decrees addressed to the provinces were transmitted through their SHUGO (military governors).

By extension from the method of publication, the term *kabegaki* came to be used for the laws and regulations (*hatto* and *okitegaki*) themselves. Some domainal codes (BUNKOKUHŌ) and household precepts (KAKUN) of the Sengoku period (1467–1568) incorporate the term in variants of their titles: for example, Ōuchike Okitegaki (ŌU-CHIKE KABEGAKI), the domainal code of the great Ōuchi *daimyō* house of western Honshū; Sagarashi Hatto (Sagarake Kabegaki), the domainal code of a Sengoku daimyō family in Higo Province (now Kumamoto Prefecture); and Asakura Takakage Jōjō (Asakura Eirin Kabegaki; see ASAKURA TOSHIKAGE, 17-ARTICLE CODE OF), a set of household precepts attributed to Asakura Takakage (also known as Asakura Toshikage; 1428–81), the daimyō of Echizen (now part of Fukui Prefecture). Another well-known code called by the term is Ōsakajō Kabegaki, promulgated in Ōsaka Castle in 1595 on the orders of the national unifier TOYOTOMI HIDEYOSHI and containing a set of regulations for the court nobility, the military aristocracy, and the religious establishment. *George* ELISON

Kabo Reform

(J: Kōgo Kaikaku). Common title for the program to modernize the Korean government and society, instituted at Japanese insistence in 1894. (*Kabo* [J: *kōgo*] is the designation for 1894 in the sexagenary cycle.) Japan's goals were to force Korea to abandon its traditional ways and at the same time lay the groundwork for increased Japanese influence on the peninsula. The most significant reforms were the establishment of a cabinet system of administration and the replacement of Korea's five-century-old civil and military examination system with government schools training candidates for officialdom in Western categories of knowledge. Some initial success and Korean cooperation were undermined by the assassination of Queen MIN in 1895 and the flight of King KOJONG to the Russian legation in 1896. Russian influence became dominant in Korea as a result and remained so until the RUSSO-JAPANESE WAR of 1904–05. See also KOREA AND JAPAN: early modern relations.

C. Kenneth QUINONES

kabuki

One of the three major classical theaters of Japan, together with the NŌ and the puppet theater (BUNRAKU). Kabuki started in the early

Kabuki——Sukeroku yukari no edo-zakura

The hero Sukeroku (played by Ichikawa Danjūrō XI) striking a pose, or *mie,* when challenged by an enemy. His makeup is in the *kumadori* style known as *mukimiguma* and his purple headband the badge of a fashionable Edo man. Written and first performed in 1713 by Ichikawa Danjūrō II. One of the 18 plays known as the *kabuki jūhachiban.*

17th century as a kind of variety show given by troupes of itinerant entertainers; by the Genroku era (1688–1704), it had grown into an artistically mature theater. During the rest of the Edo period (1600–1868), it was the most popular form of stage entertainment among the townspeople and is still performed today.

Origin of Kabuki——The beginning of kabuki is ascribed to OKUNI, a female attendant at the Izumo Shrine (a major Shintō place of worship), who in 1603 on the dry bed of the river Kamogawa in Kyōto led her company (mostly women) in a light theatrical performance featuring dancing and comic sketches. Okuni's production was a brilliant success, far surpassing the other traveling companies of female entertainers of that period. In fact, her own show gained nationwide recognition and began being identified as "kabuki," a term connoting its "unusual," "shocking," and "out of the ordinary" character. The name soon became synonymous with this theatrical tradition.

The strong attraction of *onna* kabuki (women's kabuki), which Okuni had popularized, was largely due to its sensual dances and erotic scenes. Because fights frequently broke out among the spectators over these entertainers, who also practiced prostitution, the Tokugawa shogunate in 1629 finally banned all female entertainers from appearing in these kabuki performances. Thereafter, *wakashu* kabuki (young men's kabuki) achieved striking success, but, like its predecessor, the authorities strongly disapproved of the corrupting influence of these shows which continued to create public disturbances; moreover, they were alarmed by the rising interest in male prostitution. These young entertainers, who had not yet reached their majority (which at that time was 15), were also selling sexual favors.

Kabuki after 1652——In 1652, *wakashu* kabuki was forbidden. To further implement its new policy, the shogunate required that a basic change must appear in kabuki performances before they were permitted to continue. In short, kabuki must use KYŌGEN, a type of farce play accompanying the Nō, for the basis of its performances. In it realistic dialogue and stylized acting were both highly developed.

The members of the *yarō* kabuki (men's kabuki), who now began to replace the younger males, were required to cut off their forelocks. This action announced publicly that they were of legal age. Furthermore, they would have to prove to the authorities that their kabuki presentations did not depend upon the display of youthful physical charms on the stage and that they were serious

Kabuki——Onnagoroshi abura no jigoku

The murder scene in *Onnagoroshi abura no jigoku* (Woman-Killer's Oil Hell) in which Yohei (Kataoka Takao) kills Okichi (Bandō Tamasaburō), the mistress of an oil shop. The realism of *sewa-mono* (domestic plays) is enhanced in this scene by the oil with which the characters become soaked as they fight. Written by Chikamatsu. First performed in 1721.

artists who would not demean themselves by engaging in prostitution.

Although details on the years immediately following the government decrees in 1652 are fragmentary, the stern official action seems to have had a sobering effect on the kabuki theater. The three decades leading up to the Genroku era are dotted with significant progress. In the 1660s, a broad platform extending from the main stage to the center of the auditorium developed, the forerunner of the later *hanamichi*, the familiar auxiliary stage on which the performers make their entrances and exits. In 1664, two theaters located respectively in Ōsaka and Edo (now Tōkyō) made use of the draw curtain, which brought unlimited theatrical possibilities to the previously curtainless stage by permitting the lengthening of the plays and providing the freedom to allow complicated scene changes. In the meantime, the role of the ONNAGATA (female impersonator) gradually developed into an important theatrical role requiring years of discipline and training—far removed from the early crude imitations by young males dressed as women. By the mid-17th century, the major cities of Kyōto, Ōsaka, and Edo were permitted to build permanent kabuki playhouses where performances could be scheduled year round. The simple playlets borrowed from Nō, *kyōgen*, and early JŌRURI (puppet theater) plays were gradually supplanted by works especially written for the kabuki stage. The plots became longer and more involved, the number of roles increased, and their staging and preparation required greater planning and effort.

By 1673, Ichikawa Danjūrō I (1660–1704; see ICHIKAWA DANJŪRŌ) had made his debut on the stage of the Nakamuraza (Nakamura Theater) in Edo. He created the *aragoto* ("rough business") plays which always featured courageous heroes who displayed superhuman powers in overcoming evildoers. Danjūrō I's portrayal of these bold, masculine characters helped define and establish the basic taste for these plays possessed by the townspeople of Edo, the capital of the Tokugawa military government.

Genroku Era Kabuki—When the Genroku era began, the major division of kabuki into *jidai-mono* (historical plays), *sewa-mono* (domestic plays), and *shosagoto* (dance pieces) was already established. In the Kyōto–Ōsaka area (Kamigata), the realistic acting style (*jitsugoto, wagoto*) of SAKATA TŌJŪRŌ I (1647–1709), who was enormously popular for his portrayal of romantic young men, clearly was the most appealing to the public taste of this region. Yoshizawa Ayame I (1673–1729), his contemporary, together with other accomplished artists, firmly consolidated the status of the *onnagata* as the

cornerstone of the kabuki theater. For playwriting, the collaboration of CHIKAMATSU MONZAEMON (1653–1724), the renowned dramatist, and Tōjūrō I in a series of outstanding kabuki plays contributed significantly to the public recognition of the playwright as a vital profession that now demanded years of apprenticeship and hard work. In Edo, the extraordinary presence of Danjūrō I during the late 17th century, which included his excellence as both a performer and a dramatist, added to the proud prestige of the Edo kabuki theater. In the area of kabuki playwriting, Danjūrō I, who wrote under the pen name of Mimasuya Hyōgo, was regarded as the equal of the great Chikamatsu, though they differed in their themes and subject matter.

Kabuki and the Puppet Theater—The spectacular success of kabuki in the Kyōto–Ōsaka area during the late 17th century was soon followed by a period of comparative inactivity which lasted until the middle of the next century. The immediate cause for the doldrums was the rising influence of the puppet theater. Soon after 1700 Chikamatsu left the kabuki theater to devote the rest of his career to writing puppet plays. In this dark period for kabuki, the *maruhon-mono* (kabuki adaptations of puppet plays) became the vogue in an effort to stem the tide of spectators flocking to attend the puppet theater. Even the theatrical elements of the puppet theater, including the uneven movements of the manipulated dolls, were imitated by kabuki actors. Kabuki had for a time lost its dominant position as the favorite theater entertainment. The musical accompaniment for the puppet plays, consisting of chanters and musicians, was transported to the kabuki stage. Among the early examples of the *maruhon-mono*, Chikamatsu's *Kokusen'ya kassen* (1715; tr *The Battles of Coxinga*, 1951) was one which enjoyed tremendous popularity in both the Kyōto–Ōsaka area and Edo when it was performed soon after its presentation as a puppet play. The works of later writers which are regarded as masterpieces in both theaters include: *Sugawara denju tenarai kagami* (1746, The Secrets of Sugawara's Calligraphy), *Yoshitsune sembon-zakura* (1747, The Thousand Cherry Trees of Yoshitsune), and *Kanadehon chūshingura* (1748, The Treasury of Loyal Retainers; tr *Chūshingura*, 1971).

In Edo, however, the undiminished power of the Ichikawa Danjūrō family and the traditional preference for kabuki plays in the *aragoto* style upheld kabuki's dominant position. Nevertheless, the tight logical structure of the puppet plays and their realistic portrayal of the characters eventually cast their influence on the Edo kabuki theater.

Kabuki Music and Dance—During the 18th century, the rise of the Tokiwazu (see TOKIWAZU-BUSHI) and Tomimoto schools of narrative music and the NAGAUTA school of Edo, as distinguished from the Kyōto–Ōsaka faction, enriched kabuki performances. Later, in the early 19th century, the Kiyomoto (see KIYOMOTO-BUSHI) school flourished at the expense of the Tomimoto school, which rapidly declined. The first half of the 19th century represented the golden age of KABUKI MUSIC.

This development of narrative music was accompanied by the spectacular growth of the *shosagoto*. Such actors as Nakamura Nakazō I (1736–90), an Edo actor specializing in male roles, and Segawa Kikunojō III (1751–1810), an *onnagata* of the Kyōto–Ōsaka area, brought the kabuki dance to its peak of professional accomplishment. Nakazō I was especially celebrated as the kabuki actor who wrested away the traditional monopoly by the *onnagata* of *shosagoto* pieces and opened this major area to performers of male roles.

After enjoying immense popularity during the first half of the 18th century, the puppet theater rapidly declined in the Kyōto–Ōsaka area and kabuki recaptured the support of the townspeople. In the meantime, the cultural center of Japan had gradually shifted from this region to Edo. In this period of transition, one of the notable playwrights who continued to bolster the Kamigata kabuki was Namiki Shōzō I (1730–73; see NAMIKI SHŌZŌ), better known as the inventor of the *mawaributai* (revolving stage).

A pupil of Shōzō I, the dramatist Namiki Gohei I (1747–1808; see NAMIKI GOHEI), helped to transplant the realism traditionally associated with the plays of the Kyōto–Ōsaka area to Edo. Although Gohei I was already well established as a kabuki playwright in Ōsaka, he left for Edo in 1794 with Sawamura Sōjūrō III (1753–1801), an Edo actor. Gohei I's plays laid the foundation for the development of the realistic *sewa-mono* plays, later called *kizewa-mono* ("bare" domestic plays), which were perfected by Tsuruya Namboku IV (1755–1829; see TSURUYA NAMBOKU), and further refined by Segawa Jokō III (1806–81) and Kawatake MOKUAMI (1816–93). Along with Sakurada Jisuke I (1734–1806; see SAKURADA

JISUKE), Gohei I elevated the Edo *sewa-mono* to a mature dramatic form.

Decline of Edo Kabuki—— By the time Tsuruya Namboku IV had written his *Tōkaidō Yotsuya kaidan* (1825, The Ghost Story of Tōkaidō Yotsuya; tr *Les Spectres de Yotsuya,* 1979), the ultimate masterpiece in the *kizewa-mono* style, kabuki as a dramatic art had passed its peak and began to show signs of a general decline. The public now demanded more violence, torture, murder, and shockingly explicit love scenes on the stage. The plays were often based on stories popularized by novelists and storytellers. These productions became increasingly elaborate with acrobatic feats, quick role changes, and ingenious stage mechanisms in order to delight the capricious audience.

After the death of Namboku IV in 1829, kabuki did not produce any prominent playwrights until the mid-1850s when Jokō III and Mokuami appeared. Their early successes also followed the popular trend to the *kizewa-mono*-type plays which skillfully intermingled brutality, eroticism, and macabre humor and presented colorful characters from the underworld. Mokuami further extended this theme by creating the *shiranami-mono* (thief plays) which had robbers, murderers, confidence men, and cunningly vicious women as the leading roles.

Mokuami and the Meiji Period—— The Meiji Restoration of 1868 brought down a feudalistic society which had lasted for over 250 years: a demise that meant the total collapse of a familiar social order that was divided by class into farmers, merchants, artisans, and above them all, the *samurai.* Deprived of its customary social setting, kabuki theater suddenly found itself out of touch with the contemporary world. Thus, for kabuki the Meiji period (1868–1912) represented a constant struggle with the uncertainties of the rapidly changing times, one which might end in its extinction.

During the early years of Meiji, Mokuami attempted the *zangiri-mono* ("cropped hair" plays), *sewa-mono* in a modern setting. His efforts were not very successful. The traditional warrior in his customary topknot and *kimono* seemed to have far greater appeal for the spectators than the new Japanese soldier wearing a smart Western uniform and a fancy military cap. Also, the *onnagata* dressed in Western attire and sporting a chapeau could not possibly match the idealized femininity as embodied in his appearance in a traditional Japanese costume and hairdo. The "modern" *sewa-mono* displayed only caricatures of contemporary life. Among Mokuami's major works, his *sewa-mono* in a Tokugawa setting remain the popular favorites. With his death in 1893, kabuki lost its last great dramatist, a man who was still a product of the late Edo period.

Post-Meiji Kabuki—— In their valiant effort to preserve the kabuki tradition, actors such as Ichikawa Danjūrō IX (1838–1903) and Onoe Kikugorō V (1844–1904; see ONOE KIKUGORŌ) spent their later careers encouraging the stage presentation of renowned kabuki plays and also teaching their inherited acting techniques to the younger generation of actors.

Their immediate successors, who included Kikugorō VI (1885–1949), Matsumoto Kōshirō VII (1870–1949), and Nakamura Kichiemon I (1886–1954) also attempted to maintain the spirit and integrity of the traditional kabuki performances. But unlike Danjūrō IX and Kikugorō V, the new generation experimented with kabuki plays by writers from outside the kabuki theater. They also performed in Japanese translations of Western plays by such authors as Shakespeare, Chekhov, or Ibsen and in contemporary dramas by Japanese playwrights which are based on the Western theatrical tradition. By combining these diverse dramatic forms, the modern kabuki performers expanded their acting skills far beyond traditional limits.

The major kabuki playwrights after Mokuami were born in the Meiji period and were no longer professionally affiliated with the kabuki theater. OKAMOTO KIDŌ (1872–1939), MAYAMA SEIKA (1878–1948), HASEGAWA SHIN (1884–1963), and KUBOTA MANTARŌ (1889–1963)—all identified with *shin kabuki* (new kabuki) plays, a form written after the Meiji period—were equally recognized for their accomplishments in journalism, drama criticism, novel writing, and writing for the contemporary Japanese theater. Their kabuki plays are usually in the modern vernacular form and freely incorporate the elements of pictorial realism and detailed character study derived from the Western dramatic tradition.

Post-World War II Kabuki—— Within a decade after 1945, Kikugorō VI, Kōshirō VII, and Kichiemon I passed away. As the deaths of Danjūrō IX and Kikugorō V in the late Meiji period had symbolized the end of the Tokugawa kabuki tradition for the spectators who had witnessed the pre-Meiji performances, so this series of

Kabuki——Shibaraku

A classic *mie* from the flamboyant hero of *Shibaraku* (played here by Onoe Shōroku) as he makes his dramatic entrance. His brilliant costume and special makeup (*sujiguma* style) are vital ingredients of the *aragoto* ("rough business") style characteristic of such larger-than-life heroic figures. First performed in 1697. One of the *kabuki jūhachiban.*

deaths brought home to those who had survived the great war the realization that the legacy of prewar kabuki must also recede into the past.

Nonetheless, during the same decade some of the following actors assumed leadership in the kabuki theater: Bandō Mitsugorō VIII (1906–75), Morita Kan'ya XIV (1907–75; see MORITA KAN'YA), Ichikawa Danjūrō XI (1909–65), Matsumoto Kōshirō VIII (1910–82), Nakamura Kanzaburō XVII (b 1910), Onoe Shōroku II (b 1913), Onoe Baikō VII (b 1915), and Nakamura Utaemon VI (b 1917; see NAKAMURA UTAEMON).

Jitsukawa Enjaku III (b 1921), Nakamura Jakuemon IV (b 1920), Nakamura Shikan VII (b 1928), Nakamura Tomijūrō V (b 1929), Nakamura Senjaku II (b 1931), Sawamura Tanosuke VI (b 1932), and Sawamura Sōjūrō IX (b 1933) represent the next generation of performers. They established their professional careers after the mid-1950s.

At the present time still younger actors such as Ichikawa Ennosuke II (b 1939), Matsumoto Kōshirō (b 1942), Nakamura Kichiemon II (b 1944), Bandō Tamasaburō (b 1950), Ichikawa Ebizō X (b 1951), Onoe Tatsunosuke I (b 1951), and Nakamura Kankurō V (b 1955) have reached various stages of accomplishment. While the members of this group belong to some of the foremost acting families, the proper assessment of their professional stature lies in the future.

Kabuki and Other Traditional Dramas—— During its formative years, especially after the mid-17th century when the government laid down its stringent orders for reform, kabuki borrowed important elements from the other classical theaters—particularly *kyōgen,* Nō, and the puppet theater. The strongest single influence came from *kyōgen* which served as a kind of model for reorganizing the basic structure and aim of the kabuki theater. By closely concentrating on the dialogue, acting technique, and the sense of realism found in the *kyōgen* performances, kabuki managed to move away from a kind of variety show highlighting dancing and music toward a well-defined dramatic theater. *Kyōgen* plays were frequently performed on the kabuki stage as parodies of the original works and they continued to be popular in expanded versions, even into the Genroku era when kabuki had already established itself as a recognized theatrical form.

Kabuki had an obvious debt to the Nō theater in the Nō's familiar roof-covered stage. This feature was kept until the early 18th century although kabuki modified the Nō stage by adding the draw

Kabuki —— Kyō-ganoko musume Dōjōji

The beginning of Kiyohime's (the snake demon's) dance at the temple Dōjōji. First performed in 1753, this *shosagoto* (dance piece) is one of the major *onnagata* dance roles; it is performed here by Nakamura Utaemon VI.

curtain, *hanamichi,* and other innovations. Many Nō plays were adopted for the kabuki stage with the plot, scenic design, costume, and the elegant mood evoked by the graceful movements found in the original work subtly blended into a new dramatic form, which was now performed for the common people rather than the members of the aristocratic class.

The puppet theater also helped kabuki to develop into a dramatic theater. The early kabuki plays had been short, often improvised, with rudimentary plots and few characters. The narrative element, which served as the backbone of the puppet theater and had already been refined as part of the *katari-mono* (narrative tradition) that had flourished in medieval times, was a significant contribution. The structure, unity, and coherence found in the puppet plays and based on an earlier narrative tradition provided kabuki with a rich source of ready-made plays to shore up its own meager repertory. During the last half of the 17th century, when kabuki deliberately embarked on the road to an artistically relevant theater, many adaptations of plays from the puppet theater were prominently featured. Today, half of the plays presented on the kabuki stage are adaptations of plays from the puppet theater, an indisputable proof of its powerful influence on kabuki throughout history.

Types of Kabuki Plays —— Among the three categories of kabuki plays, the *jidai-mono* and the *sewa-mono* contain principally dramatic presentations while the *shosagoto* consists of mainly dancing or pantomimic scenes. The *jidai-mono* often staged contemporary events relating to the members of the samurai class but underwent certain modifications to satisfy the government censors. In order to deal with such sensitive themes as political conspiracy or scandalous affairs involving the ruling elite, the names and places had to be changed or vaguely disguised and the setting of the actual incidents moved to an earlier period of history. This practice of reshaping factual events occurred throughout the Edo period and invariably turned the *jidai-mono* into a mixture of fact and fantasy.

The *sewa-mono* tradition started as a kind of news report offering a reenactment on stage of the latest sensational event or topic of interest among the townspeople. A shocking double suicide by desperate lovers might be presented a few days later as a kabuki play with popular stars in the leading roles. Such themes treating the affairs of the common people were staged more factually and realistically than those found in the *jidai-mono*. The structure of some plays became rather complicated when the principal characters were part of a combined historical and domestic play and they were made to assume different names as the action shifted in the interwoven story line between the two developing separate time frames. For example, in *Sukeroku yukari no edo-zakura* (1713; tr *Sukeroku,* 1975), the 12th-century Soga brothers of the *jidai-mono* portion also appear disguised as commoners of the Edo period in the *sewa-mono* scenes.

"World" of Kabuki —— In the West, an underlying theme or an idea may provide continuity and coherence to a dramatic work. A major unifying factor behind a kabuki play lies in its *sekai* (world), the established setting from which the characters and the plots are derived. The *sekai* may be a particular historical period, fictional world from one of the classical tales, or a Tokugawa setting involving a notorious *shinjū* (love suicide) or a sensational scandal. But in the kabuki theater even plays based on the latest events immediately undergo further refinement and modification as new versions on the original theme are presented on the stage. For example, the celebrated romance of Kyūemon and Matsuyama, originally set down in literary form during the early 18th century by KI NO KAION (1663–1742), a playwright for the puppet theater, has built up its own independent tradition with a *sekai* containing all the later variations on the same theme. Although the spectators are exposed to a blend of these familiar settings—even a mixture of the historical and contemporary—such bold conventions enrich the dramatic possibilities on the kabuki stage.

Kabuki and Tokugawa Thought —— Again, the kabuki theater often incorporates prevailing notions of the Tokugawa society as dramatic agents to promote the progress of a play. For example, *inga ōhō* (law of retributive justice), a Buddhist notion, may finally drive a rascal to his destruction or restore happiness to a long suffering woman. The notion of MUJŌ (sense of impermanence), also derived from Buddhism, may serve as a constant reflection on the truth that nothing in the universe remains forever, illustrated by the fall of a powerful military leader or the demise of a proud family which has prospered for generations. Moreover, certain ethical notions such as duty, obligation, and filial piety, based on Confucian tradition, may come into direct conflict with personal desires and passions, leading to a series of dramatic situations. The frequent use of these devices may appear contrived and even unimaginative; they are, nevertheless, deeply rooted conventions in kabuki playwriting.

Staging of Kabuki —— The production of kabuki plays depends largely on the accepted conventions regarding the gestures and movements of the actors, scenery, properties, costumes, wigs, makeup, sound effects, and so on. Furthermore, the staging may differ according to the category of plays. For instance, the *jidai-mono* require more elaborate scenes—many often take place in a huge mansion or a magnificent palace—and a larger cast of performers. In contrast, the *sewa-mono,* which generally portray the lives of the townspeople, are presented in a more realistic manner and situated in a more familiar environment. In the *shosagoto,* the singers and the musicians appear on the stage as well as the dancers. In order to facilitate the footwork of the performing actors and to improve the resonance of the floor area, *okibutai* (platforms made of polished Japanese cypress with hollow bottoms) are used to cover the regular surface of the stage floor. As a rule, the *maruhon-mono* offer the greatest degree of stylization in their performances. The lyrical and musical aspects in the original puppet plays render a rhythmic pattern of speech to the *maruhon-mono*. However, the presence of chanters and musicians in these adapted versions for the kabuki theater sets a limit to the extent of realism possible on the stage.

Kabuki and Formalized Behavior —— The close observance of the proprieties gives a certain stylized character to kabuki presentations. On the stage, the *shimote* (stage left) is regarded as a place of honor occupied by people of high rank, guests, and important messengers or official representatives. The *kamite* (stage right) is meant for others of lower rank and members of the household; most entrances and exits take place on this side, mainly by the *hanamichi*. During the Edo period, etiquette among members of different social status and between men and women required careful attention to speech, manner of dress, and behavior. In the *jidai-mono,* this same ceremonial aspect adds color, elegance, and a graceful atmosphere to the various scenes as witnessed in the *Kanadehon chūshingura*. Although the *sewa-mono* does not display as much formalized behavior, even the lives of the ordinary townspeople called for far closer attention to the accepted rules of conduct than in contemporary Japanese society.

Performances of Kabuki —— Today both matinee and evening programs of kabuki are scheduled throughout the year. During the Edo period, however, these performances were held between sunrise and sunset because the government, fearing the outbreak of fire, prohibited programs after dark. From the Meiji period the use of gaslight, permitting both afternoon and evening performances, affected the pattern of theater attendance and also the content of the scheduled programs. When the theater was an all-day affair, a full-length *jidai-mono* and *sewa-mono* along with a *shosagoto* could be presented on a single program. Today the average length of a kabuki performance is about five hours including intermissions; hence, the offerings have become considerably shortened and limited mostly to favorite acts and scenes from complete plays together with a dance piece. This has been the general policy at the Kabukiza (Kabuki Theater) which opened in 1889 in Tōkyō. The National Theater, built in 1966, follows a more traditional approach by attempting to present a full-length play within a single program.

Acting Roles—— The many unique features of the kabuki theater, which were developed during its formative years, are still very much in evidence; others added later have also become an integral part of the established tradition. By the Genroku era, the roles assigned to kabuki actors were already divided broadly into male and female, character or personality type, age, social position, and so on. Among them, the most distinctive roles go to the *onnagata,* who plays the female—young girl, middle-aged woman, and older woman. Types of female roles include the housewife, samurai lady, heroic woman, and wicked woman. All efforts since the Meiji period to replace the *onnagata* with actresses have failed although women occasionally co-star with kabuki actors in newly written kabuki plays. Within the current repertory of kabuki plays, the roles of Agemaki, the courtesan, in *Sukeroku yukari no edo-zakura* and Masaoka, the loyal wet nurse, in *Meiboku sendai hagi* (1777, The Disputed Succession) are regarded as among the most challenging for the fully experienced *onnagata.*

The *tachiyaku* (leading male actor) can also perform many different roles such as the virtuous hero, evil courtier, wicked samurai, handsome lover, or unscrupulous rake. Some versatile performers played both male and female roles and their acting repertory expanded to include many diverse roles. The majority, however, tended to limit their roles to a more modest number, which became hereditarily identified with their professional names.

Acting Style—— In the *kata* (form), the stylized gestures and movements of the kabuki actors, the strong influence of a long theatrical tradition is graphically illustrated. Since the *kata* is not subject to rejection at the whim of the performer, its forceful presence has helped to maintain the artistic integrity of kabuki. There is, for example, the *tate* (stylized fighting), a skillfully choreographed series of spectacular movements representing combat and danced either by an individual or a group of performers. The *roppō* ("all directions") refers to a form of dramatic exit by the main character often used on the *hanamichi* and involves boldly exaggerated movements. The *mie* (striking an attitude) is a *kata* in which an actor momentarily pauses to emphasize a high point in a scene, assumes a mighty pose, and glares defiantly often with eyes crossed. These terms apply more often to the *jidai-mono* plays which deal with the members of the warrior class and where larger-than-life situations are always expected. However, the *sewa-mono* may also contain equally formal instances of the *kata* even in the rather casual movements of actors as they walk, stand talking, or quietly sit on the stage.

Kabuki Dialogue—— The spoken lines in kabuki plays may range from the extremely stylized to the very realistic. Generally, the *jidai-mono* contains more formalized speech whereas the *sewa-mono* leans heavily toward colloquial speech. Nonetheless, a certain 7-5 syllabic pattern (similar to that of classical Japanese poetry) with a distinct rhythm and tempo is closely identified with kabuki. Its powerful effect is evident, for example, during the crucial movements of a *jidai-mono* play in the *aragoto* style when the main character must deliver the *tsurane* (declamation), a long speech meant to show off his elocutionary skill. The *maruhon-mono* is particularly noted for its famous lines in the 7-5 pattern.

Stage Assistants—— In addition to the regular performers, the *kōken* (stage assistant) serves a valuable function on stage. He is especially important in the dance pieces where he must attend to the dancer's costume, provide or remove the necessary props, and offer any other such help, all in full view of the audience. During the demanding *hayagawari* (quick costume change), the *kōken* must carefully follow the movements of the dancer, all the while remaining closely behind him, and at the crucial moment quickly remove a layer of clothing or rearrange the costume so that other patterns and colors will be revealed. The *kōken* is dressed either in a traditional costume or entirely in black, a costume typical for his job.

Kabuki: Actor-Centered Theater—— For the kabuki audience, the main attraction is the performer, not the plot or the fidelity to the original text of the play. They come to see their favorite stars in well-known roles often handed down within an acting family from one generation to the next. For example, the famous play, *Sukeroku yukari no edo-zakura* was originally written in the 18th century by Ichikawa Danjūrō II (1688–1758) and was also first performed by him in the leading role of Sukeroku. In the years following, the

Kabuki ——— Kanjinchō

A scene from *Kanjinchō* depicting the loyalty of Benkei (Matsumoto Kōshirō VIII, left) to his master Minamoto no Yoshitsune as he attempts to smuggle him past a checkpoint to safety. The pine tree backdrop visible at the rear is traditionally used for *kabuki* plays adapted from the Nō theater. One of the *kabuki jūhachiban.*

Kabuki ——— Meiboku sendai hagi

Masaoka, the loyal wet nurse in *Meiboku sendai hagi,* holding back her tears for her dead son until her enemies have left the room. This challenging role, played here by Nakamura Utaemon VI, is usually reserved for the *tateoyama,* the leading *onnagata* actor in a troupe.

audience continued to appreciate its performance by the successors of Danjūrō II due to the subtle combination of the traditional in style with the unique flair found in the latest version.

Kabuki has been an actor-centered theater since its inception; the playwright has assumed a secondary position, writing plays that would enhance the popularity and prestige of the leading stars. Unlike the puppet theater, whose plays from the early 17th century were usually published and the authorship clearly known, the kabuki play scripts were regarded as the property of the theater where the dramatist worked and throughout the Edo period remained handwritten. Kawatake Mokuami was the first kabuki playwright whose dramatic works were printed and sold to the public.

Kabuki Acting Families—— Each actor belongs to an acting family by whose name he is identified. Professionally, he is part of a closely knit hierarchical organization, headed by one of the leading actors, and in this "family," the members spend years of apprentice-

Kabuki——Aoto-zōshi hana no nishiki-e

The Shiranami robber gang lining up on the *hanamichi*, the ramp extending into the audience toward the left side of the theater, which serves both as a secondary stage and as the means by which the actors often make their dramatic entrances and exits. A second *hanamichi* toward the right of the stage is also used in some plays.

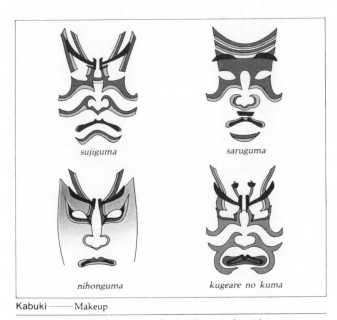

sujiguma   *saruguma*

nihonguma   *kugeare no kuma*

Kabuki——Makeup

Four examples of the *kumadori* style of makeup used in *jidai-mono* (historical plays). The first, *sujiguma*, is being worn by the hero of *Shibaraku* in the photograph on page 92.

ship under strict discipline and training. Each actor remains faithful to his assigned position within the group until he is able to advance in rank. In this context, the *shūmei* (name-assuming ceremony), held periodically, in which an actor is bestowed a new professional name indicating a higher rank, takes on an important significance. Although today the kabuki actor is hired by a giant theatrical enterprise and receives a salary, the *shūmei* nevertheless represents recognition by his peers of the increased power and influence he has acquired within the acting fraternity.

In Tokugawa times, the actors were also classified according to rank within the theater to which they belonged. In each theater, the function of the *zagashira* (troupe leader) was performed by the *tachiyaku* (leading male actor); the *tachioyama* (leading female impersonator), also an actor of the highest distinction, looked after the affairs of his specialized group of performers. The rest of the troupe was grouped into three main classifications in descending order under the *tachiyaku* and *tateoyama*. In theory, any actor was able to advance to the highest position but pedigree and family influence always played a critical part in the ultimate success of an individual actor.

Social Position of Actors——Before the Meiji period, the members of the acting profession were officially regarded as social out-

casts closely identified with the KAWARAMONO ("dry riverbed people") and unworthy of living among the rest of humanity. They were compelled to live in relative isolation; their professional and private lives were closely watched and regulated by the authorities. This stigma which was attached to the kabuki theater resulted from the official notion that it was a corrupting force and that, like the licensed pleasure quarters, it was an *akusho* ("evil place"); hence, the actors and prostitutes were treated harshly. After the Meiji Restoration, however, this discriminatory policy was dropped and the actors finally joined the ranks of the ordinary citizen. Today, the most accomplished members of the kabuki stage are designated as LIVING NATIONAL TREASURES by the government and accorded official honor and wide public recognition.

Kabuki Stage——Certain permanent physical features of the kabuki theater determine the character of the staging. The *jōshikimaku* (standard curtain), a draw curtain displaying black, green, and persimmon-colored vertical stripes presents a unique spectacle. It is drawn open from stage right to left to the usual accompaniment of the sound of wooden clappers. This curtain also serves as a backdrop for brief scenes given before or after the performance on the main stage.

Regarded as a Japanese invention, another striking aspect of the kabuki stage is the *mawaributai*. This is a large, circular platform, flush with the main stage, which can be rotated to permit a second scene to be performed simultaneously with the scene already progressing on the same stage or allow a quick flashback to be given.

The *hanamichi*, a ramp passing through the audience to the back of the theater, serves as a secondary stage as well as a means of entry and exit for the performers. It can assume the guise of a corridor, waterway, or a road, where dramatic action can take place concurrently with the scene presented on the main stage. Action can also occur solely on the *hanamichi* with the *jōshikimaku* closed. In some scenes, a double *hanamichi*, created by the addition of a second ramp placed at stage left parallel to the permanently fixed *hanamichi* (at stage right), expands the dramatic action to include the theater seating area. For example, in *Futatsu chōchō kuruwa no nikki* (The Diary of Two Butterflies in the Pleasure Quarters), an adaptation of a puppet play, the two *hanamichi* represent the banks of a river and the audience becomes the "river." As the actors speak to each other from its "banks," the spectators are effectively drawn into the dramatic situation.

Costume, Wig, and Makeup——Costume, wig, and makeup are carefully matched in accord with the nature of a role. In general, the costumes in *jidai-mono* are more stylized and elegant, befitting the members of the nobility and the samurai class. By contrast, the prevailing fashions of society at large during the Edo period are portrayed rather realistically in the *sewa-mono* plays. The costumes appearing in the *shosagoto* dance pieces are especially noted for their color, design, and workmanship.

The wigs are divided into male and female and, further, into subclasses according to age, historical period, social status, occupation, and other considerations. Some wigs are made for special effects: during an intense dramatic scene the hairdo of the *gattari* ("let down") wig comes apart; the *sabaki* ("scattering") wig has a topknot which becomes undone in a fierce fighting scene.

In the *sewa-mono*, as a rule, the makeup is more realistic than the *jidai-mono*. The *onnagata* wears heavier makeup in roles of young women, court ladies, and courtesans. The roles of older women require less makeup in both *jidai-mono* and *sewa-mono*. The actors playing the roles of a young man in a *sewa-mono* and a dashing military hero in a *jidai-mono* are heavily made up—the one to accentuate his handsome features and the other to underscore the nobility and virtue of his character. Perhaps the outstanding example of makeup on the kabuki stage is the *kumadori*, an established set of mask-like styles numbering about a hundred and used in the *jidai-mono* type of plays. For drawing the *kumadori*, the basic colors are red and blue, the first expressing passion, virtue, or superhuman powers, and the second expressing jealousy, fear, and other negative traits which reveal the evil aspects of a character. Other *kumadori* represent deities and demons. In short, makeup varies widely according to roles and is a complex, sophisticated art.

Future of Kabuki——Kabuki as a performing art appears quite secure for the foreseeable future. In 1966, the National Theater (seating capacity: 1,756) opened with strong government support. Kabuki performances are given there most months of the year, and a school for training young kabuki performers and stage technicians outside the traditional familial framework is an integral feature of the establishment.   *Ted T. TAKAYA*

- **Synopses of some major kabuki plays**

Aoto-zōshi hana no nishiki-e (Benten the Thief). Popular title *Benten Kozō*. By Kawatake Mokuami, 1862. *Sewa-mono*. Recounts the exploits of Benten Kozō Kikunosuke, a handsome young rogue skilled at disguises, and the rest of his gang, the Five Thieves (Shiranami Gonin Otoko, an alternative title of the play). The high point of the play is the Hamamatsuya Scene of Act III, one of kabuki's most famous "extortion scenes" (*yusuriba*). Benten, dressed as the daughter of a noble house and accompanied by his confederate Nangō Rikimaru, appears at the draper's store Hamamatsuya. Cleverly provoking an injury, the two demand money in compensation but are thwarted by a samurai who has been watching their performance. In the scene's climax Benten throws off his female attire and proclaims himself an accomplished criminal. That, however, is but the first stage of a sting operation: the samurai who exposed the swindle is in actuality Nippon Daemon, the chief of the gang of Five Thieves. Other famous scenes are the Imosegawa Riverbank Scene of Act IV, with its lineup of the Five Thieves declaiming their identities, and the Gokurakuji Scene of Act V, a spectacular acrobatic fight (*tachimawari*) of one against many which takes place on the rooftop of a temple and ends with the outnumbered Benten's suicide and Nippon Daemon's capture.

Dōjōji See *Kyō-ganoko musume Dōjōji*.

Kagamijishi (The Lion at the New Year's Banquet). Original title *Shunkyō kagamijishi*. By Fukuchi Ōchi and others, 1893. *Shosagoto* in two contrasting parts. At a New Year's banquet in the ladies' quarters of Edo Castle, the young attendant Yayoi performs a graceful dance until, picking up the hand puppet of a lion, she is possessed by the lion's spirit and driven from the scene. She reappears in lion makeup and puts on a spectacular show of the great beast twirling its mane.

Kanadehon chūshingura (tr *The Treasury of Loyal Retainers*, 1971). Popular title *Chūshingura*. By Takeda Izumo II, Miyoshi Shōraku, and Namiki Senryū, 1748. *Jidai-mono* with important *sewa-mono* elements; originally for *jōruri*. Based on the celebrated FORTY-SEVEN RŌNIN INCIDENT of 1701–03 but transposed into the world of the TAIHEIKI in the early years of the Muromachi period (1333–1568), it recounts in 11 acts how the villainous KŌ NO MORONAO (in the actual incident, Kira Yoshinaka) humiliated En'ya Hangan (the *daimyō* Asano Naganori of Akō), provoking him into drawing his sword in the shogunal palace of Kamakura (Edo)—an act for which Hangan was sentenced to commit suicide—and how Ōboshi Yuranosuke (Asano's chief counselor ŌISHI YOSHIO) and 46 other loyal retainers of Hangan avenged their lord's death. The celebrated play has many high points. The tense drama of Hangan's disgrace and suicide is complemented by the pathos of the death of his former retainer Hayano Kampei (Kayano Sampei), who commits suicide needlessly when he imagines himself guilty of having accidentally killed his father-in-law, Yoichibei. In the meantime Kampei's wife, Okaru, has been sold by Yoichibei into prostitution, consenting in order to obtain funds for her husband's vendetta against Moronao. She plays an important part in the great Ichiriki Teahouse Scene of Act VII: Yuranosuke, who has taken up a life of debauchery in order to lull his enemies into a false sense of security, at first suspects Okaru of spying on him, but she proves her loyalty and helps her brother Teraoka Heiemon (Terasaka Kichiemon) dispatch Moronao's real spy, Kudayū. The play has two *shosagoto* episodes, the journey scene (*michiyuki*) of the young lovers Okaru and Kampei as well as that of Konami and her stepmother Tonase to the residence of Konami's fiancé, Yuranosuke's son Rikiya (Ōishi Chikara), in Yamashina near Kyōto. In the Yamashina Scene of Act IX, Konami is spurned by Rikiya's mother because it was her father, Kakogawa Honzō (Kajikawa Yosōbei), who prevented Hangan from killing Moronao in the shogunal palace. Honzō himself appears on the scene and is run through with a spear by Rikiya; before he dies, however, he reveals his true sympathies by handing over the plan of Moronao's mansion. The play concludes with the band of loyal retainers breaking into the mansion and routing Moronao out of his hiding place; Yuranosuke takes the archenemy's head with the sword Hangan had used to slit his belly,

and the 47 *rōnin* march off to present it at their lord's grave.

Kirare Yosa See *Yowanasake ukina no Yokogushi*.

Kuruwa bunshō (A Story of the Pleasure Quarters). Also known as *Yūgiri Izaemon*. Derived from the Yoshidaya Scene of the *jōruri* play *Yūgiri Awa no Naruto* by Chikamatsu Monzaemon, 1712; first performed in kabuki in 1808. *Sewa-mono*. Izaemon, the son of a wealthy Ōsaka merchant, is disinherited for his dalliance with the courtesan Yūgiri, who then accepts a new patron. The destitute Izaemon, reduced to wearing a paper kimono even on New Year's Eve, comes to rebuke Yūgiri for her unfaithfulness. The two are reunited even as news arrives that Izaemon has been reinstated to his former position of wealth. The role of Izaemon is a parade piece for the Ōsaka-type *nimaime* (beau-actor), a lovable fop.

Kyō-ganoko musume Dōjōji (The Dancing Girl at the Temple). Popular title *Musume Dōjōji*. By Fujimoto Tobun and others, 1753. Based on the Nō play *Dōjōji*. *Shosagoto*. Recounts the outcome of the maiden Kiyohime's unrequited love for Anchin, a priest of the temple Dōjōji. As a new temple bell is being dedicated at Dōjōji, a beautiful dancer named Hanako appears at the gate and begs permission to enter. Although the temple is ordinarily closed to women, Hanako's pleas and beauty prevail, and the priests let her come inside. There she performs a series of brilliant dances, bemusing the priests. At the climax she leaps inside the bell, only to reappear metamorphosed into a horrible serpent, the true form of the spurned Kiyohime. In the finale a superhuman figure appears who quells this demon (see the summary of *Oshimodoshi* in KABUKI JŪHACHIBAN). The dazzling sequence of dances, coupled with the rapid changes of magnificent costume, make this piece an ideal platform for displaying the skills of the accomplished *onnagata*.

Meiboku sendai hagi (The Choice Wood of a Former Era). Popular title *Sendai hagi*. Earliest version by Nagawa Kamesuke, 1777. *Jidai-mono*. The story refers and the title alludes to a succession dispute which disturbed the Sendai domain of the 1660s, the DATE SŌDŌ; but the setting is transposed into an earlier era, the Muromachi period (1333–1568). Two scenes remain in the kabuki repertory. In one, a villainous group of retainers, foremost among them the evil counselor Nikki Danjō and the vicious lady-in-waiting Yashio, conspires to do away with Tsurukiyo, the young son of their incompetent lord, only to be foiled by loyal retainers such as the wet nurse Masaoka. Masaoka, who prepares Tsurukiyo's food herself for fear lest he be poisoned, succeeds in outmaneuvering Yashio only at the cost of her own son, who is stabbed by Yashio when he eats some doctored cakes meant for Tsurukiyo. The true nature of Nikki Danjō is exposed in the Under the Floor Scene, where the *aragoto* ("rough business") superman Arajishi Otokonosuke tracks down a huge rat and strikes it on the head; the rat scurries away with a list of conspirators, and moments later Nikki Danjō appears in a puff of smoke, a bleeding wound on his forehead and the list clamped between his teeth.

Seki no to See *Tsumoru koi yuki no seki no to*.

Soga no taimen (The Soga Confrontation). *Jidai-mono*. Generic title for a set piece that was a fixture of the New Year's program of Edo kabuki from the early 18th to the late 19th century, being rewritten under a different title each year to give a new twist to the familiar story. Depicted in this short scene is an incident from the popular epic SOGA MONOGATARI, namely, the initial confrontation between the Soga brothers Jūrō and Gorō and their enemy Kudō Suketsune. The earliest known version, *Tsuwamono kongen Soga*, was presented by Ichikawa Danjūrō I in 1697; the variant most frequently presented today bears the title *Kotobuki Soga no taimen*. However, it is not the plot but the festive beauty of the tableau that makes this play noteworthy, for at the climax, the entire range of lead actors strikes a set pose (*mie*).

Sonezaki shinjū (tr *The Love Suicides at Sonezaki*, 1961). By Chikamatsu Monzaemon, 1703. *Sewa-mono*; originally for *jōruri*. Based on an actual incident that was the talk of Ōsaka, this play recounts the tragic love story and death pact of the shop clerk Tokubei and the courtesan Ohatsu, who are driven to suicide by a friend's betrayal. The master of the shop where Tokubei works, his uncle Kuemon, has arranged a marriage for him with the niece of Kuemon's wife but Tokubei, heedless of his obligations (giri) to them, surrenders to his passion (ninjō) for Ohatsu and refuses to comply. Kuemon thereupon tells Tokubei to settle his accounts and clear out. Tokubei, however, has dipped into the shop's money and made a foolish loan to his friend Kuheiji. Asked to return the money, Kuheiji denies having borrowed it and accuses Tokubei of having used a stolen seal on the IOU. Ohatsu herself is taunted for ruining Tokubei's future. After a secret reunion at Ohatsu's and a pathos-filled michiyuki (journey) to Sonezaki Wood, Tokubei stabs Ohatsu and then slashes his own throat as a temple bell tolls. The passage recited by the chanter to accompany the michiyuki scene is regarded as one of the lyrical masterpieces of the Japanese traditional theater.

Tsumoru koi yuki no seki no to   (The Snowbound Barrier of Love). Popular title Seki no to. By Takarada Jurai, Toba Yarichō, and Nishikawa Senzō, 1784. Shosagoto with TOKIWAZU-BUSHI accompaniment. Based on legends associated with the Six Poetic Sages (ROKKASEN). The play recounts how Kuronushi's plan to usurp control over the country is foiled by Munesada and his lover Komachi through the magical aid of the courtesan Sumizome, the spirit of a cherry tree in human form. Under the assumed name Sekibei, Kuronushi has retired to a snowbound barrier station deep in the mountains; in a small hut nearby, Munesada and Komachi slowly realize that the barrier official is in fact their mortal enemy. Komachi is sent to get help, and Munesada, over some sake, closely questions Sekibei. After Munesada withdraws, the inebriated Sekibei prepares to chop down the cherry tree that is blossoming outside his guardhouse, but when he lifts his axe to strike, he is rendered immobile by a supernatural force. Sumizome then appears and engages Sekibei in banter about the pleasure quarters until she seduces him into revealing his identity; the two then engage in a fierce duel and Kuronushi is vanquished.

Yoshitsune sembon-zakura   (The Thousand Cherry Trees of Yoshitsune). Popular title Sembon-zakura. By Takeda Izumo II, Miyoshi Shōraku, and Namiki Senryū, 1747. Jidaimono; originally for jōruri. The play's ostensible hero is MINAMOTO NO YOSHITSUNE, who defeats the Taira in the TAIRA-MINAMOTO WAR only to be forced to flee before the jealous wrath of his elder brother MINAMOTO NO YORITOMO, angered (according to this play) when the heads of three Taira generals sent him by Yoshitsune prove to be false. The three defeated Taira—Tomomori, Koremori, and Noritsune—are the three key figures of this drama; supposed dead, they have been hiding in disguise. In the Daimotsu-no-Ura Scene of Act II, still performed to appreciative audiences today, the ferryman at the port where Yoshitsune plans to cross over to Kyūshū turns out to be TAIRA NO TOMOMORI, the admiral who lost the climactic Battle of DANNOURA; defeated by Yoshitsune once again, he leaps into the sea with a huge anchor attached to his waist. The popular Act III, including the famous Sushiya Scene, deals with the attempt of the sushi shopkeeper Yazaemon, a Taira loyalist, to safeguard Taira no Koremori, his wife, and their young son; that attempt appears to be frustrated by Yazaemon's son Gonta, whom the father thereupon mortally stabs only to discover that, far from killing Koremori and delivering Koremori's consort and heir into the hands of the enemy, Gonta has in fact substituted a false head and sacrificed his own wife and child to fool the pursuers. The brilliant dance scenes of Act IV, the michiyuki (journey), and the At Kawazura's Residence Scene are perhaps the best-known parts of the play. Protected by a faithful retainer named Satō Tadanobu, Yoshitsune's beautiful mistress SHIZUKA GOZEN travels to Yoshino to meet her lover. A samurai who looks identical to the retainer and calls himself Satō Tadanobu appears, but when he denies having traveled with Shizuka, it is realized that Shizuka was in fact accompanied by a fox in human form. This fox has been following Shizuka because she has a drum made from the skin of its parents. Impressed with the animal's filial piety, Yoshitsune gives it the drum and honors it with his own Minamoto name; in turn, the fox helps Yoshitsune repel Taira no Noritsune and his group of warrior-monks, who have staged a surprise attack.

Yowanasake ukina no Yokogushi   (Yosa the Carved). Popular title Kirare Yosa. By Segawa Jokō II, 1853. Sewamono; based on an actual incident. Acts II, III, and IV (the last of these called the Gen'yadana Scene) remain in the kabuki repertory and recount the love story of the handsome rogue Yosaburō, adopted son of the wealthy Izuya family of Edo, and the former geisha Otomi. When a natural son is born to the Izuya, Yosaburō purposely enters a life of dissipation in order to allow the child to become the heir, but is sent to recuperate at a seaside resort. There he meets Otomi, and a torrid affair results between the two despite the fact that she remains the kept woman of Akama Genzaemon. Genzaemon, the boss of a gang of gamblers, soon discovers the pair and orders his hoodlums to carve up Yosaburō's handsome face. Otomi leaps into the sea and is presumed dead, while the disfigured Yosaburō is set free for a ransom. Subsequently known as Kirare Yosa (Yosa the Carved), he teams up with Komori Yasu (Yasu the Bat, so named for his facial tattoo) and embarks on a career of petty crime. When this career leads the pair to a spot in Edo called Gen'yadana, the paths of Otomi and Yosaburō cross again. Otomi, who was saved from the ocean by a passing ship, has been set up in a house there as the mistress of her rescuer, Tazaemon. As the scene opens, she is seen returning from her bath and going about her toilette in this house. Komori Yasu enters to get money from her while Yosa, ignorant of her identity, waits outside. The ensuing moment of mutual recognition between Yosaburō and Otomi is one of the most electric in kabuki; but their reunion is interrupted by Tazaemon, and Yosaburō, hastily identified as Otomi's younger brother to avoid embarrassment, is sent away with a paltry gift of money.

▬▬——James R. Brandon, tr and ed, Kabuki: Five Classic Plays (1975), contains a translation of Sukeroku. Engeki hyakka daijiten (Heibonsha, 1960–62). Earle Ernst, The Kabuki Theatre (rev ed, 1974), a standard reference work on kabuki as a dramatic art. Gunji Masakatsu, Kabuki nyūmon (rev ed, 1962). Gunji Masakatsu, Kabuki, tr John Bester (1968), a concise summary of kabuki beautifully and copiously illustrated. Hachimonjiya Jishō, ed, Yakusha rongo (1776) tr Charles J. Dunn and Bunzō Torigoe as Actors' Analects (1969), views of kabuki by actors of the Genroku era. Aubrey S. and Giovanna M. Halford, The Kabuki Handbook (1956), contains summaries of important kabuki plays. Kabuki nempyō (Iwanami Shoten, 2nd ed, 1948). Kawatake Shigetoshi, Kabuki shi no kenkyū (1943). Meisaku kabuki zenshū (Sōgen Shinsha, 1968–73). Nihon engeki kenkyū shomoku kaidai (Heibonsha, 1966). A. C. Scott, The Kabuki Theatre of Japan (1953), introduction to the history, music, dance, and acting.

kabuki jūhachiban

(literally, "eighteen KABUKI numbers"). An inventory compiled by the actor Ichikawa Danjūrō VII (1791–1859; see ICHIKAWA DANJŪRŌ) of the most notable plays, acts, and scenes from plays in the repertory of the Ichikawa acting-family dynasty, the most illustrious in kabuki history.

The plays are: Fuwa (1680), Narukami (1684), Shibaraku (1697), Fudō (1697), Uwanari (1699), Zōbiki (1701), Sukeroku (1713), Uirō-uri (1718), Ya no ne (1720), Oshimodoshi (1727), Kan U (1737), Kagekiyo (1739), Nanatsumen (1740), Kenuki (1742), Gedatsu (1760), Jayanagi (1763), Kamahige (1769), and Kanjinchō (1840). Of these only six are often performed in the modern repertory: Narukami, Shibaraku, Sukeroku, Ya no ne, Kenuki, and Kanjinchō. Only the last, a one-act play, is complete in itself; the other five are single acts from long plays. All of the other twelve titles have been reconstructed and revived in modern times but have not found a place in the repertory.

With the exception of three plays (Uirōuri, Nanatsumen, and Jayanagi) the central character is a larger-than-life hero who acts and declaims in an exaggerated, unrealistic style called aragoto ("rough business"). A specialty of the Ichikawa line, this bombastic style came to be seen as typical of the Edo (now Tōkyō) kabuki, in contrast to the realistic mode favored in the Kyōto–Ōsaka area.

Narukami was part of a play written by Danjūrō I (1660–1704). In it, a Buddhist monk called Narukami (literally, "thunder god"), incensed at the emperor for withholding the privilege of performing rites of ordination from him, decides to get even. Through supernatural powers, he imprisons the rain-causing dragon, and a severe drought follows. The distressed emperor then sends a beautiful court lady to the monk's hermitage deep in the mountains to seduce him. She succeeds, releases the dragon, and flees. When Narukami awakes from a drunken stupor and finds it to be raining and the woman gone, he flies into a towering rage and vows vengeance.

In *Shibaraku* (One Moment), a ruthless courtier is about to execute the members of a clan whose lands he has expropriated. As the lord's minions prepare to carry out his commands, a voice calls from offstage "One moment!" A superhuman figure, dressed in a costume and wig calculated to make him five-times human size, makes his way down the *hanamichi* (a ramp connecting the stage to the rear of the theater). He frees the captives, excoriates the villain for his oppression of the weak, and proceeds to dispatch him with an eight-foot sword.

Sukeroku is named after the hero of the play, a chivalrous commoner who bests a vicious warrior for a courtesan's favors. In the process he recovers for his lord an heirloom sword stolen by the villain; it is revealed at the end of the play that he is actually a *samurai* disguised as a commoner to facilitate the search. The action takes place in the Yoshiwara pleasure quarters. Sukeroku makes his entrance when the villain, having been rebuffed by a courtesan, threatens to turn ugly. It is one of the great entrances in kabuki. The role of Sukeroku requires an actor equipped to give dash and panache to speech and movement. Three quarters of the way along the ramp, he stops, turns to the audience, and delivers a monologue introducing himself. In early kabuki, all the main actors did this, but this is the only example that has survived into modern times.

Ya no ne (The Arrowhead) has as its central character the historical figure Soga Gorō (1174–93) who, with his brother Jūrō (1172–93), avenged the death of his father. As the key figures in a vendetta, the brothers became two of the most popular figures in tales (see SOGA MONOGATARI) and in every form of Japanese theater. In the kabuki, it has been *de rigueur* since ca 1700 for the New Year's program to include a play on the Soga theme. In *Ya no ne*, Gorō is polishing a giant arrowhead when he falls asleep. In a dream, his brother Jūrō appears and pleads for help; he is in a dangerous situation. Gorō springs awake, seizes the horse of a peasant passing by, and dashes off to rescue his brother.

Kenuki (The Tweezers) was originally act 3 of a longer play called *Narukami Fudō kitayama-zakura*, and is a classic example of a kabuki plot—the usurpation by an evil faction in a feudal domain of the privileges of the house. When a prolonged drought prostrates the nation, the emperor commands the Ono family to present to him the card on which the renowned poetess ONO NO KOMACHI, an ancestress of the Ono clan, wrote a poem which possesses the magic power of causing rain. To its consternation, the Ono family discovers that the poem is missing. The main line of the plot in *Kenuki* involves the daughter of the family who is engaged to be married but postpones the ceremony on account of a singular affliction: her long hair stands on end. Her fiancé's family sends an emissary to investigate the reason for the delay. It is this emissary who is the central figure in the play. The unraveling of the mystery begins when a pair of tweezers he has been using rights itself when he lays it down. He suspects it is a magnet, installed in the attic of the young girl's apartment, that has been drawing her hair up when it attracts the ornaments in her coiffure. He is sure of this when he ascertains that iron ornaments have been substituted for silver ones. He exposes the villains who were anxious to prevent the marriage and who have stolen the poem as well, and the wedding plans proceed.

Kanjinchō (The Subscription List) is arguably the most popular play in the kabuki repertory. A play dealing with the exploits of BENKEI, the legendary retainer of MINAMOTO NO YORITSUNE (1159–89), the most tragic (and therefore the most romantic) figure in Japanese history—a brilliant general hounded to death by an insanely jealous elder brother—was written and enacted by Danjūrō I, but does not survive. The play as now presented was recast as an adaptation of the NŌ play *Ataka* by Danjūrō VII in 1840. It deals with Yoshitsune's flight north in the guise of a porter to Benkei and four retainers disguised as monks. The band arrives at the Ataka barrier where the official, Togashi, is required to confirm the authenticity of the passports of all travelers. The party is without such passes. Benkei hopes to be waved through if they profess to be itinerant monks collecting funds for a prominent temple. Togashi sees through the ruse but, moved by Benkei's display of devotion for his master, allows them to pass. One of Togashi's men, however, becomes suspicious of the porter who looks too delicate. To fore-

stall further questioning by Togashi, Benkei belabors Yoshitsune with his staff. Impressed once again by Benkei's presence of mind, Togashi authorizes their passage. Once safely past the barrier, Benkei begs forgiveness of his master who, far from chastizing the retainer, praises him. The party, except for Benkei, makes a swift exit. Benkei exits making stylized leaps and hops in *aragoto* style, expressing his triumph and joy at their escape.

Oshimodoshi (The Shoving Back) and *Uirōuri* (The Salve Vendor) are now embedded in other plays. *Uirōuri* was hardly more than an excuse to allow Danjūrō II (1688–1758), famous for the rapidity and clarity of his delivery, to entertain the audience with a monologue describing the efficacies of a popular salve. This salve peddler found his way into the play *Sukeroku*, where, to provide an effective foil for Sukeroku, he delivers his lines in a realistic manner. *Oshimodoshi* is now the final scene in several plays and dances in which an evil spirit runs amuck. As the raging demon begins to storm down the ramp, a superhuman figure, made tall by clogs and carrying a freshly-cut bamboo stalk as a weapon, enters from the opposite side of the ramp and, by striking a number of fierce poses and uttering loud threats, succeeds in intimidating the angry spirit which retreats to the stage and is overcome.

Fuwa deals with the rivalry between the two most notorious rakes of the early 17th century—Fuwa Banzaemon and Nagoya Sanzaburō. The play no longer exists in its original form, but adaptations of it are part of the modern repertory. The setting is the Yoshiwara pleasure quarters. Fuwa and Nagoya meet, exchange words over their favorite courtesan, and are about to draw swords when a brothel madam steps in and restrains them.

Fudō, a play by Danjūrō II in which Fudō (Skt: Acala; the bodhisattva who is unmoved by passion) figured, was so popular that the deity was reincarnated in other plays, eventually entering as the final scene in the play of which *Kenuki* and *Narukami* are components (i.e., *Narukami Fudō kitayama-zakura*). In *Fudō*, the apparent evil in the monk Narukami is resolved by making him take the form of this god after it has released his malevolence.

The most intriguing among the 18 titles is *Uwanari* (Ambush of the Second Wife), which comes from the medieval custom of a rejected first wife and her relatives thrashing a second wife. In this play, the spirit of the first wife wreaks vengeance on her philandering husband by entering the body of their daughter, who then punishes the interloper.

Zōbiki (Towing the Elephant) introduced a note of exoticism to the kabuki stage. Elephants were rare in Japan, historical documents recording only three such beasts in Japan before 1700. In this play, a duel of strength between the hero and the villain ends in the hero's dragging and flinging an elephant about, and triumphing.

Kan U is named after Kan U (Ch: Guan Yu or Kuan Yü), a heroic supporter of one of the three rivals contending for supremacy in the China of the 3rd century AD (later, he became the Chinese god of war). A Japanese general assumes his shape in order to reveal the sinister conspiracy of and to defeat a general who takes the form of another Chinese military figure.

Kagekiyo deals with the exploits of Taira no Kagekiyo (d 1196?), who caught the imagination of Japanese dramatists for his stubborn resistance to MINAMOTO NO YORITOMO, the mortal enemy of the Taira family. The rare revival of *Kagekiyo* today is based on a version staged in 1778, the 1739 production having been lost or superseded. In it, Kagekiyo, a captive of the Minamoto, refuses to divulge the whereabouts of the Taira treasures. The captors bring his wife and daughter before him and threaten to torture them. Kagekiyo explodes in fury, tears apart the bars of his prison, and allows his family to escape while he engages in a furious battle with the enemy.

Nanatsumen (Seven Masks) was a pretext for Danjūrō II to indulge in his skill in making lightning onstage changes. In this scene, he assumed the character and guise of seven different personages. The plot itself was apparently of little consequence. This scene has not found a place in the modern repertory.

The plot of *Gedatsu* (Redemption) was almost completely lost by the time of Danjūrō VII. Only references to it in historical documents as having Kagekiyo's ghost as the central character, and the lyrics of the dance section remained. Revived in recent times, Kagekiyo appears as an apparition haunting a bell that emits no sound. The ghost is attacked, but it disappears under the bell as it crashes to the ground. When the ghost materializes, a monk enters to deliver it from its suffering, but fails. However, the robe of the Taira-family chieftain's daughter, who has taken the tonsure, is placed over the ghost, and it finally achieves salvation and disappears.

Of *Jayanagi* (The Serpent Willow) only the sketchiest outline remains. The main character is a priest for whom a beautiful woman dies. Her spirit possesses the priest, and he utters her passionate regret at not having been able to consummate her love for him.

Kamahige (A Shave with a Sickle) again has Kagekiyo as the main character. While traveling incognito, Kagekiyo takes refuge with a swordsmith who recognizes his guest and, on the pretext of wanting to shave his guest's beard, attempts to kill him with a sickle. But Kagekiyo, being immortal, foils his enemy.

◾——Faubion Bowers, *Japanese Theatre* (1954). James R. Brandon, *Kanjinchō and the Zen Substitute* (1966). James R. Brandon, *Kabuki: Five Classical Plays* (1975), contains translations of *Sukeroku, Kenuki, Narukami,* and *Fudō.* Gunji Masakatsu, *Kabuki jūhachiban shū* in *Nihon koten bungaku taikei,* vol 98 (Iwanami Shoten, 1965). Kawatake Shigetoshi, *Kabuki meisakushū II,* in *Edo bungaku sōsho* (1936). Kawatake Shigetoshi, *Kabuki jūhachiban* (1944). Kawatake Shigetoshi, *Kabuki jūhachiban shū* in *Nihon koten zensho* (Asahi Shimbun Sha, 1952). Toita Yasuji, *Kabuki jūhachiban kō* (1955).   Frank T. MOTOFUJI

kabuki music

A variety of vocal and/or instrumental music which has accompanied dances or enhanced dramatic situations in the popular KABUKI theater from the 17th century to the present.

Early History——The first kabuki theaters used singing plus the drums and flute of the classical NŌ drama. The lyrics of surviving pieces and the plebeian nature of the theater show that this kabuki music was derived from popular and folk forms. By the 17th century, the major melodic instrument in kabuki was the three-stringed plucked lute called the *samisen* or SHAMISEN. Throughout the 18th and 19th centuries, a great variety of *shamisen* musical styles appeared both on the kabuki stage and in the neighboring amusement quarters. This music differed in repertoire, in the size and sound of the *shamisen,* and in the vocal style of the singers. The constant elaboration of kabuki productions also included the use of new percussion instruments derived from folk and religious sources. Overall kabuki showed the kind of creative eclecticism indicative of good theater music.

Music Types——The kinds of *shamisen* music used in kabuki can be divided first into those that are primarily narrative (called *jōruri* or *katarimono*) and those that are lyrical (called *utamono*). Though historically almost every genre of *shamisen* music has appeared on stage, only four are common today. The dominant lyrical genre is NAGAUTA ("long song"), while KIYOMOTO-BUSHI, TOKIWAZU-BUSHI, and GIDAYŪ-BUSHI are classified as narrative music. The names of the narrative forms are derived from those of the musicians who first created them (Kiyomoto Enjudayū [1777–1825], Tokiwazu Mojidayū [1709–64], and Takemoto Gidayū [1651–1714]). Each genre in kabuki is performed by different musicians, since their lineages and styles are different.

Another set of *shamisen* musicians are those who perform various old popular lyrical genres (like *hauta* and KOUTA) offstage or work with other offstage musicians in special effects needed for a given scene. Their music, along with that of their percussion and flute-playing colleagues, is called offstage *(geza)* music. The drummers and flutists who perform on stage with the other *shamisen* genres are known collectively as the HAYASHI, while the term for all music performed on stage is *debayashi.*

Performance Practice——Kabuki actors almost never sing or play music. The offstage music *(geza)* is usually played from a small room at the stage-right corner. It has windows covered by bamboo curtains so that the musicians can observe action on the stage or the ramp (the *hanamichi*) while not being seen themselves. On stage musicians *(debayashi)* are arranged according to the design of a given set. In a piece derived from a Nō play the *shamisen* players and singers are usually on a dais across the back of the stage, with the flutists and drummers placed at floor level in front of them. If a play is in the style of a puppet-theater (BUNRAKU) piece, the *shamisen* players and a *gidayū* chanter are seated on a special dais placed just beyond the stage-left apron, or behind a bamboo curtain in an alcove above the stage-left entrance of the set. Some plays use several genres of music on stage in the same scene. Such joint *(kakeai)* productions place the *shamisen* and singers by genre on different sections of the stage. If the normal onstage *hayashi* percussion ensemble also is needed, it is placed offstage.

Functions——Music on stage is generally used to accompany dance. Like analogous traditions elsewhere in the world, the music responds subtly to the meaning of the text and the needs of the choreography. Offstage music has many functions. It may accompany specific stage actions, set moods, establish locations or even weather conditions, identify characters, create sound effects, signal formal units, or reflect the unspoken thoughts of the actors. The manner in which each of these functions is served is quite specific, so that an experienced listener acquires a natural feel for the kind of theatrical message the music is communicating.

Fight scenes, for example, may be enhanced by dramatic percussion activity from offstage. However, in kabuki these scenes often progress into a rather slow formalized dance (a *dontappo*) complete with a *shamisen* tune. The most effective support of a specific stage gesture or pose is created by the clack of two wooden sticks (*ki* or *hyōshigi*), struck on a wooden board at stage left at the precise moment of the movement. These same sticks struck together signal the opening or ending of a scene and always have a dramatic impact on kabuki audiences.

Moods, locations, and weather are often interlaced in kabuki music. The most obvious mood music is the sense of danger which, in kabuki, is generated by slow ominous beats of a very large barrel drum (the *ōdaiko*). If light percussion and a famous old popular song from the Kansai area are heard from the offstage room, one knows that the curtain will open to reveal an Edo-period geisha house in Kyōto or Ōsaka. The sound of horse bells and the pack-horse driver's song "Eight Miles over the Hakone Pass" will combine with a large drum pattern which imitates the rolling sound of waves to indicate that the scene is along the seashore on the Tōkaidō Road. If a different drum pattern had been used one would know that it had been raining or, with another pattern, snowing. A kabuki aficionado would even note whether it was a heavy or light rain or snowfall. In all these cases, the audience is not necessarily overtly aware of the messages the music is sending. Like movie music, these kabuki traditions are so conventionalized that viewers respond automatically. The performers themselves are able to recall the correct choice and placement of such conventions by reference to "secret" professional books *(tsukechō)* which mark the text of plays with special signs or short instructions.

Sound effects such as bird calls or echoes in mountain valleys require even less conscious listening. It is also easy to sense the courtly nature of music that may accompany the entrance of some nobleman, or the songs in praise of beauty sung as a courtesan appears with her entourage, though it may be difficult to understand the words. This also is the challenge of the songs called *meriyasu* which are used to reflect upon a character's mood or thoughts. Because of such songs, it is possible for an actor to stand pensively while the audience can absorb his inner emotions without the use of monologues or soliloquies.

Form——The forms of kabuki plays are quite varied, and there are even some without any music. The dramatically functional music mentioned above is generally not directly related to the form of a play. Thus we will discuss here only the traditions of pieces which are primarily used for dance. Conventionally, they follow the so-called kabuki dance form though there is great variation.

The fundamental structure of such dances and their music is tripartite; they have an introductory section (*jo* or *deha*), a "scattering" (*ha* or *chūha*) or increase in complexity, and finally an increase in speed and density (*kyū* or *iriha*). The introductory section traditionally contains at least two subdivisions. First there is an instrumental or vocal prelude (often called the *oki*) which assists in setting moods or identifying places or characters. The actual dancer usually enters in a section that follows (*michiyuki*). The middle section will at some point have two subsections also: a highly lyrical portion (*kudoki*) and a change into a more lively dance style (*odoriji*). The subdivisions of the last section include a more intense music (*chirashi*) which leads to a final cadence pattern (*dangire*), whose music and dance postures tell the audience that a grand ending is about to happen. The orchestration, tonalities, and melodic styles of each of these sections are sufficiently standard and distinctive so that one can easily feel the forward motion of the music from start to finish even though, unlike most Western traditions, the music is through-composed, i.e., one does not hear specific themes played at the start of a piece and then developed.

Perhaps the most striking fact for Western musicians is that these beautifully effective and complex musical structures are communally composed. The singer and *shamisen* player are responsible for their own parts, while the percussion and offstage music are added in consultation with the head of the guild of percussionists (the *hayashi-gashira*) and the actors and directors of the performance. If performers from a different guild play the same piece, the result may be audibly different. Thus, there is no "correct" rendition of a piece such as one thinks of in the case of a Western symphony. Instead there may be several correct ways in which music can operate in a kabuki performance. There is no improvisation, only a thorough, viable tradition through which music can become a truly integrated part of a brilliant theatrical form.

—— William P. Malm, *Nagauta: The Heart of Kabuki Music* (1963); "Music in the Kabuki Theater," in *Studies in Kabuki,* ed, James Brandon, William P. Malm, and Donald Shively (1978).

William P. MALM

kabunakama

Monopolistic trade associations sanctioned by both the Tokugawa shogunate and various *daimyō* domains during the Edo period (1600–1868). *Nakama* meant an association of merchants in the same trade who banded together with official approval to restrict access to trade and to set prices; their loyalty to the group was enforced by shared commercial interests and a code of ethics. *Kabu* meant a "share" or membership in such an association. In theory, each member held only one *kabu,* symbolized by a wooden placard called a *kabufuda;* the number of members was strictly limited, although a member could on occasion sell or even lend his share with the group's permission. In return for the right to monopolize a trade or some aspect of it, the *kabunakama* made "contributions" (known as MYŌGAKIN) to the authorities.

Exclusive, monopolistic trade associations called ZA had flourished under official patronage in the Muromachi period (1333–1568), but most of them had been abolished during the 16th century (see RAKUICHI AND RAKUZA). In the late 17th century, however, the Tokugawa shogunate came to recognize the usefulness of such associations for regulating trade and began to approve them in Edo (now Tōkyō), Ōsaka, and other major cities. Many were approved for convenience in policing their activities, but several, such as the TO-KUMI-DOIYA in Edo and the NIJŪSHIKUMI-DOIYA in Ōsaka, were given monopolistic rights in order to stimulate business by reducing competition. During the so-called Tanuma period (1767–86) there was a conspicuous increase in the number of *kabunakama,* whose "contributions," now regularized as annual taxes, became an important source of official revenue. In Ōsaka alone, there were 129 *kabunakama.*

In the hinterlands of Ōsaka and other areas with highly developed commercial economies, rural merchants (ZAIGŌ SHŌNIN) formed local groups called *zaikata kabu* in opposition to the monopolistic control of the market by the *kabunakama,* but they eventually became subservient to the *kabunakama* in the cities. *Kabunakama* came under increasing criticism, and during the KANSEI REFORMS (1787–93) many of them were dissolved in recognition of the economic evils they had fostered. Nevertheless, the shogunate saw fit to increase the rights of certain *kabunakama.* Of particular note are its actions during the Bunka–Bunsei era (1804–31), when in the hope of improving the flow of goods from Ōsaka, the largest supply market, to Edo, the largest center of consumption, it further bolstered the monopoly of the Tokumi-doiya.

During the TEMPŌ REFORMS (1841–43) the shogunate dissolved all *kabunakama,* blaming them for the upward spiral of prices. But this action resulted in an even greater inflation, and in 1851 the senior councillor (*rōjū*) ABE MASAHIRO decided to revive the *kabunakama* system. In contrast to earlier practice, however, rural merchant associations were included in the network, the limits on membership were removed, and payment of *myōgakin* was no longer exacted. The monopoly aspects of *kabunakama* were correspondingly weakened, and the associations were abolished soon after the Meiji Restoration of 1868.

TSUDA Hideo

Kaburagi Kiyokata (1878–1972)

Japanese-style painter. Leading modern master of genre painting; specialized in *bijinga* (pictures of beautiful women). Real name Kaburagi Ken'ichi. Born in the Kanda district of Tōkyō. His father was president of the newspaper *Nichinichi shimbun* and a writer of popular novels. In 1891 Kaburagi entered the studio of Mizuno Toshikata (1866–1908) and began the study of UKIYO-E; he was soon producing illustrations for various newspapers and magazines. In 1901 he helped found the Ugōkai (1901–12), an organization that sought to revive genre painting. In 1902, at the first Ugōkai exhibit, Kaburagi unveiled *Ichiyō joshi no haka* (1902, The Tomb of Higuchi Ichiyō), a painting that revealed the direction Kiyokata was to take in his modern *ukiyo-e:* the treatment of contemporary themes coupled with a nostalgia for the passing of the Meiji period (1868–1912). When the Bunten exhibitions were established in 1907, Kaburagi gave up illustrations in order to paint full time and exhibit at the Bunten. In 1916 with HIRAFUKU HYAKUSUI, MATSUOKA EIKYŪ, Yūki Somei (1875–1957), and Kikkawa Reika (1875–1929), he helped found the Kinreisha, a group of artists who became the nucleus of the Japanese-style painting (NIHONGA) associations in Tōkyō. Kaburagi succeeded in synthesizing traditional art styles and technical mastery with a psychological insight into the nature of his changing times. ITŌ SHINSUI and Yamakawa Shūhō (1898–1944) were among his pupils. He was appointed a member of the Imperial Fine Arts Academy (Teikoku Bijutsuin) in 1929, was appointed artist for the imperial household (*teishitsu gigeiin*) in 1944, and was awarded the Order of Culture in 1954.

Aya Louisa McDONALD

kabushiki kaisha → joint-stock company

kabutogani → horseshoe crab

Kachikachi yama

(Kachikachi Mountain). Folktale about the mischievous deeds of a TANUKI (raccoon dog, a badger-like creature), a common trickster figure in Japanese folklore. A *tanuki* teases an old man and woman who become so angry that they threaten to make soup out of him. The *tanuki* deceives the old woman and kills her. He then assumes her shape, gives the old man soup made from the old woman, and escapes. A rabbit comes along and decides to avenge the old woman; he persuades the *tanuki* to carry some firewood and sets fire to the twigs with a flintstone. (The *kachikachi* of the title refers to the sound of striking flints.) He then irritates the *tanuki's* burns by applying a spicy bean-paste mixture and finally tricks the *tanuki* into boarding a boat made of mud, which immediately sinks. The first and second portions of the story were originally separate but were combined sometime during the Edo period (1600–1868). In some versions, the trickster is represented by a wolf or a monkey.

SUCHI Tokuhei

kachōga → bird-and-flower painting

Kada no Arimaro (1706–1751)

KOKUGAKU (National Learning) scholar and WAKA poet of the Edo period (1600–1868). Born in Kyōto, he was the nephew and adopted son of KADA NO AZUMAMARO, whom he succeeded in service to the shogunate. Official displeasure over the unauthorized publication of Arimaro's *Daijōe bemmō* (1739), a study of the sacred harvest ritual performed by emperors, led to his being temporarily placed under arrest. In opposition to the views of KAMO NO MABUCHI and TAYASU MUNETAKE, in whose service he had once been employed, he advocated the more refined *waka* poetry style found in the anthology SHIN KOKINSHŪ over that of the MAN'YŌSHŪ. His *Kokka hachiron* (1742) was the foremost work on poetics of its time.

Kada no Azumamaro (1669–1736)

KOKUGAKU (National Learning) scholar and poet. Born into a priestly family which had for generations served at the Fushimi Inari Shrine in Kyōto, he was educated in the traditions of WAKA poetry and Shintō scholarship. After serving three years in the court of Emperor Reigen (1654–1732; r 1663–87), he was summoned to Edo (now Tōkyō) to collate historical records and provincial documents held in the shogunal library. He also gave private lectures on the KOJIKI, NIHON SHOKI, and MAN'YŌSHŪ and published works on Shintō studies and Man'yō poetics. Considered one of the founders of the Kokugaku tradition, he urged that it be officially adopted in place of Confucianism as the ethical underpinning of the state. In 1728, after devolving his archival duties onto his heir KADA NO ARIMARO, he petitioned the shogunate to establish a center for national studies. His student, KAMO NO MABUCHI, built upon his mentor's achievements by synthesizing Azumamaro's intuitive approach to scholarship with the philological methods of KEICHŪ. Azumamaro's *waka* are collected in *Shun'yōshū* (1798); a modern edition of his complete works, *Kada zenshū,* appeared in 1928.

Kadena

Town on the island of Okinawa, Okinawa Prefecture. Approximately 81 percent of Kadena is occupied by an American air base. The town's economy is almost wholly dependent on the American base. Small amounts of sugarcane and pineapple are produced. Pop: 14,095.

Kades, Charles Louis (1906–)

American lawyer; government official. As deputy chief of the Government Section of SCAP (the headquarters of the Allied Occupation of Japan) from 1945 to 1949, he played a leading role in making and carrying out OCCUPATION policies for Japan's constitutional and legal reforms and the purge of wartime officials. He was considered by some Japanese and Americans as a liberal or "New Dealer" in political and economic outlook. Born in Newburgh, New York, he graduated from Cornell University in 1927 and from Harvard Law School in 1930. He practiced law in New York and was assistant general counsel of the Treasury Department in 1941–42. After military service he returned to law practice in New York and became a partner in the law firm Hawkins, Delafield & Wood.

Richard B. FINN

Kadokawa Publishing Co, Ltd

(Kadokawa Shoten). One of Japan's leading publishing houses. Founded in 1945 by Kadokawa Gen'yoshi (1917–75), a scholar of Japanese literature and student of ORIKUCHI SHINOBU. The company originally focused on the publishing of belles lettres. When Kadokawa's son Haruki (b 1942) became the second president of the company, he ventured into the publishing of paperback editions, and initiated for the first time in Japan the production of a single work in book and film form, supported by coordinated advertising on television and radio. His activities have changed the publishing house into a multimedia publishing organization.

KOBAYASHI Kazuhiro

Kadoma

City in central Ōsaka Prefecture, central Honshū, contiguous with Ōsaka. Kadoma has traditionally been known for its lotus roots *(renkon),* used in Japanese cooking. Matsushita Electric Industrial Co, Ltd, established here in 1933, is the chief manufactory. Pop: 138,901.

Kadoya Shichirobei (1610–1672)

Overseas trader of the early Edo period (1600–1868). Born in Matsuzaka in Ise Province (now largest part of Mie Prefecture) to a family of successful shipping merchants who had been favored by the government for three generations. In 1631, at age 21, he sailed to Annam (now Vietnam) and settled in a Japanese community near Tourane (now Da-nang). When in 1633 the Tokugawa shogunate prohibited Japanese citizens from leaving Japan (see NATIONAL SECLUSION), Shichirobei chose to stay abroad and continued to ship local products to Japan. Japan's closed-door policy was more strongly enforced from 1636, so for nearly 30 years there was no communication with Shichirobei. During the Kambun era (1661–73) regulations were eased, and Shichirobei was once again able to get letters through to Japan. According to these, he had married a woman related to the king of Annam, they had had a son, and Shichirobei had become a leader of the Japanese community. Shichirobei resumed trading between the two countries, and his son took over the business after his death. His widow continued to write letters to Japan for some years.

kadozuke

Entertainers who go door-to-door performing for food (usually uncooked rice) or money. The performance itself is also called *kadozuke.* From earliest recorded times, people dressed as gods would visit each house at certain seasons of the year to offer the blessings of the gods to its occupants. The religious significance gradually faded, but the custom persisted as an entertainment for a reward. Since World War II, *kadozuke* have greatly diminished in number. Their ranks include seasonal visitors, such as the SHISHI-MAI groups and *daikoku* dancers, whose performances are to guarantee good fortune for the year, and year-round *kadozuke,* whose performances usually are more for entertainment than for religious purposes.

MISUMI Haruo

Kaehwap'a

(J: Kaikaha; Enlightenment Faction). Also referred to as the Independence Party. A political clique organized by Koreans to promote Westernization and independence from China; formed in the aftermath of the IMO MUTINY of 1882, with a number of young Koreans who had traveled abroad providing the nucleus. Two of the leaders, KIM OK-KYUN and PAK YŎNG-HYO, had traveled to Japan and had come under the influence of the pro-Western scholar FUKUZAWA YUKICHI; some Korean historians also link the group to the Korean Confucian school of "practical studies" *(sirhak).* The group clashed with the SUGUP'A, a conservative, pro-Chinese group in the Korean government, in a Japanese-supported attempt to seize power in 1884 (see KAPSIN POLITICAL COUP). The unsuccessful coup led to a resurgence of conservative, pro-Chinese political forces and a period of Chinese dominance in Korea that ended only with China's defeat in the Sino-Japanese War of 1894–95. See also KOREA AND JAPAN: early modern relations. *C. Kenneth QUINONES*

Kaei sandai ki

(Record of Three Generations of Flowery Rule). A record of the Muromachi shogunate. Also called *Muromachi ki* or *Buke nikki.* The identity of the author is unknown, but it is presumed that he was a shogunate secretary. The work covers the period from 1367 to 1425 during the rule of the three shōguns ASHIKAGA YOSHIMITSU (r 1369–95), Yoshimochi (r 1395–1423), and Yoshikazu (r 1423–25). It is an especially valuable source for understanding the structure of the Muromachi shogunate, its relations with the Southern Court (see NORTHERN AND SOUTHERN COURTS), and economic matters such as *tansen* (see TANSEN AND TAMMAI) and HANZEI.

G. Cameron HURST III

Kaempfer, Engelbert (1651–1716)

German physician and historian. Born 16 September 1651 at Lemgo in the duchy of Lippe (now North Rhine-Westphalia), Germany, Kaempfer received an excellent medical and humanistic education at German, Dutch, Polish, and Swedish schools and universities before leaving Stockholm in March 1683 as secretary of a Swedish embassy to Persia. Not wishing to return to war-torn Germany when the embassy was over, Kaempfer entered the service of the Dutch East India Company, spending the years 1686–88 at Bandar Abbas (Gombrun, Persia) and its vicinity. A serious illness did not prevent him from compiling much valuable medical, historical, and archaeological information about Persia.

Reaching Batavia (now Djakarta, Indonesia) in 1689, he left for Japan via Siam (now Thailand) in May of the following year. In September 1690 he arrived at Nagasaki to take up the post of physician at the Dutch factory, or trading agency, on the island of DEJIMA in Nagasaki Harbor. He soon won the trust of his Japanese interpreters by plying them liberally with liquor and prescribing remedies for their own illnesses and those of their friends. A young student-interpreter, who remained with him for two years, became fluent in Dutch and supplied Kaempfer with a great deal of information on Japan. In 1691 and 1692 Kaempfer accompanied the annual tribute mission (EDO SAMPU) by the Dutch factory chief to the shōgun's court at Edo (now Tōkyō). His meticulous accounts of these journeys are the most widely quoted Western sources on these Dutch trips through the Inland Sea and along the highway Tōkaidō.

The amount of valuable and accurate information to be found in Kaempfer's two-volume *History of Japan* (1727–28) is astonishing. More than a century ago, Th. R. H. McClatchie commented on the surprising accuracy of Kaempfer's description of the baffling and intricate layout of EDO CASTLE. More impressive tribute was paid by the Nagasaki interpreter Aoki Okikatsu (1762–1812), stating in his *Tōmon jissaku* (1804) how "terrible" he found it that Europeans had acquired such precise information about Japan from Kaempfer's book. Despite the ban against foreigners acquiring any materials on Japan, Kaempfer contrived to smuggle out a collection of books, manuscripts, and maps that were fairly representative of the kind of literature available in Japan during the Genroku era (1688–1704). In an essay appended to the second volume of his posthumously published *History*, Kaempfer discussed the implementation and the results of the Tokugawa shogunate's NATIONAL SECLUSION policy. He concluded that the island empire "was never in a happier condition than it now is, governed by an arbitrary monarch, shut up, and kept from all commerce and communication with foreign nations." The historical sections are of no great value, as Kaempfer took too much of Japanese mythology on trust. But the bulk of the work forms an unrivaled description of Genroku Japan. The *History* subsequently appeared in French (1729), Dutch (1733), and German (1777–79) editions. It remained the standard European work on Japan until the publications of the works of Izaak TITSINGH and Philipp Franz von SIEBOLD in the 19th century.

In November 1692 Kaempfer sailed from Nagasaki to Batavia and returned to Europe in the following year. In April 1694 he took his medical degree at Leiden and then settled at Lemgo as physician to the prince of Lippe. In 1712 he published *Amoenitatum Exoticum*, containing, like his Leiden thesis, a miscellany of Persian, Japanese, and Indian medical, botanical, and other topics, including treatises on acupuncture and moxibustion. After Kaempfer's death at the age of 65, all his books and manuscripts, including the Japanese materials, were purchased by Sir Hans Sloane (1660–1753) and became part of the original collection of the British Museum in 1759. Copies of the *History* soon found their way to Japan. SHIZUKI TADAO translated Kaempfer's essay on the desirability of continuing the National Seclusion policy, which Shizuki himself advocated.

━━━Engelbert Kaempfer, *The History of Japan*, tr J. G. Scheuchzer, 2 vols (1727–28, repr 1906). John F. Bowers, *Western Medical Pioneers in Feudal Japan* (1970). *C. R. BOXER*

kaeshi

(paying back; literally, "return"). Gift or favor given in return for same. In some cases, Japan has relatively formal and explicit rules as to what should be paid back, and when and how. For funeral gifts (*kōden;* see CONDOLENCE GIFTS) that it has received, for example, the bereaved family must give a return gift equivalent to about one-third to one-half the value of the *kōden.* Gifts given in situations of social equality always require a return gift. Thus if a person has received a wedding gift, he or his family must give a gift of equivalent value when the giver or a member of the giver's family marries. Similarly, if one has received a farewell gift upon leaving for an extended trip, one is expected to give a farewell gift of equivalent value when the giver or a member of his family leaves on a long trip. Thus the giving of a gift of equivalent value symbolizes equal status. When return of an equivalent gift is not required, as in the case of the midyear gift (CHŪGEN) or the year-end gift (SEIBO), a hierarchical relationship is usually involved, in which an inferior gives to his social superior to express gratitude for a past favor. In short, the act of gift-giving is itself the return.

Relationships maintained through expenditure of money, time, and other resources are not easily forgotten. These customs express and create mutual trust, as well as the obligation of readiness to help each other, sometimes felt more strongly when reciprocity is entailed. As such they are an important part of the Japanese social network. See also GIFT GIVING. *Harumi BEFU*

kaezeni

(money exchange). Also called *kaesen* or *kawashi.* Method of payment by means of a bill of exchange called SAIFU employed during the Kamakura (1185–1333) and Muromachi (1333–1568) periods. It originated in the 13th century mainly as a substitute for the payment of rice and other taxes (NENGU) from landed estates (SHŌEN) in remote areas to their proprietors in Kyōto; it was especially convenient since currency was not standard at the time. The business of money exchange was handled by specialized merchants called *kaezeniya* or *saifuya.* With the development and expansion of commercial activities, the *kaezeni* system came to be widely used in general business transactions. At a time when the transport of money and goods was dangerous and difficult, this form of payment facilitated the growth of economic exchange between widely separated regions.

Kaga

City in southwestern Ishikawa Prefecture, central Honshū, on the Sea of Japan. Kaga developed as a castle town during the Edo period (1600–1868). It produces silk fabrics known as Kaga *habutae* as well as conveyors and bicycle chains. The town is also noted for its KUTANI WARE. Hot springs (Katayamatsu and Yamashiro) and tombs dating from the 5th century (at Hōōzan and Kitsuneyama) attract visitors. Pop: 65,281.

Kagaku Gijutsu Chō → Science and Technology Agency

Kagami Kenkichi (1868–1939)

Businessman who developed the general insurance industry in Japan. Born in Gifu Prefecture. Graduate of Tōkyō Higher Commercial School (now Hitotsubashi University). Kagami joined TOKIO MARINE & FIRE INSURANCE CO, LTD, in 1891 and became chairman in 1925. He is credited with transforming Tokio Marine into a large firm with an international reputation. He also became chairman of Meiji Fire & Marine in 1922, of Tōmei Fire & Marine in 1925, and of Mitsubishi Marine & Fire in 1933. He was concurrently chairman of NIPPON YŪSEN and MITSUBISHI TRUST & BANKING CORPORATION.

TATSUKI Mariko

Kagami Shikō (1665–1731)

HAIKU poet from Mino Province (now part of Gifu Prefecture), one of the ten major disciples of BASHŌ. He is credited for his part in consolidating Bashō's teachings into a coherent poetic theory and for popularizing haiku and Bashō's work throughout the country. He wrote *Kuzu no matsubara* (1692), the first critical essay on Bashō's style, and coedited *Zoku sarumino* (1698), the last item in the collection HAIKAI SHICHIBUSHŪ. In the process of popularizing haiku in the provinces after Bashō's death, his own poetry lost the essential loftiness and subtlety of his master's style. The Mino school, which he founded, was later ridiculed for its facile, vulgarized version of the orthodox style. Shikō remains, however, the foremost theorist of haiku, as evidenced in such critical works as *Haikai jūron* (1719) and *Jūron ibenshō* (1725).

Kaga no Chiyo (1703–1775)

HAIKU poet. Born in Kaga Province (now part of Ishikawa Prefecture). The precocious daughter of a scroll mounter, she had already gained fame by the time she was 18, when she attracted the attention of KAGAMI SHIKŌ, a prominent disciple of BASHŌ, who was visiting the area. Little is known about the rest of her life, except that she became a nun in her later years and was referred to as Chiyo Ni (the Nun Chiyo). *Chiyo Ni kushū* (1763) and its sequel, *Matsu no koe* (1771), are collections of her poems.

Kaga Otohiko (1929–)

Novelist; psychiatrist. Real name Kogi Sadataka. Born in Tōkyō. Graduate of Tōkyō University Medical School. After working in several Tōkyō hospitals, he went to Paris to study from 1957 to 1960. He gained recognition as a writer with *Furandoru no fuyu* (1966), a novel based on his experiences in France. As a writer also trained as a psychiatrist, he explores in his works those areas of insanity which he claims only fiction can reach. Other works include "Bungaku to kyōki" (1971), a critical essay, and *Kaerazaru natsu* (1974), a novel.

Kagawa Gen'etsu (1700–1777)

Physician and founder of the Kagawa school of obstetrics. Also known as Kagawa Shigen; original family name Miura. A native of Hikone, Ōmi Province (now Shiga Prefecture), Kagawa studied medicine of the classicist school (*koihō*) in Kyōto. In one instance of severe prolongation of delivery of a baby, he used an iron hook taken from a paper lantern. This episode was said to be the nation's first case of forceps delivery. He also made feasible other methods for facilitating delivery and published his findings in a two-volume work, *Sanron* (1766). See also MEDICINE: history of medicine.

YAMADA Terutane

Kagawa Kageki (1768–1843)

WAKA poet and theorist. Founder of the Keien school of *waka.* Born in the Tottori domain (now Tottori Prefecture), he distinguished

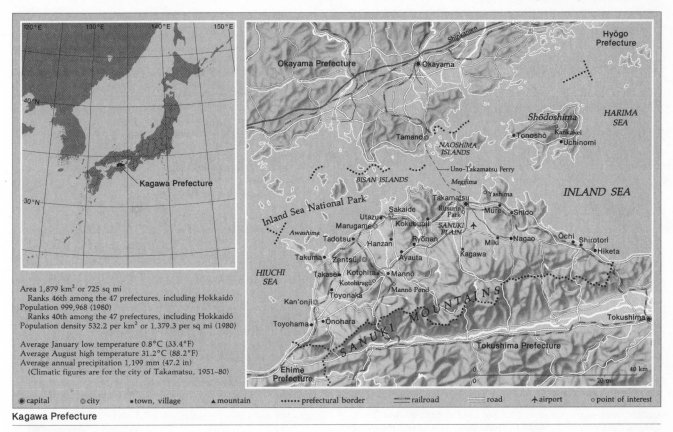

Area 1,879 km² or 725 sq mi
  Ranks 46th among the 47 prefectures, including Hokkaidō
Population 999,968 (1980)
  Ranks 40th among the 47 prefectures, including Hokkaidō
Population density 532.2 per km² or 1,379.3 per sq mi (1980)

Average January low temperature 0.8°C (33.4°F)
Average August high temperature 31.2°C (88.2°F)
Average annual precipitation 1,199 mm (47.2 in)
  (Climatic figures are for the city of Takamatsu, 1951–80)

◉ capital   ○ city   • town, village   ▲ mountain   ••••• prefectural border   ▭▭ railroad   ▭▭ road   ✦ airport   ○ point of interest

Kagawa Prefecture

himself as a poet at an early age and at age 25 went to Kyōto, where he studied under and was adopted into the family of Kagawa Kagemoto, an orthodox court poet of the conservative Nijō school of waka. Kageki's true mentor, however, was the unconventional poet OZAWA ROAN, who advocated simplicity, intelligibility, and the use of everyday language in poetry. In time, Kagawa's views came to diverge from those of Kagemoto, and he severed relations with him although he kept the family name. He was criticized by both the orthodox school of court poets, known as the dōjō (a term applied to privileged nobles who could appear before the emperor), and poets of the Edo school, followers of the teachings of KAMO NO MABUCHI who advocated the lofty style of the 8th-century MAN'YŌSHŪ, but gradually built up a following of poets all over Japan. His group, which came to be known as the Keien school, dominated waka poetic circles through the end of the Edo period. Central to Kageki's poetics is the idea of shirabe, the spontaneous flow of verse in harmonious response to feelings evoked by a particular scene or object. He stressed direct, sincere emotion as the source of all poetry and spurned intellectually contrived embellishment based on theory and lacking the immediacy of experience. He admired KI NO TSURAYUKI and other KOKINSHŪ (ca 905) poets for what he considered to be their natural, uncluttered elegance. His own waka, though somewhat limited in scope, embody his precepts. Kageki was later reviled by Meiji-period (1868–1912) poets such as MASAOKA SHIKI, who declared the lingering influence of the Keien school to be the greatest obstacle to the development of a waka tradition appropriate to the new age. His principal waka collection is Keien isshi (1828); his principal critical works include Niimanabi iken (1811), Kokin wakashū seigi (1823), and Kagaku teiyō (1850).

Kagawa Prefecture

(Kagawa Ken). Located in northeastern Shikoku and bounded by the Inland Sea to the north, east, and west, and Ehime and Tokushima prefectures to the south. The SANUKI MOUNTAINS cover the southern part of the prefecture, and the northern area is composed largely of coastal lowlands. Numerous small Inland Sea islands also fall within Kagawa's territory. As the main transport link between Shikoku and Honshū, the city of TAKAMATSU has become the economic and administrative center of the Shikoku region. The climate is generally mild and dry, except in the rainy season in June and early July.

Known after the TAIKA REFORM of 645 as Sanuki Province, it developed as a rice-producing area and later added salt, sugar, and cotton to its economy. In the Edo period (1600–1868) it was divided into small domains, with some areas under the direct rule of the Tokugawa shogunate. The present prefectural name and boundaries were established in 1888.

Agriculture is dominated by the production of rice, livestock, and fruit. Kagawa once led Japan in salt production, but the salt fields were closed in 1972. Fishing is also important. Manufacturing industries are not highly developed and consist of light industries such as food processing, textiles, and paper, as well as some heavy industries such as shipbuilding.

Tourist attractions include seashore areas which are part of the INLAND SEA NATIONAL PARK, KOTOHIRA SHRINE in Kotohira, and RITSURIN PARK in Takamatsu. Area: 1,879 sq km (725 sq mi); pop: 999,968; capital: Takamatsu. Other major cities include SAKAIDE and MARUGAME.

Kagawa Shūtoku (1683–1755)

Physician of the classicist school (koihō). Also known as Kagawa Shūan or Ippondō. Born in Harima (now Hyōgo Prefecture), he studied medicine with GOTŌ KONZAN and Confucianism with ITŌ JINSAI. Kagawa advocated "jui ippon," the doctrine that Confucianism and medical art originated from the same principles. See also MEDICINE: history of medicine.   YAMADA Terutane

Kagawa Toyohiko (1888–1960)

Christian social reformer and labor leader. Born in Kōbe, he was baptized while attending middle school in Tokushima Prefecture. He studied subsequently at Meiji Gakuin and Kōbe Shingakkō and for two years at Princeton Theological Seminary. Upon returning to Japan in 1917, he devoted himself to helping the poor in Kōbe.

A versatile, resourceful Christian, Kagawa advocated a kind of "social gospel" modeled, in part, on guild socialism. He was handicapped by constant illness, but possessed boundless energy, an encyclopedic mind, and a charismatic personality. Among his numerous publications was Shisen o koete (1920, Crossing the Deathline; tr Before the Dawn, 1924), a strongly autobiographical novel centering on a hero who, after a troubled childhood and adolescence, decides to work for the poor in the slums of Kōbe. Another was *Himmin shinri no kenkyū* (1915), an in-depth study of "the psychology of the poor" based on firsthand knowledge and data collected while he lived in the slums.

Kagawa was also active in the labor movement until the failure of the large-scale dockyard (Mitsubishi) strikes in Kōbe in 1921 led to its radicalization. For his labor activities he was briefly imprisoned in 1921. He then turned his attention to the farmers' movement and worked to establish agricultural cooperatives. Kagawa was also one of the most prominent mass evangelists Japan produced, and from the mid-1920s played an important role in interdenominational endeavors, such as the Save One Million Souls and the Kingdom of God movements. A pacifist, he was harassed by the military during World War II. After World War II, he was active in the world federation movement.

📖 ——*Kagawa Toyohiko zenshū* (Kirisuto Shimbunsha, 1962–64). George B. Bikle, Jr, *The New Jerusalem: Aspects of Utopianism in the Thought of Kagawa Toyohiko* (1976). Yūzō Ōta, "Kagawa Toyohiko (1888–1960) as a Pacifist," in John F. Howes and Nobuya Bamba, ed, *Pacifism in Japan* (1978). Sumiya Mikio, *Kagawa Toyohiko* (1966). J. M. Trout, *Kagawa: Japanese Prophet* (1959).

Yūzō Ōta

Kageki Shakai Undō Torishimari Hōan → Draft
Law to Control Radical Social Movements

Kagerō nikki

The *Kagerō nikki* (tr *The Gossamer Years*, 1964) is the diary, or memoirs, of a lady who lived in the middle and late 10th century and who is known as the mother of Michitsuna (Fujiwara no Michitsuna no Haha). The author was born to a cadet branch of the Fujiwara family. Her father, Tomoyasu, rose to the rank of provincial governor. She was married to a distant kinsman, FUJIWARA NO KANEIE, who was at the end of his life head of the Fujiwara family and the most powerful statesman in the land. Kaneie was the father of FUJIWARA NO MICHINAGA, under whose guidance, in the early decades of the following century, the Fujiwara hegemony had its greatest day. Her only son had a moderately successful career at court, but was never a serious rival of his brilliant half-brother.

The *nikki* covers twenty-one years, 954 through 974, and is chiefly concerned with the author's unhappy marriage. It is not known when she was born, but by 954 she had reached nubile age. Probably she married young, for she seems to have been a great beauty. The *Sompi bummyaku* of the Muromachi period (1333–1568) describes her as one of the three great beauties of the day. Very soon after the opening of the first of the three books into which the *nikki* is divided, Kaneie commences paying court, and soon they are married. As a secondary wife in a system of uncodified polygamy, her position was uncertain, and the *nikki* soon turns to her reasons for feeling betrayed and rejected. The story is one of great unhappiness. Her son brings satisfaction, her marriage only frustration and bitterness. She goes on pilgrimages and threatens to become a nun, and at the end of the third book is completely estranged from Kaneie.

The title comes from the passage with which the first book concludes. Looking back over the fifteen years covered in that book, the author finds her life as insubstantial as the *kagerō*, of which "gossamer" is a possible meaning. The first book is the shortest of the three, and each of the other two books covers only three years. The synoptic nature of the first book suggests less a diary than a set of memoirs. The other two books are more like a day-to-day journal which might properly be called a diary. It seems likely that she began writing in about 970, described the early years of her marriage in summary form, and thereafter kept something resembling a diary. The third book closes on an uncertain note, as of a preliminary draft. Like the other two books, however, it ends on New Year's Eve, and the likelihood is that not much if anything has been lost. Looking ahead to a lonely life on the outskirts of the city, the author probably thought the matter of her *nikki* at an end. It is not known when she died. By the end of the century she would have lived a long life for the time.

The *nikki* is unique among surviving works of the 10th century. In the prologue the author announces her purpose: to describe her difficulties, that her readers may know how life is for a well-born lady. It is a bold and unprecedented undertaking, and it succeeds. The reader may not feel that he has had an unprejudiced description of the case, but it is a vivid description. Although there is no specific evidence that MURASAKI SHIKIBU read the *nikki*, the closeness of

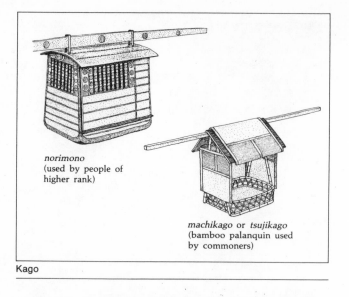

norimono
(used by people of higher rank)

machikago or *tsujikago*
(bamboo palanquin used by commoners)

Kago

court society and its appetite for literature makes the likelihood very great. More than any other surviving document of the 10th century, it could have awakened Murasaki Shikibu to the possibilities of real life as matter for fiction.

📖 ——Kakimoto Susumu, *Kagerō nikki zenchūshaku* (1966). Kawaguchi Hisao, *Kagerō nikki* in Nihon koten bungaku taikei, vol 20 (Iwanami Shoten, 1957). Kita Yoshio, *Zenkō kagerō nikki* (1961). Murakami Etsuko, *Kagerō nikki* (1963). Oka Kazuo, *Michitsuna no haha* (1943). Edward Seidensticker, tr, *The Gossamer Years* (1964). Tsugita Jun and Onishi Yoshiaki, *Kagerō nikki shinshaku* (1960).

Edward G. SEIDENSTICKER

kageyushi

(audit officers). Extrastatutory officials (RYŌGE NO KAN) appointed to supervise the rotation of official personnel, particularly provincial governors (KOKUSHI); the post was established sometime during the Enryaku era (782–806) and attached to the Ministry of Central Imperial Affairs (Nakatsukasashō). *Kageyu* referred to *kageyujō*, documents certifying that the former incumbents were not guilty of fiscal malfeasance; these were given by new appointees, after inspection, to their predecessors, who then submitted them to the central government. Friction arose over the granting of these certificates, especially in the case of provincial governors, who were often guilty of misappropriating funds or falsifying tax records. The *kageyushi* were originally established to investigate such matters, but in time their auditing duties extended to other areas as well. *Kageyushi* remained in office throughout the Heian period (794–1185) except between 806 and 824, when they were replaced by the Rokudō *kansatsushi* (investigators for the Six Circuits); but in the latter part of the period, with the rise of the provincial military aristocracy and the central government's loss of provincial control, their functions gradually became nominal.

kago

Traditional means of conveyance, especially for one person, consisting of a covered palanquin suspended from a single long pole which was carried on two men's shoulders. Originally constructed of bamboo, *kago* were later also made of wood. Only the back and front of the palanquin were covered, with the sides open or equipped with foldup screens. *Kago* came into use during the middle of the Muromachi period (1333–1568) and developed into an important mode of transportation during the Edo period (1600–1868) when there appeared several variations in form and construction materials. Types of *kago* and occasions for their use were controlled by the Tokugawa shogunate and depended on the social status of the rider. Elaborate *kago* known as *norimono* were decorated in lacquer finish and limited in use to court nobles, *daimyō*, physicians, and high-ranking priests.

INAGAKI Shisei

kago

General term for various kinds of woven baskets made of plant material such as AKEBI (*Akebia quinata*; a variety of woody vine),

Kagoshima

Downtown Kagoshima with Kagoshima Bay and Sakurajima, an active volcano, in the background.

BAMBOO, cane, or wisteria vine; it also refers to baskets made from woven leather strips or metal wire. *Kago* are roughly woven, though some show a certain intricacy of design and are comparatively large in mesh and size. This differentiates them from more finely meshed, woven containers like sieves *(zaru)*. *Kago* remains have been excavated in Japan from as long ago as the Jōmon period (ca 10,000 BC–ca 300 BC), and well-made *kago* are preserved in the 7th- and 8th-century collections of objects from all over Asia housed in the SHŌSŌIN treasure house in Nara. The varieties and uses of *kago* are numerous: as containers and winnowers in sericulture and agriculture; creels in fishing; back baskets for transporting goods; WARIGO (a traditional lunch box), TSUZURA (clothes boxes), or storage containers in the home. See also BAMBOO WARE. MIYAMOTO Mizuo

Kagome Co, Ltd

Food processor, concentrating on tomato products, juices, and sauces. Industry leader in the processing of tomatoes. Founded in 1899 when it began producing sauce from tomatoes of its own cultivation. A pioneer in its field, it eventually gained a nearly monopolistic share of the market for tomato products. In order to ensure a steady supply of produce, cultivation is conducted on a contractual basis by farmers in both Japan and Taiwan. The company has also moved into the fields of fruit drinks and instant foods. Sales for the fiscal year ending March 1982 totaled ¥68.5 billion (US $284.6 million) and capitalization was ¥2.9 billion (US $12 million). The head office is located in Nagoya.

kagome kagome

Children's game. The child who is "it" crouches in the middle with his eyes closed while the others hold hands and circle around him singing *kagome, kagome*. At the end of the song all crouch down and the one in the middle tries to guess who is directly behind him. If he guesses correctly, the one whose name he called becomes the next "it," and the game is repeated. *Kagome* probably comes from the word *kagamu* (to stoop or crouch) or from *kakomu* (to surround). SAITŌ Ryōsuke

Kagoshima

Capital of Kagoshima Prefecture, southern Kyūshū, on Kagoshima Bay. The city prospered as a castle town after a castle was constructed by the SHIMAZU FAMILY in 1602. Devastated during World War II, the city has fully recovered. Food-processing, wood crafts, and the weaving of Ōshima *tsumugi*, a silk fabric, are the major occupations. Its principal farm products are vegetables and fruits. Kagoshima is the terminus of several national highways and lines of the Japanese National Railways; it is also the point of departure for ships leaving for Okinawa and other of the Nansei Islands. A part of the KIRISHIMA–YAKU NATIONAL PARK, with SAKURAJIMA, a volcanic island (linked by lava flows to the Ōsumi Peninsula), soaring up in Kagoshima Bay, the city has been compared to Naples, of which it is a sister city. The people of the area have long been known for their Spartan virtues and spirit of independence; many

leaders of the Meiji Restoration, such as SAIGŌ TAKAMORI and ŌKUBO TOSHIMICHI, were born here. Shiroyama, a hilly section of the city, was the site of the last battle of the SATSUMA REBELLION (1877), an uprising by former *samurai* who were disgruntled with the Meiji government. Other spots of interest are the remains of Tsurumaru Castle, the garden Iso Kōen, and a museum next to the garden displaying objects associated with SHIMAZU NARIAKIRA's attempts at modernization in the 1850s. Pop: 505,077.

Kagoshima Bay

(Kagoshima Wan). Also known as Kinkō Bay. Deep bay on the southern coast of Kyūshū between the Satsuma and Ōsumi peninsulas, southern Kagoshima Prefecture. The active volcano SAKURAJIMA, linked to the Ōsumi Peninsula by lava flows, juts into the northern section of the bay. An important area for shipping, the bay is also the site of a large storage base for crude oil. Kagoshima Bay forms the center of the Kirishima–Yaku National Park. Width: 10–20 km (6.2–12.4 mi); length: approximately 70 km (43.5 mi); deepest point: approximately 200 m (656 ft).

Kagoshima Bombardment

(Satsuei Sensō). Exchange of cannon fire between a British naval squadron and the Satsuma domain (now Kagoshima Prefecture) in Kagoshima, on 15 August 1863 (Bunkyū 3.7.2). In September 1862 a British subject was killed by Satsuma *samurai* (see RICHARDSON AFFAIR); Britain responded with demands for indemnities of £100,000 from the Tokugawa shogunate and £25,000 from Satsuma in addition to the execution of the murderers. Satsuma refused to pay, and in August 1863 a squadron of seven British warships entered Kagoshima Bay to negotiate directly. After several days of fruitless talks, the British seized three Satsuma steamers anchored offshore. In the exchange of fire that followed, large parts of the city of Kagoshima were destroyed, but the British also suffered substantial losses and were forced to retreat when a typhoon struck, leaving over 60 dead and injured. Although the outcome was hailed as a Satsuma victory, Satsuma became convinced of the superiority of Western military technology, and Britain, surprised by the heavy losses, decided on a peaceful settlement. An agreement was reached in December; Satsuma promised to punish the murderers and pay the indemnity (most of which it borrowed from the shogunate).

Kagoshima Juzō (1898–1982)

Dollmaker and poet. Born in Fukuoka Prefecture. Kagoshima created the *shiso* doll, made by applying layers of paper (WASHI) to unglazed pottery. He first exhibited his work at the Imperial Academy Art Exhibition in 1936. He also made finely crafted ceramic dolls. In 1961 he was designated a LIVING NATIONAL TREASURE. Kagoshima was also active in the ARARAGI group of TANKA poets. In 1973 he was awarded the Third Order of the Sacred Treasure and published a book about his dollmaking, *Juzō tōgei ningyō*. YAMADA Tokubei

Kagoshima Prefecture

(Kagoshima Ken). Located on the southern end of Kyūshū and bordered by Kumamoto and Miyazaki prefectures to the north, the Pacific Ocean to the east and south, and the East China Sea to the west. Includes several island groups to the south. The southern portion of the prefecture is divided by Kagoshima Bay into the Satsuma and Ōsumi peninsulas. The terrain consists mostly of low hilly areas, with a few large volcanos, including KIRISHIMAYAMA, SAKURAJIMA, and KAIMONDAKE. The climate is warm with frequent precipitation. The southern islands are generally flat, with the exception of YAKUSHIMA and AMAMI ŌSHIMA; MIYANOURADAKE on Yakushima is the highest mountain in the Kyūshū region. The vegetation on these islands is subtropical. Typhoons are frequent.

Remains of both Jōmon (ca 10,000 BC–ca 300 BC) and Yayoi (ca 300 BC–ca AD 300) cultures attest to its early settlement. In early historical times the area was part of Hyūga Province and was inhabited by the KUMASO and HAYATO tribes. In the Nara period (710–794) the area was administratively divided into the provinces of Satsuma and Ōsumi. From the latter part of the Heian period (794–1185) until the Meiji Restoration (1868) it was under the control of the SHIMAZU FAMILY. Because of its location, it was among the first areas in Japan to come into contact with Europeans in the 16th century. Its geographical isolation also encouraged a spirit of in-

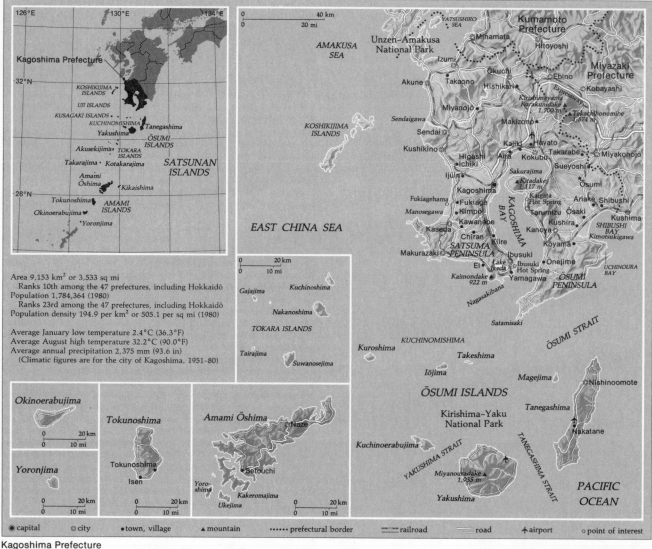

Kagoshima Prefecture

Area 9,153 km² or 3,533 sq mi
Ranks 10th among the 47 prefectures, including Hokkaidō
Population 1,784,364 (1980)
Ranks 23rd among the 47 prefectures, including Hokkaidō
Population density 194.9 per km² or 505.1 per sq mi (1980)

Average January low temperature 2.4°C (36.3°F)
Average August high temperature 32.2°C (90.0°F)
Average annual precipitation 2,375 mm (93.6 in)
(Climatic figures are for the city of Kagoshima, 1951–80)

dependence from the Tokugawa shogunate, and several Satsuma men, such as SAIGŌ TAKAMORI and ŌKUBO TOSHIMICHI, were leaders in the Meiji Restoration and the establishment of the modern Japanese state. The present prefectural boundaries were established in 1896.

Kagoshima's economy remains predominantly agricultural: the main crops are rice, sweet potatoes, and vegetables. Local specialty crops are sugar cane, citrus fruits, tea, and tobacco. Livestock farming and forestry are also important. General economic stagnation and low income levels, however, have led to a steady decline in Kagoshima's population since 1955.

Tourist attractions include KIRISHIMA–YAKU NATIONAL PARK and the subtropical vegetation and giant cryptomeria trees of Yakushima. Area: 9,153 sq km (3,533 sq mi); pop: 1,784,364; capital: Kagoshima. Other major cities include SENDAI, KANOYA, and NAZE.

kagura

A type of performance or ritual of Shintō origin that dates from early times and is still found widely in contemporary Japan. In popular usage, kagura means any performance—often one of masked dancing—that is part of the annual festival of a local Shintō shrine. To scholars of the performing arts, however, kagura is one of three primary categories in a widely accepted classification system of Japanese FOLK PERFORMING ARTS (minzoku geinō). In this context kagura is essentially the invocation of gods followed by the performance of song or dance or both, the whole event serving as prayer for the prolongation or revitalization of man's life. In

contemporary usage the emphasis of the word generally falls upon its performance aspect, and the original ritual purpose may be lost sight of.

The forms of kagura are extremely diverse. They are usually grouped into two large categories: the kagura performed at the imperial court or in major shrines closely related to it (mikagura), and what is performed outside the court (sato kagura). The latter is further subdivided into miko kagura, which involves the dances of Shintō priestesses; Ise kagura, in which boiling water is offered to the gods; Izumo kagura, in which objects are held while dancing; and shishi kagura, which involves a lion dance. This diversity is made even richer by differences due to geographical, historical, and other factors.

The Nature of Kagura——Kagura is documented from at least the early part of the 9th century, and it is assumed that even before these earliest records, the evocation of KAMI (Shintō gods) in a community setting was practiced in Japan—with or without the concomitant performance aspect. The very etymology of the word kagura underscores the close connection of performance with ritual. Although kagura is written with two Chinese characters whose meanings are "god" and "music," the word itself is Japanese and has an etymology independent of the characters. There is a measure of current agreement that it is a contraction of kamu (an older form of kami) and kura, a word that in addition to its modern sense of "storehouse" had an older one of a special or sacred place. According to this interpretation, the word kagura means the god's place or residence. This idea of the god's (temporary) place or dwelling expressed directly in Chinese characters and pronounced as a Sino-Japanese word, becomes shinza, another term often used in discussions of *kagura*. The concept lying behind *kagura*, then, is a rite to invoke the presence of a god or gods. *Kami* are present within the community during *kagura*; their invocation and later their dispatch are key moments in the temporal sequence of events.

In order to show that *kagura* is also a prayer for the prolongation of life, it is necessary to introduce yet another concept.

The Chinkon ritual. In ancient times there was a belief that the soul—which departed the body at death—could be kept from leaving or even resummoned after leaving the body by means of various rituals, including the performance of song or dance. These rituals are referred to by the general term *chinkon,* which means literally to quiet or pacify a spirit. There is a possible early reference to *chinkon* in Chinese records of the late 3rd century AD, which mention song and dance when describing Japanese customs concerning death. The account in the KOJIKI of how the sun goddess AMATERASU ŌMIKAMI was lured from her hiding place in a cave by the performance of a dance is thought by some to be a representation in myth of this belief. Dances similar to the one described in the *Kojiki* were later performed at the imperial court by women who claimed descent from the dancer of the myth, and a record of AD 807 identifies these dances as *chinkon.* According to this interpretation, *chinkon* rites, dance, or shamanistic trance had a role to play in the revitalization of the withdrawn sun goddess. As annual ceremonies and observances of the imperial court were being put together and regularized, rituals of the *chinkon* type had an important role to play.

Chinkon before it was standardized into a court ritual bears a basic resemblance to certain other Shintō rites and to *kagura*: all share the same framework or basic outline. The order of events in religious observances by Shintō lay groups (see MIYAZA), for example, is first to establish a sacred place, which is both a place of performance and a temporary residence of the *kami*; this is done by constructing a *shinza* (a place or object that is supposed to be the temporary residence of the god) in the house of a special person of the community. The next step is to transfer to the area, or to invoke there, the tutelary deity of the specific group involved in the event. Thereafter the members assemble to eat and drink together before putting on various types of performing arts. Afterwards the tutelary god is returned to his normal shrine home. There may be a second drinking event and meal, again accompanied by songs and dance. This second set may take place at a different location. The older and more basic form of *kagura* also shares elements of this pattern: establish a place for and invoke the god, celebrate formally by eating and drinking, have performance events, send off the god, and then perhaps repeat the drinking, eating, and performance section in a more relaxed setting.

Summoning and dispatching *kami* and gaining the revitalization of energy bestowed through participation in such an occasion are central characteristics of *chinkon* festivals, of *miyaza* observances, and of the older form of *kagura*. Dance and song are performed to increase the effectiveness of the event. Originally the nature of these was not rigidly prescribed. Sometimes the program was a selection of whatever music, dance, or masked performances were already popular at the period outside the *kagura* context. Certain types of masked dances, however, did develop within *kagura* itself, and these correspond to its basic nature as an occasion of a god's epiphany. Despite the freedom with which the performance repertory could be adjusted, even to accommodate popular taste, the framework itself, *kagura* in its comprehensive definition, is invariable. At a later period the performing arts section became standardized and specialized into the various forms of *kagura* enumerated in the accepted classification.

The Forms of Kagura——At an early period the term *kagura* referred to several types of performance in the imperial court or in closely related shrines. The honorific form *mikagura* is now used to distinguish this type of *kagura*. At one time performers of *mikagura* included courtiers as well as court musicians. Today it is the responsibility of the musicians of the imperial household. *Kagura* was performed on a wide range of occasions throughout the year. Today the most important is that of the Daijōe (or DAIJŌSAI), a ceremony held in the year when a new emperor is enthroned, and the annual Naishidokoro *mikagura*, named after the place in the court where it was formerly performed. The Daijōe was formerly held in the 11th and the Naishidokoro *mikagura* in the 12th lunar months. (They are now held in November and December, respectively.) The Naishidokoro *mikagura* was first performed very early in the 11th century, and by that century's end it had apparently become an annual event.

Kagura performed outside the court or its immediate sphere is called *sato kagura* or *minkan kagura* (village or provincial *kagura*). *Sato kagura* can be divided into four types: *miko kagura*, Ise *kagura*, Izumo *kagura*, and *shishi kagura*.

Miko kagura (priestess *kagura*) was originally a dance leading up to shamanic possession and the delivering of an oracle. It is the earliest of the performing arts of the *kagura* type that can be seen in the Japanese countryside today. The choreography of the dance as it can be seen today reflects circular movements and dance figures repeated in the four directions which probably characterized the dance of a female shaman at an early period. A god, invoked by the dancer in *kagura*, delivered a prophetic utterance through his medium. Dance to the accompaniment of music was a way of bringing the dancer into the state of possession that preceded the utterance. Refined and choreographed versions of this dance—what we now call either *miko kagura* or *miko mai* (priestess dance)—were early performed at the major shrines of Ise, Izumo, and Kasuga. In time the dance, which was originally a means of possession, came to be interpreted, even at many smaller shrines, as a prayer offered on behalf of the devout.

Ise *kagura*, which spread from the Grand Shrine of Ise in Mie Prefecture, though it is no longer performed there, is characterized by song and the offering of boiling water *(yudate)* as a way of invoking the gods. It is also called *yudate kagura* and *shimotsuki kagura* (*kagura* of the 11th lunar month). The rite of boiling water is but one of many events found in Ise *kagura*. Others include a type in which the performer wears a mask and, as a god, recites a blessing or engages in a traditional dialogue, perhaps with an unmasked representative of the local people to whose festival this deity has come. Dances related to SHAMANISM and YAMABUSHI rites are also common. The order of events can vary from place to place. For example, in a festival called Fuyu Matsuri (Winter Festival) at Sakambe in Nagano Prefecture, *yudate* rites offered to many different gods are performed together as a sequence one after another, whereas in the nearby HANA MATSURI group of festivals the same event, offering boiling water with prayers, is interspersed among others of quite a different origin, such as events with masked performers.

Izumo *kagura* is a performance type that spread from shrines in the Izumo area in Shimane Prefecture. Here too there is a core of continuity despite regional or individual differences: the type is characterized by unmasked dances with objects held in the hand and masked dance-dramas based upon mythological events. Both are accompanied by the music of drums, flute, and perhaps cymbals and song. So far as present evidence allows us to judge, the prototype of what scholars call Izumo *kagura* was a performance at the Sada Shrine of Izumo; the type spread throughout Japan during the Edo period (1600–1868). At Sada the principal dance is one in which new rush mats destined to become the main object of worship in each of the shrines of the large complex are held by the dancer as he dances. Dancing with the mat is a way of returning the god to the shrine in an annual ritual of renewal. The second element, masked dances, is a way of holding the attention of audiences and adding greater interest to the festival than the unmasked dances, with held objects alone, could command.

In *shishi kagura* (lion *kagura*) the central religious practice is the use of the lion-head mask. The most representative types of lion *kagura* are *yamabushi kagura* and *bangaku* of the Tōhoku and Ise *daikagura* groups (the latter not to be confused with the Ise *kagura* discussed above). In these the lion-head mask is considered the true presence of the god. In the Ise and Izumo *kagura* types, *kami* are temporarily manifested during the performance; in lion *kagura*, the god is present in the mask and the performers carry him about with them. The mask was once carried from place to place as troupes stopped at farmhouses to perform rites such as rites for fire prevention. In lion *kagura*, too, an extensive repertory of masked dances and dramas developed, which in time became the main attraction of a program.

——Bunkachō, ed, *Minzoku geinō: Kagura* (1970). Geinōshi Kenkyūkai, ed, *Kagura, Bugaku,* vol 1 of *Nihon shomin bunka shiryō shūsei* (1974). Frank Hoff, "Shinto and the Performing Arts," in Frank Hoff, *Song, Dance, Storytelling: Aspects of the Performing Arts in Japan* (1978). Honda Yasuji, *Kagura,* vol 1 of *Nihon no minzoku geinō* (1966). Honda Yasuji, "Yamabushi *kagura* and *bangaku*: Performance in the Japanese Middle Ages and Contemporary Folk Performance," *Education Theatre Journal* (1974). *Minzoku geinō kenkyū bunken mokuroku,* in *Engekigaku* (March 1976), contains extensive bibliography. Gerhild Müller [Endress], *Kagura: die*

Lieder der Kagura-Zeremonie am Naishidokoro (1971), bibliography included. Yamaji Kōzō, *Kagura,* vol 1 of *Nihon no koten geinō* (1969).

Frank HOFF

kagura uta

The songs *(uta)* of Shintō ritual dance (see KAGURA). More specifically a fixed body of ancient court songs in the musical style of GAGAKU to be sung at special concerts with a primarily vocal program. Most of these songs were originally the property of Shintō ceremony. Gradually, however, *kagura uta* came to be presented at ceremonial court banquets of informal character, and in the 9th century they were incorporated in the DAIJŌSAI accession ceremony. *Kagura* songs performed at this ceremony are recorded in the imperial poetic anthologies KOKINSHŪ (early 10th century) and SHŪI WAKASHŪ (early 11th century). During the 11th century the *kagura* concert evolved into an independent institution and became an annual event in the form of an all-night session held in December outside the palace sanctuary of the Holy Mirror (Naishidokoro). By this time a fixed repertory, which was subsequently used for all *kagura* ceremonies, had been established. Later additions were minimal. Of the pieces not included in this standard collection only a few have survived to the present day.

Modern performances generally consist of short selections from the standard repertory, which includes about 88 pieces. All extant repertory manuscripts arrange these according to the same program schedule: (1) *niwabi*—the introductory fire song; (2) *torimono*—songs on the various requisites of religious dancing such as a branch of the holy SAKAKI tree; (3) *karakami*—interlude with songs on the god of that name; (4) *saibara*—pieces in the style of folk songs; and (5) the finale consisting of miscellaneous selections, including morning songs.

All *kagura* songs consist of two parts: *moto* (the rise) and *sue* (the close), to be sung by two groups sitting opposite each other. In the *torimono* category, *moto* and *sue* are textually independent verses set in TANKA (31-syllable Japanese classical verse; see also WAKA) format. In other categories, the two choral groups either share in the recitation of one *tanka* or exchange modified *tanka* and other verse forms antiphonally. Accompanying instruments are the *wagon,* or six-string zither; the *kagurabue,* a six-hole horizontal flute; the HICHIRIKI, a kind of oboe; and the *shakubyōshi,* or wooden clappers, which are played by two singers themselves. In modern *kagura* the mode is *ichikotsuchō* (*ryo* scale on D). There are distinct differences among the various categories of song (*torimono, saibara,* etc) in meter, style of singing, and instrumental arrangement. See also EARLY JAPANESE SONG; MUSIC, TRADITIONAL.

——Gerhild Müller [Endress], *Kagura: Die Lieder der Kagura-Zeremonie am Naishidokoro* (1971). Nishitsunoi Masayoshi, *Kagura uta kenkyū* (1941).

Gerhild ENDRESS

Kahokugata

Lagoon in the northwestern part of the city of Kanazawa, Ishikawa Prefecture, central Honshū. As a result of a land reclamation project initiated in 1964 and completed in 1970, two-thirds of the lagoon has been converted into land that is now used for rice cultivation. It is known for its white swans. Area of original lake: 23 sq km (9 sq mi); circumference: 25 km (16 mi).

kai-awase

A shell-matching game popular among the aristocrats of the Heian period (794–1185). Different kinds of clamshell were used. One half shell of each clam was placed outside-up, and the players competed in selecting the matching halves from a separate pile. Later, each half shell was painted or inscribed with lines of WAKA poetry, and players had to choose matching shells to complete a picture or poem. With the decline of court power in the late Heian period, the game lost its popularity, but it was the ancestor of such pastimes as *utagai* and *utagaruta,* which became popular in the Edo period (1600–1868). See PLAYING CARDS.

Saitō Ryōsuke

Kaibara Ekiken (1630–1714)

Confucian scholar of the Edo period (1600–1868). Kaibara was born into the family of a retainer of the Fukuoka domain (now part of Fukuoka Prefecture). He entered the service of the domainal lord Kuroda Tadayuki but in 1649 came into disfavor with Tadayuki and

was deprived of his stipend and forced to become a RŌNIN. During this period he traveled to Nagasaki to study medicine and botany. In 1656 his stipend was restored by the new *daimyō* Kuroda Mitsuyuki. Under orders from Mitsuyuki, Kaibara studied for 10 years in Kyōto, where he met the Confucianist KINOSHITA JUN'AN and Mukai Genshō (1609–77), a scholar of *honzōgaku,* the study of medicinal herbs. He spent the rest of his life in the service of the Fukuoka domain.

From his interest in Confucianism (in his later years he was to deviate from the then dominant Zhu Xi [Chu Hsi] school [SHUSHIGAKU] and claim that *li* [J:*ri*] and *qi* [*chi;* J:*ki*] were inseparable) and natural science Kaibara expounded a philosophy that emphasized experience and practical knowledge. The scope of his scholarship, which went beyond Confucianism to encompass medicine, folk studies, history, geography, and education is reflected in his various works. In 1708 he wrote *Yamato honzō* in which he recorded, classified, and examined 1,300 kinds of medicinal herb from China and Japan. He followed this with *Wazoku dōjikun,* a five-volume work dealing with concrete methods of child education. In 1713 he wrote YŌJŌKUN, a work on health improvement that drew from Japanese and Chinese sources. ONNA DAIGAKU, a widely read manual for the moral training of women, has been mistakenly attributed to Kaibara.

Katagiri Kazuo

kaidō

(main highways). Term for trunk highways developed before the modern period. Their number, location, rank, and importance varied from period to period. In the Nara (710–794) and Heian (794–1185) periods, there were seven government-administered highways linking the Nara and Kyōto area with the outlying provinces. A network of post stations (see EKISEI; SHUKUEKI) was established to provide for the needs of travelers. The San'yōdō, connecting the capital region with the western provinces, was the most important. During the Kamakura period (1185–1333), the San'yōdō was superseded in importance by the Tōkaidō, the eastern seaboard route linking Kyōto and Kamakura, the headquarters of the Kamakura shogunate. By this time much of the traffic west of Kyōto had shifted to the water route along the Inland Sea. In the Edo period (1600–1868) the TOKUGAWA SHOGUNATE maintained five main highways (GOKAIDŌ) under its direct control to link the provinces with the shogunal capital at Edo (now Tōkyō). Included were the Tōkaidō and four newly established routes. POST-STATION TOWNS were designated to supply food, lodging, and horses. These highways became the scene of much transport and travel, most notably by *daimyō,* who were obliged to make periodic journeys to Edo (see SANKIN KŌTAI). In recent years modern highways have been built on or near the courses of the old *kaidō.* The original names are still popularly used to identify the routes.

Kaidōki

Travel diary of the Kamakura period (1185–1333). Author unknown. Record of a journey from Kyōto to Kamakura, probably taken in April 1223 along the highway TŌKAIDŌ. Self-reflective in tone, the work includes elegant passages capturing the pathos of such historical events as the JŌKYŪ DISTURBANCE of 1221 as well as philosophical ruminations on various tenets of Amida Buddhism. Not only is it considered, along with the TŌKAN KIKŌ, a major work of travel literature for the beauty of its *wakan konkō* prose style—classical Japanese with a heavy admixture of words and phrases from classical Chinese literature—but it is also an important source of historical information on Kamakura Buddhism and government.

kaieki

Term for *samurai* declassment during the Edo period (1600–1868). Originally *kaieki* referred to the transfer or dismissal from office of a *shōen* (estate) administrator (SHOKAN). Later, during the Kamakura (1185–1333) and Muromachi (1333–1568) periods, it referred to dismissal of JITŌ (military land stewards) and other samurai officials and gradually to deprivation of samurai status itself. The Tokugawa shogunate used the term *kaieki* specifically to mean deprivation of rank and samurai or *kuge* (court noble) status. Loss of status usually entailed diminution or confiscation of one's fief, and the shogunate used *kaieki* as a major instrument of political control. *Kaieki* was imposed for violation of regulations such as the BUKE SHOHATTO, for failure to assure stable succession in one's house (see OIE SŌDŌ), and for other political or military reasons. It was enforced most widely between 1600 and 1652, when 197 *daimyō* houses were declassed and lands assessed at 16,000,000 *koku* (see KOKUDAKA) were redistributed by the first three Tokugawa shōguns in order to eliminate incompetent, uncooperative, and overly powerful lords and to consolidate their own hegemony. Many lesser samurai were similarly declassed, by action of both the shogunate and the daimyō, whose house codes also incorporated *kaieki* clauses.

Conrad TOTMAN

Kaientai

(Naval Auxiliary Force). Name of trading and shipping company organized by SAKAMOTO RYŌMA, a *samurai* from the Tosa domain (now Kōchi Prefecture) who was active in the movement to overthrow the Tokugawa shogunate in the final years of the Edo period (1600–1868). In 1864, with help from the Satsuma domain (now Kagoshima Prefecture), a stronghold of the antishogunate movement, Sakamoto and 20 other samurai who had abandoned their domains gathered in Nagasaki and formed a small organization known simply as the Shachū (Company). With a small fleet of ships at its command, it bought goods, in particular arms, from Western traders in Nagasaki for Satsuma and Chōshū (now Yamaguchi Prefecture), another domain active in the antishogunate movement. In 1866 Sakamoto succeeded in bringing together the two rival domains in the so-called SATSUMA-CHŌSHŪ ALLIANCE.

The following year Sakamoto reestablished ties with his native domain, and his organization, renamed the Kaientai, received Tosa's official support. It was disbanded in 1868, soon after Sakamoto's assassination in Kyōto by shogunate henchmen.

Kaifūsō

The oldest Japanese anthology of *kanshi*, poems written in Chinese by Japanese poets (see POETRY AND PROSE IN CHINESE). According to the preface, it was compiled in 751, some years before completion of the *Man'yōshū* (759), the oldest extant anthology of Japanese poetry, or WAKA. There are a number of hypotheses concerning authorship of the *Kaifūsō*. It has been variously ascribed to ŌMI NO MIFUNE, Fujii no Hironari (fl ca mid-8th century), and ISONOKAMI NO YAKATSUGU, but in fact the author is unknown. The *Kaifūsō* contains 120 poems by 64 poets, covering almost 100 years from the reign of Emperor Tenji (r 661–672) until the reign of Empress Kōken (r 749–758). The poems are arranged in chronological order. There are poems by imperial princes, including Prince Ōtomo (see Emperor KŌBUN), Prince Kawashima (657–691), and Prince Ōtsu (663–686); nobles, including FUJIWARA NO FUHITO, Fujii no Hironari, and Isonokami no Otomaro (d 750); and a number of Buddhist monks. Nine of them (four princes, four monks, and one noble) are introduced by short biographies; the others are represented only by their poems, in most cases by one or two. The largest number of poems by a single author is six for Fujiwara no Umakai (694?–737). Twenty authors of the *Kaifūsō* are known also as poets of the *Man'yōshū*.

The poems of the *Kaifūsō* are traditionally Chinese in wording, phrasing, and metrical pattern. Most of them are composed in five-word verses forming eight-line stanzas. The anthology includes only seven stanzas of seven-word verses. The number of stanzas with five- and seven-word verses corresponds exactly with the *Wen xuan* (*Wen hsüan*; J: *Monzen*), the great Chinese anthology of the Six Dynasties period (220–589) that seems to have served as a model for the *Kaifūsō*. The poems of the *Kaifūsō* were composed for the most part on the occasion of court festivities; they are rich in stereotypes, only a small portion of them reflecting deeper feelings of the poet (e.g., the poem of Isonokami no Otomaro in exile).

The *Kaifūsō* attests to the great influence of Chinese literature and thought in early Japanese court life: the poems in this anthology could not have been composed without knowledge of the Chinese Confucian classics, Taoist philosophers, and poetical works. The *Kaifūsō* had some successors in Japanese court poetry, the earliest of them coming out together at the beginning of the 9th century: *Ryōunshū* (814; see SAGA, EMPEROR), BUNKA SHŪREISHŪ (818), and KEIKOKUSHŪ (827).

■——Kojima Noriyuki, ed, *Kaifūsō*, in *Nihon koten bungaku taikei*, vol 69 (Iwanami Shoten, 1964). Bruno H. Lewin, "Isonokami no Otomaro und seine chinesische Dichtung im Kaifūsō," in *China, Kultur, Politik und Wirtschaft: Festschrift A. Hoffmann* (1976). Okada Masayuki, *Nihon kambungaku shi* (rev ed 1954). Ōno Tamotsu, *Kaifūsō no kenkyū* (1957). *Bruno H.* LEWIN

Kaigai Tokō Kinshi Rei

(Prohibitions of Foreign Voyages). Major steps in the formation of the Tokugawa shogunate's NATIONAL SECLUSION (Sakoku) policy in the 1630s. These were not discrete regulations but were included in administrative directives dealing comprehensively with the control of foreign trade and of Christianity, sent by the shogunate's senior councillors (*rōjū*) in Edo (now Tōkyō) to its commissioners (*bugyō*) in the port city of Nagasaki. One of these directives, dated 1633, prohibited Japanese travel to foreign lands except on trading vessels endorsed by the *rōjū* (see HŌSHOSEN); Japanese residing overseas, except for those cast abroad by mischance who returned within five years, were forbidden on pain of death to reenter the country. Another directive, dated 1635, eliminated even those exceptions. Once having issued this Draconian directive, however, the Tokugawa regime in actuality countenanced the repatriation of castaways. Moreover, two overseas destinations remained legally open to certain rigidly circumscribed groups of Japanese in spite of the general prohibition of foreign travel. They were Ryūkyū, which after 1609 was not a sovereign foreign country but a dependency of the *daimyō* of Kagoshima, and Pusan in Korea, where the daimyō of Tsushima maintained a trading factory ("Japan House"; Kor: Waegwan; J: Wakan) from 1611 throughout the Edo period (1600–1868).

George ELISON

Kaigetsudō school

School of UKIYO-E painters and print artists in Edo (now Tōkyō) during the first half of the 18th century, specializing in large-scale paintings and prints of courtesans. Kaigetsudō Ando (also known as Kaigetsudō Yasunori) was the founder of the school, followed by his pupils Anchi (Yasutomo), Dohan (Norishige), Doshin (Noritatsu), Doshu (Noritane), and Doshū (Norihide), all using the Kaigetsudō name and flourishing during the 1710s.

Kaigetsudō Ando, the first master of the Kaigetsudō school, was an *ukiyo-e* painter in Asakusa, Edo. Nothing is known of Ando's actual training but certain influences are clearly evident in his work: most notably the influence of Hishikawa MORONOBU and his pupils, and SUGIMURA JIHEI. The works of the Kyōto illustrators Yoshida Hambei (fl ca 1664–89) and Ōmori Yoshikiyo (fl ca 1702–16) should also be compared with the early Kaigetsudō paintings. In addition the Kambun *bijin*, or genre paintings of courtesans in the mid-17th century, might well be considered the direct inspiration for Ando's majestic female figures (see KAMBUN MASTER).

Kaigetsudō Ando seems to have been active from some time shortly after 1700 until the year 1714, when he became enmeshed (probably as a go-between) in the EJIMA INCIDENT, a scandal involving the principal lady-in-waiting to the mother of the shōgun Tokugawa Ietsugu and a handsome *kabuki* actor—for which all the principals were banished forthwith from Edo. As might be expected in the work of the founding genius of a school, Ando's paintings reveal an originality, strength, and freshness that is seldom mirrored with perfection in the work of even his finest pupils.

Although their genre paintings were unsurpassed in their day, the Kaigetsudō masters are known today primarily for their work as print designers. However, only 23 designs, all from the 1710s, are extant, some in unique examples; they are sought by collectors the world over. No prints are known by the founder of the school, Ando; what remains is entirely the work of his pupils Anchi, Doshin, and Dohan. The occasional prints of the Kaigetsudō school have come to symbolize the spirit of *ukiyo-e* and of their period.

■——Richard Lane, *Kaigetsudō* (1959). Richard Lane, *Images from the Floating World* (1978). *Richard* LANE

Kaigo Tokiomi (1901–)

Educator. Born in Ibaraki Prefecture; graduate of Tōkyō University, where he later became professor of education. A leading theoretician who played a major role in postwar educational reforms, he served as chairman of the Japanese Society for the Study of Education from 1959 to 1973, contributing greatly to its growth. Kaigo's scholarly works center upon Japanese education during the Meiji period (1868–1912). His best-known works include a history of education in Japan, *Nihon kyōiku shōshi* (1940), and a study of the drafting of the IMPERIAL RESCRIPT ON EDUCATION, *Kyōiku chokugo seiritsushi no kenkyū* (1965). *Takakuwa* YASUO

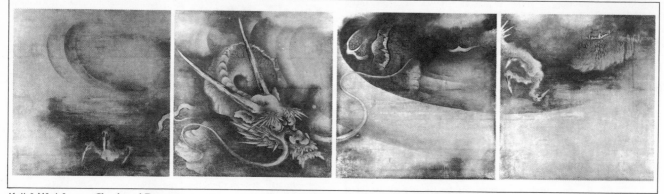

Kaihō Yūshō———Clouds and Dragons

One of a pair of dragons. Originally sliding-door panels in the abbot's quarters at Kenninji, Kyōto. Ink on paper. Height 198 cm. Ca 1600.

Kaigun Denshūjo

Training center for the study of navigation and other maritime technology, established in Nagasaki in 1855; the first naval-officer training school in Japan. In 1853 the Tokugawa shogunate lifted its longtime prohibition against building large oceangoing vessels and instituted plans for a modern Western-style navy. Holland, the only Western nation in contact with the secluded island nation, donated the steamship *Kankō maru* and sent 22 Dutch officers and crewmen to teach at the new school. There were about 200 students, from both the shogunate and the various *daimyō* domains. KATSU KAISHŪ, ENOMOTO TAKEAKI, GODAI TOMOATSU, and SANO TSUNETAMI were among the many prominent graduates of the school. In 1859 the school was absorbed into the naval training facility at Tsukiji in Edo (now Tōkyō).

Kaigun Heigakkō → Naval Academy

Kaigunshō → Navy Ministry

Kaihaku Goshi Shinrei → Shōtoku Nagasaki Shinrei

Kaihō school

(Kaihōha). A family of painters, started by KAIHŌ YŪSHŌ, that continued for seven generations until the end of the Edo period (1600–1868). Yūshō developed a highly individualistic style that set him apart from contemporary painters, but from Yūsetsu (1598–1677), the second generation, on, the family style is hardly distinguishable from that of the dominant KANŌ SCHOOL. Besides the many masterpieces left by Yūshō, who was by far the best in the line, Yūsetsu left some paintings worthy of note, such as the *Clouds and Dragons* set on sliding doors at Rinshōin, a subtemple of Myōshinji in Kyōto. Following Yūsetsu, successive generations were represented by Yūchiku (1654–1728); Yūsen, who died in his fifties in the Gembun era (1736–41); Yūzō, who received the court title of *hokkyō* in 1766; Yūtoku (fl 1818–30); and Yūshō (1817–68). Few paintings by the generations after Yūsetsu are extant.

Robert T. SINGER

Kaiho Seiryō (1755–1817)

Political economist of the Edo period (1600–1868) of *samurai* background, he spent most of his life pursuing studies of the growing commercial economy. Kaiho was born in Edo (now Tōkyō), the son of a high-ranking retainer of the Miyazu domain (now part of Kyōto Prefecture). He studied with the Confucian scholar Usami Shinsui (1710–76), a disciple of OGYŪ SORAI, but he refused to restrict himself to one school of thought, preferring to develop his own ideas. Kaiho was a pragmatist, and in contrast to others of his class who eschewed commercial activity, he held that samurai should take advantage of the money economy to enrich their domains. A thoroughgoing mercantilist, he even saw the lord-vassal relationship as ultimately a commercial contract. As practical measures, he advocated the establishment of domainal monopolies (HAN'EI SEMBAI)

and of cottage industries in samurai households. At the same time he proposed a more realistic system of rewards and punishments to bolster the authority of domainal governments. After briefly serving the domains of Owari (now Aichi Prefecture) and Miyazu, Kaiho traveled around the Kantō region and the western provinces, and in his later years settled in Kyōto, where he founded his own academy.

KATAGIRI Kazuo

Kaihō Yūshō (1533–1615)

One of the masters of Azuchi-Momoyama period (1568–1600) painting; a versatile, independent artist and the founder of the KAIHŌ SCHOOL. Yūshō was either the third or fifth son of Kaihō Zen'emon Tsunachika, a military commander who served ASAI NAGAMASA of Ōmi Province (now Shiga Prefecture). He was sent as a child novice to Tōfukuji, a major Zen temple in Kyōto, and thus was spared when in 1573 the rest of his family was destroyed by ODA NOBUNAGA's campaign against the Asai clan. Yūshō was at that time already 41, and it was then that he is said to have left the temple to become a layman and later a professional painter, even though an artist's social rank was then far inferior to that of a *samurai*.

He is variously described as having studied under KANŌ MOTONOBU or KANŌ EITOKU. Although none of Yūshō's extant paintings can be positively dated earlier than his mid sixties, his "early" work shows strong Kanō influence. It appears that he was connected with TOYOTOMI HIDEYOSHI in midcareer, and later with the imperial family (Prince Katsura in particular). Yūshō's name appears often in imperial diaries, and several of his works have come down to us in imperial collections. That Yūshō's circle was wide is attested to by the inscriptions on his paintings written by Zen priests from most of the major Kyōto Zen temples, feudal lords, imperial family members, and other artists.

Yūshō worked in both ink on paper and ink and color on a gold ground, although ink paintings form the greater part of his extant work. His output includes examples from the two main currents in Momoyama-period painting: the one deriving from Chinese INK PAINTING and the other from highly colored native Japanese YAMATO-E decorative painting. Yūshō borrowed elements from both traditions and put them together in new and unexpected ways. A notable example is his introduction of decorative elements like gold clouds, intricate fabric designs, and bright mineral pigments into the otherwise ink-brushwork-dominated Chinese subject matter of the *Four Pleasures*, a pair of folding screens at Myōshinji.

Most of Yūshō's works were large-scale paintings on sliding doors or folding screens; many of the smaller paintings, now mounted as hanging scrolls, were originally painted as single panels for folding screens. A major part of Yūshō's extant work consists of a large series of sliding-door paintings executed for KENNINJI in Kyōto. Five rooms of the abbot's quarters contain *Landscape*, *Four Pleasures*, *Seven Sages in a Bamboo Grove*, *Birds and Flowers*, and *Clouds and Dragons*; all are in monochrome ink except for some color in the *Four Pleasures* sequence. The *Seven Sages in a Bamboo Grove* sequence is notable for the way Yūshō enlarged the size of the figures and thereby minimized the landscape setting. The figures are drawn in a broad, rounded line, derived from Yūshō's study of the Chinese Southern Song (Sung; 1127–1279) painter Liang Kai (Liang K'ai). Another Yūshō characteristic that sets him apart from the

Kanō school is his use of wet washes without contour lines for landscape elements, as seen in the *Landscape* set.

Yūshō's more colorful side is best represented by the three pairs of folding screens, two of figures and one of flowers, in the Myōshinji, and by two pairs of screens, *Pines on a Beach (Hamamatsuzu)* and *Drying Fishnets (Aboshizu),* in the Imperial Household Collection, Tōkyō National Museum.

📖——Kawai Masatomo, *Yūshō/Tōgan,* vol 11 of *Nihon bijutsu kaiga zenshū* (Shūeisha, 1978). Takeda Tsuneo, *Tōhaku/Yūshō,* vol 9 of *Suiboku bijutsu taikei* (Kōdansha, 1977). Takeda Tsuneo and Kawai Masatomo, *Kenninji,* in *Shōhekiga zenshū,* 10 vols (Bijutsu Shuppansha, 1968). Robert T. SINGER

Kaikaha → Kaehwap'a

Kaikei (fl late 12th–early 13th century)

Sculptor of Buddhist images in the Kamakura period (1185–1333). A member of the KEI SCHOOL, he was the disciple of KŌKEI, and along with Kōkei's son UNKEI, was considered one of the outstanding sculptors of his time. Kaikei was commissioned by his religious mentor, the monk Chōgen (1121–1206), to create works for the reconstruction of the temple TŌDAIJI in Nara. Among his extant works are the statue of Sōgyō Hachiman and the statue of AMIDA, both housed in Tōdaiji, and the image of MIROKU in the Boston Museum of Fine Arts. His style, known as the An'ami style, while realistic, is more graceful and elegant than that of other members of his school. See also BUDDHIST SCULPTURE.

Kaikei Kansa In → Board of Audit

Kaikō Ken (1930-   )

Novelist, essayist, journalist. Also known as Kaikō Takeshi; most English translations of his works have appeared under the latter name. A member of the generation of young Japanese writers known as the "pure postwar group" *(junsui sengo ha),* who came on the literary scene in the late 1950s and early 1960s, Kaikō has achieved success as both a writer of fiction and a journalist. Kaikō's work runs closely parallel to the mainstream of international fiction at midcentury, as revealed by his deep concern for social urgencies and his frequent use of reportage techniques. His fiction is multifaceted, but one of its main themes is the self versus the crowd or organization—that faceless, mindless amalgam which robs a person of his individuality. Although he was a highly regarded literary talent in the 1960s, Kaikō's interest in fiction abruptly declined in the 1970s. Since then he has produced a stream of uneven journalism and nonfiction, the best of which is a considerable body of documentary material on the Vietnam War that he gathered as a special correspondent.

The son of an elementary schoolteacher, Kaikō was born in 1930 in the city of Ōsaka. Here he grew up, attending local schools, losing his father at an early age, and reaching adolescence at the close of World War II amid the bombing raids that devastated the city. For Kaikō, the years after the war were ones of great hardship. With his father dead, poverty compelled him to support the family. In 1948 he was admitted to Ōsaka City University, where he enrolled in the law department. He was habitually absent from class because he had to take on odd jobs to earn a living. While in school Kaikō read avidly the works of KAJII MOTOJIRŌ, KANEKO MITSU-HARU, and NAKAJIMA ATSUSHI; he also began translating (Louis Aragon and Sherwood Anderson) and writing fiction, which he published in several local little magazines. During this time he met and married the poet Maki Yōko (real name Kotani Shōko; b 1923). Kaikō graduated from college in 1953 and moved to Tōkyō. In 1954 he joined the advertising department of Suntory, Ltd, the whiskey distiller, as a copywriter, an experience which markedly influenced his personal writing style. He established a reputation in the advertising world but resigned from Suntory in 1957 to devote his energies to his own writing.

Meanwhile, his literary career had begun in 1953 when, with the help of Sasaki Kiichi (b 1914), he published "Na no nai machi" (Nameless City) and a handful of other short stories in KINDAI BUN-GAKU. He first attracted critical attention with the publication in SHIN NIHON BUNGAKU of the short story "Panikku" (1957; tr "Panic," 1977), about a dedicated public servant employed in the

forestry section of a prefectural administration who encounters higher-level bureaucratic bungling, corruption, and intractability during his attempt to rid a small town of an infestation of rats. Kaikō's real literary recognition came with "Hadaka no ōsama" (1957; tr "The Naked King," 1977), a story about the pressures brought on young schoolchildren by the Japanese educational system, which won the highly prestigious Akutagawa Prize.

With his reputation thus established, Kaikō turned out a series of stories and novels that were praised for their powerful descriptive language and bold probing of contemporary life. The theme of Kaikō's early works was basically existentialist: people are impeded from being themselves by subjective and objective circumstances. He was greatly concerned with the establishment's denigration of the individual, and his earlier fiction shows a distaste for authority and bureaucracy. His first novel, *Nihon sammon opera* (1959, A Japanese Threepenny Opera), deals in tragicomic fashion with a group of vagrants in Ōsaka immediately after World War II who barely eke out a living by selling scrap metal. *Robinson no matsuei* (1960, Robinson's Descendants) is a fictional account of a company of settlers sent to Hokkaidō from ravaged urban districts to take up farming in the waning months of the war. Kaikō's best novel, *Kagayakeru yami* (1968; tr *Into a Black Sun,* 1980), is a full-blooded, hard-hitting, and intensely moving evocation of Vietnam in the mid-1960s as told by a Japanese journalist experiencing firsthand the atrocities of war. Cast in haunting language that goes beyond mere reporting, it is set against the Vietnam conflict before heavy American involvement. The best of all Kaikō's prose, it won the Mainichi Book Award. A less successful but seriously intentioned autobiographical novel, *Aoi getsuyōbi* (1969, Blue Monday) delineates the consequences of urban alienation with subtle compassion and imaginative power. A more recent novel, *Natsu no yami* (1971; tr *Darkness in Summer,* 1973), which has been highly acclaimed by Japanese critics and by Western critics in its English translation, recounts the love affair between an expatriate Japanese woman living in Europe and a reporter. It is perhaps the most beautifully written of all his books but lacks the power of *Kagayakeru yami.*

Apart from his collected essays on the Vietnam War and Japan's pressing social problems in the journalistic and nonfiction vein, Kaikō has written a series of books on fishing, of which he is a passionate exponent, in the form of travelogues. His works have been translated into English and a number of Slavic languages. The collected works fill 12 volumes, and he is regarded as one of the leading writers of postwar Japan.

📖——Kaikō Ken, *Kaikō Ken zenshū,* 12 vols (Shinchōsha, 1973–74). Kaikō Takeshi, *Kagayakeru yami* (1968), tr Cecilia Segawa Seigle as *Into a Black Sun* (1980). Kaikō Takeshi, *Natsu no yami* (1972), tr Cecilia Segawa Seigle as *Darkness in Summer* (1973). Kaikō Takeshi, *Panikku* (1957) and *Ryūbōki* (1959), tr Charles Dumas in *Panic, and the Runaway* (1977). Dennis M. SPACKMAN

Kaikoku → Opening of Japan

Kaimondake

Also called Satsuma Fuji. Conical volcano in eastern Satsuma Peninsula, Kagoshima Prefecture, Kyūshū. Jutting out of the sea, it forms a double volcano with a lava dome on the top. Part of Kirishima-Yaku National Park. A subtropical botanical garden is located in its foothills. Height: 922 m (3,024 ft).

Kainan

City in northwestern Wakayama Prefecture, central Honshū, of the Kii Channel. Once a center of traditional crafts including Kuroe lacquer ware, Japanese umbrellas, and palm fiber goods, Kainan is today an industrial city with oil-refining, chemical, and textile plants on reclaimed land along the coast. Pop: 52,529.

Kainō Michitaka (1908–1975)

Legal scholar; lawyer. Prominent leader of the movement to modernize the Japanese court system after World War II. Born in Nagano Prefecture, he studied at Tōkyō University. After graduating in 1930, he stayed on as research assistant in the law department, immersing himself in specialized studies of civil and sociological jurisprudence. His early research culminated in two ambitious books: *Iriai no kenkyū* (1943, A Study of the Right of Commonage), an elaborate historical treatment of the issues involved in claims to the right of use of undivided open land (iriaiken), which won the first Mainichi Book Award, and Hōritsu shakaigaku no shomondai (1943, Various Problems in Sociological Jurisprudence).

Kainō taught at Chūō University for a brief period, and was a professor at Waseda (1949–54) and Tōykō Metropolitan (1954–64) universities. After World War II he served as legal counselor for the International Military Tribunal for the Far East during the Tōkyō WAR CRIMES TRIALS, where he became acquainted with modern Anglo-American litigation procedure. On the basis of this experience he roundly criticized traditional litigation methods and juridical procedure, making a significant contribution to the modernization and democratization of the Japanese court system.

Kainō believed that the people possess certain fundamental constitutional and civil rights. This belief inspired a spate of articles and books on the protection of people's rights, including Shimin no jiyū (1951, People's Freedoms) and Jiyū to kyōfu (1952, Freedom and Fear). In 1964 he gave up his academic post so that he could act as attorney for the side of the farmers in the much publicized Kotsunagi Incident in Iwate Prefecture, a dispute over commonage rights to open lands in a small village, which had dragged on between farmers and landowners for some three generations. Late in life, Kainō became deeply involved in the study of pollution-related legal issues. He was a respected teacher and prolific scholar, and his constant emphasis on people's rights had considerable effect on the study and teaching of legal science.

Kaionji Chōgorō (1901–1977)

Novelist. Real name Suetomi Tōsaku. Born in Kagoshima Prefecture. Graduate of Kokugakuin University. He began to write while teaching Japanese at a high school. A man with a broad knowledge of Japanese history, he wrote grand-scale, lyric historical novels, often about warriors, as in Taira no Masakado (1954–57) and Ten to chi to (1960–62), both of which became popular television series. His earlier novel Tenshō onna gassen (1936) won the Naoki Prize.

Kairakuen

Municipal park in Mito, Ibaraki Prefecture. With KENROKUEN and KŌRAKUEN one of the three most celebrated landscape gardens in Japan. It was built by TOKUGAWA NARIAKI as a private retreat and was completed in 1842. The park is known for its ume (Japanese plum) blossoms, which attract visitors from late February to March. Area: 7.5 hectares (18.5 acres).

Kaisakuhō

(Laws of Cultivation). Administrative reforms enacted largely between 1651 and 1656 in the Kaga domain (now Ishikawa and Toyama prefectures). The Kaisakuhō strengthened and consolidated the control of the MAEDA FAMILY over the domain and established a framework of local government and agricultural administration that, except for a few years early in the 19th century, remained fundamentally unaltered until the abolition of the domainal system in 1871. While the Kaisakuhō is representative of the tendency toward centralized daimyō control evident throughout Japan, the Maeda family's implementation of a fixed land-tax rate, not adjusted to fluctuations in crop yields (see JŌMEN), was highly innovative. The new local government and tax administration also placed an unusual degree of responsibility on peasant, rather than samurai, officials. Although there were isolated instances of peasant opposition, the reforms were on the whole effective and were copied by several other domains.

The Kaisakuhō were promulgated by Maeda Toshitsune (1593–1658), regent for his young grandson, MAEDA TSUNANORI. Toshitsune's reforms were motivated by concern over economic problems in his domain. His retainers were not deriving a steady income from their landholdings. His peasants had suffered from some retainers' demands for higher taxes and, more recently, from major crop failures in 1641 and 1642. Furthermore, Toshitsune wished to increase the domain's revenues and control over landholding retainers.

From 1651 to 1656, the domainal authorities reevaluated the putative yield (KOKUDAKA) of each village and made an intensive effort to incorporate all recently reclaimed land into their tax registers.

Based on sample cuttings (bugari or tsubogari) and extensive discussions with peasant officials, a uniform tax rate (heikimmen) for each village was established. Earlier, even on land of the same quality within a given village, the tax rate had varied depending on the authority and judgment of the retainer or domainal tax collector (daikan) in assessing the tax annually (kemihō). The new fixed tax rate generally constituted a tax increase and could be reduced only in cases of severe crop failure. Various tax-rice transport fees and labor dues were also standardized, and miscellaneous taxes on fishing rights, sake brewers, and the like, were reassessed.

Concomitantly, in 1654 the domain prohibited direct administration by a retainer of his landholdings. All land taxes and other dues were now set and collected for the retainers by the domainal administration. The domain also took jurisdiction over civil and criminal proceedings in the areas held by the retainers. In return for this loss of control, the retainers were guaranteed a stable income.

A measure of relief was also provided for the peasants. They were excused from the debts incurred during earlier crop failures or exempted from interest payments. In order to reduce usury, the domain arranged to lend peasants money or rice at the relatively low interest rate of 20 percent a year. The domain also invested large sums in irrigation and riparian works to increase agricultural productivity. To ensure that the land tax burden would be distributed equitably among the peasants of each village, the custom of periodic land redistribution (denchiwari or warichi) was extended and standardized so that each landholder would hold land of good, average, and poor quality in proportion to the ratio of these grades of land throughout the village.

To increase the efficiency of tax assessment and collection, tax functions were taken from the county commissioner (kōri bugyō) and vested in a new official, the kaisaku bugyō (cultivation commissioner). Tomuragumi (districts) were enlarged to include 30 to 50 villages, and officials were selected from among the district administrators (tomura) to form a new level of peasant official, the gofuchinin tomura, who supervised the district administrators. Special officials were appointed as assistants to the tomura to oversee taxation of reclaimed land. Tax collection, too, was entrusted in 1653 to a peasant official, the tomura daikan.

■——Sakai Seiichi, Kaisakuhō no kenkyū (1978). Wakabayashi Kisaburō, Kaga han nōseishi no kenkyū, vol 1 (1970).

Philip BROWN

kaisen

(literally, "circuit ships"). Cargo ships used from around the 14th century for transport and trade within the Japanese archipelago. Kaisen were most active during the Edo period (1600–1868). Typical of vessels of this type were the higaki kaisen and taru kaisen, which transported goods between the Kyōto–Ōsaka area and Edo (now Tōkyō), and the kitamaebune, which made the rounds from Ōsaka-Kyōto and the coastal areas of the Inland Sea to Ezochi (now Hokkaidō). Many of the Edo-period kaisen were called sengokubune from the fact that they could carry as much as 1,000 koku (1 koku = 0.28 cu m or 10 cu ft) of cargo.

Cargo ships came into regular use around the 8th century to transport tribute to the capital in Kyōto. With the rise of the SHŌEN (estate) system in the 10th century, kaisen were used to forward the rice tax (nengu) to absentee proprietors in Kyōto. As commerce prospered and markets developed during the 14th century, kaisen were used to transport commercial goods. Other kaisen plied the Inland Sea engaging in itinerant trade. Kaisen were usually 50- to 60-ton vessels. In the 15th and 16th centuries harbors were built to accommodate a growing sea trade. Some of the busier ports were SAKAI (in Ōsaka Prefecture) and Hyōgo (west of Kōbe); Onomichi and Akamagaseki (now Shimonoseki) on the Inland Sea; Obama, Tsuruga, and Mikuniminato (now Mikunichō, Fukui Prefecture) on the Sea of Japan; and Kuwana and Ōminato on the Pacific coast. In about the 15th century kaisen shikimoku (maritime regulations) were issued to regulate marine transportation practices such as the disposition of cargo in case of shipwreck.

At the beginning of the 17th century the TOKUGAWA SHOGUNATE and various daimyō made a concerted effort to develop new sea routes to facilitate the transport of tax rice to Ōsaka and Edo. By order of the shogunate, KAWAMURA ZUIKEN opened two new routes—the higashi mawari (eastern circuit), which connected ports on the Sea of Japan and Edo by way of the Tsugaru Strait and the Pacific, in 1671; and the nishi mawari (western circuit), which con-

nected the Sea of Japan ports with Ōsaka by way of the Shimonoseki Strait and the Inland Sea, in 1672. It was about this time that the *higaki kaisen, taru kaisen,* and *kitamaebune* became active. *Higaki kaisen* were used by SAKAI MERCHANTS to transport cotton, oil, *sake,* vinegar, and soy sauce to Edo. From the end of the 17th century they were managed by the NIJŪSHIKUMI-DOIYA in Ōsaka and the TOKUMI-DOIYA in Edo. *Taru kaisen* were used mainly to transport *sake* from Ōsaka to Edo. The two types of ship competed vigorously for cargo. *Kitamaebune* were vessels commissioned to sail the western circuit. With a cargo of *sake* and miscellaneous goods, they sailed from Ōsaka as far north as Matsumae and Hakodate and brought back herring, kelp *(kombu),* and other marine products. Owners of these vessels often owned the cargo as well and made enormous profits. *Kaisen* were gradually supplanted by steamboats, which appeared in the latter half of the 19th century.
📖——Furuta Ryōichi, *Kaiun no rekishi* (1961). Yunoki Manabu, *Kinsei kaiun shi no kenkyū* (1979). *TANJI KENZŌ*

kaishi

(literally, "bosom paper"). Also known as *tatōgami* (folded paper). A fine-grained crepe paper carried in the breast-fold opening of the KIMONO and used for tissue paper *(hanagami)* and letter writing. The word also refers to the paper originally used in court circles when composing WAKA and *renga* (see RENGA AND HAIKAI) poetry. This paper came in different colors and sizes, according to one's sex and social rank, and elaborate rules of etiquette determined how it should be folded and how poems should be inscribed. Court dress codes required that men carry white *kaishi* and women carry red *kaishi.* The *kogikushi* paper used in the TEA CEREMONY is also called *kaishi.* *ENDŌ TAKESHI*

Kaishintō → Rikken Kaishintō

Kaitakushi

(Hokkaidō Colonization Office). Government office of the early part of the Meiji period (1868–1912) charged with the administration and development of Hokkaidō. Recognizing the strategic importance and productive potential of Ezochi (or EZO), as Hokkaidō and islands farther north were then called, the Meiji government established the Kaitakushi in August 1869 and renamed the area Hokkaidō and Karafuto (Sakhalin). Under the provisions of the Treaty of ST. PETERSBURG (1875), Sakhalin became a Russian possession, and the Kuril Islands were placed under the jurisdiction of the Kaitakushi. The Colonization Office had its headquarters in Sapporo and was headed by a director *(chōkan)* and a vice director. After the appointment as director of KURODA KIYOTAKA from the former domain of Satsuma (now Kagoshima Prefecture), the office became a stronghold of former Satsuma *samurai.*

In 1872 the Kaitakushi was allotted a budget of ¥10 million, to be spent over a period of 10 years. It employed many foreign advisers to initiate various government-sponsored enterprises, introduce new agricultural techniques, and assist in the building of roads and railways. It founded the Sapporo Agricultural College (now Hokkaidō University) to educate young men and to carry out agricultural experiments. The office actively promoted settlement in Hokkaidō by facilitating group migration of former samurai, especially from northeastern Japan, who were recruited into a militia system (TONDENHEI) responsible for farming and defense. It also brought in convicts as an additional source of labor.

Most of the development, however, was concentrated in the Sapporo area and never progressed beyond the experimental stage. Moreover, the indigenous AINU people were summarily deprived of their fishing, hunting, and land rights, and thus of their entire livelihood. Most of the confiscated land was designated government property or property of the imperial household. In 1881 a major scandal erupted over the proposed sale of the Kaitakushi's assets at a nominal price to a private consortium. The HOKKAIDŌ COLONIZATION OFFICE SCANDAL OF 1881 resulted in a major upheaval in the central government (see POLITICAL CRISIS OF 1881) and the abolition of the Kaitakushi in the following year. Three prefectures—Hakodate, Sapporo, and Nemuro—were created in 1882, but in 1886 these were done away with and the entire island of Hokkaidō became one political unit with a prefectural form of government. *TANAKA AKIRA*

Kaitakushi Scandal of 1881 → Hokkaidō Colonization Office Scandal of 1881

Kaitei Ritsurei

(Revised Statutes). Criminal code drawn up in 1873 as an amendment and supplement to the SHINRITSU KŌRYŌ (1870). In contrast to the earlier code, which was largely a codification of 17th-century Chinese legal concepts, the Kaitei Ritsurei was influenced by Western, in particular French, criminal codes. Penalties were not only standardized and made lighter but changed to conform with modern penal practices. Both codes remained in effect until the new Criminal Code of 1880 (effective 1882) replaced them.

Kaiten

Special naval attack weapon used by the Japanese navy during World War II. Also known as the "human torpedo," the weapon was a vessel 15 meters (49.2 ft) in length and 1 meter (3.3 ft) in diameter, with a top speed in excess of 30 nautical miles per hour and a carrying capacity of one-and-one-half metric tons (1.7 short tons) of explosive charge and one man. Kaiten were first produced in the summer of 1944 (some 420 were made by the end of the war). Beginning in November, they were loaded on submarines and used to attack American ships in harbor at Ulithi Atoll, Iōjima, and Okinawa. Results were poor, mainly because of the high losses suffered by carrier submarines. During the last months of the war they were attached to bases in southern Japan in preparation for the anticipated Allied invasion. *ICHIKI TOSHIO*

Kaitokudō

Also known as Kaitoku Shoin. School for commoners founded in Ōsaka in 1724 with financial support from a group of Ōsaka merchants. Because the shōgun TOKUGAWA YOSHIMUNE encouraged the education of commoners, the school later received shogunal support. The Confucian scholar MIYAKE SEKIAN was appointed its first head. He was succeeded by Nakai Shūan (1693–1758), who had played an important role in founding the school. The school also occasionally admitted those of *samurai* background. The curriculum was based on the philosophy of Zhu Xi (Chu Hsi; see SHUSHIGAKU) and used the Confucian classics as its texts. It also included introductory expositions of Wang Yangming's doctrines (see YŌMEIGAKU). The school reached its peak under Shūan's son, Nakai Chikuzan (1730–1804), who restricted the curriculum to the Zhu Xi school. It began to decline after his death and was finally closed in 1869.

Kaizei Yakusho

(Tariff Convention). Trade agreement signed on 25 June 1866 by the Tokugawa shogunate and Great Britain, France, the Netherlands, and the United States. Under the terms of the agreement, drafted by the British minister Sir Harry PARKES, import tariffs, which had been set by the ANSEI COMMERCIAL TREATIES (1858) at 5 to 35 percent of average selling price, were reduced to a uniform 5 percent of declared value to be paid in silver. The agreement further abolished charges on foreign ships entering and leaving Japanese ports, allowed construction of foreign warehouses in Japanese cities, and exempted foreign goods from domestic transport duties. It greatly weakened the shogunate's control of foreign trade and at the same time deprived it of revenues, especially with the fall in the price of silver. Not until 1894 was this agreement supplanted by more equitable trade treaties. See also UNEQUAL TREATIES, REVISION OF.

Kaizō

General-interest magazine published between 1919 and 1955 by Kaizōsha, a publishing firm founded by innovative newspaperman YAMAMOTO SANEHIKO. It was launched in April 1919 during the heyday of TAISHŌ DEMOCRACY in Japan following World War I. With the growing tide of economic and social unrest in the early 1920s, *Kaizō* became a major forum for Marxist and socialist debate. Among its early regularly featured contributors were such leading socialist thinkers as SAKAI TOSHIHIKO, YAMAKAWA HITOSHI, ŌSUGI SAKAE, KAWAKAMI HAJIME, and KAGAWA TOYOHIKO. The guiding force behind the magazine was Yamamoto, who served as longtime editor-in-chief. He attracted attention in publishing circles with his unique approach to journalism. A far-sighted individual, Yamamoto invited such foreign luminaries as Bertrand Russell and Albert Einstein to contribute articles which appeared in *Kaizō*, making it a leading proponent of new trends in thought and science. *Kaizō* was, along with CHŪŌ KŌRON, an important influence on public opinion of its day. It was also a major publishing outlet for literature. Featured in its pages were novels and short stories by many of the top writers of the time, and it was long regarded as the doorstep to popularity for aspiring young writers. It carried such well-known masterpieces of modern Japanese literature as *Ummei* by KŌDA ROHAN, *An'ya kōro* by SHIGA NAOYA, *Aru otoko* by MUSHANOKŌJI SANEATSU, and many others. The parent company Kaizōsha specialized in publishing small, softbound editions of books by leading writers of the time, which became known as "one-yen novels." In 1942 *Kaizō* ran afoul of the military government, and publication was eventually suspended in 1944. It began republishing in 1946 but was not able to muster the same spirit that characterized it before the war. As the result of an internal labor dispute it ceased publication in 1955.

Kaizuka

City in southwestern Ōsaka Prefecture, central Honshū. Kaizuka developed as a temple town of the temple Gansenji in the late 1500s and later as a producer of and wholesale center for Izumi cotton cloth. Its modern textile industry centers on Unitika, Ltd. Metal, machinery, and foodstuffs are also produced. Pop: 81,162.

Kajii Motojirō (1901–1932)

Short story writer and example par excellence of a *bungaku seinen* ("literary youth") of the Taishō period (1912–26), young bohemians like Kajii who created the numerous coterie magazines *(dōjin zasshi)* that dominated the age. Although overshadowed by greater literary figures such as AKUTAGAWA RYŪNOSUKE, TANIZAKI JUN'ICHIRŌ and SHIGA NAOYA, they shared in their influences—Tolstoy, Baudelaire and Poe—and in their great intellectual dilemma, i.e., how to reconcile the activist demands of Marxism, newly introduced to Japan, with their basic orientation toward aestheticism.

Born in Ōsaka, Kajii attended the Third Higher School in Kyōto from 1919 to 1924 and Tōkyō University from 1924 to 1927. He founded the coterie magazine *Aozora* (Blue Skies) along with other Third Higher School graduates, including Tonomura Shigeru (1902–61), KITAGAWA FUYUHIKO, MIYOSHI TATSUJI, Yodono Ryūzō (1904–67) and Nakatani Takao (b 1901). The first issue appeared in January 1925 and featured Kajii's maiden work, "Remon" (The Lemon), the story of how the simple beauty of a lemon helps dispel the ennui of the young first-person protagonist. It was followed in February by "Shiro no aru machi ni te" (In a Castle Town).

Recurrent bouts of tuberculosis forced Kajii to interrupt his studies, and in 1926 he moved to Yugashima on the Izu Peninsula to convalesce. There he became acquainted with the young novelist KAWABATA YASUNARI and the poet HAGIWARA SAKUTARŌ, thus establishing his first contacts with the literary establishment. He continued to write for *Aozora* until its demise in June 1927 when he began publishing in other literary journals such as *Shi to shiron* (Poetry and Poetics) and *Bungei toshi* (Literary Capital). The works of this period reflect the wild poetic vision of Baudelaire whom Kajii had read through Arthur Symon's English translations.

Later on, under the influence of Marxism, he planned to go and live among the day laborers of Tōkyō, but was unable to because of illness and returned to Ōsaka to be cared for by his family. With the help of his old school friends, a collection of his first 18 short stories was published under the title *Remon* in 1931. His last work, *Nonki na kanja* (The Carefree Patient) appeared in the magazine CHŪŌ KŌRON in January before his death in March 1932. It was his first novella, and the only work for which he commanded a fee. Recognition of his talent came only after his death, especially in the 1950s when his works enjoyed a revival among young readers, and Yodono Ryūzō edited the much acclaimed collection of Kajii's correspondence titled *Wakaki shijin no tegami* (Letters of a Young Poet) which was published in 1955. Nakatani Takao's biography, published in 1961, provides a delightful portrait of Kajii's salad days at Third Higher School.

Kajii's style combines the realism and attention for detail characteristic of Shiga Naoya and the love of the fantastic of Baudelaire and Poe. Although his last works are somber in tone due to his diminishing health, they retain a vibrant "passion for despair" *(zetsubō e no jōnetsu)* which is the hallmark of this young bohemian's gemlike stories.

━━━━Kajii Motojirō, *Kajii Motojirō zenshū*, 3 vols (Chikuma Shobō, 1966). Ishikawa Hiroshi, *Kajii Motojirō ron* (1964). Nakatani Takao, *Kajii Motojirō* (1961). Sudō Matsuo, *Kajii Motojirō kenkyū* (1971). William J. TYLER

Kajima Corporation

(Kajima Kensetsu). Firm engaged in a wide variety of operations ranging from design, engineering, and construction to land development. Founded in 1840 and established in its present form in 1930, it is Japan's largest general construction company. The firm has built over 140 major dams, as well as underground power plants, highways, airports, subways, large-scale docking facilities, seaports, undersea tunnels, and bridges. It built the first Japanese skyscraper, and controls a large share of the market for the construction of such facilities as nuclear power plants, steel mills, and petrochemical plants. Kajima has participated in over 250 projects in 37 nations, including planning for the development of various types of industrial infrastructure in Southeast Asia, the Middle East, Africa, and Central and South America, while in Europe and North America it has contributed to plans for city development. The company controls 15 subsidiary firms in the fields of engineering, commerce, publishing, and motion pictures, and, in addition, has real estate companies in the United States, Brazil, and Indonesia and a financial firm in the Netherlands. In the fiscal year ending November 1981 it received orders valued at ¥1 trillion (US $4.5 billion), while total sales were ¥813.9 billion (US $3.7 billion), of which 57 percent was derived from construction, 37 percent from public works projects, and 6 percent from development projects. Four percent of sales were gained in the overseas market. In the same year capitalization stood at ¥38.2 billion (US $170.7 million). The corporate headquarters are located in Tōkyō.

Kajimaya

Wealthy Ōsaka merchant house of the Edo period (1600–1868); founded by Masanori (also called Kyūemon), who started a ricepolishing business in 1625. Prospering greatly, the family business later expanded to include money-changing, and in 1731 the Kajimaya were permitted to become brokers in the DŌJIMA RICE MARKET. The family, which developed several branches, also made extensive loans to *daimyō* (see DAIMYŌ LOANS). Like many other merchant houses, the Kajimaya had difficulty adjusting to the new circumstances after the Meiji Restoration (1868) but survived to establish the Kajima Bank in 1887.

Kajiwara Kagetoki (?–1200)

Warrior of the Kamakura period (1185–1333). Although Kagetoki initially fought on the Taira side in the TAIRA–MINAMOTO WAR, he rescued MINAMOTO NO YORITOMO at the Battle of Ishibashiyama and became one of his most trusted vassals, governor of several provinces, and an influential member of the Board of Retainers (SAMURAI-DOKORO). He fought under MINAMOTO NO YOSHITSUNE in the destruction of the Taira but later turned against him, calumniating him to Yoritomo and contributing to the growing rift between the two brothers. After Yoritomo's death in 1199, Kagetoki served briefly as an elder adviser to MINAMOTO NO YORIIE, the second shōgun; but when he slandered the prominent vassal Yūki Tomomitsu (1168–1254) he earned the wrath of the Wada, Miura, and other leading warrior houses of the Kamakura shogunate. Ousted from office, he planned to go to Kyōto to support Takeda Ariyoshi as shōgun but was discovered and killed in fighting in Suruga (now part of Shizuoka Prefecture). He is portrayed in popular literature as articulate, arrogant, and altogether treacherous.

G. Cameron HURST III

Kajiwara Shōzen (1265?–1337?)

Buddhist priest and scholar of Chinese medicine. Born in Sagami Province (now Kanagawa Prefecture). Little is known of Shōzen's life apart from the fact that he practiced medicine in Gokurakuji, Kamakura. Based on his reading of more than 2,000 Chinese works on medicine and his own experience, he wrote *Ton'ishō* (1303, Jottings on Medicine), a book in simple syllabic Japanese, and *Man'*-

anhō (1315, Prescriptions for Felicity), a revised version in classical Chinese. The two books are representative of the medical science of the latter part of the Kamakura period (1185–1333).

Kajiyama Toshiyuki (1929–1975)

Novelist. Born in Seoul, Korea. Graduate of Hiroshima Higher Normal School (now Hiroshima University). Author of popular mysteries and erotic novels. Worked as an investigative reporter and gained recognition with his documentary-style novel *Kuro no shisō-sha* (1962, The Black Test Model Car). The work explores the backroom dealings of rival automobile manufacturers and led to a boom in industrial spy novels. Another representative work is *Akai daiya* (1962–63, Red Diamonds).

Kakamigahara

City in southern Gifu Prefecture, central Honshū, on the river Kisogawa. The site of an airport and aircraft plant since World War II, Kakamigahara also produces automobiles and textiles. Pop: 114,751.

kakari-musubi

Rule of grammatical agreement in the CLASSICAL JAPANESE language. When a certain grammatical particle or *joshi* (the *kakari*) occurs in the middle of a sentence, a particular verb-adjective conjugational form (the *musubi*, literally, "tying up") corresponding to that particle is used at the end of the sentence. The particles *zo, namu, ya,* and *ka* require the *rentaikei* (attributive) form of the verb at the end of the sentence, while the particle *koso* requires the *izenkei* (perfective) form of the verb. The term *kakari-musubi* is usually applied only to these special cases in which a conjugation other than the usual *shūshikei* (sentence final) form of the verb is required; but some grammarians feel that the same grammatical principle is at work in the general correspondence between the particles *wa* and *mo* and the *shūshikei* form of the verb. *Kakari-musubi* became established during the Heian period (794–1185) but gradually ceased to function, appearing now only in a few dialects of modern Japanese. *Uwano Zendō*

kakashi

(scarecrows). Figures or objects set up in fields to frighten away birds and animals that damage crops. Various kinds of *kakashi* have been used in Japan from time immemorial. One kind is the human-shaped figure through which the divine power of the god of the fields (TA NO KAMI) is believed to manifest itself. In its presence farmers offer prayers for abundant crops in the spring and of thanksgiving after the harvest. It is typically made of straw, dressed in old clothing, and holds a bow and arrow. Chunks of rotting meat, clumps of hair or fur or other objects that give off a repulsive smell are also used as scarecrows. Other kinds include the use of frightening noises such as bird rattles (NARUKO) or small mechanisms that fire blank shots periodically. Bright, shiny materials such as tin cans and aluminum foil placed about the fields also fulfill this function. *Noguchi Takenori*

Kakegawa

City in southwestern Shizuoka Prefecture, central Honshū, on the river Sakagawa. A castle town and post-station town during the Edo period (1600–1868), Kakegawa is known for its tea, *shiitake* (a variety of mushroom), and roses. Musical instruments and transport-related machinery are also produced. *Kuzufu,* a grass cloth used traditionally for sliding doors *(fusuma)* and recently for wallpaper, has been made here since the Edo period. Tourist attractions include the ruins of Kakegawa Castle and Sayo no Nakayama Park. Pop: 64,843.

Kakei Katsuhiko (1872–1961)

Scholar of civil law and constitutional theory; Shintō thinker. Born in Nagano Prefecture, Kakei graduated from the law department of Tōkyō University in 1897 and went on to postgraduate research in Germany, where he studied under Otto Friedrich von Gierke (1841–1921), noted theorist of the Germanist school of historical jurisprudence, among others. He became assistant professor in 1900 and full professor in 1903 at Tōkyō University, where he lectured on such subjects as administrative law, constitutional law, and legal theory. Possessed of a strong religious bent, after close encounters with Christianity and Buddhism he converted to the ancient Shintō belief as set forth by the mid-19th-century line of the KOKUGAKU (National Learning) theorists MOTOORI NORINAGA, HIRATA ATSUTANE, and others. Kakei attempted a systemic explanation of history as depicted in the KOJIKI (712), the oldest extant history of Japan, and advocated a so-called Japanese world view. Because of his rather eccentric behavior, such as performing the Shintō handclapping ceremony in his office before proceeding to the classroom to present a lecture, he is generally regarded as having been an anachronistic thinker. A conservative scholar who advocated the theory that the emperor equals the state *(tennō soku kokka),* he survived the purge during the 1930s of academics and others following the hue and cry surrounding MINOBE TATSUKICHI and the emperor-as-organ theory (TENNŌ KIKAN SETSU) and was appointed to the Bunkyō Shingikai, a prewar advisory council of the Ministry of Education. In 1944 he traveled to Manchukuo, the puppet state established by the Japanese army in Manchuria, and delivered his lecture "Kami nagara no michi" (The Way Dictated by the Gods) to the Manchurian emperor. He published a number of books on Shintō and constitutional jurisprudence such as *Koshintō taigi* (1912, The Noble Road of Ancient Shintō), *Kokka no kenkū* (1913, Study of the State), *Kami nagara no michi* (1925), and *Dai Nippon teikoku kempō no kompongi* (1936, The Basic Meaning of the Constitution of the Empire of Japan). *Nagao Ryūichi*

kakekomidera

(refuge temples). Also known as *enkiridera* (divorce temples). From the 13th through 19th centuries, certain convent-temples offered refuge to women fleeing their husbands; after serving in such a temple for two full years, a woman could be granted the right of divorce by the commissioners of temples and shrines *(jisha bugyō)* despite her husband's objection. In normal circumstances a woman could seek a legal divorce only if her husband disappeared or committed a serious crime, although a husband could obtain a divorce with comparative ease. The best-known temple of this kind, TŌKEIJI in Kamakura, was founded in 1285. Mantokuji, in what is now Gumma Prefecture, was founded for this purpose in the 13th century. In the latter part of the Edo period only Mantokuji and Tōkeiji were officially recognized as refuge temples, but Tōkeiji alone is said to have harbored about 2,000 absconding wives in the 150 years before new divorce laws were instituted by the Meiji government in 1873. See also DIVORCE.

kakekotoba

("pivot word"). A type of wordplay or pun in which a word or series of syllables has multiple meanings depending on how it is parsed. For example, in this poem from the HEICHŪ MONOGATARI (mid-10th century, The Tale of Heichū), the syllables *tatsu* mean "gain a reputation," when read with the preceding phrase *na nomi* and river Tatsuta when read with the following phrase as *Tatsuta no kawa:*

Uki na nomi	This autumn as
Tatsuta no kawa no	I brood upon the shame
Momijiba wa	That stains my name
Mono omou aki no	The river Tatsuta's colored leaves
Sode ni zo arikeru	Rage red upon my tear-soaked sleeves.

Although *kakekotoba* appear in the MAN'YŌSHŪ (compiled ca 759), the oldest anthology of Japanese verse, the literary device known as MAKURA KOTOBA ("pillow words" or conventional epithets) was more common in early poetry. *Kakekotoba* reached their fullest development in the 9th century, tending to replace *makura kotoba,* with the decline of the CHŌKA, or long poem, and predominance of the brief 31-syllable TANKA, or short poem, form. By telescoping multiple meanings within a minimum number of syllables, the *kakekotoba* allowed for complexity of thought and emotion in an abbreviated poetic form. The *kakekotoba* later came to be exploited as a technique for heightening language in the genres of prose fiction and drama as well as in various poetic forms such as linked verse (*renga;* see RENGA AND HAIKAI). *Susan Downing Videen*

kakemono

(hanging scroll). Painting or calligraphy mounted with strips of luxurious fabric on flexible backing paper so that it can be rolled up for storage. In contrast to *makimono* (handscrolls), which are unrolled laterally on a flat surface and can be viewed by only one or two persons at a time, *kakemono* are designed to be used as part of the interior decoration of a room. Since the Muromachi period (1333–1568), *kakemono* have been the major artwork on the wall of the *tokonoma,* the alcove especially designed for the display of prized objects. In contrast to wall paintings *(shōhekiga)* and folding screens *(byōbu)*, *kakemono* can be easily changed to suit the season or the occasion.

The scroll was introduced to Japan in the early part of the Heian period (794–1185) in the form of Buddhist paintings and scriptures from the Asian continent. The early *kakemono* were hung over Buddhist altars or in religious halls, but eventually the form was secularized and used in the decorative scheme of residential architecture, where the *tokonoma* was evolved to exhibit them. The preferences of tea masters during the late Muromachi period greatly influenced the form, since the major object of contemplation in the tearoom is the scroll displayed in the alcove. Preferred subjects for scroll paintings are landscapes, flowers and birds, and figures; in calligraphy, the more valued scrolls display writing by virtuous men or respected priests and various lines of poetry by famous poets.

Calligraphy and painting are closely related in Japan. From the beginning it has been common practice to add *gasan,* or inscriptions, to scroll paintings. *Gasan* include prose and poetry, original compositions, and passages from classical texts. Some are written by the painter himself, some by friends and admirers. They are usually signed and bear the seal of the writer. Early Zen priests frequently wrote words of encouragement on the paintings they presented to disciples as certificates of achievement, and in the early 15th century a major form of pictorial expression was the *shigajiku* ("poetry-painting scroll"), which combined poetry with landscape painting. In the 17th century, the *haiga* form appeared, a composition integrating HAIKU poetry and impromptu painting. Some *gasan* are more highly prized than the paintings on which they appear; these were occasionally cut from their original format and remounted as independent *kakemono.*

Kakemono are sometimes made in matching sets according to subject matter. For example, a dragon and a tiger make a natural pair *(tsuifuku* or *sōfuku);* iconic paintings are suitable as triptychs *(sampukutsui);* landscapes of the 4 seasons are mounted in sets of 4; the "Eight Views of Xiao (Hsiao) and Xiang (Hsiang)" in sets of 8; and genre scenes of the 12 months in sets of 12.

The mounting of a painting or calligraphy is called *hyōsō,* and the craftsman is called a *hyōsōshi. Hyōsō* vary according to subject and style of the work and the use to which it will be put, but the style called Yamato *hyōsō* can be considered standard. In Yamato *hyōsō* the artwork *(honshi),* on paper or silk, is put on a backing of paper and adorned with strips of fine material *(kire* or *kireji)* such as gold or silver brocade, damask, silk gauze, and sometimes embroidery. The mounting is divided into three horizontal zones and, for variety, the fabric of the middle zone contrasts with that of the upper and lower zones. The most sumptuous materials are used for the areas of decorative focus: the *ichimonji* (accenting bands above and below the work of art) and the *fūtai* (two ornamental strips that hang from the top of the *kakemono).* The roller serves as a weight to hold the *kakemono* flat when it is hanging and as a spindle for rolling the scroll when it is stored. It is made of rich material such as ivory, sandalwood, ceramic, crystal, or an elaborately embossed lacquer called *tsuishu.* The *kakemono* is lifted to its position with a *kakemonokake,* a pole that has a forked tip.   Carolyn WHEELWRIGHT

kakeya

Accounting agents of the Edo period (1600–1868), generally based in Ōsaka, who handled accounts at the warehousing offices (KURAYA-SHIKI) of the shogunate and *daimyō* where tax rice and other commodities were sold. These agents were given the authority to hold the money obtained and to make monthly remittances to the domains or the daimyō residences in Edo (now Tōkyō). In times of bad harvest or extraordinary expenditures, *kakeya* lent money at interest to the daimyō, holding warehouse goods as security (see DAIMYŌ LOANS). Although the *kakeya* were not *samurai,* the services they rendered were so vital that they were given various privileges of the samurai class. Among the most powerful *kakeya* were the KŌNOIKE FAMILY.

Kakemono

A *kakemono* with an ink painting on silk as its decorative focus. Mounting 1 m 45 cm × 65 cm.

Kakeya Sōichi (1886–1947)

Mathematician. Known for his work on the properties of algebraic and simultaneous integral equations. Born in Hiroshima Prefecture, he graduated from Tōkyō University. After teaching at Tōhoku University and studying in the United States, he became a professor at Tōkyō University in 1935. He became the first director of its Institute of Statistical Mathematics in 1944.

Kakiemon ware

(kakiemon-de). Porcelain ware. A type of underglaze blue and white or polychrome overglaze enameled porcelain made in Arita, Hizen Province (now Saga and Nagasaki prefectures), from 1643 on. According to traditional accounts, Sakaida Kizaemon (1596–1666) made Japan's first polychrome porcelains at his family's Nangawara kiln in 1643 with overglaze pigments imported from China. The pigments came from an Imari ceramics merchant, Higashijima Tokuzaemon, who was the first to export Kakiemon ware. It is said that in 1644 Kizaemon was renamed Kakiemon by his domainal lord in appreciation for a porcelain ornament that he had made in the form of two persimmons *(kaki)*. Since Chinese influences on typical blue and white and polychrome Kakiemon pieces are mainly traceable to Kangxi (K'ang-hsi) era (1666–1722) porcelains, what was being produced at the Kakiemon kiln between 1643 and around 1670 is still unclear. After 1672 Kakiemon ware was imitated by other Japanese potters, after 1700 in China, and in the 18th century throughout Europe, starting with Meissen, Germany, in 1728. Although traditional designs were retained, quality dropped after the death of Kakiemon VI (1690–1735).

Typical forms include dishes, bowls, bottles, and jars, some tea-bowls, incense burners, and flower vases, as well as candlesticks, ewers with handles, teapots, and, mostly for the Western market, ornamental figures. At their best, Kakiemon pieces have a milk-white body, an almost transparent mat glaze full of bubbles with a glossy sheen, and spur marks on the base. In polychrome pieces soft orange red and azure blue predominate, sometimes with light yellow, light green, aubergine, and brown. The sensitively drawn naturalistic designs executed in a sharp brush line with or without black outlining typically occupy a third of the available space. Bird-and-flower motifs are most common and popular designs such as quail and millet, tiger and bamboo, deer and maple, and plover and waves derive from TOSA SCHOOL and KANŌ SCHOOL painting, pattern books, and lacquerwork, respectively. Kakiemon XIII (1906–82) and his son (b 1934) have carried on the family tradition.

Frederick BAEKELAND

kakiire

A system of nonpossessory collateral for loans in the Edo period (1600–1868). Also called *hikiate*. In contrast to *shichiire* (pawnage), *kakiire* did not involve transfer of the possession of the collateral to the creditor and instead required only a written pledge. Real estate, movable property, and human beings could all be offered as *kakiire* collateral. When real estate was used, the loan documents carried a statement to the effect that in the case of default, possession of the collateral would revert to the creditor or that the debt would be redeemed by the proceeds from selling the collateral. In legal proceedings, however, *kakiire*, unlike *shichiire*, was accepted only as a *kanekuji* (money suit), which received less legal protection than a *honkuji* (main suit), and the creditor was given only the protection afforded in common financial claims. After the beginning of the Meiji period (1868–1912), *kakiire* pledges of human beings were prohibited and a guarantee of preferential rights of redemption was provided for *kakiire* involving real estate. In addition, the creditor was granted the right to obtain possession of the collateral in case of default. With the enactment of a new Civil Code in 1898, *kakiire* was abolished and a mortgage system of nonpossessory collateral was established. *KOYANAGI Shun'ichirō*

Kakinomoto no Hitomaro (fl ca 685–705)

Most important poet of the MAN'YŌSHŪ, the earliest anthology of Japanese verse, and one of the most esteemed poets in Japan. Despite his poetic preeminence, Hitomaro's life is obscure. He was a low-ranking member of the courts of Empress JITŌ (r 686–697) and Emperor MOMMU (r 697–707). From the internal evidence of his poems we can surmise that he made trips to various places, including Iwami (now Shimane Prefecture) and Tsukushi (now Kyūshū), and that he had at least two wives.

Hitomaro's canon also presents problems. His authentic poems appear in the *Man'yōshū*, which also includes poems attributed to a *Hitomaro kashū* (Hitomaro collection), a SHIKASHŪ (personal poetry collection) no longer extant and not necessarily composed exclusively of verses by Hitomaro. Poems attributed to Hitomaro in later anthologies (e.g., SHIN KOKINSHŪ, 3:190) are commonly suspect on various grounds. A conservative view of his canon allows for 17 CHŌKA (long poems) from the first three books of the *Man'yōshū*; and over 60 *tanka* (short poems; see WAKA), almost entirely from the first four books and often used as *hanka* (envoys) to the long poems.

Excluding many poems attributed to him and ignoring some poems of lesser interest, we are left with others of such quality as to explain why many people consider Hitomaro the greatest Japanese poet. His art is at once the most natural and complex in the *Man'yōshū*. He masters techniques—complex parallelism, pillow words (MAKURA KOTOBA), overture-like paeans to the divinity of the land or royal line, irony—which he employs to reveal our human condition. He infuses public events with personal emotion and universalizes the intimate.

Two of Hitomaro's public poems relate to the JINSHIN DISTURBANCE of 672. *Man'yōshū* poem 2:199–201 mourns Prince Takechi who, as son of the sovereign, TEMMU, commanded the victorious forces in the Jinshin War and served as prime minister and heir apparent under the subsequent reign of his mother, JITŌ, dying before he could succeed her. This *chōka* is the longest in the collection (149 lines, with two envoys) and is unique in its vivid description of battle scenes. Some time after that war, Hitomaro visited Ōmi (now Shiga Prefecture) and the ruins of the rival court there which Prince Takechi had overwhelmed in 672. In *Man'yōshū* poem 1:29–31 Hitomaro questions why a capital was perversely established so far away, mourning the waste, the irreparable loss of people and their aspirations. Cape Kara may abide at the site, "But though it wait throughout the ages, / The courtiers' pleasure boats will not return." Such kind irony marks Hitomaro's poetry.

A poem still richer in humanity and irony concerns the body of a dead man found on an island near present-day Shikoku (2:220–22). Hitomaro begins by praising the divinity of the shore he left, recounts his experience in a typhoon, and finally relates his discovery of a man drowned in the storm and cast ashore on Samine. In the gales the body is pillowed on rocks while the surf "Pounds ever in from off the sea." Samine, "The isle so beautiful in name," is cruel and yet part of a divine landscape. Hitomaro presumes the man had a wife who would, if she could, be gathering greens for him on the island: "But is their season not now past?" By such indirection Hitomaro alludes the more powerfully to the man's death.

More personal poems include two *chōka* on the death of one wife (2:207–209, 210–212) and two on parting from another (2:131–133, 135–137). The first elegy depicts the poet distractedly visiting a market his wife frequented. He stands vainly calling out her name, waving his sleeves—yet not a single person even looks like her. Hitomaro's parting poems probably imply his being recalled to the capital for other service. The first *chōka* concludes with the poet's wretched thought on crossing the mountains which hide his wife from view: "I wish these mountains would bow down." The second poem is especially lovely in its imagery and in Hitomaro's characteristically skillful integration of the envoys with the *chōka*.

Foremost among *Man'yōshū* poets, Hitomaro remains, along with SAIGYŌ and BASHŌ, one of the three most esteemed poets in Japanese history; and no other Japanese poet is so accessible to the non-Japanese reader.

■——The standard study of Hitomaro is by Saitō Mokichi, *Kakinomoto Hitomaro*, 5 vols (1934–40). For a more recent large-scale view with discussion of scholarship, see Aso Mizue, *Kakinomoto Hitomaro ronkō* (1962). More recently there has appeared a study of wide appeal by one of the foremost specialists, Nakanishi Susumu, *Kakinomoto Hitomaro* (1970). On the *Hitomaro kashū* there is Kanda Hideo, *Hitomaro kashū to Hitomaro den* (1965). For translations and criticism in English, see Robert H. Brower and Earl Miner, *Japanese Court Poetry* (1961), chap. 4; Earl Miner, *An Introduction to Japanese Court Poetry* (1968), chap. 3; and Ian Hideo Levy, *The Ten Thousand Leaves*, vol 1 (1981), the first of a four-volume translation of the *Man'yōshū*. *Earl MINER*

kakitsubata → irises

Kakogawa

City in southern Hyōgo Prefecture, western Honshū, on the river Kakogawa. Kakogawa developed as a post-station town on the highway San'yōdō and as a river port during the Edo period (1600–1868). Now part of the Harima Coastal Industrial Zone, it produces woolens, fertilizer, steel, silk thread, and linen. Many burial mounds (KOFUN) have been discovered here, indicating that the area was settled in ancient times. Pop: 212,232.

Kakogawa

River in Hyōgo Prefecture, central Honshū, flowing southward and emptying into Harima Sea at the border of the cities of Kakogawa and Takasago. A delta is formed at the lower reaches. It winds through a grain belt; the water is used for drinking, irrigation, and industry. Length: 84 km (52 mi); area of drainage basin: 2,220 sq km (857 sq mi).

kakoimai

(stored rice). Rice stored by order of the Tokugawa shogunate and many *daimyō* during the Edo period (1600–1868) for use during famines, to stabilize rice prices, or for military purposes. The rice was stored in sheaves *(momi)* to prevent spoilage and so was sometimes called *kakoimomi*; it was also known as *okigome* or *tsumegome*. The practice of reserving rice for military use had long been in existence, but it was in 1683 that the shogunate first ordered daimyō domains to set aside a stipulated percentage of their annual rice crop for use during famines. Daimyō began issuing similar orders on their own initiative, especially after the KYŌHŌ FAMINE of the 1730s. It is estimated that by 1843 rice reserves totaled 880,000 *koku* (1 *koku* = about 180 liters or 5 US bushels; see KOKUDAKA) in domainal warehouses, 550,000 *koku* in shogunate granaries, and 230,000 *koku* in the city of Edo (now Tōkyō).

Kakuban (1095–1143)

Buddhist priest of the SHINGON SECT. Regarded as the founder of the Shingi ("new interpretation") branch of Shingon. Born in Fujitsu in Hizen Province (now part of Saga Prefecture), Kakuban entered monastic life as a child and in 1108 became a monk at the temple NINNAJI in Kyōto. In 1121 he was ordained a Shingon master (*ajari*; Skt: *ācārya*) there, receiving the *dembō kanjō* or *kanjō* (Skt: *abhiseka*: an initiation ceremony for transmitting truth *[dharma]*) from the eminent master Kanjo (1057–1125) of the Hirosawaryū school. Kakuban also received the *dembō kanjō* from several other schools within the Shingon tradition, which varied chiefly concerning ritual observance. He also practiced asceticism at the Shingon establishment on Mt. Kōya (KŌYASAN) and elsewhere.

Kakuban aspired to a spiritual revival of the teachings of KŪKAI, the founder of the Shingon tradition, and succeeded in obtaining the patronage of the retired sovereign TOBA and establishing in 1132 the Dai Dembōin hall on Mt. Kōya, where Kūkai had spent his last years. Furthermore, in 1134 he was put in charge of KONGŌBUJI, the main temple of the monastery complex on Mt. Kōya. His reform movement, however, met stiff resistance from the clerical establishment at Kongōbuji and TŌJI in Kyōto, the latter then being the central temple of the Shingon sect. Kakuban resigned from the post in 1135 and went into a long seclusion. As the antagonism between Kakuban's followers and the conservative faction grew, Kakuban and his disciples finally left Mt. Kōya in 1139 and settled at the temple Emmyōji at Negoro (in what is now Wakayama Prefecture), about 25 km (15.5 mi) northwest of Mt. Kōya, where he ended his rather short life.

Kakuban integrated Pure Land worship, which was then gaining popularity even among Shingon Buddhists, into Shingon teachings, holding that each person, upon realizing oneness with Mahāvairocana (DAINICHI) Buddha in his own life, can embody the Pure Land. He was above all concerned, however, for a spiritual reinvigoration of the Shingon tradition. (The posthumous title of Kōgyō Daishi was given him by Emperor Higashiyama in 1690.)

The Dai Dembōin was eventually moved to Negoro by Raiyu (1226–1304), whose school, with a different theological perspective concerning the nature of Mahāvairocana, came to be known as the Shingi branch. The school held Kakuban as its founder. The Dai Dembōin (now known as Negoroji) prospered greatly during the Muromachi period (1333–1568) but was reduced to ashes by the warlord TOYOTOMI HIDEYOSHI in 1585. For the two main divisions within the Shingi branch, see HASEDERA and CHISHAKUIN.

◼︎——*Kōgyō Daishi denki shiryō zenshū*, 3 vols (1942). Kushida Ryōkō, *Kakuban no kenkyū* (1975). Tomita Gakujun, ed, *Kōgyō Daishi zenshū* (1935). TSUCHIDA Tomoaki

kakubei-jishi

A dance common in the Edo period (1600–1868); performed by one or several young boys who wore lion (*shishi*) headdresses, and high GETA (clogs). Beating on small drums, they went through a routine of acrobatic stunts to the accompaniment of flute and drum. The dance is also known as *echigo-jishi* from its place of origin in Kambara, Echigo Province (now Niigata Prefecture); *kakubei* has been variously explained as the name of the originator or a corruption of Kambara. It influenced the music and dance of the time, some of its features being incorporated into the *kabuki* dance repertory. See also SHISHI-MAI; KADOZUKE. MISUMI Haruo

Kakuda

City in southern Miyagi Prefecture, northern Honshū, on the river Abukumagawa. Kakuda developed as a castle town and collection point for rice and silk cocoons transported on the Abukumagawa. Kakuda's mainstay is agriculture, centering on dairy farming, rice, vegetables, tobacco, and mulberry trees. Factory construction has also increased in recent years. Pop: 33,733.

Kakuijima

Island in the eastern Inland Sea, off southeastern Okayama Prefecture; largest of the Hinasa Islands. This mountainous island was used as a hunting ground for the lords of the domain of Okayama, and wild deer roam the island even today. Chief activities today are the cultivation of mandarin oranges and fish. Area: 10.3 sq km (3.98 sq mi).

kakun

(household precepts). Instructions composed by the head of a household for members of his family or group; an exposition of the values and modes of action that the author considers requisite to the success of the person or persons addressed and the prosperity of his house. Documents classifiable in this broad category have a long history in premodern Japan, one that extends from the "Assorted Private Teachings" (Shikyō Ruijū) of the 8th-century *udaijin* (minister of the right) KIBI NO MAKIBI and the "Admonitions" (Kujō Ujō-

Kakubei-jishi

A *kakubei-jishi* troupe in the village of Tsukigata in the Nishi Kambara district of Niigata Prefecture. The swastika is a common Buddhist symbol.

shō Ikai) of the 10th-century *udaijin* Fujiwara no Morosuke (908–960) to a multitude of prescriptions of conduct for *samurai*, townsman, and farmer households of the Edo period (1600–1868). Regulations issued for religious institutions are also sometimes called *kakun*, as in the case of Rinsen Kakun, compiled in 1339 for the monastic community of the Rinsenji, a Zen temple in Kyōto, by its founding abbot, MUSŌ SOSEKI. *Kakun* are closely related to the hortatory type of another broad category, OKIBUMI, testamentary documents that are similarly concerned with the perpetuation of a family's or religious institution's interests; *okibumi* tend to be less elaborate statements than *kakun*, but a precise distinction between the two documentary forms cannot be drawn in all cases.

Kakun of the Kamakura period (1185–1333) and Muromachi period (1333–1568) are excellent illustrations of the ethical and political attitudes of the dominant samurai class. The earliest extant examples are Rokuhara Dono Gokakun (ca 1247) by the important official of the Kamakura shogunate Hōjō Shigetoki (1198–1261; shogunal deputy in Rokuhara, 1230–47) and Gokurakuji Dono Goshōsoku, likewise attributed to him. The former document instructs the author's young son Nagatoki (1229–64) on how to conduct himself in society (many of the 43 articles deal with etiquette); it urges him to be circumspect, to handle subordinates prudently, and to take heed of his reputation among outsiders. The latter, in 99 articles, is more general in tone and has a pronounced Pure Land Buddhist coloration; it stresses the virtues of uprightness (*shōjiki*) and piety and maintains that a man should by his twenties "become accomplished in the arts," from his thirties into his fifties "perfect his moral being" and "devote himself to government," and from the age of sixty "abandon all else but earnest prayers for the afterlife and do the NEMBUTSU." Another early medieval example is the fragment of a *kakun* written in about 1275 by Shigetoki's nephew Hōjō Sanetoki (1224–76), founder of the great library KANAZAWA BUNKO, for the guidance of his son Sanemasa (1248–1302); it is noteworthy for its dyspeptic analysis of conditions in a household where "subordinates slight the superior," its caution against employing "frauds, fops, and flatterers," and its legalist dictum, "Government is nothing other than being firm and clear in dispensing rewards and punishments."

Representative *kakun* of a later period are Asakura Takakage Jōjō (see ASAKURA TOSHIKAGE, 17-ARTICLE CODE OF), attributed to Asakura Takakage (1428–81), the *daimyō* of Echizen (now part of Fukui Prefecture); SŌUNJI DONO NIJŪIKKAJŌ, attributed to HŌJŌ SŌUN, the founder of the Later Hōjō family (see HŌJŌ FAMILY) of Odawara; and a number of letters written by MŌRI MOTONARI (1497–1571), the conqueror of a vast domain in western Honshū, for the edification of his sons Mōri Takamoto (1523–63), Kikkawa Motoharu (1530–86), and Kobayakawa Takakage (1533–97). Motonari repeatedly tells the three to stick together in order to preserve the Mōri house and name inviolate into future generations; he reflects on the history of the house and discourses on policy matters; in a letter to Takamoto composed some time after his conquest of Suō and Nagato provinces (now Yamaguchi Prefecture) in 1557, he discusses the difficulties of ruling the newly acquired domain in the face of hostility from provincial barons (KOKUJIN) and disaffection among the vassals of an extended houseband, lamenting that the threat of enemies on all sides has forced him to postpone promulgating the "requisite firm laws and regulations" (ariyō no hatto, seitō).

Motonari's recognition that laws are the requisite means for the control of a daimyō domain sheds light on the relationship between kakun and kahō (house laws; more specifically, Sengoku kahō, house laws of the Sengoku period, 1467–1568), a term synonymous with BUNKOKUHŌ (domainal law codes). Kakun are expressions of the "house" as a private entity, whereas kahō or bunkokuhō are representations of the "house" as a public, legal person. Although some kakun, most notably Asakura Takakage Jōjō, contain distinct regulatory elements and therein resemble kahō, and bunkokuhō contain hortatory elements and digressions on ethics, therein resembling kakun, a distinction between these two documentary forms is not difficult. Household precepts in essence offer advice, setting down ideal rules to guide the behavior of a person or a group. In contrast, kahō or bunkokuhō are meant to be binding regulations, legal instruments to be applied in the governance of a domain.

📖——Kakehi Yasuhiko, Chūsei buke kakun no kenkyū (1967). Ishii Susumu, Ishimoda Tadashi, et al, ed, Chūsei seiji shakai shisō: I, in Nihon shisō taikei, vol 21 (Iwanami Shoten, 1972). Carl T. Steenstrup, Hōjō Shigetoki (1198–1261) and his Role in the History of Political and Ethical Ideals in Japan (1979).   George ELISON

Kakunodate

Town in eastern Akita Prefecture, northern Honshū. A castle town during the Edo period (1600–1868), Kakunodate retains several samurai residences. It is now the commercial and cultural center of the area and known especially for its articles—boxes, tea cannisters and the like—made from wild cherry bark. Pop: 16,906.

Kakure Kirishitan

(Hidden or Clandestine Christians). Christian believers of the Edo period (1600–1868) who survived the Christian prohibition edicts of the Tokugawa shogunate after 1614 and whose descendants escaped detection during succeeding waves of persecution (see PERSECUTIONS AT URAKAMI). Another term, Hanare Kirishitan (Separated Christians), though associated with Kakure Kirishitan, refers specifically to the descendants of old Christians whose faith survived the NATIONAL SECLUSION period but who refused reconciliation with the Roman Catholic Church after the abolition of Christian prohibition laws in the mid-19th century. Pockets of Hanare Kirishitan still exist in Japan.

The Kakure Kirishitan phenomenon is closely related to the implementation of the Tokugawa government's seclusion policy by which all threats to the unity of the nation and the primacy of the Tokugawa house were to be eliminated. In 1614 there were at most 300,000 baptized members of the Catholic church as founded by Portuguese missionaries after the visit of the Jesuit priest Francis XAVIER to Japan in 1549. The expulsion of the Catholic clergy which was decreed in 1614, and the general persecution of Christianity which followed, were designed to eliminate the foreign faith from Japan. The response of some of the faithful to persecution was to declare their faith and embrace martyrdom. As official policy increased in severity, however, most Christians concealed their belief and went underground. They devised ways for preserving and continuing their faith and produced a peculiarly indigenous religion of great strength. In certain notable cases, groups of Christians chose total community emigration to remote areas in the islands and coastal regions of western Kyūshū, where it was relatively easier to remain hidden from surveillance.

The shogunal Inquisition Office (Kirishitan Shūmon Aratame Yaku; see SHŪMON ARATAME), established in 1640, aimed at total extermination of Christians. The practice of efumi (trampling on holy pictures; see FUMIE), instituted in 1629 as a means of identifying believers, was well established by 1640 especially in areas of known concentrations of Christians. Small groups of priests secretly entered the country after 1636, but they were quickly detected and eliminated. The final blow came with the establishment in 1687 of Christian family investigation (Kirishitan ruizoku aratame), which introduced surveillance of descendants of detected Christians to the fifth or sixth generation in the case of males (depending on whether the line of descent was through a child of the original Christian born before his denial of the faith or after). From the standpoint of the Roman Catholic hierarchy the Church in Japan ceased to exist with the death or official banishment of the remaining priests. Thus from 1637, in matters of faith and practice, Christian communities were wholly dependent on lay leadership. Between 1640 and 1670 there

were fewer martyrdoms but increasing numbers of Christians in hiding. Christians, deprived of priestly ministry, nevertheless succeeded in establishing a faith and liturgy which functioned without the traditional institutions of the Catholic church.

When Japan was opened to international communication in the mid-19th century, the extent to which the Kakure Kirishitan had survived their 250 years of isolation became apparent. More than 30,000 believers in the old faith (mukashi Kirishitan) from the Amakusa Islands (now part of Kumamoto Prefecture), the island of Hirado (now part of Nagasaki Prefecture), and Hizen (now Saga and Nagasaki prefectures) either presented themselves in such newly established Catholic centers as Ōura Cathedral (1864) at Nagasaki or, choosing to remain separate, were identified in surrounding districts. Many maintained this separateness even after prohibition edicts were abolished in 1873.

Hidden Christians conformed with Tokugawa shogunate requirements in all outward behavior. They registered with family Buddhist temples (dannadera; see DANKA), received temple certificates of Buddhist conversion (kishōmon), made written assurances (kishōmon), and paid their dues. They permitted Buddhist priests to conduct funeral services, though frequently chanting Christian prayers simultaneously and in secret as a countermeasure, a rite known as modoshi, or service of undoing. They participated in the annual efumi, believing that the Act of Contrition performed afterward absolved them from sin.

The necessity for camouflaging Christianity to conform with acceptable Buddhist and Shintō customs led to the development of a particular structure for the preservation of doctrine and the continuation of practice. For mutual protection the Kakure Kirishitan gathered into communal or subcommunal units (mon), developed from the Portuguese confraternities and Tokugawa GONINGUMI (literally, "five-man groups," a system of joint responsibility shared by five household groups). In certain areas, such as the island of Ikitsuki, near Hirado, they divided further into smaller groups called gossha or kakiuchi ("within the walls").

The leader of each neighborhood group was called chōkata (elder), an office customarily handed down from father to son; women were excluded from holding any office. The chōkata kept records and was responsible for proper recognition of the church calendar, liturgical acts, and transmission of prayers and teachings to smaller groups and to posterity. The leaders of the smaller groups, the mizukata (baptizer), were appointed for 10 years. Their responsibility involved the administration of baptism, the only sacrament of the church administered by laymen. Marriage was not celebrated as a sacrament and though monogamy was encouraged, divorce and close intermarriage were not uncommon. The most sacred obligation of the mizukata after his baptismal duties was the verbal transmission to his successor of the precise form of the baptismal rite in Latin, a duty faithfully performed with remarkable accuracy throughout the seclusion period.

At the village level a kikikata (hearer) transmitted the faith to smaller family groups, while the oshiekata (teacher or catechist) held high prestige. It was he who was responsible for the orashio or orashū (prayer; from the Latin oratio), the focal point of the devotional life of the Christian community.

In the absence of any priest or printed manuscript, such as those put out in the 16th century by the JESUIT MISSION PRESS at Nagasaki, the entire body of doctrine and liturgy was passed on by word of mouth. However, transcriptions of acts of devotion, summaries of the faith, and sections of the liturgy including the Apostles Creed were confiscated in 1822 at Urakami in Kyūshū. These were clearly recorded from the oral tradition interpreted by the oshiekata. Humble people, often themselves illiterate, thus maintained a reasonably accurate knowledge of the faith, reciting the Ave Maria, Salve Regina, and Pater Noster with little variation throughout a wide geographical area. In districts protected by distance from gross interference by officialdom, such as Ikitsuki Island and the Gotō Archipelago, it was possible to recite devotions more openly. The chanted prayers and divine law of the orashio—sometimes melodies corresponding closely to the original Gregorian chants—and liturgies of Dochirina kirishitan (Doctrina Christian; Nagasaki edition, 1600) were sung. This musical tradition and such artistic devices as the hidden altar, concealed crosses, and the Maria Kannon, a statue of the Buddhist goddess of mercy depicted as a mother with child in arms, nurtured and perpetuated a faith sufficiently strong to survive two centuries of prohibition.

📖——Anesaki Masaharu, Kirishitan shūmon no hakugai to sempuku (1925). Richard H. Drummond, A History of Christianity in

Japan (1971). Ebisawa Arimichi, *Kirishitan no kenkyū* (1942). Kataoka Yakichi, *Kakure Kirishitan* (1967). Minagawa Tatsuo, *Oratio Christianorum Occultorum in Insula Ikitsuki* (1976).

Maida S. COALDRAKE

Kakushin Kurabu

(Reform Club). A small political party formed in November 1922 by former members of the RIKKEN KOKUMINTŌ, who were joined by independents and disaffected members of the KENSEIKAI. Headed by INUKAI TSUYOSHI, its 45 members included OZAKI YUKIO and SHIMADA SABURŌ. The Kakushin Kurabu represented the most liberal wing of the Diet at a time when the dominant RIKKEN SEIYŪKAI party was at the height of its power. Its goals were to achieve universal suffrage, to reduce the size of the military, and to abolish the system that allowed only generals and admirals on active duty to head the war ministries (GUMBU DAIJIN GEN'EKI BUKAN SEI). Like the Seiyūkai and the other major party, the Kenseikai, the Kakushin Kurabu drew its main support from the urban middle class and prosperous farmers. In 1924 it joined with the Seiyūkai and the Kenseikai in forming the second MOVEMENT TO PROTECT CONSTITUTIONAL GOVERNMENT and ousted the cabinet of KIYOURA KEIGO. Inukai subsequently served as minister of communications in the coalition cabinet of KATŌ TAKAAKI, who succeeded Kiyoura. Members of the club became divided over the passage of the repressive PEACE PRESERVATION LAW OF 1925, and lacking a firm financial base, the club dissolved in 1925, when most of the members, led by Inukai, joined the Seiyūkai.

Kakuyū → Toba Sōjō

Kakuzenshō

A collection of studies and documents on esoteric Buddhist rituals and iconography compiled by the SHINGON SECT monk Kakuzen from approximately 1176 to 1217. In addition to ritual and historical documents of the Shingon sect, this collection's 128 volumes include line drawings and writings on Buddhist iconography, which Kakuzen collected from his direct study of temple images and conversations with senior monks.

kama

(sickle). The sickle is known to be one of the oldest harvesting tools and has been used in many parts of the world since ancient times. In Japan, the use of the sickle first began in the Yayoi period (ca 300 BC–ca AD 300) and became widespread by the latter part of the Kofun period (ca 300–710). Over the centuries it became an indispensable harvesting tool and is still used by Japanese farmers today. The basic Japanese sickle has a crescent-shaped blade attached to a short wooden handle, but there is considerable variation depending on the locale. A straight wide blade is common in the Kantō (eastern Honshū) region around Tōkyō, while in the Kansai (Kyōto–Ōsaka) region the blade is considerably thinner and crescent-shaped. Regardless of region, the Japanese sickle is distinguished by the positioning of the blade, which is attached at nearly a right angle to the handle. In addition to its agricultural uses, it also often serves as an offering to the deities in local harvest festivals.

NOGUCHI Takenori

Kamada Ryūō (1754–1821)

SHINGAKU scholar of the latter part of the Edo period (1600–1868). Born in Kii Province (now Wakayama Prefecture). He was adopted by his uncle Kamata Issō, who had studied with TESHIMA TOAN, a disciple of ISHIDA BAIGAN, the founder of Shingaku. Kamada also studied with Teshima and traveled throughout the Kyōto–Ōsaka region spreading the teachings of Shingaku. As a Shingaku scholar, he was exceptional in that he tried to invigorate that school of thought with his knowledge and understanding of Western science (particularly astronomy and medicine) and of Buddhism.

kamado

Traditional Japanese stove; an earthen, stone, brick, or cement oven-like structure designed with a hollow center in which fuel is burned to provide heat and with openings on the top surface for holding

Kamakura——Tsurugaoka Hachiman Shrine

Established in 1063 as an extension of the nearby Iwashimizu Hachiman Shrine, the Tsurugaoka Shrine was moved to its present site in 1191 as the tutelary shrine of the Minamoto family. Shown are the Maidono (Dance Pavilion) and, behind it, the main building of the shrine.

pots and kettles *(kama)*. Also known as *hettsui* or *kudo* in some locales.

Kamado are known to have been in use in Japan from the Kofun period (ca 300–710). There are two types: movable and fixed (the latter usually being built into the earthen floor of the kitchen area). Since the *kamado* is the source of fire for cooking and heating in the home, an altar dedicated to the *kamadogami* (literally, "oven deity") is often installed nearby (see also SHINTŌ FAMILY ALTARS). This deity is regarded both as the god of fire and of the home, and in western Japan is called Kōjinsama (see KŌJIN). Like the hearth in the West, the *kamado* has been looked upon as the symbolic center of the home in Japan; in the past, when a branch house of a family was established (for example by marriage), fire from the *kamado* of the main house was used to light the fire in the new house. The word *kamado* is also used synonymously with wealth in several Japanese idiomatic expressions.

MIYAMOTO Mizuo

Kamagaya

City in northwestern Chiba Prefecture, central Honshū. Formerly a farming area, it is now a suburb of Tōkyō, with a flourishing machinery industry. Pear-picking in nearby orchards is a popular tourist attraction. Pop: 76,157.

Kamaishi

City in southeastern Iwate Prefecture, northern Honshū, on Kamaishi Bay. An important steel producing center since 1858 when the metallurgist ŌSHIMA TAKATŌ constructed Japan's first Western-style blast furnace. It has Japan's largest iron ore deposits, discovered in 1727; magnetite, pyrite, and copper are also mined. Its port is used by deep-sea fishing boats. Pop: 65,250.

Kamakura

City in southeastern Kanagawa Prefecture, central Honshū, 45 km (28 mi) southwest of Tōkyō. Overlooking Sagami Bay and favored with a mild climate, Kamakura is an exclusive residential area for commuters to Tōkyō. Its historical importance dates to the 12th century, when MINAMOTO NO YORITOMO chose it as the seat of the Kamakura shogunate, Japan's first military government. Kamakura remained the political center of the country until the shogunate was destroyed in 1333. Among its many historical sites are the TSURU-GAOKA HACHIMAN SHRINE, built by Yoritomo; the Zen Buddhist temples KENCHŌJI, ENGAKUJI, Jōchiji, Jufukuji, and Jōmyōji, collectively known as the Kamakura GOZAN; Myōhonji of the Nichiren sect; Kōmyōji of the Jōdo sect; and TŌKEIJI. Famous Buddhist images include the bodhisattva Kannon at the temple Hasedera and the DAIBUTSU (great Buddha; 11.5 m or 37.7 ft) at Kōtokuin, the second largest among such statues in Japan. The Prefectural Art Museum and the City Museum of Kamakura are located in the precincts of the Tsurugaoka Hachiman Shrine. Pop: 172,612.

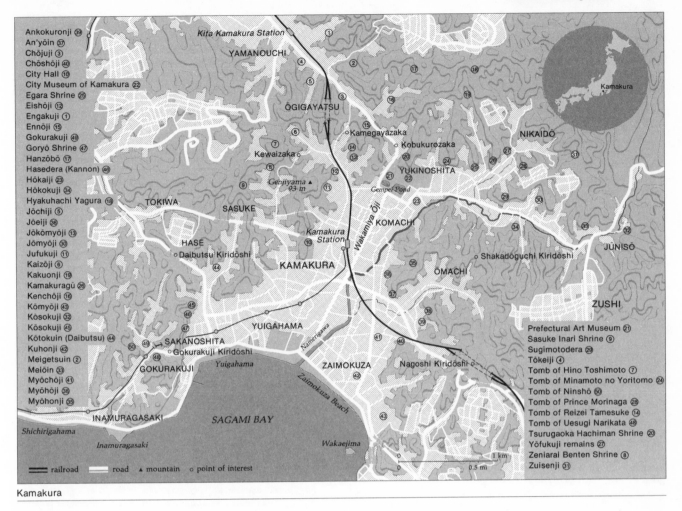

Ankokuronji ㊟	Prefectural Art Museum ㉑
An'yōin ㊲	Sasuke Inari Shrine ⑨
Chōjuji ③	Sugimotodera ㉙
Chōshōji ㊵	Tōkeiji ④
City Hall ⑩	Tomb of Hino Toshimoto ⑦
City Museum of Kamakura ㉒	Tomb of Minamoto no Yoritomo ㉔
Egara Shrine ㉕	Tomb of Ninshō ㊿
Eishōji ⑫	Tomb of Prince Morinaga ㉘
Engakuji ①	Tomb of Reizei Tamesuke ⑭
Ennōji ⑮	Tomb of Uesugi Narikata ㊽
Gokurakuji ㊾	Tsurugaoka Hachiman Shrine ⑳
Goryō Shrine ㊼	Yōfukuji remains ㉗
Hanzōbō ⑰	Zeniarai Benten Shrine ⑧
Hasedera (Kannon) ㊻	Zuisenji ㉛

Kamakura

Kamakura bakufu → Kamakura shogunate

kamakura-bori

(Kamakura carving). A lacquer technique in which lacquer is applied to a carved wooden base. The term is derived from the town of Kamakura in Sagami Province (now Kanagawa Prefecture), the most important place of its manufacture. The distinctive feature of *kamakura-bori* is the carved wooden base. *Kamakura-bori* should be distinguished from the technique of carving the lacquer itself, which it was initially intended to resemble. In time, *kamakura-bori* became an important lacquer technique in its own right, particularly during the 19th and 20th centuries. Examples of *kamakura-bori* are usually executed in red or, more rarely, in black lacquer, with traditional floral and geometric designs. According to tradition, the 13th-century artist Kōun was the first to use this technique, utilizing Chinese models. Although *kamakura-bori* is thought to have originated during the latter part of the Kamakura period (1185–1333), there are few surviving pieces that predate the 16th century. Julia HUTT

Kamakura Gozan → Gozan

Kamakura history → history of Japan

Kamakura ōzōshi

Military chronicle in three volumes, believed to have been written late in the Muromachi period (1333–1568), although its authorship and exact date are unknown. It describes political events in the Kantō region between 1379 and 1479, focusing on the office of the Kamakura KUBŌ, the governor-general of the Kantō, and the KANTŌ KANREI, his principal assistant. Since it continues the account of the TAIHEIKI, the famous chronicle covering the period of 1318–67, and corrects errors found in the earlier work, it is sometimes called the *Taihei kōki* (Postscript to the *Taiheiki*).

Kamakura period

Historical period (1185–1333) roughly corresponding to the lifespan of the KAMAKURA SHOGUNATE (1192–1333); named after Kamakura, where the government was located. Historians agree on 1333, the year the shogunate was destroyed, as the end of the period, but alternative dates have been proposed to mark the beginning (this encyclopedia has adopted 1185). The imperial court gave official recognition to the de facto military rule of MINAMOTO YORITOMO in 1192 by conferring on him the title SHŌGUN; but it was in 1180 that Yoritomo established his base in Kamakura, and in 1185 that the Minamoto conclusively defeated the rival TAIRA FAMILY at the Battle of DANNOURA. It was also in 1185 that Yoritomo was given imperial permission to appoint SHUGO (constables or military governors) and JITŌ (land stewards), offices that were to be the distinguishing features of shogunate government. The years 1185 to 1568, encompassing both the Kamakura and Muromachi periods, are often characterized as medieval or early feudal. See HISTORY OF JAPAN: Kamakura history.

Kamakura shogunate

(Kamakura *bakufu*). Japan's first military or warrior government; established by MINAMOTO NO YORITOMO in Kamakura. Although many scholars (and this encyclopedia) date the beginning of the shogunate from 1192, when Yoritomo was given the title of SHŌGUN, the bakufu itself, the warrior governmental organization, had been set up in 1180, and the system of appointed governors (shugo) and stewards (jitō) by which it controlled the country began in 1185. It can thus be said to have ruled for almost 150 years from the early 1180s to its overthrow in 1333. The Kamakura shogunate's main area of control was the eastern provinces, far removed from the imperial capital of Kyōto. Its support came from warrior bands which had previously been under the control of either the imperial court or the proprietors of various SHŌEN (landed estates). Its appearance marked a major turning point in Japanese history, representing the first in a series of military governments that ruled Japan until the collapse of the TOKUGAWA SHOGUNATE and the restoration of direct imperial rule in 1868.

The Establishment of the Shogunate——In 1180 Minamoto no Yoritomo raised forces in Izu Province (now part of Shizuoka Prefecture) in rebellion against the TAIRA FAMILY, which had gained control of political affairs in Kyōto. He succeeded in organizing vast numbers of warriors and having them pledge fidelity to him as GO-KENIN (housemen).

After defeating a large Taira force at the Battle of FUJIGAWA that year, Yoritomo established a bakufu (literally "tent government") and consolidated his control over the eastern provinces. By the end of 1183 Yoritomo's generals had expelled the Taira from Kyōto, and his de facto control of these eastern provinces was recognized by the imperial court. In 1185 he sought and received from the court the right to appoint SHUGO (military governors) in each province and JITŌ (land stewards) in the *shōen* throughout the country. This meant that Yoritomo now had control of both military and police powers, and it is from 1185 that the Kamakura period is usually dated. In 1192 Yoritomo was given the title of *seii tai shōgun* ("barbarian-subduing generalissimo"; usually abbreviated as shōgun), which from that time became the standard appellation of the head of the military government.

The Character of the Shogunate——The two supporting pillars of the shogunate were the lord-vassal relationship between Yoritomo and his *gokenin* and the system of regional control provided by the network of *shugo* and *jitō*. After his right to nominate the *jitō* had been officially recognized by the imperial court, Yoritomo used these *jitō* appointments as the means of rewarding his vassals with land. This system, based on the combination of the lord-vassal relationship and the bestowal of land, has been described by many historians as feudal *(hōkenteki)*.

Two facts must be noted, however. First, the right of *jitō* appointment did not initially extend to all estates throughout the country but was restricted to the eastern provinces, the former territory of the Taira family, and to territory confiscated from those who had rebelled against Yoritomo. This fact was also reflected in the power relationship between the shogunate and the imperial court and between the shogunate and the nobility and temples which owned the great estates. Particularly in this early period, the power of the shogunate was far from being strong and nationwide. The right to appoint *jitō* in the Kinai, or capital area, and western provinces did not come until the triumph of the shogunate over the imperial court in the JŌKYŪ DISTURBANCE of 1221. Second, the bestowal of land took the form of appointment to the post of *jitō*, or more precisely, the bestowal of *shiki* (land rights), which consisted of both the official position which had been established under the *shōen* system and the revenues which went along with it. This granting of land rights thus differed distinctly from the *daimyō* system of later times, under which land was directly bestowed. In this respect one may say that the Kamakura shogunate was based on a compromise division of power with the aristocratic proprietors of the *shōen*.

The Development of the Shogunate——Because of the central role that Yoritomo played in the establishment of the shogunate, the shogunate in its early period was necessarily a one-man rule. He did set up the SAMURAI-DOKORO, the MANDOKORO, and the MONCHŪJO to handle, respectively, the control of the *gokenin*, general and financial affairs, and legal matters. After Yoritomo's death in 1199, his successor MINAMOTO NO YORIIE, and MINAMOTO NO SANETOMO, Yoriie's successor, were both young and lacking in leadership, and their mother Masako (HŌJŌ MASAKO) took on the role of guardian. Through her, the HŌJŌ FAMILY, of which she was originally a member, took control of the shogunate as SHIKKEN (shogunal regent) and the Hōjō regency was established.

When the Jōkyū Disturbance, in which the retired emperor Go-Toba attempted to recover political power from the shogunate, ended in defeat, the preeminence of the shogunate in governmental matters was firmly established. The shogunate formulated the legal precedents of the military government in the GOSEIBAI SHIKIMOKU, and strengthened its institutional structure by setting up the Council of State (HYŌJŌSHŪ), a supreme governing body made up of 11 *gokenin* (there were later around 15 members). Under the Hyōjōshū was the *hikitsukeshū* (see HIKITSUKE), a group of coadjutors to deal with land claims.

In the late 13th century, at around the time of the MONGOL INVASIONS OF JAPAN, unmistakable signs of change appeared in the politics of the regency. The council system gradually declined, the vast majority of the *gokenin* were deprived of political influence, and the direct descendants of the main branch of the Hōjō family,

Kamakura shogunate——Table 1

The Kamakura Shōguns	
Shōgun	Term of office
1. Minamoto no Yoritomo (1147–1199)	1192–1199
2. Minamoto no Yoriie (1182–1204)	1202–1203
3. Minamoto no Sanetomo (1192–1219)	1203–1219
4. Kujō Yoritsune (1218–1256)	1226–1244
5. Kujō Yoritsugu (1239–1256)	1244–1252
6. Prince Munetaka (1242–1274)	1252–1266
7. Prince Koreyasu (1264–1326)	1266–1289
8. Prince Hisaaki (1276–1328)	1289–1308
9. Prince Morikuni (1301–1333)	1308–1333

NOTE: The Minamoto line ceased to exist in 1219; thereafter, there was no succession. Hōjō regents selected tractable members of court families and brought them to Kamakura to be installed as shōguns.

Kamakura shogunate——Table 2

Shikken of the Kamakura Shogunate	
Shikken (shogunal regent)	Term of office
1. Hōjō Tokimasa (1138–1215)	1203–1205
2. Hōjō Yoshitoki (1163–1224)	1205–1224
3. Hōjō Yasutoki (1183–1242)	1224–1242
4. Hōjō Tsunetoki (1224–1246)	1242–1246
5. Hōjō Tokiyori (1227–1263)	1246–1256
6. Hōjō Nagatoki (1229–1264)	1256–1264
7. Hōjō Masamura (1205–1273)	1264–1268
8. Hōjō Tokimune (1251–1284)	1268–1284
9. Hōjō Sadatoki (1271–1311)	1284–1301
10. Hōjō Morotoki (1275–1311)	1301–1311
11. Hōjō Munenobu (1259–1312)	1311–1312
12. Hōjō Hirotoki (1279–1315)	1312–1315
13. Hōjō Mototoki (d 1333)	1315
14. Hōjō Takatoki (1303–1333)	1316–1326
15. Hōjō Sadaaki (1278–1333)	1326
16. Hōjō Moritoki (d 1333)	1327–1333

known as the *tokusō*, and the private family council, the YORIAI, came to monopolize power.

At around this time, an exchange economy emerged, based on the increase of surplus produce made available by the shift to intensive farming. The status of the subordinate lower peasantry rose, and such professions as those of the TOIMARU, who acted as go-betweens in transportation and consignment sales, and the *kashiage*, who handled loans and the exchange of currency, enjoyed increasing prosperity. In contrast, there were increasing numbers of *gokenin* who, unable to adapt themselves to the changing times, lost their property and faced destitution. The Mongol invasions had required great personal sacrifices, but because it was a war of defense there was no confiscated territory to distribute to retainers as rewards. Dissatisfaction with the Hōjō grew, and in 1333 the Kamakura shogunate was overthrown by Emperor Go-Daigo (see KEMMU RESTORATION). See also HISTORY OF JAPAN: Kamakura history.

Ishii Susumu

Kamanashigawa

River in western Yamanashi Prefecture, central Honshū, originating in the northern Akaishi Mountains and flowing in a southerly direction. It joins the FUEFUKIGAWA in the Kōfu Basin to form the FUJI-

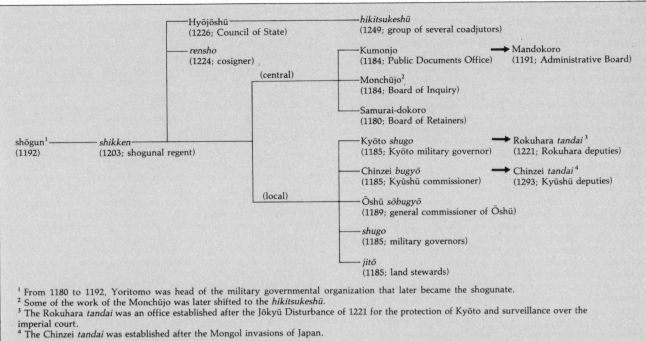

Organization chart (Kamakura shogunate):

shōgun[1] (1192) ——— shikken (1203; shogunal regent)

- Hyōjōshū (1226; Council of State)
  - hikitsukeshū (1249; group of several coadjutors)
- rensho (1224; cosigner)

(central)
- Kumonjo (1184; Public Documents Office) ——➤ Mandokoro (1191; Administrative Board)
- Monchūjo[2] (1184; Board of Inquiry)
- Samurai-dokoro (1180; Board of Retainers)

(local)
- Kyōto shugo (1185; Kyōto military governor) ——➤ Rokuhara tandai[3] (1221; Rokuhara deputies)
- Chinzei bugyō (1185; Kyūshū commissioner) ——➤ Chinzei tandai[4] (1293; Kyūshū deputies)
- Ōshū sōbugyō (1189; general commissioner of Ōshū)
- shugo (1185; military governors)
- jitō (1185; land stewards)

[1] From 1180 to 1192, Yoritomo was head of the military governmental organization that later became the shogunate.
[2] Some of the work of the Monchūjo was later shifted to the hikitsukeshū.
[3] The Rokuhara tandai was an office established after the Jōkyū Disturbance of 1221 for the protection of Kyōto and surveillance over the imperial court.
[4] The Chinzei tandai was established after the Mongol invasions of Japan.
NOTE: Figures within parentheses indicate year of establishment.

Kamakura shogunate———Organization of the Kamakura shogunate

KAWA. It has been the site of frequent floods in the past. The water is used for irrigation. Length: 64 km (40 mi).

kamasu

A bag made by folding a length of hemp cloth or straw matting in half and sewing up the sides. Large ones were used for transporting and storing coal, fertilizer, grain, salt, and so forth. Small ones were used as tobacco pouches and purses. Making the bags was mainly a task of farming households during the agricultural off-season, but with the recent increased availability of paper bags, the use of *kamasu* has decreased dramatically.   MIYAMOTO Mizuo

Kamba Falls

(Kamba no Taki). Located in the town of Katsuyama, northern Okayama Prefecture, western Honshū. It is on a minor tributary of the river Asahigawa. The surrounding area is known for spring and autumn foliage and is inhabited by wild monkeys. Height: 140 m (459 ft); width: 27 m (89 ft).

Kambara Ariake (1876–1952)

Poet. Real name Kambara Hayao. Born in Tōkyō. He contributed much to the development of modern Japanese poetry and was a devotee of Dante Gabriel Rosetti. *Kusawakaba* (1902), his first collection of poetry, contains lyrical pieces, ballads, and sonnets. *Dokugen aika* (1903), another collection of his poems, also shows lyrical and sonnet influences. He studied symbolism through the works of Arthur Symons (translated into Japanese by UEDA BIN) and, along with SUSUKIDA KYŪKIN, became a leading figure in Japanese symbolist poetry in the 1890s. A collection of his symbolist poems, *Shunchōshū*, was published in 1905. He later published translations of European poets as well as works of literary criticism.

Kambayashi Akatsuki (1902–1980)

Author. Real name Tokuhiro Iwaki. Born in Kōchi Prefecture. Graduate of Tōkyō University. He started to write fiction while working as an editor of the magazine KAIZŌ and after publishing *Bara nusubito* (1932), a collection of short stories, he began to devote himself to writing full time. He is a typical autobiographical fiction writer, his works deriving from his personal life and family affairs. He is particularly known for his series of short stories dealing with his affection and care for his wife who died after a long mental illness. His works include "Anju no ie" (1938) and "Sei Yohane Byōin nite" (1946), both short stories.

kambun

Compositions in classical Chinese, comprising prose and poetry and including the products of foreign authors writing in Chinese, mainly Koreans and Japanese. *Kambun* specifically excludes vernacular Chinese, which was in any case seldom committed to writing until the present century. In Japan classical Chinese is normally read by a standard method of translation called *kundoku* (literally, "reading in translation"). This convention is so deeply rooted in the teaching of classical Chinese that most Japanese who study that language understand it in the *kundoku* version; hence, in its widest and popular acceptation, the term *kambun* embraces both the Chinese original and its *kundoku* rendering into Japanese. But the implication of *kambun* reaches further, for classical Chinese ranks with Japanese as a major literary and linguistic factor in the formation of traditional Japanese culture. Until late in the 19th century classical Chinese occupied a position in Japan analogous to that which Latin enjoyed to the end of the 17th century in Europe, as the written language of scholarship, high literature, and religion. Its study made up the core of higher education during the Edo period (1600–1868), and today *kambun* is still taught in high schools as part of the curriculum.

Origin of the Term——The two Chinese characters which the Japanese pronounce *kambun* (Ch: *hanwen*) signify literally "Han writing" or "Han literature," in reference to the literature of the Han dynasty, which ruled China from 206 BC to AD 220. This is the sense in which the term is used by the Chinese, who until recently have referred to their written language simply as *wen* (literally, "the writing"). After the fall of the Han, however, foreign conquerors of China habitually distinguished themselves from their subjects by using *han* as a descriptive prefix to designate things Chinese, after the title of the dynasty which had been the sole representative of China to the frontier peoples during the previous 400 years; hence *hanren* (*han-jen*; people of Han) for the Chinese people and *hanwen* (Han literature) for Chinese literature. This practice was continued by the two major conquering dynasties of later times, the Mongol Yuan (Yüan; 1279–1368) and the Manchu Qing (Ch'ing; 1644–1912). Thus the extension of the dynastic title Han to designate China as a whole is of foreign origin and not characteristic of the native population.

For their part, the Japanese followed native Chinese usage throughout most of the history of their experience with classical Chinese. *Bun*, the Japanese pronunciation of *wen*, by itself sufficed to denote classical Chinese; it was *the* written language, while written Japanese was distinguished from it derivatively by prefixing *wa* (Japan) or *koku* (native) to *bun*. It was only in the 1870s that *kambun* began to appear in book titles and school curricula and to supersede *bun* as the designation of classical Chinese. This may indicate in a small way Japan's growing consciousness of a larger world; for it was precisely at this time, in the first decade following the Meiji Restoration, that the Japanese had to take seriously the existence of Western languages and literatures and to view their own language as well as classical Chinese in comparison with them.

Method of Reading Kambun —— Although the *kundoku* method of reading *kambun* results in a translation, its purpose is not so much to convert Chinese into Japanese as to provide the Japanese reader with minimum clues through his own language sufficient to enable him to make a basic sense of the text. These clues are of two kinds: those which elucidate the grammar of the Chinese by means of Japanese particles and inflections, and those which show how to rearrange the Chinese word order to correspond to Japanese, which has a quite different word order. The former are supplied in Japanese syllabic signs (KANA) on the right side of the vertical column of Chinese words or graphs, and are called *okurigana* (literally, "dispatching *kana*") or *soegana* ("appended *kana*"). The latter appear on the left side of the column and are called *kaeriten* (transposition marks). These are five varieties of *kaeriten*. One of them consists of a simple checklike mark ∨ which can be placed between any two graphs to indicate that they are to be read in reverse order. This is the most frequently used mark. The other four varieties are four sequences of ordinal signs that are used to show in what order the Chinese words are to be read in the Japanese sentence in cases where it is necessary to move them two or more places. More than one sequence is needed because in more complex sentences there are sometimes grammatical sequences enclosed within other grammatical sequences. The four sequences of signs are 一 , 二 , 三 , etc (the numbers 1, 2, 3, etc); 上 , 中 , 下 (upper, middle, lower); 甲 , 乙 , 丙 , etc (a sequence corresponding to A, B, C, etc); and 天 , 地 , 人 (heaven, earth, man). The sequences are given here in order of priority of use. If only reversals of adjacent words are necessary, only the checklike mark is used; if to this is added the transposition of one sequence of words, the 1, 2, 3 symbols are used; if a second sequence—sandwiching this—must be transposed, the upper, middle, lower, sequence is superimposed; and so on. The members of each sequence are always placed in the Chinese sentence in reverse order and never out of order, though a higher sequence often encloses a lower one and is thus interrupted, as for example: *lower; 3, 2, 1; middle, upper.* The higher the sequence the more other sequences it can enclose; the standard pattern containing all the sequences appears as follows: *man C lower 3 2 1 middle upper B A earth heaven.* To convert a Chinese sentence marked in this manner into Japanese word order, the reader restores the members of the sequences to their proper order and arranges the sequences from lower to higher: *1, 2, 3; upper, middle, lower; A, B, C; heaven, earth, man.* At the same time he must make sure to preserve in the Japanese sentence the original order of any unmarked graphs that precede any member of a sequence; and if a member of a sequence consists of two characters with a check between them, he must invert them before reading them in sequence. Most Chinese sentences can be handled by checks alone or by the two lower sequences; sentences requiring the A, B, C sequence are infrequent, and those which require *heaven, earth, man* are extremely rare. This method represents the outcome of centuries of experimentation, which reached completion only shortly before 1600.

The style of Japanese generated in the manner described above is called *kundoku kambun* (literally, "translated Chinese"). It has two general peculiarities. One of these is that the language itself is CLASSICAL JAPANESE (i.e., the vocabulary, spelling, and morphology reflect the language of the aristocratic class of the 9th century). The other general characteristic is that, being a partial as well as a literal translation, it preserves a strong flavor of Chinese. It is replete with such Chinese rhetorical devices as the double negative and with many characteristically *kambun* words and phrases. Many of these found their way into the written classical Japanese language as a whole as part of the general influence of *kambun* on Japanese.

Cultural Influence of Kambun —— The influence of *kambun* on Japanese culture was effected both through its content and through its position in Japan as the representative of an advanced civilization. *Kambun* secular literature—in the form of classical, philosophical, ethical, and historical works as well as literary essays and poetry—enriched the intellectual and aesthetic life of a progressively widening circle of the population from the late 6th century until well into the 20th; and in the fields of ethics, history, essay writing, and poetry

Japanese authors have made no small contribution to this heritage. On the other hand, *kambun* religious literature, in the form of Buddhist scriptures and commentaries, remained a property of the monasteries and was popularized only partially and, it seems, superficially. Moreover, its influence diminished with the secularization of Japanese society which began in the 17th century. In effect, through its content, *kambun* kept Japan in unremitting intellectual contact with one of the world's great civilizations and continued to be influential precisely for that reason until new intellectual currents both in China and in the world at large reduced its status in the present century.

Further, the exalted position which *kambun* held in Japan as a written language until late in the 19th century had an enormous impact on the evolution of the Japanese language. The system for writing Japanese today, which calls for a varying proportion of Chinese loanwords and the native vocabulary to be represented by graphs, with the remainder including particles and inflections written in *kana,* is the outgrowth of a condition that set in as early as the 10th century; most authors were less than competent in Chinese and consequently tended to lapse into their native language while at the same time endeavoring to keep the manuscript looking like Chinese. The result was a hybrid written form of Japanese, in principle no different from *kundoku kambun,* which could stand for Chinese in learned writing. On the other hand, it cannot be denied that this effect of *kambun* in opening the resources of classical Chinese for the enrichment of the Japanese language has resulted in a literary medium of great expressive and stylistic versatility. See also POETRY AND PROSE IN CHINESE; CHINESE LITERATURE AND JAPANESE LITERATURE.

—— E. Sydney Crawcour, *An Introduction to Kambun* (1965). Roy Andrew Miller, *The Japanese Language* (1967). Yamagishi Tokuhei, ed, *Nihon kambungaku shi ronkō* (1974).

Robert L. Backus

Kambun Master (fl ca 1660–1673)

(Kambun Kyoshō). The name given to the anonymous mentor of the UKIYO-E pioneer Hishikawa MORONOBU. It was at one time assumed that all of the *ukiyo-e*-style book illustrations and prints done in Edo (now Tōkyō) during the second half of the 17th century were the work of Moronobu. Modern research, however, has established the identity of at least two other important *ukiyo-e* artists of that time, the Kambun Master and SUGIMURA JIHEI.

The Kambun Master, who left no signed works, receives his name from the Kambun era (1661–73) in which he flourished. He was the first artist of Edo *ukiyo-e* and Moronobu's mentor, though it is not known whether the latter ever studied under him directly. His work consists of at least 50 illustrated books and several dozen prints—many of these in the SHUNGA (erotica) genre, which constituted one of the main subjects of the limited editions in early *ukiyo-e* printing. While not the complete artist and teacher that Moronobu was, the Kambun Master did create that uniquely Edo style that formed the basis for Moronobu's consolidation of the nascent *ukiyo-e* school.

—— Richard Lane, *Shunga Books of the Ukiyo-e School: Series II and III—Moronobu and the Kambun Master* (1974, 1976). Richard Lane, *Images from the Floating World* (1978). *Richard Lane*

Kameda Bōsai (1752–1826)

Also known as Kameda Hōsai. Confucian philosopher, poet, calligrapher, and painter in the *nanga* or literati style (see BUNJINGA). Born in Kōzuke (now Gumma Prefecture). When Bōsai was a child, his family moved to Edo (now Tōkyō), where he studied Confucianism. His first teacher was Inoue Kinga (1732–84); he later studied with Inoue Randai (1705–61), a leader in the new eclectic Kogaku school of Confucianism of the late 18th century. Bōsai proved an excellent pupil and he soon opened a Confucian school of his own. He was forced to close his school, however, when Matsudaira Sadanobu, the leader of the KANSEI REFORMS, decreed that only the Zhu Xi (Chu Hsi) school of Confucianism should be considered orthodox.

Bōsai thereafter led a free and unfettered life in and around Edo, sometimes living with farmers, whom he helped in times of trouble and famine. In later years he devoted himself more and more to the arts, and his home became a gathering place for literati friends. Bōsai was especially famous for his calligraphy, which somewhat resembled that of his friend the monk RYŌKAN. He particularly excelled in cursive script, where he displayed a combination of fluency and tension with a strong sense of asymmetrical balance. He contributed inscriptions to many paintings, including those of his friends SAKAI HŌITSU of the Rimpa school and TANI BUNCHŌ of the *nanga* school. Bōsai's paintings, generally of landscapes, were published in wood-block form in *Kyōchūzan* (Mountains of the Spirit) and much admired for their delicate color and semiabstract composition.

Stephen ADDISS

Kamegaoka site

Archaeological site of the Final Jōmon period (ca 1000 BC–ca 300 BC); located in Kamegaoka, Kizukuri Chō, Aomori Prefecture, on a low hill and the surrounding lowlands. First discovered in 1623 and excavated many times since the 19th century, the site has yielded STONE TOOLS, JŌMON FIGURINES, beads, and the Final Jōmon Kamegaoka-type pottery, distinguished by its artistic cloud motifs, for which it serves as the type site. Unusual recoveries of BONE ARTICLES, wooden objects, and lacquer ware have also been made from the lowland peat stratum that is typical of many sites in northeastern Japan. See also JŌMON POTTERY; JŌMON CULTURE.

■——Shimizu Junzō, *Kamegaoka iseki* (1959). *ABE Gihei*

Kameido Incident

The murder of militant laborers in the working-class district of Kameido in Tōkyō on the night of 4 September 1923 by military police. Martial law had been declared in the wake of the catastrophic TŌKYŌ EARTHQUAKE on 1 September, and amidst rumors that Koreans and leftists were rioting, police arrested many innocent Koreans, socialists, and labor union members. At the police station in Kameido, an area with a particularly active labor movement, over 700 were detained. On the night of 4 September, 10 labor union members and four other men who were part of a temporary patrol group were imprisoned and killed by military police. Their deaths were not reported in the news until 10 October. Members of the Nihon Rōdō Sōdōmei (Japan Federation of Labor) led a protest movement, and the following February a memorial service was held in honor of the victims. After the Kameido Incident and the murder of the anarchist ŌSUGI SAKAE and his common-law wife ITŌ NOE about the same time, the labor movement turned to gradualism and reformism.

Kamei Katsuichirō (1907–1966)

Literary critic. Born in the city of Hakodate, Hokkaidō, the eldest son of a banker, Kamei graduated from Yamagata Higher School in 1926 and entered Tōkyō University, where he majored in aesthetics. Soon after entering the university, he joined the SHINJINKAI (New Man Society), a Marxist study group. In February 1928 he joined the Kyōsan Seinen Dōmei (Communist Youth League), and in April of that same year he was arrested and imprisoned on political charges. In prison, Kamei renounced his Marxist beliefs, through the process that came to be known as TENKŌ, and was consequently released in the fall of 1930, after having served two and a half years.

In 1932, Kamei became actively involved in the PROLETARIAN LITERATURE MOVEMENT by joining the Nihon Puroretaria Sakka Dōmei (Japan Proletarian Writers' League) as a Marxist literary critic. His recognition of the discrepancies between the league's and his own artistic convictions led him to participate in the founding of the progressive literary journal *Genjitsu* (Reality) in 1934. The publication in the same year of his first book, a collection of literary essays entitled *Tenkeiki no bungaku* (Literature of a Changing Period), marked the end of his interest in the proletarian literary movement. In 1935 Kamei and YASUDA YOJŪRŌ, a friend and fellow member of the *Genjitsu* staff, founded the coterie NIHON RŌMANHA (Japanese Romantic School) out of their disillusionment with proletarian literature.

Inspired by Yasuda and stimulated by the rising tide of nationalism sweeping the country at the time, Kamei converted from a Marxist to a nationalist and became deeply interested in traditional Japanese culture and history, as is reflected in his "return to Japan" series: *Yamato koji fūbutsushi* (1943, A Pilgrimage to Old Temples in Yamato), *Shinran* (1944, Shinran), and *Shōtoku Taishi* (1946, Prince Shōtoku). Kamei reestablished his position in the post–World War II literary world with his autobiography, *Waga seishin no henreki* (The Pilgrimage of My Spirit), in 1949.

Kamei's journalistic sense, clear prose style, and relevant selection of topics made him one of the most widely read essayists in Japan after the war. He received the Yomiuri Literary Prize in 1951

for his critique on civilization entitled *Gendaijin no kenkyū* (1950, A Study of Modern Man). In 1959 he began writing his lifework entitled *Nihonjin no seishin shi kenkyū* (A Study of the Spiritual History of the Japanese People), for which he received the Kikuchi Kan Prize in 1965. This last project, however, remained incomplete as Kamei had written only 4 of the projected 12 volumes before his death in 1966.

■——Kamei Katsuichirō, *Kamei Katsuichirō zenshū* (Kōdansha, 1974). Kamei Fumihiko, *Tsuisō Kamei Katsuichirō* (1967). Tonegawa Yutaka, *Kamei Katsuichirō: sono jinsei to shisaku* (1967).

Tomone MATSUMOTO

Kameoka

City in central Kyōto Prefecture, west of Kyōto. A provincial capital *(kokufu)* during the Nara period (710–794), it later came under the rule of AKECHI MITSUHIDE, who built a castle here in 1579. During the Edo period (1600–1868), Kameoka was a POST-STATION TOWN on the highway San'indō. Today it is a commercial center of the Kameoka Valley, though once its principal occupation was farming. Textile and precision instrument industries are rapidly developing. Tourist attractions include the boat ride down the rapids of the river Hozugawa as far as Arashiyama in Kyōto. Paintings by MARUYAMA ŌKYO may be seen at the temple Kongōji. Pop: 69,410.

Kameyama

City in northern Mie Prefecture, central Honshū. Kameyama developed as a castle town and post-station town on the Tōkaidō, the main highway during the Edo period (1600–1868). The area is known for its rice, tea, and decorative candles. Pop: 33,486.

Kameyama, Emperor (1249–1305)

The 90th sovereign *(tennō)* in the traditional count (which includes several nonhistorical emperors); reigned 1260–74; a son of Emperor GO-SAGA. In accord with Go-Saga's wishes, Kameyama, who was his father's favorite, replaced his elder brother Emperor GO-FUKAKUSA, who was forced to abdicate. After his own abdication he continued to rule from retirement during the reign of his son Emperor GO-UDA, further frustrating the ambitions of Go-Fukakusa. However, Go-Fukakusa's son succeeded Go-Uda as Emperor FUSHIMI, beginning the tradition of alternating succession to the throne between the senior Jimyōin line (descended from Go-Fukakusa) and the junior Daikakuji line (descended from Kameyama). This practice was eventually made official by the KAMAKURA SHOGUNATE. Kameyama took holy orders in 1289 and in 1291 converted his palace into a Zen temple; it later became the temple NANZENJI.

G. Cameron HURST III

kami

Term used to refer to the divine in Shintō religion and therefore translated as divinity, deity, god, spirit, or supernatural force. This term offers a range of meanings and connotations so diverse that any translation out of context proves inadequate. The word *kami* is of uncertain origin and has traditionally been interpreted by the Japanese to denote a superior and mysterious force of either creative or destructive character, which resides in natural elements, animals, and certain human beings, causes ambivalent feelings of fear and gratitude, and is the focus of ritual behavior.

As Shintō evolved, a number of distinctions were established within the great and little traditions of this religious system. The first distinction of importance is that between *amatsukami* (heavenly divinities), such as AMATERASU ŌMIKAMI and IZANAGI and IZANAMI, and *kunitsukami* (earthly divinities), such as ŌKUNINUSHI NO MIKOTO and Ōyamatsumi no Kami (the deity of mountains). It can be said, though it is not always the case, that the heavenly divinities form the core of the mythological pantheon reflecting the politico-religious superiority of the ruling clans and that these divinities tend to be ancestral and anthropomorphic, whereas the earthly divinities tend to be linked to lesser sociopolitical groups, to have other functions (agricultural and economic), and tend to remain local, tutelary, and not necessarily anthropomorphic. In some cases, these different aspects merged while retaining subtle colorations indicative of their origins.

Kami are for the most part worshiped in shrines, in ritually defined spaces at particular times, and this is true for both traditions.

Worship includes more or less austere mental and physical preparations, purification, offerings of food, expression of the community's gratitude and desires in special language, offerings of dances and music, and so forth. See FESTIVALS.

Whereas heavenly divinities tend to reside in the High Celestial Plain (TAKAMAGAHARA) and to be worshiped at shrines formerly supported by the imperial household and by the great clans, the earthly divinities tend to reside in natural phenomena (spatial environment) and to manifest themselves either spontaneously (apparition, possession, oracle) or through summoning by priests (invocation) at regular intervals determined by mythical historical events or by the agricultural timetable (temporal environment). The number of these divinities varies—tradition refers to it as "The Eight Hundred Myriads"—and although the divine tends to pervade the cosmos, religious practitioners and communities distinguish specific purposes, names, titles, and ranks, the result being a more or less systematic hierarchy, in the dynamic organization of which the fundamental concerns of Japanese culture can be recognized.

Though, on the whole, *kami* appear to be benevolent if properly worshiped, it is not always the case. Some of the great natural calamities were attributed to the spirits of humans who had been wrongly accused and had therefore committed suicide or died in exile, leaving in the cosmic mechanism a "vengeful spirit" (GORYŌ) of a disruptive character needing to be pacified and transformed into a benevolent force of civilization. Such was the case of SUGAWARA NO MICHIZANE (Karai Tenjin) and many others. A divinity that is wronged or ill-treated manifests its wrath in varied forms; this fierce divine response, called *tatari*, once identified, has to be propitiated or exorcised. (In this particular area, esoteric Buddhism and Shintō merge in many ways.) Each *kami* is endowed with a particular force, or will, called *tama*, which is generally thought to have a "coarse" aspect *(aramitama)* and a "gentle" aspect *(nigimitama)* and is worshiped accordingly in ritual.

As Shintō evolved largely together with Buddhism and Confucianism, philosophical and ethical characteristics appeared; an emphasis was put on the interiorization of ritual, leading to the belief that the true residence of the divine was less its material support *(goshintai)* than the heart-mind. This was directly connected to basic Shintō notions of the manifestation of the divine in human behavior: honesty, purity, rectitude. Within the Shintō-Buddhist syncretic systems created around the 10th century, particular Shintō divinities were associated with particular Buddhist divinities (see HONJI SUIJAKU). Not surprisingly, the definition of *kami* changed accordingly, and by the end of the 15th and 16th centuries initiates were looking for the "*kami*-nature" of the Buddha. Attempts have been made to establish an all-encompassing *kami* at the very top of the pantheon as an ultimate cosmic principle (see SUIKA SHINTŌ; STATE SHINTŌ), but they failed, and many *kami* retain their local and historical character, as a result of historical, political, religious, and cultural interrelations with men. See also UJIGAMI; ONI; TA NO KAMI; MOUNTAINS, WORSHIP OF; YAMA NO KAMI.

Allan G. GRAPARD

Kamichika Ichiko (1888–1981)

Writer and politician. Born in Nagasaki Prefecture. In 1912 she joined the feminist group SEITŌSHA while still a student at Tsuda College; this membership was strongly disapproved by the school authorities and it also caused her dismissal from a teaching post in Aomori. She then became a reporter for the newspaper *Tōkyō nichi-nichi shimbun* (now the *Mainichi shimbun*). In 1916 she precipitated a notorious scandal (the so-called Hikage Teahouse Incident) when she stabbed and wounded her lover, the anarchist ŌSUGI SAKAE, because he had begun living with ITŌ NOE. After two years in prison, she continued her writing and her commitment to socialism, joining such groups as the Nihon Fēbian Kyōkai (Japan Fabian Society). In 1935 she edited with Suzuki Atsushi (who was her husband from 1920 to 1937) the magazine *Fujin bungei* (Women's Literary Arts). After World War II she served from 1953 to 1969 in the House of Representatives as a Japan Socialist Party member, campaigning against prostitution and for human rights. Her works include *Kamichika Ichiko jiden: Waga ai waga tatakai* (1972, The Autobiography of Kamichika Ichiko: My Loves and My Battles).

kamidana → Shintō family altars

Kami Fukuoka

City in southern Saitama Prefecture, 30 km (19 mi) from Tōkyō. Formerly a farming area, it is now a residential town for commuters to Tōkyō. Pop: 57,929.

Kamikawa Basin

Cattle grazing on a hillside east of the city of Asahikawa.

kami fūsen → paper balloons

Kamigumi Co, Ltd

Firm engaged chiefly in harbor transport, but also in warehousing. It is first among harbor transport companies in the major port cities of Kōbe, Tōkyō, Yokohama, Nagoya, and Ōsaka. The forerunner of the company was a cooperative of stevedores established when Kōbe was opened to foreign traders in 1867. In recent years the firm has concentrated its resources on investments aimed at rationalizing stevedoring operations and on construction of modern warehouses. Sales for the fiscal year ending September 1981 totaled ¥93.9 billion (US $408.3 million) and capitalization was ¥11 billion (US $47.8 million). The corporate headquarters are located in Kōbe.

kamikakushi

(literally, "hiding by the spirits"). The sudden and unexplained disappearance of a person from home was, until about two generations ago, believed to be the work of demons called TENGU, of foxes, and of other malevolent spirits. When someone fell victim to *kamikakushi*, it was customary for the entire community to conduct a search of the village and neighboring mountains with ringing of bells and beating of drums. It was believed that the victim—usually a sickly child—had been carried off to the world of spirits *(reikai)*, and that he would return after a day or two, or even after several years. The phenomenon has been explained as a form of somnambulism.

INOKUCHI Shōji

Kamikawa Basin

(Kamikawa Bonchi). In central Hokkaidō. Bounded by the Kitami and Ishikari mountains on the east and the Teshio and Yūbari mountains on the west, this fault basin consists of a floodplain on the upper reaches of the river Ishikarigawa. First developed in 1891 by colonist militia *(tondenhei)*, the area is one of the northernmost regions of rice cultivation in Japan. It also produces vegetables. The major city is Asahikawa. Area: approximately 450 sq km (174 sq mi).

kamikaze

Meaning literally, "wind of the gods" or "divine wind," *kamikaze* has been used as a "pillow word" (MAKURA KOTOBA, a literary term) for the province of Ise (now Mie Prefecture). The term was also applied to a strong prevailing wind off the coast of Ise and several neighboring provinces. However, in modern usage, *kamikaze* refers to the storms that twice destroyed much of the invading Mongol armadas off the northwestern coast of Kyūshū and forced them to withdraw in 1274 and 1281 (see MONGOL INVASIONS OF JAPAN). To the Japanese of the time, the storms represented divine intervention by the gods of ISE SHRINE. The myth of the *kamikaze* was never forgotten by the Japanese, reinforcing their belief that their land was protected by the Shintō gods. During World War II the term *kamikaze* was applied to the pilots who attacked Allied ships in suicide dives in explosive-laden planes. See KAMIKAZE SPECIAL ATTACK FORCE.

Kyotsu HORI

Kamikōchi

Taishō Pond, one of the valley's scenic attractions, with the volcano Yakedake visible in the distance. The pond was formed in 1915 when lava flows from Yakedake dammed the river Azusagawa.

Kamikaze Special Attack Force

(Kamikaze Tokubetsu Kōgekitai, or Tokkōtai). General name given to units of specially trained pilots who attacked Allied ships in suicide dives toward the end of World War II. Named for the *kamikaze* or "divine wind" that had repelled the MONGOL INVASIONS OF JAPAN in the 13th century, they were used when it became apparent that conventional means of attack could not prevent the Allied fleet from retaking the Philippines. The first Kamikaze attack took place on 25 October 1944, when five navy Zero fighters, each carrying a 250-kilogram bomb, plunged into American warships and transports off the coast of Leyte. Encouraged by the results, Vice Admiral Ōnishi Takijirō of the First Air Fleet, who had conceived the idea, hastily recruited new suicide forces. Army air force units soon followed suit. For the next 10 months, from the landing of the Allied forces on Leyte until Japan's surrender in August 1945, and especially in the Battle of Okinawa, the Japanese employed in suicide attacks more than 2,000 planes. By one count, 2,198 pilots and 1,192 planes were sacrificed. Of the pilots, some were teenagers (many of them college students) with only seven weeks of flight training. According to figures released by the United States after the war, 34 ships were sunk and 288 damaged by these "suicide squads."

Besides airplanes, the Japanese prepared other types of suicide weapons to defend the Japanese mainland, and some of them were put to use late in the war in a last frantic attempt to forestall defeat. They included a manned torpedo, which proved quite effective in disrupting a supply route; a manned glider equipped with high explosives and propelled by a rocket, which was nicknamed "baka bomb" (foolish bomb) by Allied soldiers; a motorboat with explosives on its bow; a small submarine; and a bomb carried by frogmen.

Kyotsu HORI

Kamikōchi

Scenic valley in western Nagano Prefecture, central Honshū. On the river Azusagawa and surrounded by HOTAKADAKE, YAKEDAKE, and other mountains, it became famous when the British geologist, Walter WESTON, wrote about it in 1891. It is noted for its beautiful alpine scenery, hot springs, and ponds. It is considered the best starting point for mountain climbing in the Northern Alps (Hida Mountains). Height: 1,500 m (4,920 ft).

Kaminoyama

City in central Yamagata Prefecture, northern Honshū. Known since the 15th century as a hot springs resort, the city prospered as a castle town and post-station town during the Edo period (1600–1868). Primarily a farming area producing rice, grapes, and persimmons, Kaminoyama also has silk-reeling plants and factories manufacturing pharmaceuticals and cast iron products. It is a base camp for climbing the peaks of Zaōzan, a range of mountains. There is a museum commemorating the *tanka* poet SAITŌ MOKICHI, who was born here. Pop: 38,533.

Kami Suwa Hot Spring

(Kami Suwa Onsen). Located near Lake Suwa, in the city of Suwa, central Nagano Prefecture, central Honshū. A simple thermal spring; water temperature 65–80°C (149–176°F). The volume of water is large, averaging 15,000 cu m (529,500 cu ft) a day. The highlands KIRIGAMINE and TATESHINA KŌGEN attract many visitors.

Kamitsukasa Shōken (1874–1947)

Author. Real name Kamitsukasa Nobutaka. Born in Nara Prefecture. While working as a journalist for *Yomiuri shimbun,* he began writing essays and short stories, the earlier ones being colored by the local Ōsaka culture of his youth. Many of his later works, which focus on the lives of the poor and helpless, reflect the influence of his socialist friends such as SAKAI TOSHIHIKO and KŌTOKU SHŪSUI. Works include *Hamo no kawa* (1933), a novel.

Kamiyama Sōjin (1884–1954)

Movie actor. Real name Kamiyama Mitsugu. Born in Miyagi Prefecture, he studied at the Tōkyō Drama School and joined the SHINGEKI (new theater) movement. He went to the United States, won acclaim for his role as a Mongolian prince in *The Thief of Baghdad* (1923), and was popular with audiences for his exotic charm. Returning to Japan, he played leading roles in SHIMAZU YASUJIRŌ's *Ai yo jinrui to tomo ni are* (1931, Love, Be with Mankind) and Shimizu Hiroshi's *Tōyō no haha* (1934, Mothers of Asia). Although Shōchiku Motion Pictures tried to promote his name, unlike HAYAKAWA SESSHŪ, who was successful both at home and abroad, he never attained great popularity as an actor in Japan. He lived his last years in seclusion in Itō, on the Izu Peninsula. *ITASAKA Tsuyoshi*

Kamiya Sōtan (1551–1635)

Famous merchant and tea connoisseur of the Azuchi–Momoyama (1568–1600) period and early part of the Edo (1600–1868) period; along with SHIMAI SŌSHITSU the representative Hakata townsman of his age. The Kamiya family's wealth and prominence in the trading city of Hakata (modern Fukuoka) were established by Sōtan's grandfather Jutei, who in the late 1520s began exploiting the rich IWAMI SILVER MINE in Iwami Province (now part of Shimane Prefecture) with smelting techniques newly introduced from China and Korea. Aside from metallurgy, the Kamiya were also active in wax and textile manufacture. Sōtan fortified this position by forming close ties with the national unifier TOYOTOMI HIDEYOSHI, who was eager to obtain Hakata's support in his Kyūshū expedition of 1587 and later used the city as a supply base for his INVASIONS OF KOREA IN 1592 AND 1597. Sōtan's tea diary, *Kamiya Sōtan nikki,* offers interesting glimpses into the relationship between the two men and the interplay of politics, commerce, and the tea ceremony characteristic of the period. In 1599, a year after Hideyoshi's death, Sōtan's privileged position in Hakata was confirmed by the *daimyō* KOBAYAKAWA HIDEAKI. With the establishment of the Tokugawa regime after the Battle of SEKIGAHARA the next year, however, Hakata was reduced to an appendage of the castle town of Fukuoka built by KURODA NAGAMASA, and Sōtan, overshadowed nationally by the emergence of privileged merchants close to the Tokugawa, also lost his prominent role in the administration of local affairs. See also HAKATA MERCHANTS. *George* ELISON

kamiyui

Traditional-style hairdresser. *Kamiyui* first appeared early in the Edo period (1600–1868) when diverse and complex men's HAIRSTYLES required professional care. In the late 18th century a separate profession of women's hairdressers developed in order to serve women. Hairdressers practiced either in their own shops or visited private residences, and famous salons developed in large cities like Edo (now Tōkyō) and Ōsaka. SHIKITEI SAMBA wrote descriptions of *kamiyui* in his *Ukiyodoko.* In 1871 the DAMPATSUREI law forbade the traditional *chommage* (topknot) for men, and Western-style barbers began to appear. *INAGAKI Shisei*

Kammon gyoki

(Record of Things Seen and Heard). Also known as *Kammon nikki.* The diary of the imperial prince Fushimi no Miya Sadafusa (1372–1456). His original manuscript, in 44 fascicles, survives almost complete. The diary chronicles the period 1416 to 1448 (entries for some nine years are missing) and ranges over a variety of subjects from personal matters to court affairs, town gossip, and political events during the heyday of the Muromachi shogunate.

G. Cameron HURST III

Kammon Strait

(Kammon Kaikyō). Also known as Shimonoseki Strait. Narrow strait between the city of Shimonoseki, Yamaguchi Prefecture, western Honshū and the city of Kita Kyūshū, Fukuoka Prefecture, northern Kyūshū. It connects the western Inland Sea and the Sea of Japan. It has been a vital point in marine transportation and a crossroad of land and maritime transportation in western Japan since ancient times. An underwater tunnel for the Japanese National Railways' San'yō Main Line was completed in 1942, a state road tunnel in 1958, and a Shinkansen (a super-speed train) tunnel in 1975. A highway bridge spanning the strait was completed in 1973. Narrowest point: 0.6 km (0.4 mi); widest point: 2.5 km (1.6 mi); depth: 10–21 m (33–69 ft).

Kammu, Emperor (737–806)

The 50th sovereign (tennō) in the traditional count (which includes several nonhistorical emperors); reigned 781–806. Eldest son of Emperor Kōnin (709–782; r 770–781). Because his mother was a commoner of Korean origin, Kammu was not originally in the line of succession, but he was named crown prince in 772 through the efforts of his father-in-law, the court official Fujiwara no Momokawa (732–779). During his long reign Kammu moved the capital first from Nara to NAGAOKAKYŌ and then to HEIANKYŌ (Kyōto), carried out extensive campaigns against the aborigines in the north, reformed the provincial administrative system, and dispatched officials to audit the tax registers. Although he opposed the economic and political power of the Buddhist establishment, he was a generous patron of the monks SAICHŌ and KŪKAI, who introduced new forms of Buddhism from China. Kammu was a vigorous ruler, and the power and prestige of the throne reached a peak during his reign.

G. Cameron HURST III

Kammuriyama

Also called Kamuriyama. Mountain at the junction of Hiroshima, Shimane, and Yamaguchi prefectures, western Honshū; the principal peak of the Kammuriyama Mountains, west of the Chūgoku Mountains. Surrounded by an extension of the KIBI KŌGEN highland, it is a monadnock with level land on its summit. Height: 1,339 m (4,392 ft).

Kamo

City in central Niigata Prefecture, central Honshū. Its name comes from the KAMO SHRINES in Kyōto which came into possession of this area in 794. It developed as a market town in the middle ages. Industries include the manufacture of electrical appliances, textiles, and furniture. It is also Japan's largest producer of paulownia chests. Pop: 36,705.

Kamochi Masazumi (1791–1858)

KOKUGAKU (National Learning) scholar. Born in the Tosa domain (now Kōchi Prefecture), he never left the domain but communicated by letter with scholars in Ōsaka and Edo (now Tōkyō). For the most part self-educated, he received an appointment as librarian and professor at the official school of the Tosa domain. He spent 30 years completing his chief work, the voluminous Man'yōshū kogi, an exhaustive compilation of previous annotations on the 8th-century anthology MAN'YŌSHŪ.

Kamogawa

City in southern Chiba Prefecture, central Honshū, on the Pacific Ocean. The commercial center of the area and a base for deep-sea fishing, Kamogawa also produces citrus fruit and vegetables. Tourists are drawn to its scenic offshore islands. Pop: 31,680.

Kamogawa

River in the city of Kyōto, Kyōto Prefecture, central Honshū, originating in the Tamba Mountains and flowing south to join the KA-

Kamo no Chōmei

Detail of an imaginary portrait by Tosa Hirokane. Hanging scroll. Colors on paper. 56 × 36 cm. 15th century. Jingū Bunko, Ise, Mie Prefecture.

TSURAGAWA. When the palace at the new capital city of HEIANKYŌ (now Kyōto) was constructed at the end of the 8th century, the river's course was altered to flow east of the palace. It was a line of defense for Kyōto in ancient times and was used for river transportation and dyeing (yūzen-zome). Parks have been constructed on the dry areas of the riverbed. Length: 35 km (22 mi).

Kamo no Chōmei (1156?–1216)

Poet, critic, and essayist in the troubled transitional years between the Heian (794–1185) and Kamakura (1185–1333) periods. Kamo no Chōmei has come to typify the literary recluse who abandons the world for a life of refined tranquillity in a small mountain hut.

Poet and Literary Critic——Chōmei's early skill in music and poetry ushered him into the literary world of FUJIWARA NO TOSHINARI, FUJIWARA NO SADAIE, and SAIGYŌ. A poetic disciple of the priest SHUN'E (1113–ca 1190?), the son of MINAMOTO NO TOSHIYORI, Chōmei cultivated a complex style, examples of which appear in the SHIN KOKINSHŪ (1205, New Collection of Ancient and Modern Times) and other imperial anthologies, as well as in his personal collection of verse (SHIKASHŪ), the Kamo no Chōmei shū.

In 1200 Chōmei presented to ex-Emperor GO-TOBA (1180–1239) a 100-poem sequence entitled Shōji ninen nido hyakushu (Second Hundred-Poem Sequence of the Shōji Era). In the following year Go-Toba appointed Chōmei to the newly established Bureau of Poetry (Wakadokoro).

It was, however, as a literary critic and aesthetician that Chōmei truly excelled. His Mumyōshō (post-1211, Nameless Notes) consists of 78 chapters of varying length covering a wide range of topics: the history and nature of the WAKA (classical Japanese poetry) tradition, current usages, personal behavior, and aesthetic principles. In the manner of most poetic treatises (karon), it is written in the question-and-answer format and informs by illustrative example rather than by sustained argument. Noteworthy is Chōmei's advocacy of the aesthetic ideal of YŪGEN (literally, "mystery and depth"). The quality of yūgen exists, Chōmei says, when much feeling is expressed through few words, when the ordinary suggests elegance and rare beauty through a style of surface simplicity, and when "an unseen world hovers in the atmosphere of the poem."

The Elderly Recluse——Temperamentally, Chōmei seems always to have been a solitary and peripatetic individual. In his early 30s he left his ancestral home to live in a small cottage near the river Kamogawa in Ōhara, northeast of Kyōto. From his travels a fragmentary poetic diary, Iseki (ca 1186, Accounts of Ise), remains. His name has also been spuriously linked to two later travel accounts, the Kaidōki (ca 1223, Sea Route Journal) and Tōkan kikō (ca 1242, Trip to the Eastern Barrier), attributions resting perhaps on Chōmei's trips to Kamakura to visit the shōgun-poet MINAMOTO NO SANETOMO (1192–1219).

Chōmei's taste for worldly success seems to have paled altogether when in his late 40s he was denied a hereditary post at the KAMO SHRINES, and in 1204 he became a Buddhist monk and secluded himself in the mountains of Ōhara. In 1209 he removed to Toyama on Mt. Hino (Hinoyama), south of Kyōto near Uji, where he constructed a small hut reminiscent of the abode of the Indian sage

Vimalakīrti described in the sutra bearing his name (Skt: *Vimalakīr-tinirdeśa;* J: *Yuimagyō*). There he lived in quiet elegance awaiting death, a few rolls of scripture, poetry, and music on his shelves, and with a *koto* (13-stringed Japanese zither) and lute to while away the hours when he was not invoking the name of the Buddha AMIDA or observing nature in his solitude. Chōmei immortalized this experience and defined for later generations the ideal of the literary recluse (much as his contemporary, Saigyō, created the model of the itinerant poet) in his most famous work, the *Hōjōki* (1212, The Ten Foot Square Hut or An Account of My Hut). Chōmei's brief "jottings" (*zuihitsu*) begin with a Buddhistic lament on the world's inconstancy (MUJŌ) and on the vanity of human projects, proceeding with descriptions of the natural and human calamities of the times surrounding the epic struggles between the Taira and Minamoto families during the last decades of the 12th century. Similarities in style and content suggest that the work may have been modeled on a short essay in Chinese, the *Chiteiki* (982, Pond Bower Notes) by YOSHISHIGE NO YASUTANE (ca 931–1002). But whatever its antecedents, literary or religious, Chōmei's short commentary on life has become a landmark in Japanese literary and philosophical consciousness.

Chōmei's last work was probably the collection of Buddhist exemplary tales (*setsuwa;* see SETSUWA BUNGAKU) known as the *Hosshinshū* (ca 1214, Collection of Religious Awakenings), 102 stories of persons who abandoned the world or whose lives illustrated some popular moral. This collection and the *Hōjōki* both reflect a Tendai-oriented Amidism which relies on good works as well as faith, unlike the PURE LAND BUDDHISM of HŌNEN and SHINRAN which was about to sweep the country. And, as literary Buddhists had been arguing for centuries, Chōmei saw poetry and music as possible avenues to religious realization. Kamo no Chōmei died in his little hut in 1216, a bright lingering afterglow from the radiance of Heian culture.

———Hilda Katō, "The *Mumyōshō* of Kamo no Chōmei and its Significance in Japanese Literature (together with an English translation of the *Mumyōshō*)," *Monumenta Nipponica* 23.3–4 (1968). Donald Keene, ed, *Anthology of Japanese Literature* (1955). A. L. Sadler, *The Ten Foot Square Hut and Tales of the Heike* (1928). Marian Ury, "Recluses and Eccentric Monks: Tales from the *Hosshinshū* by Kamo no Chōmei," *Monumenta Nipponica* 27.2 (1972). Yanase Kazuo, ed, *(Kōchū) Kamo no Chōmei zenshū* (Fuzambō, 1940; repr Kazama Shobō, 1956).   *Robert E. MORRELL*

Kamo no kurabeuma

Horse race held every year on 5 May at the Kami-Gamo Shrine in Kyōto (see KAMO SHRINES) as a supplicatory rite for a rich harvest and peace. Modeled on a race that used to be held at the Imperial Palace, it was first held on the fifth day of the fifth month of 1093. It was subsequently held every year, using horses that were sent as offerings to the shrine from various localities around the country. Following the ŌNIN WAR (1467–77), the race was discontinued for a time, but it was eventually revived and has continued to the present day. Twenty colorfully dressed riders line up on the right and left and, after first paying homage at the main shrine building, take turns racing their horses two by two. The starting point is a flowering cherry tree and the finish line is a maple tree. A drum beat signals a victory for the left while a ringing bell indicates a victory for the right.   *INAGAKI Shisei*

Kamo no Mabuchi (1697–1769)

KOKUGAKU (National Learning) scholar and WAKA poet; known for his important contributions to the development of the National Learning school through his studies of the ancient Japanese classics, particularly his commentaries on the MAN'YŌSHŪ (Collection for Ten Thousand Generations or Collection of Ten Thousand Leaves), the oldest anthology of Japanese verse, compiled late in the 8th century. By combining the comparative philological research methods of KEICHŪ (1640–1701) with the ethical system of KADA NO AZUMAMARO (1669–1736), his two predecessors, Mabuchi established a new era in classical literature and linguistics scholarship. In an attempt to revive the ancient spirit of the classics that predated the introduction of Buddhism and Confucianism into Japan, Mabuchi emphasized a Shintō creed of simplicity and spontaneity. Also a brilliant poet, he favored the so-called *Man'yō* style and attempted, unsuccessfully, to revive the CHŌKA ("long poem"). His literary name was Agatai.

Mabuchi, the son of a Shintō priest, was born in the province of Tōtōmi (now part of Shizuoka Prefecture). From an early age he received training in *waka* composition, at which he demonstrated remarkable proficiency, and the Japanese classics. He excelled as well in the study of Confucianism and Chinese learning, all of which contributed to his later success as a scholar and poet. In 1733 he moved to Kyōto, leaving behind his wife and children, to study formally with Kada no Azumamaro. After three years Azumamaro died, and in 1737 Mabuchi moved to Edo (now Tōkyō), where he eventually set himself up as a teacher of the classics. In 1746 Mabuchi succeeded Kada no Arimaro (1706–51), the nephew of Azumamaro, as tutor in Japanese literature to TAYASU MUNETAKE (1715–71), son of the shōgun TOKUGAWA YOSHIMUNE (r 1716–45). During his term of service to the Tayasu family, Mabuchi was influential in furthering studies of the Japanese classics; he wrote commentaries not only on the *Man'yōshū* but on the ISE MONOGATARI (mid-10th century; *Tales of Ise*) and the TALE OF GENJI (ca 1000). He retired from active service in 1760 at age 63 and concentrated his efforts thereafter on writing and teaching. Most of Mabuchi's books and tracts date from this period.

Mabuchi's poetry was at first patterned after the style of the SHIN KOKINSHŪ (ca 1205), an imperial anthology of *waka,* whose poems were written in an elegant, polished style. Later he came to prefer the lofty style and "manliness" (*masuraoburi*) of *Man'yōshū* poetry. He sought to renew interest in the *chōka,* a long poetic form that had virtually disappeared from Japanese court poetry, but met with few who shared his enthusiasm for this once venerable form of verse. To Mabuchi's way of thinking, the composition of poetry was of equal importance with classical scholarship as a means of gaining insight into the minds of the poets of old. Toward the end of his life, he turned to simpler poetic utterance, as found in such ancient historical records as the KOJIKI (712, Records of Ancient Matters).

Mabuchi's major contribution to the Kokugaku tradition, however, was made as a scholar, not as a poet. His scholastic achievements were the result of a strong desire and determination to penetrate the world of the ancient poets. This culminated in the systematic series of exhaustive explanations and interpretations of the *Man'yōshū* that make up his magnum opus, the *Man'yōkō* (1760–68). In the *Man'yōkō,* Mabuchi elaborates on each poem of each book of the *Man'yōshū,* by reflecting on the year of its composition and then comparing, deciphering, and reconstructing the texts. He discusses not only the linguistic aspects of the *Man'yōshū* but also its literary value. His study is still regarded as the finest piece of *Man'yōshū* scholarship of the premodern era. Other works by Mabuchi are the *Kanjikō* (1757), *Genji monogatari shinshaku* (1758), *Niimanabi* (1765), and a five-volume set of commentaries in the Kokugaku tradition which include the *Bun'ikō* (1762), *Kaikō* (1764), *Kokuikō* (1765), *Shoikō* (1765), and *Goikō* (1769). Among the disciples of Mabuchi were MOTOORI NORINAGA (1730–1801)—his chief disciple and successor as leader of the Kokugaku movement—KATŌ CHIKAGE (1735–1808), KATORI NAHIKO (1723–82), and MURATA HARUMI (1746–1811).

———Kamo no Mabuchi, *Kōhon Kamo no Mabuchi zenshū: Shisōhen* (Kōbundō, 1942). Kamo no Mabuchi, *Kamo no Mabuchi zenshū,* 25 vols (Zoku Gunsho Ruijū Kanseikai, 1977–). Inoue Minoru, *Kamo no Mabuchi no gakumon* (1943). Inoue Minoru, *Kamo no Mabuchi no gyōseki to monryū* (1966). Koyama Tadashi, *Kamo no Mabuchi den* (1938). Saegusa Yasutaka, *Kamo no Mabuchi* (1962). Tabayashi Yoshinobu, *Kamo no Mabuchi kashū no kenkyū* (1966). Yamamoto Yoshimasa, *Kamo no Mabuchi ron* (1963).
          ŌTA Yoshimaro

kamoshika

(Japanese serow). *Capricornis crispus.* A primitive herbivorous animal of the family Bovidae found only in Japan. The *kamoshika* inhabits the high mountain areas of Honshū, Shikoku, and Kyūshū, usually singly or in pairs. It resembles a mountain goat in shape, but is smaller, with a combined head and body length of about 1 meter (39 in) and a shoulder height of about 70 centimeters (28 in). It is usually brown in color, but some are white or black. Both sexes have horns, about 14 centimeters (6 in) long, with pointed ends. The doe bears a single fawn in the spring. The *kamoshika's* chief natural enemy is the Asiatic black bear or moon bear (*Selenarctos thibetanus*). It was once hunted extensively for its fur and horns, and its numbers decreased alarmingly. It is now a protected species, however, and has been steadily reestablishing itself. See illustration on following page.   *IMAIZUMI Yoshiharu*

Kamo Shrines

(Kamo Jinja). Two independent but closely associated Shintō shrines in Kyōto: the Kamo Wakeikazuchi Jinja (popularly Kami-Gamo Sha) in Kita Ward, dedicated to the deity Kamo Wakeikazuchi no Kami and the Kamo Mioya Jinja (Shimo-Gamo Sha) in Sakyō Ward, dedicated to the deities Tamayorihime no Mikoto (the mother goddess of Wakeikazuchi) and Kamo Taketsunumi no Mikoto (the father god of Tamayorihime). According to the tradition of the Kamo Shrines, they were built at their present locations in 678, although their origins are said to go back to the reign of the legendary first emperor, Jimmu. After the capital was moved from Nagaoka to Kyōto in 794, the shrines enjoyed great popularity because of the protection they provided to the city. During the Heian period (794–1185) they were endowed with numerous estates, and the succeeding shogunates were also lavish with their patronage. The shrines have been numbered among the greatest shrines of the country. In addition to the famous festival, the AOI FESTIVAL, which is a colorful annual event in Kyōto, both shrines hold numerous annual ceremonies. *Stanley* WEINSTEIN

kampaku

Imperial regent for an adult emperor as opposed to SESSHŌ, regent for a minor emperor. An extrastatutory office modeled after an office variously mentioned in Chinese historical documents. The *kampaku* assisted the emperor in carrying out the general duties of government. The first to take the title was Fujiwara no Mototsune (836–891), who was appointed *kampaku* in 887 to assist Emperor Kōkō (r 884–887) after having ruled as de facto regent since 884. He and his adoptive father FUJIWARA NO YOSHIFUSA had already served as *sesshō,* and their descendants thereafter held a monopoly on these titles, establishing what historians call REGENCY GOVERNMENT. The Fujiwara hold on the office lasted until the Kamakura period (1185–1333), when members of the GOSEKKE, five branch families of the Fujiwara (i.e., the Konoe, Kujō, Nijō, Ichijō, and Takatsukasa families), were appointed to the post. Apart from these, only TOYOTOMI HIDEYOSHI and his son TOYOTOMI HIDETSUGU were named *kampaku.* The political power of the *kampaku* declined with the institution of the INSEI system of government by retired emperors in the 11th century, although the office itself lasted until the Meiji Restoration of 1868.

Kampan Batabiya shimbun

The first newspaper to be published continuously in Japan. It was put out by the Tokugawa shogunate in the latter part of the Edo period (1600–1868) and was devoted to the translation of foreign news items. Publication started in 1862, but the paper was short-lived, 23 issues appeared in succession between January and February of that year before it ceased publication. Translations for the paper were done at the Institute for the Study of Western Books (Yōsho Shirabesho; see BANSHO SHIRABESHO) from selected news stories taken from a Dutch colony publication in Batavia (now Djakarta), the *Javasche Courant.* Hoping to still the current of antiforeigner sentiment that was prevalent in the late Edo period, the paper gave the public access to what had heretofore been privileged information of the shogunal officials. The government had the publisher Yorozuya Heishirō produce and sell the paper which was printed on sheets folded in half and 10 to 12 pages in length. News articles were divided according to country. After the *Kampan Batabiya shimbun* ceased publication in 1862, the government attempted publishing the *Kampan kaigai shimbun* from August to September of that same year.

Kampō → Official Gazette

kampu

Official orders *(fu)* issued by either the Grand Council of State (DAJŌKAN) or the Office of Shintō Worship (Jingikan) to their subordinate offices under the RITSURYŌ SYSTEM of government established in the late 7th century. The term most often referred to *dajōkampu,* orders issued by the Dajōkan, the chief administrative organ of the central government. The form of *kampu* was prescribed by the Kushikiryō (Forms for Official Correspondence). When transmitting an imperial edict to central government bureaus, *kampu* were added to the text of the edict; when sent to provincial offices, the edict was

Kamoshika

quoted in the *kampu. Kampu* were also issued by the Dajōkan independently of imperial edicts. They were always signed by two officials of the Benkankyoku (Controllers' Office). Although *kampu* had become an empty formality by the later part of the Heian period (794–1185), they continued in use until the early years of the Meiji period (1868–1912), when political power was restored to the imperial court. YAGI *Atsuru*

Kampūzan

Composite volcano in the central Oga Peninsula, western Akita Prefecture, northern Honshū; composed of pyroxene andesite. Skiing is available. It is part of the Oga Quasi-National Park. Height: 355 m (1,164 ft).

Kamuikotan

Canyon in the city of Asahikawa, central Hokkaidō. Formed by the river Ishikarigawa, the canyon is famous for its rugged scenery and fantastically shaped rocks. In ancient times it was believed to be the abode of the gods and thus unapproachable. In the vicinity are remains of pit houses used by primitive inhabitants. Length: approximately 10 km (6.2 mi).

Kamura Isota (1897–1933)

Novelist. Born in Yamaguchi Prefecture. He attended middle school only briefly and eventually went to Tōkyō, where he became an editor of the coterie magazine *Fudōchō.* One of his duties in this capacity was to take down from dictation the writing of KASAI ZENZŌ, an author of the so-called naturalist school, who encouraged Kamura in his own writing. Most active in the 1920s, Kamura is known as a writer of autobiographical novels (see I-NOVEL) who exposed his personal life to a degree that was extreme, even for this genre. His works include "Gōku" (1928) and "Tojō" (1932).

kan

An important Japanese concept referring to a form of intuitional cognition. *Kan* encompasses a number of attributes including intuition, the so-called sixth sense, premonition, a knack for doing things, inspiration, and sudden realization. *Kan* is considered essential in many spheres of Japanese life which involve certain traditional skills or techniques, such as the martial arts and artistic endeavors. This traditional concept was examined by the psychologist Kuroda Ryō (1890–1947), who attempted to identify and establish *kan* as an essential concept in Japanese psychology. During the 1930s, when experimental research in psychology was just beginning in Japan, Kuroda became dissatisfied with Western psychology, which he felt focused on the study of consciousness (*ishiki*) and the unconscious (*muishiki*) to the neglect of another important cognitional realm which is, along with consciousness, an evident psychological given. Kuroda described this realm with the term *kan* and, drawing on traditional Eastern thought, envisioned his psychological research as

Kana——Table 1

Modern hiragana and katakana and the Chinese characters from which they derive

Hiragana

(left to right: syllable; character; *sōgana*; modern *hiragana*)

a 安ああ	ka 加かか	sa 左ささ	ta 太たた	na 奈奈な	ha 波はは	ma 末まま	ya 也やや	ra 良らら	wa 和わわ
i 以いい	ki 幾きき	shi 之しし	chi 知ちち	ni 仁にに	hi 比ひひ	mi 美みみ		ri 利わり	i(wi) 為ゐゐ
u 宇うう	ku 久くく	su 寸すす	tsu 川つつ	nu 奴ぬね	fu 不ふふ	mu 武むむ	yu 由ゆゆ	ru 留るる	
e 衣ええ	ke 計けけ	se 世せせ	te 天てて	ne 祢ねね	he 部へへ	me 女めめ		re 礼れれ	e(we) 恵ゑゑ
o 於おお	ko 己ここ	so 曽そそ	to 止とと	no 乃のの	ho 保ほほ	mo 毛もも	yo 与よよ	ro 呂ろろ	o 遠をを
									n 无んん

Katakana

(left to right: syllable; character; modern *katakana*)

a 阿ア	ka 加カ	sa 散サ	ta 多タ	na 奈ナ	ha 八ハ	ma 万マ	ya 也ヤ	ra 良ラ	wa 和ワ
i 伊イ	ki 幾キ	shi 之シ	chi 千チ	ni 二ニ	hi 比ヒ	mi 三ミ		ri 利リ	i(wi) 井ヰ
u 宇ウ	ku 久ク	su 須ス	tsu 川ツ	nu 奴ヌ	fu 不フ	mu 牟ム	yu 由ユ	ru 流ル	
e 江エ	ke 介ケ	se 世セ	te 天テ	ne 祢ネ	he 部ヘ	me 女メ		re 礼レ	e(we) 慧ヱ
o 於オ	ko 己コ	so 曽ソ	to 止ト	no 乃ノ	ho 保ホ	mo 毛モ	yo 與ヨ	ro 呂ロ	o 乎ヲ
									n 尔ン

NOTE: This table contains the complete 48-character syllabary for both *hiragana* and *katakana*, including the symbols for *wi* and *we*, which were removed from the official *kana* list in 1946. These 48 characters alone are not sufficient to express all the syllables of Japanese. For other syllables diacritical marks or combinations of *kana* are used. See Table 2.

---

a study of *kan* rather than of consciousness. In his book *Kan no kenkyū* (1933, *A Study of Kan*), Kuroda examined the concept of *kan* along with two synonymous terms, *kaku* and *kotsu*, comparing these to consciousness. (According to Kuroda, *kan* is a colloquial equivalent of *kaku*, which happens to have other, unrelated connotations, and he therefore focused on the term *kaku* in his study.)

In Kuroda's theory, although both consciousness and *kan* are experienced by the self as psychological givens, *kan* differs from consciousness in several respects, which Kuroda discussed under eight headings. *Kan* is likewise differentiated from the subconscious *(kaishiki)* and the unconscious in that *kan* is an evident reality recognized by the self, although there are some similarities between *kan* and the subconscious.

Kuroda discerned two distinct aspects of *kan*. The first is an intuitive power revealed in cognition and judgment. This intuition differs from logic and analysis; the latter use a reportable thinking process as their medium, whereas intuition uses no such medium and perceives directly. This aspect of *kan* resembles the Western notion of intuition. A second aspect is *kotsu* (a knack or physical skill), which manifests itself in the handling of objects or in other voluntary acts. It is *kotsu* which Japan's artists and artisans have traditionally sought to attain in their works and performances; this is a product of cumulative effort and experience which does not come about without hard work and discipline. In common parlance, however, these two nuances of *kan* are not distinguished. See also SA-TORI.　　　　　　　　　　　　　　　　　　*Hoshino Akira*

kana

A general term for a number of syllabic writing systems developed in Japan, all based on Chinese characters *(kanji)* used to express the sounds of Japanese rather than the meanings of individual words. (The etymology of *kana* is *kari* "temporary, nonofficial, nonregular" plus *na* "name" or "writing," an expression of the feeling that the use of Chinese characters not for their meaning but for their pronunciation was "not regular." The word *karina* or *kana* was originally used in contrast to *mana* "real or regular writing," the latter referring to Chinese characters used as units of meaning.)

Since *kana* can express all the sounds of Japanese, the language can be written entirely in *kana*. However, the normal practice is to use a mixture of Chinese characters and *kana*; the Chinese characters are used to express the meanings of most words (from which the

pronunciation can be inferred) and the *kana* to write inflectional endings, grammatical particles, and certain words officially designated not to be written in characters (see JAPANESE LANGUAGE: writing system). Two sets of *kana* are used in the present-day Japanese writing system: *hiragana*, a cursive form (and the one commonly used for native words and any words of Chinese origin not to be written in characters), and *katakana*, a noncursive form; the latter can be used in place of *hiragana*, but it is most typically used to write LOANWORDS from European languages. Both *katakana* and *hiragana* derive from an earlier set of *kana* known as *man'yōgana*, and *hiragana* in particular derives from the cursive form of *man'yōgana* known as *sōgana*.

Man'yōgana——*Man'yōgana* are a set of unmodified Chinese characters that were once used as phonetic symbols to represent Japanese syllables. As the name suggests, *man'yōgana* (man'yō + kana) was the writing system used in the MAN'YŌSHŪ, an 8th-century anthology containing poems from the 5th century to 759 AD. Most attempts to write Japanese prior to the Heian period (794–1185) fall into the category of *man'yōgana*. Thereafter *man'yōgana* gives way to other forms of *kana*.

The *Man'yōgana* differs from the two currently used *kana* systems in at least three important aspects. First, there is no one-to-one relationship between syllables and characters. There were 87 syllable types in 8th-century Japanese (88 in the language of the KOJIKI) but over 970 Chinese characters were used to write them. For example, over 40 Chinese characters were utilized interchangeably to write the syllable *shi*, and 32 were used for the syllable *ka*.

Second, the Chinese characters were used as written in Chinese, without modification or simplification. For this reason a text written in *man'yōgana* superficially resembles a text in Chinese; however, because many of the letters are used only for their pronunciation and not for their meaning and since the language represented is Japanese, the text is likely to be unintelligible to a Chinese speaker.

Third, the types of character pronunciation represented in *man'yōgana* are more varied than in *hiragana* and *katakana*, including the *on* reading and *kun* reading of the character as well as the type of reading called *gisho* (literally, "playful writing").

The *on* reading is a Japanized version of the Chinese pronunciation for the character. For example, the Chinese character 阿, which means "mountain ridge," was pronounced ʔa in the rising tone in Middle Chinese—the language of Chang'an (Ch'angan) around 600 AD. The Japanese used this character to represent

Kana——Table 2

How kana are combined with diacritical marks to express voiced consonants and the unvoiced bilabial stop (p)										

(left to right: syllable; *hiragana*; *katakana*)

ga	が	ガ	za	ざ	ザ	da	だ	ダ	ba	ば	バ	pa	ぱ	パ
gi	ぎ	ギ	ji	じ	ジ	ji	ぢ	ヂ	bi	び	ビ	pi	ぴ	ピ
gu	ぐ	グ	zu	ず	ズ	zu	づ	ヅ	bu	ぶ	ブ	pu	ぷ	プ
ge	げ	ゲ	ze	ぜ	ゼ	de	で	デ	be	べ	ベ	pe	ぺ	ペ
go	ご	ゴ	zo	ぞ	ゾ	do	ど	ド	bo	ぼ	ボ	po	ぽ	ポ

How kana are combined to write syllables involving postconsonantal *y* gliders														

(left to right: syllable; *hiragana*; *katakana*)

kya	きゃ キャ	sha	しゃ シャ	cha	ちゃ チャ	nya	にゃ ニャ	hya	ひゃ ヒャ	mya	みゃ ミャ	rya	りゃ リャ
kyu	きゅ キュ	shu	しゅ シュ	chu	ちゅ チュ	nyu	にゅ ニュ	hyu	ひゅ ヒュ	myu	みゅ ミュ	ryu	りゅ リュ
kyo	きょ キョ	sho	しょ ショ	cho	ちょ チョ	nyo	にょ ニョ	hyo	ひょ ヒョ	myo	みょ ミョ	ryo	りょ リョ

gya	ぎゃ ギャ	ja	じゃ ジャ					bya	びゃ ビャ	pya	ぴゃ ピャ		
gyu	ぎゅ ギュ	ju	じゅ ジュ					byu	びゅ ビュ	pyu	ぴゅ ピュ		
gyo	ぎょ ギョ	jo	じょ ジョ					byo	びょ ビョ	pyo	ぴょ ピョ		

the syllable [a] in Japanese. The Chinese character 安 , which means "peace" or "tranquillity," was pronounced ʔan in the even tone in Middle Chinese; it also came to be used to represent the Japanese syllable [a] by cutting off the final *n*. These two are among seven or eight Chinese characters used for the syllable [a].

The *kun* reading is the pronunciation of a Japanese word with the same meaning as the Chinese character. For example, the Chinese character 吾 , which means "I," was pronounced ŋo in the even tone in Middle Chinese. The 8th-century Japanese word for "I" was *a*. The character was assigned the latter pronunciation as a *man'yōgana,* and thus it too was used to represent the syllable [a]. To cite another example, the character 足 , which means "foot," was pronounced tsiok in the checked tone in Middle Chinese. The 8th-century Japanese word for "foot" had two forms, the bound form *a-*, and the free form *ashi*. The Chinese character for "foot" was also utilized to represent the [a] syllable in Japanese.

The *gisho* or playful writing involves, among other things, onomatopoeia. An example is the two-character combination of 蜂音 . The first character, 蜂 , means "bee" or "wasp" and was pronounced pʰjoŋ in the even tone in Middle Chinese; the second 音 , pronounced ʔjəm (even tone), meant "sound." The sound or buzzing of bees was apparently represented as *bu* in 8th-century Japanese, and the two characters together were used to represent the Japanese syllable [bu]. Similarly 牛鳴 , "mooing of cows," represented the syllable [mu] and 馬鳴 , "neighing of horses," represented the syllable [i].

Of the three varieties of readings just cited, the *on* reading is the most frequently used, and the *gisho* reading is the least frequent. These distributional characteristics clearly anticipate later trends. Modern *kana* systems are almost totally made up of the *on* readings of the Chinese characters from which they are derived. See also the section on the *Man'yō* writing system in MAN'YŌSHŪ.

Sōgana——*Sōgana* consists of the Chinese characters of the *man'-yōgana* system written in the *sō* or cursive style (see SHOTAI). Three differences between the modern *kana* (i.e., *katakana* and *hiragana*) and *sōgana* are: (1) in *sōgana,* as in *man'yōgana,* there is no one-to-one correspondence between syllables and characters, the number of the latter exceeding the former; (2) Chinese characters are used in their full cursive forms and not in stylized, reduced cursive forms such as those associated with *hiragana;* and (3) the *kun* as well as *on* readings are reflected in the pronunciation. What characterizes *sōgana* is its cursive or *sō* form, and it is an intermediate stage of simplification between the fully regular or *kai* (noncursive) form of the Chinese characters that is used in *man'yōgana* and the totally stylized modern *hiragana*.

Katakana——In its modern, standard form, *katakana* is a system of 48 syllabic writing units for writing non-Chinese loanwords, onomatopoeia, emphasized words, and the names of flora and fauna. The *kata* in *katakana* means "partial," "not whole," "fragmentary." It is so named because many of the *katakana* are a part and not the whole of a Chinese character.

In its earlier stages, *katakana* was used as a mnemonic device for pronouncing Buddhist texts written in Chinese. Next appeared Japa-

nese texts such as the *Tōdaiji fujumon kō* (early 9th century), written in a mixture of Chinese characters and *katakana*. This writing system is called *kanamajiri bun* (sentences mixing *kana* and characters). By the middle of the 10th century, anthologies of Japanese verse (WAKA) such as the GOSEN WAKASHŪ (955–966) came to be written in *katakana* and by the 12th century collections of folktales such as the KONJAKU MONOGATARI came to be written in a mixture of Chinese characters and *katakana*. In this way the use of *katakana* spread from Buddhist Chinese texts to Japanese poetic texts and then to Japanese prose texts.

Among the earliest extant examples of *katakana* are those found in a copy, dated 828, of *Jōjitsuron,* a Buddhist text in Chinese, where they are used as mnemonics for pronunciation. At first, as in *man'yōgana,* there were more than one *katakana* that could be used in writing any one syllable, but by the Muromachi period (1333–1568) a one-to-one correspondence between *katakana* and the syllables of Japanese had gradually been established; the currently used forms were standardized in 1900. Formerly used variant *katakana* symbols that differ from the standardized forms are called *itai-gana* (variant *katakana*) or *kotai-gana* (old *katakana*).

Hiragana——In its modern, standard form, *hiragana* is a system of 48 syllabic writing units for writing indigenous Japanese words as well as Chinese loanwords that cannot be written with the 1,945 characters officially approved for general use (see TŌYŌ KANJI; JŌYŌ KANJI). *Hira* means "commonly used," "easy," "rounded." *Hiragana* is so named because the letters are considered rounded and easy compared to the full forms of the original Chinese characters. *Hiragana* is a more simplified and stylized form of the *sōgana* or cursive form of *man'yōgana*. In its early forms *hiragana* was used by women, while the unsimplified Chinese characters were used by men; for this reason, the earliest *hiragana* was also called *onnade* (women's hand).

As early as 762, some *hiragana*-like letters occurred, but it was in the Heian period that *onnade* began to appear widely. In the early Heian period, the high frequency items among the complete set of *sōgana* were chosen, and a near one-to-one relationship between the resulting set of *hiragana* and the syllables of Japanese was established. By the end of the 9th century *onnade* ceased being a system limited to women and became an accepted orthographic device to record poems. When the imperial poetic anthology *Kokin wakashū* (KOKINSHŪ; ca 905) was written in *onnade, hiragana* gained full status as an officially recognized system.

As the artistry of poetic composition became more elaborate, the early one-to-one relationship was lost and, as in the case of *man'yōgana,* more than one *hiragana* came to be used for a syllable. It was not until 1900 that the principle of one *hiragana* for one syllable was restored. In 1946 the *kana* symbols for *wi* and *we* were removed from the active list. (The *kana* for *i* and *e* adequately represent them since the actual pronunciation of Japanese had ceased to distinguish *wi* from *i,* and *we* from *e* by the 14th century.) Formerly used variant *hiragana* are called *hentai-gana*.

Kana Orthography (Kanazukai)——Orthographic prescriptions involving *kana* are called *kanazukai* (*kana* usage). A need for *kanazukai* occurred when a sound change created two or more formerly

Kana

Example of *man'yōgana* from a Kamakura-period copy of the 8th-century poetic anthology *Man'yōshū.* Shown here is the opening poem, attributed to the late-5th-century emperor Yūryaku. The text is written entirely in Chinese characters, with glosses supplied by later scholars. Nishi Honganji, Kyōto.

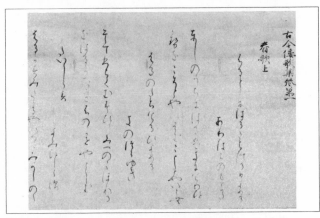

Kana

Opening section of the first book of the *Kokin wakashū.* Shown are several poems, written entirely in *hiragana,* on the seasonal theme of spring. Detail of one page from the collection known as the *Kōya-gire* ("Mt. Kōya fragments"), the oldest extant copy of the anthology. Mid-11th century. Gotō Art Museum, Tōkyō.

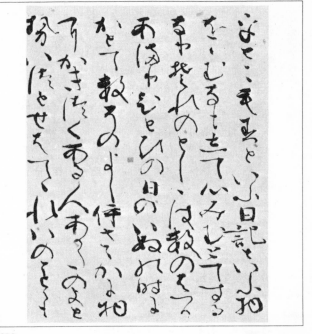

Kana

A passage from the 10th-century *Tosa nikki* by Ki no Tsurayuki written in a mixture of *hiragana* and Chinese characters. From a copy made in 1235 by Fujiwara no Teika. Sonkeikaku Library, Tōkyō. National Treasure.

distinct syllables which had come to be pronounced alike. For example, the syllables, *i, wi,* and *hi* were distinct in the Nara and in the early Heian periods. An h between two vowels came to be pronounced [w], and [w] became lost before vowels except [a] and [o]. This meant that in the late Heian period there were three *kana* symbols, *i, wi,* and *hi,* which represented [i] in the noninitial position. For this reason, by the late Heian period, there arose the need for *kanazukai,* or a convention about which one of the two or more *kana* should be used to represent a syllable such as [i].

There are at least two ways to solve a problem of this nature. One is to follow the usage of an earlier period that is somehow regarded as golden, classical, or before corruption. This is the "historical" approach. According to this approach, in order to establish *kanazukai* for [i], one needs to study the pre-Heian usage and state when to use the *kana i,* when to use the *kana wi,* and when the *kana hi,* retaining all three in the system. The other norm is the new pronunciation. This may be called a contemporary or phonetic approach. According to this solution, one would simply stop using letters no longer needed. To establish *kanazukai* for [i], the *kana* for *wi* would be eliminated from the *kana* inventory, and the *kana* for *hi,* though retained in the inventory (since [hi] is distinct from [i] at the beginnings of words), would not be used in the noninitial position.

The most important *kana* orthographies are: (1) the Teika *kanazukai* (the orthography of Fujiwara no Teika), (2) the *rekishiteki kanazukai* (historical orthography), (3) the *jion kanazukai* (an or-

thography concerned with representing the pronunciation of Chinese characters borrowed into Japanese), (4) the *jōdai kanazukai* (orthography of 8th-century Japanese), (5) *gendai kanazukai* (the current orthography). (1) is a mixture of the historical and contemporary approaches. (2), (3), and (4) are historical, and (5) is almost completely contemporary.

Teika kanazukai. The orthographic convention proposed by Fujiwara no Teika (FUJIWARA NO SADAIE; 1162–1241) and by his followers including Gyōa of the 14th century. Teika was born in a period when an earlier /h/ (probably [Φ]) between two vowels had changed to [w], and the [w] was lost before vowels except [a] and [o]. In his time, there was more than one *kana* symbol for the syllables [i], [ye], and [wo]. In an intervocalic position, there were *i, wi, hi* for [i]; *e, we, he* for [ye]; and *o, wo, ho* for [wo]. Teika apparently had no intention of making rules for the general public, but wrote down for his own reference what he considered to be a possible statement about when to use eight *kana* symbols: *o, wo, e, we, he, i, wi,* and *hi.* The principle Teika followed in his work *Hekian* (also known as *Gekanshū*) was a contemporary approach for *o* and *wo* and a historical one for the remaining six *kana* symbols. The *kana o* was to be used for a low pitched [wo] and *wo* for a high pitched [wo]. For the remaining six symbols he cited "classical" or early Heian and earlier examples.

Later in his *Kanamoji-zukai* (after 1363) Gyōa gave further illustrative examples covering not only the eight symbols Teika treated, but also six more symbols: *wa, ha, ho, u, hu,* and *mu.* In an inclusive sense the orthographic prescription implicit in the works of Teika and Gyōa and their followers is called Teika *kanazukai.*

Rekishiteki kanazukai. The orthographic convention proposed by KEICHŪ (1640–1701) and by his followers. In addition to the sound changes that necessitated the Teika *kanazukai,* another set of changes took place before Keichū's time. By the end of the Muromachi period [d] changed to [dz] before [i] or [u], [dz] changed to [z], and [z] changed to [ž] before [i]. This means that the earlier *di* (ぢ) and *zi* (じ) fell together, and so did the earlier *du* (づ) and *zu* (ず). (The sound distinctions among these four symbols cannot be expressed in the system of romanization used elsewhere in this encyclopedia.) These four *kana* symbols (known as *yotsugana*) created an additional area of orthographic confusion. Keichū, who extensively examined literature from before the middle of the Heian period, noticed that the Teika *kanazukai* did not always agree with the classical examples. Being unaware that Teika, Gyōa, and others

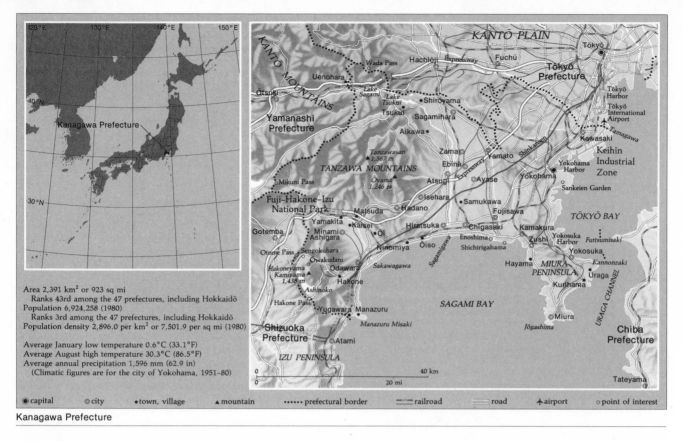

Area 2,391 km² or 923 sq mi
Ranks 43rd among the 47 prefectures, including Hokkaidō
Population 6,924,258 (1980)
Ranks 3rd among the 47 prefectures, including Hokkaidō
Population density 2,896.0 per km² or 7,501.9 per sq mi (1980)

Average January low temperature 0.6°C (33.1°F)
Average August high temperature 30.3°C (86.5°F)
Average annual precipitation 1,596 mm (62.9 in)
(Climatic figures are for the city of Yokohama, 1951–80)

◉ capital   ◎ city   • town, village   ▲ mountain   ••••• prefectural border   ══ railroad   ═══ road   ✈ airport   ○ point of interest

Kanagawa Prefecture

used both historical and contemporary approaches, Keichū wrote *Waji shōran shō* (1693) to correct the "mistakes" of Teika. Keichū's historical approach gained support among scholars of the Japanese classics and influenced MOTOORI NORINAGA (1730–1801) through *Kogentei* (1764), a work by Katori Nahiko (1723–82). Scholars in the classicist school were prominent in the Meiji government, and Keichū's historical orthography was adopted in the elementary school curriculum and continued to be taught until 1946.

Jion kanazukai. The orthographic convention concerning how to represent the *on* readings of Chinese characters by means of *kana*. The *jion kanazukai* may be considered a part of the *rekishiteki kanazukai*, since it is a convention based on the historical approach, in writing *on* readings that became homonymous. For example, the Chinese ending -au changed to ou when borrowed into Japanese and later to o: (ō).

The Chinese -waŋ changed to wau in Japan, then to o:. The Chinese -ap changed to ahu, to au, to ɔ:, then to o:. The Chinese -au changed to ɔ:, then to o:. Thus many characters borrowed from Chinese came to have long o: (ō) endings. The following are some examples:

Character	Middle Chinese	18th-cent Japanese	Jion Kanazukai
口	k'ɔu	ko: (kō)	ko u
広	kuaŋ	ko: (kō)	ku wa u
甲	kăp	ko: (kō)	ka hu
交	kău	ko: (kō)	ka u
劫	kïap	ko: (kō)	ko hu

Much of the *jion kanazukai* was established in Motoori Norinaga's *Jion kanazukai* (1774), which relied on works on Chinese phonology by MONNŌ (1700–1763), who in turn relied on a late-Tang-dynasty (T'ang; 618–907) rhyme table, *Yunjing* (*Yün-ching*; J: *Inkyō*). Motoori's reputation as a classical scholar resulted in the adoption of the *rekishiteki kanazukai* (including the historically oriented *jion kanazukai* for *on* readings) in the elementary school curriculum until 1946.

Jōdai kanazukai. Orthographic convention of 8th-century Japanese using *man'yōgana*. That there were a greater number of distinctions in types of syllables in 8th-century Japanese than in the Japanese of the Edo period (1600–1868) was detected by Motoori Norinaga in the course of his study of the *Kojiki,* and later his stu-

dent ISHIZUKA TATSUMARO (1764–1823) made an extensive investigation of not only the *Kojiki,* but also the NIHON SHOKI and *Man'yōshū* to support his teacher's hypothesis. Basically they noted that in the 8th-century documents there were two mutually exclusive groups of *man'yōgana* characters for the following 13 syllables: *e, ki, ke, ko, so, to, nu, hi, he, mi, me, yo,* and *ro.* It was not until HASHIMOTO SHINKICHI (1882–1945) that the *jōdai kanazukai* phenomenon was interpreted as a possible indication that the 8th-century vowel system was different from later systems. The number of vowels in terms of surface phonemics postulated for the Nara period (710–794) became a lively issue in the 1970s. Matsumoto Katsumi and Roland Lange posited 5, HATTORI SHIRŌ 6, and Ōno Susumu 8 (Ōno later modified this to 4). Problems of the reconstitution of the phonological picture of the 8th century aside, it is true that as a transcriptional or orthographic convention an eight-way distinction among vowels did exist. If a number smaller than eight is to be postulated for the 8th-century vowel system of Japanese, the *jōdai kanazukai* phenomenon may be regarded as just that, namely nothing more than an orthographic convention not faithfully reflecting the actual pronunciation of the Nara period.

Gendai kanazukai (current orthography) or *shin kanazukai (new orthography).* An orthographic convention which originated with Cabinet Order (Naikaku Kunrei) No. 88 and Cabinet Announcement (Naikaku Kokuji) No. 33 of 16 November 1946. It is an attempt to replace the *rekishiteki kanazukai,* which is largely based on the Heian usage, with a system that represents the pronunciation of contemporary Japanese. However, the *gendai kanazukai* is not fully representative of the pronunciation of today's Japanese in at least three areas. One is the area of three grammatical particles: [wa] for topic, [o] for object, and [e] for direction, are written *ha, wo,* and *he* respectively, preserving the practice of the *rekishiteki kanazukai.* The second is in the writing of the long o vowel. The long vowel ō or [o:], which developed from earlier *oho* or *owo* is written *oo,* as in *ookii* "big," *tooi* "distant," *too* "ten." Other cases of long o are written *ou.* The third is in the choice of either *di, du,* or *zi, zu* in the first syllable in the second member of a compound. When the simplex begins with a [t], the second member is to be written with *di* (ぢ), or *du* (づ). Otherwise *zi* (じ) or *zu* (ず) is to be used (in either case, the actual pronunciations are *ji* and *zu,* respectively). For example, *hana* (はな) "nose" plus *ti* (ち) "blood" is to be written *hanadi* (はなぢ) "nosebleed," not *hanazi* (はなじ). (The pronunciation is *hanaji.*) With the exception of these inconsistencies, the *gendai kanazukai* is a more phonetically oriented *kana* orthography than any of its recent predecessors.

📖——Hashimoto Shinkichi, *Moji oyobi kanazukai no kenkyū* (1949). Komatsu Hideo, *Iroha uta* (1979). Komatsu Shigemi, *Kana* (1968). Ōno Susumu and Shibata Takeshi, ed, *Iwanami kōza: Nihongo*, vol 8 (Iwanami Shoten, 1977).   *Haruo AOKI*

Kanagaki Robun (1829–1894)

Author and journalist. Real name Nozaki Bunzō. Born in Edo (now Tōkyō). Inheriting the farcical tradition from the late Edo period (see GESAKU), he excelled in humorous descriptions of the confusion resulting from the introduction of Western culture in the early years of the Meiji period (1868–1912). He tried unsuccessfully to turn to more serious writing, then worked for a number of newspapers, establishing himself as an able feature reporter. His principal works are *Seiyō dōchū hizakurige* (1870–76) and *Agura nabe* (1871–72).

Kanagawa Prefectural Museum of Modern Art

(Kanagawa Kenritsu Kindai Bijutsukan). Located in Kamakura, Kanagawa Prefecture. A museum that collects and exhibits Japanese and foreign art from the 19th century to the present. Opened in 1951, the museum has played an active part in the contemporary art field, organizing important exhibitions of Japanese and Western art and publishing excellent catalogs. It has purchased Japanese paintings, prints, and sculpture, as well as Western prints.
Laurance ROBERTS

Kanagawa Prefecture

(Kanagawa Ken). Located on the southern edge of the Kantō Plain in central Honshū and bounded by Tōkyō on the north, Tōkyō Bay on the east, Sagami Bay on the south, and Shizuoka and Yamanashi prefectures on the west. The terrain of the western part of the prefecture is mountainous, and the southern and eastern sections are coastal plains. Principal rivers are the SAGAMIGAWA, flowing south through the center of the prefecture into Sagami Bay, and the TAMAGAWA, which flows eastward into Tōkyō Bay. The climate is generally mild, especially along the southern coast.

The area was known as Sagami Province under the ancient provincial system (see KOKUGUN SYSTEM). The city of KAMAKURA served as the seat of the Kamakura shogunate from 1192 to 1333, and during the Edo period (1600–1868) the area became a vital transportation link between Edo (now Tōkyō), the seat of the Tokugawa shogunate, and the western half of Japan. The arrival of Commodore Matthew PERRY off the coast of URAGA in 1853 and the signing of the Kanagawa Treaty ushered in a new era in the nation's history. The prefecture's present name was established in 1876, but its boundaries were not settled until 1893. Although it suffered severe damage in the TŌKYŌ EARTHQUAKE OF 1923 and during World War II, it has developed into one of Japan's major industrial centers. Industries include machinery, electrical equipment, food processing, chemicals, and steel. Many of the factories are concentrated along Tōkyō Bay in KAWASAKI and YOKOHAMA. Yokohama also ranks as one of Japan's leading ports for international trade.

The Hakone area in southwestern Kanagawa is part of the FUJI-HAKONE–IZU NATIONAL PARK. Kamakura is known for its enormous statue of the Buddha (DAIBUTSU) and numerous historical sites. The mountains of Tanzawa and the beaches of Sagami Bay attract many vacationers. Area: 2,391 sq km (923 sq mi); pop: 6,924,-258; capital: Yokohama. Other major cities include Kawasaki, YOKOSUKA, FUJISAWA, SAGAMIHARA, and HIRATSUKA.

Kanagawa Treaty

Officially, Treaty of Peace and Amity between the United States and the Empire of Japan (Nichibei Washin Jōyaku). Signed 31 March 1854 at Kanagawa (now Yokohama, Kanagawa Prefecture) following the visit of Commodore Matthew C. PERRY to Japan. The treaty included the following terms: (1) the ports of Shimoda and Hakodate would be opened to American ships; (2) provisions would be supplied to these vessels; (3) shipwrecked sailors would receive good treatment; and (4) an American consulate would be established in Shimoda. A most-favored-nation clause was also included: both nations agreed to extend to each other any favorable trading terms

offered in subsequent agreements to third parties. Conclusion of the treaty between Tokugawa shogunate officials and Perry signaled the end of Japan's 200-year policy of NATIONAL SECLUSION; the shogunate concluded similar treaties with the British that same year, with the Russians in 1855, and with the Dutch in 1856. See OPENING OF JAPAN.

Kanai Noburu (1865–1933)

Economist. Born in what is now Shizuoka Prefecture. After graduating from Tōkyō University in 1885, he studied governmental approaches to social problems in Germany and England. Becoming a professor at Tōkyō University in 1890, he followed the German model in advocating governmental legislation of social policy. He became the first dean of the School of Economics at his alma mater in 1919. He was one of the seven professors involved in the so-called SHICHIHAKASE JIKEN at the outbreak of the Russo-Japanese War. Among his books are *Shakai keizaigaku* (1902, Social Economics) and *Shakai mondai* (1892, Social Problems).
YAMADA Katsumi

Kan'ami (1333–1384)

Full name: Kan'ami Kiyotsugu. Early NŌ (SARUGAKU) actor and playwright, and the father of the celebrated ZEAMI. One source says he was a nephew of the *samurai* warrior KUSUNOKI MASASHIGE. Kan'ami founded the Yūzaki troupe, from which the modern KANZE SCHOOL claims descent. After a life of touring he died following a performance at the Sengen Shrine (sacred to the deity of Mt. Fuji) in 1384.

Kan'ami's historic triumph came in Kyōto in 1374, when he danced *Okina* for the shōgun ASHIKAGA YOSHIMITSU. This was the first time a ruler had deigned to watch the then plebeian *sarugaku*. The secret of Kan'ami's success is said to have been that he introduced into *sarugaku* the highly popular *kusemai*, a lively song and dance form. He was a great artist, and Zeami gave him the highest possible praise. Indeed Zeami in his early critical writings claims only to pass on his father's teachings. No plays by Kan'ami survive intact, but masterpieces based on his originals include *Eguchi, Motomezuka*, and *Matsukaze*.
Royall TYLER

Kanamori Tokujirō (1886–1959)

Government official and politician. Born in Aichi Prefecture. After graduation from Tōkyō University in 1912, Kanamori entered the Ministry of Finance and in 1934 was appointed director-general of the Cabinet Legislative Bureau (Hōseikyoku). He resigned from his post two years later under attack from rightists for supporting the constitutional theories of MINOBE TATSUKICHI (see also TENNŌ KIKAN SETSU). In 1946 he became minister of state in the first YOSHIDA SHIGERU cabinet. In this capacity he was responsible for answering inquiries from the Diet on the draft of the new CONSTITUTION, a particularly difficult task in that, although the constitution was in fact an entirely new document, it was presented to the nation as a revision of the Meiji Constitution of 1889. Many of the questions focused on Japan's KOKUTAI (state structure or "national polity") and on the new symbolic role of the emperor; Kanamori is still remembered for his response to the latter point: the emperor would remain "the center of national aspirations." With the promulgation of the constitution in 1947, he resigned and later served as the first head of the NATIONAL DIET LIBRARY.
ITŌ Masami

kanamugura

(Japanese hop). *Humulus japonicus*, an annual climbing vine of the mulberry family (Moraceae), which grows wild in fields, empty lots, and along roadsides throughout Japan. Its hard stem and stalks have short spines, and its opposite palm-like leaves resemble those of the hop plant and are coarsely toothed. The *kanamugura* is dioecious; male flowers are pale yellow and bloom in long clusters in autumn; female flowers are small and cone-like. The fruits (achenes) are egg-shaped and 5 milimeters (0.2 in) long. Along with other weed vines generically called *mugura* in Japanese, the *kanamugura* has appeared in literature since ancient times in descriptions of desolate dwelling places.
MATSUDA Osamu

Kanaya

Town in central Shizuoka Prefecture, central Honshū, on the river Ōigawa. Kanaya developed as a POST-STATION TOWN during the Edo period (1600–1868). Tea is cultivated on the nearby upland MAKINOHARA and the town produces tea-processing machinery. It is also the site of the National Research Institute of Tea. Pop: 21,857.

Kanazawa

Capital of Ishikawa Prefecture, central Honshū. The political, economic, and cultural center of the Hokuriku region (the part of central Honshū that faces the Sea of Japan). Kanazawa developed during the 15th century as a virtually autonomous temple town of the Ikkō sect (see JŌDO SHIN SECT). The Ikkō sectarians were destroyed in 1580 by Sakuma Morimasa, who built a castle here in 1580. The city thereafter came under the rule of the powerful MAEDA FAMILY, who acted as patrons of the arts and learning. Kanazawa is still known for its KUTANI WARE, *kaga yūzen* (printed silk), MAKI-E (a type of decorated lacquer ware), and embroidery. Modern industries include textiles and machinery. Spared by the bombings of World War II, it retains much of its character as a castle town; tourist attractions are KENROKUEN, a garden begun in the early 19th century by the MAEDA FAMILY and now a park, and the remains of Kanazawa Castle. Pop: 417,681.

Kanazawa Bunko

(Kanazawa Library; also known as the Kanesawa [or Kanezawa] Bunko). Library in Kanazawa Chō, Kanazawa Ku, in the city of Yokohama, Kanagawa Prefecture; with the ASHIKAGA GAKKŌ library, it was one of the two most important centers of learning in medieval Japan. The library was opened in 1275 by Hōjō Sanetoki (also known as Kanezawa [or Kanesawa] Sanetoki; 1224–76), a grandson of HŌJŌ YOSHITOKI, second regent *(shikken)* of the Kamakura shogunate (1192–1333). Sanetoki was from his youth intent on learning and aspired to acquire all existing books in Chinese and Japanese; he succeeded in amassing a collection of classics, histories, poetry, essays, novels, and medical and astrological texts that was unrivaled in Japan. He housed the collection in his villa at Kanesawa (now Kanazawa Ku, Yokohama). The library was enlarged by his son Hōjō (Kanazawa) Akitoki (1248–1301) and grandson Kanezawa Sadaaki (1278–1333). Sanetoki's great-grandson Kanezawa Sadamasa (d 1333) left the area to serve as shogunal deputy in Kyōto (Rokuhara *tandai*) and allowed the library to decline.

The collection was open to the members of the Kanezawa family, scholars, and priests, but books did not circulate. The library included an office, a reading room, and a stack area containing some 20,000 ancient books, 7,000 manuscripts, and many other articles valuable to scholarship. Among its holdings are the *Issaikyō* (Complete Collection of the Buddhist Scriptures) copied in the Liu-Song (Sung) period (420–479) in China, an 11-headed Kannon (Goddess of Mercy), a Śākyamuni, a Miroku, and other Buddhist images designated as Important Cultural Properties, and the manuscript of *Tsurezuregusa* by the essayist YOSHIDA KENKŌ, who was one of the many regular users of the library.

For a period the library was called Shōmyōji Bunko, after a neighboring temple that maintained it and housed portions of the collection. Some of the valuable holdings were lost or scattered to other libraries after the fall of the Kamakura shogunate and the destruction of the Hōjō family in 1333. In 1601 TOKUGAWA IEYASU moved a portion of the collection to his Fujimitei library (now the Imperial Household Library) in Edo Castle. MAEDA TSUNANORI and other Tokugawa vassals acquired some of the Japanese books, but the bulk of the Buddhist texts remained at the Shōmyōji. The collection is now housed in a new building and is administered by the Kanagawa prefectural government. *Theodore F. WELCH*

Kanazawa Plain

(Kanazawa Heiya). Located in western Ishikawa Prefecture, central Honshū. Situated along the Sea of Japan, it consists of alluvial fans of the river Tedorigawa and the floodplain of the river Saigawa, with high sand dunes along the coast. Two lagoons, Kahokugata and Shibayamagata, are located in the interior of this rice-producing region. Around the city of Kanagawa, commercial, industrial, and residential areas are expanding. The major cities are Kanazawa and Komatsu. Area: 760 sq km (293 sq mi).

kana-zōshi

Kana-zōshi properly means a book in *kana,* i.e., in genuine Japanese rather than in Chinese or in a sinicized style. In literary history *kana-zōshi* are popular works published between 1600 and 1682, the date of SAIKAKU's *Kōshoku ichidai otoko* (The Life of an Amorous Man). They number roughly 200 and account for most of the nonscholarly or nonclassic books printed during their time. *Kana-zōshi* were succeeded by the genre of popular literature known as UKIYO-ZŌSHI, the first example of which is the above work by Saikaku.

Tokugawa rule, once established, brought peace to Japan at last. With new opportunities for wealth and culture, people were eager not only for pleasure but for self-improvement. Indeed many laws encouraged study, and the means for a diffusion of knowledge were at hand. For one thing movable type had reached Japan from Korea at the close of the 16th century. No matter if the Japanese soon found it easier to print their cursive script, with copious illustrations, from whole-page blocks; the movement was under way and bookstores began to appear. For another thing there were many poor but educated men quite willing to teach a paying public. *Kana-zōshi* authors were often *samurai* of modest rank whose livelihood in peacetime was uncertain; others were monks, physicians, or even needy court nobles. Confucian scholars wrote *kana-zōshi* with missionary intent. However, none of the *kana-zōshi* authors were themselves common townsmen. It was not until the center of printing moved to Ōsaka in the late 17th century that a townsman literature began to develop in its own.

Few *kana-zōshi* are well-constructed stories; some provide only the thinnest fictional setting for static exposition of a message, while others resemble rambling gossip. There are tales of desperate romance; stories of merchants who made good; Buddhist homilies; Confucian portraits of ideally noble women; guides to the pleasure quarters; parodies of the classics; and even a very successful translation of Aesop's *Fables* (ISOHO MONOGATARI). Many offer, besides entertainment, religious and ethical instruction or practical information. For example, a *kana-zōshi* author might work into his hero's trip down the highway TŌKAIDŌ all sorts of sermons, curious incidents, and tips on what to see and how best to travel.

As literature, *kana-zōshi* lack distinction. Many do make important ideas or intriguing experiences accessible to an unsophisticated public, but in the process they reduce the subtle to the pedestrian. *Kana-zōshi* may draw upon the language of the NŌ theater, for example, but they turn the poetry of Nō into melodrama. They also explain deep Buddhist paradoxes in terms of stock morality. They constantly admonish the man in the street to look to his neighbor, keep law and custom, work hard, and so find peace. Though commendable, such a message is not yet the realm of art, any more than the counterpart levity that some *kana-zōshi* display.

Five relatively early *kana-zōshi* are typical of many: *Uraminosuke* (after 1612, author unknown), a tale of tragic love between a young gallant and a princess; *Chikusai* (ca 1632, attributed to Tomiyama Dōya; 1585–1634), the travels of a quack doctor along the Tōkaidō; *Kiyomizu monogatari* (1638, A Tale of Kiyomizu, by Asayama Soshin; 1589–1664), a debate in which Confucianism bests Buddhism—a Buddhist refutation entitled *Gion monogatari* appeared a few years later; *Kashōki* (1642, Worth A Laugh, by Joraishi, dates unknown), a miscellany of reflections on the failings of the age; and *Nise monogatari* (after 1640, Fake Tales, author unknown), a minute parody of the classic ISE MONOGATARI (mid–10th century, tr *Tales of Ise*, 1968). Of particular interest are such works as *Ukiyo monogatari* (after 1661, Tales of the Floating World) by ASAI RYŌI (d 1691), at once the best and the most prolific of the *kana-zōshi* authors. This Pure Land Buddhist monk was perhaps Japan's first professional writer.

◼ ——Aoyama Chūichi, *Kinsei zenki bungaku no kenkyū* (1966). Donald Keene, *World Within Walls* (1976). Noda Hisao, *Kinsei shōsetsu shi ronkō* (1961). *Royall TYLER*

Kanchūki

The diary of the Kamakura-period (1185–1333) courtier Kadenokōji Fujiwara no Kanenaka (1244–1308), who worked in the KURŌDO-DOKORO (Bureau of Archivists). The title *Kanchūki* is taken from an alternative pronunciation of the first and last characters of his name. The diary is also known as *Kanenaka Kyō ki* and *Kanenaka ki*. Only later copies of the diary are extant, and the original number of volumes is unknown. It is a record of the period 1268–1300, but there are many missing sections. The entries are accurate and valuable, covering matters relating to SHŌEN (landed estate) disputes, the MONGOL INVASIONS OF JAPAN, relations between the imperial court and the Kamakura shogunate, and the alternating succession between the Daikakuji and Jimyōin branches of the imperial house.

G. Cameron HURST III

Kanda Aqueduct

(Kanda Jōsui). In Tōkyō, central Honshū. Extends from Inokashira Pond to Sekiguchi through the Takaido, Nakano, and Yodobashi districts of Tōkyō. One of the three main aqueducts of Edo (now Tōkyō) during the Edo period (1600–1868), its construction was initiated in the late 16th century on the orders of Tokugawa Ieyasu. It supplied water to the Kanda, Nihombashi, and Kyōbashi districts. Length: approximately 17 km (11 mi).

Kanda Festival

(Kanda Matsuri). Major festival of the KANDA SHRINE in Tōkyō. The gods presently enshrined are Ōnamuchi no Mikoto and Sukunahikona no Mikoto. However, according to popular legends, the shrine was originally built to placate the angry spirit of the rebel TAIRA NO MASAKADO (d 940). During the Edo period (1600–1868), this festival and the SANNŌ FESTIVAL at the HIE SHRINE enjoyed the special patronage of the shōgun. After a shogunal decree of 1681, the Kanda and Hie shrines observed their festivals in alternate years, with a smaller observance called a "shadow festival" (kage matsuri) held in the off years. Originally held on 15 September, the Kanda Festival now takes place on 15 May. Parishioners parade floats (DA-SHI), wagons filled with dancers (yatai), and portable shrines (MIKO-SHI) through a large area of downtown Tōkyō. Ōtō Tokihiko

kandaka

(valuation in terms of kan). A means of designating the tax value of agricultural land in the latter part of the Kamakura period (1185–1333) and Muromachi period (1333–1568). Kandaka was the amount of tax revenue derived from the land as expressed in a monetary unit called kammon (kan-mon). (When the tax value of land was expressed in terms of EIRAKUSEN, another currency widely circulated during the same period, it was referred to as EIDAKA.) At a time when units of measurement were not nationally standardized, this system provided a widely recognized method of stating the amount and value of land. Although the tax value of land was stated as a specific amount of currency, the tax was not necessarily paid in cash; rather, agricultural or other products of a value equivalent to the cash amount due were frequently collected. The kandaka system of land valuation was gradually replaced throughout most of Japan, beginning about 1582, with the enactment of TOYOTOMI HIDEYOSHI's major land survey (see KENCHI). From this time on, land value was generally expressed in terms of the amount of rice that could in theory be produced on it (KOKUDAKA).

Philip BROWN

Kanda Kōhei → Kanda Takahira

Kanda Shrine

(Kanda Jinja). A Shintō shrine, also popularly called Kanda Myōjin, in Chiyoda Ward, Tōkyō, dedicated to Ōnamuchi no Mikoto (see ŌKUNINUSHI NO MIKOTO) and Sukunahikona no Mikoto, two deities concerned with pacifying the Japanese islands in mythic times. In the medieval period (13th–16th centuries), however, the shrine was closely associated with the propitiation of the spirit of TAIRA NO MASAKADO, a rebel against the central government who was killed in 940. During the Edo period (1600–1868) the shrine became extremely popular with residents of downtown Edo (now Tōkyō). In order to give the shrine a more national character, the deity Sukunahikona was enshrined in 1934 in place of Masakado, whose shrine hall had been destroyed in the earthquake of 1923. Its celebrated festival, known as the Kanda Matsuri (KANDA FESTIVAL), is held on 15 May in alternate years. Stanley WEINSTEIN

Kanda Takahira (1830–1898)

Also known as Kanda Kōhei. Scholar and bureaucrat. Born in what is now Gifu Prefecture. At a time when Japan was still closed to foreigners (see NATIONAL SECLUSION), Kanda applied himself to

WESTERN LEARNING, the body of knowledge that had come into Japan through Dutch traders, and became a teacher at the BANSHO SHIRABESHO, the shogunate school for Western studies. After the Meiji Restoration (1868) he worked for the new government, doing research on economics and government. Kanda was also a member of the MEIROKUSHA, the society of scholars who introduced Western thought to Japan in the early part of the Meiji period (1868–1912). His proposal and implementation of the LAND TAX REFORM OF 1873–1881 and his work in setting up organs of local government firmly established his reputation. He was appointed to the House of Peers in 1890. His most important work, Keizai shōgaku (1867, Introduction to Economics), essentially a translation of William Ellis' Outlines of Social Economy, is the earliest Japanese book about Western economics. Kanda was father-in-law of the educator Kanda Naibu (1857–1923).

Kanebō, Ltd

Company engaged in the manufacture and sales of textiles, cosmetics, pharmaceuticals, and industrial and housing materials. It is the second largest producer of cosmetics in Japan. The company began as a small spinning mill in Tōkyō in 1887, gradually branching out into the spinning, weaving and finishing of cotton, wool, silk, and rayon, as well as the production of nylon, polyester, and acrylics. Kanebō's printed fabrics are noted for their high quality and creative designs. Products such as Belleseime synthetic suede, Belltron antistatic nylon, and Lufnen flame-retardant acrylics are popular on the Japanese market. In the cosmetics field, the company has recorded more than 10 percent growth annually in both sales and profits in the 1970s. It has over 100 subsidiaries in Japan and overseas, including 17 affiliates and subsidiaries in the United States, Brazil, Indonesia, and other countries. Sales for the fiscal year ending April 1982 totaled ¥276.3 billion (US $1.1 billion), distributed as follows: acrylics 7.1 percent, polyester 15.8 percent, cosmetics 30.5 percent, nylon 10.5 percent, wool 13.3 percent, cotton 8.1 percent, rayon staples 4.7 percent, silk 1.4 percent, pharmaceuticals 3.7 percent, industrial materials 2.2 percent, and other products 2.7 percent. The company was capitalized at ¥20.4 billion (US $83.3 million) in 1982. Corporate headquarters are located in Ōsaka.

Kaneda Masaichi (1933–   )

Professional baseball pitcher and manager. Born in Aichi Prefecture of Korean parents. He left high school without graduating and joined the Kokutetsu Swallows professional baseball team as a pitcher in 1950. During his 20 years as a professional player, Kaneda set a new world record of 4,490 strikeouts and a new Japanese record of more than 20 victories a year for 13 consecutive seasons (1951–64). From 1964 he played with the Yomiuri Giants until his retirement in 1969, soon after pitching his 400th victory. He served as manager of the Lotte Orions from 1972 to 1978.

TAKEDA Fumio

Kanegafuchi Chemical Industry Co, Ltd

(Kanegafuchi Kagaku Kōgyō). General chemical manufacturer whose chief products are vinyl chloride and soda. The company was formed in 1949 from the seven chemical factories of the Kanegafuchi Spinning Co (now KANEBŌ, LTD). With the successful mass production of vinyl chloride resin, the firm expanded its business to include production of butanol and electrolytic soda. With the development of its acrylic fabric Kanekalon in 1957, the company entered the synthetic-fiber field and in the 1960s, with the development of processing methods for oils and fats and the manufacture of petroleum protein, it moved into the foodstuff field. However, petroleum protein is no longer produced in Japan, although its technology was exported to Italy. The company is the largest Japanese producer of vinyl chloride monomer and has developed a unique technology for the production of the monomer styrene and heat resistant resin. Kanegafuchi Chemical has subsidiaries in Belgium, the Philippines, and Indonesia. Sales for the fiscal year ending March 1982 totaled ¥160 billion (US $664.7 million) and capitalization stood at ¥11.4 billion (US $47.3 million). The main office is in Ōsaka.

Kan'eiji

Temple in Ueno Park, Daitō Ward, Tōkyō, belonging to the TENDAI SECT of Buddhism. The Kan'eiji was built in 1625 (Kan'ei 2) at the urging of the influential monk Tenkai (1536?–1643), who convinced the shōgun TOKUGAWA IEMITSU that a temple should stand to the northeast of Edo Castle, since it was commonly believed that evil spirits emanated from that direction. Thus Kan'eiji was to perform the same function for Edo Castle that ENRYAKUJI performed for the Imperial Palace in Kyōto. Kan'eiji was richly supported by the Tokugawa family; seven Tokugawa shōguns were interred there. Many of the imposing temple structures were built by *daimyō* wishing to demonstrate their loyalty to the Tokugawa family. Until modern times it was customary to choose as abbot a member of the imperial family who had taken holy orders. Most buildings were destroyed in the BOSHIN CIVIL WAR of 1868.   *Stanley* WEINSTEIN

kan'ei jigyō haraisage

(sale of government enterprises). The sale of certain factories, mines, and other enterprises by the Meiji government to private interests, mainly in the 1880s. It became official policy as part of the financial retrenchment program adopted in November 1880 and marked a major shift in government economic policy from direct state involvement in the economy to promotion of private industry through technical guidance and subsidies. Since the immediate object was to help restore government finances, the initial list of enterprises scheduled for sale was restricted largely to GOVERNMENT-OPERATED FACTORIES that were running deficits, and the terms of sale were relatively stiff. As a result, there were few takers. After 1884, however, financial considerations became less pressing as the MATSUKATA FISCAL POLICY began to show results. The government accordingly relaxed the terms of sale and added such profitable operations as mines to the list of enterprises for sale. In addition, although the government had originally been prepared to sell its enterprises to anybody with sufficient funds, after 1884 it sought only buyers with demonstrated business ability. The state thus sold off many of its enterprises, with the principal exception of military and communication works, to such established concerns as MITSUI, MITSUBISHI, and FURUKAWA at low prices and on long-term installment plans. The sale helped these so-called SEISHŌ, or businesses with political connections, to develop into the giant business combines known as ZAIBATSU. But the fact that most of the enterprises sold by the state had been losing money and that the buyers were already proven entrepreneurs suggests that private initiative rather than government favoritism was the key to the success of the sale.

📖 ——Kobayashi Masaaki, *Nihon no kōgyōka to kangyō haraisage* (1977). Thomas C. Smith, *Political Change and Industrial Development in Japan: Government Enterprise, 1868–1880* (1955).

kan'ei kōjō → government-operated factories, Meiji period

Kan'ei shoka keizu den

(Kan'ei House Genealogies). The first comprehensive collection of the genealogies of *daimyō* and *hatamoto* (direct shogunal vassals) houses; named for the year of its completion, Kan'ei 20 (1643). Compiled by order of the Tokugawa shogunate under the direction of the Confucian scholar HAYASHI RAZAN, the work was based on genealogies submitted by the daimyō and hatamoto houses themselves. The genealogies were classified into four groups according to the prominent ancient lineages from which the houses claimed descent: Seiwa Genji (see MINAMOTO FAMILY), Taira (see TAIRA FAMILY), Fujiwara (see FUJIWARA FAMILY), and miscellaneous. The detail and accuracy of the individual genealogies vary greatly.

Kaneko, Josephine Conger (1872–1939)

American feminist, socialist, and journalist who married a Japanese and helped to inform Americans about Japanese women. Born in Centralia, Missouri, she studied at Christian College (Columbia, Missouri) and at Ruskin College (Trenton, Missouri), where she majored in and taught vocal music. As a girl she learned the printing and publishing business from her elder brother Ernest, who owned a local newspaper, and at the same time she began writing poetry. From 1903, when she became a member of the Socialist Party, until 1905, she was on the editorial staff of *Appeal to Reason,* a popular socialist paper published in Girard, Kansas. In 1905 she married a Japanese socialist, Kaneko Kiichi (1876–1909), who had studied at Harvard and become a reporter for the *Chicago Socialist Daily.* In

June 1907 she and her husband founded in Chicago a monthly magazine, *The Socialist Woman* (renamed *The Progressive Woman* in 1909). This magazine, which was unique for its frequent coverage of Japanese women, served as the official organ of the Women's National Committee of the Socialist Party until 1912, when it lost party support and changed its name to *The Coming Nation.* After *The Coming Nation* was discontinued in 1914, she worked as editor of *Home Life Magazine* and *The Mother's Magazine* until about 1920. Her major publications include *Stray Thoughts* (1901), *Little Love and Nature Poems* (1903), *Woman's Slavery* (1913), and *Woman's Voice: An Anthology* (1918).   KOKUBO *Takeshi*

Kaneko Kentarō (1853–1942)

Government official and public figure whose career spanned a period from the late 1870s to the early 1940s. Born to a *samurai* family in the Fukuoka domain (now part of Fukuoka Prefecture), in 1871 he went to the United States and enrolled at Harvard College, from which he was graduated in 1878 after having studied political science, economics, and law. On his return the same year to Tōkyō he became a lecturer in the preparatory course at Tōkyō University. In 1880 he was appointed a secretary in the GENRŌIN (Senate).

In 1884 he became involved in the task for which he became most famous, the drafting of the Meiji CONSTITUTION. He was assigned to the Seido Torishirabe Kyoku (Office for the Investigation of Institutions), the name given to the government office that was responsible for the drafting of the constitution. He was associated with ITŌ HIROBUMI, who was in charge of the enterprise, INOUE KOWASHI, and ITŌ MIYOJI. His relationship with Itō Hirobumi had a profound effect on his career.

In 1885 Kaneko became secretary to Itō, who in that year became Japan's first modern prime minister. In 1886 he was appointed a lecturer at Tōkyō University. Two years later he was again secretary to Itō, now the self-appointed president of the Privy Council, which he had set up to review the draft constitution before its promulgation in 1889.

In 1890 Kaneko was named to the House of Peers, which had just convened under the new constitution, and was made its secretary. Four years later he was appointed vice-minister of agriculture and forestry. In 1898 he was named minister of agriculture and commerce in the third Itō cabinet, and in 1900 minister of justice in the fourth Itō cabinet. However, his record was not distinguished, and he never again served as a cabinet minister. Although he was associated with the RIKKEN SEIYŪKAI, Itō's political party, he did not become a leading party politician.

During the RUSSO-JAPANESE WAR (1904–05), he was sent to Washington, DC, to act as a spokesman for his country. There he became a friend of Theodore Roosevelt. In 1906 he was appointed a member of the Privy Council; he served until his death. In his later years he wrote several books on the Meiji Constitution, dealing particularly with its origins. He also chaired the committee (Ishin Shiryō Hensan Kai) responsible for compiling documents concerning the Meiji Restoration.

Kaneko was made a baron in 1900 for his distinguished contributions to the state, a viscount in 1907 for his services in Washington during the Russo-Japanese War, and a count in 1934 for his work on the compilation of restoration documents. He received an honorary degree from Harvard University.   *John M.* MAKI

Kaneko Mitsuharu (1895–1975)

Poet, essayist, novelist. A poet who said in his youth, "to oppose is to be alive" (quoted from the 1917 poem "Hantai"), Kaneko elevated skepticism to an art. His revulsion against "people," power, tradition, war, and colonialism is forcefully expressed in a small but monumental book of poems, *Same* (1937, Shark). During World War II, he alone among the major poets wrote antiwar poems, most of which were published in *Rakkasan* (1948, Parachute), *Ga* (1948, Moths), and *Oni no ko no uta* (1949, Songs of a Devil's Child).

Born Ōshika Yasukazu, the third son of a *sake* dealer and speculator, Kaneko was adopted by a well-to-do family and brought up in Tōkyō and Kyōto. Beginning in 1914, he attended Waseda University, Tōkyō School of Fine Arts (now Tōkyō University of Fine Arts and Music), and Keiō University, but finished none of them. In 1916 he met several poets and wrote his first poems. That same year his adopted father died, and Kaneko inherited a considerable fortune, which he quickly spent—partly for publishing his first book of poems, *Akatsuchi no ie* (1919, A House of Red Clay), and partly for travel abroad. Going to Europe in 1919 as an apprentice to an antique dealer, he settled in a suburb of Brussels and stayed there until the end of 1920. During this Belgian stay, he studied art, read Verhaeren, Baudelaire, and Leconte de Lisle, among others, and wrote poetry. Some of these poems were published in *Koganemushi* (1923, A Golden Beetle). This book, which Kaneko wished to have regarded as his first, is unique among his many volumes of poetry in betraying, almost to an awkward degree, an indebtedness to European poetry, especially Parnassian.

In 1924 Kaneko, by then with no income, met and soon married Mori Michiyo (b 1901), a poet and novelist. The understanding between them that their marriage should not impede their individual freedom led to Mori's having an extramarital affair in 1927. The difficulties they experienced because of this incident, as well as their financial problems, impelled them to go abroad in 1928. Their travels, which took them to Shanghai, Hong Kong, several Southeast Asian countries (mostly colonies at that time), and Paris, lasted until 1932. Unlike Kaneko's first European trip, this trip was full of hardship, and it gave him a different perspective, providing him with ample writing material. It is touched upon in the *Same* poems; the prose account, *Marē Ran'in kikō* (1940, Malay–Dutch East Indies Travelogue); and autobiographical works like *Dokuro hai* (1971, Skull Bowl), *Nemure Pari* (1973, Sleep, Paris), and *Nishi higashi* (1974, West East). This trip also helped deepen Kaneko's sense of alienation, especially since he returned to a changed Japan where he found himself almost forgotten. After World War II, the about-face made by the Japanese in their attitude toward Americans and Englishmen reinforced his alienation.

With his reputation established as an outsider, Kaneko became more prolific. At the same time he developed a distinct, often experimental style, which combined earthy description, veiled erudition, and the tone of a perpetual complainer. His later poems are often wordy and formless, but in most the poet's remarkable narrative skill sustains the reader's interest. Notable among his postwar books of poetry are *Ningen no higeki* (1952, The Tragedy of Man), an autobiographical sequence incorporating prose elements, which won the Yomiuri Literary Prize; *Suisei* (1956, Force of the Water), his technically most experimental book; *IL* (1965, He), an allegory with Christ as the protagonist, for which he received a Rekitei Poetry Prize; and *Wakaba no uta* (1967, Songs on Wakaba; expanded 1974), a collection of poems about his granddaughter.

Among his prose works are *Shijin* (Poet, serialized in 1956, revised and published in book form in 1973), an autobiography, *Zetsubō no seishin shi* (1965, A History of Desperate Souls), and *Nipponjin no higeki* (1967, Tragedy of the Japanese); the last named are both attempts to explore the Japanese national character. He also wrote extensively on poetry and translated Verhaeren, Rimbaud, Baudelaire, and Aragon.

◼——Kaneko Mitsuharu, *Kaneko Mitsuharu zenshū* (Shōshin Sha, 1956–64). Kaneko Mitsuharu, *Kaneko Mitsuharu zenshū* (Chūō Kōron Sha, 1975–77). *Hiroaki* SATŌ

Kaneko Naokichi (1866–1944)

Pre–World War II entrepreneur and chief manager of SUZUKI SHŌTEN. Born in what is now Kōchi Prefecture, Kaneko joined Suzuki Shōten in Kōbe in 1886, transforming it from a small sugar importer into a leading general trading firm that rivaled MITSUI and MITSUBISHI in scale during the economic boom of World War I. Suzuki Shōten collapsed during the FINANCIAL CRISIS OF 1927; however, TEIJIN, LTD, KŌBE STEEL, LTD, and ISHIKAWAJIMA–HARIMA HEAVY INDUSTRIES CO, LTD, all companies fostered by Kaneko under the aegis of the giant trader, went on to become leading corporations in their own right. *KATSURA Yoshio*

Kanematsu–Gōshō, Ltd

One of the leading Japanese GENERAL TRADING COMPANIES. Founded in 1889, it assumed its present name in 1960 at the time of the merger of F. Kanematsu & Co, Ltd, and the Gōshō Co, Ltd. Starting as textile traders, both developed into general trading companies; the nontextile division now accounts for over 78 percent of the firm's trading volume. The firm's activities range from straight trading to acting as a land developer. The company has 80 overseas and 20 domestic offices; 34 affiliates operate overseas and 100 in Japan. Sales for the fiscal year ending March 1982 totaled ¥3.3 trillion (US $13.7 billion), distributed as follows: textiles 22 percent;

metals 16 percent; machinery and construction 14 percent; fuels 28 percent; foodstuffs 10 percent; and chemicals, general merchandise, lumber, and paper 10 percent. Exports amounted to 15 percent; imports 24 percent; overseas sales 10 percent; and domestic sales 51 percent. The firm was capitalized at ¥8.9 billion (US $37 million) in 1982. The company's main offices are located in Tōkyō and Ōsaka.

Kanemi kyō ki

Diary of Yoshida Kanemi (1535–1610), head of the branch of Shintō known as Yoshida Shintō. Entries date from 1570 to 1610, with occasional gaps. The author, who was responsible for various official ceremonies in Kyōto, was able to observe at close hand important events and figures at a time when the city was the center of political change. The military takeover of Kyōto by ODA NOBUNAGA and his death at Honnōji, the construction of Ōsaka Castle and Jurakudai by TOYOTOMI HIDEYOSHI, Hideyoshi's military expeditions to Odawara and Nagoya and his land surveys, are some of the events described. References to NŌ, *renga* (see RENGA AND HAIKAI), and the tea ceremony also make the diary a valuable source of information on the arts of the period.

Kanemi Oil Poisoning Incident

(Kanemi Yushō Jiken). The world's largest and first major episode of food poisoning by polychlorinated biphenyls (PCBs). It took place in 1968, affecting 13,000 persons who had consumed contaminated cooking oil produced by the Kanemi Sōko Co. Victims experienced chloracne, a severe skin disease, as well as cardiovascular and central nervous system disorders. By 1978 the government had officially designated 1,614 sufferers of the disease, including 51 deaths.

The contamination occurred in February 1968 during Kanemi's manufacturing of cooking oil from rice bran. PCBs, used as a heat-transfer medium in a deodorizing process, leaked from stainless steel pipes into the cooking oil mixture. It is believed that the PCBs were overheated which produced corrosion in the pipes and created pinhole leaks.

At the end of February, 2,000,000 chickens fell sick, of which 400,000–500,000 died. The Ministry of Agriculture and Forestry traced the cause to a Kanemi by-product added to chicken feed but neither identified the poison nor notified the Ministry of Health and Welfare of possible food contamination. The chicken poisoning became known as the "dark oil incident."

During the spring and summer of 1968, people throughout western Japan became ill. In October a sufferer brought a sample of Kanemi rice bran oil to a health center for testing because he believed it was contaminated. Soon thereafter a reporter for the newspaper *Asahi shimbun* scooped the story and reported the oil disease in the national media. In November the contaminant was identified as PCBs, a toxic chlorinated organic chemical and the same contaminant found in the Kanemi by-product added to chicken feed.

In October 1977, more than nine years after their tragedy had begun and eight-and-a-half years after entering court, 44 victims of Kanemi oil disease won a total legal victory against the companies involved: Kanemi Sōko, producer of the oil, and Kanegafuchi Chemical, manufacturer of the PCBs. The Fukuoka District Court found both companies guilty of negligence under civil law and instructed them to pay the plaintiffs ¥682 million (US $2.5 million). A similar decision was rendered by the Kokura branch of the same district court, which in March 1978 awarded 729 plaintiffs ¥6.08 billion (US $28.8 million) in damages to be paid by the two companies. The Kokura decision denied only one of the plaintiffs' major points, ruling that the local and national governments (codefendants in the trial) were not legally responsible for causing the massive food contamination. The two court cases significantly advanced the concept of "product liability" in Japan. In May 1978, however, Kanegafuchi was appealing both decisions.

◼——Fujiwara Kunisato, *PCB osen no kiseki* (1977). Norie Huddle and Michael Reich, *Island of Dreams: Environmental Crisis in Japan* (1975). Isono Naohide, *Kagaku busshitsu to ningen, PCB no kako, genzai, mirai* (1975). Gensyu Umeda, "PCB Poisoning in Japan," *Ambio* (August 1972). *Michael R. REICH*

Kanenaga, Prince (1329–1383)

(Kanenaga Shinnō). A son of Emperor GO-DAIGO who fought on for his father after the failure of the KEMMU RESTORATION; also known as Prince Kaneyoshi. Go-Daigo's restoration of direct imperial rule had been cut short by the revolt of one of his generals, ASHIKAGA TAKAUJI. Takauji had set up a member of a rival line of the imperial family as emperor in 1336, and Go-Daigo had established the Southern Court at Yoshino in the same year (see NORTHERN AND SOUTHERN COURTS). In 1338 the young Kanenaga was sent to Kyūshū to command forces loyal to the Southern Court. Making his way along the Inland Sea, the prince arrived at Satsuma Bay in 1342, and with the aid of several local warlords, by 1361 he was in control of most of Kyūshū. Ashikaga Takauji dispatched the general IMAGAWA SADAYO to destroy his power, and in 1375 the defeated prince withdrew to Yabe in Chikugo Province (now Fukuoka Prefecture), where he died in obscurity.

Kanesawa Bunko → Kanazawa Bunko

Kanesawa Sanetoki → Kanazawa Bunko

Kaneshige Tōyō (1896–1967)

Potter. Born Kaneshige Isamu in the Imbe district of the city of Bizen, Okayama Prefecture, to a family said to have been making BIZEN WARE since the Azuchi–Momoyama period (1568–1600). Tōyō inherited the family kiln in 1915, a time when poverty was forcing his fellow potters to lower their standards or abandon their kilns.

The Azuchi–Momoyama period had been Bizen's golden age, when potters achieved an ideal balance between spontaneity and refinement that was lacking in the decorative products of the Edo period (1600–1868). Tōyō conducted exhaustive research and experiments on firing in an effort to recreate the quality of the Azuchi-Momoyama wares, and eventually he succeeded. Intricate bird and animal sculptures comprise his earlier work, while wheel-thrown TEA CEREMONY vessels with simple contours and rugged surfaces characterize his later pieces. The acclaimed master of Bizen-ware production, Tōyō was declared one of the LIVING NATIONAL TREASURES by the government in 1956. He has exhibited and taught in the United States. He helped to organize the Nihon Dentō Kōgeikai (Japanese Traditional Craft Association) in 1967. His son Michiaki is a Bizen potter.   *Jeanne* CARREAU

kangaku

(government school). A general term for government institutions of higher learning as opposed to private ones. In the Nara (710–794) and Heian (794–1185) periods, the term referred to the government-established Daigaku (see DAIGAKURYŌ) in the capital and the *kokugaku* in the provinces in contrast to the educational facilities of Buddhist temples and private schools for the aristocracy such as the KANGAKUIN. In the Edo period (1600–1868) it referred to the official Confucian teaching authorized by the Tokugawa shogunate, that is, the Zhu Xi (Chu Hsi) school of Confucianism (SHUSHIGAKU) and to the academy of this school, the SHŌHEIKŌ. During and after the Meiji period (1868–1912) it was used to refer to universities and colleges set up by the national government.   *Etō Kyōji*

Kangakuin

Private educational facility established for students in the DAIGAKURYŌ by the Fujiwara family during the Heian period (794–1185). Founded by Fujiwara no Fuyutsugu in 821, this boarding school (also known as Daigaku Bessō) undertook the education of Fujiwara family heirs to prepare them for a career in the bureaucracy. For instructors, they enlisted the doctors (HAKASE) from the Daigakuryō. With the rise of the Fujiwara family, it became the best-organized private school of the day. When the family's power waned at the end of the 13th century, the institute also began to decline, though it lasted until the final years of the Kamakura period (1185–1333).   *Etō Kyōji*

kangeiko

The term for rigorous training exercises performed early in the morning or at night during midwinter, especially during the one-month cold period from 6 January to 3 February. Followers of Buddhism and Shintō carried on this practice in ancient times, and it became part of the traditional training program in both the martial

and performing arts. It is still practiced at KENDŌ and JŪDŌ halls for promoting mental conditioning. At the KŌDŌKAN martial arts hall, midwinter training is still observed as an annual event dating from the Meiji period (1868–1912); lifestyles having changed, however, it is now performed in the afternoon.   *TOMIKI Kenji*

Kanghwa, Treaty of

(Kōkatō Jōyaku). Korea's first modern treaty with Japan, signed on the island of Kanghwa on 27 February 1876. The treaty resulted from Japan's application in Korea of the same tactics of "gunboat diplomacy" used earlier by Commodore Matthew C. PERRY to open Japan in 1854. Japan was determined to secure trade rights and political influence in Korea, which had for centuries been a tributary state under Chinese suzerainty. Seen in historical perspective, the bilateral treaty led to the SINO-JAPANESE WAR OF 1894–1895 and was a step toward Japan's ultimate annexation of Korea in 1910. A reluctant Korea was forced to accept the modern international relationship dictated by Japan; in this sense, the treaty signaled the beginning of Korea's painful process of modernization.

Since the Japanese INVASIONS OF KOREA IN 1592 AND 1597, the Yi dynasty (1392–1910) had maintained friendly relations (Kor: *kyorin*; J: *kōrin*) with the Tokugawa shogunate. The Confucian policy of *kyorin* prescribed graded relations between peoples on the basis of sincerity, trust, propriety, and respect. After the Meiji Restoration of 1868, the new government in Tōkyō sent an envoy to Pusan with an official letter announcing to the Korean government the end of the Tokugawa shogunate and the restoration of imperial rule. The envoy was Sō Yoshitatsu, lord of the island of TSUSHIMA, through which Japan's relations with Korea had been principally conducted during the Edo period (1600–1868). The Korean government refused to accept the Japanese overture, however, on the grounds that Japan's claim to an imperial government was improper according to the principles of *kyorin*. Korea was at that time under the rule of the TAEWŎN'GUN, the powerful and xenophobic regent for his son King KOJONG; until the end of the regency in 1873, Japan's efforts to open Korea met with little success. The Korean refusal to establish relations with Meiji Japan led to a debate among the Japanese leadership, lasting from 1870 to 1873, in which one faction advocated a military expedition (see SEIKANRON); but in the end it was the judgment of the Meiji oligarchs (*genrō*) that Japan was not ready to engage in a foreign military adventure. Following the Taewŏn'gun's forced retirement in 1873, the Korean government became more responsive to Japan's diplomatic initiatives. Nevertheless, Japan chose to resort to a demonstration of military force to achieve its objective. In 1875 three gunboats were sent into the Yellow Sea, ostensibly to survey Korean coastal waters. When the gunboat *Un'yō* was fired upon off the coast of Kanghwa Island, near Seoul, it quickly fought back and proceeded to capture a Korean fortress. The Meiji government then ordered two gunboats to Pusan "to protect Japanese citizens" and demanded that Korea conclude a formal commercial treaty with Japan.

The treaty was negotiated on Kanghwa in February 1876. The Japanese mission, led by KURODA KIYOTAKA as ambassador extraordinary and minister plenipotentiary and by INOUE KAORU as vice-minister, was accompanied by three gunboats and three armed transport ships in anticipation of military resistance. Korea was taken by surprise by this massive show of force so close to its capital. The Korean government sent Sin Hŏn as minister of reception and Yun Cha-sŭng as vice-minister to negotiate peace with Japan. The negotiations began on 11 February; Japan demanded an apology for the Kanghwa "incident" of the previous year and presented a prepared treaty text of 13 articles, to which the Korean government was asked to respond within 10 days. After minor revisions, the treaty was signed on 27 February; it contained 12 articles and an expression of Korea's regret over the Kanghwa incident. The deleted article dealt with Japan's demand for most-favored-nation treatment, which the Korean government deemed unnecessary on the grounds that Korea would not conclude treaties with any Western nations. The most important stipulations of the treaty may be summarized as follows: Korea was recognized as an independent and sovereign nation possessing equal rights with Japan; an exchange of diplomatic representatives on the ministerial level was arranged; the opening of Pusan and two additional ports for trade with Japan was agreed upon; and Japan's right to establish consulates in three Korean ports with extraterritorial jurisdiction over Japanese nationals was recognized. In reaction to the unequal terms of this treaty, conservative and moderate Korean scholar-officials sent a flood of memorials to the throne in protest, but to no avail. However, the treaty had ushered Korea into the modern world of nation–states, and the one–time "hermit kingdom" now confronted the age of imperialism in East Asia. As for Japan, it gained international recognition for opening Korea on the basis of Western diplomatic principles and for the successful challenge to China's traditional relations with its tributary state.

■——Okudaira Takehiko, *Chōsen kaikoku kōshō shimatsu* (1935). Tabohashi Kiyoshi, *Kindai nissen kankei no kenkyū* (1940, repr 1972). *Fujiya* KAWASHIMA

Kanginshū

(Songs Sung in Tranquility). A collection of 311 songs of the type known as KOUTA. Compiled in 1518; the identity of the editor is unknown. Three-quarters of the songs were chosen from what was sung on private occasions, while the remainder came from the repertoires of diverse performance groups popular in the latter part of the Kamakura period (1185–1333) and in the Muromachi period (1333–1568). Fifteen percent of the latter are from the NŌ theater. This is the first extant collection of *kouta*, a genre that developed in the Muromachi period. It is difficult to give a concise characterization of *kouta*. Shorter than what was sung in the Kamakura period, it has no fixed prosodic pattern, though a stanza of 7-5-7-7 syllable lines predominates. Love is a main theme. Songs in the anthology are grouped first into those on the seasons, then into those on love. The basic guidelines to this system were inherited from traditional collections of WAKA. An additional influence upon the editor was a sense of various relationships possible between adjacent songs, fostered by the practice of linked verse (see RENGA AND HAIKAI). The use of both a Chinese and a Japanese preface is a further inheritance from the imperial collections of *waka* poetry. The former sketches the development of song both in China and in Japan. We also learn something about the editor's motives in undertaking the collection from its prefaces. An example of the characteristic wit between the sexes, which is but one element of its songs, can be seen in number 85: "Remembering/ Is really forgetting, isn't it . . . / You do not have to recall/ What you have not first forgotten."

■——"Kanginshū", tr Frank Hoff as "Private Music," in *Song, Dance, Storytelling: Aspects of the Performing Arts in Japan,* Cornell University East Asian Papers (1978). Asano Kenji, *Kanginshū kenkyū taisei* (1968). *Frank* HOFF

kangō bōeki → tally trade

Kang Youwei (K'ang Yu-wei) (1858–1927)

(J: Kō Yūi). A Chinese Confucian scholar and leader of the Hundred Days' Reform (June–September 1898), Kang Youwei reinterpreted Confucianism to provide a sanction for institutional change. Looking to reforms in Meiji Japan as a model, he led a movement for constitutional monarchy that rivaled the revolutionary movement of SUN YAT-SEN and HUANG XING (Huang Hsing) before the 1911 Revolution.

In 1895 Kang sent to the emperor Guangxu (Kuang-hsü; r 1875–1908) of the Qing (Ch'ing) dynasty (1644–1912) a memorial bearing the signatures of hundreds of scholar candidates gathered in Beijing (Peking) for civil service examinations. This memorial urged the emperor to embark on a series of reforms and to reject the Treaty of SHIMONOSEKI, which had concluded the SINO-JAPANESE WAR OF 1894–1895. Kang's action inaugurated a reform movement among the educated elite that was to culminate in the famous Hundred Days' Reform, in which the emperor issued a stream of edicts following Kang's ideas, which were based on the Meiji experience. He wrote a history of modern Japan for the edification of the emperor, using the accounts written by WANG TAO (Wang T'ao) and HUANG ZUNXIAN (Huang Tsun-hsien).

The reforms were cut short in a coup d'etat by the empress dowager Cixi (Tz'u-hsi; 1835–1908), and Kang fled to Japan, where he was well received by ŌKUMA SHIGENOBU, foreign minister and founder of the SHIMPOTŌ (Progressive Party), and by Prince KONOE ATSUMARO, founder of the Tōa Dōbunkai (East Asia Common Culture Society). Ōkuma had approved of Kang's reform attempts, since he believed that Japan should repay its cultural debt to China by forestalling Western encroachment, thus giving China time to modernize its institutions. The Japanese Ministry of Foreign Affairs provided some of the funds for Kang's subsequent travels around the world in search of support from overseas Chinese for reform in China. Japanese like MIYAZAKI TŌTEN attempted to bring Kang together with Sun Yat-sen, but Kang refused to deal with a man he considered an uneducated antimonarchist. Kang competed with Sun for the support of overseas Chinese until the overthrow of the Qing dynasty in the 1911 Revolution, after which his continued advocacy of constitutional monarchy and of Confucianism as the state religion became increasingly irrelevant.

■——Jung-pang Lo, ed, *K'ang Yu-wei: A Biography and a Symposium* (1967).

Kan Hasshū

(Eight Provinces of Kantō). An old designation used to refer collectively to the eight provinces that comprised what is now known as the KANTŌ REGION. They are Musashi, Sagami, Kazusa, Shimōsa, Awa, Kōzuke, Hitachi, and Shimotsuke provinces, corresponding to the present-day prefectures of Tōkyō, Saitama, Kanagawa, Chiba, Gumma, Ibaraki, and Tochigi.

kan'i jūnikai

("12 grades of cap rank"). The first system of courtly ranks (i) in Japan. Different colored caps (*kan* or *kammuri*) were used to designate each of the 12 ranks. Devised by Prince SHŌTOKU, it was promulgated in 604 as part of his effort to create a strong imperial bureaucracy. In contrast to the earlier hereditary titles (KABANE) based on clan membership, the *kan'i jūnikai* system was designed to reward individual merit and promote loyalty to the emperor. Ranks were named after the six Confucian virtues: *toku* (moral excellence), *jin* (benevolence), *rei* (decorum), *shin* (fidelity), *gi* (righteousness), and *chi* (wisdom); and each of these was subdivided, making 12 ranks in all. Caps of a dark or light shade of purple, green, red, yellow, white, and black were used to indicate rank and entitled the wearer to corresponding privileges at court. The *kan'i jūnikai* system was replaced by a 13-rank system in 647 and the use of caps to indicate rank was abolished in 701 with the adoption of the more elaborate court hierarchy created under the RITSURYŌ SYSTEM. See also COURT RANKS.

Kan'in, House of

(Kan'in no Miya). One of the four princely houses during the Edo period (1600–1868), the other three being Fushimi, Arisugawa, and Katsura. The house was established in 1710 at the recommendation of the scholar-statesman ARAI HAKUSEKI, with a son of Emperor Higashiyama (1675–1709; r 1687–1709) as its first head. The family died out after five generations but was revived in 1872, when a scion of the house of Fushimi, Prince Kotohito (1865–1945), was adopted. In 1947, along with other princely houses, the Kan'in family was relegated to commoner status.

kanji

(Chinese characters). The ideographs of ancient Chinese origin that are still used in China and Japan and were formerly used in other areas influenced by Chinese culture such as Korea and Vietnam. (In North Korea, Chinese characters have been entirely supplanted by the native Korean alphabet [see KOREAN LANGUAGE]; in South Korea they are still used for writing Chinese words. In Vietnam they have been supplanted by the Roman alphabet.)

Chinese characters are ideographs in that essentially each character or graph symbolizes a single idea and, by extension, the sound (i.e., spoken word or morpheme) associated with that idea. For example, the Chinese character 一 represents an idea that is pronounced "one" in English, *yi (i)* in modern standard Chinese, and *ichi, itsu,* or *hitotsu* in Japanese. The character 犬 is "dog" in English, *quan (ch'üan)* in Chinese, and *ken* or *inu* in Japanese. In ancient Chinese each word consisted of a single syllable represented by one character; thus the characters were originally, properly speaking, logographs in that one character represented both the meaning and sound of an entire word. However, in the course of the centuries compound words became more and more common, with the result that the one-to-one correspondence between word and character weakened. Characters continued to represent single syllables, and monosyllabic words continued to exist; however, in compound words characters became word-building units, some of which could no longer stand alone.

Modern printed form	kōkotsu moji "oracle bone" characters	kimbun bronze inscription	kato moji tadpole characters	daiten greater seal script	shōten lesser seal script	reisho clerical style	kaisho standard style	gyōsho semicursive style	sōsho cursive style or "grass writing"
女 (woman)						女	女	女	女
心 (heart)						心	心	心	心
楽 (music; pleasure)						樂	樂	樂	樂

Kanji——Standard examples of the various character styles

In Japan, Chinese characters are used in combination with the Japanese phonetic script known as KANA. Although any word can be written in the phonetic script, words of Chinese origin are normally written in Chinese characters alone as in Chinese, one character per Chinese syllable; however, the Japanese pronunciations of these Chinese syllables are often bisyllabic. In writing native Japanese words, Chinese characters are used either singly or in combination to indicate the meaning—and, by association, the sound—of the word. In the case of inflected words, the Chinese character or characters represent the stem of the word, inflectional suffixes being added in the phonetic script. Thus in Japanese a number of pronunciations are possible for most characters, the choice being dictated by context. For example, in the case of 一 , the first of the two characters cited above, *ichi* and *itsu* are two Japanese versions of the Chinese pronunciation (based on earlier pronunciations in Chinese), while *hitotsu* is the Japanese word for "one." The latter is written with the final syllable *tsu* represented in *kana*, thus: 一つ . In the case of 犬 , *ken* is the Japanese pronunciation of the Chinese word; it is a bound form, used in compound words, while *inu*, the Japanese word, can be used independently. See also the section on the writing system in JAPANESE LANGUAGE.

Types of Chinese Characters——Chinese characters were classified by Xu Shen (Hsü Shen) of the Later Han dynasty (25–220) into six types, which he called the Six Scripts (Liu Shu; J: Rokusho). Only the first four of these are really different types of characters, the other two being extended or "borrowed" uses of characters of these four types. The first two of the four main types are simple characters. Characters of type one are pictographs (Ch: *xiangxing* or *hsiang hsing*; J: *shōkei*), being originally pictorial representations of the things indicated—e.g., 日 (originally written ☉) "sun," 山 "mountain," 川 "river." Characters of type two are diagrammatic (Ch: *zhishi* or *chih-shih*; J: *shiji*), i.e., symbolic representations of concepts or ideas—e.g., 一 "one," 二 "two," 上 (originally written ⌐) "top, above," 下 (originally written ⌐) "bottom, below." Types two and three are complex characters, combinations of two or more simple characters of either type. In type three, "combined meanings" (Ch: *huiyi* or *hui-i*; J: *kaii*), two simple characters are combined to indicate the meaning of a word—e.g., 明 "bright" (composed of 日 "sun" and 月 "moon"), 男 "man" (composed of 田 "field" and 力 "strength"), 信 "belief, trust" (composed of 人 "person" and 言 "word, speech"). In type four, phonetic characters (Ch: *xingsheng* or *hsing-sheng*; J: *keisei*), one element of the character suggests the general area of meaning and the other indicates the sound—e.g., 梅 Ch: *mei* (J: *bai, ume*) "plum" (composed of 木 "tree" and 每 , a character of unrelated meaning [it is used here only for the sound] that is pronounced *mei* in Chinese; hence "the tree that is pronounced *mei*"), 鯉 Ch: *li* (J: *ri, koi*) "carp" (composed of 魚 "fish" and 里 , another character being used as the phonetic element; hence "the fish that is pronounced *li*"). Xu Shen's remaining two categories consist of extended usage of existing characters of the first four types to represent words other than (or in addition to) the ones with which they were originally associated. In type five, "extension" (Ch: *zhuanzhu*

or *chuan-chu*; J: *tenchū*), one character is used to represent a word of the same or similar meaning, but different pronunciation, and thus acquires an additional pronunciation—e.g., 楽 Ch: *yue* (*yüeh*; J: *gaku*) "music," which when pronounced *le* (J: *gaku*) means "pleasure, enjoyment"; 悪 Ch: *wu* (J: *o*) "to hate," which when pronounced *e* (J: *aku*) means "bad." In type six, "borrowing" (Ch: *jiajie* or *chia-chieh*; J: *kasha*), a character is used to represent phonetically a word with the same sound but different meaning—e.g., 萬 Ch: *wan* (J: *man; sasori*) "scorpion," used to write the word *wan* (J: *man*) "ten thousand"; 豆 Ch: *dou* (*tou*; J: *tō;* a raised serving dish), used to write the word *dou* (*tou*; J: *tō, mame*) "beans."

There is also a seventh type, consisting of a limited number of characters coined in Japan by combining elements from existing Chinese characters. These are known as *kokuji* or domestic characters. Two examples are 働 (*dō, hataraku*) "work" (composed of 人 "person" and 動 "move") and 峠 (*tōge*) "mountain pass" (composed of 山 "mountain," 上 "up," and 下 "down").

The total number of characters in MOROHASHI TETSUJI's *Dai kanwa jiten* (Great Chinese-Japanese Character Dictionary) is around 50,000. The majority of these are complex characters of the phonetic (J: *keisei*) type, made up of one element which indicates the general area of meaning and another which indicates the Chinese pronunciation. The existence of such a large number of characters of this type led to the traditional Chinese dictionary arrangement—still used in Morohashi's and other modern Japanese character dictionaries—in which characters with the same meaning element are grouped together so that they can be looked up by referring to a table of meaning elements. In the traditional Chinese arrangement there are 214 of these meaning elements, which are known in English as radicals and in Japanese as *bushu*. Characters of the other four main types are arbitrarily assigned a radical. It is often difficult to tell at a glance which element in a given character is its radical, and many prefer to use one of the other types of indexes provided in Japanese dictionaries, in which characters are listed by their possible pronunciations or by their total number of strokes when written. See also DICTIONARIES.

Character Styles——The oldest known Chinese characters are the so-called oracle bone characters engraved on tortoise shells and animal bones that have been unearthed from archaeological sites assigned to the Shang (or Yin) dynasty (1766 BC–1027 BC) in China. These shells and bones, which are estimated to date from about the 13th century BC, were used by rulers in divinations to determine matters of policy or ritual, the oracle being read from the cracks formed when they were subjected to intense heat. The characters scratched on them are a record of the divination. The oracle bone characters became the subject of full-scale research only in the late 19th century, and they have not yet been completely deciphered. However, it is clear that they are early versions of the Chinese characters used today, though their shapes are simpler and there is considerable variation in the way a given character is written. While simple types of characters (pictographs and diagrammatic characters) predominate, there are also complex characters of the other two types described above, and the oracle bone characters thus represent a fairly advanced stage in the development of the Chinese writing system.

A variety of standardized styles for writing the characters flourished and declined during the course of Chinese history, with the chief styles now still in use developing by the 5th and 6th centuries AD. In the bronze and stone inscriptions of the Zhou (Chou) dynasty (1027 BC–256 BC) the characters of the oracle bones have already been standardized and systematized to a certain degree. These characters are known in Japanese as *kimbun* and *sekibun*, respectively. Another style developed during the Zhou dynasty is that of the so-called tadpole characters (J: *kato moji*), which were written on bamboo or wooden slips in lacquer by means of a stylus. The decorative style known as greater seal script (J: *daiten*) became the standard style during the latter part of this period. During the Qin (Ch'in) dynasty (221 BC–206 BC) an official standardization of the writing system resulted in a refinement of the greater seal script; this is known as the lesser seal script (J: *shōten*). Scribes of the Former Han dynasty (206 BC–AD 8) wrote in an angular, straight-lined style known as the clerical script (J: *reisho*), which developed, during the Later Han dynasty (25–220), into the style known in Japanese as *kaisho*. The angular *kaisho* style remains to this day the standard, noncursive form for Chinese characters. During the 5th and 6th centuries the diffusion of writing on paper by means of brush and ink resulted in the semicursive style known in Japanese as *gyōsho* and the fluid cursive style known as *sōsho* or "grass writing." The *gyōsho* style—and to a more limited extent, the *sōsho*—continue to be used widely along with the *kaisho*. Some of the older styles, particularly the seal scripts and the clerical script, are still occasionally used for decorative purposes.

In both China and Japan, forms of the characters that deviated from the standard forms by the omission or addition of strokes (or by writing one character on the analogy of another), thereby making them easier to remember or to write, came into fairly wide use. These abbreviated or simplified characters are known in Japanese as *zokuji* or popular characters. Eventually the growing use of printing brought on greater standardization, but the abbreviated forms did not disappear entirely, and some of them became the basis for the abbreviated characters now on the officially approved list of characters for general public use in Japan. Modern Japanese typefaces for printing include several styles modeled on the styles current in China during the Song (Sung; 960–1279), Ming (1368–1644), and Qing (Ch'ing; 1644–1912) dynasties and named accordingly.

On and Kun Readings —— Since in the Japanese writing system Chinese characters can be used to write either words of Chinese origin or native Japanese words, the pronunciations that can be assigned to them in reading fall naturally into two categories: (1) the Japanese imitations or approximations of the sound of the original Chinese syllable and (2) the native Japanese word that translates the meaning of the character. The former are called *on* readings (*on yomi*), *on* being written with a character that means "sound" (i.e., the original Chinese sound); these are often referred to in English as "Sino-Japanese" readings. The latter are called *kun* readings (*kun yomi*), *kun* being written with a character that originally meant "to interpret the meaning" (i.e., the meaning of the character as expressed by the Japanese word).

A single character may have two or three possible *on* readings, based on the Chinese pronunciations of different periods or regions. Most of these readings fall into three groups: *go on* (the Wu pronunciation), *kan on* (the Han pronunciation), and *tō on* (the Tang [T'ang] pronunciation). The last two names are somewhat misleading since they seem to refer to, but do not actually derive from, the Han and Tang (618–907) dynasties of China. *Go on* are the earliest pronunciations of the Chinese characters in Japan, i.e., those introduced to Japan during the 6th century and before, when the Chinese writing system was brought in along with Buddhism. *Man'yōgana*, the early Japanese writing system of the poetry anthology *Man'yōshū* and other 8th-century works (in which Chinese characters are used phonetically to write Japanese words; see the section on the Man'yō writing system in MAN'YŌSHŪ), is based largely on *go on* readings.

Kan on are new pronunciations introduced from China during the 7th and 8th centuries. They are approximations of the contemporary pronunciation of the Tang dynasty capital at Chang'an (Ch'ang-an) in the north of China and are markedly different from the older *go on*. It is commonly assumed that the *go* (Wu) pronunciation derived from the Wu region (named after an ancient kingdom) in the lower Yangzi (Yangtze) River area; however, it is not

known for certain that Chinese was first introduced into Japan from that area, and it is possible that the differences between *go on* and *kan on* result as much from intervening sound changes within the Chinese as from regional or dialectal differences. There was an effort to make *kan on* the official pronunciation, but it never completely supplanted *go on* since the older pronunciation was already deeply embedded in Buddhist usage and in many commonly used loanwords.

Tō on consist of pronunciations introduced much later, representing Chinese pronunciations of the Song dynasty and after (they are sometimes referred to as *sō on* [Song pronunciations]). These pronunciations are the closest of all to the pronunciations of modern Chinese. They appear, however, in only a limited number of isolated words, not having been assimilated into Japanese to the same degree as the earlier types of pronunciations.

There is also a miscellaneous category of *on* readings called *kan'yō on* (customary or established *on*); these consist of pronunciations that for various reasons (one being confusion with similar characters) deviate from the pronunciation expected in one of the above categories. Standard Japanese character dictionaries label the various *on* readings for a character by type. Although not all characters have all possible types of *on* readings, quite a number have two or more. For example, the character 行 "to go, behavior, exercise" is pronounced *gyō* (go on), *kō* (kan on), and *an* (tō on), as in *shugyō* (training), *ryokō* (travel), and *andon* (paper lantern on a stand). The character 若 "young" is pronounced *nya* (go on), *nyaku* (also go on), and *jaku* (kan on), as in *hannya* (wisdom), *rōnyaku* (young and old), and *jakunen* (youth).

Both of the above characters also have more than one *kun* reading. Since *kun* readings are translations of the meaning of the character into Japanese, and since there are often various shades of meaning depending on context or on whether the character is being used as a noun or a verb, it sometimes happens that a number of Japanese words have become associated with a particular character. To cite three rather extreme examples, the character 上 "top, above" has a total of 10 readings (2 *on* and 8 *kun*), while the characters 下 "bottom, below" and 生 "sprout, be born, live," etc have 2 *on* readings and 10 *kun* readings each. Most characters, however, have only one or two readings of each type, and some have no *kun* readings or (in the case of "domestic characters" or *kokuji*) no *on* readings. A special type of *kun* reading remains to be mentioned. This is the type called *jukuji kun* (compound-word *kun*) or *ateji* ("ad hoc writing"), in which two or more characters as a compound are translated by a single Japanese word. Two examples are 今日 "today," a compound that can be read in *on* readings as *konnichi*, but which translates into Japanese as the single word *kyō*, and 大人, two characters meaning "big person," which are translated into Japanese by the one word *otona* (adult).

Number of Characters in Use —— The number of Chinese characters currently used in Japan is limited to a small percentage of the 40,000 to 50,000 contained in the larger dictionaries. A list of characters called TŌYŌ KANJI (Chinese characters for daily use) was selected by the Ministry of Education in 1946, limiting the number of characters for official and general public use to 1,850. In 1981 this list was superseded by a similar but larger one (the JŌYŌ KANJI) containing 1,945 characters. This list is intended as a guideline—for use in publications intended for the general public and in setting basic standards for public school education—it being recognized that a greater number of characters is needed in specialized areas. However, even when unrestricted by the *jōyō kanji*, no document employs more than 5,000 characters, most using below 2,000. As for the number of characters known by educated people, if individuals from several generations were sampled the number would probably extend to approximately 3,000. ———— YAMADA Toshio

kanjiki

Special footgear or crampons used for walking on snow, ice, or mud. Those used for walking on snow or ice are traditionally made of wooden hoops with rope straps and metal cleats. TAGETA, or wooden clogs, are used for working in rice paddies. ———— MIYAMOTO Mizuo

kanjō bugyō

(commissioners of finance). The principal financial officials of the Tokugawa shogunate. The post had a long ancestry in various fiscal offices used by warrior regimes from the Kamakura period (1185–1333) onward. The Tokugawa shogunate's Office of Finance (Kanjōsho) was replicated on a smaller scale in most *daimyō* domains, and because shogunate and daimyō domains alike were perennially faced with fiscal problems, these offices were subject to more modification and expansion and generated a greater body of administrative rules and regulations than any other of the Edo period (1600–1868).

In the Tokugawa shogunate the office was usually staffed by four men of relatively high HATAMOTO rank. In 1721–22, in one of many attempts to improve the shogunate fisc, the shōgun TOKUGAWA YOSHIMUNE divided the tasks of the four commissioners, assigning two of them responsibility for fiscal matters as *kattekata* and the other two charge of judicial affairs as *kujikata*. Directly responsible to the individual senior councillor (RŌJŪ) who held the special title of *kattegakari rōjū*, the four officers supervised an army of subordinates that totaled over 5,000 lesser officials, assistants, and petty office personnel. Most of this staff served in the tax-collection offices of intendants (DAIKAN and GUNDAI) that were scattered about the shogunate's own domains (TENRYŌ). Others were in offices responsible for adjudicating legal disputes that involved residents of shogunate lands or that crossed such jurisdictional boundaries as those of daimyō domains. Others worked in the central offices of tax administration, stipend disbursement, and recordkeeping. Still others were engaged in supervising mining and minting operations, commercial levies and licensing, foreign trade at Nagasaki, land mensuration and assessment, forest administration, highway and river utilization, and warehouse management. In times of crisis such as crop failure, famine, riot, conflagration, earthquake, or volcanic eruption, commissioners of finance were commonly assigned emergency responsibility with authority to oversee relief and reconstruction work. Because the office of *kanjō bugyō* was of such central importance to the shogunate, its occupants were usually among the most able and most powerful figures in the regime and exerted great influence on all levels of policy making and implementation. See also KANJŌ GIMMIYAKU.

Conrad TOTMAN

kanjō gimmiyaku

(comptrollers). Investigative officials of the Tokugawa shogunate (1603–1867) first appointed in 1682 and reestablished in 1712 after a 13-year hiatus. The post was usually filled by four middle-ranking HATAMOTO who had served as shogunal intendants (DAIKAN) and were knowledgeable about financial matters. They served one-year terms and were responsible to the senior councillors (RŌJŪ). Assisted by small staffs of subordinates, two of the comptrollers maintained surveillance over fiscal matters (as *kattekata*) and two over judicial matters (as *kujikata*). They usually worked in Edo (now Tōkyō) but could travel about the country on investigations and were authorized to report malfeasance directly to the *rōjū* when necessary.

Conrad TOTMAN

Kankakei

Gorge in the eastern part of the island of Shōdoshima, Kagawa Prefecture, Shikoku. It is known for its strangely shaped rocks, formed by erosion, and for its spectacular autumn foliage. Located within the Inland Sea National Park.

Kankoku Tōkanfu → Resident General in Korea, Office of

Kankyōchō → Environment Agency

Kannamesai

An annual rite in which the emperor makes both direct and indirect offerings of newly harvested rice to AMATERASU ŌMIKAMI, the divine imperial ancestress at the ISE SHRINE. Kannamesai, which literally means "the festival in which the deities taste [the new rice]," is one of the most important rites in the imperial calendar and, according to tradition, has been observed, with few interruptions, since the founding of the Ise Shrine (thought to have been in the 3rd century). It is first described in the TAIHŌ CODE (enforced 702) and further elaborated in the ENGI SHIKI (927; tr *Engi-shiki, Procedures of the Engi Era*, 1970–72). Although originally celebrated in September,

since 1889 the Kannamesai has been performed over a three-day period beginning on 15 October, following the Kammisosai (rite of presenting new clothes to the Inner Shrine) on 14 October.

Prior to the ceremony, the emperor dispatches representatives to Ise to make offerings there. The ceremony begins with a rite (called *miura*) to confirm the ritual purity of the celebrants and participants. Then the sacred food, known as *yuki ōmike* ("pure and sacred rice") consisting of new rice and sacred rice wine *(miki)* and other food, all specially prepared, is offered first at the Outer Shrine (Gekū) of Ise at 10:00 PM on the night of the 15th and again at 2:00 AM in the morning of the 16th; the offering of the new rice is then repeated at the Inner Shrine (Naikū) at 10:00 PM on the night of the 16th and at 2:00 AM on the morning of the 17th. The ceremony is concluded with the recitation of written addresses by the imperial representative and then by the high priest. This is followed by the presentation of sacred offerings; first of various cloths *(heihaku)* and then *tamagushi* (tree branches with cloth streamers). The last ceremony is held at the Outer Shrine at 2:00 PM on the 16th and at the Inner Shrine at 2:00 PM on the 17th, each followed by a performance of a sacred dance *(mikagura; see KAGURA)* in the evening. On the 17th at the Imperial Palace, the emperor, accompanied by other members of the imperial family and a number of specially chosen individuals, worships in the direction of Ise *(yōhai)* and then he makes his own offering at the Kashikodokoro ("Place of Awe") in the palace. See also NIINAMESAI; DAIJŌSAI.

Kannō Disturbance

(Kannō no Jōran, 1350–52). A violent conflict between the shōgun ASHIKAGA TAKAUJI and his younger brother ASHIKAGA TADAYOSHI that split the early Muromachi shogunate into warring factions. The initial point at issue was the great influence of the general KŌ NO MORONAO on state affairs. Failing to displace Moronao from his brother's counsels, Tadayoshi in the autumn of 1350 (Kannō 1) broke with Takauji and launched a campaign against him and Moronao in the name of the Southern Court of Yoshino, the great antagonist of the Ashikaga regime (see NORTHERN AND SOUTHERN COURTS). When Moronao was killed early in 1351, harmony between the brothers was seemingly restored; the end of that year, however, witnessed the bizarre spectacle of the Ashikaga shōgun Takauji taking up the colors of the Southern Court in order to legitimize a march on Kamakura in pursuit of the disaffected Tadayoshi. Early in 1352 another show of reconciliation ended with Tadayoshi's sudden death.

Kannon

(Skt: Avalokiteśvara; Ch: Guanyin or Kuan-yin). Also known in Japanese as Kanzeon or Kanjizai. Together with JIZŌ, one of the most popular of all BODHISATTVAS in Japan. This bodhisattva, the personification of infinite compassion, is believed to deliver all beings from any sort of danger when the name Kannon, meaning "the one who hears their cries," is invoked.

Kannon has long been popular in Chinese and Japanese Buddhism, regardless of sect. PURE LAND BUDDHISM regards Kannon as the major attendant of the Buddha AMIDA (Skt: Amitābha). Kannon can assume any incarnate form, male or female, in accordance with the station of the worshiper, provide protection in the present life, and finally help transport the faithful after death on a white lotus to Amida's Pure Land.

In one chapter of the LOTUS SUTRA, Kannon is depicted in 33 different incarnations. Kannon in female form became especially popular as a bodhisattva for women who desired to become mothers or who wanted reassurance during childbirth. This chapter of the Lotus Sutra, which is sometimes called "Kannongyō" and often recited independently of the rest of the sutra, has been chiefly responsible for the immense popularity of Kannon.

Stories of miracles or testimonial records of Kannon's powers rose to prominence during the 5th century in China and the 8th century in Japan, and pilgrimages to famous Kannon images have been popular for many centuries.

As Avalokiteśvara in India, Kannon was originally male. The origin of Kannon's feminine iconographic representation is the subject of speculation and controversy among scholars. Images of Kannon are predominantly female, the most popular being the White-Robed Kannon (Byakue Kannon) found in Tang (T'ang; 618–907) China from the 8th century and in Japan from the 10th century. The earliest iconographic sketch of a White-Robed Kannon dates to the

Kannon

The gilt wood image of Kannon housed in the Yumedono (Hall of Dreams) at Hōryūji in Nara Prefecture. Popularly known as the Guze Kannon, it represents a form of Kannon as universal savior. It holds in its hands a Sacred Jewel (*hōju*; Skt: *cintāmaṇi*) on a lotus mount. Camphor wood. Height 197 cm. 7th century. National Treasure.

Kan no Wa no Na no kokuō no in

The seal's handle and face. Gold. Base 2.4 cm square. Fukuoka Art Museum. National Treasure.

first half of the 13th century. The most famous images in Japan, designated as National Treasures, are the 7th-century wooden image of Kannon in the Hall of Dreams (Yumedono) at the temple HŌRYŪJI in Nara, and the array of 1,001 small statues of the Thousand-Armed Kannon in the 12th-century temple SANJŪSANGENDŌ in Kyōto. Maria Kannon, a syncretic form of Kannon and the Virgin Mary, was secretly revered by Japanese Christians (see KAKURE KIRISHITAN), primarily in Kyūshū, during the Edo period (1600–1868).

——*Kannon zenshū*, 10 vols (Yūkōsha, 1939–41). Yoshiko Dykstra, "Tales of the Compassionate Kannon: The *Hasedera Kannon genki*," *Monumenta Nipponica*, 31.2 (1976). Hayami Tasuku, *Kannon shinkō* (1970). C. N. Tay, "Kuan-yin: The Cult of Half Asia," *History of Religions* (November 1976). *Diana* PAUL

Kanno Suga (1881–1911)

Anarchist. Born in Ōsaka, the daughter of a traveling mine operator. After a three-year forced marriage, she became a journalist in 1902 and the next year joined the KYŌFŪKAI (Japan's branch of the Woman's Christian Temperance Union). While working for a socialist newspaper in Wakayama Prefecture, she began living with the leftist ARAHATA KANSON in 1906; arrested with him and imprisoned for nearly two months in the RED FLAG INCIDENT OF 1908, she came to believe in the need for violent revolution. While Arahata remained in prison, she began living with the anarchist KŌTOKU SHŪSUI, and she was again imprisoned briefly for helping him publish in 1909 two issues of a magazine called *Jiyū shisō* (Free Thought), which were both banned by the government. She left Kōtoku when she thought him too moderate politically, but both were implicated in the HIGH TREASON INCIDENT OF 1910, an alleged plot to assassinate the emperor Meiji. She and Kōtoku, along with 10 other men, were sentenced to death and hanged in 1911. Her short diary written during her last imprisonment was later published under the title "Shide no michikusa" (1950, Grasses by the Road to Death).
——Kanzaki Kiyoshi, ed, *Taigyaku jiken kiroku*, vol 1: *Gokuchū shuki* (Jitsugyō no Nihon Sha, 1950), contains Kanno Suga's "Shide no michikusa."

Kannoura

District in the town of Tōyō, eastern Kōchi Prefecture, Shikoku. It was a fishing port in the Edo period (1600–1868), and is now a base for offshore fishing, including bonito and tuna, and a shipping port for lumber and marine products. Many scenic islands and inlets are found along the coast.

Kan no Wa no Na no kokuō no in

(seal of the king of the state of Na of Wa, [vassal] of Han). A gold seal (see SEALS) discovered in 1784 on Shikanoshima in Chikuzen Province (now Fukuoka Prefecture). Found by a farmer in his rice field, it was presented through the district authorities to the Kuroda family, lords of the Fukuoka domain, whose descendants still own it. The base of the seal measures 2.4 centimeters (0.95 in) square and 0.9 centimeters (0.4 in) in height. The handle, carved in the shape of an animal with a snake's head, stands 1.5 centimeters (0.6 in) high, for a total height of 2.4 centimeters (0.95 in). The inscription consists of five Chinese characters, written in *shōten* or "lesser seal script"; rendered into Japanese, it reads: *Kan no Wa no Na no kokuō* (King of the state of Na of Wa [Japan], [vassal] of the Han [dynasty]). It is known that seals of this design were commonly given to "barbarian" rulers by the Han dynasty (206 BC–AD 220) of China. Moreover, the "Basic Annals" of the Chinese work *Hou Han shu* (History of the Latter Han Dynasty) record a presentation of tribute by the king of the Wa state of Na in AD 57, and the chapter "Records of the Eastern Barbarians" in the same work reports that he was given a seal. It is widely accepted that this is the very seal mentioned in the Chinese records, although some scholars regard it as spurious. KITAMURA Bunji

kannushi

A general designation for Shintō priests; the terms *kannushi* and *shinkan*, often refer to Shintō priests in general, although because of the lack of centralization in Shintō, priestly functions, ranks, titles, and names vary greatly depending upon individual shrines as well as on the period of history.

Originally, the term *kannushi* was used to designate those who performed a priestly function in religious ritual, mediating between the people and the divine. *Kannushi* became an institution at some of the larger shrines, such as the Kamo, Iwashimizu, Kasuga, and Matsunoo shrines, during the Heian period (794–1185), when *kannushi* were made the head priests.

Once established, the position of *kannushi* tended to be transmitted hereditarily, as is often the case in Japanese religion. This is how some major priestly families (*shake*) emerged, each connected with a particular shrine; famous ones are the Nakatomi, Imbe, Usa, Kamo, Shirakawa, Yoshida, and Aso families. The hereditary transmission of priestly functions may have reinforced the local character of Shintō and prevented the unification of the religion. The Yoshida family attempted to unify Shintō at the beginning of the 16th century under its own syncretic doctrines with its own system of conferring authorization and transmitting esoteric teachings. The attempt had considerable success among small shrines in rural areas until it was abolished by the newly established Meiji government in 1868 (see YOSHIDA SHINTŌ).

At small village shrines there was no institution of professional priesthood prior to the Edo period (1600–1868). Rather, there was the MIYAZA and *tōya* system in which lay people, often the heads of

Kanō Eitoku——Chinese Lions

A six-panel folding screen in colors on a gold ground. The dramatic appearance of the mythical lions and the monumental scale typify Eitoku's mature style. 225.0 × 459.5 cm. Late 16th century. Imperial Household Agency.

powerful households, presided by turns over the annual village festival. There is the suggestion in this of the original form of the *kannushi* role.

As the administrative head of a shrine, the designation *gūji* came to replace that of *kannushi*, although the former term remains in general use. The hierarchy headed by the *gūji* is made up of the second-ranked *negi* and the third-ranked *gonnegi*. At the ISE SHRINE *negi* specialized in the ritual expression of supplications to the divinities; at other main shrines the position was created to serve more general functions as well.   *Allan G. GRAPARD*

Kanō Eitoku (1543–1590)

KANŌ SCHOOL painter. Real name Kanō Kuninobu. The eldest son of Kanō Shōei (1519–92); grandson of KANŌ MOTONOBU, from whom he received his initial artistic training. Contemporary diaries indicate that Eitoku was the most sought-after artist of his day; his dramatic, monumental style of color-and-gold screen and wall painting for the decoration of castles and palaces during the Azuchi-Momoyama period (1568–1600) became a legacy for generations of Japanese artists.

Eitoku lived in a turbulent age of warfare and political instability, and many of his major works for the military leaders of the age—paintings for AZUCHI CASTLE built for ODA NOBUNAGA and for the Jurakudai and ŌSAKA CASTLE built by TOYOTOMI HIDEYOSHI—were destroyed shortly after their completion. Nevertheless, by the early 20th century, numerous paintings in Kyōto temples had been attributed to Eitoku; but scholarship by Tsuchida Kyōson, Doi Tsugiyoshi, Takeda Tsuneo, and others has helped to separate authentic Eitoku paintings from those of his followers and those from contemporaneous ateliers, such as those of the HASEGAWA SCHOOL and KAIHŌ SCHOOL.

An example of Eitoku's early style can be seen in the panel paintings *(fusuma-e)* in the Jukōin, the memorial chapel in the DAITOKUJI complex built in 1566 while Eitoku was in his early 20s. His painting of *The Four Elegant Pastimes (Kinki shoga zu)* is in the detailed style favored by many 15th-century Muromachi artists. However, *Birds and Flowers (Kachōzu)*, though indebted to the Motonobu mode, incorporates elements of Eitoku's monumental style. The birds and landscape elements are large and painted with a broad, vigorous brush. The integrity of the picture plane is paramount, with little interest in background elements or spatial depth.

Another important surviving work done in the detailed style associated with YAMATO-E painting is his *Scenes in and around Kyōto (Rakuchū rakugai zu)*, screens in the Uesugi Collection, Yamagata Prefecture. These screens are unquestionably by Eitoku, since they have been preserved in the same collection since their presentation by Oda Nobunaga to UESUGI KENSHIN in 1574. This popular genre subject depicts the yearly customs and festivals of Kyōto and its environs from a panoramic, bird's-eye point of view.

From about 1576 to 1579 Eitoku devoted his energies to the Azu-

chi Castle project. Following its completion he was awarded the honorary priest rank of *hōin*. Although Eitoku's most illustrious projects from the 1580s for Ōsaka Castle (ca 1584), the Sentō Palace of retired emperor Ōgimachi (ca 1584–86), Hideyoshi's residence Jurakudai (ca 1587), TŌFUKUJI (1588), Tenzuiji (1589), and the Imperial Palace (ca 1589–90) have perished, a group of works of varying degrees of authenticity illuminate Eitoku's activity during this final decade of his life. These include a pair of hanging scrolls, *Xu You* and *Chao Fu* (Hsü Yu and Ch'ao Fu; J: *Kyoyū* and *Sōfu*; Tōkyō National Museum) and two screens, *Chinese Lions (Karajishi zu*; Imperial Household Collection), and *Cypress Trees (Hinokizu*; Tōkyō National Museum). The latter two works typify Eitoku's developed style: the motifs are simplified, the scale is large and almost theatrical in depiction, the brush strokes are broad, rough, and lively, and the colors are vibrant and vivid in contrast to the gold leaf of the background. Eitoku died while working on the Imperial Palace commission in Kyōto.

——Doi Tsugiyoshi, *Motonobu, Eitoku*, vol 8 of *Suiboku bijutsu taikei* (Kōdansha, 1974). Doi Tsugiyoshi, *Kanō Eitoku, Mitsunobu*, vol 9 of *Nihon bijutsu kaiga zenshū* (Shūeisha, 1978). Takeda Tsuneo, *Kanō Eitoku*, tr H. Mack Horton and Catherine Kaputa (1977).   *Catherine KAPUTA*

Kanogawa

River in Izu Peninsula, Shizuoka Prefecture, central Honshū, originating in the AMAGI PASS and flowing north to empty into Suruga Bay at the city of Numazu. A flood control canal was constructed after the great flood of 1958, caused by the Kanogawa typhoon. The Tagata Plain, through which it flows, is the prefecture's largest strawberry-producing area. Numerous hot springs, including Shuzenji and Yugashima, are located along the gorges of its upper reaches. Length: 48 km (30 mi).

Kanō Hōgai (1828–1888)

KANŌ SCHOOL painter. Born in Chōfu, Nagato Province (now part of Yamaguchi Prefecture), he was the son of Kanō Seikō, who served as a painter for the local *daimyō*. In 1846 Hōgai was sent at the domain's expense to Edo (now Tōkyō) to study painting with Kanō Shōsen'in (1823–80). He returned home in 1856. In 1859 he received a commission to do ceiling paintings for the inner citadel of Edo Castle. Later, one of his paintings was selected for the 1876 Paris international exposition. Despite these honors he suffered financial difficulties and had to earn his living from other pursuits, including casting iron, reclaiming land, and running a writing-utensil store. His troubles were exacerbated by the social and economic uncertainties around the time of the Meiji Restoration (1868). In 1877 Hōgai returned to Tōkyō and worked for the SHIMAZU FAMILY from 1879 to 1882, where he had ample opportunity to study works by classical artists such as SESSHŪ TŌYŌ, SESSON SHŪKEI, and KANŌ

Kanō Motonobu——Bird-and-flower paintings at Daisen'in

Detail of one of a set of sliding-door paintings now mounted as hanging scrolls. Colors on paper. 174.5 × 139.5 cm. Ca 1513. Daitokuji, Kyōto.

TAN'YŪ. The American art critic Ernest F. FENOLLOSA was impressed by Hōgai's work at the Second Domestic Painting Competitive Exhibition (Naikoku Kaiga Kyōshinkai) in 1884, bought several of his paintings, and they became close friends. Fenollosa, Hōgai, HASHIMOTO GAHŌ, and OKAKURA KAKUZŌ participated in the Kangakai (Painting Appreciation Society), which played an important role in inspecting and drawing attention to important classical art objects in Kyōto and Nara. Hōgai adapted techniques of Western painting such as the use of bright colors and chiaroscuro to the tradition of Buddhist painting. His best-known paintings are *Deva Seizing a Demon* (1886), based on a Tan'yū work, *Fudō Myōō* (1887), and *Merciful Mother Kannon* (1888), which shows the influence of Western religious paintings.   *Frederick* BAEKELAND

Kanō Jigorō (1860–1938)

Educator; founder of the Kōdōkan school of JŪDŌ. Born in Settsu Province (now Hyōgo Prefecture); graduate of Kaisei Gakkō (now Tōkyō University). A disciple of the Tenjin Shin'yō and the Kitō schools of *jūjutsu,* Kanō transformed what had been primarily a martial art into a sport with spiritual and educational value. He established the Kōdōkan school of *jūdō* in Shitaya, Tōkyō, in 1882 and helped spread *jūdō* throughout Japan as well as abroad. In 1909 he became the first Japanese member of the International Olympics Committee (IOC); in 1912 he led the Japanese delegation to Japan's first Olympics in Stockholm in 1912. He also helped found the JAPAN AMATEUR SPORTS ASSOCIATION and served as its first head. He served as president of Tōkyō Higher Normal School and taught at the Peers School. He died in 1938 on his way back from an IOC meeting in Cairo, where he had won approval for Tōkyō as the site of the 1940 Olympics, an event that was never held.   TAKEDA *Fumio*

Kanō Kōkichi (1865–1942)

Scholar. Born in what is now Akita Prefecture. Kanō graduated from Tōkyō University, where he studied mathematics and philosophy. He served as principal of the First Higher School (Daiichi Kōtō Gakkō) in Tōkyō and as the first chairman of the humanities department at Kyōto University. A thoroughgoing rationalist, he taught that God, free will, and the imperishable soul were the three great delusions of mankind. After resigning from Kyōto University in 1908, he engaged in art appraisal, while continuing to read widely. His interest in the scientific thought of the Edo period (1600–1868) led to the discovery of two original thinkers, ANDŌ SHŌEKI and SHIZUKI TADAO.   TANIKAWA *Atsushi*

Kanō Masanobu (1434–1530)

Painter. Traditionally called the founder of the KANŌ SCHOOL of painting. Masanobu was the eldest son of Kanō Kagenobu, a warrior from the village of Kanō in Izu Province (now Shizuoka Prefecture) who also painted. It is not clear who gave Masanobu his

formal training as a painter, although most scholars now believe that he, like OGURI SŌTAN, studied with SHŪBUN at the temple SHŌKO-KUJI in Kyōto. The *Inryōken nichiroku,* a log kept by one of the subtemples of Shōkokuji during the mid-15th century, lists a KAN-NON and RAKAN wall painting for the Unchōin subtemple painted by Masanobu in 1463. Many other works by Masanobu are mentioned in the *Inryōken,* including posthumous portraits of leading nobles, monks, and military men such as FUJIWARA NO YOSHI-TSUNE, Kisen Shūshō (1423–93), and ASHIKAGA YOSHIMASA. These paintings were in polychrome and ink, as were the Buddhist votive paintings by Masanobu also mentioned in this record.

What is unusual is that, apart from the painting done for the Ganseiin in 1492 and *The Eight Views of Xiao and Xiang (Hsiao and Hsiang)* for the GINKAKUJI, few ink paintings by Masanobu are documented. Yet Masanobu is renowned today as an ink painter in the Zen-inspired Muromachi style (see INK PAINTING). His most important surviving works are a folding screen, *Bamboo and White Crane,* in the Shinjuan, DAITOKUJI; a hanging scroll of Hotei (Ch: Budai or Pu-tai) with inscription by Keijo Shūrin (1440–1518) in the Kuriyama Collection, Tōkyō; and a hanging scroll, *Zhou Maoshu (Chou Mao-shu) Admiring Lotus Blossoms,* in the Nakamura Collection, Tōkyō. Though based on the monochrome ink style of Shū-bun, Masanobu's paintings have a clarity and secular appeal distinct from more directly Zen-inspired works. The *Bamboo and White Crane* screen contains fundamental elements of the full-fledged Kanō school style: a decorative interest in large-scale, two-dimensional forms lucidly defined with prominent ink contours.

The Kanō school's formal alliance with the ruling military regime began in 1481 when Masanobu succeeded Sōtan as the official painter *(goyō eshi)* of the Muromachi shogunate. However, it was not until the next generation, when leadership fell to Masanobu's son KANŌ MOTONOBU, that Kanō painting was codified into a distinct style and enjoyed a broad base of support.

📖——Matsushita Takaaki, *Ink Painting,* tr Martin Collcutt (1974). Watanabe Hajime, *Higashiyama suibokuga no kenkyū* (1948).   *Catherine* KAPUTA

Kanō Mitsunobu (1561 or 1565–1608)

KANŌ SCHOOL painter. Son of KANŌ EITOKU and author of a gentle, elegant version of the Azuchi–Momoyama period (1568–1600) color-and-gold painting style. The earliest recorded mention of Mitsu-nobu is in conjunction with the important AZUCHI CASTLE commission of 1581 given to his father, Eitoku. He also worked with Eitoku on such exclusive painting projects as the Jurakudai, ŌSAKA CASTLE, and the Imperial Palace in Kyōto.

When Eitoku died while working on the Imperial Palace, Mitsu-nobu took command of the project and became the head of the family. But he lacked the authoritative leadership and political acumen of Eitoku, and after 1590, many important commissions from TOYOTOMI HIDEYOSHI were awarded to the rival HASEGAWA SCHOOL. Mitsunobu, however, was in charge of the painting project for Nagoya Castle in Hizen Province (now part of Saga and Nagasaki prefectures) in Kyūshū, erected around 1592 as an advance base for Hideyoshi's Korean campaign. In 1600 he executed a series of paintings for the Kangakuin subtemple of the Miidera (in what is now Shiga Prefecture). These sumptuous paintings of flowering trees and cypress in color on gold leaf illustrate Mitsunobu's style of delicately drawn natural forms rhythmically arranged across long sliding door panels. More elaborate examples of Mitsunobu's rich style, delicate designs, and graceful draftsmanship, complemented by exquisite use of color and gold leaf, are found in his paintings for the Chikubu-shima Shrine on an island in Lake Biwa.

📖——Doi Tsugiyoshi, *Motonobu, Eitoku,* vol 8 of *Suiboku bijutsu taikei* (Kōdansha, 1974). Doi Tsugiyoshi, *Kanō Eitoku, Mitsunobu,* vol 9 of *Nihon bijutsu kaiga zenshū* (Shūeisha, 1978). Takeda Tsuneo, *Kanō Eitoku,* tr H. Mack Horton and Catherine Kaputa (1977).   *Catherine* KAPUTA

Kanō Motonobu (1476–1559)

KANŌ SCHOOL painter; the eldest son and heir of KANŌ MASANOBU. He is credited with establishing the orthodox style of the Kanō school and securing its position as the leading school of Chinese-inspired painting in Japan. He inherited from his father the position of painter-in-attendance *(goyō eshi)* to the Ashikaga shōgun and later became the chief painter *(edokoro azukari)* at the Imperial

Court Academy. Extant paintings and literary records testify to Motonobu's artistic lineage in Zen-inspired Chinese INK PAINTING *(suibokuga)*, his training in the indigenous Japanese painting tradition or YAMATO-E, and his familiarity with Chinese polychrome BIRD-AND-FLOWER PAINTING *(kachōga)*. His genius enabled him to practice each of these stylistic traditions independently, but he is best known for his *fusuma-e* (sliding-door paintings) that integrated all the above in his own style.

Motonobu's works are known for their dramatic simplicity. Subtleties of Chinese brushwork were transformed into patterns of viscous contour lines and texturing strokes, often reinforced by additions of saturated color, or washes of color and gold. His compositions thus mark a turning point in the process of assimilating foreign models, not least because his style developed in response to the need for bold, easily comprehended designs suitable for decorating interior architectural screens *(fusuma)*. By reducing the elements of his screen compositions to large-scale patterns of ink, or ink and color, Motonobu created sensuous visual effects superbly attuned to the architectural scale of the format.

Two sets of bird-and-flower sliding-door paintings (now hanging scrolls) executed for the Daisen'in at the temple DAITOKUJI (ca 1513) and for the Reiun'in at the temple MYŌSHINJI (1543), best illustrate Motonobu's accomplishment. Both sets demonstrate his stylistic range, and more critically, the reconciliation of principles of design derived from *yamato-e*, and motifs and techniques derived from *suibokuga* and polychrome bird-and-flower painting. With so unorthodox a meeting of native and foreign heritages, the orthodox *wakan* ("Japanese-Chinese") style of the Kanō school was born.

Motonobu enjoyed the patronage of clients of every social class. Attributions that are accepted today as authentic reflect his range only partially. Much documentation provides evidence of his lifelong relationship with the shogunal house, of his ability to work in any style, format, or genre that suited his patrons' requirements, and of the degree to which his style became the standard manner for decorating temple and palace interiors. Sometime during the 1530s he was granted the honorary title *Echizen no kami* by the Ashikaga shōgun and he also held the honorific priestly title *hōgen*, awarded to artists of highest repute. He commanded unprecedented fees for enormous projects, among them the now lost screen paintings produced during more than a decade of activity at the Jōdo Shin sect temple ISHIYAMA HONGANJI in Ōsaka. His works graced Shintō shrines as well as Buddhist temples, the residences and guest rooms of priests, *daimyō*, and aristocrats, and even were sent to China as gifts to show Japan's artistic maturity and independence.

At the time of his death, Motonobu left in Kyōto a studio of disciples well equipped to transmit his style to successive generations of artists. Motonobu's grandson KANŌ EITOKU further developed and perfected the style Motonobu originated.

📖——Yamaoka Taizō, *Kanō Masanobu, Motonobu*, vol 7 of *Nihon bijutsu kaiga zenshū* (Shūeisha, 1978). Doi Tsugiyoshi, *Motonobu, Eitoku*, vol 8 of *Suiboku bijutsu taikei* (Kōdansha, 1974).
Gail Capitol WEIGL

kan on

(the Han pronunciation). One of the several varieties of *on* readings of Chinese characters (KANJI) as used in Japan. *On* readings are Japanese approximations of the way the characters were pronounced in Chinese, and for any one character there may be two or three possible *on* readings (reflecting the Chinese pronunciations of different periods and different regions). As opposed to *go on*, the pronunciations introduced to Japan in the 6th century and before along with the Chinese writing system and Buddhism (and thought by some to reflect the Chinese pronunciations of the lower Yangzi [Yangtze] River area), *kan on* are pronunciations introduced during the 7th and 8th centuries by envoys and students newly returned from China. *Kan on*, which often differ markedly from *go on*, reflect the contemporary Chinese pronunciations of the Tang (T'ang) dynasty (618–907) capital at Chang'an (Ch'ang-an). *Kan on* were declared the official pronunciations in Japan in 793 as part of an attempt to have them supersede the older pronunciations. However, *go on* had already become deeply entrenched in Buddhist usage and in many commonly used words; furthermore, the influx of new Chinese halted when the sending of envoys to China ceased in the late 9th century. As a result, *kan on* did not replace *go on* completely. Instead it came to exist alongside *go on*, becoming established especially in newly introduced words and in certain academic contexts. See ON READINGS.
YAMADA Toshio

Kan'onji

City in southwestern Kagawa Prefecture, Shikoku, on the Hiuchi Sea. Principal activities are sardine and shrimp fishing, marine-food processing, and the cultivation of rice, tobacco leaves, and mandarin oranges. Textile mills and agricultural machine plants are also located here. The southwestern section of the city is a thriving commercial area. Pop: 44,928.

Kanō Sakujirō (1885–1941)

Novelist. Born in Ishikawa Prefecture. Graduate of Waseda University. A representative writer of the so-called naturalist school in the decade beginning in 1910 (see NATURALISM). While editor of *Bunshō sekai*, a literary magazine, he wrote *Yo no naka e* (1918), an autobiographical description of life in a poor fishing village like his own hometown in Ishikawa. Works include *Yakudoshi* (1911) and *Chichi no nioi* (1941), collections of short stories.

Kanō Sanraku (1559–1635)

Painter. Leader of the Kyōto KANŌ SCHOOL of painting in the early part of the Edo period (1600–1868). Born Kimura Mitsuyori. His father is said to have been a Kanō-style painter and retainer of the warlord TOYOTOMI HIDEYOSHI. Sanraku was trained in Kyōto and became a protégé of KANŌ EITOKU, the leading master of the Kanō school. He became an adopted member of the Kanō family through marriage to Eitoku's daughter. When Kanō Shōei, Eitoku's immediate successor, died in 1592, the leadership of the Kanō school became the shared responsibility of Sanraku and KANŌ MITSUNOBU. With the latter's death in 1608, Sanraku became the head of the school.

Sanraku's name was associated with an unwieldy number of paintings until the 1930s, when efforts of art historians narrowed the number of likely attributions down to a handful. Among the paintings that scholars today consider to be Sanraku's masterpieces are two pairs of six-fold screens in private collections: *Birds of Prey* and the *Imperial Mirror*. Both are Chinese-style ink paintings. The Imperial Mirror theme derives from illustrations in a book on good government published in China in 1573 and in Japan in 1606. More of Sanraku's paintings of birds can be seen in the sliding-wall paintings in the temple Daikakuji in Kyōto. The Daikakuji also has Sanraku's well-known paintings of tree peonies and other plant-and-animal themes, executed in color and gold, which were once considered to be works by earlier Kanō masters. The sliding-wall paintings at the temple Shōdenji in Kyōto show Sanraku's treatment of the famous Chinese landscape theme Eight Views of the Xiao (Hsiao) and Xiang (Hsiang) Rivers (SHŌSHŌ HAKKEI), executed in ink and brushed gold. Finally, there is his four-fold screen *Battle of the Carriages* (now in the Tōkyō National Museum), done in the native YAMATO-E manner, in colors and gold leaf, based on a chapter in the 11th-century novel TALE OF GENJI.

📖——Doi Tsugiyoshi, *Kanō Sanraku, Sansetsu*, vol 12 of *Nihon bijutsu kaiga zenshū* (Shūeisha, 1976). Glenn T. WEBB

Kanō Sansetsu (1589–1651)

Leader of the Kyōto KANŌ SCHOOL of painting from 1635 until his death. Details of his early life are not known, but he is thought to have been born in Kyūshū (according to some sources he was born in 1590) and brought up by Kanō-school artists in Kyōto. He became KANŌ SANRAKU's principal disciple and ultimately his son-in-law, adopted son, and successor.

Sansetsu began a compilation on the history of Japanese painting from his notes on 183 artists, which his son Kanō Einō (1634–1700) edited and published in its final form in five volumes in 1693 as the *Honchō gashi*. After his death, Sansetsu's fame as a painter diminished, perhaps in large part because beyond a few small signed and dated works made routinely for shrines and temples, only one important work was actually signed by Sansetsu: the pair of screens, entitled *Winter Seascape with Birds*, now in a private collection. Recent scholarship, however, has attributed a sizable number of major works to Sansetsu, such as the series of ink monochrome wall paintings in the Shōden'in Shoin, formerly a building within the temple Kenninji in Kyōto but now located at Urakuen, a park near Nagoya. Other attributions include the four eight-fold screens at the temple Zuishin'in in Kyōto; these are colorful figure paintings on the Orchid Pavilion theme, illustrating the famous party hosted by the

4th-century Chinese poet-calligrapher Wang Xizhi (Wang Hsi-chih). The now famous cycles of sliding-door paintings in color and gold leaf at the Myōshinji subtemple Tenkyūin are also thought to have been executed by Sansetsu. From his works it is apparent that Sansetsu stayed close to Chinese models, which he refined and often adapted to a large-scale format with a delicacy that became the hallmark of Kyōto Kanō-school painting from his time on.

📖 ——Doi Tsugiyoshi, *Kanō Sanraku, Sansetsu*, vol 12 of *Nihon bijutsu kaiga zenshū* (Shūeisha, 1976). Tsuji Nobuo, *Shōhekiga zenshū: Tenkyūin* (Bijutsu Shuppan Sha, 1966).   *Glenn T. Webb*

Kanō school

A school of professional artists, patronized from the latter part of the Muromachi (1333–1568) through the Edo (1600–1868) periods by successive military governments. The Kanō were the most enduring and influential of the so-called Japanese schools of Chinese painting *(kanga).*

History——The first important Kanō master and founder of the school, KANŌ MASANOBU (1434–1530), was a follower of the Buddhist Nichiren sect. He emigrated to Kyōto sometime prior to the 1460s from his native village of Kanō, in the Izu–Suruga region (now Shizuoka Prefecture), where his father, Kagenobu (fl ca 1435), had been active as a minor artist of the warrior class. In Kyōto, Masanobu trained under the painter-priest SHŪBUN (d ca 1460) at the atelier of the temple SHŌKOKUJI. Shōkokuji was at that time a bastion of the conservative Chinese Southern Song (Southern Sung; 1127–1279) and Yuan (Yüan; 1279–1368) academic style, which had become, under the patronage of the Ashikaga shōguns, the mainstream of Muromachi INK PAINTING *(suibokuga).* During the 1480s Masanobu inherited the position accorded to leading masters of the Shōkokuji studio, that of painter-in-attendance, or *goyō eshi,* to the Muromachi shogunate. Thus not only was an impeccable *kanga* lineage established as the stylistic foundation of Kanō painting, but also their position was established as the first strictly secular and professional artists to practice and benefit from the stylistic tradition and patronage previously controlled by Zen painter-priests. From these modest beginnings, the Kanō school was to grow into a vast network of artists, linked by family ties or by training, who held hegemony for nearly 250 years over public and private commissions from the shogunate, affluent monasteries, provincial lords, and merchants newly risen to wealth and social prominence.

Of considerable interest in this regard are the activities of Masanobu's eldest son, KANŌ MOTONOBU (1476–1559). It was Motonobu who assured the Kanō school continuing prosperity, for he created the orthodox Kanō style, instituted a studio system that ensured in perpetuity the professionalism of Kanō-trained artists, and expanded his social and political connections to include all upper strata of Muromachi society. At the foundation of his work and that of his followers was versatility of manner, ranging from formal to informal modes of ink painting and indigenous Japanese painting (YAMATO-E) of the purest stamp to the style that was to mark the Kanō school at its most orthodox: a monumental *wakan* (literally, Japanese-Chinese) style that synthesized elements drawn from *kanga* and *yamato-e.*

Motonobu's grandson KANŌ EITOKU (1543–90) furthered the fortunes of the school, not least by forging a style of SCREEN AND WALL PAINTING *(shōbyōga)* that proved the classic expression of the heroic and parvenu spirit of the Azuchi–Momoyama period (1568–1600). Most of his contemporaries, even when they were not of his studio, were influenced by the style associated with Eitoku's name, and his immediate followers were heirs to a stylistic tradition, professional stature, and military patronage unalterably cemented in Eitoku's generation. His son-in-law KANŌ SANRAKU (1559–1635) in Kyōto and grandson KANŌ TAN'YŪ (1602–74) in Edo (now Tōkyō) continued what had become, by the second half of the 16th century, a Kanō history that in outline assumes the form of major figures emerging in successive ages, each of whom served as the pivot for a complex community of Kanō and Kanō-trained artists.

Kanō Lineage——The continued prosperity of the Kanō school was due in part to the inimitable training and professional connections afforded by Kanō workshops. The success of the Kanō artists must be laid in part to a studio system, as yet not fully researched, that encouraged the preservation of stylistic norms during fallow periods, when major talents had not yet emerged to assume the role of taste makers for successive military regimes. Thus, to outline the history of the Kanō through a focus on the achievements of key Muromachi, Azuchi–Momoyama, and Edo figures is convenient but

also misleading. Kanō history and genealogy indeed show the successive rise to prominence of masters whose names are synonymous with major commissions, and hence, whose artistic productions, presumably, were seminal. But such an overview neglects the contributions of lesser Kanō figures, the satellites of Motonobu, Eitoku, Sanraku, and Tan'yū, respectively. Further, the history of the major achievements of the early leading Kanō artists has been largely reconstructed from questionable attributions, many of them the recorded opinions of Tan'yū and his followers, and from records of the tragically lost cycles of wall paintings that once embellished the castles and palaces of Azuchi–Momoyama and Edo military lords. It was the less illustrious Kanō artists who preserved and expanded the heritage, either through practicing the styles established in the generations of their forebears or through exploring new directions, both of style and subject matter, in response to changing social conditions and patronage.

The importance of a system of transmitting achievements from one generation to the next is demonstrated by the activities of Motonobu's son, Shōei (1519–92). His was a talent sufficient for preserving the tradition Motonobu had constructed, and thus his work served as a bridge to the innovative achievements of Eitoku, who would emerge as Motonobu's true successor. In like manner, Eitoku's sons KANŌ MITSUNOBU (1561 or 1565–1608) and Kanō Takanobu (1571–1618) would prove the conservators of the Kanō heritage for the next generation.

A proliferation of Kanō and Kanō-trained artists occurred during the early Edo period, when Takanobu's sons Tan'yū and Naonobu (1607–50) established the Kajibashi and Kobikichō branches, respectively, of the Kanō line in Edo, while a third son, Yasunobu (1613–85), later adopted by Mitsunobu's son Sadanobu (1597–1623), founded the Nakabashi line in Edo. These orthodox and blood-related lines, the so-called *okueshi* ("painters of the inner shogunal quarters"), monopolized shogunal patronage; their leading pupils, collectively known as *omoteeshi* ("painters of the outer shogunal quarters"), founded a host of additional Kanō lines, such as the Hamachō branch in Edo established by Minenobu (1662–1708), second son and pupil of Naonobu's son and heir, Tsunenobu (1636–1713). Still other pupils, the *machieshi* ("town painters"), formed a third type of Kanō lineage. These artists were active throughout Japan, and the proliferation of Kanō studios and workshops safeguarded the official Kanō position as painters in service to the government.

The strength of the Kanō studio system was demonstrated in the few breaks that did occur in the pattern of inheritance in the blood-related familial line. For example, in the Azuchi–Momoyama period, Eitoku's adopted son-in-law Sanraku transmitted the stylistic innovations he pioneered and the academic orthodoxy he inherited to the Kyōto line that briefly flourished under his son-in-law KANŌ SANSETSU (1589?–1651) and grandson Einō (1631 or 1634–1697 or 1700). And in the Edo period, Kanō Kōi (1569?–1636), the capable pupil of Mitsunobu, and very possibly the author of the lighter ink-wash style associated with Tan'yū's name, took over the education of Takanobu's sons after their father's untimely death.

Stylistic and Thematic Range——The peaks and transitions of Kanō history demonstrate not only the merits of their studio and patronage system, but also the talent and creativity of Kanō artists in forging and preserving painting styles expressly suited to the political and social spirit of military regimes. Although the majority of the great painting cycles produced by leading masters are lost, and the authenticity of many extant works remains doubtful, surviving paintings and records of commissions are sufficient to document Kanō contributions to the general history of Japanese painting. These include the innovation of period styles, as well as the exploration of new subject matter, chiefly in the monumental landscape, figure, and bird-and-flower compositions that were the chief strength and glory of the school.

As professional painters, Kanō artists produced works of every variety, on formats ranging from fans and handscrolls (EMAKIMONO) to hanging scrolls (KAKEMONO) and votive plaques (EMA). To neglect these productions is to neglect the strong undercurrent that best illustrates the stylistic and thematic range of Kanō painting. Thus, it is notable that with the inception of the school, a tradition of painting in the orthodox *yamato-e* style was instituted and would find expression in such works as Motonobu's handscroll *Seiryōji engi emaki,* Tan'yū's handscroll *Tōshōgū engi emaki,* and the monumental screens *Rakuchū rakugai zu (Scenes in and around Kyōto;* Uesugi Collection, Yamagata Prefecture) and *Battle of the Carriages* (Tōkyō National Museum), attributed to Eitoku and Sanraku, respectively. Through the preservation of traditional *yamato-e,* in part by adapting it to new themes, Kanō artists were able to assume a leading role as painters to the imperial court as well as to the shogunate. Examples of these new themes are the screens depicting *Craftsmen of Various Trades,* attributed to Eitoku's pupil Yoshinobu (1552–1640), the *namban* screens (see NAMBAN ART), and the screens illustrating the *Festival of Hōkoku Shrine* by Shōei's pupil, Naizen (1570–1616). More significantly, Kanō artists were able to create a unique style of genre painting by synthesizing compositional and thematic elements derived from *yamato-e* and brushwork and landscape motifs derived from *kanga.* This achievement is best demonstrated by the remarkable screens *Maple Viewing at Takao* (Tōkyō National Museum) by Kanō Hideyori (fl ca 1564–77) and *Merrymaking under the Cherry Blossoms* by Eitoku's youngest brother, Naganobu (1577–1654). Both currents pioneered the tradition of genre painting (see FŪZOKUGA) that flourished during the Edo period at the hands of Kanō masters and anonymous Kanō-trained *machieshi,* as well as through the efforts of pupils who left the school to inaugurate their own styles, masters such as KUSUMI MORIKAGE (ca 1620–ca 1690) and HANABUSA ITCHŌ (1652–1724).

Kanō Ink Painting —— The *kanga* roots of Kanō painting, as pioneered by Masanobu and firmly established by Motonobu, were also a source both of stylistic innovation and of conservatism in the hands of the gifted Kanō masters and their lesser-known and often anonymous assistants or pupils. The Kanō ink painting (*suibokuga*) lineage can easily be traced from Motonobu's 1543 cycle of wall paintings at the Myōshinji subtemple Reiun'in, where he demonstrated mastery of Chinese landscape, bird-and-flower, and figural themes in the formal, informal, and cursive modes of ink painting, through the vast number of extant Kanō *suiboku* paintings dated from the late Muromachi through the Edo periods. Indeed, so varied were the ink styles Kanō artists practiced, with all the professional assurance of their academic training, and so prolific was the production of Kanō studios, that a survey of only the most generic works and cycles of monumental paintings would result in an exhaustive catalog of *suiboku* themes and techniques. From the vigorously brushed and grandiose composition of Eitoku's 1566 bird, flower, and landscape sliding-wall paintings at the Jukōin, Daitokuji, to Sanraku's more conservatively managed Eitoku-style *Pine and Hawk* sliding-wall painting at the Shōshinden, Daikakuji, thence to the modest academic elegance of Tan'yū's monumental sliding-wall paintings produced for the *hōjō,* Daitokuji and Naonobu's "grass-style" landscape screens, each generation of Kanō masters preserved the *kanga* foundation of their tradition by mastering and reinterpreting the standard models, both Chinese and Japanese, of Muromachi *suibokuga,* while at the same time adapting their ink styles and subject matter to the requirements of their patrons.

In general, however, it can be said that the Kanō ink-painting tradition pioneered in the Muromachi period played a secondary role in the Azuchi–Momoyama period and was revived to become the mainstream of Kanō painting through the efforts of Tan'yū and his brothers, under the patronage of the Tokugawa shogunate. Tan'yū's genius for reviving the 15th-century *suibokuga* roots of the school was so marked that his reputation has suffered an undeserved identification with the tedious conservatism of much of the work of his followers. That Tan'yū charted a course that became the Kanō fashion for the age, as had Motonobu and Eitoku before him, is demonstrated in part by the degree to which he revived the hegemony of the Kanō school as the orthodox, government-sponsored school of ink painting par excellence.

It is further demonstrated by the so-called Tan'yū copies, the accumulated copies and sketches of the Chinese and Japanese models that informed the Kanō tradition. The art-historical consciousness demonstrated by the "Tan'yū copies" was developed further by one of the earliest Japanese art histories, *Honchō gashi* (1693), compiled by Sansetsu's son Einō (first published in 1678 under the title *Honchō gaden*). A 19th-century member of the school, Asaoka Okisada (1800–56), continued this aspect of the Kanō heritage in *Koga bikō.* But the Kanō tradition of progressive experimentation is also present in Tan'yū's work, particularly in his descriptive nature studies, wherein he anticipated the naturalistic style of the MARUYAMA-SHIJŌ SCHOOL.

Kanō Screen Painting —— All the trends of Kanō painting, from *suibokuga* to *yamato-e,* from *kanga* to genre painting, from conservatism to progressivism, are best represented by the monumental paintings for which the school is most noted. Here, military patronage was the key, albeit not the exclusive factor in the rise to prominence of Kanō men who pioneered new styles of screen and wall painting. It is the "three great brushes" of Kanō painting—Mo-

tonobu, Eitoku, and Tan'yū—together with the fourth central figure, Sanraku, who emerge as successive authors of the mainstream styles of screen and wall painting associated with military patronage of the mid-16th through the 18th centuries.

Eitoku created a heroic style that is one of the chief glories of the Kanō tradition. He was the genius whose vision spawned a style that was to influence strongly the rival HASEGAWA SCHOOL and KAIHŌ SCHOOL but that, except for a brief revival at the hands of Tan'yū and Naonobu, would be abandoned by Eitoku's immediate circle and followers. Eitoku's brother Sōshū (1551–1601), son Mitsunobu, and pupil Sanraku adhered more closely to the judicious brushwork and compositional arrangement of smaller-scale motifs—and hence to the more elegant mood, characteristic of a late Muromachi Motonobu style—than they did to the bold designs associated with Eitoku. Eitoku's vision, as reconstructed from records of the grand painting cycles he designed for warlord ODA NOBUNAGA at Azuchi Castle from 1576 to 1580, and for TOYOTOMI HIDEYOSHI at both Ōsaka Castle in 1583 and Jurakudai in 1587, and as preserved in the Jukōin *Birds and Flowers of the Four Seasons* and the Tōkyō National Museum's *Cypress Trees* screen, showed the fullest possible exploitation of the monumental dimensions of the wall plane. His compositions of heroically proportioned and broadly stroked single-theme motifs sweeping across multiple panels established the classic formula for the decoration of shogunal and imperial audience halls and residences. But the grandeur of his conceptions did not outlive his own era. Thus, in Sanraku's *Red Plum Blossoms* sliding-wall paintings at the *kyakuden* (quest hall) at Daikakuji, or in Tan'yū's *Pine and Hawk* panels at Nijō Castle, one finds the preservation of Eitoku's effective exploitation of the single-theme motif, but without either the kinetic breadth of his brushwork or the bold exuberance of his juxtaposed patterns of ink or ink in combination with color and gold.

Far more characteristic of the next generation, and of the subsequent history of the school, are the more fragmented compositions of Mitsunobu, Sanraku, and Sansetsu. In the former's bird-and-flower panels at Kangakuin, Miidera, in Sanraku's *Peonies* panels at Daikakuji, or in Sansetsu's cycle of bird-and-flower paintings at the Tenkyūin, Myōshinji, smaller-scale, naturalistically described motifs are articulated with elegant brushwork and deeply saturated color against a ubiquitous gold ground, the whole producing quiet, yet splendidly patterned and decorative effects that recall the origins of Kanō painting in classical *yamato-e* and *kanga* of the Song (Sung; 960–1278) and Yuan (Yüan; 1279–1368) periods.

Art Historical Significance —— By the Edo period the Kanō studies were synonymous with an inherited heterodox tradition that included *kanga, yamato-e, wakan,* and genre painting; *kanga*-style ink painting nevertheless represented the mainstream associated with the school in its capacity as the conservator of the past. The school indeed became almost exclusively identified with academic conservatism, not only in its adherence to the standard themes and orthodox methods of brushwork and composition that had been transmitted from past generations, but also from the art-historical consciousness that had been developed by later Kanō artists, critics, and art historians. It was thus that the Kanō tradition remained viable for much longer than any of the other important schools of painting that arose in Japan. In part through the force of individual talents, but perhaps more significantly through the force of superb academic training and widespread patronage, as well as stylistic flexibility and professionalism, the Kanō school enjoyed unparalleled eminence in the Edo-period art world. The success of the Kanō school was transmitted even into the Meiji period (1868–1912), when KANŌ HŌGAI (1828–88) and HASHIMOTO GAHŌ (1835–1908), both of whom were trained in the Kobikichō Kanō studio, helped to found the Painting Appreciation Society (Kangakai) and Tōkyō Bijutsu Gakkō (now Tōkyō University of Fine Arts and Music), where Hashimoto, the last of the Kanō artists, taught his unique stylistic blend of Kanō and Western techniques.

📖 —— Doi Tsugiyoshi, *Momoyama Decorative Painting,* tr Edna Crawford (1977). Takeda Tsuneo, *Kanō Eitoku,* tr H. M. Horton and C. Kaputa (1977). Tōkyō National Museum, *Kanōha no kaiga* (1980). Yamane Yūzō, *Momoyama Genre Painting,* tr John M. Shields (1973).
Gail Capitol WEIGL

Kanō Tan'yū (1602–1674)

The foremost KANŌ SCHOOL painter of the Edo period (1600–1868). Real name Kanō Morinobu. The eldest son of Kanō Takanobu (1571–1618) and grandson of KANŌ EITOKU. In 1617 he was requested by the Tokugawa shogunate to come to Edo (now Tōkyō) as an official artist, and in 1621 he was given a large residence in the Kajibashi district of Edo, where he established an atelier. In his position as *goyō eshi* (official painter), he was engaged by the Tokugawa shōguns, major temples, and *daimyō* to work on the most prestigious painting commissions of his day. Among his most important early large-scale commissions were EDO CASTLE (1622), ŌSAKA CASTLE (1623–24), NIJŌ CASTLE (1626), NAGOYA CASTLE (ca 1634), and TŌSHŌGŪ in Nikkō (1634–36). At the temple NANZENJI alone he painted portions of the interior decorations of four subtemples, in addition to the main temple buildings. Not only was Tan'yū a prolific artist, he was also adept in a variety of techniques: large-scale screen paintings, including color-and-gold compositions in the Momoyama style; monochrome ink compositions inspired by Muromachi-period (1333–1568) prototypes; paintings in the YAMATO-E style similar to those of the TOSA SCHOOL, and Chinese-style hanging scrolls. His most famous work in the *yamato-e* style is the *Tōshōgū engi*, a set of five scrolls executed in 1639 and 1640 depicting the life of the shōgun TOKUGAWA IEYASU. It was shortly after this commission that he was awarded the honorary title *hōgen* and took the artistic name *(gō)* of Tan'yū. In 1662 Tan'yū received the title of *hōin*, the highest honorary rank bestowed on painters.

In addition to his painting activities, Tan'yū was highly respected as a connoisseur of old paintings, particularly works in the Chinese style. Late in his life Tan'yū began to keep a pictorial record of the paintings brought to his studio for authentication. These miniature drawings *(shukuzu)* range from rough, quickly executed sketches to finished miniature studies. Tan'yū usually made a comment beside each sketch recording the date, provenance, authenticity, and price. These connoisseur's sketches provide important research material for the study of Chinese and Japanese painting prior to the 17th century and supplement our knowledge of now scarce originals.

📖——Takeda Tsuneo, *Kanō Tan'yū*, vol 15 of *Nihon bijutsu kaiga zenshū* (Shūeisha, 1978).　　　　　*Catherine* KAPUTA

Kanoya

City in Kagoshima Prefecture, Kyūshū. Sweet potatoes, rice, tea, and peanuts are grown. Stock breeding and dairy farming are also important. A base for the Japanese naval air force until the end of World War II, it is today the site of an air base for the Maritime Self Defense Force. Pop: 73,243.

kanrei

(shogunal deputy). Also called *kanryō*. High official post in the MUROMACHI SHOGUNATE (1338–1573). Its occupant assisted the shōgun in all important government affairs, especially in mediating between the shogunate and the increasingly powerful SHUGO (provincial military governors). It is believed that the office was formalized and its title changed from the more loosely used *shitsuji* to *kanrei* in 1362, when it was assumed by Shiba Yoshimasa (1350–1410). The *kanrei* office was not hereditary like the post of SHIKKEN or shogunal regent in the preceding Kamakura shogunate, but was rotated among members of the SHIBA FAMILY, HOSOKAWA FAMILY, and HATAKEYAMA FAMILY, who were thus known as the Sankanrei or "three deputies." See also KANTŌ KANREI.

kanreki

(celebration of a person's 60th birthday). Also called *honke-gaeri*. According to the traditional way of counting age (see JIKKAN JŪNISHI), one cycle is completed in 60 years, and from the 61st year, another sexagenary cycle is repeated. The celebration of *kanreki* began in the medieval period (13th–16th centuries) and became popular during the Edo period (1600–1868). On the day of a person's 60th birthday, relatives and friends are invited to a celebratory feast; presents are usually given. In some areas it is customary for the person to wear something red, red being traditionally the color for infants' clothes and hence symbolizing the beginning of a new cycle. Until recently, a man of 60 was regarded as being old. He was expected to retire from all official positions and relinquish the position of family head to the eldest son, becoming, with his spouse, an INKYO (retired person). In addition to the 60th birthday, the 70th *(koki)*, 77th *(kiju)*, 88th *(beiju)*, and 99th *(hakuju)* birthdays are also celebrated. There are certain localities where the year of a person's *kanreki* is actually regarded as inauspicious.

Kanrin maru

The first modern warship to cross the Pacific under Japanese command. Purchased from Holland in 1857 by the Tokugawa shogunate, the *Kanrin maru*, a 300-ton, three-masted, screw-propelled steamer, was used to train a new Western-style navy in Japan. In 1860, under the command of Admiral KIMURA YOSHITAKE and Captain KATSU KAISHŪ, the *Kanrin maru* accompanied the ship taking the Tokugawa embassy to the United States to ratify the 1858 HARRIS TREATY (see UNITED STATES, MISSION OF 1860 TO). It took 37 days to complete the trip between Shinagawa and San Francisco. Although Kimura and Katsu received considerable assistance from Lieutenant John Mercer BROOKE and his crew, who were returning to the United States aboard the *Kanrin maru*, the voyage was nonetheless a great achievement for the Tokugawa navy, which had been formed less than five years earlier.　　*M. William* STEELE

Kanroku (fl early 7th century)

Buddhist priest from the Korean kingdom of PAEKCHE who came to Japan in 602, during the reign of Empress SUIKO. According to the 8th-century chronicle *Nihon shoki*, Kanroku brought with him a calendar and books on astronomy, geography, and astrology; he lectured on those subjects at the temple GANGŌJI in Yamato (now Nara Prefecture). Although it is not certain which calendar Kanroku employed, it is generally agreed that he was the first to teach calendrical science in Japan. When the government in 624 established an official Buddhist hierarchy to oversee monks and nuns, Kanroku was appointed its first primate *(sōjō)*.　　*KITAMURA Bunji*

Kansai

A term loosely applied to the area centering on the cities of Ōsaka, Kyōto, and Kōbe. It is sometimes defined as coterminous with the KINKI REGION, but the latter is an official geographical designation with clearly defined boundaries. The term "Kansai" is rather a cultural and historical one, the definition of which has changed over the years. Kansai (literally, "west of the barrier") was first used in the 10th century in contradistinction to the word Kantō. Kantō ("east of the barrier") referred to the area east of the barrier station (SEKISHO) at Ōsaka (in what is now Shiga Prefecture, not to be confused with the major city of the same name) and hence Kansai referred to the area west of the station. From the Kamakura period (1185–1333) the dividing line between Kantō and Kansai was marked by the three barrier stations at Suzuka (in what is now Mie Prefecture), Fuwa (in what is now Gifu Prefecture), and Arachi (in what is now Fukui Prefecture). It was later fixed further east at the barrier station at Hakone (in what is now Kanagawa Prefecture). The term is also used to describe local speech patterns (as in Kansai *ben* or Kansai *namari*), and manners and customs, and thus closely resembles *kamigata*, another word used loosely to cover the Kyōto–Ōsaka area. In broader usage, Kansai includes Shikoku and the CHŪGOKU REGION. See also KINAI.

Kansai Electric Power Co, Inc

(Kansai Denryoku). Company supplying electricity to most of Ōsaka, Kyōto, Nara, Shiga, Wakayama, and Hyōgo prefectures, and parts of Fukui, Gifu, and Mie prefectures. It is the second largest of the nine major electric power companies in Japan, after the TŌKYŌ ELECTRIC POWER CO, INC. The company was established in 1951, when it took over the distribution network of the Kansai Electric Supply Co, Ltd, in the Kyōto–Ōsaka region, and the power generation operations of the Japan Electric Generation & Transmission Co. Electric power resource development was intensified in the following decade, and in 1964 the company successfully completed the KUROBE DAM No. 4 hydroelectric plant, said to be the most difficult construction project in the history of Japan. In the 1960s, after the advantages of thermoelectric generation became evident, the company erected several colossal steam-generating plants.

Kansai Electric has led in nuclear power development in Japan. It was the first Japanese power company to put a nuclear power plant in operation, at Mihama, and it has since built six atomic reactors at Takahama and Ōi with a generating capacity of 4.5 million kilowatts, accounting for some 35 percent of the country's total nuclear capacity of 12.7 million kilowatts. To meet the increasing demand for electric power, the company is constructing large-scale steam-generating plants in Hyōgo and Wakayama prefectures and increasing its capacity at the Takahama and Ōi nuclear power plants. It is also converting its thermoelectric plants from oil to coal. Total power output was 21.5 million kilowatts in 1979, of which 55 percent was generated by thermoelectric plants, 24 percent by hydroelectric plants, and 21 percent by nuclear power plants, reflecting a high ratio of nuclear power generation. The company operates a total of 136 hydroelectric plants, 15 thermoelectric plants, and 3 nuclear power plants. Annual revenue totaled ¥1.9 trillion (US $7.9 billion) in 1980; capitalization stood at ¥359.7 billion (US $1.5 billion) in that year. Corporate headquarters are located in Ōsaka.

Kansai Paint Co, Ltd

Leading paint manufacturer. Founded in 1918. In 1926 it initiated domestic production of lacquer, a major factor in its subsequent growth. The present strength of the firm is based on its production of industrial paint for motor vehicles and on its extensive national sales network. Concentrating efforts on creating new technology and developing the export market, it has set up joint venture factories in Indonesia, Thailand, and Singapore to establish a base for sales throughout Southeast Asia. In the fiscal year ending in March 1982 total sales were ¥116.8 billion (US $485.2 million), of which 74 percent came from the sale of synthetic resin paints, and capitalization was ¥6.7 billion (US $27.8 million). The corporate headquarters are located in Ōsaka.

Kan Sazan (1748–1827)

Confucian scholar and writer of Chinese verse. Real name Kan Shinsui. Born in the province of Bingo (now Hiroshima Prefecture). Deeply influenced by Song (Sung) poetry, his realistic evocations of everyday life display a lucid and original style which bore considerable weight in western Japan among poets who wrote in Chinese. He opened a school, the Kōyō Sekiyō Sonsha, in his home province, which a great number of students attended, including the famous poet and historian RAI SAN'YŌ. His principal works include the prose piece *Fude no susabi* (1857) and a renowned anthology of his poetry, *Kōyō sekiyō sonsha shi* (1812, 1823).

Kansei chōshū shoka fu

(Revised Kansei Genealogies). An official compilation (1812) by the Tokugawa shogunate of the genealogies of *daimyō, hatamoto*, and other Tokugawa vassal houses. The project grew out of plans made during the Kansei era (1789–1800) to add a supplement to the earlier compilation KAN'EI SHOKA KEIZU DEN (1643). All major vassals were directed to submit their genealogies for the new compilation by the junior councillor *(wakadoshiyori)* Hotta Masaatsu (1758–1832), who directed about 60 scholars, including YASHIRO HIROKATA and HAYASHI JUSSAI. The project took 14 years to complete. The *Kansei chōshū shokafu*, though unreliable for the period before 1600, is valued particularly for its detailed and highly accurate record of family histories for the Edo period (1600–1868).

Kansei Gakuin University

(Kansei Gakuin Daigaku). A private, coeducational university located in Uegahara, in the city of Nishinomiya, Hyōgo Prefecture. The school was founded in Kōbe in 1889 by Walter R. Lambuth, a missionary of the Southern Methodist Episcopal Church in America (now United Methodist Church). In 1910 the Japanese, American and Canadian Methodist churches became joint sponsors of the school and in 1929 the campus moved to its present location. University status was granted in 1932. The university has maintained a close relationship with Southern Methodist University, Dallas, Texas. It has faculties in theology, humanities, sociology, law, economics, commerce, and science as well as its Industrial Research Institute. Enrollment in 1980 was 13,483.

Kansei Reforms

(Kansei no Kaikaku). The Kansei Reforms (1787–93; Temmei 7–Kansei 5) were the second of three reform programs undertaken by the Tokugawa shogunate, falling between the KYŌHŌ REFORMS and TEMPŌ REFORMS of the 1720s and 1840s. MATSUDAIRA SADANOBU, chief senior councillor *(rōjū shuseki)* from 1787 to 1793, was their architect and implementor. Because many *daimyō* followed his example, the term also refers to all domainal reforms of the period. The shogunate's reforms were carried out against a background of widespread bureaucratic corruption, natural disasters, numerous peasant uprisings and urban riots, and severe financial distress created by a 50 percent drop in revenues and steep inflation.

The reforms achieved administrative efficiency at the center through a major purge of officials at all levels. They restored power to the senior councillors (RŌJŪ) from the chamberlain (SOBAYŌNIN), who had held it during the preceding regime under TANUMA OKITSUGU. They ensured ideological uniformity and a renewed service ethos among shogunate personnel through the so-called Ban on Heterodoxy (Kansei Igaku no Kin). Although the ban has often been misunderstood as a nationwide suppression of academic freedom, in fact it merely limited the curriculum of the shogunal academy (SHŌHEIKŌ) to a particular school of Neo-Confucianism that subsequently served as the basis for a new examination system for shogunal retainers.

In the countryside the reforms restored tax farming, built up rice reserves for bad years, and abolished the abusive collector guilds of licensed merchants *(osameyado)*, intermediaries between the taxpaying villages and the shogunal storehouses. Peasants, who had flocked to urban areas in search of work, were ordered to return to the land (see HITOGAESHI). But rural reconstruction was inadequate and ultimately did not succeed in stemming the growing disaffection of the peasantry from the ruling class and the emergence of illegal rural entrepreneurs.

The shogunal capital of Edo (now Tōkyō), which had proven vulnerable during a four-day rice riot in July 1787, was the focus of the Kansei Reforms. Sadanobu enacted a monetary reform that included the recoining of silver pieces, a qualitative revaluation of the gold currency, and a quantitative reduction of the copper currency. By manipulating the official rate of exchange, he strengthened Edo's financial position vis-à-vis Ōsaka and reduced the upward pressure on commodity prices. He further bolstered Edo's economic independence from Ōsaka by developing the *sake*, oil, cotton, and paper industries in Edo's hinterland, the Kantō region.

Economic redress also required assuring the circulation of capital and stabilizing prices, especially the rice price, which was controlled by a clique of merchants and moneylenders. The Decree of the Cancellation of Debts (KIENREI) of 1789 was a complex measure that alleviated the plight of shogunal vassals through outright cancellation of debts older than 20 years, amortization of others at lower rates, and reduction of interest rates on future loans. The decree broke the independent power of Edo's official rice broker-bankers (FUDASASHI) by subjecting them to shogunate control. They were made managers of the Loan Agency (Saruyachō Kashikin Kaisho) established as a joint venture between the old entrepreneurs and the shogunate. Using a fund of private and public capital, these financial purveyors *(kanjōsho goyōtashi)* stabilized the rice price through massive buying and selling.

The reforms checked inflation further by means of a decree lowering the prices of a number of consumer goods (thus negatively affecting the producers), reducing by 10 to 20 percent the house and land rents in Edo, and cutting township expenses through the newly established Edo Office for Town Affairs (Edo Machikaisho; see SHICHIBUKIN TSUMITATE). The savings were rechanneled as disaster funds, rebates to the landlords, and capital to purchase rice.

Traditionally the Kansei Reforms have been viewed as a reactionary reversal of Tanuma's expansionist mercantilism. Sadanobu, indeed, abolished a number of guilds and monopolies, curtailed foreign trade, abandoned plans to develop Ezo (now Hokkaidō), and regulated consumption through sumptuary laws. But Tanuma had also issued such laws, and some of his measures were continuations from the Kyōhō Reforms, while some of Sadanobu's innovations were implementations of Tanuma's initiatives. The rally-rout-rally picture of the Kyōhō–Tanuma–Kansei eras, dramatized by Tanuma's ouster and Sadanobu's slogan "Return to the Kyōhō Reforms," obscures strong continuities in the growing social dislocations of 18th-century Japan. The Kansei Reforms, although perhaps conservative, provided temporary remedies and pulled the Tokugawa polity and its Edo heartland through a serious crisis. They revitalized the bureaucracy, restored financial solvency, and provided formal structures to harmonize the interests of the influential merchants and the needs of the ruling class. They reduced feudal-bourgeois tensions, but they did not check social and economic developments in the countryside that in the long run further undermined Tokugawa society.

🔳 ——Herman Ooms, *Charismatic Bureaucrat: A Political Biography of Matsudaira Sadanobu* (1975). Tsuda Hideo, *Hōken shakai kaitai katei kenkyū josetsu* (1970).   Herman OOMS

kanshi → poetry and prose in Chinese

Kantei style

(Kanteiryū). A style of calligraphy conceived in 1779 by Okazakiya Kanroku, an employee of the theatrical company Nakamuraza. Its thick, curved strokes form compact characters with few open areas between them, suggesting a "full house," and it quickly won favor in the theatrical world. Easily recognized from a distance, the style was used in posters advertising the productions of *kabuki* troupes as well as in writing their playbooks. To this day the style is used in kabuki posters and in bills *(banzuke)* announcing the ranking of *sumō* wrestlers.

Kantō

The major event of the TANABATA FESTIVAL as celebrated in the city of Akita, Akita Prefecture, from 5 August to 7 August; also, the bamboo poles hung with lanterns used in this event. Twenty-four or 46 paper lanterns are suspended from nine horizontal cross-poles attached to a long, vertically-held bamboo pole. At night, brightly costumed young men balance these long poles on their palms, shoulders, and foreheads as they parade through the city to the accompaniment of drums and chanting. Neighborhood groups compete for the best technique of holding the *kantō* aloft. *INOKUCHI Shōji*

Kantō Auto Works, Ltd

(Kantō Jidōsha Kōgyō). One of the three largest manufacturers of passenger car bodies in Japan. Founded in 1946, it is affiliated with TOYOTA MOTOR CORPORATION. Other product lines include prefabricated houses, marine containers, sailing dinghies, and cruisers. Sales for the fiscal year ending March 1982 totaled ￥223.7 billion (US $929.7 million), and capitalization stood at ￥3.2 billion (US $13.3 million). Corporate headquarters are located in Yokosuka, Kanagawa Prefecture.

Kantō Daishinsai → Tōkyō Earthquake of 1923

Kantō Earthquake → Tōkyō Earthquake of 1923

Kantō Electrical Construction Co, Ltd

(Kantō Denki Kōji). Affiliate of TŌKYŌ ELECTRIC POWER CO, INC. Founded in 1944, the firm is chiefly engaged in the installation of electric systems and in related construction. Over half of the company's work is electrical-power construction projects performed under contract to Tōkyō Electric Power and other companies. Moving into the overseas market, it has set up a branch in Hong Kong and a business office in Singapore. In the early 1980s the firm was concentrating on overseas contracts, and planned to enter the field of nuclear power. In the fiscal year ending March 1982 the firm completed construction projects earning ￥244 billion (US $1 billion), of which indoor circuitry constituted 35 percent, power lines 35 percent, and other projects 30 percent. In the same year capitalization stood at ￥3.5 billion (US $14.5 million).

Kantōgun → Guandong (Kwantung) Army

Kantō kanrei

(shogunal deputy for the Kantō region). Official post created in Kamakura by the Muromachi shogunate (1338–1573) to assist the members of the ruling Ashikaga family who served as governor-generals of the Kantō region (Kantō *kubō* or Kamakura *kubō*; see KUBŌ). After the appointment of Uesugi Noriaki (1306–68) as Kantō *kanrei* in 1363, the post was held in rotation by members of the four branches of the powerful UESUGI FAMILY, who retained the title until the end of the 16th century, long after they had become independent of shogunal control.

Kantō loam

Four thick layers of ash laid down by several volcanoes, chiefly Fujisan, Asamayama, Harunasan, Yatsugatake, and Hakoneyama, to form the KANTŌ PLAIN around present-day Tōkyō. The layers and their eras of deposition are: the Tama loam, 300,000 to 200,000 years ago; the Shimo Sueyoshi loam, 200,000 to 100,000 years ago; the Musashino loam, 100,000 to 30,000 years ago; and the Tachikawa loam, 30,000 to 10,000 years ago. The surface of the plain is black humus, one meter (3.3 ft) thick, formed in the last 10,000 years, a period of greatly reduced volcanic activity. Artifacts of the JŌMON CULTURE (ca 10,000 BC–ca 300 BC) are found at the bottom of the humus layer, and those of the PALEOLITHIC CULTURE (pre–10,000 BC) occur throughout the underlying Tachikawa loam, during the time the land bridges were broken and the Japanese islands started to take shape. See also HISTORY OF JAPAN: prehistory.

🕮 ——Kantō Rōmu Kenkyū Gurūpu, ed, *Kantō rōmu: Sono kigen to seijō* (1965). *J. Edward KIDDER, JR.*

Kantō Mountains

(Kantō Sanchi). Mountain system in the western Kantō region, central Honshū. It runs north to south through Nagano, Gumma, Saitama, Yamanashi, Kanagawa, and Tōkyō prefectures for a distance of about 130 km (81 mi). There are numerous peaks in the range including KOBUSHIGADAKE (2,483 m; 8,144 ft), Kokushigatake (2,592 m; 8,502 ft), and KIMPUSAN (2,595 m; 8,512 ft), the highest in the range. The central part of the mountains forms part of Chichibu-Tama National Park.

Kantō Plain

(Kantō Heiya). Located in central Honshū. The largest plain in Japan and on the Pacific seaboard, it occupies more than half the entire Kantō Region. Diluvial uplands covered with volcanic ash known as the KANTŌ LOAM layer spread over more than half of this plain; the remainder consists of alluvial areas and the deltas of the rivers Tonegawa, Arakawa, and Tamagawa. Lakes and marshland, such as Kasumigaura and Imbanuma respectively, lie on the lower Tonegawa, and on the Pacific seaboard are the sandy beaches of Kujūkurihama, Kashima, and Shōnan. The entire region is undergoing rapid change as land is reclaimed in Tōkyō Bay and as the hills are turned into residential areas for the swelling Tōkyō metropolitan area that includes Tōkyō, Yokohama, Kawasaki, and their suburbs. The principal products are rice, vegetables, fruits, and flowers. Area: 15,000 sq km (5,790 sq mi).

Kantō region

(Kantō *chihō*). Located in east central Honshū, consisting of Tōkyō, Chiba, Saitama, Kanagawa, Gumma, Ibaraki, and Tochigi prefectures. This is Japan's most heavily populated region and is the political, economic, and cultural center of the nation. The regional center is the metropolitan area that includes Tōkyō, Yokohama, Kawasaki, and Chiba.

The region is dominated by the Kantō Plain, the largest plain in Japan, which is crisscrossed by numerous rivers, including the TO-NEGAWA. The plain is bordered on its northern and western sides by the Mikuni and Kantō mountains, in which numerous volcanoes belonging to the Fuji and Nasu volcanic zones are scattered. The Abukuma Mountains extend from the TŌHOKU REGION to the northeastern part of the Kantō Plain near the Pacific Ocean. The plain also includes numerous lowland and upland areas. The Bōsō and Miura peninsulas are almost entirely hilly. The Izu and Ogasawara islands in the Pacific to the south of Tōkyō are also included in the Kantō region.

In ancient times the region was considered a frontier, and it was not until the establishment of the Kamakura shogunate in 1192 that the region began to be developed. The designation of Edo (now Tōkyō) as the seat of the Tokugawa shogunate (1603–1867) led to its further development. Edo was renamed Tōkyō after the Meiji Restoration of 1868.

The term "Kantō" (literally, "east of the barrier") originally referred to the area east of the barrier station (SEKISHO) at Ōsaka in what is now the city of Ōtsu, Shiga Prefecture (not to be confused with the city of Ōsaka); the term was used in contradistinction to the KANSAI region west of the station. The border between the two areas was set during the Kamakura period (1185–1333) at the three barrier stations at Suzuka (in what is now Mie Prefecture), Fuwa (in what is now Gifu Prefecture), and Arachi (in what is now Fukui Prefecture). The border was later set much further east at the barrier station at Hakone (in what is now Kanagawa Prefecture).

The Tōkyō–Yokohama district in the center of the region is Japan's leading commercial and industrial area. It forms the KEIHIN INDUSTRIAL ZONE and is noted for the production of chemicals, chemical fibers, petrochemicals, machinery, and metals, as well as for its textile, food processing, electrical machinery, steel, and publishing industries. The Keiyō Coastal Industrial Region extends eastward from Tōkyō into Chiba Prefecture, where steel, petrochemical, and petroleum refining industries have been developed on a large scale. The Kashima Coastal Industrial Region in Ibaraki Prefecture is rapidly becoming an important area for heavy and chemical industries, and the village of Tōkai is the center of Japan's atomic power energy program. Traditional industries such as sericulture, textiles, flour milling, and *sake* brewing are located in the interior of the Kantō Plain.

Agriculture plays a declining but still important role in the region's economy. Extensive truck farming is carried out on the Kantō Plain near Tōkyō, and vegetables, potatoes, beans, and fruit are cultivated in the upland parts of the plain. Low-lying arable land throughout the region is used for the production of rice. Coastal fishing in the Pacific Ocean and Tōkyō Bay has declined rapidly in recent years because of vastly increased catches by deep-sea fishing trawlers and because of increased pollution due to factory and urban wastes and the great expansion of reclaimed land in Tōkyō Bay. Five national parks, Fuji–Hakone–Izu, Nikkō, Jōshin'etsu Kōgen, Chichibu–Tama, and Ogasawara, are in the region. Area: 32,289 sq km (12,464 sq mi); pop: 34,893,778.

Kantōshū → Guandong (Kwantung) Territory

Kan U (?–219)

(Ch: Guan Yu or Kuan Yü). The powerful Chinese general of Shu (Szechuan) who became a popular subject for Japanese ink painters. During the Three Kingdoms (220–265) he was deified as a protector of warriors in China. With the diffusion of secular Confucian culture in Edo-period Japan (1600–1868), Guan Yu's military exploits became a popular pictorial theme.　　　*Carolyn* WHEELWRIGHT

Kanuma

City in central Tochigi Prefecture, central Honshū. Kanuma developed in the Edo period (1600–1868) as a post-station town on the highway leading to the mausoleum of TOKUGAWA IEYASU in Nikkō. Known for its wood household furnishings (*tategu*) since before World War II, the city now has lumbering, metal, and machine industries. Azaleas and strawberries are also cultivated. Pop: 85,159.

Kanzaki Paper Mfg Co, Ltd

(Kanzaki Seishi). Company specializing in production of processed paper products such as art paper and coated paper. Formerly the art-paper division of the monopolistic ŌJI PAPER CO, LTD, it became an independent company following the breakup of Ōji in 1948 under the Occupation policy that aimed at dispersing the holdings of monopolies. Concentrating its efforts on the development of special paper products, the company mainly produces quality printing paper, carbonless paper, and thermal paper. The company maintains sales offices in West Germany and Australia. Sales for the fiscal year ending March 1982 totaled ¥118.5 billion (US $492.3 million), while capitalization stood at ¥5.9 billion (US $24.5 million). The company's 15 percent export rate was the highest among Japanese paper manufacturers. The head office is in Tōkyō.

Kanzan and Jittoku

(Ch: Hanshan and Shide or Han-shan and Shih-te). Legendary Tang (T'ang) dynasty (618–907) eccentrics who became popular subjects in Chinese and Japanese INK PAINTING. Hanshan (literally, "cold mountain") was a poet-recluse in the Tiantai (T'ien-t'ai) mountain region of Zhejiang (Chekiang), near the temple of Guo qinqsi (Kuoch'ing-ssu), where his friend Shide worked in the kitchen and supplied him with leftover food. Shide (literally, "foundling") had been an abandoned child retrieved and reared by the Chan (Ch'an; J: Zen) master Fenggan (Feng-kan; J: Bukan), another unconventional personality, who often rode about on a tiger. The whimsical antics of these characters signified the spirit of Zen unworldliness.
　　　Carolyn WHEELWRIGHT

Kanzashi

Kanzashi (hair ornaments) of the Edo period. The drawings are of *kanzashi* in the collection of the Suntory Museum of Art, Tōkyō.

Kanzanji

Resort area on the shore of Lake Hamana in the city of Hamamatsu, western Shizuoka Prefecture, central Honshū. The temple Kanzanji, reputedly built by the priest KŪKAI, is famous as a site for moonviewing. An observatory, ropeway, and hot spring are also located in this area.

kanzashi

Ornaments used in traditional Japanese HAIRSTYLES. Early examples made of animal bone and believed to date from the latter part of the JŌMON PERIOD have been discovered. The immediate ancestor of the *kanzashi* is said to be the *kazashi*, a hair ornament of the medieval period (13th–16th centuries). During the 18th and 19th centuries, as new hairstyles became popular, *kanzashi* came into wide use, and many were products of fine artistic workmanship. Materials such as wood, bamboo, tortoise shell, ivory, glass, and metal were used. See also KŌGAI.　　　HASHIMOTO *Sumiko*

Kanze Motokiyo → Zeami

Kanze Motomasa (1394?–1432)

NŌ actor and playwright. Also known as Kanze Jūrō. Motomasa succeeded his father ZEAMI as head of the KANZE SCHOOL, or troupe, in 1422, when Zeami nominally became a monk. Zeami saw in him supreme genius. Unfortunately, from 1429 on Zeami and Motomasa were replaced at all important ceremonial performances by On'ami (Kanze Saburō Motoshige, 1398–1467), Zeami's nephew and rival. Then in 1432 Motomasa died. Grief-stricken, Zeami lamented his death in *Museki isshi* (1433, A Page on the Ruin of a Dream). In this document Zeami praised Motomasa as one who, despite his youth, had already understood that Nō (literally, "accomplishment") means to do nothing superfluous, and he spoke of Motomasa's death as the end of his own art. Motomasa's plays are tragic, but the *shite* (principal player) in them is never a phantom. The best known are *Yoroboshi* and the heartrending *Sumidagawa*.　　　*Royall* TYLER

Kanze Nobumitsu (1435–1516)

NŌ actor and playwright. Also known as Kanze Kojirō. Nobumitsu himself was never head of the KANZE SCHOOL or troupe, but instead assisted his older brother Masamori and Masamori's son. The ŌNIN WAR (1467–77) had so completely disrupted the troupe that in 1470, the year of Masamori's death, a performance for the emperor had to be supplemented by amateur warrior-actors because not enough Kanze actors could be assembled. Under such circumstances Nobumitsu was obliged to labor for the very survival of the Kanze-school Nō.

Nobumitsu's plays, which include *Funa Benkei*, *Dōjōji*, *Momijigari*, and *Rashōmon*, are among the most enduringly popular in the repertoire. Since Nobumitsu took principally *waki* (subordinate actor) roles, many of his plays give the *waki* unusual prominence. They are generally far more showy and ornamental than the plays of the celebrated actor-playwright ZEAMI, and some unabashedly extol the warrior virtues. Indeed Nobumitsu's style could be said to foreshadow that of KABUKI.　　　*Royall* TYLER

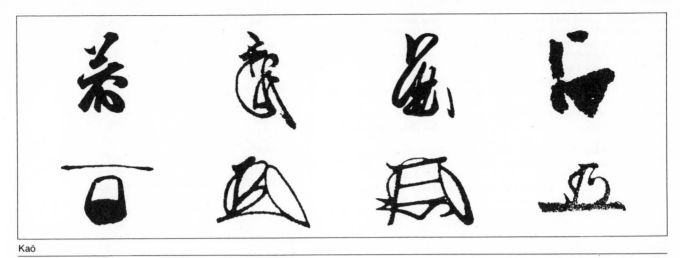

Kaō

The *kaō* of a number of historical figures. Top, left to right: Shunkan (1142?–1179), a Buddhist monk of the Shingon sect; Shinran (1173–1263), the founder of the Jōdō Shin sect of Buddhism; Emperor Go-Toba (1180–1239; r 1183–98); Rankei Dōryū (1213–1278), a Chinese monk who became a leader of Zen in Japan. Bottom, left to right: Issan Ichinei (1244–1317), a Chinese Zen monk and founder of Gozan literature; Ashikaga Takauji (1305–1358), the founder of the Muromachi shogunate; Oda Nobunaga (1534–82), the prime mover of Japan's 16th-century reunification; Tokugawa Ieyasu (1543–1616), the founder of the Tokugawa shogunate.

Kanze school

(Kanzeryū). One of the five major *shite kata* (principal player) schools (or troupes) of professional NŌ theater actors. The school is directly descended from the Yūzakiza (Yūzaki troupe), one of the four original SARUGAKU Nō troupes of the Kamakura period (1185–1333). Established during the Nambokuchō period (1336–92), its name derives from the childhood name of its founder, the early Nō master KAN'AMI. Kan'ami and his talented actor-playwright son ZEAMI were patronized by the third Muromachi shōgun ASHIKAGA YOSHIMITSU; this offical favor enabled the Kanze to surpass other rival schools. During the rule of the hegemon TOYOTOMI HIDEYO-SHI (1537–98), the Kanze troupe was eclipsed by the KOMPARU SCHOOL. This was, however, only a temporary loss of influence, and during the Edo period (1600–1868) the Kanze school ranked fore-most among Nō schools. After the Meiji Restoration (1868), Kanze Kiyotaka, the 22nd hereditary head of the troupe, moved with the deposed shōgun TOKUGAWA YOSHINOBU to Shizuoka. Meanwhile, Umewaka Minoru I (1828–1909) actively headed a splinter group in Tōkyō, laboring to revive the fortunes of Nō. In 1921 the Umewaka family branch ceded from the Kanze school, only to rejoin it later. The school is presently led by Kanze Motomasa (b 1930), the 25th hereditary head. The Kanze school is known for its elegant and colorful style of acting. KIKKAWA *Shūhei*

kao

(literally, "face"). An important concept in Japanese interpersonal relationships. The word *kao* is used in a number of idioms with implications similar to those of the Chinese word *mianzi* (*mien-tsu*; J: *mentsu*) and the English word "face." If a person has a wide circle of acquaintances, his *kao* is "broad" *(kao ga hiroi),* or if he is influential, his *kao* "works" *(kao ga kiku).* When a person "smears his *kao* with dirt" *(kao o yogosu)* or his *kao* is "smashed" *(kao o tsubusareru),* he is disgraced. When one's face is saved, one's *kao* is "made to stand" *(kao o tateru). Kao* is almost synonymous with *memboku* (Ch: *mianmu* or *mien-mu;* "face"). *Memboku* may also be "lost," "injured," "sullied," "ruined," "crushed by treading," or "smeared with ash," as when one's honor is blighted and one's dignity destroyed. *Memboku* may also be "left standing" or "maintained" when a person has kept his dignity. What is signified by these words is the individual's social self or the self as properly presented to the public. To maintain one's good reputation and to avoid shame to one's name has long been a cardinal principle of personal conduct in Japan.

——David Ho, "On the Concept of Face," *American Journal of Sociology* 81 (1976). Hiroshi WAGATSUMA

kaō

(monograms). Personal marks or signs that developed from signatures and were used in place of signatures on a vast range of docu-

ments, public and private. The word *kaō* is a compound of two Chinese characters: *ka,* or "flower," and *ō,* "to impress one's signature"; together they convey the sense of "a beautiful, flowerlike signature." *Kaō* were later called *kakihan,* the element *kaki* meaning "to write," and *han,* "to distinguish," in this case, "to distinguish self from others," for *kaō* had developed into important marks of identification.

During the 8th and 9th centuries all official documents were signed by the person responsible for them. Signatures were usually in the formal, regular script, but even when they were not, they were always quite legible. On private correspondence, however, one was free to write in the running or cursive styles, and the stroke order and basic shape of characters might be altered until they were no longer immediately recognizable. Such highly individualized, often illegible, signatures were called *kaō.* Far more than simply an expedient, they resulted from the desire for unique personal marks that could not be imitated.

Kaō first appeared about the same time that the *hiragana* syllabary was being developed by a similar process of abbreviation of Chinese characters (see KANA). Throughout the Heian period (794–1185), *kaō* were based upon the actual characters of a person's name and thus might be described as artistic signatures; yet because they were not legible to others, they resembled monograms. Usually the two characters forming a personal name were written in a highly cursive hand run together to form a single mark, a style favored by the court nobility through the Muromachi period (1333–1568).

During the Kamakura period (1185–1333) a new type of *kaō* appeared, used by the military aristocrats: portions of the two characters that made up a name were joined together to form a "new" character, which was written cursively. Originally *kaō* had been used in place of signatures, but this practice changed with the rise of the military: *kaō* became marks of identification, the sole means of confirming the authenticity of a document. They were used with or without signature.

During the Muromachi period new types of *kaō* appeared. Some persons no longer based their *kaō* upon their actual names, but chose instead a single, favorite character. Zen monks deviated even further from tradition: their *kaō* were elegantly stark combinations of dots, lines, or circles with a distinctly Zen Buddhist flavor whose originality lay not so much in shape as in the boldness and vigor of the brush.

The Sengoku period (1467–1568) brought further variety. The two characters of a name might be joined together, a single character might be reversed or inverted, or a *kaō* might be based upon the family rather than the personal name. Sometimes characters were even replaced by pictures, and *kaō* became a vehicle for the expression of a personal belief or ideal.

In the Edo period (1600–1868) *kaō* changed completely, becoming what can be called a "personality graph." In the space between two parallel lines, circles, dashes, and dots would be drawn to correspond with a person's nature as analyzed according to the ancient

Chinese doctrines of *yin* (J: *in*) and *yang* (J: *yō*) and the Five Elements (see OMMYŌDŌ). Shōgun TOKUGAWA IEYASU (1543–1616), the first to use such a *kaō*, was followed in this practice by most ranking members of the military class. It was necessary to turn to specialists for the creation of such *kaō*, and once the "correct" design was established, it was reproduced exactly, and without individual expression. From the time of the eighth shōgun TOKUGAWA YOSHI-MUNE (1684–1751), it was customary to have the *kaō* design carved into a wooden seal from which rubbings could be taken. *Kaō* lost their original meaning and significance and became little different from seals.

After the Meiji Restoration (1868), the government tried to reinstate the original purpose of *kaō* by ordering that all *daimyō* personally sign them. Soon after that the government ruled that *jitsuin*, or registered seals, be used on all important documents. *Kaō* were seldom used after this ruling (see SEALS).

Kaō are often the only clue to the identity of the author and the authenticity of certain documents. The study of *kaō*, carried out within the larger field of DIPLOMATICS ("the study of old documents"), is of immeasurable importance.

——Iki Hisaichi, *Zōtei Nihon komonjogaku* (1976). Nakamura Naokatsu, *Nihon komonjogaku* 3 (1977). Ogino Minahiko, "Komonjogaku ni okeru kaō," *Komonjo kenkyū* (1968). Satō Shin'ichi, "Kaō shōshi," *Sho no Nihon shi* 9 (1976). Tōkyō Daigaku Shiryō Hensanjo, ed, *Kaō kagami* (1964).　　　　　　　*Noburu* HIRAGA

Kaō Corporation

(Kaō Sekken). Chemical firm producing chiefly soaps, basic cosmetics, and household goods such as detergents, but also industrial products such as plasticizers and edible oils. It is first in the industry in the production of synthetic detergents and a leading manufacturer of surface active agents and fatty acids. Founded in 1887 as Nagase Shōten, it developed domestic production of high-grade soap. Within five years of its inception the firm had established a solid base for commercial growth by creating a national market for its products through the use of newspaper advertising and billboards along railways. After World War II it initiated manufacture of cosmetic, pharmaceutical, and chemical products. Employing a unified distribution system regulating all phases of production and inventory control, the company manages its national network of 84 sales firms and automated factory warehouses by a computer in its main office. It has also adopted a strict system of quality control whereby new products developed in its three research laboratories reach production only if they gain a 60 percent rate of support in market surveys. In addition to 8 wholly owned domestic factories, Kaō Corporation has established in cooperation with foreign firms 17 overseas and 4 domestic joint venture companies which produce and sell manufactured goods. Sales for the fiscal year ending March 1982 totaled ¥280.6 billion (US $1.2 billion), of which sale of household products constituted 85 percent, and products for industrial use 8 percent. In the same year the export rate was 2 percent and capitalization was ¥9.9 billion (US $41.1 million). Corporate headquarters are in Tōkyō.

Kaō Ninga (fl early 14th century)

Painter whose name is known from two signature seals found on some ink paintings dating from the first half of the 14th century. A painting is listed in the *Koga bikō*, an early-19th-century dictionary of painters, as bearing the signatures "Kaō" and "Ryōzen," providing support for the tradition that these two signatures represent the same artist; nevertheless, this theory is now largely rejected on stylistic grounds, and the considerable number of paintings bearing the Ryōzen signatures are usually regarded as the work of a different master. Another, more problematical, possibility is that Kaō Ninga was actually the famous Zen priest Kaō Sōnen, the abbot of temple Kenninji in Kyōto who journeyed extensively in China and died in 1345. However, the fact that Kaō Ninga made use of the small seal bearing the name "Ninga" below the larger seal "Kaō" in a number of paintings, and that the name "Ninga" includes the character *ga* ("felicitations"), suggests on the basis of contemporary custom that Kaō may have been a professional Buddhist painter or *ebusshi* associated with the TAKUMA SCHOOL. This would distinguish him from the high-ranking priest Kaō Sōnen.

These confusions about the possible identity of Kaō in no way detract from present-day estimates of his importance as an artist. Such paintings as the hanging scroll depicting the Chinese Zen ec-

Kappa

Detail of a drawing of *kappa* by the Japanese-style painter Ogawa Usen (1868–1938). From a collection published in 1938.

centric Hanshan (J: Kanzan) in the Hattori Collection, Tōkyō, demonstrate a seemingly casual freedom of line, which, with rapid ink-wash passages, conveys a quality of spontaneity and humor that is profoundly expressive both of the subject and of the spirit of Zen Buddhism.

——Tanaka Ichimatsu, *Kaō, Mokuan, Minchō*, vol 5 of *Suiboku bijutsu taikei* (Kōdansha, 1974). Yoshiaki Shimizu and Carolyn Wheelwright, ed, *Japanese Ink Paintings from American Collections: The Muromachi Period* (1976). Tanaka Ichimatsu, *Japanese Ink Painting; From Shūbun to Sesshū*, tr Bruce Darling (1972).

　　　　　　　Lloyd CRAIGHILL

kappa

An amphibious supernatural creature said to inhabit Japan's waters. Thought to be a transformation of a water deity. The description and name of the *kappa* vary from region to region. Generally, the *kappa* is believed to be about the size and shape of a 12- or 13-year-old child, with a face much like a tiger with a snout; its hair is bobbed, and a saucer-like depression on top of the head contains water. When the supply of water diminishes, the *kappa*'s supernatural power on land is impaired. The *kappa*'s slippery body is covered with blue-green scales and emits a fishy odor. It has webbed feet and hands. Human beings can recognize the *kappa* by its ability to rotate arm and leg joints freely. In other variations, *kappa* have beaks and wings or resemble turtles or otters. Although in some areas *kappa* help with rice-planting or irrigation, usually they prey on humans and animals. In particular the *kappa* delights in grabbing its victim and tearing out the liver through the anus. The *kappa* is also said to be fond of cucumbers and partial to SUMŌ wrestling. AKUTAGAWA RYŪNOSUKE wrote a popular novel entitled *Kappa*.　　　　　　　*Inokuchi* SHŌJI

Kapsin Political Coup

(Kōshin Jihen). An unsuccessful attempt by members of the Korean KAEHWAP'A (Enlightenment Faction) with the support of the Japanese to seize control of the Korean government in December of 1884 (Kapsin in the sexagenary year designation system used at the time). Led by KIM OK-KYUN and PAK YŎNG-HYO, the Kaehwap'a promoted the rapid Westernization of Korea following the model of Japanese modernization. Thwarted by the pro-Chinese SUGUP'A (Conservative Faction) then in control of the government, the young reformers seized the royal palace on 4 December and held it for three days before their revolt was put down by Chinese garrison forces. The Japanese legation was burned and 40 Japanese were killed; Kim, Pak, and other coup leaders fled to Japan. Japan received reparations and an apology from Korea in the Treaty of SEOUL in January 1885, while China and Japan agreed to withdraw troops from Korea in the TIANJIN (TIENTSIN) CONVENTION in April 1885. See also KOREA AND JAPAN: early modern relations.

C. Kenneth QUINONES

kara-e

(Chinese-style painting). A term often contrasted with YAMATO-E (Japanese-style painting). In its earliest 8th-century use, kara-e referred to works done by Chinese artists of the Tang (T'ang) dynasty (618–907) that were imported to Japan. Its meaning was subsequently extended to copies of Chinese paintings done by Japanese artists, and then to Japanese depictions of Chinese scenery or representations of Chinese subjects. Throughout the Heian period (794–1185), kara-e carried overtones of the dignity and opulence of Tang China in contrast to the familiarity of themes from Japanese literature. Consequently, wall paintings of Chinese sages enhanced the solemnity of official rooms in the Imperial Palace, and views of Lake Kunming (K'un-ming) or prancing Chinese horses added splendor to ceremonial occasions. While using the term kara-e only in reference to subject matter, Japanese artists gradually transformed these colorful Tang painting models into the style associated with the ambiance of the Heian court.

During the 13th and 14th centuries, ink paintings by Chinese artists of the Song (Sung; 960–1279) and Yuan (Yüan; 1279–1368) dynasties began to enter Japan. Japanese of the period called these newly imported Chinese paintings kara-e in contrast to the continuing Heian style. By the early 15th century, when the enthusiasm for Chinese things was widespread, the Japanese had begun to make stylistic distinctions between yamato-e polychrome paintings of traditional themes and kara-e ink monochrome paintings of newly introduced themes. Kara-e retained its exalted associations until the new wave had been thoroughly assimilated by Japanese artists of the late 15th and 16th centuries. The resulting Chinese-based styles were called kanga ("Chinese painting"). In the common parlance of the Edo period (1600–1868), kara-e designated the colorful style of Tang China; yamato-e referred to the classical Heian style evolved from it; and kanga indicated the Japanese translation of Song and Yuan painting styles.

Carolyn WHEELWRIGHT

Karafuto → Sakhalin

Karafuto-Chishima Kōkan Jōyaku → St. Petersburg, Treaty of

Karagoromo Kisshū (1743–1802)

KYŌKA poet. Real name Kojima Gen'nosuke. Born in Edo (now Tōkyō) to a samurai family, he was an advocate of delicately humorous verse evincing the technical intricacy and classical grace of traditional WAKA. With ŌTA NAMPO and Akera Kankō (1740–1800) he headed a group of kyōka poets formed of both samurai and townsmen (chōnin). Kyōka first became popular in Edo following the publication of Nampo's Manzai kyōkashū, a collection characterized by a hedonistic style and mordant wit, but in the stricter social atmosphere brought on by the KANSEI REFORMS, the more reserved kyōka of Kisshū and Kankō came into vogue. Kisshu's works include the anthologies Kyōka wakabashū (1783) and Suichikushū (1802).

Karai Senryū (1718–1790)

Anthologist and eponymous founder of the poetic genre senryū. Real name Karai Hachiemon. Born in Edo (now Tōkyō). A town official in Edo's Asakusa district, in his forties he became a master of the maeku zuke ("verse-capping"; see ZAPPAI AND SENRYŪ) style of haikai and was soon so prominent that verses approved and anthologized by him came to be known as senryū. From 1757 until his death he selected and published poems in annual collections known as Senryūhyō mankuawase. These volumes include some 80,000 out of the more than 2.3 million verses judged by Senryū. His disciple Goryōken Arubeshi chose from among these poems 756 that could be understood separately without their maeku couplets and published them under the title of Haifū yanagidaru in 1765, establishing

the 17-syllable form as an independent genre, the modern senryū. Editions of Senryūhyō mankuawase and Haifū yanagidaru continued to be put out under different editors until 1797 and 1838(?) respectively. Senryū is the only genre of Japanese literature that is named after a person.

Kara Jūrō (1941–)

A leading "post-postwar" playwright, director, and actor. Kara, whose legal name is Ōtsuru Yoshihide, graduated from the theater department of Meiji University. He organized the Jōkyō Gekijō (Situation Theater) troupe in 1963 and began to write plays. The group subsequently acquired a distinctive red tent that could be readily set up anywhere in the city or country. This red tent became both the symbol and the prime vehicle for realizing Kara's goal of integrating contemporary theater with everyday life.

Kara's theatrical ideal seeks a return to that time when actors were wandering beggars and their performances were without any trace of gentility or artful precocity. In the red tent, Kara's actors share with their audiences the frenzy and celebration found historically in shrine festivals. He and his Korean wife, Yi Yŏng-son (known in Japan as Ri Reisen), perform the lead roles in concert with one of the strongest acting ensembles in the world.

The dialogue in Kara's plays is a highly literary, humorous amalgam of nonsense words and onomatopoeia, incessant puns, current slang, and unexpected images and allusions. His plots are strings of singular events which are permutations of a few common themes. Persona drifts easily from one character to another. Kara often reworks his archetypal characters through a series of plays. The earth mother Koshimaki Osen, a role identified with Yi Yŏng-son, appears as a recurring character in a series of plays that includes Giri ninjō i ro ha ni ho he to hen (1967, The ABC's of Obligation vs Feeling) and others. A similar cycle is Jon Shirubā (1965, Long John Silver).

Other representative works reveal Kara's universal sources: Aribaba (1967, Ali Baba), Kyūketsu ki (1971, The Vampire Princess), Nito monogatari (1972, A Tale of Two Cities), and Bengaru no tora (1973, Bengal Tiger). Kara has made one feature film on his own, Ninkyō gaiden: Genkainada (The Sea of Genkai: A Chivalrous Legend). He also writes popular songs and short novels.

◾——Kara Jūrō no sekai, Bessatsu shimpyō (Autumn 1974).

J. L. ANDERSON

Karakhan, Lev Mikhailovich (1889–1937)

Soviet diplomat. Born in Tiflis and graduated from the University of St. Petersburg, Karakhan was politically active as a Menshevik in the Russian Social Democratic Labor Party. During the October Revolution in 1917, he joined the Bolsheviks and assumed a series of posts in the People's Commissariat for Foreign Affairs, rising quickly to the position of deputy commissar. He issued the "Karakhan Manifestos" of 25 July 1919 and 27 September 1920, which renounced privileges and concessions acquired by the tsarist regime in China. As envoy to China (1923–26), Karakhan negotiated treaties which established Soviet diplomatic relations with China (31 May 1924) and with Japan (20 January 1925). In 1928 he negotiated a fisheries convention with Japan. Karakhan continued to serve as a Far Eastern expert in the Foreign Affairs Commissariat until his arrest and execution during the Stalin purges. See also RUSSIA AND JAPAN.

◾——George Alexander Lensen, Japanese Recognition of the USSR (1970).

John J. STEPHAN

Karako site

Archaeological site of the Yayoi period (ca 300 BC–ca AD 300); located in alluvial lowlands of Nara Prefecture. Karako Pond in the center of the site was first excavated in 1936–37; the many types of YAYOI POTTERY that were unearthed were subsequently assigned to five categories or phases that have since served as the standard typology for Yayoi pottery of the Kinki region (the seven prefectures centering in the Kyōto-Ōsaka-Nara area) and as a reference-point for such wares throughout Japan. Karako was also the first site to yield wooden artifacts and agricultural implements that shed light on the daily life of Yayoi peoples. Especially notable were pedestaled bowls turned on a lathe (ROKURO). Also excavated were PIT HOUSES, storage-pit and ditch remains, and a variety of BONE ARTICLES and STONE TOOLS. Excavations in 1977 produced both clay and stone molds for casting bronze bells (DŌTAKU). See also YAYOI CULTURE; ARCHAEOLOGY.

ABE Gihei

karamatsu → larch, Japanese

kara-ori

A heavy, profusely decorated brocade cloth (NISHIKI); also, the short-sleeved *kimono* made of this cloth. The three-harness ground twill of unglossed threads that forms the background is often enhanced by gold or silver foiled thread woven into a pattern. Long strands of thick, glossy silk, appearing much like loose embroidery, stand out against the ground in multicolored designs. The name *kara-ori*, or "Chinese weave," implies the complexity of the technique, not necessarily the country of origin.

During the 15th and 16th centuries the upper classes, both men and women, wore *kara-ori*, often under a broad-sleeved cloak. A special style of *kara-ori*, around 1600, became the basis of the subsequent NŌ theater costume, with which the term is primarily associated today. In the Nō theater, this garment is used as an outer robe in women's roles: for young women's costumes, brightly patterned robes include the color red (*iroiri*), while older women's costumes contain more subdued colors (*ironashi*). The designs generally have floral associations: a field of autumn grasses, maple leaves floating downstream, wisteria hanging over lattice fences, or a collage of flowers of all seasons. The kimono may be covered with an overall pattern, or it may be divided into blocks of contrasting colors and patterns: two blocks along the back seam (*katamigawari*) or 4 to 16 alternating blocks (*dangawari*). These horizontal squares of different ground colors are effected by tie-dyeing the warp.

The standard method of wearing *kara-ori* is to wrap it tightly over the hips, secure it with a band, and loosely fold the upper portion over the chest (*kinagashi*). It is never worn bound with a stiff, broad *obi*, as were the softer materials popular from the 17th century on. Sometimes one sleeve of the *kara-ori* is slipped off the shoulder to provide easier movement (*nukisage*), or the hem may be hiked up to knee level (*tsuboori*), exposing a soft underkimono. When worn in combination with broad divided skirts (*ōguchi*), the *kara-ori* is secured at the waist and allowed to fall over the skirts as a cloak. See THEATRICAL COSTUMES.

📖——Fujishiro Tsugio, *Shashin de miru nō no shōzoku* (1972). Japan Society, *Tokugawa Collection: Nō Robes and Masks* (1977). Kitamura Tetsurō, *Nō shōzoku*, no. 46 of *Nihon no bijutsu* (March 1970). Monica BETHE

Karasumaru Mitsuhiro (1579-1638)

WAKA poet and court noble of the early part of the Edo period (1600-1868). Classified as a member of the conservative Nijō school. Studied poetry under his father-in-law, HOSOKAWA YŪSAI, from whom he received the secret, orally transmitted poetic tradition known as the KOKIN DENJU. He is regarded as the moving spirit behind the poetic revival following the wars of the 16th century. Combining classical conventions with a detachment and freedom of spirit, perhaps the result of his Zen training, he provides a bridge between the *waka* style of traditional court poetry and that of the Tokugawa period. He is also known for his calligraphy. Principal works include *Kōyō wakashū* (published posthumously in 1669) and *Jiteiki* (ca 1602).

karate

(literally, "empty hand"). Art of self-defense that uses no weapons and relies instead on arm strides (*uchi*), thrusts (*tsuki*), and kicks (*keri*). *Karate* was historically most widely practiced in China and Okinawa and thus is not considered one of the traditional Japanese MARTIAL ARTS; it is, however, loosely referred to as such outside of Japan.

Origins——Legend places the origin of *karate* in India, where it is said to have been developed by a prince some 5,000 years ago. There is inconclusive evidence that some form of bare hand combat was practiced in China and India in ancient times. Current forms of *karate* developed from a style of Chinese boxing called *quanfa* (*ch'üan-fa*, literally, "rules of the fist"; known as kung fu in the West; J: *kempō*), which was transmitted, according to tradition, by the Indian Buddhist monk Bodhidharma (d ca 532) along with ZEN (Ch: Chan or Ch'an) Buddhist teachings to Chinese disciples at Shaolin temple (J: Shōrinji) in the southern province of Henan (Honan). The method of self-defense traced to these beginnings is called Shōrinji *kempō* in Japan; it had spread widely through China by the time of the medieval Ming dynasty (1368-1644), but it was suppressed in the Qing (Ch'ing) period (1644-1912) because it was used

Karate

A successful thrust by the contestant on the left wins a decision.

by a secret society aspiring to reestablish Ming rule. The subsequent development of *karate* took place primarily in OKINAWA.

Commercial and cultural intercourse between China and the RYŪKYŪ ISLANDS (now Okinawa Prefecture) dates back to ancient times. The Okinawans were seafarers and conducted much of the trade along the China coast and in Southeast Asia. By the mid-14th century, Okinawa had entered into a tributary relationship with China, which it maintained in one form or another until modern times. It is not known when Chinese fighting styles were transmitted to the islands; probably over the course of the centuries, Chinese techniques (referred to in Japanese as *tōde*; literally "Tang [T'ang] hand") merged with indigenous techniques (called *te*; literally, "hand") to produce the *karate* style. Unarmed combat was developed rapidly after Okinawa was unified in a single kingdom in the 1420s, after which carrying weapons was forbidden. The prohibition of weapons was continued by the Shimazu clan of Satsuma, which asserted control over the islands in 1609. *Karate* developed thereafter in a context of some secrecy, but it was sustained as the primary method of self-defense. The word *karate* was initially a variant reading of the characters for *tōde*, but the characters were changed early in the 20th century.

Modern Development——A *karate* club was established at a middle school in Okinawa in 1905 after the islands had become a prefecture of modern Japan, and the sport thereafter began to emerge from obscurity. It became known throughout mainland Japan in 1922, when Funakoshi Gichin, an Okinawan master, performed a demonstration in Tōkyō under the sponsorship of the Ministry of Education. In the following years, Mabuni Kenwa, Motobu Chōki, and Miyagi Chōjun helped spread *karate* throughout the country. In the late 1920s, a *karate* club was founded at Keiō Gijuku (now Keiō University), and thereafter the development of the sport centered on the universities. Two schools developed, one of which emphasized strengthening the body, and the other, quick movements. Numerous styles (*ryū*) have emerged over the years, the principal ones being the Shōtōkanryū, founded by Funakoshi; Gōjūryū, founded by Miyagi; the Shitōryū, founded by Mabuni; and the Wadōryū, founded by Ōtsuka Hironori.

After World War II, *karate* and the other martial arts went into a period of decline that lasted until around 1955. After that point, the sport increased in popularity, and it is more widespread now than at any other time in history. A federation of student *karate* organizations was established in 1962; it now has more than 180 participating schools and 7,000 student members. Since then similar organizations have been established for corporate clubs, the Self Defense Forces, and for the general public. The various styles each operate their own schools, often with a considerable amount of rivalry and disputes over secret techniques.

A general federation of the *karate* organizations in Japan was established in 1964, after *karatedō* (the Way of *karate*) as a well-developed method of body training had achieved a large following abroad. Its principal concerns have been the unification of groups, establishment of a unified form, uniform rankings, awarding of ranks, a system of honors, establishment of rules for competition, and cooperative affiliations. Another concern is contacts with associations in foreign countries, including France, Great Britain, Germany, Brazil, and the United States.

Technique and Contests——The three main techniques of *karate* are strikes, thrusts, and kicks. A distinction is made between offensive and defensive techniques. Offensive techniques are divided into three main categories: thrusts (using the fist, elbow, crown of the head, and palm of the hand); strikes (fist, blade of the hand, palm of the hand, arm); kicks (sole of the foot, blade of the foot, kneecap). These techniques are modified according to the position of one's opponent. There are various parrying methods corresponding to each of the offensive methods; these require instant turns at the moment of the attack.

There are two sections in *karate* competitions: form *(kata)* competition and sparring *(kumite)* matches. The three classes of practice methods to be mastered are basic, form, and sparring. Sparring practice is also divided into three stages: basic, free-style one-knuckle, and free-style. Those who advance to the free-style sparring level can enter matches. Sparring matches take place in an eight square meter court and last two to three minutes. If there is no decision, the time is extended. Accurate and effective striking, thrusting, and kicking are crucial to winning decisions. When an athlete exhibits the appropriate tempo, great energy, and mental power in a correct pose, a full point is awarded. Even when a move is not perfect, it is considered in the final score. The position of the face, neck, and torso are decisive in the scoring. The *karate* move must stop before a critical part of the opponent's body is hit. There are other actions considered fouls since they violate the spirit of *karate*.

Form competitions usually take place on a court with a wooden floor, whose dimensions are not fixed. A designated routine may be judged on its own for credit or as part of a competition. If for credit, the judges assign points to the routine performed, and a decision is made on the basis of accumulated points. In a competition, both athletes perform the assigned routine simultaneously and the judges decide which is superior. Sometimes the athlete is permitted to choose the style to be demonstrated. Judgments are based on the correctness of the sequence of the forms, strength, flexibility of the body, tempo of the performance, and whether power, spirit, and concentration are evident. *Tomiki Kenji*

Karatsu

City in northwestern Saga Prefecture, Kyūshū, on Karatsu Bay. Important as the point of embarkation for Korea in ancient times, Karatsu became a castle town in 1602. After the Meiji period (1868–1912), it developed as a port for shipping coal from Karatsu Coalfield and as a base for fishing. Principal industries are the manufacture of machine tools and construction materials and the processing of foodstuffs and seafood. It is especially noted for its traditional KARATSU WARE. The coastal area is part of the Genkai Quasi-National Park. Other tourist attractions are the ruins of Karatsu Castle and the NIJI NO MATSUBARA, a stand of pines on the bay. Pop: 77,712.

Karatsu ware

(karatsu-yaki). Collective name for diverse ceramics produced south of the city of Karatsu, an ancient port in Hizen Province (now Saga Prefecture), Kyūshū. Over 100 kilns produced high-fired stonewares from the mid-16th century for shipment in great quantities to the rest of Japan. Often with a finely crackled, hard feldspathic glaze, many pieces had underglaze painted designs of simple reeds and flowers or patterns. The smaller pieces were all wheel thrown and had trimmed, unglazed foot rims. Despite their great diversity, the Karatsu style can be identified according to three major types: plain Karatsu *(muji karatsu)* having a single glaze; Korean Karatsu (Chōsen *karatsu)* combining an opaque white glaze *(madara* or *namako)* with a dark brown or black iron glaze; and underglazed decorated Karatsu *(ekaratsu)* using a milky or semitransparent glaze over iron oxide painted underglaze designs.

Certain unpretentious Karatsu pieces caught the attention of masters of the TEA CEREMONY. Some pieces were fashioned specifically for that use. The majority of Old Karatsu *(kokaratsu)* pieces extant today have been preserved because of their status as tea ceremony wares.

Extensive nomenclature is not unusual for tea ceremony wares from major kiln sites. The emphasis on diversity and distinctiveness in tea ceremony wares resulted in numerous designations of different types of Karatsu. Names were derived from: the glaze (black or *kurokaratsu,* and yellow or *kikaratsu),* resemblance to other Japa-

nese or Chinese wares *(seto karatsu, temmoku karatsu);* presumed relationship to Korea (Chōsen *karatsu),* type of decoration *(horikaratsu, mishima karatsu, hakeme karatsu, ekaratsu),* shapes *(kutsu chawan* or "shoe bowl"), and so on.

In the late 16th century, Karatsu was affected by political events when the hegemon TOYOTOMI HIDEYOSHI established residence in Kyūshū to direct his two campaigns in Korea. His tea master FURUTA ORIBE accompanied him. The first written record of Karatsu is in Oribe's tea diary *Koshoku zensho,* where he recorded using a Karatsu flower vase *(hanaire)* on 23 February 1603. At that time *bushidō,* the way of the warrior, and *chadō,* the way of tea, were inseparable for the *daimyō* and *samurai.* Korean tea ceramics were greatly prized and Japanese orders for Korean pieces were common. The warriors of the Korean campaigns brought back to Japan large numbers of Korean potters. The result was a phenomenal acceleration of ceramic production. The Korean potters introduced the fast-turning kick wheel. The high-fired climbing kiln, *noborigama,* was already in use in Japan. It was made more efficient in its firing and at some sites, such as Shiinomine, was enlarged to as many as 20 chambers. Although household wares remained the principal Karatsu product, most kilns fired some pieces for the tea ceremony, and kilns such as Fujinkawachi Chinotani catered to tea demands.

In the early part of the Edo period (1600–1868), the admiration of Korean ware and the immigration of Korean potters fostered the assumption that Karatsu was Korean in style. Korean Karatsu, the dark-and-light-glazed type, was probably called "Korean" to give it prestige, although it resembles no known Korean ceramic. Oku Gōrai wares were thought to have been imported from Korea until their shards were uncovered at Karatsu sites; legends persist about *hi bakari* ("fire only") Karatsu tea bowls made by immigrant potters using Korean clay and glaze, only the firing being Japanese.

One of the earliest kilns, Handōgame, operated from at least the mid-16th century. Production reached its peak in the early 17th century. In the first quarter of that century kaolin was discovered in Kyūshū, opening the way for many of the kilns to convert to porcelain manufacture. Among those that continued Karatsu production, Ochawangama remains active today. Nakazato Tarōemon XII (b 1895), a descendant of the early potters and one of Japan's LIVING NATIONAL TREASURES, retired as principal Karatsu potter of Ochawangama in November 1969. Now known as Muan, he makes ceramics of a style other than Karatsu. Nakazato Tarōemon XIII (b 1923), his oldest son, continues the production of Karatsu ware in the ancient, traditional style.

📖——Harada Tomohiko and Nakazato Tarōemon, *Karatsu, Takatori* (1969). Mizumachi Wasaburō and Nabeshima Naotsugu, *Karatsu* (1963). *Johanna BECKER*

karayuki san

(literally, "one who goes to China," i.e., abroad). Japanese women who went to work as prostitutes in such places as Siberia, Manchuria, China, Southeast Asia, the South Pacific, India, and even America and Africa after the Meiji Restoration of 1868. While *karayuki san* came from all parts of Japan, the majority were natives of western Kyūshū, particularly the impoverished Amakusa area, where the term originated. Their exact number is unknown, but it may have been as many as 100,000. Girls in early adolescence were either sold by their parents or unwittingly signed themselves over to procurers *(zegen),* who then sold them to overseas brothels, where they worked as maids until they could become prostitutes in their midteens. Conditions were such that most women died before age 30. Nevertheless, many of them retained feelings of filial piety and loyalty to Japan, sending money home to help support their former households and donating money to Japan in times of war. Some eventually started their own businesses abroad and thus contributed to founding Japanese overseas communities.

The height of *karayuki san* prostitution was around the time of the Russo-Japanese War (1904–05). After World War I, as Japan assumed the role of a major world power, the government suppressed the traffic in prostitutes in order to forestall international criticism, and the number of *karayuki san* decreased greatly. Following the MANCHURIAN INCIDENT of 1931, some former *karayuki san* were called upon by the Japanese army and navy to serve as prostitutes *(ianfu)* for Japanese forces, although about 80 percent of the more than 100,000 *ianfu* were Korean. After Japan's surrender in 1945, *karayuki san* as such completely disappeared. Their plight has recently been brought to the attention of the public by several books; the best known is Yamazaki Tomoko's *Sandakan hachiban shōkan* (1972, Brothel Number Eight at Sandakan), which was made into a film in 1975. See also MURAOKA IHEIJI; YAMADA WAKA.

Chiyoko ISHIBASHI

Karikachi Pass

(Karikachi Tōge). Located in the northern Hidaka Mountains, central Hokkaidō. The pass offers a panoramic view of the Tokachi Plain and serves as the watershed between it and the Ishikari Plain. The railway tunnel under the pass is the longest (5,790 m or 18,991 ft) in Hokkaidō's railway system. Altitude: 644 m (2,112 ft).

Kariya

City in central Aichi Prefecture, 24 km (15 mi) southeast of Nagoya. Kariya developed as a castle town early in the 1800s. It was rapidly industrialized after the opening of the Japanese National Railways' Tōkaidō Main Line and the establishment of the Toyota Spinning Co by Toyoda Sakichi in 1923. Many Toyota-affiliated plants manufacturing steel, automobiles, machine tools, and other products are located here. Pop: 105,643.

Karlgren, Bernhard (1889–1978)

One of the great philologists of the 20th century. Born in Jönköping, Sweden. When he was still in high school, he became interested in linguistic studies and mapped some dialects of his province, which became the subject of his first publication, *Folksägner från Tveta och Mo härader, upptecknade på folkmål* (1908). He continued his language studies at Uppsala University, where he studied the Nordic languages, Greek, and Russian. Upon graduation in 1908 he turned to Chinese and in 1910 left for field work in China, spending 18 months in Northern China (Taiyuan or T'ai-yüan), comparing dialects and beginning the work of reconstructing ancient Chinese. The revolution in 1911 forced him to cut short his stay, and he returned via Siberia to Sweden. There he continued his work on Chinese phonology and published his monumental work *Etudes sur la phonologie chinoise* (1915–26). The first 388 pages were presented as a doctoral thesis at Uppsala University (1915). Parts of the work have been translated into Chinese and also into Japanese (Japanese tr, Takata Hisahiko, *Gendai Shina hōgen no kijutsu onseigaku,* 1942).

In this work Karlgren reconstructed Chinese as it was spoken around AD 600, basing his work on Sino-Japanese (the Japanese pronunciation of Chinese words). This reconstruction he called Ancient Chinese. Later he undertook the reconstruction of Archaic Chinese, the language of about 800 BC. His results were presented in *Grammatica Serica, Scripts and Phonetics in Chinese and Sino-Japanese* (1940).

Karlgren received in 1918 a personal chair of Far Eastern Linguistics and Culture at the University of Göteborg, where he stayed until 1939. He was president of the university between 1931 and 1936. China and the Chinese language were of course his main interests here, but it should be noted that while at Göteborg Karlgren established the first Japanese program in the Scandinavian countries; the first student in Japanese graduated in 1923. In 1939 Karlgren was appointed to a professorship in Stockholm serving as the director of the Museum of Far Eastern Antiquities. In 1945 he began to teach Chinese at the University of Stockholm, where he remained until his retirement in 1958.

Karlgren has written on history, religion, and archaeology as well as linguistics. From 1929 to 1978 he was associated with *The Museum of Far Eastern Antiquities Bulletin,* to which he contributed almost annually, especially in the fields of historical linguistics and the dating of ancient Chinese bronzes.

📖 ——Else Glahn, "A List of Works by Bernhard Karlgren," in *The Museum of Far Eastern Antiquities Bulletin,* vol 28 (1956).

Olof LIDIN

karō

(literally, "house elders"). Sometimes called TOSHIYORI (and in the Tokugawa shogunate known as RŌJŪ), *karō* were the highest-ranking officials in the governments of *daimyō* during the Edo period (1600–1868) and had general responsibility for the administration of domainal affairs. Usually drawn from vassal families of high rank and long service to the daimyō's family, two to four *karō* commonly held office at one time, some being stationed at domain headquarters and others at the daimyō's mansion *(yashiki)* in Edo (now Tōkyō).

Conrad TOTMAN

Karuizawa

Town in eastern Nagano Prefecture, central Honshū, on a plateau 900–1,100 m (2,952–3,608 ft) high on the southern slope of Mt. Asama (Asamayama), the highest active volcano in Japan. A post-station town during the Edo period (1600–1868), since the late 1800s Karuizawa has grown rapidly as a fashionable summer retreat, with many villas, hotels, inns, golf courses, skating rinks, and other facilities. Tourist attractions include SHIRAITO FALLS and ONIOSHIDASHI, a massive flow of lava formed by the eruption of Mt. Asama in 1783. Pop: 14,195.

Karurusu Hot Spring

(Karurusu Onsen). Located in southwestern Hokkaidō. A simple thermal spring containing radium; water temperature 38–56°C (100–133°F). Situated along the upper reaches of the river Chitose-gawa, it was discovered in 1886. The name "Karurusu" is derived from the fact that its water is similar to that of a hot spring in Carlsbad (J: Karurusubaddo), Czechoslovakia. State-operated skiing grounds are located in the vicinity.

karuta → playing cards

kasagake

("hat-hanging"). Form of mounted archery. Originating in the Heian period (794–1185), the term derives from the fact that archers initially shot arrows at a straw hat *(kasa).* As a martial sport, *kasagake* flourished in the Kamakura period (1185–1333) along with YABUSAME and INUOUMONO. Bowmen galloped their horses down a course, from the midpoint of which they shot arrows at a leather-covered wooden target, 50 centimeters (about 20 in) in diameter, usually set up at a distance of about eight bow lengths to the side of the course. Teams were sometimes determined by lot and ceremonial exhibitions were performed at Shintō shrines. The arrows were called *kaburaya* and had hollow, bullet-shaped, wooden heads which whistled as they flew towards the target. Interest in the sport declined midway in the Muromachi period (1333–1568).

INAGAKI Shisei

Kasai

City in central Hyōgo Prefecture, western Honshū, on the river Kakogawa. Known traditionally for its *banshū-ori* (a cotton fabric), *tatami* matting, and *goza* (straw mats), Kasai's more modern industries include electrical appliances and textiles. The temple Ichijōji, which dates from the 7th century, and the Gohyaku Rakan (500 Arhats), a group of some 428 stone Buddhist images, draw visitors. Pop: 51,052.

Kasai Zenzō (1887–1928)

Novelist. Born in Aomori Prefecture. Received primary education only. Kasai moved frequently, working at various jobs in Aomori Prefecture and Hokkaidō before he settled in Tōkyō in 1905 and became a follower of TOKUDA SHŪSEI. His novels, written in the autobiographical naturalist style of the early 20th century (see I-NOVEL), describe his struggles with loneliness and illness, exacerbated by poverty. Major fiction includes *Kanashiki chichi* (1912), *Akuma* (1912), and *Kohan shuki* (1924).

Kasa jizō

("The Bamboo-Hat Jizō"). Folktale. A poor but kind-hearted old couple find that they have no money to buy rice cakes for the New Year. The old man makes bamboo hats and sets off in the snow to sell them. On his way to town, he sees six statues of JIZŌ (the guardian deity of children) standing in the snow. Feeling sorry for the statues, he covers their heads with the bamboo hats and returns home. That night the statues reward him by leaving a huge mound of rice cakes at the gate. The folktale is based on the popular belief that gods come to visit on New Year's Day (see ŌTOSHI NO KYAKU). The number of Jizō statues differs from version to version.

SUCHI Tokuhei

Kasama

City in central Ibaraki Prefecture, central Honshū. Kasama was a castle town and post-station town during the Edo period (1600–1868). It became a shrine town with the establishment of the Inari Shrine in the Meiji period (1868–1912). Rice cultivation, dairy farming, and gardening flourish; stone quarrying is also important. Utensils for the tea ceremony, flower vases, and *sake* containers called Kasama ware are produced here. Pop: 31,226.

Kasa no Kanamura (fl ca 715–733)

Poet and courtier of the early part of the Nara period (710–794). Nothing is known about him apart from what can be gleaned from brief headnotes and footnotes to his poems in the MAN'YŌSHŪ (ca 759). An important poet of the so-called third period of *Man'yō* poetry, he was one of a group of "poets laureate" during an age when poetry was being transformed from an art close to the ancient bardic tradition to a literary accomplishment of the entire court class. Of the 45 poems—11 CHŌKA (long poems) and 34 *tanka* (short poems; see WAKA)—associated with him in the *Man'yōshū*, 30 (8 *chōka* and 22 *tanka*) are specifically labeled as his; the others are indicated as from the Kanamura Collection *(Kanamura kashū)*, and are believed to have been by him. His poems are chiefly about public occasions, including celebrations of imperial visits to villas and resorts in various provinces. He also wrote elegies on the deaths of imperial princes, his best poem being a 29-line *chōka* with two envoys *(hanka)* on the death of Prince Shiki (d 716).

When compared with the greatest poets of the *Man'yō* era, Kanamura falls into the second rank; indeed, it has been said of him that his salient characteristic is the lack of any salient characteristics. His *chōka* display the tendency of the age to turn increasingly from public expression to a more private lyricism, a mode which conflicts with the formal pillow words (MAKURA KOTOBA) and other conventional language which he derives from the bardic word hoard. Nevertheless, he has attracted the interest of modern scholars because he is one of the last of the poets laureate of the *Man'yō* age, and because some of the elements of his verse are suggestive of folk song and the oral tradition.

🔲——Robert H. Brower and Earl Miner, *Japanese Court Poetry* (1961). Ian H. Levy, *The Ten Thousand Leaves* (1981–).

Robert H. BROWER

Kasaoka

City in southwestern Okayama Prefecture, western Honshū. Aside from its chemical and textile industries, the manufacture of *tansu* (wooden chests) and hats are important. Steel industrial complexes are also being constructed here. Farm products are flowers, notably pyrethrum, and fruit and poultry. Kanaura Bay is noted as a breeding ground for HORSESHOE CRABS. Pop: 61,917.

Kasaya Yukio (1943–)

Ski jumper; the first Japanese to win a gold medal in the Winter Olympics. Born in Hokkaidō; graduated from Meiji University. Kasaya took first place in the 1966 "Universiade Games" and second place in the 70-meter ski jump in the 1970 world championship meet held in Czechoslovakia. In the 1972 Sapporo Winter Olympics, he won first place in the 70-meter jump. TAKEDA Fumio

Kaseda

City in southwestern Kagoshima Prefecture, Kyūshū. The economic center of southwestern Kagoshima, it is known for its *shōchū*, native Japanese spirits distilled from rice or sweet potato, and its man-made gems. Rice, tobacco, mandarin oranges, grapes, tea, and vegetables are grown. Cattle raising also flourishes. The sand dunes on the coast, a part of FUKIAGEHAMA, attract tourists. Pop: 25,393.

kasen-e

("pictures of immortal poets"). Idealized portraits of famous Japanese poets drawn from the artists' imaginations, but following set conventions; usually painted in a series. A popular theme in the indigenous YAMATO-E painting tradition, especially in the Kamakura period (1185–1333) through the Muromachi period (1333–1568). The tradition originated in the early 12th century, when pictures of the illustrious late-7th-century poet KAKINOMOTO NO HITOMARO became popular with courtiers who venerated him as the patron saint of poetry, in the hope of gaining some of his genius. Although single portraits of Hitomaro remained popular, sets of portraits also appeared, used to illustrate two famous anthologies of WAKA poems: the *Sanjūrokunin sen* (ca 1008, Selection of Thirty-Six Poets) assembled by FUJIWARA NO KINTŌ, and the *Jidai fudō uta-awase* (Competition of Poems of Different Periods) compiled by the retired emperor GO-TOBA in the early 13th century. The term *kasen-e* is generally used to refer to these sets of paintings.

The 36 poets selected by Kintō became a popular subject, but other selections of 36 poets were also painted (see SANJŪROKKASEN). The earliest extant illustrated versions of Kintō's selection are two sets of handscrolls: the *Satake-bon* and the *Agedatami-bon*, both traditionally attributed to FUJIWARA NO NOBUZANE (ca 1176–ca 1265) although without concrete evidence. By the time these handscrolls were painted, the conventional formula had been established: the 36 poets are presented in sequence, each identified by his or her formal name, a brief genealogy, and one *waka* poem. The stiff-figure style is reminiscent of earlier periods, but the variety of facial expressions used to impart mood and personality to the poets is clearly in the tradition of early Kamakura-period portraiture.

In his *Jidai fudō uta-awase*, Go-Toba presented an imaginary competition between one hundred ancient and contemporary poets. Illustrated handscrolls show the conventionalized figures of the poets, painted as though from life, arranged in 50 pairs, with each poet represented by three poems. Many paintings of this subject were done in simple ink outlines (HAKUBYŌGA); a later variation was the *mokuhitsu* ("wood-brush") drawing, done in ink with a flattened stick rather than the usual soft brush.

From the 13th through the 15th centuries, Japan was swept by a wave of Chinese cultural influence that accompanied the introduction of Zen Buddhism to Japan. For the Kyōto artistocracy, however, the tradition of *kasen-e* provided a link with indigenous painting traditions that remained essentially unbroken. *Kasen-e* appeared in other formats besides the handscroll, including single paintings in series and albums. The *kasen-e* of these times were often amateur, uninspired productions, but two 36-poets manuscripts of the 14th century stand out for their refreshingly irreverent tone and lively depiction of the venerated poets: the *Narikane-bon* and the *Go-Toba In-bon*, named after the supposed calligraphers of each set.

Artists of the Edo period (1600–1868) picked up and reinterpreted the theme of *kasen-e* in strikingly new ways. Ogata KŌRIN (1658–1716) exploited the decorative possibilities by showing the 36 poets arranged on a twofold screen. The BUNJINGA (literati painting) artist Yosa BUSON (1716–84) and his followers carried the humorous potential of the theme to its extreme expression in their sketchy, caricature-like poet portraits.

Perhaps because of the cumbrous nature of the *Jidai fudō uta-awase*, it was not as popular with Edo artists. Instead, a card game was devised based on the HYAKUNIN ISSHU, a long-neglected poetry anthology by FUJIWARA NO SADAIE (Fujiwara no Teika; 1162–1241). The 100 cards used in this game, each depicting a poet with a representative poem, are a type of modern *kasen-e*, now the common cultural property of the Japanese people. The game is still widely enjoyed, especially at New Year's.

🔲——Mori Tōru, *Sanjūrokkasen-e*, vol 19 of *Nihon emakimono zenshū* (Kadokawa Shoten, 1967). Mori Tōru, *Uta-awase-e no kenkyū* (1970). Shirahata Yoshi, *Kasen-e*, no. 96 of *Nihon no bijutsu* (May 1974). Maribeth GRAYBILL

kashi → oaks

kashiage

Also called *kariage*. Usury or usurers of the Kamakura period (1185–1333) and early part of the Muromachi period (1333–1568). Having emerged in response to the development of a money economy, usurers became conspicuous in the Kamakura period, when many shogunal vassals *(gokenin)* fell deeply in debt to them and were forced to sell their estates. In 1239 the shogunate forbade estate stewards *(jitō)* to appoint creditors as their deputies, and in 1240 it not only prohibited the purchase of vassals' lands by usurers but also proclaimed that such properties would be confiscated. Such measures did little to check this profitable business, however, and it continued throughout the Muromachi period under the name DOSŌ.

Kashihara

City in northwestern Nara Prefecture, central Honshū. According to tradition, Kashihara was the site where JIMMU, Japan's legendary first emperor, is said to have been enthroned. Historical sites include the remains of the ancient capital FUJIWARAKYŌ, the mausolea of several emperors, and Kashihara Shrine. Many residents commute to Ōsaka. Pop: 107,320.

Kashihara Shrine

(Kashihara Jingū). A Shintō shrine in the city of Kashihara, Nara Prefecture, dedicated to the spirits of the legendary first emperor, JIMMU, and his consort, Himetataraisuzuhime no Mikoto. Built in 1889 to commemorate the founding of the Japanese nation, the shrine was refurbished and further expanded in 1940 to celebrate the 2,600th anniversary of Jimmu's supposed accession to the throne. The shrine is situated on the southeast slope of the mountain Unebiyama, the legendary site of the enthronement of Jimmu. The main shrine hall was originally part of the Kyōto palace. The annual festival is held on 11 February, the traditional date for Jimmu's enthronement, which is a national holiday (formerly called Kigensetsu, now Kenkoku Kinembi). *Stanley* WEINSTEIN

Kashii Shrine

Shintō shrine in the Kashii district of the city of Fukuoka, Fukuoka Prefecture, Kyūshū, dedicated to the spirits of the legendary emperor Chūai and the legendary empress JINGŪ. Originally an imperial mausoleum, it was converted into a shrine in the second half of the 11th century. The shrine was richly patronized by the imperial family. Customarily a new emperor sent an emissary to the shrine announcing his succession to the throne. The main hall, which is built in a unique architectural style known as the *kashii-zukuri,* has been designated a National Treasure. An annual festival is held on 29 October. *Stanley* WEINSTEIN

Kashikojima

Small island in Ago Bay, town of Ago, southeastern Mie Prefecture, central Honshū. It is separated from the mainland by a strip of water only 20 m (66 ft) wide. A center of pearl culture and the site of the National Pearl Research Laboratory. Area: 0.7 sq km (0.3 sq mi).

Kashima

City in southwestern Saga Prefecture, Kyūshū, on the Ariake Sea. The city developed in the Edo period (1600–1868) as a castle town of a branch family of the lords of Nabeshima domain. Local products are rice, mandarin oranges, *sake,* dairy goods, seaweed *(nori),* and processed seafood. Its modern industries include machinery, pharmaceuticals, and ready-made suits. Asahigaoka Park, known for its cherry blossoms, and Yūtoku Inari Shrine draw visitors. The city is the base for climbing the mountain TARADAKE. Pop: 35,007.

Kashima

Town in southeastern Ibaraki Prefecture, central Honshū, on the Pacific Ocean. The town developed as a shrine town around the KASHIMA SHRINE. Farm products include rice, sweet potatoes, and watermelon. In recent years, it has become a center of the Kashima Coastal Industrial Zone, producing steel, petrochemicals, metals, and machinery. The town is a part of Suigō–Tsukuba Quasi-National Park. Pop: 38,822.

Kashima Sea

(Kashima Nada). Arm of the Pacific Ocean, off Ibaraki Prefecture, central Honshū. Extends approximately 70 km (43 mi) from the mouth of the river Nakagawa to the cape Inubōzaki. The meeting of cold and warm currents makes this area a rich fishing ground for mackerel and sardines, and the coastal regions abound in shellfish. The Kashima Coastal Industrial Zone is located along the southern section of the coast.

Kashima Shrine

(Kashima Jingū). Shintō shrine in the Kashima District of Ibaraki Prefecture, dedicated to Takemikazuchi no Mikoto. This deity is believed to have descended to the Japanese islands together with Futsunushi no Kami (see KATORI SHRINE), ahead of NINIGI NO MIKOTO, the grandson of imperial ancestress AMATERASU ŌMIKAMI, to arrange for the transfer of the land to Amaterasu Ōmikami's descendants. The deity was also a clan deity (UJIGAMI) of the FUJIWARA FAMILY. Because this deity has been associated with military prowess as well as with the imperial cause, the shrine has been richly supported both by successive emperors and by warriors and has been the most influential shrine in the Kantō area. An annual festival is held on 1 September. On 2 September of every 12th year the shrine observes the colorful ritual of sending a portable shrine (MIKOSHI) down the river Tonegawa to the Katori Shrine and back again. See also KASUGA SHRINE. *Stanley* WEINSTEIN

Kashima Yarigatake

Mountain on the border between Toyama and Nagano prefectures, central Honshū. One of the Hida Mountains. Composed of granite, the summit is divided into two peaks. The narrow northern ridge is marked by a series of deep sawtooth notches. The mountain is part of Chūbu Sangaku National Park. Height: 2,889 m (9,476 ft).

Kashiwa

City in northwest Chiba Prefecture, central Honshū. A post-station town on the highway Mito Kaidō during the Edo period (1600–1868), it developed into a commercial center with the opening of railway lines in the Meiji period (1868–1912). It is now primarily a residential district for commuters to Tōkyō, although vegetables are still grown in the outlying areas. There is also a textile industry. Pop: 239,199.

Kashiwabara Hyōzō (1933–1972)

Novelist. Born in Chiba Prefecture. Graduate of Tōkyō University. Professor of German literature at Meiji Gakuin University and later at Tōkyō University of Fine Arts and Music. He first earned recognition with "Tokuyama Michisuke no kikyō" (1967, The Homecoming of Tokuyama Michisuke), which was awarded the Akutagawa Prize. This story is a humorous account of the struggles of an old ex-army general like Kashiwabara's own grandfather. His works, written in plain narrative style, are on the whole autobiographical. The primary aim of his writing is a reconstruction of the formative events in the process of his intellectual development as a young man. Other works include his long autobiographical novel *Nagai michi* (1969, The Long Road) and *Berurin hyōhaku* (1972, Wanderings in Berlin).

Kashiwagi Yoshimaru (1860–1938)

Also known as Kashiwagi Gien. Christian thinker and pastor. Born in what is now Niigata Prefecture, Kashiwagi attended the Tōkyō Normal School (later Tōkyō University of Education) and graduated from the Dōshisha (now Dōshisha University), where he came under the influence of NIIJIMA JŌ. He became a pastor in the Annaka Church in Gumma Prefecture in 1897 and gave himself to the ministry there until his death. From 1898 until 1936 he published the *Jōmō kyōkai geppō* (Jōmō Church Monthly; 459 issues), advocating Christian pacifism and commenting on public affairs. He opposed both the Sino-Japanese War of 1894–95 and the Russo-Japanese War (1904–05) on the grounds that war was waged for the benefit of the military and the ruling class. Kashiwagi always sided with the oppressed, as demonstrated in his support of the villagers in the ASHIO COPPER MINE INCIDENT, and even when his outspoken views led to the banning of his monthly on seven separate occasions, he abided by his convictions. *TANAKA Akira*

Kashiwara

City in southeastern Ōsaka Prefecture, central Honshū. Kashiwara flourished from ancient times as a town on the routes connecting Nara and Ōsaka. Traditional handicrafts include dyeing, bleached cotton, and shell products. Chemical and machinery plants have recently been constructed. Principal farm products are grapes, strawberries, and vegetables. A cluster of ancient tombs (KOFUN) at Matsuoka and cave dwellings at Takaida are noteworthy. Pop: 69,836.

Kashiwazaki

City in central Niigata Prefecture, central Honshū, on the Sea of Japan. A post-station town on the highway Hokuriku Kaidō during the Edo period (1600–1868), it developed as an oil town with the discovery of oil in nearby Nishiyama in the Meiji period (1868–1912). Machinery, metal, foodstuffs, and lumber-processing industries flourish. Its beaches and hot springs draw tourists. Pop: 83,499.

Kashiyama & Co, Ltd

Manufacturer and wholesaler of ready-made garments. Established in 1947. Its clothes bear the trade name Onward. The leading domestic producer of ready-made men's wear, it also produces women's and children's wear as well as clothing in the native Japanese style. The firm manufactures uniforms for government agencies and major companies, including Japan Airlines. As a manufacturer of a wide variety of fashions, it has considerable marketing power among department stores. Kashiyama has subsidiary firms in New York, Paris, and Rome, and has concluded numerous technology exchange agreements with overseas manufacturers and designers. Sales for the fiscal year ending February 1982 totaled ¥172.4 billion (US $733.1 million) and capitalization stood at ¥6.2 million (US $26.4 million). The corporate headquarters are located in Tōkyō.

kasho

Certificates of passage used from the Nara (710–794) to the Azuchi–Momoyama (1568–1600) periods. *Kasho* granted the bearer permission to pass through a barrier station (SEKISHO) or gave him exemption from tolls and served as a means of regulating internal traffic. Initially issued by the Capital Offices (Kyōshiki) or by provincial governors, they were also used for personal identification. From the Kamakura period (1185–1333) onward, when tolls (SEKISEN) were levied at barriers, *kasho* came to mean a certificate of waiver issued by the shogunate, a *daimyō*, or a large religious institution. Exemption from tolls was a privilege usually granted to wealthy merchants and others with political influence. In the Edo period (1600–1868), when barrier stations resumed the function of control of travel rather than toll collection, passage certificates came to be called *tegata*. Among various types of *tegata*, those permitting movement of firearms into Edo (now Tōkyō) and of women out of Edo were most stringently regulated. The term *kasho* remained in use, however, as in *kasho-bune*, the licensed freight boats that plied the river Yodogawa in the Kyōto–Ōsaka region.

kasō

The physical aspect (i.e., location, direction, construction) of buildings according to the art of geomancy. The basic concepts of geomancy (Ch: *fengshui*) originated in China during the Shang (Yin) dynasty (16th to 11th centuries BC) and was practiced, along with astrology and other forms of divination, in predicting the flooding of the Yellow River, in laying out palaces and cities, and in carrying on daily activities, e.g., determining directional taboos (KATATAGAE) and taboo days. In Japan *kasō* was used in the planning of two early capitals, FUJIWARAKYŌ (694–710) and HEIJŌKYŌ (710–784) and so was probably introduced to Japan from the continent around that time. After the Taika Reform of 645, an office called the Ommyōryō (see OMMYŌDŌ) was established. Although it was primarily an office for astronomical and calendrical studies, it included in its activities *kasō* divinations in determining the geographical orientation of buildings and streets in the capital.

An example of *kasō* still practiced today is *kimon*, referring to the inauspicious direction, i.e., northeast. In both Kyōto and Edo (now Tōkyō) Buddhist temples were built to the northeast, the *kimon* direction, to protect the cities against evil forces (ENRYAKUJI on Mt. Hiei [Hieizan] in Kyōto and KAN'EIJI at Ueno in Edo). *Kimon* is also believed to be an unlucky direction in houses. Not only the position and direction of the house itself but those of the front gate, the entrance, the toilet, the bathroom, etc, are also sometimes taken into consideration.   SEIKE Kiyosi

Kasori shell mounds

Archaeological site of the Middle (ca 3500 BC–ca 2000 BC) to Late (ca 2000 BC–ca 1000 BC) Jōmon period; located in Kasori Chō, the city of Chiba, Chiba Prefecture, on a Pleistocene terrace cut by the river Miyakogawa. The site covers an area extending about 400 meters (1,312 ft) north to south and about 200 meters (656 ft) east to west and consists of two tangential ring-shaped SHELL MOUNDS and many smaller middens with deposits up to 2 meters (6.6 ft) thick. Excavations since 1887 have yielded PIT HOUSES, flexed burials (see PREHISTORIC BURIALS), STONE TOOLS, BONE ARTICLES, and pottery. In 1923 a distinction was made between Middle (Kasori E type) and Late (Kasori B type) JŌMON POTTERY, and for the first time it was recognized that Jōmon pottery variations represented temporal change. A museum at the site displays the strata and artifacts from these typical south Kantō shell mounds.   ABE Gihei

Kasuga

City in northwestern Fukuoka Prefecture, Kyūshū. Formerly a farming village, during World War II it was the site of numerous munitions plants. After the war it became a military base for the American OCCUPATION forces. Returned to Japan in 1972, the city serves as a base for the Self Defense Forces. Many of its residents commute to Fukuoka. The city is also known for the SUKU SITE, where Yayoi-period (ca 300 BC–ca AD 300) burial jars were excavated. Pop: 65,838.

Kasugai

City in northwestern Aichi Prefecture, central Honshū, contiguous with Nagoya to the northeast. Numerous paper and electrical appliance factories were established after World War II, although peaches and cactus are still cultivated in its hilly areas. There are huge apartment complexes. Mitsuzōin, a TENDAI SECT temple built over 300 years ago, is located here. Pop: 244,114.

Kasuga Ikkō (1910–   )

Politician. Born in Gifu Prefecture, Kasuga studied at a communications school and worked for the government telephone office in Nagoya before founding a firm which made musical instruments. After serving in the Aichi Prefectural Assembly, he was elected in 1952 to the House of Representatives as a candidate of the JAPAN SOCIALIST PARTY. Identified with the right wing of the JSP, he left in 1960 to help form the DEMOCRATIC SOCIALIST PARTY, becoming secretary in 1967 and serving as chairman from 1971 to 1977. He is noted for his skillful political maneuvering and his eloquence.

Kasuga no Tsubone (1579–1643)

Nurse of TOKUGAWA IEMITSU, the third Tokugawa shōgun. Given name Fuku. A daughter of Saitō Toshimitsu, a retainer of AKECHI MITSUHIDE, she married and bore three children. She was asked by the shogunate to become Iemitsu's nurse and accepted the position after her husband Inaba Masanari divorced her. Through her skillful maneuvers Iemitsu became shōgun in 1623, and she later exerted great influence within the shogunate's domestic establishment, managing to put the entire women's quarters (ŌOKU) under her control.

Kasuga Shrine

(Kasuga Taisha). Shintō shrine in the city of Nara, dedicated to the deities of three shrines associated with the Fujiwara family: the KASHIMA SHRINE (the deity Takemikazuchi no Mikoto), the KATORI SHRINE (the deity Futsunushi no Kami), and Hiraoka Jinja (in the city of Higashi-Ōsaka; the married deities Amenokoyane no Mikoto and Hime no Kami). Kasuga Taisha was founded in 709 by FUJIWARA NO FUHITO to protect the new capital at Nara, on which construction was to begin the following year. Originally, the Fujiwara installed in the Kasuga Shrine their own clan deity from the Kashima Shrine. The Kasuga Shrine thus functioned as both a clan shrine and a national shrine. Around 768 the shrine, which had been on the nearby mountain Mikasayama, was moved to its present location nearer the capital. The sacred symbol (*shimboku*, literally, "sacred wood") of the Kasuga Shrine was often carried into Kyōto in the 11th and the 12th centuries by protesting shrine servants (JINNIN) and WARRIOR-MONKS (*sōhei*) of the nearby KŌFUKUJI, a major Buddhist temple associated with the shrine, in an effort to intimidate the government. The Kasuga Shrine was lavishly endowed with a large estate throughout Japanese history, and it has developed numerous branch shrines elsewhere in the country. The shrine is noted for its unique style of architecture (kasuga-zukuri) and the many deer that inhabit the park around it. The deer are considered sacred messengers from the gods and often constitute a symbolic element in the so-called Kasuga mandara (see MANDALA). The annual festival (Kasuga Matsuri), which was started in 850 as an imperial festival and has been counted as one of the nation's most important festivals, is now celebrated on 13 March. The subshrine Wakamiya, or Kasuga Wakamiya Jinja, has also been a renowned shrine with its grand festival (Ommatsuri) now held on 17 December.   Stanley Weinstein

Kasugayama

Hill in the eastern part of the city of Nara, Nara Prefecture, central Honshū. It has been regarded since ancient times as a sacred abode of various deities; its sacred trees have never been cut. At the foot of the hill is KASUGA SHRINE. Kasugayama is part of Nara Park. Height: 496 m (1,627 ft).

Kasukabe

City in eastern Saitama Prefecture, central Honshū, on the river Furu Tonegawa about 35 km (22 mi) north of Tōkyō. During the Edo period (1600–1868), it prospered as a post-station town and market town along the highway Nikkō Kaidō. It is now a residential town for commuters to Tōkyō, although its traditional products such as chests (tansu), battledores (HAGOITA), and clogs (GETA) continue to be manufactured. Pop: 155,556.

Kasumigaura

Lake in southeastern Ibaraki Prefecture, central Honshū. Japan's second largest lake after Lake Biwa. Located within Suigō–Tsukuba Quasi-National Park. During the Edo period (1600–1868) it flourished as a transportation route when the lake port of Ogawa was a shipping center of rice to Edo (now Tōkyō). Catches include pond smelt, eels, carp, crucian carp, prawns, goby, and corbicula. Pearl culture is also conducted. The water is used for industrial purposes by factories in the Kashima Coastal Industrial Zone. Area: 178 sq km (68.7 sq mi); circumference: 138 km (86 mi); depth: 7 m (23 ft).

kasuri

(ikat). A kind of cloth, typically of hemp, ramie, or cotton, with hazed patterns of reserved white against a deep indigo-blue ground, popular for farmers' and merchants' clothing from the mid-18th to the beginning of the 20th centuries. The patterns are made by selectively reserving sections of thread to be used for warp or weft from the dye (as by binding some sections tightly with thread) in such a way as to produce, when woven, a predetermined pattern in the finished cloth.

There are several important early examples of thread-resisted textiles in Japan: fragments of 7th and 8th century Buddhist ritual banners of complex polychrome warp ikat, probably from western Asia; flat plaited ceremonial scarves (hirao) worked with resist-dyed elements, the earliest dating from the Heian period (794–1185); simple, block-patterned warp ikats (shimekiri) used for kosode (an early form of KIMONO) and NŌ costumes, the earliest extant example dating from the late 16th century.

Although produced by the same technique, these textiles are quite different from, and had little or no influence on, the subsequent development of kasuri weaving as it is known today.

In the 14th century ikat was introduced to the Ryūkyū (now Okinawa) islands from the south. The techniques and motifs developed there formed the basis of later Japanese kasuri weaving. Kasuri was introduced to Japan proper in the form of annual tribute payments from Ryūkyū to Satsuma (now Kagoshima Prefecture) in the early 17th century. Feudal lords and their retainers used these textiles for their fashionable kosode garments (see CLOTHING).

The development of kasuri weaving in Japan was spurred by demands from well-to-do city merchants. The earliest recorded kasuri weaving in Japan was in the remote Sea of Japan province of Echigo (now Niigata Prefecture), which in the 1660s added kasuri motifs to the ramie cloth woven for sale and further distribution

Kasumigaura

Traditional fishing boats of a type once common on Kasumigaura. Lines stretch from the upper spar and from both bow and stern to drag a net for the lake's freshwater smelt. The boats have now been largely replaced by power vessels, and the few remaining are principally tourist attractions.

Kasuri

A Meiji-period (1868–1912) example of picture kasuri (e-gasuri) from Tottori Prefecture. Dark blue and white cotton cloth for quilting.

through the port city of Ōsaka. Stimulated by the new widespread availability of cotton and a growing market economy, the late 18th century saw a rapid proliferation and popularization of kasuri weaving throughout the country and the emergence of particular local characteristics. Patterns ranged from hazy mottlings of white on a deep blue ground through simple abstracted representational forms (arrows, flying birds, wells) and geometric motifs (including Chinese ideographs) to complete, nonrepeating pictures and even landscapes executed in weft kasuri. The complex tying calculations necessary for the e-gasuri (picture kasuri) were facilitated by the invention of the e-dai, or picture stand. On this, a mother thread was wound to the width of the cloth and the length of one pattern repeat, the desired picture drawn or stenciled on it. The mother thread was then rewound on a large tying frame and the markings on it used to tie subsequent groups of weft threads quickly and accurately.

The 19th and early 20th centuries saw the development of increasingly complex patterns, a proliferation of technical innovations, such as Kokubo Kintarō's foot-powered wrapping machine in Kurume, Kyūshū, in 1909 and the emergence of small cottage industries to manufacture cotton kasuri cloth by hand. Most of these cottage industries were later replaced by modern factories that apply advanced cloth-dyeing techniques to warp or weft yarns or both before they are woven. The postwar period has seen a resurgence of interest in the most basic of the old kasuri processes, and today kasuri weaving is done by various types of weavers throughout the country. Kasuri cloth is woven in two of the three local textile areas named by a 1975 law to promote traditional handcraft industries: Kurume manufactures cotton e-gasuri and Niigata Prefecture produces fine asa-gasuri with small hand-tied motifs.

🔲 ——"Aizome no kasuri," special issue of *Senshoku to seikatsu* (Summer 1974). Mary Dusenbury, "Kasuri: A Japanese Textile," *Textile Museum Journal* (1978). Fukui Sadako, *Nihon no kasuri bunka shi* (1973). Mary DUSENBURY

Katagami Noburu (1884–1928)

Literary critic, scholar of Russian literature. Born in Ehime Prefecture. Pen name Katagami Tengen. Graduate of Tōkyō Semmon Gakkō (now Waseda University), where he studied Russian and where he later became a member of its faculty. He published frequently in naturalist periodicals, later turning more toward humanism and idealism. In 1913 a collection of his literary criticism, *Sei no yōkyū to bungaku,* was published. His second visit to Russia in 1924 reinforced his developing interest in the proletarian movement. He later became a pioneer of left-wing literary criticism. His principal works are *Shizen shugi no shukanteki yōso* (1910), *Mugen no michi* (1915), and *Naizai hihyō ijō no mono* (1926), all literary criticism.

katagi

(character, turn of mind, spirit). An important concept of character in Japanese traditional popular psychology. The word originally meant a wooden board with carved designs used to print designs on paper and cloth. It later came to mean customs and habits, and eventually, the spirit, traits, or type of mind, common to members of an occupational, age, or status group. Stories describing the *katagi* of members of various social categories (such as sons, daughters, mistresses, tea ceremony masters, merchants, and artisans) constituted a genre *(katagi-mono)* of popular literature in the Edo period (1600–1868). *Katagi* among artisans *(shokunin katagi),* for example, was characterized by a fastidious devotion to one's work and pride in one's product, to the point of ignoring profit. It also implied a lack of social tact, indifference to complicated interpersonal relations, honesty and naivete, and a tendency to spend money soon after earning it without thought for the future. The *katagi* of such groups as farmers, merchants, students (in general, and of a specific school), artists, scholars, as well as of native inhabitants, of various prefectures have been described. *Hiroshi WAGATSUMA*

Katagiri Katsumoto (1556–1615)

Warrior of the Azuchi–Momoyama (1568–1600) period and early part of the Edo period (1600–1868). Katsumoto gained fame as one of the "Seven Spears" (Shichihon'yari) of the national unifier TOYOTOMI HIDEYOSHI in the 1583 Battle of SHIZUGATAKE; in 1595, having been granted domains yielding 10,000 *koku* (see KOKUDAKA), he attained *daimyō* status. After Hideyoshi's death in 1598, Katsumoto drew close to the future shōgun TOKUGAWA IEYASU and through his backing obtained an influential position in the household of Hideyoshi's heir, TOYOTOMI HIDEYORI. Fully dependent on his patron Ieyasu, who promoted Katsumoto to a 28,000-*koku* fief at Tatsuta in Yamato Province (now the town of Ikaruga, Nara Prefecture) in 1601, he became in effect the Tokugawa agent within the Toyotomi family's stronghold at Ōsaka Castle. Katsumoto, who in all likelihood assumed this double role unwittingly, found himself caught in the conflict between the Toyotomi and the Tokugawa that came to a head with the SHŌMEI INCIDENT (1614), in which Hideyori was accused of disrespect toward Ieyasu. He went to SUMPU (now the city of Shizuoka) to plead Hideyori's case before the nominally retired Ieyasu but returned to Ōsaka as the bearer of an unacceptable ultimatum; informed that Ōsaka hard-liners, such as ŌNO HARUNAGA and KIMURA SHIGENARI, suspected him of treason and planned to assassinate him, he barricaded himself in his quarters but two weeks later was permitted to leave the castle unharmed. Ieyasu ordered him to take part in the two Ōsaka campaigns of 1614–15 (see ŌSAKA CASTLE, SIEGES OF), which ended in the Toyotomi party's destruction. Katsumoto was rewarded by the increase of his domains to 43,000 *koku,* but he died a mere three weeks after the fall of Ōsaka Castle. *George ELISON*

katakana → kana

katakiuchi

Blood revenge for the killing of an elder relation or, less often, a feudal superior. This type of vendetta was regularly justified in Japan by reference to the Chinese Confucian classics. The *Nihongi* (or NIHON SHOKI, 720), for instance, echoes such classic Confucian moral pronouncements as that found in the *Li ji (Li chi; The Book of Rites):* "No one should live under the same Heaven as his father's enemy." Although in Chinese practice emphasis was on revenge for reasons of filial or at least family piety (despite one reference in the *Li ji* to revenge for the killing of an "intimate friend"), in premodern Japan, Chinese classical statements on revenge also served to justify vengeance for the murder of a feudal superior. Contrary to the common impression, based on the countless retellings of the FORTY-SEVEN RŌNIN INCIDENT of 1703, only two vendettas recorded in the Edo period (1600–1868) were carried out to revenge a feudal superior's murder.

How common *katakiuchi* was in ancient Japan is not known, for lack of documentary records. The archetype of the practice was for centuries the revenge exacted by the two Soga brothers in 1193, whose legend has been celebrated in literature from the SOGA MONOGATARI down to modern times. The cult of the vendetta rapidly gained momentum in the medieval period, and increasingly during the Edo period. Indeed, between 1600 and 1868, the number of recorded cases exceeds 100. At first *katakiuchi* was almost exclusively a matter for the warrior class, but by the 19th century as many, if not more, avengers were from other classes. Some pursuers continued seeking their enemy for many years, in the face of enormous difficulties and hardships.

From at the latest some time in the Zhou (Chou) dynasty (1027–256 BC), Chinese had debated the legality and social acceptability of blood revenge. So too in Japan, though a desire for blood revenge was considered laudable as a demonstration of Confucian filial piety (or feudal loyalty), the exacting of private vengeance could constitute an infringement of public authority. Thus, especially in the Edo period, a vendetta was only legal if it followed strict rules. A would-be avenger had to secure permission from his own domain's *(han)* authorities and then inform them of his success, if achieved in his domain. If the murderer had already fled to another domain, then in theory a representative of the shogunate had to second the original domain's permission and then be informed by the avenger of his success. If the proper authorities, upon learning of the revenge, determined that the avenger had kept to these rules, then they imposed no punishment. Indeed, the avengers were often feted and rewarded by their home authorities. Perhaps the most noteworthy feature of the Japanese practice of blood revenge is that the vendetta was not allowed to continue after the first revenge was taken. Furthermore, acts of revenge could only be aimed at the original murderer, not another member of his household.

Though *katakiuchi* flourished right up to the opening of Japan to the West, the Meiji government could not countenance the continuance of a practice that allowed avengers to usurp one of the functions of central authority, public justice. In 1873 a government decree formally declared blood revenge to be illegal. However, despite the changes Japanese society has undergone since then, vengeance as a subject of drama remains just as popular today as it was in the Edo period.

🔲 ——Douglas E. Mills, "Kataki-uchi: The Practice of Blood Revenge in Pre-modern Japan," *Modern Asian Studies* 10 (1976). *Li Chi,* tr James Legge as *The Li Ki* (1885, repr 1960). *Nihon shoki,* tr W. G. Aston as *Nihongi: Chronicles of Japan from the Earliest Times to A. D. 697* (1896, repr 1956). *Douglas E. MILLS*

katakuri

(trout lily or dogtooth violet). *Erythronium japonicum.* Also known archaically as *katakago.* A perennial herb of the lily family (Liliaceae) growing wild mainly in wooded mountain areas throughout Japan. The rhizomes are white, succulent, scaly, and several of them lie in clusters deep under the ground. Early in spring a soft stalk (scape) sprouts 20–30 centimeters (8–12 in) high, and a flower grows at the summit and a pair of leaves at the lower middle of the scape. The leaves are narrowly ovate, purple-spotted, and 6–12 centimeters (2.5–5 in) long. The flower faces sideways or downward and measures 4–5 centimeters (1.5–2 in) across. The flowers have six perianth lobes and are reddish purple.

The boiled young leaves and cooked bulbs are edible, but the bulbs, harvested from May to June when the flower and leaves are gone, have generally been used to make a starch called *katakuriko,* which is used for food as well as for medicinal purposes. Dissolved in boiling water it is used as an aid for intestinal problems. Most of the starch now sold as *katakuriko* is made from white potatoes or sweet potatoes. *MATSUDA Osamu*

katanagari → sword hunt

Katano

City in northeastern Ōsaka Prefecture, central Honshū. Formerly a rice-producing area, it is now a residential town for commuters to Ōsaka. The Kisaichi section is known for its strawberries and hiking courses. Pop: 61,425.

Kataoka Chiezō (1903–1983)

Actor; real name Ueki Masayoshi. Born in Gumma Prefecture. At age nine he joined the Kataoka Youth Theater run by a *kabuki* actor, Kataoka Nizaemon, and performed his first stage role in *Chūshingura*. He had entered the kabuki world directly, but rebelling against the lineage system, decided to become a movie actor. He starred in numerous films produced by MAKINO SHŌZŌ's Makino Puro (Makino Productions), among them Nakajima Hōzō's *Mange jigoku* (1927), and gained popularity as a handsome swordsman. However, conflicts arose with Makino over Kataoka's rivalry with his contemporary ARASHI KANJŪRŌ. In 1928 he set up an independent production company, and despite various financial problems before its dissolution in 1937, the company produced several excellent works, such as INAGAKI HIROSHI's *Tenka taihei ki* (1928), *Mabuta no haha* (1931, Visions of Mother), and *Ippon gatana dohyōiri* (1931, A Sword and the Sumo Ring), and Itami Mansaku's *Kokushi musō* (1932, Peerless Patriot). In the post–World War II era, he starred in a number of box-office successes such as Inagaki's *Dokuganryū Masamune* (1942), UCHIDA TOMU's *Chiyari Fuji* (1955, Bloody Spear at Mt. Fuji), and Matsuda Sadaji's (also known as Matsuda Teiji) *Ninkyō Tōkaidō* (1958). *ITASAKA Tsuyoshi*

Kataoka Kenkichi (1843–1903)

Politician active during the Meiji period (1868–1912). Born into a *samurai* family in the Tosa domain (now Kōchi Prefecture), he rose quickly in the domain's bureaucracy. In 1868 he joined a squad of Tosa soldiers under the command of ITAGAKI TAISUKE and fought in the BOSHIN CIVIL WAR. In 1869, the year after the MEIJI RESTORATION, he assumed command of the Tosa division of imperial bodyguards stationed in Tōkyō. Between 1871 and 1872 he traveled widely in America and Europe on a mission sponsored by the Tosa domain to study foreign military systems. Upon his return he was appointed a captain in the Japanese navy, largely because of his support of SAIGŌ TAKAMORI's plan to invade Korea (see SEIKAN-RON). In 1874, after the Korean scheme had failed, Kataoka renounced his government office and returned to Kōchi. Earlier, in 1873, he and other Tosa men had formed a paramilitary organization, the Kainan Gisha, with the aim of maintaining readiness in case of a national emergency. This was the parent organization of the RISSHISHA political society that Kataoka and Itagaki established in Kōchi in the spring of 1874. Thereafter he was active in promoting the FREEDOM AND PEOPLE'S RIGHTS MOVEMENT. In 1875 he helped Itagaki form the AIKOKUSHA, which attempted to unite political societies throughout the nation. In 1877, as representative of the Risshisha, he presented a petition to the government demanding a national assembly. Three years later he presented another petition, this time as the representative of the LEAGUE FOR ESTABLISHING A NATIONAL ASSEMBLY. Kataoka was also a key figure in the organization of Japan's first political party, the JIYŪTŌ, in 1881. Later, in 1887, he was involved in widespread antigovernment agitation that culminated in a petition he presented to the government demanding a lighter tax burden, revision of the so-called Unequal Treaties (see UNEQUAL TREATIES, REVISION OF), and freedom of speech, press, and assembly (see SANDAI JIKEN KEMPAKU MOVEMENT). He was arrested and imprisoned for these activities but was pardoned in the amnesty following the promulgation of the new constitution in 1889. After the Diet was established in 1890, Kataoka won election to the House of Representatives and continued to win reelection until his death. He was initially a member of the Jiyūtō, but after its dissolution in 1895, he was instrumental in the formation of the KENSEITŌ. Similarly, in 1900 he played an important role in the formation of the RIKKEN SEIYŪKAI. *M. William STEELE*

Kataoka Teppei (1894–1944)

Novelist. Born in Okayama Prefecture. A college dropout, he started to write while working for several newspapers. In 1924 he participated in *Bungei jidai*, a coterie magazine that gave birth to a group of talented new writers popularly known as the SHINKAN-KAKU SCHOOL (School of New Sensibilities). He became one of the leading figures in the group, but his interest soon turned to the leftist PROLETARIAN LITERATURE MOVEMENT. Imprisoned because of his involvement with the Communist Party, he left the movement in 1934. In his later years, he wrote popular fiction. Works include "Tsuna no ue no shōjo" (1927) and "Aijō no mondai" (1931), both short stories.

kataribe

A hereditary occupational group (BE) that specialized in reciting orally transmitted texts at court ceremonies in ancient times. The appearance of clan (UJI) names like Kataribe no Kimi and Kataribe no Obito in 7th- and 8th-century documents seems to indicate that such groups existed in the provinces as well. According to the legal formulary ENGI SHIKI (927), during the Nara (710–794) and Heian (794–1185) periods *kataribe* were summoned from several provinces to recite at the court on the occasion of enthronement and thanksgiving (DAIJŌSAI) ceremonies. Although what they recited has never been clear, it may be surmised that it had to do with legendary feats of military valor, such as passages from the chronicles KOJIKI (712) and NIHON SHOKI (720) describing the exploits of Emperor JIMMU. The members *(kataribe)* of this occupational group were long thought to have held official positions, but this has been conclusively disproved by the historian TSUDA SŌKICHI. A blind reciter named HIEDA NO ARE, who is mentioned in the preface to the *Kojiki* as having recited genealogies for the benefit of its compilers, was perhaps a forerunner of these *kataribe*. *KITAMURA Bunji*

katashiro

An object employed as a scapegoat in the exorcism of ritual impurities or evil influences (see KEGARE) in Shintō rites. The malignant influences are drawn into the *katashiro,* which is then floated away or burnt. *Katashiro* are also termed *hitogata* (literally, "dolls"), from their common occurrence in the form of dolls or human effigies, or *nademono* ("things for rubbing"), from the practice of rubbing the scapegoat against the worshiper's body to absorb evil influences. Formerly, the observance of the DOLL FESTIVAL on the third day of the third month included a "Snake Day Exorcism" in which a doll made of grass or paper was rubbed against the body and then set adrift on a river. The Suma chapter of the TALE OF GENJI relates that Prince Genji hired an *ommyōji* (see OMMYŌDŌ) ritualist to conduct this Snake Day rite. Purificatory rites employing *katashiro* occur throughout Japan during the NAGOSHI observance held on the last day of the sixth month according to the old lunar calendar. Local tutelary shrines distribute paper *katashiro* among their parishioners; the names and ages of family members are written upon the *katashiro,* which are then returned to the shrine for purification. The *mamako nagare* rite, conducted in certain parts of Gumma Prefecture on the same day, consists of casting a large straw doll holding a long wooden sword into a river. *ŌTŌ Tokihiko*

katatagae

Taboos about directions, based on OMMYŌDŌ, the ancient Chinese body of knowledge that sought to explain natural phenomena in terms of the *yin-yang* theory. During the Heian period (794–1185), it was customary to stay overnight at another place if one had to travel in the direction from one's home that was presided over by the god Nakagami (also known as Nagagami). Nakagami was believed to govern people's fortunes, both good and bad. He descended from heaven on a certain day, traveled from one direction to another in a prescribed order for a total of 44 days, and returned to his celestial abode for 16 days. The cycle was repeated endlessly, and it was in order to avoid Nakagami that *katatagae* was observed. It was considered safe to travel in any direction while the god was in heaven. A passage in the *Makura no sōshi* (late 10th century; The Pillow Book) describes how, in order to circumvent a directional taboo, the author SEI SHŌNAGON made a preliminary overnight stop at another's house before continuing on a pilgrimage to the temple Kuramadera. *ŌTŌ Tokihiko*

Katayama Sen (1860–1933)

A pioneering social worker, trade union organizer, and leader of radical political parties and movements. His active career extended from the latter part of the Meiji period (1868–1912) to the early part of the Shōwa period (1926–). After the Sino-Japanese War (1894–95) he was widely known to politicians, intellectuals, and working people in Japan, but after World War I began in 1914, he was even more broadly acclaimed as one of the foremost revolutionaries in all Asia.

Katayama was born Yabuki Sugatarō in what is now Okayama Prefecture. He and his older brother were left to their mother's care when their parents separated in about 1864. At about age 19, he was adopted by the Katayama family and took the personal name Sen. In 1881 he moved to Tōkyō to obtain an advanced education, believing that this was the key to a coveted government position.

His stay in Tōkyō was a disappointment. After flirting with Christianity, he moved on to the United States in 1884. For close to 10 years, he went from school to school pursuing vaguely defined educational goals. The capstone was a stay at Andover Theological Seminary and Yale Divinity School. More important than Katayama's formal schooling was his conversion to "socialistic" ideas then being spread by several Protestant Christian denominations. Following a trip to England and Scotland to observe local social work, he returned to Japan at the end of 1895.

In 1897 he became director of Kingsley Hall in Tōkyō, Japan's first modern settlement house. A few months later, he was chosen as a "leader" in Japan's budding trade union movement. Katayama also became editor of *Rōdō sekai (Labor World),* Japan's first trade union newspaper. The bilingual (Japanese and English) newspaper published its final—the 100th—number in 1904. An unsympathetic state quickly stifled the movement, and Katayama and like-minded dissidents shifted their action to the educational (propagandistic) area. Just before the Russo-Japanese War (1904–05) Katayama joined with KŌTOKU SHŪSUI and others in forming several socialistic groups and parties, some of them pacifistic. In December 1903 Katayama went to the United States and Europe for two years. His socialist, and more specifically his antiwar, lectures and writings won him international fame. Back in Japan he found the socialist movement sorely split. For many years because of intramovement quarrels few Japanese followed his ideological view.

Going back to the United States in September 1914, Katayama became a permanent expatriate. He lived in San Francisco and dabbled in socialist politics. In the fall of 1916 he was invited to New York City by the well-financed left-wing socialist S. J. Rutgers. Katayama was reborn politically and, casting aside his usual caution, immersed himself in the wrangles that flared after the Bolshevik Revolution (November 1917) broke out. This strife centered on the founding of the American Communist Party, and Katayama and several others were called upon to bring contending factions into line. In time he learned more about Bolshevism, which he had earlier espoused.

Late in 1921 Katayama went to Moscow to attend the forthcoming meeting of the First Congress of Toilers of the Far East. He was given a hero's welcome by the Bolsheviks, who sensed the magic of the Katayama name in their revolutionary struggle. Save for occasional trips abroad, he remained in Moscow until his death on 5 November 1933. He was thrust forward as an expert on Japanese revolutionary affairs and as a spokesman for the struggling masses of Asia. As such he was repeatedly appointed to the prestigious Presidium of the Third or Communist International, in his lifetime the only Asian so honored. He was buried in the Kremlin Wall. ◼――Katayama Sen, *Jiden* (1922, repr 1954). Katayama Sen, *Hansen heiwa no tame ni* (1954). Jane Degras, ed, *The Communist International, 1919–1943: Documents,* 2 vols (1956–60). Hyman Kublin, *Asian Revolutionary: The Life of Sen Katayama* (1964), detailed bibliography. Ōkōchi Kazuo, *Reimeiki no Nihon rōdō undō* (1955). Hyman KUBLIN

Katayama Tetsu (1887–1978)

Politician and socialist leader; prime minister 1947–48. Born in Wakayama Prefecture. Graduate of Tōkyō University. Under the influence of ABE ISOO, and from his own conviction as a Christian, Katayama became interested in socialism and social reform. He established a law office in Tōkyō and helped to settle labor disputes. In 1926 he joined Abe in forming the SHAKAI MINSHŪTŌ (Socialist People's Party). He was elected to the Diet in 1930 and in 1932 joined the SHAKAI TAISHŪTŌ (Socialist Masses Party), which was formed when the Shakai Minshūtō merged with other leftist parties. He left the party in protest over the expulsion of the Rikken Minseitō politician Saitō Takao (1870–1949) from the Diet for making an antimilitary speech.

Immediately after World War II, Katayama helped to form the JAPAN SOCIALIST PARTY, and after the party's victory in the first general election under the new constitution, he headed a coalition cabinet in 1947, becoming Japan's first socialist prime minister. With the encouragement of OCCUPATION authorities he created a new Ministry of Labor, revised the criminal code and Labor Standards Law, enacted the Antimonopoly Law, and oversaw the dissolution of the *zaibatsu,* or financial combines. Katayama came under growing criticism from the left wing of his party for his price and wage controls; the cabinet coalition, moreover, was shaky, and he resigned after eight months. He withdrew from all official positions in the JSP and acted in an advisory capacity, aligning with the right wing after the 1951 split and helping to form the DEMOCRATIC SOCIALIST PARTY in 1960. He retired from politics in 1963 after his defeat in the elections.

katazome

(stencil dyeing). Textile-dyeing method. The process involves placing a cut stencil over the cloth and applying glutinous rice paste-resist *(nori)* over it. When dry, the uncovered areas of the cloth are hand-dyed. This type of dyeing allows for the production of either a repeated or a continuous pattern. Other methods include resist stenciling both sides of the fabric and then vat dyeing *(chūgata);* and direct dyeing by adding dye to the paste-resist before stenciling *(utsushizome).*

Stencils *(katagami)* have traditionally been made in Shiroko, near Ise, where this craft specialty has been maintained. They are most often made of *kōzo* (paper mulberry). Stencils are treated with a prepared persimmon juice *(shibu)* and after they dry are hung in a smokehouse. Stencil paper can be cut with precision, it tolerates repeated use and rinsing, and it does not warp. Knife-cut stencils have a characteristic flowing line and, in general, after the paste-resist dries, the cloth is brush-dyed so that colors flow into one another, causing a misty blurring effect known as *bokashi.*

Stencils were used in dyeing from at least the later part of the Muromachi period (1333–1568). The earliest extant example is a hemp *kimono (katabira)* with a KOMON (small-dot) design, said to have belonged to the military leader UESUGI KENSHIN. Stencil dyeing became well established in the Azuchi–Momoyama period (1568–1600), and by the Genroku era (1688–1704) technical development was rapid. Along with the rise of the merchant class, there grew a great demand for *komon*-designed cloth for *kimono;* other popular patterns included shark's hide, plover, tortoiseshell, geometric shapes, and bamboo. The so-called Edo *komon,* named after Edo (now Tōkyō) to contrast it with the YŪZEN cloth of Kyōto, consists of an overall pattern of small white dots on a muted, solid-colored ground. *William G. MORTON*

Katō Chikage (1735–1808)

Also known as Tachibana Chikage. KOKUGAKU (National Learning) scholar and WAKA poet. Born in Edo (now Tōkyō), the son of the scholar and minor city official Tachibana Enao, he studied with KAMO NO MABUCHI, one of the most respected *kokugaku* scholars at that time. After his teacher's death in 1769, Katō came to be recognized as a leading figure in *kokugaku* scholarship. Serving in a number of official posts for the shogunate until he was forced to retire from office in 1788, Katō also earned a reputation as a major poet of the so-called Edo school of *waka* with his elegant, urbane compositions. Principal works include a major commentary on the MAN'YŌSHŪ, the *Man'yōshū ryakuge* (1796–1812), which remains in high esteem today, and a collection of his *waka, Ukeragahana* (1802).

Katō Gen'ichi (1890–1979)

Physiologist known for his theory concerning nerve excitation and conduction. Born in Okayama Prefecture. Graduate of Kyōto University and professor at Keiō University. Katō succeeded in isolating (or extirpating) single nerve fibers, and at the International Congress of Physiology in Rome in 1932 he demonstrated by means of motion pictures that the intensity and the conduction rate of excitation of nerve fibers was without decrement. Ishikawa Hidezurumaru (1878–1947) of Kyōto University criticized Katō's theory, which led to a general dispute. Katō wrote *Seirigaku* (1925, Physiology), the first systematic textbook on physiology in Japanese. See also BIOLOGY. *NAGATOYA Yōji*

Katō Hajime (1900–1968)

Ceramist. Best known for his reworking of late-Ming-dynasty (1368–1644) Chinese polychrome porcelain styles. He was born in the city of Seto, a ceramic center in Aichi Prefecture. He started his career as a ceramics designer but soon became a potter. He served at the Gifu Prefectural Ceramics Research Station from 1926 to 1939 and opened his own kiln in Yokohama in 1940. Thereafter, he divided his time between potting and teaching. From 1955 to 1964 he was a professor at Tōkyō University of Fine Arts and Music, where he helped to organize one of the best ceramic departments in Japan. His impressive exhibition record includes yearly entries at the Teiten (1927–35), the Nitten (1950–58), and the Japan Traditional Crafts Exhibition (1954–66); his many prizes include grand prizes at the 1938 Paris international exposition and the 1939 Brussels World's Fair and the Chūnichi Cultural Prize in 1952. He became president of the Japan Crafts Society in 1966. An authority on what is known as Oribe ware (see FURUTA ORIBE), he wrote a volume on it for the ceramics reference series Tōki zenshū (1959).

Katō Hajime made outstanding MINO WARE and SETO WARE pottery and he particularly excelled in delicate Oribe-style pieces. His highly accomplished porcelains include imaginative recreations of Chinese Song (Sung) dynasty (960–1279) white porcelain; colorful green-and-yellow-ground works with gold or silver decoration; strongly designed red, green, and yellow pieces (aka-e); subtle but strong underglaze-red works; and the first successful revival of the Ming-dynasty yellow-ground decorated pieces overglazed in red. In 1961 he was honored as one of the LIVING NATIONAL TREASURES for his polychrome porcelains.　　　　　　　　Frederick BAEKELAND

Katō Hiroharu (1870–1939)

Admiral. Also known as Katō Kanji. Born in what is now Fukui Prefecture; graduate of the Navy War College. After serving as head of the college, he attended the WASHINGTON CONFERENCE of 1921–22 as a member of the delegation headed by KATŌ TOMOSABURŌ. Katō unsuccessfully opposed the proposed 10:10:6 ratio for capital ship tonnage for the United States, Great Britain, and Japan, insisting instead on a 10:10:7 ratio. In 1925 Katō was appointed commander in chief of the Combined Fleet. As head of the naval command at the time of the LONDON NAVAL CONFERENCES, he opposed signing the disarmament treaty. Hoping to obstruct its ratification, Katō appealed directly to the emperor, and when the cabinet of HAMAGUCHI OSACHI ratified the treaty, Katō accused the prime minister of interfering with the navy's prerogative of supreme command (see TŌSUIKEN). After retiring from the navy in 1935, he established ties with ultrarightist elements in the army and agitated for expansion of the military.

Katō Hiroyuki (1836–1916)

Political thinker and educational official of the Meiji period (1868–1912), remembered as a scholarly apologist for the statist trend of the Meiji government, chiefly through his introduction into Japan of German studies and Social Darwinism. In a long, distinguished career in scholarship and public affairs Katō served the government as president of Tōkyō University (1877–86 and 1890–93), head of the Imperial Academy (1905–09), and variously as lecturer to the emperor, adviser to the Imperial Household Ministry, and member of the Senate (GENRŌIN) and House of Peers.

Born into an impoverished samurai family in the Izushi domain in Tajima Province (now northern Hyōgo Prefecture), Hiroyuki left the local samurai school at the age of 16 for Edo (now Tōkyō) to study Western military science under SAKUMA SHŌZAN and WESTERN LEARNING with Ōki Nakamasu from 1852 to 1859. As a teacher at the shogunate's BANSHO SHIRABESHO and Kaiseijo (both schools for Western studies) between 1860 and 1868, he became the first Japanese to undertake the study of German language and thought.

Starting as a proponent of individual liberties based on the concept of natural rights, Katō had attacked feudal institutions in Tonarigusa (1862, The Grass Next Door) and commended Western constitutionalism and democratic politics in Rikken seitai ryaku (1868, Survey of Constitutional Systems), Shinsei taii (1870, Outline of True Government), and Kokutai shinron (1875, New Thesis on the National Polity). In 1874 he joined the MEIROKUSHA society of Westernizing intellectuals.

Having also translated J. C. Blüntschli's Allgemeines Staatsrecht (tr Kokuhō hanron, 1872), however, Katō was drawn both intellectu-

ally and by virtue of his position to a statist point of view. He opposed a popular assembly in 1874 on the grounds of prematurity and from 1882 onward, disavowing his earlier books, took upon himself the major Western-style philosophical defense of state supremacy against the FREEDOM AND PEOPLE'S RIGHTS MOVEMENT, finding in Darwin, Spencer, Haeckel, and Buckle the ingredients for his own evolutionary, historically positivist interpretation of the Japanese polity. He propounded his doctrines of the organic state and of rights acquired through the survival of the fittest most notably in his Jinken shinsetsu (1882, A New Theory of Human Rights) and in his bilingual Kyōja no kenri no kyōsō/Der Kampf ums Recht des Stärkeren und seine Entwicklung (1893, The Struggle for the Right of the More Powerful).

In his later years, Katō also developed a utilitarian doctrine of morality based on enlightened self-interest, and delivered a blistering attack on the Christian religion as superstition and a threat to the unity of the Japanese state, in Kirisutokyō no gaidoku (1911, The Poison of Christianity).

📖——Ishida Takeshi, Meiji seiji shisō shi kenkyū (1954). Kōsaka Masaaki, Meiji shisō shi in Kōsaka Masaaki chosakushū, vol 7 (Shisōsha, 1969), tr David Abosch as Japanese Thought in the Meiji Era (1958). Matsumoto Sannosuke, "Katō Hiroyuki," in Naramoto Tatsuya, ed, Nihon no shisōka (1954). Tabata Shinobu, Katō Hiroyuki (1959).　　　　　　　　　　　　　　　　Ivan P. HALL

Katō Kanji → Katō Hiroharu

Katō Kiyomasa (1562–1611)

Daimyō of the Azuchi-Momoyama period (1568–1600). A man of obscure origins, Kiyomasa is said to have been born in Nakamura (now part of the city of Nagoya) in Owari Province (now part of Aichi Prefecture), the native village of the national unifier TOYOTOMI HIDEYOSHI; their mothers were supposedly related. He served Hideyoshi from an early age, gained fame as one of his "Seven Spears" (Shichihon'yari) at the Battle of SHIZUGATAKE in 1583, and was that year awarded a fief assessed at 3,000 koku (see KOKUDAKA). Kiyomasa made a spectacular advance to major daimyō status in 1588, when Hideyoshi assigned him and KONISHI YUKINAGA the task of restoring strict order in Higo (now Kumamoto Prefecture), a province that had the previous year been the scene of a massive uprising of local samurai (KOKUJIN). Higo was divided between the two, and Kiyomasa was allotted a 250,000-koku domain centering on Kumamoto Castle. In 1592 Yukinaga and Kiyomasa led the two main prongs of the first of Hideyoshi's invasions of Korea (see INVASIONS OF KOREA IN 1592 AND 1597), Kiyomasa's force advancing across the Tumen River into Manchuria; when the tide turned against the Japanese, Yukinaga was one of those advocating a peace settlement, while Kiyomasa remained a stubborn member of the war party, for a time incurring Hideyoshi's disfavor and being recalled to Japan. In 1597 Kiyomasa again led an invasion force into Korea, but the Japanese withdrew after Hideyoshi's death the following year. Kiyomasa, whose rivalry with Yukinaga was exacerbated by their incompatible religious affiliations (Katō was as fervent a Nichiren Buddhist as Konishi was a Christian), naturally took the side of TOKUGAWA IEYASU when Yukinaga emerged as a leader of the daimyō league opposing the future shōgun in 1600; he helped to secure northern Kyūshū for Ieyasu's party as Konishi and his allies were being defeated at the Battle of SEKIGAHARA, and after the Tokugawa victory he was rewarded by the augmentation of his fief with most of Yukinaga's former holdings, becoming the master of a 520,000-koku domain. For all that, Kiyomasa remained loyal to Hideyoshi's memory and intent on protecting the interests of his heir TOYOTOMI HIDEYORI; he died after conducting Hideyori safely through a meeting with Ieyasu, before relations between the Toyotomi and Tokugawa families had deteriorated to the point of an armed conflict (see ŌSAKA CASTLE, SIEGES OF).　　　　　　George ELISON

Katō Kōmei → Katō Takaaki

Katō Kyōtai (1732–1792)

Late-18th-century HAIKU poet from Nagoya. Originally a samurai in the service of the Tokugawa branch-house in Nagoya, at age 28 he decided to pursue a career as a haiku poet. He first studied under teachers from the Mino school; later, along with Yosa BUSON, he became a central figure in the movement to reform haiku along the lines that had been established by BASHŌ. It is worth noting, for instance, that he was responsible for the first printing of the *Kyoraishō* (1775), an authoritative record of Bashō's teachings as set down by his disciple Kyorai. Similarly, in *Aki no hi* (1772), a collection of verse sequences by Kyōtai and his disciples, he included an unpublished manuscript of verses composed by Bashō and others during a visit to Nagoya in 1688. As a haiku master, Kyōtai's influence was greatest in the Nagoya area, but he was also active in Yosa Buson's haiku circles in Kyōto. Some 1,153 of his verses are collected in the *Kyōtai kushū* (1809).

Katō Michio (1918–1953)

Playwright. Born in Fukuoka Prefecture. Graduate of Keiō University. While a student, he became interested in drama. Inspired by the Japanese classics, he wrote *Nayotake* (1946), a poetic play based on the ancient tale TAKETORI MONOGATARI. After World War II, he joined Bungakuza, a modern theater group, and started writing plays characterized by an antirealism that reflected the influence of the French playwright Jean Giraudoux. His life ended in suicide. Other plays are *Episōdo* (1948) and *Omoide o uru otoko* (1951).

Katori Nahiko (1723–1782)

KOKUGAKU (National Learning) scholar and poet. Born in Shimōsa (now Chiba Prefecture). Studied *kokugaku* under KAMO NO MABUCHI and in 1765 published *Kogentei*, a dictionary of classical words. In his WAKA verse, collected in *Nahiko kashū* (1777), he employed the archaic diction of the 8th-century poetry anthology MAN'YŌSHŪ.

Katori Shrine

(Katori Jingū). Shintō shrine in the city of Sawara, Chiba Prefecture, dedicated to Futsunushi no Kami, a clan deity (UJIGAMI) of the FUJIWARA FAMILY. The date of the origin of the shrine is not known, but its central deity, along with the deity (Takemikazuchi no Mikoto) of the Kashima Shrine, was installed by the Fujiwara in the KASUGA SHRINE in the 8th century. The shrine, which was believed to offer protection to military men, was patronized by both the Fujiwara family and the court. An annual festival is held on 14 April; it is celebrated in a particularly colorful fashion on 15 April every 12th year, when shrine parishioners, dressed in traditional warrior garb, transport a portable shrine (MIKOSHI) up the river Tonegawa to KASHIMA SHRINE and back. *Stanley* WEINSTEIN

Katō Sawao (1946–)

Gymnast. Born in Niigata Prefecture; graduate of Tōkyō University of Education. Lecturer at Tsukuba University. He took first place in the men's individual combined exercises (all-around) at the 1968 Mexico Olympics and then again at the 1972 Munich Olympics. In the 1976 Olympics in Montreal he won the gold medal in the parallel bars and led the Japanese men's gymnastics team to its fifth consecutive team championship. *TAKEDA Fumio*

Katō Shizue (1897–)

Feminist and politician, known for her promotion of FAMILY PLANNING. Born in Tōkyō, the first daughter of Hirota Ritarō, a former *samurai* who became a prominent engineer. In 1914 she graduated from the Joshi Gakushūin (Peeresses' School) and married Baron Ishimoto Keikichi. Her husband worked for two years as an engineer at the Mitsui coal mines in Kyūshū, and Shizue greatly sympathized with the sufferings of the workers there. Then, following her husband to the United States in 1919, she met the birth control advocate Margaret SANGER (she was later instrumental in inviting Sanger to Japan to lecture). Shizue herself, on her return to Japan the next year, began to campaign for birth control and other women's rights.

After her husband left her to go to Manchuria, Shizue supported herself and her two sons through writing and other work, making lecture tours in the United States in 1932 and 1936. Her continued efforts for social reform, including family planning campaigns, led to a brief arrest in 1937. Her work also brought her in contact with the labor leader Katō Kanjū (1892–1978); they married in 1944. In the first postwar election in 1946, Shizue, as well as her husband, was elected to the House of Representatives as a candidate of the JAPAN SOCIALIST PARTY. She was then elected to the House of Councillors

in 1950, remaining a member until 1974. She also helped to lead the Nihon Kazoku Keikaku Remmei (Family Planning Federation of Japan) from its founding in 1954. She has also campaigned for environmental preservation. She wrote two autobiographies: *Facing Two Ways* (published in English only, 1935) and *Hitosuji no michi* (1956, A Straight Road).

Katō Shūichi (1919–)

Literary critic, novelist, medical doctor. Born in Tōkyō; graduate of Tōkyō University. Taught at the University of British Columbia and Freie Universität Berlin, and later at Sophia University, Tōkyō. After World War II, he embarked upon a literary career with *1946 bungakuteki kōsatsu* (1947), a collection of essays published as a combined effort with NAKAMURA SHIN'ICHIRŌ and others. Among his writings are an antiwar novel, *Aru hareta hi ni* (1949), a collection of essays on Japanese culture, *Zasshu bunka* (1956), his autobiography, *Hitsuji no uta* (1968), and a collection of essays on Japanese art, *Shōshin dokugo* (1972). *ASAI Kiyoshi*

Katō Shūson (1905–)

HAIKU poet. Real name Katō Takeo. Born in Tōkyō. Graduate of Tōkyō Bunrika Daigaku (now Tsukuba University). While working as a middle school teacher in the late 1920s, he contributed to *Ashibi*, a haiku magazine, and became a disciple of its chief editor MIZUHARA SHŪŌSHI. He shifted, however, from the lyrical style of the Ashibi group to a more abstract and introspective mode of expression. As a poet of the so-called "human quest" school of abstract haiku in the mid-1930s and as the founder in 1940 of the magazine *Kanrai*, he exerted a significant influence on young haiku poets after World War II. He also contributed to the study of Bashō, the famous 17th-century haiku poet.

Katō Takaaki (1860–1926)

Also known as Katō Kōmei. Statesman and politician. Born Hattori Sōkichi, second son of a retainer of the Owari domain (now part of Aichi Prefecture), he was separated from his parents early in life, going to live with his paternal grandparents in Nagoya where opportunities for schooling were better. At the age of 13 he was adopted by a distant relative of higher status, Katō Buhei. A bright student, he early excelled in English and entered the government-run Tōkyō Foreign Language School. Upon graduation, Katō entered the Tōkyō Kaisei Gakkō, soon incorporated into the newly established Tōkyō University. He studied English law and in 1881 graduated at the head of his class. Throughout his life he remained an anglophile, with particular admiration for the English parliamentary system, regarding it as the model on which the Japanese system should be patterned.

Despite the opportunities open to him, Katō chose not to enter government service. Instead he entered the Mitsubishi company and enjoyed the patronage of IWASAKI YATARŌ, the company's founder. He was chosen in April 1883 to study abroad in England; while there, he was affiliated with a wealthy Liverpool merchant, learning much about the marine transport business. In June 1885 he returned home and became an assistant manager in the Mitsubishi home office. The following year, he married Iwasaki's eldest daughter.

Public Life —— Feeling somewhat confined at Mitsubishi, he turned to government service in 1887, becoming private secretary for Foreign Minister ŌKUMA SHIGENOBU in 1888. He also participated in plans for the revision of the Unequal Treaties (see UNEQUAL TREATIES, REVISION OF). This was followed by a short affiliation with the Finance Ministry, but in 1894 he returned to the Foreign Ministry and was appointed minister to Britain. Over the next few years, he worked diligently to build the foundation of an Anglo-Japanese alliance but, because of a disagreement over foreign policy, left his post in February 1900. The ANGLO-JAPANESE ALLIANCE was concluded two years later, and though Katō rejoiced in its realization, he lamented that it had been so long delayed.

When the RIKKEN SEIYŪKAI party was organized by ITŌ HIROBUMI in 1900, Katō had declined an invitation to join but had accepted an appointment as foreign minister in the Itō cabinet set up in October. He began to entertain political ambitions from about 1902 when he was elected a Diet member from Kōchi Prefecture. With his background as a bureaucrat and diplomat, however, he was somewhat lacking in the arts of political astuteness and maneuvering. Moreover, he was known for his arrogance and to the end never captured the popular imagination. In 1904 he purchased the newspaper *Tōkyō nichinichi shimbun* hoping to use it as a vehicle for his political views; but the results fell short of his goals, and he sold the newspaper a few years later.

In January 1906 he became foreign minister again in the SAIONJI KIMMOCHI cabinet but resigned in less than two months because of a disagreement over policy. In 1908 he became minister to Britain once more, and it was largely through his efforts that the Anglo-Japanese Alliance was revised in July 1911. In January 1913 he became foreign minister in the cabinet of KATSURA TARŌ, but the cabinet fell in February. In April Katō entered Katsura's party, the RIKKEN DŌSHIKAI, becoming at first senior manager and then leader of the party upon the death of Katsura that year.

After participating in the formation of the Ōkuma Shigenobu cabinet in April 1914, Katō became foreign minister and was greatly responsible for various cabinet policies, including Japan's decision to participate in World War I. This decision greatly angered the GENRŌ (elder statesmen), with whom he had not fully consulted. Ōkuma helped to patch up the situation, but the dissension between Katō and the *genrō* broke out anew when in January 1915 Katō sent the so-called TWENTY-ONE DEMANDS to China, arousing fierce opposition both at home and abroad over this Japanese attempt to secure hegemony over China. Undaunted, Katō pushed through with negotiations, securing Chinese acquiescence to an ultimatum in May. With *genrō* anger rekindled, Katō managed to escape the uncomfortable situation by resigning shortly afterward during the bribery scandal of Home Minister ŌURA KANETAKE. The Dōshikai continued to support the Ōkuma cabinet, and during 1916 Ōkuma himself began to promote Katō's succession to the premiership. This was unacceptable to the *genrō*, however, and Katō was bypassed when Ōkuma resigned. In the meantime, the Dōshikai, Chūseikai, and Kōyū Kurabu had merged, and Katō was selected president of the newly formed party, the KENSEIKAI. The party built its program around extension of suffrage and opposition to the *genrō*.

Katō was sensitive to the great changes that had taken place throughout the world as a result of World War I, especially the growing power of the "masses," and he spoke often of a need to inculcate in these "masses" the notion of duty and a spirit of cooperation. In general, the Kenseikai advocated concession to growing popular demands for reform, including stabilization of the people's livelihood, the labor problem, education, civil rights, and constitutional government. Katō at first had reservations about the immediate granting of universal suffrage, feeling that preparation was necessary for the exercise of such a privilege, but he later indicated that he would not be averse to proposing a universal suffrage bill in the 1920 Diet if members of his party were in favor of it.

Premiership —— In January 1924 a nonparty cabinet under KIYOURA KEIGO was formed, and the Kenseikai joined with the Seiyūkai and KAKUSHIN KURABU in a MOVEMENT TO PROTECT CONSTITUTIONAL GOVERNMENT. In the May 1924 election the opposition parties captured an absolute majority; the Kiyoura cabinet resigned, and Katō became premier, presiding over a three-party cabinet.

The major goals of the new cabinet were the passage of universal suffrage, "enforcement of official discipline," administrative and financial retrenchment, and reform of the House of Peers. Compared with other cabinets of the Taishō period (1912–26), the legislative accomplishments of the Katō cabinet and the 50th Diet were noteworthy. The record was not one of unrelieved success, however, reflecting the continued need for political compromise. The Universal Manhood Suffrage Law of April 1925 granted the vote to all male citizens over the age of 25 who had resided in their districts for one year and who were not indigent. This law was balanced by the passage two months earlier of a long-pending piece of legislation, the PEACE PRESERVATION LAW OF 1925 (Chian Iji Hō). Aimed at repressing communism, anarchism, and other forms of extreme radicalism, the passage of this law probably eased the way for Katō to push through other legislation. The cabinet also achieved modest reform of the House of Peers but ran into trouble with other goals like retrenchment. In the summer of 1925 internal friction in the cabinet resulted in its resignation en masse. Katō was asked to remain in office, and a new Kenseikai cabinet was formed under him in August.

Katō had been in a state of declining health since a fall in 1922, and in January 1926 his condition worsened. Urged by his doctors to rest, he refused, realizing his party's weak position in the Diet. He

died on 28 January, having been made a count and decorated with the Supreme Order of the Chrysanthemum.

🖢 —— Peter Duus, *Party Rivalry and Political Change in Taishō Japan* (1968). Itō Masanori, ed, *Katō Takaaki*, 2 vols (1929, repr 1970). Kondō Masao, *Katō Takaaki* (1959). Katō Takaaki Den Kankō Kai, ed, *Katō Takaaki den* (1928). Nagaoka Shinjirō, "Katō Takaaki ron," *Kokusai seiji* 1 (1966). Sharon A. MINICHIELLO

Katō Takeo (1877–1963)

Banker. Born in Tochigi Prefecture. After graduating from Keiō Gijuku (now Keiō University), Katō joined Mitsubishi Gōshi Kaisha's banking division (now MITSUBISHI BANK, LTD) in 1901. He became the bank's president in 1943 and concurrently served as a director in the central office of the MITSUBISHI *zaibatsu*, where his power was exceeded only by IWASAKI KOYATA's. After World War II Katō played a quiet but crucial role in the regrouping of the Mitsubishi group's firms. ASAJIMA Shōichi

Katō Tōkurō (1898–)

Ceramist. Famous for his reproductions of Azuchi–Momoyama-period (1568–1600) TEA CEREMONY wares. Born in Seto, Aichi Prefecture, to an old potting family, he learned traditional techniques as a child and became an independent potter at the age of 15. In 1935 he established his present kiln in Nagoya. His excavations and studies of the kiln sites that produced old MINO WARE, SETO WARE, and KARATSU WARE have helped him make pieces that are very similar to the ancient wares. Since 1950 he has exhibited widely and traveled abroad with Japanese craft delegations, even exchanging works with Pablo Picasso. He has conducted research into Persian and Majorcan ceramics. Tōkurō played an important role in founding the Japan Ceramics Society (1947) and the Japan Crafts Society (1955) and was active in these and other organizations until 1960, when he became involved in a major scandal. In 1959 a pot thought to date from the Einin era (1293–99) was given the designation of Important Cultural Object; when doubts about the pot's origin were raised by a group of ceramic researchers, Tōkurō, who was a member of the committee that accorded the designation, declared that he himself had made the pot in 1937. The designation was removed and Tōkurō resigned from all his official positions.

Tōkurō has had an outstanding exhibition record. He is also a prolific author of articles and books on ceramics. His finely glazed and modeled Shino, Oribe, yellow and black Seto, Karatsu, IGA WARE, and SHIGARAKI WARE pieces are thought by many to reach the benchmarks set by the older wares that were their inspiration.

🖢 —— Katō Tōkurō, *Genshoku tōji dai jiten* (Tankōsha, 1972). Frederick BAEKELAND

Katō Tomosaburō (1861–1923)

Admiral; prime minister (1922–23). Born in the Aki domain (now part of Hiroshima Prefecture). Graduate of the Imperial Naval Academy. During the Russo-Japanese War (1904–05), he participated in the Battle of TSUSHIMA as chief of staff under Admiral TŌGŌ HEIHACHIRŌ. After serving as navy vice-minister and commander of the Kure Naval Station in 1915, he was named navy minister in the second ŌKUMA SHIGENOBU cabinet. He remained in that post in the TERAUCHI MASATAKE, HARA TAKASHI, and TAKAHASHI KOREKIYO cabinets. In 1921 Katō headed Japan's delegation to the WASHINGTON CONFERENCE and there signed the Naval Limitation Treaty of 1922, which established a 10:10:6:3.5:3.5 ratio of capital ship tonnage for Great Britain, the United States, Japan, France, and Italy. Named prime minister in 1922 to succeed Takahashi, he formed a cabinet composed mainly of bureaucrats and members of the House of Peers. He implemented the decisions of the Washington Conference, decommissioning 11 warships and reducing army personnel by 60,000. He also saw to the withdrawal of Japanese troops stationed on the Shandong (Shantung) Peninsula since World War I. Katō died in office in August 1923.

Katō Works Co, Ltd

(Katō Seisakusho). Manufacturer of construction machinery, including oil hydraulic power shovels and large truck cranes. Leading domestic producer of the latter. Founded in 1935, the firm initially manufactured internal combustion locomotives and all types of industrial vehicles. However, after World War II it turned to construction and stevedoring machinery, and has been successful in building a large export trade with communist nations. The firm is noted for its oil hydraulic technology. Sales for the fiscal year ending October 1981 were ¥82 billion (US $355 million), of which export sales accounted for 35 percent, and capitalization was ¥2.2 billion (US $9.5 million). Corporate headquarters are in Tōkyō.

Katsu Awa → Katsu Kaishū

Katsu Kaishū (1823–1899)

Statesman active during the period of transition from the Tokugawa shogunate to the new Meiji government. Also known as Katsu Rintarō and Katsu Awa. Early in his career he was instrumental in the formation of what eventually became the modern Japanese navy. At the time of the MEIJI RESTORATION in 1868 he acted as the chief negotiator for the Tokugawa shogunate, supervising its demise and ensuring that the transfer of power took place in an orderly, peaceful fashion.

Born in Edo (now Tōkyō) in 1823, Katsu was the eldest son of an impoverished, low-ranking retainer of the shogunate. From childhood he was trained in the art of swordsmanship and was encouraged to study Western military science. He mastered Dutch and by 1850 was able to open his own school, having gained a reputation as an expert in Western military technology.

The arrival of Commodore Matthew PERRY in Japan in 1853 altered Katsu's career. Katsu submitted a memorial stressing the need to improve coastal defense and to establish a school of Western military studies. He was given official appointment as a translator dealing with foreign affairs, and in 1855 was sent with a group of shogunal retainers to the KAIGUN DENSHŪJO in Nagasaki for naval training under Dutch instructors.

In 1859 the shogunate decided to send to the United States the KANRIN MARU, a Japanese warship built by the Dutch, to accompany the mission to ratify the HARRIS TREATY. Katsu was appointed captain and in the spring of 1860 sailed the first modern Japanese ship across the Pacific (see UNITED STATES, MISSION OF 1860 TO).

Upon returning to Japan, Katsu was appointed commissioner of warships (gunkan bugyō) in 1862. With the aim of creating a national navy, Katsu established the Kōbe Naval Training Center and recruited men regardless of their domainal affiliations. By 1864, however, Katsu's criticism of Tokugawa leadership placed him in political disfavor; he was dismissed and the training center at Kōbe was dismantled.

In 1866 Katsu was reappointed commissioner of warships and was called upon to negotiate a peace settlement between the shogunate and the Chōshū (now Yamaguchi Prefecture), the most extremist of the antishogunate domains. Katsu's conciliatory efforts were undermined when the shōgun TOKUGAWA YOSHINOBU arbitrarily reversed his policy and put into effect a series of reforms to strengthen the shogunate's position.

Yoshinobu's reforms came too late. Under attack from the powerful Satsuma (now Kagoshima Prefecture) and Chōshū domains, the shogunate collapsed in late 1867. Some Tokugawa retainers argued for a last-ditch resistance, but Katsu argued that surrender was the only realistic course of action. Eventually Katsu's argument was accepted. On 10 February 1868 Katsu was appointed minister of naval affairs and soon afterward commander-in-chief of military affairs, an ad hoc office that gave him control of all Tokugawa military forces.

On 5 and 6 April Katsu conducted negotiations with the chief spokesman of the imperial forces, SAIGŌ TAKAMORI. Saigō demanded the total dismemberment of Tokugawa political and military power. Katsu countered by presenting a series of proposals that would allow the Tokugawa family to retain considerable autonomy. Katsu's arguments were persuasive, and since the British minister Harry PARKES had earlier cautioned Saigō against a harsh policy, Saigō was forced to concede. He called off the attack on Edo, and on 3 May Edo Castle was surrendered to the imperial forces without incident.

Civil war had been avoided, and Tokugawa participation in the new government seemed ensured. But the SHŌGITAI, a squad of prowar Tokugawa retainers, refused to accept the humiliation of defeat and initiated hostilities in Edo on 4 July. After a brief battle the imperial forces were victorious, and Katsu's compromise settlement was destroyed. On 13 July the Tokugawa family was stripped of its vast landholdings and ordered to leave Edo to take up residence in the province of Suruga (now part of Shizuoka Prefecture). Katsu followed his lord into exile.

From 1872 to 1875 Katsu returned to government service as the Meiji government's minister of the navy, one of the more prominent of the many Tokugawa retainers who served the new regime. He spent the remainder of his life in scholarly pursuits, primarily as editor of a series of documents constituting a detailed history of the army, navy, treasury, and foreign relations of the Tokugawa shogunate. In 1887 he was awarded the title of count. Numerous other honors were also bestowed on him in recognition of his service to the nation at the time of the Meiji Restoration.

■ ———Katsube Mitake, ed, Katsu Kaishū zenshū, 23 vols (Keisō Shobō, 1970–82).   M. William STEELE

Katsukawa school

(Katsukawaha). School of UKIYO-E founded by KATSUKAWA SHUNSHŌ; flourished in the latter half of the 18th century. Because its branch schools produced numerous yakusha-e (portraits of actors), the Katsukawa school was referred to as the school of yakusha-e masters. In contrast to the traditional style of the TORII SCHOOL, the style of the Katsukawa school was realistic; and the school helped establish the nigao-e style ("likeness portrait" style) of yakusha-e. However, the school was overshadowed by the UTAGAWA SCHOOL and gradually fell into decline.

Katsukawa Shun'ei (1752–1819)

UKIYO-E illustrator, print designer, and comic artist, specializing in portraits of SUMŌ wrestlers and KABUKI actors. The artist, whose given name was Isoda Kyūjirō, was a latecomer to ukiyo-e. His first prints, portraits of actors modeled on the work of his teacher KATSUKAWA SHUNSHŌ, were not published until 1782, and his subsequent prints designed in the 1780s reveal a slow, and occasionally painful, search for a personal style.

The Katsukawa artists had, in the 1780s, a virtual monopoly on full-color woodblock portraits of kabuki actors. Monopoly led to demand, and in 1790, after Shunshō had entered retirement, and Shunkō, his eldest pupil, had fallen ill, the task of meeting these demands fell upon Shun'ei, who drastically simplified his style of composition and drawing. After an interval in 1792 when he seems to have met the actor-painter Taga Ryūkōsai in Ōsaka, Shun'ei simplified his drawing style even further and began designing prints with broad, simple expanses of color, which influenced SHARAKU, UTAGAWA TOYOKUNI, and the other actor portraitists of the 1790s, and lent his own prints the qualities of serenity and pathos that set his work apart. He designed the first mica-ground portraits of actors in 1794, months before Sharaku, and an outstanding series of 20 or more full-length portraits of actors against gray backgrounds in scenes from the play Chūshingura (Treasury of the Loyal Retainers) the following year. In 1796 he collaborated with Toyokuni and UTAGAWA KUNIMASA on an important series of large heads of actors and designed several more full-length portraits of actors, but afterwards his portraits became fewer and less inspired and in 1800 he stopped designing actor prints altogether. In the remaining years of his life he designed many portraits of wrestlers, often coarse to the point of caricature, and several comic prints, which give us some idea of the comic painting style he is said to have invented, of which no examples seem to have survived. Shun'ei used the secondary name Kutokusai and had several pupils, the most distinguished being Katsukawa Shuntei (1770–1820).   Roger KEYES

Katsukawa Shunshō (1726–1792)

Painter and UKIYO-E print designer. Active in Edo (now Tōkyō) during the 1760s through the 1780s, Shunshō is noted for his realistic portraits of kabuki actors, sumō wrestlers, and legendary warriors. He was the primary force behind the Katsukawa school of ukiyo-e artists.

Shunshō was born in the Kamigata (Kyōto–Ōsaka) region; his family name was Fujiwara, and his given name Yōsuke (later Yūsuke). He came to Edo early in his life and studied haikai poetry and painting under various teachers including Miyagawa Shunsui. As a painter, he first called himself Miyagawa (and Katsumiyagawa) but eventually settled on the name Katsukawa Shunshō. Throughout his long career, he signed his paintings and prints using various names such as Jūgasei, Kyokurōsei, Ririn, and Rokurokuan. Because of the jar-shaped seal containing the character "Hayashi" which he used while in the employ of Hayashiya Shichiemon, he is also known as Tsuboya, or Tsubo Shunshō (from the Japanese word for jar, *tsubo*).

From early in the 1760s, fully utilizing the multicolor technique refined by HARUNOBU, Shunshō began producing dynamic actor prints that dominated the field and succeeded in filling the void left by the demise of the TORII SCHOOL of actor prints.

Shunshō revolutionized kabuki actor portraiture by assigning each actor individual features by which he was readily recognizable. Almost caricatures, his actors with characteristic facial features relieved the public from the monotony of having to identify their favorite actors by their leading roles, costumes, or family crests.

Shunshō also specialized in depicting actors in masculine, action-filled roles; rarely did he produce prints of *onnagata*, or actors in feminine roles. In a similar vein, he produced numerous *sumō* and warrior prints that are dynamic and powerful. His many pupils—all with names that begin with "Shun"—include Shunchō, Shundō, Shun'ei, Shunjō, Shunkō, Shunzan, and Shunrō (later Katsushika HOKUSAI). *James T. KENNEY*

Katsura Detached Palace

Shown are the four sections of the main house (right to left): the Old Shoin, the Middle Shoin, the Music Room, and the New Shoin.

Katsuki Yasuji (1905–)

Physiologist. Born in Ishikawa Prefecture. Graduate of Tōkyō University. Professor at the Tōkyō Medical and Dental University. Katsuki carried out research on the auditory mechanism and made notable contributions in the field of sensory physiology and the development of the auditory function. He received the Order of Culture in 1973. *NAGATOYA Yōji*

Katsumoto Seiichirō (1899–1967)

Literary critic. Born in Tōkyō. Graduate of Keiō University. A Marxist, he became involved in the PROLETARIAN LITERATURE MOVEMENT in the late 1920s. He lived in Germany from 1929 to 1933, attending the 1930 Comintern International Writers' Conference in Kharkov. After returning to Japan in 1933, he devoted his energies to the study of modern Japanese literature. In 1936 he helped found the Japan P.E.N. Club, but two years later he was expelled from the organization for his political views. After World War II he served as chairman of the Japan Commission for UNESCO and lectured at Keiō and other universities. His principal works of criticism are *Zen'ei no bungaku* (1930) and *Kindai bungaku nōto* (1948).

Katsunuma

Town in northeastern Yamanashi Prefecture, central Honshū. It developed as a post-station town on the highway Kōshū Kaidō in the Edo period (1600–1868). The area is Japan's oldest wine producing center and has been known for its grapes since the Edo period. Its numerous wineries and vineyards attract tourists. Pop: 8,632.

Katsunuma Seizō (1886–1963)

Physician. Born in Shizuoka Prefecture. Graduate of Tōkyō University. He elaborated on the histochemical study of oxidase. In 1919 he described oxidoreductases (redox enzymes) in cells histocytologically and clarified their relationship to tissue iron. For this work he received the Imperial Prize of the Japan Academy in 1926. He also carried out comprehensive studies on geriatrics and aeromedicine. He was a member of the Japan Academy from 1944 and became president of Nagoya University in 1949. He received the Order of Culture in 1954. *ACHIWA Gorō*

katsuo → bonito

Katsurada Fujio (1867–1946)

Pathologist. Born in Kaga Province (now Ishikawa Prefecture) and graduated from the University of Utrecht. A pioneer in the field of parasitology in Japan, Katsurada is known for his research on distomiasis, an endemic disease in Okayama Prefecture, and for his discovery of *Schistosoma japonicum* (1904). He was awarded the Japan Academy Prize in 1918 for his work on schistosomiasis japonica. He taught at Okayama Igaku Semmon Gakkō (now Medical Faculty of Okayama University). *ACHIWA Gorō*

Katsura Detached Palace

(Katsura Rikyū). Originally a 17th-century country villa of the Hachijō no Miya family, an imperial princely family, located west of Kyōto; presently maintained by the Imperial Household Agency. Situated on the west bank of the Katsura River (Katsuragawa), the estate includes a main house, or hall, with special quarters for imperial visits, four smaller pavilions for entertaining in the variously located gardens, several belvederes for viewing the landscape, and a small Buddhist chapel. The compound, which is about 69,000 square meters or 17 acres in area, contains a large pond for boating, several islands connected by bridges and paths, and extensive plantings that highlight the four seasons. The principal structure represents a highly crafted style of wooden architecture, called SHOIN-ZUKURI, and is often cited as one of Japan's finest examples of residential construction.

The Katsura site has a long history as a country retreat for the aristocracy of Kyōto, but when Prince Toshihito of the Hachijō no Miya family (1579–1629) began to visit the location, none of the present buildings were extant. A letter written ca 1619 describes "a little teahouse in a melon patch," and a painting of the same period shows only a few thatch-roofed buildings clustered around a pond. Prince Toshihito built the original section of the present main house and some of the other buildings between ca 1620 and ca 1625. Prince Toshihito's son Prince Toshitada (1619–62) is credited with construction of most of the rest of the present buildings between ca 1640 and ca 1655, using deliberately rustic details for the teahouses and garden pavilions.

The original section of the main house (built by Prince Toshihito) is known as the Old Shoin (Ko Shoin). The sections known as the Middle Shoin (Chū Shoin), Music Room (Gakki no Ma), and New Shoin (Shin Shoin) were added by Prince Toshitada, the New Shoin being specially built in anticipation of a visit from the retired emperor Go-Mizunoo. (The visit did not actually take place until 1658. After Prince Toshitada's death Go-Mizunoo visited the villa again, in 1663.) The main house taken as a whole contains several moderate-size rooms (averaging 3.7 × 9 m; 12 × 30 ft) with mat floors (tatami) and painted sliding wall panels (fusuma). The rooms are informally arranged along a diagonal axis, and the verandah that runs across the entire south facade appears sawtoothed in plan. The gardens were carefully planted to be viewed from the main house, and the interior and exterior spaces are visually integrated. The first room of the New Shoin (Shin Shoin) includes an imperial dais, a fine example of the SUKIYA-ZUKURI style of architecture with its reading desk, bookshelves in an ell shape, and lowered lacquered ceiling.

Of the remaining pavilions on the man-made hills and islands of the estate, the ones called the Gepparō and the Shōkintei were built by Prince Toshihito. Prince Toshitada built the pavilions called the Shōkatei and the Shōiken as well as the small Buddhist chapel called the Enrindō and rebuilt the older Gepparō and Shōkintei. The Gepparō immediately east of the Old Shoin contrasts by its smaller scale and rustic construction with the polished elegance of the main house. The name Gepparō (literally, "moon-wave tower") derives from a verse by the Chinese poet Bo Juyi (Po Chü-i). Other buildings and garden arrangements are similarly associated with familiar names of people and places in Chinese and Japanese literature or reproduce in miniature actual famous places. For example, a small man-made peninsula in a section of the pond recreates the beach at AMANOHASHIDATE on the Sea of Japan, one of the so-called three most famous views in Japan. The Shōkatei resembles a typical rustic teahouse of the type once found along roadsides in Japan for the refreshment of travelers, and the structure of the Shōkintei copies aspects of a typical country farmhouse (see MINKA). Such literary associations and adaptations of rural architectural styles formed an integral part of early 17th-century aristocratic aesthetics. Retired emperor Go-Mizunoo created a similar garden at the SHUGAKUIN DETACHED PALACE.

Katsura Detached Palace has been popular among European and American architects of the 20th century, especially Bruno TAUT, who were impressed by the simplicity in overall form, the use of natural materials, the interpenetration of interior and exterior spaces, and the richness of detail. The estate can be visited by permission of the Imperial Household Agency.

■ ——— Akira Naitō and Takeshi Nishikawa, *Katsura: A Princely Retreat*, tr Charles S. Terry (1977). Naomi Ōkawa, *Edo Architecture: Katsura and Nikko*, tr Alan Woodhull and Akito Miyamoto (1975). Kenzō Tange and Yasuhiro Ishimoto, *Katsura*, tr Charles S. Terry (1972).   Bruce A. COATS

Katsuragawa

River in western Kyōto, Kyōto Prefecture. A section of a longer river that originates in the Tamba mountains and flows into the Yodogawa. The Katsuragawa is that part of the lower reaches of the river between ARASHIYAMA and the point where it joins the Yodo-gawa. The section above Arashiyama as far as Kameoka is called the Hozugawa, and the part above Kameoka is called the Ōigawa. The Katsuragawa has been used for transportation and irrigation since ancient times. A dyeing industry has developed along the river. Numerous ancient tombs and remains of Nagaokakyō Palace are located along the river. Length: 31 km (19 mi).

Katsuragawa Hoshū (1751–1809)

Physician and scholar of WESTERN LEARNING. Together with MA-ENO RYŌTAKU and SUGITA GEMPAKU, he undertook the first transla-tion into Japanese of a Western anatomy book, *Ontleedkundige Tafelen* (1734, Anatomical Tables), a Dutch version of the German work *Anatomische Tabellen* (1722) by Johann Adam Kulmus (1689–1745). Their translation was published as *Kaitai shinsho* (New Book of Anatomy) in 1774. Hoshū was from an early age involved in the mainstream of discourse between Japanese intellec-tuals and the Dutch, the only Westerners allowed in Japan. Carl Peter THUNBERG, a physician stationed at the Dutch trading post in DEJIMA, wrote admiringly of Hoshū, as did the trade commissioner Izaak TITSINGH. In 1777 Hoshū became physician to the shōgun, the sixth member of the Katsuragawa family to be so appointed. He also taught at the Igakukan, the Tokugawa shogunate school of medicine. Among his works are *Hokusa bunryaku* (1794), written by order of the shōgun, which chronicled the adventures in Russia of the shipwrecked sailor DAIKOKUYA KŌDAYŪ, and *Roshia shi* (1794, Russian Report), a work intended to serve as an aid in devising coastal defense strategy.

Katsurahama

Coastal area located on Urado Bay in the southern part of the city of Kōchi, central Kōchi Prefecture, Shikoku. White-sand beaches lined by pines and rocks and reefs are notable. The area has developed into a tourist and resort spot in recent years, and many visitors come to view the moon over the bay in autumn. An aquarium and a bronze statue of SAKAMOTO RYŌMA are located here. Length: ap-proximately 700 m (2,296 ft).

Katsura Kogorō → Kido Takayoshi

Katsura-Taft Agreement

Memorandum signed by American Secretary of War William How-ard Taft and Japanese Prime Minister KATSURA TARŌ on 29 July 1905, immediately before the termination of the RUSSO-JAPANESE WAR. The agreement included Japanese recognition of US sover-

eignty in the Philippines, endorsement of close working relations between the two countries to ensure peace in East Asia, and Ameri-can recognition of Korea as a Japanese protectorate. The agreement, which was kept secret until 1924, was not legally binding and was merely meant to clarify relations between the United States and Japan, an emergent world power.

Katsura Tarō (1847–1913)

Army general and politician of the Meiji period (1868–1912) who held key positions in the military high command and was prime minister from 1901 to 1906, 1908 to 1911, and 1912 to 1913. Through the ANGLO-JAPANESE ALLIANCE of 1902, the RUSSO-JAPANESE WAR of 1904–05, and the annexation of Korea (see KOREA, ANNEXATION OF) in 1910, all carried out under Katsura's prime ministership, Japan became a major imperialist power in East Asia. At the end of his career, despite the disapproval of his patron and men-tor, YAMAGATA ARITOMO, Katsura founded a political party, the RIKKEN DŌSHIKAI (or Dōshikai), to contest the growing strength of the RIKKEN SEIYŪKAI (or Seiyūkai), the majority party in the lower house of the Diet.

He was born in the castle town of Hagi in the domain of Chōshū (now Yamaguchi Prefecture) on 28 November 1847, the eldest son of a *samurai* family. At 17 he joined the movement in Chōshū against the Tokugawa shogunate and, as captain of a company and deputy commander of a battalion, fought in some of the major campaigns leading to the overthrow of that regime. He was given imperial recognition in August 1868 for his meritorious service. Following the MEIJI RESTORATION (1868), Katsura studied military science in Germany between 1870 and 1873. Two years later he was appointed military attaché to the Japanese embassy in Germany, where he served until 1878. From 1884 to 1885 he again visited Europe, ac-companying a mission led by Minister of the Army ŌYAMA IWAO, to study military systems.

Katsura's advancement in the army was swift. Promoted to ma-jor general in 1885, he served as adviser to the chief of the Bureau of General Affairs and commissioner of the General Staff and then as vice-minister of the army. After serving as general of the Third Division under the command of Yamagata Aritomo during the SINO-JAPANESE WAR OF 1894–1895, Katsura was appointed gover-nor-general of Taiwan in 1896 and then army minister in successive cabinets from 1898 to 1900. During these years Katsura assisted Yamagata and Ōyama in the general reorganization of the national army on the German model. Administrative procedures, structure of command, and military education were all unified and stream-lined within a national system. Katsura was often praised for the close attention he gave to details regarding budget, conscription, and salary schedule.

Between 1901 and 1913 Katsura was a conspicuous figure on the political scene as prime minister. He directed the signing of the Anglo-Japanese Alliance in 1902, a treaty much prized because a Western power and an Asian nation had reached an international agreement as equals. The treaty specifically protected Japan's flank on the high seas, allowing for greater concentration on the mounting threat of tsarist Russia on the East Asian continent. Equally momen-tous was the Russo-Japanese War of 1904–05, in which an Asian nation defeated a Western power on the field of battle. It gained for Japan the status of an imperialist power possessing "special inter-ests" in Manchuria and Korea. In 1910, again under Katsura's prime ministership, Korea was annexed. Under Katsura, Japan secured those territorial boundaries agreed upon by government leaders to be necessary for the maintenance of national independence and in-tegrity.

In domestic politics, Katsura engaged in a complex struggle for power with the Seiyūkai. He sustained his prime ministerships through a compromise arrangement with the party. The Seiyūkai agreed to vote for Katsura's budget in the lower house, and in return Katsura promised to support the president of the Seiyūkai, SAIONJI KIMMOCHI, as his successor as prime minister. This period, there-fore, is often referred to as the Katsura–Saionji decade, with the premiership alternating between the two men. However, it was pri-marily HARA TAKASHI, the secretary-general of the Seiyūkai, with whom Katsura worked out the compromise arrangement. Recogniz-ing Hara's use of this relationship to expand and solidify the Sei-yūkai, Katsura in 1913 organized a party of his own, the Dōshikai, to contend with the Seiyūkai.

Despite Katsura's powerful position as military leader and prime minister, the support of the Seiyūkai in the lower house was essential to his political success, as he had little other base of public support. Indeed, Katsura became increasingly unpopular during his prime ministerships. In 1905, following the Russo-Japanese War, large crowds rioted in Tōkyō to protest his handling of the Treaty of PORTSMOUTH (see HIBIYA INCENDIARY INCIDENT). Katsura was accused of sacrificing the wishes of the people who had fought the war and given their lives. As a general from Chōshū, Katsura was seen as an egregious leader of selfish domainal and military clique politics (see HAMBATSU; GUMBATSU). The army was alleged to be not the people's army but the private tool of Chōshū generals like Katsura.

In 1910 Katsura gained further notoriety through his handling of the socialist movement. Responding to rumors that a group of anarchists were plotting the assassination of the emperor, Katsura rounded up leftists in a heavy-handed and harsh manner (see HIGH TREASON INCIDENT OF 1910). KŌTOKU SHŪSUI and 11 others were executed, despite misgivings voiced by the press and by political groups. This incident added to the chorus of criticisms about Katsura's capabilities as a leader of state.

Throughout this period landowners, heads of small- and medium-sized industries, and common laborers all complained bitterly about land, business, and consumption taxes. They especially pointed to the military expenditures, which appeared needlessly inflated in a time of peace. Doubts about Katsura's ability and sincerity mounted steadily through the early 1910s and exploded once again into popular riots in late 1912 and 1913, shortly after the death of Emperor Meiji, in what is known as the TAISHŌ POLITICAL CRISIS. Katsura was suspected of using the new Taishō emperor, a young man of dubious mental powers, to have himself appointed prime minister for the third time and then using this office to carry out an expansion of the army by two whole divisions. Also suspect was his plan to convert the railway system in Japan from narrow- to broad-gauge lines to accord with those already in existence in Manchuria. The response from the public was instantaneous and angry. All that had been said of Katsura since 1905 appeared true: he was ruthless in his manipulation of the throne; his efforts to bolster the army were made at the expense of the people. A MOVEMENT TO PROTECT CONSTITUTIONAL GOVERNMENT was organized by journalists and politicians and quickly spread throughout the country.

During these months of raucous demonstrations and protest meetings, Katsura became thoroughly discredited. He was mercilessly challenged by politicians, the press, and unruly crowds. As the crisis deepened, instead of compromising, Katsura chose to confront the Seiyūkai by organizing a rival party, the Dōshikai. Hara Takashi responded in kind and, backed by the Movement to Protect Constitutional Government, turned to meet Katsura's challenge. Hara objected to Katsura's plan to expand the size of the army and, in particular, to revise the railway system, which, through the pork-barrel politics of local railway construction, was a crucial part of Hara's own scheme to develop his political party. During the political crisis, Katsura, despite his many achievements in transforming Japan into an imperialist power, felt the brunt of an enraged public. On 11 February 1913 he was finally forced to resign as prime minister. Shortly afterward he became ill and died in October of the same year.

Katsura's admirer and biographer, TOKUTOMI SOHŌ, one of the most eminent and prolific journalists of that era, believed Katsura was blessed with common sense and wisdom. In Tokutomi's eyes no other politician of the Meiji period could compare with Katsura in terms of his accomplishments in government and military administration. It was this same Katsura, however, who was unable to meet the challenge of new political forces in the Diet and in the streets of cities throughout the country during the Taishō Political Crisis.

■——Tokutomi Iichirō, *Seijika to shite no kō* (1913). Tokutomi Iichirō, *Kōshaku Katsura Tarō den*, 2 vols (1917).   *Tetsuo NAJITA*

katsura tree

(katsura). *Cercidiphyllum japonicum*, a deciduous tree of the family Cercidiphyllaceae which grows wild in mountainous regions throughout Japan. It is known for the beauty of its spring and autumn foliage. The trunk grows erect and reaches a towering height of about 27 meters (88.5 ft) with a diameter of about 1.3 meters (4.3 ft). The leaves are opposite, broadly ovate, heart-shaped at the base and slightly pointed at the tip, with serrated edges; they measure about 3–7 centimeters (1.2–2.8 in) in length and width and are whitish beneath, with 5–7 palmate veins. The tree is dioecious, and flowers are wrapped in bracts in the axils, growing before the leaves in

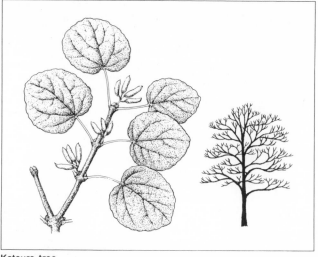

Katsura tree

late spring. The flowers are naked and lack petals. Male flowers have numerous stamens with red anthers.

At the AOI FESTIVAL held each May in Kyōto, branches of *katsura* are used to decorate the oxen and horses, apparently because *katsura* leaves resemble those of the *futaba aoi* plant (*Asarum caulescens*), which is used for this festival, and from which the festival takes its name, but also probably because the *katsura* was long regarded as a sacred tree. The wood is lightweight and warp-resistant and has wide uses in construction and carpentry. The tree has a pleasant fragrance, and the leaves are used to make incense; the bark, which contains tannin and resists decay, is used as roofing material. The katsura tree was exported to the United States in 1878. It has also been introduced to Canada and Germany.

MATSUDA Osamu

Katsushika Hokusai → Hokusai

Katsushika Ward

(Katsushika Ku). One of the 23 wards of Tōkyō. Between the rivers Arakawa and Edogawa. A former farming area, today Katsushika Ward is a residential area undergoing rapid industrialization. Tourist attractions are Mizumoto Park and the temple Shibamata Taishakuten. Pop: 420,175.

Katsu Shintarō (1931–   )

Actor and director. Real name Okumura Toshio. Born in Tōkyō, he made his debut in Tasaka Katsuhiko's *Hana no byakkotai* (1954, White Tiger Brigade). But it was as the reckless outlaw Asakichi in Tanaka Tokuzō's *Akumyō* (1961, The Rogue), that he won popular acclaim. His masterly performance as the blind swordsman, Zatōichi, in the film series (begun in 1962) of the same name, firmly established his reputation. He also starred in Masumura Yasuzō's *Heitai yakuza* (1965, Hoodlum Soldier). In 1967 he founded his own Katsu Productions.   *ITASAKA Tsuyoshi*

Katsuta

City in eastern Ibaraki Prefecture, central Honshū, on the river Nakagawa. Formerly a farming village, Katsuta has become an industrial town since the establishment of a plant by Hitachi, Ltd, in 1940. Pop: 92,620.

Katsuura

City in southeastern Chiba Prefecture, central Honshū, on the Pacific Ocean. Favored with good natural harbors, Katsuura is principally a fishing port, with the largest catch in the prefecture after Chōshi. The morning fish and vegetable market is said to have a history of 300 years. The view from OSENKOROGASHI, a precipice, draws many visitors. Pop: 25,462.

Kawabata Yasunari

Kawabata in May 1961.

Katsuyama

City in northeastern Fukui Prefecture, central Honshū, on the river Kuzuryūgawa. It developed as a castle town in the Edo period (1600–1868) and as a terminus for river transportation. Originally a tobacco-growing region, Katsuyama was the home of a textile industry during the Meiji period (1868–1912). Today, synthetic fiber industry flourishes. Farming is prevalent in the surrounding areas. Pop: 30,853.

Kauffman, James Lee (1886–1968)

American lawyer and teacher. Born in Pennsylvania, he studied at Princeton and at Harvard, where he earned an LLB in 1911. From 1913 to 1919 he taught English and American law at Tōkyō University. He later founded an architectural firm and was responsible for the Marunouchi Building and other modern structures in Tōkyō. After World War II he worked for Japan's economic recovery, giving advice to the Supreme Commander for the Allied Powers (SCAP) and facilitating the introduction of foreign capital. He was decorated by Japan with the Order of the Sacred Treasure, 2nd Class, and the Order of the Rising Sun, 3rd Class.

Kawabata Bōsha (1900–1941)

HAIKU poet. Real name Kawabata Nobukazu. Born in Tōkyō. Although he aspired to be a Western-style painter, studying with the noted Meiji artist KISHIDA RYŪSEI, pulmonary tuberculosis prevented him from realizing his plans. Around 1920 he became a disciple of TAKAHAMA KYOSHI, the leader of the school of traditional haiku associated with the magazine HOTOTOGISU, and contributed frequently to the magazine. Although he adopted Kyoshi's basic style of objective description of flowers and birds, Bōsha's haiku contain bold metaphors and have a spirit of religiosity. His principal haiku collection is *Kegon* (1939).

Kawabata Gyokushō (1842–1913)

MARUYAMA–SHIJŌ SCHOOL painter and book illustrator. Real name Kawabata Takinosuke. Born in Kyōto to a family of lacquerers. As a youth he studied with the Maruyama-school painter Nakajima Raishō (1796–1871); at this time he also studied BUNJINGA (literati painting) with Oda Kaisen (1785–1862). In 1866, after making a sketching tour throughout Japan, he settled in Edo (now Tōkyō), where he experienced severe financial difficulties. He briefly studied Western-style painting with Charles WIRGMAN in Yokohama. But it was not until he won a gold medal at the first Domestic Exposition (Naikoku Kangyō Hakurankai) in 1877 that he received recognition.

Gyokushō's work soon became very popular and he served in many official positions; he screened the Japanese-style paintings submitted to the world's fairs in Paris (1900) and St. Louis (1904). He taught Japanese-style painting at the Tōkyō Bijutsu Gakkō (now Tōkyō University of Fine Arts and Music) from 1890 to 1912. In 1909 he established his own painting school. In 1896 he was ap-

pointed an artist for the imperial household *(teishitsu gigeiin)* and he also received commissions from the influential and wealthy MITSUI family. His style tended to employ strong outlines contrasting with areas of color and wash, a compromise between the softer, traditional Kyōto approach and Western realism. For this reason, Gyokushō was both an exhibitor and judge at conservative exhibitions, such as the Japan Fine Arts Association (Nihon Bijutsu Kyōkai) and the government-sponsored BUNTEN, as well as at more progressive exhibitions, such as the Japanese-style Painting Society (Nihonga Kai). He had many pupils, of whom Yūki Somei (1875–1957) and HIRAFUKU HYAKUSUI are the best known.　　*Frederick* BAEKELAND

Kawabata Ryūshi (1885–1966)

Japanese-style painter and principal advocate of *kaijō geijutsu* ("art for the exhibition place"), a philosophy that emphasized the public nature of art. Real name Kawabata Shōtarō. Born in Wakayama Prefecture, he moved to Tōkyō in 1895. He studied Western-style painting (YŌGA) at the studios of the White Horse Society (HAKUBA-KAI) and the Pacific Painting Society (Taiheiyō Gakai), doing illustrations for magazines and newspapers on the side. He traveled to the United States in 1913, and he visited the oriental galleries of the Boston Museum of Fine Arts. Upon his return to Japan in 1914 he took up Japanese-style painting (NIHONGA). Although he was a regular exhibitor at the Inten, the annual art exhibitions of the reorganized Nihon Bijutsuin (JAPAN FINE ARTS ACADEMY), he withdrew in 1928 and formed his own group, the Seiryūsha, based on the philosophy of *kaijō geijutsu*. In 1930 he was awarded the Asahi Culture Prize and in 1959 the Order of Culture. In 1963 the Ryūshi Kinenkan, an exhibition hall displaying his paintings, was opened on the grounds of his private estate. The Seiryūsha disbanded in 1966 after Ryūshi's death.

Kawabata Yasunari (1899–1972)

One of the finest of modern Japanese novelists; the only Japanese to be awarded the Nobel Prize in literature (1968). Kawabata was born in Ōsaka. The loneliness of his childhood—he was to describe himself as "an expert at funerals"—may account for the melancholy nature of his writings. He was orphaned at an early age and soon lost his only sister and the grandmother with whom he lived. The death of his grandfather, his last near relative, is described in his earliest surviving work, "Jūrokusai no nikki" (Diary of a Sixteen-Year-Old), published without alteration as a fragment of a boyhood diary.

For some years thereafter he lived in school dormitories in suburban Ōsaka. In 1917 he entered the First Higher School in Tōkyō, and in 1920, the English literature department of Tōkyō University. A year later he transferred to the Japanese literature department. He graduated in 1924. His literary activities as a student attracted the attention of such eminent literary figures as KIKUCHI KAN, and he was one of the earliest contributors to Kikuchi's magazine, BUNGEI SHUNJŪ.

The literary group of which he was a member was named the SHINKANKAKU SCHOOL (Neosensualist school). Its models were said to be foreign, and indeed Kawabata was well read in avant-garde European literature, with which his fondness for startling images and abrupt transitions has something in common. He was also a student of Japanese literature. His sad themes and frequent ellipses have very ancient origins. The felicitous meeting of the traditional and the modern which establishes him as an important writer is already to be seen in his juvenilia.

The novelist MISHIMA YUKIO once described Kawabata as "the eternal traveler." Kawabata once said of himself that he was chiefly attracted by "islands in a distant sea." The first of several travelers' lodgings that are important to his writing was one on the Izu Peninsula south of Tōkyō. "Izu no odoriko" (tr "The Izu Dancer," 1955), published in two installments in 1926, made him famous. It tells of a despondent high-school student who, on a walking trip down the Izu Peninsula, makes friends with the young dancer of the title and returns to Tōkyō in much improved spirits. It is based upon his first visit to Izu and is held to be representative of the "neosensualist" Kawabata. The effect is indeed sensual, but the story is successful because of the dashes of melancholy and even bitterness that cut through what might otherwise be cloying sweetness.

One is struck by the fact that Kawabata left so many of his writings unfinished. His notions of form were such that the incidents along the way were more important than the conclusion. Because of this predilection he was fond of likening himself to a practitioner of *renga,* or linked verse (see RENGA AND HAIKAI). Even works which may seem finished to the reader may not have seemed so to Kawabata himself. "Izu no odoriko" is an example. He thought of adding more detailed descriptions of the natural background, and so, perhaps, bringing it nearer the main currents of his later writing. Another striking aspect of the Kawabata novel is the delicate balance between the actors and the background against which the action takes place. Human life seems very fragile and precarious, and constantly on the point of fading away into nature.

In his early professional years Kawabata was the chief exponent of a form called *tanagokoro no shōsetsu* or "palm-of-the-hand story," which might more freely be rendered "vignette" or "short, short story." He thought of the form as peculiarly Japanese, in the tradition of HAIKU. Some of his best stories are in collections called *Tanagokoro no shōsetsu.* For a period of some two decades, beginning soon after his graduation from Tōkyō University, Kawabata regularly wrote critical reviews of new writing. His part in discovering new writers was considerable. From a later period, his most important "find" was probably Mishima, who looked to Kawabata as his teacher. He also busied himself in cinema. His script for *Kurutta ippeiji* (1926, A Page of Madness), directed by KINUGASA TEINOSUKE, has become a classic of the experimental cinema.

Asakusa, Snow Country, War Years—— From the late 1920s the Asakusa district in Tōkyō, then the most lively of the plebeian entertainment districts, became for Kawabata an island in a distant sea. His most significant "Asakusa piece" is *Asakusa kurenaidan* (Scarlet Gang of Asakusa), serialized in 1929 and 1930, with an unfinished sequel in 1934 and 1935. The influence of Edo literature is so strong as to make it seem almost imitative; *Kurenaidan* is not typical Kawabata. The investigation of lonely lives on the edges of the Asakusa demimonde, however, brings it close to the central preoccupations of Kawabata's writing. His most famous essay, "Matsugo no me" (1933, Eyes in their Last Extremity), is from the same period. It is a meditation on death, another of his central preoccupations, and it was much discussed at the time of Kawabata's own death. *Suishō genso* (1931, Crystalline Fantasy) is his main exercise in stream-of-consciousness writing. If there is too much of Edo in *Asakusa kurenaidan,* there is too much here of the European avant-garde, and again imitation might be alleged. Both experiments were of a sort that Kawabata seems to have found uncongenial.

The next traveler's lodging or distant island to become important in his writing was the "snow country" along the Sea of Japan. It is the setting for *Yukiguni* (tr *Snow Country,* 1956), which is generally numbered among his masterpieces, and parts of which were published in several magazines from early 1935. After some rewriting it appeared in book form in 1937. There were subsequent additions and an attempt at a conclusion that did not satisfy Kawabata. Not until 1948 was the final version published in book form.

This method of composition, episode upon episode over considerable periods of time and in a manner suggesting free association and the methods of *renga,* is typical of Kawabata. So too is the inconclusiveness of the episode at length designated the final one. Although the chronological sequence is complex, the plot is simple, telling of an affair between a Tōkyō dilettante and a mountain-town *geisha,* for him desultory and for her unrewarding, and of the man's resolve not to visit the snow country again. So fleeting and insubstantial is the affair that lyrical evocation of the mountain background almost seems to be Kawabata's principal concern. The meeting of the traditional in the form and in the natural description and of the modern in the theme and characterization is most effective.

Never a prolific writer, Kawabata published little during the war years. The first installment of *Meijin* (tr *The Master of Go,* 1972) appeared in 1942. Again with additions and rewriting over the years, the work was not published in book form until 1954. It is a delicately fictionalized account of a *go* match which took place in 1938, and which Kawabata reported for a major newspaper. The "master" of the title entered the match, which was to be his last, as an undefeated champion, and lost. The defeat of the master is made to seem the defeat of a great tradition, and it can be seen as an oblique comment on Japan's disastrous defeat in 1945, by which Kawabata was deeply affected. In one of his most celebrated statements, he said shortly after the defeat that his writings must thenceforth be limited to elegies.

Postwar Years—— Kawabata's postwar career was, on the surface and through most of its course, a bright and busy one. He was among the recognized leaders of the literary world. As president of the Japan P.E.N. Club and one of the more frequently translated of modern authors, he had gained considerable international fame even before he was awarded the Nobel Prize in 1968. After the award he was elevated by the mass media to the status of celebrity, and the difficulty of pursuing his work in such circumstances has been averred in explanation of his death.

His two most important postwar works, *Sembazuru* (tr *Thousand Cranes,* 1959) and *Yama no oto* (tr *The Sound of the Mountain,* 1970), were written around the same time. The first installment of *Sembazuru* appeared in 1949, and the work was, to all appearances, finished in 1951. In 1953, however, with a short story treating the same characters, Kawabata began what seems to have been intended as a sequel of considerable length. It was never finished.

The first installment of *Yama no oto* also appeared in 1949, and the last in 1954. The gradual accretion of the two works is typical of Kawabata's methods. *Sembazuru* was brought to what may seem an adequate conclusion, then continued, and finally left dangling. Kawabata himself said that *Yama no oto* was finished, though it ends on an uncertain note, and could as well have ended at various places along the way. In the irrelevance of the very notion of "conclusion" to Kawabata's important writing lies much of its strength. It places him where he thought of himself as belonging, in a very old lyrical tradition.

Sembazuru centers upon the tea ceremony, and upon hopeless love. The hero is drawn to the mistress of his deceased father, and after her suicide, to her daughter, who flees from him. At the end of the 1951 version, the hero is left alone with a remarkably unpleasant teacher of the tea ceremony, also a former mistress of his father's. The tea ceremony seems to be present not so much to provide a beautiful foil for ugly human affairs as to emphasize Kawabata's fascination with death. People die, but the vessels of the tea ceremony remain, still bearing the marks of the dead.

Yama no oto, also a tale of impossible love, is set in Kamakura, Kawabata's home from 1936 to his death. The hero is an old man who has little affection for his children, and for whom his wife is an object of a certain wry amusement but not of passion. He is strongly drawn to someone whom he cannot have, his daughter-in-law, and over much of the action hovers the ghost of someone whom he could not have, his sister-in-law. At the end of the story he thinks of going back to the old family home, but it is typical of Kawabata's writing that the action in the story does not see him on his way. The characterization is vivid, but, as in *Yukiguni,* the characters seem always on the point of merging with the natural background. The play between the two is reminiscent of the TALE OF GENJI *(Genji monogatari)* in which, along with the Buddhist writ, Kawabata recognized his deepest roots. He wrote movingly of the solace he derived from the *Tale of Genji* during the war years.

Last Years, Death, Achievement—— In his last years Kawabata became a master of what might be called the literature of the aged. *Yama no oto* is an example. An even better example is *Nemureru bijo* (tr *House of the Sleeping Beauties,* 1969), a novelette or long story published in several installments in 1960 and 1961. It tells of the ultimate in unrealizable love. An old man frequents a most unusual house of pleasure, which purveys drugged maidens to old men no longer capable of possessing them sexually. Old men spend nights fondling girls and going no further, and the girls are too deeply drugged to respond.

Nemureru bijo and other works of Kawabata's late years also feature a withdrawal from society. Kawabata experimented with increasingly extreme aspects of isolation. The most extreme example, perhaps, is "Kataude" (tr "One Arm," 1969), published serially in 1963 and 1964. (Serial publication of a short story is an eccentricity which accorded well with Kawabata's methods of composition.) In it a man spends a night with the severed but still living arm of a young girl. For the man as well as for Kawabata, society has withered quite away, and attempts to bring it back in his last writings are somehow wanting in conviction.

Three years and some months after the Nobel award, Kawabata died an untimely and even now inadequately explained death. On the evening of 16 April 1972, he was found dead in a gas-filled room in an apartment he owned not far from his Kamakura home. Everything suggested suicide, and the consensus is that he died by his own hand. There was no suicide note, however, and among his close associates there are those who still argue accident. The fascination with death that runs through his writing suggests less an active courting of death than a willing and almost affectionate acceptance.

Anders Usterling of the Swedish Academy, who made the presentation address at the Stockholm ceremonies in 1968, chose to dwell chiefly upon *Koto* (the Ancient Capital), a novel about Kyōto published serially in 1961 and 1962. He said in part: "In the postwar wave of violent Americanization his novel is a gentle reminder of the necessity of trying to save something of the old Japan's beauty and individuality for the new." Kawabata was certainly aware of "the old Japan's beauty," and to set down something of the old before it disappeared was among his reasons for studying Kyōto and writing the novel. Yet the Swedish view of Kawabata does not do justice to his subtleties. He is made to seem a sweeter and gentler sort of writer than in fact he was. A strain of bitterness and even of ugliness runs through his writing, making it clear that his view of tradition was not so simple as Usterling implied. If his eye was on traditional beauty, it was also on death and decay, in a manner less regretful than accepting. The sense of decay is very modern, the acceptance very traditional, and in the joining of the two lies Kawabata's strength.

As early as 1934, in a survey of his career thus far, Kawabata acknowledged his debt to the West but affirmed his fundamental loyalty to the East: "I have been baptized in the literature of the West, and indeed I have imitated it; but, my roots in the East, I have not once lost my direction these 15 years." In a famous statement set down in 1947 he reaffirmed his traditionalism, but made it clear that the traditional was not, for him, merely the pretty and gentle. The chief ingredient was acceptance itself. "The sadness and the melancholy are not such that one confronts them in the open Western manner. I have not once experienced sorrows and torments of the Western sort. Not once have I seen in Japan the Western sort of emptiness and decadence."

■——Works by Kawabata: *Kawabata Yasunari zenshū*, 19 vols (Shinchōsha, 1969–74). Translations: *Yukiguni* (1935–48), tr *Snow Country* (1956); *Meijin* (1942–54), tr *The Master of Go* (1972); *Sembazuru* (1949–51), tr *Thousand Cranes* (1959); *Yama no oto* (1949–54), tr *The Sound of the Mountain* (1970); *Nemureru bijo* (1960–61), tr *House of Sleeping Beauties* (with "Birds and Beasts" and "One Arm"; 1969); all the above tr Edward G. Seidensticker. *Mizuumi* (1954), tr Reiko Tsukimura as *The Lake* (1974). *Utsukushisa to kanashimi to* (1961–63), tr Howard S. Hibbett as *Beauty and Sadness* (1975). Works about Kawabata: *Bungei tokuhon Kawabata Yasunari* (1977). Hasegawa Izumi, *Kawabata Yasunari ronkō* (1965). Hasegawa Izumi, *Kawabata Yasunari bungaku e no shiten* (1971). Hayashi Takeshi, *Kawabata Yasunari kenkyū* (1976). Hōjō Makoto, *Kawabata Yasunari, bungaku no butai* (1973). Inamura Hiroshi, *Kawabata Yasunari, geijutsu to byōri* (1975). Mishima Yukio, "Eien no tabibito," and other essays on Kawabata, in *Mishima Yukio hyōron zenshū* (Shinchōsha, 1966). Saegusa Yasutaka, *Kawabata Yasunari* (1961). Shindō Sumitaka, *Kawabata Yasunari* (1976). Takeda Katsuhiko and Hasegawa Izumi, ed, *Kawabata bungaku kaigai no hyōka* (1969). Yamamoto Kenkichi, ed, *Kawabata Yasunari* (1959).

Edward G. SEIDENSTICKER

kawabiraki

("river opening"). Annual festival celebrating the beginning of summer. Held in a number of cities, including Ishinomaki in Miyagi Prefecture and Niigata and Nagaoka in Niigata Prefecture. The festival in the Ryōgoku section of Tōkyō is particularly famous and has a long, intermittent history. In the Edo period (1600–1868) the festival occurred on the 28th day of the fifth month of the lunar calendar and marked the start of a three-month period during which city dwellers went out to enjoy the cool of evening. Since the Meiji period (1868–1912) the festival has been celebrated on the third Saturday in July with an elaborate display of fireworks near the Ryōgoku Bridge along the Sumida River (Sumidagawa). The term *kawabiraki* also refers to the opening day of the river fishing season.

INOKUCHI Shōji

Kawachi Nagano

City in southern Ōsaka Prefecture, central Honshū. Metal and *sake*-brewing industries are active. The city is also known for its toothpicks. Farm products include rice and mandarin oranges. Tourist attractions include the temple Kanshinji, associated with the warrior KUSUNOKI MASASHIGE, and the temple Emmeiji, said to have been founded by KŪKAI, and known for its maples. Pop: 78,573.

Kawagoe

City in central Saitama Prefecture, central Honshū. Kawagoe developed as a castle town around Kawagoe Castle, constructed by Ōta Dōshin and his son ŌTA DŌKAN. The city retains traditional warehouse-style merchant houses built with wattle and daub (*dozōzukuri*). Chemical and foodstuff industries thrive. Sweet potatoes are grown in the area. Tourist attractions are the Kitain temple, associated with the TOKUGAWA FAMILY, and the Kawagoe Festival in October. Pop: 259,317.

Kawaguchi

City in southeastern Saitama Prefecture, central Honshū. The river Arakawa separates the city from Tōkyō. The principal occupation of the city is iron casting, which developed during the Edo period (1600–1868). Machinery, textiles, and electrical appliance industries are also well developed. In recent years it has virtually become a suburb of Tōkyō. The Angyō section in the northeastern part of the city is known for its BONSAI and tree nurseries. Pop: 379,357.

Kawaguchi Ekai (1866–1945)

Buddhist monk, scholar, and explorer. Born in Sakai. He studied at INOUE ENRYŌ's institute of philosophy known as the Tetsugakukan and in 1890 became a monk of the ŌBAKU SECT of Zen Buddhism in Tōkyō. He twice embarked on trips to Tibet, India, and Nepal in search of original Sanskrit and Tibetan Buddhist texts. His first trans-Himalayan journey in 1897 was noteworthy because it came at a time when travel there was restricted. On his second sojourn in India and Tibet (1905–13), he exchanged with the Dalai Lama complete sets of Japanese and Tibetan Buddhist texts. He returned to Japan in 1916 with more than 200 Sanskrit books, Buddhist statuary and paintings, as well as botanic specimens and folk craft items. Kawaguchi, known for his progressive views, renounced his priestly status in 1935. He taught at Taishō University. Among his publications are *Chibetto ryokōki* (1904), which was published in London in 1909 in an English version titled *Records of a Tibetan Journey*, and a Tibetan grammar book; he did not complete work on a planned Tibetan-Japanese dictionary.

Kawaguchi, Lake

(Kawaguchiko). In southeastern Yamanashi Prefecture, central Honshū. One of the FUJI FIVE LAKES, it is located directly north of Mt. Fuji (FUJISAN) and was created by a dam formed by lava flows. It is a base for climbing Mt. Fuji. A tourist attraction is the upside-down image of Mt. Fuji reflected in the lake; this is known as *sakasafuji*. Area: 6.1 sq km (2.3 sq mi); circumference: 17 km (11 mi); depth: 14.6 m (47.9 ft); altitude: 831 m (2,726 ft).

Kawaguchi Matsutarō (1899–)

Novelist, playwright, stage and film producer. Born in Tōkyō. Raised in a poor family, he completed elementary school and left home at age 14. He started to write while working in various ways to support himself. He established himself as a writer of popular fiction in 1935, winning the first Naoki Prize for his short story "Tsuruhachi Tsurujirō" (1934). His serialized novel *Aizen katsura* (1936–38), a melodramatic love story about a nurse and a doctor, gained him tremendous popularity. Since 1947 he has been on the board of directors of DAIEI CO, LTD, a motion picture company. In 1965 he was elected to the Japan Academy of the Arts.

Kawahara Keiga (ca 1786–ca 1860)

A painter of Edo-period (1600–1868) Western-style pictures (see WESTERN-STYLE PICTURES, EARLY), who sometimes signed his works in roman letters "Tojosky," a Westernization of his given name Toyosuke. Keiga was a native of Nagasaki; his early artistic training was acquired as an apprentice in his family's print shop. His father, who achieved minor recognition as a painter of the Western manner, was a confrere of Araki Gen'yū (1728–94), the official appraiser of paintings (*kara-e mekiki*) in Nagasaki. Gen'yū's heir, Ishizaki Yūshi (1768–1846), also held the government office of *mekiki* and chronicled the artifacts and activities of the Hollanders residing on the island of DEJIMA in Nagasaki Bay. Keiga became

Yūshi's disciple at an early age and established a lifelong relationship with his popular and prosperous mentor.

Yūshi's sponsorship permitted Keiga access to Dejima and opportunity to examine directly Western prints and paintings. By the age of 30 Keiga had mastered the art of portrait painting and had executed many superb portraits modeled after 18th-century European miniatures. The likeness of Hendrick DOEFF, director of the Dutch factory at Dejima from 1803 to 1817, represents perhaps the finest of Keiga's attempts in this genre.

Keiga's maturity as an artist may be said to date from the time of his association with Dr. Philipp von SIEBOLD (1796–1866), a German physician who arrived in Japan in 1823. Over a period of six years Keiga painted innumerable illustrations to complement von Siebold's extensive botanical and ethnological studies. The majority of paintings that have survived are album illustrations in the von Siebold collection. Other works include portraits both secular and religious, landscapes, *ukiyo-e* paintings, and woodblock prints. His pictures reflect in varying degrees the amalgamation of European and indigenous YAMATO-E styles. Some represent quite unusual experimentations with themes found in European prints, such as his copies and adaptations of *Les Grimmaces*, an album by the French lithographer L. L. Boilly (1761–1845). Additional influence and training may have come from Carl Hubert de Villeneuve, von Siebold's painter assistant, although, with little surviving evidence, this association remains speculative.

Scandal involving von Siebold's attempt to smuggle from the country maps of the Japanese coastline brought an end to Keiga's official relationship with Dejima in 1829. After a brief exile from Kyūshū, Keiga returned and changed his name to Taguchi. His son adopted the name Taguchi Rokoku. During the last 30 years of his life Keiga devoted his efforts to portraits, festival paintings, and occasional prints, such as the series depicting the mission of the Russian Admiral PUTIATIN to Japan in 1853. Continued association with Yūshi brought commissioned projects, including the painting of the coffered ceiling of Kannonji in Nagasaki in 1846, in which he chose as themes botanical studies executed in traditional *yamato-e* style. The works are signed both by Yūshi and Keiga and bear the seal Keiga used during this period, "Tanemi." The same seal appears on Keiga's last known painting, a portrait of Nagashima Kiku, dated to 1860, the year of the artist's presumed death at the age 75.

📖——Cal French, *Through Closed Doors: Western Influence on Japanese Art* (1977). Tetsurō Kagesato, ed, *Phillip Franz von Siebold's Ukiyo-e Collection* (National Museum of Ethnology, Leiden), vol 3, pt. 2 (Kōdansha, 1978). Kaneshige Mamoru, "Shīboruto to Kawahara Keiga," *Nagasaki dansō* 52 (December 1971). Kaneshige Mamoru, "Dejima deiri no eshi Kawahara Keiga," *Nihon bijutsu kōgei* 7.430 (July 1974). Koga Jūjirō, *Nagasaki kaiga zenshi* (1944). Kuroda Genji, *Nagasaki keiyōga* (1932). *Michael Lee* BROWNE

Kawahigashi Hekigotō (1873–1937)

HAIKU poet. Real name Kawahigashi Heigorō. Born in Ehime Prefecture. While still in middle school, he began writing haiku under the guidance of his friend MASAOKA SHIKI, a leader in the modern haiku movement. He contributed many haiku to *Hototogisu*, the magazine founded by Shiki in 1897, becoming, along with TAKAHAMA KYOSHI, one of Shiki's two most important disciples. After Shiki's death in 1902, however, he left the magazine, disagreeing with Kyoshi's conservative style. He advocated a more progressive form, commonly referred to as *shinkeikō* (new trend) haiku, which discarded both the traditional metric pattern of 5–7–5 syllables and the use of "season words" *(kigo)*. His principal works include the collection of travel essays *Sanzenri* (1906) and the haiku collection *Hekigotō kushū* (1916).

Kawai Eijirō (1891–1944)

Scholar and publicist. Born in Tōkyō. Kawai studied political science at Tōkyō University under Onozuka Kiheiji (1870–1944), who became his lifelong mentor. From 1920 to 1939 Kawai taught social and industrial relations policy in the faculty of economics at Tōkyō University.

Kawai's main interest was political philosophy, because it offered theoretical grounds for social reform. He was particularly influenced by the political thought of Thomas Hill Green (1836–82), an English idealist who emphasized the importance of self-realization of the individual. Kawai believed that Japan's social problems created by industrialization must be solved without recourse to either commu-

nism or state absolutism, because these extremes of the left and the right exalted the class or the state rather than the individual.

While still a student, Kawai learned about the desperate living conditions of Japanese industrial workers. To help promote their well-being he became a factory inspector in the Ministry of Agriculture and Commerce, which was in charge of labor problems. The labor legislation he advocated, however, was too progressive for the ministry. When his superiors rejected the position paper he wrote for the Japanese delegation to the first conference of the International Labor Organization (1919), he resigned from government service and became a university professor. His experience in the bureaucracy convinced him that Japan's national interests, both real and imagined, would always preclude attempts at social reform from above and that for government officials the state's rights were sacrosanct, but not those of the individual.

Kawai came to advocate, along the lines of the British Labour Party, extensive public ownership of the means of production. A combination of idealist moral philosophy and socialist economic programs subject to parliamentary control was Kawai's prescription for social reform in Japan. His "idealist socialism" was a form of opposition to Marxism and communism. Realizing the power and intransigence of the Japanese government, however, he hoped for a united front of Marxists and non-Marxist socialists to improve the life of workers. This hope never materialized. When Marxists were forced underground or into prison after the Great Depression in the 1930s, Kawai was one of the few men who remained free and openly willing to oppose the nationalist extremism that had begun to dominate the government.

Kawai courageously resisted the "fascist" trend of the 1930s in a March 1936 article denouncing the attempted coup d'etat (FEBRUARY 26TH INCIDENT) by army officers in the previous month. Despite the nationalists' resentment against this work, Kawai continued to voice his dissent from Japan's increasingly totalitarian politics.

For this he was indicted in 1938. The charge was dissemination of dangerous ideas from the West in violation of the PUBLICATION LAW OF 1893. He was forced to surrender his faculty position. The Kawai Eijirō case became the biggest "thought trial" of the time, lasting for six years and ending in his conviction. He died soon afterward. Throughout his protracted struggle against fascism, Kawai single-mindedly asserted that no societal institutions, including the government, had value in and of themselves, and that they were merely the means to the highest goal of human life, that is, self-realization and perfection of human character and capabilities as a form of individualism to which even socialism was the means.

📖——Kawai Eijirō Zenshū Kankō Kai, ed, *Kawai Eijirō zenshū*, 24 vols (Shakai Shisō Sha, 1967–70). Egami Teruhiko, *Kawai Eijirō den* (1970). *Atsuko* HIRAI

Kawai Gyokudō (1873–1957)

Japanese-style painter. Real name Kawai Yashisaburō. Born in Aichi Prefecture. He went to Kyōto in 1887 to study with KŌNO BAIREI, a teacher of the MARUYAMA–SHIJŌ SCHOOL of painting. After seeing a painting by HASHIMOTO GAHŌ, a master of the KANŌ SCHOOL, at an exhibit in Kyōto in 1895, he went to Tōkyō to study under him. In 1907 he was chosen as a judge for the first annual Ministry of Education exhibit, the Bunten. He was invited to teach at the Tōkyō Bijutsu Gakkō (now Tōkyō University of Fine Arts and Music) in 1915 and was elected a member of the Imperial Fine Arts Academy (Teikoku Bijutsuin) in 1919. In 1940 he received the Order of Culture. The genius of Gyokudō's style resulted from a masterful blending of the techniques of the Shijō and Kanō schools. Most of his paintings are preserved and exhibited at the GYOKUDŌ ART MUSEUM in Ōme, outside Tōkyō.

Kawai Kanjirō (1890–1966)

Artist-potter; friend of HAMADA SHŌJI. Kawai was born in Shimane Prefecture but spent most of his adult life in Kyōto. His kiln and traditional Japanese house there are now a museum. The house contains antique Japanese and Korean furniture and folk crafts, and the museum has a representative selection of Kawai's ceramics and sculpture.

Kawai studied pottery making under ITAYA HAZAN in the Ceramics Department at Tōkyō Industrial College, where Hamada was a fellow student. After his graduation in 1914, Kawai was hired as an engineer at the Kyōto Ceramics Testing Institute; Hamada joined him in 1916 and they conducted a series of 10,000 glaze experiments there.

In 1919, Kawai and Hamada made a trip to Korea and Manchuria, collecting and studying the ceramics and other folk art of those areas. In 1926, while visiting the mountain monasteries on KŌYA-SAN, Kawai, Hamada, and the influential philosopher–art critic YA-NAGI MUNEYOSHI determined to found a crafts society. They organized the Nihon Mingei Kyōkai (Japan Folk Art Association), which began publishing the crafts magazine *Kōgei* in 1931 and opened the JAPAN FOLKCRAFT MUSEUM in Tōkyō in 1936. The three men traveled throughout Korea in 1936 and 1937, collecting Korean folk art for the new museum.

Kawai's ceramics before World War II remained close to the Japanese and Korean folk-art traditions, with considerable influence from English slip-decorated folk pottery via Hamada's and Kawai's friend Bernard H. LEACH, the English potter. After the war, Kawai developed his own distinctive, personal style of ceramic art. His slab-mold bottle-vases and boxes are prized for their original, sculpturesque shapes. These pieces often have lively, high-relief, slip-trailed decoration touched with various brightly colored glazes. Kawai is also noted for his skillful use of two particular glazes, *gosu* (poorly refined cobalt-oxide blue with interesting iron-oxide brown inclusions), and *shinsha* (underglaze copper red). See also FOLK CRAFTS. Robert MOES

Kawai Michi (1877–1953)

Educator and Christian activist. Born in Mie Prefecture into a family of Shintō priests of the Ise Shrine. She attended a mission school in Sapporo; later, aided by NITOBE INAZŌ, she was able to attend Bryn Mawr College in Pennsylvania. Graduating in 1904, she returned to Japan, taught at Tsuda Eigakujuku (now Tsuda College), and helped TSUDA UMEKO and others to establish Japanese branches of the Young Women's Christian Association (YWCA). She became the first director-general of the Japanese YWCA and often represented it abroad. Her belief in Christianity was strengthened by her friendship with the Christian leader UEMURA MASAHISA. In 1929 she founded Keisen Jogakuen (now Keisen Jogakuen Junior College). After World War II, she worked in the Ministry of Education to help establish Japan's system of two-year junior colleges. Her works include *My Lantern* (1939), written in English.

Kawai Musical Instruments Mfg Co, Ltd

(Kawai Gakki Seisakusho). Manufacturer and vendor of musical instruments such as pianos, electronic organs, harmonicas, and guitars. Second in both domestic and world markets to NIPPON GAKKI CO, LTD. Founded in 1927, it was established in its present form in 1951. The firm has shown swift growth based on a national direct sale system, the operation of music and physical fitness classrooms, and subscription sales. It has subsidiary companies in the United States and West Germany, Canada and Australia and exports to over 50 foreign countries. Sales for the fiscal year ending May 1982 totaled ¥71.8 billion (US $303 million), of which the sale of pianos accounted for 53 percent, music and physical fitness classrooms 18 percent, electronic organs 13 percent, other instruments 12 percent, and other sources 4 percent. In the same year the export ratio was 17 percent and capitalization stood at ¥3.6 billion (US $15.2 million). The corporate headquarters are located in the city of Hamamatsu in Shizuoka Prefecture.

Kawai Sora (1649–1710)

HAIKU poet of the early Edo period. A disciple of BASHŌ. Born in Shinano Province (now Nagano Prefecture). As a young man, he served the *daimyō* of the Nagashima domain of Ise Province (now Mie Prefecture) as a *samurai*. After retiring early from this position, he went to Edo (now Tōkyō), where he studied SHINTŌ and WAKA. As Bashō's disciple and manservant, he accompanied his master on several journeys, including the one that resulted in Bashō's *Oku no hosomichi (The Narrow Road to the Deep North)*. Sora's diary of that journey is indispensable for the study of this famous work.

Kawai Suimei (1874–1965)

Poet. Real name Kawai Matahei. Born in Ōsaka Prefecture. He gained recognition for his romantic and lyrical poems which appeared in the literary magazine *Bunko* during his 13-year editorship through 1907. Influential in poetry circles of the late Meiji period, he encouraged such younger poets as YOKOSE YAU, KITAHARA HA-

KUSHŪ, and KAWAJI RYŪKŌ. Around 1910 he began to write poems in the spoken language and became a leader in the movement for free-verse poetry written in modern Japanese. He was elected to the Japan Art Academy (Nihon Geijutsuin) in 1937. His principal collections include *Mugenkyū* (1901) and *Tōei* (1905).

Kawai Tsugunosuke (1827–1868)

Official of the Nagaoka domain (now part of Niigata Prefecture). As a youth he studied with SAKUMA SHŌZAN, and after traveling to Nagasaki, then the only port open to foreign countries, he called for an end to the Tokugawa shogunate's long policy of NATIONAL SECLUSION. Within his domain, he assisted the *daimyō* in carrying out financial reforms. At the time of the BOSHIN CIVIL WAR (1868–69) accompanying the overthrow of the shogunate, he recommended that, in consideration of its historic ties to the Tokugawa, Nagaoka remain neutral, but when the domain's stance was interpreted as hostility by a general of the imperial army, Kawai decided to fight. He died of wounds incurred while trying to recover Nagaoka Castle, which had been captured by imperial forces.

Kawaji Hot Spring

(Kawaji Onsen). Located near the upper reaches of the river Kinugawa, northwestern Tochigi Prefecture, central Honshū. A simple thermal spring; water temperature 42–47°C (108–117°F). Located within Nikkō National Park, the site has been in continual use since the Edo period (1600–1868). Scenic spots in the area include Lake Ikari and the gorge called Ryūōkyō. Several inns and souvenir shops are located in the resort.

Kawaji Ryūkō (1888–1959)

Poet and critic. Real name Kawaji Makoto. Born in Tōkyō. Graduate of the Tōkyō School of the Arts (now Tōkyō University of Fine Arts and Music), where he studied Japanese painting. His free verse poem "Hakidame" (later renamed "Chirizuka") and others of his poems published in 1907 had a great impact on Japanese poetic circles as the first poems to be composed in the modern spoken language. After 1920 Kawaji wrote increasingly intellectual poetry, discarding lyricism for witty technique. He received the 1957 Japan Art Academy Award for his poetry collection *Nami* (1957). Other works include the poetry collections *Robō no hana* (1910) and *Ayumu hito* (1922) and numerous essays on art.

Kawaji Toshiakira (1801–1868)

Official of the Tokugawa shogunate (1603–1867); together with his brother INOUE KIYONAO, a major participant in the events that terminated Japan's two centuries of NATIONAL SECLUSION. Kawaji distinguished himself as an administrator and rose rapidly in the shogunate hierarchy. The pragmatism of his teacher, SATŌ ISSAI, and close association with FUJITA TŌKO, EGAWA TARŌZAEMON, WATANABE KAZAN, and other scholars inspired him with a deep interest in international affairs. In 1852 he was appointed commissioner of finance (*kanjō bugyō*) and placed in charge of coastal defense. The following year he was sent to Nagasaki to negotiate with the Russian envoy Evfimii Vasil'evich PUTIATIN, who sought to open commercial relations with Japan. In 1855 he concluded a treaty of friendship with Russia modeled after the KANAGAWA TREATY, which had recently been signed with Commodore Matthew PERRY of the United States. In 1858 Kawaji accompanied HOTTA MASA-YOSHI to Kyōto in an unsuccessful attempt to win imperial sanction for the HARRIS TREATY. Kawaji was placed under house arrest in 1859 by the great elder (*tairō*) II NAOSUKE for supporting the losing faction in the 1858 shogunal succession dispute, but he returned to prominence after Ii's assassination in 1860. As commissioner of foreign affairs (*gaikoku bugyō*) he was active in shaping the foreign policy of the shogunate. He committed suicide on the day after Edo Castle, the seat of the Tokugawa regime, was surrendered to imperial forces.

Kawakami Bizan (1869–1908)

Novelist and poet. Originator of the so-called *kannen shōsetsu* (idea or concept fiction). Born Kawakami Akira in Ōsaka. As a youth, he moved to Tōkyō with his parents and, graduating from high school, entered the law school of Tōkyō University in 1888. A year later he transferred to the literature department, but eventually withdrew. Bizan had already become associated with such writers as OZAKI KŌYŌ and YAMADA BIMYŌ and in late 1886 had joined the group known as the KEN'YŪSHA. But he turned away from it around 1893 and began to associate with the *Bungakukai* (a literary magazine) writers and later, around 1914, with the literary group known as the Ryūdokai.

Bizan's earliest works fall into two categories. The first comprises HAIBUN, *kyōbun* (see KYŌSHI AND KYŌBUN), and other short pieces filled with florid descriptions, ornate allusions, puns, and word plays, written in a fancy, eloquent style. This category was crowned by *Futokoro nikki* (1897), a *haibun*-style travel account considered Bizan's masterpiece and still highly regarded today.

Melodramatic love tales in the regular Ken'yūsha vein, also composed in a rich, beautiful style, constituted the second category. Their form is loose, characterization superficial, plots fragmented, and tone romantic. Bizan was never able to free himself completely of these tendencies.

"Sodezukin" (1892) contains the earliest indications of Bizan's next phase. His fiction remained unrealistic and poorly structured, but a darkening tone and a mood of deep pessimism began to emerge. The beginnings of Bizan's social criticism—especially his antipathy to wealth, power, greed, and corruption—were also visible in limited degree. Such elements became central to Bizan's next period.

The brief *kannen shōsetsu* period is generally limited to 1895, including such works as *Ōsakazuki, Shokikan, Uraomote,* and *Yamishio,* an unfinished novel later retitled *Ajirogi.* These works, with which Bizan achieved his highest critical acclaim, were vaguely anchored in philosophical concepts and contained a blend of bitter misanthropy and slashing social censure. Politicians, businessmen, and the wealthy were savagely criticized.

From 1897 to 1900 Bizan largely returned to the formulas of 1892–94. Romantic and domestic tragedies recorded the conflict between love and lust, the troubled relationships between men and women. Permeating everything was a tone of somber gloom and hopelessness. It is not surprising these stories were poorly received.

Bizan's works of 1902–03 could be viewed as an extension of the *kannen shōsetsu,* or as nebulous forerunners of the *shakai shōsetsu* (social novel). All of them are set in agricultural villages and focus on the inhabitants and their lives. Major themes concern local poverty, feudal customs, village ostracism, rural-urban conflicts, and struggles between landowners and tenant farmers. The tone occasionally approaches that of later proletarian fiction.

Bizan's final period continued to center on social and domestic problems, but due to his reading of Zola and his closeness with the Ryūdokai, displayed some influence from NATURALISM. *Kannon iwa* (1903–07), his second best work *Harin* (1907)—his closest approach to psychological realism—and other novels exhibit the standard naturalistic concentration on sex. Passion, lust, promiscuity, and adultery all make obligatory appearances. But the naturalistic elements are very tenuous.

The relatively short yet prolific career of Bizan manifests the inability of almost all the Ken'yūsha members to make a significant break with old patterns already enshrined in obsolete models. Bizan made a determined effort, but the shortcomings of his fiction are obvious. Settings increase in realism but usually remain exercises in stylistic prowess cleverly stapled into the linear movement of the text. Characterization, best realized in the feminine roles, is stereotyped and sentimental. External delineation predominates, and only rarely is psychological development encountered. Plots, even when intent on objective realism, turn out subjective and romantic. Structure is sketchy and disjunctive in most cases. No really unified or detailed theses surface from Bizan's narrow themes. Philosophical views and social criticisms, perhaps better termed soured idealism or rancorous disenchantment, tend to be expressed in obtrusive fragments or in blatant tirades and preachments. Ideas and concepts overpower or disrupt structure when abruptly inserted.

Bizan was too serious, ambitious, and artistic to remain satisfied with outdated practices. He wished to explore the meaning of existence, plumb the depths of the psyche, expose the hypocrisy of society, and turn romanticism toward realism. Though Bizan never scaled these heights nor became a first-rate writer, the trends he experimented with were not unimportant in the development of the modern novel. Without him, the maturation of modern prose fiction might have been a slower process. *Thomas E. SWANN*

Kawakami Gen'ichi (1912–)

Businessman. Born in Shizuoka Prefecture. Graduated from Takachiho Commercial School (now Takachiho Commercial University). Kawakami joined NIPPON GAKKI CO, LTD, in 1937. He replaced his father, Kawakami Kaichi (1885–1964), as president in 1950 and made the Yamaha brand name well known throughout the world. In 1955 he separated the motorcycle division from his company and turned it into an independent firm, YAMAHA MOTOR CO, LTD. A great devotee of musical education, Kawakami established the Yamaha Music Foundation, which now operates a nationwide chain of music schools. *MAEDA Kazutoshi*

Kawakami Hajime (1879–1946)

Marxian economist. Professor of economics at Kyōto University from 1908 to 1928, Kawakami was instrumental in introducing Marxism into Japan in the period following World War I. Although his decision to embrace Marxism came relatively late in his life, in 1919 at the age of 40, it may be traced to his search as a young man for solutions to the ethical and social problems created by Japan's industrialization.

Born in Iwakuni, Yamaguchi Prefecture, on 20 October 1879, the eldest son of a former *samurai,* Kawakami was imbued at an early age with a sense of patriotic nationalism and political responsibility. A product of elite schooling, he graduated from the Law Faculty of Tōkyō University in 1902, bent on a career in government service. Between 1902 and 1905 he taught economics in the Faculty of Agriculture of Tōkyō University and at the Peers' School (see GAKUSHŪIN UNIVERSITY). In 1905 he published the first Japanese translation of E. R. A. Seligman's *The Economic Interpretation of History* (1902) and a series of articles entitled "Shakaishugi hyōron" (A Critique of Socialism), which established his reputation as a social critic.

Disappointed in his political ambitions and disturbed by evidence of poverty and government neglect, in January 1906 Kawakami briefly entered a Buddhist religious sect known as Mugaen (Garden of Selflessness). He was subsequently moved by a mystical religious experience and became determined to devote himself selflessly to the common good. His economic research thereafter was guided by his attempt to reconcile the individualist ethos of capitalism with his newly established ethics of absolute selflessness. This effort eventually led him to embrace Marxism and to work for the Communist Party.

Following a brief career as editor of *Nihon keizai shinshi* (Japan Economics Journal), Kawakami joined the faculty of Kyōto University as a lecturer in economics. In 1913 he received a Ministry of Education fellowship for study in Europe. Although the outbreak of war interrupted his overseas stay, a firsthand encounter with poor people in England rekindled his interest in the problem of economic injustice and led him to write his most famous work, and one of the most famous of the time, *Bimbō monogatari* (Tale of Poverty). Serialized in the newspaper *Ōsaka asahi shimbun* in 1916 and published in book form in 1917, *Bimbō monogatari* was Kawakami's last major publication before his conversion to Marxism. His account of the existence of poverty in the industrialized nations of the West and his depiction of economics as a humanistic science helped to popularize the study of economics in Japan and attracted many students to his side in the 1920s. With the founding of his own journal, *Shakai mondai kenkyū* (Research in Social Problems), in 1919, Kawakami, now a full professor, determined to study Marxism.

Although he quickly became recognized as the leading Japanese authority on Marxist thought, Kawakami's persistent call for moral as well as institutional reform and his failure to view history in terms of dialectical materialism led critics to question his understanding of Marxism. A series of academic exchanges in the 1920s with two of his major critics, KUSHIDA TAMIZŌ, his former student, and FUKUMOTO KAZUO, leader of the newly reorganized Japan Communist Party, forced Kawakami to revise his interpretation of Marxism. Under pressure from Fukumoto, he also felt compelled to engage in revolutionary practices.

Political suppression of "dangerous thought" on campus eventually jeopardized Kawakami's academic position, and in 1928 he was forced to resign from the university. Afterward, he worked with ŌYAMA IKUO to reorganize the Labor-Farmer Party (RŌDŌ NŌMINTŌ) under the abbreviated name Rōnōtō. In 1930 he ran unsuccessfully for election to the Diet on the New Labor-Farmer Party (Shin Rōnōtō) ticket. Two years later, at the request of the Japan Communist Party, he translated the new Comintern *Theses,* published in the party organ *Akahata* (Red Flag). Now openly identified as a communist supporter, Kawakami became a target of the Home Ministry's efforts to suppress the communist movement. Accused of being a leader of the Communist Party in violation of the PEACE PRESERVATION LAW OF 1925, he was arrested in January 1933, several months after joining the party, found guilty, and sentenced to five years in prison, even though his lawyers argued that he had been merely a participant in the party—an offense liable to only two years' imprisonment. The sentence was eventually commuted to four years, and he was released in 1937.

Kawakami spent the remaining years of his life in seclusion, writing an autobiography that became a best-seller immediately after World War II. It reveals that he had not completely renounced his religious quest; rather, he viewed his reluctant participation in politics as the highest form of selflessness and called himself a "special Marxist."

■——Kawakami Hajime, *Kawakami Hajime chosakushū*, 12 vols (Chikuma Shobō, 1964–65). Kawakami Hajime, *Shakai mondai kenkyū*, 12 vols (1974–75). Amano Keitarō, *Kawakami Hajime hakase bunkenshi* (1956). Gail Lee Bernstein, *Japanese Marxist: A Portrait of Kawakami Hajime, 1879–1946* (1976). Furuta Hikaru, *Kawakami Hajime* (1959). Ōuchi Hyōe, *Kawakami Hajime* (1964). Suekawa Hiroshi, ed, *Kawakami Hajime kenkyū* (1965). Sumiya Etsuji, *Kawakami Hajime* (1962).   *Gail Lee* BERNSTEIN

Kawakami Jōtarō (1889–1965)

Politician. Born in Tōkyō; graduate of Tōkyō University. Influenced by KINOSHITA NAOE, he became interested in socialism. He was elected to the House of Representatives (1928) as a member of the prewar Nihon Rōnōtō (Japan Labor–Farmer Party). He participated in forming the postwar Japan Socialist Party (Nihon Shakaitō) but was barred from office under the OCCUPATION PURGE for having served in the IMPERIAL RULE ASSISTANCE ASSOCIATION (Taisei Yokusankai). As soon as he was depurged in 1951, he became chairman of the right wing *(uha)* of the Japan Socialist Party and resigned after both wings were reunited in 1955. After the assassination of ASANUMA INEJIRŌ in late 1960, he became chairman of the party, resigning in 1965 due to ill health.

Kawakami Otojirō (1864–1911)

Actor; theatrical entrepreneur; principal originator of the SHIMPA theatrical tradition. Born in Hakata (now in Fukuoka Prefecture), Kawakami moved with his family to Tōkyō, where he was—in succession—a novice Buddhist priest, disinterested college student, servant, policeman, and vagabond. He then joined the FREEDOM AND PEOPLE'S RIGHTS MOVEMENT (Jiyū Minken Undō) as a traveling agitator. This led to frequent arrests for his radical speechmaking. After a brief apprenticeship to a traditional storyteller, Kawakami became a humorous balladeer in YOSE (Japanese vaudeville theater). His talking song *Oppekepei bushi*, in which he ridiculed the new social and political elite, brought him national fame.

Inspired by Sudō Sadanori (1867–1907) who in 1888 had turned to staging crude dramas as a means to disguise his political speeches, Kawakami organized his fellow agitators into a theatrical troupe in 1891. This group barnstormed the country with contemporary political plays performed in a style that imitated KABUKI. In 1893 Kawakami traveled to Europe to study theater and switched to producing apolitical melodramas upon his return. His 1894 productions of the murder mystery *Igai* (Surprise) and its sequels established Kawakami as a leading theater reformer. During the Sino-Japanese War (1894–95), Kawakami dominated the entire Tōkyō theater season with his spectacular staging of patriotic plays set in the battle zones. Other box-office successes followed.

Kawakami ran for a seat in the Diet in 1898 but lost. Disappointed, he embarked on an adventurous tour of America and Europe with his wife Sadayakko (1872–1946) and a small troupe. Between 1899 and 1903, the Kawakami company made three tours abroad with a repertoire composed principally of kabuki adaptations. Although some Japanese observers disliked their interpretations, the company's work was held in highest regard by foreign critics and by such professionals as Henry Irving, Eleonora Duse, Hugo von Hofmannsthal, Vsevolod Meyerhold, and Loie Fuller.

Between 1903 and 1906, Kawakami staged and starred in Japan's first professional productions of Shakespearean and other European plays in translation. He gradually abandoned acting to concentrate on reforming the way in which plays were produced and theaters managed in Japan.

Kawakami Sadayakko was a popular Tōkyō *geisha*, a favorite of the political leader ITŌ HIROBUMI, when she married Otojirō in 1891. She accompanied her husband on his tours abroad, and when the troupe's two female impersonators died in Boston during the winter of 1899–1900, she took over all of the female leads. Although she had no formal training or previous experience as an actress, Sadayakko's performances in this and the two later tours were held by European observers to be equal to those of leading actresses of the day such as Sarah Bernhardt. Back in Japan, Sadayakko became the first female star of the new theatrical age, although most historians consider MATSUI SUMAKO Japan's first truly modern actress. Sadayakko and her husband were also pioneers in the formal training of actresses, and she was the founder of the children's theater movement in Japan.

■——Louis Fournier, *Kawakami and Sada Yacco* (1900). Yanagi Eijirō, *Shimpa no rokujūnen* (1948).   J. L. ANDERSON

Kawakami Sadayakko → Kawakami Otojirō

Kawakami Sōroku (1848–1899)

Army general. Born in the Satsuma domain (now Kagoshima Prefecture), the son of a *samurai*. Early in his career, he fought for the imperial side in the BOSHIN CIVIL WAR of 1868 and helped to quell the SATSUMA REBELLION of 1877 as commander of the 13th Regiment. Kawakami studied military science in Europe on two separate occasions, once with the German General Staff, then under Field Marshal Helmuth von Moltke. During the SINO-JAPANESE WAR OF 1894–1895, he served as the senior army staff officer at Imperial Headquarters (DAIHON'EI) and distinguished himself as a brilliant strategist.   KONDŌ Shinji

Kawakami Tetsutarō (1902–1980)

Critic. Born in the city of Nagasaki. Graduate of Tōkyō University in economics. A friend of the critic KOBAYASHI HIDEO, Kawakami wrote perceptive criticism on literature, music, and religion from a symbolist viewpoint and translated French literature and literary criticism. His critical essay, *Nihon no autosaidā* (1959), won the sixth Shinchōsha Prize. In 1961 he received the Japan Art Academy Award and the following year was made a member of the academy.

Kawakami Tōgai (1827–1881)

Literati painter; early scholar of Western painting (YŌGA). Born in Shinano Province (now Nagano Prefecture), he went to Edo (now Tōkyō) at age 15 and studied literati painting (BUNJINGA) with Ōnishi Chinnen (1792–1851). Between 1856 and 1868 Tōgai worked at the Bansho Shirabesho, the shogunate school for the study of European science and technology, studying and lecturing on Western painting. After the Meiji Restoration (1868), Tōgai was employed by the ministries of education and the army. He established a private art studio and school for the study of Western-style painting, the Chōkō Dokuga Kan, in the Okachimachi district of Tōkyō, where he instructed Koyama Shōtarō (1857–1916), Matsuoka Hisashi (1862–1943), TAKAHASHI YUICHI, and others who were to become early leading masters of *yōga*.

Kawamoto Kōmin (1810–1871)

Also known as Kawamoto Yukitami. Scholar of WESTERN LEARNING. Born in Settsu (now part of Hyōgo Prefecture), he studied medicine in Edo (now Tōkyō) and later opened a practice there. With the establishment in 1856 of the BANSHO SHIRABESHO, the shogunal school for Western studies, he was appointed as an instructor in physics and chemistry. At the same time, he advised SHIMAZU NARIAKIRA, the *daimyō* of the Satsuma domain (now Kagoshima Prefecture), on the manufacture of armaments, chemicals, and machinery. Apart from several treatises on chemistry, Kawamoto wrote the 15-volume *Kikai kanran kōgi* (1851–56, Observing the Waves in the Sea of Ether, Expanded), based on Johannes Buijs's *Natuurkundig Schoolboek* and *Volks-Natuurkunde*, in which he gave simple explanations of electricity, optics, thermal dynamics, and other subjects. He also experimented with photography, using methods similar to the daguerreotype.

Kawamura Zuiken (1617–1699)

Wealthy merchant of the early Edo period (1600–1868). Born to an impoverished family in the province of Ise (now Mie Prefecture), at the age of 12 Zuiken went to Edo (now Tōkyō), where with ingenious tact and foresight he worked his way up and established himself in the lumber business. In the rebuilding of Edo that followed the great MEIREKI FIRE of 1657, his business made enormous profits. In addition, Zuiken developed new water routes for transporting rice from northeastern Honshū to Edo and devised means of controlling the river Yodogawa in the Ōsaka region. In recognition of his contributions he was made a direct shogunal vassal (hatamoto).

Kawanabe Gyōsai (1831–1889)

Also known as Kawanabe Kyōsai. UKIYO-E artist and painter, sometimes called the second HOKUSAI. Real name Kawanabe Nobuyuki. Born to a samurai family in Koga, Shimōsa Province (now part of Ibaraki Prefecture), and brought up in Edo (now Tōkyō). At age 7 he entered the atelier of the ukiyo-e master UTAGAWA KUNIYOSHI and, from the age of 11, he studied with KANŌ SCHOOL artists, first Maemura Dōwa (d 1841) and later Kanō Dōhaku Chinshin (d 1851). From around 1858–59 he established himself as an independent artist in the Hongō section of Edo. Gyōsai was greatly influenced by his study of the history of Japanese and Chinese painting, including early ukiyo-e, and by the irreverent humorous sketches of the 12th-century monk-painter TOBA SŌJŌ. He was arrested and imprisoned for several months in 1869 for caricatures politically offensive to the newly established Meiji government. His independence and powerful artistic style, together with a tremendous productivity, made him one of the most popular figures of his day. He participated in the Vienna Exposition of 1873 and the Paris Exposition of 1878. Among his many pupils was the English architect Josiah CONDER. Gyōsai's extant prints and paintings are numerous. Among his illustrated books are the Gyōsai gadan (1887), Kyōsai gafu (1860), and the Gyōsai manga shinseki (date unknown). *Aya Louisa McDONALD*

Kawanakajima, Battles of

(Kawanakajima no Tatakai). A series of inconclusive engagements fought between the armies of two of the most prominent daimyō of the Sengoku period (1467–1568), UESUGI KENSHIN of Echigo Province (now Niigata Prefecture) and TAKEDA SHINGEN of Kai Province (now Yamanashi Prefecture), in the same locale between the rivers Chikumagawa and Saikawa in northern Shinano Province (now Nagano Prefecture). The conflict between the two was instigated by Shingen's advance into that strategic area, which put him on the borders of Kenshin's domain; and Kenshin initially took the field in 1553 in response to urgent pleas for assistance from Ogasawara Nagatoki (1514–83) and Murakami Yoshikiyo (d 1573), petty barons of northern Shinano whom Shingen had conquered. The exact number of clashes has been the subject of considerable debate. The current consensus is that there were five: in 1553, 1555, 1557, 1561, and 1564. Only the second and fourth were substantial battles; the fifth, in particular, amounted to nothing more than a sally on the part of Kenshin's forces. The fame of these combats is attributable less to their influence on the course of events, which was small, than to the imagination and rhetoric of Edo-period (1600–1868) compilers of chronicles and treatises on "military science," beginning with the KŌYŌ GUNKAN (ca 1625), a diffuse paean on the exploits of the house of Takeda. In these accounts, which influenced popular literature, the ruthless warlords Kenshin and Shingen are romanticized as chivalrous heroes, and the Battles of Kawanakajima are transformed from haphazard frays into epic encounters. *George ELISON*

Kawanishi

City in southeast Hyōgo Prefecture, western Honshū. Situated on the river Inagawa, Kawanishi developed as a land and river transportation center. Local products utilizing the clean river water are leather goods and yūzen-zome (a dyed cloth). Modern industries include precision machinery. Kawanishi is now a rapidly growing suburb of Ōsaka. Pop: 129,834.

Kawanoe

City in eastern Ehime Prefecture, Shikoku, on the Hiuchi Sea. The focal point of land and sea transportation since ancient times, a com-

missioner's office (bugyōsho) of the Tokugawa shogunate was established here in the Edo period (1600–1868) to oversee the Besshi Copper Mine and the highway Tosa Kaidō. Its paper industry is said to have been developed during the 18th century, and together with neighboring Iyo Mishima, is second only to that of Fuji in Shizuoka Prefecture. Pop: 37,213.

kawaraban

Commercial newssheets of the Edo period (1600–1868). It is thought that the name kawaraban ("roof-tile print") derives from the fact that engraved roofing tiles were once used as printing plates; early on, however, the tiles were replaced by woodblocks. The oldest extant kawaraban dates from 1615 and was printed in Kyōto to inform the populace of TOKUGAWA IEYASU's great military victory at Ōsaka over the forces of TOYOTOMI HIDEYORI. The earliest presses were clandestine operations producing crude newssheets 24.1 by 12.7 centimeters (9.5 by 5 in) in size and written in a burlesque and doggerel style. Later, large bookstores, which customarily doubled as printshops, published single or occasionally multiple newssheets of a similar size reporting ribald gossip from the bordello districts and the double suicides of courtesans and their lovers. When the shogunate forbade such reportage, they chronicled recent calamities and vendettas or accounts of praiseworthy deeds. When a tidal wave swept across the main highway (TŌKAIDŌ) connecting Kyōto with Edo (now Tōkyō) in 1854, and an earthquake and fire devastated Edo in 1855, a multitude of newssheets sprang forth to report the tragic details. In the last years before the collapse of the shogunal regime, articles dealing with the political situation began to appear. The newssheets were sold in the streets by hawkers who read out selected passages to attract buyers, giving rise to the alternate appellation yomiuri or "sell by reading" (now the name of a leading newspaper). Kawaraban flourished until the introduction of Western-style daily newspapers early in the Meiji period (1868–1912). *David DUTCHER*

Kawaradera remains

Site of Kawaradera (also known as Gufukuji), an important temple in the ancient capital FUJIWARAKYŌ; located in the village of Asuka, Nara Prefecture. The year of construction is not clear, though the Fusō ryakki, a 12th-century history, states that the temple was built in 655. A palace called Kawara no Miya is thought to have existed in the same area, and both are believed to have been closely connected with Emperor TENJI. The Kawaradera was prominent throughout the Nara period (710–794) but began to decline after it was designated a subtemple of the TŌJI in the 9th century. Excavations of the site in 1957 and 1958 revealed the plan of the original temple compound: the great south gate and middle gate, the west main hall pagoda, an enclosing corridor, the middle main hall, the lecture hall, and the east and west priests' quarters. See also BUDDHIST ARCHITECTURE. *KITAMURA Bunji*

kawaramono

("dry riverbed people"). A term used during the premodern age for members of the lowest stratum of Japanese society. They traditionally lived along kawara (dry riverbeds) and often performed the most menial tasks, such as sweeping roads and collecting night soil. Some worked as gravediggers, wigmakers, tanners, and comb makers—all occupations that involved contact with corpses and carcasses. Hence, kawaramono as a whole were stigmatized according to customary religious beliefs as unclean and unfit to mingle with the rest of society.

Among the kawaramono, there was a variety of entertainers—singers, dancers, musicians, acrobats, puppeteers—who performed on the dry riverbed, a place where the government did not demand a share of their receipts or require official permission to set up facilities for public viewing. Consequently, prior to the Edo period (1600–1868), these free, unrestricted areas gradually developed large entertainment centers: the Shijō-Gawara ("Fourth Street Dry Riverbed") district on the river Kamogawa in Kyōto, later known for its kabuki theaters, is the most familiar example.

The close identification of kabuki actors with kawaramono remained strongly fixed in the public mind throughout the Edo period. Moreover, the shogunate, which regarded the kabuki theater as a necessary evil, considered these actors as undesirables and closely supervised their food, clothing, residence, travel, and social activi-

Kawasaki

A large petrochemical complex in Kawasaki.

ties. This discriminatory policy continued until the Meiji Restoration (1868). Another term, *kawara kojiki* ("dry riverbed beggars"), equally derogatory, was also applied to kabuki actors during the same period.

📖——Hayashiya Tatsusaburō, *Chūsei geinō shi no kenkyū* (1960). Hayashiya Tatsusaburō, *Kabuki izen* (1954).

Ted T. TAKAYA

kawara nadeshiko → fringed pink

Kawasaki

City in northeastern Kanagawa Prefecture, central Honshū; separated from Tōkyō by the river Tamagawa. The center of the KEIHIN INDUSTRIAL ZONE. During the Edo period (1600–1868), it developed as a post-station town and as a temple town of the KAWASAKI DAISHI. Industrialization of the city started in 1907 with the construction of factories on the banks of the Tamagawa. From 1913, a coastal industrial district was created on land reclaimed from Tōkyō Bay. After World War II, petrochemical and other industrial complexes were established in the city. Today, oil and coal products, electrical machinery and appliances, steel, cars, cement, chemicals, and flour are produced. The port of Kawasaki is one of the largest ports in Japan, importing oil, iron ore, coal, and foodstuffs. Located between Tōkyō and Yokohama, the city is also a center for land transportation. The city has developed into a dormitory suburb of the cities of Tōkyō and Yokohama. Tourist attractions are the temple Heigenji, popularly known as Kawasaki Daishi, Mukōgaoka Amusement Park, and Inadazutsumi, an area on the banks of the Tamagawa famous for its cherry blossoms. Pop: 1,040,698.

Kawasaki Chōtarō (1901–)

Novelist. Born in Kanagawa Prefecture. In the early 1920s he associated with anarchist poets and participated in the founding of the anarchist poetry magazine *Aka to kuro* in 1923, although he soon turned away from the anarchist movement as a result of the political oppression after the TŌKYŌ EARTHQUAKE OF 1923. He began writing semiautobiographical novels and short stories, attracting the attention of KIKUCHI KAN and other established writers. After World War II he achieved prominence as a result of his sentimental short stories depicting the love affair of an old man and a prostitute. His works include the novel *Michikusa* (1934) and the short stories "Makkō Chō" (1950) and "Hōsenka" (1952).

Kawasaki Daishi

Formally Heigenji. Popular temple in the city of Kawasaki, Kanagawa Prefecture, belonging to the Chizan branch (see CHISHAKUIN) of the SHINGON SECT of Buddhism. According to tradition, Heigenji was built in 1127 by an exiled warrior, Hirama Kanenori, who recovered from the sea a wooden image of KŪKAI (popularly known as Kōbō Daishi; 774–835), the founder of the Shingon sect. (The Heigen of the temple's name is an alternate pronunciation of the Chinese characters for the name Hirama.) The image, which is housed in the temple, is thought to help worshipers in warding off evils (*yakuyoke*). The Kawasaki Daishi was completely destroyed in an air raid in 1945 but is now largely restored. Because of its proximity to Yokohama and Tōkyō, the temple draws great numbers of visitors during the three-day New Year's holiday, usually far more than the number of New Year's visitors to other major temples or shrines in Japan. Festivals attracting large numbers of devotees are held on the 21st day of January, March, May, and September.

Stanley WEINSTEIN

Kawasaki disease

(*kawasakibyō*; acute febrile mucocutaneus-lymph-node-syndrome; MCLS). Acute disease with fever and exanthema which mainly attacks infants (male:female = 1.5:1) under four years old; named after Kawasaki Tomisaku, who reported the syndrome in 1967. It should not be confused with the so-called Kawasaki asthma caused by air pollution in the city of Kawasaki (see POLLUTION-RELATED DISEASES). The disease is characterized by six main symptoms: (1) high fever that lasts for more than five days; (2) hyperemia of both conjunctiva bulbi; (3) redness, dryness, and bleeding of the lips; (4) swelling of neck lymph nodes; (5) exanthema of the body; and (6) redness of palms and soles and desquamation membranosa from the tops of the fingers and toes after swelling of the hands and feet. Patients sometimes suffer continuously from aneurysma of the coronary artery and obliteration by thrombosis as sequelae, and some of them may die suddenly from thrombosis of the coronary artery. According to a national survey in January 1977, 11,980 persons in Japan were reported as having been affected. Although its cause has not yet been discovered, aspirin therapy is recognized as being effective.

Nose Takayuki

Kawasaki Heavy Industries, Ltd

(Kawasaki Jūkōgyō). Major manufacturer of ships, industrial machinery, engines, aircraft, motorcycles, rolling stock, and industrial plants. An important member of the Kawasaki group. Its forerunner was the Kawasaki Tsukiji Shipyard, established in 1878 in Tōkyō by Kawasaki Shōzō. Kawasaki also opened the Kawasaki Hyōgo Shipyard in Kōbe in 1886, and in 1896 the two were merged to form the Kawasaki Shipyard Co. The company took its present name in 1939. With the boom in war industries and shipbuilding during World War I, the company expanded quickly and branched out into the manufacture of steel plates, machinery, marine transport equipment, aircraft, and land-based steel structures. In 1919 KAWASAKI KISEN KAISHA, LTD, became independent of its parent company, followed by Kawasaki Car Mfg Co, Ltd, in 1928, the Kawasaki Aircraft Co, Ltd, in 1937, and the KAWASAKI STEEL CORPORATION in 1950.

The company developed original technologies through the construction of large-size tankers and liquefied natural gas (LNG) carriers. In 1969 it absorbed Kawasaki Car Mfg Co and Kawasaki Aircraft Co to recover its former position as a comprehensive heavy manufacturer producing rolling stock, aircraft, and machinery. In the 1970s it placed heavy emphasis on the development of overseas markets for plant exports. Kawasaki-brand motorcycles, produced through technology acquired from the manufacture of ship engines, are exported in great volume. Kawasaki has 10 overseas subsidiaries and 9 offices in the Philippines, Brazil, the United States, and elsewhere. Sales for the fiscal year ending March 1982 totaled ¥764.4 billion (US $3.2 billion), ranking third among heavy manufacturers, after MITSUBISHI HEAVY INDUSTRIES, LTD, and ISHIKAWAJIMA-HARIMA HEAVY INDUSTRIES CO, LTD. Of the total sales, ships accounted for 21 percent, machinery 16 percent, industrial plants 29 percent, engines 19 percent, aircraft 7 percent, and rolling stock 8 percent. The export ratio was 57 percent in 1978. Sales declined in the three years before 1980 because of the recession in the shipbuilding industry. The company was capitalized at ¥66.1 billion (US $274.6 million) in 1982. Corporate headquarters are located in Kōbe.

Kawasaki Kisen Kaisha, Ltd

Leading Japanese ocean freight carrier. Its ships operate abroad under the name K Line. It is affiliated with both KAWASAKI HEAVY INDUSTRIES, LTD, and KAWASAKI STEEL CORPORATION. Established in 1919 when it was separated from Kawasaki Shipbuilding Co (forerunner of Kawasaki Heavy Industries), the firm offers comprehensive ocean freight service, including container ships, specialty ships, and tankers, in addition to conventional freighters, on regular and tramp routes. Scheduled ships operate on 8 container routes and 10 conventional routes covering all parts of the world. Tramp ships and tankers also carry freight worldwide. The firm owns 59 ships totaling 3.5 million deadweight tons and operates approximately 140 others for an aggregate of 10 million deadweight tons. Sales for the fiscal year ending March 1982 were ¥381.9 billion (US $1.6 billion) and capitalization was ¥22.4 billion (US $93 million). The corporate headquarters are located in Tōkyō.

Kawasaki Natsu (1889–1966)

Feminist and educator. Born in Nara. A graduate of Tōkyō Women's Higher Normal School (now Ochanomizu University), she taught writing there and at other leading women's schools, including Tōkyō Women's Christian College and Tsuda College, where she encouraged the students' political interests. In 1921 she joined with the poet YOSANO AKIKO and others to found the coeducational Bunka Gakuin (Culture Academy) for training in creative arts. From 1921 to 1934, she wrote an influential advice column for the newspaper *Yomiuri shimbun*. She also participated in major prewar women's movement groups such as the SHIN FUJIN KYŌKAI and the FUSEN KAKUTOKU DŌMEI, working with the feminists HIRATSUKA RAICHŌ and ICHIKAWA FUSAE. She even secretly helped leftists such as the labor activist TATEWAKI SADAYO and the writer MIYAMOTO YURIKO. During World War II she was appointed to several committees concerned with welfare and women's problems, in the government's effort to gain the cooperation of prominent women. After the war, in 1947, she was elected to the House of Councillors and helped organize peace-movement and social-reform activities, especially the Nihon Fujin Dantai Rengōkai (Japan Federation of Women's Groups) in 1953, and the annual Mothers' Conferences (Hahaoya Taikai), which began in Japan in 1955.

Kawasaki Steel Corporation

(Kawasaki Seitetsu). A leading steelmaker. Its volume of production ranks among the top five Japanese steelmakers. Its forerunner was the steel mill established in 1906 in Kōbe by Kawasaki Shipbuilding Co (currently KAWASAKI HEAVY INDUSTRIES, LTD, a separate company). The corporation became independent of Kawasaki Heavy Industries as a result of the enterprise reconstruction and reorganization law in 1950. It is a leading member of the Kawasaki group.

In 1951 the corporation constructed an ultramodern integrated-process steel mill in the city of Chiba with technology imported from overseas. With an annual production of 500,000 metric tons (about 551,000 short tons) of blister steel, the mill started operating in 1953 and the corporation expanded from a medium-sized steel material and special steel manufacturer to a giant steel producer. Later, a larger steel mill was constructed in Mizushima (Okayama Prefecture) and began operations in 1973. As a result, the corporation's annual production of blister steel rose to 12 million metric tons (13.2 million short tons). It currently has overseas offices in New York, Houston, Los Angeles, London, Düsseldorf, Bangkok, Singapore, Manila, Caracas, Rio de Janero, Saō Paulo, and Victoria. In the Philippines it also jointly operates a sintering plant and a limestone mine. In Brazil the corporation is involved in mining iron ore and is providing capital and expertise in the construction of the Tubaron steel mill. Sales for the fiscal year ending March 1982 totaled ¥1.3 trillion (US $5.4 billion), of which plates and sheets constituted 55 percent; pipes 20 percent; rods, bars, and shapes 9 percent; and other products 16 percent. The export ratio was 44 percent and the corporation was capitalized at ¥134.4 billion (US $558.3 million) in the same year. Corporate headquarters are in Kōbe.

kawase kaisha

(exchange companies). Financial institutions—forerunners of modern Japanese banks—established in 1869 under the auspices of the Meiji government as part of its program to promote foreign trade. Together with the TSŪSHŌ KAISHA (commercial companies), whose operations they were meant to finance, the *kawase kaisha* were set up under the direction of government commercial offices (*tsūshōshi*) in eight cities: Tōkyō, Ōsaka, Kyōto, Yokohama, Kōbe, Niigata, Ōtsu, and Tsuruga. The government drafted rich merchant houses (see SEISHŌ) such as MITSUI and ONO-GUMI to participate in the

kawase kaisha, advanced the companies large sums of money, and guaranteed their loans to the *tsūshō kaisha*. Besides lending money these firms engaged in such activities as banknote issue and currency exchange. With the passage of the National Bank Ordinance in 1872 (see NATIONAL BANKS), the Yokohama Kawase Kaisha became the Second National Bank (Daini Kokuritsu Ginkō), and the other *kawase kaisha* were dissolved.　　　　TANAKA Akira

Kawashima Takeyoshi (1909–　　)

Legal scholar; specialist in the CIVIL CODE and the sociology of law. Born in Gifu Prefecture. A 1932 graduate of Tōkyō University, where he studied the Civil Code under WAGATSUMA SAKAE, Kawashima joined its faculty in 1934 and became a full professor in 1945. He served as chairman of the Japan Private Law Association (Nihon Shihō Gakkai) and as a member of the Legislative Council of the Ministry of Justice (Hōsei Shingikai). Since his retirement from Tōkyō University, he has practiced as an attorney.

Kawashima's 1949 work *Shoyūken hō no riron* (Theory of the Law of Ownership) greatly influenced post–World War II legal education. He has also been a leader in the postwar development of the relatively new field of legal sociology, being noted especially for his study *Nihon shakai no kazokuteki kōsei* (1948, The Familial Structure of Japanese Society). Other works include *Iriaiken no kaitai* (1958–68, Anatomy of the Right of Commonage) and *Nihonjin no hōishiki* (1966, The Legal Consciousness of the Japanese). The publication under Kawashima's editorship of the 10-volume *Hōshakaigaku kōza* (1972–73, Lectures in Legal Sociology) raised the level of research in that field to new heights.　　　　ISHIMURA Zensuke

Kawashō Corporation

(Kawatetsu Shōji). Trading firm specializing in iron and steel manufactured goods. Its sales volume for these products is the largest in the domestic market. Directly affiliated with KAWASAKI STEEL CORPORATION, it was founded in 1954 when the trading department of the parent firm was made independent. In addition to iron and steel products, the company handles the domestic sale as well as the export and import of iron ore, coke, and other raw materials. Together with the parent firm, Kawashō mines dolomite in the Philippines and participates in an iron ore mining project in Brazil. The firm also has subsidiary companies in Thailand and Singapore, which manufacture and sell iron and steel products. In Hong Kong, West Germany, Canada, and the United States there are affiliated corporations handling export and import operations. In recent years Kawashō has diversified into such fields as lumber, chemicals, coal, and machinery. Sales for the fiscal year ending September 1981 totaled ¥1.069 trillion (US $4.65 billion) and capitalization stood at ¥3.8 billion (US $16.8 million). The corporate headquarters are located in Ōsaka.

Kawatake Mokuami → Mokuami

kawauso

(otter). *Lutra lutra whiteleyi*. The *kawauso* is a subspecies of the common Eurasian otter, of the family Mustelidae. It is small in size, with a head and body length of about 70 centimeters (28 in) and a tail of about 45 centimeters (18 in). Until about 50 years ago *kawauso* were common in rivers, streams, swamps, and lakes throughout Hokkaidō, Honshū, Shikoku, and Kyūshū, but reckless hunting and contamination of rivers and streams are thought to have exterminated them in freshwater areas by about 1950. At present a limited number of individuals inhabit the coast of southwestern Shikoku, where they make nests in seaside rocks and catch fish and crabs in the sea. The *kawauso* is now designated as a protected species, but protective measures have shown little success.

IMAIZUMI Yoshiharu

Kawazu, Seven Falls of

(Kawazu Nanadaru). Located on the upper reaches of the river Kawazugawa, Izu Peninsula, Shizuoka Prefecture, central Honshū. All seven falls are located within 2 km (1.2 mi) of each other south of Amagi Pass. The biggest waterfall is Ōdaru Falls, with a height of 27 m (89 ft) and a width of 7 m (23 ft).

Kaya

A region of southern Korea where some tribes formed a league named Kaya in the 4th or 5th century. Many Japanese scholars refer to the area as Mimana and claim it was controlled by Japan in the Yamato period (ca 300–710). A wedge of land between the ancient Korean kingdoms of SILLA and PAEKCHE, it was conquered by Silla in two stages in 532 and 562. See also KOREA AND JAPAN: premodern relations.　　　　　　　　　　　　C. Kenneth QUINONES

Kayaba Industry Co, Ltd

(Kayaba Kōgyō). Japan's largest manufacturer of shock absorbers and hydraulic equipment. Its brand name is KYB. Established in 1935, the company supplies products and services utilizing hydraulic technology for the machinery of the automobile, motorcycle, special-purpose vehicle, construction, agricultural, industrial vehicle, aircraft, and shipbuilding industries. It has a sales subsidiary in the United States, as well as production bases for shock absorbers in four countries. Sales for the fiscal year ending March 1982 totaled ¥101 billion (US $419.6 million), and it was capitalized at ¥6.9 billion (US $28.7 million). The head office is in Tōkyō.

kayari

Smoke to drive away insects such as mosquitoes and gnats. The word kayari appears in the Wamyō ruiju shō (931–937), Japan's first encyclopedia. At first branches of the kaya (Japanese nutmeg tree) or sawdust mixed with sulphur were burned to create smoke. Mugwort (yomogi) was used by farming families. In the latter half of the 19th century, pyrethrum (jochūgiku), a kind of chrysanthemum, was cultivated, ground into a powder, and burned to ward off insects. This powder was eventually pressed into a spiral form called katori senkō, and in this form remains in wide use today. The word kayari is frequently used in haiku as a seasonal term denoting summer.　　　　　　　　　　　　MIYAMOTO Mizuo

Kaya Seiji (1898–　　)

Physicist who explored the properties of ferromagnetic crystals. Born in Kanagawa Prefecture, he graduated from Tōhoku University in 1923. Kaya became a professor at Tōkyō University in 1943 after teaching at Hokkaidō University for 13 years. After World War II he played a key role in the founding of the SCIENCE COUNCIL OF JAPAN (Nihon Gakujutsu Kaigi) for the purpose of restructuring Japan's educational and research systems. He served as president of Tōkyō University from 1957 to 1963 and received the Order of Culture in 1964.

Kaya Shirao (1738–1791)

HAIKU poet of the late 18th century. Born in Shinano Province (now Nagano Prefecture), he was active in the effort to bring BASHŌ's haiku back into favor, and his influence extended from the Kantō region to the provinces of northern and western Japan. In his essay Kazarinashi (1771, Without Artifice), he rejected subjectivism and technical artifice in haiku in favor of direct, natural expression. His uncompromising devotion to his art inspired a host of bright young disciples who became leading poets of the next generation.

Kazan, Emperor (968–1008)

The 65th sovereign (tennō) in the traditional count (which includes several nonhistorical emperors); reigned 984–986. Eldest son of Emperor Reizei (950–1011; r 967–969); his mother was a daughter of Fujiwara no Koretada (924–972) who served as regent to his successor. During Kazan's reign, his maternal relatives Fujiwara no Yoshichika (956–1008; son of Koretada) and Koreshige (953–989) enjoyed great influence, incurring the wrath of the main line of the Fujiwara family. Consequently, when Kazan became despondent over the death of his favorite consort, FUJIWARA NO KANEIE had his son Michikane persuade him to abdicate and installed Emperor ICHIJŌ (Kaneie's grandson) on the throne, thus paving the way for total control of the succession by the Fujiwara regents (see REGENCY GOVERNMENT). Kazan retired to the temple Kazanji and became a Buddhist priest.　　　　　　　　　　G. Cameron HURST III

Kazo

City in northeastern Saitama Prefecture, central Honshū, on the river Furu Tonegawa. A market town in the Edo period (1600–1868), Kazo has long been known for its cotton textiles. Its special products include carp streamers (koinobori) for CHILDREN'S DAY and JŪDŌ wear. Pop: 47,590.

kazoku → peerage

kazoku kokka

("family-state"). A term likening the national structure of Japan to that of an extended family with the EMPEROR as its head and his subjects as his children. It was used from the Meiji period (1868–1912) through World War II to justify the absolute authority of the emperor.

Kazuno

City in northeastern Akita Prefecture, northern Honshū, on the river Yoneshirogawa. In addition to farming and commerce, copper mining at the Osarizawa Mine is an important occupation. A part of Towada–Hachimantai National Park, the city has several hot springs and a Jōmon-period (ca 10,000 BC–ca 300 BC) site consisting of stone circles (see ŌYU STONE CIRCLES). Pop: 45,627.

Kazu, Princess (1846–1877)

(Kazu no Miya). Sister of Emperor Kōmei (r 1846–67) and wife of the 14th Tokugawa shōgun, Iemochi. She was the object of a political marriage arranged by the senior councillors (rōjū) ANDŌ NOBUMASA and KUZE HIROCHIKA as part of the attempt to bolster the shogunate's tottering prestige by more closely associating it with the imperial court in Kyōto (see MOVEMENT FOR UNION OF COURT AND SHOGUNATE). The marriage (which took place in March 1862) was pushed through although Princess Kazu was already betrothed to an imperial prince, ARISUGAWA NO MIYA TARUHITO, but it did not have the desired effect. Rather, antishogunate radicals were so enraged by the event that a group attempted to assassinate Nobumasa (see SAKASHITAMON INCIDENT).

When Iemochi died in 1866 Princess Kazu remained in Edo (now Tōkyō) and became a Buddhist nun. When the Tokugawa shogunate was overthrown by imperial forces in 1867–68 (see MEIJI RESTORATION) she pleaded before the new government for lenient treatment of the Tokugawa family.

kebiishi

(imperial police). An extrastatutory office (RYŌGE NO KAN) established by Emperor SAGA (r 809–823) to maintain order in the capital. The word kebiishi refers to the individual officials and by extension to the force they constituted. Like another extrastatutory institution, the KURŌDO-DOKORO (Bureau of Archivists), the kebiishi were set up by Saga to forestall attempts, such as the KUSUKO INCIDENT, to usurp the throne. Their highest rank was bettō, to which one person was appointed. Other ranks included suke, jō, and sakan, the number of whom varied over time. These officials gradually assumed wide-ranging powers to arrest, try, and punish offenders, not only in Kyōto but in the provinces as well, taking over many of the functions of the Board of Censors (Danjōdai), the Ministry of Punishments (Gyōbushō), and the Office of Municipal Affairs (Kyōshiki). After the establishment of the Muromachi shogunate (1338–1573), the functions of the kebiishi were absorbed by the head of the Samurai-dokoro or Board of Retainers.

Keenan, Joseph Berry (1888–1954)

American chief counsel for the Allied prosecution in the WAR CRIMES TRIALS of Japanese wartime leaders in Tōkyō. Born in Pawtucket, Rhode Island, he graduated from Brown University in 1910 and from Harvard Law School in 1913. He served with the US armed forces in France during World War I, practiced law in Ohio, and entered the US Justice Department in 1933, where he won a reputation as a "gang-busting" attorney. He was appointed chief prosecutor for the Tōkyō trials in 1945. He was the author, with Brendan F. Brown, of *Crimes against International Law* (1950).

Richard B. Finn

kegare

(ritual impurity or defilement). The concepts of clean and unclean, pure and impure, have been of cultural and social significance in Japan from ancient times up to the present. One special characteristic of the concept of *kegare* held by the Japanese in ancient times was its close ties to the concept of TSUMI (sin or crime). Thus good was understood as pure and clean, while evil implied something dirty which defiled or contaminated the good. Consequently, the two concepts were fused in the compound word *tsumi-kegare*, inclusive of all that was abhorred by the Shintō deities (KAMI). Another characteristic of things considered sinful and unclean is that they can be passed from one person to another through direct contact. Hence, persons thought to have been contaminated were required to undergo purification (MISOGI) or to separate themselves from everyday life for a set period of time. Through such actions it was believed that individuals could be released from their state of contamination and restored to their original state of purity.

Among Japanese myths, the story of the visit of Izanagi no Mikoto to the land of the dead is the prototype for this process. Izanagi, overcome by longing for his deceased wife Izanami no Mikoto, goes to visit her in the land of the dead. After his meeting with Izanami, who is defiled by death, the *kegare* most abhorred by the ancient Japanese, it is necessary for Izanagi to undergo purification by lustration. See IZANAGI AND IZANAMI.

Various types of *kegare* are enumerated in such Shintō writings as the NORITO and ENGI SHIKI, and the prescriptions for purification are also set forth. These form the basis of the notion of *kegare*, which can be divided into several categories. The first category of *kegare* includes things unclean from a sanitary viewpoint, e.g., human excrement, garbage, decomposing matter, stagnant water, and so on. The second category involves human blood. It covers a wide range of possibilities from causing bloodshed or incurring wounds to bleeding at childbirth and menstruation. The third category involves everything related to death. This is inclusive not only of human death but also the death of animals. Killing or wounding birds and beasts and cooking them for food also comprise *kegare*. Fourth, subjection to all sorts of natural disasters was also considered a form of *kegare*. This category is inclusive of events wherein human beings and other creatures suffer injury due to natural calamities: human beings being bitten by insects or snakes, domestic animals being attacked by wild beasts, or crops being ravaged by harmful insects. Fifth are all actions which serve to disturb life in human society. In the *norito* are enumerated various crimes against agriculture, such as destroying the paths along the ridges between rice fields, obstructing the water for irrigation, and disturbing other people's fields. In later ages, looting, embezzlement and misappropriation, robbery, fire and arson, and the like also came to be regarded as *kegare*. In the area of sexual acts, incest and bestiality were treated as *kegare* but other sex acts were not.

The concept of *kegare* detailed above is believed to have been established during the period from ancient times to the Heian period (794–1185). Examples, especially *kegare* involving death and blood, abound in the literary works, diaries, and other writings of the Heian aristocracy. However, opinions are divided as to whether this notion of *kegare* was diffused among all social strata in ancient times. All that can be said with certainty is that, according to various documentary records, at the very least the people of the upper class in ancient times were extraordinarily sensitive to these sorts of *kegare*.

For ancient as well as modern Japanese, the phenomena surrounding death and blood lie at the heart of *kegare*. If someone in the family should die, it was required that the survivors wear mourning for a set period of time. In ancient times, at the death of an emperor, close relatives and retainers wore mourning for several years. The period of mourning among the common people in modern times is much briefer, in most cases 49 days, a figure said to be derived from the influence of Buddhism. During this period of mourning the individual must refrain from participating in relations with the Shintō deities, e.g., visiting shrines. In modern times it has been Buddhism that has had the function of purifying people of the *kegare* of death and of setting to rest the spirits of the dead.

The *kegare* concerning blood was largely connected with women. Above all, the occasions of childbirth and menstruation were considered to be in a state of *kegare* and ranked with death in being most abhorred by the Shintō deities. It was not at all rare for

Kegon Falls

the very presence of women to be considered *kegare* from the standpoint of some ritual observances.

Hoshino Eiki

Kegon Falls

(Kegon no Taki). Located in northwestern Tochigi Prefecture, central Honshū, on the river Daiyagawa, which has its source in Lake Chūzenji. This is Japan's most famous and most frequently visited waterfall. An elevator takes visitors to the bottom of the gorge for a spectacular view of the descending water. Part of Nikkō National Park. Height: 97 m (318 ft).

Kegon sect

One of the schools that flourished in the early centuries of Japanese Buddhist history and one of the six sects of NARA BUDDHISM, the Kegon (Ch: Huayan or Hua-yen) school was introduced from China first by the Chinese monk Daoxuan (Tao-hsüan; J: DŌSEN, 702–760) and then by the Korean monk known in Japan as Shinjō (d 742). ROBEN, a priest of the temple TŌDAIJI in Nara, was an early expert on the school's basic scripture, the *Kegonkyō* (Skt: *Avataṃsakasūtra*); the monk-scholars GYŌNEN of Tōdaiji and Kōben (MYŌE) of KŌZANJI in Kyōto were considered the highest authorities during the Kamakura period (1185–1333). Although the school later fell into inactivity, there have been a number of outstanding scholars of the sutra—which is germane to various Japanese Buddhist doctrines—including the monk Sōshun (also known as Hōtan; 1659–1738). Today, Tōdaiji in Nara is the central temple of this small sect, with 47 other temples.

Tsuchida Tomoaki

Kehi Shrine

(Kehi Jingū). Shintō shrine in the city of Tsuruga, Fukui Prefecture, dedicated to Izasawake no Mikoto and six other deities. According to tradition, Izasawake was worshiped by Homudawake no Mikoto (the personal name of Emperor ŌJIN; late 4th to early 5th century) on the instruction of his mother, the empress JINGŪ, during a visit to this area after her successful campaign in Korea. The Kehi Jingū soon became the largest shrine in the region and beginning with an imperial offering in 691 was the frequent recipient of gifts from the court. It also enjoyed particular patronage from warrior families. The shrine, which is noted for its huge four-legged gateway *(torii)* built in 1645, has its annual festival on 4 September.

Stanley Weinstein

Keian Genju (1427–1508)

Zen priest of the RINZAI SECT, one of those responsible for the spread of Zhu Xi (Chu Hsi) Neo-Confucian learning (SHUSHIGAKU) in the regional domains of late medieval Japan. Born in Nagato Province (now part of Yamaguchi Prefecture). Genju came in contact with Neo-Confucianism in the course of his early training in Kyōto in the great Rinzai monasteries known as the GOZAN. He went to China as a member of the 1465 embassy headed by Ten'yo Seikei, the abbot of KENNINJI (one of the Gozan). After that mission's return in 1469, Genju remained behind to deepen his knowledge of the Confucian classics. When Genju came back to Japan in 1473, the country was in the throes of the ŌNIN WAR, and he could not proceed to Kyōto; accordingly, he sought refuge with several lords in Kyūshū, to whom he preached Buddhism and taught Neo-Confucianism. His most prominent patron was Shimazu Tadamasa (d 1508) of Satsuma (now part of Kagoshima Prefecture), who endowed a temple for him. The lineage of Zhu Xi Neo-Confucian studies established by Genju is known as the Satsunan school, after Satsuma Province.

Keian Incident

(Keian Jiken). An unsuccessful coup d'etat against the Tokugawa shogunate in 1651 (Keian 4); also known as the Yui Shōsetsu Disturbance after the name of its leader, who headed a group of masterless samurai (rōnin). The number of rōnin in the shogunal capital of Edo (now Tōkyō) had increased during the rule of TOKUGAWA IEMITSU, who had dispossessed many daimyō, depriving their samurai of sustenance. YUI SHŌSETSU, a teacher of "military science," apparently attracted some of these drifters by promising to find them employment with Tokugawa Yorinobu (1602–71), the lord of Kii Province (now Wakayama Prefecture). Iemitsu's death and the accession of the 10-year-old TOKUGAWA IETSUNA as shōgun in 1651 were deemed opportune by the plotters, who intended to create a crisis by blowing up the shogunate's arsenal and setting fire to Edo. Shōsetsu, accompanied by a band of 10, planned at the same time to burn SUMPU (now the city of Shizuoka) and occupy the shogunate's sacred shrine at Kunōzan, outside that town. The putsch was discovered before any of these actions could be undertaken, possibly because of an indiscretion on the part of Shōsetsu's lieutenant, MARUBASHI CHŪYA. Informers reported the cabal to the shogunal senior councillor (rōjū) MATSUDAIRA NOBUTSUNA, Chūya and his group were captured and executed in Edo, and Shōsetsu committed suicide in Sumpu. He left behind a note disclaiming the intention to overthrow the shogunate and insisting that he intended only a remonstrance against bad government. Shōsetsu and Chūya became heroes of popular literature and theater. The Keian Incident was the subject of several 17th- and 18th-century works of the genre JITSU-ROKUMONO (historical fiction), among which Keian taiheiki is the most famous, and inspired the kabuki play Kusunokiryū hanami no makubari by Kawatake MOKUAMI.   George ELISON

Keian no Ofuregaki

(Instructions of the Keian Era). Ordinance directed toward farmers, issued in 1649 (Keian 2) by the shōgun TOKUGAWA IEMITSU. Comprising 32 articles and written from a Confucian point of view, the ordinance instructed peasants on morality in their everyday life and especially on the virtue of obedience. The ordinance also extolled self-sufficiency and frugality; farmers were told to wear cotton instead of silk, to eat less valuable grains rather than rice, and even to refrain from tobacco, sake, and tea. It also went into particulars such as what seeds to buy, how to care for tools, or when to cut grass. It is clear that these instructions were designed to ensure proper and prompt payment of taxes (NENGU); in fact, the ordinance states that "once he paid his taxes, there was no calling as easy as a peasant's."

keibatsu

A clique (BATSU) in which access to political or economic power is controlled through marriage alliances between influential families. Often a man of a less influential family marries a daughter of a more influential one. This kind of marriage alliance has a long history in Japan as it has elsewhere in the world, the most notable instances in Japan being the marriage politics of the Fujiwara family during the Heian period (794–1185) and the marriage alliances of warring daimyō families, particularly during the 16th century. The word keibatsu, however, came into prominence in the last quarter of the 19th century and the first quarter of the 20th century, when the family system played an important role in political and industrial circles and when career diplomats and other bureaucrats often advanced

themselves by means of strategic marriages. Examples of keibatsu are the relationships established by marriages between the Iwasaki family (businessmen) and the Gotō family (politicians), between the Hatoyama (politicians) and the Ishibashi (businessmen), and between the Itō and the Suematsu (politicians). Other families such as the Mitsui, the Shibusawa, the Kuhara, and the Aikawa through this practice built up powerful family groups as the industrialization of Japan proceeded. The arrangement of loveless marriages for the purpose of creating exclusive, highly influential cliques has in recent years been strongly criticized in Japan as antidemocratic. A related term, mombatsu, is often used interchangeably with keibatsu; however, mombatsu is broader, referring to cliques based on various kinds of family connection.   IWAI Hiroaki

keichō

Also called daikeichō or daichō. Tax registers compiled in ancient Japan as part of the effort to introduce a uniform tax system under the TAIKA REFORM (645). Each year provincial governors ordered the heads of households to compile registers (shujitsu) listing the number of people in the household, their age, sex, physical characteristics, and, most important, which members were taxable and which were exempt. This information was reported to the provincial officials, who compiled summaries (keichō) and forwarded them to the Grand Council of State (Dajōkan) at the capital. These registers, which were revised every six years, formed the basis for government land allotment (see HANDEN SHŪJU SYSTEM) and taxation. The system was discontinued in the 9th century. See also HOUSEHOLD REGISTERS.   Philip BROWN

Keichō kemmon shū

(Things Seen and Heard in the Keichō Era [1596–1615]; more properly called Kembunshū). A collection of anecdotes by Miura Jōshin (1565–1644). A samurai in the employ of the Hōjō of Odawara, Jōshin lost his sustenance with the fall of that daimyō house in 1590 (see ODAWARA CAMPAIGN), turned to the life of a merchant in Edo (now Tōkyō), and eventually entered religion. The main value of his Kembunshū is in its copious if unsystematic depiction of the ordinary life of Edo as it was being transformed from a backwater to a metropolis at the dawn of the 17th century: it contains sketches of such events as the introduction of a water supply, the foundation of the Yoshiwara pleasure quarters, and early kabuki performances. The collection's preface and postscript are both dated Keichō 19 (1614), but incidents that occurred after that date are also included in the contents; the author evidently made additions as he was editing his life's work, which also includes the storybooks (kana-zōshi) Junrei monogatari (1614, A Pilgrim's Tale) and Sozoro monogatari (1641, A Rambling Tale), as well as Kembun gunshō (1667, Extracts from Military Tales) and HŌJŌ GODAI KI (The Five Generations of the House of Hōjō). Indeed, much of his other literary product is duplicated in the Kembunshū, which circulated in manuscript in the Edo period (1600–1868).   George ELISON

Keichū (1640–1701)

Shingon priest, scholar, and poet. Born at Amagasaki in Settsu Province (now part of Hyōgo Prefecture) into a disowned samurai family called Shimokawa. As a child Keichū showed great intellectual aptitude, entering the Buddhist priesthood at the age of 11. Apart from Buddhism, his studies included classical Chinese and Japanese literature, and Shittan (Skt: SIDDHAM; a script used to write Sanskrit). Keichū's friendship from his mid-twenties with the renga (linked verse) master SHIMOKŌBE CHŌRYŪ (1624–86) was of great importance, as it seems to have influenced him toward an attitude critical of unauthenticated tradition—an attitude that later formed the basis of his scholarship. For financial reasons Keichū spent the greater part of his life within the Buddhist order, though there was a period of about 10 years from about 1670 when he was able to devote himself entirely to studying. It was after this, during the remaining 20 years of his life, that almost all of Keichū's works were written.

Keichū is known primarily for his academic writings, which fall into two broad categories: classical commentaries and language studies. It should be noted that there is a close link between the two categories: Keichū's research into KANA (the Japanese phonetic syllabary) usage, for example, directly resulted in important progress in the interpretation of old texts. The most important of the classical commentaries is undoubtedly *Man'yō daishō ki* (ca 1683–90), a work considered to be on a level with MOTOORI NORINAGA's *Kojiki den* (completed 1798); even today, *Man'yō daishō ki* is quoted by modern scholars. This commentary on the MAN'YŌSHŪ was undertaken by Keichū at the request of TOKUGAWA MITSUKUNI of Mito (now part of Ibaraki Prefecture). Keichū also wrote commentaries on such works as the *Genji monogatari* (TALE OF GENJI), KOKINSHŪ, and ISE MONOGATARI. His main works on language relate to *kana* usage; the most important of these is WAJI SHŌRAN SHŌ (completed 1693; published 1695). As a result of his *Man'yōshū* studies, Keichū had perceived the consistent usage of *man'yōgana* (Chinese characters used phonetically)—within the limits of the 47 signs of the IROHA POEM—in the *Man'yōshū* and other early works such as WAMYŌ RUIJU SHŌ (10th century). His insistence that *kana* usage be based on that in the ancient literature arose not only from a desire to correct the historically inaccurate Teika *kana* usage (see KANA), but also from his conviction that the level of knowledge had declined since the ancient period, which for him represented some sort of golden age, and that the ancient system of writing was somehow nearer the Truth. His research in both Japanese language and literature may be seen as an attempt to rediscover the Truth and Wisdom of the ancient period. It is, moreover, possible to reconcile Keichū's research with his religious beliefs: those beliefs were eclectic, since Keichū was a follower of Dual Shintō (Ryōbu Shintō), and also subscribed to Confucian teachings. Keichū composed several volumes of poetry, including the *Manginshū*, completed in the Jōkyō era (1683–87). His poetry, however, is of relatively minor importance.

All Keichū's academic writings are characterized by an objective spirit of independent inquiry very much in contrast with the traditional attitude toward scholarship. This new objectivism, based on empirical and inductive procedures, formed the methodological basis for research among the later KOKUGAKU (National Learning) scholars, including Motoori Norinaga. For this reason, the significance of Keichū's work extends beyond the respective fields of language and literature into the history of Japanese scholarship and thought.

Traditionally the Kokugaku movement was regarded as centering around four main scholars: KADA NO AZUMAMARO, KAMO NO MABUCHI, Motoori Norinaga, and HIRATA ATSUTANE. Keichū was not normally included, partly it seems because his writings are characterized by a Buddhist viewpoint that was considered incompatible with the stand of the Kokugaku scholars. Minor points such as this, however, do not substantially affect the magnitude of Keichū's contribution to the beginnings of the Kokugaku movement; recently, moreover, there has been a reappraisal of Keichū's work by Japanese scholars, and the importance of his role in the early development of Kokugaku is now generally recognized.

Keichū's disciples included Kaihoku Jakuchū and Andō Nariakira. The high level of his scholarship was recognized by Motoori Norinaga, who was influenced considerably by Keichū's writings.
▰ ——Keichū, *Keichū zenshū*, 16 vols (Iwanami Shoten, 1973–). Hisamatsu Sen'ichi, *Keichū* (1963).   *Christopher SEELEY*

Keidanren

(abbreviation of Keizai Dantai Rengōkai; Federation of Economic Organizations). One of Japan's four main business organizations (the other three being NIKKEIREN, the JAPAN COMMITTEE FOR ECONOMIC DEVELOPMENT, and the JAPAN CHAMBER OF COMMERCE AND INDUSTRY). Keidanren has as members about 110 industry-wide groups representing major industries such as mining, manufacturing, trade, finance, and transportation in addition to about 807 of Japan's largest corporations.

Keidanren was established in 1946 as part of a general reorganization of business groups. In its early years, the effectiveness of its leadership was limited due to large-scale dislocations in the Japanese economy created in part by the purge of business leaders, the ZAIBATSU DISSOLUTION program, and the economic deconcentration measures carried out by the Allied Occupation authorities. In 1952, however, Keidanren absorbed the Japan Industrial Council (Nihon Sangyō Kyōgikai) and considerably increased both its size and influence.

Keidanren's principal functions are to adjust and mediate differences of opinion among its various member industries and businesses, and to submit proposals to the government regarding policies to stimulate the economy. It also promotes international exchanges on business matters between private citizens. To carry out these functions, Keidanren has a total of 32 permanent committees and

consulting organs, including committees concerned with general policy, energy, economic cooperation, trade policy, and marine development. It also has ad hoc committees on defense production and space exploration. Internationally, Keidanren conducts an active program of economic diplomacy on a nongovernmental level through conferences with American and European business leaders and groups such as the Special Committee on Europe, the Japan–Brazil Businessmen's Economic Committee, the Committee on Cooperation with Africa, and the Committee on Cooperation with Indonesia.

As Keidanren is the spokesman for big business in Japan, its proposals and demands have exerted a strong influence in Japanese political life. This power was clearly demonstrated in 1955 when the business community, in particular, Keidanren, demanded that the two conservative parties, the Japan Democratic Party (NIHON MINSHUTŌ) and the Liberal Party (JIYŪTŌ), merge to form a large conservative party. The result was the birth of the LIBERAL DEMOCRATIC PARTY. Keidanren's influence was also evident at the time of the revision of the United States–Japan Security Treaty in 1960 when it, together with the other three main economic organizations, issued a statement calling for a change in the political climate. This helped bring about the fall of the Kishi government and the installation of the Ikeda cabinet. On the other hand, during the severe inflationary period following the OIL CRISIS OF 1973, when faced with public criticism of big business, President UEMURA KŌGORŌ of Keidanren revealed the federation's weakness when he stated that Keidanren was not empowered to be the command headquarters of the business world and so could not control the activities of individual enterprises.

In a survey conducted among union members of the Federation of Independent Unions of Japan (CHŪRITSU RŌREN) and the General Council of Trade Unions of Japan (SŌHYŌ) in September 1979, the respondents named Keidanren as the most powerful organization in Japanese politics and society.   *HIRATA Masami*

keigo → honorific language

Keihan Electric Railway Co, Ltd

(Keihan Denki Tetsudō). Private railway company engaged in the transportation of passengers between Ōsaka and Kyōto. Established in 1906. During World War II it was absorbed by the Hankyū Electric Railway Co (now HANKYŪ CORPORATION), but was again made independent in 1949. With the increase in population in the area between Ōsaka and Kyōto, the company's earnings have grown, not only from the railway line, but also from its expanded businesses, which include housing developments, department stores, and leisure facilities along the line. The company controls 89.5 kilometers (55.5 mi) of trackage. At the end of March 1982 annual income totaled ¥72.9 billion (US $302.8 million), of which 51 percent came from rail service and capitalization was ¥13.9 billion (US $57.7 million). Corporate headquarters are located in Ōsaka.

Keihin Electric Express Railway Co, Ltd

(Keihin Kyūkō). Chiefly a railroad company, it also sells real estate and operates a bus line, hotels, and recreation facilities. Its main rail line runs through the industrial area between Tōkyō and the two cities of Kawasaki and Yokohama, extending as far as the Miura Peninsula in Kanagawa Prefecture. Total trackage is 83 kilometers (51.6 mi). Founded in 1898 as Daiichi Electric Railway Co, it merged with TŌKYŪ CORPORATION during World War II, but regained independent status in 1948. The firm controls 39 affiliated companies. Sales for the fiscal year ending March 1982 totaled ¥83.9 billion (US $348.5 million), of which its railway accounted for 45 percent, its bus line 17 percent, and other sources 38 percent. In the same year capitalization stood at ¥14.6 billion (US $60.7 million). The head office is in Tōkyō.

Keihin Industrial Zone

(Keihin Kōgyō Chitai). Extends along the shores of Tōkyō Bay and the interior. Tōkyō, Kawasaki, and Yokohama are its principal cities. It ranks first in Japan in the value of industrial goods produced. Factors that contributed to its growth are its proximity to Japan's greatest consumer markets and labor force and to the ports of Tōkyō and Yokohama. The heart of the zone is the coastal industrial belt on reclaimed land between Kawasaki and Yokohama, where giant steel mills, oil refineries, petrochemical plants, shipyards, primary food processing plants, thermoelectric plants, and other plants are located. Automobile, electric machinery, secondary food processing, and precision machine industries are located in the interior. The country's largest publishing houses and printing plants are located in the Tōkyō area. Parallel to the expansion of the Keihin Industrial Zone, coastal areas in Chiba and Ibaraki prefectures, respectively called the Keiyō Coastal Industrial Region and the Kashima Coastal Industrial Region, have been developed, with numerous steel mills, oil refineries, and thermoelectric plants. Since the 1970s, however, the zone has been plagued by overpopulation, air and water pollution, and a shortage of industrial water, thus causing many plants in the central part of the zone to relocate.

Kubota Takeshi

Keikō, Emperor

The legendary 12th sovereign (tennō) in the traditional count (which includes several other nonhistorical emperors); in the account given in the chronicle NIHON SHOKI (720) he is supposed to have reigned AD 71–130, an implausibly early period. He is said to have greatly extended the authority of the imperial court through marriage alliances and warfare. After establishing his court in the Yamato region, he reputedly led an expedition to Kyūshū to suppress an uprising of the KUMASO tribes. When they rose again, he dispatched his son, Prince YAMATOTAKERU, to chastise them and later to subdue the EZO tribes of northern Honshū. What is believed to be his tomb survives in the city of Tenri, Nara Prefecture.

Keikokushū

Early-Heian-period (794–1185) anthology of verse and prose in Chinese. Compiled under the supervision of Yoshimine no Yasuyo at the command of Emperor Junna in 827, it is one of the three imperial anthologies in Chinese along with Ryōunshū (814) and Bunka shūreishū (818). Originally 20 chapters, only 6 are extant. Covering 120 years, the work includes contributions by 178 authors in a variety of literary forms and styles.

Keiō University

(Keiō Gijuku Daigaku). A private coeducational university located in Minato Ward, Tōkyō. Founded by FUKUZAWA YUKICHI in 1858 as a private school for the study of Dutch and organized as a private university in 1890. It was the first private university established in the modern period, and now maintains faculties of literature, economics, law, commerce, medicine, and engineering. It offers correspondence curricula in letters, economics, and law. The university is also known for its School of Medicine and for the following institutes and laboratories: Institute of Cultural and Linguistic Studies, Institute of Journalism, Institute of Physical Education, Institute of Information Science, Keio Economic Observatory, Pharmaceutical Laboratory (School of Medicine), Research Laboratory of Diet and Nutrition (School of Medicine). Enrollment was 23,561 in 1980.

keiretsu

A group of affiliated private business enterprises; often, the loose groupings of former subsidiaries of the giant ZAIBATSU (financial and industrial combines) that have appeared since the zaibatsu dissolution program following World War II. The former zaibatsu keiretsu include the Mitsui keiretsu, the Mitsubishi keiretsu, and the Sumitomo keiretsu. Other forms of keiretsu include kin'yū (finance), shihon (capital), and kigyō (enterprise). A more general term for such affiliations is ENTERPRISE GROUPS.

A kin'yū keiretsu is a group of companies that have their highest borrowing from the bank that gives the grouping its name. Professor Nakamura Takafusa sees these groups as an outgrowth of the pattern of bank financing established during World War II for the so-called munitions companies. The BANKING SYSTEM provides the bulk of corporate funds in postwar Japan and plays a more important role than shareholders' equity in CORPORATE FINANCE. Thus, many Japanese observers attribute a great deal of significance to the grouping of companies around a "primary" bank. Given the scale of postwar capital needs, however, a major corporation may have significant capital borrowing from 20 to 30 different banks, and a corporation will not infrequently change its primary source of funding.

A shihon keiretsu is a group of companies with a common parent company. The many subsidiaries of Matsushita Electric form a group of this sort. The parent company in a shihon keiretsu typically holds 20 to 50 percent of the stock of the SUBSIDIARY COMPANIES.

A kigyō keiretsu is a group of companies that do subcontract work for the same firm. Large manufacturing companies often engage many small and medium enterprises as SUBCONTRACTORS, which are considered part of a keiretsu if they do the bulk of their business with one firm.

As keiretsu, SUMITOMO, MITSUI, and MITSUBISHI are substantially different in form from their zaibatsu predecessors. First and foremost, there are no top HOLDING COMPANIES to serve as command centers for the groups. Holding companies were outlawed by the ANTIMONOPOLY LAW (see ZAIBATSU DISSOLUTION). Coordination of keiretsu activities is achieved through "presidents' clubs," made up of the presidents of the most important companies in each group. It is important to note that this means that coordination is conducted by companies that are not in a hierarchical relationship to each other. GENERAL TRADING COMPANIES and keiretsu banks also serve a coordinating function in these groups.

Ownership ties among keiretsu companies are weaker than those in the prewar zaibatsu. Intercompany shareholding tends to be on the order of 3 to 5 percent. Typically, the two service organizations, the bank and the general trading company, have the strongest ownership ties with the other keiretsu companies. With 1977 amendments to the Antimonopoly Law, bank holdings are again restricted to a maximum of 5 percent of equity, as they were under the original form of the law.

In contrast with the prewar period, bank lending and borrowing occur across keiretsu lines. Further, trading companies may no longer bind companies to purchases and sales through them alone. "Sole agency contracts" were outlawed by the Antimonopoly Law. Companies are thus free to use the trading company of their own group for a portion of their transactions in combination with the services of other trading companies.

A shihon keiretsu is likely to have much stronger ownership ties than a keiretsu formed from former zaibatsu companies. The ties resemble the type of ownership pattern seen in the former zaibatsu. The most important point of distinction between the two is the size of the member companies: former zaibatsu keiretsu consist of major corporations, whereas the members of a shihon keiretsu are likely to be small and medium enterprises.

▬——Richard E. Caves and Masu Uekasa, "Industrial Organization" in Hugh Patrick and Henry Rosovsky, ed, Asia's New Giant: How the Japanese Economy Works (1976). Eleanor M. Hadley, Antitrust in Japan (1970). Keizai Chōsa Kyōkai, Keiretsu no kenkyū (annual). Kōsei Torihiki Iinkai, ed, Shuyō kaisha ni okeru shihon keiretsu no jōkyō (issued irregularly). Eleanor M. Hadley

Keisai Eisen (1790–1848)

A popular and prolific painter, book illustrator, and designer of UKIYO-E woodblock prints; a playwright, novelist, biographer, and amateur historian. Real name Ikeda Yoshinobu. Eisen was born in the Hoshigaoka district of Edo (now Tōkyō), the son of Ikeda Yoshiharu, a poet, calligrapher, and devotee of the tea ceremony. His earliest works are thought to be two illustrated novelettes published in 1808 and 1809 signed Keisai Shōsen; he adopted the name Eisen in 1816. He wrote plays as Chiyoda Saiichi, fiction as Ippitsuan Kakō, biography as Mumeiō, and historical essays as Kaedegawa Shiin. He designed erotica (SHUNGA) as Insai and Insai Hakusui and is said to have used the name Keisai, Kokushunrō, and Hokutei or Hokkatei on conventional pictures, although no works signed Hokutei or Hokkatei are presently known. As a child he studied with the painter Kanō Hakkeisai; in his twenties he worked under the ukiyo-e painter Kikukawa Eiji and studied Chinese painting and the work of HOKUSAI, whom he greatly admired. Today he is remembered for hundreds of prints of young women: brazen, distant, somewhat harsh, yet intimate, elegant, graceful, and subtly aroused. He is also remembered for many distinguished SURIMONO and landscape prints, and numerous erotic books and albums. As a writer he is best remembered for Mumeiō zuihitsu (1833, Essays of a Nameless Old Man), a manuscript revision of Ukiyo-e ruikō, a compilation of biographies that is one of the most valuable sources of information about artists of the ukiyo-e school. In his lifetime he was admired for his prints, paintings, and book illustrations, and for the fiction that occupied more and more of his attention during the last two decades of his life. Although there is some disagreement over the date of his death, 1848 is now generally accepted.

Eisen's autobiography was written in 1833. Close to that date he became proprietor of the Wakatakeya, a brothel in the Nezu district of Edo. The brothel burned and Eisen was accused of misappropriating another man's seal and absconding. These events may explain the interruption of Eisen's important set of landscape prints *Kiso Kaidō rokujūkutsugi* (1835, 69 Stations of the Kiso Kaidō Road) for which Eisen designed 24 plates, but which HIROSHIGE was asked to finish. In the late 1830s, Eisen withdrew from print design and spent more time writing miscellanies and fiction.

🕮 ——Jūzō Suzuki, *Makki ukiyo-e* (1969), tr John Bester as *The Decadents* (1969).

Roger KEYES

Keisatsu Yobitai → National Police Reserve

Kei school

(Keiha). A group of sculptors of Buddhist images active in the Kamakura period (1185–1333). These sculptors belonged to the Shichijō workshop (BUSSHO) in Nara and traced their ancestry to the 11th-century sculptor JŌCHŌ. Since they often took *kei* as part of their names, they became known to later generations as the Kei school. Their realistic style and depictions of virile, muscular male torsos gained the approval of warriors in the Kamakura period. As represented in the works of important sculptors like KŌKEI, UNKEI, KAIKEI, and TANKEI, the Kei school flourished over the older EN SCHOOL and IN SCHOOL. The Kei school lasted through the Edo period (1600–1868) despite its gradual lapse into mannerism.

Keisei Electric Railway Co, Ltd

(Keisei Dentetsu). Railroad and real estate company. Established in 1909, it also operates a bus line and an amusement park. The firm's main rail line connects the new Tōkyō International Airport in Narita, Chiba Prefecture, with the metropolitan area. Its special express trains carry passengers nonstop from the airport to Tōkyō. Total trackage is 89.5 kilometers (55.9 mi). Keisei Electric Railway has the largest network of bus routes in Chiba Prefecture and, jointly with MITSUI REAL ESTATE DEVELOPMENT CO, LTD, built an amusement park called Tōkyō Disneyland. Sales for the fiscal year ending March 1982 totaled ¥64.6 billion (US $268.4 million), of which its sale of real estate earned 25 percent, railway 43 percent, buses and other vehicles 27 percent, and other activities 5 percent. In the same year capitalization was ¥13.6 billion (US $56.5 million). Corporate headquarters are in Tōkyō.

keishi

(house stewards). Clerks who administered the household affairs of imperial princes, regents, court nobles, high-ranking officials, and other great men of the Heian period (794–1185). Also known as *ietsukasa*. The term came to be used in warrior houses as well, and with the rise of WARRIOR GOVERNMENT under the Kamakura shogunate (1192–1333), functionaries in such governmental organs as the Administrative Board (MANDOKORO), the Council of State (HYŌ-JŌSHŪ), the High Court (Hikitsukeshū), and the Board of Inquiry (MONCHŪJO) were all designated *keishi*. The Muromachi shogunate (1338–1573) adopted substantially the same system. The term never lost its original meaning of house steward, however, and as late as the end of the Muromachi period, warlords (SENGOKU DAIMYŌ) still referred to their household administrators as *keishi*.

KOYANAGI Shun'ichirō

Keitai, Emperor (first half of the 6th century)

The 26th sovereign *(tennō)* in the traditional count (which includes several nonhistorical emperors). According to the chronicle NIHON SHOKI (720) he is supposed to have reigned 507–531, but these dates are rejected by modern scholars. According to the *Nihon shoki*, when Emperor Buretsu (latter half of the 5th century) died without an heir, the court military leaders ŌTOMO NO KANAMURA and Mononobe no Arakabi (see MONONOBE FAMILY) discovered Keitai either at Mio in Ōmi Province (now Shiga Prefecture) or at Mikuni in Koshi Province (later Echizen Province, now part of Fukui Prefecture) and installed him as emperor. Although he was alleged to be a fifth-generation descendant of Emperor ŌJIN (late 4th to early 5th

century), some scholars have speculated that he was unrelated to the original imperial house. In any case, in the *Nihon shoki* it is said that opposition to him in the Yamato court was so strong that 20 years passed before he entered Yamato. Among the events attributed in the chronicle to his troubled reign are the loss (in 512?) of four districts of KAYA, the supposed Japanese enclave in Korea, and the Rebellion of IWAI in Kyūshū. In his last years, Japan is said to have been torn by civil wars.

KITAMURA Bunji

Keizai Dōyū Kai → Japan Committee for Economic Development

keizai kanchō

(economic agencies). Government ministries and agencies concerned with economic policies, in particular, the MINISTRY OF FINANCE, the MINISTRY OF INTERNATIONAL TRADE AND INDUSTRY (MITI), and the ECONOMIC PLANNING AGENCY (EPA).

The Ministry of Finance plays an important role in the formation of the national budget and in any revisions of the tax system. Budget bills prepared by this ministry are rarely revised by the Diet, as they are prepared in close cooperation with the party in power. The ministry also provides supervision and guidance for banks and securities companies.

MITI provides supervision and guidance for individual industries and is responsible for the formulation and enforcement of international trade policies. In discussions of economic policies, MITI tends to represent the views of industry; in turn, MITI is influential in the industrial world through its ADMINISTRATIVE GUIDANCE powers.

The EPA is charged with the coordination of economic policies, as well as the preparation of long-term economic plans, annual economic forecasts (in conjunction with the preparation of the national budget), and the WHITE PAPER ON THE ECONOMY. The agency is also responsible for the coordination of various policies relating to commodity prices and economic life.

In addition to these three main government organs, there are many others which deal with economic matters. Public works projects are handled primarily through the offices of the MINISTRY OF CONSTRUCTION and the MINISTRY OF TRANSPORT. In many cases, the Japanese government attempts to control business fluctuations through the manipulation of public works expenditures rather than tax revenues, so that the economic role of these agencies is quite important. The Statistics Bureau of the Prime Minister's Office prepares various economic statistics, while the MINISTRY OF LABOR is charged with responsibility for employment policies. The MINISTRY OF FOREIGN AFFAIRS, MITI, the EPA, and the Ministry of Finance divide among themselves the responsibility for overseas economic aid.

KATŌ Masashi

Keizai Kikaku Chō → Economic Planning Agency

Keizan Jōkin (1268–1325)

Monk of the SŌTŌ SECT of Zen Buddhism. Born in Echizen Province (now Fukui Prefecture). As a child, he entered the Buddhist order at the temple EIHEIJI where he studied under Gikai (1219–1309), a disciple of DŌGEN. Later he also studied esoteric Buddhist tradition in Kyōto. His outstanding virtue attracted many admirers and he was active in disseminating Sōtō teachings at various places including the temples Jōmanji in Awa Province (now Tokushima Prefecture) and Daijōji in Kaga Province (now Ishikawa Prefecture). In 1321 he founded the temple SŌJIJI, to which Emperor Go-Daigo contributed an imperial plaque. Along with Eiheiji, Sōjiji became a center of the sect. Keizan had many noteworthy disciples and helped establish firmly Japanese Sōtō Zen. His writings include the well-known collection of monastic rules *Keizan oshō shingi* and a collection of his speeches titled *Denkōroku*.

MATSUNAMI Yoshihiro

Kellner, Oscar (1851–1911)

German agricultural chemist. Invited by the Japanese government as an instructor, he traveled to Japan in 1881 and taught agricultural chemistry at Komaba Agricultural School. While he was studying soils and fertilizers, the school developed into the Tōkyō Agricultural and Forestry School (now part of Tōkyō University). He is regarded as the founder of Japanese agricultural chemistry, because during his 11 years' stay he laid the foundations of agriculture and agricultural science study in Japan. His method of nutritional analysis of livestock feed, which he worked out after returning to Germany, is called Kellner's feeding standard and was used for a long time in the Japanese cattle industry. *KATŌ Shunjirō*

Kellogg–Briand Pact

(Fusen Jōyaku). Agreement signed in Paris on 27 August 1928 by Japan and 14 other countries, denouncing "recourse to war for the solution of international controversies"; also known as the Pact of Paris. Its terms derived from the June 1927 proposal of French Foreign Minister Aristide Briand to the American government to bar all war between their respective governments and from American Secretary of State Frank B. Kellogg's reply that other countries join them in such an agreement. The pact was initially signed by 15 nations, including France, Germany, Great Britain, Italy, and the United States. Later, 48 other nations joined them.

Japan was requested to sign the pact in April 1928. Because of continuing political and military uncertainty in China, particularly after Chiang Kai-shek's Northern Expedition of 1926–27, the Japanese government had reservations about the pact. It was unwilling to deny itself the right to intervene militarily in Chinese affairs in order to protect its nationals in China and its interests in Manchuria. Such military intervention, it insisted, would be for self-defense, the sole reason recognized by the pact as acceptable for waging war. Another problem arose because of the pact's claim that its signatories agreed to the terms "in the names of their respective peoples." Many Japanese criticized this wording as a direct assault on the sovereignty of the Japanese emperor, and eventually Kellogg exempted Japan from this condition. After the Privy Council ratified the pact in June 1929, Japan proceeded to invade Manchuria in 1931 (see MANCHURIAN INCIDENT).

kemari

Also known as *shūkiku*. Traditional game in which several people form a circle and kick a ball to prevent it from falling to the ground. It is thought to have come to Japan from China, and there are records of its being played at the imperial court as early as the mid-7th century. *Kemari* achieved wide popularity among the *kuge* (court nobles) during the Nara (710–794), Heian (794–1185), and Kamakura (1185–1333) periods. The game later gained popularity among both warriors and commoners. The playing field was known as the *kakari* and consisted of an area about 3 meters (10 ft) square, with one tree (a willow, a cherry, a pine, and a maple) planted at each of the four corners. Groups of four, six, or eight players wearing leather shoes shouted as they kicked the *mari*, a deerskin ball 24 centimeters (9.4 in) in diameter. The game became increasingly formalized toward the end of the Heian period, as style and etiquette took on more importance than the actual outcome of the game. *INAGAKI Shisei*

kemi

(or *kemmi*; crop inspection). An Edo-period (1600–1868) procedure for inspecting crop yields in order to calculate the amount of land tax (HONTO MONONARI). In principle the inspections occurred annually. Crop inspections were carried out from the Kamakura period (1185–1333) onward, but they did not become widespread until the late 16th century, when they are thought to have been systematized through nationwide implementation of TOYOTOMI HIDEYOSHI's land survey (see KENCHI).

Inspections were made by officials of different levels. In the Tokugawa house lands (TENRYŌ) inspections by village officials of the yield of each plot in the village were called *naiken*. A *kokemi* was an investigation of yields by the shogunal intendant's (DAIKAN) assistant, who reviewed and checked the reports that village officials prepared by taking sample cuttings (*tsubogari, bugari*) in the village. If the *daikan* himself checked the work of his representative in a similar manner, it was called *ōkemi*.

Among the various inspection and tax-adjustment methods, the following were the most important. In the *sebiki kemi* a standard amount of tax rice was assessed per unit of land. If the yield fell, an area of land producing the amount of tax to be forgiven was subtracted from the total land area of the village. This method was incapable of keeping pace with long-term yield increases because the tax assessment was constant. The *arige kemi* was most likely to

reflect crop conditions accurately because the tax rate was based on crop sampling. *Ukemen'i* involved interviews of the peasants by domain officials as to the condition of the crops, without any formal standardized inspection. In the *tōmi kemi* an official scrutinized the entire village from a single vantage point and assessed the yield impressionistically. These and other inspection methods were frequently combined.

Since the tax assessments were based on each year's crop yields, these methods are often considered to have been fairer to the peasants and more efficient for the *daimyō* than the JŌMEN (fixed tax rate) system, which is thought to have become more common from the early 18th century. Peasants were not penalized for crop failures, and the daimyō could increase tax revenues in proportion to rising crop yields. Nevertheless, the change to the *jōmen* system is thought to have permitted peasants to accumulate a surplus and to have been a major source of rural economic growth in the 18th and 19th centuries.

This evaluation ignores problems inherent in some of the inspection methods and the difficulties in implementing even the most accurate of them. *Ukemen'i* and *tōmi kemi* lacked any specific measurement of crop yields and were frequent sources of dispute between villagers and the *daikan*. *Arige kemi*, conducted by means of *naiken, koken*, and *ōkemi*, was probably the most accurate method, but it required great expense of time and labor and could not be repeated frequently.

These forms of tax assessment were discontinued with the implementation of the Meiji LAND TAX REFORM OF 1873–1881. *Philip BROWN*

Kemmu nenchū gyōji

Three-volume work completed about 1334 (Kemmu 1) describing annual events and ceremonies at the imperial court and compiled by order of Emperor GO-DAIGO. It was an attempt to revive discarded court ceremonies on the occasion of the KEMMU RESTORATION (1334). In contrast to similar works up to that date, the book was written in Japanese instead of classical Chinese. It was known by a variety of names before the present title was chosen in the Edo period (1600–1868). The work is a valuable source for understanding the ideals of the Kemmu Restoration and the most common yearly events in the court calendar. *INAGAKI Shisei*

Kemmu nenkan ki

(Chronicle of the Kemmu Era). A record of the Kemmu era (1334–36) during the reign of Emperor GO-DAIGO, who had succeeded in retrieving political power from the Kamakura shogunate in the KEMMU RESTORATION. Compiled anonymously in about 1336, it includes the government's administrative regulations, dispositions concerning SHŌEN proprietary rights, lists of officials, legal decisions, and transcriptions of the so-called NIJŌGAWARA NO RAKUSHO, satirical verses about the government and general fashions of the time. It is thus an important source of information about the Kemmu Restoration government.

Kemmu Restoration

(Kemmu no Chūkō). The attempt by Emperor GO-DAIGO in 1333–36 to restore direct imperial rule following the overthrow of the Kamakura shogunate. Kemmu refers to the era name (*nengō*) that Go-Daigo inaugurated in 1334. Go-Daigo's policies proved hopelessly reactionary, and within three years his restoration government was in turn overthown by ASHIKAGA TAKAUJI, who established the Muromachi shogunate.

The concept of imperial restoration in Japanese history derives from the enduring belief, rooted in ancient myths recounting the divine origins of Japan and its people, that a single dynastic line descended from AMATERASU ŌMIKAMI, the sun goddess, was mandated to rule the land eternally. In fact, however, emperors have seldom exercised any real power since the early 9th century. Yet the ideal of restoring power to the throne has periodically been advanced in Japanese history as a rationale by one group (imperial loyalists) to seize rule from another group ("bad ministers," who are accused of arrogating powers that rightfully belong to the emperor). Usually, as in the cases of the MEIJI RESTORATION of 1868 and the movement of rightists for a "SHŌWA RESTORATION" in the 1920s and 1930s, there has been little opportunity for the emperor himself to serve as anything more than a symbol. Yet in the Kemmu Restoration of the 14th century Emperor Go-Daigo played the central role and was determined to reclaim the powers of direct rule that he perceived to have been exercised by emperors in the past.

The Seeds of Restoration —— Despite the founding of the KAMAKURA SHOGUNATE in 1185 and the further expansion of its power in the early 13th century, the ancient régime of court and courtiers in Kyōto retained a considerable economic basis in landed estates (SHŌEN) and the potential, at least, to reassert itself politically. For practical purposes, however, the court was totally subordinated to Kamakura's will following the unsuccessful attempt in 1221 by the retired emperor GO-TOBA to overthrow the shogunate (see JŌKYŪ DISTURBANCE). Thereafter even the succession to the throne was dictated by Kamakura. It was therefore essentially the shogunate's fault when, upon the death of the retired emperor GO-SAGA in 1272, no firm decision was made as to which line the succession should go to—that of his older son, the former emperor GO-FUKAKUSA, or his younger son, the emperor KAMEYAMA.

The shogunate may, in fact, have preferred to have the Kyōto court in a divided state at a time when its attention was largely directed toward defense against the MONGOL INVASIONS OF JAPAN of 1274 and 1281. An antishogunate movement centered in the court would have sorely taxed the resources of the Kamakura regime. Moreover, the shogunate could scarcely have imagined the difficulties that would eventually result from its failure to settle the imperial succession dispute in its early stages.

By the end of the 13th century, when the threat of invasion finally subsided, the shogunate had generally accepted the practice of alternate succession to the throne by members of the senior (Go-Fukakusa or Jimyōin) and the junior (Kameyama or Daikakuji) lines. The imperial house had by this time divided into two distinct branches, with separate economic holdings in estates, and the bitterness of their rivalry had become so intense and had so divided the ministerial families at court that reconciliation seemed virtually impossible.

The Restoration —— By the time Go-Daigo ascended the throne in 1318, the quality of Kamakura rule had declined greatly, and Go-Daigo determined not only to end alternate succession but also to overthrow the "eastern barbarians" in Kamakura and restore imperial power. An antishogunate plot was uncovered in Kyōto in 1324 (see SHŌCHŪ CONSPIRACY), and in 1331 Go-Daigo himself was arrested and sent into exile for conspiring against Kamakura (see GENKŌ INCIDENT). But the loyalist tide was not thereby turned, and within two years the shogunate was suddenly and dramatically overthrown by the betrayal of two of its leading generals, Ashikaga Takauji and NITTA YOSHISADA, scions of the two main branches of the Minamoto family.

Go-Daigo returned triumphantly to Kyōto in 1333 to "restore" imperial power. Historically, there were three groups that could be identified as having successively arrogated such power: the Fujiwara regents (see REGENCY GOVERNMENT), the senior retired emperors (see INSEI), and the shōguns of the warrior government in Kamakura. The junior branch of the imperial family had already abolished the office of senior retired emperor, and Go-Daigo now resolutely refused either to appoint a Fujiwara regent or to bestow the title of shōgun upon a warrior leader. In selecting the name Go-Daigo ("The Latter Daigo"), he clearly expressed his desire to model his regime on that of Emperor DAIGO, who had ruled from 897–930, before the Fujiwara had fully consolidated their control over the throne.

Although Go-Daigo interpreted the overthrow of the Kamakura shogunate as a mandate for imperial restoration, he was ill-prepared to deal with the realities and needs of the warrior-dominated society that had evolved since the 12th century. The most conspicuous failure of the restoration government was its inability to adjudicate efficiently and fairly the land disputes that were so common among provincial warriors. Yet even had Go-Daigo and his ministers been more competent in this and other areas of administration, they would probably have been unable to survive as a government much beyond the three years of the Kemmu Restoration. For underlying the veneer of restoration were profound conflicts of interest and ambition among the great warrior chieftains of the land, especially Ashikaga Takauji and Nitta Yoshisada.

Takauji and Yoshisada were both generously rewarded for their roles in bringing about the Kemmu Restoration; but whereas Yoshisada became a principal figure in the restoration government, Takauji remained almost entirely aloof from Kyōto affairs. So conspicuous was his absence from Go-Daigo's central councils that, according to one chronicle, people at the time spoke pointedly of the phenomenon of government "without Takauji" (Takauji nashi).

Failure of the Restoration —— Takauji coveted the title of shōgun (more formally, *seii tai shōgun*), which MINAMOTO NO YORITOMO had received from the court in 1192 to grace his position as founder of the Kamakura shogunate and which had subsequently been held by the titular heads of the shogunate even after the rise of the HŌJŌ FAMILY to power as shogunal regents (*shikken*). From Takauji's conduct at this time and later, it is obvious that he aspired to succeed to the role of military hegemon of the country. Go-Daigo, however, steadfastly refused to comply with Takauji's wishes, even when the Ashikaga leader directly requested that he be made shōgun in 1335 as part of a commission to chastise remnants of the shogunate's supporters who had risen in the east.

Shortly thereafter the court accused Takauji, who had remained in the east after putting down the uprising, of flouting its will and dispatched an army under Nitta Yoshisada, Takauji's arch rival. Thus began the conflict that within a year led to the overthrow of the restoration government, the flight of Go-Daigo to Yoshino, and the establishment by Takauji of the Muromachi shogunate in Kyōto. At this time began the long struggle known as the war between the courts, lasting from 1336 until 1392, which pitted the Southern (Yoshino) Court of Go-Daigo and his descendants of the junior branch of the imperial house against the Northern Court of the senior branch, situated in Kyōto and supported by the Ashikaga shōguns (see NORTHERN AND SOUTHERN COURTS).

Historical Assessment of the Restoration —— Go-Daigo's Kemmu Restoration was little more than an anachronistic pause between the overthrow of the first shogunate and the founding of the second. Yet it gave rise to the only major dynastic schism in Japanese history, and later generations of historians, especially from the Edo period (1600–1868) on, felt impelled to deal with the fundamental issue of imperial legitimacy that had been raised by Takauji's treatment of Go-Daigo and by the subsequent division of the court into northern and southern branches. To nationalistic historians of the modern age the very concept of divided sovereignty was anathema, and they insisted that only one court—the northern or the southern—could be regarded as legitimate. The issue was not officially settled until 1911, when the government of Prime Minister KATSURA TARŌ, seeking to settle a dispute over how the dynastic schism of the 14th century should be treated in primary-school textbooks, decreed that the Southern Court of Go-Daigo, who had never freely relinquished the throne, had been the legitimate imperial seat during the period 1336–92. One reason why this decision was especially popular at the time was that it historically justified, so to speak, the conduct of men such as Nitta Yoshisada and KUSUNOKI MASASHIGE, who had given their lives for Go-Daigo's cause and had been apotheosized as the greatest of Japan's loyalist heroes. See also NAMBOKUCHŌ SEIJUN RON.

—— H. Paul Varley, *Imperial Restoration in Medieval Japan* (1971). Hayashiya Tatsusaburō, *Nambokuchō* (1957). Kubota Osamu, *Kemmu chūkō* (1965). Murata Masashi, *Nambokuchō shi ron* (1959). Satō Shin'ichi, *Nambokuchō no dōran* (1965).

H. Paul VARLEY

Kemmu Shikimoku

(Kemmu Code). Code of basic governmental principles and policies promulgated in 1336 (Kemmu 3) by ASHIKAGA TAKAUJI, founder of the Muromachi shogunate (1338–1573). Drawn up by a commission of scholars and officials in consultation with Takauji, the code is neither a treatise on legal theory nor a compilation of statutes but a modest list of general precepts for the guidance of the ruling class. It comprises 17 articles that enjoin frugality, maintenance of law and order, respect for property rights, selection and reward of officials on the basis of merit and honesty, scrupulous fairness in judicial decisions, resistance to the influence and demands of courtiers and monks, and attention to the grievances of the poor. In form, the Kemmu Shikimoku is modeled on the SEVENTEEN-ARTICLE CONSTITUTION issued by Prince SHŌTOKU in 604, and in content it is comparable to the GOSEIBAI SHIKIMOKU (1232), the rigid military code of the Kamakura shogunate (1192–1333); but it is less moralistic and didactic than the former and less complex and specific than the latter.

Kempō Chōsakai → Commission on the Constitution

Kempō gige

(Commentary on the Constitution). Official commentary on the Meiji CONSTITUTION and the IMPERIAL HOUSEHOLD LAW; published under the general supervision of ITŌ HIROBUMI in 1889. The actual author, however, was INOUE KOWASHI, one of the original drafters of these laws, who worked with the advice of the PRIVY COUNCIL and other scholars and officials who had been involved in the drafting of the constitution.

Kempō Mondai Kenkyūkai → Constitutional Problems Study Group

Kempō satsuyō

A treatise on the Meiji Constitution, published in 1923 by MINOBE TATSUKICHI, professor of administrative law at Tōkyō University, in which he advanced the theory that the emperor was an organ of the state (TENNŌ KIKAN SETSU). In opposition to conservative scholars like HOZUMI YATSUKA and UESUGI SHINKICHI, who saw the emperor as absolute and mystically identified with the body of the state, Minobe described the state as a legal person possessing both sovereignty and the authority to rule, the emperor being merely the highest organ of the state and holding the ultimate right to perform executive functions. Minobe's theory was the prevalent legal interpretation of the constitution until the 1930s, when it was denounced by militarists and rightists associated with the movement to "clarify the national polity" (see KOKUTAI DEBATE). Minobe came under attack in the Diet, and his works were proscribed in 1935.

ken

(literally, "fist"). Any of a number of games for two or more persons, played by extending the fist, the open hand, a number of fingers, and so forth. The commonest form of ken resembles the familiar "scissors-paper-rock." Some form of ken was probably brought to Nagasaki from China at the beginning of the Edo period (1600–1868). Ken games became popular among the common people and were often played at drinking parties. The best-known forms of the game include kazuken, kitsuneken (also called tōhachiken), and janken. In kazuken ("numbered fist"), one player tries to match, by guessing, the number of fingers extended by the other player. In kitsuneken ("fox fist"), the hand shape representing the hunter beats the fox, the village headman beats the hunter, and the fox beats (outwits) the village headman. Janken is the children's game of "scissors-paper-rock." The players call out "jan, ken, pon" and, as in other nations, make one of three forms with one hand: stone (closed fist), scissors (two fingers extended), or paper (hand opened flat). Stone beats scissors, scissors beats paper, and paper beats stone. Janken is often played to determine who shall be "it" in games of tag or who shall go first in selecting teams.

SAITŌ Ryōsuke

kenchi

A general term applied to cadastral surveys in Japan, particularly from the 16th century through the Edo period (1600–1868). Surveys that registered cultivated land for purposes of administration and taxation were carried out either by government officials or privately by landed proprietors from early historic times. These were given a variety of names. During the medieval period (13th–16th centuries) the term *kenchū* was most commonly used. Under the Kamakura shogunal rule (1192–1333), the shōgun's superior provincial agents (SHUGO) were ordered to collect cadastral records (*kenchū*) from local officials in both the *kokugaryō* (public lands) and the SHŌEN (private estates). These province-wide registers were referred to as ŌTABUMI, and they served as the basis for certain province-wide imposts. Only a few such registers survive, the earliest from 1223, and their reliability and use are not fully known.

During the last half of the Muromachi period (1333–1568), and particularly with the appearance of the so-called SENGOKU DAIMYŌ after 1500, new land registrations, now called *kenchi,* were initiated by the large military lords. Such surveys were as yet not carried out systematically, nor did most DAIMYŌ have the power to intrude their own survey teams onto lands held in fief by their vassals or by powerful religious proprietors. Thus the usual practice was for the daimyō to require the submission of cadastral documents from the fief and estate holders themselves, a procedure known as *sashidashi.* Increasingly the Sengoku daimyō came to rely on *kenchi* figures as a means of extending their control over the land and manpower of their domains. A more accurate knowledge of the productive capacities of their vassals' holdings, for instance, gave the daimyō a more reliable basis on which to recruit military service. Moreover,

since many daimyō, by claiming to be successors to the Muromachi-period *shugo,* sought to collect domain-wide surtaxes, it was important to have accurate information on the total cultivated area of their domains. Among the Sengoku daimyō, the most powerful, such as the IMAGAWA FAMILY of Suruga and Tōtōmi provinces (now parts of Shizuoka Prefecture), the TAKEDA FAMILY of Kai and Shinano provinces (now Yamanashi and Nagano prefectures), and the Later HŌJŌ FAMILY of Odawara (in what is now Kanagawa Prefecture), were noteworthy for their reliance on the *kenchi* as a tool in local governance. But no Sengoku daimyō achieved complete cadastral control of all land in his domain. This was not to happen until a national hegemonic power of sufficient magnitude had combined with the daimyō to form a more powerful force at the local level. By that time, however, the daimyō had had to give up a significant portion of their local autonomy to superior national military authority.

Soon after his entrance into Kyōto in 1568, ODA NOBUNAGA ordered a full survey of lands in Ōmi Province (now Shiga Prefecture), a province adjoining the home province of Yamashiro (now part of Kyōto Prefecture) and the future location of his castle headquarters at Azuchi. In the next few years, as Nobunaga extended his conquests, other provinces in central Japan were cleared of hostile forces and superfluous castles, and local civil and military proprietors were obliged to submit cadastral records on their landholdings. In most cases Nobunaga did not send his own surveyors to conduct the actual survey, but in certain instances he did dispatch his own cadastral commissioners *(kenchi bugyō)* to check for accuracy.

It was under TOYOTOMI HIDEYOSHI that the system of land registration that was to remain in use throughout the early modern period was designed and enforced on a national scale. Although Hideyoshi alone cannot be credited with the series of surveys begun in 1582 and extended into the 1590s, it is common practice to call this national effort the Taikō *kenchi.* (TAIKŌ is the title by which Hideyoshi was known in his later years.) The Taikō *kenchi* literally worked a revolution in land administration and tenure practices in Japan. By virtue of its comprehensiveness, it swept away all previous systems of landholding. The national military hegemon now stood as the sole possessor of the rights of proprietorship throughout Japan. All superior land rights—i.e., the rights to administer, tax, and adjudicate—whether of the daimyō, the court nobility, or religious institutions, were held under the vermilion seal of the military hegemon.

Kenchi were carried out in a variety of ways. In many parts of the country, where daimyō local power was strongly entrenched, Hideyoshi allowed the daimyō to conduct their own surveys according to his announced specifications. This was the case for the TOKUGAWA, Ukita, CHŌSOKABE, and MŌRI families. In other instances Hideyoshi sent his own survey commissioners to oversee, or to do the job directly. The approach depended on the balance of power at the moment. For example, in 1587 Hideyoshi's forces invaded Kyūshū and defeated the armies of the SHIMAZU FAMILY of Satsuma Province (now part of Kagashima Prefecture). But Hideyoshi felt obliged to permit the Shimazu daimyō to retain most of his holdings, requiring only the submission of detailed land registers presumably based on newly conducted land surveys. By 1592, however, having won suzerainty over all the daimyō of Japan, Hideyoshi felt strong enough to order the survey of Shimazu lands by a team of his own choosing headed by his trusted vassal daimyō ISHIDA MITSUNARI. Ishida used 30 of his own retainers as survey overseers. The Shimazu domain, covering two and a half provinces of southern Kyūshū, was completely resurveyed in roughly six months' time. The resulting figure for the productive capacity of the entire domain came to 578,733 *koku.* (The KOKU was a dry measure for grain roughly equivalent to about 180 liters or 5 US bushels.)

One feature of the Taikō *kenchi* was that it imposed upon the country a new set of standard measures for surface area and dry volume. The effort to unify weights and measures throughout Japan was one of Hideyoshi's main policy objectives. For volume, he adopted the existing Kyōto dry measure *(kyōmasu;* approximately 1.8 liters or 3.8 US pints) as the standard for the *koku* size by which to measure tax rice. For area he adopted a measure of his own devising. The *tan* (a unit measuring roughly 0.12 hectare or 0.3 acre), which had been historically calculated at 360 *bu (bu:* a unit measuring roughly 3.34 sq m or 4 square yards), was set by Hideyoshi at 300 *bu,* thereby decreasing the *tan* by one-sixth to an area of roughly 0.1 hectare or 0.25 acre. On paper this new measure increased the number of *tan* in Japan by one-sixth. It has been suggested that this change had the hidden purpose of extracting a larger tax by increasing the number of *tan,* but that is to misunderstand the new basis on which taxes were assessed. Taxes under the new system were no longer based on historically set amounts per *tan*. Instead, taxes were calculated as a certain percentage of the estimated yield of the land, and for this purpose the size of the *tan* was immaterial. Of much greater importance as a device to increase tax volume was the fact that the *kenchi* program penetrated all parts of the country systematically so as to bring to light fields that up to then had been "hidden" either intentionally or inadvertently.

Not only was the Taikō survey systematic and far-reaching, it brought into being a new system of land registration and taxation. The new surveys did three things: they identified and measured each unit of cultivated land, wet or dry; they assessed the quality of land, using the four ratings superior (*jō*), medium (*chū*), poor (*ge*), and very poor (*gege*), and calculated the productive capacity in units of *koku (kokumori)*; and they identified and recorded the name of the cultivator or owner. As mentioned above, an important innovation of the system was that land parcels, instead of being assessed a set amount, were recorded by yield (*taka*). Yields were measured in units of rice, either actual, in the case of paddy land, or by calculation, in the case of dry fields. The unit of measure being the *koku*, the total tax assessment base for a village (i.e., the sum total of *koku* figures for all land registered in the names of the village's members) was called the village's KOKUDAKA. These figures in turn became the basis of a systematic tax collection procedure. A daimyō now levied taxes as a certain percentage of the yield figures of the villages in his domain. The *kenchi* also provided the national overlord with new powers of political control. With a fairly accurate map of the location and productive capacity of the country's agricultural land base, Hideyoshi and his successors were able to adjust wealth to status among the military aristocracy more precisely. Daimyō were now ranked according to size of domain measured in *kokudaka*. Only now did daimyō come to be defined as military proprietors holding lands assessed at no less than 10,000 *koku*.

The enforcement of the Taikō *kenchi* program did more than provide a systematic registration of the land, it had numerous political and social ramifications. First, with respect to the relationship between the daimyō and the national overlord, since the daimyō were now granted their domains in terms of agreed-upon *kokudaka* totals, the identification of a daimyō with any specific location lost much of its significance. This facilitated the practice initiated by Nobunaga, perfected by Hideyoshi, and continued by the Tokugawa shogunate (1603–1867) whereby the national hegemon could move daimyō from location to location for strategic or political purposes.

The *kenchi* had a profound effect upon the *samurai* and land-cultivating classes. Prior to the enforcement of the new survey, rural society was organized in both two and three tiers. In the daimyō's own "granary lands," central authority was exercised not through enfeoffed vassals but directly by his house bureaucracy, manned by salaried samurai retainers. In the remainder of the domain, daimyō authority was exercised only indirectly through the daimyō's enfeoffed vassals. In most instances these vassal samurai lived in the countryside, where they administered the villages that they held in fief. Throughout the 16th century, the daimyō made concerted efforts to convert their vassal housemen into the more dependent variety. As the warfare between daimyō became increasingly severe, and especially after the introduction of firearms from Europe in the middle of the century, there was a strong tendency for the rural samurai to move physically into the daimyō's CASTLE TOWNS. And, although in some cases and for varying lengths of time fiefholding vassals were permitted to continue direct management of their fiefs, setting the amount of the annual rice dues and having it delivered directly to their castle-town storehouses, this practice met increasing opposition from the daimyō and was largely discontinued during the first half-century of Tokugawa rule. In other words, all cultivated land, all villagers and their affairs came to be administered by the daimyō's administrative offices. The two-tier structure of the daimyō's granary lands had become the norm for the entire domain.

Although there were several reasons for the flow of rural samurai (the middle tier) into the daimyō's castle towns, the *kenchi* was a major contributing cause, for it presented to the rural samurai two clearcut choices: to remain on the land and be classed as farmers (HYAKUSHŌ) or to preserve samurai status by moving to the daimyō's castle. The result was an irreversible legal separation of the samurai from the farming class—a phenomenon called *heinō bunri* by Japanese historians. The withdrawal of the entire samurai class of lower landed military gentry from the land and its conversion into an urban-dwelling, military-administrative officer corps attached to national and regional centers of administration had a profound effect

upon the Japanese nation for the next two and a half centuries. Samurai were no longer landowners. They were no longer identified by locality of fief but rather simply as officials of a certain number of *koku* stipend in service to the shōgun or to a particular daimyō. They could not acquire private landed wealth. Their income could be improved only by increases in stipend as a result of meritorious service to shōgun or daimyō.

The *kenchi* had a profound effect upon the cultivator class as well. Under the *kenchi*, land was recorded plot by plot in village (*mura*) units, and taxes were imposed on the basis of the total *kokudaka* of each village. Each village was made accountable for tax payments as a corporate entity through its headman (SHŌYA), whose job it was to allocate the tax burden within the village. The *kenchichō* (land register) literally defined the village. Important to the villagers, also, was the fact of registration, which accomplished two things. It identified for each plot of village land the individual responsible for payment of the tax due on the plot. It also confirmed the villager's right to work the plot without jeopardy. The first condition put certain restrictions on the villager's use of the land (the right to alienate or to convert to other purposes). The second condition provided the villager with security of occupancy that bordered on ownership. The *kenchi* thereby gave new legal status to an entire class of landholding farmers, the *hyakushō*, who, by virtue of being recorded in the village register, became what might be called copyholders. Most significantly the *hyakushō* as a class were protected from the private interference of a military gentry and placed under the uniform bureaucratic governance of shogunal or daimyō administrations.

Because of the complex social and institutional consequences of the Taikō *kenchi*, modern historians have debated over several matters of interpretation. The Taikō *kenchi* debate (*Taikō kenchi ron*) has focused attention on the two problems of motivation and result. Aside from the obvious intent to increase the efficiency and effectiveness of land registration and taxation, did Hideyoshi and the other Sengoku daimyō intend to restructure society by drawing the samurai off the land and creating the semi-autonomous village? And, whether intended or not, what were the major social results of the *kenchi*, and how are they to be interpreted?

The current debate, which was most animated during the late 1950s and 1960s, was started by the publication of works by Araki Moriaki. Araki, having made a study of original *kenchichō* documents, proposed that the Taikō *kenchi* was responsible for working a feudal revolution (*hōken kakumei*). This resulted from Hideyoshi's intent that the *kenchi* should serve as a means of freeing the "small peasants," who up to that time had been held in a form of household slavery in large patrimonial peasant households. Most scholars agree that, during the 16th and early 17th centuries, village society became less subservient to the few great landholding families that dominated village life, and that former dependents or bound families (FUDAI) were increasingly able to become independent cultivators as rural samurai withdrew into the daimyō's castle towns. But many have argued against ascribing to Hideyoshi an intent to create a new class of "small independent cultivators." Araki has seen in Hideyoshi's edict of 1587, in which he stated that "ordinary farmers (*hirabyakushō*) shall not be held in service by leading farmers (*otonabyakushō*) or by rural officials (*shōkan*) even for one moment," an effort to destroy the hierarchy of classes in the pre-*kenchi* village. This he presumably accomplished by registering land in the names of dependent cultivators as though they were independent (owner) cultivators. But an examination of *kenchichō* from several different parts of Japan indicates that there were many differences in the ways that *kenchi* were compiled, and studies of wealthy rural families have shown that the new method of registration had very little effect on their holdings or social status. In fact other scholars, including Hayami Akira, maintain that the *kenchichō* encouraged the continued existence of *yakke* (families with a history of service in positions of authority in the villages).

Whatever the true intent of the Taikō *kenchi*, the work was a mammoth undertaking, occupying the energies of Japan's rulers for many years. By their very nature cadastral surveys are never finished, since the land base is continually changing. There is no firm evidence that before Hideyoshi's death in 1598 all provinces had been subjected directly to the Taikō *kenchi*. Comprehensive orders had been given out, and since by 1591 all daimyō were under his authority and subject to these orders, they had presumably complied. In any case, if there were neglected areas, the succeeding Tokugawa regime discovered them. *Kenchi* programs were initiated several times by the Tokugawa authorities, so that for most parts of

Japan the registers compiled under the Tokugawa regime up to the 1690s became the standard cadastral base (hondaka) for tax purposes. New fields added to the tax registers between the 1690s and 1720s were called "old new fields" (ko shinden), and those added to the registers during the 1720s were known simply as "new fields" (shinden). The use of the kenchichō as the basic cadastral document for land tax purposes came to an end with the LAND TAX REFORM OF 1873–1881. Nationwide surveys conducted between 1875 and 1878 became the basis for the modern transformation of land ownership and land tax practices under the Meiji government.

◼︎ —— Araki Moriaki, Bakuhan taisei shakai no seiritsu to kōzō (1959). John W. Hall and Marius B. Jansen, ed, Studies in the Institutional History of Early Modern Japan (1968). John W. Hall and Toyoda Takeshi, ed, Japan in the Muromachi Age (1977). Akira Hayami, "Epanouissement du 'Nouveau Régime Seigneurial' aux 16ᵉ et 17ᵉ Siècles: Le cas des Daimyō Asano," Keiō Economic Studies 1 (1963). Miyagawa Mitsuru, Taikō kenchi ron, 3 vols (1957–63). Guy Moréchand, " 'Taikō kenchi.' Le cadastre de Hideyoshi Toyotomi," Bulletin de l'Ecole Française d'Extrême-Orient 53.1 (1966). Osamu Wakita, "The Kokudaka System: A Device for Unification," Journal of Japanese Studies 1.2 (1975).   John W. HALL

kenchiku girei

The collective term for various religious and magic ceremonies and rites observed in the process of building a house. Such ceremonies are conducted in order to foretell whether the house, from the start of construction to completion, will meet disaster or be completed without mishap, and to invoke divine protection in keeping misfortune from falling on the house while under construction. Kenchiku girei are said to have originated in the Heian period (794–1185) under the influence of the Chinese cosmological concept of yin-yang. They were most scrupulously observed during the Edo period (1600–1868). The rites are performed in the following order during the construction of a house.

First comes the jichinsai, or groundbreaking ceremony. Before actual construction of the house is started, a ceremony is held to invoke peace on the construction site, the work, and the building to be constructed. Four bamboo branches are erected on the construction site and a shimenawa (straw rope) is tied around them to form a square. A Shintō priest is then called in to purify the site. Next is the koyairi, or erecting of a work hut, sometimes referred to as chōna hajime (starting work with an adze). A work hut is built at the outset of construction to celebrate the start of work. This is followed by the rite of ishibatsuki, or solidifying the foundation. Stones and rocks, which make up the foundation of the house, are pounded solidly into the ground. Completion of the foundation is celebrated by making rice cakes (mochi) of pounded glutinous rice. Fourth is the muneage or tatemae, the setting up of the framework of the house. When the framework is erected, sacred paper strips (GOHEI) are tied to the ridge pole to invoke the blessing of the gods. Rice cakes are then thrown from the ridge of the house to people who have gathered below. This in turn is followed by tōryō okuri, or seeing the master carpenter home. After the frame of the house has been erected, the master carpenter, who heads the team of carpenters working on the house, is ceremonially escorted back to his home. Bales of rice and barrels of sake are placed in front of the master carpenter's house in thanks for the erection of the framework. The shinchiku iwai celebrates completion of the house. Kayu (rice gruel) is cooked and poured over the pillars of the newly constructed house. Finally comes the ceremony of yautsuri, or moving into the new house. When people moved into a newly constructed house, the first object to be moved was predetermined by the custom of the particular region. In Tōkyō this first object was the omoto, a type of plant; in other regions it was the Shintō family altar (kamidana), or a wooden tub used to pickle vegetables, or a horse or cow. Generally the only kenchiku girei observances performed today are the jichinsai and the muneage.   Ōtō Tokihiko

Kenchōji

Head temple of the Kenchōji branch of the RINZAI SECT of Buddhism, located in the city of Kamakura, Kanagawa Prefecture. Kenchōji was founded in 1249 by the fifth Kamakura shogunal regent (SHIKKEN), Hōjō Tokiyori (1227–63), to serve as a major Zen center in Kamakura for RANKEI DŌRYŪ (Ch: Lanqi Daolong or Lan-ch'i Tao-lung, 1213–78), a distinguished Chinese Zen master who had arrived in Japan three years earlier. The site was selected by Toki-

yori's teacher, the famous Zen monk ENNI (1202–80), who sought to establish in Japan a Zen temple modeled after the great Chinese monastery on Jingshan (Ching-shan) in Hangzhou (Hangchow), where Enni had studied. Construction of the main temple buildings was begun in the year 1251 and completed two years later. Rankei was installed as the founding abbot of Kenchōji, which was ranked first among the five great Zen monasteries in Kamakura and was designated a kiganjo, i.e., a temple at which prayers were to be offered regularly for the well-being of its patron, the Hōjō family. In 1258, the sixth Kamakura shogunal regent, Hōjō Nagatoki (1229–64), presented Kenchōji with a complete set of the Buddhist canon in memory of his deceased wife.

Over the centuries Kenchōji suffered extensive damage from fires and earthquakes, but was rebuilt after each disaster. The last catastrophe to strike was the great Tōkyō Earthquake of 1923, which destroyed virtually the entire temple aside from the main gate (sammon), built in 1775, and the lecture hall (hattō), built in 1814. Several of the other buildings that collapsed in the earthquake, such as the Buddha hall, originally built in the Kambun era (1661–73), and the worship hall (shōdō), originally built in 1458, have since been restored.

The Hōjō family exempted Kenchōji from taxes, as did Toyotomi Hideyoshi (1536–98), the 16th-century military dictator, who forbade his troops to enter the temple precincts. The Tokugawa shōguns likewise looked on Kenchōji favorably and assisted in the reconstruction of the buildings that had suffered in various fires. The temple boasts a superb collection of paintings, calligraphic scrolls, and images, many of which have been designated National Treasures.   Stanley WEINSTEIN

Kenchōji-bune

Ship sent on a trade mission to the Yuan dynasty (1279–1368) of China in 1325 by the Kamakura shogunate (1192–1333). The shogunate authorized the mission and provided protection for its passage in return for a share of the profits, which were to be used to rebuild Kenchōji, a Zen temple at Kamakura that had been burned in 1315. The mission was a predecessor of the more famous TENRYŪJI-BUNE trade missions.

kendan

Also known as kendan sata. Policing and adjudication authority, including the power to pursue, arrest, incarcerate, try, and sentence criminals, legally vested in various officials from late in the Heian period (794–1185) through the Muromachi period (1333–1568) and arrogated by local magnates in times of disruption. In the Heian period, provincial governors (KOKUSHI) exercised this authority in the public domains, and landed proprietors, who had been granted certain immunities (FUYU AND FUNYŪ), had jurisdiction in their estates (SHŌEN). Beginning in the Kamakura period (1185–1333) kendan powers were divided, by an intricate formula, among the Board of Retainers (SAMURAI-DOKORO), the shogunate-appointed provincial military governors (SHUGO), and estate stewards (JITŌ). Shugo held police powers over murderers and rebels (see DAIBON SANKAJŌ), and jitō were responsible for apprehending robbers, arsonists, gamblers, and other miscreants. Jitō were jealous of their kendan privileges, because they could exercise armed force and could share in the confiscated wealth of the criminals. Their frequent abuse of these powers was to be a source of contention between them and shōen proprietors, with the latter gradually losing control.

kendō

(the Way of the sword). Japanese fencing based on the techniques of the two-handed sword of the samurai. Before the Shōwa period (1926–), it was customarily referred to as kenjutsu or gekken. Kendō is a relatively recent term which implies spiritual discipline as well as fencing technique.

In all probability, fencing with the single-edged, straight-blade sword was introduced from Sui (589–618) or early Tang (T'ang; 618–907) China. In the 9th century, combat on horseback led to the use of longer curved blades, and the increased length made it necessary to abandon the one-handed Chinese style of swordfighting for a two-handed style. With the establishment of the Kamakura shogunate in the late 12th century and the ascension to power of a martial aristocracy, the cultivation of sword skills flourished. Midway into the Muromachi period (1333–1568), there arose the custom of accomplished swordsmen opening schools in order to teach fighting skills and to preserve their traditions. From the ŌNIN WAR (1467–77) until 1600, a nearly unbroken period of civil war, *kenjutsu* was practiced by performing *kata,* formal attack and parrying exercises, sometimes with an oaken training sword.

With the establishment of nationwide peace by the Tokugawa shogunate in the early 17th century, *kenjutsu* went into a decline; it was no longer essential for survival and the moral and spiritual element became prominent, drawing on Confucianism, Shintō, and Buddhism, especially Zen. *Kenjutsu* became an element for training the mind and body. The number of schools increased to more than 200, and in the latter half of the 18th century, protective equipment and bamboo training swords *(shinai)* were introduced, making possible unrestrained competition without bloodletting.

Following the Meiji Restoration (1868), the practice of *kenjutsu* again went into a temporary decline, but in 1879 the Tōkyō police force instituted a *kenjutsu* course, and in 1895 the Dai Nihon Butokukai (All Japan Martial Virtue Society) was established to encourage *kenjutsu* and other martial arts. In 1911 *kenjutsu* was included in middle-school physical education programs.

In 1912 a committee was organized to assemble a body of training forms from among the *kata* of the foremost schools. With slight variations, these are retained today. In 1939 *kendō* became a regular course for the upper grades of primary schools. At the end of World War II, the Occupation authorities banned *kendō* on the basis of its use before the war to cultivate militarism. But following the end of the Occupation period in 1952, the All Japan Kendō Federation (Zen Nihon Kendō Remmei) was established, and in 1957 the practice of *kendō* was returned to Japanese middle schools.

The weapon is a hollow cylinder made of four shafts of split bamboo. It is bound with a leather grip and cap at its tip and with a leather thong or silk or nylon cord wound three times around the bamboo cylinder, one end fixed at a point just below the tip and the other attached to the hilt to prevent the four shafts from collapsing when striking. The length for junior high school students is 112 centimeters (3.7 ft), high school students 115 centimeters (3.8 ft), and adults 118 centimeters (3.9 ft). Fencers are protected by a *men* (face mask), which is secured to the head over a cotton towel which is bound to the head with two cords. The trunk of the body is protected by the *dō* (chest protector). The thighs are protected with five overlapping quilted panels, the *tare,* and the hands with padded mittens *(kote).*

Training is based on a variety of movements of attack and defense known as *waza.* Most fundamental are stance, footwork, cuts, thrusts, feints, and parries. Practice may consist of a drill on one or more special techniques, but *keiko* (free style practice) is most common. There are *kakari keiko* (sustained practice), in which students are compelled to attack over and over again, and *shiai keiko* (match practice), which is normally conducted before a tournament.

A match lasts five minutes, extensions, three. The winner is the first to score the first two out of three points. If only one point has been scored in regulation time, that person is the winner. The first to score a point in an extension period is the winner. Points are scored by the prescribed "cuts," which are limited to the center of the head or oblique cuts to the temple accompanied by the call *men* (face), cuts to either side of the trunk with the call *dō* (chest), and a cut to the right wrist at waist level or, when both hands are raised, cuts to either wrist with the call *kote.* The only thrust is made to the throat with the call *tsuki.* Both length and width of the match area may vary from 9 meters (29.5 ft) to 11 meters (36 ft). There are three referees.

Kendō has the following grades: six classes *(kyū)* of beginners graded from six up to one. Above these are *yūdansha* (rank holders) on a scale from 1 to 10. There are three teaching degrees: *renshi* requiring a minimum of 3 years at the 5th *dan* (rank) and limited to persons over 24 years of age; *kyōshi,* a minimum of 7 years as *renshi* and over 31 years of age; and *hanshi,* a minimum of 20 years as *kyōshi* and over 55 years of age. Each prefecture has a *kendō remmei* (federation) which may make promotions up to the fifth *dan.* Higher promotions are made by the Zen Nihon Kendō Remmei. The overall controlling organization is the International Kendō Federation founded in 1970. It observes the standards and rules of the All Japan Kendō Federation but has a multinational board of directors which oversees triennial international tournaments.

■——All Japan Kendō Federation, comp, *Fundamental Kendō* (1974). Iho Kiyotsugu, *Kendō* (1976). R. A. Lidstone, *Kendō* (1964). Mitsuhashi Shūzō, *Kendō* (1972). Nakano Yasoji, Tsuboi Saburō,

Kendō

A match is won with a one-handed thrust to the throat.

Zusetsu kendō jiten (1970). Nakano Yasoji, ed, *Gendai kendō kōza,* 3 vols (1971). Nakano Yasoji, *Kendō no tanoshimikata* (1972). Junzō Sasamori and Gordon Warner, *This is Kendo* (1964). Shigeoka Noboru, *Nihon kendō kata* (1977). Shōji Munemitsu, *Kendō hyakunen* (1966). Tominaga Kengo, *Kendō gohyakunen shi* (1972). Yamada Jirōkichi, *Nihon kendō shi* (1960). Benjamin H. HAZARD

kenin

(servant; houseman). A term widely used in ancient and medieval times to describe someone who had entered into a client relationship with a court noble or warrior chieftain. In the 7th and 8th centuries *kenin* were one of the five classes of servants of aristocratic families (see SEMMIN). In the Heian period (794–1185) *kenin* were attached as servants to the houses of major nobles and warrior leaders. Service in the latter case was normally military in nature, and these *kenin* are usually referred to as housemen. In the Kamakura (1185–1333) and Edo (1600–1868) periods the vassals of the shogunate were called GOKENIN (honorable housemen).

G. Cameron HURST III

kenka ryōseibai

Principle according to which both parties in a private fight are punished. This principle was first institutionalized in the Nambokuchō (Northern and Southern Courts) period (1336–92), when the Ashikaga shogunate (1338–1573) issued the interdict Kassen Togamegoto (1350) in order to prevent the increasing fights among *samurai.* According to Kassen no Toga no Koto, when two samurai engaged in a fight over territorial rights before the shogunate's judgment had been delivered, the shogunate confiscated all the land of the samurai who had started the fight and half the land of the one who had been forced into the fight. This law was reissued by the Muromachi shogunate in 1516. After the Ōnin War (1467–77), SENGOKU DAIMYŌ (warlord) families such as the Date, Takeda, Mōri, and Chōsokabe established similar codes in their domains. During the Sengoku (Warring States) period (1467–1568) *kenka ryōseibai* was applied not only to samurai but also to priests and commoners. In the Edo period (1600–1868), when a peaceful hierarchical structure was established, the practice continued, although the principle was not officially part of the KUJIKATA OSADAMEGAKI, the fundamental code of the Tokugawa shogunate. The strength of *kenka ryōseibai* as a concept is illustrated by the public sympathy toward the 47 samurai who avenged the forced suicide of their lord, Asano Naganori, who had attacked the lord Kira Yoshinaka (see FORTY-SEVEN RŌNIN INCIDENT).

Kennaiki

Full title *Kenshō In Naifu ki.* The diary of Madenokōji Tokifusa (1394–1457), a Muromachi-period (1333–1568) courtier who became inner minister (*naidaijin* or *naifu*) in 1445; Kenshō In is his posthumous title. The diary originally covered the years 1417 to 1455, but only the portion (50 vols) for 1428 to 1447 survives. *Kennaiki* is a very important source for the study of early Muromachi courtier society and such incidents as the assassination of the shōgun ASHI-

migimen shōmen hidarimen

men

keikogi

do

kote kote
tare

hakama

shinai

nodo

mune

migikote
migidō

hidarikote

hidaridō

Armor and dress

Point-scoring targets
of *datotsu* (strikes and
thrusts)

jōdan (overhead)
posture

hassō (eight-phase)
posture

waki (side)
posture

chūdan (middle) posture

gedan (low) posture

Kendō —— Armor and basic postures

The 10th abbot, ENNI, renovated the temple and further promoted Zen teachings. It was only after the 11th abbot, RANKEI DŌRYŪ, assumed office in 1259 that Kenninji became a monastery exclusively for Zen. In 1334 it was designated as one of the GOZAN temples, the five most important Zen monasteries patronized by the Kamakura and Muromachi shogunates, and from 1380 it ranked third in importance.

Although Zen was known to those Japanese monks who had studied in China during the Heian period (794–1185), it was not until Eisai built Jufukuji in Kamakura (1200) and Kenninji in Kyōto that it became an independent school. This would not have been possible had Eisai not allied himself with the shogunate founded by the Minamoto in Kamakura and decided to compromise with the Tendai and Shingon sects. In order to justify the establishment of a Zen monastery in the capital, Eisai argued in *Kōzen gokoku ron* (1198, Propagation of Zen for the Protection of the Country) that Zen teachings promoted the general welfare and national security.

Many notable monks received their training at Kenninji over the years, for example, DŌGEN (1200–1253), who later studied in China, accompanying Eisai's successor Myōzen, and MUSŌ SOSEKI (1275–1351), who served as a spiritual adviser to numerous political leaders and did much to enhance the position of Zen Buddhism. During the Muromachi period (1333–1568) Kenninji was a leading center of GOZAN LITERATURE, and a number of outstanding practitioners of this literature served terms in the abbacy, including SESSON YŪBAI (30th abbot), CHŪGAN ENGETSU (42nd), BETSUGEN ENSHI (44th), and GIDŌ SHŪSHIN (55th). In the 16th century Kenninji experienced a period of decline but regained its status during the Edo period (1600–1868). In 1872, when the Rinzai sect was reorganized into seven branches, Kenninji was designated as the headquarters of the Kenninji branch.

Over the years temple buildings were destroyed by fire and reconstructed so that most of the present buildings date from the Edo period. It houses a number of finely executed screen paintings (*fusuma-e;* see SCREEN AND WALL PAINTING) by the 16th-century artist KAIHŌ YŪSHŌ, as well as paintings by Tawaraya SŌTATSU and HASEGAWA TŌHAKU.

T. James KODERA

kenrei

(prefectural governor). Title for the governor of a prefecture, in use from 1871 to 1886. With the return of domain registers to the new imperial government *(hanseki hōkan)* a year after the MEIJI RESTORATION of 1868, the former *daimyō* had been designated governors *(chiji)* of their domains. In 1871 the government decided to abolish the feudal domains altogether and institute a prefectural system (see PREFECTURAL SYSTEM, ESTABLISHMENT OF); at that time the title for prefectural governors was changed to *kenrei* or *gonrei,* although the governors of Tōkyō, Kyōto, and Ōsaka continued to be called *chiji.* Appointed by the central government, the *kenrei* was in full charge of the administrative business of his prefecture. In 1886 the system of local administration was revised, and the title of a prefectural governor was changed back to *chiji.*

Kenrei Mon'in Ukyō no Daibu shū

(The Poetic Memoirs of Lady Daibu). A collection of 359 poems arranged in basically chronological order and furnished with often long prose headnotes *(kotobagaki),* so that the whole reads as a short lyrical autobiography. The memoirs consist of two volumes, the first of which describes Lady Daibu's early days at court in the service of Empress Tokuko, later known as Kenrei Mon'in (1155–1213). She writes of her love affairs with the noted poet and portrait painter FUJIWARA NO TAKANOBU and with Taira no Sukemori, a grandson of TAIRA NO KIYOMORI. It is the affair with Sukemori that forms the main theme of her work. The second volume tells of the death of Sukemori in the TAIRA–MINAMOTO WAR and her attempts to overcome and forget her grief. She continues with an account of her reentry into service at the court of Emperor GO-TOBA in about 1193 and describes the grief and longing for the past that were roused by the familiar sights of the court. Each volume contains a long sequence of mediocre poems with no prose interruption, recreating the moods of the two major periods of her life. An epilogue consisting of an exchange with the poet FUJIWARA NO SADAIE (Fujiwara no Teika) helps to date the work as no later than 1233. Although some of Lady Daibu's poems are outstanding and 23 of them were included in imperial anthologies, she cannot be considered more than a minor poet. Her memoirs, however, have enjoyed a quiet, steady

KAGA YOSHINORI and the Shōchō no Doikki (see TSUCHI IKKI), a peasant uprising in Ōmi Province (now Shiga Prefecture).

G. Cameron HURST III

Kenninji

ZEN monastery of the RINZAI SECT located in Higashiyama Ward, Kyōto; established by EISAI (or Yōsai), who served as its first abbot. In 1202 the shōgun MINAMOTO NO YORIIE commissioned Eisai to found a monastery in the southern part of Kyōto. Eisai modeled it on the Baizhang (Pai-chang) monastery in China, built during the Tang (T'ang) dynasty (618–907) and the first to institute uniquely Zen monastic codes. Construction was completed in 1205, and it was named Kenninji after the era (Kennin) in which it was built. Eisai transmitted the teachings of the Rinzai (Ch: Linji or Lin-chi) sect of Zen Buddhism, but from the outset he was careful to combine Zen with SHINGON SECT and TENDAI SECT teachings in order to avoid antagonizing the two dominant Japanese Buddhist establishments of the day.

popularity, in part because of their moving portrayal of grief and in part because of their connection with the epic events of the Taira-Minamoto War and their depiction of the suffering of war from a woman's point of view.

📖 ——*Kenrei Mon'in Ukyō no Daibu shū*, tr Phillip T. Harries as *The Poetic Memoirs of Lady Daibu* (1980). *Phillip T.* HARRIES

kenrikin → key money

Kenrokuen

Garden in Kanazawa, Ishikawa Prefecture, central Honshū. One of the three most famous gardens in Japan (the others being KAIRA-KUEN and KŌRAKUEN). It was laid out in 1822 as the garden of the *daimyō* Maeda Narinaga. The Ishikawa Prefectural Art Museum is located within the garden. Area: 10 hectares (25 acres). See photo at GARDENS.

Kensei Hontō

(True Constitutional Party). Political party formed in November 1898 by the former SHIMPOTŌ faction of the KENSEITŌ. In December 1900 ŌKUMA SHIGENOBU became the Kensei Hontō president. The following year 34 members left the party out of opposition to its support for the fourth ITŌ HIROBUMI cabinet's proposal to increase taxes to pay for BOXER REBELLION expenses. In 1903 it allied with Itō's party, the RIKKEN SEIYŪKAI, to oppose the first KATSURA TARŌ cabinet's proposal to increase taxes for naval armaments and in so doing helped to bring down the 17th Diet. In December 1907 Ōkuma resigned from the party presidency. In the 1909 election the party won 65 seats as against the Seiyūkai's 204. Its own factional disputes still unresolved, it decided to merge with other Diet groups, including the Yūshinkai, the Mumeikai, and the Boshin Kurabu, to form the RIKKEN KOKUMINTŌ in March 1910. See also POLITICAL PARTIES.

Kenseikai

(Constitutional Association). Political party founded in October 1916 through a merger of the RIKKEN DŌSHIKAI, CHŪSEIKAI, and Kōyū Kurabu. Its 197 seats in the House of Representatives immediately made it the majority party and nourished the expectation that its president, KATŌ TAKAAKI, would be named prime minister by the elder statesmen (GENRŌ). The appointment instead of General TERAUCHI MASATAKE and his subsequent dissolution of the Diet in the face of a Kenseikai no-confidence motion initiated a decade of political isolation for the Kenseikai. It won only 121 seats in the 1917 election and 110 in the 1920 election. No member was invited to join a cabinet until 1924, when it allied with the RIKKEN SEIYŪKAI and KAKUSHIN KURABU to bring down KIYOURA KEIGO's nonparty cabinet and won more than 150 Diet seats to become the majority party in the election later that year. With Katō heading a three-party coalition cabinet (GOKEN SAMPA NAIKAKU), the Kenseikai favored international cooperation and further domestic political reform. In 1925 it reduced the number of army divisions, opened diplomatic relations with the Soviet Union, and criticized the army's SIBERIAN INTERVENTION of 1918–22 while reforming the House of Peers and admitting only members of political parties to its cabinets. Its liberal reputation, however, was sullied by its passage of the repressive PEACE PRESERVATION LAW OF 1925.

The accession of General TANAKA GIICHI to the presidency of the Seiyūkai in 1925 drew Seiyūkai members out of this coalition cabinet, and Katō's second cabinet consisted solely of Kenseikai members. Upon Katō's sudden death in January 1926, WAKATSUKI REIJIRŌ succeeded him as party president and prime minister. His negotiations with the Seiyūkai and SEIYŪ HONTŌ in January 1927 temporarily eased the pressure for a new election, but Wakatsuki was forced to resign when the Privy Council quashed his proposal to aid banks in financial distress. In June 1927 the party merged with the Seiyū Hontō to form the RIKKEN MINSEITŌ. See also POLITICAL PARTIES.

Kenseitō

(Constitutional Party). Political party of the latter part of the Meiji period (1868–1912). Formed in June 1898 by an alliance of the JI-YŪTŌ (Liberal Party) and the SHIMPOTŌ (Progressive Party), with

ŌKUMA SHIGENOBU as president. Following the dissolution of the Diet by ITŌ HIROBUMI, whose cabinet had been unsuccessful in its efforts to increase taxes, the Jiyūtō, headed by ITAGAKI TAISUKE, and the Shimpotō decided to join forces. The new party called for the safeguarding of constitutional government, expansion of trade, a balanced budget, a party cabinet, and diffusion of education. Ōkuma and Itagaki were ordered to form a new cabinet. In the election that followed, the Kenseitō won a majority. Ōkuma filled the posts of foreign minister and prime minister, while Itagaki became home minister. Members of the old Jiyūtō faction, however, felt they had not been given their share of cabinet appointments. Intraparty tension increased when the old Jiyūtō faction joined Yamagata and other conservative elements in accusing Minister of Education OZAKI YUKIO of lese majesty for his "Republic Speech" in which he had said that Japan would be headed by the president of either MITSUI or MITSUBISHI if it were a republic. Even after Ozaki's resignation, the two factions could not decide on his successor. With the resignation of Itagaki, the cabinet dissolved barely four months after its formation. The former Jiyūtō faction reorganized as the new Kenseitō, with Itagaki as its head, and the Ōkuma faction reformed as the KENSEI HONTŌ (True Constitutional Party). The new Kenseitō became increasingly conservative, supporting the policies of the new nonparty cabinet formed by Yamagata, and in 1900 it was absorbed by Itō's RIKKEN SEIYŪKAI (Friends of Constitutional Government Party).

Kensei Yōgo Undō → Movement to Protect Constitutional Government

Kensetsushō → Ministry of Construction

Kenshō (fl 1161–1207)

WAKA poet, scholar, and Buddhist prelate; an adopted son of FUJI-WARA NO AKISUKE and a leader of the conservative Rokujō school of poets and scholars. Kenshō is better known for his commentaries on the MAN'YŌSHŪ, KOKINSHŪ, and other classical anthologies and for his critical treatises than for his own poetic compositions. He participated as both poet and judge in several major poetry contests, where he served as a principal proponent of Rokujō poetic ideals; his disputes with JAKUREN over poetic theory on the occasion of the "Poetry Contest in 600 Rounds" (*Roppyakuban uta-awase*) of 1193 are particularly famous. Thirteen of his poems are included in the seventh imperial anthology of court poetry SENZAI WAKASHŪ (ca 1188, Collection of a Thousand Years).

kentōshi → Sui and Tang (T'ang) China, embassies to

ken'yakurei

(sumptuary edicts). Edicts issued during the Edo period (1600–1868) by the Tokugawa shogunate and domain governments with the aim of enforcing frugality. Issued with increasing frequency, the regulations specified how to retrench finances and went into particulars about dress, food, housing, and almost every other aspect of life. See also KEIAN NO OFUREGAKI; KYŌHŌ REFORMS; KANSEI REFORMS; TEMPŌ REFORMS.

Ken'yūsha

Literary coterie. Formed in February 1885 as a casual fraternity of college students to dabble in literature, the Ken'yūsha became Japan's first major modern literary clique. The coterie journal the group published, *Garakuta bunko* ("Library of Odds and Ends"), launched the careers of several major novelists before the group dissolved in 1903.

Evolution (1885–1890) —— The four charter members, ranging in age from 17 to 19, were OZAKI KŌYŌ (1867–1903), YAMADA BIMYŌ (1868–1910), Ishibashi Shian (1867–1927), and Maruoka Kyūka (1865–1927). All were students of leading universities and shared a youthful but urbane taste in literature. Under the group name, Ken'yūsha ("Friends of the Inkstone"), they inaugurated their journal, *Garakuta bunko*, which first circulated among friends in hand-written copies and later was printed for private distribution. By the time the magazine went on sale (16 issues, May 1888–February 1889), membership had swollen to 85, including KAWAKAMI BIZAN

Kenzan

Teabowl with a bold design of a flowering plum tree. Low-fired transparent glaze over iron-oxide decoration on a white slip ground. Height 8.7 cm. Late 17th or early 18th century. Umezawa Memorial Gallery, Tōkyō.

(1869–1908) and IWAYA SAZANAMI (1870–1933), soon joined by Emi Suiin (1869–1934). Shortening its name to *Bunko* (nos 17–27, March–October 1889), the journal attracted new members, one of whom was HIROTSU RYŪRŌ (1861–1928) and guest contributors such as KŌDA ROHAN (1867–1947). Bimyō, having made his commercial debut ahead of the others with an acclaimed short story, "Musashino," and a GEMBUN ITCHI (unity of spoken and written languages) style of his own creation, left the Ken'yūsha in 1888 for a new and rival fiction journal, *Miyako no hana*. Although between 1889 and 1892, the Ken'yūsha published three more periodicals, *Shōbungaku, Edo murasaki,* and *Senshi bankō,* the vital force propelling the Ken'yūsha into an unprecedented position of power was Kōyō, who proved to be not only a prolific writer of extremely popular stories in a pioneering style but also a competent manager of practical affairs. He took charge of the prestigious literary section of the newspaper YOMIURI SHIMBUN in 1889 and influenced the editorial policies of two great publishing houses, HAKUBUNKAN and Shun'yōdō, enabling him to advance the careers of Ken'yūsha writers.

Zenith (1891–1903)——Members who had established a reputation, particularly through the ambitious fiction series, *Shincho hyakushu* (A Hundred New Volumes) inaugurated by Yoshioka Shosekiten in 1889, found themselves besieged by flocks of aspiring young writers begging to be disciples. Out of this second generation of Ken'yūsha members and associates emerged authors whose historical significance ultimately matched or surpassed that of the first generation: IZUMI KYŌKA (1873–1939) and TOKUDA SHŪSEI (1871–1943) from the Kōyō school; NAGAI KAFŪ (1879–1959) under the auspices of Sazanami and Ryūrō; and TAYAMA KATAI (1872–1930), a protégé of Suiin. While schooling and launching such future luminaries, Ken'yūsha climbed to the peak of its influence and creativity, several among the older members producing major works and establishing literary genres of their own. The undisputed leader, Kōyō, championed a return to the realism of Ihara SAIKAKU (1642–93) whose influence is apparent in *Kyaramakura* (1890, Aloeswood Pillow), introduced the genre of the psychological novel with *Sanninzuma* (1892, Three Wives) and *Tajō takon* (1896, Much Love Much Regret), and ended his career with the crowning statement of Ken'yūsha style, *Konjiki yasha* (1897–1902; tr *The Golden Demon*, 1905), in which he explored the conflict between social and personal values. The versatile Sazanami promoted the development of creative juvenile literature with *Koganemaru* (1891, Golden Boy) and established it as a legitimate genre through extensive editorial activity. Before he was driven to suicide, Bizan turned from his early romantic lyricism to the indictment of evils of the social system in such stories as "Uraomote" (1895, Inside Outside), originating, with Kyōka, the genre known as the *kannen shōsetsu* (idea or concept fiction), which flourished after the Sino–Japanese War (1894–95). The *shinkoku* (or *hisan*) *shōsetsu* (dismal, or harrowing fiction) was born with "Kurotokage" (1895, Black Lizard), written by the cynical Ryūrō, who authored another Ken'yūsha mas-

terpiece, "Imado shinjū" (1896, Double Suicide at Imado). Toward the turn of the century, the Ken'yūsha began to lose popularity and with the death of Kōyō cohesive organization was lost.

Significance——The Ken'yūsha's contribution to literature can be traced ultimately to its transitional nature. Ken'yūsha writers expanded literary horizons in a number of ways: (1) they replaced didactic presentation of personified abstract concepts such as virtue and vice with a realistic portrayal of the human dilemma; (2) through observation of contemporary society and meticulous descriptions, they brought to literature a degree of psychological depth, analytical insight, and social perspective, rendering it more immediately significant to the reading public and acceptable to intellectuals; (3) they consummated stylistic innovations such as *gazoku setchū bun* (synthesis of poetic and vernacular dictions) which was well suited to deal with the transitional and eclectic Meiji culture, and *gembun itchi* forms like the durable ". . . *de aru*" style that Kōyō used; (4) they contributed to the development of *taishū bungaku* (POPULAR FICTION), the *katei shōsetsu* (home novel), and the FŪZOKU SHŌSETSU (novel of manners). If most of the works written by its members now seem elaborate but maudlin melodramas, Ken'yūsha will still stand prominently as the last monument dedicated to indigenous aesthetic and literary traditions before the mainstream of Japanese literature entered fully into the Western-oriented phase of its evolution.

■——Collection of Ken'yūsha works in Japanese: *Ken'yūsha bungaku shū*, in *Meiji bungaku zenshū*, vol 22 (Chikuma Shobō, 1969). Translations: Hirotsu Ryūrō, "A Lover's Suicide at Imado (synopsis)," *Japan P.E.N. News* vol 13 (October 1964). Iwaya Sazanami, *The Crab's Revenge* (1938). Iwaya Sazanami, *Iwaya's Fairy Tales of Old Japan* (1914). Iwaya Sazanami, *Japanese Fairy Tales* (1953). Izumi Kyōka, "A Tale of Three Who Were Blind," tr Edward Seidensticker, in Donald Keene, ed, *Modern Japanese Literature* (1956). Ozaki Kōyō, *The Golden Demon*, tr Arthur Lloyd (1905). Works about the Ken'yūsha: James R. Morita, "Garakuta Bunko," *Monumenta Nipponica* 24.3 (1969). Fukuda Kiyoto, *Ken'yūsha no bungaku undō* (1950). Ikari Akira, *Kōki Ken'yūsha bungaku no kenkyū* (1958). Ikari Akira, *Ken'yūsha no bungaku* (1961).

Chieko MULHERN

Kenzan (1663–1743)

Also known as Ogata Kenzan. Real name Ogata Shinsei. Potter, painter, and younger brother of the famous Edo-period (1600–1868) artist Ogata KŌRIN. He was the third son of Ogata Sōken (1621–87), a wealthy Kyōto textile merchant among whose patrons were members of the imperial court nobility. Kenzan was related through his great-grandfather to the notable 16th- and early-17th-century calligrapher, ceramist, and lacquer-ware designer HON'AMI KŌETSU.

The Ogata home was a center of animated artistic activity and discussion, and in this atmosphere Kenzan's talented brother Kōrin showed early promise as a painter and designer, but the retiring Kenzan showed a scholarly disposition and devoted his attention to the study of Chinese and Japanese poetry. Nevertheless, contacts with the current generation of potters at the Takagamine artists' colony founded by Kōetsu began to draw his attention to the ceramic arts, and to the Kōetsu-related RAKU WARE tradition in particular.

Kenzan built a scholarly retreat near the kiln of the prominent Kyōto potter NONOMURA NINSEI, and contacts with Ninsei and his sons were also instrumental in moving Kenzan toward an active career as an artist. In 1699 Kenzan established a kiln of his own at Narutaki, northwest of Kyōto, on land provided by a member of the court nobility. Since the northwesterly direction is called *inui,* Kenzan called the kiln Inuiyama (Northwest Mountain). The same characters used to write Inuiyama can be read *kenzan,* which became his best-known art name and the name by which he is known to history.

His brother Kōrin joined him after his debut as a ceramic artist and some of the finest surviving examples of Ogata ceramic art are the result of their collaboration. Kōrin sometimes did designs in a Chinese literati-painter style in bold blackish iron-oxide brush strokes on a ground of white slip, with the potting and poetic inscriptions provided by Kenzan, but the results of this kind of cooperation were so harmonious that they appear to be products of a single artistic impulse. Kenzan took a very deferential attitude toward his brother's abilities as a painter, but Kenzan's paintings were outstanding in their own right, and some of the square plates he made and inscribed with landscapes and poetic inscriptions are certainly the equal of the collaborative pieces.

Kenzan was no businessman, and by 1712 he was forced for financial reasons to give up his adventurous and creative work at Narutaki. He opened a pottery retail store in Kyōto and rented facilities for the production of what were generally more routine pieces that emphasized the strong overglaze enamel colors popularized by Ninsei. In 1731 he left the capital to accept the patronage of a priestly aristocrat in the city of Edo (now Tōkyō). This financial reprieve, although coming late in life, gave him a new creative impetus and he remained active in scholarly and artistic endeavors until his death.

Kenzan is notable, even among the highly versatile artists of the RIMPA tradition, for his imaginative combination of the poetic sensibilities of the Chinese literati-painter tradition with the decorative verve and invention of the great Japanese artist-artisans who flourished in the 17th and early 18th centuries. See also KYŌTO CERAMICS.

📖——Ryōichi Fujioka, *Tea Ceremony Utensils,* tr Louise Allison Cort (1973). Masahiko Satō, *Kyoto Ceramics,* tr Anne Ono Towle and Usher P. Coolidge (1973). Tanaka Sakutarō and Nakagawa Sensaku, *Tōgei,* vol 19 of *Genshoku Nihon no bijutsu* (Shōgakukan, 1967). Lloyd CRAIGHILL

Kenzō → Takada Kenzō

kenzuishi → Sui and Tang (T'ang) China, embassies to

keppan

("blood seal"). A fingerprint stamped with blood drawn from one's fingertip; affixed on or beside a signature to show one's responsibility for and adherence to the terms of various contractual and ceremonial documents. This custom, which can be traced back to the 14th century, became popular among the warrior class during the Sengoku period (1467–1568), a time of war and treachery. During the Edo period (1600–1868), it spread to other social classes and was used, for example, to seal pledges of love. As variations, people might sign in blood *(kessho shohan)* or write the entire text *(ketsubun* or *kessho)* in a mixture of India ink and blood or in blood only.

Kerama Islands

(Kerama Rettō). Small group of islands approximately 30 km (19 mi) west of the main island of Okinawa. Made up of some 20 small islands clustered around the larger islands of Tokashikijima and Zamamijima. There is active coastal fishing but relatively little farming because of the hilly terrain.

Kesennuma

City in northeastern Miyagi Prefecture, northern Honshū, on the Pacific coast. A fishing port since ancient times, Kesennuma also has several seafood processing plants. It is a part of the Rikuchū Coast National Park. Pop: 68,559.

keshin → avatar

Ketsumeidan Jiken → League of Blood Incident

ketsuzei ikki

("blood tax" riots). Also called *chōhei hantai ikki.* Riots by peasants in opposition to the CONSCRIPTION ORDINANCE OF 1873. The government tried to dismiss the riots as the result of a misinterpretation on the part of peasants of the word *ketsuzei* (literally, "blood tax," but actually a metaphor for compulsory military service) in the official notice, it being rumored that the blood of conscripts would be taken and sold to foreigners. The peasants' grievances were real, however, for conscription would drain the villages of necessary labor. The new ordinances on compulsory education and the LAND TAX REFORMS OF 1873–1881 added further to their burdens. More than 15 riots took place, mostly in western Japan, in which peasants attacked and burned government offices, schools, and police stations. The riot in Fukuoka Prefecture involved some 30,000 people.

The riots were eventually quelled by forces made up of former *samurai,* the leaders were executed, and more than 16,000 others were punished.

keyaki → zelkova

key money

(kenrikin). A payment by the lessee (tenant) of a specified sum to the lessor (landlord) at the commencement of a lease agreement for land or structures as a premium which is not returned to the lessee upon the expiration of the lease; sometimes referred to as fee money *(reikin)* or honorarium *(shakin).* The practice of requiring a lessee to pay key money originated in the large urban areas of Japan and has no legal basis. Whether a lessee is required to pay key money theoretically depends upon the mutual agreement of the parties in the lease agreement, but in reality, if a lessor requests such a fee as a condition of the lease contract, it is very difficult for a lessee to refuse. The amount of key money is usually set unilaterally by the landlord.

The reasons for paying key money vary, and accordingly, the legal consequences of such payments also vary. In a lease of land or a building for business purposes, key money is often paid as compensation for the benefit the lessee obtains in acquiring the lease of a preferred business location. In a lease for residential purposes, key money may be a prepayment of part of the rent or compensation to the lessor for granting consent, which is legally required, to the assignment of a lease right by a lessee to a third party. The nature of the payment, and thus its legal consequences, is established by the language of the contract and the amount of the payment. See also DEPOSIT MONEY. KAI Michitarō

K. Hattori & Co, Ltd

(Hattori Tokeiten). Firm engaged in the sale of watches and clocks made by Seikō-affiliated plants. Its sales volume for timepieces is the largest in the world. Founded in 1881 by HATTORI KINTARŌ, in 1892 it established a manufacturing concern, Seikōsha Co, Ltd, and initiated production of Seikō-brand wall clocks; it later established two other plants, Daini Seikōsha Co and Suwa Seikōsha Co. In 1895 it began to produce pocket watches, in 1899 table clocks, and in 1913 wristwatches. During World War II it produced precision weapons, but resumed production of timepieces after the war and attained domestic leadership in the field by building a nationwide network of retail outlets. The firm with its plants supplied the official timing devices used in the 1964 Tōkyō Olympics, establishing its reputation worldwide and creating a basis for the expansion of export sales. In recent years the firm has begun mass production of higher-grade wristwatches employing advanced microelectronic technology. A unique feature of the company is the administrative separation of the functions of manufacture and sales, the former being in charge of the three manufacturing plants. In 1968 the firm set up its first overseas sales company in Hong Kong, followed by similar companies in New York, Düsseldorf, London, and other cities. Through Daini Seikōsha and Suwa Seikōsha, it has established manufacturing facilities in Singapore and other Southeast Asian countries. In the fiscal year ending in March 1982, annual sales were ¥364.8 billion (US $1.5 billion), of which the sale of watches accounted for 76 percent, clocks 13 percent, special machinery 4 percent, and jewelry and other goods 7 percent. In the same year the export ratio was 50 percent and capitalization stood at ¥4.8 billion (US $19.9 million). Corporate headquarters are in Tōkyō.

ki

An important concept in Japanese traditional popular psychology and in interpersonal relationships. The word *ki,* which means loosely "mind," "spirit," or "heart," is used in a number of idiomatic expressions to describe various states of mind. The use of the word *ki* occurs in over 40 such expressions which may be classified roughly into the following categories. (1) Consciousness, awareness, or sanity: when a person becomes insane, it is said that his *"ki* is out of kilter" *(ki ga kuruu);* when he faints, his *"ki* becomes distant" *(ki ga tōku naru);* when he gets distracted, his *"ki* becomes scattered" *(ki ga chiru).* (2) Interest, intention, or volition: when an individual is willing, his *"ki* proceeds" *(ki ga susumu);* when he loses his initial interest, his *"ki* changes" *(ki ga kawaru).* (3) Mood, feelings, or emotions: when a person feels depressed, his "*ki* sinks or becomes closed" *(ki ga shizumu/fusagu);* when he is nervous, his "*ki* becomes ruffled" *(ki ga kusha kusha suru).* (4) Temperament, heart, or mind: of a quick-tempered person it is said that his "*ki* is short" *(ki ga mijikai);* of a timid person that his "*ki* is small" *(ki ga chiisai);* of a good-natured person that his "*ki* is good" *(ki ga ii);* of a patient person that his "*ki* is long" *(ki ga nagai).* In some expressions *ki* is used as an object, for example, a person "moves his *ki* around" *(ki o mawasu)* when he makes a conjecture about another person, or he "drops his *ki*" *(ki o otosu)* when he is disappointed. However, in most expressions it is *ki,* not the individual, that is the subject of the statement. When a person is patient, it is not *he* but the *ki* (in him) that is long. When an individual feels depressed it is not *he* but *ki* that sinks.

📖——Takeo Doi, "Japanese Language as an Expression of Japanese Psychology," *Western Speech* 20 (1956).

Hiroshi WAGATSUMA

Kiaochow concession → Jiaozhou (Kiaochow) concession

Ki Baitei (1734–1810)

A painter of the literati (BUNJINGA) manner. A native of Ōtsu in Ōmi Province (now Shiga Prefecture) and disciple of BUSON (1716–84), both in painting and *haiku* poetry, Baitei was often referred to as Ōmi Buson and Ōtsu Buson. Baitei spent most of his life in the area of Ōtsu known as Konan, and many of his paintings executed from 1783 bear the name Konan as part of the signature. Names appearing most frequently on his art are Baitei, Baitei Ki Jibin, Konan Kyūrō, and in his late years, Kyūrō Sanshō. His most commonly used seals are Bai Tei and Jibin. In February of 1909, a memorial exhibition of his work was held at the temple Chōjuji, Ōtsu, to commemorate the 100th anniversary of his death.

Baitei's paintings show much of the lyricism found in the work of Buson, though in general they are less meticulously executed, their rough brushwork giving the impression of tremendous power and dramatic energy. His specialty was landscape painting, but he numbered among his accomplishments *haiga* (haiku paintings), *giga* (humorous paintings), ŌTSU-E (folk-style pictures from Ōtsu), *bijin* (beautiful women), and *kyōga* (satirical paintings). He published many of his works in woodblock-illustrated books, the finest of which is *Kyūrō gafu,* an important reference for the study of his art. The woodcuts relate closely to his painting style and reveal the strong influence of Buson as well as the dramatic inclination of Baitei's original genius.

📖——Cal French, *The Poet-Painters: Buson and His Followers* (1974).

Cal FRENCH

kiba minzoku setsu → horse-rider theory

Kibi Kōgen

(Kibi Highland). Series of low-lying mountains. Southern corner of the Chūgoku Mountains. Extends from Okayama Prefecture to Hiroshima Prefecture, western Honshū. Part of a larger highland extending from Hyōgo Prefecture to Yamaguchi Prefecture. In the valleys are paddy fields, while in the uplands are limestone quarries and cement plants. Stock farming and vegetable farming flourish on the highland. Elevation: 200–600 m (656–1,968 ft).

Kibi no Makibi (693–775)

Scholar-official of the Nara period (710–794). Born into a powerful family of the Kibi region (now part of Okayama Prefecture), in 717 he was sent, with the scholar ABE NO NAKAMARO, the priest GEMBŌ, and others, to study in China (see SUI AND TANG CHINA, EMBASSIES TO), where he gained a degree of literary fame. In 735 he returned to Japan with Gembō, bringing back many books, musical instruments, weapons, Buddhist images, and sutras. Makibi and Gembō became influential in government under the regime of TACHIBANA NO MOROE, but after the rise to power of FUJIWARA NO NAKAMARO, they were both demoted. In 752 Makibi was again sent to China, this time to invite the Chinese monk GANJIN to teach in Japan. On his return in 754 he was assigned to DAZAIFU, the government headquarters in Kyūshū, where he supervised the building of

the fortification ITOJŌ. In 764 Makibi played a central role in the suppression of a civil disturbance led by Nakamaro and was promoted to minister of the right *(udaijin).* However, with the death of Empress Shōtoku (Empress KŌKEN) and the ensuing succession dispute, he retired from office in 771. Makibi was well versed in the Confucian classics as well as in astronomy, military science, and law; he also directed the construction of the temple TŌDAIJI. He wrote a book of admonitions, *Shikyō ruijū,* for the edification of his descendants. His first trip to China is depicted in the scroll *Kibi Daijin nittō ekotoba.*

KITAMURA Bunji

Kibuneyama

Mountain in northern part of the city of Kyōto. Noted for its forests of cedar. It is the site of Kibune Shrine, dedicated to the god of rain. It has numerous hiking trails. Height: 700 m (2,296 ft).

kibyōshi

(literally, "yellow covers"). A major form of GESAKU literature, the generic designation for all prose fiction from the mid-18th century to the end of the Edo period (1600–1868). One of the main subgenres of the KUSAZŌSHI (grass books), a distinctive genre of popular illustrated fiction produced mainly by writers and artists in the city of Edo (now Tōkyō) ranging from juvenile tales to elaborate stories that flourished from the late 18th century to the mid-1880s. The name *kibyōshi* derives from the bright yellow color of these jacketed booklets, as does the name for earlier species of the *kusazōshi* genre, e.g. the *kurobon* (black books) and *aohon* (green books), out of which the *kibyōshi* developed.

The format of the *kibyōshi* is a five-by-seven-inch (thirteen-by-eighteen centimeter) bound pamphlet of woodblock-print illustrations with narrative and dialogue inscribed in the blank spaces in the drawings. The pamphlet contains five double pages and is bound in a yellow cover; most stories are made up of three such pamphlets. Similar picture books, much cruder and addressed to the semiliterate and children, had been available since the 1720s. What sets the *kibyōshi* apart from those earlier works in addition to the new format is the content of somewhat greater sophistication, which made it suitable for adult readers. Humor, wit, parody, irony, satire, and allegory are prominent elements. Among the illustrators were such prominent UKIYO-E artists as TORII KIYONAGA and UTAGAWA TOYOKUNI.

The *kibyōshi* emerged as a distinct category of fiction with the instant success of an illustrated story titled *Kinkin sensei eiga no yume* (1775; tr *Mr Glitter 'n' Gold's Dream of Splendor,* 1970) which promptly created a vogue in Japan for stories in a similar vein. *Kinkin sensei* was written and illustrated by Kurahashi Kaku (1744–89), a samurai who wrote many *kibyōshi* using the pen name KOIKAWA HARUMACHI. The story is an adaptation of the NŌ play *Kantan,* which had been modeled on a classic Chinese story. Kinkin, an impoverished commoner on his way to the great city of Edo in quest of wealth and happiness, falls asleep while he is waiting for millet cakes to be served at a wayside inn. He dreams of falling heir to a vast inheritance; he squanders it all by indulging himself in every conceivable extravagance, and, by the dream's end has been reduced to his original state of penury. Kinkin is made aware of the vanity of his ambition and promptly returns to his home as a much wiser man. Although the story is didactic, the setting is the world of teahouses, *geisha,* and courtesans. This background gave it an aura of modernity that made it attractive to readers, especially the townspeople, of the Edo period.

The best *kibyōshi,* certainly the most pungent ones, were written in the decade before 1791, the year in which the fury of the program of moral austerity initiated by the reformist MATSUDAIRA SADANOBU was directed at writers of fiction. The most provocative writers of that period were Tōrai Sanna (1749–1810), whose *Kiruna no ne kara kane no naru ki* (1785, Don't Cut Down the Tree Whose Root Bears Gold) parodies poverty by depicting a millionaire who glorifies poverty but fails in his attempt to attain it, and SANTŌ KYŌDEN, best known for his *Edo umare uwaki no kabayaki* (1785, Spitchcocking the Edo-born Philanderer), about a vainglorious swain who fails miserably in his attempt to acquire a reputation as a suave, sensuous man of leisure, and *Kōshijima toki ni aizome* (1789, Confucian Stripes Dyed a Timely Indigo), a caricature of the way the reformist government stressed Confucian ethics. The *kibyōshi* indeed became an instrument for lampooning the government.

Bumbu nidō mangoku-dōshi (1788, Sifting for Practitioners of the Dual Paths of Literary and Martial Learning) of HŌSEIDŌ KISANJI, for instance, was a devastating satire on samurai mores and the futility of policies aimed at raising them; it was consequently banned by the Tokugawa shogunate. Kyōden was also among those writers who were punished for literary transgression and thereafter tended to avoid controversial issues.

The *kibyōshi* were, above all, entertaining and inexpensive. The extent of their popularity may be deduced from the fact that more than two thousand titles were published between 1775 and 1806, after which the reader's preference shifted to the GŌKAN (bound volumes), doubtless the most lavish and elaborate form of illustrated fiction ever devised in any country.

■ ——James T. Araki, "The Dream Pillow in Edo Fiction, 1772–81," *Monumenta Nipponica* 25.1–2 (1970). Mori Senzō, *Kibyōshi kaidai* (1972). Leon M. Zolbrod, *"Kusazōshi:* Chapbooks of Japan," *The Transactions of the Asiatic Society of Japan,* 3rd ser, vol 10 (1968).   James T. ARAKI

Kida Minoru (1895–1975)

Writer, anthropologist. Real name Yamada Yoshihiko. Born in Kagoshima Prefecture; graduate of Keiō University in economics. From 1933 to 1939 he studied sociology at the University of Paris and worked as a reporter for Agence France Presse, the French wire service. His *Kichigai buraku shūyū kikō* (1946), a novel in essay form satirizing various aspects of postwar Japanese society, received the 1948 Mainichi Book Award. In 1958 Kida published a complete translation of the French naturalist Jean Henri Fabre's 10-volume work on insects, *Souvenirs entomologiques.* He also translated a number of French works on sociology.

Kido Kōichi (1889–1977)

Politician. Grandson of KIDO TAKAYOSHI, one of the leaders of the Meiji Restoration (1868). Born in Tōkyō; graduate of Kyōto University. Kido held several minor bureaucratic posts before becoming minister of education in the first KONOE FUMIMARO cabinet (1937) and home minister in the Hiranuma Kiichirō cabinet (1939). As lord keeper of the privy seal (NAIDAIJIN) from 1940, he was supposed to stay out of politics; nevertheless, in July of that year he called a meeting of JŪSHIN (senior statesmen) and recommended that Konoe succeed YONAI MITSUMASA as prime minister, thereby assuming the unofficial role formerly carried out by the GENRŌ (elder statesmen). He did so again in 1941, on the eve of the Pacific War, this time recommending that TŌJŌ HIDEKI succeed Konoe. Kido is generally credited with persuading the government toward the end of the war to accept the conditions of the POTSDAM DECLARATION. Sentenced by the International Military Tribunal (see WAR CRIMES TRIALS) to life imprisonment as a class-A war criminal, he was released in 1955 for reasons of ill health. His diary, the *Kido nikki* (1966), which he kept from January 1930 to December 1945 and was presented at the trials to clear his record, is an extremely important historical source for the last days of World War II.

Kido Kōin → Kido Takayoshi

Kido Shirō (1894–1977)

Film producer. Born in Tōkyō. Graduating from Tōkyō University in 1919, he joined the studios of Shōchiku Motion Picture Company (see SHŌCHIKU CO, LTD). Becoming the head of the Shōchiku Kamata studio in 1924, he actively encouraged OZU YASUJIRŌ, KINOSHITA KEISUKE, and other directors to make films with an optimistic humanitarian content. Such films appealed especially to female audiences and were labeled as "Ōfuna-style" movies after the site of Shōchiku's Ōfuna studios in Kanagawa Prefecture. With the expansion of the second Sino-Japanese War in China his films came increasingly under criticism for being too frivolous. Nonetheless, in 1940 he became the president of the Nan'yō Eiga Kyōkai and in 1943, he became the chairman of the Dai Nihon Eiga Kyōkai, two film organizations that promoted the war effort. After World War II, Shōchiku revived the Ōfuna-style movie with such films as Ōba Hideo's *Kimi no na wa* (1953, What Is Your Name?) and Kinoshita Keisuke's *NIJŪSHI NO HITOMI* (1954, Twenty-Four Eyes). Kido was appointed president of Shōchiku in 1954.   ITASAKA Tsuyoshi

Kidōtai → Riot Police

Kido Takayoshi (1833–1877)

Also known as Kido Kōin. Statesman of the Meiji period (1868–1912); with SAIGŌ TAKAMORI and ŌKUBO TOSHIMICHI, he is known as one of the "three heroes" of the MEIJI RESTORATION of 1868. As representative of the Chōshū domain (now Yamaguchi Prefecture) he negotiated the secret alliance (1866) with the powerful Satsuma domain (now Kagoshima Prefecture) that eventually overthrew the Tokugawa shogunate; his initiatives between 1868 and 1871 as a Meiji government official brought about the abolition of the feudal system and the creation of a centralized bureaucratic state. For the eloquence of his state papers, he is denominated "the pen of the Restoration."

Kido's career was the briefest among Meiji leaders, yet it divides into distinct periods. During the first period, from the mid-1850s to 1865, as an imperial-loyalist *(sonnō)* swordsman he schemed against the Tokugawa shogunate, aided at times by his *geisha* lover Ikumatsu. (This image of Kido as a romantic figure has been celebrated in films; during his own lifetime it was the theme of a stage production in Yokohama.) In the second period, 1865–74, Kido emerged as a statesman who influenced the course of the nation in his roles as a Chōshū official, until 1868, and afterward as a privy councillor in the new national government. In the final period, 1874–77, Kido became the cabinet's conscience, acting as an in-house critic of the rapid pace of modernizing reforms, which impoverished farmers and SHIZOKU (former *samurai*) in the localities. He also held a concurrent post in the Imperial Household Ministry to oversee the moral education of the young emperor MEIJI.

Chōshū Samurai —— Kido was born in the Chōshū castle town of Hagi into the samurai household of the domain physician Wada Masakage. Although the family stipend was only 20 *koku* (1 *koku,* a measure of rice, equals about 180 liters or 5 US bushels; see KOKUDAKA), the impressive family mansion with two entrances—one for warrior patients, the other for townsmen—attested to the father's lucrative practice. At the age of seven, the son was taken into the 150-*koku* Katsura family in a deathbed adoption that, according to existing regulations, led to reduction of their stipend to 90 *koku.* Until 1865 he was known as Katsura Kogorō. To his natural father, with whom he continued to live, Kido owed an interest in Dutch studies (see WESTERN LEARNING) and some affluence; to his adoptive father he owed his relatively high social status. His rank qualified him for an orthodox education in literature and the military arts at the Meirinkan, the domain school. Subsequent attendance at the private academy of YOSHIDA SHŌIN, the ideologue of the proimperial movement, introduced him to imperial loyalism and to lower samurai whose leadership Kido ultimately assumed.

In 1852 Kido went to Edo (now Tōkyō) to study swordsmanship with Saitō Yakurō (1798–1871). Saitō's students were preoccupied with politics, however, and Kido established ties with loyalists from Mito (now part of Ibaraki Prefecture) and other domains. Serving with Chōshū forces assigned to coastal defense against the United States squadron of Commodore Matthew C. PERRY in 1853–54, Kido became both patriotic and interested in Western military science. He studied artillery with EGAWA TARŌZAEMON, a shogunate military reformer, and after observing foreign shipbuilders at Shimoda and Nagasaki, designed the first Western-style schooner to be constructed (1856) in Chōshū.

Restoration Activist —— After 1858, in his dual role as Chōshū official and a moderate in the clique of loyalist samurai, Kido acted as a liaison between the radical lower-samurai loyalists and the regular domain bureaucracy. In 1862 he fell under shogunate suspicion for his ties with Mito loyalists who had attempted to assassinate the senior councillor *(rōjū)* ANDŌ NOBUMASA and was transferred from Edo to Kyōto. There he joined the inner circle of Chōshū officials who guided their domain to a loyalist-exclusionist SONNŌ JŌI policy.

Chōshū's failures to control the imperial court soon clouded Kido's career. As chief domain officer in Kyōto, he failed to obtain advance warning of the COUP D'ETAT OF 30 SEPTEMBER 1863, in which Satsuma and Aizu drove Chōshū forces out of the city. Again, though he considered the attempt premature, he was involved in the HAMAGURI GOMON INCIDENT of 20 August 1864, a suicidal Chōshū charge on the Imperial Palace. On defeat Kido went into hiding with the geisha Ikumatsu, who later became his wife. Presently he took flight, posing as a shopkeeper in Tajima Province (now part of Hyōgo Prefecture) for several months.

He was summoned back to Chōshū when the radical clique under TAKASUGI SHINSAKU regained control of the domain in 1865. The success of the coup rested with the *shotai* (units made up of samurai and farmers), which had overwhelmed regular domain forces. Takasugi and Kido now deployed the *shotai* against the shogunate armies that pressed a punitive expedition against Chōshū in 1865–66; under the slogans Full Independence of Central Control and Reliance on Arms, Takasugi and Kido led the Chōshū forces to victory (see CHŌSHŪ EXPEDITIONS). (Mōri Takachika [1819–71], the daimyō of Chōshū, conferred on Kido the new name of Kido Kanji, altered to Kido Jun'ichirō in 1866 and to Kido Takayoshi in 1869.) Under the strong encouragement of SAKAMOTO RYŌMA, the loyalist from the Tosa domain (now Kōchi Prefecture), Kido negotiated a secret anti-Tokugawa alliance with Satsuma in 1866, partly to acquire English arms through Satsuma's collusion (see SATSUMA-CHŌSHŪ ALLIANCE).

When Takasugi died in 1867, Kido became Chōshū's available man. He was senior in age and rank to other loyalists; he had been uninvolved in factional struggles within the domain, and above all, he had survived the turbulent 1860s, which decimated Chōshū's loyalist leadership.

Meiji Councillor—— Following the overthrow of the Tokugawa shogunate and the restoration of imperial rule, Kido became the chief Chōshū spokesman in the new government, itself largely a Satsuma-Chōshū creation (see HAMBATSU). Under various titles he promoted policies of centralization and modernization, most notably as SANGI (councillor) in 1870–74 and 1875–76. He shared in drafting the CHARTER OATH, the new government's statement of principles. He also initiated the movement to abolish the semiautonomous domains. He personally directed the surrender of domain registers *(hanseki hōkan)* in 1869 and worked for the abolition of domains and the establishment of prefectures in 1871 (see PREFECTURAL SYSTEM, ESTABLISHMENT OF). He recognized that feudal Japan was no match for the modern, centralized states of the West. He also saw the need to strengthen central authority against discontented samurai, those cast adrift by defeat in the BOSHIN CIVIL WAR of 1868–69 as well as those inadequately rewarded for victory. He was unreceptive to the demands of the samurai-peasant units of Chōshū, personally quelling their 1870 revolt.

Kido was ambivalent toward the West. He both feared and admired the Western powers and sought to modernize his own nation through imitation. As associate ambassador to the United States and Europe with the IWAKURA MISSION (1871–73), he was able to study firsthand Western political and educational systems. On his return home he presented a memorial on constitutional government, to be established gradually on the German model, which he thought better suited to Japan. It was the first formal proposal on the subject by a high government official.

The trip abroad also convinced Kido that priority should be given to internal development, and in the cabinet debate of October 1873 he and the peace faction barely defeated the war faction of Saigō Takamori, who espoused an expedition against Korea (see SEIKANRON). Quoting from the ancient Chinese philosopher Mencius, Kido stressed his social concern: the masses were destitute, and war would halt reform programs to improve their lot. Kido remained consistently prudent in foreign policy, and in May 1874 he resigned in protest against the TAIWAN EXPEDITION OF 1874, which nearly embroiled Japan in war with China.

Cabinet Critic—— Following the ŌSAKA CONFERENCE OF 1875, a meeting of government leaders that endorsed a gradual move toward constitutional government, Kido returned to the government as councillor. In June he presided over the ASSEMBLY OF PREFECTURAL GOVERNORS. A conference with proto-legislative powers, it was a limited start toward popular participation in government.

In 1876 Kido expressed dissatisfaction with policies that, by building up the central government at the expense of the localities, had alienated *shizoku* and peasants. He secured minor modification of the system of enforced capitalization of *shizoku* pensions in 1876 (see CHITSUROKU SHOBUN). His efforts did not prevent an uprising by former samurai in Chōshū (see HAGI REBELLION) but probably minimized its scope. In the wake of peasant riots in Mie and Ibaraki prefectures in 1877, Kido pressed successfully for reducing the new land tax from 3 to 2.5 percent of assessed land value (see LAND TAX REFORM OF 1873–1881).

In his last years Kido oversaw the young emperor Meiji's education. He admonished the monarch not to neglect his studies and to be socially concerned. Kido advised the emperor during his northeast tour of 1876 to be more attentive in receiving local officials.

During the SATSUMA REBELLION of 1877, Kido persuaded the emperor to ride through the streets of Kyōto despite inclement weather to inspire the populace and to visit the war wounded.

Kido was a man of many talents. He preferred the traditional arts, excelling in calligraphy and poetry, enjoying the tea ceremony and *gidayū-bushi* chanting.

After 1873 Kido lost the dominant position in the government to the taciturn but more forceful Ōkubo. Ill health, absence from the seat of power after his resignation in 1874, and the defection of his chief protégés had forced Kido into a secondary position. His diary, kept from 1868 to 1877, the year of his death, reveals an increasingly discontented politician. Despite his criticisms, he did maintain the unity of the government and supported the suppression of the Satsuma rebellion that threatened its order.

📖 ——Kido Takayoshi, *Kido Takayoshi nikki,* ed, Tsumaki Chūta, 3 vols (1932). Sidney D. Brown and Akiko Hirota, "The Self-Image of an Early Meiji Statesman: Through the Diary of Kido Takayoshi, 1868–1877," *Selected Papers in Asian Studies,* Western Conference, Association for Asian Studies, 1 (1976). Albert M. Craig, "Kido Kōin and Ōkubo Toshimichi: A Psycho-Historical Analysis," in Albert M. Craig and Donald H. Shively, ed, *Personality in Japanese History* (1970). Ōe Shinobu, *Kido Takayoshi* (1968). Tanaka Sōgorō, *Kido Takayoshi* (1941). Tsumaki Chūta, *Shōgiku Kido Kō den,* 2 vols (1927). Tsumaki Chūta, ed, *Kido Takayoshi monjo,* 8 vols (1929–31). *Sidney DeVere BROWN*

kienrei

Debt moratoriums declared by the Tokugawa shogunate (1603–1867) to save its retainers from destitution. The retainers habitually sought cash advances against their rice stipends from FUDASASHI (rice brokers); these debts, with interest, rose beyond the retainers' ability to pay. The shogunate attempted to control interest rates and *samurai* expenditures, but the debts continued to mount. In 1789 the senior councillor *(rōjū)* MATSUDAIRA SADANOBU canceled all debts to *fudasashi* incurred before 1784, a total of some 1,200,000 *ryō.* Debts incurred between 1784 and 1789 were deferred and were to be paid off in annual installments at a low rate of interest. The shogunate decreed another *kienrei* in 1843 as part of the TEMPŌ REFORMS, and various *daimyō* instituted similar orders at different times. The *kienrei* were at best palliative measures, not a solution of the problem. Many *fudasashi* were bankrupted, and most of those who survived refused to lend money.

Ki family

An influential family (UJI) of ancient Japan. They claimed descent from Ki no Tsunu no Sukune, son of TAKENOUCHI NO SUKUNE, a legendary warrior of the YAMATO COURT (ca 4th century–ca mid-7th century). According to the early chronicle KOJIKI (712), the latter was the common ancestor of the HATA, Kose, SOGA, Heguri, Ki, and other prominent families. It is difficult, however, to accept this lineage as genuine, and the scholar TSUDA SŌKICHI considers it an invention of the Soga family; the SHINSEN SHŌJIROKU, a 9th-century genealogy, lists the Ki and Soga families as descended from the imperial line. The Ki, like the Soga, had a long history of diplomatic and cultural relations with the Asian continent. After the TAIKA REFORM of 645, several members of the Ki family attained high rank at the court, but in general the family tended to produce scholars and literary men such as KI NO TSURAYUKI and KI NO TOMONORI. *KITAMURA Bunji*

kigen

(era). A chronological system in which events are dated from a specified base year; also, the base year itself or the period of time reckoned from it. Examples include the Christian era, based on the year of Christ's birth, and the Islamic era, based on the year of the *hegira* (Mohammad's flight from Mecca to Medina in AD 622). In 1872, four years after the Meiji Restoration, the Japanese government officially inaugurated the use of the "imperial era" *(kōki),* reckoned from 660 BC, the year in which the legendary first emperor, JIMMU, was said to have ascended the throne. According to the imperial era, AD 1980 would have been *kigen* (or *kōki*) 2640; but since the end of World War II the system has rarely been used.

It is generally understood that the designation of 660 BC as the beginning of the imperial era was made by Prince SHŌTOKU when he compiled the histories TENNŌKI AND KOKKI in the early 7th century AD. In accordance with certain augural beliefs borrowed from China, the prince and his associates extrapolated backward from AD 601 (Suiko 9), a year considered auspicious in the sexagenary cycle (JIKKAN JŪNISHI), and arrived at 660 BC as a suitable year for the founding of the imperial dynasty. To fix the inception of the dynasty at such an early date was, of course, historically untenable. In archaeological terms, 660 BC belongs to the Final (Latest) Jōmon period (ca 1000 BC–ca 300 BC), a time for which there is no evidence of any kind of political organization, much less national unification. The date was doubtless chosen in part to give Japan a history comparable in length to that of China.

In any case, the reckoning of historical dates from the year of Jimmu's accession was used only infrequently. The method traditionally preferred was based on an emperor's reign or, later, on the use of era names (NENGŌ; see also PERIODIZATION; CALENDAR, DATES, AND TIME). A notable exception was the practice among Buddhists of computing from the year of Buddha's death. If that year is fixed at 949 BC, the year AD 1052 (Eishō 7; *kigen* 1712; 8th year of Emperor Go-Reizei) was the year 2001 in this system; but the year chosen for Buddha's death varied widely according to sect and period.

With the increase in contact with the West toward the end of the Edo period (1600–1868) and the introduction of the Western calendrical system, Japanese attention paradoxically turned once again to the imperial era. TOKUGAWA NARIAKI, a staunch advocate of restoring direct imperial rule, urged that 1840, or *kigen* 2500, should be a year of great national celebration. His view was accepted by many, for it served to emphasize the antiquity of Japan's history compared to that of the Western nations.

At the time the Meiji government instituted the imperial era, it also calculated the date of Jimmu's accession as the first day of the first (lunar) month. Converted to the Gregorian calendar as 29 January, it was established as a national holiday and in 1873 officially named Kigensetsu (the date was later changed to 11 February). Underlying these measures was the government's desire to build as quickly as possible a modern nation-state, with the unbroken imperial line as the symbol of national unity. The holiday was abolished in 1948, partly in response to OCCUPATION directives to expunge all traces of nationalism and militarism but especially in response to Japanese public opinion. The abolition was opposed by conservative elements, who succeeded in 1966 in having the holiday restored as Kenkoku Kinembi, or Founding-of-the-Nation Day. See KIGENSETSU CONTROVERSY.　　　　　　　　　　　*MAYUZUMI Hiromichi*

Kigensetsu controversy

Postwar debate over the revival of Kigensetsu (also known as Kenkoku Kinembi, or Founding-of-the-Nation Day) as a national holiday. There had always been an argument as to the validity of dating the founding of Japan from the legendary enthronement of Emperor JIMMU in 660 BC (designated as year 1 of the traditional Japanese calendar; see KIGEN); and the computation of the first day of the first month of that year as 11 February in the Gregorian calendar was even more controversial. By declaring in 1872 that the 11th of February would thenceforth be a national holiday to commemorate the founding of the Japanese empire, the leaders of the new Meiji government hoped to give further legitimacy to the imperial institution. In 1948 the *kigen* system of dating and most traditional holidays were abolished; Kigensetsu in particular had come to be associated with the "emperor system" and with the excesses of nationalism during the pre–World War II period. Therefore, when Prime Minister YOSHIDA SHIGERU in 1951 made known his desire to revive Kigensetsu as soon as Japan recovered its national sovereignty, there was strong opposition, especially from leftists and intellectuals who saw it as an attempt to limit freedom of thought. Nevertheless, in 1966 a bill was passed declaring 11 February, Kenkoku Kinembi, a national holiday.

Kiguchi Kohei (1873–1894)

Soldier and war hero of the SINO-JAPANESE WAR OF 1894–1895. Born in Okayama Prefecture. He was serving as private first-class in the 12th Regiment and as bugler at a battle in what is now Ansŏng Province in Korea, when he was wounded in the chest. Using his rifle as a crutch, he continued to sound the charge signal until he died. His heroic death was cited in moral and ethics primers for schoolchildren until the end of World War II.　　*KONDŌ Shinji*

Kihara Hitoshi (1893–　　)

Geneticist. Born in Tōkyō. Graduate of Hokkaidō University. He became a professor at Kyōto University in 1927. His most important research concerned the cytogenetics of wheat. He succeeded in tracing the original ancestry of wheat. His other research includes work on the seedless watermelon and the sex chromosomes of *suiba* (a variety of sorrel). He founded the Kihara Institute for Biological Research in 1942 and served as director of the National Institute of Genetics. He was awarded the Order of Culture in 1948.　　*SUZUKI Zenji*

Kiheitai

(Irregular Militia). A crack volunteer militia unit organized by the Chōshū domain (now Yamaguchi Prefecture) in 1863 in anticipation of an attack by the Western powers. Formed by TAKASUGI SHINSAKU, the unit comprised 300 to 400 men of all social classes, including peasants, from Chōshū and other domains. Leaders were chosen for ability rather than hereditary status, and the unit was characterized by strict discipline, Western-style training, and an extremely high caliber of leadership. Initially this elite corps included archers and lancers, but it was later equipped with rifles, which gave it the remarkable effectiveness for which it became known. Funds were contributed by the Chōshū government and privately by wealthy farmers and merchants.

The Kiheitai first saw action against the forces of the four Western powers during the SHIMONOSEKI BOMBARDMENT in 1864. It completely routed the armies of the Tokugawa shogunate during the second Chōshū Expedition in 1866. Always the principal support of the proimperial reformist faction in Chōshū, it later overthrew the proshogunate conservative faction that had taken control of the domainal government late in 1864 and joined the imperial forces in defeating the shogunal armies in the BOSHIN CIVIL WAR (1868). The Kiheitai was disbanded in 1869 after the establishment of the Meiji government.

The success of this mixed unit against armies composed entirely of *samurai* was an important factor in the establishment of universal conscription in Japan. Indeed, the CONSCRIPTION ORDINANCE OF 1873 was drafted by YAMAGATA ARITOMO, a former commander of the Kiheitai.

Kihira Tadayoshi (1874–1949)

Also known as Kihira Masami. Philosopher. Born in Mie Prefecture, he graduated from the Department of Philosophy of Tōkyō University in 1900. In 1919 he became a professor at the Peers' School (now Gakushūin University) and from 1932 to 1943 was an active member of Kokumin Seishin Bunka Kenkyūjo (Institute for Research on National Spirit and Culture), a government-operated organ for the propagation of nationalist ideology. Kihira pioneered the Japanese study of Hegel's philosophy and wrote a book on epistemology, *Ninshikiron* (1915). Later he tried to integrate traditional Japanese thought and Western philosophical methods but gradually became disenchanted with German idealism, particularly its concept of nationhood. After the publication of *Gyō no tetsugaku* (Philosophy of Spiritual Discipline) in 1923, he concentrated solely on the Japanese spiritual tradition, and championed nationalist philosophy in such publications as *Nihon seishin* (1930, The Spirit of Japan).　　*TAKAHASHI Ken'ichi*

Kii Channel

(Kii Suidō). Between eastern Shikoku and the western coast of the Kii Peninsula, Wakayama Prefecture, central Honshū, connecting the Inland Sea and Ōsaka Bay with the Pacific Ocean. Because of its strategic position, this is a major shipping artery. Length: 50 km (31 mi); width: 30–50 km (19–31 mi).

Kii Mountains

(Kii Sanchi). Mountain range covering the Kii Peninsula in Nara, Wakayama, and Mie prefectures, central Honshū. The highest peak is Hakkenzan (1,915 m or 6,281 ft). With one of the highest precipitation rates in Japan, the area has abundant water resources. The mountains of the Kii Peninsula are covered with forests of cryptomeria and cypress, and lumbering is important. Yoshino–Kumano National Park and Kōya–Ryūjin Quasi-National Park are the area's main attractions.

Kii Peninsula

(Kii Hantō). Located in the southern Kinki region, central Honshū. Jutting out into the Pacific Ocean, it encompasses Mie, Nara, and Wakayama prefectures. The greater part of the peninsula is covered by the rugged Kii Mountains. Heavily indented coasts surround the peninsula. There is heavy precipitation with the annual rainfall of the city of Owase exceeding 4,000 mm (158 in). The principal industries are forestry in the mountainous districts and fishing and tourism in the coastal regions.

kiji → pheasants

kijiya

Traditional woodworkers who mainly produced round wooden objects such as bowls, trays, and KOKESHI dolls, using a lathe (ROKURO). Also called *kijishi*, *kijibiki*, and *rokuroshi*. They built temporary huts in the mountains as base camps for collecting wood, changing locations when the proper kind of wood became scarce. Their traditional base was in the Ogura valley of Ōmi Province (now Eigenji Machi, Kanzaki District, Shiga Prefecture). The two shrines located there are dedicated to the supposed *kijiya* ancestor, Prince Koretaka (844–897), first son of Emperor Montoku (r 850–858). *Kijiya* credit the prince with the invention of the lathe. Lathe workers are mentioned in such early records as the SHŌSŌIN documents (8th century) and the ENGI SHIKI (927). The lathe-made, miniature wooden pagodas (the Hyakumanki Shōtō) at the temple HŌRYŪJI in Nara Prefecture are early examples of their work. With the clarification of forest ownership rights after the Meiji Restoration (1868), *kijiya* were unable to traverse the mountains freely, and so turned to valley agriculture or woodworking in the city for their livelihood. The contribution of *kijiya* to Japanese crafts is noteworthy, as several of the areas now famous for LACQUER WARE or WOODENWARE, including *Aizu-nuri* of Fukushima Prefecture, developed around *kijiya* communities.   MISUMI Haruo

Kikaishima

Island approximately 25 km (16 mi) east of the island of AMAMI ŌSHIMA, Kagoshima Prefecture, Kyūshū. One of the AMAMI ISLANDS, it is a rather flat island surrounded by coral reefs. The climate is subtropical and some 90 percent of the island is arable. The chief activities are sugarcane and vegetable cultivation, stock raising, and sugar production. The special product of the island is Ōshima *tsumugi* (pongee). Area: 56 sq km (22 sq mi).

kikajin

Immigrants from the Asian continent (particularly the Korean peninsula) who settled in early Japan. The term refers especially to the immigrant group led by YUZUKI NO KIMI from the Korean state of PAEKCHE in about AD 400. The term *kika*, meaning to change country of allegiance, was applied to this group in the chronicle NIHON SHOKI (720). The term *kikajin*, as first defined in the RYŌ NO SHUGE, a collection of early 8th-century legal commentaries, follows earlier Chinese usage and reflects a certain ethnocentrism with connotations of "grateful change of allegiance" (J: *kinka naiki*) to new rulers; therefore, many scholars today prefer a more neutral term like *toraijin* ("people from overseas") or *ijūmin* (immigrants). Historians have commonly used the term *kikajin* to refer, also, to several generations of the newcomers' descendants.

The principal source materials, including the KOJIKI, *Nihon shoki*, *Shoku nihongi*, KAIFŪSŌ, GENKŌ SHAKUSHO, SHINSEN SHŌJIROKU, and FUDOKI, suggest that the *kikajin* came for a variety of reasons: to escape war and political persecution, to earn a better livelihood in a country that was potentially rich but still undeveloped and sparsely populated, and to meet the demand in Japan for their knowledge and skills. Most probably came voluntarily, but historical records also say that especially skilled or learned men and women were sometimes "presented" by Korean rulers to the Japanese sovereign. There is also mention of Korean captives brought back after military expeditions. In the 7th century more than 100 Chinese taken captive in Korea were settled in Mino Province (now part of Gifu Prefecture); it is said that they provided military advice to the future emperor TEMMU during the JINSHIN DISTURBANCE of 672.

Many immigrants and their descendants were appointed to important positions in diplomacy, military affairs, and Buddhist and Shintō establishments, while others were leaders in economic development. Many formed wealthy families or clans (UJI) in the ASUKA region and other parts of the country, and many attained high court rank, especially after the late 7th century. In the *Shinsen shōjiroku* (an early 9th century listing of the genealogies of the nearly 1,200 families with official rank in the capital and the five Kinai [central] provinces), 324 of the 1,059 families listed are specified as being of immigrant origin. Emperor KAMMU (r 781–806) proudly acknowledged descent from the royal house of the Korean state of Paekche through his mother, Takano no Niigasa (d 789).

Arrivals of the continental immigrants can be classified, for the most part, into three roughly definable periods. Aside from the virtually certain arrival of large numbers of pre-4th-century immigrants lost to written history, the newcomers in the first historical mass movement appear to have come around the end of the 4th and the beginning of the 5th century, a period of political turmoil in China and the Korean states, settling mainly in the Kinai region. They included the scholar WANI (ancestor of the Kawachi no Fumi clan) from Paekche; a large group led by Yuzuki no Kimi, ancestor of the HATA FAMILY; and a large group led by Achi no Omi, ancestor of many of the AYA FAMILY and its branches, such as the SAKANOUE FAMILY. The immigrants of this period are linked to the introduction of silkworm culture, horse breeding, SUE WARE, and other economic innovations and public works.

A second and longer, less pronounced phase of immigration from the continent may be identified with the period from the late 5th century until the beginning of the 7th century. Many immigrants from this second phase are associated with the development of learning, government administration and technology, as well as the BE system of organized economic production. In the latter part of this period, some of the newcomers, like SHIBA TATTO, are identified with the introduction and spread of BUDDHISM. Largely anonymous immigrant artisans of the earlier part of this period are often referred to in the *Nihon shoki* as *imaki no tehito* (newly arrived artisans) or *imaki no ayahito* (newly arrived immigrants).

The latter part of the 7th century was a period of large-scale immigration as a result of the warfare and political changes that accompanied the unification of Korea by the kingdom of SILLA in the 660s. Many of the *kikajin* of this period, including former nobles from the defeated kingdoms of Paekche and KOGURYŌ, were given tax-exempt lands in Musashi and other eastern provinces. Many of them and their descendants, like the progeny of earlier immigrants, gained distinction in various branches of religious and secular studies, poetry, music, medicine, metallurgical and other technologies, and law and government. Many were sent by the government to study in China or Korea.

Relatively few immigrants arrived after the middle of the 8th century. Over the years the various immigrant groups changed their names, dispersed geographically, and through intermarriage and cultural assimilation gradually lost whatever distinguishing traits they might once have had.

📖 ——Bruno Lewin, *Aya und Hata: Bevölkerungsgruppen Altjapans Kontinentaler Herkunft* (1962). Kim Tarusu (Talsu), *Nihon no naka no Chōsen bunka*, 6 vols (1970–1976). Seki Akira, *Kikajin* (1966). Shiba Ryōtarō et al, ed, *Kodai Nihon to Chōsen* (1974). Ueda Masaaki, *Kikajin* (1965).   William R. CARTER

Kikakuin Jiken → Planning Board Incident

Kikawada Kazutaka (1899–1977)

Businessman. Born in Fukushima Prefecture. Graduate of Tōkyō University. In 1926 Kikawada joined Tōkyō Dentō Kabushiki Kaisha (reorganized as TŌKYŌ ELECTRIC POWER CO, INC, in 1951). After World War II Kikawada devoted himself to realizing private ownership of the electric power industry in cooperation with nine regional companies under the leadership of MATSUNAGA YASUZAEMON. He became director of Tōkyō Electric Power Co in 1951 and president in 1961. Kikawada became chairman of the JAPAN COMMITTEE FOR ECONOMIC DEVELOPMENT (Keizai Dōyū Kai) in 1963. He also served as chairman for the Economic Council, an advisory organ for the ECONOMIC PLANNING AGENCY, from 1966 to 1977.   TOGAI Yoshio

Kike wadatsumi no koe

Collection of letters and other writings of Japanese students who died in World War II; published posthumously in 1949 by an ad hoc committee organized by survivors. An English translation, *Hearken to the Ocean's Voice!*, appeared in 1968. The book has been translated into many other languages, including French, German, Korean, and Esperanto. The committee was later formally organized as the Sembotsusha Gakusei Kinen Kai (Association for a Memorial to Students Fallen in Battle), although it is more popularly known as the Wadatsumikai. It has been active in various peace campaigns.

HARADA Katsumasa

Kikkōman Corporation

Japan's largest soy sauce producer. Kikkōman also produces and sells wine, other sauces, and processed food; it is expanding its restaurant chains in Japan and overseas. Its predecessor was the Noda Shōyu Co, established in 1917 by the Mogi family and others. In 1957 it established Kikkōman International, Inc, a sales subsidiary, in San Francisco. With the rapid increase in demand for soy sauce in the United States, it established Kikkōman Foods, Inc, a soy sauce manufacturing plant in Walworth, Wisconsin, in 1972. In 1979 Kikkōman Trading Europe, GmbH, was established as a European sales subsidiary for soy sauce and other foods. Kikkōman also produces and distributes wines and enzymes for medicinal purposes, manufactured with its own brewing technology. In addition, through agreements with overseas food manufacturers, it produces Del Monte tomato products, Ragu spaghetti sauce, Lea & Perrins worcestershire sauce, Ocean Spray cranberry products, and Coca-Cola. Kikkōman Shōyu's long-range goal is to become a completely diversified food producer. In 1981 sales totaled ¥128.9 billion (US $588.7 million), of which soy sauce constituted 62 percent, processed food 19 percent, alcoholic beverages 12 percent, sauces 5 percent, and others 2 percent; the export ratio was 1 percent. Capitalization stood at ¥8 billion (US $36.5 million) in the same year. The head office is in Noda, Chiba Prefecture.

kiku → chrysanthemums

Kikuchi

City in northern Kumamoto Prefecture, Kyūshū, on the river Kikuchigawa. The base of the Kikuchi warrior family from the 10th to the 14th century, Kikuchi also prospered as a village on the route connecting Kumamoto with Hita. Principal products are rice, chestnuts, and *shiitake* (Japanese mushrooms). Sericulture, brewing, and lumbering are also active. Tourist attractions include a hot spring, Kikuchi Gorge (part of Aso National Park), Kikuchi Shrine and other sites associated with the Kikuchi family. Pop: 28,460.

Kikuchi Dairoku (1855–1917)

Mathematician and educational administrator noted for his contribution in furthering the study of mathematics in Japan. Born in Edo (now Tōkyō). After attending the BANSHO SHIRABESHO, the shogunal institute for Western studies, he studied in England from 1866 to 1868. In 1870 he again went to England to study physics and mathematics at Cambridge University. After returning to Japan in 1877, he became a professor at Tōkyō University, where he later founded the mathematics department. He devoted his energies to the furthering of mathematics education in Japan and helped to improve geometry education at secondary schools. His *Shotō kikagaku kyōkasho* (1881, Elementary Geometry Textbook) was the most widely used textbook in Japan until the end of World War II. Kikuchi served as president of Tōkyō University (1898–1901), minister of education (1901–03), and the first head of the INSTITUTE OF PHYSICAL AND CHEMICAL RESEARCH. After retirement he involved himself in examining the applicability of the American educational system in Japan and advocating the adoption of the liberal arts college system. He is also known for his research into WASAN, or the native mathematics of Japan.

TERASAKI Masao

Kikuchi family

Warrior family based in the Kikuchi district of Higo Province (now Kumamoto Prefecture) in Kyūshū. Although the Kikuchi claimed

descent from Fujiwara no Takaie (974–1044), it is more likely that they were descended from a warrior who fought under Takaie during the Jürchen (TOI) invasion of northern Kyūshū in 1019. The heroism of Kikuchi Takefusa in the defense of Kyūshū against the second of the MONGOL INVASIONS OF JAPAN in 1281 is depicted in the famous scroll *Mōko shūrai ekotoba* commissioned by his fellow warrior Takezaki Suenaga. Takefusa's grandson Taketoki was killed during the GENKŌ INCIDENT of 1331 fighting for Emperor GO-DAIGO, and thereafter the Kikuchi served the Southern Court (see NORTHERN AND SOUTHERN COURTS). After the two courts were reunited in 1392, however, the Kikuchi declined, and they were ultimately destroyed by a powerful *daimyō* house, the ŌTOMO FAMILY. Later a branch family, the Mera, revived the name.

G. Cameron HURST III

Kikuchi Kan (1888–1948)

Author, playwright, editor and founder of the influential monthly BUNGEI SHUNJŪ. Real name Kikuchi Hiroshi. Born in Takamatsu, Kōchi Prefecture, into a poor family of *samurai*-scholar ancestry. A precocious writer, he won prizes in two essay contests (one metropolitan, one national) before he turned 20. In 1908 he was admitted to the tuition-free Tōkyō Higher Normal School (later Tōkyō University of Education) but was expelled after one year for misconduct. The following year he entered the National First Higher School (now part of Tōkyō University), where he became friends with many future authors, most notably AKUTAGAWA RYŪNOSUKE, YAMAMOTO YŪZŌ, and KUME MASAO. He was forced to leave school, however, after he was wrongly accused of involvement in a minor theft incident in the school dormitory. He went on to study at Kyōto University, where he majored in English literature, in particular, modern Irish drama, graduating in 1916. In 1914, while still at Kyōto University, he was invited to become a member of the group that published the third series of SHINSHICHŌ, a literary coterie magazine of Tōkyō University students, which had been reactivated that year by his former higher school classmates. He contributed some of his first one-act plays to the magazine. The coterie was reorganized in 1916; (the magazine it published is known as the fourth series of *Shinshichō*), and Kikuchi continued to contribute one-act plays. One of these plays was *Chichi kaeru* (1917; tr *The Father Returns*, 1925), which was inspired by *The Return of the Prodigal* by the English playwright John Hankin and which became a classic of Japan's modern creative theater. The plays he wrote for the magazine attracted little attention at the time, however, and the magazine was discontinued in early 1917, only one of the members of the coterie, Akutagawa, having achieved any fame. While working as a reporter for the newspaper *Jiji shimpō*, Kikuchi turned to writing short stories and established himself in this genre with "Mumei sakka no nikki" (1918, The Diary of an Unknown Writer), a fictionalized account of his jealousy of the success of his friend Akutagawa, and "Tadanao Kyō gyōjō ki" (1918; tr "On the Conduct of Lord Tadanao," 1961), a modern interpretation of the 17th-century tyrant MATSUDAIRA TADANAO. In 1920 his *Shinju fujin* (Madame Pearl), a monumental modern popular novel and the first of numerous melodramatic works, was serialized simultaneously in two large newspapers in Ōsaka and Tōkyō. In the same year *Chichi kaeru* was staged at a major commercial theater in Tōkyō. The play created a sensation because of its originality, and he achieved belated recognition as a playwright.

In 1923 he launched his own magazine, *Bungei shunjū*, partly motivated by his concern over the increasing aggressiveness of Marxist writers (see PROLETARIAN LITERATURE MOVEMENT). Although the magazine suffered a temporary setback due to losses incurred in the TŌKYŌ EARTHQUAKE OF 1923, it quickly recovered and grew into a popular magazine with unprecedented circulation. During the 1920s and 1930s he was considered the champion of moderate journalism as well as the "grand shōgun" (*ōgosho*) of the Japanese literary world. After World War II, he was forbidden by the OCCUPATION authorities to run for public office or to hold a government or civil service job for his supposed role as a leader of public opinion sympathetic to Japan's wartime military government.

One of Kikuchi's greatest contributions to Japan's literary world was the establishment of two important literary prizes, the Akutagawa Ryūnosuke Literary Prize (abbreviated as the Akutagawa Prize) and the Naoki Sanjūgo Literary Prize (abbreviated as the Naoki Prize). The two LITERARY PRIZES, instituted in 1935 as memorials for his two close friends, served as models for numerous similar awards and remain today the most prestigious of all Japanese literary awards. Kikuchi's talent in the field of journalism is illustrated by his creation of the *taidankai* (dialogue) and *zadankai* (round-table talk) formats, which he used as the basis of magazine articles. Both formats are still extremely popular in Japanese journalism. He was instrumental in forming what later developed into the Professional Writers' Guild of Japan, and he used his magazine to help further the careers of younger writers.

■ ——Works by Kikuchi: *Chichi kaeru* (1917), tr Glenn W. Shaw as "The Father Returns," in *Tojuro's Love and Four Other Plays* (1925). *Daini no seppun* (1925). "Irefuda" (1921). *Kikuchi Kan zenshū*, 15 vols (Chūō Kōron Sha, 1937). *Okujō no kyōjin* (1916), tr Yozan Iwasaki and Glenn Hughes as "The Madman on the Roof," in Donald Keene, ed, *Modern Japanese Literature* (1956). "Onshū no kanata ni" (1919), tr John Bester as "The Realm Beyond," in *Japan Quarterly* 7.3 (1960). "Rangaku kotohajime" (1921). "Tadanao kyō gyōjō ki" (1918), tr Geoffrey Sargent as "On the Conduct of Lord Tadanao," in *Today's Japan* 6.3 (1961). *Tōjūrō no koi* (1919), tr Glenn W. Shaw as "Tojuro's Love," in *Tojuro's Love, and Four Other Plays* (1925). Works on Kikuchi: *Bungei shunjū sanjūgo-nen shi kō* (1959). Eguchi Kan, *Waga bungaku hansei ki* (1953). Nagai Tatsuo, *Kikuchi Kan* (1961). KOKUBO Takeshi

Kikuchi Seishi (1902–1974)

Nuclear physicist and a leader in the development of nuclear physics in Japan. Born in Tōkyō, the fourth son of mathematician and educator KIKUCHI DAIROKU, he graduated from Tōkyō University in 1926. He continued his work at the INSTITUTE OF PHYSICAL AND CHEMICAL RESEARCH (Rikagaku Kenkyūjo), and in 1928 he was successful in producing cathode ray diffraction in a mica crystal. The same feat had been accomplished only a short time before by G. P. Thomson in Britain and by C. J. Davisson and L. H. Germer in the United States; Davisson and Thomson received the Nobel Prize in 1937 for this work. Kikuchi served as the first director of the Tōkyō University Institute for Nuclear Study and also directed the construction of two cyclotron facilities at Ōsaka University. He received the Order of Culture in 1951.

Kikumura Itaru (1925–)

Novelist. Real name Togawa Yūjiro. Born in Kanagawa Prefecture. Graduate of Waseda University. Worked as a newspaper correspondent in the Philippines and China for the *Yomiuri shimbun* during World War II. In 1957 his short story "Iōjima" (Iwo Jima) was awarded the Akutagawa Prize. Kikumura's works often deal with the uncertainties that his generation experienced because of the war and the distorted perception of life such uncertainties had given them. His writing ranges from fiction to documentary and from mystery to biography. His works include *Aa Etajima* (1958) and *Shōsetsu Ikeda Daisaku* (1969).

Kiku no Sekku → Chrysanthemum Festival

Kikuta Kazuo (1908–1973)

Popular stage and radio playwright; show-business innovator. Kikuta began his career as a writer of short comedies for small theaters in the Asakusa amusement area of Tōkyō. His first success, at age 22, was a parody of the KABUKI classic *Kanadehon chūshingura* titled *Akō gishi meimei den,* which he created for the leading Asakusa comedian, Enoken (ENOMOTO KEN'ICHI).

In 1933, Kikuta became the house playwright for the Warai no Ōkoku (Kingdom of Laughter) troupe headed by FURUKAWA ROPPA. The strong dramatic construction of his plays made Kikuta the leader of the prewar "script first" school of comedy. His *Hana saku minato* (1943, The Port Where Flowers Bloom), a tale of two grifters (played by Enoken and Roppa) who try to cheat simple fishermen, was the outstanding comedy of the war years. It became a postwar standard.

During the Occupation period, Kikuta turned from stage comedy to write three immensely popular dramatic serials for radio: *Kane no naru oka* (1947–50, The Hill Where the Bell Resounds), *Yama kara kita otoko* (1945, The Man from the Mountains), and *Kimi no na wa* (1952–54 What's Your Name?).

Kikuta became the head of the stage division of the TŌHŌ CO, LTD, in 1955. Among his innovations at Tōhō, he set up HASEGAWA KAZUO's "Tōhō Kabuki" to integrate the classic form with contem-

porary popular theater. He also imported the idea of the unlimited theatrical run and thereby broke with the Japanese tradition of booking a show for a fixed period (seldom more than a month) regardless of its popularity. In 1959, Kikuta's comedy, *Gametsui yatsu* (Crafty Rascal) set a long-run record of 10 months in Tōkyō.

His cosmopolitan touch was evident in the Tōhō stage musicals he wrote during the early 1950s such as *Morugan Oyuki* (Oyuki Morgan) which starred Koshiji Fubuki as the *geisha* who married into the J. P. Morgan family. Having revolutionized the indigenous musical theater, Kikuta began to produce Japanese versions of Broadway musical comedies such as *My Fair Lady* after 1960 as yet another step toward his lifetime goal of providing Tōkyō with the world's widest range of theatrical experiences.

■ ——Kikuta Kazuo, *Shibai-zukuri yonjūnen* (1968).

J. L. ANDERSON

Kikutake Kiyonori (1928–)

Architect. Born in Fukuoka Prefecture. After graduation in 1950 from Waseda University, he worked first for Takenaka Kōmuten Co, Ltd, and then in the firm of Murano and Mori. In 1953 he opened his own office. In the course of producing buildings of great formal invention, he has also articulated a distinctive design methodology and left his mark on Japanese domestic architecture. In 1960 Kikutake helped found the Metabolist group, with the architect KUROKAWA KISHŌ, which attempted to express the dynamic, cyclical quality of urban growth. He designed futuristic marine cities which were partly realized in the Aquapolis for the Okinawa Exposition (1975). His buildings include Sky House (1957), his private residence, Hotel Tōkōen (1964), and the Kurume Civic Center (1969).

WATANABE Hiroshi

Kikutake Sunao (1880–1937)

Journalist known for his antimilitary views; pen name Rokko. Born in Fukuoka Prefecture, in 1903 he joined the newspaper *Fukuoka nichinichi shimbun* after graduating from Waseda University. As editor (1911) and later as managing editor (1926), he was known for the moral integrity rather than the analytical incisiveness of his editorials. In 1932, at the time of the attempted coup d'etat by army officers (see MAY 15TH INCIDENT), when public sentiment favored the "patriotism" of the conspirators, Kikutake steadfastly criticized the military for acting outside legitimate political channels. Until his death, despite severe denunciation of both himself and his newspaper by local military authorities, he persisted in his criticism.

ARASE Yutaka

kikyō

(balloonflower or Chinese bellflower). *Platycodon grandiflorum.* A perennial herb of the family Campanulaceae which grows wild in grassy mountain highlands throughout Japan and is also cultivated as an ornamental plant. It is found in much of the temperate zone of Asia. The roots are thick, succulent, and yellowish white. Its straight stems grow over a meter (39 in) and exude a white sap when injured. The leaves are alternate and lanceolate-oblong, with margins acutely serrate, and undersides whitish green. In August and September it opens bluish purple bell-shaped flowers with five lobes at upper leaf modes; the corollas measure 4–5 centimeters (1.6–2 in) in diameter. There are also garden varieties with white and pink flowers and a miniature variety. It is one of the seven flowers of autumn *(aki no nanakusa).* In Chinese pharmacological practice its root is used to prepare a cough medicine and expectorant. In mountain villages roots are eaten either pickled or boiled then fried. See also TSURIGANE NINJIN. MATSUDA Osamu

Kimbusenji

Head temple of the Kimbusen Shugen Honshū, a sect of the Buddhist–Shintō ascetic tradition, SHUGENDŌ, located in Yoshino district (see YOSHINOYAMA), Nara Prefecture. According to tradition, the temple was founded by EN NO GYŌJA (late 7th century), a semi-legendary mountain ascetic. The temple was expanded in the Jōgan era (859–877) by the Shingon monk Shōbō (832–909), who made it a center for Shugendō practices. Thereafter the influence of the Kimbusenji grew and came increasingly into conflict with KŌYASAN, the headquarters of the Shingon sect. Kimbusenji is known to have offered a haven to Prince MORINAGA (1308–35) and then to his father Emperor GO–DAIGO (r 1318–39) during their campaign to restore imperial rule (see KEMMU RESTORATION); it was thus at one time the seat of the Southern Court.

The chief divinity enshrined in the main hall, the Zaōdō, is Zaō Gongen, who is believed by devotees to represent the ferocious aspect of Buddha, capable of suppressing all evil. The main hall and the gate (niōmon) were built in the 15th century and are designated as National Treasures. Kimbusenji was affiliated with the Tendai sect when Shugendō was suppressed in 1872 by the government but became an independent religious organization after World War II.

Stanley WEINSTEIN

Kim Gu (1876–1949)

(J: Kin Kyū). Also known as Kim Ch'angam and Kim Ch'angsu. A leader of the Korean independence movement and the post–World War II struggle for unification. An Andong Kim clansman from Hwanghae Province just north of Seoul, he joined the Tonghak religion the year before the sect's 1894 rebellion (see TONGHAK REBELLION). He fought both Chinese and Japanese suppressors of the rebellion during the SINO-JAPANESE WAR OF 1894–1895. Kim was arrested in 1896 and convicted of murdering a Japanese soldier in retaliation for the assassination of Queen MIN; he escaped from prison in 1898 and lived in hiding for a while before returning to his studies. He studied Buddhism, and then became a Christian in 1903. He was again arrested in 1911 in conjunction with a plot to kill TERAUCHI MASATAKE, the Japanese governor-general of Korea, and he was held in prison until 1917.

Kim helped to organize the anti-Japanese demonstrations of 1 March 1919 (see SAMIL INDEPENDENCE MOVEMENT), after which he fled to Shanghai. There he served the PROVISIONAL GOVERNMENT OF KOREA in various capacities and formed the Korean Independence Party. He was associated with a number of anti-Japanese terrorist actions. With the support of Chiang Kai-shek, Kim established a military academy for Koreans in Nanjing (Nanking) and organized a Korean division, which eventually fought with the Chinese Nationalist army against the Japanese during World War II.

Kim returned to Korea as president of the provisional government in November 1945. His dream of leading a united and independent Korea from Japanese colonialism into the modern world was undermined by superpower rivalry and squabbling among Korean political factions. His moderate coalition, the Minjuŭiwŏn (Democratic League), called upon the United States, the USSR, and the United Nations to disengage from Korea so that the nation's citizens could determine their own fate without foreign influence. Kim attended a reunification conference in the Soviet-controlled north in 1948, against the wishes of the American military government and Syngman RHEE (Yi Sŭng-man). He was assassinated by a South Korean military officer in June 1949. See also KOREA AND JAPAN: early modern relations. *C. Kenneth* QUINONES

Kimigayo → national anthem

Kimiidera

Popular name of the temple Nagusazan Gokokuin, located in the city of Wakayama, Wakayama Prefecture. The temple belongs to the Guze Kannon branch of the SHINGON SECT of Buddhism. It is said to have been founded in 770 when the Chinese priest Ikō (Ch: Weiguang or Wei-Kuang) came to Japan and donated an image of the Senju Kannon (Avalokiteśvara with a Thousand Arms) to the temple. The chief deity enshrined is the Jūichimen Kannon (Avalokiteśvara with Eleven Faces), a statue carved by Ikō. Because there are three holy springs within the temple compound, the temple is known as Kimiidera, or the Miidera of Kii (Kii Province, now Wakayama Prefecture) to differentiate it from the MIIDERA in Ōtsu, Ōmi Province (now Shiga Prefecture). It was designated an imperial temple during the rule of the retired emperor GO-SHIRAKAWA (1127–92). Many of the original buildings are still intact. Approached by a flight of over 200 stone steps, the temple's magnificent view of the city of Wakayama and the island of Awaji has attracted many visitors since ancient days. Kimiidera is also famous as the second of the so-called 33 Kannon temples in western Japan.

Kim Il-sŏng (1912–)

Also written Kim Il-sung (J: Kin Nissei). Born Kim Sŏng-ju (sometimes spelled Kim Sung-chu). Premier of the Democratic People's Republic of Korea (DPRK; North Korea) from 1948 to 1972; DPRK president since 1972. Born near P'yŏngyang, capital of North Korea. Kim's father was arrested in 1917 for involvement in the anti-Japanese Korean National Association. The family emigrated to Manchuria after his father's release in 1920. Kim Il-sŏng returned to Korea for schooling in 1923, but his father's second arrest by Japanese police in 1925 brought him back to Manchuria where he entered the Jilin (Chi-lin) Middle School. Joining the Communist Youth League in 1927, he was arrested some time between 1928 and 1930 because of anti-Japanese activities and was elected the league's secretary in 1929. He entered the Chinese Communist Party in 1931 because the Korean Communist Party (KCP) had been disbanded by a 1928 Comintern directive.

Kim Il-sŏng rose to prominence as the leader of an anti-Japanese guerrilla group called the Kapsan Faction that operated in Manchuria and northern Korea between 1932 and 1940. At some point during this period he adopted the name of a famous Korean patriot and noncommunist guerrilla leader, Kim Il-sŏng.

Kim retreated into Siberia after some success against the Japanese along the Manchurian-Korean border between 1936 and 1937. By 1941 he commanded the Korean People's Liberation Army attached to the Soviet army, which attacked the Japanese from base camps in Soviet Siberia.

Kim returned to Korea in September 1945 under the name Kim Sŏng-ju as commander of the Korean contingent of the Soviet occupation forces. On 3 October 1945, a week after the assassination of Hyŏn Chun-hyŏk, leader of Marxists in Korea during World War II, Kim Sŏng-ju appeared in P'yŏngyang under the name Kim Il-sŏng, and was elected first secretary of the Korean Communist Party's Central Bureau. He became premier of the DPRK when it was established in September 1948. See also KOREA AND JAPAN: relations with the Republic of Korea.

🕮 —— *Brief History of the Revolutionary Activities of Comrade Kim Il-sung* (P'yŏngyang, Foreign Languages Publishing House, 1969). Young Hoon Kang, "Kim Il Sung: Mysterious North Korean Leader," in Rodger Swearingen, ed, *Leaders of the Communist World* (1971). Ilpyong J. Kim, *Communist Politics in North Korea* (1975). *C. Kenneth* QUINONES

Kimi Pass

(Kimi Tōge). Located on the border of Ōsaka and Wakayama prefectures, central Honshū, bisecting the Izumi Mountains. The ancient route Kōya Kaidō, extending from Ōsaka to the mountain KŌYASAN, was built along the pass. The pass was crowded with pilgrims to Kōyasan in former days. A railroad, constructed in 1915, now runs through tunnels under the pass. Height: 438 m (1,437 ft).

Kimitsu

City in southwestern Chiba Prefecture, central Honshū, on Tōkyō Bay. Known early on for its seaweed (nori), Kimitsu is now part of the KEIHIN INDUSTRIAL ZONE. The mountains to the southeast, including Kanōzan, belong to a prefectural natural park. Pop: 77,286.

Kimmei, Emperor (509–571)

The 29th sovereign (tennō) in the traditional count (which includes several nonhistorical emperors). According to the chronicle NIHON SHOKI (720) he reigned from either 531 or 539 to 571 and was the third son of Emperor KEITAI. On Keitai's death, Kimmei is said to have contested the succession with his elder half-brothers, emperors Ankan and Senka, in a dispute provoked by rival factions in the court. For several years it is not clear who actually ruled, or whether two or more emperors ruled jointly or separately. In any case, Ankan and Senka soon died, leaving Kimmei in sole possession of the throne. Again according to tradition, it was during his reign (in either 538 or 552) that BUDDHISM was introduced from Korea, causing a conflict between the pro-Buddhist SOGA FAMILY and anti-Buddhist MONONOBE FAMILY that was not resolved for decades. Kimmei's foreign policy was unsuccessful; KAYA, the Japanese enclave in Korea, was engulfed by the state of SILLA in 562.

KITAMURA Bunji

Kimono——Woman's kimono

Woman wearing an unlined summer *kimono* made of silk gauze. Worn with white *tabi* and thonged *zōri* as footwear, it is a semiformal kimono suitable for going calling.

Kimono——Man's kimono

Man wearing a wool *kimono* and *haori*. A winter kimono, this is relatively informal dress that might be worn at home or on the street. Dark-colored *tabi* and *geta* complete the ensemble.

Kimmon Incident → Hamaguri Gomon Incident

kimoiri → shōya

Kim Ok-kyun (1851–1894)

(J: Kin Gyokukin). An early advocate of Korea's Westernization; organizer of the KAEHWAP'A (Enlightenment Faction or Independence Party). He was born to a Ch'ungch'ŏng Province branch of the Andong Kim clan. Passage of the higher civil service examination *(munkwa)* in 1872 was followed by a decade of routine service in the central administration. Sent to Japan in 1881 to study the Meiji government, he fell under the influence of FUKUZAWA YUKICHI's interpretation of Westernization and pan-Asianism. He and other Koreans formed a political group, the Kaehwap'a, and set out to lead Korea's Westernization. Encountering resistance in Korea, yet urged on by sympathetic Japanese, the group attempted unsuccessfully to seize control of the Korean government in 1884 (see KAPSIN POLITICAL COUP). Kim fled to Japan, where he remained until 1894. That year he left for Shanghai, where he was assassinated by a Korean government agent. See also KOREA AND JAPAN: early modern relations.　　　　　　　　　　　　　　*C. Kenneth* QUINONES

kimono

The word *kimono* (literally, "clothing") is usually used in the narrow sense to refer to the traditional Japanese wrap-around garment with rectangular sleeves used by both men and women, which is made of vertical panels of cloth stitched together and is bound with a sash (OBI). In this sense the word does not include the half-length jacket *(haori)* or the full-length underrobe *(juban)*. It is occasionally used in the broad sense as a term for clothing or for the native dress in general as opposed to Western-style clothing *(yōfuku)*. The predecessor of the kimono is the *kosode* ("small sleeves"), which was worn as an undergarment from about the Nara period (710–794) and as the outer garment of everyday apparel from about the mid-16th century. The term kimono gained favor over *kosode* only in the 18th century. For a more detailed history of kimono, see CLOTHING.

In the 17th century the heretofore narrow sash wound above the hips was replaced in the case of women by a broad and stiff sash bound just beneath the breasts. The growing wealth of townspeople in the Edo period (1600–1868) contributed to the flourishing of tradesmen engaged solely in the making and decoration of kimono cloth, which was treated like an artist's canvas and figured with hand-brushed dyes or worked with brocade. The elegance of kimono bought by affluent merchants for their wives or paramours is reflected by government prohibitions in 1683, 1689, and 1721 on excessive expenditures on women's kimono. Similar sanctions were laid down against men's kimono made from lustrous *habutae* silk; this was allowed only to members of the *samurai* class, and commoners were enjoined to wear kimono of hemp or cotton. However, the prohibition was not strictly enforced, and by the early 19th century *habutae* was the accepted cloth for the apparel of wealthy townsmen.

In the Meiji period (1868–1912) many men began wearing Western-style clothes, reserving kimono for formal occasions or when relaxing at home. Beginning in 1870, government workers were required to wear Western-style suits of clothes, and at the Meiji emperor's court similar rulings were enacted for ordinary wear at court for both men (1872) and women (1886). It is only since the beginning of the Shōwa period (1926–) that the new style of dress has become popular among women in general. Today most women wear kimono mainly for social and ceremonial events or when performing certain traditional arts. Children and young men and women may wear kimono for such occasions as NEW YEAR, the SHICHIGOSAN festival, Adulthood Day (see GEMPUKU), graduations, and WEDDINGS.　　　　　　　　　　　　　　*TERAI Minako*

Men's Kimono——The ceremonial kimono for men is made of black *habutae* silk, the sole decoration being the family CREST *(mon)* in white which appears on the back, on both front panels, and on each sleeve; this and other garments with crests are called *montsuki*. Over this kimono is worn a *haori* (jacket) and *hakama* (pleated trousers or skirt). For less formal wear, the kimono and *haori* may be made of wool. For summer, either a light-weight cotton kimono *(yukata)* or linen knee-length shorts and upper garment *(jimbei)* are worn at home. In winter, a cotton-quilted robe called *tanzen,* often striped, may be worn at home over a kimono.

Women's Kimono——Women wear different formal kimono for festive occasions and for mourning. The wedding costume is particularly dazzling, consisting of a long outer robe *(uchikake),* generally white, though red is also common. It is lavishly decorated with embroidery or brocade depicting auspicious symbols like the crane and tortoise. Two layers of white robes (*kakeshita*) are worn underneath. The bride also has her hair done in the style known as *bunkin shimada* and wears a white hood called *tsuno-kakushi* (literally "horn covering").

Married women's kimono for festive occasions are made of black or dark silk crepe (*chirimen*). Called *edozuma* or *tomesode*, this type of kimono has the family crest, and, in addition, a design on the front and hem. Young unmarried women wear *furisode*, kimono with sleeves as long as 1 meter (3.3 ft) and an overall design that usually runs diagonally from the shoulder down to the hem. Usually a special *obi* of double width but folded once, known as *maruobi*, is worn with *edozuma* and *furisode* kimono. For funerals, a plain black *montsuki* kimono and white underkimono are worn with a black *obi* and black accessories.

Formal or semiformal kimono may have either no design, a small overall print, or a free design (*tsukesage*). On more formal occasions a black *montsuki haori* jacket of the type worn at funerals may be added, or an *ebaori* jacket, which has a dyed, woven, embroidered, or painted design.

Other Kimono——Traditional work clothes for both men and women, in broader usage also called kimono, were often designed in a two-piece style for practicality and comfort. The terms *yamagi* ("hill wear") and *noragi* ("field wear") are still used today. The most common traditional work clothes consist of a short top called *kogin* or *hadako* worn with baggy trousers called *mompe* or *karusan*. Accessories include a covering for the back of the hands (*tekkō*) and gaiters (*kyahan*). These are worn by farmers and laborers, though Western-style work clothes are more common today. For some types of work a short coat (*hanten* or *happi*) is worn; this is often designed with the emblem or name of the employee's company displayed prominently on the back and front. A coverall apron (*kappōgi*), which protects the kimono sleeves is widely used in the kitchen, even over Western clothes, and is perhaps the housewife's most typical garment.

Style and Tailoring——The material for making kimono comes in *tan*, or rolls, of about 11 meters (12 yd) in length and 36 centimeters (14 in) in width, which is enough material for one adult's kimono. The fabric is cut in eight pieces: the main sections (*migoro*), front sections (*okumi*), sleeves (*sode*), and collar and over-collar (*eri* and *tomoeri*). The material is cut and sewn along the warp, with the seams always the same width, regardless of the size of the person. The sleeves may vary in length and are sewn in a rectangle or curved along the bottom edge.

For women's kimono, the length is about 20 centimeters (8 in) longer than the height of the woman. This extra length (*ohashori*) is tucked under the *obi* so that the fold shows about 4 or 5 centimeters (about 2 in) below the *obi*. The underarm portions of sleeve seams are left unstitched.

Men's kimono should also be longer than the wearer's height, but the excess material is tucked and sewn around the waist so that it is invisible when covered by the *obi*. The underarm seams are completely sewn up. Children's kimono are tucked at the shoulder and waist so that they can be let out as the child grows.

Kimono may be unlined (*hitoe*), lined (*awase*), or cotton-quilted (*wataire*). Unlined kimono are worn from June through September; for everyday wear, stencil-dyed cotton *yukata* are most common. For street or formal wear, materials such as silk gauze (RO AND SHA) or fine linen (*jōfu*) are used. Lined kimono are worn from October through May and are mainly made of silk or wool. Today, synthetic materials are often used for both lined and unlined kimono, and one-layer wool kimono are often worn in winter. Cotton-quilted kimono are for midwinter and are only worn at home.

How to Wear Kimono——Generally one dresses in the following order: *tabi* (socks worn with traditional thonged ZŌRI footwear); top undergarment and wrap-around underskirt; and underkimono (*nagajuban*), which is tied tightly with a wide belt (*datemaki*). The *nagajuban* has a collar (*han'eri*), usually white, which should show about 2 centimeters (1 in) above the collar of the kimono which is worn over it. The kimono is fitted on the body with all the seams straight: the length is adjusted by folding excess material around the waist, and the whole is anchored with many ties before the *obi* is put on. The left side is lapped over the right in front; the opposite is done only when dressing a body for burial. The technique of donning kimono and *obi* was traditionally passed on from mother to daughter, but today women often go to a special school to learn how to achieve the correct effects.

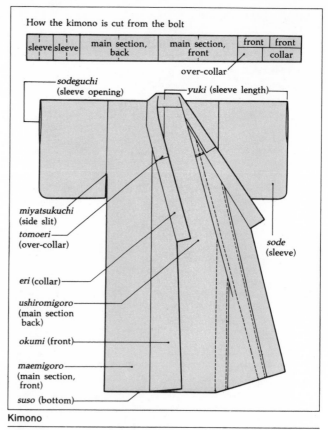

How the kimono is cut from the bolt

| sleeve | sleeve | main section, back | main section, front | front | front |
| | | | | | collar |

over-collar

sodeguchi (sleeve opening)

yuki (sleeve length)

miyatsukuchi (side slit)

tomoeri (over-collar)

sode (sleeve)

eri (collar)

ushiromigoro (main section back)

okumi (front)

maemigoro (main section, front)

suso (bottom)

Kimono

All adults' kimono are cut in eight sections from one roll of cloth about 36cm (14 in) wide and 11 meters (12 yd) long, (top); as the seams are cut straight and always the same width regardless of the wearer's size, no cloth is left over. No fasteners are used and the kimono is held in place using tightly wound cords and/or a sash (*obi*).

Caring for Kimono——A silk kimono is usually not cleaned as a whole unit but is first taken apart along the seams; since these are straight and usually hand-sewn, this is not difficult. The sections are washed and then laid out on thin bamboo sticks (this method is called *shinshibari*) or stretched on a board to dry (*araihari*). Since silk kimono should not be cleaned very often, daily care is important. After every wearing the kimono should be hung on a straight-armed hanger (*ikō* or *emonkake*) and aired. The collar, sleeve ends, and bottom hem should be hand-cleaned frequently. For storage, the kimono is folded in a set order along the seams, wrapped in special paper (*tatōgami*), and laid flat in a drawer. Kimono are aired and dried after the annual rainy season in early summer. See also TEXTILES, CARE AND PRESERVATION OF. *Ōtsuka Sueko*

Kimpishō

(Summary of Court Practices). A three-volume compilation of material pertaining to court appointments and ceremonial, completed in 1213 or 1221. Also known as *Kinchūshō*, *Juntoku In mishō*, or *Kenryaku gyoki*. The author of the work was the emperor JUNTOKU. The contents cover details of administrative practice as well as of annual observances, festivals, ceremonies, edicts, and the like. Because of this detail, *Kimpishō* became a model for later generations. *G. Cameron Hurst III*

Kimpokusan

Mountain on the island of Sado, Niigata Prefecture, off central Honshū; the island's highest peak. It is a young mountain composed of pyroxene andesite and liparite. Tracts of alpine rose flourish, along with other alpine flora. Kimpokusan Shrine is on the summit. It is part of Sado–Yahiko Quasi-National Park. Height: 1,172 m (3,844 ft).

Kimpusan

Mountain on the border between Yamanashi and Nagano prefectures, central Honshū; composed of granite. It was formerly a source of quartz, a noted product of Yamanashi Prefecture, but the supply is now exhausted. Height: 2,595 m (8,512 ft).

Kim Tae-jung (1926–)

(J: Kin Daichū). Often transliterated Kim Dae-jung. South Korean politician; New Democratic Party candidate for president of the Republic of Korea (ROK) in 1971. Kim nearly defeated incumbent PAK CHŎNG-HŬI in the April 1971 presidential election, in which he ran on a platform calling for neutralization of the Korean peninsula, equitable distribution of wealth, and elimination of government corruption. Persisting in his criticism of Pak's administration, he moved to Tōkyō after a new constitution gave Pak broad powers in October 1972. On 13 August 1973 he was kidnapped from a Tōkyō hotel and reappeared in Seoul one week later. The Japanese public was outraged at what was considered an infringement of Japan's sovereignty after Tōkyō police identified the kidnappers as agents of the Korean Central Intelligence Agency. The ROK government denied any involvement, and the ensuing diplomatic crisis was only partially resolved by a formal apology to the Japanese government by Korean Prime Minister Kim Jong-p'il. Kim Tae-jung became an internationally known political dissident because of the incident and his subsequent imprisonment. Though released from jail in 1979, he was accused of instigating an uprising in his hometown of Kwangju in South Chŏlla Province in May 1980. The South Korean military regime that seized power after Pak Chŏng-hŭi's assassination used excessive force in subduing the city's inhabitants and imprisoned Kim Tae-jung for sedition. He was convicted by a military court, but his life was spared as a result of intense international pressure on the Korean government. See also KOREA AND JAPAN: relations with the Republic of Korea.   C. Kenneth QUINONES

Kim Tal-su (1919–)

Novelist. Born in Korea. Two years after his father's death, he went to Japan with his mother at the age of ten. He worked his way through Nihon University, and then worked as a newspaper reporter for *Kanagawa shimbun* until the outbreak of World War II. After the war, he edited a Japanese-language news magazine about Korea called *Minshu Chōsen*. He turned to fiction with the novel *Genkainada* (1954), based on his experiences as a Korean reporter during the war years. His works capture, often with humor and grace, the dilemma of the Koreans who suffered during the Japanese occupation of their country and those who presently must live with the discrimination against them prevalent in Japan. Recently his interests have turned to investigations of archaeological sites of Korean origin in Japan, some of which are considered important in comparative archaeology. Other works include *Pakutari no saiban* (1958), which was nominated for the Akutagawa Prize.

Kimura Hisashi (1870–1943)

Astronomer. The first director of the Latitude Observatory of Mizusawa from 1899 to 1941, he was known for discovering the Z-term of latitude variation (in addition to the already known X- and Y-terms). Born in Ishikawa Prefecture, he graduated from Tōkyō University. In 1937 he became one of the first recipients of the Order of Culture.

Kimura Kaishū → Kimura Yoshitake

Kimura Ki (1894–1980)

Literary historian and critic. Born in Okayama Prefecture. After graduating from Waseda University, he worked for a publisher in Tōkyō and began writing critical essays and fiction. During the period of liberalism in the 1920s, he participated in the tenant-farmers movement and was a founding member of the Japan Fabian Society and Japan Labor–Farmer Party (NIHON RŌNŌTŌ). At the same time he joined the Meiji Bunka Kenkyūkai (Society for the Study of Meiji Civilization) organized by the liberal scholar YOSHINO SAKUZŌ. Working as an editor for the society's periodical and other publications, he established himself as an authority on the cultural history

of the Meiji period (1868–1912). His works include *Shimabara bishōnen roku* (1927), an historical novel, and *Nichibei bungaku kōryūshi no kenkyū* (1960), a monumental study of literary exchanges between the United States and Japan.

Kimura Motoo (1924–)

Geneticist. Born in Aichi Prefecture. A graduate of Kyōto University. He has been a staff member of the National Institute of Genetics since 1949, engaging in research in population genetics. Based on recent findings concerning the mutation level of DNA molecules, he opposed the theory of natural selection current since the time of Darwin and in 1968 advocated a "neutral" theory of evolution. He received the Weldon Prize for his studies in population genetics. In 1976 he was awarded the Order of Culture.   SUZUKI Zenji

Kimura Shigenari (1592?–1615)

A warrior of uncertain provenance who served TOYOTOMI HIDEYORI, son of the national unifier TOYOTOMI HIDEYOSHI, and was one of the Toyotomi party's stalwarts in its tragic final showdown with the Tokugawa regime in 1614 and 1615 (see ŌSAKA CASTLE, SIEGES OF). During the Tokugawa armies' first assault on Hideyori's Ōsaka Castle in the so-called Winter Campaign, Shigenari distinguished himself in what was perhaps the campaign's sharpest field encounter, his troops fighting the forces of the *daimyō* UESUGI KAGEKATSU and Satake Yoshinobu (1570–1633) to a draw at the Shigino-Imafuku perimeter on 26 December 1614 (Keichō 19.11.26). According to the popular story, when an armistice was concluded the next month, Shigenari—a mere youth in the presence of the land's most powerful personages—dared to demand that the retired shōgun TOKUGAWA IEYASU reimpress his seal of blood (KEPPAN) on the truce document. The story, however, is apocryphal, as it was actually the shōgun TOKUGAWA HIDETADA to whom Shigenari was sent as ambassador. When the conflict was resumed in the Summer Campaign of 1615, Shigenari and his troop of 4,700 sallied from Ōsaka Castle in an attempt to surprise the shogunate's main force on the march but were intercepted in the area of Wakae by the detachment of TŌDŌ TAKATORA and Ii Naotaka, and in the ensuing encounter, which took place on 2 June 1615 (Keichō 20.5.6), Shigenari was killed. Ōsaka Castle fell the next day.   George ELISON

Kimura Yoshitake (1830–1901)

Also known as Kimura Kaishū. Retainer of the Tokugawa shogunate who advocated the creation of a modern navy during the 1860s. Born in Edo (now Tōkyō). Kimura held numerous minor posts within the military bureaucracy of the shogunate before his appointment as supervisor of the Nagasaki Naval Training Academy (KAIGUN DENSHŪJO) in 1856. Thereafter he became interested in naval expansion. In 1859 he was promoted to the newly created office of commissioner of warships (*gunkan bugyō*) and was commanding officer aboard the KANRIN MARU when it sailed across the Pacific in 1860, the first Japanese vessel to do so. Throughout the 1860s Kimura and KATSU KAISHŪ, another Tokugawa naval officer, submitted proposals for the modernization of the shogunate navy. In 1867 they succeeded in establishing a program of naval training with English instructors, but the collapse of the shogunate in 1868 terminated these arrangements. Kimura declined the invitation of the new Meiji government to help build a modern navy, preferring to lead a life of ease devoted to writing.

Kinai

(Capital Provinces). General term for the provinces surrounding the ancient capitals of Nara and Kyōto in the old provincial system. It is a Japanese rendering of an old Chinese term that referred to the 1 million square *ri* (ca 448,900 sq km) area centered on the imperial residence. In Japan until the mid-7th century the term was loosely applied to the general region around the imperial capitals in YAMATO (now Nara Prefecture). The area was officially defined at the time of the TAIKA REFORM of 645 to include specifically the four home provinces of Yamato, Yamashiro (now part of Kyōto Prefecture), Kawachi (now part of Ōsaka Prefecture), and Settsu (now part of Hyōgo Prefecture). Later, with the creation of Izumi Province from part of Kawachi, the home provinces came to number five. Under the RITSURYŌ SYSTEM of administration instituted in the late

7th century, residents of the Kinai enjoyed special privileges including full exemption from the craft-produce tax paid in lieu of corvée labor (yō) and half exemption from the textile tax (chō; see SO, YŌ, AND CHŌ). See also GOKI SHICHIDŌ.

Kin Bay

(Kin Wan). Inlet of the Pacific Ocean, on the eastern coast of the main island of Okinawa, Okinawa Prefecture. Bounded by Kimmisaki, a cape on the north, and the Yokatsu Peninsula on the south. The bay is studded with many small islands.

Kinchū Narabi ni Kuge Shohatto

(Laws Governing the Imperial Court and Nobility). Laws issued by the Tokugawa shogunate in 1615 to regulate the imperial court and Kyōto nobility; drafted by the Buddhist priest SŪDEN. Issued at the same time as the laws governing the daimyō (BUKE SHOHATTO) and religious institutions (Jiin Hatto), these regulations defined the proper role and limits of the emperor and his court. The emperor was to occupy himself with scholarship and the arts, and the political role of the court was limited to tasks assigned by the shogunate. Thus, although the shōgun in theory derived his authority from his appointment by the emperor, these regulations clearly placed the court under the shōgun's command and were a major step in the Tokugawa effort to put all potential rivals under strict shogunal control.   *Ronald P. Toby*

Kindai bungaku

(Modern Literature). Literary journal published from January 1946 to August 1964. Founded after World War II by a newly formed coterie of critics and writers, it became a central pillar of modern literary criticism and helped restore some sense of intellectual order during the chaotic postwar period by critically examining events of the recent past. Its original members were HONDA SHŪGO, HIRANO KEN, ARA MASAHITO, Sasaki Kiichi (b 1914), Yamamuro Shizuka (b 1906), HANIYA YUTAKA, and ODAGIRI HIDEO. Later participants included NOMA HIROSHI, UMEZAKI HARUO, SHIINA RINZŌ, ABE KŌBŌ, KATŌ SHŪICHI, and SHIMAO TOSHIO. Having experienced the collapse of the PROLETARIAN LITERATURE MOVEMENT and its aftermath, Kindai bungaku coterie members opposed the Shin Nihon Bungaku Kai (New Japanese Literature Society; see SHIN NIHON BUNGAKU) in its attempt to establish a new leftist literary movement. The two groups engaged in an inconclusive debate about politics and literature, with Ara Masahito and Hirano Ken taking the centrist position that literature should be free of ideological constraint. Kindai bungaku broke new ground in the study of modern Japanese literature in critical articles reassessing works by writers like SHIMAZAKI TŌSON and AKUTAGAWA RYŪNOSUKE. It provided an outlet for experimental works by new writers and nurtured a new generation of critics. Kindai bungaku was, until its demise, one of the foremost critical literary magazines of its time.

Theodore W. Goossen

Kindaichi Kyōsuke (1882–1971)

Philologist. Born in Morioka, Iwate Prefecture. He graduated from Tōkyō University where he became professor of linguistics; he later served as professor of Kokugakuin University. Kindaichi devoted much of his career as a scholar to the study of the AINU LANGUAGE, especially as a vehicle of Ainu literature and its attendant reflection of Ainu cultural history. He left numerous publications on Ainu language studies, including Ainu jojishi yūkara no kenkyū I–II (1931), a valuable written record of Ainu oral literature as recounted in the epic tradition of the yūkara. His studies of the Japanese language are also well known, and he was awarded the Imperial Prize and Order of Culture. Among his other principal works is Kokugoshi keitō ron (1938, On the Systems of the History of the Japanese Language). He was chief compiler of the Japanese-language dictionary Meikai kokugo jiten (1943, rev ed, 1952), and a three-volume collection of his selected works is found in Kindaichi Kyōsuke senshū (1960–62). See also JAPANESE LANGUAGE STUDIES, HISTORY OF.

Uwano Zendō

kindergartens → preschool education

Kinkakuji —— The Kinkaku (Golden Pavilion)

Originally built in the late 14th century as part of the villa of the shōgun Ashikaga Yoshimitsu, the Kinkaku survived until the 20th century only to perish by fire in 1950. The structure shown is a reconstruction completed in 1955.

Kingu

(King). Popular general-interest monthly magazine founded in 1925 by NOMA SEIJI, the president of KŌDANSHA, LTD, who launched it with the promotional slogan, "Japan's most entertaining and enlightening magazine." Geared for the general reading public, it featured special sections on literature, humor, fashion, human interest stories, sports, and new trends, as well as extensive coverage of current news. The press run for the first issue was 740,000 copies; in 1927 the circulation exceeded one million copies. Its name was changed to Fuji in 1943. Renamed Kingu in 1946, it ceased publication in 1957.

Kinkai wakashū

Commonly called the Kinkaishū ("The Collection of the Kamakura Minister of the Right"). The personal poetry collection of MINAMOTO NO SANETOMO (1192–1219), accounted by some critics to be one of Japan's best poets and by others a poet of mediocre talent. His reputation is influenced by the romantic and tragic circumstances of his life: the second son of MINAMOTO NO YORITOMO, founder of the Kamakura shogunate, he became shōgun in 1203, following the illness and forced retirement of his elder brother, Yoriie, who was murdered in 1204; he was embroiled in political factions and rivalry with supporters of his brother's son and was assassinated in mysterious circumstances on the steps of the Tsurugaoka Hachiman Shrine in Kamakura. The earliest version of his collection is thought to have been compiled by Sanetomo himself before 1213 and was probably sent to his teacher, FUJIWARA NO SADAIE (Fujiwara no Teika), for comment. It appears to have been a collection of practice poems, for there are many sequences of poems having the same topic and with only the smallest variations in wording. A second and larger version containing 716 poems was compiled on the basis of the earlier version probably soon after his death.

Compelled by his position to live in the military capital of Kamakura, and thus cut off from the center of poetic activity at court, Sanetomo trained himself largely by study of poetic treatises and anthologies, so that the bulk of his poetry is purely imitative of the dominant SHIN KOKINSHŪ style of his day. He experimented with archaic diction, particularly that of the MAN'YŌSHŪ (ca 759), but the lack of direct supervision and of direct involvement in poetic circles often led to excessive sentimentality and bizarre effects rather than successful originality. However, his best poems, which were written in his later years, show a burgeoning mastery of his own style, a keen appreciation of simple details from life, and a refreshing boldness and freedom in the use of words. About 20 of these successful poems exist to secure his reputation and suggest that, had he lived longer, he might have become a truly first-class poet.

Phillip T. Harries

Kinkakuji

(Temple of the Golden Pavilion). Formally known as Rokuonji. A temple in Kita Ward, Kyōto, belonging to the SHŌKOKUJI branch of the RINZAI SECT of Zen Buddhism. Kinkakuji is built on the site of an estate of the aristocrat Saionji Kintsune (1171–1244) at the foot of the Kitayama Mountains; the third Muromachi shōgun, Ashikaga Yoshimitsu (r 1369–95), took possession of the estate in 1397 with the intention of turning it into an elegant retreat. Over the next 10 years various buildings, including a three-storied pagoda and a seven-storied pagoda, were erected at an enormous cost. The whole complex, which was called Kitayama-dono (Kitayama Palace), was the de facto center of Ashikaga power at the time, since Yoshimitsu's successor as shōgun, Yoshimochi, was only eight years old when he succeeded to that office. After Yoshimitsu's death in 1408, the Kitayama-dono was converted into a temple in accordance with his last wishes and given the name of Rokuonji, Rokuon being Yoshimitsu's posthumous religious title. The great Zen master Musō Soseki (1275–1351) was designated the honorary first abbot. Successive abbots were generally selected from high ranking military or aristocratic families.

The Kinkakuji suffered severe damage during the ŌNIN WAR (1467–77) but was largely restored owing to the efforts of the ninth Muromachi shōgun, Ashikaga Yoshihisa (r 1473–89). Only two of the original buildings, the Kinkaku (Golden Pavilion) and the Fudōdō (Fudō Hall) survived the conflagration that swept the temple around 1565. Although some reconstruction took place subsequently, the Kinkakuji gradually fell into disrepair because of a decline in revenues during the Edo period (1600–1868). With the advent of the Meiji period (1868–1912) the temple underwent extensive renovations. The Kinkaku—the only vestige from the time of Yoshimitsu—was completely destroyed in 1950 in a fire set by a youth who sought to protest the degradation and commercialization of Buddhism. The writer MISHIMA YUKIO fictionalized these events in his celebrated novel *Kinkakuji* (1956; tr *The Temple of the Golden Pavilion*, 1959). An exact reproduction of the original Kinkaku building was completed in October 1955.

The Kinkaku is a gilded three-story structure. The ground floor (known as the Hōsuiin) is built in the SHINDEN-ZUKURI architectural style, and has at the rear altars with images of the Buddha AMIDA with two flanking bodhisattvas, Musō Soseki, and Yoshimitsu. The middle floor (the Chōonkaku) is representative of the *buke-zukuri* (*samurai*-style) architecture and holds images of the bodhisattva Kannon and the Four Heavenly Kings (Shitennō). The top floor (the Kukyōchō) follows the *shariden* (a type of Buddhist temple building) architectural style and originally contained images of Amida with 25 attendant bodhisattvas, which were all lost during the 16th century. More than half of the Kinkakuji precincts is taken up by a fine landscape garden, which has a large pond at its center interspersed with oddly shaped rocks and islets. The temple is also noted for its rich collection of art treasures. See also KITAYAMA CULTURE.

Stanley WEINSTEIN

Kinkazan

Island 1 km (0.6 mi) southeast of the Oshika Peninsula, eastern Miyagi Prefecture, northern Honshū; composed of granite with sea-eroded cliffs. The Koganeyama Shrine, located here, commemorates the guardian god of gold, silver, and other valuables. Wild monkeys and deer inhabit the island. Area: 9 sq km (3 sq mi).

Kinki Electrical Construction Co, Inc

(Kinki Denki Kōji). Firm chiefly engaged in electrical construction, but also in construction of production plants and installation of air conditioning systems and instrumentation. It is the second largest firm in the industry behind KANTŌ ELECTRICAL CONSTRUCTION CO, LTD. It was founded in 1944 with the merger of over 50 electrical construction companies, initially to erect power lines for KANSAI ELECTRIC POWER CO, INC. But in 1982 60 percent of its income derived from other private and public construction projects. The firm has set up joint venture companies in Singapore, Indonesia, and Malaysia and accepts contracts for overseas projects. Sales for the fiscal year ending March 1982 totaled ¥216.8 billion (US $900.6 million), of which the laying of indoor circuitry accounted for 56 percent, erection of power lines 35 percent, and other projects 9 percent. In the same year capitalization was ¥4.3 billion (US $17.9 million). The head office is in Ōsaka.

Kinki Nippon Railway Co, Ltd

(Kinki Nippon Tetsudō; commonly called Kintetsu). Largest private railroad firm, also engaged in the operation of bus lines and department stores and in the sale of real estate. The company's rail lines connect Ōsaka with such major tourist and commercial centers as Kyōto, Nara, Ise, and Nagoya. It transports an average of two million passengers daily. Founded in 1910 as the Nara Railway Co, Ltd, it offered service between Ōsaka and Nara; in 1938 work was completed on an extension of its trunk line connecting Ōsaka with Nagoya. The company assumed its present name in 1944, and through a merger in 1963 it initiated service from Kyōto to Nara and Ōsaka. The Kintetsu group, of which Kinki Nippon Railway is the central firm, includes approximately 170 companies with combined annual earnings of ¥1.5 trillion (US $7.1 billion) for the fiscal year ending September 1981, engaged in such activities as sea and land transport, operation of hotels, sale of real estate, travel and tourism, manufacture, construction, advertising, and insurance. Overseas, Kintetsu Enterprises Co of America operates hotels and restaurants and leases buildings in San Francisco. Kinki Nippon Tourist Co, Ltd, an affiliate of Kinki Nippon Railway, has set up four subsidiaries, one of which is Kintetsu International Express, Inc, and another affiliate, Kintetsu World Express, Inc, has formed three subsidiary companies, among which is Kintetsu World Express, Inc. Sales for the fiscal year ending March 1982 totaled ¥145.8 billion (US $605 million), of which earnings from its railroad division constituted 75 percent, from its bus line 7 percent, and from real estate and other enterprises 18 percent. In the same year capitalization stood at ¥53.3 billion (US $221.4 million). The head office is in Ōsaka.

Kinki region

(Kinki *chihō*). Located in west central Honshū and consisting of Ōsaka, Hyōgo, Kyōto, Shiga, Mie, Wakayama, and Nara prefectures. Traditional center of government and culture of Japan since the beginning of recorded history and today the nation's second most important industrial region.

The region's northern part is dominated by the Chūgoku Mountains and the Tamba Mountains, and the steep Kii Mountains lie to the south on the Kii Peninsula. The land is generally low between these ranges, with many small basins where such cities as Kyōto and Nara are located. There are numerous coastal plains on the Inland Sea, Ōsaka Bay, and the Kii Channel, including large ones at Ōsaka and Himeji. The Kii Peninsula has some of the heaviest precipitation in Japan and is warm even in winter. The northern part of the region faces the Sea of Japan and is noted for its heavy snowfall in winter. Rain is rather scarce in the central lowlands.

The Kyōto–Nara area was the political center of Japan in ancient days, but it lost its political significance after the Meiji Restoration of 1868, when the capital was moved to Tōkyō. The Ōsaka–Kōbe district is the center of commerce and industry for western Japan. It is dominated by chemical and heavy industries, including iron and steel, metalworking, vehicles, machinery, chemicals, and petrochemicals. Rice production and sericulture are important in the north; lumbering and fishing are important on the Kii Peninsula. Citrus fruits are grown throughout the region, especially on the Kii Peninsula; there are many truck farms on the Ōsaka Plain. Kōbe is one of the country's most important ports.

Under the Kinki Region Development Law (1963) a sweeping development plan was implemented to make the Kinki region comparable to the TŌKYŌ METROPOLITAN AREA in economic and cultural importance. As the location of the ancient capitals of Kyōto and Nara, it has many famous temples, shrines, scenic spots, and historical relics, attracting great numbers of foreign tourists every year. It is the location of four national parks (Ise-Shima, Yoshino-Kumano, Inland Sea, and San'in Coast) as well as of seven quasi-national parks. Principal cites include Ōsaka, Kyōto, and Kōbe. See also KANSAI REGION. Area: 33,033 sq km (12,751 sq mi); pop: 21,209,310.

kinki shoga

(Ch: *qinqi shuhua* or *ch'in-ch'i shu-hua*). A Chinese painting subject illustrating the four accomplishments of the cultivated Chinese gentleman: music (specifically, playing the Chinese stringed instrument called the *qin*), the game of GO (Ch: *qi*; also called *weiqi*), CALLIGRAPHY (Ch: *shu*), and painting (Ch: *hua*). Depicted in China since ancient times, the theme was established in Japan by the end of the

15th century and became a popular subject related to the diffusion of Confucian ideas during the Edo period (1600–1868).

Carolyn WHEELWRIGHT

kinkyōrei → anti-Christian edicts

Ki no Kaion (1663–1742)

A leading dramatist for the PUPPET THEATER who wrote about 50 JŌRURI plays—mostly *jidaimono* (historical plays). Real name Enami Kiemon. Born in Ōsaka. Kaion and his contemporary CHIKAMATSU MONZAEMON are often mentioned as professional rivals, but Chikamatsu was by far the superior in both playwriting ability and popularity. Kaion's broad interest in Japanese literature and poetry and Chinese studies earned him great respect among intellectual circles, but his puppet plays tended to be rather dry and highly moralistic, even if technically proficient.

Unlike Chikamatsu's, Kaion's plays are seldom performed on the current stage. His serious contribution to the puppet theater can be appreciated only after a close textual analysis of his extant works and the exploration of their bearing on the subsequent course of Japanese theatrical history. In 1708, for example, he introduced the now familiar romance of Kyūemon, the wooden-bowl dealer, and Matsuyama, the courtesan, in *Wankyū sue no Matsuyama* (Wankyū and Matsuyama), and soon thereafter he described for the first time the tragic love affair of Sankatsu, the umbrella dealer, and Hanshichi, the courtesan, in *Kasaya Sankatsu nijūgonen ki* (Sankatsu and Hanshichi). Both of these stories were later developed into major KABUKI dramas by other playwrights.

▬ ——Donald Keene, *World Within Walls: Japanese Literature of the Pre-Modern Era, 1600–1867* (1976). Kuroki Kanzō, "Ki no Kaion kenkyū," *Nihon bungaku kōza,* vol 10 (Shinchōsha, 1931). Sonoda Tamio, *Jōruri sakusha no kenkyū* (1944). *Ted T.* TAKAYA

Kinokawa

River in northern Wakayama Prefecture, central Honshū, originating in Nara Prefecture, where it is known as the Yoshinogawa. It flows west through the Wakayama Plain, a rich farming area, to enter the Kitan Strait at the city of Wakayama. Many dams have been constructed along the river since World War II. The water is used for irrigation and for industrial purposes. Length: 136 km (84 mi); area of drainage basin: 1,730 sq km (667.8 sq mi).

Kinokuniya Bunzaemon (late 1660s?–1734?)

Wealthy merchant of the middle Edo period (1600–1868). He was probably born in Kii Province (now Wakayama Prefecture) and became a lumber merchant in the Hatchōbori district of Edo (now Tōkyō). He secured exclusive rights to supply building material for the main halls of the temple Kan'eiji in Ueno, the largest and most influential in Edo. As an official purveyor to the shogunate, Bunzaemon was able to obtain choice lumber and maintain a flourishing business. Other stories credit his fortunes to his success in shipping tangerines from his native Kii to Edo.

Bunzaemon was famed for his extravagant living. His guests included the highest shogunate officials, such as YANAGISAWA YOSHIYASU, who reciprocated his hospitality with special privileges. A generous patron of the theater and entertainment world, he ransomed Miuraya no Kichō, the most famous courtesan of the time. It was said that when he went boating on the river Sumidagawa he set afloat gold and lacquer cups to surprise the people downstream. Such behavior made him a favorite subject of contemporary literature. Bunzaemon's fortunes began to decline with the fall from power of Yoshiyasu and especially after an official contract he had won to mint coins was abruptly canceled. He spent his final years in relative austerity, writing and painting at his home in the Fukagawa district of Edo.

Kinosaki

Town in northern Hyōgo Prefecture, western Honshū, on the river Maruyamagawa. Known for its hot spring since the 8th century, Kinosaki is perhaps most closely associated with the works of SHIGA NAOYA: *An'ya kōro* (1921–37; tr *A Dark Night's Passing,* 1976) and "Kinosaki nite" (1917; tr "At Kinosaki," 1956). Located nearby are Hiyoriyama coastal park and the GEMBUDŌ cave. Pop: 5,303.

Kinoshita Chōshōshi (1569–1649)

WAKA poet. Born in Owari (now part of Aichi Prefecture). Nephew of Kita no Mandokoro, the wife of TOYOTOMI HIDEYOSHI (1537–98), Chōshōshi was in 1594 granted the lordship of Obama Castle in Wakasa (now part of Fukui Prefecture) but before the Battle of SEKIGAHARA (1600), uncertain with which side to ally himself, he fled to the outskirts of Kyōto, where he lived in seclusion. Though deprived of his domain by TOKUGAWA IEYASU (1543–1616), victor at Sekigahara, Chōshōshi subsequently married his daughter to Ieyasu's fifth son Nobuyoshi and formed other connections with important members of Ieyasu's family, thus enabling him to lead a life of elegant ease. Chōshōshi associated with various well-known cultural figures of the day. He was a student of the *waka* master HOSOKAWA YŪSAI (1534–1610) and the Neo-Confucian scholar FUJIWARA SEIKA (1561–1619). In addition, he was on amicable terms with ANRAKUAN SAKUDEN (1554–1642), an anecdotist and Buddhist priest; KOBORI ENSHŪ (1579–1647), an architect and a connoisseur of ceramics, *waka,* calligraphy, and the tea ceremony; and HAYASHI RAZAN (1583–1657), a Neo-Confucianist. Knowledgeable in both the Chinese and Japanese classics, Chōshōshi nevertheless wrote in a fresh and uniquely personal style which attracted numerous imitators. Although it received harsh criticism from traditionalists such as MATSUNAGA TEITOKU (1571–1653), his verse, collected in *Kyohakushū* and *Wakasa no Shōshō Katsutoshi Ason shū,* influenced the poetry of BASHŌ (1644–94) and was a pervasive force in the development of Edo-period (1600–1868) progressive *waka.*

Kinoshita Jun'an (1621–1698)

Neo-Confucian scholar of the early Edo period (1600–1868). Born in Kyōto, he studied with MATSUNAGA SEKIGO, a disciple of FUJIWARA SEIKA. After a brief stay in Edo (now Tōkyō), he returned to Kyōto, where he remained for the next 20 years, until he was invited to the Kanazawa domain (now Ishikawa Prefecture) by MAEDA TSUNANORI, the enlightened *daimyō* of that domain. In 1682 he was appointed a Confucian scholar to the shogunate and lecturer to the shōgun TOKUGAWA TSUNAYOSHI. Thenceforth he commuted between Kaga and Edo, acquiring a reputation as an outstanding teacher who tried to develop the individual talents of each student. His many disciples included the scholar-statesmen ARAI HAKUSEKI, MURO KYŪSŌ, AMENOMORI HŌSHŪ, and MIYAKE KANRAN.

Kinoshita Junji (1914–   )

One of Japan's foremost modern playwrights. Between 1940 and the late 1970s Kinoshita wrote over 40 plays for stage and radio, in general taking subjects either from Japanese folklore or from contemporary history. He has also published many important works on the theory of the stage.

Kinoshita Junji was born in Tōkyō but in 1921 moved with his family to Kumamoto in western Japan, where he spent most of his school days. In 1936 he returned to Tōkyō to study English literature at Tōkyō University and specialized in Elizabethan drama under the famous scholar of English NAKANO YOSHIO. Like many of his fellow students, Kinoshita watched performances of Shakespeare and modern Japanese plays given by the two main left-wing SHINGEKI (new drama) groups of the time. Simply to attend performances by these groups was regarded by students and intellectuals as a form of symbolic protest against the increasingly militarist character of the Japanese government. Kinoshita's interest was particularly drawn to the socialist realist plays of KUBO SAKAE. Until 1938 Kinoshita intended to become a scholar specializing in the history of drama, but the incident of that year involving KAWAI EIJIRŌ convinced him that academic life might mean having to compromise some of his principles. With much encouragement from the actress YAMAMOTO YASUE, Kinoshita decided to make playwriting his career.

Kinoshita's first work was *Fūrō* (1934, Wind and Waves), staged in 1954. It is a realistic historical drama set in Kumamoto and traces the anxious pursuit of new ideals by a young *samurai* in the first decade of the Meiji period (1868–1912). Soon afterward Nakano Yoshio encouraged him to read YANAGITA KUNIO's *Zenkoku mukashibanashi kiroku* (Complete Compendium of Japanese Legends), and in this work Kinoshita found material for a new type of modern play, later to be known as *minwageki* (folktale play). Kinoshita wrote three such plays in 1943, including one, *Tsuru nyōbō* (The Crane Wife), which was rewritten later into the famous *Yūzuru* (1949; tr *Twilight Crane,* 1956).

In the immediate postwar years Kinoshita published several *minwageki,* a translation of *Othello,* and three radio plays, and participated in the founding of a new *shingeki* group, Budō no Kai (Grape Society). It was this group that henceforth performed all Kinoshita's *minwageki,* including *Yūzuru* in October 1949. *Yūzuru,* one of the most popular postwar plays in Japan, generated a widespread interest in Japan's heritage of folktales which culminated in the founding of the Minwa no Kai (Folktale Society) in 1952 (Kinoshita was a founder-member).

Kinoshita continued to write *minwageki,* but he was also experimenting with plays set in contemporary Japan; *Yamanami* (1949, Mountain Range), *Kurai hibana* (1950, Dark Sparks), *Kaeru shōten* (1951, Ascension of a Frog). In the *minwageki* the ancient past had proved capable of moving Japanese audiences; Kinoshita considered that there was much in the present which should move them also, and these three plays can be seen as transitional between the *minwageki* and the *gendaigeki* (plays of the present) for which Kinoshita is also famous. During the early 1950s Kinoshita also became known as a leading spokesman on the modern Japanese theater and its problems. In 1957, two years after a spiritually invigorating trip to India, the Middle East, Europe, Russia, and China, Kinoshita published *Onnyoro seisuiki* (The Rise and Fall of Onnyoro). Based on a play Kinoshita had seen in China, it tells the story of an overweening bully who destroys two of three scourges afflicting a village only to be mortified to learn that the third is himself.

With its riots against renewal of the United States–Japan Security Treaty, 1960 was for Kinoshita, as for many other Japanese intellectuals, a year of great trauma. Kinoshita's plays from now on reflect his concern with individuals who are forced to decide how to stand against the momentum of history. *Okinawa* (1961), *Ottō to yobareru nihonjin* (1962, A Japanese Called Ottō), and *Fuyu no jidai* (1964, The Winter Season) are Kinoshita's most famous *gendaigeki* of the time. Ottō (the Soviet code name for OZAKI HOTSUMI), by his involvement in the Sorge spy ring (see SORGE INCIDENT), commits treason in an attempt to stop Japan's drift to war. *Shimpan* (1970; tr *The Judgment,* 1979) examines the problem of war guilt. In 1966 Kinoshita published his only novel, *Mugen kidō* (Track without End), describing a day in the lives of three train drivers, during which man is dominated by dehumanizing machine technology. During the 1970s Kinoshita wrote a number of important theoretical works and published a complete translation of Shakespeare's plays. In addition his own playwriting has taken another new direction. His long-standing interest in the Japanese language as a medium for drama combined with his search for a truly dramatic hero led him to the medieval romance HEIKE MONOGATARI (The Tale of the Heike). Kinoshita discerned a natural drama in the language of this medieval classic and experimented with group and individual recitation of it. A series of gramophone records was released in 1969 entitled *Heike monogatari ni yoru gundoku: Tomomori* (Group Readings from *Heike monogatari:* Tomomori). Kinoshita also found in the same work a character, Tomomori, whose personality and predicament exactly met his ideas on the dramatic hero as they had evolved over several decades. In 1977 Kinoshita completed a full-length play with Tomomori as its hero, *Shigosen no matsuri* (The Dirge of the Meridian), which combined the recitation of the *Heike monogatari* with a reconstruction of the final downfall of the Taira.

Apart from a considerable corpus of plays, Kinoshita has been a prolific writer on many aspects of drama. He admires and has extensively studied Western drama, especially Greek tragedy, Shakespeare, and Synge. His playwriting career has been an untiring search for a new Japanese drama and the wide variety of play types that he has written shows how intense this search has been. Kinoshita has paid particular attention to the technical side of playwriting and production. He has often experimented with the Japanese language (notably in *Yūzuru* and *Ottō to yobareru nihonjin*) in an attempt to impart to it a dramatic quality that he believes it generally lacks. Kinoshita's stature as a playwright, however, depends mainly on his conception of the dramatic hero. In many of Kinoshita's plays the hero is placed in an environment or against forces that are bound to overwhelm him, but Kinoshita is not interested in characters who are affected negatively by this. The concept of resistance is central to Kinoshita's thought. It was something that he discovered in Greek myths but found lacking in Japanese folktales. Kinoshita himself resisted in the 1960 anti–Security Treaty demonstrations. His aim is to strike at the consciences of his audience and to stimulate them to recreate for themselves in their own contexts the spirit of resistance being portrayed on the stage. Theatrically and intellectually Kinoshita Junji has been a major force in postwar *shingeki.*

——Works by Kinoshita Junji: *Kinoshita Junji sakuhinshū* (Miraisha, 1962–71). *Kinoshita Junji hyōronshū* (Miraisha, 1972). "Shigosen no matsuri," *Bungei* (January 1978). Works about Kinoshita Junji: Eric J. Gangloff, "Kinoshita Junji: A Modern Japanese Dramatist," PhD dissertation, University of Chicago (1973).

Brian POWELL

Kinoshita Keisuke (1912–)

Film director. Kinoshita's eclectic choice of subjects and styles makes him difficult to classify, but he is especially fond of themes related to contemporary social problems. He has treated these social problems as comedy, in *Karumen kokyō ni kaeru* (1951, Carmen Comes Home), and as tragedy, in *Nihon no higeki* (1953, A Japanese Tragedy). These and other of his films examine the foibles of postwar Japanese society with serious, though often satiric, concern.

Kinoshita's most successful and famous film is NIJŪSHI NO HITOMI (1954, Twenty-Four Eyes), about what befalls a teacher and her class of 12 pupils over the course of three decades and the devastation of World War II. The film delivers a strong polemic against war and develops an affecting portrait of each member of the class. It is also a prime example of what has been termed Kinoshita's devotion to the ideals of innocence and purity, which appear frequently in his films.

Nijūshi no hitomi won the Kinema Jumpō Award as the best film of 1954. Kinoshita has won that award for two other films as well: *Ōsoneke no asa* (1946, Morning for the Ōsone Family) and *Narayama-bushi kō* (1958, The Ballad of Narayama). A hallmark of Kinoshita's work is his fondness for long, panoramic, postcardlike shots that give the viewer a feel for the setting of his films.

Throughout most of his career Kinoshita has worked for the same studio (SHŌCHIKU CO, LTD) and with the same staff, which has included his brother Chūji as composer and his brother-in-law as cinematographer.

——Audie Bock, *Japanese Film Directors* (1978).

David OWENS

Kinoshita Mokutarō (1885–1945)

Physician, poet, playwright, novelist. Real name Ōta Masao. Born in Shizuoka Prefecture. Kinoshita began writing poetry while he was a student in the Medical School of Tōkyō University. In 1908 he became a member of PAN NO KAI, a group of poets and artists which included KITAHARA HAKUSHŪ and YOSHII ISAMU. He contributed novels, dramas, and poems to journals such as *Subaru* and *Okujō teien,* and by the time of his graduation in 1911 he had established his reputation as a writer. The theme of his works was usually the conflict between intellect and emotions and the sorrow deriving from it. In 1916 he became a hospital director in Manchuria and traveled extensively in China. Upon returning to Japan, he served as professor of dermatology at several universities, including Tōkyō University. In 1941 he received the Légion d'Honneur of France for his contributions to dermatological studies. His complete works are collected in the *Kinoshita Mokutarō zenshū,* 12 vols (Iwanami Shoten, 1948–51).

James R. MORITA

Kinoshita Naoe (1869–1937)

Novelist, socialist, Christian pacifist, and in his later years proponent and practitioner of an indigenous form of meditation. He graduated from Tōkyō Semmon Gakkō (now Waseda University). Kinoshita was one of the few vocal "outsiders" of the late 19th and early 20th centuries. A blend of youthful republicanism and humanitarian idealism, fueled by a fascination with Cromwell and by the Sermon on the Mount, he found expression in journalism, first in the provincial town of Matsumoto (in what is now Nagano Prefecture) where he was born, and then in Tōkyō. Soon he joined one of the small groups of intellectuals out of whose interest in Western socialist ideas organized Japanese socialism was later born. In a flood of forcefully written articles he attacked a wide range of social abuses, and in a country with little tradition of public speaking quickly became known too as an eloquent orator, whose speeches generated great excitement, though they were often halted in midstream as "dangerous" by the police, who invariably attended his meetings. War seemed to him totally incompatible with the spirit of Christianity, and he was not afraid to say so in public during the Sino–Japanese War of 1894–95, when patriotic support for the war was universal in Japan. That he did not suffer for his views was no doubt because they appeared absurd and so aroused no significant support.

The most striking affirmation of both his socialism and his pacifism is his first novel, *Hi no hashira* (1904; tr *Pillar of Fire,* 1972), for which he is best remembered today. It was written almost on the spur of the moment, to fill a vacant serial column in his newspaper. Though technically a great advance on the so-called political novels of the 1880s, its literary status is not high: the story is too much a simple matter of right versus wrong, the characters too thin. Yet this tale of a nonviolent Christ-like socialist and editor, whose insistence on the stupidity of war isolates him not only from his church but even from the workers whose cause he has espoused, is written with such love and fury that its very naiveté makes a greater impact than, for example, the "proletarian" fiction of the 1920s. Remarkably, despite the fact that the book appeared during the Russo–Japanese War (1904–05), and that its leading villains were caricatures, only thinly disguised, of prominent real-life statesmen, Kinoshita was still not molested by the authorities. *Hi no hashira,* however, was banned in 1910, and not republished in full until 1950.

Kinoshita published several other novels and collections of essays. He also compiled, in 1900, a memorable series of reports on the pollution caused by poisonous effluent from the giant Ashio Copper Mine northeast of Tōkyō (see ASHIO COPPER MINE INCIDENT). This pollution gave rise to one of the most notorious political and industrial scandals of the Meiji era, if not of the entire modern period. Kinoshita's newspaper reports from the contaminated areas, inspired in part by a meeting with TANAKA SHŌZŌ, the courageous politician who had for years been campaigning doggedly but with only modest success on behalf of the peasant victims of the effluent, were later published as a book, and constitute what may be the first systematic indictment of environmental pollution ever made.

From about 1910, however, he began to feel a need for an inwardness which his writing and political activity could not satisfy. Acknowledging a debt to both Christianity and Buddhism ("Christ and the Buddha are two flowers blooming on a single stem"), he spent the rest of his life as a near-recluse, advocating the form of meditation known as *seiza* (sitting in silence). This withdrawal in early middle age from an active to a contemplative life was no eccentricity: he was choosing to follow an ancient and well-understood tradition.

📖 ── Kinoshita Naoe, *Kinoshita Naoe chosakushū,* 15 vols (Meiji Bunken, 1968–73). Kinoshita Naoe, *Hi no hashira* (1904), tr with biographical introduction as *Pillar of Fire* (1972). Yamagiwa Keiji, *Kinoshita Naoe* (1955). Yanagida Izumi, *Kinoshita Naoe—Nihon kakumei no yogensha* (1961).   *Kenneth* STRONG

Kinoshita Rigen (1886–1925)

TANKA poet. Real name Kinoshita Toshiharu. Born in Okayama Prefecture. Graduate of Tōkyō University. Together with his classmates SHIGA NAOYA and MUSHANOKŌJI SANEATSU, he founded the literary magazine *Shirakaba* (see SHIRAKABA SCHOOL) in 1910. He shared in the philosophy of the group that came to be associated with the magazine, and his poetry, written in the colloquial language but in an elegant style, has an undertone of humanism and confidence in mankind. His poetry collections include *Kōgyoku* (1919) and *Ichiro* (1924).

Kinoshita Takafumi (1789–1821)

Late Edo-period WAKA poet from Bitchū Province (now Okayama Prefecture). While still a youth he went to Kyōto to study *waka* with KAGAWA KAGEKI and became his leading disciple. Though they both saw the need for a new style in *waka,* they did not thoroughly agree on what was to be done, and their relationship was further strained by personality conflicts. Kageki modeled his poetry on the KOKINSHŪ, for example, while the greatest influence on Takafumi's poetry collection, *Sayasaya ikō,* is that of the MAN'YŌSHŪ. "Hinkyū hyakushu," a series of 100 poems on poverty included in the collection, is particularly original and noteworthy.

Ki no Tomonori (fl ca 900)

Classical (WAKA) poet, one of four courtiers commanded by Emperor DAIGO (855–930; r 897–930) to compile the first imperial anthology of native poetry, the KOKINSHŪ (completed 905). Of somewhat obscure origins, Tomonori appears to have been a relatively low-ranking official. Contemporary sources reveal that in 897 he held the post of secretary of the province of Tosa (now Kōchi

Prefecture), and that he became a junior private secretary at court the following year. A headnote to poems 1078 and 1079 in the GOSEN WAKASHŪ indicates that he held no position at court before the age of 39 or 40, and it is thought that he was already well along in years by the time he was appointed as joint compiler of the *Kokinshū.* Nevertheless, the honor of the appointment shows that he was highly regarded as a poet. It is clear from the fact that the *Kokinshū* contains poems by KI NO TSURAYUKI and MIBU NO TADAMINE lamenting his death that he died before the anthology was completed. Tomonori's personal collection is very small, numbering in its present form only some 72 poems. On the other hand, the *Kokinshū* contains 46 of his poems, and a score more are found in other imperial anthologies from the *Gosen wakashū* on. These show him to have been a skillful poet in the style of courtly elegance popular in his day, and some of his subjective questionings and witty conceits are classic examples of their kind.

📖 ── Robert H. Brower and Earl Miner, *Japanese Court Poetry* (1961).   *Robert H.* BROWER

Ki no Tsurayuki (872?–945)

One of the leading WAKA poets of the Heian period (794–1185). Born into a family of the middle aristocracy and of poets. Sources differ as to his year of birth, some giving 859, 883, or 884. Tsurayuki served in official capacity both at the imperial court and in the provinces. In his thirties he was appointed head of the imperial library and in 945, when he was over 70, he was put in charge of the bureau of palace repairs, having advanced to junior fourth rank, a position which allowed him direct access to the palace. As to his provincial posts, in 917 Tsurayuki was appointed vice-governor of Kaga (now part of Ishikawa Prefecture), and later of Mino (now part of Gifu Prefecture), and in 930 at the age of about 50, governor of Tosa (now Kōchi Prefecture). Tsurayuki's career, particularly his provincial duties, reflect a common fate of members of the middle aristocracy (fifth rank and up). His advancement to the fourth rank of the high aristocracy relates less to his family background than to his reputation and talents as a poet.

Tsurayuki's first appearance as a poet in an official capacity dates back to the two poetry contests (UTA-AWASE) of the Kampyō era (889–898), the Koresada Shinnō Ke Uta-awase and Kampyō no Ontoki Kōkyū Uta-awase. By the Engi era (901–923), Tsurayuki had become a poet at court, where he had to compose poems in poetry contests, for adornment on folding screens *(byōbu uta),* on festive occasions, and in court ceremonies. In 905 the ruling emperor of the time, Daigo, entrusted Tsurayuki, among other leading poets, with the compilation of Japan's first imperial anthology of poetry—the *Kokin wakashū* (or KOKINSHŪ). That he wrote one of two prefaces suggests his leading role in its compilation. Tsurayuki's preface, which was in Japanese (the other was in Chinese) and called *Kokin wakashū jo,* was written in KANA (the Japanese syllabary) and constitutes the first known critical work on poetry in the Japanese language. In the preface Tsurayuki points out the basic functions and qualities of poetry and then gives his critical views on the poetry of six leading poets of his time. Tsurayuki says that ARIWARA NO NARIHIRA had "too much heart and too few words," reflecting his own basic differentiation between *kotoba* (diction) and *kokoro* (heart) in poetry. In spite of the shortcomings Tsurayuki accused his fellow poets of, they were later revered as the Six Poetic Geniuses (ROKKASEN), probably by the mere fact that they were mentioned in this preface.

Tsurayuki's *kana* preface to the *Kokin wakashū* also reflects the period, with its reemphasis on native elements in Japanese culture, as opposed to the overwhelming influence of Chinese culture in the 9th century. This reevaluation of the Japanese heritage finds further expression in Tsurayuki's *Tosa nikki.*

The *Tosa nikki* (Tosa Diary) describes Tsurayuki's return voyage in 934–935 to the Kyōto capital from Tosa in Shikoku, as if written by a real or fictitious female companion. She records the sad departure of the governor, the pain of separation from a dead daughter buried in Tosa, the dangers of the voyage by boat, and the joy of approaching the capital—all in the chronological sequence of a personal diary. Fifty-seven *waka* mark the emotional high points of the diary. In spite of the hardships and dangers of the voyage (pirates, storms, and so forth), the *Tosa nikki* includes some humorous passages. The inclusion of *Tosa nikki* poems in imperial anthologies of poetry under Tsurayuki's name led to the theory that Tsurayuki must have written the *Tosa nikki* through the persona of a female companion, since it was uncommon for a man to write a diary of an official voyage in *kana*. Tsurayuki's disguise may also have been prompted by his daughter's death in Tosa. She is mentioned significantly both at the beginning and end of the diary. That this was Tsurayuki's possible attempt to write a diary in memory of his daughter may explain the attention to children and to children's poems, as well as the passages in which the author tries to see the world through the eyes of a child.

Other works by Tsurayuki are the prefaces of the collection *Ōigawa gyōkō waka* and of the anthology *Shinsen wakashū*, both written in *kana*. About 500 poems have been preserved in imperial anthologies (the *Kokinshū* includes over 100) and in private collections such as the *Tsurayuki shū*.

🔲 ——Robert H. Brower and Earl Miner, *Japanese Court Poetry* (1961). Earl Miner, tr, *Japanese Poetic Diaries* (1969), contains a translation of *Tosa nikki*.   Herbert E. PLUTSCHOW

kinran and ginran

(gold brocade and silver brocade). Sumptuous fabric made by weaving a pattern into twill, satin, or gauze cloth with either gold or silver leaf, or gold or silver thread. The technique was introduced from China into Japan through the port city of Sakai during the late 16th century and later transmitted to the Nishijin weaving district of Kyōto. These fabrics are used for Buddhist priests' robes, costumes for NŌ plays, and traditional accessories such as bags and sashes (OBI) worn with KIMONO.   Yasuko YABE

kinroku kōsai

Public bonds issued in 1876 by the Meiji government in commutation of the hereditary stipends *(chitsuroku)* of nobles and members of the former *samurai* class. Earlier, in 1873, the government had offered the option of a lump-sum payment, half in cash and half in bonds. In 1876 it decided to commute all stipends into public bonds on a sliding scale. The interest rates of these bonds and their dates of maturity varied according to the amount of the original rice stipend. Many of the poorer former samurai, who had no business experience, were forced to sell their bonds at a loss. See CHITSU-ROKU SHOBUN.

Kinsei kijin den

(Tales of Unusual Men of Our Day). A collection of biographical sketches and anecdotes on more than 100 outstanding men of the Edo period (1600–1868); written by Ban Kōkei (1733–1806), a poet and Japanese classics scholar, illustrated by Mikuma Katen, and published in 1790. Most of the subjects were *samurai* and men of letters, but sketches of hermits, farmers, and townsmen were also included. It met with such great success that a second collection, written by Katen with Kōkei's help, was published in 1798. *Kinsei kijin den* exerted a strong influence on later Japanese literature, particularly the genre known as KIBYŌSHI.

Kinshi Kunshō

(Order of the Golden Kite). Award given by the emperor to members of the military before World War II for bravery in action. First given on 11 February 1890 to commemorate the traditional anniversary of the accession of the legendary first emperor, JIMMU, it had seven different ranks. The order takes its name from the golden kite that supposedly helped Emperor Jimmu to subdue his foes by blinding them with its dazzling feathers.   KONDŌ Shinji

kinship

The basic pattern of the Japanese kinship system is bilateral. Both the paternal and maternal sides are symmetrically referred to and addressed by the same terms, as in the Anglo-American pattern. In standard Japanese, the term for uncle is *oji*, for aunt *oba*, and for cousin *itoko*. Differences from the Anglo-American categories are found only in the terms for siblings. Both brothers and sisters are differentiated according to relative age: *ani* for elder brothers and *otōto* for younger brothers; likewise, *ane* for elder sisters and *imōto* for younger sisters. The term *kyōdai* includes both brothers and sisters. The range of kinship terms extends to first cousins.

Another characteristic of the Japanese use of kinship terms is found in the equation of cognates and affines: spouses of uncles, aunts, and siblings are referred to and addressed by the same term

as those related by blood, and the same range and terms apply to the cognates and affines of one's spouse. As reflected in this usage of kinship terms, the Japanese tend to conceptualize their kinship universe without differentiating between cognates and affines. This is closely related to the concept of the IE (household), the members of which are grouped as a distinctive social unit. A set of relatives called *shinrui* (or *shinseki*) is conceptualized in terms of households rather than individuals. The *shinrui* includes a certain number of households whose family members are related to one through the bilateral extension of kinship, normally including first cousins. Although it is not a constant group of kin, it has important functions: it is the *shinrui* who assemble and are indispensable for weddings and funerals. A circle of *shinrui* is recognized as a set of households, not simply as an aggregation of relatives, and the functions of *shinrui* are performed as by households, not as by individuals.

Composition of the Shinrui —— The *shinrui* of the individual members of a household tend to be congruent with the *shinrui* of the household head rather than genealogical networks traced out from each individual member. The recognition of kinship itself with reference to each individual does not necessarily establish a *shinrui* relationship by itself. It is the kin of the household, not of the individual, that is most significant socially. Therefore the range of the *shinrui* for an individual gradually changes as his status alters in the household. For example, the head of a household sees the composition of his *shinrui* change at two major events: his father's funeral and his son's marriage. Some *shinrui* members appear for the former but disappear from the latter, and in place of them, new *shinrui* members appear. The former were those *shinrui* recognized with reference to his father and the latter, with reference to his son. The funeral of his parent would be the last occasion on which his distant *shinrui* through his parents (such as his parents' cousins) come to his household. His son's wedding marks the beginning of an association with *shinrui* new to him. In the case of a woman, before her marriage her *shinrui* is recognized as that of her father; if she moves to the household (or village) of her husband upon her marriage, the *shinrui* of her husband stand closer to her, while her previous *shinrui* relationships tend to fade; finally, after the retirement of her husband as head of the household or after the death of her husband, her *shinrui* will gradually frame itself about that of her son, while contact with her husband's distant *shinrui* will diminish. Contact with these distant *shinrui* is normally ended on the death of cousins, nephews, and nieces.

In theory the number of *shinrui* members would constantly increase by the marriage of members of the households involved in the *shinrui* relationship, and at the same time, the death of individuals would decrease their number. Hence the range of a *shinrui* is kept fairly constant with reference to a household, though its composition gradually changes.

The *shinrui* relationship will not extend along the simple lines of relatedness through cognatic and affinal relationships. The recognition of a *shinrui* or its outer limit is precisely governed by the economic and moral rights and obligations of the members to each other. Among the members of a *shinrui*, the degree of gradation has significance according to the closeness of the relationship. In the grading there is no discrimination between the paternal and the maternal sides, and cognates and affines are placed in the same grade. In fact, the household from which the wife came stands as one of the most important *shinrui* to the husband's own household, no less important than the household of his married siblings.

Local familiarity combining with socioeconomic obligation, which makes it possible to maintain constant intercommunication, seems an important factor for recognition of the *shinrui* relation. The range of *shinrui* also differs according to social strata: a wealthy household tends to have a broader range of *shinrui*, while the poorer sector of the community tends to have a narrower range. When members of a *shinrui* reside far apart, they usually cease to interact, yet a wealthy household will maintain contact with quite distant *shinrui*. The maintenance of the *shinrui* relationship thus tends to depend largely upon the location of a household and its economic standing.

Dominant Tendency of the Male Side —— The Japanese kinship system is often labeled "patrilineal" in sociological literature. This erroneous description derives from the tendency toward dominance of the male side accompanying virilocal marriage (in which wives come to live with husbands' families after marriage), which became the dominant pattern in the feudal age and after. During the Edo period (1600–1868), when the *ie* institution became prevalent, it was advantageous for management of a household that the head be succeeded by his son, who had been his active collaborator. Among *samurai* as well as among farmers it became the ideal pattern that the head of the household be succeeded by his own son. As a result, patrilocal marriage became the predominant pattern in the society. However, in the absence of a son, normally the daughter's husband became an adopted son-in-law, assuming the position of *de jure* as well as *de facto* successor of his wife's father. As the Japanese never had a patrilineal descent system with its pattern of exogamous marriage as did China or Korea, the adoption of a son-in-law was widely practiced. According to data collected in one remote hill village, one-third of the total number of household heads were adopted sons-in-law. In general, whether an adopted son-in-law was related to the head or not was not important to consider. In the presence of such a widespread custom, therefore, the Japanese kinship system should not be called patrilineal in the usage of current social anthropology.

After the introduction of surnames among commoners following the Meiji Restoration of 1868, it became the general practice for children to take the father's surname. Upon marriage women changed their surnames to that of their husbands, except when husbands became adopted sons-in-law and changed their surnames to that of their wives' fathers. It should be pointed out that this custom is rarely found among Chinese and Koreans, who follow the patrilineal system in which surnames are based strictly on patrilineal descent lines.

Another phenomenon that sometimes gave the impression that the Japanese had a patrilineal system was the existence of a special type of local group called *dōzoku* in sociological literature. A *dōzoku* is a set of households which split off from an original one: the original household is called the *honke* and the branch household is called the *bunke*. The *dōzoku* group was normally created around the households of brothers, so that it gave the impression of being a patrilineal group. However, here too, some branch households were created by adopted sons-in-law. At the same time, a brother who became an adopted son-in-law in another household which was not already in a *dōzoku* did not become a member. Thus, strictly speaking, the *dōzoku* cannot be called a patrilineal descent group. Rather it is a collection of households that maintain specific relationships centered on the original one from which they split off. In comparison with a *shinrui*, the composition of a *dōzoku* demonstrates a greater tendency toward the male links since it is a collection of households linked through the fission of the household(s). It is a lineally organized group clearly demarcated from others, while *shinrui* is a set of households recognized in reference to a particular household. *Shinrui* may be found across the boundaries of village communities, but *dōzoku* are mostly confined to the same village community. Therefore, *dōzoku* and *shinrui* may overlap each other but not be identical. Moreover, *shinrui* are found in all strata of the population and regions of Japan, but the creation of *dōzoku* was limited by local economic and historical conditions, and the degree of cooperation with the *honke* also differs from one case to another.

Importance of Women in the Kinship Network —— The predominance of virilocal marriages, including the *dōzoku* organization, offers an impression of the dominance of the male line in Japanese kinship in spite of its bilateral character. Indeed it is always father and eldest brother who occupy higher seats than mother and sister in a gathering of *shinrui;* and relatives of the father's (husband's) side are given priority on formal occasions. However, it is interesting and necessary to indicate another side of this picture—the importance of women. It is the mother, wife, and sisters who play the key role in communication among relatives, especially in the functions of *shinrui,* which are mostly carried out and maintained by these women.

For example, in an agricultural community, the head of a household in need of assistance requests help without hesitation from households such as his wife's natal household (wife's brother); his sister's household (sister's husband); his mother's natal household (mother's brother or his son); father's sister's household (father's sister's son) in preference to his own brother's household. It is clear that all these households are related through women who were once members of his own household, whether they live in the same village or in neighboring villages. Villagers talk about what a handicap it is if one has no sister. It is a man's sister who comes to help at once when somebody becomes ill in his house.

It is the general tendency in a community, whether it be rural or urban, that kinship relations are constantly kept up by sisters and wives. This often leads to a household having more effective links with relatives on the wife's side. This is the latent and informal side

of the Japanese kinship system at work. Today, virilocal marriages are rapidly decreasing, except in farming households. With the decline of the traditional formality, it has become an emergent tendency among young people that they visit the wife's natal house first, more frequently, and for longer periods than the husband's. Thus the recent tendencies disclose the latent importance of women in the Japanese kinship system and strengthen the interpretation of its essential nature as bilateral.

📖 ——Nakane Chie, *Kinship and Economic Organization in Rural Japan* (1967). R. J. Smith, "Japanese Kinship Terminology: The History of a Nomenclature," *Ethnology* 1 (1962).　　NAKANE Chie

Kinshō-Mataichi Corporation

Trading firm handling iron, steel, nonferrous metals, and textiles. Founded in 1960 through the merger of Kinshō, a trading firm handling metals and former MITSUBISHI Corporation affiliate, and Mataichi, an old Ōsaka trading firm dealing with textiles. Kinshō-Mataichi subsequently grew into a comprehensive trading company, adding new products such as foodstuffs, machinery, fuels, and synthetic goods. Overseas it has 11 offices and 3 subsidiary companies. Sales for the fiscal year ending March 1982 totaled ¥286.5 billion (US $1.2 billion) and capitalization was ¥1.6 billion (US $6.6 million). The head office is in Tōkyō.

Kintarō

Popular figure in Japanese folklore. Kintarō (Golden Boy) was the childhood name of Sakata no Kintoki, one of the four trusted followers of the warrior MINAMOTO NO YORIMITSU. Although Sakata seems to have been a historical figure, appearing in the 11th-century anthology KONJAKU MONOGATARI, he is depicted in later stories as having been the son of a YAMAMBA (mountain witch), born on Mt. Ashigara, and as being a prodigy of Herculean strength who wrestled with bears and other beasts. Kintarō appears in 17th- and 18th-century ballads (JŌRURI) and KABUKI plays, often by the name of Kaidōmaru. The tales of his supernatural birth, his red complexion, and his possession of a hatchet said to be the thunder-god's weapon, all point to a connection with belief in the thunder god—the ensurer of a bountiful crop—that was probably indigenous to the Ashigara area. Kintarō may be seen as a combination of a local fertility god and the historical figure Sakata.　　SUCHI Tokuhei

Kinugasa Teinosuke (1896–1982)

Film director. Initially famous as one of the first great innovators of Japanese cinema, later noted for his lavish and spectacular productions.

Kinugasa began his acting career as an ONNAGATA (female impersonator) with several SHIMPA theater troupes. He continued as an *onnagata* at the Nikkatsu (see NIKKATSU CORPORATION) film studio beginning in 1917 where a great many films of *shimpa* performances were being produced. Kinugasa appeared in as many as 44 films in a single year. Actresses began to replace *onnagata,* however, and in 1922, Kinugasa led a futile strike of the actors who had taken female roles.

With his acting career at an end, Kinugasa immersed himself in other aspects of the film industry. He wrote his first screenplay in 1920, and directed his first feature in 1923. At the time he also belonged to a group of artists and writers whose members included the writer KAWABATA YASUNARI. Kawabata collaborated on Kinugasa's first independent project, *Kurutta ippeiji* (1926, A Page of Madness). The film revolves around a woman incarcerated in an asylum and her remorseful husband who has taken a menial job at the asylum to be near her. Kinugasa did not employ conventional narrative techniques, but sought instead to convey the sensations of insanity through visual imagery and editing techniques.

Kinugasa's other important film of this period was the last production of his own company. *Jūjiro* (1928, Crossroads), like *A Page of Madness,* defied conventional methods in presenting the story of a man who believes he has killed a rival in a duel. Images from the man's past merge with those of his present condition as he lies wounded in refuge. It is considered a seminal work of Japanese cinema.

Following his hard-won and unconventional artistic success in the 1920s, Kinugasa became a very conventional director, though one of great skill. Following the war he specialized in lavish costume dramas and remakes of some of his earlier films. Of this body of work, only one film is well known: *Jigokumon* (1953, Gate of Hell), the first successful Japanese color film. It won the Grand Prix at the Cannes Film Festival in 1953 and the Academy Award as Best Foreign Film in 1955. The film is an elegant exercise in style which recreates for the cinema the pictorial quality of Japanese scroll paintings.　　　　　　　　　　　　　　　　　　　　　　*David* OWENS

Kinugawa

River in Tochigi and Ibaraki prefectures, central Honshū. Originating in the Taishaku Mountains in northwest Tochigi Prefecture and flowing south, it joins the Tonegawa at the city of Mitsukaidō. Numerous dams, including the Kawamata and Ikari, and many hot springs such as Kinugawa and Kawaji are located along the upper reaches. The water is utilized for drinking, irrigation, and electric power. Length: 176.7 km (109.7 mi); area of drainage basin: 1,760.6 sq km (679.6 sq mi).

Kinugawa Hot Spring

(Kinugawa Onsen). Located near the Kinugawa Gorge, northwestern Tochigi Prefecture, central Honshū. A simple thermal spring; water temperature 34–53°C (93–127°F). Located within Nikkō National Park, it is one of the most famous spas in the Kantō region, abounding in numerous natural scenic spots such as the gorge called Ryūōkyō.

Kin'yō wakashū

(Collection of Golden Leaves; the full title is usually abbreviated to *Kin'yōshū*). The fifth imperial anthology (*chokusenshū*) of classical Japanese poetry. Ordered in 1124 by the retired emperor SHIRAKAWA (1053–1129; r 1073–87); drafts completed between 1124 and 1127; standard version is the second draft. Compiled by MINAMOTO NO TOSHIYORI; 10 books. The number of poems varies depending on draft and manuscript copy; second draft commonly has 712 poems, third draft, 648.

Compilation——The compiler, Minamoto no Toshiyori, was an original, daring, and often eccentric poet who found it hard to please his imperial patron, not to mention his poetic opponents. Shirakawa refused to accept his first two drafts, and he submitted his only manuscript copy of the third draft, probably expecting another rebuff. Surprisingly, it was immediately accepted by the former emperor, who kept it, and Toshiyori was thus deprived of his text. It is for this reason that the second draft became the commonly circulated version, the third existing today only in fragmentary form. At all events, it is well that the second draft became standard, because this version contains the most interesting poetry. Toshiyori gave considerable prominence to the new poetry of natural description, both his own and that of other contemporaries and poets of the recent past, and thus contributed to the increasing acceptance and valuation placed upon the style. The *Kin'yōshū* is an important precursor of the great imperial anthologies of the late 12th and 13th centuries, which represent the fullest development and efflorescence of the poetry of descriptive symbolism.

Structure——Toshiyori showed a disregard for tradition by making the anthology the shortest to date and by limiting it to 10 books instead of the 20 considered standard since the first imperial anthology, the KOKINSHŪ (ca 905, Collection of Ancient and Modern Times). The obvious explanation is that he could not find enough poems he judged of sufficient quality to justify a larger format, although the results suggest that he did not search as widely or as diligently as he might have done. Another departure was the inclusion in the last book of a major subcategory headed *renga*, "linked poems"—standard five-line, 31-syllable poems of which one person had composed the first three lines and another the last two. These were an ancestor of the later extended forms of linked verse, and had never before been considered worth including in imperial anthologies. Another characteristic—indicative of a general trend rather than the compiler's peculiar tastes—is the relative increase of verse composed on set topics (*dai*) and a corresponding decrease in poems on situations and occasions in real life.

Major Poets——Poetry of Toshiyori's own generation and the previous one accounts for the bulk of the anthology, with only about one-tenth by older poets. Noticeable partiality is shown toward Toshiyori's own relatives and intimates of Shirakawa and his two main consorts, while the outsiders—poetic conservatives and political opponents—are given short shrift. In terms of numbers of poems included, the most important figures are: Toshiyori himself, 37 poems; his father MINAMOTO NO TSUNENOBU, 27; Fujiwara no Akisue, 20; Fujiwara no Tadamichi and Fujiwara no Nagazane, 15 each; and FUJIWARA NO AKISUKE, 14. Likewise, women poets, more prominent than men in the previous anthology, are given much less importance.

Reputation——The anthology came under violent attack from the conservatives, who objected to its title, its format, and its choice of poems. Thus Toshiyori was subjected to the same treatment his father Tsunenobu had meted out to FUJIWARA NO MICHITOSHI, compiler of the preceding imperial anthology, in his *Nan goshūi* (1086, Errors in the *Go shūishū*). In later centuries, however, the *Kin'yōshū* came to be admired as a collection of much intrinsic interest and as an important milestone in the development of descriptive symbolism.

■——Robert H. Brower and Earl Miner, *Japanese Court Poetry* (1961).　　　　　　　　　　　　　　　　　　　*Robert H.* BROWER

kinza, ginza, and zeniza

The gold (*kin*), silver (*gin*), and lesser coin (*zeni*) mints (*za*) of the Tokugawa shogunate (1603–1867). Today the major commercial district of Tōkyō is named Ginza after the silver mint that was situated in that area from 1612 to 1800.

Control of money and commerce was important to political leaders from the late Muromachi period (1333–1568) onward. As TOKUGAWA IEYASU extended his power during the 1590s and 1600s, he set up mints as part of his larger strategy to regularize commercial and political life and establish direct control over the output of gold and silver mines. Initially there were several mints, and they were relocated as Ieyasu wished. At one time or another during the two decades before his death in 1616 gold and silver mints were located in Sumpu (now the city of Shizuoka), Fushimi, Edo (now Tōkyō), Kyōto, Nagasaki, Sado, and Ōsaka. Later, however, their activities were centered in Edo and Kyōto. The mints were periodically convulsed by charges of corruption and consequent punishment of their heads and reorganization of their operations, and after an incident of corruption in 1800 both *kinza* and *ginza* were consolidated in Edo. Minting activities were run as hereditary monopolies under the supervision of the commissioners of finance (KANJŌ BUGYŌ). GOTŌ MITSUTSUGU and his descendants were the principal figures in the shogunate mints, in charge of both gold and silver minting at first, losing control of the *ginza* during the 1670s but exercising control over gold, silver, and most lesser coin minting from 1765 until the dissolution of the mints in 1869.

The *kinza* dates from 1594, when Ieyasu ordered Gotō Mitsutsugu to mint gold coins (KOBAN and *ichibu kin*; ŌBAN were minted there from 1601). Mitsutsugu was a descendant by adoption of Gotō Yūjō (1440?–1512?), who had minted gold for the Muromachi shogunate, and his heirs became the hereditary heads of the gold mint with the title *gokingin aratameyaku* and after 1705 *gokin aratameyaku*.

The main mint was situated in Edo, moving about the Nihombashi–Hongō–Asakusabashi vicinity in response to periodic fires and reorganizations. Other *kinza* were situated on the island of Sado (site of the SADO MINES) until the Kyōhō era (1716–36), and in Kyōto until the Kansei era (1789–1801).

In return for running the mint, the Gotō family head was paid a stipend of 200 *ryō* and 20 *fuchi* (see MONEY, PREMODERN), and enjoyed the right to wear a sword and use his surname (MYŌJI TAITŌ) and to ride a horse. He also derived substantial income from his commission on recoinage. Together with three subordinate officials, he supervised the acquisition and assessment of bullion and old gold, the minting operation itself, the denomination, assay, and issuance of coins, and the maintenance of mint records. Because of the central function of money in government affairs, members of the Gotō family frequently played an influential role in shaping official economic policy.

Ieyasu established a *ginza* in Fushimi in 1601 with Gotō Mitsutsugu and Sueyoshi Toshikata (1526–1607) supervising and Daikoku (Yuasa) Sakuhei (d 1636; later known as Daikoku Jōze, or Daikoku the "sealer" or "certifier") in charge of the actual minting process. In 1608 the Fushimi mint was moved to Kyōto, where it functioned until 1800 under the descendants of Daikoku Jōze, all of whom took his name. In 1606 Ieyasu established a second *ginza* at

Sumpu and six years later moved it to Edo, where another line of the Daikoku family supervised the minting and assaying of the shogunate's silver coins, notably the silver *isshu, nishu,* and *ichibu.* Until 1800 a third *ginza,* producing coinage for foreign trade, was located in Nagasaki.

From their origins until the Empō era (1673–81) all *ginza* operations were directly responsible through Gotō to the senior councillors *(rōjū).* During the Genroku era (1688–1704), however, they were placed directly under the *kanjō bugyō.* The Daikoku Jōze of Edo were then titled *gogin aratameyaku* and given a seat of honor in Edo Castle directly after that of Gotō.

During the 18th century *ginza* operations grew, administrative posts proliferated, and mint supervisors *(toshiyori yaku),* who were the Daikoku's chief assistants and chosen from among the mint's 50-odd craftsmen, exercised considerable power and were punished periodically for illegal practices. In 1765 Gotō was again placed in a supervisory role, but during the 1790s especially serious charges of corruption were leveled against the Edo Daikoku Jōze himself, leading to abolition of his family line and temporary dissolution of all *ginza* operations throughout the country. In 1800, however, the shogunate reopened the Edo *ginza* under the Kyōto Daikoku Jōze. It was located in new quarters in Nihombashi and soon began growing again. In 1819 the mint acquired over three acres of additional space in Asakusabashi for smelting operations, and in following years it added another five acres of space. It was reorganized briefly in the 1860s and abolished a year after the Meiji Restoration of 1868.

The *zeniza* was first established in 1636, when the shogunate ordered a copper mint established in Edo and another at Sakamoto in Ōmi Province (now Shiga Prefecture). During the following century coin use increased dramatically, and a great variety of copper and iron coins were minted on a contractual basis at many temporary mints around the country. A resulting decline in currency values prompted the shogunate in 1745 to reduce coin output by shutting down all *zeniza* and then placing all *zeni* minting under *kinza* and *ginza* control. A new *zeniza* was erected in Edo, and from the 1770s onward all copper, iron, and brass coins were produced under *kinza* and *ginza* supervision, mostly at the Edo mint.

■ ——Taya Hiroyoshi, *Kinsei ginza no kenkyū* (1963). Toyoda Takeshi and Kodama Kōta, *Ryūtsūshi* (1), in *Taikei nihonshi sōsho,* vol 13 (Yamakawa Shuppansha, 1969).   Conrad TOTMAN

Kira Yoshinaka (1641–1703)

Official of the Tokugawa shogunate who was killed by ŌISHI YO-SHIO and his band of 46 men in the famous FORTY-SEVEN RŌNIN INCIDENT. Born in Edo (now Tōkyō). Belonging to one of a select group of families (KŌKE) responsible for shogunate protocol and enjoying close ties with the powerful YANAGISAWA YOSHIYASU, Kira was widely disliked for his arrogance. In April 1701, on the occasion of a reception for imperial messengers in Edo Castle, he was slightly wounded by Asano Naganori (1665–1701), *daimyō* of Akō (now part of Hyōgo Prefecture), who believed that Kira had deliberately kept him ignorant of fine points of etiquette. To draw a sword in the shogunal castle was a serious offense, and Asano was immediately deprived of his domain and ordered to commit suicide. Kira was not even reprimanded, although he was later relieved of his office. Asano's retainers, led by Ōishi, vowed vengeance, and in 1703 they finally killed Kira at his home. Kira has been vilified in the extensive popular literature about the incident.

kiri → paulownia

kiribi

Sacred fire, principally for ceremonial or ritual use, ignited by friction, such as rubbing together pieces of cypress *(hinoki)* wood, or by striking flint. In ancient times special wooden mortar and pestle sets were also commonly used for starting fires, especially at Shintō shrines. Fire struck in this manner was believed to be sacred and the sparks were believed to have a purifying effect on persons and objects. Today, the fire used in ceremonies at the ISE SHRINE is still ignited by mortar and pestle. The related custom of scattering sparks on a person about to leave the house is still observed by some members of the tradition-bound world of the *geisha* and other entertainers.   TSUCHIDA Mitsufumi

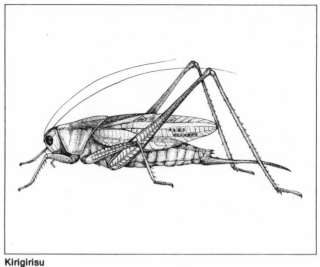

Kirigirisu

Kirigamine

Highland northwest of Lake Suwa, central Nagano Prefecture, central Honshū. Shield-shaped and covered with grass, it is used for flying gliders. Skiing and camping are popular. It has several beautiful marshlands including Yashimagaike and Kamagaike, and is part of Yatsugatake Chūshin Kōgen Quasi-National Park. The main peak is Kurumayama (1,925 m; 6,314 ft). Average elevation: 1,700 m (5,576 ft).

kirigirisu

(katydid). *Gampsocleis buergeri.* Insect of the order Orthoptera, family Tettigoniidae. The Japanese *kirigirisu* is green or light brown with black spots on the forewings. The body is long with very long antennae and hind legs. The adult has a body length of about 40 millimeters (1.6 in). It is seen from summer through late autumn in grassy plains and dry riverbeds; it chirps day and night. There are about 40 species of the same family among the Japanese *kirigirisu,* including the *yabukiri (Tettigonia orientalis),* *tsuyumushi (Phaneroptera falcata),* *umaoi (Hexacentrus japonicus),* and *kutsuwamushi (Mecopoda nipponensis).* The male insect of all species makes a sound by rubbing the sound organs of the forewings.   NAKANE Takehiko

It is thought that in ancient times the word *kirigirisu* was used to refer to CRICKETS, which are now called *kōrogi.* It has also been suggested that *kirigirisu* was the common name for insects that chirp in autumn and that only in the Heian period (794–1185) did the word take on its present meaning of katydid.   SAITŌ Shōji

kirikane

Thin gold- or silver-leaf decorative technique used on paintings and lacquerware; also, the gold and silver used. Introduced to Japan in the Nara period (710–794) from Tang-dynasty (T'ang; 618–907) China. From the Heian period (794–1185) through the Kamakura period (1185–1333) this technique was widely and effectively used on Buddhist paintings and statuary to add to their splendor and grandeur. The earliest known example of *kirikane* is found on the 7th-century Shitennō images in the *kondō* (main hall) of the temple HŌRYŪJI in Nara.

For use in paintings, two or three sheets of thin gold leaf are baked into one leaf, which is then placed on a deerskin surface and shredded with a bamboo knife into strips approximately one millimeter (0.04 in) wide. The strips are then applied with glue and brush. In the 12th century the *sunago* technique of sprinkling very fine pieces of gold leaf was invented; this technique can be seen in the *Heike nōkyō* scrolls dedicated by the TAIRA FAMILY and kept in the ITSUKUSHIMA SHRINE in Hiroshima Prefecture.

The use of *kirikane* for lacquerware can be traced to the Nara-period technique known as *hyōmon,* a type of inlay that employed gold or silver pieces approximately 0.02 to 0.05 millimeters (0.0007 to 0.0019 in) thick and about 1 millimeter (0.04 in) in diameter.

Generally, these thin pieces were applied to lacquer to highlight or add variety to a design; the piece was then sprinkled with lacquer powder and polished. The oldest known *kirikane*-decorated lacquerware is the inside surface of the lid of an inkstone box *(suzuri)* with a design of small chrysanthemums, owned by the TSURUGAOKA HACHIMAN SHRINE in Kamakura. See also MAKI-E.

Nakasato Toshikatsu

kirimai

Rice stipend given to *daimyō* or shogunal retainers who did not hold fiefs (CHIGYŌ) that yielded tax income; also known as KURAMAI. As most daimyō strengthened direct control over their domains throughout the Edo period (1600–1868), their retainers, including many of the highest rank, lost their fiefs and received a rice stipend instead. Before 1723, stipendiaries *(kuramaitori)* directly under the shogunate collected their stipend in equal installments in the spring, summer, and winter. Thereafter they received one-fourth of their stipend in the spring and summer and half during the winter. Although the entire stipend was usually specified in terms of rice alone, part of it was frequently paid in cash according to the official exchange rates. *Samurai* employed brokers (FUDASASHI) for these transactions and turned with increasing frequency to these brokers for loans.

Philip BROWN

Kirin Brewery Co, Ltd

(Kirin Bīru). Producer chiefly of beer, but also of soft drinks and food products. With over 60 percent of the market share in recent years, it is the largest Japanese beer brewer. A member of the MITSUBISHI group of companies, it was established in 1907 when it took over the facilities of its predecessor Spring Valley Brewery, Japan's first producer of beer, founded in 1869. In 1928 it initiated production of a soft drink, Kirin Lemon, and in the 1930s established overseas companies in Korea and Manchuria. During World War II production was reduced because of the difficulty of obtaining raw materials. After the war Kirin was third in the industry, behind ASAHI BREWERIES, LTD, and Nippon Breweries, Ltd (now SAPPORO BREWERIES, LTD). But through the expansion of production and aggressive promotional efforts within a nationwide network of sales outlets, it was able to overtake its competitors and since 1954 has been the industry leader. Seeking product diversity, the firm established in 1972 Kirin–Seagram Ltd, in cooperation with Joseph E. Seagram & Sons, Inc, for the production of distilled liquors and initiated production of dairy products and tomato juice. Kirin has joint venture companies in Brazil and Australia for the production of soft drinks and malt, and in the United States has invested in Coca-Cola bottling companies. The firm has 3 offices overseas and 14 plants, 5 hop handling centers, and 1 research laboratory in Japan. Kirin has also established theaters in a number of regional cities for the presentation of children's plays and publishes the Kirin Life Library series of books. Sales for the fiscal year ending January 1982 totaled ¥985 billion (US $4.4 billion), of which the sale of beer contributed 93 percent and soft drinks and other products 7 percent. In the same year capitalization stood at ¥40 billion (US $178.1 million). The head office is in Tōkyō.

Kirishima Volcanic Zone

(Kirishima Kazantai). Volcanic zone extending south from ASOSAN, a volcano in Kumamoto Prefecture, Kyūshū, to northern Taiwan via the Ryūkyū Islands. The major volcanoes in the zone are Asosan, SAKURAJIMA, and KIRISHIMAYAMA. Volcanically active during the Cenozoic era from the end of the Tertiary period to the Quaternary period; ash and lava from the zone's volcanoes spread over a large area of central and southern Kyūshū. The volcanic ash called *shirasu* is widely found in Kagoshima Prefecture.

Kirishima–Yaku National Park

(Kirishima–Yaku Kokuritsu Kōen). Situated in southern Kyūshū in Kagoshima and Miyazaki prefectures. The scattered regions of the park include volcanoes, some still active, mountains, lakes, caldera lakes, forests, and an island off the southern Kyūshū coast. The Kirishima Volcanic Group, consisting of 23 volcanoes, 15 craters, and 10 caldera lakes, is dominated by the two outstanding peaks of Karakunidake (1,700 m; 5,576 ft) and TAKACHIHONOMINE (1,574 m; 5,163 ft). The latter is sacred to the Japanese because it is the spot where the god Ninigi no Mikoto is said to have descended from heaven. To the northwest is the highland EBINO KŌGEN, with an average altitude of 1,200 m (3,936 ft), rich in various species of plants and flowers, including the wild Kirishima azalea *(miyama kirishima)*, native to Kyūshū. A cluster of resorts, known as Kirishima Hot Spring, is located in the southwest of the region. South of Kirishima are the SATSUMA PENINSULA and ŌSUMI PENINSULA, with KAGOSHIMA BAY in between. KAGOSHIMA, the principal city in southern Kyūshū, lies on the bay halfway down Satsuma Peninsula, directly opposite SAKURAJIMA, a peninsula with an active volcano, where fruit trees and Sakurajima *daikon* (a giant spherical radish) thrive on the sheltered northern slopes. At the tip of the Satsuma Peninsula is Ibusuki Hot Spring, renowned for hot volcanic mud baths; Lake IKEDA, the largest freshwater lake in Kyūshū; and the mountain KAIMONDAKE (922 m; 3,024 ft). Sixty km (37 mi) south of Ōsumi Peninsula lies YAKUSHIMA, a round island with a cluster of peaks rising sharply from sea level, the highest being MIYANOURADAKE (1,935 m; 6,347 ft). The island is noted for its forests of gigantic cedars *(yakusugi)*, some over 1,000 years old. Area: 540 sq km (208 sq mi).

Kirishimayama

Volcanic group on the border between Kagoshima and Miyazaki prefectures, Kyūshū. Twenty-two simple volcanoes and one composite volcano forming an unusual volcanic group. One of the group, Shin Moedake, erupted in 1959. There are 15 volcanoes with perfect craters and 10 crater lakes. The mountains are covered with mixed forests. On the summits grow rare plants such as *miyamakirishima* (a kind of rhododendron) and the Japanese green alder. Hot springs abound in the foothills. Kirishimayama is the center of KIRISHIMA-YAKU NATIONAL PARK and its highest peak is Karakunidake (1,700 m; 5,576 ft).

Kirishitan → Kakure Kirishitan

kirishitan-ban → Jesuit mission press

Kirishitan daimyō → Christian daimyō

Kirishitan monogatari

(Tales of Christians). An anonymous chapbook dated 1639 (Kan'ei 16), the progenitor of a profuse genre of fictional narratives dealing with early Japanese Christianity. The work begins with a grotesque portrayal of the first missionary to arrive in Japan, denigrates basic Christian practices, depicts a one-sided debate between the Christian apologist FABIAN and an expert in Buddhist doctrine, and ends with a semihistorical account of the SHIMABARA UPRISING. Subsequent exemplars of this vulgar literature abandon historicity altogether and concentrate on describing the magical arts and other sinister devices by which "southern barbarian" (NAMBAN) *bateren* (Christian priests) and their native helpers attempted to ensnare Japan in the web of an imperial conspiracy emanating from the Land of Yaso (Jesus). The most popular variants bore titles such as *Kirishitan shūmon raichō jikki* (A True Account of the Christian Religion's Advent to Our Empire) and *Nambanji kōhai ki* (after 1695; The Rise and Fall of the Temple of Southern Barbarians). These chapbooks were widely read throughout the Edo period (1600–1868) and constituted the single most important element in the formation of the propagandistic image of Christianity as the "pernicious faith" *(jashūmon)*. An English translation of *Kirishitan monogatari* is included in George Elison, *Deus Destroyed: The Image of Christianity in Early Modern Japan* (1973).

George ELISON

Kirishitan Yashiki

(Christian Mansion). The seat of the Tokugawa shogunate's anti-Christian inquisition (see SHŪMON ARATAME), located in Kobinata in Edo (now Tōkyō). It was originally the villa of the shogunate's inspector-general *(ōmetsuke)* Inoue Masashige (1585–1661), a former Christian who was the first to hold the inquisitor's post (1640–58). The Kirishitan Yashiki was officially designated a prison for Christian missionaries around 1646, housing under protective custody the Jesuits of the so-called Second Rubino Group, captured off the coast of Kyūshū in 1643, who had apostasized under torture. The "fallen padre" *(korobi bateren)* Giuseppe Chiara, also known as Okamoto San'emon (d 1685), is the best known of the group. After its last member died in 1700, the Kirishitan Yashiki was destined to be the prison of only one other missionary, Giovanni Battista SI-DOTTI, who was incarcerated there from 1709 until his death in 1714. Thereafter the Kirishitan Yashiki fell into disuse; the prison building burned in about 1725 and was not rebuilt; the establishment was abolished in 1792 together with the office of the inquisition, which was no longer considered necessary. An interesting summary of the routine of the place in its heyday may be found in *Sayō yoroku* (1672–91, Record of Investigation of Heretics), the diary of one of the guards, translated into German by Gustav Voss, S.J., and Hubert Cieslik, S.J., together with *Kirishito ki,* the records of the inquisitor Inoue (*Monumenta Nipponica Monographs,* 1940).

George ELISON

kirisute gomen

(permission to kill). A privilege enjoyed by the *samurai* class during the Edo period (1600–1868) whereby they were permitted to kill members of the lower classes (farmers and townsmen) on serious provocation, especially on points of honor. (Samurai were the only class permitted to bear arms during this period.) If a death resulted from the exercise of this prerogative, the samurai was expected to report his action to the authorities; he could be punished if he were found to have exceeded his rights.

Kiritake Monjūrō II (1900–1970)

Master puppeteer in the BUNRAKU puppet theater of Japan. Born in Ōsaka Prefecture, Monjūrō became a disciple of the noted puppeteer Yoshida Bungorō III in 1909 and embarked on a career which brought him recognition as one of Japan's great puppet operators. Monjūrō was acclaimed especially for his masterful handling of puppets cast in various feminine roles, among them princesses, warriors' wives, young girls, and courtesans. Monjūrō's activities extended beyond the Bunraku stage to include popularization of puppetry as an art and experimentation with puppetry theatricals set to Western music. In 1965 he was designated a LIVING NATIONAL TREASURE.

MOTEGI Kiyoko

Kiroku Shōen Kenkeijo

(Office for the Investigation of Shōen Documents). Better known in English as the Records Office, from the Japanese abbreviation Kirokusho. An extrastatutory office established by Emperor GO-SANJŌ in 1069 to investigate the legality of the documentation of private landed estates (SHŌEN) in an attempt to regulate the illegal acquisition of land by noble houses and religious institutions. It had some effect but disappeared after Go-Sanjō's death. The office was revived in 1156 by Emperor GO-SHIRAKAWA and came to function as the body that adjudicated land disputes between local officials and *shōen* proprietors. It was revived again in 1187 at the behest of MINAMOTO NO YORITOMO. During Emperor Go-Daigo's KEMMU RESTORATION (1333–36) the Records Office became the central organ of the imperial government.

G. Cameron HURST III

Kiryū

City in eastern Gumma Prefecture, central Honshū. Long known for its fine silks, Kiryū rivals Kyōto's Nishijin district both in quality and quantity. In addition to textiles, Kiryū's electric appliance, automobile parts, machine, and metal industries have made rapid progress in recent years. Pop: 132,888.

Kiryū Yūyū (1873–1941)

Liberal journalist. Born Kiryū Masatsugu in Ishikawa Prefecture. Graduated from the law department of Tōkyō University. After years as an editor for various newspapers, he became editor in chief of the *Shinano mainichi shimbun,* and drew attention with his editorial policies of antimilitarism and liberalism. In 1933 his editorial "Kantō bōkū daienshū o warau" (In Ridicule of the Grand Tōkyō Air Raid Maneuvers) invited strong opposition from organizations such as the Veterans' Association, and he was forced to resign. The next year he began *Tazan no ishi,* a privately circulated magazine in Nagoya. Though it was banned repeatedly, he continued his antifascist activities until his death.

ARASE Yutaka

Kisarazu

City in western Chiba Prefecture, central Honshū, on Tōkyō Bay. Kisarazu prospered in the Edo period (1600–1868) as a port for ships bound to and from Edo (now Tōkyō). A naval base during World War II, after the war it became a base for the Self Defense Forces. Land has been reclaimed to create an industrial zone. The city is connected to Yokohama and Kawasaki by ferries. Shōjōji, a temple made famous in a nursery song, is located here. Pop: 110,711.

Kisegawa

River in eastern Shizuoka Prefecture, central Honshū. It originates in the city of Gotemba at the eastern slope of Mt. Fuji (Fujisan) and flows south, converging with the Hakone Canal, to join the Kanogawa at the city of Numazu. Gorges along the upper reaches are a scenic attraction. Length: 32 km (20 mi).

Kishibojin

Also known as Kishimojin, or Karitei, from the Sanskrit Hārītī; guardian deity of children. She is said originally to have been a malevolent goddess who ate the children of others, although she had 100 of her own. In order to chastise her, Buddha hid her youngest and favorite child. When she went to him to ask its whereabouts, he admonished her, and she repented and was converted to Buddhism. In Japan childless women pray to Kishibojin to become pregnant, and she is regarded as the tutelary deity of safe childbirth and conjugal harmony. She is also thought to protect children from harm and disease. Although Kishibojin is sometimes represented as a demon, she is more often depicted as a beautiful celestial being robed in silken garments, with a pomegranate in her right hand and her favorite child in her left. In paintings she is often pictured with children. As the guardian deity of the LOTUS SUTRA, she is especially venerated by followers of the NICHIREN SECT.

ŌTŌ Tokihiko

Kishida Ginkō (1833–1905)

Pioneer journalist of the Meiji period. Real name Kishida Ginji. Born in what is now Okayama Prefecture. Kishida assisted James Curtis HEPBURN in the compilation of his Japanese-English dictionary. Together with HAMADA HIKOZŌ he published one of Japan's first modern newspapers, the *Kaigai shimbun.* In 1872 he became a reporter for another paper, the *Tōkyō nichinichi shimbun* (now the MAINICHI SHIMBUN), where he achieved great popularity with his articles, which were written in the spoken language rather than the classical Japanese that was normal in newspapers of the time. He was one of Japan's first modern war correspondents, covering the Taiwan Expedition of 1874. He left the newspaper in 1877 to become a businessman. He was the father of the well-known Western-style painter KISHIDA RYŪSEI.

ARASE Yutaka

Kishida Kunio (1890–1954)

The finest playwright in Japan during his generation, who did much to raise the standards of modern theater during the prewar period. Born in Tōkyō. Kishida graduated from the Army Academy in 1912 and studied in Paris with the celebrated French director Jacques Copeau in 1921 and 1922. Returning to Japan, he spent the rest of his career composing plays and writing critical essays in an attempt to create a theater responsive to the literary and humanistic values he felt to be important. He was one of the founders of the Bungakuza (Literary Theater), an important theatrical troupe that began its activities in 1939. Among his plays are short poetic sketches of considerable charm such as *Kamifūsen* (1925; tr *A Paper Balloon,* 1965) as well as longer comedies of manners, such as *Ochiba nikki* (1927; tr *Fallen Leaves, a Diary,* 1961) and *Sawa shi no futari musume* (1935, Mr. Sawa's Two Daughters), which portray with wit and considerable irony the emotional attitudes of the Europeanized upper-middle classes in prewar Japan. Kishida can well be credited with the creation of stage dialogue in modern Japanese theater; his plays are eloquent and wholly colloquial.

Kishida Kunio zenshū (Shinchōsha, 1955) contains texts of plays and critical writings. Details of Kishida's life and work can be found in J. Thomas Rimer, *Toward a Modern Japanese Theater* (1974). See also SHINGEKI.

J. T. RIMER

Kishida Ryūsei (1891–1929)

Painter. Born in Tōkyō, the son of the progressive journalist KI-SHIDA GINKŌ (1833–1905). He left school in 1908 to study Western-style painting with KURODA SEIKI at the White Horse Society (HA-KUBAKAI) studio. His earliest works, exhibited beginning in 1910 at the BUNTEN, the annual Ministry of Education art exhibition, show the influence of Kuroda's plein-air style. Through his friendship with the writer MUSHANOKŌJI SANEATSU, he became involved with the White Birch school (SHIRAKABA SCHOOL), a literary group whose journal was instrumental in disseminating in Japan the currents of contemporary French art, cubism and fauvism. Strongly influenced by these Postimpressionist trends, Kishida formed the Fyūzankai (Fusain Society; 1912–13) with the artists Saitō Yori (1885–1959), Kimura Shōhachi (1893–1958), Yorozu Tetsugorō (1885–1927), and Takamura Kōtarō (1883–1956). In 1915 he founded the Sōdosha (1915–22) along with Kimura and Nakagawa Kazumasa (b 1893). Around 1917, Kishida began to be noticeably influenced by the realism of Northern Renaissance painting, especially Dürer and Van Eyck. His well-known series (1918–24) of portraits of his daughter Reiko successfully combines the seemingly disparate elements of photographic realism and decorative surface effect. In the early 1920s Kishida abruptly shifted his focus to Japanese-style painting (nihonga) and began a serious study of the heritage of East Asian art, from Chinese painting to UKIYO-E. For a brief time in the 1920s he exhibited with another artists' group, the Shun'yōkai. Later, after he moved to Kamakura in 1926, he became associated with the artists Kondō Kōichiro (1884–1962) and Tsuda Seifū (1880–1978) and their circles. — *Aya Louisa McDonald*

Kishida Toshiko (1863–1901)

Writer and political activist, often called Japan's first woman orator. Also known as Nakajima Toshiko; pen name, Nakajima Shōen. Born in Kyōto into a family of cloth merchants, she so excelled in her study of Chinese and Japanese classics that she became in 1880 the first girl of commoner background to serve as a companion to Empress Shōken (1850–1914), wife of Emperor Meiji. In 1882 she suddenly left the court and began a series of speaking tours with associates of the new political party JIYŪTŌ (Liberal Party). (See also FREEDOM AND PEOPLE'S RIGHTS MOVEMENT.) Her calls for greater political participation by all Japanese, both men and women, attracted much attention, and once in 1883 she was briefly imprisoned. In 1884 she married a Jiyūtō leader, NAKAJIMA NOBUYUKI, and together they continued political agitation until such activity was restricted by the PEACE PRESERVATION LAW OF 1887. She then taught at the Ferris Girls' School in Yokohama and continued to contribute poems and essays to the progressive women's magazine JOGAKU ZASSHI. She traveled abroad with her husband when he was appointed ambassador to Italy in 1892. She was also known as a practical businesswoman who made a fortune in real estate and as a brilliant conversationalist who won the friendship of the leading oligarch ITŌ HIROBUMI. Her works include *Shōen Nikki* (1903, Shōen's Diary).

Kishi Nobusuke (1896–)

Bureaucrat, politician, and prime minister (February 1957 to July 1960). Kishi was born in 1896 in Yamaguchi Prefecture, the second son of Satō Hidesuke and brother of another prime minister, SATŌ EISAKU. He took the name Kishi when adopted into his uncle's family. Upon graduation from Tōkyō University (1920), Kishi entered the Ministry of Agriculture and Commerce and soon became a leader of the so-called new bureaucrats (shinkanryō), who were skilled professionals, interested in economic planning, and willing to cooperate with the military. From 1936 to 1939 he served in varied capacities in the government of the puppet-state of MANCHUKUO, entrusted with the task of making it a strong industrialized dependency of Japan.

In 1939 and 1940, on the eve of World War II, Kishi was vice-minister of commerce and industry, supervising the conversion of peacetime industries into wartime industries. A member of the cabinet of TŌJŌ HIDEKI from 1941 through 1944, he was in charge of Japan's economic mobilization in the war against the United States. Imprisoned by the OCCUPATION authorities as a war criminal, he emerged as a leader of the democratic movement after his release in 1948.

In 1953 Kishi was elected to the House of Representatives as a member of the LIBERAL PARTY (Jiyūtō), but later he aligned with

HATOYAMA ICHIRŌ to become secretary-general of the Japan Democratic Party (NIHON MINSHUTŌ). Kishi was the main architect of the conservative coalition, the LIBERAL DEMOCRATIC PARTY (LDP), formed in November 1955, and became its secretary-general. In 1957 Kishi became prime minister after serving briefly as foreign minister in the cabinet of ISHIBASHI TANZAN, who narrowly defeated him in the 1956 LDP presidential election.

As prime minister Kishi promoted revision of the United States–Japan Security Treaty in hopes of restoring independent diplomacy for Japan and cementing close relations with the United States. He obtained its ratification in the absence of opposition parties who boycotted the Diet debates (May 1960). His high-handed tactics incurred wide public protest and he was eventually forced to resign.

Since 1960 Kishi has remained a member of the House of Representatives and leader of those LDP members who advocate maintaining close ties with South Korea and Taiwan. Known for his conservatism, Kishi sees a key to Japan's security and prosperity in close cooperation with the United States and noncommunist Pacific nations. See also UNITED STATES–JAPAN SECURITY TREATIES. — *David J. Lu*

Kishi Seiichi (1867–1933)

Leading figure in Japanese amateur sports; lawyer. Born in Shimane Prefecture; graduate of Tōkyō University. In 1921 he became the second president of the JAPAN AMATEUR SPORTS ASSOCIATION. He also served as a member of the International Olympic Commission and headed the Japanese athletic delegations to both the 1928 (Amsterdam) and the 1932 (Los Angeles) Olympics. In accordance with his will the ¥1 million he left to the Japan Amateur Sports Association was used to build the Kishi Memorial Sports Hall. — *Takeda Fumio*

Kishiwada

City in southern Ōsaka Prefecture, central Honshū, on Ōsaka Bay. The base for the Wada family, supporters of the Southern Court during the dynastic schism of the period of Northern and Southern Courts (1336–92), Kishiwada was a castle town of the Okabe family during the Edo period (1600–1868). Since the late 1800s Kishiwada has been known for its Izumi cotton. More recently, industrial complexes for lumber, steel, and metal production have been constructed on reclaimed land. Farm products include rice, onions, and mandarin oranges. The remains of Kishiwada Castle and the annual Kishiwada Danjiri Festival draw tourists. Pop: 180,317.

Kiska

One of the American Aleutian Islands occupied by Japanese forces during World War II, in June 1942; it was renamed Narukami Island. After ATTU fell to American forces in May 1943, the Imperial Japanese Navy went to great pains to evacuate its considerable garrison on Kiska, succeeding on the fifth try despite round-the-clock radar surveillance by American destroyers. It was the only major attempt by the Japanese to relieve a garrison during the war. — *Otis Cary*

Kisodani

Valley on the upper reaches of the river Kisogawa, southwestern Nagano Prefecture, central Honshū. The highway Nakasendō passed through this long and narrow valley which bustled with travelers and processions of daimyō journeying between Edo (now Tōkyō) and their fiefs in the Edo period (1600–1868). Today the Chūō Main Line of the Japanese National Railways and National Route No. 19 pass through the valley. Contains a forest composed mainly of Japanese cypress, counted as one of the three most beautiful forests in Japan.

Kiso Fukushima

Town in southwestern Nagano Prefecture, central Honshū. Located in the KISODANI (Kiso Valley) on the highway Nakasendō, the town was the site of a shogunate commissioner's office (bugyōsho) and a toll barrier (sekisho) during the Edo period (1600–1868). It was also known for its horse fair, held three times a year, and for its herbal medicine. More recently, it relies on its lumber, woodwork, and musical instruments (notably violins) industries. Tourist attractions are a folk museum and several hot springs. Kiso Fukushima is the base for pilgrims climbing the sacred mountain ONTAKESAN. Pop: 10,213.

Kisogawa

River in Nagano, Gifu, Aichi, and Mie prefectures, central Honshū. It originates in the northern Kiso region, flows southwest between the Hida and Kiso mountains to form the Kisodani (Kiso Valley), and empties into Ise Bay. It flows through a granite plateau, creating gorges, and enters the Nōbi Plain near the city of Inuyama, where frequent floods have inundated the plain. Regions along the river are covered with Kiso cypress (Kiso *hinoki*) and are counted as one of the three most beautiful forest areas of Japan. Numerous WAJŪ (farming settlements protected by circular embankments) are found along the lower reaches. The water is used for drinking, irrigation, electric power, and industry. Popular tourist attractions include the gorges called NEZAMENOTOKO and ENAKYŌ and the area referred to as the Japan Rhine. Length: 193 km (120 mi); area of drainage basin: 5,020 sq km (1,938 sq mi).

Kiso Mountains

(Kiso Sammyaku). Mountain range. Part of the Nihon Arupusu (JAPANESE ALPS); referred to as the Chūō Arupusu (Central Alps) because of its location. It runs northeast to southwest for about 100 km (62 mi) in Nagano Prefecture, central Honshū. It is noted for its towering, rugged peaks and its cirques. The highest peak in the range, KOMAGATAKE (2,956 m; 9,696 ft), is rich in alpine flora.

Kiso Yoshinaka → Minamoto no Yoshinaka

kissaten → coffee houses

Kitabatake Akiie (1318–1338)

Prominent supporter of the attempt by Emperor GO-DAIGO to reassert imperial rule over Japan (see KEMMU RESTORATION). The eldest son of the courtier and imperial loyalist author KITABATAKE CHIKAFUSA, Akiie was in 1333, the year of the overthrow of the Kamakura shogunate, appointed by Go-Daigo as civil governor of Michi no Oku, with responsibility over the vast provinces of Mutsu (now Fukushima, Miyagi, Iwate and Aomori prefectures) and Dewa (now Akita and Yamagata prefectures) in northern Honshū. As a sign of Go-Daigo's intent to maintain central control over that northernmost region of Japan, he was also given the ancient title Chinjufu shōgun (general of the Headquarters for the Pacification of Ezo) in 1335. That year, however, Go-Daigo's erstwhile supporter, the future shōgun ASHIKAGA TAKAUJI, turned against him, and Akiie was called to the emperor's assistance. In a three-week campaign, early in 1336, Akiie marched his troops the great distance from his headquarters at Taga (now the city of Tagajō, Miyagi Prefecture), assaulted Kyōto, and expelled Takauji from the capital city. Upon Akiie's return north, Takauji regained the initiative, defeated Go-Daigo's other armies, and installed the rival emperor Kōmyō (1322–80; r 1336–48) of the Northern Court in Kyōto. By early 1337 Takauji had founded the Muromachi shogunate, and Go-Daigo had fled to the Southern Court at Yoshino (see NORTHERN AND SOUTHERN COURTS). Early in 1338 Akiie again marched an army to the capital region, defeating a blocking force in Mino (now part of Gifu Prefecture); but his exhausted troops could not maintain themselves against the Ashikaga, and Akiie fell in battle against Takauji's general KŌ NO MORONAO in the area of Sakai. The remonstrance Akiie addressed to Go-Daigo on 3 June 1338 (Engen 3.5.15), a week before his final defeat, is perhaps as famous as the unprecedented grand scale of his campaigns over vast distances. *George ELISON*

Kitabatake Chikafusa (1293–1354)

Courtier, scholar, and prominent political figure of the period of the NORTHERN AND SOUTHERN COURTS (1336–92). Scion of the Murakami branch of the MINAMOTO FAMILY, Chikafusa was in 1325 appointed *dainagon* (great counselor) and invested with offices emblematic of that family's headship (Genji no Chōja). In 1330, however, he took the tonsure upon the death of an imperial prince he served as tutor. In 1336, after the apparent failure of the so-called

KEMMU RESTORATION, the attempt by Emperor GO-DAIGO to reassert direct imperial rule, Chikafusa counseled Go-Daigo to leave Kyōto, taking the imperial regalia with him, and establish a separate court at Yoshino; he thereby contributed to the beginning of a severe dynastic schism. Thereafter he engaged himself in the effort to rally provincial support for the cause of Go-Daigo and his Southern Court, at first in Ise (now part of Mie Prefecture) and from 1338 in the eastern region of Hitachi (now part of Ibaraki Prefecture). His effort defeated by the forces of the MUROMACHI SHOGUNATE, which supported the rival Northern Court, and by his own adamant refusal to recognize the claims of provincial barons, Chikafusa fled to Yoshino in early 1344 and was appointed to ministerial rank by Emperor Go-Murakami (1328–68; r 1339–68). Under Chikafusa's leadership, the Southern Court recaptured Kyōto in 1352 but was able to hold it for only three weeks. Chikafusa is famed as the author of the classic imperial loyalist history JINNŌ SHŌTŌ KI (Chronicle of the Direct Descent of Divine Sovereigns), composed in Hitachi between 1339 and 1343. His other major works are Gengenshū (a Shintoist account of Japan's origins) and SHOKUGENSHŌ (a study of official posts in Japanese history); he also enjoys a reputation as a poet. *George ELISON*

Kitabatake family

Court nobles and later *daimyō* of the Sengoku period (1467–1568). Founded by Nakanoin Masaie, the family was descended from the Murakami branch of the MINAMOTO FAMILY, who had generally remained in Kyōto to serve as court ministers. Masaie's great-grandson KITABATAKE CHIKAFUSA and his son KITABATAKE AKIIE are best remembered for their strong support of Emperor GO-DAIGO in the 1333 KEMMU RESTORATION. In 1335 Kitabatake Akiyoshi (d 1383), another son of Chikafusa, became governor *(kokushi)* of Ise (now Mie Prefecture), where the family maintained its power until Kitabatake Tomonori (1528–76) was defeated by ODA NOBUNAGA in 1576.

Kita Daitōjima

Island approximately 350 km (217 mi) east of Okinawa. One of the Daitō Islands. A coral island with steep cliffs. The central part is level land composed of limestone. Some 46 percent of the island is arable and is utilized for sugarcane production. Area: 13.9 sq km (5.37 sq mi).

Kitadake

Mountain in western Yamanashi Prefecture, central Honshū, in the northern part of the AKAISHI MOUNTAINS. It is Japan's second highest mountain; one of the three-mountain group called SHIRANE SANZAN, along with Ainodake and Nōtoridake. It is composed primarily of argillite and phyllite. It has a great variety of alpine flora and fauna. With a 600 m (1,968 ft) face, the Kitadake buttress on the mountain's eastern slopes is popular with rock climbers. Height: 3,192 m (10,470 ft).

Kitagawa Fuyuhiko (1900–   )

Poet and film critic. Real name Taguro Tadahiko. Born in Shiga Prefecture. Graduate of Tōkyō University. He started to write poems under the influence of French surrealists and Dadaists in the early 1920s and founded the magazine *Shi to shiron* (1928). A participant in the proletarian literary movement of the late 1920s, he combined his avant-garde poetry with his political ideology. The result was a unique kind of antiwar poetry, collected in *Sensō* (1929). He remained in the forefront of the development of modern poetry. More recently he has written film criticism. His poetry collections include *Iyarashii kami* (1936) and *Jikkenshitsu* (1941).

Kitagawa Morisada → Morisada mankō

Kitagawa school

(Kitagawaha). A school of UKIYO-E artists active late in the Edo period (1600–1868). Its origin, as an offshoot of the Toriyama Sekien school, can be traced to the master printmaker UTAMARO (1753–1806), who was acclaimed for his highly sophisticated prints of beautiful women *(bijinga)*. Although Utamaro's prominence ensured the school's success in the Kansei era (1789–1801), none of his many followers, including Utamaro II, Tsukimaro, and Fujimaro, could match his brilliant style. The Kitagawa school disappeared soon after Utamaro's death, unable to compete with newer, rival schools.

Kitagawa Utamaro → Utamaro

Kitahara Hakushū (1885–1942)

A versatile poet recognized both for his TANKA and modern poetry and an influential figure in poetry circles during the early 20th century. Real name Kitahara Ryūkichi. Born the first son of a prosperous *sake* brewer in Fukuoka Prefecture, Kitahara was brought up with indulgence. The first book of poetry he read with passion was SHIMAZAKI TŌSON's *Wakanashū* (1897, Collection of Young Herbs), an early collection of poems in the *shintaishi* (new form poetry) style (see LITERATURE: modern poetry), but like most poets of the period, he began by publishing *tanka*. In 1904 he moved to Tōkyō, where his poems immediately won praise. Two years later he joined the Shinshisha (New Poetry Society) and became a leading contributor to its magazine, *Myōjō* (Bright Star). In 1908, along with several other poets and Western-style painters, he formed the PAN NO KAI (The Pan Society), which, after adding a number of musicians and actors, soon became the most important gathering of "aesthetes."

In 1909 Kitahara published his first book of poems, *Jashūmon* (Heretics). Written in the alternating five- and seven-syllable verse, the book is rather weak in content, its main concern being a somewhat contrived exoticism. However, because of its rich imagery and dazzling diction, *Jashūmon*, along with YOSANO AKIKO's *tanka* collection *Midaregami* (1901; tr *Tangled Hair*, 1971), is credited with liberating the senses and imagination in modern Japanese poetry. That same year he started, with some friends, the literary magazine *Okujō teien* (Roof Garden), the first of several influential magazines he headed.

In 1911 he published his second book of poems, *Omoide* (Memories). Written about the same time as the poems in his first collection, *Omoide* is a brilliant evocation of a child's world and compares with NAKA KANSUKE's famous novel, *Gin no saji* (1913; tr *The Silver Spoon*, 1976). His introduction, entitled "Waga oitachi" (How I Was Brought Up), is one of the finest examples of belles-lettres of the period. The book, highly praised by two eminent men of letters of the time, UEDA BIN and NAGAI KAFŪ, continues to delight readers. For Kitahara himself *Omoide* was important, for out of it grew his innumerable poems for children.

In 1912 Kitahara was convicted of adultery and jailed for two weeks. The incident is touched on in his first collection of *tanka*, *Kiri no hana* (1913, Paulownia Blossoms), which was welcomed as a fresh stimulus to the *tanka* form. More important, the experience gave a religious turn to Kitahara's outlook. This is evident in *Shinju shō* (1914, Selection of Pearls), which consists mainly of one-line poems, and in *Hakkin no koma* (1914, Platinum Top), which includes poems in WASAN (Buddhist prayer) form. Kitahara's religious feelings led him to a state of "oriental simplicity" (*tōyōteki kotan*), to which he gave expression in *Suibokushū* (1923, Collection of Ink Drawings), a book of modern poems, and in *Suzume no tamago* (1921, Sparrow Eggs), a book of *tanka*. His interest in early classical poetic forms, which began while he was writing the *Shinju shō* and *Hakkin no koma* poems, culminated in *Kaihyō to kumo* (1929, Seals and Clouds), in which he experimented with forms from the KOJIKI and other ancient books.

Kitahara remained active even after nearly going blind in 1937, and he published almost 200 books in his lifetime. He also brought out a number of poetry magazines, notably *Chijō junrei* (Earthly Pilgrimage), to which HAGIWARA SAKUTARŌ, MUROO SAISEI, and ŌTE TAKUJI, among others, contributed. Others were *Ars; Shi to ongaku* (Poetry and Music); and the *tanka* magazine *Tama*. In addition, he was poetry editor of the children's magazine *Akai tori* (Red Bird). Many of his poems for children were set to music by YA-MADA KŌSAKU, and some remain popular today.

■ ——Kitahara Hakushū, *Kitahara Hakushū sakuhinshū*, 9 vols (Kawade Shobō, 1952). *Hiroaki* SATŌ

Kitahara Takeo (1907–1973)

Novelist; critic. Born in Kanagawa Prefecture. While still a student at Keiō University, he published his first novel and also his transla-

tions of Jean Cocteau and Raymond Radiguet. His early novels center on his first wife, who died in a mental hospital; one of them, *Tsuma* (1938, Wife) became a candidate for the Akutagawa Prize. His second wife was novelist UNO CHIYO; together they published from 1936 the successful women's fashion magazine called *Sutairu*. Many of his later novels depict promiscuous women vainly searching for love in the decadent city. Kitahara established himself as a commentator on issues concerning women as well as a critic of contemporary fiction. *James R.* MORITA

Kitahara Tasaku (1870–1920)

Marine scientist; oceanographer. A graduate of Tōkyō University, where he studied zoology. Kitahara implemented numerous projects dealing with marine resources and technology in the belief that the development of the fishing industry should be based on scientifically sound oceanographic investigation. He designed various marine instruments that bear his name and discovered Kitahara's law which states that the area where two ocean currents come together is where schools of fish gather. His published works include *Gyoson yawa* (1921). *ARUGA Yūshō*

Kita Ibaraki

City in northeastern Ibaraki Prefecture, central Honshū, on the Pacific Ocean. The city was formerly a coal-producing area, occupying the southern part of the JŌBAN COALFIELD; the closing of the mines has led to a drastic decrease in the population, although efforts are being made to introduce new industries. Artists, such as OKAKURA KAKUZŌ and YOKOYAMA TAIKAN, have built their summer homes on the IZURA coast, noted for its sea-eroded cliffs. Pop: 47,672.

Kita Ikki (1883–1937)

Leader of the movement for national socialism during the Taishō (1912–26) and Shōwa (1926–) periods. Born in Sado in Niigata Prefecture; real name Kita Terujirō. He attended Waseda University in Tōkyō as an auditor and developed an interest in evolutionary and socialist thought. While in Tōkyō he became friends with KŌTOKU SHŪSUI, SAKAI TOSHIHIKO, and other thinkers of the HEIMINSHA, a socialist organization.

The revolutionary situation in China consumed most of Kita's time and energy from 1911 to 1919. Before the Chinese Revolution of 1911 Kita became a member of the United League (Tongmeng Hui or T'ung-meng Hui), a Chinese revolutionary group, and made use of his acquaintance with SONG JIAOREN (Sung Chiao-jen) and others of its leaders who had studied in Japan. He journeyed to China at the outbreak of the revolution and attempted to take part. Following Song Jiaoren's assassination in 1913, the Chinese government of YUAN SHIKAI (Yüan Shih-k'ai) ordered Kita to leave China when he attempted to publicize the true facts surrounding Song's death. Kita returned to China from 1916 to 1919 but left after the failure of the MAY FOURTH MOVEMENT. In 1915–16 Kita wrote and privately circulated his *Shina kakumei gaishi* (Unofficial History of the Chinese Revolution), in which he criticized Japanese activists who placed too much reliance and support on SUN YAT-SEN, whom Kita saw as a superficial user of Western slogans. Kita felt that the Chinese revolutionaries should work for a better balance of Western and Oriental ideologies.

In 1919 Kita helped to form the YŪZONSHA, an ultranationalist organization founded by ŌKAWA SHŪMEI and others, and became one of the leading theorists of what came later to be called the fascist movement. Thereafter he devoted his time to writing and various RIGHT WING activities. He took part in muckraking in connection with various financial and political scandals of the time and at the same time maintained relations with some financial combines (ZAI-BATSU), receiving contributions from IKEDA SHIGEAKI, KUHARA FU-SANOSUKE, and other prominent businessmen.

Kita's political philosophy is discussed in two of his books, *Kokutai ron oyobi junsei shakai shugi* (1906, National Polity and Pure Socialism) and *Nihon kaizō hōan taikō* (1923, An Outline Plan for the Reorganization of Japan). In these works Kita advocated an "Asian nationalism," through which Japan would lead a united and free Asia. The welfare of Asia, however, first depended on a radical revision of Japan and Japanese society. This reconstruction of Japan was to be achieved through a military coup to rid Japan of its existing leadership and substitute an authoritarian regime based on the promise of a direct relationship between the emperor and the people. The emperor would then suspend the constitution, declare martial law, and authorize the formation of a National Reorganization Diet, free of control by corrupt politicians and businessmen. The Diet would nationalize Japan's principal industries, confiscate excess wealth, put limitations on private property, and enact a land reform program that would benefit impoverished farmers. When this process was completed, Kita claimed, the nation would be strengthened, the economic well-being of all Japanese—especially farmers and workers—would be protected, and Japan could proceed on its mission of "civilizing" Asia through a vigorous course of expansionism.

Kita was convinced that the Japanese were missing their destiny because of incompetent leadership. He never wavered from his belief in a unique Japanese national mission. The two propositions that run like threads through his writings are Japan's evolution toward a socialism identical with the national polity (KOKUTAI) in its modern form and Japan's destiny as the bearer of liberation to other societies suffering under Western imperialism. If existing leaders and institutions did not recognize the validity of these propositions, the only recourse was revolution to put Japan back on its destined evolutionary track. These threads give his thought a consistency over time that belies contentions of a "shift" from socialism to fascism. Kita Ikki does not epitomize the content of the early-20th-century Japanese intellectual's encounter with Western ideas but rather the agonies that this encounter produced and the struggle to resolve them. Kita's ideas contributed to the ideological background for those army officers who advocated the carrying out of a "SHŌWA RESTORATION" and led the unsuccessful 1936 revolt known as the FEBRUARY 26TH INCIDENT. Kita was arrested for complicity in planning the revolt, and after trial by a military court, he was executed by an army firing squad in 1937. ▨ —— Kita Ikki, *Kita Ikki chosakushū*, 3 vols (Misuzu Shobō, 1959–72). Tanaka Sōgorō, *Kita Ikki* (1959). George M. Wilson, *Radical Nationalist in Japan: Kita Ikki, 1883–1937* (1969).

George M. WILSON

Kitakami

City in southern Iwate Prefecture, northern Honshū, on the river Kitakamigawa. Kitakami formerly flourished as a river port and as a post-station town on the highway Ōshū Kaidō. Rice and fruit growing and stock raising are the traditional principal occupations. Industrialization is also in progress. The area is known for a sword dance called Futago Oni Kembai. Pop: 53,647.

Kitakami Basin

(Kitakami Bonchi). In Iwate Prefecture, northern Honshū. Flanked by the Kitakami and Ōu mountains, it consists of piedmont alluvial plains below the fault scarps of the Ōu Mountains, diluvial uplands, and the narrow flood plain of the river Kitakamigawa. Rice is cultivated on the uplands and the flood plain, and apple orchards abound on the levees and lower hills. The major cities are Morioka and Ichinoseki. Length: approximately 180 km (111.8 mi); width: approximately 10–20 km (6.2–12.4 mi).

Kitakamigawa

River in Iwate and Miyagi prefectures, northern Honshū. It originates in the mountain Nanashigureyama in northern Iwate Prefecture and flows south between the Kitakami and Ōu mountains, creating a longitudinal valley. After winding through the Sendai Plain, it enters the bays of Ishinomaki and Oppa in Miyagi Prefecture. It is the largest river in the Tōhoku Region. It was important for the transportation of goods before the Japanese National Railways Tōhoku Main Line was opened. The Kitakami Basin and Sendai Plain are fertile grainlands of Miyagi and Iwate prefectures. Numerous dams have been constructed on the river and its tributaries for flood prevention, electric power, and irrigation. Length: 249 km (155 mi); area of drainage basin 10,200 sq km (3,937 sq mi).

Kitakami Mountains

(Kitakami Sanchi). Plateau-like mountain range extending 250 km (155 mi) from Aomori Prefecture to Miyagi Prefecture, northern Honshū. There are numerous peaks over 1,000 m (3,280 ft); the highest peak is Hayachinesan (1,914 m; 6,278 ft). The mountains end abruptly at the Pacific Ocean, forming a beautiful backdrop for Rikuchū Coast National Park.

Kita Kyūshū

A waterfront industrial area in Kokurakita and Tobata wards.

Kitakata

City in northwestern Fukushima Prefecture, northern Honshū. Kitakata developed as the site of a shogunate commissioner's office *(bugyōsho)* and as a market town in the Edo period (1600–1868). Industries include traditional *sake* brewing and lacquer ware, as well as aluminum smelting. Farm products include rice and hops. Kitakata is the gateway to the Bandai Kōgen highland and the Iidesan Mountains. Pop: 37,555.

Kita Kyūshū

City in northern Fukuoka Prefecture, Kyūshū. Located on the Sea of Japan. In 1963 the five cities of Moji, Kokura, Wakamatsu, Yawata, and Tobata merged to become Kita Kyūshū. The city consists of seven wards. Until the first half of the Meiji period (1868–1912), the area was composed of fishing and farm villages, with the exception of the castle town of Kokura and the port and post-station town of Kurosaki in Yawata. With the development of the Chikuhō Coalfield, Moji and Wakamatsu became ports for shipping coal. In 1901 the government-operated YAWATA IRON AND STEEL WORKS (now Nippon Steel Corporation, a private corporation) was founded in Yawata, providing impetus for industrial development in the area. Today the steel and iron, chemical, machinery, ceramics, and electrical appliance industries dominate the 30 km (19 mi) coastline extending from Kammon Strait to Dōkai Bay. Many factories have been built on reclaimed land and reclamation on the coasts of Moji and Wakamatsu was in progress during the early 1980s. Food-processing is also active. Moji is connected directly with SHIMONOSEKI on Honshū by an undersea tunnel and bridge. Served by the port of Kita Kyūshū and Kita Kyūshū Airport, the city is the main approach to the island of Kyūshū. Local attractions include HIRAODAI, with limestone caves, Hobashirayama, a hill with an excellent view of both the city and the sea, Tōminohana, a cape that is part of Genkai Quasi-National Park, and the annual Kokura Gion Daiko festival. Area: 473.82 sq km (182.89 sq mi); pop: 1,065,084.

Kitami

City in northeastern Hokkaidō. Kitami was first settled in 1897 by government-sponsored colonist-militia (TONDENHEI). Today it is the political, commercial, and educational center of the Kitami region. Principal industries are flour processing, sugar refining, dairy farming, lumber, furniture, and pulp. It is the nation's largest producer of peppermint and menthol. The city is the gateway to the mountain DAISETSUZAN and AKAN NATIONAL PARK. Pop: 102,915.

Kitami Mountains

(Kitami Sanchi). Mountain range in north central Hokkaidō. The highest peak is Muriidake (1,876 m; 6,153 ft). The mountains have been mined extensively for a variety of minerals. The range is covered by dense primeval forests as well as forests utilized by major lumber companies.

Kitamori Kazō (1916–)

Protestant theologian. Born in Kumamoto. Kitamori studied at the Lutheran Theological School, Tōkyō, and Kyōto University. He has been a professor at Tōkyō Union Theological Seminary since 1949. Kitamori was deeply influenced by Martin Luther and the philosopher Tanabe Hajime (1885–1962). The central concept of his theology, the pain of God, combines in a paradoxical way the wrath of God against the sins of humanity and the love of God toward humans who are sinners; when this divine pain becomes manifest in the crucified Christ, man is forgiven and human salvation is achieved. Among his many writings are *Kami no itami no shingaku* (1946; tr *Theology of the Pain of God*, 1961), which has been translated into several languages and *Shūkyōkaikaku no shingaku* (1960, *Theology of the Reformation*). See also CHRISTIANITY.

TOKUZEN Yoshikazu

Kita Morio (1927–)

Novelist and neurologist. Real name Saitō Sōkichi. Born in Tōkyō, second son of Saitō Mokichi, the well-known WAKA poet and psychiatrist. Graduated from Tōhoku University Medical School. He became interested in writing after World War II. In 1960 his *Yoru to kiri no sumide* won the Akutagawa Prize. Also published in 1960 was *Dokutoru Mambō kōkai ki*, a best seller based on his travels and experience as a ship physician. The first of his popular "Doctor Mambō" series, it was followed in 1961 by *Dokutoru Mambō konchū ki* and in 1968 by *Dokutoru Mambō seishun ki*. A serious but humorous treatment of modern Japanese life characterizes his style. Other major works include *Nireke no hitobito* (1964), a fictional account of three generations of his family based on recollections of his youth, which received a Mainichi Book Award.

Kitamoto

City in eastern central Saitama Prefecture, central Honshū. Predominantly a farming district until the late 1950s, it has rapidly become an industrial and residential center. The area is noted for its chrysanthemums and orchids. Pop: 50,888.

Kitamura Kigin (1624–1705)

Classical scholar and WAKA and HAIKU poet of the early Edo period. Born in Ōmi Province (now Shiga Prefecture). A student of *haiku* masters YASUHARA TEISHITSU and MATSUNAGA TEITOKU, he sought to preserve the authority of the declining Teimon school of *haikai*, producing works on haiku composition and for a time instructing the young BASHŌ in the art. He also wrote valuable commentaries on most of the major Japanese classics. He later became the official *waka* instructor of the Tokugawa shogunate. His principal works include *Yama no i* (1648), *Shin zoku inu tsukubashū* (1667), *Genji monogatari kogetsu shō* (1673), and *Makura no sōshi shunsho shō* (1674).

Kitamura Kusuo (1917–)

Olympic swimmer. Born in Kōchi Prefecture; graduated from Kyōto University. At the age of 14 he won the 1,500–meter freestyle at the 1932 Los Angeles Olympics with a time of 19:12.4, an Olympic record which stood unchallenged for 20 years. The record-setting achievements of Kitamura and 16-year-old MIYAZAKI YASUJI were widely publicized at the time.

TAKEDA Fumio

Kitamura Rokurō (1871–1961)

Actor. Born in Tōkyō. He first appeared on stage in 1892. He later moved to Ōsaka and founded the drama group Seibidan, which successfully produced *Shibijin* (1900, Dead Beauty) at the Asahi Theater. He returned to Tōkyō in 1906 and along with II YŌHŌ became one of the great actors of the SHIMPA theater. His teaching methods were strict and demanding, but he was also exacting about his own acting. Known for his sensitive portrayal of women, Kitamura's greatest dramatic success was in *Onna keizu* (Genealogy of Women). His only film appearance was in *Noroi no fue* (1958, The Cursed Flute). In 1947 he became a member of the JAPAN ART ACADEMY and in 1955 was designated one of Japan's LIVING NATIONAL TREASURES *(ningen kokuhō)*.

ITASAKA Tsuyoshi

Kitamura Sayo (1900–1967)

Religious leader; founder of the religious movement known as Tenshō Kōtai Jingū Kyō. Sayo was the wife of a farmer in Tabuse, Yamaguchi Prefecture. After experiencing personal troubles, she claimed, in 1944, to hear a divine voice. After World War II she declared herself to be the only daughter and shrine of the goddess Tenshō Kōtaijin (i.e., the sun goddess, AMATERASU ŌMIKAMI) and began preaching and faith-healing. Sayo was regarded by her followers as the goddess herself incarnate, and a religious organization, the Tenshō Kōtai Jingū Kyō, was established in 1946. She was known for her skillful use of words and everyday imagery in gaining adherents and preparing them for the divine age. Sayo's words and deeds are recorded in *Seisho* (1951, 1967). Since her followers (40,000 as of 1980) express their blissfulness in free-style dancing, her religious movement is popularly known as the "dancing religion" *(odoru shūkyō)*. The organization has gained a following among overseas Japanese. Her granddaughter Kiyokazu (b 1950) succeeded her as head of the organization in 1968.

TSUCHIDA Tomoaki

Kitamura Tōkoku (1868–1894)

Poet, essayist, and leader of the *Bungakukai* literary coterie. Tōkoku deserves his prominent position in the history of modern Japanese literature less for what he accomplished than for what he initiated and for what he came to symbolize. In a brief five years of activity, from 1889 to 1894, he sowed the seeds for a number of later developments in Japanese literature and thought.

Born in Odawara in Kanagawa Prefecture in 1868, Tōkoku received a strict feudal upbringing at the hands of his very traditionminded grandparents. When he was 13 he finally went to live with his parents in Tōkyō. At an early age he became interested in the FREEDOM AND PEOPLE'S RIGHTS MOVEMENT and conceived the ambition of becoming "another Christ, consecrating all my energies to politics." Very quickly disillusioned with the politics of the day, however, he next determined to become a writer and to serve society as "a Japanese Hugo."

At the age of 16 he entered Tōkyō Semmon Gakkō, which was later to become Waseda University, enrolling first in the political science department but transferring almost immediately to the English literature department. He withdrew from school, however, before graduation. At the age of 18 he met and fell in love with Ishizaka Mina, the daughter of a prominent leader in the People's Rights Movement, and they were married the following year. Under Mina's influence, Tōkoku became a Christian. Though baptized a Presbyterian, he soon gravitated toward the Quakers. He interpreted for the foreign missionaries and even served for a time as an evangelist himself.

At the age of 20 he wrote his first long poem, "Soshū no shi," which has a plot and theme very similar to Byron's "The Prisoner of Chillon." It was the first Japanese poem of any great length to be written in free verse. Shortly afterwards Tōkoku wrote another long poem in free verse, "Hōraikyoku," which, while much influenced by Byron's "Manfred," is a strange blend of Christian and Buddhist notions of life, death, love, and the self. Between 1892 and 1894 he contributed a large number of short essays to two magazines, *Bungakukai*, the publication of the first group of avowedly "romantic" writers in Japan, of which Tōkoku was the acknowledged leader; and *Heiwa*, the organ of the first Japanese pacifist movement, which Tōkoku himself edited.

Tōkoku's finest essays are those that concern what he called "the inner life": "Naibu seimei ron," "Jinsei ni aiwataru to wa nan no i zo," and "Takai ni taisuru kannen." In his earlier essays Tōkoku exalts what he calls "the life-espousing view" of the West and contrasts it with the nihilistic "life-denying view" of traditional Buddhist and Shintō Japanese tradition. In the later essays, however, particularly in "Bambutsu no koe to shijin," it is the latter that has the greater hold upon him. He became progressively discouraged and depressed, and in December 1894 at the age of 25 he took his own life.

Though Tōkoku's work fills fewer than 1,000 pages in the large-print, less-than-octavo edition of his complete works, Japanese critics consider him to be a figure of some importance in modern Japanese literature. In his essays on the inner life Tōkoku pointed out the nihilistic tendencies of traditional Japanese culture, and he turned to the West—especially to Byron, Carlyle, Emerson, and to Christian thought in general—for a more hopeful view of life that would rescue the individual self from eventual annihilation. Thus he is one of the first writers in Japanese literature to explore the nature and potentialities of the individual self and to try to integrate a philosophy of self into an overall view of life. For this reason one critic has called his essay "Naibu seimei ron" the starting point of modern Japanese literature.

With a keen eye for the good in his own tradition and in that of the West, Tōkoku tried to fuse the two traditions into a coherent, harmonious whole that would transcend East and West. The task was too great for him, and he did not succeed. But his tremendous passion and sincerity, together with the intensity of his short life ending in tragic suicide, make him a fit symbol of the tragic tension that is felt through much of Japanese literature: the tension between an impersonal nihilistic approach to life and society that draws men away from human relationships, and a more human approach that desperately searches for a way to love and to engage in human affairs. A number of later writers, particularly SHIMAZAKI TŌSON, were influenced by Tōkoku and developed further in their own work the themes that had occupied him in his short lifetime.

📖 ——Works by Tōkoku: *Tōkoku zenshū*, 3 vols (Iwanami Shoten, 1950). Works about Tōkoku: George B. Bickle, "Kitamura Tōkoku's Search for Salvation," *Thought* (1973). Funabashi Seiichi, *Kitamura Tōkoku* (1942). Hiraoka Toshio, *Kitamura Tōkoku kenkyū* (1967). Hiraoka Toshio, *Zoku Kitamura Tōkoku kenkyū* (1971). Francis Mathy, "Kitamura Tōkoku: The Early Years," *Monumenta Nipponica* (1963). Francis Mathy, "Kitamura Tōkoku: Essays on the Inner Life," *Monumenta Nipponica* (1964). Francis Mathy, "The Meaning of Tōkoku," *Hikaku bungaku* (1964). Francis Mathy, "Kitamura Tōkoku: Final Essays," *Monumenta Nipponica* (1965). Nihon Bungaku Kenkyū Shiryō Kankō Kai, *Kitamura Tōkoku* (1972). Odagiri Hideo, *Kitamura Tōkoku ron* (1971). Sakamoto Hiroshi, *Kitamura Tōkoku* (1957). Sasabuchi Tomoichi, *Kitamura Tōkoku* (1957). *Francis* MATHY

Kitano Shrine

(Kitano Temmangū). A Shintō shrine, also known as Kitano Jinja and Kitano Tenjin, in Kamigyō Ward, Kyōto, dedicated to the spirits of the scholar and court official SUGAWARA NO MICHIZANE (845–903), his wife, and his son. Shortly after Michizane's death in Dazaifu, Kyūshū, a series of disasters struck the capital, Kyōto. It was soon believed that these misfortunes were the work of Michizane's vengeful spirit (*onryō*; see GORYŌ) chafing at the injustices that he had suffered at the end of his career. To placate his spirit, the court conferred upon him the name Karai Tenjin (God of Thunder). The Kitano Shrine was built on the 44th anniversary of his death. As the patron of scholarship and calligraphy, Michizane has had an enormous following, as can be seen from the large number of Tenjin shrines dedicated to him throughout Japan (see TEMMANGŪ). In addition to the annual festival on 4 August, special ceremonies are held during the year. Among the many treasures owned by the shrine is the famous *Kitano Tenjin engi*, a scroll (EMAKIMONO) depicting the life of Michizane and the building of the shrine. See also DAZAIFU SHRINE. *Stanley* WEINSTEIN

Kitaōji Rosanjin (1883–1959)

Artist-potter. Real name Kitaōji Fusajirō. Born in Kyōto. One of the few Japanese potters to achieve international recognition, having had two major exhibitions abroad (San Francisco, 1964; New York City, 1972). During the past few years his reputation in Japan and the high prices collectors are willing to pay for his ceramics have continued to rise.

An illegitimate child, Rosanjin became an orphan at a very young age and was shuttled from one foster home to another. Yet he managed to establish himself as a calligrapher, an art in which he displayed considerable talent. This skill with the brush was to serve him well in painting designs and calligraphy on ceramics later in his career. From 1915 to 1917 Rosanjin studied porcelain production at a Kutani kiln in Kanazawa (see KUTANI WARE). He subsequently moved to Kita Kamakura and eventually built his own kiln there. He began to design and produce ceramics partly through his passion for fine Japanese food (he owned a restaurant in the Akasaka district of Tōkyō) and his conviction that the ceramics of his day were inadequate for serving it.

In 1936, Rosanjin left the restaurant and turned to making ceramics full time. Rosanjin imitated an astonishing assortment of earlier Japanese wares, creating his own individual, contemporary

versions. Most of his output before World War II consisted of porcelain, inspired by Imari blue-and-white (see ARITA WARE) as well as Kutani overglaze enamel wares. After the war he concentrated on stoneware in the manner of various old Japanese wares such as BIZEN WARE and MINO WARE.

The potter HAMADA SHŌJI criticized Rosanjin as "merely a decorator, not a potter" because assistants did much of the routine production work, though in fact this practice had been standard in earlier periods. In any case, Rosanjin designed all his own pieces, closely supervised the throwing, and did the brushwork decoration himself. His best pieces blend painting or calligraphy and ceramic vessels into powerful, poetic, unified artistic statements. *Robert* MOES

Kitao Shigemasa (1739–1820)

UKIYO-E illustrator and print designer, calligrapher, and poet. The artist was born in Edo (now Tōkyō), the eldest son of a bookseller, Suharaya Saburobei, but left the family business to a younger brother in order to be an artist. He seems to have been self-taught and to have taken the family name Kitao, and the working name Shigemasa. His first signed work, an illustrated book, was published in 1760, followed by several actor portraits, most of which were printed in three colors. In 1765 he designed a full-color calendar print, which he signed Karan, a name he had received from his teacher of *haikai* (see RENGA AND HAIKAI) verse, Tani Sogai. In the late 1760s he designed a series of narrow vertical prints, influenced by HARUNOBU, illustrating the Six Tama Rivers (Mutamagawa), and in the early 1770s, he collaborated with UTAGAWA TOYOHARU and KATSUKAWA SHUNSHŌ on a set of 12 prints depicting pastimes associated with months of the year. This led to two further collaborations with Shunshō, a set of 12 prints on the subject of sericulture, and a three-volume book of portraits of courtesans, *Seirō bijin awase sugata kagami* (Mirror Images of the Greenhouse Beauty Contest), published in 1776, which is one of the masterpieces of the Japanese illustrated book. Around this time Shigemasa designed the solemn and dignified full-size color prints of *geisha*, which influenced both ISODA KORYŪSAI and TORII KIYONAGA and which are perhaps his greatest contribution to *ukiyo-e*.

Shigemasa's career as a commercial print designer seems to have ended around 1780, but he continued to be active as a book illustrator, a poet, a calligrapher, and a designer of SURIMONO prints, an activity that he pursued until the end of his life, frequently signing these prints Kōsuisai. His pupils included Keisai Masayoshi (1764–1824), Kitao Masanobu (better known as the writer SANTŌ KYŌDEN), and KUBO SHUMMAN. *Roger* KEYES

Kita Sadakichi (1871–1939)

Historian. Born in Tokushima Prefecture; graduate of Tōkyō University. In 1899 he founded the Nihon Rekishi Chiri Kenkyūkai (Japan Historical Geography Society) and began to publish the journal *Rekishi chiri*. As an official of the Ministry of Education he edited history textbooks to be used in all elementary schools of the national educational system, but he resigned in 1911 after coming under attack by rightists for having implied that the present imperial family was descended from the Northern Court (see NAMBOKUCHŌ SEIJUN RON). He also stirred controversy with his theory that buildings of the temple HŌRYŪJI in Nara, reputed to be the oldest wooden structures in the world, were not the original edifices. He founded the journal *Minzoku to rekishi* (Race and History). He was also one of the first to study the BURAKUMIN, Japan's largest minority group.

Kita school

(Kitaryū). One of the five major *shite kata* (principal player) schools (or troupes) of professional NŌ theater actors. Founded by Kita Nagayoshi (professionally known as Kita Shichidayū; 1586–1623). The school was officially recognized by the second Tokugawa shōgun Hidetada (1579–1632), making it the youngest of the five leading Nō acting troupes, the others being the KANZE SCHOOL, HŌSHŌ SCHOOL, KOMPARU SCHOOL, and KONGŌ SCHOOL. Though not born into a family of Nō actors, Shichidayū studied Komparu-school Nō from his childhood and became a skilled actor. Early in his career he was patronized by the hegemon TOYOTOMI HIDEYOSHI and served for a time as troupe head (*tayū*) of the Kongō school with which he also had close ties. His acting style derived mainly from the Komparu school, but he adapted the strong points of the various schools in perfecting an independent acting style. The school was patronized by the Tokugawa shogunate in the Edo period (1600–1868), and many of the *daimyō* studied Kita-school Nō. It declined, however, with the advent of the Meiji period (1868–1912). Kita Roppeita (1874–1971), the 14th hereditary troupe head, revived the school, and it continues to perform today.   KIKKAWA *Shūhei*

Kitaura

Lake in southeastern Ibaraki Prefecture, central Honshū. Situated east of Lake Kasumigaura, Kitaura developed from an inlet. The water is used for industrial purposes by the Kashima Coastal Industrial Area. Catches include pond smelt, crucian carp, and carp. Area: 38.5 sq km (14.8 sq mi); circumference: 87 km (54 mi); depth: 9 m (29.5 ft).

Kita Ward

(Kita Ku). One of the 23 wards of Tōkyō. South of the river Arakawa. Many metal, textile, printing, machinery, and chemical plants are located in the ward. Former military areas in Akabane are now the site of housing complexes and schools. Pop: 387,256.

Kitayama culture

(Kitayama *bunka*). The culture of the early part of the Muromachi period (1333–1568), particularly of the period from 1369 to 1408, when the third Muromachi shōgun, ASHIKAGA YOSHIMITSU, ruled, first as shōgun and, after 1395, as retired shōgun. It is named for the location of Yoshimitsu's villa at Kitayama in the northern part of Kyōto. Encompassing recent cultural influence from China and the native cultures of both the court nobility and the newly-risen warrior class, Kitayama culture found expression in a remarkably wide range of artistic accomplishments. Its chief ornaments were the cultivated Zen literature of the Five Mountains (GOZAN LITERATURE); monochrome INK PAINTING, strongly influenced by Chinese painting of the Song (Sung; 960–1279) and Yuan (Yüan; 1279–1368) periods and exemplified by JOSETSU and MINCHŌ; the perfection of NŌ drama by KAN'AMI and his son ZEAMI; linked verse (*renga*; see RENGA AND HAIKAI); and an eclectic architecture incorporating both the Japanese court style and the Chinese Tang (T'ang) dynasty (618–907) style, the former epitomized by Yoshimitsu's official residence, the Hana no Gosho (Palace of Flowers) and the latter by the Golden Pavilion (KINKAKUJI). Indeed, all of the arts flourished in this period, fostered by the social stability of the times and by Yoshimitsu's generous patronage. Kitayama culture is often compared with the HIGASHIYAMA CULTURE of the reign of the eighth Muromachi shōgun, ASHIKAGA YOSHIMASA.

Kitazato Shibasaburō (1853–1931)

Bacteriologist. Born in what is now Kumamoto Prefecture. Graduate of the Kumamoto Igakkō (a medical school) and Tōkyō University. From 1885 to 1891, Kitazato studied bacteriology under Robert Koch in Germany and in 1889 succeeded in obtaining a pure culture of *Clostridium tetani*, the bacterium that causes tetanus. Returning to Japan in 1892, he established the Institute for Infectious Diseases, a private research institution, with the assistance of FUKUZAWA YUKICHI. As its first president, he devoted himself to the study of bacteriology and serological therapeutics. In 1894 he went to Hong Kong during an outbreak of the bubonic plague and discovered *Pasteurella pestis*. When his institute was put under the jurisdiction of the Ministry of Education in 1914 without prior consultation, he resigned from his post. The following year he and his colleagues established the Kitazato Institute. Kitazato was the first dean of the Faculty of Medicine of Keiō University, served in the House of Peers, and became the first president of the Japan Medical Association.   TANAKA *Akira*

Kitazono Katsue (1902–1978)

Poet. Real name Hashimoto Kenkichi. Born in Mie Prefecture. Graduate of Chūō University. In the late 1920s he associated with several avant-garde poetry coteries and wrote experimental surrealistic verses which established him as a leading poet. He founded the poetry magazine *VOU* in 1935. He is also known for his translations of Paul Éluard and Stéphane Mallarmé. His poetry collections include *Shiro no arubamu* (1929) and *Kuroi hi* (1951).

kite, black

(*tobi*). *Milvus migrans*. A large hawk of the family Accipitridae. Its total length is around 64 centimeters (25 in). Its tail is notched and its color is blackish brown except for white spots at the base of the primary wing feathers, visible when in flight. Its distribution extends throughout Eurasia, as well as Africa and Australia; it is usually found as a resident bird in all parts of Japan northward from Kyūshū and is especially common along the seashore and at river mouths. Soaring on spread wings, it searches for the carcasses of small animals and fish, then dives sharply to seize them with its claws. It makes its nest by piling dead branches at the top of a large tree.   TAKANO *Shinji*

The NIHON SHOKI (720) says that when Japan's legendary first emperor, Jimmu Tennō, was fighting to conquer the Yamato region, a glittering golden kite alighted on his bow and flashed like lightning so that his enemies were defeated. The Order of the Golden Kite (KINSHI KUNSHŌ), a citation for exceptional military service awarded between 1890 and 1945, took its name from this legend.

Since kites eat the remains of small animals and kitchen waste, they have long been valued as scavengers in Japan; it is said that at times the bodies of rats were purposely thrown into the street for kites to carry away. Because they have been so common in both cities and the countryside, kites often appear in proverbs and folk sayings.   SANEYOSHI *Tatsuo*

kites

(*tako; ikanobori; ika*). Japan's kites are among the most spectacular in the world, treasured as much for their aesthetic worth as for the pleasure they give as toys. The traditional kite consists of a light bamboo or wood frame over which is affixed paper painted with various bold motifs, ranging from faces of legendary war heroes to brilliant geometric patterns; in the hands of a skilled craftsman, the Japanese kite becomes a work of art. Japanese kites are made in many sizes, from miniature kites of only a few square inches to immense ones of over a thousand square feet, and in many different shapes. Many of them require considerable skill in handling if they are to be airborne successfully. Japanese kites possess a history of association with folk religion and figure in a number of famous military adventures. Today's kites are a source of pleasure for this reason as well, for they draw upon, and to some extent preserve, traditional legend.

Kites in Premodern Japan —— Kites are a worldwide phenomenon familiar to most peoples. It is difficult to ascertain with confidence whether or not kites in Japan were indigenous or an importation or both. Most kite historians see China as the ultimate source for the kite as it developed in Japan. Some have suggested a Malayo-Polynesian origin; however, if Japan's kites are indeed the result of diffusion from abroad, then geographical and cultural proximity makes China the most likely primary source.

The earliest mention of kites in Japan is a citation in the 10th-century WAMYŌ RUIJU SHŌ, a dictionary of Chinese characters compiled by poet-scholar MINAMOTO NO SHITAGAU. The dictionary provides Japanized pronunciations of the Chinese words written by two sets of characters, both denoting a contrivance "made of paper in the shape of a hawk, which rides the wind and flies well": *shirōshi* ("paper venerable hawk") and *shien* ("paper kite," i.e., paper hawk). Since these Chinese words for "kite" appear in the *Wamyō ruiju shō* without an accompanying native Japanese word, some scholars have been encouraged to argue that the kite was introduced from China.

The words *ikanobori* and its shortened version *ika* are considered the oldest Japanese terms for "kite." In the illustrated encyclopedia WAKAN SANSAI ZUE of 1712, *ikanobori* and *ika* are cited as the standard Japanese readings for the characters "paper hawk." The current Japanese word *tako* derives from Kantō-region speech of the Edo period (1600–1868). *Tako* eventually replaced *ika* in the standard language, but Edo-period studies already acknowledged that *ika* was the original term and *tako* its variant. Both words make punning reference to a common premodern kite shape: *ika* is a homophone for the word meaning "squid," and *tako* for the word meaning "octopus." The *Wakan sansai zue* and other pictorial records of the Edo period depict kites with oval frames and long tails resembling tentacles, features already suggested in the wordplay of kite terminology. The Chinese character now used to write "kite" (*tako*) in Japan is a Japanese coinage composed of an element meaning "wind" and an element meaning "scrap of cloth."

Folklorists and kite historians, approaching the past through the regional festivals and observances of today, attribute an ancient religious function to kites. The relationship binding kites to the myriad KAMI (gods, deities, spirits) of Japan's indigenous SHINTŌ religion is apparently an old one. Kites have been interpreted as prayers in concrete form linking heaven and earth and as offerings to the gods. As such they have been identified with a number of universal archetypal roles, among them protection against evil; insurance of good health, good fortune, and good harvests; celebration and thanksgiving; and the supplication for sturdy, productive offspring.

The Nara-period (710–794) gazetteer *Hizen no Kuni fudoki* describes a shaman who sets aloft a contrivance which rides the wind to a distant place. This may have been a kite, though it is described as a "banner." The shaman constructs a shrine on the spot where it lands and purifies the region. Modern kites in Akita and Aomori prefectures, painted with devillike ONI figures, are thought to be survivals of the folk belief that kites serve to purify and to ward off evil. Until the early years of the Meiji period (1868–1912), families in the city of Kakuta, Miyagi Prefecture, fashioned small kites bearing their names and on New Year's Day set them aloft in the nearby mountains, cutting their strings, as an offering to the local *kami;* this was intended to insure safety and prosperity through the ensuing year. Modern kite meets held at a number of shrines in Kanagawa Prefecture include as their final event the burning of a giant kite, which is offered to the shrine *kami* as a plea for a good harvest. Kites are associated especially with children for reasons deeper and older than their current role as a toy. In some rural areas grandparents still present their grandchildren with a celebratory kite *(engi-dako)* at their *hatsu-zekku* (a child's first DOLL FESTIVAL or CHILDREN'S DAY; see SEKKU), a practice which probably preserves an earlier connection between kites and children's good health.

Kites also have a military history. Stories abound in which kites serve as signals, message-carriers, and even primitive airborne transport for daredevil warriors. Although most of these stories are probably apocryphal, many are certainly within the realm of possibility. During the LATER THREE YEARS' WAR (1083–1087), a retainer of the besieged Kiyohara no Iehira is said to have communicated with his lord by kite. (Local legend in Shizuoka Prefecture relates that in the early 1500s the lord of Suruga used kites to signal from his castle.) In one legend the famous hero MINAMOTO NO TAMETOMO (1139–77), exiled to the island of Ōshima in the Izu Islands, constructs a huge kite to bear his son back to Honshū. Perhaps the most popular kite escapade, which made its way onto the KABUKI stage as NAMIKI GOHEI's *Keisei kogane no shachihoko* (1782, Stealing the Golden Fishscales), concerns the landholder-turned-robber Kakinoki Kinsuke (also known as Kakinomura Kinsuke). In 1712 Kinsuke is supposed to have boarded a great kite in order to steal the golden scales from the fabulous dolphinlike fish on the ridgepole of NAGOYA CASTLE.

The Edo period saw the emergence of kites as a popular form of amusement largely detached from traditional associations. If the illustrations in contemporary woodblock prints are any indication, there were times when the skies of Edo (now Tōkyō) were literally filled with kites. Kite historians have delineated a kite enthusiasm in the Japan of the late Edo period as an outgrowth of the same social climate which gave rise to UKIYO-E woodblock prints. A taste for kites seems to have arisen among wealthy members of the CHŌNIN (merchant) class, who further popularized them and speeded their entry into society as a whole. Kite battles *(tako-gassen)* in particular attracted enthusiastic crowds and, periodically, the wrath of public officials. Huge kites, deployed by teams of operators often stationed on opposite banks of a river, were pitted against each other to the wild approval of spectators. By the end of the Edo period, kites enjoyed a broad popular base.

The brilliantly painted kite known today developed after the GENROKU ERA (1688–1704). Although there is some indication that earlier kites were painted, most apparently were not decorated to any remarkable extent. However, by the end of the 17th century families of the warrior class began to have their children's kites illustrated with dragons or Chinese lions in imitation of the TOSA SCHOOL and KANO SCHOOL paintings on the *fusuma* (sliding doors) and hanging scrolls of their homes. The warrior figures prevalent on late Edo kites are believed to have developed as a *chōnin* phenomenon. Wealthy merchants derived much pleasure from the various military romances in vogue at the time and apparently transferred this enthusiasm to kites. By the 1780s kite painting had reached such ostentatious proportions that the government attempted to forbid overly luxurious kites; in retaliation, kite fanciers began to

Kites

Two traditional Japanese kites. Top: The Rokugō hawk, a Tōkyō kite first popular around the end of the 19th century. Bottom: A hexagonal fighting kite *(rokkaku-dako),* painted with the face of a warrior, from Sanjō, Niigata Prefecture. Colors on paper.

commission simple yet gorgeous kites adorned with sumptuous renditions of Chinese characters denoting "dragon" *(ryū),* "orchid" *(ran),* and "crane" *(tsuru).*

By the close of the Edo period, kites from Edo had made their way into the provinces as a form of souvenir carried home by traveling warriors and merchants. Most popular as souvenirs were the *nishikie-dako,* which featured *ukiyo-e* subjects and were fancied by warrior households, and the ironic *yakko-dako* favored by merchant families, which depicted a warrior's manservant *(yakko)* with his arms outspread in a silly pose. Both of these are viewed as the prototypes of various modern regional kites.

Kites in Modern Japan —— The modern Japanese kite has its roots firmly planted in the Edo period, when its standard shapes and motifs were established. Some kites depict legendary heroes in a way that emphasizes their bravery and good deeds. Others, like the kites from Hachijōjima which feature Tametomo, humorously comment on kite legend. The great majority of kites have a story to tell through the imagery of their decoration; many are witty visual puns.

Aside from abstract geometric motifs, four categories of subject are common as kite decoration. Most prominent is the warrior hero of legend or drama, for example, the tragic hero MINAMOTO NO YOSHITSUNE. Folk images also find their way onto kites; the *daruma* doll (see DARUMA FAIRS) is a popular figure, as are the comic masks OKAME and HYOTTOKO. Various Chinese written characters and Japanese *kana* syllables form another category of designs. For many kite fanciers, birds and insects—especially the ever-popular cicada—present the most entertaining subjects, as they dictate the form of the kite itself.

The Japanese kite shape has come a long way since its original form as a schematic bird or an oval with fluttering tails. Today kites are fashioned in a variety of two-dimensional and three-dimensional shapes; many are equipped with brightly colored tails. Intricate box kites, linked kites, and tube kites are among the most popular. Kites painted with figural motifs generally remain square, oblong, or hexagonal in shape but are constructed so as to flap and flutter, which gives them a three-dimensional quality. Kites are built to ride and buck with the wind, sometimes spinning in circles or shooting from side to side. Undulating *mukade-dako* ("centipede" kites), formed of jointed sections, are the most complex of the kites based on bird or insect form. Kites are also built to create noise by flapping and snapping; they are frequently fitted with hummers or whistles, which produce anything from a deep rumble to a high-pitched whine. The combined effect of color, shape, motion, and sound is spectacular.

Kites continue to figure in a number of traditional observances. In many parts of Japan, they are flown on New Year's Day. Kites are given to children and flown in March and May, coinciding with the Doll Festival and Children's Day, and Japan's major kite events take place in these months. In some areas kites are even set aloft during the Buddhist BON FESTIVAL.

Kite battles still attract an enthusiastic following. The annual *tako-gassen* staged in early May at Hamamatsu in Shizuoka Prefecture and in early June at Shirone in Niigata Prefecture are famous throughout Japan. The Hamamatsu event is said to have originated in the 16th century, when a great kite was launched to celebrate the birth of a local feudal lord's son. Square kites, 3.3 meters (11 ft) on each side and weighing about 10 kilograms (22 lb), are equipped with specially prepared hemp kite strings designed to rip and cut; the object is to disable and down the opponent's kite.

The Shirone event apparently resulted from an 18th-century fiasco, when a celebratory great kite built by one village crashed in a neighboring village, causing consternation followed by retaliation. Manned by teams of 7 to 15 men stationed on each side of a local river, kites measuring 7 by 5 meters (23 by 16.4 ft) and weighing 40 kilograms (88 lb) are pitted against each other; the object is to pull the opponent's kite out of the sky and into the river.

The launching of enormous kites *(ōdako)* rivals kite wars as a popular spectacle. The city of Hōjūbana in Saitama Prefecture is renowned for the immense kite it sends aloft annually on 3 and 5 May. The coordinated teamwork of 50 men is required before the kite, approximately 15 by 11 meters (49 by 36 ft) and weighing about 800 kilograms (1,760 lb), lifts skyward in ponderous majesty. The Hōjūbana *ōdako* is said to have originated in 1782, when the monk Jōgen flew a grant kite to augur the coming silk harvest. By the Meiji period (1868–1912) the Hōjūbana *ōdako* was an established tradition, and great kites have been set aloft annually at Hōjūbana for at least 100 years. Not to be outdone, in March of 1980 the city of Shirone broke the Guiness world record for kites by launching a kite measuring 19.07 meters by 14.10 meters (63 by 46 ft).

Kites as a Folk Craft—— Because kites are appreciated as works of art, they are collected by some as a form of folk craft. While many are certainly flown, they are also treasured as examples of popular folk art. This is particularly true of kites produced today in various parts of Japan by kitemakers who have endeavored to preserve traditional methods and motifs. Many of Japan's regional kites date back to types established during the Edo period. Like KOKESHI dolls and other folk crafts, kites are valued as representative products of certain regions and evoke a sense of the old Japan.

The *tsugaru-dako,* for example, is produced in Aomori Prefecture and is noted for its colorful figural decoration; it is also renowned for the deep roar it emits when airborne, so similar to that of a bomber that the kite was banned during World War II. The *noshiro-berabō* of Akita Prefecture bears a grotesque male or female face with lolling tongue. Fukushima Prefecture produces the peculiar Aizu *karabito-dako,* which depicts the scowling face of a "southern barbarian" (see NAMBAN). Niigata Prefecture's best-known kite is the Shirone *rokkaku-dako,* a brilliantly painted hexagonal fighting kite which participates in the Shirone kite war.

Chiba Prefecture is famous for its noisy Kazusa *karabito-dako,* a spindle-shaped kite which emits a tremendous growl when flown, and for its kimono-shaped *sode-dako* with warrior motifs. Continuing an Edo tradition, Tōkyō produces the well-known *yakko-dako* and the gorgeous *edo-dako,* which recalls the *nishikie-dako* of the 18th century.

Aichi Prefecture's *sakurei-dako* are fashioned in the forms of insects and birds. The Taisha *iwai-dako* of Tottori Prefecture depicts the Chinese characters for "crane" *(tsuru)* and "tortoise" *(kame).* As its name implies, it is connected with IZUMO SHRINE (Izumo Taisha). Kaga Prefecture is known for its squid-shaped Takamatsu *ika-dako.* The giant, round *wanwan-dako* of Tokushima Prefecture is well known as one of the largest kites made in the world.

Fukuoka Prefecture produces the *kaminari dōjin,* a kite which depicts dragons and devillike figures on a flat body with complex curvilinear borders. The *nagasaki-hata* of Nagasaki Prefecture is popular for its elegant designs in blue, red, and white and for its flaglike form; famous as a fighting kite, it is equipped with kite strings fitted with broken glass in order to disable the kites of opponents. Nagasaki also produces the exotic *baramon-dako,* a wild-looking kite decorated with grimacing faces and ornate robes; it is said to have been introduced from India by Portuguese traders of the 16th century.

📖——*Bijutsu techō bessatsu: Tako o tsukuru* (Winter 1982). Clive Hart, *Kites: An Historical Survey* (1967). Hiroi Tsutomo, *Tako* (1973). Niisaka Kazuo, *Tako no hanashi* (1981). David Pelham, *The Penguin Book of Kites* (1976). Saitō Tadao, *Tako no katachi* (1971). Tal Streeter, *The Art of the Japanese Kite* (1974). Tawara Yūsaku and Sonobe Kiyoshi, *Nihon no tako* (1970).   Tal STREETER

Kitsuki

City in northeastern Ōita Prefecture, Kyūshū, on north Beppu Bay. Kitsuki developed as the base of the Kitsuki family, who built a castle here in 1250. Kitsuki is known for its *shichitōi,* a reed used for *tatami* mats. Mandarin oranges are also grown. Pop: 21,994.

Kiuchi Sekitei (1724?–1808)

Mineralogist and collector of fossils and stone-age tools and other archaeological artifacts. A native of Ōmi Province (now Shiga Prefecture), from an early age he was fond of collecting unusual rocks. From about 1750 Kiuchi traveled throughout Japan, collecting and classifying stones and artifacts. He published his findings in *Unkonshi* (15 vols, 1773–1801; Treatise on Rocks) and left several other works in manuscript.

Kiuchi Shinzō (1910–   )

Scholar of human geography and urban studies specialist. Born in Tōkyō, Kiuchi graduated from Tōkyō University in 1935. He became professor of geography at Tōkyō University and was visiting professor of geography at the University of Chicago. Active in Japanese and international geographical circles, he served as president of the ASSOCIATION OF JAPANESE GEOGRAPHERS and the Japan Society for Urbanology, as vice-president of the TŌKYŌ GEOGRAPHICAL SOCIETY and the International Geographical Union, and as vice-chairman of the organizational committee of the International Geographical Congress. Among his published works are: *Toshi no chirigakuteki kenkyū* (1949, Geographical Studies of Cities), *Toshi chirigaku kenkyū* (1951, Study of Urban Geography), *Chiiki gairon* (1968, Introduction to Regional Studies), and *Toshi chirigaku genri* (1979, Principles of Urban Geography). He was the recipient of the Karl Ritter silver medal from the Geographische Gesellschaft zu Berlin in 1959 and the George Davidson Prize from the American Geographical Society.   NISHIKAWA Osamu

Kiuchi Sōgorō → Sakura Sōgorō

Kiwanis Club

The first Japanese chapter of the Kiwanis Club was established in 1964 in Tōkyō. In 1968 the Japan Kiwanis Committee was organized and charter clubs were formed in Nagoya, Ōsaka, Hiroshima, Kōbe, Sendai, Sapporo, Yokohama, Takamatsu, and Fukuoka. Kiwanis clubs organize lectures and do much to promote local craftsmanship and various charities. They publish a semiannual bulletin called *Kiwanis Japan.* Membership in 1979 was 1,050.   HOMMA Yasuhei

Kiyokawa Shōji (1913–   )

Olympic swimmer. Born in Aichi Prefecture; graduated from Tōkyō Shōka Daigaku (now Hitotsubashi University). In the 1932 Los Angeles Olympics he took the gold medal in the men's 100-meter backstroke. The silver and bronze medalists were also Japanese, marking the first time Japan took all the medals in one Olympic event. At the Berlin Olympics in 1936, he took third place in the backstroke event. As a result of his achievements, as well as those of other Japanese swimmers, Japan received international attention as a nation of champion swimmers. Since 1966 he has been a member of the International Olympic Committee.   TAKEDA Fumio

Kiyomizudera

Temple of the HOSSŌ SECT of Buddhism; located on a high hill in Higashiyama Ward, Kyōto. Kiyomizudera, also known as Seisuiji, was founded about 798 by the monk Enchin with support from SA-KANOUE NO TAMURAMARO (758–811), a general who fought several hard campaigns to bring eastern Japan under the control of the central government.

According to one account of the founding of the temple, Enchin first arrived in Higashiyama in 778 as a wandering ascetic. An eccentric layman named Gyōei, who was a devotee of the bodhisattva Kannon (Skt: Avalokiteśvara), invited Enchin to share his hermitage, which stood next to a waterfall. While on a hunting expedition, Tamuramaro happened to pass the waterfall where Enchin was performing his daily ablutions. After hearing a lecture from Enchin on the evils of taking life, Tamuramaro became his disciple. In 798 the two men erected at the site of the hermitage a temple which they named Kiyomizudera (Temple of Clear Water) to house a newly made image of the Eleven-faced Kannon (Jūichimen Kannon; see KANNON). In 804 they successfully petitioned for a grant of land to provide an income for the temple and requested that Emperor Kammu (r 781–806) serve as an honorary patron. Three years later a certain Lady Miyoshi presented Kiyomizudera with her mansion, which was dismantled and moved to the temple precincts, where it was rebuilt as the main hall.

When private ownership of temples was prohibited in 810, Kiyomizudera, which had been under the control of Tamuramaro's family, was designated a national temple, at which prayers were to be offered for the protection of the empire, although for a long while descendants of Tamuramaro continued to hold important temple positions. Over the centuries the buildings were repeatedly destroyed by fires, earthquakes, and warfare. Because of its close affiliation with the temple KŌFUKUJI in Nara, Kiyomizudera became a frequent target for attack by Kōfukuji's great rival, ENRYAKUJI, and the latter's ally, the YASAKA SHRINE, which on several occasions joined forces to demolish Kiyomizudera.

The last major fire to strike the temple occurred in 1629. Reconstruction was begun two years later at the order of the third Tokugawa shōgun, Tokugawa Iemitsu (in office 1623–51) and completed in 1633, from which time many of the present buildings date. Although the temple prospered throughout the Edo period (1600–1868), its fortunes declined with the advent of the Meiji period (1868–1912), which ultimately led to the closing of many of its subtemples. Kiyomizudera now consists of seven halls, a three-story pagoda, and several minor structures. The main hall, one end of which is built out over a cliff, has a spacious veranda which affords a panoramic view of Kyōto. Kiyomizudera is the 16th of the 33 places of pilgrimage sacred to Kannon in western Japan.

Stanley WEINSTEIN

Kiyomizu ware → Kyōto ceramics

kiyomoto-bushi

Type of music for KABUKI, accompanied by SHAMISEN and other instruments. It was developed by Kiyomoto Enjudayū (1777–1825) out of the prevailing *tomimoto-bushi* style, the first performance being in 1814, at the Ichimuraza, Edo (now Tōkyō). Compositions by Enjudayū which are still performed include *Yasuna, Kasane,* and *Toba-e.* The line was continued by his son Enjudayū II (1801–55) and his descendants, and by several branch lines. Enjudayū I and II also performed in compositions written for them by Kawaguchi Onao (d 1845), formerly a *geisha* in the Yoshiwara, and proprietress of a restaurant in the Yagembori district. Her works include *Ume no haru* (1827) and the well-known *Hokushū* (1818), the text of which was written by the learned ŌTA NAMPO (1749–1823). Other early *kiyomoto* were written for plays by Tsuruya Namboku IV (1755–1829; see TSURUYA NAMBOKU), the author of many successful works. Thus *kiyomoto,* like several other forms of late Edo culture, combined elements from the worlds of literature, kabuki, and the demimonde. Of some 300 *kiyomoto* pieces, 40 have been maintained in the repertoire, including *Kanda-matsuri, Bun'ya, Seigaiha, Unohana, Sumidagawa,* and *Yoshiwara suzume.* The leading performers of modern times are Kiyomoto Shizudayū (b 1898), Enjudayū VI (b 1926), and Umekichi III (b 1932).

Kiyomoto has a more narrative character than NAGAUTA or TO-KIWAZU-BUSHI, also music of the kabuki theater. It uses a medium-sized *shamisen,* and the general effect of the music is light and cheerful. The vocal tessitura is high, and the singer uses a declamatory, nasal style of delivery. Some characteristic musical figures are the ones called *kaeshi* and *otoshi,* and various other small details of

enunciation and ornament contribute to the definition of the style. Historically, *kiyomoto* has been one of the most adaptable forms of kabuki music; this has helped to ensure its survival, and to make it attractive to dancers. In the late 19th century it had some influence on Edo KOUTA.

📖——Gunji Masakatsu, ed, *Kiyomoto,* vol 8 of *Hōgaku taikei* (1970). Ninchōji Tsutomu, *Kiyomoto kenkyū* (1930).

David B. WATERHOUSE

Kiyonaga → Torii Kiyonaga

Kiyono Kenji (1885–1955)

Pathologist and anthropologist. Born in Okayama Prefecture. The son of a medical doctor, Kiyono graduated from Kyōto University in 1909. He studied in Germany from 1912 to 1914 under the German pathologist Ludwig Aschoff at the University of Freiburg. His specialty was the study of vital staining, and he is said to have first established this discipline in Japan. He was a professor at Kyōto University from 1921 to 1938, where he lectured on microbiology and pathology. Beginning around 1919 Kiyono excavated a large number of ancient SHELL MOUNDS throughout Japan in an effort to clarify the racial characteristics of Stone Age man in Japan. He concluded that the Stone Age people of Japan were partly of Korean origin and that they were the direct ancestors of the present Japanese people.

Kiyooka Takayuki (1922–   )

Poet; novelist. Born in Dairen (Ch: Dalian or Ta-lien) in China. His father was a railway engineer. He graduated from Tōkyō University, where he majored in French literature; later he taught French at Hōsei University. He is one of the few surrealist poets in Japan. *Kōtta honoo* (1959) is a collection of his poems. In the 1960s he began writing novels; *Akashiya no Dairen* (1969) won the Akutagawa Prize for the same year. He has also produced news documentaries and written film criticism. Other works include *Nichijō* (1962), a poetry collection, and *Furūto to ōboe* (1971), a collection of short stories.

Kiyosato

District in the town of Takane, northwestern Yamanashi Prefecture, central Honshū. Situated on a plateau 1,300 m (4,264 ft) high in the eastern foothills of YATSUGATAKE. The people of this district engage in the cultivation of agricultural products and dairy farming. With an excellent view of Yatsugatake, Mt. Fuji (Fujisan), and the mountains of the Southern Alps, Kiyosato has developed as a resort.

Kiyosawa Kiyoshi (1890–1945)

Journalist and specialist on foreign affairs. Born in Nagano Prefecture. Kiyosawa traveled to the United States in 1906 and studied at Whitworth College in Spokane, Washington, after which he worked as a reporter for Japanese-language newspapers in Seattle and San Francisco. He returned to Japan in 1920 and continued to work as a journalist for the *Asahi shimbun, Hōchi shimbun, Chūō kōron,* and other publications. As a liberal he advocated cooperation with Western powers, particularly the United States and Britain, and supported the internationalist diplomacy of SHIDEHARA KIJŪRŌ. His wartime diary, published as *Ankoku nikki* (3 vols; 1954), provides information on the activities of Japanese political leaders such as KONOE FUMIMARO and HATOYAMA ICHIRŌ. A work on Japanese diplomacy, *Nihon gaikō shi* (1941), is still highly regarded.

Kiyose

City in northern Tōkyō Prefecture. Formerly a farming village, Kiyose has witnessed a large population increase with the construction of many housing projects and residences since the 1950s. It is also the site of numerous hospitals and convalescent homes. Pop: 61,915.

Kiyosumiyama

Hill in the town of Amatsu Kominato, southern Bōsō Peninsula, Chiba Prefecture, central Honshū. It is the site of a Nichiren sect temple, Seichōji (also known as Kiyosumidera). The temple is surrounded by a dense forest, that has been used as an experimental station by the agriculture department of the Tōkyō University. Kiyosumiyama is a part of Minami Bōsō Quasi-National Park. Height: 383 m (1,256 ft).

Kiyoura Keigo (1850–1942)

Politician. Prime minister (1924). Born in what is now Kumamoto Prefecture, he attended the Kangien, a school founded by the Confucian scholar HIROSE TANSŌ. Kiyoura joined the justice ministry in 1876 and helped to draft the PEACE PRESERVATION LAW OF 1887. Allied with the clique headed by YAMAGATA ARITOMO, he successively became minister of justice in the second MATSUKATA MASAYOSHI cabinet (1896) and the second Yamagata cabinet (1898). He was concurrently justice minister, home minister, and commerce and agriculture minister in the first KATSURA TARŌ cabinet (1901). In 1906 he was made a member of the Privy Council, becoming president in 1922. In January 1924 Kiyoura formed a cabinet; opposed in principle to party government, he drew heavily from the House of Peers. He was attacked by the KENSEIKAI, RIKKEN SEIYŪKAI, and the KAKUSHIN KURABU political parties (see MOVEMENT TO PROTECT CONSTITUTIONAL GOVERNMENT), and barely five months later he and his cabinet were forced to resign.

Kiyozawa Manshi (1863–1903)

Buddhist priest and philosopher. He attempted to reform the JŌDO SHIN SECT of PURE LAND BUDDHISM by combining the school's teachings of salvation through reliance on Buddha with stoic self-discipline. Kiyozawa was born in Nagoya, the eldest son of Tokunaga Naganori, a low-ranking *samurai* in the service of the Owari branch of the Tokugawa family and also a practitioner of Zen. His mother was a devout follower of the Ōtani branch of the Jōdo Shin sect. In 1878 Kiyozawa entered the priesthood. Educated first at a Jōdo Shin sect academy established by the Ōtani branch in Kyōto, he later attended Tōkyō University, where he studied Western philosophy with Ernest F. FENOLLOSA and Ludwig Busse (1862–1907). While working for a graduate degree in philosophy of religion, he taught French history at the First Higher School in Tōkyō and philosophy and psychology at Tetsugakkan, which later became Tōyō University. He moved to Kyōto in 1888 to serve as head of a middle school which was financially supported by his sect at the time, and about the same time he married, taking his wife's family name, Kiyozawa. In 1890 he resigned his position and devoted himself to a life of religious austerity and scholarship.

Recovering from a two-year bout with tuberculosis which he had contracted in 1894, Kiyozawa initiated reforms aimed at spiritually reinvigorating and democratizing the Ōtani branch of the Jōdo Shin sect through the publication of a journal titled *Kyōkai jigen* (A Timely Admonition to Religious Circles). The proposals he and his supporters made, however, met with stiff opposition from conservative elements within the Ōtani branch. This led him to retreat to a temple in Aichi Prefecture to study the early teachings of Gautama Buddha collected in the Āgamas, SHINRAN'S KYŌGYŌSHINSHŌ and TANNISHŌ, and Epictetus' *Discourses*. From Epictetus Manshi learned Stoicism, which helped to sustain him during his long illness. It also convinced him of the need for moral fiber, a quality that he found lacking in Jōdo Shin teachings, which emphasized the singular importance of reliance on the saving grace of the "other power" (TARIKI), that is, Amitābha (J: AMIDA) Buddha.

In 1898 Manshi was invited by the newly appointed chief abbot of the Jōdo Shin sect to be his tutor in Tōkyō. In 1901 he became the first dean of Shinshū University after its move from Kyōto to Tōkyō (now Ōtani University, relocated in Kyōto). The *seishin shugi* (spiritualism) movement that he founded in Tōkyō in these later years was deeply rooted in Manshi's dialectic: the synthesis of Stoic rigor and Shinran's teachings of *tariki*. Manshi finally fell victim to tuberculosis, just before his 41st birthday.

His major works include: *Shūkyō tetsugaku gaikotsu* (1892, A Skeletal Outline of the Philosophy of Religion); *Tarikimon tetsugaku gaikotsu shikō* (1892, A Draft Outline of the Philosophy of Tariki); *Zaishō zange roku* (1894, A Record of Repentance during Illness); and *Waga shinnen* (1903, My Faith).

▬——*Kiyozawa Manshi zenshū*, 8 vols (1953–57). Wakimoto Tsuneya, *Kindai no bukkyōsha* (1967).   T. James KODERA

Kiyū shōran

(Diversions for One's Amusement). A compendium of miscellaneous information written by Kitamura Nobuyo (1784–1856), a scholar and bibliographer of prodigious memory and immense learning; published in 1830 in 12 volumes with an appendix. The work consists mainly of excerpts from works read by the author with his own commentaries. Covering a large number of topics ranging from clothing and deportment to music, festivals, language, and trade, the encyclopedic work is a rich source of information on the manners and customs of urban commoners during the Edo period (1600–1868).

Kizokuin → House of Peers

Kizugawa

River in southern Kyōto Prefecture, central Honshū, joining the Yodogawa at the southern part of the Kyōto Basin. Known as Izumigawa in antiquity, it has been remembered in poems and songs. It was used to transport lumber when the palaces in the capitals of FUJIWARAKYŌ and HEIJŌKYŌ were being constructed. Length: about 45 km (28 mi).

know-how

(*nō-hau*). The English colloquial expression "know-how," in the sense of technical knowledge or trade secrets, has come into daily use in the Japanese business world, especially in disputes involving technology transfer or licensing contracts between Japanese and foreign companies. No trade secrets law has yet been developed in Japan to protect the owner of valuable technical know-how, customer lists, or other kinds of trade secret against their misappropriation or unauthorized disclosure. Neither the CIVIL CODE nor the penal code (see CRIMINAL LAW) of Japan, unlike those of some European countries, contains remedies against trade secret misappropriation. Civil remedies can be sought under the general tort provisions of the Civil Code, but injunctions cannot be obtained, and even the awarding of damages is generally considered to require a liberal construction of the code. The dearth of legal precedents resulting from so few court decisions dealing with trade secrets further emphasizes the need for satisfactory legislation.

The owner of trade secrets or know-how must try to protect himself through various security measures and contractual arrangements. In *Forseco Japan, Ltd v Okuno et al.* (Hanrei Jihō [no. 624] 78, Nara Dist. Ct., 23 October 1970), the plaintiff obtained a temporary injunction order from the court against his former employees who had established a competing company in violation of their employment contracts which forbade competition. By rejecting the respondents' argument that the contracts were an unconstitutional infringement on their freedom of choice of occupation, the court upheld the use of contracts as protection against trade secret misappropriation.

But the still pressing need for satisfactory legal remedies is shown by another court case, the only one considering the legal status of trade secrets. In *Deutsche Werft A. G. v Chūetsu-Waukeshiya, Inc.* (17 Kakyū Minshū 769, Tōkyō High Ct., 5 September 1966), a German licenser of know-how to an American company appealed to the Tōkyō High Court a district court decision that refused to order temporary injunction against the use of know-how by the American licensee's joint venture company in Japan. The High Court dismissed the appeal, holding that "know-how has property value and yet it has not been recognized as a legal right." See also INTANGIBLE PROPERTY RIGHTS.   DOI Teruo

ko

(household). Smallest administrative unit of the KOKUGUN SYSTEM of land division that was inaugurated by the RITSURYŌ SYSTEM of government in the mid-7th century. The *ko* (also known as *gōko*) was a subunit of the *ri* (hamlet or village, later renamed *gō*), 50 *ko* making up one *ri* or *gō*. The *ko* served as the basic unit for the allocation of land (see HANDEN SHŪJU SYSTEM) and various taxes (see SO, YŌ, AND CHŌ). *Ko* differed in size, ranging from around 10 to 100 people and, in addition to husbands, wives, parents, and children, also included such people as cousins, nephews, nieces, other relatives and close friends called *kikō*, slaves, and vassals. Thus it may be thought of as a legal fiction differing from the IE (household), or naturally occurring family group.

Each *ko* was entered into a family register *(koseki).* During the Nara period (710–794), the family register ordinarily included, in addition to the *koshu* or household head's family, several families whose heads were relatives of the *koshu.* These subhouseholds were called *bōko* (houses) or *betsubo.* During the Nara period, the *bōko* was regarded as the basic unit for levying taxes.

Since the *ko* was an administrative unit and the position of the *koshu* was based on public law, the household head did not have the same legal rights vis-à-vis other household members as the *koshu* under the Meiji Civil Code. He did not, for example, have the right to withhold approval of a member's marriage or the right to designate the place of residence.

Starting with the code of 670 (KŌGONEN-JAKU), the drawing up of household registers was, in principle, carried out every six years. However, the practice fell into disuse in the middle of the Heian period with the collapse of the *ritsuryō* system. Thereafter, until modern times, nothing resembling the family register existed. See also HOUSEHOLD REGISTERS.　　　　　　　　*UEDA Nobuhiro*

Koban

Koban of the Edo Period				
Name	Period minted	Period in use	Weight	Net gold content
Keichō *koban*	1601–1695	1601–1738	17.85 gm or 0.63 oz	84.29%
Genroku *koban*	1695–1716	1695–1717	17.85 gm or 0.63 oz	57.37%
Kenji *koban*	1710–1714	1710–1719	9.38 gm or 0.33 oz	84.29%
Shōtoku *koban*	1714	1714–1738	17.85 gm or 0.63 oz	84.29%
Kyōhō *koban*	1716–1736	1716–1860	17.85 gm or 0.63 oz	86.79%
Gembun *koban*	1736–1819	1736–1827	13.13 gm or 0.46 oz	65.71%
Bunsei *koban*	1819–1828	1819–1842	13.13 gm or 0.46 oz	56.41%
Tempō *koban*	1837–1858	1837–1860	11.25 gm or 0.40 oz	56.77%
Ansei *koban*	1859–1860	1859–1874	9.00 gm or 0.32 oz	56.78%
Man'en *koban*	1860–1867	1860–1874	3.30 gm or 0.12 oz	56.78%

NOTE: The names of *koban* derive from those of the eras in which they were first minted except Kenji *koban,* which derives from a Chinese character that appears on the coin.
SOURCE: Tōkyō Daigaku Shiryō Hensanjo, ed, *Tokushi biyō* (1966).

kō

Religious or fraternal associations which originally developed from lecture meetings on Buddhist sutras and later spread among the Shintō faithful as well. *Kō* have exerted a large influence, with some being organized by religious leaders for the propagation of their faith and others being organized regionally for some economic or educational purpose.

Kō such as the Saishōkō, Ninnōkō, and the Hokkekō, all lecture meetings on Buddhist sutras, were popular among the aristocracy during the Nara (710–794) and Heian (794–1185) periods. The institution spread rapidly among the general populace during the Kamakura period (1185–1333). Several Buddhist *kō* formed at this time, such as the Daishikō and the Amidakō, survive to this day. Within Shintō, the Isekō and the Kumanokō are among the oldest and the largest. Many Shintō sects which became independent in the Meiji period (1868–1912), such as the Izumo Ōyashirokyō and the Ontakekyō, could not have done so without the structural base provided by their *kō.* Many *kō* are regional organizations, with those related to SHUGENDŌ (mountain worship) being particularly prominent. Also associated with mountain worship are the Fujikō or Fuji associations. The *daisankō,* associations for the purpose of sending a representative on a pilgrimage for the collective benefit of all the members, developed in both Buddhism and Shintō. The *kō* also came to function as mutual assistance associations, leading to the development of the *tanomoshi* and the MUJIN, both *kō* for financial assistance. The Ebisukō and Daikokukō are examples of this type of *kō,* which developed as early as the Kamakura period and flourished with the rise of commerce in the Edo period (1600–1868).
　　　　　　　　UEDA Kenji

kōan

(Ch: *gongan* or *kung-an*). Literally, "public cases." The conundrums or propositions used by the RINZAI SECT (Ch: Linji or Lin-chi) of Buddhism as an aid to meditation and enlightenment. The collection of *kōan* began in the Song (Sung) period (960–1279) in China; the two classics are the *Blue Cliff Records* (Hekiganroku; Ch: Biyan-lu or Pi-yen-lu, 1125) and the *Gateless Gate* (Mumonkan; Ch: Wu-menguan or Wu-men-kuan, 1228). "Does a dog have Buddhanature?"; "What is the sound of one hand clapping?"; and "Buddha preached 49 years, and yet his broad tongue never once moved" are typical *kōan.* The rational impasse created by these seemingly unsolvable *kōan* paradoxes helps to free the mind from its normal conceptual frame and open the novice to a pure encounter with reality-as-is. In Japan, the *kōan* tradition was systematized by HAKUIN. The Rinzai tradition claims *kōan* as effecting the true "sudden enlightenment" but the SŌTŌ SECT tradition gives less validity to it. See also ZEN.　　　　　　　　*Whalen LAI*

Kōan Chōsa Chō → Public Security Investigation Agency

kōan jōrei

(prefectural public safety ordinance). A generic term for ordinances made by local governments for the regulation of assemblies, parades, and other types of demonstration. Before World War II this type of popular gathering was controlled by the PUBLIC ORDER AND POLICE LAW OF 1900 (Chian Keisatsu Hō). This law was abolished immediately after the war and since then no national law has replaced it. At least some branches of the Occupation administration advised respective local governments to enact their own by-laws to replace the sweeping Public Order and Police Law. Most *kōan jōrei* require that permits for public meetings or demonstrations be obtained from the police or respective public safety commissions a certain number of days before the day of the proposed gathering. Thus *kōan jōrei* inevitably involve the controversial issue of whether they are an unconstitutional "previous restraint" on FREEDOM OF ASSEMBLY as guaranteed by article 21 of the 1947 constitution. In 1960 the Supreme Court, in upholding the validity of the Tōkyō ordinance, did away with doubts about their constitutionality. See TŌKYŌ ORDINANCE DECISION.　　　　　　*OKUDAIRA Yasuhiro*

Kōa Oil Co, Ltd

(Kōa Sekiyu). Oil-refining firm affiliated with Caltex Co. The company was established in 1933 for the domestic production of high-grade lubricating oil, but later turned to the production of airplane fuel and other materials to meet military demand. Following World War II, Caltex bought a 50 percent interest in the company and supplied it with crude oil, which it refined and sold to NIPPON OIL CO, LTD. In 1955 it joined with companies of the Mitsui group to establish MITSUI PETROCHEMICAL INDUSTRIES, LTD, to which it now supplies raw materials at the petrochemical complex in Iwakuni in Yamaguchi Prefecture. Kōa was an early distiller of petroleum coke, which it sells through MITSUBISHI CORPORATION. Sales for the fiscal year ending March 1982 were ¥630 billion (US $2.6 billion) and capitalization stood at ¥6.0 billion (US $24.9 million). The main office is in Tōkyō.

koban

Gold coins with a face value of one *ryō* (a standard monetary unit), in general circulation during the Edo period (1600–1868). *Koban* were thin coins, elliptical in shape (3.5 × 7.5 cm or 1.4 × 3 in) and weighing about 4.76 *momme* (17.85 gm or 0.63 oz). The earliest *koban* issued in large quantities and circulated nationwide were the Keichō *koban.* These were issued by order of TOKUGAWA IEYASU. They were 84.29 percent gold, and thus at the time one *ryō* equaled 15.0 grams of gold. *Koban* were recalled and reissued 9 times during the Edo period in order to increase their number while reducing their gold content. As with the larger ŌBAN coins, this practice substantially debased their value; at times the gold content of a *koban* (and thus a *ryō*) fell aas low as about 1.8 grams of gold. See also KINZA, GINZA, AND ZENIZA; MONEY, PREMODERN.

kōban

(usually translated as "police box"). *Kōban*—or more correctly *hashutsujo* in urban areas and *chūzaisho* in the countryside—are the primary mechanism of police deployment in Japan. All of Japan is divided into jurisdictions for police stations, whose areas are further subdivided into jurisdictions for police boxes. *Kōban* are manned by police officers on a shift system. They range in size from those in quiet residential areas with one or two men per shift to the over-50-man mammoth *kōban* found in several Tōkyō entertainment districts, which resemble small police stations. *Kōban* usually have an office with desks and chairs in the front part and sleeping quarters and storage areas in the rear or upstairs. Police officers *(omawari san)* sit on duty in the office area to assist callers and patrol the surrounding neighborhood on foot or bicycle; they are required to visit each home in the *kōban's* jurisdiction twice a year. New policemen fresh out of police school are always given *kōban* duty as their first assignment.

Chūzaisho, which outnumber *hashutsujo* about two to one, are found in rural areas. A typical *chūzaisho* is a small house in which a police officer (called a *chūzai san*) lives with his family with an office attached to the front for handling police business. The policeman and his entire family, to an extent, are responsible for policing the village community. His relationship to the villagers is often quite intimate and is considered the ideal of police-community relations. As Japan continues to urbanize, however, *chūzaisho* are slowly being transformed into *hashutsujo* in areas near encroaching cities because of the increasingly heavy burden of police work on the lone police officer. See also POLICE SYSTEM. *Walter AMES*

kobanashi

(literally, "little story"). A term used in a general sense to refer to a variety of brief humorous stories popular from the 17th to the 19th century and in a restricted sense to designate a specific kind of short humorous story, the Edo *kobanashi,* produced in Edo (now Tōkyō) during the last quarter of the 18th century.

Humorous stories of varying length, often with a didactic slant, appear in several very early works, both Buddhist and secular, but it was not until the 17th century that collections of stories of this kind began to emerge as a unique and separate literary genre having the sole purpose of providing amusement for its own sake. Initially called *karukuchihon* (books of light-mouthed stories) in the Kyōto-Ōsaka area and *otoshibanashibon* (books of punch-line stories) in Edo, these compilations ultimately came to be known collectively and generically as *hanashibon* (talk books) and later in popular usage as *shōwahon* (books of funny stories) or *kobanashibon* (books of short humorous stories).

Approximately 1,000 *hanashibon* were published during the 200 years or so in which the genre was in vogue. One of the earliest compilations of such stories was the *Seisuishō* (Laughs to Wake You Up), traditionally attributed to the priest ANRAKUAN SAKUDEN (1554–1642). Completed in manuscript form by 1623 (according to the accompanying preface) and containing more than 1,000 stories (not all of which are humorous) arranged within 42 thematic rubrics, the *Seisuishō* is the largest work in the genre and certainly the most significant progenitor of those that followed. It was very likely preceded by one other collection, and possibly by two—the *Gigen yōkishū* (Collection of Jokes to Buoy Up the Spirits) and the *Kinō wa kyō no monogatari* (Events of Yesterday, the Tales of Today), anonymous works of far lesser scope and thematic coverage, presumably compiled by one or more members of military hegemon Toyotomi Hideyoshi's (1537–98) OTOGISHŪ (companion entertainers).

The first works to appear following the *Seisuishō* were intended for the amusement of the well-educated and not specifically for the newly rising CHŌNIN, or townsmen. Among them were *Hyaku monogatari* (1659, One Hundred Tales) attributed to ASAI RYŌI and *Shikatabanashi* (1659, Tales Told with Gestures) compiled by Nakagawa Kiun (1636–1705). Some of these works consisted of stories that were designed not merely to be read at one's leisure but to be told aloud, and hence they infused new vigor into the tradition of oral storytelling that had always been a common mode of diversion among all classes of society.

Toward the end of the 17th century, there was a shift in the authorship of the *hanashibon* from the literati writers of KANA-ZŌSHI, a variety of popular fiction of the 17th century, to members of the townsman class. Giving impetus to this trend was the emergence, in the three great centers of urban culture—Kyōto, Ōsaka, and Edo—of a new form of public plebian entertainment consisting of solo recitations of humorous stories. By 1681 Tsuyu no Gorobei (1643–1703) was reportedly staging performances on the more heavily traveled streets of Kyōto and at various popular gathering places in the city. At approximately the same time, similar performances were being offered in Ōsaka by Yonezawa Hikohachi (d 1714), and

somewhat later in Edo by Shikano Buzaemon (1649–99), the first to achieve prominence as a professional teller of humorous stories in eastern Japan. Apparently stimulated by the success of their performances (a small admission fee was charged), the new enterprising storytellers soon turned to publishing a series of *hanashibon* that presumably recorded the essence of their respective repertories.

As a result of a lack of innovation, there ultimately came a temporary decline in the popularity of the storyteller and in the *hanashibon* as a genre. But in 1772 the publication of *Kanokomochi* (Ricecakes of a Fawn), compiled by the KYŌKA ("mad verse") master Kimuro Bōun (1708–83) resulted in an immediate revival of the *hanashibon* genre in Edo. Bearing the unmistakable stamp of Edo pertness—the so-called *edomae*—Bōun's stories provided a model for the best of the *kobanashi* that followed. The next year, the success of *Kanokomochi* was duplicated by *Kiki jōzu* (Good at Listening), a work produced by the UKIYO-E artist Komatsuya Hyakki (dates unknown). These two works ushered in the so-called Golden Age of the *hanashibon,* and for the next decade as many as 15 new works in the genre appeared each year.

With the resurgence of the *hanashibon* genre came a subsequent revival of the art of comic storytelling. In 1786 Utei Emba (1743–1822), *kyōka* master and writer of GESAKU (light) fiction, with the collaboration of several other *gesaku* writers and *kyōka* devotees, including ŌTA NAMPO, Sakuragawa Jihinari (1762–1833), and SHIKATSUBE MAGAO, began to sponsor social gatherings devoted to the performance of the humorous story. So successful were these meetings that similar convocations (called *otoshibanashi no kai* or *hanashi no kai*) began to be held in Edo (and later in the Kyōto-Ōsaka area as well) on a regular basis, and it was not long before the vogue spread through all levels of Edo society. In spite of edicts issued by the Tokugawa shogunate forbidding such assemblies on the grounds that they were a source of moral corruption, public interest in this activity, either as spectator or amateur performer, continued to grow, and the convocations surreptitiously went on as before, now disguised as meetings devoted to readings in the classics and light fiction. From these groups there issued a large number of *hanashibon* that consisted essentially of stories presented at the *hanashi no kai* gatherings. At the same time, several of the more talented members of these groups took what had begun as a social diversion and turned it into a profession, thus eventually giving rise to the establishment of a new and still popular performing art that later in the 19th century came to be called RAKUGO (a variant reading for one of several ways in which *otoshibanashi* was written in Chinese characters). With the rise of professionalism in the art of comic storytelling there came a final decline in the *hanashibon* as a published genre, and the long humorous story *(nagabanashi)* eventually replaced the much shorter *kobanashi* form as the focal point of *rakugo* performances. This development did not spell the demise of the *kobanashi* but merely relegated it to the subordinate position it still occupies as a device to warm up an audience for appreciation of the long story and its inevitable concluding punch line.

—— R. H. Blyth, *Japanese Humour* (1957). R. H. Blyth, *Oriental Humour* (1959). Kojima Teiji, *Rakugo sambyakunen* (1966). Koshiba Chiichi, "Hanashibon," in *Zōho kaitei Nihon bungaku daijiten* (Shinchōsha, 1949–52). Maeda Isamu, *Kamigata rakugo no rekishi* (rev ed, 1966). Mutō Sadao, *Edo kobanashi jiten* (1965). Okada Toshio, ed, *Edo shōwashū,* vol 100 in *Nihon koten bungaku taikei* (Iwanami Shoten, 1966). Okitsu Kaname, *Nihon bungaku to rakugo,* in *Gendai no kyōyō,* vol 33 (Ōfūsha, 1970).

Miles K. McELRATH

Kobayakawa Hideaki (1582–1602)

Daimyō of the Azuchi–Momoyama period (1568–1600). A nephew of Kita no Mandokoro (1548–1624), wife of the national unifier TOYOTOMI HIDEYOSHI, and adopted as Hideyoshi's son, Hideaki was by 1594 readopted by Kobayakawa Takakage (1533–97), the daimyō of a domain assessed at 307,000 *koku* (see KOKUDAKA) at Najima in Chikuzen (now the city of Fukuoka), and at his retirement the next year succeeded to this domain. In 1597 Hideaki was appointed commander *(sōdaishō)* of Hideyoshi's invasion forces in Korea (see INVASIONS OF KOREA IN 1592 AND 1597), but the next year he incurred Hideyoshi's disfavor and was saved only by the intercession of the future shōgun TOKUGAWA IEYASU, being demoted to a 120,000-*koku* fief at Kitanoshō in Echizen (now the city of Fukui). In 1599, the year after Hideyoshi's death, he was restored to his previous domain in northern Kyūshū. In the Battle of SEKIGAHARA in 1600, Hideaki nominally adhered to ISHIDA MITSUNARI, and his contingent occupied an important position in the "Western Army";

he had, however, sent secret pledges to Ieyasu, and at a crucial point in the battle he attacked and routed the detachment of his supposed ally Ōtani Yoshitsugu (1559–1600), thus ensuring Ieyasu's victory. Hideaki was rewarded with a 510,000-*koku* domain at Okayama, the former possession of another erstwhile ally, UKITA HIDEIE; two years later, however, he died without issue.   *George* ELISON

Kobayashi

City in southwestern Miyazaki Prefecture, Kyūshū. The area is known for its rice, cultivated in the lowlands, and its cattle, raised in the foothills of the Kirishima volcanic range. Grapes and sweet potatoes are also grown. Pop: 40,033.

Kobayashi Ataru (1899–1981)

Businessman. Born in Yamanashi Prefecture. After studying at Waseda, Indiana, and London universities, he joined the Isawa Bank in his native prefecture. In 1929 he moved to Fukoku Chōhei Hoken (now Fukoku Mutual Life Insurance Co), where four years later he became the general manager. He was made president of the JAPAN DEVELOPMENT BANK upon its establishment in 1951, and served as chairman of the board for ARABIAN OIL CO, LTD, and JAPAN AIR LINES CO, LTD. He was a strong supporter of mainstream conservative politicians, including YOSHIDA SHIGERU and IKEDA HAYATO, and was counted among the four most powerful leaders in the postwar business-industrial community. See SAKURADA TAKESHI; MIZUNO SHIGEO; and NAGANO SHIGEO.   ITŌ *Hajime*

Kobayashi Hideo (1902–1983)

Critic. Kobayashi has exerted great influence on Japanese literature since the 1930s and helped to establish criticism as an independent literary form, concerning himself with the classical and modern literature of Japan and with critical studies of Dostoevsky, Mozart, and the impressionist school of painters.

He was born in Tōkyō in 1902 and was graduated from Tōkyō University, where he studied French literature. Inspired by his reading of Rimbaud, Baudelaire, and Valéry, and by the SHIRAKABA SCHOOL novelist SHIGA NAOYA, Kobayashi became a critic. He made his debut by publishing a prize-winning essay, "Samazama naru ishō" (All Manner of Designs), in a contest sponsored by the magazine *Kaizō* in 1929. In the late 1920s, the Japanese literary world was swept by a wave of interest in Marxist and post–World War I avant-garde literature. Kobayashi was critical of both schools, particularly the "deception through ideas" perpetrated by proletarian literature, and he chose instead to write about such contemporary Japanese novelists of the time as Shiga Naoya and YOKOMITSU RIICHI. He was unique among critics in emphasizing the individualistic nature of literature and pointing out that literature in Japan was in a state of crisis.

After the MANCHURIAN INCIDENT in 1931 and the ascendance of militarism, proletarian literature and modernism went into a state of decline, leaving the Japanese literary world without direction. Under such conditions, Kobayashi joined with KAWABATA YASUNARI, TAKEDA RINTARŌ, HAYASHI FUSAO, and others in 1933 to launch the literary journal *Bungakukai*. He believed that literature should be more relevant to society and advocated the practice of wide-ranging criticism. He published *Watakushi shōsetsu ron* (1935), a vigorous attack on the Japanese I-NOVEL (*watakushi shōsetsu*), which had shaped the mainstream of modern Japanese literature since the early 1900s. He also completed *Dosutoefusukī no seikatsu* (1935–37), a critical biography of Dostoevsky.

In 1937, war with China broke out, and Kobayashi traveled to the continent as a special correspondent to cover the hostilities. He also took to writing social commentary for newspapers, working to fulfill what he felt was his social responsibility as a literary art critic. The latter experience gave him new confidence in the culture and ethos of the Japanese and diverted his interest from the war.

Following the outbreak of World War II, Kobayashi completely reversed himself by ceasing to write modern criticism and social commentary. He turned to the traditional arts and literature of Japan, particularly the literature of the medieval period as represented by such figures as SAIGYŌ and MINAMOTO NO SANETOMO, and withdrew to the world of beauty and classical literature. His new interests are reflected in a collection of essays entitled *Mujō to iu koto* (1946, On *mujō*).

Japanese literature saw great changes after the defeat in 1945, but Kobayashi showed little interest in Japan's new postwar literature or

in literary criticism. He searched, instead, to discover the possibilities of the human spirit and began long studies on the lives and works of artists throughout the world. His chief works include *Mōtsuaruto* (1946), on the life of Mozart, *Gohho no tegami* (1951–52), a study of the letters of Van Gogh, and *Kindai kaiga* (1954–58), on modern painters. He also continued his study of Dostoevsky, viewing his existentialist thought as an outpouring of "pure conscience," and published studies of *Crime and Punishment* and *The Idiot*. Although Kobayashi's method of criticism went against the main current of literary criticism in postwar Japan, he held fast to his ideas and showed a deepening appreciation of the Japanese mind, sensibility, and historical traditions.

In the 1960s, Kobayashi began his study of MOTOORI NORINAGA, the 18th-century scholar of National Learning (KOKUGAKU), publishing a critical biography of him in 1977. He is a member of the Japan Arts Academy (since 1959) and a recipient of the Order of Culture (1967). His collected works are in *Kobayashi Hideo zenshū* (Shinchōsha, 1978–79, 13 vols).

📖 ——Etō Jun, *Kobayashi Hideo* (1962). Kamei Hideo, *Kobayashi Hideo ron* (1972).   YOSHIDA *Hiroo*

Kobayashi Ichizō (1873–1957)

Businessman and politician. Born in Yamanashi Prefecture. Graduate of Keiō Gijuku (now Keiō University). Kobayashi joined MITSUI BANK, LTD, in 1893. He participated in the establishment of Minoo Arima Railway (now HANKYŪ CORPORATION) in 1906, becoming president in 1927 and chairman in 1934. He developed a unique way of managing the railroad company by combining it with housing and land developments, an amusement park, and a department store. Kobayashi became involved in the entertainment business by establishing the TAKARAZUKA KAGEKIDAN (Takarazuka Girls' Opera Company) and TŌHŌ CO, LTD, in 1913. While holding executive positions in electric power and railroad companies, Kobayashi served as commerce and industry minister in the second Konoe cabinet (1940) and as state minister in the Shidehara cabinet (1945).
          MAEDA *Kazutoshi*

Kobayashi Issa → Issa

Kobayashi Kiyochika (1847–1915)

Painter, illustrator, and UKIYO-E print designer; one of the first traditional artists to formally study Western painting; particularly noted for his atmospheric landscapes and reportorial prints published during the Sino-Japanese War of 1894–95 and the Russo-Japanese War of 1904–05.

Kiyochika was born in the Asakusa district of Edo (now Tōkyō), the ninth and last son of a government warehouse supervisor named Kobayashi Mohei. On the death of his father in 1862, Kiyochika was recognized as the most capable member of the family and was entrusted with its leadership in spite of his age. In the late 1860s, following the restoration of the emperor, the shōgun's warehouses failed and Kiyochika retired to Shizuoka with his mother and lived there for some time in poverty. When his mother died he determined to return to Tōkyō but stopped en route at Yokohama where he met Shimooka Renjō (1822–1914), the pioneer of photography in Japan, and Charles WIRGMAN, the expatriate English painter, who taught him the rudiments of Western oil painting. After arriving in Tōkyō, he acquired more skill in Japanese-style painting from KAWANABE GYŌSAI and SHIBATA ZESHIN.

The 100 or more horizontal landscape prints for which he is most remembered today, and which have earned him the title of the HIROSHIGE of the Meiji period (1868–1912), were published between 1876 and 1881, mostly by Matsuki Heikichi and Fukuda Kumajirō. During this period he also began to contribute illustrations to magazines, and from 1885 on, illustrations for books and monthly periodicals occupied much of his time. During the wars with China and Russia, Kiyochika was an active propagandist, designing caricatures to disparage the enemy and heroic triptychs to glorify the Japanese. These triptychs, with their snowfalls, sudden explosions, and bursts of light, have pictorial and technical qualities that link traditional woodblock prints of the *ukiyo-e* school with modern "creative prints" or *sōsaku hanga*. In the last years of his life, Kiyochika traveled extensively throughout Japan, painting and sketching. He fell ill on one of these journeys and died on 28 November 1915.

Kiyochika's only pupil was Inoue Yasuharu, or Yasuji (1864–89), who designed many landscapes, some in Japanese style, others in a more Western style. Over a quarter of Yasuharu's more than 130 quarter-block, or postcard-sized, views of Tōkyō are reduced copies of larger prints by Kiyochika, and others may have been based on his teacher's sketches or designs. He died very young, and all his prints, which were signed either Tankei or Yasuji, were published in the 1880s.

Another artist, Ogura Ryūson, designed a few landscapes in Western style which were published in 1880 and 1881. They are obviously modeled on Kiyochika's landscapes, but the direct relation between the two men is unclear. *Roger* KEYES

Kobayashi Kokei (1883–1957)

Japanese-style painter (real name Kobayashi Shigeru); born in Niigata Prefecture. Orphaned at an early age, he went to Tōkyō in 1899 to study with the painter Kajita Hanko (1870–1917). Fellow students were MAEDA SEISON and Okumura Dogyū. His paintings in this period show a gradual change from representational art to the more decorative styles of YAMATO-E and RIMPA. Traveling to Europe with Maeda in 1922, he made a copy of the *Admonitions of the Instructress to the Palace Ladies*, attributed to the 4th-century Chinese painter Gu Kaizhi (Ku K'ai-chih), at the British Museum. With a renewed interest in ancient East Asian art, he produced one masterpiece after another in the so-called neoclassic style, based on a study of traditional *yamato-e* scrolls (see EMAKIMONO). He taught at the Tōkyō Bijutsu Gakkō (now Tōkyō University of Fine Arts and Music) from 1944 to 1950 and was awarded the Order of Culture in 1950.

Kobayashi Masaki (1916–   )

Film director noted for works that criticize Japanese social mores. Kobayashi was educated at Waseda University in philosophy. He joined Shōchiku Studios (see SHŌCHIKU CO, LTD) in 1941, but was drafted into the military in January of 1942. He was taken prisoner in Okinawa, an experience that served as the subject for his first feature film, *Kabe atsuki heya* (1953, The Thick-Walled Room). This film set the tone for his work in its assertion that many men who were punished as war criminals after World War II were victims of a vicious system that let the real criminals go unpunished. He pursued in subsequent films this theme of the cruel and corrupting force that a rigid social order has over ordinary men. The most notable of these films are *Ningen no jōken* (1959–61, The Human Condition), a three-part, nine-and-one-half-hour work on the struggle of a soldier to survive World War II with his values intact; and *Seppuku* (1962, Harakiri), a critical examination of the 17th-century warrior code of ethics. *Seppuku* is universally recognized as his finest film. *Kaidan* (1964, Kwaidan), adapted from several tales of Lafcadio HEARN, also garnered international attention. His film, *Kaseki*, was made in eight one-hour installments for Japanese television in 1973 and then reedited and released in a three-and-a-half hour theatrical version. *Kaseki* concerns a man's reexamination of his values as he confronts his own mortality.

Kobayashi is the nephew of the late actress and director TANAKA KINUYO. *David* OWENS

Kobayashi Takiji (1903–1933)

Author. The most famous of the writers in the PROLETARIAN LITERATURE MOVEMENT in Japan. His entire output consisted of short stories and novellas, all of which were expurgated when printed or banned outright until after World War II.

He was born in Akita Prefecture, to a poverty-stricken family. With the assistance of a brother, Takiji's father migrated north with his family to Otaru in Hokkaidō, where he opened a small bakery in the poor section of town. In 1916 Takiji entered Otaru Commercial School, where he developed an artistic and literary talent. He organized a literary society which published the works of its members through 1920. In 1921, again with the support of his uncle, he entered Otaru Higher Commercial School. In the aftermath of the Russian Revolution, the 1920s in Japan coincided with the reemergence of the proletarian movement. The appearance in 1920 of the influential proletarian journal *Tane maku hito* (The Sowers) is testament to the liberal climate of the times in artistic circles.

In 1924, after graduating from school, Takiji found employment as a bank clerk. On the side he founded and edited the magazine *Clarté* with friends. This name was taken from the novel written by the French war writer Henri Barbusse (1873–1935). The *Clarté* Movement he founded espoused PACIFISM, social equality, and intellectual internationalism.

Takiji's humanitarianism focused initially on the principles espoused by the SHIRAKABA SCHOOL, but he became critical of its tenets and veered toward the realistic style of Russian writers like Dostoevsky and Gorky and of the Japanese proletarian writer HAYAMA YOSHIKI. Some of his early works dealt with the lives of prostitutes. With one such woman he formed a lifelong relationship based on a deep sympathy for her wretched circumstances.

The year 1927 marked the turning-point in Takiji's commitment to proletarian causes. He joined a group studying social problems, supported the labor union movement in Otaru, and threw in his lot with the proletarian literary movement. He secretly took part in the organizing of two strikes in that year, one on behalf of tenant farmers, the other of stevedores. But on 15 March 1928, leftists were rounded up throughout Japan (see MARCH 15TH INCIDENT). In Otaru 13 members of the Japan Communist Party were arrested. Takiji then wrote his first major work "Senkyūhyakunijūhachinen sangatsu jūgonichi" (The Fifteenth of March, 1928), in which he described the activities of the underground and the arrest and torture of its leaders. The work was published the same year in *Senki* (Battle Flag), the organ of the All-Japan Federation of Proletarian Arts. The magazine was banned, but eight thousand copies were sold before the crackdown. Takiji's literary fame grew, but police surveillance became more intense.

In the story "Bōsetsurin" (The Snowbreak), completed in 1929 but not published until 1947 when the manuscript copy was discovered, he described the intolerable conditions of the settlers along the river Ishikarigawa in Hokkaidō and their ultimate rebellion against their lot. In 1929 Takiji also wrote "Kani kōsen" (tr "The Factory Ship," 1973), the most celebrated work in Japanese proletarian literature. It deals with the brutal conditions under which several hundred men and boys slave aboard a factory ship in the Okhotsk Sea. Their gradual awakening under the guidance of organizers to their own strength in unity forms the core of the story. The initial attempt at a strike fails because of a lack of solidarity among the men; the majority of them hang back as they watch the strike leaders being taken off the ship by armed sailors of a cruiser of the Imperial Navy. But this outcome serves to disillusion and awaken those who had believed that the navy was there only to protect the factory ships and the workers; the men are now aware of the link between capitalism and militarism and the resultant exploitation of workers. The organization is better for the second strike. It succeeds, and management is forced to capitulate.

Takiji had read an account of such a strike two years earlier and had done considerable research on the incident. When he submitted the story to the publishers, he said that he had intentionally created no single hero in the story, that the collective hero was the workers, and that he had deliberately adopted a simple style so that the story would be accessible to the least educated. When "Kani kōsen" was published, it created a furor and enhanced Takiji's reputation. About 15,000 copies were sold before it was suppressed. It appeared only in a bowdlerized edition until 1948.

In 1929 Takiji wrote "Fuzai jinushi" (tr "The Absentee Landlord," 1973), which was also based on an actual event that took place in 1926 when a group of tenant farmers, protesting the inequitable assessment of fees, took their case to court, carried out public demonstrations in which they were joined by labor unions, and won their case. As in "Kani kōsen," a group of unorganized laborers, gradually awakened through indoctrination to their power, bring the absentee landlord, whose authority had been absolute, to his knees. An interesting feature in this story is the extent to which the farm women also participate in the rallies and demonstrations. Unlike "Kani kōsen," however, "Fuzai jinushi" was not a critical success.

His bank's role as an agent in the exploitation of farmers and land in Hokkaidō was exposed by Takiji in "Fuzai jinushi." The result was that, late in 1929, he was summarily dismissed from his post. He then went underground. On 20 February 1933, he was lured to a rendezvous by an undercover police agent and arrested. He was tortured during interrogation and died the same day.

Other representative works are "Higashi Kutchan kō" (1928, Journey to East Kutchan), "Kōba saibō" (1930, Factory Cell), "Orugu" (1931, The Organizer), "Yasuko" (1931), "Numajiri Mura" (1932, Numajiri Village), "Tōseikatsusha" (1932, Life in the Communist Party), "Tenkeiki no hitobito" (1932, Men in Transition), and "Chiku no hitobito" (1933, Men of the Zone).

📖 ——Works by Kobayashi: *Kobayashi Takiji zenshū,* 15 vols (Shin Nihon Shuppansha, 1968–69). *The Cannery Boat and Other Japanese Short Stories* (1933). *The Factory Ship, and the Absentee Landlord,* tr Frank T. Motofuji (1973). Kubokawa Tsurojirō, *Kobayashi Takiji* (1950). Kurahara Korehito, *Kobayashi Takiji kenkyū* (1948). Kurahara Korehito, *Kobayashi Takiji to Miyamoto Yuriko* (1953). Odagiri Hideo, *Kobayashi Takiji* (1954). George Shea, *Left-wing Literature in Japan* (1964). Tezuka Hidetaka, *Kobayashi Takiji* (1963).   Frank T. MOTOFUJI

Kōbe

Capital of Hyōgo Prefecture, western Honshū, and one of Japan's leading ports. Overlooking ŌSAKA BAY and sheltered on the north by the Rokkō Mountains (Rokkōzan). It has a mild and dry climate. Its importance as a port goes back to the Nara period (710–794), when it was known as Hyōgo. It prospered in the trade with China and particularly in the 15th and 16th century TALLY TRADE with the Ming dynasty. Under the ANSEI COMMERCIAL TREATIES (1858) Kōbe was designated an open port, although for political reasons it was not opened until several years later. In total value of import and export trade Kōbe ranks second in Japan, after Yokohama.

Kōbe is the largest industrial city in the prefecture, producing ships, railway cars, steel and iron, textiles, matches, and rubber, as well as *sake.* It is served by three major Japanese National Railways lines, the Tōkaido Main Line, the San'yō Main Line, and the super-speed Shinkansen, as well as by National Route No. 2 and the Hanshin Expressway. The city is known for its cosmopolitan atmosphere; the central shopping areas at Motomachi and "Sanchika-town," an underground mall, are especially popular. The Hakutsuru Art Museum houses Chinese and Japanese art. The complex of hot springs on Rokkōzan and numerous historical sites are also of interest. Area: 540.92 sq km (208.8 sq mi); Pop: 1,367,392.

Kōbe Steel, Ltd

(Kōbe Seikōsho). Integrated manufacturer of iron and steel. Japan's fifth largest producer of crude steel and largest producer of welding rods, the firm also manufactures heavy machinery and copper and aluminum products. Established in Kōbe in 1905 as a division of Suzuki Shōten, it became a subsidiary of that company in 1911. The firm grew rapidly because of the Japanese navy's increased demand for steel during World War I. The company subsequently began production of various types of industrial machinery. In 1921 it took over Harima Shipbuilding Co from Teikoku Steamship Co, Ltd. In 1929 Harima was set up as an independent company, eventually becoming ISHIKAWAJIMA–HARIMA HEAVY INDUSTRIES CO, LTD. Suzuki Shōten went bankrupt in 1927, but thanks to new products developed by its engineering and rolling mill divisions and to rising military demand in the 1930s, Kōbe Steel was able to recover its position in the industry. Today it controls a network of 22 overseas factories and employs 70,000 workers. Following World War II it set up four new companies: Shinkō Electric Co, Ltd, from its former heavy electric machinery division; Shinkō Shōji Co, Ltd, from its iron and steel sales division; Shinkō Engineering Co, Ltd, from its engineering division; and Shinkō Wire Co, Ltd, from its steel wire division. In the parent firm a manufacturing system was also established for four types of products: steel, welding rods, heavy machinery, and aluminum and copper. With the completion of the first blast furnace at the Kakogawa (Hyōgo Prefecture) steel plant in 1970, Kōbe Steel began manufacturing pig iron for steel-making and, with the introduction of sheet metals, became an integrated steel manufacturer. The firm has joint venture companies in Brazil, Canada, India, Nigeria, Qatar, Venezuela, and in several countries in Southeast Asia. Sales for the fiscal year ending March 1982 totaled ¥1.18 trillion (US $4.9 billion), of which sales of iron, steel, and welding rods constituted 63 percent; machinery 22 percent; and aluminum and copper products 15 percent. In the same year the export rate was 24 percent and capitalization stood at ¥101.2 billion (US $420.4 million). The head office is in Kōbe.

Kōbe University

(Kōbe Daigaku). A national, coeducational university located in Nada Ward, in Kōbe. Originally the Kōbe Higher Commerce School, founded in 1902, it became Kōbe University of Commerce in 1929, and then Kōbe University of Economics in 1944. Kōbe University was established in 1949 by combining this school with Hyōgo Higher School, Kōbe Technical College, Hyōgo Normal School, and Hyōgo Youth Normal School. Later Kōbe Medical College and Hyōgo Agricultural College merged with the university.

Kōbe

Houses in Ikuta Ward built by foreign residents in the late 19th century.

The university is known for its Research Institute for Economics and Business Administration. It maintains faculties of letters, education, law, economics, business management, science, medicine, engineering, and agriculture. Enrollment was 8,773 in 1980.

Kōbō Daishi → Kūkai

Kobori Enshū (1579–1647)

Prominent tea master, pottery connoisseur, garden designer, and architect; also a calligrapher and poet. Born in Ōmi Province (now Shiga Prefecture), the son of the commissioner of public works *(fushin bugyō)* under the national unifier TOYOTOMI HIDEYOSHI, Enshū himself served as *fushin bugyō* under the first three Tokugawa shōguns. In his youth he studied the tea ceremony with FURUTA ORIBE and later founded his own school of tea ceremony for courtiers and *daimyō.* He is reputed to have designed several famous teahouses in Kyōto, including those at the Ryōkōin and Kohōan subtemples of the DAITOKUJI. Tea gardens that offer varied views from every point along the path to the teahouse, such as those at the Konchiin subtemple of the NANZENJI and the KATSURA DETACHED PALACE, profited by his advice if not his design. His name has also been associated with the construction of several of the more famous castles and palaces in the Kyōto area, among them NIJŌ CASTLE. As a tea master, Enshū patronized a number of kilns, and his taste influenced the techniques and materials used in producing tea wares. Seven types of pottery became particularly associated with his name: Shitoro ware, Zeze ware, Kosobe ware, AGANO WARE, TAKATORI WARE, ASAHI WARE, and Akahada ware. He is known to have practiced the art of flower arrangement as well. Among his students was the calligrapher and painter SHŌKADŌ SHŌJŌ.

Kobotoke Pass

(Kobotoke Tōge). Located on the border of southwestern Tōkyō and Kanagawa prefectures, central Honshū. Situated northwest of the mountain TAKAOSAN, it was formerly a pass on the road Kōshū Kaidō, and remains of a former barrier station *(seki)* can still be seen. Presently the Chūō Main Line of the Japanese National Railways runs through tunnels under the pass. Several hiking courses are located around the pass. Altitude: 590 m (1,935 ft).

Kōbu Gattai Undō → Movement for Union of Court and Shogunate

Kōbun, Emperor (648–672)

The 39th sovereign *(tennō)* in the traditional count (which includes several nonhistorical emperors); said to have reigned January–August 672. Known to history as Prince Ōtomo, he was the eldest son and designated heir of Emperor TENJI. Soon after Tenji's death in early 672, however, Ōtomo was challenged for possession of the throne by his uncle Prince Ōama, who had raised armies in the provinces (see JINSHIN DISTURBANCE). Within six months Ōtomo was defeated and obliged to commit suicide. Prince Ōama ascended the throne as Emperor TEMMU in the following year.

Although the NIHON SHOKI (720) makes no mention of Prince Ōtomo's enthronement, the compilers of the DAI NIHON SHI (1657–1906) asserted that he had formally acceded as Emperor Ōtomo shortly before the rebellion. In 1870 Emperor MEIJI concluded that Ōtomo had indeed reigned for several months during 672 and gave him the posthumous name Kōbun. This ill-fated ruler is thought to have had literary talent; two poems ascribed to him, composed in classical Chinese, survive in the anthology *Kaifūsō* (751). KITAMURA Bunji

Kobunjigaku

(School of Ancient Rhetoric). One of the schools of Confucianism in the Edo period (1600–1868). Its most outstanding exponent was OGYŪ SORAI, who opposed the teachings of Wang Yangming (see YŌMEIGAKU) and Neo-Confucianism (SHUSHIGAKU) as well as the Kogigaku school (School of Ancient Meaning) of ITŌ JINSAI and claimed that the purpose of Confucian scholarship was the understanding of the original Confucian classics through the close study of the meaning of ancient words. Other representative scholars of the school were HATTORI NANKAKU and DAZAI SHUNDAI. The school was also known as the Ken'engaku school, an allusion, through alternate pronunciations of the Chinese characters involved, to Kayabachō, the district of Edo (now Tōkyō) in which Sorai lived.

kōbusen

(more correctly, Kōbu *tsūhō,* Kōbu currency). Chinese copper coins cast during the Hongwu (Hung-wu; J: Kōbu) era (1368–98) of the Ming dynasty. The coins were of five different sizes, with denominations ranging from 1 *mon* to 10 *mon,* and were imported during the Muromachi period (1333–1568). Together with EIRAKUSEN, coins of the Yongle (Yung-le) era (1403–24), they remained in use until the beginning of the Edo period (1600–1868). Chinese coins were used in Japan throughout the Kamakura (1185–1333) and Muromachi periods; although the number in circulation was never very great, they were accepted as sound currency in business transactions (see ERIZENI). In the late Muromachi period facsimiles of *kōbusen,* called *kajikisen,* were cast in Japan.

kobushi

Magnolia kobus. A deciduous tree of the family Magnoliaceae which grows wild in mountainous regions throughout Japan and is also widely planted as an ornamental. Its distribution also includes the southern part of Korea. It reaches a height of about 8 meters (26 ft), and the erect trunk grows numerous branches. The twigs are green and give off a pleasant scent when broken. The leaves are alternate and oval. The fragrant white flowers open at the branch tips before leafing in spring and have six petals, each about 6 centimeters (2.5 in) long. After flowering, the tree bears fruits which split open in autumn to reveal red seeds hanging from white strings.

A variety called *kitakobushi,* which grows wild in mountainous areas of the Sea of Japan coast in Hokkaidō and northern and central Honshū, has larger flowers and leaves than those of the *kobushi.* The *shidekobushi (M. stellata),* said to be native to China, is also widely planted in Japan. It generally resembles the *kobushi* but has large reddish white flowers with 12–18 slender petals.

The *kobushi* was exported to the United States and England in the early 19th century as an ornamental tree. In recent years it has attracted attention as a handsome and vigorous tree which is tolerant of pollution. MATSUDA Osamu

Kobushigadake

Also called Kobushidake. Mountain at the junction of Saitama, Yamanashi, and Nagano prefectures, central Honshū. It forms the watershed between the rivers Shinanogawa and Arakawa. In the Chichibu Mountains, it is part of CHICHIBU–TAMA NATIONAL PARK. The highest point is Sampōzan (2,483 m; 8,144 ft).

kobushin

Vassals of the Tokugawa shogunate, largely HATAMOTO or GOKENIN with fiefs or stipends of less than 3,000 *koku* (1 *koku* = about 180

liters or 5 US bushels; see KOKUDAKA) of rice, who were assigned to no official posts because of age, illness, or incompetence. The term means literally "minor construction" and was originally applied to vassals assigned to such work as the repair of castles rather than military duties. Divided into 6 to 12 groups, they were at first supervised by the Edo Castle administrators (RUSUI) and, after 1719, by the shogunal senior councillors (RŌJŪ).

Kobutori jijii

("The Old Man Who Lost His Wen"). Folktale. An old man with a wen on one of his cheeks comes upon a company of carousing demons (ONI; TENGU in some versions) and entertains them with song and dance. As a reward the demons remove his wen. Hearing of this, his neighbor, also afflicted with a wen, decides to perform for them too, but he is so clumsy that the angry demons put a wen on his other cheek. This comic tale is found in the 13th-century UJI SHŪI MONOGATARI and in the *Seisuishō,* a collection of humorous stories published in the 17th century. SUCHI Tokuhei

Kōchi

Capital of Kōchi Prefecture, Shikoku, on Urado Bay. The city developed as a castle town after a castle was constructed in 1603 by YAMANOUCHI KAZUTOYO. Kōchi is today the main economic, cultural, and transportation center of the prefecture. Cement, steel, chemicals, lumber, shipbuilding, paper, and foodstuff industries flourish. Rice and vegetables are grown in the rural districts. Tourist attractions are the ruins of Kōchi Castle, Godaisan Park, the scenic coastline of KATSURAHAMA, and Tosa Shrine, built by CHŌSOKABE MOTOCHIKA. Pop: 300,830.

Kōchi Plain

(Kōchi Heiya). Located in central Kōchi Prefecture, Shikoku. Bordering the Pacific Ocean and separated by step faults from the Shikoku Mountains in the north, it consists of alluvial sediment of the rivers Monobegawa and Niyodogawa. In the Nankai Earthquake of 1946, the center of the flood plain sank approximately 1 m (3 feet). A warm climate allows two rice crops a year in some areas; vegetables are grown in greenhouses. The major city is Kōchi. Area: approximately 140 sq km (54 sq mi).

Kōchi Prefecture

(Kōchi Ken). Located in southern Shikoku and bounded by Ehime Prefecture to the northwest, Tokushima Prefecture to the northeast, and the Pacific Ocean to the south. The terrain consists of the Ishizuchi Mountains, with small level areas concentrated along rivers. The climate is among the warmest in Japan, with heavy precipitation. Subtropical vegetation flourishes in the southern coastal regions.

It was known as Tosa Province under the ancient provincial system (see KOKUGUN SYSTEM). During the Sengoku period (1467–1568) it came under the control of several warrior families, including the Chōsokabe and the Yamanouchi. In the latter part of the Edo period (1600–1868) *samurai* from Tosa, such as SAKAMOTO RYŌMA and NAKAOKA SHINTARŌ, were prominent in the movement to overthrow the Tokugawa shogunate. The prefecture's present name dates from 1871, and its current boundaries were established in 1880.

Agriculture is the main occupation, and Kōchi is one of the few places in Japan with a climate that permits the harvesting of two rice crops annually (in some areas). Forestry and fishing are also important. Apart from woodworking and papermaking, which draw on the prefecture's abundant lumber resources, there is very little industry.

Tourist attractions include the coastal scenery of the cape ASHIZURIMISAKI (the main attraction of ASHIZURI–UWAKAI NATIONAL PARK), the cape MUROTOZAKI, the KATSURAHAMA seacoast, and the unspoiled mountain areas to the north. Kōchi is also known as a center for the breeding of fighting dogs. Area: 7,107 sq km (2,743 sq mi); pop: 831,283; capital: Kōchi. Other major cities include NANKOKU, TOSA, and NAKAMURA. See map on following page.

kōchō jūnisen

(twelve coinages of the imperial court). Twelve types of copper coin minted in ancient Japan; they were issued by the court during the

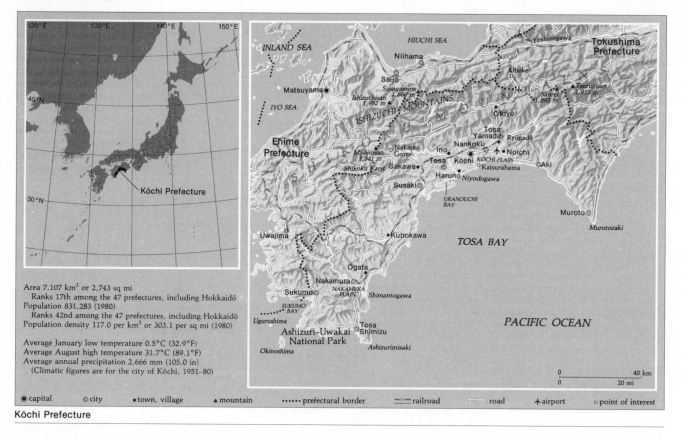

Area 7,107 km² or 2,743 sq mi
  Ranks 17th among the 47 prefectures, including Hokkaidō
Population 831,283 (1980)
  Ranks 42nd among the 47 prefectures, including Hokkaidō
Population density 117.0 per km² or 303.1 per sq mi (1980)

Average January low temperature 0.5°C (32.9°F)
Average August high temperature 31.7°C (89.1°F)
Average annual precipitation 2,666 mm (105.0 in)
  (Climatic figures are for the city of Kōchi, 1951–80)

◉ capital　　◎ city　　● town, village　　▲ mountain　　••••• prefectural border　　═══ railroad　　═══ road　　✦ airport　　○ point of interest

Kōchi Prefecture

Nara (710–794) and Heian (794–1185) periods to demonstrate its authority to the people. The first Japanese coins, called WADŌ KAIHŌ, were modeled on those of the Chinese Tang (T'ang) dynasty (618–907) and were minted in 708 (Wadō 1); they were circular, with a square hole in the center and four Chinese characters inscribed on one side. In the following 250 years, 11 other types of coin appeared, all similar to the Wadō *kaihō*: Mannen *tsūhō* (760), Jingū *kaihō* (765), Ryūhei *eihō* (796), Fuju *shimbō* (818), Jōwa *shōhō* (835), Chōnen *taihō* (848), Jōeki *shimpō* (859), Jōgan *eihō* (870), Kampyō *taihō* (890), Engi *tsūhō* (907), and Kengen *taihō* (958). These names are in fact the inscriptions on the coins; the first two characters in each case are either auspicious phrases or the names of the eras (see NENGŌ) in which the coins were issued, while the last two are various terms for "currency." The coins circulated only in a limited area around the capital and were used exclusively by the aristocracy: commoners still used grain and cloth as media of exchange. The use of these coins diminished as the power of the court declined. After the minting of 958, Japanese coins gradually disappeared, and imported Chinese coins (SŌSEN; KŌBUSEN; EIRAKUSEN) were used increasingly until the end of the 16th century, when the Japanese resumed the official minting of coins.

Kōda Aya (1904–　　)

Novelist; essayist. Born in Tōkyō, the second daughter of the novelist KŌDA ROHAN. She established her name as an essayist after World War II, when she wrote a series of articles about her late father, for whom she had long kept house, including "Shūen" (1947, Last Moments). She went on to write autobiographical fiction and won the Yomiuri Literary Prize for her story "Kuroi suso" (1954; tr "The Black Kimono," 1960). Other works include *Nagareru* (1955, To Flow), about an aging *geisha*; *Otōto* (1956–57, Younger Brother), and the essay collection *Chigiregumo* (1956, Tattered Clouds). She received the Japan Art Academy Award for *Nagareru* in 1956.

Kōdaiji maki-e

A type of MAKI-E lacquer ware popular in the Azuchi-Momoyama period (1568–1600). Named after the temple Kōdaiji in Kyōto, which owns some of the most important examples of this ware. Kōdaiji *maki-e* designs are often clear representations of flowers or

grasses, rather than whole landscapes, and are highly ornamental. The lacquer surface is frequently divided into contrasting fields, each with its own design.

The most famous examples of Kōdaiji *maki-e* are a pair of miniature shrines dated 1596 now located in the temple Kōdaiji and dedicated to the hegemon TOYOTOMI HIDEYOSHI and his wife. Other notable examples are part of the interior decoration of the main hall of the Tsukubusuma Shrine in Shiga Prefecture and the Sambōin hall of the temple DAIGOJI in Kyōto. Eventually Kōdaiji *maki-e* came to be applied more widely for household implements and utensils. A related type of lacquer ware, known as *namban maki-e* ("southern barbarian" *maki-e*), was designed mainly for export.

Characteristic Kōdaiji *maki-e* designs employ *hira maki-e* ("level sprinkled-picture"), in which gold or silver flakes are sprinkled onto black lacquer; although this is normally covered with a coat of raw lacquer and ground down to a flat surface, here it is left without being polished or ground down. This technique results in a distinctive gold tone and is known as *makihanashi* ("left as sprinkled"). Additional design elements may be added by "needle drawing" *(harigaki)*. These techniques are frequently used in combination with sprinkled gold or silver dust, *nashiji* ("pear-skin ground"), used in the decoration as well as the background. See also LACQUER WARE.

NAKASATO Toshikatsu

Kodai kenkyū

(The Study of Ancient Times). A collection of essays by folklorist ORIKUCHI SHINOBU, published in three volumes, 1929–30. One volume deals with Japanese literature, the other two with FOLKLORE STUDIES. The essays present Orikuchi's views, based on his profound knowledge of the early Japanese language, concerning basic Japanese traits as reflected in folklore and early literature. The literature volume includes original studies on such subjects as the 8th-century poetry anthology MAN'YŌSHŪ, the TALE OF GENJI, and SETSUWA BUNGAKU ("tale literature"); the volumes on folklore contain many seminal essays for the then newly developing discipline. Also included are extensive studies of ancient religious beliefs as revealed in folk customs. In addition, there are Orikuchi's reports on his research trips to Okinawa and to the island of Iki, which are highly valued as resource documents.

ŌTŌ Tokihiko

Kodaira

City in central Tōkyō Prefecture. A flourishing village on the highway Ōme Kaidō in the Edo period (1600–1868), from the 1920s it was the site of military installations, schools, and factories. The land occupied by military installations is now the site of large factories and housing complexes. Hitotsubashi University, Tsuda College, and Musashino Art University are located here. Pop: 154,610.

Kodaira Kunihiko (1915–)

Mathematician. Known internationally for his extensive work in various fields of mathematics including harmonic analysis, differential operators, complex analytic manifolds, and algebraic geometry. Born in Tōkyō, he received from Tōkyō University a mathematics degree in 1938 and a physics degree in 1941. In 1949 Kodaira was invited to the Institute for Advanced Study at Princeton University, and, until his return to Japan in 1967 to teach at Tōkyō University, he taught at Princeton, Johns Hopkins, and other American universities. He received the Fields Medal in 1954 and the Order of Culture in 1957. See also MATHEMATICS, MODERN.

Kodama Gentarō (1852–1906)

Army general. Born in Suō Province (now part of Yamaguchi Prefecture). Kodama fought in the BOSHIN CIVIL WAR, and, after the Meiji Restoration (1868), in the Saga and Satsuma rebellions (see SAGA REBELLION and SATSUMA REBELLION). As head of the Army Staff College, together with Major Klemens MECKEL, a German adviser, he worked for the adoption of the German military system. He served in the SINO-JAPANESE WAR OF 1894–1895, and afterward, as governor-general of Taiwan, he distinguished himself as an excellent administrator. Kodama was appointed army minister in the fourth ITŌ HIROBUMI cabinet (1900), remaining in that post in the succeeding KATSURA TARŌ cabinet, while concurrently serving as minister of both home affairs and education. Promoted to full general in 1904, during the RUSSO–JAPANESE WAR of 1904–05 he served under Commander in Chief ŌYAMA IWAO as chief of general staff of the Manchurian Army, and assisted General NOGI MARESUKE in the capture of Port Arthur. In 1906 he was named chief of the Army General Staff Office. *Mutsu Gorō*

Kodama Yoshio (1911–)

Right-wing leader. Born in Fukushima Prefecture and raised in Tōkyō. He was involved in right-wing politics from his youth, being imprisoned on two separate occasions (1931, 1932) for threatening acts against senior statesmen. In 1937 he went to Manchuria (then the puppet state of MANCHUKUO) and North China on a fact-finding mission for the Foreign Ministry. In 1941 he was commissioned by the Naval Air Force to set up a network (known as the "Kodama Kikan") in Japanese-occupied Shanghai to procure war matériel. After World War II, Kodama was imprisoned by the OCCUPATION authorities as a class-A war criminal. Released in 1948, he resumed his right-wing political activities. He quickly became a powerful behind-the-scenes manipulator, using capital he had amassed during the war to finance conservative parties and politicians. In 1976 he was prosecuted for his involvement in the LOCKHEED SCANDAL. *Harada Katsumasa*

kōdan

A genre of oral storytelling. Initially termed *kōshaku*, since the Meiji period (1868–1912) it has been known as *kōdan*. The word is used to refer to either the art or the story itself. Though considered with RAKUGO (humorous anecdotes) to be the most important of the recitational arts (at one time its popularity exceeded that of *rakugo*), it languished after the late Meiji period in the face of competition from new amusements such as NANIWA-BUSHI (ballads sung to musical accompaniment), movies, and records. Since World War II, because of its dated material and a dearth of new performers, it has declined even more. Until 1974 the Hommokutei, a performance hall in Tōkyō's Ueno district, was the center of efforts to preserve the art, but the troupe was subsequently rent by dissension; now there are four schools, with only a few performers.

Originally, lectures on historical and literary texts given before high-ranking personages were known as *kōshaku*, and these developed into the entertainment now known as *kōdan*. Because of this heritage, even today, the narrator always sits behind a desk, marking the rhythm of his words with a fan or wooden clappers. Though artists no longer read from texts, recitals are still called "readings."

During the Muromachi period (1333–1568) generals and *daimyō* sought to educate themselves by having scholars or members of their coterie of companions (*otogishū*) give lectures or relate tales. Much of their material came from GUNKI MONOGATARI, or medieval war tales. In the Edo period (1600–1868) masterless samurai (*rōnin*) in Kyōto and Ōsaka supported themselves by reciting stories to audiences of townsmen. Because they recited mostly from the TAIHEIKI, the 14th-century military romance, they were commonly called *Taiheiki* readers. They are considered to be the first *kōshaku-shi* or *kōshaku* performers. The first professional *kōdan* artist was Nawa Seizaemon; under government license he established a recitation hall called Taiheikiba at Akasaka Mitsuke in Edo (now Tōkyō) in 1700. The recitations were mainly derived from historical tales and martial chronicles, and the narrators prided themselves on their knowledge of history. In the latter half of the 18th century they enlarged their repertory to include incidents in the lives of townsmen, succession disputes in daimyō households, and the like. At the close of the Edo period, recitations concerning the lives of townsmen became more realistic, with dialogue being used to express the emotions of lovers. During the same period tales of vendettas, thieves, and heroic protectors of the downtrodden became popular. After the Meiji Restoration (1868) newly created material helped make *kōdan* more popular than ever. At one time there were as many as 50 recitation halls in Tōkyō alone. The number decreased drastically after the Tōkyō Earthquake (1923), but even so there remained six or seven halls in Tōkyō early in the Shōwa period (1926–).

Though initially *kōdan* were recitations of historical events, fictional elements were gradually added. It is quite evident that *kōdan* and Edo-period novels and dramas drew from each other. Midway in the Meiji period stenographic transcriptions of *kōdan* were made. These later gave rise to an independent form of "written" *kōdan*, which were anthologized in collections such as the TACHIKAWA BUNKO, and it was from these that the contemporary genre of popular fiction (*taishū bungaku*) evolved. *Nagai Hiroo*

Kōdansha, Ltd

One of Japan's largest publishing houses. The forerunner of Kōdansha was the Dai Nippon Yūben Kai (Greater Japan Oratorical Society), established in November 1909 by NOMA SEIJI (1878–1938). The society published its first magazine *Yūben* (Oratory) in February 1910 under the slogan "justice will fall if oratory declines." Noma also helped establish an oratorical club at the Tōkyō University law school, where he was employed as a clerk. He drew up plans to publish the speeches made in the club and in time became the editor and publisher of these speeches. The pre–World War II publishing activities of Kōdansha were based on Noma's confidence in the value of personal communication, exemplified by the slogans, "from mouth to mouth" and "from people to people."

Kōdansha was established in 1911 in order to publish a second magazine, called *Kōdan kurabu*. *Yūben* was to be an academic magazine, while *Kōdan kurabu* was to be recreational. Following the publication of these two magazines, Noma successively inaugurated other popular magazines, including SHŌNEN KURABU (1914), *Omoshiro kurabu* (1916), *Gendai* (1920), *Fujin kurabu* (1920), and *Shōjo kurabu* (1923). With the establishment of the magazine KINGU in 1925, Noma combined the names of the two publishing firms and renamed his company the Dai Nippon Yūben Kai Kōdansha. In 1926, Noma added *Yōnen kurabu*, the last of the so-called "Nine Magazines of Kōdansha." Kōdansha's magazines accounted for 70 percent of total magazine circulation in prewar Japan. *Kingu* was promoted as "the most interesting, the most instructive, the most inexpensive, and the most widely circulated magazine in Japan." Noma's aspiration was not only to make *Kingu* the best-selling magazine in Japan, but also to combine in it the recreational aspects of *Kōdan kurabu* and the more serious qualities of *Yūben*. Noma was thoroughly successful with *Kingu*, and the magazine was Kōdansha's most important publication during this period.

Kōdansha's publishing activities aimed at two standards: the "interesting" and the "instructive." Through this approach, Noma succeeded in creating a unique Japanese type of publication directed at the popular masses. After 1927, Noma advocated the theory that magazines should be of service to the country. To commemorate the anniversary of the issuance of the IMPERIAL RESCRIPT ON EDUCATION, Noma established the Kingu Prize to be given to persons who served the country well. A total of 6,862 persons were awarded this prize. During the 1930s, Noma's approach was called Kōdansha Bunka ("Kōdansha Culture") in contrast with the Iwanami Bunka ("Iwanami Culture" exemplified by IWANAMI SHOTEN PUBLISHERS) which was supported by intellectuals who were critical of Kōdansha's publications. The writer TOKUTOMI SOHŌ dubbed prewar Kōdansha a "privately operated Ministry of Education," and it is no exaggeration to say that Kōdansha contributed much to the education of the general masses that the government's Ministry of Education could not accomplish.

Japan's defeat in World War II destroyed completely the value system on which Kōdansha's publishing activities had relied and led to demands, particularly by the JAPAN BOOK PUBLISHERS ASSOCIATION, to investigate Kōdansha for the role it played in the war effort. This shook Kōdansha to its very foundation, and the crisis was only weathered by the resignation en masse of the company's officials, the discontinuation of the magazines Gendai and Kōdan kurabu, and the reorganization of the management system. NOMA SHŌICHI became Kōdansha's new president, but he was purged by the Allied Occupation authorities and prohibited from engaging in public activity. Until Noma was depurged in 1949, Kōdansha published without a president and rumors abounded that Kōdansha was on the verge of bankruptcy due to deteriorating business. When Noma returned to office, he led a drastic modernization and streamlining program that brought the company out of the worst crisis since its establishment.

The inauguration of the literary magazine Gunzō in 1946, SHISŌ NO KAGAKU in 1954, and the publication of NAKANO SHIGEHARU's best-seller Muragimo, also in 1954, reflect Kōdansha's concentrated efforts to change its prewar image. The 1957 discontinuation of Kingu, Kōdansha's best-selling prewar publication, after a vain attempt to adapt to the postwar situation, was symbolic of the change that had taken place. The publishing house changed its name in 1958 from Dai Nippon Yūben Kai Kōdansha to the current Kōdansha. The magazine Nippon was published from 1958 to 1966 without great success. As of 1982, Kōdansha was publishing 34 magazines, including monthlies and weeklies: for general readers, WASEDA BUNGAKU, Gendai, Shōsetsu gendai, Gunzō, Sōkai, Besuto kā gaido, Rikujō kyōgi, Shūkan gendai, and Chekkumeito; for women, Fujin kurabu, With, Wakai josei, and Yangu redī; for children and teenagers, Nakayoshi, Tanoshii yōchien, Otomodachi, Dizunīrando, Mimi, TV magajin, Gekkan shōnen magajin, Bessatsu shōjo furendo, Biggu myūjikku, Shūkan shōnen magajin, and Shōjo furendo. The most recent addition was Quark, a popular science magazine. Of the above magazines, the only one remaining from the prewar period was Fujin kurabu. The daily Nikkan gendai began publishing in 1975. The fundamental direction of Kōdansha since the war has been the pursuit of comprehensive mass publication and sales appropriate to postwar Japanese society. Compared with prewar days, Kōdansha has placed increased weight on the publication of books: in 1980, Kōdansha published a total of 1,565 titles and ranked first among Japan's publishers. But the central activity of the company remains the publication of mass magazines. Kōdansha established Kōdansha International, Ltd, which publishes English-language books, in 1963. Corporate earnings in 1980 were ¥100 billion (US $441 million), one of the highest in the publishing industry in Japan.

📖 ——Kōdansha, ed, Kōdansha no ayunda gojūnen (1959).

KAKEGAWA Tomiko

Kōda Rohan (1867–1947)

Novelist and poet. An idealist writer, Rohan was a leading figure in the Japanese literary world during the period of transition from premodern literature at the close of the 19th century. He captured much of the vitality and constructive idealism of Japanese society then in the early stage of modernization. Writing in a pithy pseudoclassical prose style modeled on that of the great 17th-century master Ihara SAIKAKU, Rohan was the last of a breed of well-educated men of letters in the classical East Asian tradition and a precursor of Japanese romanticism and symbolism.

Life——Rohan, born Kōda Shigeyuki in 1867 in Edo (renamed Tōkyō the following year), was the son of a minor samurai serving the Tokugawa shōgun. The Kōda family also produced other prominent offspring: the explorer GUNJI SHIGETADA (1860–1924,

Rohan's brother), the pianist and imperial tutor Kōda Nobu (1870–1946, sister), the scholar Kōda Shigetomo (1873–1954, brother), the violinist and imperial tutor Andō Kōko (1878–1963, sister), and the novelist KŌDA AYA (b 1904; Rohan's daughter). After private preschool lessons and modern elementary school, Rohan's education was irregular for financial reasons: a year at Tōkyō First Middle School, a year at Tōkyō English School, another year at a private academy of Chinese learning taught by the eminent Confucian scholar Kikuchi Shōken (1806–86), and three years of intensive reading at Tōkyō Library. Eventually prompted by a desire to be self-supporting, Rohan graduated from the government-financed telegraphers school in 1884. His employment record is equally sporadic: telegrapher (1883–87), associate staff writer of SHIMBUN SHŌSETSU for the YOMIURI SHIMBUN (1889–90), staff novelist of the Kokkai shimbun (1890–95), editor of a fiction journal, Shinshōsetsu (1895–96), and lecturer on Japanese literature at Kyōto University (1908–09). Rohan devoted a major part of his life to an intense study of writing and scholarly study which earned him a doctorate degree in literature in 1911 and membership in the Teikoku Geijutsuin (Imperial Fine Arts Academy) in 1937. From his literary debut with "Tsuyu dandan" (1889, Dewdrops), a Christian love story set in New York, until his last work, a prodigious commentary published in 1947 on the Shichibushū (Seven Collections) of the BASHŌ school of HAIKU, Rohan produced a massive amount of writing in diverse fields. His pen name, Rohan, means companion of the dew. Rohan's life spanned successive periods of dramatic change between the Meiji Restoration of 1868 and the end of World War II. He died of pneumonia in 1947.

Works——Isanatori (1891–92, The Whaler) is Rohan's only completed novel; it focuses on the ethical issue of karma versus human conscience. Fūryū mijinzō (1893–95, The Minute Storehouse of Life), his most expansive though unfinished novel, delineates his vision of the Buddhist cosmic order by means of a "chain-link structure." Sora utsu nami (1903–05, Waves Dashing against the Sky) represents his final attempt at realistic technique and pursuit of moral self-judgment. Rohan is best-known, however, for his early idealistic short stories charged with poetic passion, metaphysical vision, fertile imagination, and affirmation of the self. "Fūryūbutsu" (1889, Love Bodhisattva), his first sensational success, sublimates love into a religious impulse in a Pygmalion story about a Buddhist sculptor and his statue-turned bodhisattva; "Tai dokuro" (1890, Encounter with a Skull) is a mysterious tale in the NŌ play tradition; it teaches equality of all beings. In the novella Gojū no tō (1891–92, The Five-storied Pagoda), Rohan's best work, the Rohanesque hero is fully developed in the character of its singleminded carpenter-architect protagonist and the symbol of his idealism in the Buddhist pagoda. "Higeotoko" (1896, The Bearded Samurai) redefines samurai loyalty in affirming life over death. Rohan's experiments in realistic techniques were less than spectacular: "Tsuji jōruri" (The Wandering Balladeer) and its sequel "Nemimi deppō" (Surprise Gunshot), both of which came out in 1891, were studies of a profligate-turned-dedicated-merchant. Rohan was, however, very effective in creating evocatively haunting tales: "Shin Urashima" (1895, New Urashima) tells of a layman's attempt at enlightenment with the aid of a demon king. "Futsuka monogatari" (1898 and 1901, Tales of Two Days) is about a visit by the wrathful ghost of Emperor SUTOKU to the poet-monk SAIGYŌ, while Dogū mokugū (1905, Clay Image, Wooden Image) unfolds an eerie tale of metempsychosis. Beginning with "Yoritomo" in 1908, Rohan fashioned a new genre of historical fiction, which became a continuing favorite of readers, a form nearly perfected in "Ummei" (1919, Destiny), which answers its own question: "Does destiny exist as an actual force?" Besides composing a quantity of haiku and WAKA (31-syllable poems), Rohan wrote several long poems, a play, juvenile literature, travelogues, essays, scholarly discourses, and commentaries.

In the history of modern Japanese literature, long dominated by the confessional I-NOVEL, a typically Japanese genre, and its superfluous self-destructive heroes, Rohan is unique in his lofty visions of the world beyond, optimistic faith in man's perfectibility, advocacy of moral fortitude, and romantic belief in the power in art (and literature) as the supreme crystallization of human will and a means to salvation. Rohan synthesized Buddhist metaphysics, Taoist mysticism, Christian humanism, Confucian activism, and Japanese aestheticism into a bright microcosm of ideals and aspirations. His heroes and heroines, endowed as they are with uncompromising conviction in response to their callings, memorialize those nameless individuals who made Japan's modernization possible. Rohan's prose style, a synthesis of poetic diction and the vernacular known as *gazoku setchū*, masculine vigor, and fiery idealism proved beyond emulation or imitation.

■ ——Kōda Rohan, *Rohan zenshū*, 41 vols (Iwanami Shoten, 1950–58). *Pagoda, Skull, and Samurai: Three Stories by Koda Rohan*, tr Chieko Mulhern (1982). Fukumoto Kazuo, *Nihon runessansu shiron kara mita Kōda Rohan* (1972). Chieko Mulhern, *Koda Rohan* (1977). Seri Hiroaki, *Bummei hihyōka to shite no Rohan* (1971). Shinoda Hajime, *Sakuhin ni tsuite* (1971). Shiotani San (Dobashi Toshihiko), *Kōda Rohan* (1965–68). Yanagida Izumi, *Kōda Rohan* (1942). Chieko MULHERN

kōden

(public fields). Also pronounced *kuden*. The type of cultivated land most stringently controlled by the state under the RITSURYŌ SYSTEM of government established in the late 7th century. At first *kōden* were defined as fields to which the cultivator was not given exclusive right of usufruct. There were three main types of *kōden*: excess land *(jōden)* remaining after the distribution of field allotments (KUBUNDEN) to individual cultivators; government land *(kanden)* supervised by the Ministry of the Imperial Household; and land set aside to award to holders of high government office, possessors of high court rank, or temples and shrines. Thus *kōden* were distinguished from SHIDEN (private fields) or lands with fixed rights of usufruct. After the above-mentioned awards, the awarded land became *shiden*, which was categorized according to recipient as follows: *shikiden* (land awarded to holders of high government office), *iden* (holders of high court rank), *jiden* (temples), and *shinden* (shrines).

However, following the establishment in 743 of a law permitting permanent possession of newly opened or reclaimed rice land (see KONDEN EISEI SHIZAI HŌ), the distinction between *kōden* and *shiden* underwent a change: all cultivated lands other than those newly developed for private use *(konden)* and those granted to religious institutions *(shinden, jiden)* were called public lands. Hence, *kubunden, jōden,* and other lands that remained under government control came to be known as *kōden*. With the development of the SHŌEN (landed estate) system during the 10th century, lands on which the central government or provincial governors *(kokushi)* could levy taxes *(denso)* or high-interest loans of seed rice (SUIKO) were designated *kōden*. In spite of these changes in strict definition, the word *kōden* seems to have been used loosely to refer to cultivated land in general, just as the term *kōmin* (public people) was applied to the entire populace. YAGI Atsuru

Kōdōha

("Imperial Way" faction). Army faction during the 1930s led by generals ARAKI SADAO and MAZAKI JINZABURŌ. Strongly supported by junior officers and partial to men from the former Saga and Tosa domains (now Saga and Kōchi prefectures, respectively), the Kōdōha stressed spiritual training, an almost mystic devotion to the emperor, and "direct action" to achieve total national reform and military success over the Soviet Union. Its struggle with a rival faction, the TŌSEIHA, intensified in 1935 when Mazaki was dismissed from his appointment as inspector general of military education for his complicity in a 1934 plot by Kōdōha officers and Imperial Army Academy cadets to murder prominent politicians (see NOVEMBER INCIDENT). In retaliation Aizawa Saburō (1889–1936), a Kōdōha officer, murdered General NAGATA TETSUZAN, a Tōseiha figure whom he blamed for Mazaki's dismissal. In February 1936 pro-Kōdōha junior officers led an insurrection to establish a military government (FEBRUARY 26TH INCIDENT). Thirteen officers and six civilians involved in the mutiny were executed, and army discipline was reinforced. Accepting personal responsibility for their misbehavior, General Araki resigned from active service, and there ensued a purge of other powerful Kōdōha members from top army posts. Control of the army then passed into the hands of the Tōseiha.

Kōdōkan

An educational foundation for the teaching and promotion of JŪDŌ. Also refers to the gymnasium belonging to the foundation. Established in Tōkyō by KANŌ JIGORŌ in 1882, its membership numbers 1.1 million, of which 6,000 are women and more than 30,000 foreigners. TAKEDA Fumio

Kōdōkan ki jutsugi

A two-volume commentary on the *Kōdōkan ki* (1838, Record of the Kōdōkan); written 1845–49 by the author of the former work, FUJITA TŌKO, a scholar of the MITO SCHOOL. Tōko had written the *Kōdōkan ki* at the behest of the Mito *daimyō* TOKUGAWA NARIAKI to set forth the educational principles of the Kōdōkan, the Mito domainal school that Nariaki planned to establish. The school opened in 1841, and, again under orders from Nariaki, Tōko wrote a detailed commentary on his earlier work. Tōko's argument that everyone, from the shōgun to the lowliest commoner, should, each according to his station, loyally serve his lord—and by extension, the emperor—was to exert great influence on the proimperial, antiforeign SONNŌ JŌI thought of the mid-19th century.

Kōetsu → Hon'ami Kōetsu

Kōfu

Capital of Yamanashi Prefecture, central Honshū. Business, cultural, and transportation center of Yamanashi Prefecture. The base of the TAKEDA FAMILY during the 16th century, Kōfu flourished as a castle town and as a post-station town on the highway Kōshū Kaidō during the Edo period (1600–1868). Its industries are foodstuffs and textiles; it is also known for its wine and crystal ware. Attractions are the park at the site of Kōfu Castle, Takeda Shrine, and Yumura Hot Spring. Pop: 199,272.

Kōfu Basin

(Kōfu Bonchi). In central Yamanashi Prefecture, central Honshū. Bounded by the fault scarps of the Akaishi Mountains on the west and the Misaka Mountains on the southeast, it consists of piedmont alluvial plains of the rivers Fuefukigawa (the upper reaches of the Fujikawa) and Kamanashigawa. Grapes and peaches flourish there and rice is grown on the flood plain. Industrial areas are rapidly growing. The major city is Kōfu. Area: approximately 190 sq km (73 sq mi).

Kōfukuji

One of the two head temples of the HOSSŌ SECT of Buddhism, located in the city of Nara, Nara Prefecture. The origins of Kōfukuji go back to 669, when Kagami no Ōkimi (d 683), consort of the statesman FUJIWARA NO KAMATARI (614–669), established a temple at the family estate in Yamashina (in what is now Kyōto Prefecture) on behalf of her ailing husband. In this temple, first known as Yamashinadera, she installed a 16-foot (4.9 m) image of Shaka (Śākyamuni) Buddha, which had been commissioned by Kamatari in 645 when he crushed the SOGA FAMILY. With the establishment of the capital at Nara in 710, the temple was renamed Kōfukuji and moved to its present location within the city.

Kōfukuji grew rapidly in size and wealth as the family temple *(ujidera)* of the powerful FUJIWARA FAMILY and soon established its dominance over the KASUGA SHRINE, also founded by the Fujiwara. In 721 Empress Genshō (r 715–724) built the famous octagonal Hokuendō—a hall dedicated to the future Buddha Maitreya (J: MIROKU). In 723 the SEYAKUIN and HIDEN'IN were established. These institutions provided medical care and refuge, respectively, for the orphaned and impoverished. In 726 Emperor Shōmu built the Tōkondō, enshrining an image of the healing Buddha Yakushi (Bhaiṣajyaguru) in the hope of bringing about Empress Genshō's recovery from illness.

From the mid-8th century until the advent of the Meiji period (1868–1912) Kōfukuji was the leading center for Hossō studies in Japan. The Hossō doctrines were brought to Kōfukuji in 735 by the monk Gembō (d 746), who had spent 18 years in China. Gembō was followed at Kōfukuji by a line of distinguished Hossō scholars who constituted the Hokuji (Northern Temple, i.e., Kōfukuji) branch of the Hossō sect, which by the end of the 11th century had triumphed over the rival Nanji (Southern Temple, i.e., Gangōji) branch. Kōfukuji was known for its finely printed wood-block editions of Buddhist texts called *kasugaban* (Kasuga editions), which were struck in honor of the deity of the Kasuga Shrine, who was looked upon as a protector of the temple. Although *kasugaban* continued to be published through the Edo period (1600–1868), their heyday was in the

13th and 14th centuries. The earliest surviving *kasugaban* dates from 1088.

Owing to its strong Fujiwara backing, Kōfukuji became the dominant force in the province of Yamato (now part of Nara Prefecture) and owned extensive estates, from which it derived great revenue. To protect its interests it maintained an army of WARRIOR-MONKS *(sōhei)*, which it did not hesitate to use in its struggles with TŌDAIJI and ENRYAKUJI after the 10th century. Kōfukuji also frequently brought pressure to bear on the imperial court and its nominal patrons, the Fujiwara, by sending its underlings (JINNIN) at the Kasuga Shrine into Kyōto carrying consecrated tree branches *(shimboku)*, an act which usually sufficed to intimidate the authorities into accepting its demands. In 1180 the Heike warrior leader TAIRA NO KIYOMORI (1118–81) had Kōfukuji razed as punishment for its involvement in a conspiracy.

Kōfukuji was rebuilt under the sponsorship of the founder of the Kamakura shogunate, MINAMOTO NO YORITOMO (1147–99), who engaged KŌKEI, UNKEI (d 1223), and other great sculptors of the time to work on the temple. Through the Muromachi period (1333–1568) there was a steady erosion in the temple's landholdings, leading to its impoverishment. In 1600 the founder of the Tokugawa shogunate, TOKUGAWA IEYASU (1543–1616), sought to revive Kōfukuji as a purely religious establishment through an annual endowment of 25,000 *koku* of rice (see KOKUDAKA), which made possible the renovation and reconstruction of many of the temple buildings. In 1717, however, a disastrous fire gutted much of the temple complex, which by then consisted of 112 buildings. With the independence of the Kasuga Shrine in 1868 and the confiscation of most of the temple precincts three years later, Kōfukuji virtually became a defunct temple. In 1872 it formally affiliated itself with the powerful SHINGON SECT, but 10 years later declared its independence as a head temple of the Hossō sect. Surviving structures include the three-story pagoda (1143), the Hokuendō (1210), the Tōkondō (1415), the five-story pagoda (1426), the Nan'endō (1789), and the Kondō (1805). Kōfukuji also houses a rich collection of art treasures (see KŌFUKUJI TREASURE HOUSE).

Stanley WEINSTEIN

Kōfukuji Treasure House

(Kōfukuji Kokuhōkan). Located at the temple KŌFUKUJI in Nara. A collection, opened in 1959, of some of the finest sculpture in Japan dating from the 7th century through the Kamakura period (1185–1333). There are pieces attributed to such Kamakura sculptors as Jōkei, UNKEI, and Kōben. The few paintings include a 14th-century Kasuga mandala. This collection is essential to the study of Japanese sculpture, but many of the pieces are occasionally on extended loan to the national museums at Tōkyō, Kyōto, or Nara.

Laurance ROBERTS

kofun

(tomb mounds). Large tombs of mounded earth built mainly for deceased members of the ruling elite during the 4th to 7th centuries. Ranging in size from 15 meters (50 ft) in diameter to 32.3 hectares (80 acres) in area, these tombs are the greatest single source of information on the social and political organization and material culture of the Kofun period (ca 300–710; see HISTORY OF JAPAN: protohistory).

Early Kofun-Period Tombs —— The appearance of tomb mound building at the end of the 3rd century in Japan is so sudden that in the early postwar period it was thought by some archaeologists that the tombs reflected either a conquest or influence from outside Japan. The identity of the contributing society was eagerly sought among the tomb-building cultures of China and northern Korea–Manchuria, but in 1952 Kobayashi Yukio (b 1911) laid to rest these ideas by demonstrating that there were no direct similarities in mound shape or burial chamber construction between Japan and the continent.

In the 1970s, two kinds of mounded burials from the preceding Yayoi period (ca 300 BC–ca AD 300) were identified. One—a square, ditched grave *(hōkei shūkōbo;* see PREHISTORIC BURIALS) found near village sites on level ground—is not thought to be the prototype of the great tomb mounds, but another—a mounded grave *(funkyūbo)* discovered on hilltops—is regarded by some archaeologists to be the direct predecessor of tomb mounds. Though the topic is controversial and has yet to be resolved, tomb mound-building is considered to be an outgrowth of native burial practices.

Kōfukuji Treasure House

One of the noted sculptures at the Kōfukuji Treasure House, this representation in painted dry-lacquer of the Buddhist guardian deity Ashura (Skt: Asura) is a major example of 8th-century style and technique. Height 152.3 cm. 734. Kōfukuji, Nara. National Treasure.

The earliest tomb mounds of the Kofun period were built in the Kinai (Kyōto–Ōsaka–Nara) region. From there, tomb building spread to northern Kyūshū through the Inland Sea region in the early 4th century. Early tombs had either round or keyhole-shaped mounds, the latter so called in English because their profiles resemble the shape of old-fashioned keyholes when the tombs are viewed from the air (see illustration). Keyhole tombs may have either front-square and rear-round mounds *(zempō kōen fun)* or front-square and rear-square mounds *(zempō kōhō fun)*. The front mounds may have originally functioned as a place for funerary rites to be carried out; the main burial is usually in the rear mound.

The first tombs were constructed on existing hilltops overlooking fertile agricultural land. Burial facilities consisted of a wooden coffin buried directly in the summit of the mound or placed in a stone chamber of the *tateana sekishitsu* (literally, "vertical hole, stone chamber") style. To build this type of chamber, a pit was sunk into the top of the mound and lined with brick-sized stones. A floor of smooth clay was prepared to receive the wood coffin; then ceiling rocks were laid to seal this pit-style chamber, and earth was mounded over the top. Clay cylinders and various funerary sculptures (see HANIWA) were often embedded in the tomb summit over the grave, and the surface of the tomb may have been paved with rocks.

The funerary goods of the early tombs are mainly ceremonial in nature, with some iron weapons and armor, an indication that the individuals buried there had considerable magico-religious powers as well as military might. Chinese-made BRONZE MIRRORS, necklaces of curved *magatama* and cylindrical beads made from precious jade and jasper, jasper ornaments resembling spindle whorls and *koto* bridges (see BEADS, ANCIENT), and unusually shaped jasper bracelets made up the main deposits.

In the late 4th century, tomb building spread further into eastern and northern Japan and to the western coastal areas. The tombs assumed a greater variety of shapes—square or gourd-shaped, formed by two round mounds joined together. Alternate burial facilities were also developed: large stone coffins were placed in the pit-style chambers or directly into the ground, and wooden coffins were embedded in prepared clay enclosures rather than stone chambers. For funerary goods, the imported bronze mirrors were joined by locally produced mirrors; there also began a trend to make jasper reproductions of functional objects such as sheathed knives, iron axe

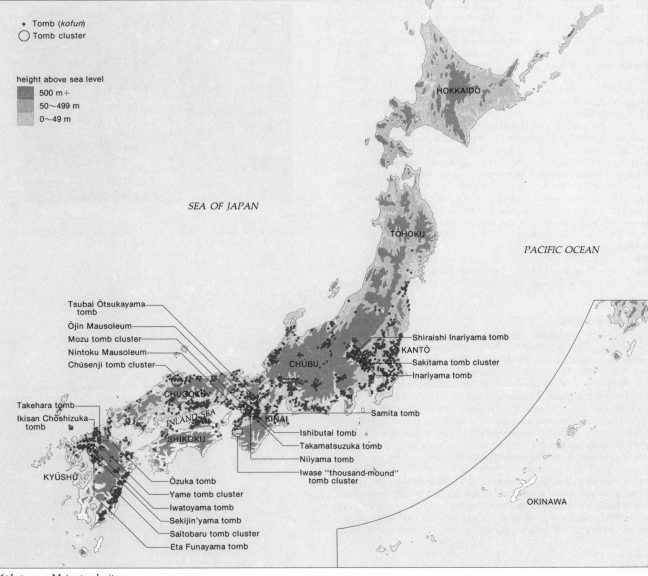

Kofun——Major tomb sites

and adze heads, and to place these in the tombs instead of the originals.

Middle Kofun-Period Tombs—— In the 5th century, the character of the tombs underwent drastic changes. Instead of being built on natural hillocks, they were mounded up from flatter terrace surfaces. Wide moats became a common feature, dramatically increasing the area of the tombs (see NINTOKU MAUSOLEUM; ŌJIN MAUSOLEUM). Accessory mounds *(baichō)* often accompany the highest status tombs of this period, acting as depositories for tremendous volumes of funerary goods. Their contents attest to both the rulers' limitless access to the resources of society and to new contacts with the Korean peninsula at this time. One of the accessory tombs of the Ōjin Mausoleum, the Ariyama tomb, alone held over 3,000 iron swords and tools. Funerary goods of imported gold ear ornaments (see EAR ORNAMENTS, ANCIENT), SUE WARE, and horse trappings (see HORSE TRAPPINGS, ANCIENT) from the continent gradually contributed to the replacement of fine jasper ornaments by coarse soapstone imitations, a decrease in the number of bronze mirrors deposited in the tombs, and the disappearance of *haniwa* from Kinai-region tombs.

A new type of tomb chamber called *yokoana sekishitsu* (literally, "horizontal hole, stone chamber") was also transmitted from the Korean peninsula in the 5th century. Equipped with a corridor entrance, this kind of chamber was oriented so that one could walk into it, rather than only being accessible through the ceiling like the pit-style chamber. To construct a corridor-style chamber, a level surface was provided on the mound and the stone chamber was then built up on the flat surface. The entrance to the corridor was positioned so that it opened onto the slope of the mound. Finally, earth was piled over the chamber, embedding it in the center of the mound (see ISHIBUTAI TOMB). The corridor allowed the tomb to be used not just once but several times, and in the late Kofun period, family tombs became quite popular.

Late Kofun-Period Tombs—— Tombs of the 6th and 7th centuries shrank in size and increased in number as they came to be used by a greater segment of the population and not just rulers. Entire hillsides were devoted to cemeteries of small, round mounds averaging 15 meters (50 ft) in diameter and each containing a corridor-style chamber (see IWASE "THOUSAND MOUND" TOMB CLUSTER; SAITO-BARU TOMB CLUSTER; YAME TOMB CLUSTER).

Funerary goods of this period are increasingly utilitarian in nature, reflecting disparities in social status or occupation of the interred. *Sue* and HAJI WARE containing food provisions for the afterlife, personal weapons and jewelry, and tools such as blacksmith's irons, etc, composed the main deposits.

Regional differences in construction and decoration are the hallmarks of these latter-day tombs. In northern Kyūshū, stone figures carved of local tuff (volcanic rock) replaced many *haniwa* images on the mounds, while bold geometric designs and animate figures were painted on the interior walls of the chambers (see ORNAMENTED TOMBS). The tombs of eastern Japan retained the grandeur of the 5th-century keyhole mounds of the Kinai region. The Kantō Plain housed a robust frontier society in the late Kofun period, and its warriors—thought to be under the influence of the YAMATO COURT (see INARIYAMA TOMB)—were buried in style in large mounded tombs. *Haniwa* manufacture, dying out in the Kinai, was transplanted to the Kantō area and flourished in its new home. *Haniwa* images reached their peak of expression at this time, reflecting the frontier mix of lavishly ornamented horses, fully armored warriors, stylishly attired nobles, and farmers, singers, and dancers of common origins. Funerary goods included gorgeous gilt bronze horse trappings, fine iron weapons, and even bronze vessels from the Korean peninsula.

With the introduction of Buddhism in the middle of the 6th century, an increasing number of the central elite had begun to build temples instead of tombs for posterity. Though some elaborate examples such as Ishibutai and TAKAMATSUZUKA TOMB are known from this period, imperial proscriptions governing the size and ostentatiousness of the tombs acted together with the new Buddhist attitudes, causing tomb-building to gradually cease during the 7th century. A great number of people from the late 5th to 8th centuries were interred in cave-like YOKOANA tombs in response to restrictions on space, labor, and sumptuary requirements. See also ARCHAEOLOGY.

📖 ——J. Edward Kidder, Jr, *Early Japanese Art: The Great Tombs and Their Treasures* (1964). Ōtsuka Hatsushige, "Kofun no hensen," *Nihon no kōkogaku,* vol 4 (1966). *Gina Lee* BARNES

Kofun period

(Kofun *jidai*). In Japanese ARCHAEOLOGY, the name of the protohistorical period characterized by the construction of large tumuli or tomb mounds (KOFUN). It is variously dated as ca 250–552, ca 300–552, ca 300–645, ca 300–710, and so forth, and it may be divided into either two or three phases: early (4th century), middle (5th century), and late (6th and 7th centuries); or early (4th and 5th centuries) and late (6th and 7th centuries). This encyclopedia has adopted the three-phase division and the dates ca 300–710 for the period; thus it is coterminous with the Yamato period and encompasses the ASUKA PERIOD (latter part of the 6th century to 710; see PERIODIZATION). The Kofun period saw the development of a class society, the rise of the YAMATO COURT, incipient urbanization, and the adoption of BUDDHISM from the Asian continent. It was preceded by the YAYOI PERIOD (ca 300 BC–ca AD 300), in which agriculture and metals first appeared in Japan, and was followed by the NARA PERIOD (710–794) of mature statehood. See also the sections on protohistory and Asuka history in HISTORY OF JAPAN. *Gina Lee* BARNES

Koga

City in western Ibaraki Prefecture, central Honshū. The base of members of the Ashikaga family, the so-called Koga *kubō,* who rebelled against the Muromachi shogunate in the mid-1400s, it developed during the Edo period (1600–1868) as a post-station town on the highway Nikkō Kaidō. Textiles, umbrellas, electrical appliances, machinery, and chemicals are produced. Farming is also a major occupation. Of interest are the remains of Koga Castle and the grave of the Confucian scholar KUMAZAWA BANZAN at the temple Keienji. Pop: 56,656.

kōgai

Long hairpins used for traditional Japanese HAIRSTYLES. Originally, *kōgai* were used by both men and women for parting and styling the hair, as well as for scratching the scalp. During the Edo period (1600–1868), they also functioned as women's hair ornaments, varying in size and decoration. *Kōgai* were made of wood, bamboo, metal, glass, tortoiseshell, or the shinbones of cranes and were sometimes decorated with gold and silver lacquerwork. See also KANZASHI. *Hashimoto Sumiko*

Koga Issaku (1899–   )

Electrical engineer. Inventor of the high-performance quartz crystal resonator (1930), which has improved the performance and reliability of communications equipment. Born in Saga Prefecture, he graduated from Tōkyō University in 1923. He took an interest in the research on quartz crystal application and devised a new cutting method that made it possible to produce crystals with excellent frequency-stability under variations in temperature. He became a pro-

Kofun

The largest tomb mound in Japan, said to be that of the emperor Nintoku (first half of the 5th century). Sakai, Ōsaka Prefecture.

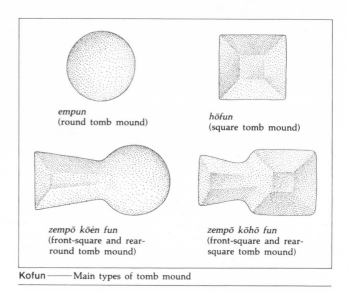

empun
(round tomb mound)

hōfun
(square tomb mound)

zempō kōen fun
(front-square and rear-round tomb mound)

zempō kōhō fun
(front-square and rear-square tomb mound)

Kofun——Main types of tomb mound

fessor at Tōkyō University in 1944 and dean of engineering in 1958. He received the Order of Culture in 1963.

Kogaku

(Ancient Learning). Revival movement in Japanese Confucianism advocating a return to the works of the ancient Chinese Confucian sages in order to understand their content correctly without resorting to the interpretations of the later scholars like Zhu Xi (Chu Hsi) and Wang Yangming (see SHUSHIGAKU; YŌMEIGAKU). YAMAGA SOKŌ (1622–85), ITŌ JINSAI (1627–1705), and OGYŪ SORAI (1666–1728) were the chief proponents of this movement, which emerged in the middle years of the Edo period (1600–1868). These men had no direct mutual bonds, but they had certain intellectual connections. They each in turn called for the same "return to the ancients." Although their teachings are known under the name of Kogakuha (School of Ancient Learning), no unified philosophical school actually existed. The movement signifies a maturity in Japanese Confucianists' attempts to understand the Confucian tradition.

When the teachings of Zhu Xi and Wang Yangming entered Japan from China by way of the Korean peninsula—the former in the Kamakura period (1185–1333), the latter toward the end of the Muromachi period (1333–1568)—the Japanese attempted to interpret them within a Japanese context. The philosophical schools of both Zhu Xi and Wang Yangming, however, did not readily yield to adaptation. As Confucian learning gradually became more influential with the beginning of the Edo period, and as the Zhu Xi school in particular gained the support of the Tokugawa shogunate, Confucian concepts had increasing significance in people's lives. Eventually there arose a feeling among some scholars that the Zhu Xi or Wang

Kofun

An example of the wall paintings found in some Late Kofun-period tombs in northern Kyūshū. This painting in the Takehara tomb, Fukuoka Prefecture, is executed in red and black on the innermost wall of the tomb. Height of painting 120 cm. 6th century.

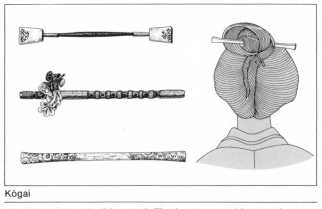

Kōgai

Kōgai (hairpins) of the Edo period. The drawings are of *kōgai* in the collection of the Suntory Museum of Art, Tōkyō.

Yangming teachings, which had evolved in the vastly different Chinese society, could not be applied to Japanese society. This led to a rejection of the Zhu Xi and Wang Yangming schools and the birth of the Kogaku movement, which promoted direct contact with the original writings of the Chinese Confucian sages. A return to the original writings of the ancients meant that the Confucian texts would gain the richer interpretations necessary for incorporation into Japanese life.

The first written work to clarify the emphasis on ancient learning was Yamaga Sokō's remarkable *Seikyō yōroku* (1665, Essentials of the Holy Teachings). Not only a Confucian scholar, Sokō was also a well-known military strategist with powerful *daimyō* as his pupils. After he criticized the Zhu Xi school, which was supported by the shogunate, he was treated with suspicion. As a military man, he placed much emphasis upon action and a spirit unbound by dogma. In his view, the Zhu Xi school, which made "principle" (Ch: *li*; J: *ri*) the metaphysical basis of all things, idealized a static otherworldly enlightenment that Sokō found hard to accept.

For Sokō, the universe was a vital entity pulsating with life but governed by certain inevitable principles *(jōri)*. The sages had comprehended these principles and presented them in the form of right conduct *(reigi)*. Sokō maintained that the aim of learning should be the mastery of these rules of right conduct, according to which people should live their daily lives. By living in accordance with the principles of right conduct, people would make contact with the vital and dynamic internal aspect of their spirits, an aspect derived from an equally vital and dynamic universe. Sokō used the word MA-KOTO (sincerity or truthfulness) to refer to a life which accorded with this internal nature. A "sincere" or "truthful" life was a life which adhered to the principles of right conduct. Since Sokō was both a

warrior and a military expert, he detailed matters concerning the proper behavior of a warrior (see BUSHIDŌ). His system of thought was based on the "Four Books" of Confucian teachings (the *Analects,* the *Mencius,* the *Great Learning,* and the *Doctrine of the Mean*), the same as those which composed the classics for Zhu Xi scholars (see FOUR BOOKS AND FIVE CLASSICS).

At almost the same time that Sokō's *Seikyō yōroku* was issued, Itō Jinsai, who had no connection with Sokō, independently proposed a return to ancient learning. The son of a Kyōto merchant family, Jinsai ran a private school for the merchant class. Jinsai's philosophy, known as *kogigaku* (study of ancient meaning), rejected the authority of the Four Books as taught by Zhu Xi. He viewed the *Great Learning* (Ch: *Daxue* or *Ta-hsüeh*) as nonorthodox and the *Doctrine of the Mean* (Ch: *Zhongyong* or *Chung-yung*) as marred with nonorthodox elements. Thus it was through the *Analects* (Ch: *Lunyu*) and *Mencius* (Ch: *Mengzi* or *Meng-tzu*) that he attempted to grasp the true essence of the ancient teaching. Jinsai's approach accordingly differed from Sokō's in that his position was based on philological study.

Jinsai emphasized the dynamism of human relations built upon mutual love and friendship in the ordinary lives of people. This led him to propose that the true way of life for a human being, the sort of life taught by the ancient sages, must be lived within these bounds of love and friendship. Jinsai used the word MICHI (Way) to describe a life lived within this framework of human relations. For Jinsai, *michi* was based upon *jin* (Ch: *ren* or *jen;* benevolence, charity). In this he referred not only to the emotional aspects of love but also to the desire to bring beneficial results to others.

Of particular importance in Jinsai's system is *chūshin* (Ch: *zhongxin* or *chung-hsin;* loyalty, fidelity), which he considered the proper basis of an ethical code in human life. In Jinsai's view, *chūshin* was a supreme form of sincerity, free of guile or deceit. When *chūshin* is realized in one's life, then *jin* will naturally follow. He noted that while Zhu Xi had preached of *kei* (Ch: *jing* or *ching;* veneration; see TSUTSUSHIMI) and Wang Yangming had valued *chi ryōchi* (attainment of good knowledge; Ch: *zhi liangzhi* or *chih liang-chih*), no mention had been made of the importance of *chūshin,* which Confucius and Mencius, according to Jinsai, had emphasized.

With Ogyū Sorai, born a generation after Sokō and Jinsai, ancient learning took on a new philosophical approach, reaching the apex of its development. Sorai rejected all philosophical works after Confucius and Mencius as consisting of subjective, factional arguments. The only reliable works were those from the "ideal" ages of the ancients or works belonging to the traditional Six Classics, including the *Book of Odes* (Ch: *Shijing* or *Shih-ching*) and the *Book of Documents* (Ch: *Shujing* or *Shu-ching*) in addition to the Four Books. Since all these works were written in the ancient rhetorical style, Sorai emphasized the study of ancient rhetoric as a means of understanding the teachings of the sages. As a result of these teachings, Sorai's theories came to be known as the School of Ancient Rhetoric (KOBUNJIGAKU).

Sorai taught that the Zhu Xi school's striving for a comprehension of *ri* (Ch: *li;* principle), which necessarily required a degree of subjectivity, was unsuitable as a basis for human conduct. According to Sorai, the true essence of the universe was only known to the ancient sages who had received superhuman powers from heaven. The sages, in order to govern humanity and protect the lives of mankind, had grasped these concepts and gone on to create the way by which mankind should live. Sorai divided this Way into rites (Ch: *li;* J: *rei*) and music (Ch: *yue* or *yüeh;* J: *gaku*). Observing rites would preserve the social order and music would inspire the human heart. According to Sorai, rites and music comprised the whole of the ancient sages' teaching. Understanding of the ancient rhetoric would bring about a concrete understanding of the rites and music described in the Six Classics.

Living in accord with the teachings of the sages, Sorai believed, meant immersing oneself in music or in the poetry which had replaced the early music. In these teachings, Sorai emphasized the emotional release that humans required, a concept not found in either Sokō or Jinsai. The rigid Zhu Xi concept of *ri,* Sorai said, made people less sensitive to their most human emotions. Sorai went on to reject the Zhu Xi and Wang Yangming view, which focused upon training the inner self to find the virtuous essence within each human being. This rejection led Sorai to affirm the usefulness of developing one's innate ability and individual traits by referring to the sages' teachings. In stressing adherence to rites, he took the view that official institutions would have to guide the citizenry toward morality, rather than depend upon each individual's attempts at betterment. The Zhu Xi school had taught that society had arisen in accordance with a heaven-bestowed *ri* that was not subject to change. Sorai countered that this heavenly, natural *ri* did not exist, and that social institutions had been formed by the sages, who were themselves human beings. Thus society was not a direct realization of heaven's principle and could therefore be modified. Sorai's rejection of Zhu Xi's *ri* strengthened the position he inherited from Sokō and Jinsai and effected a significant retreat from the thinking which recognized *ri* as the universal unchangeable.

The teachings of Sorai enjoyed a period of great popularity. His decreased emphasis on individual morality was criticized, and a movement to reassess the teachings of Zhu Xi and Wang Yangming followed. Nevertheless, after having created and accepted the Ancient Learning movement, Zhu Xi and Yangming could no longer be viewed as absolute authorities and an attempt was made to understand the ancient teachings through a blending of the arguments of Sorai, Jinsai, Zhu Xi, and Wang Yangming. These eclectic studies chose interpretations of ancient texts by trying to find what was fit for Japanese society. This attitude was more subjective than previous approaches.

The argument that only an understanding of the original classics could bring comprehension of the truth died out for the most part with the demise of Sorai's philosophical school. Nevertheless, a later scholar, MOTOORI NORINAGA, was considerably influenced by Sorai. Motoori was a leading figure in the KOKUGAKU (National Learning) movement, which tried to define the essence of Japanese native thought through study of the Japanese classics.

SAGARA Tōru

Koga kubō

("ruler at Koga"). Term applied to Ashikaga Shigeuji (1434–97) and four of his descendants from 1455 to 1583 while they held an independent power base at Koga in Shimōsa Province (now part of Ibaraki Prefecture). Shigeuji's father, Mochiuji (1398–1439), had been the last in the family to hold the title of Kamakura *kubō* (or Kantō *kubō*; governor-general of the Kantō), having been defeated by the shogunal deputy (Kantō *kanrei*) UESUGI NORIZANE and shogunate troops for openly defying the Ashikaga shogunate in Kyōto (this incident is known as the Eiryō Rebellion). The Uesugi family then became the dominant power in the Kantō region, but in 1450 they asked the shogunate to send Shigeuji to Kamakura as a figurehead governor-general. In 1454, however, Shigeuji slew Norizane's son, Noritada (1433–54) in revenge. Fleeing the Uesugi and shogunate armies sent against him, Shigeuji took a stand in Koga and called himself Koga *kubō*. He managed to hold out against the forces led by the shōgun Ashikaga Yoshimasa's younger brother Masatomo (1435–91), who established a base in Horikoshi on the Izu Peninsula and called himself HORIKOSHI KUBŌ. Shigeuji eventually made peace with the Uesugi in 1478 and with the shogunate in 1482; his heirs held the Koga area until 1583, although by then, because of intrafamily feuds, they had become completely powerless and dominated by the Go-Hōjō family (see HŌJŌ FAMILY).

Koga Masao (1904–1978)

Composer of popular Japanese music, particularly of the genre called *kayōkyoku*. Born in Fukuoka Prefecture, he attended Meiji University, where he was an active member of the mandolin club. In 1936 he was sent by the Ministry of Foreign Affairs on a goodwill mission to the United States. His sentimental melodies, such as *Kage o shitaite* (1924, Yearning for the Shadow) and *Sake wa namida ka tameiki ka* (1930, Is Wine a Tear or a Sigh), are extremely popular. From 1964 until his death he was chairman of the Japanese Society of Rights of Authors, Composers, and Publishers.

ABE Yasushi

Koganei

City in central Tōkyō Prefecture, central Honshū. A residential suburb of greater Tōkyō. Tōkyō Gakugei University, Tōkyō University of Agriculture and Technology, and Hōsei University are located here. Koganei Park is known for its cherry blossoms. Pop: 102,412.

Koganei Yoshikiyo (1859–1944)

Anatomist; anthropologist; one of the initiators in Japan of the study of physical anthropology. Born in what is now Niigata Prefecture, Koganei graduated from Daiichi Daigaku Igakkō (now Tōkyō University School of Medicine) in 1880. That same year he went to Germany, where he spent five years studying anatomy and histology. He returned home in 1885 and became a lecturer on anatomy at Tōkyō University; he was appointed to a professorship the following year. Koganei studied the anatomy and bone structure of the AINU and published his findings in *Ainu zoku no kenkyū* (1904–05), which was acclaimed for its contribution to the field of Ainu studies. He claimed that the paleolithic people of Japan were Ainu.

koganemushi → gold beetle

kōgi

("authorities"; "government"; "public" as opposed to "private"). A term widely used from the 7th century through the Edo period (1600–1868), referring primarily to public authorities such as the imperial court, the shogunate, or the *daimyō*, and secondarily to the public or society at large. The character for *kō* is also read *ōyake*, meaning a large residence. It is believed that the residence of the leader of a group or community in ancient times became associated with his authority and eventually with the imperial authority. The character for *gi* means "ceremony," "affair," or "case."

Historically, *kōgi* referred to the emperor or the imperial court from the time of the establishment of the RITSURYŌ SYSTEM of government in the 7th century until the Kamakura period (1185–1333). With the decline of imperial authority, it came to mean the shōgun (or shogunate) or the *daimyō* (i.e., whoever held political power), the former sometimes being called *daikōgi* in distinction to the latter. *Kōgi* in the sense of public place or public opinion dates from the Muromachi period (1333–1568), when it referred to the collective power of regional lords *(ryōshu)* or to a consensus among urban groups.

MIZUBAYASHI Takeshi

Kogidō

A private school for commoners founded in 1662 in the Higashi Horikawa district of Kyōto by the Confucian scholar ITŌ JINSAI (1627–1705); also known as the Horikawa Gakkō. Its teaching was centered on the exposition of such works as the Confucian *Analects, Mencius,* and the *Doctrine of the Mean* (Zhongyong or Chung-yung). Over 3,000 students came under Jinsai's direction during his 40-year teaching career. His ideas on moral education greatly influenced the academic world of the day. Jinsai's heirs continued the Kogidō after his death until the early years of the Meiji period (1868–1912).

ETŌ Kyōji

kōgi seitai ron

(argument for government by public discussion). Political argument used in the 1860s, on the eve of the MEIJI RESTORATION, calling for the adoption of elements of the Western parliamentary system into the Tokugawa shogunate; it was propounded by pro-Tokugawa factions who saw it as a means of shoring up the failing regime. After the arrival of Commodore Matthew C. PERRY in 1853, the shogunate found it increasingly difficult to act as a national government. Many *daimyō* demanded that they be allowed to participate in national affairs; at the same time, adherents of the proimperial antiforeign SONNŌ JŌI cause criticized the shogunate for opening the country to foreign intercourse without imperial sanction (see HARRIS TREATY). After the failure of the ANSEI PURGE (1858–60) to eliminate dissidents, the shogunate was forced to make concessions. During the 1860s various schemes were advanced to preserve the shogunate. One was embodied in the MOVEMENT FOR UNION OF COURT AND SHOGUNATE, while another proposed the establishment of a council of daimyō to conduct national affairs. In particular, MATSUDAIRA YOSHINAGA, daimyō of the Fukui or Echizen domain (now part of Fukui Prefecture), felt that a Western-style parliamentary system, with an upper house composed of daimyō and a lower house of *samurai* and commoners, would create a new sense of national unity and supplant the cumbersome feudal BAKUHAN SYSTEM of government. Finally in 1867 YAMANOUCHI TOYOSHIGE, daimyō of Tosa (now Kōchi Prefecture), submitted a memorial to the shōgun TOKUGAWA YOSHINOBU urging him to return his political mandate to the emperor and to support a bicameral parliamentary system. Although these ideas never materialized—the shogunate was soon overthrown by force—soon after the Restoration (1868) the emperor issued the CHARTER OATH, in which he promised a parliamentary form of government. Later, in the 1870s and 1880s, when such a system was not immediately forthcoming, the old argument for government by public discussion was used by advocates of the FREE-DOM AND PEOPLE'S RIGHTS MOVEMENT to hasten its implementation.

M. William STEELE

kōgō

Nonreigning empress (a reigning empress being called *tennō*). The title *kōgō* was reserved for the principal consort of an emperor, that is, the one who gave birth to the heir apparent. According to the RITSURYŌ SYSTEM, only women of imperial blood were eligible for that honor; but in 729 FUJIWARA NO FUHITO's daughter became *kōgō* to Emperor SHŌMU (see KŌMYŌ, EMPRESS) and the first of many Fujiwara empresses. The codes had established an office called Chūgūshiki to serve the needs of the *kōgō*, but Shōmu set up the separate office Kōgōgūshiki for Empress Kōmyō, while the Chū-gūshiki continued to serve his mother, the empress dowager. When Emperor ICHIJŌ in 1000 initiated the practice of having two empresses at once—one called *kōgō*, the other CHŪGŪ—these offices became permanent. In forms of address, honorific terms, and general deference, the *kōgō* was equal to the sovereign. The title *kōgō* was sometimes conferred as an honorary one, for example, on the wife of a deceased crown prince or on a woman (usually an imperial princess) who had given birth to an heir apparent. The title is still in use today; under the IMPERIAL HOUSEHOLD LAW, the wife of the crown prince automatically assumes it on the death of the emperor.

G. Cameron HURST III

kōgoishi

Stone fortifications of the 6th century ringing the summits of mountains in northern Kyūshū and the extreme western coast of the Inland Sea; probably built in anticipation of invasions from Korea. Called *kōgoishi* ("divine protection stones") by the archaeologist TSUBOI SHŌGORŌ, who thought they were some sort of religious sanctuaries, they are distinguished from mountain fortifications like ITOJŌ, Ōnojō, and Kiijō (all defensive outposts of DAZAIFU) by walls of cut stone as much as 3 kilometers (1.9 mi) in length. Eight *kōgoishi* have been found, of which the best examples are at Zoyama, Kōrasan, Kagenoma, and Goshogatani, all in Fukuoka Prefecture.

■——Onoyama Setsu, *Kofun to kokka no naritachi*, vol 6 of *Kodaishi hakkutsu* (1975).

J. Edward KIDDER, Jr.

Kōgon, Emperor (1313–1364)

The first sovereign *(tennō)* of the Northern Court; reigned 1331–33. Eldest son of the retired emperor Go-Fushimi (1288–1336; r 1298–1301). As a member of the Jimyōin line of the imperial family, Kōgon became crown prince under Emperor GO-DAIGO of the rival Daikakuji line in accordance with the Kamakura shogunate's policy of alternating members of the two lines on the throne. He became emperor in 1331, after the ambitious Go-Daigo, who had attempted a coup against the shogunate, was sent into exile (see GENKŌ INCIDENT). Two years later, however, Kōgon was forced to abdicate when Go-Daigo succeeded in overthrowing the shogunate and restoring direct imperial rule (see KEMMU RESTORATION). Go-Daigo's rule, in turn, quickly came to an end in 1336, when the military commander ASHIKAGA TAKAUJI revolted and established the Muromachi shogunate, placing Emperor Kōmyō (1322–80; r 1336–48), Kōgon's brother, on the throne. Go-Daigo took refuge in Yoshino (now in Nara Prefecture) and set up a separate court, referred to as the Southern Court in distinction to the Northern Court in Kyōto (see NORTHERN AND SOUTHERN COURTS). Kōgon, as retired emperor, headed the cloister government of the Northern Court for the next 15 years. He is known as a co-compiler of the poetry anthology *Fūga wakashū* (1346).

Kōgonen-jaku

(Register of the Kōgo Year). A set of household registers compiled in the year corresponding to 670, designated *kōgo* in the sexagenary cycle. Although it is no longer extant, several references to it appear in such historical sources as the *Shoku nihongi* (797) and the SHINSEN SHŌJIROKU (815). Although registers had been compiled every six years since the time of the TAIKA REFORM (645), the Kōgonen-jaku is believed to have represented the first such undertaking of nationwide scope. It listed the name and official rank-title of each household, as well as the status of each household member, includ-

ing servants. While other registers were normally destroyed after 30 years, the Kōgonen-jaku remained in use until the middle of the Heian period (794–1185) as a basic reference for verifying the antiquity of a family's social pedigree.

Michiko Y. AOKI

Kogosho Kaigi

(Kogosho Conference). The first meeting of the leaders of the new Meiji government, held in the Kogosho, part of the Imperial Palace in Kyōto, on 3 January 1868, the day of the coup d'etat that restored imperial rule (ŌSEI FUKKO). A number of court nobles, major *daimyō*, and other political activists met in the presence of Emperor Meiji to decide the future political status of the Tokugawa shōgun. A compromise faction led by YAMANOUCHI TOYOSHIGE, GOTŌ SHŌJIRŌ, and MATSUDAIRA YOSHINAGA urged that the shōgun, TOKUGAWA YOSHINOBU, should be included in the new government and tried to arrange for him to participate in the meeting. However, IWAKURA TOMOMI, ŌKUBO TOSHIMICHI, and others who had long plotted the overthrow of the shogunate refused to allow Yoshinobu to attend. Moreover, they succeeded in persuading the compromise faction that Yoshinobu must be ordered to resign all offices (he had formally returned his mandate to the emperor the previous November [TAISEI HŌKAN] but still held the court title inner minister [naidaijin]), surrender his domains to the emperor, and apologize for his lack of leadership. The intransigence of Ōkubo and Iwakura resulted in the BOSHIN CIVIL WAR.

Kogo shūi

Historical work compiled in 807 by Imbe no Hironari. The book is a collection of myths and legends dating back to the time before the reign of Emperor Jimmu, and transmitted orally through the descendants of the IMBE FAMILY. It contains material not found in the KOJIKI and NIHON SHOKI, the oldest extant histories of Japan, as well as references to the achievements of the Imbe family.

ASAI Kiyoshi

Koguryŏ

(J: Kōkuri). One of Korea's three ancient kingdoms (see KOREAN THREE KINGDOMS PERIOD) that emerged with the demise of Han Chinese colonies in the peninsula (see LELANG [Lolang]). Formed by tribes in southern Manchuria between 37 BC and 19 BC, Koguryŏ dominated the northern two-thirds of Korea from AD 313 until overwhelmed by the southeastern Korean kingdom of SILLA and Tang (T'ang) Chinese forces in 668. As a result, Japan, which had earlier sent a naval force to help PAEKCHE against Silla and China (see HAKUSUKINOE, BATTLE OF), lost whatever influence it had on the Korean peninsula.

C. Kenneth QUINONES

Kōgyō iken

(Opinions on Promoting Industry). Record of industrial production of the first 17 years of the Meiji period (1868–1912). Commissioned by the Ministry of Agriculture and Commerce, the editor, Maeda Masana (1850–1921), traveled throughout Japan to gather data. Of the total of 30 volumes completed in 1884, 14 outline policy for the promotion of industry and 16 consist of regional reports. Copies were distributed to prefectural governors. The *Kōgyō iken* is invaluable for its information on economic conditions of the early Meiji period.

Kōgyoku, Empress → Saimei, Empress

Koichijō In (994–1051)

Alternative name of Prince Atsuakira, eldest son of Emperor SANJŌ (r 1011–16) and Fujiwara no Ishi. In 1016 he was named heir apparent to Emperor GO-ICHIJŌ (r 1016–36). But Fujiwara no Shōshi (JŌTŌ MON'IN), consort of Go-Ichijō and daughter of the powerful regent *(sesshō)* FUJIWARA NO MICHINAGA, had given birth to a son, later Emperor Go-Suzaku (1009–45; r 1036–45), whom Michinaga wished to make heir apparent; and Atsuakira abdicated his position under great pressure in 1017. Michinaga treated Atsuakira generously thereafter: he was granted the palace Koichijō In, from which he took his name, and was treated like a retired emperor, enjoying great prestige and substantial wealth—notably tracts of land that came to be known as Koichijō In *goryō*—but he was never again influential in Heian court politics. *G. Cameron* HURST *III*

Koide Narashige (1887–1931)

Western-style painter; born in Ōsaka. He studied both Japanese-style painting (NIHONGA) and Western-style painting (YŌGA) at the Tōkyō Bijutsu Gakkō (now Tōkyō University of Fine Arts and Music). At the 1919 exhibit of the Nikakai (an association of artists formed in 1914 in opposition to the conservative tendencies of the BUNTEN) he received the Chogyū Prize, and in 1920 he was awarded the Nikakai Prize. After a trip to France and Germany in 1921–22, he became a member of the Nikakai. In 1924, with Nabei Katsuyuki (1888–1969) and other painters in the Kyōto–Ōsaka area, he founded the Shinanobashi Yōga Kenkyūjo (Shinanobashi Western-style Painting Study Institute) in Ōsaka. Koide is best known for his nudes.

Koikawa Harumachi (1744–1789)

Author and illustrator of KIBYŌSHI. *Samurai* of a small domain in Suruga Province (now Shizuoka Prefecture). Real name: Kurahashi Kaku. He was stationed in Edo (now Tōkyō) and, a pursuit unusual for someone of his status, studied *ukiyo-e* painting. He is credited with being the originator of *kibyōshi* (small illustrated books of prose fiction bound in yellow covers), the first one being his witty and satirical *Kinkin sensei eiga no yume* (1775). He wrote 30 *kibyōshi* but his *Ōmugaeshi bumbu no futamichi* (1789), a great popular success, was interpreted by the government as a satire on the KANSEI REFORMS. He was censured by the authorities and died the same year; according to one account, he committed suicide as a result of the censure. He also wrote KYŌKA poetry under the pen name of Saka no Ue no Furachi, and popular fiction in the SHAREBON genre, of which his *Mudaiki* (1779) is the most notable.

kōiki shichōsonken

Local councils established since 1969 by the MINISTRY OF HOME AFFAIRS for the integrated administration of large regions. Having evolved from various local administrative organizations, they now provide, with the consent of the localities concerned and with some central government subsidy, such services as road construction, waterworks, garbage disposal, and fire fighting. The standard *kōiki shichōsonken* was meant to have jurisdiction over a central city and neighboring towns and villages with a total population of 100,000. Of the 329 regions so designated, however, the average population has been about 180,000 and the average area 1,063 square kilometers (410 sq mi). *NISHIKAWA Osamu*

Koishikawa Botanic Garden

(Koishikawa Shokubutsuen). Botanical garden located in Bunkyō Ward, Tōkyō, with an adjunct in the city of Nikkō, Tochigi Prefecture. The full name is Botanical Gardens, Faculty of Science, Tōkyō University. It is maintained for research purposes and is open to the public. It was originally established as an herb garden under the Tokugawa shogunate in 1638, and after the Meiji Restoration in 1868, it was placed under the control of the Tōkyō city government. In 1877 control was transferred to Tōkyō University. Since then it has contributed greatly to research undertaken by the biology department of Tōkyō University. The trees studied by HIRASE SAKUGORŌ in his experiments leading to the discovery of the spermatozoon of the gingko tree are still growing there. See also BOTANICAL GARDENS. *SUZUKI Zenji*

Koishikawa Yōjōsho

Charitable hospital in Edo (now Tōkyō) established by the Tokugawa shogunate in 1722 at the recommendation of a local physician, Ogawa Shōsen (1672–1760), who had deposited a request in the shogunate's suggestion box (MEYASUBAKO). The hospital was located in the Koishikawa Yakuen, the shogunate's garden for medicinal herbs. Placed under the jurisdiction of the Edo city commissioners (Edo *machi bugyō*) and staffed by 20 doctors, it had accommodations for 40 (later 170) patients. Only those who had been certified by town authorities as having no means of support were admitted. In 1868 the Koishikawa Yōjōsho was made part of

the shogunate medical school (IGAKUJO) and later became the Tōkyō University Hospital.

Koishiwara ware

(koishiwara-yaki). Sometimes referred to as Koishibara ware *(koishibara-yaki)*. Pottery made in and around Sarayama, in the village of Koishiwara, Fukuoka Prefecture. The generally accepted theory is that Koishiwara pottery was started in 1682 at the instigation of the third Kuroda *daimyō*, Mitsuyuki. Pottery was produced on a small scale during the 18th and 19th centuries and consisted almost entirely of everyday wares: large pickle jars, water vessels, *sake* bottles, and so on. Glazes most commonly used were translucent honey *(ame)* and transparent *(tōmei)* over a white slip, with drips or splashes of green, white, or yellow overglazing *(uchigake* and *nagashigake)*. The slip brushmark decoration *(hakeme)* and *tobikanna* chattering are comparatively recent innovations of the 20th century. Koishiwara pots are similar to ONTA WARE in both style and glazing techniques.

There are two or three old kiln sites around Sarayama, suggesting that some potters may have fired their wares independently, but by the end of the 19th century all nine farmer-potter households were sharing two climbing kilns *(noborigama)*. However, with the depression of the 1930s, production virtually ceased and was only resuscitated after the war by the efforts of YANAGI MUNEYOSHI, leader of the folk craft *(mingei)* movement.

In 1952–53 potters mechanized clay preparation techniques, a decision that has led to considerable expansion and social change, including the breakup of the cooperative kilns. There are now almost 40 households firing kilns independently in the village of Koishiwara. Despite the introduction of electric wheels, gas- and oil-fired kilns, and chemical compounds in glazes, and although some of the more newly founded potteries do not even use Koishiwara clay, the style of throwing and decorating pots—particularly in Sarayama—has remained to some extent unaltered over the past three centuries. *Brian* MOERAN

Koiso Kuniaki (1880–1950)

Army general and prime minister (1944–45). Born in Tochigi Prefecture, graduate of the Army War College. He entered the General Staff Office in 1913 and was involved in plans to use the so-called MANCHURIAN-MONGOLIAN INDEPENDENCE MOVEMENT to Japan's advantage. As chief of the Military Affairs Bureau of the Army Ministry he played a leading role in the so-called MARCH INCIDENT of 1931, in which young army officers attempted to establish a military cabinet headed by General UGAKI KAZUSHIGE. Koiso served as minister of colonial affairs in the HIRANUMA KIICHIRŌ (1939) and YONAI MITSUMASA (1940) cabinets, and after the outbreak of World War II as governor-general of Korea (then a Japanese colony). He became prime minister after the fall of the TŌJŌ HIDEKI cabinet in July 1944. He lowered the conscription age to 17, established the Supreme Wartime Leadership Council (Saikō Sensō Shidō Kaigi) and tried to improve Japan's position in the war. But following the paralysis of production under intense American air raids, the failure of efforts to reach a peace accord through Soviet mediation, and the fall of Okinawa, he resigned. Tried as a class-A war criminal by the International Military Tribunal (see WAR CRIMES TRIALS) after the war, he was sentenced to life imprisonment and died in Sugamo Prison.

Koizumi Chikashi (1886–1927)

TANKA poet. Real name Koizumi Ikutarō. Born in Chiba Prefecture. While teaching primary school, he began to write *tanka*. First recognized by ITŌ SACHIO, he was active as a member of the ARARAGI group (founded in 1908), which played a significant role in revitalizing traditional *tanka* poetry. In his poems the sentiment that inspired him prevails over the descriptive sketch of the subject itself. His poetry collections include *Kawa no hotori* (1925) and *Okujō no tsuchi* (1928).

Koizumi Shinzō (1888–1966)

Economist. Born in Tōkyō. Graduate of Keiō Gijuku (now Keiō University). His father was Koizumi Shinkichi, who served as president of Keiō Gijuku and manager of Yokohama Specie Bank (now

Bank of Tōkyō, Ltd). After graduating from Keiō in 1910, Koizumi studied economics while teaching at his alma mater. After studying in Europe from 1912 to 1916, Koizumi became professor at Keiō and eventually served as the university's president for 15 years. Koizumi became educational adviser to Crown Prince Akihito after World War II and worked to modernize the lifestyle of the imperial family. A specialist in economic history and social thought, he was a long-time critic of Marxism. Koizumi also was a specialist in the studies of FUKUZAWA YUKICHI. Koizumi's works include *Marukusu shigo gojūnen* (1958, Fifty Years after the Death of Marx), *Rikādo kenkyū* (1934, A Study of Ricardo), and *Kyōsan shugi hihan no jōshiki* (1949, Basics in Criticism of Communism). YAMADA *Katsumi*

Koizumi Yakumo → Hearn, Lafcadio

Kojidan

(Stories about the Past). Collection of historical anecdotes believed to have been compiled about 1212-15 by Minamoto no Akikane (1160-1215). The author gathered his material from old anthologies and chronicles such as the *Shoku nihongi* (797). Written in *kiroku-tai*, a heavily Japanized style of classical Chinese, most of the tales are didactic in tone. *Kojidan* directly influenced such later works as UJI SHŪI MONOGATARI and JIKKUNSHŌ.

Kojiki

(Record of Ancient Matters). Japan's oldest extant chronicle, recording events from the mythical age of the gods up to the time of Empress SUIKO (r 593-628). The compiler, Ō NO YASUMARO, states in the preface that it was presented to the reigning empress Gemmei (661-722; r 707-715) on 9 March 712 (Wadō 5.1.28).

The *Kojiki* is divided into three sections. The first section, known as "Jindai no maki" (Book on the Age of the Gods), records the creation of heaven and earth and myths concerning the founding of Japan. It describes the descent from heaven of NINIGI NO MI-KOTO, grandson of AMATERASU ŌMIKAMI, progenitrix of the imperial line, to the mountain TAKACHIHONOMINE in Kyūshū. There is also the story of Umisachihiko, ancestor of the HAYATO people in southern Kyūshū, who gave allegiance to Hohodemi no Mikoto, grandfather of JIMMU, Japan's legendary first emperor (see MYTHOLOGY).

The second section covers the period from Emperor Jimmu through the reign of Emperor ŌJIN at the beginning of the 5th century. The third section records events from the reign of Emperor NINTOKU until the rule of Suiko in the early 7th century. Beginning with the passage in the third section dealing with Emperor Kensō (latter half of the 5th century), almost all story elements disappear, and the narrative consists mainly of records on imperial succession and the imperial family. This contrasts sharply with the NIHON SHOKI (720), in which the information beginning with the reign of Emperor Yūryaku in the latter half of the 5th century becomes increasingly detailed. The *Kojiki*, which places emphasis on myths, legends, and historical and pseudohistorical narratives, may thus be called a *furukotobumi*, i.e., a literary work dealing with matters in ancient times. The *Kojiki* is transcribed in Chinese characters *(kanji)*, since the Japanese had yet to develop their own phonetic script. The main text, in prose, is written in HENTAI KAMBUN, a hybridized form of literary Japanese that borrows heavily from classical Chinese, while the verse sequences make phonetic use of Chinese characters. The main text includes glosses indicating accent patterns, the pronunciations of characters in Japanese and Chinese, definitions of terms, and so forth. Unlike the *Nihon shoki*, however, the *Kojiki* does not present variant or supplementary versions of a story.

According to Ō no Yasumaro's preface, sometime during the latter half of the 7th century, Emperor TEMMU issued a decree stating that the TEIKI, (the genealogical record of the imperial family) and the KYŪJI (a collection of myths, legends, and songs connected with the forebears of the imperial and other leading families) had ceased to be accurate and would have to be corrected; the compilation of accurate historical records would "clarify the basis of the state and the foundations for the moral teachings of the emperors." Temmu therefore ordered the court attendant HIEDA NO ARE to commit to memory the contents of the *Teiki* and *Kyūji*. The project was interrupted for various reasons, but on 3 November 711 (Wadō 4.9.18), Empress Gemmei ordered Ō no Yasumaro to transcribe the information memorized by Are, and the completed records were presented to the court the following year.

The oldest surviving manuscript of the *Kojiki* is a scroll copied in the years 1371-72. It is known as the Shimpukuji-bon after the temple Shimpukuji in Nagoya where it is stored. The postscript to this edition notes that copies from the Kamakura period (1185-1333) existed at the time, but that no copies from the Nara period (710-794) or the Heian period (794-1185) had been found. Moreover, in other historical records from the Nara period there is no mention of the *Kojiki*. In the Edo period (1600-1868), speculation arose that the *Kojiki* had not actually been compiled in 712 but was rather a forgery from a later age. The 8th-century anthology MAN'-YŌSHŪ, however, includes quotations from the work, and the *Shōhei no shiki* (936, Private Record of the Shōhei Era) describes the *Kojiki* as Japan's oldest historical work. From the period of the NORTHERN AND SOUTHERN COURTS (1336-92) the *Kojiki*, with the *Nihon shoki* and the *Sendai kujihongi*, a Heian-period work on ancient history, came to be valued as a historical document. Scholarly research on the *Kojiki*, however, began only in the Edo period, with MOTOORI NORINAGA's *Kojikiden* being the most famous and influential study. Scholars of the KOKUGAKU school of historical studies, such as Motoori, regarded the *Kojiki* as a "classic among classics."

Concerning the compilation of the *Kojiki*, there are various views as to when the orally transmitted prototypes of the *Teiki* and the *Kyūji* were assembled for transcription and as to the connection between Hieda no Are's memorization of the documents and Ō no Yasumaro's compiling of the information. Most scholars accept TSUDA SŌKICHI's conclusion that these oral traditions were first written down in the middle of the 6th century. As for the second question, the work by Ueda Masaaki listed below provides pertinent information. In addition to being a history, the *Kojiki* is also one of the classics of Japanese literature, valuable for an understanding of the mythology, traditions, religious beliefs, and arts of Japan. See also LITERATURE: early literature.

📖——Basil Hall Chamberlain, tr, *Translation of "Ko-ji-ki," or "Records of Ancient Matters,"* 2nd ed with notes by W. G. Aston (1918). Kurano Kenji, *Kojiki zenchūshaku* (1973). Donald L. Philippi, tr, *Kojiki* (1969). Nishinomiya Kazutami, *Kojiki* (1973). Tsuda Sōkichi, *Nihon koten no kenkyū* (1963). Tsugita Jun, *Kojiki shinkō* (rev ed, 1956). Ueda Masaaki, general introduction to *Kojiki*, in *Kanshō Nihon koten bungaku*, vol 1 (Kadokawa Shoten, 1978).
 UEDA *Masaaki*

Kōjima

Island approximately 300 m (980 ft) off the southern coast of Miyazaki Prefecture, southeastern Kyūshū. The island is covered with subtropical vegetation and inhabited by over 100 wild monkeys *(Maccaca fuscata)*. These monkeys are able to swim, and they wash their food before they eat it. A team of anthropologists from Kyōto University has been studying their behavior since 1947. Area: 0.6 sq km (0.2 sq mi); circumference: about 4 km (2 mi).

Kojima Bay

(Kojima Wan). Former inlet of the Inland Sea south of the city of Okayama, southern Okayama Prefecture, western Honshū. Due to extensive reclamation, Kojima Bay has been converted into a man-made lake with a channel to the Inland Sea. Eel cultivation is carried out in the lake, and the reclaimed land is largely used for rice paddy fields.

Kojima Iken (1837-1908)

Also known as Kojima Korekata. Jurist. Born in what is now Ehime Prefecture, he participated in the movement to overthrow the Tokugawa shogunate. He joined the Ministry of Justice in 1871 and became chief justice of the Great Court of Cassation (Daishin'in) in 1891. Later he served as a member of the House of Peers (1894) and House of Representatives (1898). As chief justice of the Great Court of Cassation, he heard evidence relating to the ŌTSU INCIDENT (1891) in which the crown prince of Russia (later Nicholas II), then visiting Japan, was wounded by an escort policeman named Tsuda Sanzō at Ōtsu. Though the government put pressure on the court to sentence Tsuda to death, Kojima resisted; invoking the law of attempted murder, he imposed only a life sentence. His action was seen at the time as an affirmation of judicial independence and was highly praised, particularly since there were no Russian reprisals.

SATŌ *Kōji*

Kojima Nobuo (1915–)

Author. Born in Gifu Prefecture; graduated from Tōkyō University, majoring in English literature. Professor of English at Meiji University. As part of the earliest wave of new writers after the war, he wrote a series of stories based on his wartime experience. In 1954 his "Amerikan Sukūru" (American School), which describes with humor the helpless lot of postwar Japanese intellectuals, won the Akutagawa Prize. His humor later turned to serious criticism of the disintegration of society and the family in postwar Japan, as in *Hōyō kazoku* (1964), which received the Tanizaki Jun'ichirō Prize in 1965. Other works include *Watakushi no sakka hyōden* (1972–73), a three-volume collection of critical biographies of modern writers.

Kojima Takanori (fl 1330s)

Legendary warrior of the Nambokuchō period (Northern and Southern Courts period; 1336–92). According to the 14th-century war chronicle *Taiheiki*, he lived in Bizen Province (now part of Okayama Prefecture) and during the GENKŌ INCIDENT of 1331 raised an army in support of Emperor GO-DAIGO, who hoped to overthrow the Kamakura shogunate and restore direct imperial rule. When the captured emperor was on his way into exile, Takanori attempted to rescue him; having failed, he carved a poem on the trunk of a cherry tree near the emperor's stopping-place as a testimony of his loyalty. He remained loyal to Go-Daigo even after the failure of the emperor's short-lived KEMMU RESTORATION (1333–36). From the Meiji period (1868–1912) through the end of World War II, references to Takanori often appeared in elementary school textbooks and songs, and his story was used by the government to promote patriotism. Today it is considered doubtful whether he ever existed.

kōjin

A category of folk deities. *Kōjin* are said to cast evil spells on people and expose them to danger unless properly revered; they fall into the category of malevolent deities *(aramitama)* which are juxtaposed in the Shintō tradition against beneficent deities *(nigimitama)*. If properly reverenced, they are believed to protect worshipers. Belief in *kōjin* includes three basic types of deities. (1) A god of the kitchen fire who dislikes uncleanliness. Because of its great power, in northeastern Japan it is thought to bring vigor to new-born babies on whose foreheads soot from the kitchen fire has been rubbed. Also believed to prevent fires, it has been adopted into Buddhism as the three-headed, six-armed god *sampō kōjin,* who protects the faithful. (2) Gods worshiped outdoors in southwestern Japan and known as *jikōjin* (earth *kōjin*) that are treated in various areas as protectors of houses, family gods, or community gods. (3) A god widely worshiped as a guardian deity of horses and cattle.

Koji ruien

Government-sponsored encyclopedia of premodern Japan. Initially undertaken by the Ministry of Education at the instance of NISHIMURA SHIGEKI, the project was ultimately entrusted to the Bureau of Shintō Shrines (Jingū Shichō) and published in 350 volumes from 1896 to 1913. Information concerning Japan is arranged by topic under 30 categories based on traditional Chinese encyclopedic conventions. Following an introductory essay on each topic, relevant primary and early secondary documents, all written by Japanese authors prior to 1867, are extensively cited. A comprehensive table of contents and index contribute to the accessibility of this mammoth work, which cites many source works not generally available. A third revised edition in 60 volumes was issued by the Koji Ruien Kankō Kai in 1931–36. The Bureau of Shintō Shrines published an updated fourth edition in 51 volumes between 1967 and 1971.

UWANO *Zendō*

Kojong, King (1852–1919)

(J: Kōsō). The next-to-last monarch (r 1864–1907) of the Korean YI DYNASTY. Kojong (personal name Yi Tae-wang) ascended the throne when only 12 years old, and his father (the TAEWŎN'GUN) played a dominant role at court between 1864 and 1873. Kojong spent much of his reign trying to balance the interests of contending political cliques and foreign powers. His father sought to restore political influence to his Yi kinsmen by drawing them into government, while Kojong's wife, Queen MIN, attempted to do the same for her kinsmen. At the same time, Confucian-educated and Chinese-oriented officials contended with Japanese-oriented advocates of Westernization. Beginning in 1881, Japan vied first with China and then with Russia for influence over the Korean peninsula. Finally, in 1910, Kojong's kingdom was transformed from a Confucian monarchy into a Japanese colony (see KOREA, ANNEXATION OF).

Kojong's wife was brutally assassinated by the Japanese in 1895, and the Japanese minister ITŌ HIROBUMI used military force to pressure him into abdicating the throne in July 1907. He was succeeded by his son Sunjong (1874–1926; r 1907–10). The final humiliation came when his son Yi Ŭn (1897–1970) was forced to reside in Tōkyō, and Korean titles of royalty were replaced with Japanese titles of nobility in August 1910. Koreans erupted in violent nationalistic demonstrations against Japan on 1 March 1919, just before Kojong's funeral (see SAMIL INDEPENDENCE MOVEMENT). He is remembered as a symbol of Korean nationalism. See also KOREA AND JAPAN: early modern relations.

C. Kenneth QUINONES

kōjo ryōzoku

(public order and good morals). A basic standard of Japan's CIVIL CODE. Acts that are contrary to this standard are not valid (Civil Code, art. 90). Accordingly, primary actors and third parties may assert the invalidity of such acts and thus prevent ratification. A demand for return of a thing delivered pursuant to a JURISTIC ACT contrary to the *kōjo ryōzoku* standard is denied legal protection as a delivery in respect of illicit consideration.

Some examples from the cases of acts that have been held to be contrary to the standard follow. (1) Acts contrary to orderly property interests. Acts taking advantage of the indiscretion or financial difficulty of another and deriving unjust enrichment, by, for instance, contracting for excessive liquidated damages in case of nonfulfillment of an obligation; acts that are conspicuously speculative, such as gambling; or contracts that unduly restrict freedom of enterprise. (2) Acts contrary to public morals. Contracts of concubinage and for noncohabitation of parents and children are examples. (3) Acts that impinge on freedom or human rights. The prototypical example of this is a contract compelling the continuation of prostitution in order to discharge a prior debt. (4) Acts contrary to notions of right. Acts that require the performance of a crime (such as arrangements to ostracize amounting to criminal intimidation), and assisting in criminal acts are examples.

OKA *Takashi*

Kōjunsha

A social and political club made up of graduates of FUKUZAWA YUKICHI's Keiō Gijuku (now Keiō University) and business figures connected with the school. The club was formed in 1880 by Fukuzawa, BABA TATSUI, and others for the purpose of exchanging information and advising the government on public affairs. Membership at the time of its founding was 1,800. The club published a periodical, *Kōjun zasshi.* In 1881 members of the Kōjunsha submitted a draft constitution based on the British system as described in Alpheus Todd's *On Parliamentary Government in England* (1867–69). Ideologically close to ŌKUMA SHIGENOBU's Constitutional Reform Party (RIKKEN KAISHINTŌ) and associated reform movements, the club was later active in the MOVEMENT TO PROTECT CONSTITUTIONAL GOVERNMENT at the time of the TAISHŌ POLITICAL CRISIS of 1912–13. In the early 1980s the Kōjunsha still existed in Tōkyō as a purely social club with a membership of approximately 2,300.

Kōkaido Ō ryō hi → Kwanggaet'o monument

Kokan Shiren (1278–1346)

Zen monk of the Rinzai sect, born in Kyōto. With SESSON YŪBAI one of the two great figures in early GOZAN LITERATURE (Chinese learning in medieval Japanese Zen monasteries). While Sesson began its poetic tradition, Kokan, though also a poet, is considered the founder of its scholarly tradition. His writings include *Saihokushū,* an anthology of poems and belles-lettres; *Shubun inryaku,* a dictionary of Chinese rhymes, the first such compiled in Japan and highly popular; GENKŌ SHAKUSHO, the first history of Japanese Buddhism;

Kōkei

Completed in 1189 by the sculptor Kōkei, this monumental image of the bodhisattva Fukū Kensaku Kannon (also called Fukūkenjaku Kannon) is the main icon of the hall Nan'endō at the temple Kōfukuji in Nara. Assembled woodblock construction (yosegi-zukuri), lacquered and gilt. Height 341.5 cm. National Treasure.

Butsugo shinron, the first treatise written in Japan on the *Lankāvatāra-sūtra;* and numerous other religious treatises and literary handbooks, including several of a sectarian nature intended to prove the superiority of Zen to other Buddhist doctrines. Kokan entered monastic life as a small child and from adolescence on enjoyed a personal acquaintance with emperors and ex-emperors but was apparently without political ambitions. Fragile health prevented Kokan from ever visiting China, but he is often praised as one of the finest Japanese writers of Chinese prose after SUGAWARA NO MICHIZANE.　　　　*Marian* URY

Kōkatō Treaty → Kanghwa, Treaty of

kōke

(literally, "elevated families"). Hereditary officials of the Edo period (1600–1868); masters of rites and ceremonies for the Tokugawa shogunate. The 26 families eligible for the post included the Kira (see KIRA YOSHINAKA), ŌTOMO, HATAKEYAMA, and KYŌGOKU, all of whom traced their lineage to the Muromachi period (1333–1568). Although their stipends were less than the minimum assigned to *daimyō,* they enjoyed honorary daimyō status. They were placed under the office of the senior councillors (*rōjū*). Apart from their ceremonial functions, the *kōke* received emissaries from the imperial court and served as the shōgun's representatives at the court and at major shrines and temples, including the Ise Shrine and the Tokugawa Shrine at Nikkō.

Kōkei (fl late 12th century)

Sculptor of Buddhist images. His work strongly influenced the development of Kamakura-period (1185–1333) sculpture and enabled the KEI SCHOOL to flourish. He was the father of UNKEI and the teacher of KAIKEI, both prominent Kei-school sculptors. Kōkei often collaborated with his followers in restoration projects for major temples in the Kyōto and Nara areas, such as the temple TŌDAIJI. Among the few authenticated examples of his work are the *Fukū Kensaku Kannon* in the temple KŌFUKUJI in Nara. The strong emotions and physical movement expressed in his sculpture won favor over the elegant grace of works of the established IN SCHOOL and EN SCHOOL.

Kokei sanshō

("The Three Laughers of Tiger Ravine"; Ch: Husi san xiao or Hu-ssu san hsiao). A Chinese allegorical story illustrating that spiritual purity is not limited by artificial boundaries. The Buddhist monk Huiyuan (Hui-yüan; 334–416) practiced intense religious austerities in his monastery on Lushan, vowing never to reenter the secular world and never to cross the bridge over the bordering Tiger Ravine. However, the poet Tao Yuanming (T'ao Yüan-ming; ca 365–427) and the Taoist Lu Xiujing (Lu Hsiu-ching; ca 406–477) came to visit him and, after an evening of penetrating conversation, Huiyuan escorted his guests out. So intellectually involved were the men in their discussion that no one noticed when they crossed the stone bridge over Tiger Ravine. Suddenly realizing that Huiyuan had broken his solemn vow, the three men clasped hands and burst out laughing, understanding that Huiyuan's moral integrity was unimpaired. The story became a subject for Japanese INK PAINTING from the Muromachi period (1333–1568).

koken

Bill of sale, or deed, used from the Heian period (794–1185) to the Meiji period (1868–1912) in sales of property (*kokyaku*), particularly of real estate such as farmlands or residential lots. A *koken* was given by the seller to the buyer at the time of the transaction as legal confirmation of the sales contract, lest the validity of the transaction be challenged in future. Also called *baiken, baikenjō,* and *kokyakujō.* The many surviving documents of this type vary in format according to the periods in which they were written. Under the administrative provisions of the RITSURYŌ SYSTEM (7th–11th centuries), *koken* were official documents certified with the seals of provincial governors (KOKUSHI) or district officials (GUNJI). From the mid-Heian period onward, such certification was no longer required, and *koken* were simply exchanged by the parties concerned; in some cases, however, neighbors of the parties would add their seals in witness of the transaction. During the Edo period (1600–1868) it was required that *koken* bear the seals of town or village officials, or those of the semiofficial neighborhood leaders' groups known as GONINGUMI. After the MEIJI RESTORATION (1868) the *koken* deed system was retained by the authorities in large cities such as Tōkyō and Kyōto, and it is said to have influenced the *chiken* (title-deed) system which the Meiji government employed until 1889.

　　　　KOYANAGI Shun'ichirō

Kōken, Empress (718–770)

The 46th and 48th sovereign (*tennō*) of Japan in the traditional count (which includes several nonhistorical emperors), reigning 749–758 as Kōken and 764–770 as Shōtoku. She was the second daughter of Emperor SHŌMU and Empress KŌMYŌ. Deeply religious like her parents, in 752 Kōken officially dedicated the great image of the Buddha at the temple TŌDAIJI. She was strongly influenced by her cousin, the powerful FUJIWARA NO NAKAMARO, and following his advice abdicated in 758 in favor of Prince TONERI's seventh son, who became the 47th emperor, Junnin. When the retired empress came to favor the monk DŌKYŌ, the outraged Nakamaro rose up in arms and was soon captured and killed. Charging Junnin with responsibility for the uprising, Kōken had him deposed and exiled; she then reascended the throne in 764 as the reigning empress Shōtoku. She granted Dōkyō great power and even hoped to make the monk her successor, but courtiers such as WAKE NO KIYOMARO opposed this move because Dōkyō was not of imperial lineage. Following Shōtoku's death, he was banished by the FUJIWARA FAMILY. After this headstrong woman sovereign, no other woman was allowed to reign until the two figurehead empresses (Meishō and Go-Sakuramachi) of the Edo period (1600–1868).　　KITAMURA Bunji

kōkennin

(guardian). A person lawfully invested with the power and charged with the duty of taking care of and supervising a person incapable of administering his own affairs (CIVIL CODE, arts. 838–876). The ward of a guardianship (*kōken*) may be either a minor or an incompetent. A guardianship for a minor is established when there is no one to exercise parental authority over the minor. If the person who last exercised parental authority over the minor child did not designate a guardian by will, the family court appoints a guardian. With respect to incompetent wards, if a married person is adjudged incompetent,

Kokeshi

Examples of the ten types of *kokeshi*: (from left to right) the Tsuchiyu type; the Yajirō type; the Tōgatta type; the Narugo type; the Hijiori type; the Sakunami type; the Zaō type; the Kijiyama type; the Nambu type; and the Tsugaru type.

the spouse becomes his or her guardian. If there is no spouse, a guardian is appointed by the family court. A ward cannot have more than one guardian.

A guardian is responsible for the supervision and education of a minor ward and for the medical treatment of an incompetent ward, and also manages the ward's property and represents the ward in juristic acts concerning his or her property. A higher degree of care is required of a guardian than of a parent and, in certain cases, a supervisor of the guardian may be appointed. In addition, the family court supervises a guardian and may, under certain conditions, remove a guardian.   BAI Kōichi

kokeshi

Wooden doll with a spherical head attached to a cylindrical body having no limbs; originally a folk toy of the Tōkohu district (northeastern Japan). *Kokeshi* are thought to have originated in the early 19th century, made by woodworkers in this poorest area of Japan. Many *kokeshi* have a girl's face, with floral designs such as chrysanthemum, plum, or cherry blossoms on the body. They are classified into 10 types, according to manufacturing techniques, shape, decoration, and so forth. There were once as many as 60 different local names for the doll. Since World War II, *kokeshi* have become popular among collectors.   SAITŌ Ryōsuke

Kokin Denju

("Transmission of the *Kokinshū*"). The tradition of handing down, from teacher to chosen disciple, a body of secret teachings concerning the poems of the 10th-century classic poetry anthology KOKINSHŪ. The term *denju* refers to the transmission of secret teachings, a convention common to Buddhism and many Japanese arts.

The tradition of Kokin Denju began during the Kamakura period (1185–1333), when the *Kokinshū* had come to be regarded as the basic canon of poetry, and the Nijō and Kyōgoku–Reizei literary families, both descended from the great poet FUJIWARA NO SADAIE (Fujiwara no Teika; 1162–1241), were vying for the prestige of being considered the true heirs to his poetic tradition. The conservative Nijō version of the teachings, which was generally regarded as the authentic one, remained in the family until the time of NIJŌ TAMEYO (1250?–1338) who, for lack of an heir, handed it down to his disciple TON'A (1289–1372). Eventually it was bestowed, through TŌ NO TSUNEYORI (1401–84), on the *renga* (linked verse) poet SŌGI (1421–1502). From Sōgi it was transmitted to SANJŌNISHI SANETAKA (1455–1537) and his family, and then to HOSOKAWA YŪSAI (1534–1610) and Prince Toshihito (1579–1629), from whence came the so-called Gosho (Imperial Palace) Denju. A second line of transmission was begun when Sōgi transmitted the teachings to his disciple SHŌHAKU (1443–1527) as well, and this became known as the Sakai Denju, from Shōhaku's residence in the city of Sakai, near Ōsaka.

Despite its prestige and authority, the actual content of the Kokin Denju is the subject of much skepticism. By the 15th century it had apparently lost whatever substantial content it may have originally possessed and deteriorated to arcane trivia: the names of three birds and three plants referred to in the *Kokinshū*, for example, and the proper way to pronounce certain characters. Whatever its content, however, up to the end of the 16th century the Kokin Denju retained

however, up to the end of the 16th century the Kokin Denju retained its authority as a highly respected symbol of a strong cultural tradition.

Kokinshū

(Collection from Ancient and Modern Times). More properly known as the *Kokin wakashū* (Collection of Japanese Poems from Ancient and Modern Times). Although its compilation was already under way during the reign of Emperor Uda (r 887–897), the *Kokinshū* was officially commissioned under Emperor Daigo (r 897–930). It was completed about 905. Although the compilers of the *Kokinshū* believed that the 8th-century collection of Japanese verse, the MAN'YŌSHŪ, had also been royally commissioned, the *Kokinshū* was in fact the first in a series of anthologies of native verse compiled by royal command, the *chokusenshū* or *nijūichidai shū*, "collections from 21 eras." The *Kokinshū* is also termed the first of the *sandaishū*, collections from the 3 eras that begin the 21; and the first of the *hachidaishū*, collections of (the first) 8 eras. Next to being chosen as a compiler of such a collection, having one's poems included was the highest poetic honor.

The four compilers of the *Kokinshū* include KI NO TSURAYUKI and his cousin KI NO TOMONORI, ŌSHIKŌCHI NO MITSUNE, and MIBU NO TADAMINE. Tsurayuki wrote the Japanese preface to the *Kokinshū* and Ki no Yoshimochi (d 919) the Chinese preface. The collection was ordered so "that many matters should not be consigned to oblivion, as also the past should not be forgotten and an interest be maintained in things of long ago." To sustain this royal purpose, the collection's 1,111 poems were chosen from three principal if overlapping chronological groups: anonymous poems from older and more recent times; poems from the period of the "six poetic sages" (ROKKASEN; mid-9th century); and poems by the compilers and their contemporaries. The six poetic sages attained their status by virtue of having been discussed in Tsurayuki's preface and include: Bishop HENJŌ (17 poems); ARIWARA NO NARIHIRA (30 poems); Bun'ya no Yasuhide (5 poems); Priest Kisen (1 poem); ONO NO KOMACHI (18 poems); and Ōtomo no Kuronushi (3 poems). The compilers themselves are represented by 243 poems: Tsurayuki, with over 100, has more poems than any other poet; Tadamine, with 35, is the least represented of the compilers. Another 6 poets, including Lady ISE and Priest SOSEI, are represented by 10 or more poems each, accounting for 121 poems in all. Most of the other named poets have just a few specimens each. Something over 120 named poets are represented, including almost 100 men and almost 30 women; however, more than 450 anonymous poems, some of great attractiveness, make up the largest single group in the entire collection.

The *Kokinshū* set the practice of arranging poems not by single author canons but by topics, and the ensuing 20 royal collections use its basic organization, whether in its 20 books or in the occasional variant of 10. Pride of place and number go to the seasonal poems (books 1–6) and the love poems (books 11–15), which open the two halves of the collection. The seasons include two books on spring, one on summer, two on autumn, and one on winter (342 poems). They are followed by one book each of congratulatory, parting, travel, and acrostic poems. The five books of love poems (360 poems) are followed by a book of laments, two books on miscellaneous topics (in which no single topic such as spring or love prevails), one on miscellaneous poetic forms, and one on poems from the Bureau of Poetry (Wakadokoro). The proportions make it clear that seasonal and love poetry were considered the essential topical concerns of lyric poetry. Later collections drop acrostics and add books on such topics as Buddhism, with miscellaneous topics coming to have increasing importance.

The *Kokinshū* also pioneered in arranging poems within a given topic in meaningful sequences. The seasonal poems follow the course of natural phenomena in themselves and as ordered by annual court rites (*nenchū gyōji*, see FESTIVALS: annual events). The love poems detail the course of lovers' affairs from their inception, through countless vicissitudes of arrest and renewal, to their ends. Such progressions tend to integrate poems into larger sequences.

Systematic Japanese poetics also begin with Tsurayuki's and Yoshimochi's prefaces to the *Kokinshū*. The latter especially exhibits the influence of the great preface to the Chinese *Shijing* (Shih-ching; Book of Songs). Yoshimochi posits three poetic concepts: feeling (Ch: *qing* or *ch'ing*; J: *jō* or *nasake*); words (Ch: *ci* or *tz'u*; J: *shi* or *kotoba*); and style (Ch: *ti* or *t'i*; J: *tai*). Tsurayuki's equivalents are heart or mind *(kokoro)*, words *(kotoba)*, and style *(sama)*, although this last yields to total effect *(sugata)*. Above all, Tsurayuki's encounter with lyric poetry brought about a lyric poetic system based on affectivism and expressionism. This accounted for poet, world, reader, and expression—as any full poetics must—and was so sound that the later introduction of valued prose narrative and drama only modified without overturning it.

Japanese usually compare the *Kokinshū* with the SHIN KOKINSHŪ (ca 1205, New Collection from Ancient and Modern Times), and the later collection is conventionally preferred for its profundity. The *Kokinshū* is more original, however, and more responsive to immediate life. Its poets sought to express nature and the world in terms of the responding human heart, whereas the later collection sought to discover human significance in the world.

In these and other respects, the *Kokinshū* represents the most creative period of the Japanese court. Since its values and presumptions endured for centuries, it is the most illuminating place to begin a study of classical Japanese literature. See also WAKA; CHINESE LITERATURE AND JAPANESE LITERATURE; LITERATURE: Heian literature.

—— Many editions of the *Kokinshū* exist with commentary: Konishi Jin'ichi, ed, *Kokin wakashū* in *Shinchū kokubungaku sōsho* (Dai Nihon Yūbenkai Kōdansha, 1949). Kubota Utsubo, ed, *Kokin wakashū hyōshaku*, 3 vols (rev ed, 1960). Saeki Umetomo, ed, *Kokin wakashū* in *Nihon koten bungaku taikei*, vol 8 (Iwanami Shoten, 1958). These provide useful bibliographical information. A conspectus of recent criticism and scholarship will be found in the *Kokinshū* issue of *Bungaku* 43 (1975). Useful Western-language sources and translations include: Georges Bonneau, *Le Monument poétique de Heian: le Kokinshū*, 3 vols (Librairie Orientaliste Paul Guenther, 1933–35). Robert H. Brower and Earl Miner, *Japanese Court Poetry* (1961). Konishi Jin'ichi, Robert H. Brower, and Earl Miner, "Association and Progression: Principles of Integration in Anthologies and Sequences of Japanese Court Poetry," *Harvard Journal of Asiatic Studies* 21 (1958). Earl Miner, "Toward a New Approach to Classical Japanese Poetics," in Japan P.E.N. Club, ed, *Studies on Japanese Culture*, vol 1 (1973). *Earl* MINER

kokiroku

(ancient private records). The term *kiroku*, as used in its narrow sense by Japanese historians, is almost synonymous with "diary." The prefix *ko* (old) indicates the antiquity of the documents.

From the latter half of the 9th century, it was customary for members of the aristocracy to keep diaries. In later periods this custom spread throughout society. Large numbers of these diaries, which are central to the study of Japanese history, survive.

Some of the oldest *kokiroku* mentioned in history are IKI NO MURAJI HAKATOKO NO FUMI, an account written in the latter half of the 7th century by a traveler to Tang (T'ang) China, and *Ato no Chitoko no nikki*, a record of the JINSHIN DISTURBANCE of 672. However, these were not diaries in the ordinary sense, but private records of certain incidents, and the manuscripts themselves have been lost. The oldest extant diary manuscripts are fragments from a diary by an 8th-century copier of sutras and fragments from a *guchūreki*, a kind of almanac.

In ancient Japan, as in China, the government sponsored the compilation of official histories (see RIKKOKUSHI). The last of these,

the *Nihon sandai jitsuroku*, ends with the last year of the reign of Emperor Kōkō (r 884–887).

The diaries of the Heian period (794–1185) were almost all written by members of the imperial family or by court nobles. The emperors UDA (r 887–897), DAIGO (r 897–930), Murakami (r 946–967), and others kept diaries; of these only a few fragments or isolated sentences remain. The number of diaries written by court nobles is larger and a great many of them have been preserved almost in their entirety. The more notable ones are SHŌYŪKI, MIDŌ KAMPAKU KI, CHŪYŪKI, and TAIKI. Most of them are copies, but in some of them, such as *Midō Kampaku ki*, a large part of the original manuscript has been preserved. In the same period travel diaries were written by priests who went to study in Tang China. The more famous ones are those by ENNIN, ENCHIN, and Jōjin (1011–81).

In the Kamakura period (1185–1333) the diaries of the emperors FUSHIMI and Hanazono, as well as the GYOKUYŌ, MEIGETSUKI, and *Minkeiki* (by Hirohashi Tsunemitsu; covers 1226–67), written by nobles, are noteworthy. Diaries were also kept by shrines and temples, including the KASUGA SHRINE. As for records kept by the shogunate, only a portion of *Kenji sannen ki* remains. AZUMA KAGAMI is not an actual diary of the Kamakura shogunate; it was compiled at a much later date. Since it utilized many private records and documents as reference materials, it is still an important historical record of the shogunate of that period.

Among diaries written during the Northern and Southern Courts period (1336–92), ENTAIRYAKU, MOROMORIKI, and *Gukanki* (by Konoe Michitsugu; covers 1353–83) are notable. In the Muromachi period (1333–1568), Emperor Go-Nara's (1497–1557; r 1526–57) diary and KAMMON GYOKI by Prince Fushimi no Miya Sadafusa are important. A record of events in the court, *Oyudono no Ue no nikki*, was kept by ladies-in-waiting until the end of the Edo period (1600–1868). Among diaries written by the nobility, KENNAIKI, SANETAKA KŌ KI, and *Tokitsugu Kyō ki* are especially noteworthy. During this period, diaries written by temple officials and priests appear one after another; among them are MANSAI's *Mansai Jugō nikki*, Inryōken nichiroku (kept by the abbot of Rokuon'in, a subtemple of SHŌKOKUJI), DAIJŌIN JISHA ZŌJI KI, and TAMON'IN NIKKI (kept from 1478 to 1617 by abbots of Tamon'in, a subtemple of KŌFUKUJI). Official diaries by shogunate officials exist as well, but private diaries by *samurai* in this period have yet to be discovered.

There is a large number of diaries dating from the Azuchi-Momoyama (1568–1600) and Edo periods, many of them by court nobles, temple officials, and priests. UWAI KAKUKEN NIKKI is famous as the private diary of a samurai. An enormous number of official shogunate and domain diaries have also been preserved. Important shogunate officials, including senior councillors, *daimyō*, and samurai of various domains, left numerous records. Diaries by people from all walks of life—scholars, artists, merchants, farmers, and women—also remain. For literary diaries see NIKKI BUNGAKU.

Saiki Kazuma

Kokka

(National Flower). Influential monthly magazine specializing in East Asian, particularly Japanese, art. It was founded in 1889 by the art patron Kuki Ryūichi (1852–1931), the Japanese scholar OKAKURA KAKUZŌ, and the *Asahi shimbun* editorial writer Takahashi Kenzō (1855–98) to counterbalance what they regarded as excessive Japanese enthusiasm for Western art, and to awaken Japanese and Western interest in East Asian art. It remains one of Japan's most distinguished art journals.

Kokkai → Diet

Kokkai Kisei Dōmei → League for Establishing a National Assembly

Kokka Kōan Iinkai → National Public Safety Commission

Kokka Shintō → State Shintō

Kokka Sōdōin Hō → National Mobilization Law

kokkeibon

(literally, "funny books"). A highly heterogeneous body of comic writing, largely but not exclusively fiction, produced for the most part in Edo (now Tōkyō) from the middle of the 18th century until the end of the Edo period (1600–1868). All *kokkeibon* are humorous in intent, but not all humorous works of the period are called *kokkeibon;* those whose subject matter or format place them in other categories, such as SHAREBON and KIBYŌSHI, are not designated *kokkeibon.* Most *kokkeibon* are distinguished by the fact that they were printed originally as *chūbon,* "middle-size books" whose page size set them apart physically from other formats for fiction. A great many *kokkeibon* consist in large part of vivid, highly colloquial dialogue.

While the term *kokkeibon* itself did not come into general use until the 1820s, literary historians trace the origin of the form to the *dangibon,* books of sermons or ethical discourses *(dangi),* often satiric in tone, modeled on the sermons of proselytizing priests of the Jōdo sect. *Imayō heta dangi* (1752, Clumsy Sermons for the Modern Age) by Jōkambō Kōa, an Ōsaka physician, is the best-known work in the *dangibon* tradition. While the *dangibon,* despite their vivid, colloquial language and comic effects (including not only satire but a liberal use of puns and lewd and scatological jokes), seem to have been seriously intended efforts to provide moral lessons to a broad popular audience, the *kokkeibon* in the hands of later writers for the most part lost its didactic component.

The most important figure in the early history of the *kokkeibon* is the Dutch scholar and naturalist HIRAGA GENNAI (1728–80), whom later writers revered as the spiritual father of the form. *Nenashigusa* (1763, Rootless Grasses), a fantasy describing the efforts of Emma, the king of the netherworld, to acquire as his lover a famous young actor of the day, and *Fūryū Shidōken den* (1763), an equally fantastic "biography" of the popular contemporary storyteller Fukai Shidōken (1682–1765), set a high standard for pungent social satire. Gennai also wrote several nonfiction satiric essays that became models for similar comic essays by later writers. Gennai's perverse, sophisticated wit and scintillating style, however, are rarely seen in later *kokkeibon.*

Without question, the two writers most closely identified with the *kokkeibon* are JIPPENSHA IKKU (1765–1831) and SHIKITEI SAMBA (1776–1822). Ikku's *Tōkaidōchū hizakurige* and its sequels, which appeared between 1802 and 1822, portray the comic adventures of a pair of footloose travelers from Edo as they make their way along the famous highway Tōkaidō to Ōsaka and Kyōto. Samba's *Ukiyoburo* (1809–13, The Bathhouse of the Floating World) presents a series of vignettes of everyday occurrences in a typical public bath in Edo. Both works consist largely of dialogue, and much of their humor derives from their authors' keen sensitivity to the rhythms and quirks of contemporary spoken Japanese. Ikku's humor tends to the ribald and the slapstick, while Samba's grows out of his more subtly ironic view of human nature.

Hizakurige and *Ukiyoburo* and many similar works by Ikku and Samba and their imitators show the strong influence of RAKUGO and other contemporary comic storytelling modes. Although the *kokkeibon* from Gennai to Samba and beyond includes many examples that are not based on monologues, dialogues, or conversations— parody was a staple of *kokkeibon* writers—perhaps the most important role of the form in literary-historical terms was in showing the importance and effectiveness of paying close attention to the realistic rendering of dialogue as an element of fiction. See also GESAKU.

Robert W. LEUTNER

kokkuri

(literally, "nodding"). A type of popular divination, the Japanese counterpart of planchette or Ouija. If one wishes to find a lost object, for example, one has a medium hold the top of a tripod of loosely tied sticks over a board on which are written numbers from 1 to 10 and the 50 letters of the Japanese *kana* syllabary. As the medium, usually blindfolded, goes into a trance, the sticks begin to slide over the letters on the board and, letter by letter, a message appears. The name *kokkuri* refers to the movement of the medium, who nods involuntarily like a person dozing off. There are many variations of *kokkuri* divination. It has been popular since the middle of the Meiji period (1868–1912). See also DIVINATION.

INOKUCHI Shōji

Kokon chomonjū

Also called *Kokin chomonshū.* Collection of tales with moral lessons for the young, dating from the early part of the Kamakura period (1185–1333). Originally compiled by Tachibana no Narisue in 1254; later amended by others. The more than 700 stories, many of which also appear in the JIKKUNSHŌ, are divided into 30 categories ranging from "Buddhism," "Government," and "Loyal Retainers" to "Animals," "Thieves," and "Gambling." AKUTAGAWA RYŪNOSUKE used it as the source for some of his short stories, including "Jigokuhen" (tr "Hell Screen," 1948). See SETSUWA BUNGAKU.

kokorozuke

Token of appreciation; tip. Money or articles given, as an expression of appreciation for services, to a person of lower status, such as a maid in a Japanese-style inn, a *geisha,* or a chauffeur. Also referred to as SHŪGI. If more than a normal amount of service is desired, one gives a little more than the prevailing rate in advance, especially if this is the first or only time services are to be requested. For a person whose services one uses often, or in a place that one frequents, *kokorozuke* need not be given in advance, even if more than normal services are expected. To such a person or establishment, one would give seasonal gifts, such as CHŪGEN (at midyear) or SEIBO (at the end of the year). Money is the most common form of *kokorozuke.* It is placed in a special gift-money envelope with ornaments (MIZUHIKI and NOSHI), usually printed on the envelope. At the top of the envelope the Chinese characters for *shūgi* (literally, "in celebration") or *sunshi* ("a trifle") may be written to indicate the purpose of the gift. The characters for *kokorozuke* would never be written or printed because of that word's association with advance payment. See also GIFT GIVING.

Harumi BEFU

koku

A measure of volume or capacity, used generally for rice but sometimes for other dry substances and liquids as well. In the Edo period (1600–1868) a *koku* of grain equaled about 0.18 cubic meter, 180.39 liters, or 5.12 US bushels, theoretically enough rice to feed one person for a year. Land productivity, tax assessments, the stipends of *samurai,* and the wealth of *daimyō* were all measured in *koku* (see KOKUDAKA; KENCHI). As a measurement unit for lumber or ship capacity, the *koku* equaled 10 cubic *shaku,* or approximately 0.28 cubic meter or 10 cubic feet. As early as the 7th century, under the RITSURYŌ SYSTEM, the following hierarchy of measurement units was adopted from China: one *koku* equaled 10 *to;* one *to* equaled 10 *shō;* and one *shō* equaled 10 *gō.* The size of these units varied widely with time and place. When they were standardized by the national unifier TOYOTOMI HIDEYOSHI late in the 16th century, the *koku* was set at more than twice the size it had been in the 7th century. See also WEIGHTS AND MEASURES.

Kokubō Fujinkai → Dai Nippon Kokubō Fujinkai

Kokubu

City on Kagoshima Bay in central Kagoshima Prefecture, Kyūshū. It takes its name from the provincial temple (KOKUBUNJI) that was established here in the 8th century. The city's fame derives mainly from its tobacco, grown since 1604. A Self Defense Force base is located here. Pop: 35,436.

Kokubungaku Kenkyū Shiryōkan

(National Institute of Japanese Literature). Government center for the preservation of classical Japanese literature, forming a counterpart to the Nihon Kindai Bungakukan, the MUSEUM OF MODERN JAPANESE LITERATURE. The institute systematically surveys, collects (largely on microforms), studies, processes, preserves, and provides access to pre-1868 Japanese literature. Its main clientele is the scholarly research community, both within and without the university setting in Japan and abroad, who undertake current research in fields related to retrospective literature. The Japan Science Council was instrumental in urging the Ministry of Education to establish the center in direct response to requests from the academic community.

Although established in 1972, the institute first opened its doors to the public in July 1977, providing reference, lending, and photocopying services as well as reading space. Approximately 5,000 items of old literary works are added annually on microfilm. Forming the core of the collection is the former Historical Documents Division of the Ministry of Education, which had been created in 1951 to concentrate mainly on the collection and preservation of documents of the Edo period (1600–1868). To date some 40,000 historical documents, about 5,000 pieces of folk materials, and 800 reels of microfilmed historical documents are available for consultation. Some of the tools available for accessing the institute are: (1) Catalog of Japanese manuscripts and printed books in microfilm; (2) Catalog of periodicals, indexing more than 1,300 current serials; (3) Annual bibliography of current research in Japanese literature, covering some 5,000 journal articles and 1,000 monographs in the field of Japanese literature; (4) *Kokubungaku kenkyū shiryōkan kiyō* (Bulletin of the National Institute of Japanese Literature, annual, 1975–), and (5) *Kokubungaku kenkyu shiryōkan hōkoku* (NIJL Report, biannual, 1972–). The institute sponsors literature exhibitions and a variety of cooperative research projects. The staff numbers in excess of 80 and is located in a new five-story building in a park setting in Yutakachō, Shinagawa Ward, Tōkyō. *Theodore F.* WELCH

Kokubunji

City in central Tōkyō Prefecture. It takes its name from the provincial temple (KOKUBUNJI) that was established here in the 8th century. An agricultural district before World War II, it is now the site of precision instruments plants, homes, and colleges, including the Railway Technical Research Institute and Tōkyō College of Economics. Both the Man'yō Botanical Gardens, with plants associated with the 8th-century poetic anthology MAN'YŌSHŪ, and the remains of the provincial temple are noteworthy. Pop: 91,014.

kokubunji

(provincial temple). Temples built as state institutions by the government during the Nara period (710–794) in imitation of a similar system in Tang (T'ang) period (618–907) China. In 741 Emperor SHŌMU decreed that a *kokubunji* and *kokubunniji* (provincial nunnery) be built in each province. State funds as well as donations from major families (*uji*) financed their building, and the manpower of peasants serving the annual 60-day corvée labor (*zōyō*; see YŌEKI) was enlisted for the project. By 780 most of these temples were completed. The official name of the *kokubunji* was Konkōmyō Shitennō *gokoku no tera*, and that of the *kokubunniji* was Hokke *metsuzai no tera*, indicating that the former was built to pray for the protection of the state and the latter for the atonement of sin. Twenty monks resided in each *kokubunji*, which numbered among its buildings, the main South Gate, the main hall, pagodas, lecture hall, belfry, sutra libraries, dining hall, and monks' quarters. A bronze Śākyamuni triad (statue of Śākyamuni with two attendants) that was surrounded by statues of the Four Heavenly Kings (Shitennō) was enshrined in each main hall. The *kokubunniji*, which housed 10 nuns each, were smaller in size. In 752, the TŌDAIJI, enshrining the 16-meter high statue of Vairocana Buddha, was built in Heijōkyō (present-day Nara) as the head *kokubunji*. *MURAKAMI Shigeyoshi*

kokudainō

The practice during the Edo period (1600–1868) of paying the annual tax (NENGU) in cash instead of rice, the customary medium of payment. The *kokudainō* was used when grain transport was inconvenient or when poor harvests limited the amount of available rice. The methods of computation and the ratio of payment in kind to specie, differed from place to place. This practice greatly increased after the middle of the 18th century, as the money economy grew, but the shogunate, concerned over the shortage of stored rice (see KURAMAI), placed limitations on *kokudainō* and encouraged payment in rice.

kokudaka

(assessed tax base in terms of *koku*). An estimate of the annual yield of farmland, measured in *koku* (1 *koku* = about 180 liters or 5 US bushels) of unpolished rice; the uniform basis of land taxes through-

out the Edo period (1600–1868). Established nationwide by TOYOTOMI HIDEYOSHI at the time of his cadastral survey of 1582 to 1596 (see KENCHI), this kind of assessment remained in use until the LAND TAX REFORM OF 1873–1881. Because yield is affected by the fertility of the soil and the availability of water, paddy fields were classified in four grades with average annual yields (*kokumori*) of 1.5, 1.3, 1.2, and 1.1 *koku* for each *tan* (about 0.1 hectare or 0.25 acre) of area. Multiplying the *kokumori* of a paddy field by its number of *tan* produced its *kokudaka*, or assessed tax base. The productivity of dry fields was similarly computed. *Daimyō* levied annual taxes (NENGU) on each village as a percentage of its total *kokudaka* figure, and the shogunate exacted contributions and services from each daimyō on the basis of the total *kokudaka* figures for his domain. Reassessment was infrequent, so that farmers and daimyō alike had an incentive to improve the yield; and farm production did increase significantly during the Edo period. *Kokudaka* replaced KANDAKA (the agreed-upon annual tax calculated in terms of money), which had been used in the Kamakura (1185–1333) and Muromachi (1333–1568) periods. Because *kokudaka* was simply a tax base figure, the authorities were able to vary the amount of taxation due from the farmers by changing the tax rate *(men)*. *Kokudaka* was calculated in kind, and so it protected the farmers—though not the daimyō—from the vagaries of rice prices in an increasingly money-based economy. *John W.* HALL

Kokudochō → National Land Agency

kokufu

(provincial capitals). Seats of provincial governments under the RITSURYŌ SYSTEM of government begun in the late 7th century; also known as *fuchū* or *funai*. Located at strategic points throughout Japan, they apparently had the same "checkerboard" layout found in the capital cities HEIJŌKYŌ (Nara) and HEIANKYŌ (Kyōto) and were surrounded by earthen walls and moats. The main government offices *(kokuga)*, located in the north central section, served as the headquarters of the provincial administrators (KOKUSHI), who were responsible for collecting the central government's taxes and maintaining law and order. A government-sponsored Buddhist temple (KOKUBUNJI) and a major local Shintō shrine *(sōja* or *sōsha)* were usually situated nearby. Traces of some of these administrative centers still exist, the best-known example being in Hōfu City, the capital of Suō Province (now part of Yamaguchi Prefecture). Other modern cities whose names reflect their past history as provincial capitals include Kōfu (the seat of Yamanashi Prefecture), Fuchū in Tōkyō, and several towns called Kokufu. See also SAKU.

Kokugaku

(National Learning). A general name for the textual and exegetical study of Japanese classical literature and ancient writings which began in the 17th century. Kokugaku should be distinguished from Japanese learning on Japan in general which was then called *wagaku* (Japanese studies) or *kogaku* (ancient studies; this in turn not to be confused with KOGAKU, a school of Japanese Confucian studies). Hence, Kokugaku is sometimes more specifically defined as the philological study of Japanese classical literature and ancient writings with the aim of identifying peculiarly Japanese cultural elements or examples of a typical Japanese mentality. In the course of modern Japanese history until the end of World War II, Kokugaku also meant the study of the imperial state, devoted to the elucidation of what was seen as Japan's unique national polity of KOKUTAI. Thus, at times Kokugaku has assumed an ideological character and cannot be equated with classical studies in general.

Edo Period (1600–1868) —— Four scholars have traditionally been cited as forming the lineage of orthodox Kokugaku in the Edo period (1600–1868): KADA NO AZUMAMARO (1669–1736), KAMO NO MABUCHI (1697–1769), MOTOORI NORINAGA (1730–1801), and HIRATA ATSUTANE (1776–1843). This lineage, although beginning with Kada no Azumamaro, was conceived and propagated by Atsutane and his followers to serve their nationalist ideology, which exerted a certain influence on late Edo-period thinkers. As they conceived it, Kokugaku was the study of Japanese classics and antiquity, which was synonymous with Shintō studies. In contrast, modern philologically-oriented scholars see KEICHŪ (1640–1701) as the forerunner of Kokugaku. They define Kokugaku as an investigation of ancient Japanese thought and culture through the philological study of the classics, seeing it as having reached a high level of development in the Edo period before Norinaga. Thus, this latter approach sees in Norinaga a significant change in the nature of Kokugaku, from the philological to the ideological.

Though a monk of the Shingon sect, Keichū lived among laymen and spent his days reading classical literature. He completed the *Man'yō daishō ki,* an annotated text of the 8th-century poetry anthology MAN'YŌSHŪ at the request of TOKUGAWA MITSUKUNI, *daimyō* of the Mito domain (now part of Ibaraki Prefecture) and a patron of scholarship. In his study of this earliest extant Japanese poetic anthology, Keichū demonstrated his strong affinity for the ancient poets. He insisted that in order to understand the spirit of the ancients, one had to suspend the way of thinking of one's own time. In his view, the contemporary mind was fettered by concepts alien to the ancients and had traveled far from the naive emotions necessary for a direct, human response.

This humanistic spirit characterizes Keichū's scholarship as does his methodical explication of ancient words *(kogen).* He went back to the ancient texts to gather many examples of usage, and his definitions of ancient Japanese vocabulary were bolstered by hard evidence and seem to avoid personal interpretation. His literary studies of the *Man'yōshū,* KOKINSHŪ (the first imperial anthology, compiled in the early 10th century), and ISE MONOGATARI (a mid-10th century sequence of poetic tales) proved to be a great spiritual heritage for later classicists, along with his studies on KANA usage in his *Waji shōran shō* (Notes on the Rectification of Japanese Scripts).

Another early influence in Kokugaku studies was Kada no Azumamaro, a teacher, researcher on old documents, and scholar of the classics who came from a family of Shintō priests. Azumamaro devoted much of his life to the acquisition and bibliographical research and evaluation of ancient documents. He asked for the shogunate's sanction to found a school for Japanese studies in Kyōto, an attempt to promote National Learning that was later highly praised by Hirata Atsutane and other nationalists.

Kada no Azumamaro was the teacher of Kamo no Mabuchi, who was also from a Shintō family. Mabuchi eventually went to Edo (now Tōkyō), where he served TAYASU MUNETAKE (son of the shōgun TOKUGAWA YOSHIMUNE), an admirer of the *Man'yōshū* and himself a poet. Like Keichū, Kamo no Mabuchi studied the *Man'yōshū.* He was learned enough in ancient Japanese to be able to compose *Man'yō*-style WAKA poems and enthusiastically promoted such pursuits among other Kokugaku scholars. Mabuchi's study of the *Man'yōshū* was thus not only a scholarly effort but also an attempt to incorporate the spirit of the work into his life. He praised the "lofty and honest spirit" *(takaku naoki kokoro)* of the *Man'yōshū* poets. He emphasized that originally, before Japanese culture absorbed strong foreign influences (principally Buddhist and Confucian), *waka* had been composed to express straightforwardly the feelings of the ancient poets. Mabuchi saw truth revealed in this "lofty and honest spirit," as opposed to what he thought of as the false, artificial poetry of later times. His predilection for the world of the *Man'yōshū* became a yearning for ancient times when honest emotion was expressed with ease and vigor. This view of ancient times and of the *Man'yōshū* constituted an important aspect of the ideological basis of Kokugaku. For those who were to follow Mabuchi, the word *kodai* (ancient times) became a symbol of this longing for the spiritual origins of the Japanese people, and for a time when truth had flourished.

Motoori Norinaga was a student of Kamo no Mabuchi. Before his contact with Mabuchi, however, he had already been profoundly influenced by Keichū's literary outlook, especially concerning *waka,* and his approach to the classics. Another important factor in his background was his training in Confucianism. It was actually Norinaga's teacher of Confucianism, Hori Keizan (1688–1757), who introduced him to the thought of Keichū. Keizan is known for his correspondence with OGYŪ SORAI, Confucian scholar and advocate of *kobunjigaku* (exegetical study of ancient writings), and while a student of Keizan, Norinaga also studied Sorai's writings. (This is only one instance of the common spiritual ties that often existed among Confucian scholars and scholars of the Japanese classics in the late 17th and 18th centuries. Another example of this common ground can be seen in the Confucian scholar ITŌ JINSAI, who viewed literature as a true depiction of human life and tended, like Keichū and other Kokugaku scholars, to reject the moralistic and speculative interpretations of the classics espoused by the Zhu Xi [Chu Hsi] school of Confucianism [SHUSHIGAKU]).

Norinaga met Mabuchi in 1763. Having finished his work on the *Man'yōshū,* Mabuchi was then beginning his studies of the KOJIKI, the early-8th-century chronicle. Since he was too old to complete this major work, he expected his student Norinaga to complete the project. An important step toward deciphering such ancient works as the *Kojiki* was annotation of that treasury of the ancient Japanese language, the *Man'yōshū.* It was because Norinaga wanted to annotate the *Kojiki* that he first began his study of the *Man'yōshū* with Mabuchi.

Norinaga did not, however, agree with his teacher's literary and historical views. From the start Norinaga did not share Mabuchi's enthusiasm for the *Man'yōshū.* He also veered sharply from the prevalent Confucian and Buddhist doctrinal interpretations of classical works. Instead, Norinaga sought a more direct, spontaneous response that understood the classics as expressions of life as it had actually been lived. His tenets served to bring Kokugaku studies closer to a search for the uniquely Japanese quality of the classical works.

On the basis of his study of the TALE OF GENJI and *waka* literature, Norinaga felt that literary creation was dependent upon sensitivity to what he called MONO NO AWARE *(mono no aware o shiru kokoro).* By this Norinaga meant a sensibility genuinely and sympathetically responsive to the nuances of objects and events in the human and natural worlds. He believed that this sensibility was the principle behind all Japanese literature and insisted that literature was an artistic, not an ideological, mode of expression. Norinaga thought that the intrinsic value of literature lay in the expression of *mono no aware,* an approach that he brought to his work on the annotation of the *Kojiki.*

It took approximately 34 years for Norinaga to complete his *Kojikiden* (1764–98), the greatest annotation of a classical work in the Edo period. Norinaga stated that the *Kojiki* contained the purest record of ancient oral Japanese and so was more valuable than the NIHON SHOKI (720), a chronicle written in classical Chinese (*kambun*). In his elucidation of the *Kojiki's* myths, Norinaga again strongly rejected what he called the Chinese way of thinking (*karagokoro;* literally, "Chinese mind"), which Shintoists used in deducing dogmas from myths.

Norinaga emphasized that the *Kojiki* simply contained factual descriptions of the gods and the people of ancient times. He believed that by studying its language these historical events would be illuminated. The facts recorded in the *Kojiki* had value to Norinaga precisely because they espoused no dogmatic system or moral principles. Consequently, they faithfully described life in ancient days when people lived in peace under the gods and their descendants (i.e., the emperors) without having to refer to prescribed moral principles. He did not extol ancient times with the vehement restorationist passion of Kamo no Mabuchi. Yet Norinaga did maintain that early Japanese writings did not contain the word MICHI (way) in the sense of the right moral path precisely because they tacitly assumed a right way of living, which he called Kodō, the Way of the Ancients. Norinaga stated that because the ancient Japanese acted correctly without moralizing, ancient Japan had been superior to Confucian China.

While Kokugaku scholars in the late Edo period still lauded Norinaga's *Kojikiden* as the finest piece of Kokugaku scholarship, the focus of classical studies began to shift. Kokugaku emphasized the thought, culture, and mentality of ancient Japan prior to the introduction of such foreign teachings as Buddhism and Confucianism. Classical studies became more a means to, and an expression of, a religious quest and a religious world view. In this period, the ideological character of Kokugaku gradually strengthened, a tendency that crystallized in the work of Hirata Atsutane.

Although he never met Norinaga, Atsutane believed that he himself most closely adhered to Norinaga's thought and ideals and was his obvious successor. Formulated in the shifting historical context that existed just before the overthrow of the Tokugawa shogunate and the restoration of direct imperial rule (the MEIJI RESTORATION), Atsutane's proposed lineage of orthodox Kokugaku contrasted with Norinaga's apparent indifference to the issue of orthodoxy. In fact, Norinaga preferred to designate his studies as *kogaku* (the study of antiquity), rather than *kokugaku* (the study of the nation). Atsutane's claim of orthodoxy invested the concept of Kokugaku with an ideological character. Kokugaku, in his view, was the study of the Japanese classics and the ancient period undertaken with a nationalistic orientation that accorded with Shintō thought as he conceived it.

For Atsutane, ancient documents were not merely subjects for textual analysis, but also a means of deriving a precise world view, or determining the Shintō or Way of the gods. To establish this Way of the gods, Atsutane went back to the classical texts.

Atsutane constructed a Shintoist cosmology and world view that considered salvation of the soul after death, as well as a cosmogony (an extension of the *Sandaikō* of Hattori Nakatsune [1757–1824], Norinaga's disciple). With the *Kojiki* and *Nihon shoki* as its base, his cosmogony combined Chinese cosmology and Western astronomical ideas. Previous descriptions of Shintō beliefs had dwelt upon the many different gods in the pantheon. Unique in Atsutane's cosmogony was the importance he placed on the type of deity called *musubinokami* (god of procreation), who ruled the production of all things, preceded all things, and was the source of all existence, divine and human.

Creation and procreation became the main principles of Atsutane's cosmology. The process of the formation of the cosmos was the process of realization of the *musubinokami*'s divine will. Atsutane regarded this Japanese cosmogony not only as the truth about existence, but as a truth superior to any other nation's, although it drew upon certain foreign concepts.

This image of the world exerted a strong influence upon late Edo society. Atsutane's thought was especially welcomed by agrarian leaders, since it recognized the important role of peasants in productive work. Atsutane also had particular views about the afterlife. He stated that eternal happiness in the next life was promised to those who performed meritorious activities in this world. Atsutane's theories about salvation have certain resemblances to Christianity, but the location of his afterworld and character of its life more closely resemble those associated with ANCESTOR WORSHIP and the worship of gods in agrarian communities.

Atsutane's cosmogony and view of the afterlife inspired many thinkers in the late Edo period. His cosmogony, centering on the god of procreation, led another Kokugaku scholar of peasant origins, Suzuki Masayuki (1838–72), to a world view based on the principle of production. ŌKUNI TAKAMASA (1792–1871) and many other thinkers who played active roles in the imperial restoration movement were Atsutane's disciples. These scholars believed that the activities of people in this world, directed toward realizing the divine will of the god of procreation, should be those of a subject's obligatory duty to the emperor. A new concept of the nation, with strong emphasis on the obligation of its subjects to give reverent service to the exalted figure of the divine emperor, was thus created. Atsutane's reordering of the Japanese gods, his placement of the god of procreation at the pinnacle of the pantheon, as well as his attention to Japanese folk religion (as in the worship of UBUSUNAGAMI, the protective deity of one's birthplace) influenced local Shintō priests such as Mutobe Yoshika (1806–63).

Later Developments——Modern scholars have differed in the emphasis given to Kokugaku studies. They usually associate the philological approach with scholars up to Norinaga and the ideological perspective with Atsutane and other late Edo thinkers. Hence, Kokugaku is sometimes divided into early and late Kokugaku. However, Muraoka Tsunetsugu (1884–1946), a representative modern Kokugaku scholar, saw that even Norinaga's studies, which were essentially philological, were supported by strong ideological elements.

In the years before World War II, nationalist zealots used Kokugaku as the ideological framework for the imperial Japanese state. The scholar YAMADA YOSHIO rejected Kokugaku as a purely philological study and insisted in *Kokugaku no hongi* (1942, Principle of National Learning) that its principal goal was the "clarification of the national polity." The ideological effort to determine and propound the essence of the Japanese spirit through Kokugaku studies ended with Japan's defeat in World War II.

Such postwar studies as MARUYAMA MASAO's *Nihon seiji shisōshi kenkyū* (1952; tr *Studies in the Intellectual History of Tokugawa Japan,* 1974) have attempted to place Kokugaku, along with the various Confucian schools, in the history of premodern thought. There have recently been other studies on Kokugaku scholars' political thinking in relation to the Edo feudal system, as well as studies of thinkers with ties to agrarian society, the so-called grass-roots Kokugaku scholars of Norinaga's school, whose studies went beyond philology. Other research has centered upon Atsutane's thought and concern with the afterlife.

━━━━━Haga Noboru, *Bakumatsu kokugaku no tenkai* (1963). Haga Yaichi, *Nihon bunkengaku* (1928). Hisamatsu Sen'ichi, *Koku-*

gaku: Sono seiritsu to kokubungaku to no kankei (1941). Itō Tasaburō, *Sōmō no kokugaku* (1945). Kobayashi Hideo, *Motoori Norinaga* (1977). Koyasu Nobukuni, *Norinaga to Atsutane no sekai* (1977). Matsumoto Sannosuke, *Kokugaku seiji shisō no kenkyū* (1957). Muraoka Tsunetsugu, *Motoori Norinaga* (1928). Yoshikawa Kōjirō, *Motoori Norinaga* (1977).　　　　Koyasu Nobukuni

Kokugakuin University

(Kokugakuin Daigaku). A private, coeducational university located in Shibuya Ward, Tōkyō. Its predecessor was the Kōten Kōkyūjo, a research institute of National Learning (KOKUGAKU) and Japanese history, founded in 1882. In 1890 the school was renamed Kokugakuin, and in 1906 became a university, taking its present name. A department of Shintō studies was established in 1927. After World War II, the university expanded its faculties to include letters, law, and economics. Night courses are offered in all faculties. The university has a two-year curriculum for the training of Shintō priests. The Institute of Japanese Culture and Classics is well known. Enrollment was 10,662 in 1980.

Kokugikan

SUMŌ wrestling stadium operated by the Nihon Sumō Kyōkai, first established in the Ryōgoku area of Tōkyō, in 1909. A new stadium was built in the Kuramae area of Tōkyō, in 1954. Professional *sumō* tournaments are now held six times a year; the January, May, and September tournaments are held at Kokugikan. The stadium accommodates 12,000 persons.　　　　Takeda Fumio

Kokugo Shingikai → Council on the National Language

kokugun system

The administrative division of Japan into PROVINCES (*kuni* or *koku*) and districts (*kōri* or *gun*) under the RITSURYŌ SYSTEM of administration, which developed in the 7th and 8th centuries. Although the chronicle *Nihon shoki* (720) claims that this system was established in 646 as part of the TAIKA REFORM, Japanese scholars have recently shown that the Chinese character read *gun* did not come into use for Japanese administrative divisions until the early 8th century, at about the time of the TAIHŌ CODE (701). Under this code Japan was divided into 58 *kuni* and three island provinces (changed by the mid-9th century to 66 *kuni* and two island provinces). *Kuni* were divided into four categories according to size, and each was administered by officials appointed by the central government (see SHITŌKAN). The *gun* districts within the *kuni* were divided into five categories, also according to size; their number, which varied somewhat over time, was well over 500 and they were administered by powerful local families.

The *kokugun* system was established to strengthen the local authority of the central YAMATO COURT; by the middle of the Heian period (794–1185), however, it had been undermined by administrative difficulties and the growth of privately held estates (SHŌEN). Nonetheless, the basic territorial divisions were retained in the shogunal administrative systems of the Kamakura (1185–1333) and Muromachi (1333–1568) periods, and even to some extent in the domainal system of the Edo period (1600–1868).　　　　Kitamura Bunji

Kokuhō → National Treasures

Kokuhonsha

(National Foundations Society). Nationalist society of the 1920s and 1930s, formed by the conservative bureaucratic politican HIRANUMA KIICHIRŌ in 1924. The name *kokuhon* or "nation-based" was antithetical to the term *mimpon* or "people-based" (*mimpon shugi* was the term then used as a translation of "democracy"), hence the organization's name suggested a nationalist society that was opposed to democracy.

The organization's manifesto indicted the democratic, socialist, and labor movements as heterodoxies that threatened to undermine traditional national values. According to Kokuhonsha theorists, post–World War I Japan was on the brink of social revolution. They therefore called upon patriots to reject the popular foreign "isms" and to reaffirm their adherence to the traditional national spirit.

Members included Hiranuma's Justice Ministry colleagues and protégés SUZUKI KISABURŌ, Shiono Suehiko (1880–1949), and Hara Yoshimichi (1867–1944), followers from patriotic organizations like the Shin'yūkai, and his personal lieutenants from a group associated with the magazine *Kokuhon*, Takeuchi Kakuji (1875–1946) and Ōta Kōzō (1889–1981). Though the Kokuhonsha boasted many high-ranking officials and military officers such as ARAKI SADAO, MAZAKI JINZABURŌ, Obata Toshishirō (1885–1947), KATŌ HIROHARU, and even Admiral TŌGŌ HEIHACHIRŌ, the hero of the Russo-Japanese War, the participation of these people indicated only that they were generally sympathetic to Hiranuma's revivalist campaigns. They did not necessarily support him on political issues. Hiranuma also made a nationwide appeal for members, and by 1936 he could claim 80,000 adherents.

Hiranuma used the Kokuhonsha as a platform for airing his programs to revive the national spirit and as a base for establishing multilateral political alliances. Throughout the early 1930s he attempted, unsuccessfully, to construct Kokuhonsha-linked coalitions that would bring him the prime ministership. After the FEBRUARY 26TH INCIDENT of 1936, Hiranuma dissolved the society, finding its reputation as a fascist organization an obstacle to his political ambitions.

📖——Itō Takashi, *Shōwa shoki seijishi kenkyū* (1969).

Richard YASKO

kokujin

Also called *kunishū,* both terms meaning "provincials". Provincial barons, in general originating from the more powerful local land-holding warriors *(samurai),* especially those assigned as land stewards (JITŌ) during the Kamakura period (1185–1333). From early in the Muromachi period (1333–1568), *kokujin* were the dominant political and military figures on the local level. Since their allegiance was essential to the administration of the military governor (SHUGO), who generally lacked a base in his province of assignment, the *kokujin* frequently took advantage of the *shugo*'s weakness to expand their own influence and territorial control in the province. *Kokujin* sometimes formed confederations or leagues (IKKI) among themselves and, controlling the cultivators, provided leadership for the numerous uprisings by provincial groups (KUNI IKKI) of the 15th and early 16th centuries. By the late Muromachi period, the more powerful of these barons had succeeded in displacing the military governors and becoming autonomous territorial rulers (SENGOKU DAIMYŌ). Lesser *kokujin* became their retainers.

📖——John W. Hall and Toyoda Takeshi, ed, *Japan in the Muromachi Age* (1977). Nagahara Keiji, *Sengoku no dōran,* vol 14 of *Nihon no rekishi* (Shōgakukan, 1975). *Michael* SOLOMON

Kokumin Chōyō Rei → National Service Draft Ordinance

Kokumin Dōmei

(National Alliance). Ultranationalist political party formed in December 1932 by ADACHI KENZŌ and NAKANO SEIGŌ. When Adachi was prevented by the RIKKEN MINSEITŌ from returning to its ranks after his precipitous withdrawal in 1931, he set up his own party, the Kokumin Dōmei, consisting mostly of defectors from the Minseitō. The party advocated government control of strategic industries and financial institutions, as well as the creation of a Japan–Manchuria economic bloc. In 1934 it demanded an inquiry into the TEIJIN INCIDENT to bring down the SAITŌ MAKOTO cabinet and disgrace relatively moderate civilian politicians. In 1935 when the Yamaji Jōichi (1882–1942) faction returned to the ruling Minseitō, Kokumin Dōmei's Diet representation fell to 20 seats from its original strength of 31 seats, to 15 after the 1936 election, and to 11 after the 1937 election. In 1936 Nakano's defection to the more extremist TŌHŌKAI further depleted its ranks, and in July 1940 the few remaining members joined the IMPERIAL RULE ASSISTANCE ASSOCIATION. See also POLITICAL PARTIES.

kokumin gakkō

(national people's schools). Name given to the Japanese compulsory school system between 1941 and 1947. Influenced by the concept of

the German *Volksschule,* the idea was a product of the jingoistic atmosphere of World War II. The curriculum under the *kokumin gakkō* system was dedicated to training "loyal subjects of the emperor." Under the National People's School Order (Kokumin Gakkō Rei) of 1941, the nation's compulsory education system, which had consisted of six years of primary school, was to be reorganized to consist of eight years (six primary and two secondary). However, realization of the system was hindered by worsening war conditions, and in actual practice compulsory education remained confined to the six years of primary school. After World War II, the system was reorganized as the present elementary and secondary system under the SCHOOL EDUCATION LAW OF 1947. See ELEMENTARY AND SECONDARY EDUCATION. *SATŌ Hideo*

Kokumin Jissen Yōryō

(Guidelines for Popular Practical Morality). A set of proposed guidelines for moral education in Japan's public schools drawn up in 1951 by the minister of education, AMANO TEIYŪ. Prior to and during World War II the IMPERIAL RESCRIPT ON EDUCATION, with its emphasis on filial piety and loyalty to the emperor, had formed the basis for the nationalistic moral training course known as SHŪSHIN. This course had been withdrawn from the curriculum at the end of the war, and Amano wished to release a government document which would provide a basis for a new popular morality. His guidelines were based on a morality of individualism, but at the same time they called for love and loyalty toward society and the state. Amano was eventually forced to withdraw the proposal because of popular opposition. *NISHIMURA Makoto*

kokumin kenkō hoken → national health insurance

Kokumin Kyōdōtō

(People's Cooperative Party). Centrist political party founded in March 1947 with the merger of the People's Party (Kokumintō) and the Cooperative Democratic Party (Kyōdō Minshutō); it began with 78 members, and MIKI TAKEO was party secretary. The party's platform emphasized class harmony, cooperation, and modernization of rural areas. Party members served as ministers in the KATAYAMA TETSU and ASHIDA HITOSHI cabinets. In April 1950 the party, which had fared badly in the election of January 1949, merged with the conservative Democratic Party (MINSHUTŌ) to form the People's Democratic Party (Kokumin Minshutō). The Kokumin Minshutō, reorganized as the Kaishintō (Reform Party) in 1952, ultimately merged with the LIBERAL DEMOCRATIC PARTY (Jiyū Minshutō). *HARADA Katsumasa*

Kokumin Kyōkai

(Nationalist Association). 1. A progovernment political group organized in 1892 by SHINAGAWA YAJIRŌ, SAIGŌ TSUGUMICHI, and others. The popular parties, such as the JIYŪTŌ and RIKKEN KAISHINTŌ, that had gained control of the Diet after the first national election in 1890 had proved obstructive to the government's legislative program. To counter such opposition parties, the government resorted to dissolution of the Diet, and in the election of February 1892 it connived at massive interference by Shinagawa, who was at the time home minister in the first MATSUKATA MASAYOSHI cabinet (see also SENKYO KANSHŌ). When election interference failed to prevent the popular parties from returning a majority to the Diet, Shinagawa was forced to resign. Soon afterward, Shinagawa and other conservatives founded the Kokumin Kyōkai. In so doing, they were following the political philosophy of the oligarch YAMAGATA ARITOMO, who advocated a three-party system in which a third party loyal to the oligarchs would act as a wedge between the two opposition parties. The antiparty bias of the Kokumin Kyōkai's founders was reflected in their refusal to acknowledge that it too was a political party. In 1893, however, they sided with the opposition parties in attacking the government's plan for treaty revision (see UNEQUAL TREATIES, REVISION OF), and as a result it became identified in the popular mind as a political party. The Kokumin Kyōkai's objectives included government reform, fiscal retrenchment, and the establishment of naval shipyards and steelworks. In the years immediately preceding the Sino-Japanese War of 1894–95, the group was a major proponent of armaments expansion. In 1898 the position of the Kokumin Kyōkai as the sole progovernment faction in the Diet was weakened with the formation of an alliance between the KENSEITŌ (Constitutional Party) and the second Yamagata cabinet. The group was therefore dissolved in 1899 and reorganized as the TEIKOKUTŌ (Imperial Party).

2. Ultranationalist political group founded by AKAMATSU KATSUMARO and others in July 1933. It attacked theories skeptical of the "divine nature" of the emperor (see TENNŌ KIKAN SETSU) and strove to clean up elections. It disbanded in July 1937 to form, with other nationalistic associations, the Nihon Kakushintō (Japan Reform Party). See also POLITICAL PARTIES.

Kokumin no tomo

Review organ of the Min'yūsha (Society of the People's Friends) founded by TOKUTOMI SOHŌ in February 1887. Its name was taken from an American weekly, *The Nation,* and each issue of the magazine bore the English banner *The Nation's Friend* across the front cover. A total of 372 issues was published; first it was a monthly, then a biweekly (numbers 9 to 36), and, finally, a triweekly until the last issue in August 1898. Chiefly devoted to political, social, economic, and literary reviews, *Kokumin no tomo* carried provocative essays on contemporary cultural and social issues and had a profound influence on the thought and journalism of the succeeding generation. The magazine reflected Sohō's ideas on democracy (which he called *heimin shugi*) as well as his interest in Christian-inspired humanism and the FREEDOM AND PEOPLE'S RIGHTS MOVEMENT (Jiyū Minken Undō). It drew upon some of the best writers of the day, such as FUTABATEI SHIMEI, YAMADA BIMYŌ, TOKUTOMI ROKA, KUNIKIDA DOPPO, and UCHIDA ROAN. Not only did it occupy a leading position in the intellectual world of the 1890s, it was also the gateway to literary success for many aspiring writers. Following the Sino-Japanese War of 1894–95, Sohō shifted to a nationalistic position, and the magazine lost its following and eventually dissolved. *The Far East,* an English edition of the *Kokumin no tomo,* was published monthly from February 1896 to August 1898.

YAMARYŌ Kenji

Kokumin Seishin Sōdōin Undō → National Spiritual Mobilization Movement

Kokumin shimbun

A Meiji-period (1868–1912) political tabloid launched in Tōkyō in 1890 by writer-critic TOKUTOMI SOHŌ. In its early days the paper was popular because of its moderate approach to people's rights. After the Russo-Japanese War (1904–05), however, Sohō shifted his position and began to advocate an expansionist policy in line with that of militarists like YAMAGATA ARITOMO. Because of its support of the conservative Katsura Tarō cabinet, the *Kokumin shimbun* came to be regarded as a government mouthpiece. During the years of TAISHŌ DEMOCRACY, it came under heavy fire, and company offices were attacked by angry members of the Freedom and People's Rights Movement. The paper eventually ran into financial difficulty for which Sohō, still unmoved by the times, took responsibility and resigned from the company in 1929. Continuing to publish until 1942, when many newspapers were forced to consolidate because of wartime conditions, the *Kokumin* merged with the MIYAKO SHIMBUN to form the present TŌKYŌ SHIMBUN.

kokumin shukusha

Nationally operated lodging houses. Erected at scenic locations, these lodges have relatively new facilities that are low in cost and provide accommodations for Japanese vacationers and foreign tourists. Started in 1956, the lodges are built and maintained with long-term, low-interest loans obtained from the national government out of accumulated monies collected from national pension funds. Accommodations, dinner, and breakfast, all included in the cost, are generally Japanese-style, though a few lodges have beds and Western-style meals. Most of these lodges can accommodate an average of 110 guests; they are primarily located within national and prefectural parks. As of 1979, there were 338 national lodging houses; a listing may be obtained at local government offices. In addition to these publicly operated lodging houses, there are approximately 27,000 privately operated facilities known as MINSHUKU.

NAITŌ Kinju

Kōkuri → Koguryŏ

kokuritsu ginkō → national banks

Kokuritsu Kōbunshokan → National Archives

Kokuritsu Kokugo Kenkyūjo → National Japanese Language Research Institute

Kokuritsu Rekishi Minzoku Hakubutsukan

(National Museum of Japanese History). A museum of history and folk culture which opened in March 1983 in the city of Sakura, Chiba Prefecture. It collects and preserves Japanese historical, archaeological, and folk material and data and exhibits them to the public. It also conducts surveys and studies in the fields of history, archaeology, and folklore and assists scholars engaged in research in these fields. Its exhibitions emphasize the history of the life of the common people instead of a general display of material. The first president of the museum was Inoue Mitsusada, a historian. The museum also operates a nationwide information network. The site of the museum encompasses a total of approximately 130,000 square meters (1,391,000 square feet).

Kokuryūkai → Amur River Society

Kokusai Denshin Denwa Co, Ltd

(KDD; International Telegram and Telephone Public Corporation). Firm monopolizing telecommunication services, such as telephone, telegraph, telex, and television relay, between Japan and foreign countries. In 1953, through special legislation, it was separated from NIPPON TELEGRAPH AND TELEPHONE PUBLIC CORPORATION and established as a private enterprise (see TELECOMMUNICATIONS SYSTEMS).

In 1956, with the goal of modernizing international telecommunications, the firm initiated telex service between Japan and the United States, and in 1964, following the laying of a submarine cable, inaugurated semiautomatic telephone service. In 1967 the circuit volume between Japan and the United States was expanded by means of satellite transmission using Intelsat-11. The completion of the Sea of Japan cable in 1969 brought significant improvement to telecommunication with Europe. Automation of telex and telephone service was followed in 1978 by the inception of high-speed facsimile communication between the United States and Japan. In the early 1980s the company was working to develop the field of international data transmission and the use of submarine optical fiber cables.

In addition to its head office in Tōkyō, the firm has 17 liaison offices in major foreign cities, including New York, Washington, Paris, and London. It has international telephone and telegraph offices in Tōkyō and Ōsaka, 6 domestic transmitting and receiving stations, 2 satellite communication centers, and 4 cable landing stations. In 1980 it handled 23.4 million international phone calls, 38 million telex calls, and 3.3 million telegrams; as of December 1981 it operated 2,220 international telephone circuits, 1,754 telex circuits, and 71 telegraph circuits. Sales for the fiscal year ending March 1982 totaled ¥165 billion (US $685.4 million), of which telephone calls contributed 54 percent, telex 31 percent, and telegrams 6 percent. Capitalization was ¥16.5 billion (US $68.5 million) in the same year.

kokusaku kaisha

(government policy company). Partially government-owned enterprises established after the SINO-JAPANESE WAR OF 1894–1895 to promote industrial control, increase productivity, and develop the economies of the occupied territories. Such enterprises were established by legislation, and the government retained final approval in the selection of management. Many such enterprises were established during the 1930s. Among these were enterprises concerned with transportation, generation and transmission of electricity, natural resource development, and coal and petroleum supply. Enterprises, including an airline, a maritime transport company, and a North China development company, were also established for the development and control of occupied territories. After World War II these enterprises were either dissolved or transformed into special or government-chartered companies *(tokushu gaisha)*; examples are JAPAN AIR LINES CO, LTD, and KOKUSAI DENSHIN DENWA CO, LTD. See also PUBLIC CORPORATIONS. *Udagawa Masaru*

kokusan kaisho

(local production associations). Also called *bussan kaisho*. Offices established by domainal governments in the Edo period (1600–1868) to encourage and gain more complete control over production operations (see HAN'EI SEMBAI); they furnished loans, materials, and technical guidance. Many of them were established in the wake of the Tokugawa shogunate's KYŌHŌ REFORMS. With the growth of the commodity economy these offices came to handle sales and distribution as well, some of them establishing branches in Ōsaka and Edo (now Tōkyō). During the early 1800s *kaisho* officials attempted to increase domainal revenues by encouraging production of specialized local goods (see BUSSANGAKU) that they could sell profitably through official monopolies. Most of the *kokusan kaisho* were partly staffed by chartered merchants (GOYŌ SHŌNIN), whose wealth and financial expertise were valuable; their presence, however, was not always to the advantage of the producers. In an effort to strengthen its own finances, the shogunate prohibited domainal monopolization of products in 1842. Plans to regulate the *kokusan kaisho* in the late 1850s, however, never materialized. Frequently the *kokusan kaisho* endangered the stability of domainal economies by recklessly issuing paper money and causing severe inflation. Long-term effects on the farmers were often ignored in the rush for quick profits. The *kokusan kaisho* were abolished in 1871 together with the domains themselves.

kokusei chōsaken

The power of the national DIET to investigate matters relating to government. The 1947 CONSTITUTION of Japan states: "Each House may conduct investigations in relation to government, and may demand the presence and testimony of witnesses, and the production of records" (art. 62). In order to make this power of investigations effective, the Law concerning the Oath and Testimony by Witnesses before the National Diet (Giin ni Okeru Shōnin no Sensei Oyobi Shōgen Tō ni Kansuru Hōritsu; generally referred to as Giin Shōgen Hō) was enacted in 1947. This law compels a person to appear, testify, and produce records under oath before a House of the Diet whenever asked to do so by that House. There are some exceptions; for example, a public official may refuse to testify about confidential matters of his office or matters that gravely affect national interests. The law establishes penalties for failure to appear, failure to submit subpoenaed documents, refusal to take an oath or to testify, and perjury. How far the Diet can extend this power of investigation is undetermined and sometimes controversial.

In conducting an investigation, the Houses of the Diet are required to exercise caution so as not to usurp the function of another branch of government, especially of the judiciary, and not to violate civil liberties. The actual exercise of the Diet's power in Japan has sometimes verged on a kangaroo-courtlike investigation. In 1952, each of the Houses established by separate action a provision for unsworn witnesses *(sankōnin)*, who are required to provide information but are not compelled to take an oath. Some fear that this system of unsworn witnesses has diluted the Diet's power of investigation. *Ishimine Keitetsu*

kokushi

(provincial governors). Administrators *(shi)* of provinces *(kuni* or *koku)* in the Nara period (710–794) under the RITSURYŌ SYSTEM of government. There were four major ranks: the governor *(kami)*, vice-governor *(suke)*, commissioner *(jō)*, and inspector *(sakan)*. The title *kokushi* was originally applied to all these officials, but in later years it was used mainly to refer to the governors. Usually chosen from the central government bureaucracy, they were assigned to provincial headquarters (KOKUFU) for terms of four to six years and were given the income from state lands for their support. Their principal duties involved supervision of the militia, the police, the land registry, and the tax bureau. Beginning in the 8th century some provincial governors, while accepting the title and stipend, retained their posts at the capital and governed through deputies; these absentee governors—called *yōnin kokushi* in contrast to ZURYŌ, the

actual administrators—were common from the 9th century onward. In the 12th century, with the rise of private landed estates (SHŌEN), central authority declined; and with the establishment of warrior government by the Kamakura shogunate (1192–1333), *kokushi* became an empty title. Nonetheless, it continued to be used for its prestige throughout the Muromachi period (1333–1568), when warlords styled themselves governors, and even into the Edo period (1600–1868), when *daimyō* were given the title.

Kokushi taikei

(Compilation of Japanese History). A major collection of standard sources for Japanese history from the earliest times to the Meiji Restoration (1868), including official histories, private records, genealogies, laws, and literary works. Published in two editions from 1897 to 1966. The first series (32 vols, 1897–1904) was edited by the economist and cultural historian TAGUCHI UKICHI, and the second series, a careful revision of the first, entitled *Shintei zōho kokushi taikei* (Revised and Enlarged Compilation of Japanese History; 66 vols, 1929–66), was begun under the general editorship of KUROITA KATSUMI, professor of Japanese history at Tōkyō University.

The *Kokushi taikei* is noted for the rigorous selection, collation, and editing of documents that went into its production. The methods reflect both the native tradition of textual collation and criticism and the positivist techniques of Western historical scholarship that influenced Japanese historiography after the Meiji Restoration. The prefaces to the individual works in the *Kokushi taikei* contain information on extant manuscripts and variant texts.

kokuso

(provincial appeals; also read *kuniso*). Demands by peasants late in the Edo period (1600–1868) for the redress of grievances, particularly against the monopoly trade guilds (KABUNAKAMA). The petitioners, usually led by local merchants, presented their complaints to the *daimyō* or to the *kabunakama* authorities. In contrast to the frequently violent peasant uprisings (TSUCHI IKKI) of the time, the *kokuso* followed legal procedures. They occurred principally in the rural areas of western Japan. The first major example took place in 1823, when more than 1,000 villages engaged in cotton and rapeseed production in the Ōsaka region joined to present an appeal.

kokutai

Usually translated as "national polity," "national essence," or "national entity." In its more general sense, the term denotes the form of the state as defined by the locus of sovereignty: where sovereignty resides with a monarch, the state is a monarchy; where it resides with the people, the state is a democracy; and so on. In this sense, *kokutai* has been used to translate the German *Staatsform*. The term has been more commonly used, however, in a narrower sense, to refer to what was seen as the uniquely Japanese polity, the most important elements of which were rule by an unbroken imperial line and the concept of the state as a family, in which the relationship between the emperor and his subjects is like that between a father and his children. In its earliest Japanese occurrence, the term appears to have had a topographical sense. In the 8th-century text *Izumo no kuni no miyatsuko no kan'yogoto* we read that the god "Amenohohi no Mikoto was dispatched to inspect the (form of the) land." It is found in something like its modern sense, however, in such early Chinese works as the *Spring and Autumn Annals*, the *Guanzi (Kuan-tzu)*, and the *History of the Former Han Dynasty*.

The idea that Japan is different from all other countries in its origins and in the organization of the state is a very old one. From earliest times, there are frequent references to Japan as "the land of the gods." In the chronicle NIHON SHOKI (720), the king of the ancient Korean kingdom of SILLA is recorded as saying, "I have heard that there is to the east a land of the gods called Japan, which has a sacred king called the *tennō*." KITABATAKE CHIKAFUSA declared in his JINNŌ SHŌTŌ KI that Japan's heavenly origins and unbroken imperial line were unique and explained that this was why the Office of Shintō Worship (Jingikan) was the highest organ of the imperial government.

It was not until the Edo period (1600–1868), however, that the uniqueness of Japan's polity became a subject for scholarly discussion. Stimulated by greater knowledge of early Japanese history, scholars of the time began to feel resentment at the dominance of Confucian thought and the "worship" of all things Chinese. YA-

MAGA SOKŌ, who in the 17th century used the term *kokutai* frequently in his works, criticized himself for excessive admiration of China and neglect of the Japanese tradition. He asserted that Japan, not China, was the true "middle kingdom." Japan's ethics and system of government had not been learned from China; on the contrary, SHINTŌ led where Confucianism followed. Toward the end of the Edo period, with the rise of KOKUGAKU (National Learning) and in particular of the MITO SCHOOL of historical studies, *kokutai* became the subject of heated debate.

With the introduction of Western political ideas at the time of the Meiji Restoration (1868), *kokutai* began to be discussed in "modern" terms. KATŌ HIROYUKI, an advocate of constitutional government and natural rights, attacked the view that Japan's national polity was superior to that of any other country. In his work *Kokutai shinron* (1874, A New Theory of *Kokutai*) he stated: "Our national polity is characterized by the mean and vulgar tradition of servility . . .The emperor and the people are not different in kind: the emperor is a man, the people too are men." Katō was the first to draw a distinction between *kokutai*, or national polity, and *seitai*, or system of government, but his usage of the two terms differed from that which later prevailed.

FUKUZAWA YUKICHI, in his BUMMEIRON NO GAIRYAKU (1875), offered the following definition of the *kokutai*: "*(tai)* refers to a structure in which things are gathered together into a whole and separated from other things. *Kokutai*, therefore, refers to the grouping together of people of one race who share pleasures and pains; to the creation among them of a sense of separateness from people of other countries; to the fostering among them of warmer feelings toward one another than toward foreigners and of a greater willingness to exert themselves on behalf of one another than on behalf of foreigners. They live under one government, rule themselves, and do not wish to be under the control of another government: they are independent, and are responsible for their own weal or woe. It is what is called in the West 'nationality.'"

Legal and constitutional scholars applied themselves to the task of formulating a more exact definition of the concept. In this they were influenced by German constitutional thought. Following Katō Hiroyuki, they drew a distinction between "form of constitution" *(kokutai)* and "form of government" *(seitai)*. The nature of *kokutai* was clarified: it was based not on the locus of sovereignty as *defined* by the constitution, but on the locus of the sovereignty that *created* the constitution.

The locus of sovereignty in a given state, in the view of HOZUMI YATSUKA, was determined by national tradition, or "racial confidence." Hozumi believed that true monarchy existed only in Asia, specifically in Japan. European nations were basically democratic and republican in character, and monarchs in the West were merely presidents-for-life who ruled in the name of the people. Monarchs in Asia ruled in their own right, with their own power. It was Hozumi who developed the "family concept of the state," in which the emperor was seen as being directly descended from AMATERASU ŌMIKAMI, the sun goddess, and his subjects were regarded as an extension of the imperial family. Proponents of Hozumi's idea asserted that there were two types of state—that which evolved naturally and that which was man-made. The evolution of the "natural" state took the following course: the family grew to become a clan *(shizoku)*, the clan became a tribe *(buzoku)*, and the tribe expanded to form a state. The head of this kind of state corresponded, therefore, to the head of the family, clan, or tribe, and his prerogative *(taiken)* was merely an extension or enlargement of the father's rights over the family. The foundations of the "natural" state were thus firmer than those of the man-made state. The ideal example of the natural state was Japan, whose imperial house was literally the head family of the nation, and whose people were literally the emperor's children. This concept became the pivot of popular education from the 1890s on. The IMPERIAL RESCRIPT ON EDUCATION (1890) says: "Our Imperial Ancestors have founded Our Empire on a basis broad and everlasting and have deeply and firmly implanted virtue; Our subjects, ever united in loyalty and filial piety, have from generation to generation illustrated the beauty thereof. This is the glory of the fundamental character of Our Empire *(kokutai)*, and herein also lies the source of Our Education." Read in the schools on important occasions, the rescript was the basis of Japanese ethics for half a century.

Incidents in which some person or group was persecuted for expressing views held to be contrary to the orthodox interpretation of *kokutai* occurred frequently up to the end of World War II. The most famous was the Affair of the "Emperor-as-an-Organ-of-the-State" Theory (TENNŌ KIKAN SETSU), involving MINOBE TATSUKICHI. In February 1935, Minobe was attacked by a member of the House of Peers for describing the emperor as an "organ" of the state and subject, therefore, to constitutional limitations. Minobe made a conciliatory reply, but a clamorous campaign was launched against him. He was accused of lese majesty, some of his books were banned, and he was forced to resign his seat in the House of Peers.

The Minobe incident was representative of the new, more intense campaign against "unorthodox" ideas that had begun with the enactment of the PEACE PRESERVATION LAW OF 1925 (Chian Iji Hō). This law (the first in which the term *kokutai* was used) forbade membership in any association advocating changes in the constitution or the overthrow of the system of private property. Action hitherto directed mainly against communists and anarchists came more and more to be directed against liberals such as Minobe, whose "organ theory" was not an attack on the *kokutai* but merely a "modern" interpretation of it.

This intensified attack on heresy gave rise to the "clarification of the *kokutai*" movement *(kokutai meichō undō;* see KOKUTAI DEBATE), one result of which was the book KOKUTAI NO HONGI (1937; tr *Kokutai no hongi: Cardinal Principles of the National Entity of Japan,* 1949), published by the Ministry of Education and used as a textbook for ethics classes in schools. Written to put an end to the confusion resulting from the Minobe affair, it presented the Japanese origin myths as historical facts and was extremely xenophobic in tone, deploring the Western philosophy of individualism, which laid stress on "the abstract human being, independent of all history." The book offered no more precise definition of the *kokutai* than that it was "the everlasting rule over the Great Japanese Empire of an unbroken line of emperors in obedience to the commands of their ancestors."

As a result of Japan's defeat in World War II and the ensuing Occupation reforms, the concept of *kokutai* fell into disuse. *Kokutai* ideology has survived among some traditionalists in a rather diffuse form, but the term *kokutai* is rarely used in its prewar sense and has little meaning to most Japanese today.

——Frank O. Miller, *Minobe Tatsukichi: Interpreter of Constitutionalism in Japan* (1965). Richard H. Minear, *Japanese Tradition and Western Law: Emperor, State, and Law in the Thought of Hozumi Yatsuka* (1970). Ministry of Education, *Kokutai no hongi: Cardinal Principles of the National Entity of Japan,* tr John O. Gauntlett, ed Robert K. Hall (1949). *Graham* HEALEY

kokutai debate

(kokutai meichō mondai; literally, "debate concerning the clarification of the national polity"). A major political controversy in 1935 instigated by extremist elements in the army, right-wing politicians, and civilian groups in an attempt to discredit the theory of MINOBE TATSUKICHI (professor of law at Tōkyō University and member of the House of Peers) that the emperor was merely an organ of the state (TENNŌ KIKAN SETSU).

Minobe's theory, which had been the dominant legal interpretation of the Meiji CONSTITUTION since World War I, defined the emperor not as an absolute sovereign but as one of several organs of state. Traditionalists subscribing to an absolutist view of imperial sovereignty had been attacking liberal intellectuals for several years, when in February 1935 they took Minobe as their target. They denounced him in the Diet for violating the "national polity" (KOKUTAI), the state structure unique to Japan as embodied in the imperial institution. When Minobe refuted their charge, they promptly accused him of lese majesty. The affair escalated into a political issue, in part because the RIKKEN SEIYŪKAI, the opposition party in the Diet, tried to use it to overthrow the OKADA KEISUKE cabinet. In conjunction with right-wing organizations, the Seiyūkai initiated a campaign for "the clarification of the national polity." These groups were joined by leaders of the so-called Imperial Way faction (KŌDŌHA) in the army who, through the IMPERIAL MILITARY RESERVISTS' ASSOCIATION, helped turn the campaign into a nationwide movement. The government was finally pressured into banning three of Minobe's works; it issued statements declaring the organ theory to be "contrary to the true meaning of the national polity." Minobe himself was interrogated by the police and eventually forced to resign from the House of Peers.

The *kokutai* debate was symptomatic of a growing dissatisfaction with party government among certain elites. It also added fuel to right-wing demands for a radical reconstruction of the political order and accelerated the trend toward ultranationalist thinking in the years immediately preceding World War II.

kokutai meichō mondai → kokutai debate

Kokutai no hongi

(Cardinal Principles of the National Entity of Japan). A political tract published on 30 March 1937 by the Ministry of Education. It was regarded by the Japanese government as a statement of the fundamental principles of the KOKUTAI (national entity or national polity), the state structure unique to Japan as embodied in the imperial institution. Considered by OCCUPATION authorities to be militarist propaganda, it was banned in December 1945.

As stated in its introduction and conclusion, the avowed purpose of *Kokutai no hongi* was to combat internal turmoil, social unrest, and doubts, which were largely seen as stemming from Western influence. The mission of the Japanese people was stated in the final paragraph of the book, "to create and develop a new Japan by virtue of their immutable national entity which is the basis of the State and by virtue of the Way of the Empire which stands firm throughout the ages at home and abroad, and thereby more than ever to guard and maintain the prosperity of the Imperial Throne which is coeval with heaven and earth."

This goal was to be achieved by stimulating patriotic pride in the people for their national achievements of the past; linking this pride with myths, traditions, and historical events and persons; building a mystical belief in the divine origins and absolute authority of the imperial line; and finally, creating motivation and willingness to accept blindly any command or demand for sacrifice alleged to have come from that source.

In order to make its meaning ambiguous, *Kokutai no hongi* was written in a stylistically difficult Japanese. The text was intended for the masses, including schoolchildren, but as a propaganda instrument it also had to be convincing, or at least defensible, to intellectuals. Thus, it is full of pretentious phrases—often recognizable quotations from religious and political sources—and terms, such as HAKKŌ ICHIU (the whole world under one roof), that had acquired powerful political connotations and held esoteric meanings. Acceptance by the people was further promoted by linking the text with widely accepted philosophy and religious belief, such as Shintō, Zen Buddhism, and Confucian ethics.

In addition to the introduction and conclusion, *Kokutai no hongi* is divided into two books, the first defining the "National Entity" and the second citing the "Manifestations of Our National Entity in History." The fundamental thesis of the first book is that Japan prospers because it is blessed with a divine origin, divine leadership, and divine characteristics. The second book explores characteristics of the Japanese way of life, including the language, manners and customs, culture, education, morality, ethics, BUSHIDŌ, religious rites, the Meiji Constitution, and direct rule by the emperor, all with a view to justify the ultimate objective of the thesis, the divine mission.

Hisamatsu Sen'ichi (1894–1976), a professor at Tōkyō University and an outstanding scholar of Japanese classics, prepared the original draft in 1937. Later it was extensively edited and rewritten by two committees, one largely composed of university scholars, the other of government officials. Final editing, which involved rewriting large sections of the text, was done by Itō Enkichi, an official of the Education Ministry.

The first printing of 300,000 was soon exhausted, as all prefectural governors, university presidents and principals of *kōtō gakkō* (higher schools preparatory to the university) and *semmon gakkō* (college–level technical schools) were directed to make every effort to secure wide dissemination. Later, official editions were published by the Cabinet Printing Bureau and approximately 1.9 million copies were sold. Private presses are known to have reprinted at least 28,000 more, and at least 51,000 reproductions of the *Kokutai no hongi* appeared in other books.

◼——John Owen Gauntlett, tr, and Robert King Hall, ed, *Kokutai no hongi: Cardinal Principles of the National Entity of Japan* (1949.)

Robert King HALL

Kokutetsu → Japanese National Railways

Kokuyo Co, Ltd

Chief Japanese manufacturer of stationery, notebooks, account books, receipt pads, and other office and school supplies. Founded in 1930 by Kuroda Zentarō, the company has remained in the family's control. It has a nearly monopolistic hold on the domestic market through special contract arrangements with a nationwide network of 50,000 retail stores. In 1960 it initiated manufacture of steel desks and other office furniture and subsequently became the leader in the field. Sales for the fiscal year ending September 1981 totaled ¥139.3 billion (US $605.6 million) and capitalization was ¥5 billion (US $21.7 million). The head office is in Ōsaka.

kokyū

Long-necked bowed lute. Japan's only bowed musical instrument, the *kokyū* was derived partly from the Portuguese rebec and partly from the SHAMISEN, and entered Japan from the Ryūkyū Islands, probably at the end of the 16th century. In the 17th century it was still rare, but by the early 18th it was being widely used as a folk instrument, and spread to Edo (now Tōkyō), where by mid-century it was played in *sankyoku* (trios with *shamisen* and KOTO). During the 1780s a fourth string was added to the Edo *kokyū*. At present the instrument is little played outside the TENRIKYŌ sect.

David B. WATERHOUSE

koma → tops

komadori

(Japanese robin). *Erithacus akahige.* A bird of the family Muscicapidae, known for its rhythmical song, one section of which resembles the whinny of a horse, hence the name *komadori* ("horse bird"). It measures about 14 centimeters (5.5 in) in length and has an orange red breast. It summers in mountainous areas north of Kyūshū, preferring brush and thickets of dwarf bamboo about 1,500 meters (5,000 ft) above sea level. The *komadori* has a strong sense of territory and nests in hollows of fallen trees or crevices in cliffs. Its eggs are blue. Although it winters in southern China, it breeds only in Japan. A subspecies, the *tanekomadori (E. akahige tanensis)* is found on the Izu Islands.

TAKANO Shinji

Noted for its beautiful appearance and song, the *komadori* has been kept in homes since early times. Although celebrated with the *uguisu* (bush warbler) and *ōruri* (blue-and-white flycatcher) as one of the "three birds of Japan," it has rarely been used as a poetic or pictorial subject.

SAITŌ Shōji

Komae

City in south central Tōkyō Prefecture, central Honshū. Formerly a farming district, it is now a residential suburb of greater Tōkyō. Pop: 70,824.

Komagane

City in southern Nagano Prefecture, central Honshū, on the river Tenryūgawa. Rice and pears are grown. There is also an electronics and precision instrument industry. It is a base camp for the mountain Kiso Komagatake and the highland Komagane Kōgen, popular with climbers and campers. The temple Kōzenji, with its magnificent stand of cypresses, and the house of the Takemura family, prominent village officials during the Edo period (1600–1868), are also of interest. Population: 31,179.

Komagatake

Active conical volcano in the Nasu Volcanic Zone, Oshima Peninsula, southwestern Hokkaidō. Also called Oshima Fuji. It has erupted frequently since the Edo period (1600–1868), most recently in 1942. Its slopes are covered with broad-leaved forests. It is the dominant peak in Ōnuma Quasi-National Park. Height: 1,133 m (3,716 ft).

Komagatake

Composite volcano, in the Nasu Volcanic Zone, on the border between Akita and Iwate prefectures, northern Honshū. Also called

Komainu

A pair of *komainu* statues. The figures are usually slightly asymmetrical, and, as here, the mouth of one is always open and the other closed.

Akita Komagatake and Akitakoma. The peak Medake is in the volcano's central crater, and Otokodake is on the crater rim. Medake erupted in 1970 and 1971. On Komagatake's slopes are Nyūtō and Tazawako Kōgen hot springs. Alpine flora, designated as natural monuments, abound. Komagatake is in Towada–Hachimantai National Park. Height: 1,637 m (5,369 ft).

Komagatake

Mountain in the village of Hinoemata, southwestern Fukushima Prefecture, northern Honshū. Also called Aizu Komagatake and Aizukoma. The entire mountain is of Paleozoic strata and forms a young topography. There are deep valleys on the slopes. On the southern ridge are located swamps and ponds. Summer skiing is available because of late-lasting snow. Height: 2,132 m (6,993 ft).

Komagatake

Mountain in southwestern Nagano Prefecture, central Honshū; the highest peak in the Kiso Mountains. Also called Kiso Komagatake and Kisokoma. Composed of granite, the east and west slopes are steep. The summit's eastern side has a glacial erosion area, and the Senjōjiki cirque is famous. Alpine flora abound. There is a ropeway to Komagatake Shrine which is on the summit. Height: 2,956 m (9,696 ft).

Komagatake

Mountain on the border of Yamanashi and Nagano prefectures, central Honshū, in the northern Akaishi Mountains; composed of granite. Also called Kai Komagatake and Kaikoma. The mineral spring Yabunoyu is located in the foothills. Japanese black fritillary *(kuroyuri)*, an alpine flower, grows here. Height: 2,966 m (9,728 ft).

komainu

Mythical lion-like beasts, statues of which are customarily placed in pairs in front of the gates or main halls of many shrines and temples to repel evil. The images may be made of stone, wood, or bronze. The custom of placing *komainu* figures in front of shrines and temples is related to the similar use of images of lions in India and the Middle East; it came to Japan from continental Asia during the Heian period (794–1185).

Komaki

City in northern Aichi Prefecture, 13 km (8 mi) north of Nagoya. Komaki developed after the national unifier ODA NOBUNAGA established his base here in the 1560s. Served by several expressways, it is a satellite city of Nagoya, with rubber, machinery, and textile industries. Nagoya Airport is located to the south of the city. Of historic interest is the site of the KOMAKI NAGAKUTE CAMPAIGN (1584). Pop: 103,234.

Komaki Nagakute Campaign

(Komaki Nagakute no Tatakai). Campaign fought in 1584 by the national unifier TOYOTOMI HIDEYOSHI against the combined forces of the future shōgun TOKUGAWA IEYASU and Oda Nobukatsu (or Nobuo; 1558–1630), ODA NOBUNAGA's son; the second and final stage of the succession struggle that had broken out among Nobunaga's generals after that hegemon's assassination in 1582. In the first stage, which ended with Hideyoshi's victory at the Battle of SHIZUGATAKE in 1583, Nobukatsu took Hideyoshi's side and Ieyasu was passive. Disaffected by Hideyoshi's spectacular rise, Ieyasu and Nobukatsu formed an alliance, and in the spring of 1584 Nobukatsu flung down the gauntlet by ordering the suicide of three of his councillors for their friendliness with Hideyoshi. Nobukatsu's domain of Owari (now part of Aichi Prefecture), Iga, and Ise (now parts of Mie Prefecture) thereupon became the battleground of a drawn-out conflict that began with initial successes for Hideyoshi's "Western Army," notably the seizure of Inuyama Castle in Owari on 23 April 1584 (Tenshō 12.3.13). The "Eastern Army" of Nobukatsu and Ieyasu countered by occupying the strategic hillside position at Komaki some 10 kilometers (6 mi) away. Hideyoshi sought to break the developing stalemate by a bold stroke at Ieyasu's home province of Mikawa (now part of Aichi Prefecture), but his sluggish marching detachments were intercepted by Ieyasu at Nagakute (now the town of Nagakute, Aichi Prefecture) on 18 May (Tenshō 12.4.9) and were resoundingly defeated. The war settled into fruitless skirmishing at Komaki, and the next month Hideyoshi left Owari in order to secure his home area of Ōsaka against the threat posed by the militant Shingon monks of the temple Negoroji and the True Pure Land sectarians (see IKKŌ IKKI) of Saiga in Kii Province (now Wakayama Prefecture), as well as by the *daimyō* CHŌSOKABE MOTOCHIKA of Shikoku. That winter Hideyoshi marched on Ise, but the object of this offensive was to make peace with Oda Nobukatsu rather than conquer him. This goal was achieved on 16 December 1584 (Tenshō 12.11.15), in effect ending the Komaki Nagakute campaign, since Ieyasu welcomed the accommodation with Hideyoshi. The two great adversaries became allies early the next year, with Hideyoshi adopting Ieyasu's son Hideyasu (1574–1607; readopted into the Yūki family in 1591). With his eastern flank thereby secured, Hideyoshi was left free to pursue his plans for the reunification of Japan.

George ELISON

Komatsu

City in southwestern Ishikawa Prefecture, central Honshū, on the Sea of Japan. Komatsu developed as a castle town after a *daimyō* of the Kanazawa domain retired here in 1639. Traditionally known for its KUTANI WARE and silk, it has textile and heavy machinery industries. Attractions are Awazu Hot Spring; the temple Natadera, said to have been founded in the 8th century; and the site of Ataka no Seki, a barrier station associated with the tragic hero MINAMOTO NO YOSHITSUNE. Pop: 104,327.

Komatsubara Eitarō (1852–1919)

Journalist and statesman of the Meiji period. Born in Okayama Prefecture, he studied at Keiō Gijuku (now Keiō University). His radical stance for people's rights and critical attacks on the Meiji government in 1876 were followed by a two-year imprisonment. He entered the Ministry of Foreign Affairs in 1880 through the good offices of FUKUZAWA YUKICHI. He was appointed chief of the police department under the Home Ministry (Naimushō) in 1891, director of general affairs of the same ministry in 1899, and member of the House of Peers in 1900. In the same year he became managing editor of the *Ōsaka mainichi shimbun* (predecessor of the MAINICHI SHIMBUN) and president in 1901. He was minister of education in the second KATSURA TARŌ cabinet in 1908. A radical democrat in his youth, he was regarded as a main spokesman of the bureaucratic clique of the House of Peers in his later years.

HARUHARA Akihiko

Komatsu, Ltd

(Komatsu Seisakusho). Company engaged in the manufacture of construction and industrial machinery, steel castings, and other products. Established in 1921, the company developed Japan's first crawler-type tractor in 1931 and its first bulldozer in 1943. Today it is the second largest diversified construction-machinery manufacturer in the world, with bulldozers its main product line. The company advanced early into overseas markets and maintains a high export ratio (54 percent in 1981), with products shipped to over 150 countries. Efforts at internationalization continue, including foreign capital procurement and overseas local production. Net sales in 1981 were ¥567.4 billion (US $2.6 billion), distributed as follows: construction machinery 89 percent, industrial machinery 9 percent, and others 2 percent. The company was capitalized at ¥39.1 billion (US $178.6 million) in the same year. Corporate headquarters are located in Tōkyō.

Komatsu Sakyō (1931–　)

Novelist. Real name Komatsu Minoru. Born in Ōsaka Prefecture. Graduated from Kyōto University, majoring in Italian literature. He turned to writing science fiction in the early 1960s. With his novel *Nihon Apatchi zoku* (1964), Komatsu's reputation as a writer skilled in humor and satire became established. Possessing a broad knowledge of science, he writes in an extremely readable style. In his bestselling novel *Nihon chimbotsu* (1973; tr *Japan Sinks*, 1976), which has been made into a film, he depicts the catastrophic end of the Japanese islands by earthquake while preserving hope and sympathy for the human race.

Komatsushima

City on the Kii Channel in eastern Tokushima Prefecture, Shikoku. A port town in the Edo period (1600–1868), it is now the center of pulp, textile, and seafood processing industries. Pop: 43,638.

Komatsu Tatewaki (1835–1870)

High-ranking *samurai* of the Satsuma domain (now Kagoshima Prefecture) active in the overthrow of the Tokugawa shogunate in 1867–68; later a high official in the Meiji government. As councillor to the Satsuma *daimyō*, he was responsible for the bureaucratic reforms that made it possible for talented men of humble birth, like ŌKUBO TOSHIMICHI, to rise to positions of influence within the domainal government. He became senior elder (KARŌ) in 1862 and after 1864 was Satsuma's representative in Kyōto, acting as coordinator of the various factions in the anti-Tokugawa movement. Together with SAKAMOTO RYŌMA and others, he was instrumental in bringing about the SATSUMA–CHŌSHŪ ALLIANCE. After the MEIJI RESTORATION, Komatsu served in the Meiji government as a junior councillor (*san'yo*) and briefly as vice-minister of foreign affairs.

Kōmei, Emperor (1831–1867)

The 121st sovereign (*tennō*) in the traditional count (which includes several nonhistorical emperors). He reigned from 1846 to 1867, a turbulent time when Japan was faced with two national crises: within, the movement to overthrow the Tokugawa shogunate threatened to divide the country; without, the Western powers stood poised to open Japan by force. Kōmei was by nature conservative and in favor of continuing the 200-year policy of NATIONAL SECLUSION. After the visit by Commodore Perry and his fleet in 1853, Kōmei accepted the KANAGAWA TREATY of 1854, but he gave only grudging, conditional approval (in 1859) of the HARRIS TREATY. At the same time, he was opposed to the military overthrow of the shogunate, preferring instead to support the MOVEMENT FOR UNION OF COURT AND SHOGUNATE (Kōbu Gattai Undō). He accordingly consented to the marriage of his sister Princess KAZU to the shōgun TOKUGAWA IEMOCHI, which took place in March 1862. This conciliatory gesture further inflamed the antishogunate movement, however, and in 1863, under pressure from SONNŌ JŌI (Revere the Emperor, Expel the Barbarians) extremists, Kōmei issued an edict ordering the expulsion of all foreigners from the country. The extremists were driven out of Kyōto in the COUP D'ETAT OF 30 SEPTEMBER 1863. Political power reverted to the moderate *kōbu gattai* faction, and in 1865 the emperor gave his belated approval to the Harris Treaty and several other trade agreements, collectively known as the ANSEI COMMERCIAL TREATIES. Thereafter, the antishogunate forces openly proclaimed their intention to overthrow the military regime by force and restore political power to the emperor; but before the issue could be resolved, Kōmei died of smallpox in January 1867. It was rumored that he had been poisoned, but this was never substantiated. See also MEIJI RESTORATION.

Miki Seiichirō

Kōmeitō

(Clean Government Party). The second largest opposition party in Japan, after the JAPAN SOCIALIST PARTY. What is now the Kōmeitō began as the political wing of SŌKA GAKKAI, the large lay organization of Nichiren Shōshū, a Buddhist sect. In 1961 this evolved into the Kōmei Political Federation and on 17 November 1964 became a full-fledged party under its present name. The Kōmeitō was made independent from Sōka Gakkai in 1970, with the aim of developing into a genuine national party whose membership is open to a broad segment of the public. Voting strength in the national Diet and in local assemblies continued to grow until a substantial loss of seats in the 1972 House of Representatives election. In 1973, the 11th party convention proclaimed a middle-of-the-road platform, and from that time on the party has made a major effort to elaborate its policy positions. The party regained strength in the 1977 House of Councillors election when party candidates received 7.7 million votes, 14.2 percent of the total cast. The Kōmeitō's 56 seats in the House of Representatives and 28 seats in the House of Councillors made it Japan's second largest opposition party.

The Kōmeitō defines its official ideology as "humanitarian socialism," which it considers a new brand of socialism based on freedom and humanity that seeks to build a welfare society free from corruption, injustice, and oppression. The party's view of socialism is different from those of orthodox socialists, in that socialism is not necessarily considered superior to capitalism. Nor is socialism regarded as a stage historically more advanced than capitalism, but as a model for correcting the shortcomings in capitalism and improving its positive aspects. Specifically, the Kōmeitō supports the maintenance of the free enterprise system, but contends that corporate behavior should be more socially responsible and wealth distributed more equally.

The Kōmeitō's pragmatism is evident in both its basic policy line and action programs. Critical of the overly theoretical and idealistic stance of other opposition parties, the Kōmeitō has emphasized since its inception the importance of devising practical alternatives and taking concrete action on each issue. As a national, rather than a class-oriented party, the Kōmeitō also considers it important to reflect in its policy the aspirations and interests of various strata of the people.

Policies——The Kōmeitō's domestic policy aims at the construction of a welfare society in which the nation's economic prosperity and individual happiness are well balanced. In foreign affairs, the Kōmeitō advocates a policy of "equidistance" and "strict neutrality." Specifically, the party is opposed to Japanese intervention in armed conflicts, to expansionism in any form, and to participation in any military bloc or alliance. It also seeks to promote peaceful coexistence with all nations regardless of ideology or social and political system, and pledges full support for the charter of the United Nations. Finally, the Kōmeitō proposes the establishment of a nuclear-free zone in the Asian-Pacific region, which would prohibit production, storage, testing, and development of atomic and hydrogen weapons in all nonnuclear countries in the region.

Organization——The party's highest decision-making body is its national convention, followed by the central committee and the general assembly of Diet members. A central executive committee is at the top of the administrative setup, and it has subordinate departments to handle such areas as labor, international affairs, culture, and policy research. Party headquarters are located at Shinanomachi, Tōkyō, and there are prefectural headquarters with subsidiary branches in major cities and towns. The number of Kōmeitō members in prefectural legislatures and municipal assemblies throughout the nation was 3,455 in March 1979 and the total registered membership numbered 142,000. The Kōmeitō publishes several periodicals: its newspaper, *Kōmei shimbun*, with a daily circulation of 800,000 (1.4 million for the Sunday edition); the monthly *Kōmei gurafu* with 350,000 subscribers; and a monthly policy journal, *Kōmei*, with a circulation of 70,000 (1980).

Future Outlook——Japan has undergone a diversification of values and political ideas in the post–World War II era. In the political arena this has meant an end to the so-called one-and-a-half party system established in 1955 by the Liberal Democratic and Japan Socialist parties, and the emergence of a multiparty system. In the 1980s Japan may well enter an era of coalition government. Anticipating such an era, the Kōmeitō has mapped out plans for a coalition government of moderate, reformist parties. To make the plans a reality, the party has proposed the establishment of a national front of such parties.

kome kitte

(rice certificates). Security certificates issued during the Edo period (1600–1868) to merchants upon purchase fom *daimyō* of rice stored in the latter's warehousing offices (KURAYASHIKI) in Ōsaka and other major commercial centers. The purchaser or recipient of the certificate held title to the amount of stored rice stipulated in the document. *Kome kitte* bore the name of the warehouse and were issued in denominations of 10 KOKU (1 *koku* = about 180 liters or 5 US bushels). Though valid for only a limited time, *kome kitte* were widely circulated and became the principal instrument of rice transactions. The practice arose of redeeming part of the value of the certificate in silver rather than rice; *kome kitte* came to be used as security, and they were used increasingly in transactions involving amounts greater than their face value. As these practices spread, the market in *kome kitte* became quite confused.　　*Philip* BROWN

kome sōdō → rice riots of 1918

Kome Yokose Mēdē → Shokuryō Mēdē

kōminkan → community centers

Komiya Toyotaka (1884–1966)

Literary critic. Born in Fukuoka Prefecture. Graduate of Tōkyō University, where he majored in German literature. Professor of Tōhoku University and, after World War II, of Gakushūin University. One of the talented pupils of the Meiji novelist NATSUME SŌSEKI, he wrote mainly on the *kabuki* and Nō theater and the *haiku* poet BASHŌ. Most noted among his works are his contributions to the study of Sōseki: *Natsume Sōseki* (1938) and *Sōseki no geijutsu* (1942).　　*Asai Kiyoshi*

Kommintō

("Indigents' Party"). Also known as Shakkintō ("Debtors' Party"). Group of peasants who participated in rebellions in the western part of the Kantō region and the southeastern part of the Chūbu region from 1883 to 1885 to demand lower interest rates and partial cancellation of debts. Many of them had been genuinely impoverished by the deflationary policies of Finance Minister MATSUKATA MASAYOSHI (see also MATSUKATA FISCAL POLICY), but others were relatively well-off peasants who had come under the influence of the FREEDOM AND PEOPLE'S RIGHTS MOVEMENT. See also CHICHIBU INCIDENT.

komon

Textile pattern of fine dots made from stencils and paste-resist; also fabrics with such patterns. The dots are usually from 1 to 2 centimeters in diameter (0.4 to 0.8 in), but the finest patterns have as many as 600 to 700 dots per 3 square centimeters (1.2 sq in). Early in the Edo period (1600–1868) *komon* was used mainly on a monochrome background for *kamishimo,* the warriors' formal upper garment, and later for unlined *haori, kosode,* and *nagajuban* (see CLOTHING). Since it was particularly popular in Edo (now Tōkyō), it is also known as Edo *komon.* In the Meiji period (1868–1912) its popularity declined, but it has recently come into use again. See also TEXTILES.　　*Hosoda Kazuo*

komonjo → diplomatics

komononari

Miscellaneous taxes, as opposed to the annual land taxes (*honto mononari;* see NENGU), levied by the shogunate and the domains during the Edo period (1600–1868). These taxes were imposed on certain businesses and crafts, on produce such as tea and fish, and on peasants' exploitation of forests, mountains, and fields, which were

not covered by *honto mononari;* they were paid in rice or cash. Some *komononari* were assessed annually at a fixed rate; they were called *jō komononari* and were recorded in the village tax registers. Others were only temporary, or fluctuated in amount; these were called *uki komononari* or *ukiyaku* and were not recorded. *Komononari* assessed on various businesses were further classified as UNJŌ, MYŌGAKIN, etc. The kinds and amounts of *komononari* assessed varied from domain to domain. Like many other irregular imposts, these taxes were abolished in the course of the LAND TAX REFORM OF 1873–1881.　　*Philip* BROWN

Komoro

City in eastern Nagano Prefecture, central Honshū, on the slopes of Asamayama. A prosperous castle town and one of the POST-STATION TOWNS during the Edo period (1600–1868), Komoro is associated with the poems of SHIMAZAKI TŌSON (1872–1943). Vegetables, apples, and peaches are grown. There is also an emerging electronics industry. Kaikoen, a park on the river Chikumagawa, contains the remains of Komoro Castle and a museum in honor of Tōson. Pop: 42,355.

Komparu school

(Komparuryū). One of the five major *shite kata* (principal player) schools (or troupes) of professional NŌ theater actors. It claims descent from the Emaiza (Emai troupe; also known as the Takedaza), the oldest of the four Yamato SARUGAKU Nō troupes, which from the Kamakura period (1185–1333) had been under the patronage of the temple KŌFUKUJI and the KASUGA SHRINE in Nara. The Emai troupe's association with Nō theater is said to have first begun with Bishaō Gonnokami, the troupe head *(tayū),* who lived sometime around the Nambokuchō period (1336–92); the present name of the school is said to derive from the name of his son Komparu Gonnokami. Actor-playwright KOMPARU ZENCHIKU, son-in-law of the famous Nō actor and theorist ZEAMI, is credited with reviving the school in the mid-15th century. Komparu Zempō (b 1454), Zenchiku's grandson, is another well-known school playwright. The school flourished during the time of the military hegemon TOYOTOMI HIDEYOSHI, but declined in the Edo period (1600–1868) after the death of Zenkyoku (1549–1621). In the Meiji period (1868–1912) the school produced a number of famous actors including Sakurama Sajin (1835–1917). As of 1982, Komparu Nobutaka (b 1920) was the 79th hereditary head of the school, whose members included Sakurama Michio (b 1897), who was designated an Important Intangible Cultural Property in 1970.　　*Kikkawa Shūhei*

Komparu Zenchiku (1405–1470?)

NŌ actor and playwright. Real name Komparu Ujinobu. Zenchiku was head of the Emman'i troupe (ancestor of the modern KOMPARU SCHOOL of Nō), and was active mainly in the region of Nara. In his youth he studied with ZEAMI, the actor-playwright who transformed Nō into a classic art, and he married Zeami's daughter. He actually was Zeami's successor, but he shared in Zeami's disfavor after ASHIKAGA YOSHINORI became shōgun, and so all his life was overshadowed by On'ami, Yoshinori's favorite. In 1468, to avoid the Ōnin War (1467–77), Zenchiku retired to a hermitage near that of his friend, the Zen master IKKYŪ. A record from the year 1471 refers to Zenchiku as already deceased. Zenchiku wrote such respected critical treatises as *Kabu zuinō ki* (1456, The Essence of Song and Dance), and *Rokurin ichiro* (1455, The Six Wheels and the Drop of Dew). He also left several fine plays, including *Teika, Kamo,* and *Bashō.*　　*Royall* TYLER

Kompira → Kotohira Shrine

Kōmundo Incident

(Kyobuntō Jiken). Also known as the Port Hamilton Incident. An 1885 dispute between Great Britain and Russia over Kōmundo (J: Kyobuntō), a small island off Korea's southwest coast at the entrance to the Yellow Sea and midway between China and Japan. Russia's unsuccessful effort to lease the island in 1882 aroused British interest in its potential as a commercial and naval base in a strategic location. When British naval forces seized the island in 1885, China, Russia, and Japan immediately joined Korea in demanding their withdrawal. This was accomplished in 1887, but only after China and Russia promised Britain to neither approve nor attempt the occupation of Korean territory. Japan was greatly relieved because it viewed any foreign presence in Korea as a potential threat to its own national security.

C. Kenneth QUINONES

Komura Jutarō (1855–1911)

Foreign minister who figured significantly in such major diplomatic issues of the latter part of the Meiji period (1868–1912) as the AN-GLO-JAPANESE ALLIANCE, the RUSSO-JAPANESE WAR, and the annexation of Korea.

Born in the small southern Kyūshū domain of Obi (now part of Miyazaki Prefecture), Komura studied English at Nagasaki and then law at the Daigaku Nankō (later Tōkyō University). In 1875 the government sent him to Harvard Law School; he was graduated three years later. Upon returning to Japan via Europe in 1880, he entered the Ministry of Justice and two years later became a judge in the Great Court of Cassation (Daishin'in). In 1884 he entered the Ministry of Foreign Affairs. For nine years he served in the ministry's translation bureau and was instrumental in establishing the foreign service examination system. During those years, it is said, he covertly opposed Foreign Minister ŌKUMA SHIGENOBU's "weak-kneed" revision plans for the unequal treaties (see UNEQUAL TREATIES, REVISION OF).

In 1893 Komura became first secretary of the legation in Beijing (Peking). As Sino–Japanese relations deteriorated over the Korean issue, he urged his government to strike first and evacuated the Beijing legation without waiting for instructions from Tōkyō. During the SINO-JAPANESE WAR OF 1894–1895 he first served as civil administrator of the Japanese-occupied areas in Manchuria. Later, as chief of the Foreign Ministry's political affairs bureau, he drafted the Japanese peace demands, which sought, among other things, to expand Japan's economic claims on the continent (see SHIMONOSEKI, TREATY OF).

In October 1895 Komura was sent to Korea, where Japan and Russia were in competition for control of the royal court. In May 1896 he signed an agreement with Russia, known as the Komura-Vaeber Memorandum, allowing for joint interference in Korean internal affairs. For the next two years, as vice-foreign minister, he was engaged in issues concerning Korea, the Western powers' activities in China, the American annexation of Hawaii, and Japanese EMIGRATION to the United States.

As minister to Washington from September 1898, Komura observed the American acquisition of the Philippines and John Hay's proclamation of the OPEN DOOR POLICY in China. He also advised Tōkyō to restrain emigration to the United States. In February 1900 he was transferred to Russia. When the BOXER REBELLION broke out, he urged Japan to join the allies in suppressing it. He represented Japan in the Beijing international conference for the settlement of the incident.

In September 1901 Komura became foreign minister in the first KATSURA TARŌ cabinet. When the conflict with Russia over Manchuria mounted, he promoted a hard-line policy and helped induce Japan to conclude the Anglo-Japanese Alliance in January 1902. He conducted prewar diplomacy toward Russia with full expectation of war, and during the Russo-Japanese War (1904–05) he drafted peace terms that aimed at making Korea Japan's de facto sphere of sovereignty and southern Manchuria Japan's sphere of interest. In August 1905 he represented Japan at the peace conference convoked by Theodore Roosevelt in Portsmouth, New Hampshire. Frustrated with Russian intransigence, he decided to terminate negotiations. The leaders in Tōkyō, however, desired the immediate conclusion of the war and instructed Komura to sign the Treaty of PORTSMOUTH. The Japanese populace, bitterly dissatisfied with the treaty, rebuked him. Upon returning home, he quashed the preliminary agreement that the American railway tycoon E. H. Harriman had reached with the Tōkyō government for the joint operation of what was to become the SOUTH MANCHURIA RAILWAY. He then went to Beijing to obtain Chinese consent, as required by the Portsmouth treaty, for the transfer of Russian rights and interests in southern Manchuria to Japan and to acquire further concessions from China. Komura succeeded in forcing China to sign the Treaty of Beijing in December 1905.

In January 1906 Komura resigned as foreign minister and was appointed to the Privy Council (Sūmitsuin). In June of the same year he was named ambassador to England. In August 1908 he became foreign minister in the second Katsura cabinet. At that time he proclaimed that his basic foreign policy was to secure permanently the position that Japan had acquired in Manchuria and Korea and to persuade the Western powers gradually to recognize Japan's special position in East Asia. Accordingly, in November 1908 he arranged the signing of the TAKAHIRA–ROOT AGREEMENT with the United States, but in early 1910 he rejected the American proposal for the neutralization of the Manchurian railways. In August of the same year, Japan annexed Korea (see KOREA, ANNEXATION OF).

In 1911 Komura successfully concluded with the major powers a series of new commercial treaties, which finally restored complete tariff autonomy to Japan. In the new treaty with the United States, however, he conceded on the immigration issue, believing that Japanese emigration should be concentrated on the Asian continent. Thus, throughout his career, Komura, a representative of the second generation of leaders in Meiji Japan, vigorously promoted his country's continental expansion.

▰——Gaimushō, ed, *Komura gaikō shi*, 2 vols (1953, repr 1966). Masumoto Uhei, *Shizen no hito Komura Jutarō* (1914).

Shumpei OKAMOTO

komusō → shakuhachi

Kōmyō, Empress (701–760)

Nonreigning empress (*kōgō*); consort of the 45th emperor, SHŌMU (r 724–749). Daughter of the court official FUJIWARA NO FUHITO and the court lady AGATA NO INUKAI NO TACHIBANA NO MICHIYO, her personal names were Kōmyōshi and Asukabehime. In 729, through the influence of her family, she became the first woman not of royal blood to attain the rank of empress. Kōmyō was a devout Buddhist, and it was at her suggestion that Shōmu established government temples and convents (KOKUBUNJI and *kokubunniji*) throughout the country. She herself assumed sponsorship of the HIDEN'IN and SE-YAKUIN, charitable foundations that ministered to the poor and the sick, and was a munificent patroness of temples, especially of the HOKKEJI, chief of the *kokubunniji*. After her husband's death she dedicated some 600 valuable objects used by him and his court to the Great Buddha (DAIBUTSU) in Nara; a little more than 100 of them, including specimens of Kōmyō's own calligraphy, are preserved today in the SHŌSOIN, treasure house of the temple TŌDAIJI. Empress Kōmyō is said to have wielded the real power of government during the rule of her daughter, the empress KŌKEN.

KITAMURA Bunji

Kōnan

City in northern Aichi Prefecture, on the river Kisogawa; 17 km (11 mi) north of Nagoya. Kōnan was long known for its vegetables and sericulture, but the latter has more recently been replaced by the synthetic fiber, foodstuff, machinery, and metal industries. Pop: 92,141.

kondei

(literally, "able-bodied young men"). Militia established during the Nara period (710–794). Men between the ages of 20 and 40 with skills in archery and horsemanship were selected to serve in the provinces for periods of 60 days in exchange for temporary exemption from corvée labor (YŌEKI) and land taxes (SO, YŌ, AND CHŌ). Most of the original 300 militiamen came from families of district officials (GUNJI) or local powerholders. Although the *kondei* system was first created in 733, it was not until 792 that it replaced the earlier conscription system (*gundan*) established under the TAIHŌ CODE of 701. It attained a maximum strength of some 3,000 men, with 20 to 200 assigned to each province. By the middle of the Heian period (794–1185), however, it had drastically shrunk in number and was eventually disbanded.

Konden Einen Shizai Hō → Konden Eisei Shizai Hō

Konden Eisei Shizai Hō

(also called Konden Einen Shizai Hō). Nara-period (710–794) law that granted permanent private ownership of newly opened agricultural land to the individuals who developed it. Under the RITSURYŌ SYSTEM, instituted in the late 7th century, all land was officially owned by the government, which then distributed it for use to individual cultivators (see HANDEN SHŪJU SYSTEM). In order to encourage reclamation so that there would be enough land for an expanding population, the government in 723 enacted the SANZE ISSHIN NO HŌ, a law granting individuals ownership of reclaimed land through three generations. This law proved to be ineffective, and in 743 the Konden Eisei Shizai Hō was promulgated to encourage further land reclamation. Although the new law set some restrictions (e.g., limiting the amount of land that could be owned by an individual), it was an abandoning of the basic principle of public ownership of land as it had existed under the *ritsuryō* system. It allowed wealthy nobles and temples that owned their own labor force to amass huge private estates (SHŌEN).

kondō butsu

("gilt-bronze Buddhist image"). The Japanese bronze Buddhist images that were produced in large numbers mainly from the 6th century through the 8th century using a bronze-casting process imported from China. Japanese bronze from this time was an alloy of copper, tin, and lead mixed in unfixed proportions. Two main techniques of casting were employed. In the lost wax method a beeswax model was constructed around a small clay core. Clay was then applied to the exterior of the model to make a mold. When the mold was heated the wax burned away, allowing the molten bronze to be poured in. The second method employed a model of either clay or wood. A clay mold was made of the model, which was then pared down to form the inner core. This pared core was secured within the hollow of the outer mold and molten bronze was poured into the space between the core and the outer mold. The latter process was used especially in the casting of large images. After the casting of a statue the application of the gold to the bronze surface was accomplished through an amalgam of gold and mercury. The colossal DAIBUTSU at the temple TŌDAIJI in Nara attests to the remarkable skill of the Japanese bronze craftsmen of the 8th century. By the Heian period (794–1185), wood replaced bronze as the main sculptural material, but the bronze-casting process never completely disappeared.

Kondō Heisaburō (1877–1963)

Organic chemist and pharmaceutical scientist. Born in Shizuoka Prefecture. Graduate of the Faculty of Pharmaceutical Science, Tōkyō University. He contributed to studies on the components of medicinal plants in Japan, especially the chemistry of alkaloids. He discovered new types of alkaloid through his structural determination of menispermaceous alkaloids. These studies opened a new avenue in the field of organic chemistry. He served as army pharmacist superintendent general, as a professor at Tōkyō University and as director of the Otou Laboratory. He received the Order of Culture in 1958. *SŌDA Hajime*

Kondō Isami (1834–1868)

Shogunal loyalist and police official of the Tokugawa shogunate (1603–1867). Born into a farming family in Musashi Province (now part of metropolitan Tōkyō), he studied swordsmanship under Kondō Shūsuke, who adopted him as successor to the family name and school. In 1863 Kondō joined the SHINSENGUMI, a police force newly created to check increasing antishogunate activities in Kyōto. He became its commander after the death of two fellow leaders, and in 1864 led the Shinsengumi in a bloody attack against Chōshū *samurai* in Kyōto (see IKEDAYA INCIDENT). After the defeat of Tokugawa forces at the hands of the imperial loyalists in the Battle of TOBA–FUSHIMI in 1868, Kondō returned to Edo (now Tōkyō) and formed a shogunal loyalist unit, the Kōyō Chimbutai. He led this force in sporadic attacks against imperial strongholds in the Kantō region until his capture and execution in the late spring of 1868.

Kondō Jūzō (1771–1829)

Retainer of the Tokugawa shogunate (1603–1867) who explored EZO, as Japan's northern frontier was then called. Real name Kondō Morishige; pen name Seisai. Born in Edo (now Tōkyō). After holding a series of minor shogunate posts, in 1798 Kondō was sent with several other officials to explore and survey Ezo. Altogether he made four trips to the area, on one occasion replacing a Russian territorial claim stake on Etorofu, the largest of the Kuril Islands, with one proclaiming the island Japanese territory. In his explorations, Kondō was helped in no small measure by a resident merchant, TAKATAYA

KAHEI. He submitted several memorials to the shogunate, urging the colonization of Ezo. In 1808 he was appointed shogunal commissioner of documents *(shomotsu bugyō)*. Besides writing on geography and defense, Kondō edited *Gaiban tsūsho*, a collection of shogunate documents concerning foreign relations, and *Kenkyō ruiten*, a collection of shogunate laws.

Kondō Keitarō (1920–)

Novelist. Born in Mie Prefecture. Studied painting at Tōkyō Bijutsu Gakkō (now Tōkyō University of Fine Arts and Music) but became more interested in writing. His early stories reflect his experiences in a fishing village where he lived after World War II. His best-known short story about the sea is "Amabune" (1956, Women Divers) which was awarded the Akutagawa Prize. Later he turned to fiction concerned with sex, written for a popular audience.

Kondō Morishige → Kondō Jūzō

Kongōbuji

A Buddhist temple complex that is the central headquarters of the more than 3,600 temples in Japan belonging to the Kōyasan Shingonshū (Mt. Kōya Shingon sect) of Buddhism (see SHINGON SECT); located on Mt. Kōya (KŌYASAN) in Wakayama Prefecture. A mountaintop plain located among peaks some 1,000 meters (3,289 ft) above sea level, Mt. Kōya is one of Japan's foremost holy places; no women were allowed on the mountain until 1872.

Kongōbuji was originally the general name for all the temples and buildings on Mt. Kōya, but in 1869 two of the temples, Seiganji and Kōzanji, merged to become a single temple named Kongōbuji. The temple's origins date back to 816, when Emperor SAGA granted Mt. Kōya to the priest KŪKAI (commonly known as Kōbō Daishi; 774–835), who opened there the first training center for Shingon *mikkyō*, a new school of ESOTERIC BUDDHISM with Indian origins that he had introduced to Japan from China and further systematized. The temple suffered destruction several times because of factional disputes and fire, but it was restored after each episode.

The Daishi Kyōkai Hombu here is the administrative headquarters of the Kōyasan Shingonshū. Kūkai is interred in a mausoleum in the Oku no In, the innermost complex of Kōyasan. There he is believed still to be deep in meditation for the salvation of all beings. Kongōbuji is thus regarded as a spiritual haven beyond sectarian divisions, a place for all people who wish to be saved by "Odaishi Sama," as Kūkai is reverentially called. Its physical setting is impressive, with towering cryptomeria *(sugi)* trees several hundred years old. Some 250,000 moss-covered graves are found on either side of the path leading to the buildings; these include those of *daimyō* of the Edo period (1600–1868) and patriarchs from various Buddhist sects.

Notable structures include the *daimon*, or main entrance gate into Mt. Kōya, and the main temple building *(shuden)*, which was originally Seiganji. The latter includes the *jibutsudō*, where the mortuary tablets of emperors are placed, and the rooms known for their outstanding paintings ascribed to KANŌ TAN'YŪ, an early-Edo-period artist. The huge Kompon Daitō (Great Tower) forms the center of the mountaintop complex known as the Danjō Garan. Found within this complex are the *kondō* (main hall), the Mieidō housing an image of Kūkai, the Fudōdō constructed in 1198 and designated a National Treasure, and 13 other structures. Surrounding this complex and the *shuden* are more than 110 smaller temples, including 53 with sleeping facilities *(shukubō)*.

Kongōbuji owns the oldest (1086) and largest picture of the Death of Buddha *(nehanzu)* in Japan. Also in its possession are a manuscript copy of the tract *Rōko shiiki* in the brushwork of Kūkai himself and copies of Buddhist sutras written in gold and silver dating from 1167. These and other holdings are stored in the KŌYASAN TREASURE HOUSE.

━━Yoshito S. Hakeda, *Kūkai: Major Works* (1972). Horita Shinkai, *Kōyasan Kongōbuji*, in *Nihon no jiin*, vol 1 (1972). Ōyama Kōjun, *Kōyasan* (1963). *MATSUBARA Mitsunori*

Kongōkai

(Skt: Vajradhātu; Diamond or Thunderbolt Realm). A realm symbolizing one of two aspects of the Dharmakāya Buddha Mahāvairocana (J: DAINICHI), the central Buddha in ESOTERIC BUDDHISM, more particularly the SHINGON SECT. The Kongōkai reveals the wisdom aspect of this Buddha, who is also ultimate reality, without beginning or end. The essence of this wisdom is unchanging and indestructible, and it is powerful enough to destroy all delusions; it is therefore called diamond. The Kongōkai is further divided into five spheres of wisdom, each symbolizing a particular realm. The *Kongōkai mandara* (MANDALA of the Vajradhātu) is a pictorial representation of this world, and the *Kongōchō-gyō (Vajraśekhara-sūtra)* is the sacred text that explains the structure of the mandala. The Vajradhātu mandala is a square mandala divided vertically and horizontally into nine sections. The Kongōkai, and the TAIZŌKAI (Matrix or Womb Realm), which is the other aspect of Mahāvairocana, can be seen as either dual entities or one and the same, depending on interpretation. See also RYŌBU MANDARA. *Matsunami Yoshihiro*

Kongōsan

Also known as Kongōsen. Mountain on the border between Ōsaka and Nara prefectures, central Honshū; the highest peak in the Kongō Mountains. On its western slopes are the remains of Chihaya Castle, built by KUSUNOKI MASASHIGE in 1332. On the summit are the Katsuragi Shrine and the Buddhist temple Tempōrinji. Kongōsan is part of Kongō–Ikoma Quasi-National Park. Height: 1,125 m (3,690 ft).

Kongō school

(Kongōryū). One of the five major *shite kata* (principal player) schools (or troupes) of professional NŌ theater actors. The school claims direct descent from the Sakadoza (Sakado troupe) of the Nambokuchō period (1336–92), originally one of the four Yamato SARUGAKU Nō troupes that had been in the service of the temple HŌRYŪJI in Nara from the Kamakura period (1185–1333). According to the *Kongō keifu,* a Kongō school genealogy, the Sakadoza ended with Shirō Katsuyasu (1437–85). The present name of the school is said to derive from the childhood name, Kongōmaru, of Saburō Masaaki (1449–1526), who succeeded as troupe head *(tayū).* His grandson Shinroku Ujimasa (1507–76) is credited with reviving the school in the mid-16th century. Ukon Ujinari (1815–84), head of the school from the latter part of the Edo period (1600–1868) through the early part of the Meiji period (1868–1912), was a well-known Nō actor. The Sakado Kongō family line, however, ended with his grandson Ukyō Ujiyasu (1872–1936). Kongō Iwao (1886–1951) of Kyōto later succeeded as school head; as of 1982 his son Iwao II (b 1924) was the 25th hereditary head of the school.

Kikkawa Shūhei

Kon Hidemi (1903–)

Literary critic, novelist. Born in Hokkaidō. Younger brother of the writer KON TŌKŌ. Graduate of Tōkyō University. A student of modern French literature, he wrote critical essays for the modern theater movement and various literary groups. After serving in the army during World War II, he wrote *Sanchū hōrō* (1949), based on his wartime experiences in the Philippines. He received the Naoki Prize in 1950 for his short story "Tennō no bōshi." Since the war, as director of the Ministry of Education's art department and founder of the annual Japan Art Festival, he has been active in promoting Japanese literature and the arts both at home and abroad. He served as the first director of the government's Agency for Cultural Affairs from 1968 until he became the president of the Japan Foundation, established in 1972. His works include *Miki Kiyoshi ni okeru ningen no kenkyū* (1950), a piece of biographical fiction about the modern philosopher Miki Kiyoshi.

Konishi Raizan (1634–1716)

Haikai (see HAIKU) poet of the Edo period. Born in Ōsaka; son of an apothecary. He studied with NISHIYAMA SŌIN, the founder of the DANRIN SCHOOL of haiku, and at the age of 18 established himself as an instructor. He cultivated a friendship with the haiku poet UEJIMA ONITSURA, whose aesthetic of MAKOTO (sincerity) influenced his verse. Raizan's style is considered closer to the elegant restraint of BASHŌ than to the poetry of the Danrin group; while avoiding that group's characteristic frivolity, he profited from their freedom from the restrictive conventions of traditional WAKA and linked verse. Chief among his works is a posthumous collection of poetry and prose, *Imamiyagusa* (1734).

Konishiroku Photo Industry Co, Ltd

(Konishiroku Shashin Kōgyō). Manufacturer of photographic film, sensitized paper, cameras, optical instruments, and xerographic machines, as well as medical, printing, and industrial machinery. Japan's second largest manufacturer of photographic film after FUJI PHOTO FILM CO, LTD, the company markets its photosensitive materials and related equipment under the trade name Sakura, its cameras under the name Konica, and its copying machines under the name U-BIX. Although not established in its present form until 1936, the original firm was founded in 1873 and produced photographic and lithographic materials. The company developed extremely fine-grained film in 1974, and ultra-sensitive film and the world's first camera with automatic focusing in 1977. During the fiscal year ending April 1982 the export rate was about 53.1 percent, and annual sales amounted to ¥215 billion (US $878.1 million), of which 37.1 percent came from film, 27 percent from copying machines, 9.2 percent from cameras, 16.9 percent from photosensitive paper, and 9.8 percent from other products. In the same year capitalization was ¥11 billion (US $44.9 million). The head office is in Tōkyō.

Konishi Yukinaga (1556?–1600)

A principal lieutenant of the national unifier TOYOTOMI HIDEYOSHI; known to contemporary Europeans as the CHRISTIAN DAIMYŌ Dom Agostinho. Yukinaga's father, Konishi Ryūsa Joachim (d 1594), a merchant with interests in Kyōto and Sakai who was an early supporter of Christianity, eventually became Hideyoshi's fiscal intendant *(kurairibun daikan)* in Kawachi Province (now part of Ōsaka Prefecture). Yukinaga was adopted by an Okayama merchant, but he entered Hideyoshi's service by 1581, was entrusted with the important port of Murotsu in Harima Province (now the town of Mitsu, Hyōgo Prefecture), and became involved with maritime affairs. He distinguished himself as a fleet commander in Hideyoshi's campaigns in Kii Province (now Wakayama Prefecture) in 1585 and Kyūshū in 1587. In 1588 Hideyoshi sent Yukinaga and KATŌ KIYOMASA to restore order in Higo Province (now Kumamoto Prefecture), dividing between them a province swept by a rebellion of local *samurai* proprietors (KOKUJIN) in the previous year. Yukinaga's domain, centered at Uto, included the Amakusa Islands, where Dom Agostinho in 1589–90 had to subdue a rebellion of local barons who were his fellow Christians (see CHRISTIAN DAIMYŌ); the Amakusa Islands were later important in the SHIMABARA UPRISING of 1637–38. In May 1592 Yukinaga and Kiyomasa led the first two waves of Hideyoshi's invasion of Korea, competing for the laurels; Yukinaga's forces occupied P'yŏngyang but were checkmated by the appearance of a large Chinese army. Yukinaga remained active in Korean affairs as a diplomat and military commander until Japanese forces withdrew following Hideyoshi's death in 1598. Subsequently he joined the league of *daimyō,* led by ISHIDA MITSUNARI, that opposed the future shōgun TOKUGAWA IEYASU but met defeat in the Battle of SEKIGAHARA in 1600. As a Christian, Yukinaga refused to commit suicide and was put to death in Kyōto. His Uto domain was awarded to his rival Katō Kiyomasa. *George Elison*

Konjaku monogatari

(Tales of a Time That Is Now Past). A collection of more than 1,000 short tales said to have been compiled at a retreat in Uji, southwest of Kyōto, by a nobleman, Minamoto no Takakuni (1004–77), from tales told him by passers-by. This tradition has been discredited, partly because the work contains references to events after 1077 but mostly because, although many of the tales are evidently based on oral tradition, others derive from literary sources including Buddhist scriptures, Chinese histories, and secular Japanese works. (One of these sources seems not to have been brought to Japan until 1120.)

Possibly the work was never completed. It is divided into 31 books: 5 are about India, mostly concerning the Buddha and the growth of Buddhism; 5 about China (1 not extant), including some non-Buddhist as well as many Chinese Buddhist tales; and 21 about Japan (2 not extant), approximately evenly divided between Buddhist and secular themes. The Japanese Buddhist tales contain, among others, legends about Prince SHŌTOKU (574–622), famous priests, the founding of temples, miracles brought about by the Lotus Sutra or by Kannon or by Jizō, and instances of rebirth in Amida's Paradise. The Japanese secular tales deal with such varied subjects as the FUJIWARA FAMILY, famous warriors, tales about poems, ghosts, or criminals, but include also many humorous or gossipy, often bawdy or even grotesque anecdotes about the lives of both the nobility and the common people. Notably, the tales include no myths, and Shintō themes play a very small part.

The title is derived from the opening words of each story, the same "Once-upon-a-time" formula used in fairy tales, though in the *Konjaku monogatari* it is used indiscriminately for stories remote and near in time. Moreover the stories are told as legends, describing actual events, not as fairy tales. *Konjaku* tales can be described as "popular" because they are earthy, prosaic narratives devoid of the refined qualities (suggestiveness and understatement) of Heian court literature. They depict all classes of society, high and low alike, but they are not "folk literature." We do not know how the collection was compiled, whether by one man or by several (in recent years numerous theories have been propounded, including one that regards the compilation as a religious project organized by Takakuni) or why (it may have been a promptbook for preachers, though some of the tales are hardly edifying).

Stylistically the collection represents a transitional stage in the development of the language from the purer Japanese of the Heian period to the mixed Chinese-Japanese style of the Kamakura war tales (see GUNKI MONOGATARI). Many of the Buddhist tales, especially those of India and China, show strong evidence of their origin in texts written in Chinese. Much of the work is stereotyped and repetitious, and the moralistic commentary, however trite, at the end of each tale is tedious. Nevertheless, some of the tales are so skillfully told that one modern scholar treats them as early masterpieces of the short story. Certainly the collection is invaluable in giving a picture of Heian society not found in court literature.

The modern writer AKUTAGAWA RYŪNOSUKE (1892–1927), greatly attracted to the Konjaku collection, dealt with its material in several of his stories in his own distinctive way. Its abundant supernatural element intrigued him, as well as its plain narration unadorned with any analysis of the characters' psychology, which left him scope to adapt the tales to his own purposes. But more important was the *Konjaku monogatari*'s intensely human appeal for him. It had a "beautiful freshness" (literally, "rawness"), and he called it the "Human Comedy" of the prefeudal period. As literature, it bears no comparison with the TALE OF GENJI, yet without *Konjaku monogatari* we should have much less understanding of what people were really like in the Heian period.

📖——Translations of selected tales: Bernard Frank, tr, *Histoires qui sont maintenant du passé* (1968). Horst Hammitzsch, ed, *Erzählungen aus dem Konjaku Monogatari* (1965). Marian Ury, tr, *Tales of Times Now Past* (1979). Critical studies: Michael Kelsey, "Konjaku monogatari shū: Toward an Understanding of Its Literary Qualities," *Monumenta Nipponica* 30 (1975). Douglas E. Mills, *A Collection of Tales from Uji* (1970).   Douglas E. MILLS

konketsuji

(mixed-blood child). Those individuals who are defined by Japanese society as being of mixed blood or racially mixed parentage. This social definition may be applied to anyone of Japanese or other nationality who is the offspring of a Japanese and a non-Japanese parent, but most often the word is used to indicate a person who is of Japanese and white or black parentage.

In the post–World War II period, Japan's *konketsuji* population has been the focus of extensive group prejudice and social stigma. Much of the cultural antipathy toward these racially mixed individuals has been attributed to the considerable social and cultural tensions that emerged throughout Japan in the aftermath of World War II and the nation's American military OCCUPATION (1945–52). In addition, expressions of social prejudice and discrimination have emerged from historical traditions of "pure race" mythologies and cultural patterns of social stratification based on concepts of class, vertical group relationships, and the primacy of patrilineal descent in determining social status.

Since 1974, official government surveys have provided estimates of over 10,000 *konketsuji* living in Japan. Several private and religious social agencies have estimated their numbers to be closer to 22,000. Government authorities have also claimed that approximately 40 percent of these racially mixed individuals hold American citizenship. Virtually all such *konketsuji* have acquired this status as the offspring of legally married parents of Japanese and American citizenship, usually between Japanese mothers and American fathers. Many of the foreign citizens who have fathered *konketsuji*

have resided in Japan as US military personnel, business representatives, or students.

The remaining 60 percent of Japan's racially mixed population have been unable or have chosen not to meet the naturalization requirements for establishing US or other foreign citizenship. Of those *konketsuji* who were born out of wedlock or abandoned by their foreign fathers, many have been reared by their Japanese mothers, maternal kin, foster parents, or in the ELIZABETH SAUNDERS HOME. Consequently, many of these individuals now regard themselves as Japanese citizens. Despite the many legal and arbitrary discriminatory barriers that have often made the acquisition of Japanese citizenship status difficult (see JAPANESE NATIONALITY), these *konketsuji* are completely Japanese in their cultural/linguistic orientation and preferences. Many have been viewed by the Japanese government as "stateless" foreigners, severely restricted in their access to equal employment opportunities and ineligible for such universal benefits as free public education, child welfare assistance, and national health insurance. Several social service agencies have attempted to alleviate these problems by providing limited legal and counseling assistance.

Extensive patterns of social rejection and racial discrimination are often experienced by *konketsuji* who have been reared in broken or fatherless homes, where traditional extended family ties have been severed. This is particularly true of those children who have been identified within their respective communities as illegitimate or fatherless.

Those individuals reared in two-parent, intact family settings have enjoyed the most success in areas of social, educational, and occupational mobility. However, both gender and the socially ascribed racial identities of many *konketsuji* are also major determinants of personal success within Japanese society. Caucasian-Asian females have experienced higher levels of social acceptance and self-esteem than their male or half-black counterparts in contemporary Japanese society. See also FOREIGNERS IN JAPAN; FOREIGNERS, ATTITUDES TOWARD; KOREANS IN JAPAN; MINORITIES; MINORITY RIGHTS.   Nathan O. STRONG

Konkōkyō

One of the syncretist SHINTŌ religions (*shūgō* Shintō) founded in 1859 by Kawate Bunjirō (1814–83), a farmer of Bitchū Province (now part of Okayama Prefecture). Kawate was a deeply religious and hard-working farmer, but a series of misfortunes overtook his family, and he himself was struck by illness at the age of 42, traditionally regarded as an unlucky age (YAKUDOSHI) for men. He recovered after a prayer of supplication and apology to the divine for his disrespect in not observing his daily prayers. Through this experience his faith in Konjin was strengthened. (The origin of Konjin, a vengeful deity, is traced back to OMMYŌDŌ, a belief that was spread through activities of itinerant YAMABUSHI.)

In 1857 his brother became possessed by, and surrendered his life to, the god Konjin. Kawate became a devotee of this god and soon experienced a divine revelation. The god's words poured forth naturally from his mouth, and, toward the end of the year, he received the divine title of Bunji Daimyōjin. In 1859, following the god's instructions, Kawate quit his farmwork, took the god's name Konkō Daijin ("the great god of golden light"), converted his home into a shrine, and set forth on a life dedicated to the god. After embarking upon his religious activities, for a quarter of a century Konkō sat day and night before the god and prayed to receive, interpret, and transmit the words of the god to his followers.

Konkōkyō holds Konjin to be the parent god of heaven and earth, the god of love, calling him Tenchi Kane no Kami. Konkōkyō holds that the life of the founder, who lived following divine instructions, is in itself the doctrine and does not uphold any systematic views as to the nature of the god, the universe, or man. The doctrine of Konkōkyō can be best characterized as simple instructions for daily life, centering on the present and adhering closely to the life and occupation of the farmer and merchant classes. It teaches a life in harmony with the principle of nature and earth, and the tendency toward magic and shamanistic practices is weak. Men, because they are all children (*ujiko*) of the same god, are all equal, and god and man should help each other and work together. If man worships god sincerely, works diligently, free from selfishness, and is kind to others, he is certain to receive the god's blessings. It also denounces all superstitious practices which have burdened mankind.

By the end of the Edo period (1600–1868), Konkōkyō's teachings had spread in the well-to-do farming areas along the Inland Sea, and congregations had been organized among peasants, merchants, and artisans. Although it faced opposition from the established religious groups such as the SHUGENDŌ and suffered repression, in 1864 Konkō acquired from the Shirakawa family, ministers of Shintō affairs *(jingihaku)*, a license to conduct worship, and three years later was licensed as the priest (KANNUSHI) of the Konjin Shrine. In 1868 the divine title of Konkō was finally settled upon as *ikigami* Konkō Daijin (see IKIGAMI). However, persecutions, such as the revoking of Konkō's license as Shintō priest of the Asao domain in 1871 and orders to remove the shrine under the government policy of consolidating Japanese religions in 1873, followed. In the same year, Konkō composed the *Tenchi kakitsuke*, which states the essence of his faith as follows: "Ikigami Konkō Daimyōjin, Tenchi Kane no Kami! Pray with one mind. Your blessings are in my mind. Entrust yourself now."

From 1874 Konkō embarked upon writing his autobiography, *Konkō Daijin oboe.* In 1875 the Konkōkyō spread its teaching activities to Ōsaka and, during the first decade of the Meiji period (1868–1912), engaged in missionary activities in Kyōto and Tōkyō as well. In the process, the clarity and rationality of the teachings which characterized its early years fell away, and missionary activities, which centered on magical elements emphasizing the acquisition of worldly benefits aimed at urban workers, predominated. Throughout his life, Konkō opposed any subordination of his sect to STATE SHINTŌ. However, the officers of the organization, to thwart the sect's suppression and to legalize their teaching activities, began a movement to have the sect officially recognized, and doctrines conforming to State Shintō were created by Satō Norio (1856–1942) and others.

In 1885 Konkōkyō became the Konkō Church, belonging to the bureau of Shintō, and in 1900 its independence as one sect of SECT SHINTŌ was officially recognized. Subsequently, the church, under the banner, "Faith, loyalty and filial piety are one," advanced along the path of service to national policies under the State Shintō system, spreading its activities to Korea and China. However, it gradually stagnated into a family-centered religion. The present "Scriptures of the Konkōkyō" is based upon the *Konkō Daijin oboe, Konkō Daijin rikai,* a record of Konkō's teachings, and *Shinkai* and *Shinkun*, both of which Konkō transmitted orally in 1883. Its headquarters are in Konkō Chō, Okayama Prefecture, and it claimed about 480,000 followers in 1978.

📖 —— Education Bureau, Konkōkyō Headquarters, ed, *Konkō Daijin* (1953). Education Bureau, Konkōkyō Headquarters, ed, *Gaisetsu Konkōkyō* (1972). Murakami Shigeyoshi, *Konkō Daijin no shōgai* (1972). D. B. Schneider, *Konkōkyō: A Japanese Religion* (1962).   *Murakami Shigeyoshi*

Kōno Bairei (1844–1895)

MARUYAMA–SHIJŌ SCHOOL painter, book illustrator, and teacher. Born in Kyōto, he studied with the Maruyama school artist Nakajima Raishō (1796–1871) until the latter's death, and then with the Shijō school painter Shiokawa Bunrin (1808–77), who greatly influenced him. He also pursued the study of calligraphy and Chinese literature with the Confucian scholars Kamiyama Hōyō and Miyahara Setsuan. Bairei was instrumental in founding the Kyōto Prefectural Painting School (Kyōto Fu Gagakkō) in 1880 but left when he opened his own school in 1881. In 1888, when the Kyōto Prefectural Painting School was reorganized, he returned there for two years. He retired from teaching shortly afterward when, in 1890, he helped establish the Kyōto Art Association (Kyōto Bijutsu Kyōkai). In 1893 he was appointed artist for the imperial household *(teishitsu gigeiin)*, and from this period he was sought after as a judge at many official exhibitions. He had numerous students, including TAKEUCHI SEIHŌ, UEMURA SHŌEN, and KAWAI GYOKUDŌ. Following in the tradition of MATSUMURA GOSHUN, the founder of the Shijō school, Bairei worked in a style that relied on shading, wash, and color, rather than line. However, his style also often included the use of some outlines, realistic detail, and perspective not found in typical literati painting (BUNJINGA). His works are carefully composed with conventional subject matter, often taken from Chinese sources, and tend to lack spontaneity.   *Frederick Baekeland*

Konoe Atsumaro (1863–1904)

Political leader and pan-Asianist, scion of the KONOE FAMILY and father of the statesman and prime minister KONOE FUMIMARO. Born in Kyōto and educated at the University of Leipzig, he received

the title of prince under the modern PEERAGE system instituted in 1884 and was named to the House of Peers in 1890. Konoe openly criticized the monopoly of government power by the Satsuma and Chōshū cliques (see HAMBATSU) in the early 1890s. As the major opponent of the involvement of the nobility in party politics, he refused to align himself with the opposition parties in the Diet. In 1895 Konoe became head of the Peers' School (see GAKUSHŪIN UNIVERSITY). The following year he became chairman of the House of Peers and after his resignation in 1903 was appointed to the Privy Council.

Konoe showed great interest in Asian affairs and advocated close cooperation between Japan and other nations of Asia. In 1898 he founded the TŌA DŌBUNKAI, a society to promote a pan-Asian movement to end European influence in East Asia. Konoe pressed for resolution of czarist Russia's occupation of Manchuria following the BOXER REBELLION of 1900 and in 1903 formed the Tairo Dōshikai to incite public opinion against Russia. He died shortly before the outbreak of the RUSSO-JAPANESE WAR of 1904–05.

Konoe family

The senior of five houses (GOSEKKE) of the Northern Branch (Hokke) of the FUJIWARA FAMILY whose members were eligible for the post of regent *(sesshō* or *kampaku)*. The Konoe house was established late in the Heian period (794–1185) by Fujiwara (Konoe) Motozane (1143–66); the family took its name from the Konoedono residence of Motozane's son Motomichi (1160–1233) in Kyōto. Family members served generation after generation as regents *(sesshō kampaku)* and grand ministers of state *(dajō daijin)*, and among their number were many learned scholars, poets, and calligraphers (see KONOE NOBUTADA). At the time of the Meiji Restoration (1868) and the establishment of a new peerage *(kazoku)*, the Konoe were given the rank of prince *(kōshaku)*. Perhaps the best-known member of the family was KONOE FUMIMARO, who was the son of KONOE ATSUMARO and who served three times as prime minister in the years immediately preceding World War II. Documents, books, and art objects long in the possession of the Konoe family, are preserved in the library YŌMEI BUNKO in Kyōto.   *G. Cameron Hurst III*

Konoe Fumimaro (1891–1945)

Politician; prime minister 1937–39 and 1940–41. One of the most important political figures in Japan in the late 1930s and early 1940s. The son of KONOE ATSUMARO, he was born into an aristocratic house of the highest rank and inherited the title of prince from his father. A native of Tōkyō, he graduated from Kyōto University in 1917. Seated in the House of Peers in 1916, he served as a member of the Japanese delegation to the Paris Peace Conference in 1919 and then traveled extensively in Europe and the United States. Throughout the 1920s and early 1930s he was an active leader of the House of Peers, becoming its vice-president in 1931 and its president from 1933 to 1937. A staunch defender of the privileges of the hereditary aristocracy, he maintained that the nobility should preserve a high-minded "impartial" position as defenders of the imperial polity (KOKUTAI) from interelite rivalries, class conflict, and social unrest. Nonetheless, he urged the peers to respect Japan's representative government and refrain from obstructing its functions and so won a reputation as a far-sighted and progressive leader. Able to retain the support of a wide variety of groups, he was first nominated to the post of prime minister after the FEBRUARY 26TH INCIDENT of 1936 but declined and did not form his first cabinet until June of the following year.

Konoe had long advocated the reduction of Western influence in Asia and the enhancement of Japan's power and prestige in its place. After World War I he had publicly castigated Anglo-American internationalism as a self-interested but specious rationale for maintaining the present allocation of the world's territory and resources to their benefit and Japan's detriment. During the 1920s Konoe had promoted closer Japanese ties with Chinese nationalism, particularly in its struggle to oust Western imperialism from Asia. But when Chinese nationalists failed to support Japan's expansion on the Asian continent, Konoe supported the use of military force against China in the early 1930s, as in the conversion of Manchuria into a Japanese puppet state (MANCHUKUO). He described the seizure of Manchuria as a step toward Japan's destiny to become the leader of East Asia.

Konoe's first cabinet (4 June 1937–5 January 1939) presided over the outbreak of the SINO-JAPANESE WAR OF 1937–1945 in July 1937 and the Japanese government's initial steps toward mobilizing the populace into a "national defense state." As prime minister he pur-

Konoe Fumimaro

Konoe (left) with Tōjō Hideki on the occasion of transferral of the prime ministership to the latter on 18 October 1941.

sued the foreign policy goals he had long enunciated, insisting as a condition for peace that China recognize Japan's superior power and role as master of East Asia. Consequently, he badly overestimated Japan's ability to force China to accept its demands, and because of his inability to end the war in China on his terms he disbanded his cabinet and resigned in early 1939.

Throughout the rest of 1939 Konoe was president of the PRIVY COUNCIL and continued to play a vital mediatory role in central government politics. In early 1940 he sought the establishment of the NEW ORDER MOVEMENT and in July was reappointed prime minister. His two consecutive terms in this office (22 July 1940–18 July 1941; 18 July 1941–18 October 1941) saw a worsening of Japan's position at home and abroad. Through the IMPERIAL RULE ASSISTANCE ASSOCIATION he tried to combine the requisites of wartime mobilization with his earlier vision of integrating the populace into the political process without increasing the demands of private interest groups on the state. He therefore attempted to augment his powers as prime minister in order to control various elites and extend his personal control over a populace that might otherwise resist his government's demands. However, he seriously misjudged the willingness of the elites to subordinate their interests to his authority and his definition of the state's needs.

Abroad Konoe continued to seek the fulfillment of Japan's destiny as master of East Asia. He proclaimed the establishment of a Japan-dominated GREATER EAST ASIA COPROSPERITY SPHERE and launched a bold diplomatic plan to forestall Anglo-American resistance to this program and to alleviate Western pressure on his government to withdraw from China. He first promoted Japan's entry into a military alliance with the Axis Powers in Europe in September 1940 (see TRIPARTITE PACT), and then sought the Soviet Union's support of this accord in order to secure Japan's northern flank and deter Anglo-American intervention in China and Southeast Asia.

Konoe's miscalculations in foreign affairs proved even more costly than his errors at home. The Tripartite Pact exacerbated, rather than reduced, tension between Japan and the Anglo-American powers. Hitler's attack on the Soviet Union in June 1941 torpedoed Konoe's plans for a quadripartite alliance. When in the summer of 1941 he perceived that Japan's overseas expansion could not succeed in the face of American economic and military pressure, he proposed, in vain, a summit meeting with President Franklin D. Roosevelt. He was equally unsuccessful in his efforts to persuade his cabinet to revise the militarist policies he had originally helped to formulate. Unwilling to accept any further responsibility for Japan's dilemma, he resigned from office on 16 October. Throughout World War II he held no public office but retained enough influence to participate in the covert maneuvering of late 1944 and early 1945 that led to the resignation of his successor as prime minister, General TŌJŌ HIDEKI, and ultimately Japan's surrender. In the first postwar cabinet under HIGASHIKUNI NARUHIKO, he served as vice-prime minister and worked on an extensive revision of Japan's constitution to conform with the wishes of the OCCUPATION authorities. But they withdrew their support of his constitutional reforms and indicted him as a war criminal. On 16 December 1945, the day by which he had been ordered by the Occupation authorities to turn himself in for confinement and trial, he committed suicide.

In his memoirs, written during and immediately after World War II, Konoe emphasized his friendship for China, his opposition to a war with the Anglo-American powers, his inability to check the militaristic tendencies of the late 1930s, and his private efforts in 1945 to end the war and thus save Japan's social and political structure from complete destruction. His critics countered with the charge that, regardless of his intentions, he had been a weak and vacillating leader who had fallen under the control of the militarists. His first cabinet oversaw the outbreak of the Sino-Japanese War and his second cabinet had made foreign policy decisions that brought Japan to the start of World War II. Furthermore, his domestic policy strengthened the authoritarians, particularly through the NATIONAL MOBILIZATION LAW of 1938 and the Imperial Rule Assistance Association of 1940.

▄▄——Works by Konoe: *Heiwa e no doryoku,* ed, Tanaka Kanjirō (1946). "Saigo no gozen kaigi," *Jiyū kokumin* 19.2 (1946). *Ushinawareshi seiji,* ed, Godaiin Yoshimasa (1946), tr *Memoirs of Prince Konoye* in *Pearl Harbor Attack: Hearings before the Joint Committee on the Investigation of the Pearl Harbor Attack,* 20 (1946). Works about Konoe: Gordon M. Berger, "Japan's Young Prince: Konoe Fumimaro's Early Political Career, 1916–1931," *Monumenta Nipponica* 29.4 (1974). Gordon Mark Berger, *Parties out of Power in Japan, 1931–1941* (1977). Konoe Nikki Henshū Iinkai, ed, *Konoe nikki* (1968). Oka Yoshitake, *Konoe Fumimaro* (1972). Yabe Teiji, *Konoe Fumimaro,* 2 vols (1952). *Gordon M. BERGER*

Konoe Iehiro (1667–1736)

Courtier, master calligrapher, and cultural leader in Kyōto. Born into the highest ranking family of courtiers, Iehiro was the son of Konoe Motohiro and his wife, the daughter of Emperor GO-MIZUNOO. Iehiro himself married the daughter of Emperor Reigen (1654–1732; r 1663–87). He rose rapidly in court rank until he became regent in 1709, the youngest man ever to hold this position. As the real power was held by the shogunate in Edo (now Tōkyō), Iehiro's position was largely ceremonial; he retired in 1725 and became a monk with the name of Yorakuin.

Iehiro was a great cultural figure in Kyōto, with his own schools of tea ceremony and flower arrangement. He stressed the importance of a knowledge of the past, and with his own collection formed the core of the Konoe Collection now housed in the YŌMEI BUNKO in Kyōto. He was also a poet, painter, and garden designer, but his greatest achievements were in calligraphy. His brushwork follows the models of the previous masters of the Konoe school, but he expanded the stylistic range of his predecessors. He wrote in all of the five Chinese script styles as well as Japanese *kana;* his brushwork is at once delicate and strong, formal and loose. See also CALLIGRAPHY. *Stephen ADDISS*

Konoe Nobutada (1565–1614)

Courtier and one of the great calligraphers of his era. Nobutada was the son of the regent Konoe Sakihisa; the Konoe were the leading family among Kyōto courtiers. Nobutada held various exalted posts, but these were ceremonial, since the Tokugawa shogunate in Edo (now Tōkyō) controlled the country. Like members of his family over many generations, Nobutada developed his calligraphy following family traditions, but he also incorporated the style of Heian-period (794–1185) masters. With HON'AMI KŌETSU and SHŌKADŌ SHŌJŌ, Nobutada has been classed as one of the Kan'ei no Sampitsu ("Three Brushes of the Kan'ei Era"), although he died 10 years before the Kan'ei era (1624–44) began. His brushwork is characterized by a sense of blunt power and movement. In painting, Nobutada's simplified style puts him in the tradition of Zen painting (ZENGA). In his love of calligraphy and literature, he frequently brushed Tenjin, the deity of literature, and occasionally painted Zen subjects such as Daruma (Bodhidharma), the first patriarch of Zen.

▄▄——Haruna Yoshie, *Kan'ei no sampitsu* (1971).
Stephen ADDISS

Kōno Hironaka (1849–1923)

Political activist and politician. Born into a rural *samurai* (GŌSHI) family of the Miharu domain (now part of Fukushima Prefecture), Kōno persuaded his domain to support the imperial forces in the BOSHIN CIVIL WAR that accompanied the Meiji Restoration. He became acquainted with ITAGAKI TAISUKE, then a commander in the imperial army, and later (after reading a translation of J. S. Mill's *On*

Liberty) enlisted in Itagaki's FREEDOM AND PEOPLE'S RIGHTS MOVE-MENT to establish a national assembly. He joined Itagaki's JIYŪTŌ (Liberal Party) on its establishment in 1881. Elected chairman of the Fukushima Prefectural Assembly in the same year, Kōno in 1882 organized popular resistance to Prefectural Governor MISHIMA MI-CHITSUNE's plan to levy compulsory labor service for road-building projects (see FUKUSHIMA INCIDENT). He was arrested and imprisoned but was released in the general amnesty of 1889. In the first Diet election, in 1890, Kōno was elected to the first of 14 consecutive terms in the House of Representatives. He left the Jiyūtō in 1897 and the next year joined the rival KENSEI HONTŌ (True Constitutional Party). In 1905 Kōno helped to organize a mass meeting in Tōkyō's Hibiya Park to protest the Treaty of PORTSMOUTH just concluded with Russia. The rally led to the HIBIYA INCENDIARY INCIDENT, and Kōno was imprisoned on charges of incitement to riot but was released the next year. In 1914 Kōno became minister of agriculture and commerce in the second ŌKUMA SHIGENOBU cabinet. He spent his last years working for the UNIVERSAL MANHOOD SUFFRAGE MOVEMENT.

Kōno Ichirō (1898–1965)

Politician. Born in Kanagawa Prefecture. Graduated from Waseda University. He worked as a reporter for the newspaper *Tōkyō asahi shimbun* before his election to the House of Representatives as a member of the RIKKEN SEIYŪKAI party in 1932. In 1945 Kōno helped HATOYAMA ICHIRŌ form the Japan Liberal Party (Nihon Jiyūtō). He was barred from office by the OCCUPATION authorities from 1946 to 1951. As minister of agriculture and forestry (1954) under Hatoyama, he worked toward restoring relations with the Soviet Union. He became minister of agriculture and forestry under IKEDA HAYATO in 1961. Throughout his career he had a reputation as a realist and a man of action. His son KŌNO YŌHEI is at present active in politics.

Kōnoike family

A major Ōsaka merchant house during the Edo period (1600–1868), founded by Yamanaka Shinroku (1570–1650). The family name Kōnoike is derived from the name of the village where Shinroku first established his business. Around 1600 Shinroku, a man of *samurai* origin who became a brewer in the village of Kōnoike in Settsu Province (now part of Ōsaka Prefecture), discovered how to make clear *sake*. The demand for Kōnoike *sake* grew rapidly, for the refined product was better than the traditional milky brew, and soon Shinroku was sending it to Edo (now Tōkyō). In 1615 he sent two of his sons to establish branches in Ōsaka, then moved to the city himself in 1617 and opened a brewery. By 1625 the Kōnoike were shipping *sake* to Edo by sea, and by 1630 they were major shippers as well as brewers. Shinroku became an agent for sales of *daimyō* tax rice stored in their warehouses in Ōsaka and this gave him access to rice for his *sake* production (see KURAMAI). By 1637 the Kōnoike were engaged in making loans to various daimyō (see DAIMYŌ LOANS), and in 1650, when Shinroku died, the Kōnoike were wealthy Ōsaka merchants.

Shinroku was succeeded by his son Zen'emon (1608–93), the first of 13 generations of family heads to use the name Kōnoike Zen'emon. He expanded the shipping business to include shipments of daimyō tax rice and in 1656 opened a *ryōgae* (money changer) shop (see RYŌGAESHŌ), which became the primary business of the Kōnoike house. Zen'emon II (1643–96) succeeded his father in 1663 and expanded the *ryōgae* business. By 1670 he was a member of the 10-man advisory council of Ōsaka *ryōgae*. The business included sales of gold and copper coins, sales of silver by weight, loans, issuing and cashing money orders and drafts, and accepting cash deposits. *Ryōgae* thus served as premodern bankers. Success led to appointments as account agent (KAKEYA) for various daimyō, and the Kōnoike held the authority to conduct their financial affairs and rice sales in Ōsaka. By the end of the 17th century Kōnoike Zen'emon was among the richest merchants in Ōsaka.

Daimyō loans were a natural outgrowth of Kōnoike tax-rice shipments. The alternate attendance (SANKIN KŌTAI) system, whereby daimyō were required to reside in alternate years in Edo to attend the shōgun, increased the strain on their finances, and when short of cash they asked their Ōsaka agents for advances on tax revenues. Daimyō loans increased under Zen'emon III (1667–1736), and by 1696 he had financial dealings with 32 daimyō including the lords of Owari, Kii, Echizen, Kaga, Satsuma, Sendai, Kumamoto,

Bizen, and Tosa. Loans were at high rates of interest and normally were repaid in less than 10 years. Profits from loans were a major source of Kōnoike income as were the fees they received for services performed as daimyō agents in Ōsaka. The Kōnoike also made loans to merchants and, in 1670, merchant loans were 59 percent and daimyō loans 19 percent of total capital. By 1704 daimyō loans had dramatically increased and accounted for 73.5 percent of total house capital. In the 1720s and 1730s the Kōnoike withdrew from the less profitable *sake* and shipping business and concentrated on daimyō loans and money changing. They were also active in land reclamation and under Zen'emon III developed the famous Kōnoike *shinden* (new rice fields) in a swampy area in the province of Kawachi southeast (and now part) of Ōsaka.

Zen'emon III compiled a set of house rules, and in 1732 these became the Kōnoike house constitution (KAKUN). It regulated the business, branch houses, employees, and family conduct and also severely limited Kōnoike flexibility. Consequently, the expansion of the house under the leadership of Shinroku and Zen'emon I, II, and III did not continue under their successors. The house continued to prosper, but in the early 19th century daimyō interest payments declined and the Kōnoike were increasingly subjected to forced levies by the Tokugawa shogunate. The financial base of the house was strong enough to withstand both these levies and the shocks of the MEIJI RESTORATION of 1868, but the fortunes of the Kōnoike declined and they proved unable to take full advantage of new business opportunities. Although they assisted the Meiji government and continued to play an important role in the Ōsaka business community, the relative position of the Kōnoike was diminished in the late 19th and early 20th centuries. Active in banking, insurance, real estate, and other enterprises, they have survived, however, as prestigious members of the Ōsaka commercial community.

■ ——Johannes Hirschmeier, *The Origins of Entrepreneurship in Meiji Japan* (1964). Johannes Hirschmeier and Tsunehiko Yui, *The Development of Japanese Business: 1600–1973* (1975). Miyamoto Mataji, "The Merchants of Ōsaka," *Ōsaka Economic Papers* 7.1 (1958), 15.1 (1966). Miyamoto Mataji, *Kōnoike Zen'emon* (1958). Miyamoto Mataji, ed, *Ōsaka no kenkyū* 3 (1969), 4 (1970), 5 (1970). Miyamoto Mataji, ed, *Kamigata no kenkyū* 3 (1975). Mori Yasuhiro, *Daimyō kin'yū shiron* (1970). Sakudō Yōtarō, *Kinsei hōken shakai no kahei kin'yū kōzō* (1971). Yasuoka Shigeaki, *Zaibatsu keisei shi no kenkyū* (1970).   William B. HAUSER

Kōnoike Zen'emon → Kōnoike family

Kōno Kenzō (1901–   )

Politician. Born in Kanagawa Prefecture; graduate of Waseda University. He was elected to the House of Councillors in 1953 as a member of the Liberal Democratic Party (LDP), following a long career in business and four years in the House of Representatives (1949–53). He quickly became an influential Diet member and served as vice-speaker of the House of Councillors (1965–68) and as its president (1971–77). On his election to the latter office, Kōno disaffiliated himself from the LDP because of his belief that the position required strict impartiality. He is the brother of KŌNO ICHIRŌ and the uncle of KŌNO YŌHEI.

Kōno Michiari (fl 1280s)

Warrior of the Kamakura period (1185–1333); military governor (*shugo*) of Iyo Province (now Ehime Prefecture). In command of a contingent from Iyo in the defense of northern Kyūshū against the second of the MONGOL INVASIONS OF JAPAN (1281), with only two small boats he made a night attack on the Mongol fleet, setting several ships afire and capturing an enemy admiral. He was rewarded afterward with lands in Kyūshū and Iyo. Kōno is depicted in the *Mōko shūrai ekotoba*, a scroll commissioned by his fellow warrior TAKEZAKI SUENAGA to commemorate the battle.

Kō no Moronao (?–1351)

General of the period of the Northern and Southern Courts (1336–92). Member of a family of hereditary retainers (*hikan*) of the Ashikaga, Moronao served ASHIKAGA TAKAUJI, the founding shōgun of the MUROMACHI SHOGUNATE, as his chief executive officer (*shitsuji*) from 1336. By the end of that year, a schism had irrevocably divided the imperial household, leading to the establishment of rival NORTHERN AND SOUTHERN COURTS, the former supported by the Ashikaga. In the wars that followed, Moronao fought Southern armies with great success, destroying KITABATAKE AKIIE in 1338 and Kusunoki Masatsura in 1348; on the latter occasion, Moronao's forces occupied Yoshino, the Southern Court's capital. In shogunate politics, Moronao is identified as the leader of a "radical" faction opposed to the "legalists" headed by ASHIKAGA TADAYOSHI, Takauji's brother and his right hand in civil administration. In 1349 Tadayoshi sought to displace Moronao, who turned the tables on him in a coup d'etat. The next year, however, Tadayoshi formally adhered to the Southern Court and raised an army that occupied Kyōto early in 1351 and inflicted sharp defeats on Takauji and Moronao. Tadayoshi agreed to be reconciled with Takauji on condition that Moronao take the tonsure and withdraw from affairs; but on his way back to Kyōto in the robes of a Zen monk, Moronao was killed by troops loyal to Tadayoshi.

Moronao's image as an arrogant and irreverent parvenu was firmly established by the great 14th-century war tale *Taiheiki*. He is even more famous as the villain of the immensely popular 18th-century *bunraku* and *kabuki* play *Chūshingura* (The Treasury of Loyal Retainers), where he figures as the persecutor of the loyal retainers' lord, En'ya Hangan Takasada, whose wife had spurned his lustful advances. This story's origins are in the *Taiheiki*, but En'ya Takasada (also known as Sasaki Takasada; d 1341), the *shugo* (military governor) of Izumo and Oki provinces (now parts of Shimane Prefecture) was a historical person. *George* ELISON

Kōnosu

City in central Saitama Prefecture, central Honshū. Kōnosu developed as a post-station town on the highway Nakasendō during the Edo period (1600–1868). Now a satellite city of Tōkyō and with numerous industries, it is also known for its dolls. Pop: 57,085.

Kōno Togama (1844–1895)

Politician active during the Meiji period (1868–1912). Born into a *samurai* family in the Tosa domain (now Kōchi Prefecture), he excelled in Confucian scholarship and at the age of 15 was sent to Edo (now Tōkyō) to study under YASUI SOKKEN. He returned to Tosa in 1861 and immediately joined a local proimperial league under TAKECHI ZUIZAN. In 1863 he and others in the league were imprisoned by domain authorities for their antishogunate activities. In 1869, after the MEIJI RESTORATION, GOTŌ SHŌJIRŌ, a ranking member of the new government from Tosa, introduced Kōno to ETŌ SHIMPEI, who was working for the Ministry of Punishments (Gyōbushō), and Etō managed to secure an official appointment for Kōno. He gradually rose within the ministry to become chief justice and presided over the trial of Etō, who had broken with the Meiji government to lead the SAGA REBELLION in 1874. Kōno also tried the cases brought against the leaders of the SATSUMA REBELLION in 1878. In 1881 he was appointed minister of agriculture and commerce but was forced to retire as a result of the POLITICAL CRISIS OF 1881. Thereupon he joined with ŌKUMA SHIGENOBU to found a political party, the RIKKEN KAISHINTŌ, and served as its vice-president. In 1884 he and Ōkuma argued in favor of dissolving the party, but when outvoted they decided to leave the party. In 1888 Kōno served on the PRIVY COUNCIL, newly created to review ITŌ HIROBUMI's draft of the proposed CONSTITUTION. In 1892 he served in the first MATSUKATA MASAYOSHI cabinet as minister of agriculture and commerce and thereafter held such posts as minister of justice, home minister, and minister of education. *M. William* STEELE

Kōno Yōhei (1937–)

Politician. Founder (1976) and first chairman of the NEW LIBERAL CLUB (Shin Jiyū Kurabu), a political party. A graduate of Waseda University, he attended Stanford University in California in 1961. Previously a member of the ruling LIBERAL DEMOCRATIC PARTY (LDP), he was elected to the House of Representatives in 1967 at age 29, succeeding his late father, KŌNO ICHIRŌ, who had been a faction leader in the LDP. He became parliamentary vice-minister of education in 1973. He founded the study group Seiji Kōgaku Kenkyūjo in 1974 as his personal support organization. His political philosophy is discussed in his book, *Hakushu wa iranai: Seiji o motomete* (1976, I Need No Applause: Searching for a New Politics). *Lee W.* FARNSWORTH

Konrad, Nikolai Iosifovich (1891–1970)

Soviet orientalist. In 1912 he graduated from the Japanese-Chinese Section of the Department of Oriental Languages of St. Petersburg University and the Japanese Section of the Practical Oriental Academy. In 1912 and from 1914 to 1917 he studied in Japan. Konrad headed the Japanese language and literature sections of the Oriental Department of the St. Petersburg (now Leningrad) University, the A. S. Enukidze Leningrad Oriental Institute (1922–38), and the Moscow Oriental Institute (1941–49). He wrote a grammar of conversational and literary Japanese as well as a number of works on Japanese and Chinese literary history. Konrad was also the founder of the Soviet school of scientific translation and commentary on major texts of classical Japanese literature. He was an expert on the history of the arts of Japan, particularly drama. He edited the two-volume *Large Japanese–Russian Dictionary* (1970) and contributed valuable works to the fields of sinology and linguistics. He delved into the ancient and medieval history of Japan and other countries of the Far East as well as into common problems and laws of world history. Konrad contributed to the understanding of controversial issues in Oriental studies, rejecting the hypothesis of a slave-owning state in ancient Japan, soundly criticizing both Eurocentrism and Asiacentrism, and making comparative studies of the basic workings and characteristics of socioeconomic, historical, and cultural development in countries of the East and the West. In 1969 he was awarded the Order of the Rising Sun, the highest Japanese decoration given to foreigners.

◼ ——Works by Konrad: *Zapad i Vostok, Stat'i*, 2nd edition (1972). *Kratkii ocherk grammatiki iaponskogo razgovornogo iazyka* (1934). *Ocherki iaponskoi literatury* (1973). *David I.* GOLDBERG

konsei

A type of deity. Often referred to as *konsei sama*. The *konsei* is worshipped primarily as a god ensuring safe delivery of babies and as a god of marriage. This god is considered a variation of the *sae no kami* (DŌSOJIN). Yanagita Kunio's *Tōno monogatari* describes the widespread worship of this god. Found frequently in eastern Japan, most notably in the Tōhoku and Kantō regions, it takes the form of a phallus of stone or wood or, rarely, bronze. *Ōtō Tokihiko*

Konsei Pass

(Konsei Tōge). Located on the border of Tochigi and Gumma prefectures, central Honshū. Lying west of the Nikkō Yumoto Hot Spring in Nikkō National Park, it is famed for its spectacular views of the wooded slopes of the mountain Nantaisan. A 755-m (2,476 ft) tunnel through the pass and a toll road were completed in 1965. Altitude: 2,024 m (6,639 ft).

Konsen Highlands

(Konsen Daichi). Diluvial upland, northeast of the city of Kushiro, eastern Hokkaidō. An abrasion platform averaging about 100 m (328 ft) in elevation, covered by volcanic ash. This vast tract of land was long left untouched because of sea fog in the summer, but the land was finally cleared, and dairy farming began in 1956. Potatoes and sugar beets are also cultivated here. Area: approximately 3,500 sq km (1,351 sq mi).

Kon Tōkō (1898–1977)

Novelist, Buddhist priest, politician. Born in Kanagawa Prefecture. Elder brother of novelist KON HIDEMI. A middle-school dropout and a vagabond in his youth, he participated in the avant-garde literary movement of the 1920s led by such notable writers as KAWABATA YASUNARI and YOKOMITSU RIICHI. He was a maverick of the group and participated briefly in the so-called PROLETARIAN LITERATURE MOVEMENT before becoming a Buddhist priest in 1930. After 20 years away from the literary world, he resumed writing with the novel *Ogin sama* (1956), winner of the Naoki Prize, which made him an instant best-selling author. Most of his works are amorous anecdotes narrated with uninhibited eloquence, which often take as their setting the history and culture of Ōsaka's Kawachi region, where he lived. In 1966, as a bishop of the TENDAI SECT, he assumed the position of abbot at Chūsonji, the historic temple in Iwate Prefecture. In 1968 he was elected to the House of Councillors. Both as writer and politician, he was known for his outspokenness. Other important works include *Shundei Ni shō* (1957) and *Akumyō* (1961).

Kōrakuen

Landscape garden in Okayama, Okayama Prefecture, Honshū. It is considered an outstanding representative of the KOBORI ENSHŪ school of landscape gardening. Completed in 1700 by Ikeda Tsunamasa, the local *daimyō*, it was donated to Okayama Prefecture by the Ikeda family in 1871, and is now a municipal park. It has tea ceremony houses, five ponds, and man-made waterfalls. There are also a miniature tea plantation and rice paddy, a stage for the Nō drama, and an iris garden. Area: 13.3 hectares (32.9 acres).

Kōrakuen Garden

Municipal park in Bunkyō Ward, Tōkyō. Built around a large pond with a small island, Hōraijima, in the center, it reflects a strong Chinese influence in its design and construction. Several miniature hills represent famous Chinese and Japanese scenes from nature. The garden was originally laid out by Tokudaiji Sahei on the orders of Tokugawa Yorifusa and TOKUGAWA MITSUKUNI, *daimyō* of the Mito domain (now part of Ibaraki Prefecture), who maintained a residence in the city. It was completed in 1629. Adjoining the garden is an amusement center with a stadium, amusement park, ice-skating rink, and other sports facilities. Area: 6.85 hectares (16.9 acres).

Korea and Japan

PREMODERN RELATIONS (TO 1875)

The turbulent history of relations between Japan and the Korean peninsula apparently began when Japan and the Asian mainland were connected or just barely separated. It is clear that at least as long as 10,000 years ago various peoples came through the Korean peninsula into Japan, to be joined by others migrating from the south and still others from Siberia. During China's Han dynasty (206 BC–AD 220), there was considerable intercourse between southern Japan, southern Korea, and the Chinese colony of LELANG (Lolang; Kor: Nangnang) in northern Korea. According to one theory, a warlike, horse-riding people migrated through the Korean peninsula into Japan around the 3rd or 4th century AD. From the 4th to the mid-6th century Japan's Yamato people are thought by some to have maintained a foothold in southeastern Korea, in an area known in Japanese records as Mimana (in Korean accounts called one of the KAYA states), and it is generally agreed that there were close relations between this area and Yamato. Close ties also existed between the YAMATO COURT (ca 4th century–ca mid-7th century) and the southwestern Korean state of PAEKCHE, which sent envoys to introduce Buddhism into Japan in the 6th century. In 663 the Yamato court sent a fleet to aid Paekche against China's Tang (T'ang) dynasty (618–907), but it was defeated by Tang naval forces. When a coalition of Tang China and the southeastern Korean state SILLA conquered Paekche and the northern state of KOGURYŌ, Japan received a large influx of educated refugees from these two defeated Korean states. This helps to explain the extraordinary cultural advances made by Japan in the latter half of the 7th century. Through the Nara period (710–794) and the first two centuries of the Heian period (794–1185), Silla was the dominant maritime power in the Yellow Sea and in the Tsushima Strait, and Silla merchants transported both Korean and Japanese monks, who, with their Chinese counterparts, played an important role in introducing more Chinese culture into Japan.

After a long hiatus, there was an era of improved relations between the Korean court and the founders of the KAMAKURA SHOGUNATE (1192–1333). But this era of good will was ruptured as early as 1223, when Japanese raiders (WAKŌ) from Kyūshū began attacking Korea's southern coast. These raids continued until the Mongol forces began to mass in Korea for their attempted invasions of Japan in 1274 and 1281. A period of isolation for both nations continued until 1350, when the *wakō* again burst upon Korea and devastated its economy for over half a century (1350–1408). A leader in combating the *wakō* was YI SŎNG-GYE, and the fame and support he gained in such campaigns helped him establish the YI DYNASTY in 1392. Korean warships, much improved under the early Yi monarchs, put an end to Japanese pirate attacks except for sporadic raids, and later some trade was permitted to the Japanese. The Japanese national unifier TOYOTOMI HIDEYOSHI, intent on conquering China, invaded Korea in 1592 and 1597, but after his death Japanese troops were withdrawn. Numerous Korean artisans taken captive en-

Kōrakuen

The noted landscape garden Kōrakuen. Okayama Castle, reconstructed in 1966, is visible in the background.

hanced Japanese crafts, especially ceramics. In 1606 the Koreans accepted apologies from the shōgun TOKUGAWA IEYASU for this invasion and many Korean captives were returned; the two nations then reestablished a formal exchange of envoys and limited trade, which continued until the MEIJI RESTORATION of 1868. However, the Koreans did not wish to recognize the Meiji government; after a Japanese survey ship in Korean waters drew fire from shore batteries on Kanghwa Island, the Japanese imposed a Western-style "unequal treaty" through gunboat diplomacy in 1876.

Prehistoric and Protohistoric Relations—— At the beginning of the Pleistocene age, Japan was part of a single land mass connected to the Asian continent probably as far south as Taiwan. This land connection permitted the migration of early men into what is now Japan. Toolmakers may have arrived in Japan from the north or from what is now Korea. Up to the 3rd century BC, the characteristic cord-marked pottery of the JŌMON CULTURE, and its partly subterranean dwellings to cope with cold winters, suggest northeast Asian immigrants. Wheel-turned ceramics and polished-stone implements characteristic of Japan's YAYOI CULTURE (ca 300 BC–ca AD 300) indicate a close affinity with Korea, Manchuria, and northern China. Burial practices of southern Korea, Kyūshū, and southern Honshū also show cultural closeness. Apparently, new immigrants to Japan brought with them not only the new pottery style and methods of working stone implements but also a knowledge of bronze. Bronze objects such as mirrors were acquired through trade with the Chinese, and some bronze-casting apparently began in both Korea and Japan at that time.

The wars of conquest waged by China's state of Qin (Ch'in), beginning about 300 BC, are the most likely explanation for this migration of peoples down the Korean peninsula and into Japan, as well as for the arrival of other peoples from south and central coastal China who brought wet-rice culture into Kyūshū, southern Honshū, and southern Korea. The Chinese invasion under Emperor Wu of Han (r 141 BC–87 BC) of the semisinicized state of Chosŏn, in northwestern Korea, again caused people to flee to southern Korea and on into Japan. Physical evidence of this is found on both sides of the Korean Strait in Scytho-Siberian bronze weapons and horse trappings. Characteristic animal motifs are found on Chinese-style bronze weapons, mirrors, coins, and other articles, some of local manufacture. Furthermore, chieftains in southern Japan, some of whom were women, traded with the Chinese colonies, especially Lelang, and sent envoys to Han China. It would seem that the presence of Chinese refugees prompted such missions and an active commerce between southern Japan, Korea, and China.

It can be assumed that the larger number of the peoples who created the Yayoi culture entered Japan from Korea. They may have visited across the Korea Strait until time and tribal realignment weakened their ties. After the Han Chinese colonized northwestern Korea in 108 BC, Lelang became a trade center attracting goods and raw materials from southern Korea and western Japan, notably iron from the Naktong River Basin in southern Korea. There seems to have been a lively commerce between Kyūshū, Yamato, southern Korea, and Lelang in the 3rd century AD.

The HORSE-RIDER THEORY, promoted by Egami Namio (b 1906) and his followers in the 1960s, suggests that a mounted warrior people swept through the Korean peninsula and then sailed to Japan by the 4th century AD. Evidence for this theory includes the appearance around that time of iron armor, swords and arrowheads, and clay models (HANIWA) of warriors and horses in Japanese tomb mounds (KOFUN). These warrior people, usually identified with the Puyŏ of Manchuria, may have also constituted the ruling elite of Paekche; similarities between the deities of Paekche and Izumo Province (now Shimane Prefecture) are further evidence of cultural ties. Besides the coast of Izumo, the coast of Echizen Province (now part of Fukui Prefecture) and the Okayama Plain seem to have been sites of early Puyŏ settlements; the warrior people then apparently migrated northeastward through Honshū. The KWANGGAET'O MONUMENT of AD 414 and the legends of Empress JINGŪ refer to early Japanese battles in Korea, but the Japanese presence in Kaya may have represented ties with an ancestral territory rather than dominion over a new conquest. In any case, there is evidence of close bonds between the ruling elites in Japan and Korea.

According to Japanese accounts, Paekche annexed districts of Kaya early in the 6th century. Then, when Koguryŏ invaded Paekche in 548, Paekche allied itself with Silla and asked for Yamato assistance. Silla finally annexed the remaining Kaya territory in 562, putting an end to Yamato claims on any Korean soil. For the next 80 years, however, both Paekche and Silla alternately presented tribute to the Yamato court on behalf of the lost Kaya territory, probably because the threat of Koguryŏ encouraged them to seek ties with Yamato.

Foreign Influences and the Consolidation of the Yamato State

A new wave of immigrants from the Asian mainland began to settle in Japan from the middle of the Yayoi period. They introduced new agricultural techniques and improved such crafts as weaving and metal casting. The role of foreigners as advisers, technicians, and artisans greatly increased in the latter half of the 4th century. The principal beneficiary of such new technology among the contending kin groups (UJI) of Japan was the Yamato uji in the Nara and Kyōto area. The new immigrants, many of whom claimed Chinese descent, were called KIKAJIN (naturalized subjects) and they formed uji of their own: those descended from people of the Qin dynasty became the HATA FAMILY; those from the Han, the AYA FAMILY; and those from the state of Wu (222–280), the "new" Aya uji. This influx followed the fall of the Chinese colonies Lelang and Daifang (Tai-fang), the territory of the latter having been absorbed by Paekche.

The ties between Paekche and the Yamato court seem to have been particularly close, and Paekche sent scholars and artisans to Japan. Among these was the scholar WANI, who carried the Analects of Confucius and other texts to the Yamato court early in the 5th century, when Chinese writing was still the virtual monopoly of Chinese and Korean kikajin who worked as scribes (fuhito), interpreters, and administrators of occupational groups (BE or tomo). Their descendants continued to provide invaluable technological services to the Yamato court through the 6th and 7th centuries, and the court rewarded them with titles (often reflecting their occupations) and recognized them as members of the court hierarchy. The Yamato ruling house, which controlled by far the largest number of kikajin, had the advantage of a literate staff and accountants to help in controlling rival groups.

BUDDHISM was also important in Japan's conversion from a tribal to a bureaucratic state. Buddhism was introduced in 384 to Paekche, where it flourished. In 552 (or 538) Paekche sent to the Yamato court in Japan monks, Buddhist objects, and messages encouraging the adoption of the new faith. These gifts became the center of controversy when certain families (the MONONOBE FAMILY and Nakatomi Family) claimed that their acceptance would offend the native deities, while the SOGA FAMILY advocated experimenting with the new religion. The issue was actually a ploy in the struggle for power at court and became entangled with conflicting policies toward Paekche, Silla, and Koguryŏ. The Soga were triumphant in 587.

Even during the period of conflict there came a continual stream of Buddhist missionaries and artisans, particularly from Paekche. In addition to the Buddhist faith, they expanded or introduced various facets of Chinese arts, sciences, and political institutions. Prince SHŌTOKU built the magnificent temple HŌRYŪJI undoubtedly with the assistance of Paekche immigrants and their kikajin descendants. Such advisers also aided in drawing up the ambitious TAIKA REFORM (645), which modeled Japan's administration on that of Tang China. At the same time, Yamato's foreign relations began to deteriorate. Tang China planned a pincer attack in cooperation with Silla against

Paekche, and the Paekche capital fell in 660. However, pockets of loyal Paekche troops remained, and a Paekche prince called on the Yamato state for assistance. A Japanese fleet was dispatched but was annihilated by Tang and Silla forces in 663 in the Battle of HAKUSU-KINOE. Koguryŏ was finally conquered by Tang and Silla in 668. Koguryŏ and Paekche refugees, many from the elite, arrived in Yamato in larger numbers than any preceding immigrants. The educated were taken into the government, priests were assigned to temples being built throughout Japan, artisans were employed, and farmers were settled in the extreme north. Fearing a possible invasion from the continent, the Japanese rulers had forts constructed in western Japan with Korean expertise. Furthermore, Emperor TENJI took advantage of the continental crisis to reinforce the RITSURYŌ SYSTEM of centralized rule borrowed from China under the Taika Reform. He was aided in this by kikajin. In fact, such immigrants were so esteemed that in an 815 compilation of the genealogies of 1,182 noble families, 176 were from China, 120 from Paekche, 88 from Koguryŏ, 18 from Silla, and 11 from Kaya.

Relations with Silla——When Tang China established garrisons in Paekche and Koguryŏ, Silla felt threatened by its former ally and encouraged peoples of the defeated Korean states to revolt. In 671 Silla invaded and annexed territory that had been part of Paekche. The fighting finally broke off in 676 with Silla in control of the peninsula south of a line between Wŏnsan and the mouth of the Taedong River. While both Silla and Japan wished to benefit from the civilization of China and thus sent their envoys and tribute, they both had reason to fear its expansionist policies.

Japan depended largely on Silla's shipping (which dominated the Yellow Sea) and welcomed Silla's Buddhist monks. Out of mutual self-interest, in 676 Emperor TEMMU sent a mission to Silla, and Silla sent envoys with tribute and held political discussions. Relations were amicable until the 730s, when BOHAI (Po-hai), a state in Manchuria formed of remnants of Koguryŏ and other tribal peoples, threatened China from the northeast. China responded in 735 by again allying itself with Silla and recognizing Silla's border. Thus Silla no longer felt threatened by China and considered it unnecessary to conciliate Japan. Silla changed its name to Wăngsŏngguk, but when envoys bearing documents with the new name appeared at the Japanese court, they were reprimanded and sent back. Envoys continued to be exchanged, but the Japanese envoys were received by officials of increasingly lower rank and the Japanese themselves often rejected documents from Silla for being couched in language unsuitable for a "tributary state." However, Silla monks continued to be welcome as lecturers, and from the 750s on Silla immigrants still arrived occasionally and were settled in the Kantō Plain and what is now Gifu and Shizuoka prefectures. In 759 news arrived of the rebellion of the general An Lushan against the Tang dynasty, and Kyūshū was ordered to prepare coastal defenses. FUJIWARA NO NAKAMARO, who dominated the Japanese government at that time, realized that Silla could not expect any military support from a China beset by internal rebellion, and so he ordered the mobilization of troops in Kyūshū and other areas to build 500 warships in preparation for an invasion of Silla, apparently hoping that a foreign war would help him remain in power. By 761, 40,700 troops had been raised and 394 ships constructed, but the invasion was never begun because Nakamaro fell from power, rebelled, and was killed in 764. In a conciliatory gesture, Japanese envoys were sent to Silla with presents of gold in 804.

The political situation in Silla disintegrated during the 9th century because of repeated palace coups, and the resulting unrest in the countryside led more Silla immigrants to seek refuge in Japan. However, they were viewed with suspicion and were not treated with the respect that earlier Korean immigrants had received. Their position was made more difficult by the forays of Silla pirates against Tsushima in 811 and other islands off Kyūshū in 813 and 835.

Koreans still dominated the maritime trade in the Yellow Sea in the 830s, and CHANG PO-GO, a man of obscure background who had made his fortune in China, controlled most of Silla's trade with Japan from a strategically located island off the southwest coast of Korea. When he attempted to seize power and was assassinated, Silla's great commercial empire collapsed. In the latter half of the 9th century, central authority in Korea declined, and peasant revolts erupted. Silla piracy against Japan resumed in 869, when pirate ships entered Hakata Bay and seized tax silk. In 893 pirates raided Matsura in northern Kyūshū and in 894 attacked Tsushima with 45 ships; the Japanese, however, killed more than 300 of the raiders and seized 10 ships. This success deterred piracy for the remainder of the life of the Silla state.

Raids and Trade in the Koryŏ Period (935–1391) —— KORYŎ
began as one of the contending states carved from moribund Silla. Its founder, Wang Kŏn (r 918–943), who conquered his rivals and peacefully took over Silla in 935, sought friendly relations with Japan, but his overtures were rebuffed by the Heian court. During most of Japan's Heian period, a state of nonrecognition persisted because neither Korea nor Japan was willing to communicate in language acceptable to the other. Both countries, however, returned castaways with due courtesy. At the close of the 10th century pirates harassed Kyūshū. They may or may not have been from Koryŏ, but the Heian court believed they were.

The first trade mission in Korean chronicles was during the reign of King Munjong (r 1046–83), when, in the summer of 1073, 42 Japanese requested permission to "present" gifts, and 33 men from the island of Iki requested permission to "offer" goods to Korea's heir apparent. Both groups were granted permission to proceed to the capital. Thus trade was conducted in the language of tributary missions. In his declining years Munjong appealed to both China and Japan for physicians, and this led briefly to a somewhat more open attitude toward Japanese traders. Nonetheless, there were hardly any official missions exchanged during the 12th century. There is some evidence of unofficial trade and smuggling by natives of Tsushima along the Korean coast near the mouth of the Naktong River, but Korean officials apparently attempted to frustrate it.

During the TAIRA–MINAMOTO WAR (1180–85) in Japan, a Minamoto adherent on Tsushima who was threatened with an attack by the Taira fled to Koryŏ. After the Minamoto triumph, the Koreans provided him with a ship and sundry gifts. Thus the founders of the Kamakura shogunate were friendly toward Koryŏ, although Japan's imperial court remained hostile.

An attack on Kŭmju in 1223 is considered the first raid by Japanese pirates (wakō); other raids soon followed. Koryŏ, involved in trying to repel the Mongol invasion of Korea during the years from 1231 to 1359, sought to negotiate an end to these Japanese attacks and, fearing that the Japanese would take advantage of its preoccupation with the Mongols, fortified Kŭmju in 1251. In 1259 a Koryŏ mission went to Japan to request the suppression of wakō raids, but in 1263 Japanese attacked the island Multo in the administrative district of Kŭmju and seized a tax-rice ship destined for the capital. The Koryŏ mission protesting this raid was informed that the raiders were from Tsushima and received restitution. Again in 1256 Japanese raided the south coast of Korea, but this was the last wakō raid of the first phase, for the Mongols were massing in Korea to attack Japan and did so in 1274 and 1281 (see MONGOL INVASIONS OF JAPAN). It was the misfortune of the Koreans that they were required to provide the Mongols with ships, sailors, and troops. The Japanese, both court and shogunate, found it hard to forgive this participation, even though it was done under duress.

The second phase of the wakō raids began in 1350. Japanese began to seize tax rice shipped from the three southern Korean provinces to the capital at Songdo (now Kaesŏng) in the north. After a decade of constant losses, the rice was transported overland, but then the wakō directed their attacks at the royal granaries. Ultimately they raided throughout the country, except for the rice-poor massif of north central Korea. During the next 50 years, nearly 500 raids were recorded.

These wakō raids were at last controlled by Ch'oe Mu-sŏn (d 1395), who had learned the manufacture of gunpowder and cannons; by Ch'oe Yŏng (1316–88), who created a Korean navy; and by the nationwide signal system of smoke relays by day and fire by night to warn of wakō incursions. In the early autumn of 1380 a fleet of wakō craft variously estimated at 300 to 500 ships put into the Kŭm River estuary. The beacon signal system flashed the warning to the capital and Na Se (1320–97) was ordered to sail with the new cannons aboard the ships. The Japanese fleet was destroyed by the much smaller Korean flotilla. The naval initiative thus passed to the Koreans, and they began to recapture islands long in the hands of the Japanese. Diplomacy was also employed. Koryŏ found it more effective to deal directly with the powerful lords of western Japan and to gain their cooperation in curbing wakō based in their domains. The return of Korean captives was reciprocated with gifts, and pirates who wished to surrender were settled on plots of farmland in Korea.

The MUROMACHI SHOGUNATE (1338–1573) ordered the wakō in Kyūshū suppressed in 1381. Thus began a shift from piracy toward trade. The wakō began to turn to China, which was in the throes of

establishing a new dynasty, the Ming (1368–1644). Then Koryŏ, impelled by tensions with China and internal politics, sent a military expedition to the area north of Wŏnsan in the late 1380s. The Korean commander Yi Sŏng-gye mutinied at the Yalu River in 1388 and returned to the capital to become the de facto ruler. The wakō, however, took advantage of the northern expedition to raid on a massive scale. The Koreans countered with a punitive expedition against Tsushima, burning more than 300 ships and most of the shoreline housing.

Relations with the Yi Dynasty to 1875 —— The year 1392 marked
both the establishment of the Yi dynasty in Korea and the end of a prolonged civil war in Japan with the unification of the NORTHERN AND SOUTHERN COURTS. In the following 50 years, three of the four Yi kings were dynamic and forceful; Korea continued to strengthen its coastal defenses and navy while engaging in diplomacy and encouraging trade. The Koreans directed special attention to Tsushima, which had the anomalous status of being both a tributary of Korea (since the late Koryŏ period) and a part of the body politic of Japan, until its ties with Korea were cut after Japan's Meiji Restoration. The Muromachi shogunate attempted to suppress the pirates in Tsushima and Iki and requested in return a copy of the Korean Tripitaka, the most comprehensive collection of Buddhist scriptures then available. Sō Sadashige (d 1423), the lord of Tsushima, received a copy in 1416, but wakō from other parts of Japan continued to raid. Korea responded by launching a punitive expedition against Tsushima in 1419 (see ŌEI INVASION). The fighting was furious, for Japanese levies were called up from Kyūshū as far south as Satsuma Province (now part of Kagoshima Prefecture). Having used the stick in vain, Korea offered the carrot—in 1426 three ports were officially opened to Japanese trade and residence: Naeip'o (now Chep'o), Pusanp'o (now Pusan), and Yŏmp'o (near modern Ulsan). Between 1436 and 1474 their combined Japanese population rose from 376 to 3,105. Japanese ships came in such numbers that in 1443 a treaty was concluded with Sō Sadamori (1385–1452) allowing only 50 ships a year to call at Korean trading ports. All were to be authorized by the lord of Tsushima, with exceptions made for special missions. Initially the Muromachi shogunate and a number of powerful lords participated, but gradually the Sō FAMILY through a series of maneuvers monopolized the trade. The Sō transported Chinese and Korean goods from Korea to Japan and obtained Japanese and Southeast Asian goods to convey from Hakata to Korea. Copies of the Korean Tripitaka were sent to the Sō, the shogunate, and other powerful feudal lords. When requested, Korea also felt it expedient to contribute to the repair or building of Buddhist temples in Japan. Among the several Korean missions to Japan was that of SONG HŬI-GYŎNG (also known as Nosongdang), who left perhaps the first diary of an envoy to Japan, recording the events of his mission of 1420 in his Nosongdang Ilbon haengnok (Record of Nosongdang's Travel to Japan). Sin Suk-chu's (1417–75) mission of 1443 left one of the best records of 15th-century Tsushima, Okinawa, and Japan, as well as state papers exchanged between Korea and Japan concerning the wakō, in his Haedong jegukki (Record of the Countries of the Eastern Sea), compiled in 1471.

At the close of the 15th century the Korean court was beset by factional strife, and Japan too entered a prolonged period of civil war. The Japanese residents at the three ports of Naeip'o, Pusanp'o, and Yŏmp'o, with the connivance of Tsushima, had not adhered to the treaty agreements of 1443; when Korean authorities attempted to enforce regulations on smuggling and taxation, the Japanese residents rioted in 1510 and were expelled, but in 1512, after an apology, Naeip'o was reopened (see SAMP'O INCIDENT). Then the wakō, who had carried their raids farther and farther to the south, learned of the weakness of Korea and raided there in 1544 and 1555. The military hegemon Toyotomi Hideyoshi, who brought virtually all of Japan under his control, issued an edict forbidding piracy in 1588, but in 1589 the wakō again raided southeastern Korea.

Hideyoshi had a grandiose plan to conquer East Asia and even India, but Korea, as a vassal of China's Ming dynasty, refused to allow Japanese troops to move through the peninsula against China. Thereupon Hideyoshi launched two invasions of Korea, one in 1592 and the second in 1597 (see INVASIONS OF KOREA IN 1592 AND 1597). The first quickly overran the country, yet in the end both were frustrated by the intervention of Ming Chinese armies and the efforts of patriotic Koreans such as the naval genius YI SUN-SIN (1545–98) and the scholar-official YU SŎNG-NYONG (1542–1607).

The vast numbers of Korean artisans of all kinds taken captive in these invasions made a lasting contribution to Japanese arts, especially ceramics (see CERAMICS: Edo-period wares), and to a lesser extent printing. Korean movable type of Chinese characters was brought back as booty to Japan and was used for a time, but ultimately, for aesthetic reasons, the Japanese abandoned movable type.

With the death of Hideyoshi, the new hegemon, Tokugawa Ieyasu, sought to restore relations with Korea. He assumed a humble posture, admitted Japan's war guilt, sued for peace, returned Korean war prisoners, and agreed to punish Japanese guilty of desecrating Korean royal tombs. Korea sent envoys in 1607, and a treaty was concluded in 1609. From 1607 to 1764 there were eleven missions from Korea to the TOKUGAWA SHOGUNATE at Edo (now Tōkyō). These missions each took more than a year, and that of 1763 included 497 men. But although Japanese envoys of the Muromachi period had traveled to the Korean capital, those of the Edo period (1600–1868) were allowed to proceed no farther than the walled compound (WAEGWAN) reserved for them just north of Pusan. (See also CHŌSEN TSŪSHINSHI.) Trade was completely controlled by Tsushima and limited to 20 ships a year. However, there were various diplomatic problems, such as the wording of documents (see SHUGŌ INCIDENT), and no Korean missions went to Edo after 1764. In 1809 a new protocol was drawn up, but the Korean mission of 1811 proceeded no farther than Tsushima. Later missions were also held up, ostensibly over the wording of credentials.

After the Meiji Restoration of 1868, Japan's new government decided that relations with Korea should be taken out of the hands of the Sō family and be conducted by the new Ministry of Foreign Affairs. Tsushima notified Korea of the change in government and the new arrangement, but the Korean authorities refused to accept the new documents because they were not in accord with tradition. This impasse led to a dispute among the Meiji oligarchs, and the faction headed by SAIGŌ TAKAMORI pressed for a military solution (see SEIKANRON). Moriyama Shigeru (1842–1913), who had been involved in the Korean problem from the beginning of the Restoration, was in Pusan and Tonghae during much of 1874, attempting to improve relations between Korea and Japan. He returned to Korea again in 1875, this time offending the Koreans by wearing Western clothing, arriving on a steamship, and insisting on wording that put Japan on a par with China as suzerain of Korea. Negotiations were immediately deadlocked. Three Japanese warships, the *Kasuga, Teiu,* and *Un'yō,* began surveying the Korean coast from Pusan west and north toward Inch'ŏn. Near Inch'ŏn the *Un'yō* sent a small boat ashore to obtain drinking water on 19 September 1875. It was fired upon, as was a second boat with a flag of truce. On 21 September 1875 the *Un'yō* fired on the shore batteries of Kanghwa Island, killing about 30 Koreans. This gave Japan the leverage to "open" Korea the next year with the Western-style Treaty of KANGHWA.

■——Amakasu Ken, "The Significance of the Formation and Distribution of *Kofun*," *Acta Asiatica* (1977). James K. Ash, "Korea in the Making of the Early Japanese State," *Journal of Social Science and Humanities* (December 1971). William G. Aston, *Nihongi* (1896 repr 1956). Chester S. Chard, *Northeast Asia in Prehistory* (1974). Hilary Conroy, *The Japanese Seizure of Korea, 1868–1910, A Study of Realism and Idealism in International Relations* (1960). Egami Namio, *Kiba minzoku kokka* (1967). Namio Egami, "Light on Japanese Cultural Origins from Historical Archaeology and Legend," in *Japanese Culture and its Development and Characteristics* (1962). Woo-keun Han, *The History of Korea,* tr Kyung-shik Lee, ed Grafton K. Mintz (1971). Takashi Hatada, *A History of Korea,* tr and ed Warren W. Smith, Jr. and Benjamin H. Hazard (1969). William E. Henthorn, *A History of Korea* (1971). Kunio Hirano, "The Yamato State and Korea in the Fourth and Fifth Centuries," *Acta Asiatica* (1977). Igata Sadaaki, "Chōsen ni okeru ine saibai no kigen: Ine yurai setsu hihan," *Chōsen gakuhō* (January 1961). Mitsusada Inoue, "The *Ritsuryō* System in Japan," *Acta Asiatica* (1977). Wanne J. Joe, *Traditional Korea: A Cultural History* (1972). Tashiro Kazui, "Tsushima Han's Korean Trade, 1684–1710," *Acta Asiatica* (1976). J. Edward Kidder, *Japan Before Buddhism* (1959). Isao Komatsu, *The Japanese People: Origins of the People and the Language* (1962). Kim Ha-tai, "The Transmission of Neo-Confucianism to Japan by Kang Hang, a Prisoner of War," *Transactions of the Korea Branch of the Royal Asiatic Society* (April 1961). Yoshi S. Kuno, *Japanese Expansion on the Asiatic Continent: A Study in the History of Japan with Special Reference to Her International Relations with China, Korea and Russia,* 2 vols (1939–1940). Gari Ledyard, "Galloping along with the Horseriders: Looking to the Founders of Japan," *The Journal of Japanese Studies* (Spring 1975). M. G. Levin, *Ethnic Origins of the People of Northeast Asia* (1963). George M. McCune, "The Exchange of Envoys between Korea and Japan during the Tokugawa Period," *Far Eastern Quarterly* (May 1946).

Nakamura Hidetaka, *Nissen kankei shi no kenkyū,* 3 vols (1965–1969). A. P. Okladnikov, *The Soviet Far East in Antiquity: An Archaeological and Historical Study of the Maritime Region of the U.S.S.R.* (1965). Park Yune-hee, *Admiral Yi Sun-shin and his Turtleboat Armada* (1973). Donald L. Philippi, *Kojiki* (1964). Robert Karl Reischauer, *Early Japanese History,* 2 vols (1937). Sohn Powkey, Kim Chol-choon, and Hong Yi-sup, *The History of Korea* (1970). Arikiyo Saeki, "Studies on Japanese History: Past and Present," *Acta Asiatica* (1977). Seki Akira, *Kikajin* (1956). Suematsu Yasukazu, *Mimana kōbō shi* (1949, rev ed 1956). Suenaga Masao, *Nippon jōdai no buki* (1941). Boleslav Szcesniak, "The Kotaio Monument," *Monumenta Nipponica* (January 1951). Tamura Hiroyuki, *Chūsei Nitchō bōeki no kenkyū* (1967). Tamura Hiroyuki, *Nichirai kankei hennen shiryō* (1967). Tamura Hiroyuki, *Taiso, Teisō, Taisō jitsuroku Nitchō kankei hennen shiryō* (1967). Tamura Hiroyuki, *Seisō jitsuroku Nitchō keizai shiryō* (1968). Tanaka Takeo, *Chūsei kaigai kōshōshi no kenkyū* (1959). Ryūsaku Tsunoda, *Japan in the Chinese Dynastic Histories: Later Han through Ming Dynasties* (1951). John Young, *The Location of Yamatai: A Case Study in Japanese Historiography 720–1945* (1957).

Benjamin H. HAZARD

EARLY MODERN RELATIONS (1876–1910)

Korea and Japan enjoyed a relatively harmonious relationship for the two-and-a-half centuries of the Edo period (1600–1868), but this calm was broken with the rise of a dynamic and expansionist modern Japan following the Meiji Restoration of 1868. The history of Korean-Japanese relations during the period from 1876 to 1910 is one of Japan's aggressive challenge and Korea's meek and ineffective response. Japan broke down the wall of Korea's seclusion by gunboat diplomacy in 1876 and intervened in the Korean crisis of 1882 and 1884 with military forces, only to back down in the face of superior Chinese military strength in Korea. By 1894 Japan was determined to settle the Korean problem once and for all by eliminating the Chinese and directly controlling Korea. The resultant SINO-JAPANESE WAR OF 1894–1895 ended in Japan's favor, but because of Russia's intervention the Japanese did not succeed in controlling Korea. Japan prevailed again in a second war over Korea—the RUSSO-JAPANESE WAR of 1904–05. Korea was then converted into a protectorate and, in 1910, annexed to the Japanese empire.

The Opening of Korea——The prolonged peace between Yi-dynasty Korea and Tokugawa Japan was possible mainly because both countries subscribed to a policy of national seclusion. Only minimal diplomatic and commercial contact existed before 1876. Japanese envoys and merchants, dispatched exclusively by the feudal lord of Tsushima, carried on their business at a small depot in Pusan, called the WAEGWAN, or "Japan House," under strict supervision of local authorities. In return for the "tribute" *(chin'gong)* brought by the Tsushima envoys, the Korean government sent irregular embassies, called communication envoys *(t'ongsinsa),* to the shogunal capital Edo (now Tōkyō) on felicitous occasions. The Yi Korean policy of maintaining a harmonious relationship with Japan was referred to as cultivating a "neighborly relationship" *(kyorin),* in contrast to its policy of "subservience to the great" *(sadae),* adopted toward China.

The leaders of Meiji Japan took the initiative in changing the long-standing pattern. In an attempt to bring diplomatic and commercial relationships into line with modern practices, Japan opened negotiations at Pusan in 1868. The Korean government rejected this overture: the effective ruler of Korea, the TAEWŎN'GUN (the king's father, whose personal name was Yi Ha-ŭng, 1820–98), adamantly refused to consider any change in the status quo. This cold rebuff gave rise to a "Conquer Korea Debate" (SEIKANRON) in the high councils of the Meiji oligarchy in 1873. With the defeat of the war-oriented faction, however, the Japanese government embarked upon a policy of forcing a modern treaty on Korea through gunboat diplomacy. After provoking some initial confrontations, Japan in 1875 dispatched a fleet of six warships to the mouth of the Han River to blockade the approaches to the capital city, Seoul, and entered negotiations on a treaty that was concluded the following February. Korea meekly acceded to Japanese demands on this occasion because the antiforeign Taewŏn'gun had been eased out of power in late 1873 and more conciliatory leaders, including King KOJONG (r 1863–1907) and Queen MIN, held the reins of the government. Japan thus achieved the opening of the "Hermit Kingdom" for the first time—a feat that the French and the Americans had failed to accomplish in 1866 and 1871.

The Treaty of KANGHWA, signed on 26 February 1876, was an "unequal treaty" modeled after the Japanese treaty with Britain of 1858. Japan proclaimed that "Korea, being an independent state, enjoys the same sovereign rights as does Japan," in defiance of the centuries-old Chinese claim of suzerainty over Korea. In the remaining 11 articles Japan obtained trading concessions at three Korean ports to be opened in stages, extraterritorial rights for Japanese nationals in Korea, the right to survey the Korean coast, and an agreement to exchange envoys in the future. Through two supplementary agreements and a memorandum, Japan also gained the right to circulate Japanese currency in Korean ports and an exemption from duties on imported Japanese goods. Japanese merchants enjoyed the last-mentioned privilege until 1883.

The Treaty of Kanghwa brought about many important changes in Korean-Japanese relations. Three ports—Pusan, Wŏnsan, and Chemulp'o (now Inch'ŏn)—were opened to Japanese trade in 1876, 1880, and 1883, respectively. A full-fledged Japanese minister, Hanabusa Yoshimoto (1842–1917), opened the Japanese legation in Seoul in 1880. A large amount of Japanese goods, mainly British-manufactured cotton cloth, was introduced to Korea in exchange for an increasing volume of Korean export items, mainly foodstuffs and gold. Bilateral trade, which was nearly balanced during this period, grew from about ¥164,000 in 1875 to more than ¥3.8 million in 1881.

Modernization and the Imo Mutiny —— These changes in diplomatic and commercial relations caused major repercussions in Korean society. One of the major consequences was the development of a so-called "enlightenment" (kaehwa) or "self-strengthening" (chagang) movement in Korea. The government dispatched a 75-man diplomatic mission led by Kim Ki-su (1832–93) to Japan in 1876—the first visit since a communication envoy traveled to Edo in 1763—for the purpose of studying Japan's Westernization. This mission submitted a favorable report on its findings. The Korean king and government, however, did not embark on a vigorous program of modernization until 1880, when a second mission to Japan, headed by Kim Hong-jip (1842–1896), brought home a message of the inevitability of reform from well-meaning and Russophobic Japanese leaders and Chinese diplomat-scholars in Japan. Taking a cue from Minister Hanabusa, the Korean government in 1881 opened a protomodern foreign affairs office, the T'ongni Kimu Amun, and organized a Japanese-style military unit, called the "Special Skill Force" (Pyŏlgigun), under a Japanese drillmaster, Horimoto Reizō (d 1882). In addition, an educational mission consisting of 38 capable officials, called the "Gentry Observation Mission" (Sinsa Yuramdan), was sent to Japan in 1881 to study the details of modern Japanese institutions, including the organization of the central government, the military systems, and the customs service. The mission's report was utilized in the enlargement of the T'ongni Kimu Amun in 1882.

The Japanese "opening" of Korea also stimulated a strong anti-Japanese and anti-Western movement launched by conservative Neo-Confucian scholars. Korean conservatives regarded modernized Japan and the West as being equally barbarous. Under the assumption that all West-centered modern culture was based on Christian "heterodoxy," they organized a campaign to "defend orthodoxy in repudiation of heterodoxy" (wijŏng ch'ŏksa) in 1881. This movement, which the government rigorously suppressed, lost momentum among intellectuals by the end of 1881, but it precipitated a violent mutiny—commonly known as the IMO MUTINY—in the summer of 1882. The mutineers were primarily alienated members of the old-style army who increasingly felt discriminated against. They killed the Japanese drillmaster Horimoto, set fire to the Japanese legations, and brought the antiforeign hero, the Taewŏn'gun, back to power. The Taewŏn'gun reestablished himself in the authority structure and undid the institutional innovations of the previous years.

Both Japan and China dispatched troops to Korea to quell the mutiny and to seek reparations for losses. The Chinese expeditionary forces managed to abduct the Taewŏn'gun, whom they considered responsible for the trouble. They then restored power to the group that favored steady modernization, which consisted mainly of Min clan members. The Chinese government also tightened its control by forcing Korea to sign a trade treaty confirming China's suzerain rights, appointing a number of Chinese and European advisers to the Korean government, and maintaining a garrison force in Seoul. Japan brought a battalion of punitive forces into Seoul, demanding satisfactory reparations. Confronted by this military threat, on 30 August 1882 the Korean government signed the Treaty of CHE-MULP'O, which obliged Korea to send an apologetic mission to Japan, to pay ¥550,000 as an indemnity, and to give Japan the right to maintain "some" soldiers in Seoul to guard its legation. Through separate agreements, Japan also obtained the right to trade at Yanghwajin, a river port southwest of Seoul, an extension of the "walking areas" for Japanese merchants in the three open ports, and complete freedom of movement for Japanese officials in Korea. Finally, at Japanese request and to symbolize Korean commitment to a modernization policy, the government demolished the antiforeign stone tablets that the Taewŏn'gun had erected throughout the country in 1866.

The 1884 Coup d'Etat —— Korean-Japanese cultural contact increased after the settlement of the 1882 crisis. Many Korean officials and students visited Japan during 1882–84 to study Japan's successful method of modernization. Some of them, including KIM OK-KYUN (1851–94) and PAK YŎNG-HYO (1861–1939), who led the Korean apology mission to Japan in 1882, established personal contact with FUKUZAWA YUKICHI, the leader of the Japanese movement for "enlightenment and civilization," and with the leaders of the Liberal Party (JIYŪTŌ). Fukuzawa, enthusiastic over the budding Korean enlightenment, sent his disciples, including Inoue Kakugorō (1860–1938), to Korea to help publish a modern newspaper, the Hansŏng sunbo (Seoul Decadal) in late 1883. Also, during 1883–84, a pro-Japanese Korean faction, the KAEHWAP'A (Enlightenment Faction), was formed under the leadership of Kim Ok-kyun and Pak Yŏng-hyo. This party promoted the rapid enlightenment of the country according to the Japanese model and attracted some members of the Korean mission to the United States from 1883 to 1884. The activities of the Kaehwap'a and Fukuzawa's disciples in Seoul were thwarted, however, by the pro-Chinese SUGUP'A (Conservative Faction) in control of the government. Finding it impossible to realize reform under the pro-Chinese regime, the members of the Kaehwap'a engineered a coup d'etat on 4 December 1884, known as the KAPSIN POLITICAL COUP.

Several important Japanese in Seoul, including Minister Takezoe Shin'ichirō (1842–1917), Inoue Kakugorō, and a few sōshi ("toughs"), participated in the planning and execution of the coup, during which Japanese legation guards in Seoul aided a three-day occupation of the royal palace. The Tōkyō government, however, failed to make its stance clear to its minister in Seoul until after the coup broke out. A surprisingly adroit military action by the Chinese garrison forces, which far outnumbered the Japanese guards, turned back the coup attempt after a three-day stalemate. The Chinese military leaders in Seoul, including YUAN SHIKAI (Yüan Shih-k'ai), restored the conservative elements to power. Forty Japanese were killed and the Japanese legation in Seoul was burned again by angry Korean crowds. Nine of the Korean coup leaders, including Kim Ok-kyun and Pak Yŏng-hyo, sought refuge in Japan, while the rest of the participants were severely persecuted. The failure of the 1884 coup was a major blow to the pro-Japanese enlightenment movement in Korea.

The Japanese government dispatched its foreign minister, INOUE KAORU, as a special envoy to Seoul under heavy military guard to settle Korean-Japanese complications stemming from the abortive coup. With the signing of the Treaty of SEOUL on 9 January 1885, Inoue obtained an official apology for harm done to Japanese citizens and property, an indemnity of ¥110,000, and a promise to build and maintain army barracks for 1,000 Japanese soldiers in Seoul at Korean expense. More fundamental issues concerning the prevention of future trouble in Korea were dealt with at Tianjin (Tientsin) between the Chinese viceroy LI HONGZHANG (Li Hung-chang) and the Japanese representative ITŌ HIROBUMI. In the TIANJIN (TIENTSIN) CONVENTION (17 April 1885), China and Japan agreed to withdraw troops from Korea, to let the Korean king organize a reliable military force of his own by engaging military advisers from a third country, and to retain the right to send troops to Korea in the event of serious disturbances on the condition that such military action would be preceded by written notification. Through this convention, Japan attained the status of a joint guarantor of Korean peace on a par with China.

A decade-long peace followed the signing of the Li-Itō convention while Korea became a virtual protectorate of China as a result of intensified Chinese control through the "resident," Yuan Shikai. In order to discourage the growth of Korean nationalism, Yuan suppressed the nascent enlightenment movement and severely restricted Korean contact with foreign countries. Although Korea had concluded treaties with Japan, the United States, Great Britain, Germany, and Russia before the appointment of Yuan to the post of resident in 1885, Korea was not allowed to establish legations in the treaty nations, except in Japan and the United States. Korea opened legations in Tōkyō in 1885 and Washington, DC, in 1887. Japanese policy toward Korea from 1885 to 1894 tolerated Chinese control over Korea because China could effectively block any Russian attempt to get a foothold in the peninsula. Both China and Japan took alarm at a rumored Korean royal attempt to seek Russian protection in early 1885. In order to prevent the pro-Western Korean king and queen from engaging in a secret pact with Russia, Japan encouraged China to repatriate the Taewŏn'gun and to appoint American advisers to the Korean government, customs service, and the military. In the meantime, Japanese merchants in Korean ports actively competed with Chinese merchants who entered Korea after 1882. In the Sino-Japanese trade competition between 1885 and 1894, the Japanese maintained superiority, but the Chinese were increasingly aggressive. In 1885 Japanese trade with Korea totaled US $1.75 million, compared with US $310,000 in Chinese trade; by 1891, the figures were US $6.42 million and US $2.18 million, respectively. An increased volume of grain exports from Korea to Japan during this time provoked the so-called GRAIN EMBARGO CONTROVERSY between the two nations from 1889 to 1892. Along with a fishery dispute, this controversy remained one of the most sensitive diplomatic issues during the peaceful decade.

Sino-Japanese War of 1894–1895——Korean-Japanese relations were suddenly strained in the spring of 1894 by two incidents: the assassination of Kim Ok-kyun in Shanghai and the massive TONG-HAK REBELLION led by Chŏn Pong-jun (1853–95) in southern Korea. When news reached Tōkyō that the Chinese government was taking steps to dispatch expeditionary troops to Korea to crush the rebels, the Japanese government under Itō Hirobumi's cabinet decided also to send a large military force to Korea. Japan's decision to intervene was motivated by several factors. By this time, Japanese military leaders were confident of winning a war with China and, following the construction of the trans-Siberian railroad, which started in 1891, they were concerned about the increased likelihood of Russian involvement. The civilian leaders of Japan wanted to divert public attention from a serious political crisis precipitated by an acrimonious confrontation between the Diet and the cabinet. Prompted by these mixed motives, Japan sought a suitable casus belli against China after its troops reached Korea in early June 1894. When the Chinese and Japanese arrived at the Korean ports, the Tonghak Rebellion had temporarily subsided, but Japan insisted that its troops would not withdraw until Korea achieved satisfactory governmental reform and full independence from China. Under this pretext, Japanese troops forcibly occupied the Korean royal palace on 23 July and organized a pro-Japanese puppet regime headed by Kim Hong-jip. The Taewŏn'gun was installed as regent in order to control the pro-Western and potentially anti-Japanese king and queen. Japan then obtained a "request" from the puppet government to drive the Chinese troops from Korea. Japan declared war against China on 1 August 1894.

Japan pursued a Janus-faced policy in Korea during the Sino-Japanese War. On the one hand, the Japanese minister in Seoul, ŌTORI KEISUKE, promoted ostensibly altruistic reforms—known as the KABO REFORM—through the pro-Japanese Korean leadership. On the other hand, the Japanese government obtained the right to use Korean land and to requisition Korean labor through the Japanese-Korean Treaty of Alliance (26 August 1894). An additional agreement, called the Provisional Joint Agreement (20 August 1894), granted Japan the right to appoint Japanese advisers to the Korean government and army, to build railroad and telegraph lines, and to open new ports for trade. The Japanese cabinet adopted a policy of converting Korea into a protectorate on 17 August.

In a further effort to achieve its goal, Japan sent Inoue Kaoru as the new minister to Korea in October 1894. When Inoue reached Seoul, a large-scale anti-Japanese "righteous army" (ŭibyŏng) movement was launched by the Tonghak elements in conjunction with the Taewŏn'gun. (The Taewŏn'gun had turned against the Japanese in September 1894.) Inoue defeated the Tonghak "righteous army" by employing Japanese troops side by side with Korean government troops, deprived the Taewŏn'gun of power, and engaged in a flurry of reform activities through a Korean regime now comprising not only Kim Hong-jip but also Pak Yŏng-hyo, whom the Japanese returned from exile in the early phase of the war. The Tonghak leaders, including Chŏn Pong-jun, were arrested, tried in a mixed Korean-Japanese court, and put to death in April 1895. For the purpose of promoting Japanese-oriented reforms, Inoue arranged a loan of ¥3 million to the Korean government and installed about 40 Japanese advisers in the Korean government. Furthermore, Inoue tried to obtain a series of concessions regarding railroads, telegraph lines, open ports, and customs service by changing the Provisional Joint Agreement into full-fledged treaties. All of these efforts failed in the face of the TRIPARTITE INTERVENTION (23 April 1895) spearheaded by Russia after the conclusion of the Sino-Japanese war.

Growth of Russian Influence——The Tripartite Intervention triggered major changes in Korean politics and in Japanese policy toward Korea. With the sudden rise of Russian influence in Korea, the pro-Western King KOJONG and Queen MIN began suppressing pro-Japanese leaders. First, Pak Yŏng-hyo was driven out of the country in July 1895. Then, in October, the royal pair began dismantling the royal palace guard, called Hullyŏndae (J: Kunrentai, "Trained Force"), which had been organized and trained by the Japanese during the war, preliminary to striking a final blow against the remaining pro-Japanese elements. Faced with a total collapse of the Japanese influence so carefully built up in Korea during the war, Japan's new minister to Korea, MIURA GORŌ, engineered the assassination of Queen Min, the leader of pro-Russian forces in the court, on 8 October 1895. Miura took leadership in this macabre incident, and various groups of Japanese in Seoul, including the legation staff, legation police, garrison forces, and sōshi, took an active part. Koreans of anti-Queen Min inclination, including the Taewŏn'gun, the Hullyŏndae soldiers, and the pro-Japanese officials, also played a role. Queen Min's death allowed the return of power to pro-Japanese Korean leaders, headed by Kim Hong-jip, but the fate of their regime and of Japanese influence in Korea was rendered precarious by a new and widespread anti-Japanese "righteous army" movement organized by Neo-Confucian scholars. Riding the tide of this movement, a group of pro-Russian Korean officials succeeded in smuggling the king into the Russian legation on 11 February 1896. With this dramatic royal flight, Japanese influence in Korea came to an end, as pro-Japanese officials were either killed or sought asylum in Japan.

Korean-Japanese relations lapsed into tranquillity in the following period. The king emerged from the Russian legation in March 1897, elevated himself to emperor, and changed the name of the country from Chosŏn to the Taehan ("Great Han") Empire (see TAE-HAN EMPIRE). Behind the facade of these superficial changes, made possible by the defeat of China in the Sino-Japanese War, Korea reverted to the Confucian-style conservatism of the pre-1894 era. Against this background, the INDEPENDENCE CLUB (Tongnip Hyŏp-hoe), organized and led by Sŏ Chae-p'il (or Phillip Jaisohn, 1863–1951) and Yun Ch'i-ho (1864–1946), carried on a reform movement promoting "Korea for the Koreans" and a constitutional monarchy based on democracy, during 1896–98. Among other activities, the club organized an effective mass campaign during 1897 to stop Russian infiltration into Korea through advisers and concessions. When the club was suppressed by the conservative regime, however, no foreign power, including Japan, raised a hand in its support. Japan's failure to intervene stemmed from a shift in policy, which now emphasized two goals: negotiating with Russia concerning Japanese rights and influence in Korea, and obtaining concessions from Korea in competition with Russia, the United States, Britain, France, and Germany. Japan's negotiations with Russia led to the Komura–Waeber Memorandum in Seoul (14 May 1896), the YAMAGATA–LOBANOV AGREEMENT in Moscow (9 June 1896), and the NISHI–ROSEN AGREEMENT in Tōkyō (25 April 1898)—all related to the definition of Japanese and Russian rights in Korea with the purpose of avoiding conflict. Following 1898, when Russia adopted a PORT ARTHUR-oriented policy, Japan sought Russian acquiescence in Japanese control of Korea in return for recognition of Russian rights in Manchuria. Japan pressured Russia to come to terms on this proposal to "exchange Korea for Manchuria" by concluding an alliance with Great Britain on 30 January 1902. When Russia failed to respond to Japanese demands, Japan went to war with Russia in 1904. In the meantime, Japan secured a series of concessions from Korea, including a franchise to build the Seoul–Inch'ŏn railroad (1899) and the Seoul–Pusan railroad (1902) and the right to issue Japanese banknotes in Korea (1902), in addition to opening several new ports for trade.

Japanese Control and Annexation——Japan took swift action to overrun and control Korea at the outbreak of the Russo-Japanese War in February 1904. Ignoring the Korean declarations of neutrality announced in August 1903 and January 1904, the Japanese army secured control of Korea, and the Japanese minister, Hayashi Gonsuke (1860–1939), forced the acceptance of a protocol obliging Korea to collaborate in the war and to "accept Japanese advice for improvement of administration" on 23 February 1904. These events set the stage for Japan's renewed effort to convert Korea into a protectorate. Following another agreement signed on 22 August 1904, Japan introduced Japanese or Japanese-nominated American advisers into the Korean government. These advisers dealt with Korean finance, foreign affairs, police, army, and education in the name of reform during the war. Japan also succeeded in securing American and British consent to Japan's free hand in Korea in the wake of the war through the secret KATSURA–TAFT AGREEMENT (29 July 1905) and the second ANGLO-JAPANESE ALLIANCE (12 August 1905). The Treaty of PORTSMOUTH of 5 September 1905 confirmed Japan's "predominant" interest in Korea, including the right to "direct, protect, and supervise" the nation. Unlike in 1895, Japan was free from fear of an international intervention in converting Korea into a Japanese protectorate.

Japan dispatched Itō Hirobumi to Korea to conclude a protectorate treaty—the KOREAN-JAPANESE CONVENTION OF 1905, which was signed on 18 November 1905. Itō secured this treaty from a reluctant, albeit divided, Korean cabinet after applying military threats to the Korean rulers. Japan opened the organ of the protectorate government, the Office of the RESIDENT GENERAL IN KOREA (Kankoku Tōkan Fu), in February 1906 in accordance with the protectorate treaty. Itō assumed the post of resident general and carried out major reforms of Korean finance, the military, and the police, while fully undertaking the management of Korean foreign affairs. He changed his gradualist approach toward Korea in the middle of 1907, following the discovery of Emperor Kojong's clandestine movement to regain independence through a secret mission to the world peace conference at The Hague. Using this imperial "betrayal" as an excuse, Itō pressured Emperor Kojong to retire in favor of his imbecilic son, Emperor Sunjong (1874–1926; r 1907–10), and forcibly disbanded Korean troops during July and August 1907. By concluding an agreement with the Korean cabinet on 23 July 1907, Itō secured the right to appoint Japanese officials to the Korean bureaucracy under the level of vice-minister of the cabinet.

During the remainder of his tenure as resident general, Itō concentrated on two major goals: suppressing the nationwide "righteous army" movement against the Japanese and developing various political, military, and economic institutions to cement Japanese control over Korea. It took three years for the Japanese garrison forces, gendarmerie, and police to suppress the "righteous army" movement. While introducing a large number of Japanese officials into the Korean bureaucracy, Itō helped to develop a large-scale gendarme force (kempeitai)—composed in 1908 of 2,400 Japanese gendarmes and about 4,200 Korean assistant gendarmes—as the main security force to suppress recalcitrant Koreans. Together with two divisions of Japanese garrison soldiers in Korea, this gendarme system remained a central feature of the Japanese colonial regime in Korea. In addition, Itō helped to organize the Oriental Development Company (TŌYŌ TAKUSHOKU KAISHA) and the Bank of Korea (Kankoku Ginkō; see CHŌSEN GINKŌ) in 1908 to facilitate Japanese economic penetration. By the time Itō resigned in 1909, the Japanese were in full control of Korea's important economic sectors, including finance, banking, mining, fisheries, transportation, and communication. Japan also maintained its dominance of Korean trade during this period, although trade with Great Britain and the United States became significant after 1906.

The Japanese government decided to annex Korea on 6 July 1909, partly because of domestic pressures exerted by some ultranationalists, including the members of the AMUR RIVER SOCIETY (Kokuryūkai), and partly because of fear of international opinion raised against Japan through the agitation of American missionaries in Korea. In order to carry out annexation effectively, Japan appointed Army Minister TERAUCHI MASATAKE to the concurrent role of governor-general of Korea in May 1910. A pro-Japanese Korean political organization, the Ilchin-hoe (Advancement Society), led by Yi Yong-gu (1868–1912) and Song Pyŏng-jun (1858–1925), had campaigned for an early "merger" of Korea and Japan in late 1909. Nonetheless, Korean public opinion remained strongly anti-Japanese. Terauchi therefore augmented Japanese troops in Korea and tightened military control over Seoul before forcing annexation. He arranged the signing of the annexation treaty with a pro-Japanese prime minister, YI WAN-YONG, on 22 August 1910, after creating a state of undeclared martial law in Seoul. Korea, a proud nation that throughout its history had survived repeated foreign attempts at subjugation, thus lost its sovereignty in toto to Japan. See also KOREA, ANNEXATION OF.

Korean Reaction to Japanese Control —— Except for the members of the Ilchin-hoe, which was created during the Russo-Japanese

War under the influence of UCHIDA RYŌHEI, representing the Amur River Society, the Koreans reacted to the Japanese encroachment during 1904–10 first with suspicion and then with intense hostility. Emperor Kojong and his entourage led a series of abortive diplomatic moves to enlist the support of the Western powers for the cause of Korean independence. Particular attempts were made to persuade US President Theodore Roosevelt, the peacemaker and mediator of the Portsmouth Treaty, to intervene in favor of Korea against Japanese ambitions in 1905. Roosevelt, however, turned a deaf ear to Korean appeals in the belief that the Koreans "could not strike a blow in their own defense" against the Japanese. An increasing number of American missionaries in Korea sympathized with the Korean cause after learning about Japanese atrocities and exploitation partly through the Korean Daily News, owned by the British journalist E. T. Bethell (1872–1909). But American public opinion at home remained indifferent to Korea's fate.

The Korean masses participated in two popular attempts to rescue the country from Japanese domination during 1904–10. One was a belated educational campaign to arouse and organize patriotic sentiment against Japanese imperialism through schools, churches, newspapers, and pamphlets. A dozen political-educational societies were created as vehicles for promoting the "patriotic enlightenment" movement. The second was the previously mentioned militant "righteous army" movement. This effort drew its inspiration from the Korean resistance against the Japanese during the Japanese INVASIONS OF KOREA IN 1592 AND 1597 and from more recent examples of anti-Japanese resistance during and after the Sino-Japanese War. Its leadership came mainly from Neo-Confucian scholars and the officers of the disbanded Korean army, but its ranks were filled by peasants. It started in 1906 as a small-scale local movement, but rose to national proportions after mid-1907. The "righteous army" reached its peak strength (about 70,000) in 1908 and in the same year fought its largest number of engagements (1,451) against Japanese forces. The Japanese burned Korean villages in their all-out attempt to suppress the movement. In the four-year-long guerrilla war, the Korean resistance suffered total casualties of 17,779 deaths and 3,707 wounded, against 136 deaths and 2,777 wounded on the Japanese side. The movement continued in Manchuria after Japan's annexation of Korea.

In addition to the mass movements, many patriotic Koreans engaged in individual acts of protest, heroism, and terrorism against the Japanese. About 10 Korean officials, including Min Yŏng-hwan (1861–1905), committed suicide after learning of the conclusion of the protectorate treaty in 1905. Two Korean youths in the United States shot to death the Japanese-installed American adviser to the Korean foreign office, Durham W. Stevens (1851–1907), in San Francisco in 1907. Stevens was on a speaking tour attempting to justify Japanese actions in Korea when the outraged students caught up with him. An abortive attempt on Yi Wan-yong's life was made in Seoul in 1909. These individual acts culminated in the assassination of Itō Hirobumi by a Korean patriot and commander of a "righteous army" unit, AN CHUNG-GŬN, at Harbin, Manchuria, on 26 October 1909.

🔖——Isabella L. Bird Bishop, Korea and Her Neighbors, 2 vols (1897). Boku Sōkon (Pak Chong-gŭn), "Bin Hi gyakusatsu jiken no shorisaku o meguru shomondai," in Ōtsuka Shigakukai, ed, Higashi Ajia kindaishi no kenkyū (1967). Vipin Chandra, "An Outline Study of the Ilchin-hoe (Advancement Society) of Korea," University of Washington, Occasional Papers on Korea 2 (March 1974). Jongsuk Chay, "The Taft–Katsura Memorandum Reconsidered," Pacific Historical Review 37 (1968). Ching Young Choe, The Rule of the Taewŏn'gun, 1864–1874 (1972). Hilary Conroy, The Japanese Seizure of Korea, 1868–1910 (1960). Harold F. Cook, Korea's 1884 Incident (1972). Martina Deuchler, Confucian Gentlemen and Barbarian Envoys (1977). Raymond A. Esthus, Theodore Roosevelt and Japan (1967). Fujimura Michio, Nisshin sensō (1973). Fujiwara Yōko, "Gihei undō," Rekishigaku kenkyū 187 (1955). Hō Takushu, Meiji shoki Nikkan shin kankei no kenkyū (1969). Eugene C. I. Kim and Han-kyo Kim, Korea and the Politics of Imperialism, 1876–1910 (1967). Key Hiuk Kim, The Last Phase of East Asian World Order (1980). Kyō Tokusō (Kang Tŏk-sang), "Rishi Chōsen kaikō chokugo ni okeru Chōnichi bōeki no tenkai," Rekishigaku kenkyū 265 (1962). Kyō Zaigen (Kang Chae-ŏn), Chōsen kindaishi kenkyū (1970). Sunkeun Lee, "Historical Recollections of Korean-Japanese Relations," Journal of Social Sciences and Humanities 19 (December 1963). Young Ick Lew, "The Reform Efforts and Ideas of Pak Yŏng-hyo, 1894–1895," University of Hawaii, Korean Studies 1 (1977). Andrew Malozemoff, Russian Far Eastern Policy, 1881–1904 (1958). Marlene J. Mayo, "The Korean Crisis of 1873 and Early Meiji Foreign Policy," *Journal of Asian Studies* 31.4 (August 1972). George M. McCune, "The Exchange of Envoys between Korea and Japan during the Tokugawa Period," *Far Eastern Quarterly* 5.3 (May 1946). George A. McGrane, *Korea's Tragic Hours* (1973). Nakatsuka Akira, *Kindai Nihon to Chōsen* (1969). James B. Palais, *Politics and Policy in Traditional Korea* (1975). Seong-Rae Park, "Fukuzawa Yukichi on Korea," *Journal of Social Sciences and Humanities* 45 (June 1977). Shin Kokuchū (Sin Kuk Ju), *Kindai Chōsen gaikō shi* (1966). Shinobu Jumpei, *Kan hantō* (1901). Pow-Key Sohn, "The Opening of Korea," *Transactions of the Korea Branch of the Royal Asiatic Society* 36 (April 1960). Tabohashi Kiyoshi, *Kindai Nisshisen kankei no kenkyū* (1930). Tabohashi Kiyoshi, *Kindai Nissen kankei no kenkyū*, 2 vols (1940). T. F. Tsiang, "Sino-Japanese Diplomatic Relations, 1870–1894," *Chinese Social and Political Science Review* 17 (1933–34). Benjamin B. Weems, *Reform, Rebellion and the Heavenly Way* (1964). Yamabe Kentarō, *Nihon no Kankoku heigō* (1966). Yamabe Kentarō, *Nikkan heigō shōshi* (1966).

Young Ick LEW

JAPANESE COLONIAL CONTROL OF KOREA (1910–1945)

On 30 September 1910, shortly after the annexation of Korea by Japan, the Office of the Resident General in Korea was replaced by the Government-General of Korea (Chōsen Sōtoku Fu). This colonial government, largely controlled by the Japanese military, remained the central organ of Japanese rule until it was abolished on 15 August 1945 in accordance with the terms imposed by the POTSDAM DECLARATION. The Government-General attempted to assimilate the Korean people into the Japanese empire through indoctrination and a variety of harshly repressive measures. After 1931, the Korean government was used to mobilize Korean resources and labor for the Japanese war effort. The Japanese maintained complete control over the administration of the Korean government and suppressed all resistance through an extensive network of police and military agencies.

Colonial Administration—— The head of the colonial administration, the governor-general of Korea, was a Japanese general or admiral appointed by and directly responsible to the emperor. He was in command of the armed forces on the Korean peninsula and had broad powers of control over legislative, judicial, and executive matters. All administrative matters in Korea came within the jurisdiction of the governor-general. He had the power to establish laws, issue orders, and impose sentences of up to a year and fines of up to ¥200 for the violation of his orders. The governor-general also assumed direction of all lower-level executive offices, including judicial organs, and could annul or repeal unlawful or unjust commands or punishments.

The governor-general was assisted by a director of governmental affairs (*seimu sōkan*), and one bureau and five executive offices carried out his policies: the Bureau of the Government-General (Sōtoku Kambō), the General Affairs Section (Sōmubu), the Internal Affairs Section (Naimubu), the Finance Section (Takushibu), the Section of Agriculture, Commerce, and Industry (Nōshōkōbu), and the Judiciary Section (Shihōbu). Affiliated bureaus included a privy council (a consultative organ established to appease the former ruling class of Korea), a police affairs office, a bureau of railways, and other offices. Within the 13 traditional provincial divisions (*dō*) in Korea, the colonial government established 12 *fu* (urban prefectures) and 317 *gun* (local districts). It also set up 4,322 *men* (equivalent to the *mura* or village in Japan). To these areas were assigned various administrators (*dōchōkan, fuin, gunshu,* and *menchō*). In the early period of colonial rule, no Koreans were assigned to positions higher than *gun* administrator.

Establishment of the Colonial System—— The first period of colonial rule, from annexation until early 1919, was characterized by the forcible establishment of the institutions of control. The economic infrastructure of Korea was reformed through a number of measures, including an extensive land survey, forest and field studies, construction of communication and transportation facilities, the reform of financial and monetary systems, and the standardization of weights and measures. Korea became a market for Japanese goods and capital investment and a prime source for Japanese imports of food and raw materials. Overall, Korea was incorporated into the rapidly progressing industrialization effort already under way in Japan.

The reordering of the Korean economy was carried out under orders of the colonial administration, which were enforced by a special police force (*kempei keisatsu*, gendarmerie). This force, originally a military police force, assumed the duties of the regular police

in Korea. A network of 1,642 special police stations was established throughout the country, and large numbers of Koreans were employed as assistant *kempei* in outlying areas. Two army divisions and additional naval units were permanently stationed in Korea and garrison troops were deployed throughout the country.

The rights of Koreans to free speech, assembly, and political organization were suspended, and the Government-General dissolved 12 political organizations. It became necessary to report even such events as school athletic meets to the police station in the local jurisdiction. All existing newspapers were suppressed, and their place was taken by progovernment newspapers, including the Japanese-language *Keijō nippō* (Seoul Daily), the Korean-language *Mae il shinbo* (Daily News), and the English-language *Seoul Press*. The educational system was utilized to assimilate (*dōka kyōiku*) the Korean people into the Japanese empire. The teaching of the Japanese language was introduced, while Korean history and language were neglected, in keeping with the "ideology of extending the homeland" (*naichi enchō shugi*).

Economic policies, which formed the core of colonial rule, centered on an extensive land survey during the first period. The survey was begun shortly before annexation and continued until 1918. Landowners were required to register their holdings, but many were illiterate and unable to do so and consequently were dispossessed of their land. Land that was jointly owned by clans or villages was appropriated by the military government, as was land that was officially national property but had come under private cultivation. Large landowners tended to gain through the survey, while the bulk of small farmers lost their holdings and were forced to become tenant farmers or laborers or to migrate to Manchuria and Japan (many of the Korean residents of Japan today are descendants of these farmers). The colonial land policy aimed at preserving the semifeudal production system of large Korean farms, while establishing a parallel, modern landownership system that would reinforce Japanese control. Land that was appropriated was sold at low prices to the TŌYŌ TAKUSHOKU KAISHA (Oriental Development Company), a Japanese-government-sponsored real estate and investment company, which then sold the land to Japanese immigrants.

The displacement of Korean farmers and the transformation of the Korean economy caused widespread uncertainty and discontent, which erupted in the SAMIL INDEPENDENCE MOVEMENT that began on 1 March 1919. Though harshly suppressed, this movement continued for months, with hundreds of demonstrations throughout the country. The uprising forced Japan to make significant modifications in its system of colonial control.

Liberalized Colonial Rule—— The second period of Japanese colonial rule began after the Samil uprisings of 1919 and continued until the MANCHURIAN INCIDENT ushered in the Japanese war effort in 1931. Reform measures introduced during this period included the opening of the governor-generalship to Japanese civilians and the reestablishment of a civilian police force in place of the *kempei keisatsu*. The sections (*bu*) of the central government became departments (*kyoku*); the Police Affairs Department (Keimukyoku) and the Educational Affairs Department (Gakumukyoku) were added. In July 1920 a strictly controlled election system was established for local offices throughout the country. Restrictions on freedom of speech were reduced somewhat, and Korean-language newspapers, including *Tong'a ilbo* (Asian Daily) and *Chosŏn ilbo* (Korean Daily), and magazines made their appearance.

While the reforms were meant to appease the Korean people, the effort to assimilate Korea forcibly continued. Although civilian rule was authorized, no civilian was ever appointed to the position of governor-general. The number of police and police stations was tripled, and surveillance of the populace was made more stringent. Education policies aimed at assimilation were reinforced, and Koreans were required to learn Japanese.

After the RICE RIOTS OF 1918 in Japan, Koreans were required to produce cheap rice for export to Japan. Dry fields were turned into paddies, and Koreans were forced to subsist on low-grade cereals from Manchuria. A 15-year plan to increase rice production through land improvement, irrigation projects, and new planting methods was inaugurated, but rising interest rates and resistance by farmers forced the discontinuation of the program.

During this period many in the upper echelons of Korean society were mollified by the reforms and cooperated with the Japanese. At the same time, nationalism and class consciousness continued to grow among workers and farmers, leading to the formation of the Korean Communist Party in 1925 and the Sin'ganhoe, a coalition of independence groups, in 1927. A mass rally was held in Seoul in 1926 on the occasion of the funeral of Sunjong, the deposed emperor; a general strike was staged in Wonson in 1928; and the KWANGJU STUDENT RESISTANCE MOVEMENT occurred in 1929.

Korea after Japanese Militarization —— The Manchurian Incident of 1931 marked the beginning of the intensive militarization of Japan and was followed by the invasion of China in 1937 and World War II in 1941. During this period, Japan attempted to incorporate Korea into its war mobilization by increasing efforts at assimilation and transforming the nation into a base for its armed forces. Agricultural development became one of the key policies of the early 1930s, and some effort was made to revitalize the countryside, which had suffered a crushing blow from the depressed economy of the period; in the end, however, this effort concentrated on encouraging frugality and diligence.

In the latter part of the 1930s, the entire Korean economy was reorganized to meet the requirements of the military, and heavy and chemical industries experienced rapid development with heavy investment from Japanese enterprises. The focus was on the production of raw materials and unfinished products for use in Japan, and such industries as machine-tool manufacturing remained undeveloped.

The beginning of the Sino-Japanese War in 1937 brought a campaign for the "unification of the homeland and Korea" *(naisen ittai),* which aimed at the total Japanization of the Korean people. The Kokumin Seishin Sōdōin Remmei (League for the Mobilization of the People's Spirit) was established in 1938 to promote support for the war effort, and *aikokuhan* (patriotic groups) were created along the lines of the Japanese NEIGHBORHOOD ASSOCIATIONS as the basic units of ideological indoctrination. The government required visits to Shintō shrines and recitation of an oath of loyalty to the empire. Koreans were even required to take Japanese names in a campaign called "establishing family names and changing given names" *(sōshi kaimei).* After 1931, academic societies devoted to Korean studies were disbanded, and educational reforms in 1938 and 1942 made the use of Japanese compulsory in the schools.

In 1938 the government established a volunteer system as the first step toward conscription, which went into effect in 1942, soon after the outbreak of World War II. Earlier, in 1939, a national service ordinance authorized the conscription of Koreans for strategic industries. After 1942, when Japan began to feel a labor shortage, authorities drafted Korean laborers for work in Japanese factories, mines, and military bases; the greater part of heavy labor in Japan was performed by Koreans in the last years of the war.

Korean resistance to Japanese imperialism continued to mount after 1940. Korean soldiers deserted from the Japanese military, and conscripted laborers escaped from work camps. Overseas Koreans joined the war against the Japanese, led by KIM GU in China and KIM IL-SŎNG in Manchuria. Others, such as Syngman RHEE (Yi Sŭngman) in the United States, agitated for the independence of Korea, which was finally achieved with the end of World War II in 1945.

🔳——Asada Kyōji, *Nihon teikoku shugi ka no minzoku kakumei undō* (1973). Hisama Ken'ichi, *Chōsen nōsei no kadai* (1943). Kang Dong-jin, *Nihon no Chōsen shihai seisaku shi kenkyū* (1979). Kim So-un, *Chōsen shishū* (1954). Pak Kyong-sik, *Chōsenjin kyōsei renkō no kiroku* (1965). Yamabe Kentarō, *Nihon tōchika no Chōsen* (1971). MIYATA Setsuko

EARLY POSTWAR RELATIONS (1945–1952)

Japan's 35-year rule over Korea terminated with the end of World War II in August 1945. As Japan was occupied by the Allied Powers from that time until April 1952, when the SAN FRANCISCO PEACE TREATY came into effect, and the southern and the northern halves of Korea were also under the occupation of the United States and the Soviet Union respectively until the summer of 1948, relations between Korea and Japan were, of course, abnormal. The other major factors in early postwar relations between Korea and Japan were the development of the cold war, the establishment of the Democratic People's Republic of Korea (North Korea) and the Republic of Korea (South Korea) in 1948, and the outbreak of the KOREAN WAR in 1950.

The initial problems in the postwar relations of Japan and Korea were the repatriation of Japanese servicemen and civilians in Korea, disposal of Japanese property in Korea, and the repatriation of Koreans in Japan. Most of the approximately 200,000 Japanese servicemen and 500,000 civilians in the American-occupied southern half of Korea were smoothly repatriated by November 1945 and February 1946 respectively, but repatriation from the Soviet-occupied north, including Japanese refugees from Manchuria, was delayed. It was

only after the conclusion of a Soviet-American agreement in December 1946 that repatriation from North Korea began, but most of the 300,000 Japanese who were there at the end of the war had already escaped to South Korea by crossing the 38th parallel. The repatriation of servicemen was completed by March 1947, but the repatriation of some technical personnel was further delayed and was not completed until June 1948.

Japanese property in South Korea, both public and private, was requisitioned by the US occupation forces and was transferred to the new Republic of Korea government in September 1948. Japanese property in North Korea was placed under the jurisdiction of the North Korean Interim People's Committee through the land reform of March 1946 and the nationalization of major industries of August 1946. The Constitution of the Democratic People's Republic of Korea, adopted in 1948, provided for the confiscation of all Japanese property in North Korea.

The repatriation of Korean residents in Japan, whose number was estimated at about two million, was carried out on a larger scale than that of the Japanese in Korea, and the repatriation of most of those Koreans wishing to return to South Korea was completed by September 1946. The Koreans who remained in Japan for various reasons totaled about 600,000. Repatriation to North Korea was partially carried out in 1947, with only 351 Koreans returning; further repatriation to the north took place after 1959.

The governments of both of the new states founded on the Korean peninsula in the summer of 1948 demanded the complete demilitarization of Japan as a precaution against the revival of Japanese militarism. As the United Nations recognized the government of the Republic of Korea (South Korea), which had been organized following a general election conducted under UN supervision, as the only legitimate Korean government, Japan's relations were restricted to South Korea. The outbreak of the Korean War confirmed this policy. In a speech on 14 July 1950 Japanese Prime Minister YOSHIDA SHIGERU pledged full cooperation with the operations of the UN expeditionary forces in Korea, and throughout the war Japan played a vital role as a military supply base.

While both South Korea and Japan became important members of the anticommunist camp in the cold war, their relations were not normalized smoothly. South Korean President Syngman Rhee insisted strongly on his country's participation in the San Francisco Peace Conference. He also demanded Japan's renunciation of claims on property in Korea, pressed South Korea's claim over the disputed island of TAKESHIMA (Tokto), and demanded control over the activities of Japanese fishing boats in waters adjacent to the Korean peninsula. However, South Korean participation in the conference was not achieved, and the peace treaty signed between Japan and most of the Allied Powers on 8 September 1951 did not contain a Japanese renunciation of rights to Takeshima, while the settlement of the two other problems was left to negotiations between the two countries. The North Korean government denounced the treaty after it was signed. In January 1952, three months before the treaty became effective, South Korea issued the so-called RHEE LINE declaration, demonstrating its determination to exclude Japanese fishing boats from the waters off Korea by force. OKONOGI Masao

RELATIONS WITH THE REPUBLIC OF KOREA (1953–   )

Efforts to reestablish relations between Japan and the Republic of Korea (ROK or South Korea) were largely unsuccessful during the 1950s. Bitter memories of Japan's colonial domination of Korea, Japan's inability to adjust to Korean independence, and Syngman Rhee's strong anti-Japanese policies undermined the normalization efforts that were made. Changes in the South Korean government in 1960 set the stage for renewed talks, which bore fruit in the normalization treaty of 1965. Economic and political relations between the two countries have developed apace in the following years, although serious tensions remain that give rise to occasional disputes and diplomatic crises.

Deterioration of Relations in the 1950s —— Preliminary negotiations aimed at the normalization of diplomatic relations began in October 1951, before the Peace Treaty became effective. These talks were arranged by SCAP (the headquarters of the Allied Occupation of Japan) in Tōkyō and resulted in the convening of a plenary parley in February 1952. The negotiations progressed smoothly at first but were broken off on 25 April after becoming deadlocked on the issues of fishing rights and Japanese property claims. Japan refused to abandon its claims to property, while the ROK refused to dispense with the Rhee line. A second parley was begun in April 1953, and a third parley followed a break for the summer. Property claims again proved to be the most difficult issue, and the talks broke off on 21 October 1953, partly as a result of injured feelings on the Korean side caused by a speech by Japanese delegate Kubota Kan'ichirō.

Relations between the two countries reached their nadir in the summer of 1955, when the ROK prohibited trade with Japan and restricted travel of ROK citizens to Japan on 17 August. The most serious conflicts during this period related to Korean enforcement of the fishing restrictions imposed by the Rhee line. The ROK began seizing Japanese vessels fishing within the limits of the line in August 1952. A total of 10 boats and 132 fishermen were seized in 1952, 47 boats and 585 fishermen in 1953, 34 boats and 454 fishermen in 1954, 30 boats and 498 fishermen in 1955, and 19 boats and 235 fishermen in 1956. The number of seizures decreased after 1957; a total of 232 boats and 2,784 fishermen were seized prior to the signing of a fishing agreement in June 1965.

Tensions began to ease somewhat in 1957. Negotiations were held early in that year regarding the retraction of the Kubota statement, the renunciation of Japanese property rights in Korea, and the release of fishermen held in the ROK and undocumented Korean immigrants held in Japan. The negotiations were concluded successfully in December 1957, and the exchange of persons held by the two countries was conducted between February and March of 1958.

On 15 April 1958, the fourth session of the Japan–ROK talks opened after a lapse of four and a half years. A total of 10 regular sessions and 25 unofficial meetings were held between the two countries, but in 1959 a new problem arose: the repatriation of Korean nationals residing in Japan to the Democratic People's Republic of Korea (DPRK, North Korea) through the mediation of the International Committee of the Red Cross. The board of directors of the Japanese Red Cross society decided in January 1959 to separate the repatriation problem from politics and proceeded to map out a plan with the support of the Japanese government. Negotiations were held between the Japanese and North Korean Red Cross societies from 13 April 1959, an agreement was initialed on 24 June, and a formal document was signed on 13 August. Some 88,000 Koreans were repatriated to the DPRK between 1959 and 1967.

The South Koreans, meanwhile, registered their opposition to the repatriation of Korean nationals to the DPRK in a formal resolution of the parliament on 19 February, and demonstrations were held in various parts of the ROK. As the repatriation negotiations approached completion in Geneva, the ROK again suspended trade with Japan on 15 June 1959. The Japan–ROK talks under these circumstances focused on the status of Koreans residing in Japan; the talks were held between 11 August and 2 November, but failed to come to any conclusion. They were virtually suspended until after the April 1960 student revolt brought the fall of the Rhee government.

The Path toward Normalization——The Rhee government had considered "anticommunism" and "opposition to Japan" the two central pillars of its foreign policy. The new government, under a parliamentary cabinet headed by Prime Minister Chang Myŏn, could not ignore the pressure from the United States to normalize relations with Japan. Chang's government also thought that the establishment of cooperative relations with Japan would reinforce the economic foundation of the country. Japan, for its part, anticipated a great deal from the new government and on 6 September dispatched Foreign Minister Kosaka Zentarō to the ROK as a goodwill ambassador. This was the first official visit of a Japanese envoy to Korea since the end of World War II. The fifth series of Japan–ROK talks were opened soon after, on 25 October 1960.

The talks were suspended on 16 May 1961 as a result of the coup d'etat of Major General PAK CHŎNG-HŬI (Park Chung-hee), but the enthusiasm of the two countries for normalization was not diminished. Pak's new regime declared a foreign policy of vigorous anticommunism and close alliance with the countries of the "free world." Japanese Prime Minister IKEDA HAYATO discussed the problem of normalization with US President John Kennedy when he traveled to the United States in June 1961. The sixth session of the Japan–ROK talks opened on 20 October. On 12 November, Pak stopped in Japan en route to the United States and met with Ikeda; the two leaders promised each other they would concentrate on the successful conclusion of the negotiations.

Notwithstanding the commitments of the two governments, negotiations came to an impasse over the issues of property rights and fishing territory in March 1962. To break the deadlock, two meetings were held between Japanese Foreign Minister ŌHIRA MASAYOSHI and Korean Central Intelligence Agency Chief Kim Jong-p'il,

on 20 October and 12 November. The secret talks produced the following agreement, which resolved both the problem of property claims and economic cooperation: Japan agreed to provide the ROK with a total of $300 million in grants, $200 million in low-interest loans, and a substantial amount of private credit.

Remaining to be resolved were the issues of fishing territory, the legal status of Koreans in Japan, and territorial claims to the island of Takeshima. The year 1963 was an election year in Korea, and since the topic of fishing rights was an issue, the talks were suspended until March 1964. A movement opposing the talks began at that time among students and the opposition parties, and opposition members of the parliament threatened to resign en masse. This opposition reached a climax in a massive demonstration on 3 June 1964, which led to a declaration of martial law in Seoul. Meanwhile, the United States increased its pressure for normalization. Secretary of State Dean Rusk visited South Korea on 29 January 1964; ROK Foreign Minister Yi Dong-wŏn and US Ambassador to the ROK, Winthrop Gilman Brown, issued a joint communiqué on 17 August expressing their desire for the successful conclusion of the normalization talks; and a similar communiqué was issued on 1 October by Foreign Minister Yi and US Assistant Secretary of State William Putnam Bundy. In Japan, SATŌ EISAKU became prime minister on 9 November, and $20 million in emergency private credits were granted to South Korea on 11 December.

The seventh and concluding round of the Japan–ROK talks opened on 3 December, and the final agreements were to be worked out during a visit by Japanese Minister of Foreign Affairs Shiina Etsusaburō on 17 February 1965. Movements opposing normalization, however, began to develop in Japan. The Japan Socialist Party (JSP) presented a no-confidence motion against Shiina on 16 February, and members of the student organization ZENGAKUREN (National Federation of Student Self-Government Associations) and JSP-affiliated organizations mounted a large demonstration at Haneda International Airport on 17 February in an attempt to prevent Shiina's departure. A basic relations treaty was signed on 20 February, however, which provided the framework for normalization. The treaty declared void all treaties and agreements signed on or before 22 August 1910 (the date of the annexation of Korea to Japan), thus removing the most important point of dispute in the negotiations. Japan confirmed UN resolution 195, which specified the government of the ROK as the only lawful government in Korea.

Agreements on most of the remaining problems were initialed in Tōkyō on 3 April. It was agreed that the Rhee line would be abolished and replaced by an ROK fishing zone up to 12 miles (19.3 km) from its shores and a joint, restricted fishing zone beyond the 12-mile limit. Japan also agreed to provide a total of $120 million ($90 million for general purposes; $30 million for shipbuilding) in commercial loans to the ROK fishing industry. It was also agreed that those Koreans in Japan who had been living there prior to World War II would be given permanent resident status. Japan increased the $300 million in credits it had agreed to extend to resolve the problems of property claims and economic cooperation. The official signing of the agreements took place on 22 June 1965. The documents included one treaty, four agreements, two protocols, nine exchange documents, five minutes of agreement, two reciprocal letters, and two records of negotiations. The unresolved issue of territorial rights to Takeshima was handled with an exchange document regarding the resolution of the dispute that was exchanged just prior to the signing ceremony. See also KOREA–JAPAN TREATY OF 1965; KOREA–JAPAN TREATY OF 1965, SUPPLEMENTARY AGREEMENTS.

Postnormalization Relationship——The signing of the normalization treaty was epochal in that it resolved, at least with South Korea on the diplomatic level, the legacy of Japanese colonial control of Korea. Coming 20 years after the end of World War II, the event signified the reemergence of Japan as a political force in Asia and established a critical element of Japan's economic and security relations with the region. The treaty cemented the ROK's anticommunist foreign policy and contributed to the stabilization of the country's politics and economy. The antitreaty movements of the early 1960s dissipated following the signing of the agreements, and it appeared, as Korean President Pak Chŏng-hŭi commented on the day after the signing, that Japan and South Korea had entered a new era of mutual benefit, security, and prosperity.

In the years following normalization, a number of vehicles for cooperation were established. In September 1966, on the basis of an agreement between the leaders of the two countries, a conference of economic ministers was held at which the Japanese pledged active cooperation in the ROK's second five-year plan for economic development, which was scheduled to begin in 1967. This conference developed into a regular ministerial conference the next year, with the addition of the foreign ministers of the two countries. A private parliamentary conference was inaugurated in June 1968, followed by a private economic committee in January 1969 and a committee for the promotion of Japanese-Korean cooperation in February 1969. In the SATŌ–NIXON COMMUNIQUÉ of 1969, Japanese Prime Minister Satō stated that "the security of the Republic of Korea was essential to Japan's own security," marking another watershed in the formulation of a Japan–ROK alliance.

Closer relations were particularly evident in the economic field. Prior to normalization, economic relations had been focused on trade, but after 1965 economic and technical cooperation was initiated. Based on the 1965 economic cooperation agreement, Japan provided $172 million in grants and $104 million in loans in the five years ending 1971. Private credit amounted to $490 million for industrial plants and $551 million for the fishing industry. With this assistance, the South Korean economy registered an annual growth rate of more than 10 percent in the same five years. Japanese investments increased dramatically during the next five-year plan. By 1976 Japanese investments constituted some two-thirds of the total accumulated foreign investment since 1962. The gross national product of the ROK at the end of 1976 stood at $25 billion, with per capita income of $864.

Continuing Tensions —— Despite the emergence of a close Japan–ROK political and economic alliance after 1965, periodic crises have arisen, most notably in 1973 and 1974. The August 1973 abduction of Korean opposition leader KIM TAE-JUNG from a hotel in Tōkyō by agents of the Korean Central Intelligence Agency (KCIA) was the first serious incident to occur. Kim, who had nearly defeated Pak in a 1971 presidential election, was continuing his opposition to Pak's policies in exile in Tōkyō after Pak assumed extraordinary powers in the fall of 1972. The KCIA kidnapped him and took him back to South Korea, where he was imprisoned for a number of years. Numerous Japanese, particularly major newspapers, attacked the ROK government for violating the sovereignty of Japan, and the Japanese government's policy of cooperation with the ROK also became a target of criticism.

Korean Prime Minister Kim Jong-p'il came to Japan in November 1973 to formally apologize to the Japanese government, but criticism continued since Kim Tae-jung remained imprisoned in South Korea. Then, in the spring of 1974, two Japanese youths were arrested in South Korea on charges of aiding the antigovernment activities of Korean students. In August of the same year, Mun Segwang, a young Korean residing in Japan, attempted to assassinate Pak in Seoul. These incidents severely strained Japan–ROK relations, and Shiina Etsusaburō was dispatched to Seoul as a special envoy in September in order to prevent the severing of diplomatic relations.

The long-term effect of these incidents has been significant. On the Japanese side, relations with the ROK have increasingly come to be seen as closely linked with the struggle to reestablish democracy in South Korea. The repeated imprisonment of Kim Tae-jung and other opposition leaders, along with various scandals involving Korean government officials, have eroded popular sympathy for the ROK government. On the South Korean side, anti-Japanese sentiments have been rekindled. Japanese involvement in Korean internal affairs as well as the heavy involvement of Japanese enterprises in the Korean economy and the large number of Japanese tourists visiting South Korea, have given rise to charges that the Japanese seek to reestablish control over Korea. While the governments of the two nations have strived to maintain close and friendly diplomatic relations, political conflicts appear likely to persist.

◾ —— Kwan Bong Kim, *The Korea-Japan Treaty Crisis and the Instability of the Korean Political System* (1971). Young C. Kim, ed, *The Major Powers and Korea* (1973). Soon Sung Cho, *Korea in World Politics: 1940–1950* (1967). OKONOGI Masao

RELATIONS WITH THE DEMOCRATIC PEOPLE'S REPUBLIC OF KOREA (1953–)

The importance of the Democratic People's Republic of Korea (DPRK or North Korea) to Japan is primarily geopolitical: its proximity to China, the Soviet Union, and Japan, and its significance for the United States, which has strong political, economic, and military ties with the Republic of Korea (South Korea).

In the modern era, the Korean peninsula has been directly involved in several wars in which Japan has participated. Both the SINO-JAPANESE WAR OF 1894–1895 and the RUSSO-JAPANESE WAR of 1904–05 were sparked by clashes of interests over Korea. After the Japanese annexation of Korea in 1910, the Korean peninsula served as the corridor for the Japanese invasion of Manchuria and China proper in the 1930s. Thus, Japan perceives the stability of the Korean peninsula as essential to its own security. Japan's definition of a stable Korea would doubtless include both preventing the communization of the entire peninsula under North Korean leadership and ensuring that neither Moscow nor Beijing (Peking) become the dominant power in the area.

There are additional factors that help to underscore the importance of North Korea to Japan. Nearly half of the Koreans living in Japan identify with and support the Democratic People's Republic of Korea. Organized and led by the General Federation of Korean Residents in Japan (Kor: Choch'ongnyŏn; J: Chōsōren), they have developed substantial links with left-wing political groups and individuals throughout Japan.

In economic terms, for a resource-poor and trade-oriented country such as Japan, North Korea represents not only a source of raw materials but also a potential market. Although the potential economic payoffs to Japan are limited, the fluid international economic situation requires diversification of trading partners, and no market may be considered too small to merit serious attention.

The preceding considerations also suggest the importance of Japan to North Korea. In fact, Japan is probably more important to North Korea than vice versa. North Korea needs Japanese technology and machinery to implement its ambitious economic development plans. Moreover, the protection of North Korea-oriented Korean residents in Japan requires the cooperation of the Japanese government, which controls the frequency and volume of visits to and from North Korea. Finally, North Korea's security interests dictate the prevention of too close an alliance between Japan and South Korea, a situation which in turn underscores the need to exert political pressure on the Japanese government through solidarity with left-wing political parties, pressure groups, and "progressive" individuals.

P'yŏngyang's eagerness to normalize relations with Japan is easy to understand; however, it has not been reciprocated by Tōkyō, which has established full diplomatic relations and forged strong economic ties with Seoul. Although Japan's policy toward the two Koreas is sometimes characterized as one of "equidistance," it undeniably favors South Korea. Another frequently heard phrase, however, is germane to Korea—namely, *seikei bunri* (the separation of politics and economics); the absence of political relations has not prevented Japan and North Korea from developing economic relations.

Background —— There were virtually no relations between the two countries from the founding of the DPRK in September 1948 until after the Korean Armistice in July 1953, when North Korea began efforts to establish formal ties with Japan. On 25 February 1955 DPRK Foreign Minister Nam Il expressed a desire to normalize relations and to develop economic and cultural ties with Japan. Nam reiterated his government's position in December 1955. Although P'yŏngyang's overtures were ignored, unofficial contacts were nonetheless established in the form of visits to North Korea by members of left-wing Japanese political parties and groups.

In September 1956 indirect trade between the two countries was initiated. The total value of trade turnover from September 1956 to May 1958, mediated through Dalian (Ta-lien; J: Dairen), China, amounted to ¥3.14 billion (US $8.71 million). Trade was suspended for a year in the wake of the NAGASAKI FLAG INCIDENT, involving an insult to the national flag of the People's Republic of China in Japan. Trade resumed in June 1959 through Hong Kong, and the total value of turnover from mid-1959 to April 1961 was ¥3.58 billion (US $9.95 million). In April 1961 the Japanese government approved direct trade between Japanese firms and North Korea. Followed by further relaxation of restrictions by the Japanese government, this move led to a marked increase in trade volume.

Meanwhile, a program for repatriating Korean residents remaining in Japan from before the end of World War II was initiated in 1959, ostensibly under the auspices of Red Cross organizations in the two countries. Nearly 80,000 Koreans were repatriated in 1959 to North Korea. Both countries stood to gain from the arrangement; North Korea not only obtained much needed manpower but also scored a propaganda victory over South Korea, while Japan reduced the social and economic burdens of dealing with its Korean minority.

North Korea, however, suffered a major setback in 1965, when Japan signed a series of treaties with the Republic of Korea that normalized relations and prepared for close economic cooperation between the two countries. This development was bound to strain the already precarious relations between P'yŏngyang and Tōkyō. P'yŏngyang sharply increased its attacks on the Japanese government, accusing the latter of conspiring to reinvade Korea through economic means and of reviving militarism.

P'yŏngyang's displeasure was reflected in a 70 percent decline in the value of imports from Japan in 1966 over the previous year. Because of a sharp increase in North Korean exports to Japan in the same year, the total value of trade declined by only 11 percent. By 1968 the trade situation returned to normal and remained fairly constant—in the $50 million range—until 1972, when the value of trade jumped to $132 million, an increase of 223 percent over the previous year. A peak was reached in 1974, when the figure exceeded $360 million.

Two major factors help to explain such a dramatic increase. One was the conclusion in January 1972 of a five-year trade agreement, and the second was P'yŏngyang's decision in 1972 to begin purchases of industrial plants and machinery on a massive scale. The increase was located mainly in spiraling North Korean imports, which created huge deficits in the balance of trade.

Coupled with other factors, notably the quadrupling of crude oil prices in 1973, the worldwide economic depression, and a sharp decline in the prices of North Korea's chief export items, nonferrous metals, North Korea's "buying spree" resulted in serious payment problems. Saddled with an estimated trade debt of $1.8 billion, of which $260 million was owed to Japanese firms, North Korea in 1975 was unable to pay its bills in the world market. Although the terms of payment were renegotiated in late 1976, North Korea was reported in late 1977 to be having difficulty in meeting its obligations to Japanese firms. Symptomatic of the problem was a 54 percent decline in Japanese exports to North Korea in 1976 over the previous year. In subsequent years, however, Japanese trade with North Korea gradually increased. By 1980, the value of the two-way trade reached $570 million.

Meanwhile, North Korea continued to signal its desire to normalize relations with Japan. On numerous occasions, DPRK President KIM IL-SŎNG indicated to visiting Japanese newsmen that North Korea would be willing to improve relations with Tōkyō without insisting upon the latter's abrogation of the normalization treaty with Seoul. In effect, Kim suggested, North Korea would accept a two-Korea policy from Japan—a policy of equidistance in the true sense of the term.

For its part, the Japanese government has, as of 1980, expressed its willingness to normalize relations with North Korea, provided that China and the Soviet Union recognize South Korea. Known as the policy of "cross recognition," this policy is jointly embraced by Tōkyō and Washington, with explicit approval from Seoul. North Korea's vehement criticism of the cross recognition idea is inconsistent with both its demands for fair treatment from Tōkyō and its practice of establishing diplomatic relations with countries that simultaneously recognize South Korea. In any event, since 1972 the number of visitors between Japan and North Korea has risen dramatically; in May 1977 a North Korean parliamentary delegation led by Hyŏn Chun-Gŭk, P'yŏngyang's former ambassador to Beijing, visited Japan on a putatively nonpolitical mission.

Many problems remain in the bilateral relations of Japan and North Korea. North Korea's proclamation in August 1977 of a 370-kilometer (200-nautical mile) economic zone as well as of a military boundary extending 73 kilometers (50 nautical miles) in the Sea of Japan and 370 kilometers in the Yellow Sea created a new problem: the fishing activities and livelihood of thousands of Japanese fishermen were adversely affected. In an informal agreement signed in September 1977, North Korea agreed to permit fishing by Japanese fishermen in its economic zone outside of its military boundary for two years.

A significant variable in the evolution of Japanese-North Korean relations will be the nature and magnitude of economic and political bonds between Tōkyō and Seoul. Given the fundamentally asymmetrical nature of the respective leverages of Tōkyō and P'yŏngyang, it is unlikely that Japan will make any significant concessions.

Byung Chul KOH

Korea, annexation of

(Nikkan Heigō). Annexation of Korea by Japan on 22 August 1910; the act resolved the Meiji government's long-standing concern over how to exclude Western imperialists from Korea by absorbing it into the Japanese empire (see SEIKANRON). By the eve of the SINO-

JAPANESE WAR OF 1894–1895, Japan's policy makers were divided into two camps: ITŌ HIROBUMI led the group that advocated helping Korea to modernize so that it could resist Western imperialism. Simultaneously, government leaders like YAMAGATA ARITOMO and KATSURA TARŌ and nationalistic groups like the AMUR RIVER SOCIETY urged Japan's seizure of Korea. Japan's victories over China set in motion a series of Westernizing reforms (see KABO REFORM) in Korea. After the war Russia replaced China as Japan's rival on the Korean peninsula, but under the YAMAGATA–LOBANOV AGREEMENT the two countries agreed to preserve Korea's independence.

Once the RUSSO-JAPANESE WAR had begun in 1904, however, Japan moved military units into Korea and declared it a Japanese protectorate. Extensive reforms were initiated and Western diplomatic approval was sought for the protectorate's establishment. Nonintervention by Western powers was assured by the KATSURA–TAFT AGREEMENT of June 1905, the August renewal of the ANGLO-JAPANESE ALLIANCE, and the Treaty of PORTSMOUTH. Korea was then compelled to sign a protectorate treaty on 18 November 1905. Itō Hirobumi became resident general of a Japanese-staffed administration that paralleled the Korean bureaucracy and initiated comprehensive reform and economic development programs in February 1906.

Koreans were outraged by this arrangement because it benefited primarily Japanese immigrants and investors. Bands of armed Koreans called "righteous army" (ŭibyŏng) units challenged Japanese rule. The Korean monarch KOJONG (1852–1919; r 1864–1907) secretly authorized an appeal of the protectorate treaty before the second Hague Conference on World Peace, but this was unsuccessful and led to Kojong's forced abdication on 19 July 1907. Itō assumed complete control of the Korean government on 24 July, disbanded its army on 1 August, and installed Kojong's feeble-minded son Sunjong on the throne on 27 August.

Prime Minister Katsura Tarō informed Itō on 10 April 1909 that Korea's annexation was inevitable, and in June Itō, who resisted immediate annexation, resigned as resident general of Korea. Itō's assassination in October by AN CHUNG-GŬN only hastened implementation of annexation. Korea's prime minister, YI WAN-YONG, and Japan's minister of war, TERAUCHI MASATAKE, signed a treaty that transformed Korea into Chōsen, Japan's colony until 15 August 1945. See also KOREA AND JAPAN: early modern relations; KOREA AND JAPAN: Japanese colonial control of Korea.

——Hilary Conroy, The Japanese Seizure of Korea, 1868–1910 (1960). Eugene C. I. Kim and Han-kyo Kim, Korea and the Politics of Imperialism, 1876–1910 (1967). C. Kenneth QUINONES

Korea–Japan Treaty of 1965

(J: Nikkan Kihon Jōyaku). Formally known as the Treaty on Basic Relations between Japan and the Republic of Korea. The treaty was concluded in 1965 after 14 years of negotiations. It is the basic document concerning the normalization of relations between the governments of Japan and the Republic of Korea (South Korea) and contains a number of provisions which define the legal relationship between the two countries. After recalling "the historical background of relationship between [the] peoples [of Japan and the Republic of Korea], and their mutual desire for good neighborliness and for the normalization of the relations on the basis of the principle of mutual respect for sovereignty" (preamble), the treaty provides that diplomatic and consular relations shall be established between the two countries (art. 1). It also confirms that all treaties or agreements concluded between Japan and Korea on or before 22 August 1910, the date of the annexation of Korea to Japan, are already null and void (art. 2). On the question of the legal status of the government of the Republic of Korea and especially the question of its jurisdiction in the context of the post–World War II division of the Korean peninsula, it is confirmed that the government of the Republic of Korea is the only lawful government in Korea as specified in Resolution 195 (III) of the United Nations General Assembly (art. 3). In addition, the treaty provides that the two countries will be guided by the principles of the Charter of the United Nations in their mutual relations (art. 4).

The normalization of relations was achieved through the conclusion of a number of agreements in addition to the Treaty on Basic Relations; these covered such areas as fisheries, settlement of problems concerning property and claims, economic cooperation, the legal status and treatment of Republic of Korea nationals residing in Japan, cultural cooperation, and the settlement of disputes. All these were signed together on 22 June 1965 and should be regarded as representing one comprehensive package that constitutes the normalization of relations between Japan and the Republic of Korea.

Ōwada Hisashi

Korea–Japan Treaty of 1965, supplementary agreements

The 26 documents concerning disputes that had festered for decades between Japan and the Republic of Korea (ROK), signed on 22 June 1965 along with a Treaty on Basic Relations. The agreements involved four main areas of dispute: property claims, fishing rights, the legal rights of KOREANS IN JAPAN, and jurisdiction over the island of TAKESHIMA (Tokto). Most of these disputes arose out of the period of Japanese colonial occupation of Korea (1910–45). The colonial experience intensified long-standing animosities between the Japanese and Koreans and made the post-World War II normalization of relations a long and difficult process. The 1965 agreements thus represented a watershed in Japanese-Korean relations.

The property issue was considered during the first conference between Japan and the ROK in February 1952. At that time, the ROK government set forth a seven-point list of demands that included the return of gold and silver bullion removed to Japan from Korea during the period of colonial control, claims for various savings and compensation owed to Korean nationals during the period, and claims for Korean art objects removed to Japan. The Japanese refused to discuss the ROK claims and submitted a counterclaim to a large percentage of the disputed Korean property. With the claims of each side considered out of order by the other, the first round of negotiations was stalemated. A second attempt at negotiation, between April and July 1952, produced negligible improvement. A third round opened in October 1953, but a statement by the Japanese delegate, Kubota Kan'ichirō, so enraged the ROK delegates that they walked out, terminating the negotiations.

Over the next decade, the claims and counterclaims of the 1952 conference became increasingly amenable to negotiation, primarily because of strong US pressure and the economic policies of the Pak Chŏng-hŭi government after 1961. In late 1962 a secret agreement was reached under which Japan was to provide US $800 million in grants and government and commercial credits to the ROK. Although the secrecy of the negotiations was denounced by Koreans and Japanese, the Kim–Ōhira Memorandum, as it came to be known, provided the framework for the 1965 agreement on property claims and economic cooperation.

A second major area of dispute resulting directly from the forced withdrawal of the Japanese from Korea was the fate of Koreans who had elected to remain in Japan. The number of Koreans living in Japan had increased dramatically during the colonial period. In 1914 they numbered 3,630, but by the end of World War II some 2.4 million Koreans were in Japan, the vast majority of whom were unskilled laborers. It was nearly impossible for the Korean minority to be integrated into Japanese society, in large part because of the long tradition of prejudice and hatred between the Japanese and Korean people.

At the end of World War II, about three-fourths of the Koreans in Japan were repatriated, and the status of the approximately 600,000 Koreans remaining in Japan became an issue of contention. The ROK demanded that residents be given special status, with the full benefits of Japanese citizenship and the right to remain ROK citizens. Negotiations on the issue of the legal rights of Korean residents began in October 1951 but stalled in the late 1950s after a serious dispute arose between the ROK and Japan over the repatriation of approximately 51,000 Koreans to the Democratic People's Republic of Korea (DPRK; North Korea). Agreement was finally reached after Japan made a number of concessions, including the classification of all Koreans as nationals of the ROK and the recognition of demands concerning privileges of permanent residence, favorable treatment, and the removal of property and funds.

The fishing disputes between the two countries stemmed mainly from the refusal of Japan to negotiate fishing agreements with the ROK as required by article 9 of the San Francisco Peace Treaty. During the Allied Occupation, Japan's fishing grounds had been limited by the so-called MacArthur Line, which was to be abolished when the peace treaty became effective in April 1952. The ROK interpreted Japan's refusal to negotiate a fishing agreement as an indication that when the MacArthur Line ceased to exist the much more efficient Japanese fishing fleet would invade hitherto protected ROK fishing grounds.

In order to provide continued protection of the Korean fishing industry, ROK President Syngman RHEE (Yi Sŭng-man) in a unilat-

eral declaration on 18 January 1952 established the so-called Peace Line (known in Japan as the RHEE LINE), which placed ROK sovereign control over all natural resources adjacent to the peninsula. The line encompassed more sea territory than the MacArthur Line and stretched in some areas 200 miles (322 km) from the Korean shore. Between 1952 and 1964, more than 230 Japanese vessels were seized by the ROK in waters on the Korean side of the line.

The ensuing bilateral negotiations centered on the status of the Peace Line in international law and the seizures and detention of Japanese vessels and crews. The main factor contributing to the settlement of this dispute was the softening of the ROK position on the validity of the Peace Line and a growing desire to settle outstanding problems with Japan. By 1964 the framework for conducting the negotiations had been set. The actual agreement represented a compromise in that it allowed each country to establish an exclusive fishing zone with a 12-mile limit (19.3 km), allowed for the establishment of joint regulations, and set maximum limits with respect to the number of fishing vessels in the area, the size of the vessels, and the type of fishing. In addition, Japan extended US $120 million in commercial credits to the ROK for the development of its fishing industry. The Peace Line was not specifically mentioned, but with the agreement both sides seemed to accept it as a basis for establishing the ROK defense perimeter.

The dispute over the legal control of Takeshima (Tokto), the only area of contention that could not be resolved by negotiation, seemed to stem from its somewhat minor importance as a base for fishing operations. Barren and rocky, the island could not support a permanent population and was therefore useful only as a stopping place for fishermen. Japan claimed to have legally incorporated the island into its Shimane Prefecture in 1905 and argued that international law had been observed in that no other country had control of the island. Takeshima was surveyed and was listed publicly as Japanese territory.

Korea argued that historical precedent was on its side. The island was incorporated in 512 into the territory of Silla, one of the three kingdoms existing on the peninsula at that time. During the following centuries, frequent disputes arose between Japanese and Korean fishermen over the use of the island. Finally in 1696, as a result of Korean protests, Japan seemed to give up its claims to the area in which the island was located when it announced a decision to prohibit Japanese fishermen from participating in fishing operations in the vicinity of Takeshima.

In addition, directives concerning the disposal of Japanese territories after World War II seem to support ROK claims. After World War II, the Supreme Commander for the Allied Powers (SCAP) took responsibility for disposing of Japanese territories. In SCAPIN no. 677, SCAP classified Takeshima as an island over which Japan would not have sovereignty. Thus, South Korea seems to hold the advantage as far as supporting its claims and in fact has physical possession of the island. Japan has refused to accept the ROK position and no final agreement has been reached yet. However, the two countries did agree to continue negotiations in an exchange of notes concerning peaceful settlement of disputes.

The serious negotiations and subsequent agreements of 1965 represented an important turning point in the relations between the ROK and Japan. The fact that these agreements were received unfavorably by the citizens of both countries showed that even if the Korean and Japanese people were incapable of resolving past hatred and prejudices, at least the governments had accepted the necessity of realistic solutions to their differences. The four main disputes reviewed here were by no means the only areas of disagreement. However, the fact that problems of such magnitude, in an environment of mutual hostility, could finally be coolly discussed represented significant progress in Japan–ROK relations. The ROK scored a diplomatic victory over the DPRK by negotiating the normalization accords and received substantial economic assistance from Japan. Japan–ROK cooperation has continued, although occasional disputes continue to arise. See also KOREA AND JAPAN: relations with the Republic of Korea (1953–).

Soon Sung Cho

Korean campaigns of 1592 and 1597 → invasions of Korea in 1592 and 1597

Korean "Independence Party" → Kaehwap'a

Korean language

Han'gŭl Romanization Systems

Han'gŭl	Yale	McCune-R.	Lukoff	1959-SK	CK
ㅂ	p	p, b	p	b	p
ㅍ	ph	p'	ph	p	ph
ㅃ	pp	pp	pp	bb	pp
ㄷ	t	t, d	t	d	t
ㅌ	th	t'	th	t	th
ㄸ	tt	tt	tt	dd	tt
ㅅ	s	s	s	s	s
ㅆ	ss	ss	ss	ss	ss
ㅈ	c	ch, j	j	j	ts
ㅊ	ch	ch'	jh	ch	tsh
ㅉ	cc	tch	jj	jj	tss
ㄱ	k	k, g	k	g	k
ㅋ	kh	k'	kh	k	kh
ㄲ	kk	kk	kk	gg	kk
ㅁ	m	m	m	m	m
ㄴ	n	n	n	n	n
ㅇ	-ng	-ng	-ng	-ng	-ng
ㄹ	l	l, r	l	l, r	r
ㅎ	h	h	h	h	h
ㅣ	i	i	i	i	i
ㅟ	wi	wi	wi	wi	wi
ㅔ	ey	e	e	e	e
ㅖ	yey	ye	ye	ye	ye
ㅞ	wey	we	we	we	we
ㅚ	oy	oe	ö	oe	oi
ㅐ	ay	ae	ä	ae	ai
ㅒ	yay	yae	yä	yae	yai
ㅙ	way	wae	wä	wae	wai
ㅡ	u	ŭ	ʉ	eu	ŭ
ㅓ	e	ŏ	ø	eo	ɤ
ㅕ	ye	yŏ	yø	yeo	yɤ
ㅝ	we	wŏ	wø	weo	wo
ㅏ	a	a	a	a	a
ㅑ	ya	ya	ya	ya	ya
ㅘ	wa	wa	wa	wa	wa
ㅜ	wu	u	u	u	u
ㅠ	yu	yu	yu	yu	yu
ㅗ	o	o	o	o	o
ㅛ	yo	yo	yo	yo	yo
ㅢ	uy	ŭi	(ʉi)	eui	ŭi

NOTE: Table shows how several systems differ in representing the *han'gŭl* symbols. Minor details in each system, such as the abbreviation of *wu* to *u* after labials in the Yale system, are not mentioned. "McCune-R." refers to the McCune-Reischauer system; "Lukoff" refers to the phonemic orthography used in Fred Lukoff's *Spoken Korean*; "1959-SK" refers to the system of the Republic of Korea Ministry of Education; "CK" refers to that of the North Korean Academy of Sciences (*Cosen kwahak-wen*), as reported in the 1957 Beijing (Peking) volume *Pinyin wenci xiefa guice*.

SOURCE: Samuel E. Martin, Yang Ha Lee, and Sung-Un Chang, *A Korean-English Dictionary* (1967).

Korean-Japanese Convention of 1905

(J: Dai Niji Nikkan Kyōyaku). Also known in Korea as the Ŭlsa Treaty (Ŭlsa is the designation in the sexagenary cycle for the year corresponding to 1905) or Protectorate Treaty. The convention established Korea as a Japanese protectorate and was a major step toward Japan's 1910 annexation of Korea. ITŌ HIROBUMI presented it to the Korean cabinet, which signed it in the early morning hours of 18 November 1905 after Japanese soldiers occupied the Korean royal palace. Japan assumed complete responsibility for Korea's foreign affairs. Korean diplomats were recalled, their duties assigned to Japanese embassies, and trade in Korean ports was placed under Japanese supervision. The Residency General of Korea was established to advise the Korean government. King KOJONG sent a secret mission to the Second Hague Conference on World Peace in 1907 to contest the convention, but the effort failed. Korea's sovereignty was seriously curtailed, making annexation in 1910 essentially a le-

gal formality. See also KOREA AND JAPAN: early modern relations; KOREA, ANNEXATION OF. C. Kenneth QUINONES

Korean language

Korean is the native language of the inhabitants of the Korean peninsula; in 1982 there were about 60 million speakers. The syntax is remarkably similar to that of the Japanese language, but the phonology and morphology are markedly different. Both languages are unrelated to Chinese except as neighbors. In earlier days Korea, like Japan, borrowed heavily from the Chinese vocabulary, and the borrowed elements are used today to make up new words much as English uses Latin and Greek. That is why most of the words in the modern Korean dictionary, as in the Japanese, are made up of morphemes originally written with Chinese characters. About 10 percent of the basic vocabulary of modern Korean is of Chinese origin. The basic vocabulary of Japanese is only half so reliant on the borrowings: the Korean word for "mountain" is *san*, borrowed from an older pronunciation of Chinese *shan*, while the Japanese use their own word *yama*; the Korean word for "river" is *kang*, borrowed from an older pronunciation of Chinese *jiang (chiang)*, but Japanese use the native *kawa*.

Writing——The Koreans learned to write from the Chinese. Unlike the Japanese, they largely restricted their use of Chinese characters *(hanja* or *han-cha* or *hanmun-cha)* to the writing of classical Chinese *(hanmun)* and later used them to write Korean words of Chinese origin but not native words, so that the student of Korean is seldom baffled by multiple readings for a single character, which often trouble the student of Japanese. Most Korean names are taken from Chinese and often written in characters; when you see a surname like *Chang* further information is required to know whether the person bearing the name is likely to be Korean or Chinese. Korean place names are mostly Chinese, too, but there are exceptions such as Seoul: *sŏul* is an old Korean word meaning "capital." Native Korean words are written in a unique alphabet called *han'gŭl* (earlier also *ŏnmun*), which was promulgated by King Sejong in 1446. The alphabet provides a symbol for each phoneme of Korean. The symbols are made up of simple elements that represent the components of the phoneme. The symbols for the basic consonants are rudimentary pictures of articulatory organs (tongue, mouth, throat, teeth), with additional strokes added for those consonants thought to be more complex. The symbols for the vowels were made up of three elements to which philosophic notions were adduced: a dot round as heaven, a line low and flat like the earth, and a vertical line upright like a human. The symbols are grouped into syllable blocks that resemble the equidimensional frame of Chinese characters; traditionally these are arrayed in vertical lines starting from the top right of the page, but modern publications increasingly use horizontal lines that begin at the top left. An individual symbol adjusts its shape according to the graphic complexity of the particular syllable in which it appears.

Spelling——The *han'gŭl* symbols write phonemes and do not distinguish phonetic variants that are predictable by position. That is why one symbol is used for both the lateral *-l* of *tal* "moon" and the flap *-r-* of *tari* "leg" and why another symbol is used for the initial of both syllables of *kago* "going," the second of which is automatically voiced. In spelling out words the *han'gŭl* symbols can represent them the way they sound (phonemically), but those who already know the language find it easier to read spellings that write the words in stable basic shapes (morphophonemically). Controversies over spelling are usually concerned with the extent to which morphophonemic spellings should be used and with specific details of the grammatical analysis. The spelling systems prescribed by the Republic of Korea (ROK) and by the Democratic People's Republic of Korea (DPRK) are based on criteria devised by Korean linguists in the 1930s; they differ only in certain refinements of the established analysis. Both republics are committed to limiting or eliminating the use of Chinese characters and writing all words in *han'gŭl*. Because Korean enjoys a richer syllable structure, homonyms are less of a problem than they are in Japanese.

Romanization——Several systems of romanization are in use, each with its virtues and its drawbacks depending on the purpose to which it is put. The McCune-Reischauer romanization is intended to write Korean words (especially names) in foreign writings about Korea; the symbols represent the sounds more or less as heard by an American ear, not the native phonemes, and the spellings are faithful to the phonetic forms, not to the underlying structure shown in the *han'gŭl* orthography. Some of the works treating the Korean language as such adapt the McCune–Reischauer or a similar system to transliterate the *han'gŭl* orthography; others use the Yale system, which closely follows the native spellings and avoids the use of diacritics by representing certain vowels of diphthongal origin with digraphs (see table). In using the McCune–Reischauer system it is important to give special care to the diacritics: the apostrophe in *P'yŏngyang* and *Ch'unch'ŏn*, the breve in *Okchŏ* and *Puyŏ*. And it is important to bear in mind that the sound changes ignored by the *han'gŭl* spellings are meticulously noted: the word *to*, "province," as in *Hamgyŏng-bukto*, "North Hamgyŏng province," becomes *-do* in *Kyŏnggi-do*, "Kyŏnggi province," and *Hamgyŏng-namdo*, "South Hamgyŏng province"; the abbreviation of *Chŏlla* is not *Chŏl* but *Chŏn* as in *Chŏn-buk Taehakkyo*, "the University of North Chŏlla," since the *han'gŭl* spelling, for historical reasons, is *Chŏn-ra*.

Sounds —— Standard Korean is spoken in phrases which, like those of French, have no distinctive stress or accentuation. In the south and along the east coast the phrases and words are distinguished by melodic patterns very similar to the pitch accent of Japanese. In the central and northwestern areas the only relics of the earlier accentual system are long vowels in certain words, and even this feature is ignored by younger speakers. The phrases consist of syllables, the boundaries of which do not always coincide with those of the underlying words. Whenever possible, as in French, a final consonant is shifted over to begin the following syllable: *Talk-ida*, "It's a chicken," is pronounced *tal-gi-da; Miguk-ida*, "It's America," is *mi-gu-gi-da; Sŏul-e*, "to Seoul," is *sŏ-u-re*. There are few syllable-final consonants: *-p -t -k -l -m -n -ng*. Words and stems which end in other consonants in basic form (as before the copula *-ida* or a particle beginning with a vowel) automatically reduce these to the corresponding permitted finals: *Os-ŭl poja*, "Let's look at the clothes," *ot*, "clothes"; *Kkoch'-ŭl poja* "Let's look at the flower," *kkot*, "flower"; *Kaps-i ssada*, "The price is low," *kap*, "price"; *Ap'e sŏ-ra*, "Stand in front," *ap*, "front." The reduced consonant is subject to further automatic changes: *ot ap-man*, "just in front of the clothes," is pronounced *o-dam-man*.

The initial consonants of Korean are *p- t- ch- k-* (with the voiced allophones *-b- -d- -j- -g-* between basically voiced sounds); tense unaspirated *pp- tt- tch- kk-;* heavily aspirated *p'- t'- ch' k'-; m- n- h-;* and the two sibilants *s-* (lightly aspirated) and *ss-* (tense). The palatal quality of the affricates is widely ignored in the north and *ch- (-j-)* often sounds like *ts- (-z-)*. The spirant *-h-* is often dropped between basically voiced sounds. Initial *r-* occurs in recent loanwords, but in older words this is replaced by *n-*. In ROK orthography when a basic *r-* is pronounced nasal it is written as *n-;* in DPRK orthography *r-* is written, so that the port known to the Japanese as Rashin is spelled *Najin* in South Korea but *Rajin* in North Korea. In standard Korean the sound *n-* is suppressed before *i* or *y* and the ROK spellings reflect this, but the spelling in North Korea (where often the *y* is suppressed) writes the *n-* (or *r-* if that is basic): the word for "woman" is written *yŏja* in the south, but *nyŏja* in the north, where it is often pronounced *nŏza*. The word for "yes," earlier *nye*, is pronounced *ye* in the south, but Seoul has largely adopted the northern pronunciation *ne*. Internal *-ll-* results when basic *-l-* or *-n* is followed by basic *r-*, or when *l* is followed by *n-*, so that *il-nyŏn*, "one year," is pronounced *illyŏn*, *il-ri*, "one [mini-] league," is *illi*, and *ch'ŏn-ri*, "a thousand leagues," is *ch'ŏlli*. But *-n + n-* is pronounced *-ll-* only in dialect speech, so that *ch'ŏllyŏn* for *ch'ŏnnyŏn*, "a thousand years," is nonstandard.

The standard vowel system has three front vowels: *i* (like b<u>i</u>t or b<u>ee</u>), *e* (b<u>e</u>t or b<u>a</u>y), *ae* (b<u>a</u>t); three unrounded central or back vowels *ŭ* (p<u>u</u>t or c<u>oo</u>k), *ŏ* (b<u>u</u>tt or b<u>ou</u>ght), *a* (p<u>a</u> or <u>ah</u>); and two rounded back vowels *u* (w<u>oo</u> or b<u>oo</u>t), *o* (g<u>o</u> or b<u>oa</u>t). These may be preceded by *y* or *w*, as in *ye* (<u>ye</u>t), *yae* (<u>ya</u>p), *ya* (<u>ya</u>cht), *yŏ* (<u>yu</u>m or <u>you</u>ng); *yu* (<u>you</u> or H<u>u</u>gh), *yo* (<u>yo</u>ke); *wi* (<u>wi</u>t or <u>wee</u>), *we* (<u>we</u>t or <u>wa</u>y), *wae* (<u>qua</u>ck), *wa* (<u>wa</u>sp), *wŏ* (<u>wo</u>n). In rapid speech *-w-* is often dropped after a consonant, especially a labial, so that *ip-wŏn*, "entering hospital," is said as *ibŏn*, making it sound just like *i-bŏn*, "this time." The standard orthography also has the front rounded vowel *oe* (usually pronounced the same as *we* or *wae*) and a diphthong *ŭi*, which is often pronounced *ŭ-* or *-i-* but *e* when it represents the particle meaning "of." Speakers from some of the southern provinces do not distinguish *ŭ* from *ŏ*, nor *e* from *ae;* the latter distinction is poorly maintained even in Seoul, except for older speakers in the first syllable of a word. The vowel system of the 15th century was different in that some of the modern vowels were diphthongs with *-y* (as indicated by the *han'gŭl* symbols and the Yale romanization); there was also one more simple vowel, written with a subscript dot (called *arae-a*, "*a* on the bottom"), and the corresponding *-y* diph-

thong. This system exhibited a kind of vowel harmony such that the vowel of certain endings varied to accord with the tongue-height of the final vowel of the stem; many linguists believe this system was the result of a shift from an earlier system in which the harmony was one of tongue advancement (front and back), as in the Altaic languages.

Korean borrowed the old Chinese unreleased stops *-p -t -k* (still heard in Cantonese) as *-p -l -k;* and the old Chinese *-m -n -ng* are preserved in Korean borrowings. The velar nasal *-ng* occurs only at the end of a syllable and today it is written with the same *han'gŭl* symbol (a little circle) used for the "zero" initial of syllables that begin with a vowel or semivowel: *Yŏng-ŏ*, "English," is written with three occurrences of this little circle.

Grammar —— Koreans put their sentences together much as Japanese do. Known information, such as the subject, is freely omitted, and a sentence can be complete with just a predicate. The predicate, representing the logical proposition, comes at the end; it is preceded by various adjuncts, representing the arguments of the proposition: time, place, subject, means, indirect object, direct object—typically in that order, though the order can be changed for emphasis. The grammatical case of an adjunct, showing its relationship to the rest of the sentence, can be marked by postpositional particles, which are suffixed to noun phrases, but the nominative marker for the subject and the accusative marker for the object are often omitted in common phrases. Similar particles are used to focus attention or delimit reference. Certain of the particles have two shapes; one attaches to a word that ends in a vowel and the other to a word that ends in a consonant: *Namja-ga san-ŭl ponda* ("man–*nominative* mountain–*accusative* looks" =) "A man looks at the mountain"; *Saram-i pada-rŭl ponda* ("person–*nominative* sea–*accusative* looks" =) "A person looks at the sea." Many of the particles have counterparts in Japanese; most uses of Japanese *-wa*, "as for," are like those of the Korean particle that is pronounced *-nŭn* after a vowel and *-ŭn* after a consonant, and most uses of Japanese *-mo*, "also/even," are like those of Korean *-do* (which is romanized as *-to* after a word that ends in *p, t*, or *k*). The particle *-e* "to" corresponds to many uses of Japanese *-ni* or *-e*, "toward"; and the particle *-ŭi* (also pronounced *-e*) is virtually identical in grammar with the Japanese particle *-no*, "of," marking one noun phrase as modifying the next. Modifying expressions always precede the phrases they modify, and there are special endings, like Latin participles or the attributive *(rentaikei)* of classical Japanese, to mark the predicate of a finite sentence used to modify a noun: *pada-rŭl po-n namja* ("sea–*accusative* look–*attributive* man" =) "the man who saw the sea," *namja-ga po-n pada* ("man–*nominative* look–*attributive* sea" =) "the sea the man saw," *namja-ga pada-rŭl po-n pam-e* ("man–*nominative* sea–*accusative* look–*attributive* night" =) "on the night the man saw the sea."

There are three types of predication: the verbal expresses a process, the adjectival describes, and the nominal identifies. To identify a noun the copula *-ida* is attached, and this usually contracts to *-da* after a vowel: *Pam-ida*, "It's evening"; *Pada-da*, "It's the sea." When one noun is equated with another, the first (the identified) is normally marked with the nominative particle (where Japanese use *-wa*): *Uri-ga Han'guk saram-ida* ("we–*nominative* Korea people–*copula*" =) "We are Koreans"; *I-gŏs-i chido-da* ("this-thing–*nominative* map–*copula*" =) "This is a map." When an equation is denied, the copula attaches to the word *ani*, "no," and both the identified and the identifier are marked as nominative: *Uri-ga Miguk saram-i ani-da* ("we–*nominative* America people–*nominative* not–*copula*" =) "We are not Americans"; *I-gŏs-i chido-ga ani-da* ("this-thing–*nominative* map–*nominative* not–*copula*" =) "This is not a map." The copula and the predicated adjectives are conjugated with the same endings as the verbs but lack semantically incompatible forms such as the imperative. Verb endings can be quite long, for they consist of a series of elements that impart information over and above the proposition itself, such as whether the subject is to be specially honored (*ponda*, "sees it," but *posinda*, "an honored person sees it"); whether the action is present, future, or past; the level of respect you wish to convey toward the person hearing you. The polite expressions usually heard in the southern provinces are made with the formal endings, such as *-mnida/-sŭmnida* for statements and *-mnikka/-sŭmnikka* for questions, but in Seoul these are often replaced by the more relaxed endings that end in *-yo*, such as *-ŏ-yo* and *-ji-yo*. The expression *Yŏ-bosipsio* is a very formal way to call someone's attention; in Seoul a telephone "hello" is usually *Yŏ-bose-yo;* and a husband often addresses his wife with *Yŏ-bo*. These expressions are contractions of words meaning "See here," i.e., "Look toward me."

History——Modern Korean descends from the language of the unified Silla kingdom (7th–10th centuries AD) and the Koryŏ dynasty which followed it. Although the unified kingdom incorporated also the states of PAEKCHE and KOGURYŎ, the language of the ruling class of these early states was originally that of the northern Puyŏ people (who constituted the tribal states of Puyŏ, Koguryŏ, Okchŏ, and Ye), which was quite different from the languages spoken by the peoples of the southern tribes known as the Three Han (Ma-han, Chin-han, and Pyŏn-han), whose related dialects formed the basis for the Silla language. The term "Old Korean" has been used to refer to what was spoken on the peninsula during the first 10 centuries AD, but knowledge is largely limited to Chinese transcriptions of the names of ancient Han and Puyŏ places and persons. We know much more about Later Korean. This is usually divided into Early Middle Korean, from the 11th century up to 1446 (and the invention of han'gŭl), which is attested by a few texts that use Chinese characters to represent vernacular words; Late Middle Korean, attested by many han'gŭl texts of the 15th and 16th centuries; and Modern Korean, which dates from 1592 (the date of Hideyoshi's invasion and the Imjin war). Modern Korean is conveniently divided into Early Modern Korean (roughly 1600–1750) and Late Modern Korean, written in the second half of the 18th century and through the 19th century. The language of the 20th century is called Contemporary Korean; cultivated and studied by patriotic writers and scholars through the first half of the century despite persecution from the Japanese regime, it flourished after the liberation of Korea in 1945.

Scholars are not agreed on the prehistory of the Korean language. Many believe it is related to the Altaic group (the Tungusic, Mongolian, and Turkic languages) on the one hand; and to Japanese, on the other. It has proven difficult to marshal convincing arguments that the many lexical and grammatical resemblances among these languages are due to a common heritage rather than early borrowing. The comparativist is hindered in his research by the lack of early records for most of the relevant languages and by their geographical propinquity. Although it appears likely that there is a core of common elements in Korean, Japanese, and the Altaic languages, a definitive judgment on their genetic relationship must await the outcome of current research on the problem.

■——Kim Chin-Wu, "The Vowel System of Korean," *Language* 44 (1968). Kim Wan-jin, *Kugŏ ŭm'un-ch'egye ŭi yŏn'gu* (1971). Gari K. Ledyard, *The Korean Language Reform of 1446: The Origin, Background, and Early History of the Korean Alphabet* (1966). Lee Ki-Moon, *Kugŏ ŭm'un-sa yŏn'gu* (1972), tr Fujimoto Yukio as *Kankokugo no rekishi* (1975); tr Bruno Lewin as *Geschichte der Koreanischen Sprache* (1977). Bruno Lewin, "Japanese and Korean: The Problems and History of a Linguistic Comparison," *Journal of Japanese Studies* 2 (1976). S. E. Martin, "Lexical Evidence Relating Korean to Japanese," *Language* 42 (1966). S. E. Martin, "Problems in Establishing the Prehistoric Relationships of Korean and Japanese," *Proceedings of the International Symposium Commemorating the 30th Anniversary of Korean Liberation*, National Academy of Sciences (1975). S. E. Martin and Young-Sook C. Lee, *Beginning Korean* (1969). S. E. Martin, Y. H. Lee, and S. U. Chang, *A Korean-English Dictionary* (1968). B. Nam Park [Pak Pong-nam], *Korean Basic Course*, 2 vols (1969). S. R. Ramsey, *Accent and Morphology in Korean Dialects* (1978). *Samuel E. MARTIN*

Koreans in Japan

The presence of a large ethnic minority of Koreans in Japan, most of whom are legally aliens, is mainly a legacy of Japanese colonialism. When Japan annexed Korea in 1910, there were only about 800 Koreans in Japan. However, with the enactment in 1939 of the NATIONAL SERVICE DRAFT ORDINANCE on the eve of World War II, the number of Koreans in Japan began to show a marked increase. The Service Draft Ordinance brought forced laborers and military draftees to Japan to fill the manpower shortage incurred by the war economy. At the same time, free laborers, and poor peasants voluntarily migrated to Japan in search of employment. Of the estimated 6 million Koreans mobilized in Japan and Korea for the war effort by the Japanese government, approximately 1 million were draftees and conscripted laborers shipped to Japan between 1939 and 1945. At the end of the war, there were more than 2 million Koreans in Japan; with Japan's surrender, many were repatriated. In the late 1970s approximately 650,000 Koreans resided in Japan, constituting the largest ethnic minority. Approximately 75 percent of this population consisted of Japanese-born second- and third-generation Koreans. Many had never been to Korea, nor learned to speak Korean.

Legal and social barriers effectively keep this ethnic minority apart from the mainstream of Japanese society. Koreans were given Japanese nationality during the colonial period and retained it until 1952, when the Alien Registration Order (Gaikokujin Tōroku Rei) disenfranchised them and declared them aliens, excluded from the benefits reserved for Japanese citizens. As Japan does not recognize the principle of *jus soli*, birth in Japan does not legally assure Japanese citizenship. In some localities, Koreans have been denied access to public housing, child welfare, and aid to families with dependent children. The social welfare benefits for Koreans are limited to the bare minimum, such as national health insurance and unemployment compensation. No social security benefits are applicable to Koreans who hold permanent resident alien status.

The avenue for becoming naturalized citizens is not entirely closed to Koreans, but the legal process is so complicated and the rules for eligibility so hard to meet that only a very limited number of Koreans can qualify under the provisions of the Japanese Nationality Law (Kokuseki Hō; see JAPANESE NATIONALITY; NATURALIZATION). Nevertheless, the number of Koreans becoming naturalized seems to be rising.

Social discrimination also isolates Koreans in Japan. The Japanese look at themselves as a unique people with a history and culture distinctly different from that of other races and are often intolerant of other linguistic and ethnic groups on their soil. The employment rate for Koreans remained low even during the rapid economic growth after the war, and this situation has not changed since then. Most enterprises owned and operated by Koreans are small businesses related to the entertainment and service industries, for example, pinball parlors, restaurants, scrapyards, cabarets, and saunas. Some Koreans resort to illegitimate means to make a living, and apparently a great number of them are engaged in organized crime. There are only a few Koreans who have made fortunes in legitimate businesses competing with other Japanese industries. Some Koreans have also become very successful as professional wrestlers, baseball players, and pop singers. Not one of them uses an original Korean name.

The Korean community in Japan has been split by an ideological rivalry between supporters of North and South Korea. The Chōsen Sōren (Zainichi Chōsenjin Sō Rengō Kai; General Federation of Korean Residents in Japan) is a supporter of the Democratic People's Republic of Korea, and the Mindan (Daikan Minkoku Kyoryūmin Dan; Korean Residents Association in Japan) supports the Republic of Korea. Each organization claims to be the sole representative body of all Koreans in Japan, and both have used their influence to try to protect Korean interests in Japan. They maintain separate educational systems, cooperatives, credit unions, and other voluntary associations, and they reside in separate neighborhoods. The antagonism between the two organizations is so fierce that the chance of their uniting as a cohesive ethnic interest group is remote. This division has seriously crippled attempts to demand changes in the discriminatory policies of the Japanese government.

After many years of subjugation, humiliation, and mistreatment of Koreans, there are few signs of a new trend, although some Japanese have started to show sympathy for the Korean situation and are helping to fight prejudice and discrimination in the Japanese judicial courts.

Pak Chong-sŏk, plaintiff in *Pak Chong-sŏk v Hitachi, Ltd*, 1974, was born in Japan of Korean parents. When he finished high school in 1970, he answered a recruitment advertisement from Hitachi, Ltd, and applied for a job, using his Japanese name as he had always done. He successfully passed the examination with an above-average mark and received an official notice of his employment. As is customary in Japan, Hitachi asked him to submit a certificate of family registry. It was then that the company learned of Pak's Korean nationality. Legally, he should have used his Korean name as it appears on his alien registration card. A few days later, Pak received a letter of rejection from Hitachi, stating that Pak had committed perjury. Pak insisted that the perjury charge was merely an excuse for the company's discriminatory policy and filed a civil suit against it. When the trial ended three years later, Pak's supporters had formed an organization with more than 400 Korean and Japanese members. This group played a key role in mobilizing public opinion in favor of Pak and waged an extensive boycott against all Hitachi products.

The matter was settled in court in June 1974. "The official issuance of the hiring notice specifying the amount of salary and the date to report for work," said the judge, "constituted a consummation of a labor contract between the two parties." The court held that, "the cancellation of employment of the plaintiff should be construed as an arbitrary breach of the labor contract, which was a violation of article 3 of the Labor Standards Law and article 90 of the Civil Code of Japan." The court said that its sympathy rested with the motive of the plaintiff, because Japanese society had compelled him to hide his Korean name in order to escape discrimination.

A somewhat different case is that of Kim Kyong-dŭk (1977). In order to become a lawyer in Japan, one must successfully pass the law examination given by the Ministry of Justice, then train for two years at the Legal Training and Research Institute (Shihō Kenshūjo). In the Lawyer's Law (Bengoshi Hō) there is no specification regarding nationality (the "imperial subject clause" of the law having been deleted), and technically an alien has the right to become an attorney, provided he follows the prescribed procedure. However, the Legal Training and Research Institute has admitted aliens only on the condition that they declare intent of naturalization.

Kim was born in 1949 of Korean nationals in Japan. He graduated from the Law Department of Waseda University in 1972 and passed the law examination in October 1976. When he applied to the institute, he was rejected because he refused to declare his intention to become naturalized. Kim submitted a petition to the Japanese Supreme Court in November 1976, requesting that he not be forced to renounce his nationality in order to be admitted to the institute. He stated that he wanted to become an attorney in order to defend fundamental human rights and did not intend to become a judge or a public prosecutor in Japan. As the Korean population is the largest group of aliens in Japan, there is an acute need for Korean attorneys to handle litigation, as well as issues related to human rights. Forcing him to declare his intent to naturalize as a condition for admission to the institute was tantamount to demanding that he negate his ethnic identity.

On 2 March 1977, the Supreme Court ruled in a very brief decision that, "In the case of Mr. Kim, the question of nationality should not be a factor in denying him admission to the Legal Training and Research Institute." The court refused to elaborate any further on whether the ruling would apply to all aliens in Japan. Nevertheless, this case and *Pak* v *Hitachi* are landmark decisions in that the judicial authorities admitted the existence of discrimination against Koreans in Japan. This kind of judicial action was long overdue and has provided a cornerstone for the development of civil rights for Koreans in Japan.

📖——Changsoo Lee, "Ethnic Discrimination and Conflict: The case of the Korean Minority in Japan," in William A. Veenhoven, ed, *Case Studies on Human Rights and Fundamental Freedom: A World Survey* (1976). Changsoo Lee and George De Vos, *Koreans in Japan: Ethnic Accommodation and Conflict* (1981). Richard H. Mitchell, *The Korean Minority in Japan* (1967). Shihō Kenshūjo, ed, *Zainichi chōsenjin shogū no suii to genjō* (1955). Edward Wagner, *Korean Minority in Japan: 1905–1950* (1951). Yi Yu-whan, *Zainichi kankokujin rokujūman* (1971).   *Changsoo* LEE

Korean Three Kingdoms period

(J: Sangoku *jidai;* Kor: Samguk *sidae*). The period in Korea from approximately 300 to 668 when three states, KOGURYŎ in the north, PAEKCHE in the southwest, and SILLA in the southeast, took form and contested for control of the Korean peninsula. The era began with Koguryŏ's conquest of the Han Chinese colony, LELANG (Lolang; Kor: Nangnang), and ended with Silla's unification of the peninsula in 668. It was a period of cultural synthesis between China's Confucian tradition, Buddhism, and native Korean traditions. Chinese culture, institutions, and technology also filtered through Paekche to Japan, initiating its sinicization. See also SAMGUK SAGI; SAMGUK YUSA.   *C. Kenneth* QUINONES

Korean War

(Chōsen Sensō). A major military confrontation between the Republic of Korea (ROK), the United States, and the United Nations on one side, and the Democratic People's Republic of Korea (DPRK), the People's Republic of China, and the Soviet Union on the other side. The war began on 25 June 1950, when the DPRK sought to forcefully reunite the Korean nation, and lasted until an armistice was concluded on 27 July 1953.

Korea was divided at the 38th parallel into a Soviet-occupied north and American-occupied south at the conclusion of World War II in 1945 according to US–USSR agreements. The division was intended to be a temporary measure for facilitating the surrender of Japanese forces, but geopolitical and ideological rivalry between the

two superpowers immediately crystallized Korea's splintered polity into contending factions and thwarted all efforts to negotiate reunification. The United Nations, urged on by the United States, sought to achieve unification through a nationwide plebiscite in 1948, but this also failed when UN representatives were denied access to North Korea. Two separate governments then materialized: the Soviet aligned DPRK led by KIM IL-SŎNG in the north and the ROK, supported by the United States, recognized by the United Nations, and headed by Syngman RHEE (Yi Sŭng-man) in the south.

The situation stabilized briefly in the winter of 1949–50, as foreign troops except for some military advisers left the peninsula. Korea was considered outside the US zone of strategic interest in Asia, with US foreign policy shifting to the containment of Soviet initiatives in Europe, and the recently established People's Republic of China (PRC) preoccupied with its postwar reconstruction.

The beginning of hostilities in June 1950 thus came as a surprise to most world leaders. President Harry S. Truman ordered General Douglas MACARTHUR to rush troops from Japan to Korea in support of the ROK. The United States presented the matter to the UN Security Council with such haste that the Soviet representative, who was then boycotting the council's meetings because of its refusal to seat the PRC delegation, was unable to prevent approval of UN military intervention against the DPRK, which was designated the aggressor. Though many nations' troops fought under the UN flag, it was an American-led and -equipped army.

The war progressed through four distinct phases. During the summer of 1950 DPRK forces pushed UN and ROK forces into a small area around the southeastern port of Pusan. India tried in vain to establish a cease-fire, while the PRC called upon the United States to clarify its objectives after the US realigned itself with the Republic of China on Taiwan, stationed a fleet off the PRC's southeastern coast, and began bombing near the Manchurian-Korean border. A major troop buildup by the PRC began in southern Manchuria only after its inquiries went unanswered.

US forces launched the war's second phase on 15 September with an amphibious attack at Inch'ŏn, a port mid-point on Korea's western coast. DPRK forces crumbled into retreat as their supply lines were severed. In October UN–ROK armies struck across the 38th parallel into North Korea. Truman assured the PRC that its territory would not be invaded, but MacArthur failed to halt his troops well south of the Yalu River, China's border with Korea, when ordered to do so by the US president. He instead urged his armies northward while condoning air strikes in the PRC and even Soviet territory and discussed the possibility of ROC military cooperation with his offensive. The PRC was also quite concerned by the dramatic reversal of US policy toward Japan, its archenemy for 50 years. Japan became a staging area and supply depot for the US military effort in Korea and also received millions of dollars of contracts for supplies. US Occupation policy also shifted from an emphasis on reform to one on reconstruction of Japan as a new ally.

China responded with a massive offensive when UN–ROK armies regained Seoul, and by the summer of 1951 both sides were entrenched along the 38th parallel. The tedious negotiations to achieve the armistice continued for two years in P'anmunjŏm, until an agreement was signed on 27 July 1953, leaving Korea divided by a demilitarized zone along the 38th parallel. Casualties amounted to approximately 4 million people, including 1 million civilians on each side and 900,000 Chinese. Some 33,600 US soldiers died in the conflict.

📖——Dean Acheson, *The Korean War* (1972). Akira Iriye, *The Cold War in Asia* (1974). John W. Spainer, *The Truman MacArthur Controversy and the Korean War* (1959). I. F. Stone, *The Hidden History of the Korean War* (1952). Allen Whiting, *China Crosses the Yalu* (1968).   *C. Kenneth* QUINONES

Korea Strait

(Chōsen Kaikyō). Between the Korean peninsula and the island of TSUSHIMA, connecting the Sea of Japan and the East China Sea. This strait has long been important in transportation between Japan and the continent. In recent years it has been the site of fishing disputes between Japan and South Korea. It is a rich fishing ground in winter and spring because of the ocean currents. Narrowest point: 50 km (31 mi); deepest point: 210 m (689 ft).

Kōrin (1658–1716)

Also known as Ogata Kōrin. Real name Ogata Koretomi. Edo-period painter and designer in the RIMPA style who imbued the

Kōrin

Pair of two-panel folding screens entitled *Red and White Plum Trees (Kōhakubai zu)*. Colors and gold leaf on paper. Each screen 156.6 × 172.7 cm. Ca 1711. MOA Museum of Art, Atami, Shizuoka Prefecture. National Treasure.

classical themes of HON'AMI KŌETSU (1558–1637) and Tawaraya SŌTATSU (d 1643?) with a cool elegance and decorative sense of design that has earned him universal appeal. Even his most formalized and simplified BIRD-AND-FLOWER PAINTINGS, however, are enhanced by a lifelike naturalism based on sketches from life.

Kōrin was the second son of a prosperous and cultivated upper-class merchant, Ogata Sōken (1621–87), the proprietor of a successful Kyōto textile shop. Sōken's grandfather, Ogata Dōhaku, who had married a sister of the great Momoyama-period artist Hon'ami Kōetsu, is thought to have been the first in the family to have specialized in textile design. When Sōken died in 1687 his eldest son took over management of the shop, relieving Kōrin of any business responsibilities.

A typical personality of the Genroku era (1688–1704), the young Kōrin was a romantic but profligate playboy, enjoying the carefree life of pleasure described by SAIKAKU in his 1682 novel *Kōshoku ichidai otoko (The Life of an Amorous Man)*. Independently wealthy, skilled at classical arts like NŌ, a talented artist and witty conversationalist, Kōrin was much sought after in the highest circles of Kyōto society. Through self-indulgence and poor investments he quickly squandered his inheritance and in 1694 was forced to pawn some of the family treasures, including a lacquer box by Kōetsu.

His financial difficulties led Kōrin to take up painting as a serious profession from the 1690s, for he was already well trained in the techniques of KANŌ SCHOOL ink painting, which he had studied with Yamamoto Soken (d 1706). There is also evidence that he was already an accomplished designer at this time. Among his many designs and sketches are some for lacquer INRŌ and writing boxes that were inspired by Kōetsu, and stylish textile patterns that were widely copied and published during his own lifetime. As early as 1699 he was painting directly onto women's satin robes.

Around 1700 and again between 1709 and 1712 Kōrin collaborated with his younger brother KENZAN, who had chosen pottery as a profession. Kōrin painted quick sketches in iron oxide on the flat surfaces of the square plates his brother designed. His earliest independent work may be the abbreviated ink painting of a mischievous Hotei, one of the SEVEN DEITIES OF GOOD FORTUNE, kicking a football. Some interpret this as a humorous self-portrait of the artist "kicking off" his new career. In 1701, at age 43, Kōrin achieved official recognition with the award of the honorary title *hokkyō*.

The monochrome ink medium always remained important in his oeuvre, but he is most admired for his gorgeous screens in rich colors against a gold ground. The earliest of these are thought to be the *Iris Screens (Kakitsubatazu)* in the Nezu Art Museum in Tōkyō. Several clusters of iris are identical, executed with a stencil technique obviously adapted from the artist's early training in textile design. His first dated work is a 1704 portrait of his lifelong friend and patron, Nakamura Kuranosuke, a newly rich senior officer of the government mint. That year Kōrin moved to Edo (now Tōkyō) in search of more lucrative commissions and for seven years he served a succession of wealthy *daimyō* lords and merchant clients. His only other dated work, a long handscroll of plants and flowers,

was executed in 1705 for the daimyō of Tsugaru. The style reflects his deep understanding and study of the paintings of Sōtatsu, whom he revered and whose work he is known to have owned and copied. Kōrin's twofold screen of *Rough Waves (Hatōzu)* in the New York Metropolitan Museum of Art is also based closely on a painting by Sōtatsu but at the same time it has disquieting and ominous overtones that may reflect the artist's unhappiness during his years of self-enforced exile in Edo. It is unusual to see this darker side of Kōrin's personality. In 1711 the need for artistic freedom drove him back to Kyōto where, although eventually reduced to poverty, he produced some of his most complex and best work. His masterpiece, the screens of *Red and White Plum Trees (Kōhakubai zu)*, in the MOA Museum of Art in Atami, are thought to date from this final period.

Kōrin had three famous followers, who might have been his direct pupils: WATANABE SHIKŌ (1683–1755), Fukae Roshū (1699–1757), and TATEBAYASHI KAGEI (fl mid-18th century). A dozen others are now known only by name. There is speculation that his disciples, especially Shikō, may have executed paintings for Kōrin on occasion.

━━ Chizawa Teiji, *Kōrin* (1970). Kōno Motoaki, *Ogata Kōrin*, vol 17 of *Nihon bijutsu kaiga zenshū* (Shūeisha, 1976). *Kōrinha III*, in *Rimpa kaiga zenshū* (1979–80). Mizuo Hiroshi, *Sōtatsu to Kōrin*, tr John M. Shields as *Edo Painting: Sotatsu and Korin* (1972). Yamane Yūzō, *Kōrin kankei shiryō to sono kenkyū* (1962). Yamane Yūzō, "Ogata Kōrin and the Art of the Genroku Era," *Acta Asiatica* 15 (1968). Yamane Yūzō, *Sōtatsu to Kōrin*, vol 14 of *Genshoku Nihon no bijutsu* (Shōgakukan, 1969). *Julia MEECH-PEKARIK*

Kōriyama

City in central Fukushima Prefecture, northern Honshū. One of the POST-STATION TOWNS on the highway Ōshū Kaidō in the Edo period (1600–1868), it was rapidly industrialized after the opening of the ASAKA CANAL in the Meiji period (1868–1912). Chemicals, electrical appliances, food processing, and precision instruments are its main industries. Pop: 286,497.

Kōriyama Basin

(Kōriyama Bonchi). In central Fukushima Prefecture, northern Honshū. Bounded by the Ōu and Abukuma mountains, most of the basin consists of diluvial uplands and the flood plain of the river Abukumagawa's upper reaches. The ASAKA CANAL, constructed in 1882, has made it possible to grow rice on the uplands. The major city is Kōriyama. Area: approximately 150 sq km (57.9 sq mi).

kōrogi → crickets

Kōrokan

Government office for the reception and accommodation of foreign embassies and merchants from the 7th through the 11th century; it took its name from the Honglu Si (Hung-lu Ssu; Court of Diplomatic Reception) of the Sui dynasty (589–618) of China. The first office was established in 608 in the port of Naniwa (now Ōsaka) to receive emissaries from the Sui court. The second was established around 688 at DAZAIFU, the government headquarters in northern Kyūshū. Sometime after Heiankyō (now the city of Kyōto) became the capital in 794, a third Kōrokan was established in the southern section of that city. Separate buildings seem to have been maintained for different countries. With the decline of the RITSURYŌ SYSTEM of government and the end of regular diplomatic relations with China and the Korean state of SILLA in the 9th century, these offices fell into disuse and the buildings were used to accommodate Chinese and Korean merchants. By the 12th century they had fallen into private hands.

Kōrōkyō

(abbreviation of Kōkyō Kigyōtai Tō Rōdō Kumiai Kyōgikai; Council of Public Corporation and National Enterprise Workers' Unions). A coordinating body of nine unions of workers in public corporations and government enterprises. Its member unions include the employees of the JAPANESE NATIONAL RAILWAYS, the NIPPON TELEGRAPH AND TELEPHONE PUBLIC CORPORATION, the JAPAN TOBACCO AND SALT PUBLIC CORPORATION, and other government enterprises such as the postal and forestry services. The Kōrōkyō unions are affiliated with Japan's largest labor federation, SŌHYŌ (General Council of Trade Unions of Japan). They play a key role in the Sōhyō-led annual spring wage offensive (SHUNTŌ), despite the fact that public employees are restricted from striking or collective bargaining by the PUBLIC CORPORATIONS AND GOVERNMENT ENTERPRISES LABOR RELATIONS LAW. In fact, Kōrōkyō has led strikes and been involved in collective bargaining with the government since 1965. Many of the strikes have been for the right to strike; the strike in 1975 (see SUTO KEN SUTO) was one such, and it was particularly long and bitter. At present, however, public employees still do not have the legal right to strike. Kōrōkyō represents the left wing of the Japanese labor movement. Recently, however, there has been some talk of reorganization. The union of the Nippon Telegraph and Telephone Public Corporation, for example, has been working towards effecting ties with private unions. Total membership stood at 885,000 in 1978. *Kurita Ken*

Koryŏ

(J: Kōrai). A medieval Korean state established by Wang Kŏn (r 918–943) in 918; it became the ruling state on the Korean peninsula in 935. The Buddhist impact on Korea reached its zenith during the Koryŏ period, and the Korean government came to resemble a Chinese-style bureaucracy. A civil service examination system emphasizing the study of Confucian texts was instituted in 958. Koryŏ dynastic rule was never strong after the state withstood three invasions by the Khitan Liao dynasty of northeastern China between 993 and 1018. Contending military families usurped the monarch's authority during the 12th century only to be subdued by the Mongols in the 13th century (see MONGOL INVASIONS OF KOREA). Finally YI SŎNG-GYE rebelled against Koryŏ authority and established the YI DYNASTY in 1392. See also SAMGUK SAGI; SAMGUK YUSA. *C. Kenneth Quinones*

Kōryūji

Temple in the Uzumasa section of Ukyō Ward, Kyōto, belonging to the Omuro branch (see NINNAJI) of the Shingon sect of Buddhism. Also known as Hachiokadera, Uzumasadera, and Hatanokimidera, it is said to have been founded in 603 by a high official, Hata no Kawakatsu, to house an image of the future Buddha MIROKU (Maitreya), that he had received from Prince SHŌTOKU (574–622). On a visit to the temple in 619 Shōtoku supposedly laid the foundation beam for a pagoda and pledged his support through an endowment of paddy land. Another image that arrived from the Korean kingdom of Silla was installed in 622.

Kōryūji was originally built to serve the needs of the HATA FAMILY, a powerful family of Chinese or Korean origin living in the Yamashiro region outside Kyōto, where the temple was situated until it was moved to its present site around 794. The original Kōryūji was destroyed in a fire in 818, but was rebuilt in the Jōwa era (834–848).

Kōryūji was devastated by fire a second time in 1150 and rebuilt by imperial command 15 years later. The present lecture hall (kōdō), popularly called the Red Hall (Akadō) dates from this time. Enshrined in the lecture hall is a huge wooden seated image of Amida Buddha dating from 836, a standing image of an Eleven-faced, Thousand-armed Kannon dating from the Kōnin era (810–824), and an image of Fukū Kensaku (Amoghapāśa) Kannon dating from the Tempyō era (729–749). Another early structure is the Keikyūin, a single-story octagonal building popularly called the Inner Sanctum (Okunoin), which is roofed with Japanese cypress bark. According to tradition, the Keikyūin was originally a temporary residence built for Prince Shōtoku, which was later converted to a temple and presented to Kawakatsu. In fact, the Keikyūin was built in the Kamakura period (1185–1333) and subsequently renovated several times. It contains images of Nyoirin (Cintāmaṇi Cakra) Kannon and Prince Shōtoku, both reputedly carved by Shōtoku himself, and an image of Amida Buddha, said to have been presented to the Japanese court by the Chinese emperor Yang (r 604–617) of the Sui dynasty. Within the temple precincts is a museum built in 1923 that houses a superb collection of Buddhist sculptures, including the famous image of Miroku in contemplation, which is said to date from the first half of the 7th century and was designated the first National Treasure. *Stanley Weinstein*

Kosai

City in western Shizuoka Prefecture, central Honshū, on Lake Hamana (Hamanako). The birthplace of TOYODA SAKICHI, the inventor of the Toyoda-type loom, Kosai has long been the center of the silk-reeling and textile industries. Now its principal industries are automobile parts and precision instruments. *Nori,* a seaweed, and yellowtail are grown in the lake. Pop: 37,633.

kosaku sōgi → tenant farmer disputes

Kōsei shimpen

A partial translation into Japanese, with annotations, of the Dutch translation of M. Noël Chomel's *Agronome français: Dictionaire économique* (1709); 70 fascicles. Undertaken in 1811 by ŌTSUKI GENTAKU and other scholars under the official sponsorship of the newly created Translation Bureau (Bansho Wage Goyōgakari) of the Tokugawa shogunate, the translation was never completed, although work continued until 1839. The *Kōsei shimpen* (literally, "a new book to promote public welfare") stressed entries on the natural sciences, particularly medicine, and stimulated the development of Rangaku (Dutch studies; see WESTERN LEARNING), as studies of the West were then called.

Kōseishō → Ministry of Health and Welfare

koseki → household registers

Kose no Kanaoka (fl 9th century)

Court painter of the early part of the Heian period (794–1185) and founder of the KOSE SCHOOL. No authenticated work by him survives, though he is known to have painted portraits of the Confucian sages for the wall of the Imperial University (Daigakuryō) in 880 and a screen for a member of the powerful FUJIWARA FAMILY in 885. He introduced native subjects and a new Japanese style to the prevalent Chinese mode; as a consequence, he has sometimes been referred to as the founder of YAMATO-E painting.

Kose school

(Koseha). The earliest school of painters in Japan and one of the longest lived, originating in the 9th century and surviving into the 15th century. Paintings by early Kose masters have not survived, but fragmentary primary documents suggest that these artists played a central role in transforming the style imported from China during the 7th and 8th centuries into an inherently Japanese mode of secular art. They are credited with initiating the classical Heian-period (794–1185) style which later became known as YAMATO-E. During the late Heian period, Kose-school artists were *eshi* (professional artists) at the Kyūtei Edokoro (Imperial Court Painting Bureau); in the Kamakura period (1185–1333), a branch of the family established itself as *ebusshi* (professional priest-painters) in the EDOKORO (painting bureau) of the temple KŌFUKUJI in Nara; and in the Nambokuchō era (1336–92), another branch served the *edokoro* of the Kyōto temple TŌJI as well as the Kyūtei Edokoro of the Northern Court (see NORTHERN AND SOUTHERN COURTS).

The school began with KOSE NO KANAOKA near the end of the 9th century in the capital (now Kyōto). In contrast to the low social status of earlier painters in Japan, Kanaoka was an aristocrat bearing the titles *shinsen'en no tsukasa* and *uneme no kami* and holding the imperial court rank of junior fifth rank, lower grade *(jugoi ge)*. The subjects of Kanaoka's paintings were of Chinese derivation: in 880 he painted Confucius and his disciples on the walls of the Imperial University (Daigakuryō), and in 888 he did portraits of great Confucian scholars for the Imperial Palace. His style was essentially Chinese, based on naturalistic Tang (T'ang) dynasty works and their more delicate Korean translations, which had entered Japan during the preceding centuries of intense continental influence. Legends of the magic realism of his painting include the story of a painted horse that broke free from its wall every night to roam the neighborhood.

As for succeeding generations of Kose artists, records cite Kose no Aimi as *edokoro eshi* in 901, mention that Kose no Kintada painted screens for the Imperial Palace in 955, and report that the court considered Kose no Kimmochi a less accomplished artist than his contemporary, Asakabe no Tsunenori (fl ca 969). Numerous citations show that Kanaoka's great-grandson Hirotaka was in demand by the court of Emperor ICHIJŌ. In addition to wall paintings for the Imperial Palace, he designed textiles, painted albums and portraits, and decorated screens for members of the powerful FUJIWARA FAMILY. So solidly did Hirotaka establish the Kose school that his successors retained their central position in the Kyūtei Edokoro throughout the 11th and 12th centuries. Nobushige and his son Muneshige were highly acclaimed, although there is some disagreement about the dates of their activity. Most of these Kose artists are known only by their names and court titles.

The Kose line, faced with strong competition from Tokiwa no Mitsunaga (fl 1173) and FUJIWARA NO NOBUZANE, began to lose status at court in the Kamakura period (1185–1333). It is not surprising that in the middle of the 13th century a branch of the Kose school went to Nara, took priestly orders, and became affiliated with the painting workshops of Kōfukuji. The delicately aristocratic style of these artists is preserved in their panel paintings of Shintō gods and goddesses at the Yasumigaoka Hachiman Shrine in the temple Yakushiji in Nara, painted in 1295 by Gyōgon, a Kose artist who was an *ebusshi* at the Kōfukuji subtemple of Ichijōin. In a neighboring subtemple, Daijōin, Kose artists operated a painting bureau for 200 years. The most reliable chart of their family lineage comes from a 1472 (Bummei 4.12.23) entry in the journal of Jinson, abbot of the subtemple (see DAIJŌIN JISHA ZŌJI KI).

Not all Kose painters went to Nara. Incidental references to their activity in Kyōto continue, and they again gained recognition during the Nambokuchō period (1336–92). Besides supplying the court with artistic leadership, they were prominent in the workshops of Tōji. At the beginning of the century, Kose no Arihisa held court rank and top position in the Kyūtei Edokoro before being appointed *daibusshi* (chief Buddhist artist) at Tōji in 1325. None of his work exists today, but some of the scrolls of the *Kōbō Daishi gyōjō e* still owned by Tōji were painted by his son and successor, Yukitada, who, in 1375, was appointed *edokoro azukari* (director of the painting bureau) for the Northern Court of Emperor Go-En'yū (1359–93; r 1371–82). Several other existing paintings bearing Kose names from the 14th century verify that the artists of this school were conservators of a tradition, but that the school had lost its vitality. During the early years of the Muromachi period (1333–1568), they were absorbed into the mainstream of *yamato-e* artists.

Carolyn WHEELWRIGHT

koshi

A covered palanquin resting on long horizontal poles that were borne on the shoulders or at the hips of men. During the Nara (710–794) and Heian (794–1185) periods, only the emperor and certain imperial kinsmen rode in these conveyances, which were formally called *ren*. From the late Heian period such palanquins came to be used also by nobles and priests, and they varied in construction and decoration. Their use later extended to *samurai* and common-

ers, but in the Edo period (1600–1868) *koshi* were supplanted by the more popular KAGO. MIKOSHI, portable shrines carried in festival processions, are the only kind of *koshi* in use today.

Koshigaya

City in southeastern Saitama Prefecture, central Honshū, on the river Moto Arakawa. A market and post-station town on the highway Nikkō Kaidō in the Edo period (1600–1868), it is now an industrial and commercial center. Horticulture and poultry are important activities. Koshigaya is known for its dolls *(hina ninygō)*. Pop: 223,243.

Koshikijima Islands

(Koshikijima Rettō). Group of islands 40 km (25 mi) west of the city of Kushikino, Kagoshima Prefecture, Kyūshū. Composed of Kami Koshikijima, Naka Koshikijima, Shimo Koshikijima, and smaller islands. All the islands are hilly. The islands are frequently struck by typhoons, fishing has declined, and farming is poor. The climate is mild; Indian laurel, tree ferns, and the like flourish. Sweet potatoes and wheat are grown on terraced land; a well-known local product is lily bulbs. Area: 119 sq km (45.9 sq mi).

kōshin

A year or day designation in the sexagenary cycle, a system of Chinese origin for counting (naming) years and other calendar units (see JIKKAN JŪNISHI; CALENDAR, DATES, AND TIME: the sexagenary cycle). *Kōshin* designates any year or day that falls on the combination of *kō* (Ch: *geng* or *keng*), the 7th of the "10 stems," and *shin* (Ch: *shen*), the 9th of the "12 branches" or zodiacal symbols, hence the 57th year or day of a complete cycle of 60. The two Chinese characters with which *kōshin* is written can also be pronounced with the native Japanese reading *kanoe saru*. The word *saru* (which corresponds to the zodiacal symbol *shin*) literally means "monkey," and a *kōshin* year or day is one of the several years or days "of the monkey" in the cycle.

According to ancient Taoist tradition, the night of a *kōshin* day was the time when "three worms" (J: *sanshi*) believed to dwell in the human body would sneak out and report a person's sins to the Celestial God, a report that would result in the shortening of the person's life. To prevent this, people stayed awake on *kōshin* nights. By the Heian period (794–1185) this custom was introduced to Japan and became widespread among the general public. The practice of staying awake on *kōshin* nights was referred to as *kōshin machi* (the *kōshin* wake). Because of the designation *saru* or monkey, the *kōshin* belief in Japan became associated with the Shintō god Sarudahiko no Mikoto and with the worship of the guardian deities known as DŌSOJIN.

koshirae

(sword mountings; also known as *tōsō* or *gaisō*). The parts of a Japanese SWORD excluding the blade; these generally consist of the *tsuka* (handle), *saya* (scabbard), and TSUBA (guard). The original purpose of the mountings was to protect the blade, but in time they became increasingly ornate and functioned as status symbols or as displays of authority. *Koshirae* may be made of metal, lacquer, leather, or textiles.

The *koshirae* of the long swords *(tachi)* preserved in the 8th-century SHŌSŌIN imperial art repository display metal and lacquer work of the highest technical quality. Metal pommels *(kashira)* are characteristic of these early swords. From the Heian period (794–1185), swords for use in battle were made with slightly curved blades, and these often featured black lacquer, not only on the hilt and scabbard but on the sword guard and other metal fittings as well. This type of *koshirae* was used by warriors and monk-soldiers through the Kamakura period (1185–1333). Further developments in sword shape occurred from the Muromachi period (1333–1568) on, and with these developments *koshirae* changed as well. Sword guards in particular became more elaborate and refined, followed by the development of other accessories, most notably the *kozuka* (small knife), *kōgai* (an awl-like instrument), and *menuki* (hilt ornament).

koshiro and nashiro

Hereditary groups of workers (BE) who, along with the lands they worked on, were considered the property of the imperial family, from perhaps as early as the 5th century up to the TAIKA REFORM of 645. The two terms seem to have been used interchangeably, but when a distinction is made, *koshiro* may indicate *be* designated for the support of an imperial consort, prince, or princess, and *nashiro*, would be *be* set up in the name of an emperor without issue. In both cases, they were usually taken over from local chieftains (KUNI NO MIYATSUKO) and assigned to members of the imperial family, constituting their main source of support. Many such *be* were located in the Kantō region far to the northeast of the main imperial power base in Yamato; all were administered by TOMO NO MIYATSUKO and thus some tended to be treated as the personal property of such men rather than of the imperial family. After the Taika Reform, the members of all these *be* were considered the property of the central government and were relabeled *kōmin* ("public people").

Kōshitsu Tempan → Imperial Household Law

koshō

(page or attendant). A title used during the period of warrior rule to identify personal attendants of major leaders. During the Muromachi period (1333–1568) it referred generally to those who attended to the daily needs of warrior lords. In the Edo period (1600–1868) it denoted specific personal attendants of the *shōgun*. About 50 *nakaoku koshō* (also called *omote koshō*) attended the shōgun, assisted in ceremonies, and ran errands in those parts of Edo Castle (the *omote* or "exterior," and *nakaoku* or "middle interior") where the shōgun handled affairs of state. Another 50-odd *oku koshō* assisted the shōgun in his personal affairs and facilitated movement between his personal chambers in the "middle interior" and those of his wife and ladies in the "great interior" (ŌOKU). The *koshō* were under the authority of the junior councillors (WAKADO-SHIYORI), were directly supervised by four overseers (*tōdori*), and generally were recruited from bannermen (HATAMOTO) families.

Conrad TOTMAN

Kōshoku

City in northern Nagano Prefecture, central Honshū. Kōshoku is known for its knitted goods, foodstuff, and machine industries, as well as for its carnations and Easter lilies. The more than 50,000 apricot trees in the southeastern section attract visitors in April. Pop: 35,715.

kōshokubon

("amorous books"). A genre of popular fiction of the Edo period (1600–1868) that dealt with the amorous affairs of the merchant class and the licensed pleasure quarters. Outstanding examples are SAIKAKU's *Kōshoku ichidai otoko* (1682; tr *The Life of an Amorous Man,* 1964) and *Kōshoku ichidai onna* (1686; tr *The Life of an Amorous Woman,* 1963). Besides Saikaku, writers of these mildly erotic books included NISHIZAWA IPPŪ, EJIMA KISEKI, and Hachimonjiya Jishō (d 1745). After 1716, with increasing shogunate control of published materials, the term UKIYO-ZŌSHI, or books of the floating world, came to be used in place of *kōshokubon*.

Kōshū Kaidō → Gokaidō

Kosugi Tengai (1865–1952)

Novelist. Important forerunner of French naturalism in modern Japanese literature. Born Kosugi Tamezō in what is now Akita Prefecture. He moved to Tōkyō in 1886 and entered college, but soon withdrew. In 1891, Tengai became a student of SAITŌ RYOKUU. He joined the magazine *Shinchō gekkan* in 1897 but later transferred to the staff of *Hōchi shimbun.* Tengai was elected to the JAPAN ART ACADEMY (Nihon Geijutsuin) in 1948 in recognition of important contributions made in such works as *Hatsusugata* (1900) and *Hayariuta* (1902), whose famous prefaces were among the earliest manifestos of naturalism in Japan.

Because of his pioneer role in furthering the concept and practice of realism, in experimenting with Zola's ideas, and in pointing the

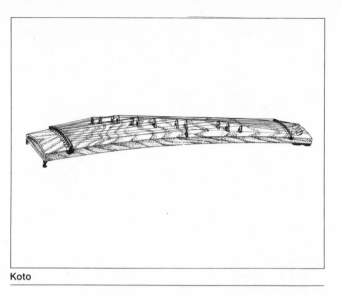
Koto

way toward fuller realization of naturalism in Japan, Tengai remains an important figure in literary history. During his naturalist phase, he attempted to divorce fiction from aesthetic and ethical utilitarianism; to pursue reality unencumbered by value judgments or set formulas; to create an objective style whereby the writer does not obtrude himself, his thoughts, or his feelings into his writings; to present characters dispassionately and uncolored by the author's likes and dislikes; and to portray detailed, starkly realistic settings.

How well Tengai actually accomplished his aims, however, is open to question. He never really followed French naturalism's demand for scientific experimentation through literature, or for art to become as acutely impersonal and analytical as science. His stylistic objectivism was mainly limited to depicting figures exclusively through their external aspects. Two-dimensional characters usually resulted, lacking any real internal or psychological development. This largely confined his realism to a copying of the extrinsic. Even his best works contain few deep views of society or humanity, and they frequently rely too heavily on coincidence and intrusion of fate. His plots contain many of the romantic elements and subjects dominating earlier Meiji novels. In practice, Tengai's literary strategy was to take a standard, complexly plotted Meiji melodrama and shackle it, through exposition, with hereditary and environmental determinism. Mechanically saddled with fateful "causes" (promiscuous parents, illegitimate birth, a theatrical background), his characters numbly acted out "effects" (infidelity, wantonness, rootless existence) until they reached a predetermined end (despair, death, loneliness). Nevertheless, Tengai's efforts were an improvement over those of most earlier writers.

Thomas E. SWANN

Kotani Kimi (1901–1971)

Cofounder and leader of REIYŪKAI, a lay religious organization. Born in the city of Miura, Kanagawa Prefecture. First married at age 17, she was widowed soon thereafter and moved to Tōkyō, where she worked as a maid. In 1924 she married Kotani Yasukichi (1895–1929). She began to receive religious instruction from his brother, Kubo Kakutarō (1892–1944; his name had been changed to Kubo by adoption), and she and the two brothers founded Reiyūkai in 1925. Kubo served as the group's director until his death in 1944, while she served as president. She assumed complete control of the organization upon Kubo's death and led it until her own death in 1971. A highly charismatic figure, Kotani became known for her successful proselytizing efforts in the 1930s and 1940s and for her faith-healing activities. She taught that suffering arises from moral deficiencies and neglect of ancestral spirits and that genuine repentance can lead to worldly benefits, including healing. Socially and politically conservative, she advocated preservation of the values of the traditional Japanese family system.

Helen HARDACRE

koto

Thirteen-stringed half-tube (semicylindrical) plucked zither. The earliest *koto* (*yamatogoto* or *wagon*) had only five strings, and was about three feet long. A sixth string was added in the Nara period (710–794). The thirteen-stringed *koto,* modeled on the Chinese

Kotohira Shrine

The main hall of the shrine. The present structure dates from the Meiji period (1868–1912).

zheng (cheng), and about six feet long, also dates from Nara times, and under the name gakusō was and is used in the court music ensemble. Starting in the late 15th century there was a series of new schools of solo koto (see SŌKYOKU). The koto is made of paulownia wood, has movable bridges for each string (and many tunings), and is played with small picks on the thumb and first two fingers of the right hand (the left meanwhile may raise the pitch of strings or modify the tone). There are special tablatures, the oldest extant being preserved in a 10th-century collection, Kinkafu. See also MUSICAL INSTRUMENTS; GAGAKU; SHICHIGENKIN.

David B. WATERHOUSE

kotobagaki

(headnotes). Prefatory notes to WAKA poems found in both imperially commissioned anthologies and private collections of verse. Intended to explain the poem's theme or the circumstances of its composition, kotobagaki were sometimes elaborate, fictional narratives, apparently written by someone other than the poet. Certain uta monogatari (poem tales) may have developed from extended kotobagaki and their poems.　Susan Downing VIDEEN

Kotohira

Town in western Kagawa Prefecture, Shikoku. Kotohira developed in the Edo period (1600–1868) as a shrine town around the KOTOHIRA SHRINE and is still a popular pilgrimage center. Pop: 13,876.

Kotohira Shrine

(Kotohiragū). Shintō shrine, popularly known as "the Kompirasan [Kompira Shrine] of Sanuki Province," in the Nakatado district of Kagawa Prefecture, Shikoku, dedicated to the deity Ōmononushi no Kami (see ŌKUNINUSHI NO MIKOTO) and to Emperor Sutoku (r 1123–42). The latter died in exile in Sanuki, where he had become a devotee of this shrine. Founded at the beginning of the 11th century, the shrine was first dedicated to Kompira Daigongen, a Buddhist-Shintō syncretic deity that had its origins in the Indian crocodile god of the Ganges, Kumbhīra. Because of the shrine's proximity to the sea, Kompira, who had been enshrined as a protector of a nearby Buddhist temple, was viewed as a benevolent deity who would look after fishermen and sailors. The deity enjoyed a great popularity during the Muromachi (1333–1568) and Edo (1600–1868) periods, and there are numerous offshoot shrines throughout the country. After the forcible separation of Buddhism and Shintō in 1868, the syncretic Kompira Daigongen was reidentified as the purely Shintō deity Ōmononushi no Kami who was described in the 8th-century chronicle KOJIKI as the god who had "come over, illuminating the sea." The annual festival is held on 10 October. See also HONJI SUIJAKU.　Stanley WEINSTEIN

kōtō jogakkō

Girls' secondary schools of the period from the late 19th century to just after World War II. The term means, literally, girls' high school, but the schools were actually counterparts of the middle schools

(chūgakkō) for boys (see ELEMENTARY AND SECONDARY EDUCATION). The earliest were the Tōkyō Girls' High School (Tōkyō Jogakkō), founded in 1872, and the Girls' High School attached to the Tōkyō Women's Normal School (Tōkyō Joshi Shihan Gakkō; now OCHANOMIZU WOMEN'S UNIVERSITY), founded in 1882. Other schools soon appeared throughout the country but, owing to the government's relative indifference to girls' education, the great majority of these were privately operated (see MISSION SCHOOLS). In 1899 the Directive on Girls' High Schools (Kōtō Jogakkō Rei) provided for the establishment of a secondary education system for girls. All primary school graduates were eligible for entrance, and the course of study was four to five years. Yet education there was designed primarily to make each student a "good wife and wise mother" (ryōsai kembo). Now, since 1947, coeducation has become the norm in public schools (see EDUCATION, FUNDAMENTAL LAW OF). See also WOMEN'S EDUCATION.　Etō Kyōji

Kōtoku, Emperor (597–654)

The 36th sovereign (tennō) in the traditional count (which includes several nonhistorical emperors); reigned 645–654. Kōtoku succeeded his sister Empress Kōgyoku (see SAIMEI, EMPRESS) with the support of his cousin, Prince Naka no Ōe (later Emperor TENJI) and Nakatomi no Kamatari (later FUJIWARA NO KAMATARI). He transferred his residence from Asuka (now Nara Prefecture) to Naniwa (now Ōsaka) and ordered work begun on the TAIKA REFORM, which was enacted the following year. Throughout his reign, policies were determined by Naka no Ōe and Kamatari; in addition to far-reaching reforms in government, land tenure, and taxation, relations with Korea and China were strengthened. Kōtoku eventually fell out with the prince, however, and, after the prince moved back to Asuka, Kōtoku died alone and forgotten in Naniwa.

KITAMURA Bunji

Kōtoku Shūsui (1871–1911)

Meiji-period (1868–1912) socialist and anarchist leader. Kōtoku Shūsui (real name Kōtoku Denjirō) was born in Nakamura, a small town in the rural Hata district of Kōchi Prefecture, on 4 November 1871. The son of a dry goods merchant, Kōtoku developed an early interest in the FREEDOM AND PEOPLE'S RIGHTS MOVEMENT. Having studied in the Confucian academy of Kido Mei, he went to Tōkyō to pursue his studies of English and to support the popular rights cause. Like other supporters of the Liberal Party (JIYŪTŌ), he was expelled from Tōkyō under the new PEACE PRESERVATION LAW OF 1887. He went to Ōsaka and became a boarding student in the home of NAKAE CHŌMIN, the popular rights advocate, the following year.

One year after graduating from the Kokumin Eigakkai, a Tōkyō school of English, Kōtoku began to write for a series of newspapers that included the Jiyū shimbun and the YOROZU CHŌHŌ. By the late 1890s his dissatisfaction with the course of Japanese development led to an interest in social problems, and in 1898 he joined KATAYAMA SEN and Murai Tomoyoshi (1861–1944) in the newly founded SHAKAI SHUGI KENKYŪKAI (Society for the Study of Socialism). In 1901 Kōtoku, Katayama, and ABE ISOO formed the SHAKAI MINSHUTŌ, Japan's first socialist-democratic party, which was quickly outlawed by the government. In the same year Kōtoku published his first major book, Nijisseiki no kaibutsu teikoku shugi (1901, Imperialism: The Specter of the Twentieth Century), and in 1903 he published Shakai shugi shinzui (The Quintessence of Socialism), which remained the leading exposition of socialism written in Japan prior to World War I.

Faced with the growing threat of war with Russia that followed the Boxer Rebellion in China, Kōtoku joined UCHIMURA KANZŌ and other writers on the staff of the Yorozu chōhō in a pacifist campaign. When the Yorozu chōhō deserted its antiwar stance, Kōtoku resigned his position and organized the weekly HEIMIN SHIMBUN, through which he continued to speak out against the RUSSO-JAPANESE WAR (1904–05). It was in this paper that he and fellow socialist SAKAI TOSHIHIKO published the first Japanese translation of Karl Marx's Communist Manifesto in the autumn of 1904. Prosecuted for violations of the PRESS ORDINANCE OF 1875, Kōtoku was imprisoned for five months in 1905. A period of intense study in prison, followed by a six-month stay in the United States (where he experienced the catastrophic San Francisco earthquake of 1906) convinced Kōtoku to abandon his former parliamentary strategy for an anarchist-syndicalist position. Back in Japan Kōtoku advocated "direct action" and a "general strike" of workers as a means of bypassing parliamentary politics. In 1907 he brought his program to the floor of the second convention of the recently organized JAPAN SO-CIALIST PARTY. Although rejected by the majority, Kōtoku's "direct action" stand split the party, and his insistence that the party remove from its platform its commitment to work "within the limits of the law" brought on the forced dissolution of the party at the hands of the SAIONJI KIMMOCHI cabinet.

After 1907, Kōtoku's commitment to "direct action" made him a source of inspiration for those who sought radical solutions to Japan's economic and social problems. At the same time, increased government pressures against those harboring "dangerous thoughts" resulted in escalating confrontations between left-wing activists and the police. In the wake of the RED FLAG INCIDENT OF 1908, in which several of Kōtoku's followers were arrested and imprisoned for parading in Tōkyō with flags inscribed with "Anarchism" and "Anarchist Communism," a group of young radicals, including KANNO SUGA, Kōtoku's common-law wife, began to plot actively the assassination of the Meiji emperor. Although only peripherally involved in the plot, Kōtoku was arrested and brought to trial for high treason in 1910. On 18 January 1911, Kōtoku and 23 of his fellow defendants were found guilty of the crime of lese majesty and sentenced to death. Six days later Kōtoku was hanged at Ichigaya Prison. Eleven of the other 23 were also actually executed. (See HIGH TREASON INCIDENT OF 1910.)

An outspoken critic of his times, Kōtoku reflected the intellectual and emotional turmoil common to Meiji thinkers and activists who tried to transform the Japanese tradition in order to use it for new political ends. Vilified in the prewar period as Japan's arch traitor, Kōtoku has been resurrected in the post-World War II years by the Japanese left as the nation's leading symbol of unflinching self-sacrifice and unmitigated opposition to an absolutist government that destroyed human dignity and freedom.

🔲——Kōtoku Shūsui, *Kōtoku Shūsui zenshū* (Meiji Bunken, 1968–72). Itoya Toshio, *Kōtoku Shūsui kenkyū* (1967). Kanzaki Kiyoshi, *Jitsuroku Kōtoku Shūsui* (1971). Nishio Yōtarō, *Kōtoku Shūsui* (1966). F. G. Notehelfer, *Kōtoku Shūsui: Portrait of a Japanese Radical* (1971). Tanaka Sōgorō, *Kōtoku Shūsui: Ichi kakumeika no shisō to shōgai* (1955). **F. G. NOTEHELFER**

Kōtō Ward

(Kōtō Ku). One of the 23 wards of Tōkyō. Between the rivers Sumidagawa and Arakawa. Nearly destroyed twice, once during the Tōkyō Earthquake of 1923 and once during World War II, Kōtō Ward recovered each time to become a busy commercial and industrial district. Principal industries are metal, machinery, chemical, foodstuff, shipbuilding, and lumber. Pop: 362,170.

kotowaza → proverbs

kotoyōka

("small eighth day"). Annual ceremonies of agrarian origin held on the 8th day of the 2nd and 12th months. Originally entailing a period of abstinence during which temporary lodgings *(yorishiro)* were set up to receive beneficent Shintō spirits, *kotoyōka* was later transformed into a ceremonial warding off of evil deities like the god of epidemic disease (Ekijin). The initial ceremony is called *koto hajime* and the final ceremony *koto osame*. Rites vary widely, but in the Kantō area woven baskets are placed atop poles, their meshes *(me)* thought to prevent visitations by HITOTSUME KOZŌ, goblins with one eye *(me)*. As in the SETSUBUN ceremony, *kotoyōka* may include placing a sprig of holly adorned with the head of a sardine over doors and windows. HARI KUYŌ, a ceremony to honor used sewing needles, is observed on the same day. **INOKUCHI Shōji**

kouta

("short songs"). Also known as Edo *kouta*. A type of popular song with SHAMISEN accompaniment. To be distinguished from Edo NAGAUTA ("Edo long songs"), the most important kind of KABUKI MUSIC. Edo *nagauta*, Edo *kouta*, such related short-song forms as *ogiebushi*, *hauta* and *utazawa*, and even other types of Edo kabuki music, are sometimes described collectively as Edo *uta*, "Edo songs," to distinguish them from Kamigata *uta*, the various chamber and stage song types associated with the Ōsaka-Kyōto region.

The Edo *kouta* has antecedents going back to the 16th century; but, like *utazawa*, it derives immediately from *hauta*, a *shamisen* song type which flourished first in the Fukagawa district of Edo (now Tōkyō) in the earlier 19th century, and was performed mainly by GEISHA. As compared with *utazawa*, *kouta* often have an instrumental postlude (instead of a prelude), the *shamisen* is plucked with the fingernails instead of with a plectrum, there is more emphasis on the *shamisen* part, the pitch is higher, and the music is too fast for dancing.

Edo *kouta* of the mid-19th century were often performed by singers of KIYOMOTO-BUSHI, who left their own imprint on its style; but in the early part of the Meiji period (1868–1912) separate lines of *kouta* singers were established by one Kumame, and her male successor Masajusai (b 1839; succeeded 1875 or 1876). After Masajusai's death the interest of literati such as OZAKI KŌYŌ (1867–1903), NAGAI KAFŪ (1879–1959), SASAKI NOBUTSUNA (1872–1963), and KUBOTA MANTARŌ (1889–1963), and the composer Yamada Shōtarō (1899–1970) helped to give new directions to the genre. At present Edo *kouta* are sung especially by geisha; and there are many professional singers, of whom the best known in this century are probably Tade Kochō (1869–1958), Kasuga Toyo (1881–1962), Motoki Sui (1888–1979), and Gotō Ichimaru (b 1906).

🔲——Yuasa Chikusanjin, *Kouta kenkyū* (1921). Victor Records, *Kamigata uta, Edo uta,* vol 11 of *Hōgaku taikei* (Chikuma Shobō and Japan Victor Co, 1971). **David B. WATERHOUSE**

kōwaka

A genre of dramatic ballads dating from the 15th century, also known as *kōwaka-mai* (*kōwaka* dances) and *mai-mai* (dances) but usually called after the child-name of Momonoi Kōwakamaru Naoaki (1403–80), who is traditionally regarded as their originator. They consist mainly of accounts of military episodes from warrior tales such as the HEIKE MONOGATARI (Tale of the Heike), recited to a musical chant. *Kōwaka* was connected with NŌ and other medieval entertainments, and provided material for later literary and dramatic works. There are 36 pieces in the traditional repertoire, but 50 extant texts, called *mai no hon* (dance books), are now known. Most of these deal with the TAIRA–MINAMOTO WAR of 1180 to 1185 (many of them with the great hero MINAMOTO NO YOSHITSUNE). Several deal with the vendetta of the Soga brothers (see SOGA MONOGATARI). Of the remainder, a few are set in other periods of Japanese history and one in ancient China.

Kōwakamaru is said to have been a musical prodigy as a child. He developed a type of music which incorporated other contemporary styles—e.g., musical recitations of the *Heike monogatari, kusemai,* and *shōmyō* Buddhist chant—and sang ballads to this new kind of music. His texts kept the original literary embellishment and occasional parts in an irregular meter, but many were also adorned with Buddhist allusions. Tradition has it that he wrote most of the pieces at the command of the retired emperor Go-Komatsu (1377–1433). What is certain is that, at its height in the late 16th and 17th centuries, *kōwaka* ranked with Nō in its popularity among the military class, and was similarly patronized by such figures as ODA NOBUNAGA, TOKUGAWA IEYASU, and his son Hidetada. It became largely forgotten by the end of the 17th century, and its main line in the province of Echizen (modern Fukui Prefecture) disappeared with the Meiji Restoration of 1868; but performances continued to be given by a few members of the Daigashira school, which had moved to the village of Ōe in modern Fukuoka Prefecture in 1582, and these were discovered by scholars in the first decade of the 20th century.

In spite of most of the names used for *kōwaka*, dance was probably a very minor element in its performances. Essentially these consist of three men standing side by side and reciting the texts in a highly stylized way to the beat of a fan or, at most, to the accompaniment of two small drums and a flute. *Kōwaka* pieces were composed in narrative form and are now declaimed either in chorus or in turn by the three performers. Following the terminology of Nō, these were originally called *tayū* (leader), *waki* (secondary player), and *tsure* (companion).

🔲——James Araki, *The Ballad-drama of Medieval Japan* (1964). Sasano Ken, *Kōwaka bukyoku shū* (1943). **P. G. O'NEILL**

Koyama Yūshi (1906–1982)

Playwright. Born in Hiroshima Prefecture; graduate of Keiō University; studied drama under KISHIDA KUNIO. His plays are uniformly set against a background of local color reflecting customs and manners of the Inland Sea region. With rich poetic sentiment he depicts the thoughts and lives of the common people. His later plays look closely at individuals who carry the scars of World War II. Two of his best plays are *Seto Naikai no kodomora* (1936, Children of the Inland Sea) and *Nihon no yūrei* (1965, Ghosts of Japan).

Kōyasan

(Mt. Kōya). Mountain in the north central Kii Peninsula, northern Wakayama Prefecture, central Honshū. On the south bank of the river Kinokawa. Kōyasan is a level uplifted peneplain surrounded by eight low peaks, including Jingamine (1,106 m; 3,628 ft) and Yōryūzan (1,009 m; 3,310 ft); it is covered with fine forests of cedar, cypress, and umbrella pine *(kōyamaki)*. The mountain is famous as the location of the temple KONGŌBUJI, constructed by the priest KŪKAI in 816, and the head temple of the SHINGON SECT of Buddhism; more than 110 other related temples are also located here. (The name Kōyasan is used to refer to Kongōbuji and the other temples here as well as the mountain itself; see following article.) It has long attracted a large number of pilgrims, but women were prohibited from climbing the mountain until 1872. It forms part of the Kōya-Ryūjin Quasi-National Park. Elevation: approximately 900 m (2,952 ft).

Kōyasan

Sometimes abbreviated as Yasan. General name for the Buddhist monastic complex of the SHINGON SECT on Mt. Kōya (Kōyasan) in Wakayama Prefecture; located about 39 km (24 mi) east of the city of Wakayama. With KONGŌBUJI as its head temple, Kōyasan has more than 110 temples and monasteries (Kongōbuji was originally a name for all the temples on the mountain, but in 1869 it was adopted as the name of a single large temple). Regarded as one of the most sacred places in Japan, Kongōbuji has traditionally been associated with KŪKAI, the founder of Shingon ESOTERIC BUDDHISM, and contrasted with HIEIZAN, the Tendai sect complex near the city of Kyōto, which centers on ENRYAKUJI.

Kōyasan is believed to have been a sacred mountain for ascetics even before Kūkai obtained imperial permission in 816 to found a religious community there, far from the capital of Kyōto. The main temple complex was built under the second abbot Shinnen (804–891). During the 10th century, Kōyasan was temporarily eclipsed by the temple TŌJI in Kyōto and also ravaged by fire (994). It was fully restored under Myōsan (1021–1106) and given patronage by the retired emperors SHIRAKAWA and TOBA, whose visits set a precedent for future sovereigns. KAKUBAN's reform movement around 1132 gave momentum to Buddhist studies at Kōyasan. As evidenced by Kakuban's attempts to integrate the belief in the Pure Land into Shingon teachings, Kōyasan at the time attracted a number of Pure Land Buddhists, who formed communities in the area. Called HIJIRI, these people included Kyōkai (1001–93), Myōhen (1142–1224), and Chōgen (1121–1206), who made Kōyasan a center of PURE LAND BUDDHISM almost rivaling Hieizan. Especially from the late 12th century, in the wake of the TAIRA-MINAMOTO WAR, aristocrats and warriors such as KUMAGAI NAOZANE and SAIGYŌ took refuge at Kōyasan, many of them joining the *hijiri* group. Also toward the close of the Heian period (794–1185), under the influence of itinerant *hijiri* (eventually called Kōya *hijiri*) the practice arose, first among the court aristocracy and later among the common people, of placing some hair or part of the ashes of a deceased person at Kōyasan. These Kōya *hijiri* went around the country, spreading Pure Land beliefs along with the cult of Kōbō Daishi (honorific title of Kūkai) and raising funds for Kōyasan; from around 1300, however, they adopted Jishū (IPPEN's Pure Land movement) with its proselytizing method of singing and dancing and eventually evolved into wandering entertainers or peddlers.

Kōyasan continued to flourish under the patronage of successive shogunates, although there were setbacks, such as the massacre of hundreds of *hijiri* and other members of Kōyasan by the hegemon ODA NOBUNAGA, threats of invasion by TOYOTOMI HIDEYOSHI (both in the late 16th century), and occasional fires (1521, 1888, 1926). During the Muromachi period (1333–1568), moreover, Kōyasan was frequently rent by internal dissension. The gyōnin (also known as *dōshū*), who, like lay brothers in Western monastic institutions, engaged chiefly in manual work to assist the clergy (*gakuryo* or *shūto*), gained power as the management of Kōyasan and its landholdings became more complex. They eventually constituted a third force (called the *gyōnin-gata*) after the *gakuryo* and *hijiri*, even encroaching upon the religious authority of the *gakuryo*. One of them, Mokujiki Ōgo (1536–1608), succeeded in establishing the temple Kōzanji in 1590 for the *gyōnin-gata* to counter the temple Seiganji, controlled by the *gakuryo*. At one point (1644–47) the temples

held by the *gyōnin* numbered several times more than those controlled by the *gakuryo*. In 1692, the *gyōnin-gata* were repressed by the Tokugawa shogunate, which exiled 627 of their leaders and demolished more than one thousand of their temples. (The shogunate also forced the *hijiri* to merge with the Shingon sect and thus put an end to their movement in 1606.) The *gyōnin* challenge continued on a minor scale until 1868, when the three divisions were abandoned and Seiganji, assuming the name of Kongōbuji, became the head temple of the entire complex. In 1872 the ban on women's entry to Kōyasan was lifted (see NYONIN KINZEI; MURŌJI).

— Gorai Shigeru, *Kōya hijiri* (1965). Miyasaka Yūshō et al, *Kōyasan shi* (1962). Takamine Shūkai et al, *Kōyasan* (1980). Toganoo Shōun, *Himitsu bukkyō shi* (1933, repr 1959).

TSUCHIDA Tomoaki

Kōyasan Treasure House

(Kōyasan Reihōkan). Located at Mt. Kōya (KŌYASAN), Kōya Chō, Wakayama Prefecture. Built in 1921, it preserves and displays important art of the Heian (794–1185) and Kamakura (1185–1333) periods owned by the temples on Kōyasan. Its holdings include paintings, calligraphy, sutras. sculpture, and Buddhist ritual objects. The collection also contains copies of the *Issaikyō* (the entire Buddhist canon), writings of KŪKAI, letters of the warriors MINAMOTO NO YORITOMO and MINAMOTO NO YOSHITSUNE, mandalas, and portraits of priests. Several of the more famous paintings of the Heian period, such as the *raigō* triptych, which depicts the descent of the Buddha AMIDA to welcome believers into the Pure Land, are rarely on exhibition, but copies of some may be on view.

Laurance ROBERTS

Kōyō gunkan

A 20-volume military treatise dating from the early years of the Edo period (1600–1868), probably ca 1625. Focusing on the illustrious military careers of two warrior generals, TAKEDA SHINGEN and his son TAKEDA KATSUYORI, the work presents a picture of the accomplishments, battle tactics, and government practices of the warrior class *(bushi)* of Kōshū (now Yamanashi Prefecture). It is the oldest existing document to use the term BUSHIDŌ ("the Way of the warrior") in examining the psychology and ideals of the warrior class. As referred to in the *Kōyō gunkan*, bushidō describes a manly spirit which places importance on justice and impartiality and which values bravery while disdaining violence. The most reliable studies single out Obata Kagenori (1572–1663), a military strategist of the early Edo period, as compiler.

SUZUKI Eiichi

koyori

A string or cord formed by twisting thin strips of Japanese paper (WASHI). Also called *kanze-yori*. Koyori are traditionally used for binding notebooks, wrapping gifts, tying up Japanese-style hairdos, cleaning pipes, and so forth. They may be woven together and then lacquered to make items such as trays, cigarette cases, and pillboxes (INRŌ).

MIYAMOTO Mizuo

Kōyō Seikō Co, Ltd

Leading manufacturer of bearings. Founded in 1921 in Ōsaka. Benefiting from military protection given to businesses in the munitions industry, it expanded rapidly. Following World War II it temporarily suspended operations, but in the 1950s resumed production of bearings. Through investment in equipment and the introduction of innovative technology the company was able to improve its products, move into the field of machine parts, and increase exports and overseas production. Kōyō Seikō controls numerous production and sales companies and joint-venture firms in Southeast Asia, India, Canada, the United States, West Germany, England, France, the Netherlands, Sweden, Spain, Australia, and Central and South America. Sales for the fiscal year ending March 1982 totaled ¥137.6 billion (US $571.6 million) and capitalization was ¥7 billion (US $29 million). The head office is in Ōsaka.

Kōzaha

("Lectures" faction). Group of Marxist theorists who supported the JAPAN COMMUNIST PARTY line, as expressed in the seven-volume NIHON SHIHON SHUGI HATTATSU SHI KŌZA (Lectures on the History of the Development of Japanese Capitalism, 1932–33). In the 1930s the Kōzaha was engaged in a dispute with members of the rival RŌNŌHA (Labor-Farmer faction) over the nature of Japanese capitalism and of the coming revolution in Japan. The Kōzaha stressed the feudal character of Japanese capitalism, arguing that the MEIJI RESTORATION of 1868 had been an incomplete revolution and had resulted in the establishment of an absolutist emperor system based on a semifeudal land system. Therefore, the group asserted, Japan's impending revolution would be a "bourgeois-democratic" upheaval, aimed at abolishing feudal landownership and overthrowing the emperor system. In its dispute with the Rōnōha, which emphasized the bourgeois character of Japanese capitalism and claimed that Japan's coming revolution would be a socialist one, the Kōzaha published its views mainly in the journals *Keizai hyōron* and *Rekishi kagaku;* the debate was also covered in the periodicals KAIZŌ and CHŪŌ KŌRON. Suspended when members of both groups were arrested in 1937 and early 1938, the dispute was resumed after World War II by heirs to the Kōzaha and Rōnōha viewpoints and remains unresolved to this day. It has had great influence in Japanese academic circles, but in its original form, as waged by the Kōzaha and Rōnōha in the context of the global economic crisis of the 1930s, it was fundamentally a dispute over revolutionary strategy and tactics. See NIHON SHIHON SHUGI RONSŌ.

Kozai Shikin (1868–1933)

Novelist and essayist. Born Shimizu Toyoko in Okayama Prefecture, raised in Kyōto. She joined in early campaigns for women's rights with FUKUDA HIDEKO, then studied at Meiji Jogakkō (Meiji Girls' School) in Tōkyō and became a contributor, under her pen name Shimizu Shikin, to the pioneering women's magazine JOGAKU ZASSHI. In 1892 she married the agricultural chemist Kozai Yoshinao (1864–1934), a professor at and later president of Tōkyō University. Her stories and essays, which centered on contemporary women's problems, appeared mainly in *Jogaku zasshi* during the 1890s. Her works include "Koware yubiwa" (1891, The Broken Ring), "Kokoro no oni" (1897, The Demon of the Heart), and "Imin gakuen" (1899, The Immigrants' School).

Kozaki Hiromichi (1856–1938)

Christian leader and educator. Born in the Kumamoto domain (now Kumamoto Prefecture), he studied at the KUMAMOTO YŌGAKKŌ, where he came under the influence of Leroy Lansing JANES and was baptized. After graduating from the Dōshisha (now Dōshisha University) in Kyōto in 1879, he went to Tōkyō, where he contributed to the founding of the Reinanzaka Church, the Japan YMCA (1880), and the magazine *Rikugō zasshi* (1880), which later became an important forum for Christian and socialist thought. He became president of the Dōshisha in 1890, and from 1899 to 1931 he served as pastor of Reinanzaka Church. During these years Kozaki also served as chairman of the Japan Council of Churches and other Protestant associations. *Tokuzen Yoshikazu*

Kōzanji

Temple in Ukyō Ward, Kyōto, belonging to the Omuro branch (see NINNAJI) of the SHINGON SECT of Buddhism. The origins of the temple are not known. It is first mentioned in a biography of Son'i (866–940), the abbot of ENRYAKUJI, who is said to have retreated for three years to Toganoodera, another name for this temple. After it fell into disrepair, the celebrated MONGAKU, a one-time warrior who had become a monk to repent the accidental killing of his lover, sought to restore the temple, but died before he could do so. Mongaku entrusted the task to the great KEGON SECT scholar MYŌE, who succeeded in obtaining a decree from the retired emperor Go-Toba (r 1183–98) authorizing the reconstruction of the temple. This was accomplished under Myōe's supervision. Kōben chose the name Kōzanji (Temple of the High Mountain) from a well-known line in the sutra *Kegonkyō* (Skt: *Avataṃsaka*). The temple became a center for both Kegon and Shingon scholarship. The temple fortunes began to decline after the Ōnin War (1467–77), but subsequently recovered through the efforts of three well-known military leaders, Oda Nobunaga (1534–82), Toyotomi Hideyoshi (1537–98), and Tokugawa Ieyasu (1543–1616), all of whom patronized the temple. Another major reconstruction took place in 1636, from which time many of the present buildings date. The temple is noted for its maple trees and tea garden, the oldest in Japan, which is said to have been begun with seeds that the Zen monk EISAI (1141–1215) had

brought from China, and for the CHŌJŪ GIGA (Scrolls of Frolicking Animals and Humans), a group of ink paintings, which is one of its treasures. *Stanley WEINSTEIN*

Kōzen gokoku ron

(On Promoting Zen and Protecting the Nation). A three-volume treatise expounding the legitimacy of ZEN Buddhism, written in 1198 by the monk EISAI, founder of the RINZAI SECT; the earliest Japanese work on Zen. Eisai had returned from China in 1191, bringing back the teachings of the Linji (Lin-chi; J: Rinzai) sect, and had advocated the revival of Buddhism through Zen practices. Although he quickly found a following among the warrior class, he encountered opposition from the older, established Buddhist sects, which denounced his teaching as heretical and urged the imperial court to suppress it. It was in response to these attacks that Eisai wrote his treatise. Drawing widely from the sutras, he explained the tenets of Zen Buddhism and asserted that Zen alone could protect Japan.

Kōzuke monuments

(Kōzuke *sampi*). Stone monuments in Gumma Prefecture (historically known as Kōzuke Province) dating from the 7th and 8th centuries. They are the Yamanoue (or Yamana) Monument and the Kanaizawa Monument, both in the city of Takasaki, and the Tago Monument in Yoshii Machi, Tano District. The Yamanoue Monument was erected by Chōri, a priest of the temple Hōkōji, as a gravestone for his mother; it is dated either 681 or 741, depending on how one interprets the sexagenary calendric dates (see JIKKAN JŪNISHI). To the east of the monument is a mounded tomb (KOFUN) with a corridor-type stone chamber. The Tago Monument commemorates the establishment in 711 of Tago no Kōri (Tago District), an event also recorded in the chronicle *Shoku nihongi* (797). The Kanaizawa Monument was erected in 726 to commemorate a pledge to the Buddhist faith taken by nine residents of the area. Although the inscriptions are written with Chinese characters, the syntax follows the Japanese language. They are highly valuable historical documents. *KITAMURA Bunji*

kū → emptiness

Kuan Yü → Kan U

kubō

A contraction of the honorific term *kuge no kata* (the character *kata* also being read *hō* or *bō*) and sometimes read *ōyakekata,* the word *kubō* originally referred to the emperor and his court. From the Kamakura period (1185–1333) through the Edo period (1600–1868) it was used by *samurai* to refer to the shōgun. During the Muromachi period (1333–1568) the term referred both to the Ashikaga shōguns and to their deputies in the Kantō region who were members of the Ashikaga family (e.g., Kamakura *kubō* [also called Kantō *kubō*]; KOGA KUBŌ; HORIKOSHI KUBŌ; see also KANTŌ KANREI). *Conrad TOTMAN*

Kubokawa Tsurujirō (1903–1974)

Literary critic. Born in Shizuoka Prefecture. Attended the Fourth Higher School (now part of Kanazawa University) in the city of Kanazawa. He participated in the small coterie magazine *Roba* and began to write critical essays. He was active in the so-called PROLETARIAN LITERATURE MOVEMENT of the 1920s and was imprisoned in 1932 for being a member of the Communist Party. His representative works include *Gendai bungaku ron* (1939) and *Saisetsu gendai bungaku ron* (1944), both critical essays on modern literature. After World War II, Kubokawa began to take a more historical approach to literature while continuing to write critical essays. His first wife, SATA INEKO, is also a writer.

Kubo Ryōgo (1920–   )

Theoretical physicist known for his early research on the statistical mechanics of rubber elasticity and for his later work in solid-state physics, particularly on magnetic resonance absorption. Born in Tōkyō, he graduated from Tōkyō University in 1941. After doing research at the University of Chicago, he became professor at Tōkyō

University in 1954. He served as dean of science from 1968 to 1971 and received the Order of Culture in 1973. His publications include *Gomu dansei* (1947, Rubber Elasticity).

Kubo Sakae (1901–1958)

Playwright, producer, novelist. Born in Hokkaidō; studied German literature at Tōkyō University. In 1926 he joined the Tsukiji Shōgekijō (Tsukiji Little Theater) and studied drama under OSANAI KAORU. Translating plays by such early 20th-century German dramatists as Kaiser, Toller, and Wedekind, he was considerably influenced by German expressionism. Kubo was active in the prewar proletarian theater movement (see PROLETARIAN LITERATURE MOVEMENT), and his staging gave subtle expression to leftist thought. Two of his best plays date from this time: *Goryōkaku kessho* (1933) and *Kazan baichi* (1937). During the war years his attention turned to stage production and theater studies. His major postwar achievement was *Noborigama* (1952), a well-received historical novel. He committed suicide in 1958.

Kubo Shumman (1757–1820)

UKIYO-E woodblock-print designer, writer, poet, painter, and craftsman in lacquer and shell work; a central figure in the development and production of the privately published prints called SURIMONO. The artist was born into the Kubota family and given the familiar name Yasubei. His father died while he was a child and he was raised by his grandfather. His first teacher was the poet and painter Katori Nahiko (1723–1782) who gave him the name Shumman, the first character of which he changed soon afterwards to prevent being taken for a pupil of the actor portraitist KATSUKAWA SHUNSHŌ. He studied *ukiyo-e* with KITAO SHIGEMASA and designed a few elegant prints in *ukiyo-e* style, most of them with a narrowly limited range of colors, in the late 1780s. He studied KYŌKA ("mad verse") with Rokujuen and eventually became a leader and judge in the Bakuro Group, designing numerous illustrations for poetry albums from the 1790s onward, to which he also contributed verse.

From the late 1790s he became increasingly interested in the design and production of *surimono,* his name or seal appearing on the works of TOTOYA HOKKEI, UTAGAWA TOYOKUNI, and other artists, in addition to his own. Shumman's son and grandson were said to have been printers, and perhaps he had some hand in their engraving and printing, since his prints display a delicacy and refinement of technique that surpass those of his contemporaries.

Shumman was a prolific painter, adopting the styles and subjects of the classical, *ukiyo-e,* and modern schools. His secondary names include Shōsadō (suggesting that he was left-handed), Nandaka Shiran, Hitofushi Chizue, Shiokarabō, and Kōzandō. *Roger* KEYES

Kubota, Ltd

(Kubota Tekkō). Manufacturer of cast iron pipe, agricultural and industrial machinery, housing equipment, building materials, and environmental control facilities. Founded in 1890 by Kubota Gonshirō and incorporated in 1930, Kubota is Japan's largest manufacturer of agricultural machinery, ductile iron pipe, and related equipment for supplying water and other utilities. Manufacturing operations are conducted at 20 plants in Japan. Kubota also has a subsidiary in Brazil and affiliates in Taiwan, the United States, Indonesia, Malaysia, Iran, Thailand, and the Philippines, engaged in the manufacture of agricultural machinery. International sales subsidiaries are located in the United States, the United Kingdom, France, and Canada, and sales affiliates in Thailand. Exports accounted for about 22 percent of the company's net sales of ¥536.2 billion (US $2.2 billion) for the fiscal year ending April 1982. The sales breakdown in that year was as follows: agricultural machinery 38 percent, pipe 32 percent, industrial machinery 9 percent, building materials and housing 8 percent, castings 8 percent, and other products 5 percent. The company was capitalized at ¥66.5 billion (US $271.6 million) in 1982. Corporate headquarters are located in Ōsaka.

Kubota Mantarō (1889–1963)

Novelist, playwright, *haiku* poet. Born in Tōkyō. Graduate of Keiō University. His first stories and plays were published in *Mita bungaku,* the organ (founded in 1910) of the Keiō University Department of Literature. By 1920 he had made his name as a writer. In 1932 he became director of the drama and music department of the

Tōkyō Broadcasting Station (now NHK), directing many radio and stage dramas. He was also a distinguished *haiku* poet. Kubota was a connoisseur of the lifestyle and culture of the old downtown area of Tōkyō (SHITAMACHI), where he lived all his life. His writing reflects in fine detail the pathos and humor and speech patterns of its denizens. His most important works are the novels *Uragare* (1917) and *Shundei* (1928) and the plays *Ōdera gakkō* (1927) and *Hanabie* (1938).

Kubota Utsubo (1877–1967)

WAKA poet and scholar of Japanese literature. Real name Kubota Michiharu. Born in Nagano Prefecture. Graduate of Tōkyō Semmon Gakkō (now Waseda University) where he later taught Japanese classics. Kubota early joined YOSANO TEKKAN's New Poetry Society (Shinshisha) and published in the magazine *Myōjō.* His many poetry collections contain both new-form poems (*shintaishi*) and CHŌKA; examples include *Mahiruno* (1905), *Tsuchi o nagamete* (1918), and *Kyonen no yuki* (1967). *Rohen* (1911), a collection of short stories, shows the influence of Japanese NATURALISM (*shizen shugi*). He was also a greatly respected scholar and published collections of criticism as well as commentaries on classical works such as the MAN'YŌSHŪ and the ISE MONOGATARI.

kubunden

(personal field allotment). The share of rice land granted by the central government to an individual in the land distribution system (HANDEN SHŪJU SYSTEM) under the RITSURYŌ SYSTEM that developed in the late 7th century. For male commoners (RYŌMIN) aged six years or more, the allotment was two *tan* (1 *tan* = about 0.12 hectare or 0.3 acre); for females it was two-thirds of that amount; for servants (KENIN) and private slaves (*shinuhi;* see NUHI) it was only one-third of the regular allotment for male or female commoners. Apart from government servants (*kanko*) and government slaves (*kannuhi* or *kunuhi*), who received the same amount of land as commoners, all grantees were obligated to pay taxes on the land (see SO, YŌ, AND CHŌ). These lands were distributed according to a census conducted every six years and were returned to the government for redistribution when the grantees died. By the early 10th century the *kubunden* system had decayed because of irregular enforcement of the law, gradual increase in privately owned lands, and tax and corvée evasion by the farmers. Most of these lands were eventually absorbed by private landed estates (SHŌEN).

Kubushiro Ochimi (1882–1972)

Feminist and Christian social reformer. Born in Kumamoto Prefecture, the daughter of a Christian minister; maiden name, Ōkubo. She graduated from Joshi Gakuin and in 1902 went to California with her parents. There she married in 1910 Kubushiro Naokatsu, (who became a Christian minister before his death in 1920). After their return to Japan, she joined in 1916 the KYŌFŪKAI (Japan's version of the Woman's Christian Temperance Union), led by her great-aunt YAJIMA KAJIKO, and became especially active in its campaigns against prostitution. As a member of the FUSEN KAKUTOKU DŌMEI she also worked for women's suffrage and was a major organizer of the 1930 Zen Nihon Fusen Taikai (All-Japan Women's Suffrage Conference). After World War II she continued to help lead the Kyōfūkai's campaigns against prostitution and for Christianity and world peace. Her autobiography is *Haishō hitosuji* (1973, Crusading against Prostitution).

kuchiei and kuchimai

A kind of miscellaneous tax added to the annual land tax (see HONTO MONONARI) during the Edo period (1600–1868). Although the rate varied from domain to domain, it was usually assessed as a 2- or 3-percent surcharge on the basic tax. When collected in rice it was called *kuchimai;* when collected in cash, it was called *kuchiei, kuchigin,* or *kuchizeni.* The tax originated in the Kamakura period (1185–1333) to compensate for loss or damage to tax rice during shipment. It was not until the late 16th century, however, that it became a common form of taxation. In the Edo period it became a regularized tax to cover the expenses of tax collectors' offices. The assessment of *kuchimai* and *kuchiei* was discontinued with the enactment of the LAND TAX REFORM OF 1873–1881. *Philip* BROWN

kuchinashi → gardenia

Kudamatsu

City in southeastern Yamaguchi Prefecture, western Honshū, on the Suō Sea. Once a flourishing port town and producer of salt, it now has chemical and heavy industries such as rolling stock, metal, shipbuilding, and oil refining. Pop: 54,804.

Kudaradera remains

Site of a temple affiliated with the Kudaraō family, descendants of the royal house of PAEKCHE who migrated to Japan in the 7th century. Located in what is now Nakamiya, in the city of Hirakata, Ōsaka Prefecture, the temple flourished from the Nara period (710–794) into the Heian period (794–1185). Excavations in 1932 and 1965 revealed that the buildings—a great south gate, central gate, eastern and western pagodas, lecture hall, main hall, corridors, and so forth—were arranged in the manner of YAKUSHIJI in an area of about 4 hectares (9.9 acres). It was further ascertained that the pagodas were encircled with stones and the main hall with rows of tiles. Recovered artifacts include numerous ROOF TILES, gilt bronze ornaments, and BUDDHA TILES.   KITAMURA Bunji

kudashibumi

A type of document used to convey orders from a superior official or office to a subordinate one. The kudashibumi originated in the Heian period (794–1185), replacing the more complicated fu stipulated by the YŌRO CODE. First used by the Controlling Boards (Benkan), the kudashibumi form came to be widely employed by the administrative office (MANDOKORO) of the Fujiwara regent's house (see REGENCY GOVERNMENT), the Retired Emperor's Office (In no Chō), and in temple, provincial, and estate (shōen) offices as well. Later, in the Kamakura (1185–1333) and Muromachi (1333–1568) periods, kudashibumi were most frequently used by the Administrative Board (Mandokoro) of the shogunate. Usually, kudashibumi had the word kudasu ("ordered") at the beginning of the text, but this form was not always followed. See also DIPLOMATICS.
          G. Cameron HURST III

kuden → kōden

Kudō Heisuke (1734–1800)

Administrator and medical doctor of the Edo period (1600–1868). The son of a physician in the service of the daimyō of the Kii domain (now Wakayama Prefecture), he was adopted by Kudō Jōan, a doctor of the Sendai domain (now part of Miyagi Prefecture). He served as a doctor of the Sendai domain from his station in Edo (now Tōkyō). There he studied Japanese and Chinese classics and became familiar with WESTERN LEARNING, the body of knowledge about European culture and science, through his friendships with KATSURAGAWA HOSHŪ, NAKAGAWA JUN'AN, AOKI KON'YŌ, and MAENO RYŌTAKU. His report AKAEZO FŪSETSU KŌ, in which he stressed the need for colonization of EZO (now Hokkaidō) in order to defend it from Russian encroachment, presaged the ideas of later advocates of national defense and northern development such as HAYASHI SHIHEI and HONDA TOSHIAKI.

kudzu → kuzu

Kuga Katsunan (1857–1907)

Journalist of the Meiji period (1868–1912). Born Nakada Minoru, the son of a Confucian scholar in the Tsugaru domain (now part of Aomori Prefecture), he was later adopted into the Kuga family. Katsunan was a pen name. He attended the law school (Hōgakkō) of the Ministry of Justice but left without graduating and became an official in the Meiji government in 1881. In 1888 he resigned in opposition to what he saw as the indiscriminate Westernization policy of government leaders eager to secure revision of the Unequal Treaties (see UNEQUAL TREATIES, REVISION OF).

In the same year he founded the newspaper Tōkyō dempō (Tōkyō Telegram). He discontinued publication the following year and started another newspaper, Nihon (Japan). In his editorials, known for their trenchancy, Kuga criticized the cliquism (see HAMBATSU) in the government and called for a nationalism based upon the united will of the Japanese people (kokumin shugi). As a result, more than 20 issues of the newspaper were suppressed by the government. He maintained close friendships with such people as MIYAKE SETSUREI. Kinji seiron kō (1891, Thoughts on Recent Politics) is his major work.
          TANAKA Akira

kugatachi

Also called kukatachi; kukadachi. A kind of trial by ordeal practiced in ancient Japan and recorded in the NIHON SHOKI (720). The process was quite similar to the ukeiyu ("hot-water vow"), in which a suspect was forced to take a small stone out of a pot of boiling water, and his guilt or innocence was determined by whether or not his hand blistered. Before the ordeal, the suspect prayed to the gods to bear witness. A somewhat similar practice, called yugishō, is recorded as late as the Muromachi period (1333–1568).
          G. Cameron HURST III

Kūge nichiyō kufū ryakushū → Kūge nikkushū

Kūge nikkushū

Full title Kūge nichiyō kufū ryakushū (Instructions on Monastic Life by Kūge). Journal kept by GIDŌ SHŪSHIN (pen name Kūge; 1325–88), a Zen priest of the period of the Northern and Southern Courts (1336–92). Of the original 48 volumes, only four chapters of excerpts survive. The excerpts cover all the years of his life, the earlier portions having been written in retrospect by Shūshin himself ·and the later portions by a disciple. The journal is useful for its information on the monastic and cultural life of the leading Zen temples (see GOZAN) of his day as well as on political events, of which Shūshin, as an adviser to the Muromachi shogunate, was a close observer.

kugyō

Also called kandachime. The highest-ranking officials at the imperial court in Kyōto during the Heian period (794–1185). Essentially, the title was restricted to officials of the third rank and higher (see COURT RANKS), but it was also applied to councillors (SANGI) who had not achieved the third rank. The term is a composite of two words: kō, which refers to the grand minister of state (dajō daijin) and the ministers of the left and right (sadaijin, udaijin); and kyō, which included all officials above the third rank, the great and middle counselors (dainagon, chūnagon), and the sangi. It was this group—comprising only about 20 men during the heyday of FUJIWARA NO MICHINAGA in the early 11th century—that governed Japan.
          G. Cameron HURST III

Kuhara Fusanosuke (1869–1965)

Mining magnate and conservative politician, whose Kuhara Mining Company eventually became Nippon Sangyō (Nissan), largest of the newer ZAIBATSU or financial combines that came into existence in the 1920s and 1930s. A native of the Chōshū domain (now Yamaguchi Prefecture), Kuhara graduated from Keiō Gijuku (now Keiō University) and joined the Fujita-Gumi, a mining company founded by his uncle FUJITA DENZABURŌ. In 1905 Kuhara purchased and modernized an old mine at Hitachi in Ibaraki Prefecture. Buying other copper mines, he formed the Kuhara Mining Company in 1912 and profited greatly from the World War I copper boom. The company's capital rose from ¥10 million in 1912 to ¥100 million by 1918, making it a major copper-producing firm. Profits were invested in new mines, zinc refining, lumber, electrical goods manufacture, and other ventures. However, the financial crisis of the 1920s slowed company growth, and Kuhara turned to politics. In 1928 Kuhara transferred company management to AIKAWA YOSHISUKE, who reorganized the administration to create Nissan. Nissan cooperated with the military in the development of Manchuria.

Kuhara was a major contributor to the RIKKEN SEIYŪKAI party, and in 1928 he was named communications minister in the TANAKA

GIICHI cabinet, in spite of vigorous opposition from Education Minister MIZUNO RENTARŌ, who resigned in protest. Kuhara strongly supported the movement in 1931 to form a coalition government with the rival party, the RIKKEN MINSEITŌ; he also favored an expansionist policy on the Asian continent and was suspected of ties with the military. In 1940, as president of the Seitō faction of the Seiyūkai, he played a willing role in its absorption by the IMPERIAL RULE ASSISTANCE ASSOCIATION. Kuhara was purged by Occupation authorities, but after 1951 he became active in negotiations for reopening relations with China. _Richard RICE_

kuiawase

The term _kuiawase_ (also called _tabeawase;_ literally, "eating together") refers to combinations of certain foods traditionally believed to cause food poisoning or illness, and the prohibitions surrounding these combinations of foods. Although there were some local variations, taboos concerning such combinations as eel and pickled plum (UMEBOSHI), TEMPURA and watermelon, eel and watermelon, and crab and persimmon were widespread. Such proscriptions probably derived from the combined influence of Chinese medical treatises of the Tang (T'ang; 618–907) dynasty, empirical observation, and superstition. _ŌTSUKA Shigeru_

kuina → rails

Kuji

City in northeastern Iwate Prefecture, northern Honshū, on the Pacific Ocean. A castle town during the Edo period (1600–1868), Kuji is now the center of a thriving lumber industry. Dairy and stock farming are also important. The construction of modern port facilities in 1968 has led to the construction of factories. Pop: 39,016.

kuji

(literally, "public matters"). Term variously used to mean political affairs, court ceremonies, or legal proceedings but mainly to indicate a major type of tax under the SHŌEN (private estate) system of land tenure that prevailed from the 9th through the 15th centuries. Tax requirements for these _shōen_ were broadly divided into _kuji_ and NENGU (rice tax); the _kuji_ category was further divided into corvée labor (BUYAKU) and miscellaneous goods (_zōkuji_) of as many as 30 different types, including marine products, bamboo, cloth, and craft items. _Kuji_ taxes, levied mainly on independent landholders (MYŌSHU), were collected by estate proprietors (RYŌSHU) as well as by their deputies (_azukari-dokoro_) and the shogunate-appointed military governors (SHUGO) and estate stewards (JITŌ).

Kujigawa

River in Ibaraki Prefecture, central Honshū, originating in the prefecture's northern mountains and emptying into the Pacific Ocean south of the city of Hitachi. The port of Hitachi is located at its mouth. Scenic gorges are found on the upper reaches of the river and paddy fields along the lower reaches. Sweetfish (_ayu_) are plentiful, and there is good hiking in the surrounding areas. Length: 118 km (73 mi); area of drainage basin: 1,500 sq km (579 sq mi).

Kujikata Osadamegaki

(Official Provisions). Important legal code of the Tokugawa shogunate (1603–1867); issued in 1742, it remained in effect until the Meiji Restoration (1868). It was compiled at the command of the shōgun TOKUGAWA YOSHIMUNE by a group of commissioners (_bugyō_) under the senior councillor (_rōjū_) Matsudaira Norimura (1686–1746), and consisted of two parts. The first outlined administrative procedures and civil regulations in 81 articles; the second set forth criminal laws and penalties in 103 articles (popularly called the Hyakkajō, or Hundred Articles). The code, which was in principle secret and issued only to designated officials, served as a guide for commissioners in passing judgments in both civil and criminal cases. Although it was directed primarily at commoners in the shogunate's own domains (TENRYŌ), some of its regulations were applicable to lesser _samurai_ as well. The code was also enforced in domains held by the shogunate's direct retainers (HATAMOTO and GOKENIN) and was adopted, with some modifications, by several other _daimyō_ for use as their own domainal code.

Kuji kongen

(Origins of Court Ritual). Book on ancient practices and precedents of the imperial court (YŪSOKU KOJITSU); written in about 1422 and attributed to the noble and scholar ICHIJŌ KANEYOSHI. Drawing on such sources as the KEMMU NENCHŪ GYŌJI, it lists the annual events observed by the imperial court in monthly order and explains their origins and historical development. The work was highly regarded by scholars of later ages and was the subject of commentaries such as _Shūshaku_, by Matsushita Kenrin (1637–1703), and _Shinshaku_, by Sekine Masana (1860–1932).

Kujō family

One of the five houses (GOSEKKE) of the Northern Branch (Hokke) of the FUJIWARA FAMILY whose members were eligible for the post of imperial regent (SESSHŌ; KAMPAKU), the Kujō were descended from Fujiwara no Tadamichi's (1097–1164) third son, KUJŌ KANEZANE. His elder brother Motozane (1143–66) had earlier founded the KONOE FAMILY, and Kanezane took the name of his Kyōto residence as his family name. The Kujō were closely linked with the Kamakura shogunate, and after the murder of MINAMOTO NO SANETOMO, the regent HŌJŌ FAMILY installed Kujō Yoritsune (1218–56) and Kujō Yoritsugu (1239–56) as the fourth and fifth shōguns. The Kujō rotated in high, but increasingly meaningless, posts with other _gosekke_ courtiers throughout the medieval age and enjoyed extensive landholdings. After the Meiji Restoration (1868), the Kujō were given the rank of prince (_kōshaku_) in the new peerage. A Kujō became the chief consort of Emperor TAISHŌ and the mother of the present emperor. _G. Cameron HURST III_

Kujō Kanezane (1149–1207)

Also known as Fujiwara no Kanezane. Courtier of the Kamakura period (1185–1333). The third son of the imperial regent (_kampaku_) Fujiwara no Tadamichi (1097–1164) and an elder brother of JIEN, the scholar-priest, he founded the Kujō family (one of the GOSEKKE or five regent families), so named after his residence in Kyōto. In 1186 he was appointed _sesshō_ (regent for a minor sovereign) and five years later, _kampaku_. Kanezane attempted to restrain retired emperors (see INSEI) from intervening in politics and to reestablish courtier government, but in 1196 he fell from power because of the intrigues of the ambitious Minamoto (Tsuchimikado) no Michichika (1149–1202) and became a priest. He spent the rest of his life in Buddhist devotions, becoming a patron-disciple of HŌNEN. Kanezane was also a man of wide learning, a connoisseur of music, and an accomplished poet; more than 20 of his poems are included in the anthologies SENZAI WAKASHŪ and SHIN KOKINSHŪ. His diary, known as GYOKUYŌ (or _Gyokukai_), is a valuable source of information on the events of his time.

Kujū Kōgen

Grassy highland on the slopes of the Kujū Volcanic Group, west central Ōita Prefecture, Kyūshū. It is a lava highland, with abundant pumice. It is used for cattle grazing and hay production. There is a plan to transform it into a tourist attraction and dairy farming area. Part of Aso National Park. Elevation: 600–1,100 m (1,968–3,608 ft).

Kujūkurihama

Sandy coastal area in northeastern Chiba Prefecture, central Honshū. Situated on the Pacific seaboard. The offcoast seas provide good fishing grounds for sardines. Kujūkurihama Plain is located inland. Designated a prefectural natural park; numerous swimming resorts are located on the coast. Length: approximately 60 km (37 mi).

Kujūsan

Mountain in central western Ōita Prefecture, Kyūshū. The highest peak in the Kujū Volcanic Group, it is also the highest in Kyūshū. It is a lava dome, composed of amphibole and andesite. It is part of Aso National Park. Height: 1,788 m (5,865 ft).

Kūkai (774–835)

Also known as Kōbō Daishi. Buddhist priest of the early part of the Heian period (794–1185) and founder of the SHINGON SECT of Buddhism. Kūkai was born into a declining aristocratic family, at Byō-bugaura in Sanuki province (now Zentsūji, Kagawa Prefecture) in Shikoku. At the age of 18 he entered the national college in the capital with the aim of becoming a statesman but withdrew after a few years. He justified his action by denouncing Confucianism and Taoism and extolling Buddhism in a provocative work entitled *Sangō shiki* (798; originally titled *Rōko shiki)*. Kūkai then pursued his Buddhist studies wandering about the country as an itinerant hermit practicing meditation.

In 804 Kūkai sailed to China as a student monk. In Chang'an (Ch'ang-an), the capital of China during the Tang (T'ang) dynasty (618–907), he studied under Huiguo (Hui-kuo; J: Keika), the patriarch of esoteric Buddhism and returned to Japan in 806 a master of esoteric Buddhist teachings. In 809, with his assumption of the abbacy of Takaosanji (now called JINGOJI), a temple in the suburbs of Kyōto, Kūkai rose to eminence as a cultural and religious leader of early Heian society.

In 819 Kūkai initiated construction of a monastic center on Mt. Kōya (KŌYASAN) for the practice of esoteric Buddhist meditation. Along with systematization of the Shingon doctrine, the completion of the monastery on Mt. Kōya was Kūkai's major concern during the remainder of his life. In 823 the emperor SAGA (r 809–823) presented Kūkai with TŌJI, the most important temple at the southern entrance to Kyōto, which became the headquarters for Shingon Buddhism. From 832 until his death, he spent most of his time on Mt. Kōya. To this day it remains the object of pilgrimage for those who believe that Kūkai has merely entered into eternal *samādhi* (meditation) and is still alive there as a savior and teacher.

In addition to the common belief that, as the inventor of the KANA syllabary, he was the father of Japanese culture, Kūkai is remembered as the originator of the pilgrimage circuit of 88 temples on Shikoku (see PILGRIMAGES), a builder of lakes, and a wandering saint who engaged in severe ascetic practices. He was also known as a poet, calligrapher, sculptor, and lexicographer who compiled the *Tenrei banshō myōgi,* the oldest extant dictionary in Japan. He founded the SHUGEI SHUCHIIN in Kyōto, the first school in Japan to enroll students regardless of social or economic status, providing free meals to both teachers and students. Although Kūkai's popularity has somewhat declined in recent times, he is still regarded as a man of genius and of profound religious experience and thought. Legends concerning him abound in Japan.

The esoteric Buddhism that Kūkai introduced to Japan was especially fashionable in court circles in China at the beginning of the 9th century. It was the latest form of Mahāyāna Buddhism, having been recently imported from India. It emphasized yogic discipline leading to direct spiritual experience and was characterized by a rich symbolism and a highly complex iconography. The practice of esoteric Buddhism fascinated the Heian intellectuals, stimulating their imagination and refining their aesthetic sensibilities, thus contributing much to the spiritual and aesthetic foundations of Heian culture.

Between his return from China and his last years, Kūkai composed about 50 religious works centering on two principal themes: the superiority of esoteric Buddhism over all other systems of thought and religion then known and the essential teachings and practices of esoteric Buddhism. Among Kūkai's fundamental ideas is the assertion that by practicing Shingon Buddhism one can realize enlightment here and now. Two of Kūkai's most significant writings systematizing the essentials of his Shingon doctrine are *Sokushin jōbutsu gi* (Meanings of Attaining Enlightenment in This Very Existence) and JŪJŪSHIN RON (Treatise on the Ten Stages of the Development of Mind).

🐚——Mikkyō Bunka Kenkyūjo, *Kōbō Daishi zenshū,* 3rd ed, 8 vols, (1967). Yoshito S. Hakeda, *Kūkai: Major Works, Translated, with an Account of His Life and a Study of His Thought* (1972).

Yoshito S. HAKEDA

Kuki

City in northeastern Saitama Prefecture, central Honshū. A market town during the Edo period (1600–1868), it is now an industrial and residential town. Special products are pears and strawberries. Pop: 54,410.

Kūkai

Imaginary portrait in wood of Kūkai by Kōshō, a sculptor of the Kei school. Height 83 cm. Ca 1233. Tōji, Kyōto.

Kuki Shūzō (1888–1941)

Philosopher. Born in Tōkyō. After graduating from the department of philosophy of Tōkyō University in 1912, Kuki went to Europe in 1922 to study with Heinrich Rickert, Henri Bergson, and Martin Heidegger. Returning to Japan in 1929, he taught the history of philosophy at Kyōto University. He engaged in a phenomenological, hermeneutical study of *iki* (see IKI AND SUI), a key concept in Japanese aesthetics, and conducted philosophical investigations into various aspects of Japanese culture. Endowed with a keen sense of aesthetic sensibility, Kuki led a life which could be described as one of "aesthetic existentialism." He also attempted to study the notion of the "accidental," a concept little developed in Western existentialism, by relating it to the human emotion of wonder. Kuki's works include *Iki no kōzō* (1930, The Structure of *Iki*) and *Gūzensei no mondai* (1935, The Problem of the Accidental). See also EXISTENTIALISM.

TANIKAWA Atsushi

Kumagai Gumi Co, Ltd

General construction firm specializing in large-scale public works projects. Founded in 1938. The company possesses a research plant for the study and development of special construction methods and machinery. It is noted for its achievements in the construction of high-rise buildings and housing tracts. It has subsidiaries and branch offices in Southeast Asia, Australia, North America, and the Middle East. In the fiscal year ending in September 1981 total sales were ¥559.0 billion (US $2.4 billion), with revenue from public works projects and general construction projects each contributing half. In the same year capitalization was ¥17.2 billion (US $74.8 million). The head office is in Tōkyō.

Kumagai Naoyoshi (1782–1862)

WAKA poet of the late Edo period. Born in the Iwakuni domain, Suō Province (now part of Yamaguchi Prefecture). Kumagai studied *waka* composition under KAGAWA KAGEKI, visiting him often in Kyōto. In his forties he severed his domain affiliation and moved to Ōsaka to devote his time to writing and teaching poetry. Regarded along with KINOSHITA TAKAFUMI as one of Kageki's leading disciples, he elaborated his master's theories in such works as *Ryōjin kōshō* (1860).

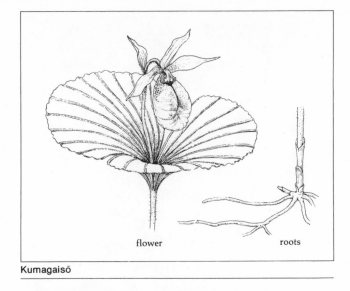

flower   roots

Kumagaisō

Kumagai Naozane (1141–1208)

Military commander who joined the Minamoto during the TAIRA-MINAMOTO WAR (1180–85). He took a leading part in the great Minamoto victory at Ichinotani (near modern Kōbe) in 1184. After the war Naozane became a disciple of the priest HŌNEN, patriarch of the JŌDO SECT of Buddhism. After a property dispute was decided against him in 1192, Naozane himself became a priest, taking the religious name Renshō. Naozane is best known for an incident recounted in the 13th-century war romance HEIKE MONOGATARI. Although tempted to spare the life of a young enemy, TAIRA NO ATSUMORI, Naozane was forced by the arrival of other Minamoto warriors to kill the youth. The story gives Naozane's remorse over this incident as the motive for his later entrance into the priesthood, but no extant historical sources support this tradition. A similar passage involving two other men occurs elsewhere in the *Heike monogatari*, suggesting that the incident is apocryphal. However, this moving story became the basis of such classic dramas as the *Nō* play *Atsumori* (ca 15th century; tr *Atsumori*, 1920) and the *bunraku* and *kabuki* play *Ichinotani futaba gunki* (1751; tr *Chronicle of the Battle of Ichinotani*, 1975).   Barbara L. ARNN

kumagaisō

Cypripedium japonicum. A perennial herb belonging to the group called "lady's slippers" of the orchid family (Orchidaceae). An indigenous Japanese species, it grows wild in mountain woods and sometimes in bamboo forests throughout Japan. The stem grows straight 30–40 centimeters (12–16 in) high from a rhizome, and fan-shaped leaves grow nearly opposite, though actually alternate. From April to May a flower stalk about 15 centimeters (6 in) high grows from the base of the leaves and opens a yellowish-white flower with a sac-shaped labiate corolla. The graceful shape of the flower and its handsome leaves have made it highly prized as a garden flower. It was introduced to Europe by the Swedish botanist C. P. THUNBERG. The closely related species *atsumorisō (C. macranthum)*, a reddish flower, is also widely found in Japan.   MATSUDA Osamu

Kumagai Taizō (1880–1962)

Medical scientist. Born in Nagano Prefecture; graduate of Tōkyō University. Kumagai is noted for his research on tuberculosis—its process of infection, its pathology, and the BCG vaccine. He served as professor and president of Tōhoku University. A member of the Japan Academy from 1943, he received the Order of Culture in 1952.   ACHIWA Gorō

Kumagawa

River in southern Kumamoto Prefecture, Kyūshū, flowing through the Kyūshū Mountains into the Yatsushiro Sea. It is the second longest river in Kyūshū after the CHIKUGOGAWA and one of Japan's swiftest. Its abundant water is used for irrigation and electric power and as industrial water for the Yatsushiro Coastal Industrial Area. The 18-km (11 mi) Kumagawa *kudari* (boating down the river) offers a memorable experience. Length: about 115 km (71 mi); area of drainage basin: 1,880 sq km (726 sq mi).

Kumagaya

City in northern Saitama Prefecture, central Honshū, on the river Arakawa. A post-station town on the highway Nakasendō in the Edo period (1600–1868), it is now an important business and transportation center in the region. Principal industries are nonferrous metal, steel, and electrical machinery. Of interest are the Uchiwa (fan) Festival at the Yasaka Shrine in July, the three-day Ebisu Festival in November, and the temple Yūkokuji, said to have been founded by KUMAGAI NAOZANE, a medieval war hero. Pop: 136,807.

Kumai Kei (1930–   )

Film director. His films, though fictions, are known for their documentary qualities. Kumai became interested in filmmaking while in college when he got a part-time job with a film company shooting on location near his university. After graduation he joined NIKKATSU CORPORATION where he assisted Hisamatsu Seiji, TASAKA TOMOTAKA, Abe Yutaka, and others on various film projects in the 1950s. His first project as a director was the fictional recreation of a famous crime that had taken place just after the war. Since then his films have been marked by their documentary realism. Two of his films, *Shinobu kawa* (1972, The Long Darkness) and *Sandakan hachiban shōkan: Bōkyō* (1974, Sandakan #8; Brothel #8) have won the Kinema Jumpō prize as best film of the year. *Sandakan hachiban shōkan: Bōkyō* was also nominated for an Academy Award.

Shinobu kawa was much praised in 1972 for its lyrical treatment of a pure old-fashioned love story that went against the prevailing movie trend toward excessive sex and violence. Kumai became seriously ill during the shooting of the film and was actually bedridden on the set. *Sandakan hachiban shōkan: Bōkyō* gained international attention for its star, TANAKA KINUYO, who won the award as Best Actress at the Berlin Film Festival. It was Tanaka's last film performance.   David OWENS

Kumamoto

Capital of Kumamoto Prefecture, Kyūshū. A provincial center since the 7th century, it flourished as a castle town with the construction of Kumamoto Castle by KATŌ KIYOMASA in 1601. It later came under the rule of the HOSOKAWA FAMILY. It was the site of a garrison *(chindai)* from the Meiji period (1868–1912) until the end of World War II. Principal industries are textiles, agricultural machinery, electrical equipment, and foodstuffs. The city is served by rail and land transportation and by an airport. Attractions are Kumamoto Castle, Suizenji Park, Tatsuta Park, the last with the grave of HOSOKAWA GRACIA, and the grave of MIYAMOTO MUSASHI in the Tatsutamachi section of the city. Pop: 525,613.

Kumamoto Plain

(Kumamoto Heiya). Located in Kumamoto Prefecture, Kyūshū. It extends from the diluvial uplands on the slopes of Asosan, a mountain to the east, where fruits and vegetables such as sweet potatoes are grown, to the alluvial lowlands that border Shimabara Bay to the west, where the largest rice crops in the prefecture are produced. The shallow beaches of the bay are rich in seaweed. Area: approximately 780 sq km (301 sq mi).

Kumamoto Prefectural Art Museum

(Kumamoto Kenritsu Bijutsukan). Located in the city of Kumamoto. One of the handsomest of the prefectural museums, it was designed by MAEKAWA KUNIO and opened in 1976. It has an active program of temporary exhibitions and special activities. Its permanent collection contains excellent objects of the Kofun period (ca 300–710) as well as contemporary paintings and prints. In spring and autumn the museum houses a special exhibition of objects from the collection of the Eisei Bunko in Tōkyō; each exhibition is accompanied by an illustrated catalog.   Laurance ROBERTS

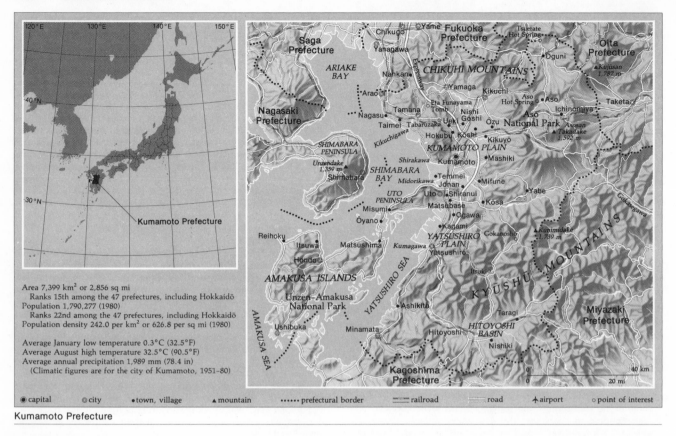

Area 7,399 km² or 2,856 sq mi
Ranks 15th among the 47 prefectures, including Hokkaidō
Population 1,790,277 (1980)
Ranks 22nd among the 47 prefectures, including Hokkaidō
Population density 242.0 per km² or 626.8 per sq mi (1980)

Average January low temperature 0.3°C (32.5°F)
Average August high temperature 32.5°C (90.5°F)
Average annual precipitation 1,989 mm (78.4 in)
(Climatic figures are for the city of Kumamoto, 1951–80)

● capital   ○ city   ● town, village   ▲ mountain   ······ prefectural border   ▭▭ railroad   ▭▭ road   ✈ airport   ○ point of interest

Kumamoto Prefecture

Kumamoto Prefecture

(Kumamoto Ken). Located in western Kyūshū and bounded to the north by Fukuoka Prefecture, to the northeast by Ōita Prefecture, to the east by Miyazaki Prefecture, to the south by Kagoshima Prefecture, and to the west by the Amakusa Sea. The southern and northeastern sections of the prefecture are mountainous, and the north central area forms a large plain which contains most of the population. Southwest of the capital of KUMAMOTO, the AMAKUSA ISLANDS extend toward the East China Sea. The climate is generally mild.

Known as Higo Province after the TAIKA REFORM of 645, it was strongly influenced by continental culture, as evidenced by the great number of ORNAMENTED TOMBS found here. The area fell under the control of a succession of warlords from the end of the Heian period (794–1185). Peasants and Christians from the Amakusa Islands took part in the great SHIMABARA UPRISING of 1637. The prefecture's present boundaries were established in 1876.

Agriculture remains the principal occupation. The main crop is rice, but a wide variety of fruits and vegetables are also grown, with mandarin oranges as the best-known specialty crop. Stock and dairy farming and forestry are important. Industrial development has been hampered by the prefecture's remoteness from major economic centers, and large factories are limited to a few of the major cities. Industrial development, however, has been accelerated in recent years.

Tourist attractions include ASOSAN, a large active volcano in the northeastern part of the prefecture, and the unspoiled coastal scenery of the Amakusa Islands, both of which are designated as national parks. The city of Kumamoto features a restored feudal castle, one of the largest in Japan, and the garden of Suizenji. Area: 7,399 sq km (2,856 sq mi); pop: 1,790,277; capital: Kumamoto. Other major cities include YATSUSHIRO, ARAO, and HITOYOSHI.

Kumamoto Yōgakkō

School established in Kumamoto in September 1871 by the Jitsugakutō, literally, the "Practical Studies" reform faction. Staffed by foreign teachers (all classes were given in English), its curriculum emphasized Western science. It was initially operated by the prefectural government but was later supported by contributions from the former daimyō of Kumamoto, Hosokawa Morihisa (1839–90), and other benefactors. Students were mainly from families of samurai

background. The best-known teacher at the school was the military instructor Leroy Lansing JANES, who took it upon himself to introduce his students to Christianity. Some 35 or 40 of these students were baptized, and in 1876 they formed the "Kumamoto Band" on Mt. Hanaoka outside Kumamoto City and signed an oath to preach the gospel "even at the sacrifice of their lives." Their action incurred the displeasure of conservatives in Kumamoto, and the school was closed later that year. The members of the band transferred en masse to the Dōshisha (now Dōshisha University) in Kyōto. Many of those who studied at the Kumamoto Yōgakkō, including EBINA DANJŌ, TOKUTOMI SOHŌ, UKITA KAZUTAMI, and KOZAKI HIROMICHI, went on to distinguish themselves as journalists, educators, and social reformers.   TANAKA Akira

Kumano

City in southern Mie Prefecture, central Honshū, on the Kumano Sea. Fishing, forestry, and horticulture are its principal industries. The city is the gateway to Yoshino–Kumano National Park. Pop: 26,062.

Kumanogawa

River in Nara, Mie, and Wakayama prefectures, central Honshū. It originates in the mountain Ōminesan, in southern Nara Prefecture, and flows south along the border of the prefectures of Mie and Wakayama to empty into the Kumano Sea at the city of Shingū. The upper reaches are known as TOTSUKAWA. A sharply winding river, it has carved its way through granite porphyry. The scenic gorge of DOROKYŌ is located on the Kitayamagawa, a tributary. Cedar and cypress forests grow along the river, and there are numerous hot springs. Length: 158 km (98 mi); area of drainage basin: 2,420 sq km (934 sq mi).

Kumano Sanzan Shrines

(Kumano Sansha). Collective name for three SHINTŌ shrines located in the Kumano district of Wakayama Prefecture. They are Kumano Hongū Taisha in Hongū enshrining Ketsumiko no Kami, that is, SUSANOO NO MIKOTO; Kumano Hayatama Taisha in Shingū enshrining Kumano Hayatama no Kami; and Kumano Nachi Taisha in Nachi Katsuura enshrining Kumano Fusumi no Kami.

From earliest times, Kumano, a mountainous area overlooking the sea, was believed to be a dwelling place of the gods (KAMI). With the propagation of PURE LAND BUDDHISM in the Heian period (794–1185), the Kumano shrines became popularly identified with the Pure Land. As a result, a large-scale syncretism took place at Kumano (see HONJI SUIJAKU). In their Buddhist context, the shrines were known as Kumano Sansho Gongen, and the enshrined *kami* were considered localized manifestations *(gongen)* of Amida Buddha and various bodhisattvas. They thus became a popular pilgrimage site, attracting many from the Kyōto court. Kumano was also a center of SHUGENDŌ mountain asceticism. In medieval times, the cult of the Kumano Sansha was spread by wandering monks (HIJIRI), shrine maidens (MIKO), and mountain ascetics (YAMABUSHI).

Miyake Hitoshi

Kumano Sea

(Kumano Nada). Inlet of the Pacific Ocean on the eastern coast of the Kii Peninsula (Mie and Wakayama prefectures), central Honshū. Extends approximately 140 km (87 mi) from the Shima Peninsula to the cape SHIONOMISAKI. The warm KUROSHIO (Japan Current) makes it an important fishing area.

Kumashiro Tatsumi (1927–)

Film producer. Born in Saga Prefecture. He aspired to be a novelist but was also interested in film, and after graduating from Waseda University in 1952, he entered Shōchiku's (see SHŌCHIKU CO, LTD) Kyōto studios as assistant director. In 1955 he transferred to the assistant director's department of the Nikkatsu (see NIKKATSU CORPORATION) movie company. He made his debut as a director with *Kaburitsuki jinsei* (1968, Life on the Front Row). It was a commercial failure, however, and stripped of his position, he worked for a while making television films. When Nikkatsu began producing pornographic films in 1971, Kumashiro worked in the genre and made such films as *Nureta kuchibiru* (1972, Wet Lips), *Ichijō Sayuri—Nureta yokujō* (1972, Ichijō Sayuri—Wet Desire), *Koibito tachi wa nureta* (1973, The Lovers Became Wet), *Onna jigoku—Mori wa nureta* (1973, Woman's Hell—The Forest Became Wet). His *Yojōhan fusuma no urabari* (1973, The Paper Lining of the Sliding Doors of a Four-and-a-half Mat Room) was chosen the best film of the year by Japanese movie magazines and praised as a masterpiece that transcended the genre of mere pornography.

Itasaka Tsuyoshi

Kumashiro Yūhi (1713–1772)

Artist of the Edo period (1600–1868). Real name Kumashiro Hi. Also known as Kamashiro Shūkō; he sometimes used the signature Yū Hi, an imitation of a Chinese name. Born into a family that served as hereditary translators *(tsūji)* for Chinese merchants in Nagasaki. Kumashiro studied painting, at first with Watanabe Shūseki, and later with Shen Nanpin (Shen Nan-p'in) from China, who taught him a new Chinese technique of painting directly from life. He is known for his use of strong colors in his paintings and also for his vigorous monochrome ink paintings. Among his many students were Mori Ransai (d 1801) and the priest Kakutei (d 1722). His *Nami ni u zu (Cormorants on the Waves)* is in the collection of the Tōkyō National Museum.

Kumaso

A tribe mentioned in early Japanese writings such as the chronicles *Kojiki* (712) and *Nihon shoki* (720). The Kumaso are believed to have inhabited the central and southern parts of Kyūshū. The name Kumaso is probably reflected in such Kyūshū place names as the former Kuma district of Higo Province (now Kumamoto Prefecture) and the Sō district of Ōsumi Province (now part of Kagoshima Prefecture). Some scholars believe that the Kumaso were identical with or racially related to the HAYATO tribe. The early chronicles contain accounts of a rebellion of the Kumaso against the YAMATO COURT, the best-known episode being their defeat by Prince YAMATOTAKERU. Although these episodes, which supposedly took place during the 4th century, are questionable as history, they are an important part of Japan's early heroic literature.

Kitamura Bunji

Kumazawa Banzan (1619–1691)

Important Confucian thinker of the Edo period (1600–1868). Born the son of a *rōnin* (masterless *samurai*) in Kyōto, Banzan entered the service of IKEDA MITSUMASA (1609–82), the *daimyō* of Bizen Province (now part of Okayama Prefecture) in 1634 but resigned in 1639. In 1641–42 he studied under NAKAE TŌJU (1608–48), founder of the Wang Yangming, or Idealist, school of Neo-Confucianism (see YŌMEIGAKU) in Japan, whose leading disciple he became. He reentered Mitsumasa's service in 1645 and was instrumental in bringing about domain governmental reforms. In 1656 he again resigned and a few years later moved to Kyōto, where he pursued a life of teaching and cultural study. In 1667 he left Kyōto, probably as a result of official disfavor and thereafter lived a life of semiexile in various provincial towns. Banzan's voluminous writings almost all date from the last period of his life. Most important are two collections of dialogues and letters (the *Shūgi washo*, primarily concerned with moral philosophy, and the *Shūgi gaisho*, concerned with social problems and politics); a treatise on contemporary strategic, political, social, and economic problems entitled *Daigaku wakumon* (Questions on the Great Learning); commentaries on the Confucian classics; and a commentary on the *Genji monogatari* (TALE OF GENJI).

Banzan was an eclectic popularizer rather than a rigorous or systematic philosopher. His thought owes much to Nakae Tōju and Wang Yangming, but he also borrowed from the Zhu Xi (Chu Hsi), or Rationalist, tradition of Chinese Neo-Confucianism (see SHUSHIGAKU). He believed that men are endowed with a faculty which enables them, through introspection, to choose and act out the right course of conduct in varying historical, geographical, and social circumstances. Thus he opposed rigid adherence to traditional Confucian ritual institutions such as the prohibition on nonagnatic adoption. Banzan also stressed the importance of empirical knowledge of the external world, particularly as it related to the samurai's conduct of administration, which led him to make acute diagnoses of many developments in contemporary society and to suggest specific remedial measures such as the resettlement of samurai on the land and the partial return to rice as the medium of exchange. His philosophical and social views influenced later Tokugawa thinking, particularly of the KOGAKU (Ancient Learning) school of the early 18th century, and of the samurai activists of the late Edo period.

▰——Kumazawa Banzan, *Banzan zenshū*, 6 vols (Banzan Zenshū Kankōkai, 1940–43). Kumazawa Banzan, *Daigaku wakumon*, tr Galen M. Fisher as "Dai Gaku Wakumon: A Discussion of Public Questions in the Light of the Great Learning," *Transactions of the Asiatic Society of Japan* 16 (1938). Gotō Yōichi, Tomoeda Ryūtarō, ed, *Kumazawa Banzan*, vol 30 of *Nihon shisō taikei* (Iwanami Shoten, 1971). Ryūsaku Tsunoda, Wm. Theodore de Bary, and Donald Keene, ed, *Sources of Japanese Tradition* (1958).

James McMullen

Kumejima

Volcanic island approximately 100 km (60 mi) west of Okinawa. There is an American radar base on the mountain Ōdake. The chief activity is sugarcane production, with some rice growing. The special product of the island is Kumejima *tsumugi*, a handspun silk with a distinctive KASURI pattern. Area: 58.7 sq km (22.7 sq mi).

Kume Kunitake (1839–1931)

Historian. Born in Saga domain (now part of Saga Prefecture). After studying at the Shōheikō, the shogunal academy in Edo (now Tōkyō), he returned to his native domain and assisted in administrative reform. In 1871 he joined the IWAKURA MISSION, the government delegation sent to Europe and the United States to observe Western institutions. In his capacity as private secretary to IWAKURA TOMOMI, the head of the mission, he compiled a five-volume account of the journey, *Tokumei zenken taishi: Beiō kairan jikki* (1878). He was appointed professor at Tōkyō University in 1888; he also assisted in the compilation of the *Dai Nihon hennenshi*, a comprehensive history of Japan, at the Shūshikyoku (now the Historiographical Institute of Tōkyō University). The publication of an article, "Shintō wa saiten no kozoku" (Shintō Is an Outmoded Custom of Worshiping Heaven), in the history journal *Shigakukai zasshi* (1891, reprinted the following year in *Shikai*) earned him the opprobrium of Shintōists, and he was obliged to resign from the university. Kume continued to write and lecture on ancient history at Tōkyō Semmon Gakkō (now Waseda University). In his scholarship Kume stressed the importance of studying old documents *(komonjo)*.

Kume Masao (1891–1952)

Novelist; playwright. Born in Nagano Prefecture. Graduate of Tōkyō University. With his classmates AKUTAGAWA RYŪNOSUKE and

KIKUCHI KAN, Kume participated in the literary coterie that published the magazine *Shinshichō*. The popularity of his play *Gyū-nyūya no kyōdai,* staged at the Yūrakuza theater in 1914, established him as a dramatist. From drama he turned to writing novels, and in 1933 he wrote the melodramatic *Tsuki yori no shisha,* which placed him on the road to becoming a best-selling author in the 1930s. Other novels include *Hotarugusa* (1918) and *Hasen* (1922). He is also known as a HAIKU poet, under the pen name Santei.

kumi

Neighborhood groups of households bound together by residential proximity and reciprocal aid. Consisting of from several to 15 households, *kumi* function as joint work and assistance subunits of the village. Together the members of a *kumi* plant rice, prepare for festivals and ceremonies, handle funerals, build and repair homes and roads, and often provide capital, credit, and especially labor for one another. In the Edo period (1600–1868), with the growth of cities, urban *kumi* called GONINGUMI were institutionalized to handle neighborhood functions. During World War II, the *kumi* were reorganized as *tonarigumi* or *rimpohan*. Different areas have alternate names for *kumi,* such as *tsubo, kaito,* or *keiyaku.*

NOGUCHI Takenori

Kumiai Chemical Industry Co, Ltd

(Kumiai Kagaku Kōgyō). Manufacturer of herbicides, fungicides, and insecticides. The largest domestic producer of agricultural chemicals, it is affiliated with the National Federation of Agricultural Cooperative Associations (Zennō). Its predecessor was a factory that produced agricultural chemicals, established in 1928 by a cooperative of mandarin-orange growers in Shizuoka Prefecture. It became an independent company in 1949 but retained affiliation with the Zennō, using local agricultural cooperative associations (*nōkyō*) as a basis for its sales network. Its herbicide, Saturn, and fungicide, Kitazinp, are exported to Southeast Asia and various Eastern Bloc nations. The firm controls subsidiary production companies in the United States, Thailand, and Brazil. Sales for the fiscal year ending October 1981 totaled ¥67.6 billion (US $292.2 million) and capitalization was ¥3.4 billion (US $14.7 million). Corporate headquarters are in Tōkyō.

kumihimo

(braiding). Silk cords or bands handcrafted by the weighted bobbin braid technique of the same name. The strands of *kumihimo* are interlaced obliquely in prescribed sequences to produce a wide variety of shapes and patterns. The number of component strands runs from four to several hundred, with each strand consisting of from 20 to more than 200 fine silk threads. *Kumihimo* is traditionally used as trim for amulet cases, ritual banners, priestly vestments, wrappings for sword hilts, and in armor as lacing, trim, shoulder straps, and belts. Today, well-dressed women use it in the form of the *obidome,* a decorative as well as functional band worn on OBI.

Kumihimo was highly developed as early as the 8th century, and examples have been preserved in the SHŌSŌIN imperial repository and in many Buddhist temples and Shintō shrines. One of the most complex types of *kumihimo* is known as *hirao*. *Hirao* are silk bands approximately 9 centimeters (3.5 in) wide and 2.4 meters (8 ft) long, color coded to denote the official rank of the wearer and worn with the formal male court costume, according to practices established in the 10th century.

The principal tools for the craft are leaded wood bobbins on which the component strand is wound, and, depending on the type of *kumihimo,* one of the following devices: *marudai* (circular-top stool), *kakudai* (square-top stool with overhead device), *takadai* (sit-in interlace loom), or *ayatakedai* (warp interlink loom). Though the exact nature of the technique employed in ancient times is not known, it is likely that similar implements were used.

📖 ——Dōmyō Shimbei, *Himo* (1963, 1973). Jules and Kaethe Kliot, *Kumihimo* (1977). Shōsōin Jimusho, *Shōsōin no kumihimo* (1973). Masako Kinoshita, "Kumihimo," in *Shuttle, Spindle and Dyepot* (Winter 1977; Summer 1980). Masako KINOSHITA

Kumoi Tatsuo (1844–1870)

Political activist of the Edo (1600–1868) and Meiji (1868–1912) periods; real name, Kojima Moriyoshi. A *samurai* of the Yonezawa domain (now part of Yamagata Prefecture), Kumoi was sent to Edo (now Tōkyō), where he studied Zhu Xi (Chu Hsi) Confucianism (SHUSHIGAKU). He represented his domain in the political maneuverings directed toward a conciliation between the Tokugawa shogunate and the imperial court (see MOVEMENT FOR UNION OF COURT AND SHOGUNATE). After the overthrow of the shogunate in January 1868, Kumoi served in Kyōto as an official of the new government. He was dismayed by the dispatch of punitive forces against those still loyal to the Tokugawa (see BOSHIN CIVIL WAR) and by the dominance of the Chōshū (now Yamaguchi Prefecture) and Satsuma (now Kagoshima Prefecture) domains in the new government, however, and he soon returned to Yonezawa to help form a league of northeastern domains (see ŌUETSU REPPAN DŌMEI) against the government. The coalition was short-lived, and in 1869 Kumoi set out again for Tōkyō, this time as his domain's representative to the Kōgisho, the newly established legislative body. He resigned shortly afterward and gathered about him samurai who were discontented with the new government. He came under suspicion of fomenting a plot to assassinate government officials in order to restore feudal government and was executed.

kumon

(official documents; clerks). A general term for documents, especially census and tax records, during the 7th and 8th centuries, when the RITSURYŌ SYSTEM of government was evolving. In the Heian (794–1185) and Kamakura (1185–1333) periods *kumon* came to mean the functionaries in noble houses and religious institutions who were in charge of drawing up and keeping documents and records. More specifically, *kumon* were one level of official appointed by the proprietors of private landed estates (SHŌEN) and specially charged with handling documents, assigning tax burdens and the like. See also KUMONJO; SHŌKAN. G. Cameron HURST III

kumonjo

Originally, departments within provincial headquarters (*kokuga*) responsible for keeping documents under the RITSURYŌ SYSTEM of government from the 7th century onward. By the middle of the Heian period (794–1185) *kumonjo* had come to refer to the offices in noble households, religious institutions, and private landed estates (SHŌEN) that were charged with keeping records. The most famous Kumonjo was that established by MINAMOTO NO YORITOMO in 1184 at his headquarters in Kamakura. He appointed ŌE NO HIRO-MOTO to head the office, known in English as the Public Documents Office, with Nakahara no Chikayoshi (1143–1208), Fujiwara (Ni-kaidō) no Yukimasa, and several other scholars working under him to handle political affairs. After Yoritomo had consolidated his control over the country, the Kumonjo was absorbed into the structure of the Administrative Board (MANDOKORO), sometime after that body was established in 1191. See also KUMON.

G. Cameron HURST III

kumosuke

Hired carriers of freight and palanquins on the major highways during the Edo period (1600–1868). The Tokugawa shogunate required the master of each post station (SHUKUEKI) to make available a specified number of porters for hire, and the quota was met by imposing a labor-service requirement (SUKEGŌ) on the local peasantry. When the service requirement was commuted to cash payment, the post stations turned to hired labor, often unsavory types who were hard to control. They were called *kumosuke,* literally, "cloud men," because they drifted like clouds with no fixed abode.

INAGAKI Shisei

Kunaichō → Imperial Household Agency

Kunaichō Shoryōbu → Archives and Mausolea Department, Imperial Household Agency

Kunashiri

Volcanic island approximately 20 km (12 mi) off the eastern coast of Hokkaidō. This long, narrow island is one of the Kuril Islands, separated from Hokkaidō by the Nemuro Strait. The fishing ports of

Tomari and Furukamappu are located on the southwestern side of the island. Ships used to run regularly between Tomari and Nemuro on Hokkaidō, but the island has been under Soviet occupation since 1945 (see TERRITORY OF JAPAN). The highest point is Chachadake (1,822 m; 5,976 ft), a composite stratovolcano. Area: 1,500 sq km (579 sq mi).

kuni ikki

Provincial uprisings of the Muromachi period (1333–1568); led by local landowners and warriors (KOKUJIN) against the military governors (SHUGO), they differed from other uprisings in their large scale and political goals. *Shugo* often lacked the territorial base and military following needed to dominate the provinces *(kuni)* to which they were assigned, and so they tried to enlist the *kokujin* as vassals. The aim of the *kokujin*, however, was to increase their own power in the province, and this they did by forming leagues (IKKI). Though *kokujin* leagues were normally temporary responses to military threats, they could be used to resist or even supersede the *shugo's* authority; such leagues were especially effective when they secured the support of the peasantry, who would cooperate in order to avoid taxation by the *shugo*. In 1429 *kokujin* and peasants rose against the *shugo* of Harima Province (now part of Hyōgo Prefecture) in the first important *kuni ikki*. The largest and best known occurred in Yamashiro Province (now part of Kyōto Prefecture) in 1485, when a similar league expelled the *shugo* HATAKEYAMA FAMILY from the southern half of the province and ruled it for the next eight years through a *kokujin* council (see YAMASHIRO NO KUNI IKKI). Scholars disagree on the contribution of the peasants and the motivation of the *kokujin* in these uprisings, but *kuni ikki* certainly hastened the rise of local political power, in which many *kokujin* emerged as autonomous territorial lords (SENGOKU DAIMYŌ). See also TSUCHI IKKI.

———David L. Davis, "*Ikki* in Late Medieval Japan," in John W. Hall and Jeffrey P. Mass, ed, *Medieval Japan: Studies in Institutional History* (1974). Kurokawa Naonori, "Chūsei kōki no nōmin tōsō: Tsuchi ikki kuni ikki," in *Kōza nihonshi*, vol 3 (Tōkyō Daigaku Shuppankai, 1970). Minegishi Sumio, ed, *Doikki*, vol 9 of *Shimpojiumu Nihon rekishi* (Gakuseisha, 1974). Nakamura Kichiji, *Tokusei to doikki* (rev ed, 1966).   Michael SOLOMON

Kunikida Doppo (1871–1908)

Poet and novelist. Real name Kunikida Tetsuo. One of the important forerunners of Japanese NATURALISM, he was nevertheless basically a romantic, known for his short stories depicting tragic incidents in the lives of common people. Doppo was born in Chōshi, Chiba Prefecture, and raised in Yamaguchi Prefecture. Illegitimate by birth, he was adopted by Kunikida Sempachi (said to be his real father). He enrolled in the English language department at Tōkyō Semmon Gakkō (now Waseda University) when he was 19 years old and already well read in literature. Three years later he was baptized by UEMURA MASAHISA and became a Christian. After becoming involved in an abortive attempt to have the college president removed, Doppo quit school and began working as a journalist and schoolteacher. With the outbreak of the SINO-JAPANESE WAR OF 1894–1895, Doppo joined the news staff of the KOKUMIN SHIMBUN as a war correspondent. In November 1895 he married Sasaki Nobuko, on whom ARISHIMA TAKEO is thought to have based his well-known novel *Aru onna* (1919; tr *A Certain Woman*, 1979), but their marriage broke up five months later. Deserted by his wife, Doppo wrote *Azamukazaru no ki* (1893–97, An Honest Diary), in which he expressed his mental anguish over his separation from Nobuko, an incident that was to color all his writing. Later he founded a small publishing house named Dopposha which went bankrupt after a few years.

Doppo made his literary debut as a romantic poet with *Doppo gin* (Doppo's Poems), a group of poems influenced by Wordsworth that appeared in *Jojōshi* (Lyric Poems), an anthology he coauthored in 1897 with TAYAMA KATAI and Matsuoka Kunio (later known as YANAGITA KUNIO). In these poems he sang his love of nature. Doppo enjoyed continuous success until his untimely death from tuberculosis in 1908.

Doppo's writing career can be roughly divided into three short periods. During the first period, 1897 to 1901, he attempted to discover the meaning of life in nature, producing such romantic short stories as "Gen oji" (1897; tr "Uncle Gen," 1956), "Musashino" (1898, Musashi Plain), "Kawagiri" (1898, The River Mist), and "Wa-

sureenu hitobito" (1898, People I Shall Never Forget). "Musashino" describes vividly the beauty of the forests, streams, and paths in Musashino which Doppo and Nobuko used to visit, while "Gen oji," based upon Doppo's own observations during his teaching days in Saeki (Ōita Prefecture), is a moving story of an old widower who brings home an orphan boy only to have the boy desert him. "Kawagiri" is a story about a teenager who leaves his country home to try to open a business in Tōkyō but who fails and returns home. He then plans to open a private school, but the very night before the school is to open, he abruptly disappears on a riverboat. In this novel Doppo demonstrates that the youth's deeds were all determined by fate: the threads of destiny led him somewhere he never expected to be. In his next work, "Wasureenu hitobito", Doppo expressed his sympathy for the plight of the poor people.

In the second period, 1901 to 1904, Doppo focused on man's fate in the universe; realistic elements became more pronounced, but the romantic undertones were not yet lost. "Gyūniku to bareisho" (1901; tr "Meat and Potatoes," 1964), from this period, is a short story presenting three different types of people—an idealist; a realist; and a third type who has only one earnest request of life, that is "to be surprised at the mystery of the universe." In "Ummei ronja" (1903, The Fatalist), Doppo's view of fatalism is well expressed by the protagonist who, confessing to a complete stranger that a supernatural power controls his fate, says, "An almost unbelievable mystical fate is playing within me." "Haru no tori" (1904; tr "Spring Birds," 1954) deals with a mute boy who loves birds and who, thinking he can fly like a bird, jumps from a castle roof and dies. In this story, Doppo's principle of "return to nature" is expressed vividly. Doppo emulates Wordsworth in idealizing the boy as embodying the true nature of humankind.

During the third period, the years 1906 to 1908, Doppo gradually moved toward naturalism. His representative works from this period are "Kyūshi" (1907, A Poor Man's Death) and "Take no kido" (1908; tr "The Bamboo Gate," 1964). "Kyūshi" is a short story, based upon an incident that Doppo actually witnessed, in which a destitute day laborer afflicted with tuberculosis commits suicide by throwing himself on the railroad tracks near Nishi Ōkubo in Tōkyō. As is the case with "Kyūshi," Doppo depicts the life of lower-class people with much compassion in "Take no kido." Although often called the forerunner of naturalism, Doppo produced these naturalistic works not because he himself desired to move in that direction, but because his romantic spirit gradually ebbed. Therefore, on the whole, it is perhaps fair to conclude that throughout his life Doppo was essentially a romanticist, for as the writer AKUTAGAWA RYŪNOSUKE once remarked of him, "the poet within him was eternally the poet."

———Collected works: *Kunikida Doppo zenshū*, 8 vols (Kaizōsha, 1930). Translations: Kunikida Doppo, "Gen oji" (1898), tr Sam Houston Brock as "Old Gen," in Donald Keene, ed, *Modern Japanese Literature* (1956). Kunikida Doppo, "Gyūniku to bareisho" (1901), tr Leon Zolbrod as "Meat and Potatoes," in *Orient-West* 9.3 (1964). Kunikida Doppo, "Haru no tori" (1904), tr Tsutomu Fukuda as "Spring Birds," in *Pacific Spectator* 8 (1954). Kunikida Doppo, "Take no kido" (1908), tr John Bester as "The Bamboo Gate," in *Japan P.E.N. News* 13 (1964). Hiroshi Sakamoto, *Kunikida Doppo* (1969). Toshihiko Satō, "Kunikida Doppo's Romanticism," *Literature East and West* 15–16 (1971–72).   Toshihiko SATŌ

Kunimidake

Also known as Ōkunimi. Mountain on the border of Kumamoto and Miyazaki prefectures, Kyūshū. The second highest peak of the KYŪSHŪ MOUNTAINS. Composed of Paleozoic limestone. Height: 1,739 m (5,704 ft).

Kuninaka no Muraji Kimimaro (?–774)

The most eminent Nara-period (710–794) sculptor of Buddhist images. The grandson of a naturalized Korean official, he supervised the making of the DAIBUTSU or Great Buddha for the temple TŌDAIJI in Nara, a project that was completed in 752. In 761 he was given administrative responsibility for the construction of the Tōdaiji itself; he retired from all official activities in 767.

Kuni no Miya

Capital of Japan from 741 to 744; situated at what is now Kamomachi Mikanohara in the southern part of Kyōto Prefecture. After the rebellion of FUJIWARA NO HIROTSUGU, Emperor SHŌMU decided to take the advice of TACHIBANA NO MOROE and move the capital from HEIJŌKYŌ (Nara) to the village of Kuni. Construction began, and the emperor moved to the new capital in 741, but in 744, before its completion, he decided to move the capital to NANIWAKYŌ. Foundation stones and tiles have been unearthed from the banks of the river Kizugawa in Kamomachi.   KITAMURA Bunji

kuni no miyatsuko

Local chieftains of the 6th and 7th centuries who governed small territories (kuni) under the jurisdiction of the YAMATO COURT. They were mostly former independent chieftains of prestigious local clans (UJI) who had submitted to the Yamato sovereign. In the early part of this period there were also local administrators called AGA-TANUSHI. It is unclear whether the agatanushi were subordinates of the kuni no miyatsuko and governed smaller territories or whether they were an older type of local administrator who were gradually replaced by kuni no miyatsuko, and the exact relation between the two has been a subject of debate among historians. Kuni no miyatsuko were often given the honorific cognomens (KABANE) kimi or atae. A few received the more prestigious cognomen omi (see UJI-KABANE SYSTEM).

At the time of the TAIKA REFORM of 645, new officials called kuni no mikotomochi or kokushi were appointed to oversee local administration. Between this time and the establishment of the KO-KUGUN SYSTEM by the centralizing ritsuryō government in the late 7th century, the older kuni no miyatsuko system was abandoned, and many former chieftains were appointed as gunji (district officials). The title kuni no miyatsuko was retained, however, designating one who exclusively presided over the Shintō rites of each kuni or province. The latter type of kuni no miyatsuko are often called shin kokuzō (new kuni no miyatsuko, kokuzō being an alternate pronunciation of the Chinese characters used to write kuni no miyatsuko) by modern historians to distinguish them from the former.

Kunisada → Utagawa Kunisada

Kunisaki Peninsula

(Kunisaki Hantō). Located in northeastern Ōita Prefecture, northeastern Kyūshū. It is bounded to the north by the Suō Sea, to the east by the Iyo Sea, and to the south by Beppu Bay. This rich agricultural region has a large annual yield of rice, mandarin oranges, tobacco, and vegetables. The highest peak, Futagosan (721 m; 2,365 ft) is included in the Inland Sea National Park. Many ancient temples and stone statues of the Buddha are on the peninsula. The major cities are Bungo Takada and Kitsuki.

Kunitachi

City in west central Tōkyō Prefecture. It is primarily a campus town and residential district, with Hitotsubashi University and Kunitachi Music College. Pop: 64,154.

kuniyaku

(literally, "provincial levies"). Taxes imposed by a provincial governor, domainal lord, or shogunate on a province or domain. Also called kokuyaku or kuniyakukin. These levies originated in the Heian period (794–1185) in the form of corvée labor for palaces, landed estates (shōen), and public-works projects such as roads and irrigation facilities. The Kamakura (1192–1333) and Muromachi (1338–1573) shogunates imposed these taxes for similar purposes in the form of cash levies and labor service.

During the Edo period (1600–1868) kuniyaku was an irregular tax collected to meet extraordinary expenses such as the shōguns' pilgrimages to their family shrine at Nikkō, repair of river dikes, and other flood-control projects. The Tokugawa shogunate established kuniyaku regulations for its own domains (tenryō) in 1720. Kuniyaku was assessed at a fixed rate of cash per 100 koku of each village's estimated rice yield (see KOKUDAKA). It was not levied nationwide. A different tax, also called kuniyaku, was assessed on craftsmen in Edo (now Tōkyō), the administrative seat of the Tokugawa shogunate; it was collected in the form of labor service (later commuted to cash) from the various craftsmen's and artisans' wards (chō) of the city.   Philip BROWN

Kuniyoshi → Utagawa Kuniyoshi

Kuniyoshi, Yasuo (1893–1953)

Painter. Born in the city of Okayama, Okayama Prefecture, he came to the United States in 1906. From 1908 to 1910 he studied painting at the Los Angeles School of Art and Design. He later settled in New York City and studied at the National Academy of Design and at the Art Students League under Kenneth Hayes Miller. His first one-man exhibition was in 1922; in 1929 his work was included in the Museum of Modern Art's "Nineteen Living American Artists" exhibition.

His early paintings and drawings are works of fantasy and gentle humor, using plants and animals as subjects, cast in subdued earth tones. In his mature work, such as I Think So (1938) and Somebody Tore My Poster (1943), languorous women predominate, drawn in melancholy moods and dark shades; he is said to have been influenced by the paintings of Jules Pascin. From around the time of World War II, his sharp social and political perceptions were given expression through highly original symbols and rich, vibrant colors.

He was an instructor at the Art Students League from 1933 and also taught at the New School for Social Research and at the artists' colony in Woodstock, New York. His work was presented in 1948 at the Whitney Museum of American Art's first major retrospective of a living artist. He was the first president of the Artists' Equity Association.

Kuno Yasu (1882–1977)

Also known as Kuno Yasushi. Physiologist. Specialist in the physiology of human perspiration. Born in Aichi Prefecture. After graduating from the Aichi Igakkō, a medical college, he studied at Tōkyō University. Kuno gained recognition after publishing The Physiology of Human Perspiration (1934) in English (the Japanese version appeared in 1946). He taught at Nagoya University from 1937 to 1955. He received the Imperial Prize of the Japan Academy in 1941 and the Order of Culture in 1963.   ACHIWA Gorō

Kunōzan

Hill in the eastern part of the city of Shizuoka, Shizuoka Prefecture, central Honshū. On the summit is a shrine dedicated to TOKUGAWA IEYASU, the first Tokugawa shōgun. The shrine is named Tōshōgū, not to be confused with the well-known shrine of the same name, also dedicated to Ieyasu, at NIKKŌ.

kun readings

(kun yomi). One of the two basic types of pronunciation of Chinese characters (kanji) as they are used in the Japanese writing system, the other being on readings. Whereas ON READINGS are Japanese approximations of the original Chinese pronunciations of the characters and occur when the characters are used to write words of Chinese origin, kun readings consist of native Japanese words that translate the meaning of the characters (the Chinese character used to write kun originally meant "to interpret the meaning"). An example is the character   "mountain" the on reading for which is san (Ch: shan) and the kun reading yama (the Japanese word for mountain). Some characters have no established kun readings, being used exclusively to write words of Chinese origin. Others have several kun readings, several native Japanese words having become associated with the character. Many of the compound words (composed of two or more characters) that are in common use in Japanese are of Chinese origin and involve the use of on readings. However, there are also many native compound words written with two or more characters, and some compounds can be read either way. An example is   "food," which can be pronounced shoku-motsu (two on readings) or tabe-mono (two kun readings). See also the section on on and kun readings in KANJI.   YAMADA Toshio

Kuo Mo-jo → Guo Moruo (Kuo Mo-jo)

Kuonji → Minobusan

Kurashiki——Kurashiki Folkcraft Museum

Consisting of three two-story traditional rice storehouses, the museum houses a collection of 10,000 art objects from around the world.

Kuo Sung-ling → Guo Songling (Kuo Sung-ling)

Kurabō Industries, Ltd

(Kurashiki Bōseki). Textile firm possessing a high level of technology in the spinning of cotton and synthetic thread. Founded in Kurashiki, Okayama Prefecture in 1888, through mergers and the absorption of lesser companies, it initiated production of wool yarn and cloth. In 1926 Kurabō founded a subsidiary firm, Kurashiki Kenshoku (now KURARAY CO, LTD), for the production of silk thread. During World War II it manufactured machinery and heavy industrial goods, but at the war's end returned to specialization in the textile industry, concentrating on the spinning of cotton and wool. It established a unified system for all stages of the production of knitwear from manufacture of raw thread to sale of the finished product. In the 1970s the firm diversified its product range and developed commercial devices for the prevention of environmental pollution. It has joint venture production companies in Brazil, Thailand, and Indonesia. Sales for the fiscal year ending April 1982 totaled ¥155.7 billion (US $635.9 million), of which sale of cotton and synthetic textiles constituted 77 percent, wool 14.5 percent, and nontextile products 8.5 percent. Its export rate was 19.8 percent and capitalization was ¥8.3 billion (US $33.9 million) in the same year. The head office is located in Ōsaka.

Kurahara Korehito (1902–)

Literary critic. Born in Tōkyō. Studied Russian at Tōkyō Foreign Language School (now Tōkyō University of Foreign Studies). After returning from a period of study in Russia, he joined a leftist arts association and worked as the leading theorist for *Bungei sensen,* a literary magazine which led the so-called PROLETARIAN LITERATURE MOVEMENT of the 1920s. In 1927 he published "Gendai Nihon bungaku to musan kaikyū" and other essays, advocating what he called "proletarian" realism in literature. These greatly influenced such writers as KOBAYASHI TAKIJI. He joined the then illegal Japan Communist Party and published underground essays on the application of Marxist principles to art. During the 1930s he spent several years in prison for his underground left-wing activities. After World War II he became an active leader in the Japan Communist Party.

Kurahashijima

Island in the western Inland Sea, southwestern Hiroshima Prefecture. Separated from the city of Kure on the mainland by the Ondo Strait. Composed of granite, but almost entirely under cultivation. A vital point of transportation in the Inland Sea in ancient days. Chief activities on the island are mandarin orange *(mikan)* cultivation, shipbuilding, and granite quarrying. Area: 69 sq km (27 sq mi).

Kurahashi Yumiko (1935–)

Novelist. Born in Kōchi Prefecture. Graduate of Meiji University. She first gained recognition for her short story on political alienation,

"Parutai" (1960; tr "Partei," 1961), which was written while she was still a student. She is known as an antirealist, influenced by Kafka and other modern European writers, and this approach is well-developed even in such early works as "Kon'yaku" (1961, The Engagement) and *Kurai tabi* (1961, Dark Journey). Other works include the essay collection *Watashi no naka no kare e* (1970, To Him Inside Me), the novels *Sumiyakisuto Q no bōken* (1969, The Adventures of Q the Charcoalist) and *Yume no ukihashi* (1971, The Bridge of Dreams), and the story collection *Hanhigeki* (1971, Anti-Tragedies), which includes "Kakō ni shisu" (tr "To Die at the Estuary," 1977).

kuramai

(granary rice). Tax rice collected from peasants by the shogunate or by *daimyō* during the Edo period (1600–1868) and stored in their granaries to be dispensed to their retainers as stipends (see KIRIMAI). The term also refers to the portion of such rice sent to various domainal warehousing offices (KURAYASHIKI) in major cities and sold on the commercial market, as distinct from *nayamai,* or rice that was handled exclusively by merchants. In Ōsaka, the largest market, about four-fifths of the rice sold was *kuramai.* The largest suppliers of *kuramai* were the granaries of the domains of Kuroda (now part of Fukuoka Prefecture), Hosokawa (now Kumamoto Prefecture), Chōshū (now Yamaguchi Prefecture) and Asano (now part of Hiroshima Prefecture), all in southwestern Japan and known collectively as "the four granaries" *(shikura);* the granaries of the Bizen (now part of Okayama Prefecture) and Kaga (now Ishikawa and Toyama prefectures) domains also played a significant role in the Ōsaka rice market. *Philip BROWN*

Kuramayama

Hill in the northern part of the city of Kyōto. Kuramadera, a temple founded in 796, is located on its slopes. The annual *himatsuri* (torch festival) held in January is widely known. Height: 570 m (1,870 ft).

Kuraray Co, Ltd

(Kurare). Manufacturer of synthetic fiber, artificial leather, and resin film. Among producers it has the largest share of the world markets in synthetic leather and goods made from polyvinyl alcohol and high molecular compounds. Founded in 1926 as Kurashiki Kenshoku, it assumed its present name in 1970. The firm was the first in the world to initiate commercial manufacture of polyvinyl alcohol fiber, establishing an integrated production system. Kuraray has also created a number of subsidiary firms to produce raw materials and is fully self-sufficient for its supply of terephthalic acid, required in the manufacture of polyester fiber. The firm has sold its polyvinyl alcohol technology to foreign firms, and since 1963 has exported three production plants to China. It has seven overseas subsidiaries, situated in the United States, the Middle East, and Southeast Asia. Adapting the technology of polymer chemistry, the company has moved into the field of fine chemicals, chiefly isoprene derivatives, and of medical products such as kidney dialysis machines. Sales for the fiscal year ending March 1982 totaled ¥195.4 billion (US $811.7 million), of which sale of textiles constituted 75 percent. Its export rate was 28 percent and capitalization stood at ¥10.6 billion (US $44 million) in the same year. The head office is in Ōsaka.

Kurashiki

City in southwestern Okayama Prefecture, western Honshū. The city flourished in the Edo period (1600–1868) as a commercial center and as a river port for the transshipment of rice. The center of a textile industry since the establishment of a spinning plant in 1888 by the father of the industrialist ŌHARA MAGOSABURŌ, it also has steel and petrochemical industries. The Ōhara Art Museum, the Kurashiki Folkcraft Museum, the Kurashiki Archaeology Museum, and the cluster of Edo-period, white-walled warehouses on the banks of the Kurashikigawa attract tourists. WASHIUZAN, a nearby hill, commands a view of the Inland Sea. Pop: 403,785.

Kurata Chikara (1889–1969)

Businessman. Second president of HITACHI, LTD. Born in Fukuoka Prefecture, he graduated from Sendai Higher Technical School (now

Tōhoku University). Kurata joined Hitachi, then a repairing division of the Hitachi mine owned by Kuhara Mining Industry. He became its president in 1947 when ODAIRA NAMIHEI, founder of the company, was purged by the Allied Occupation authorities. During a 20-year term as president and chairman, he contributed greatly to the nation's industries by developing new technologies. Under Kurata's leadership, Hitachi became an important international firm widely known for its excellent technology.　　UDAGAWA Masaru

Kurata Hyakuzō (1891–1943)

Playwright; essayist on religious subjects. Born in Hiroshima Prefecture. Because of illness, he left the First Higher School in Tōkyō without graduating. Influenced by the philosophical writings of NISHIDA KITARŌ, he became deeply interested in religious thought. Though his health remained poor through the early 1900s, before he was 25 he had published *Shukke to sono deshi* (1916; tr *The Priest and His Disciples*, 1922), a play about the early-13th-century Buddhist priest SHINRAN, which became a long-term best-seller. His best work is *Ai to ninshiki to no shuppatsu* (1922, The Beginning of Love and Understanding). This collection of essays on such subjects as love, sex, and faith remained something of a classic among young people for over a quarter of a century.

Kuratsukuri no Tori (fl early 7th century)

Sculptor of Buddhist images. Born into a saddle-making (*kuratsukuri*) family; grandson of the naturalized Chinese craftsman SHIBA TATTO (Ch: Sima Dadeng or Ssu-ma Ta-teng) and son of the Buddhist sculptor Kuratsukuri no Tasuna. He was patronized by Prince SHŌTOKU, who commissioned many of his works. In 606 he completed a large image of the Buddha Shaka (Śākyamuni), commissioned for the temple ASUKADERA by the empress SUIKO. He is best known for his Shaka Trinity in the main hall of the temple HŌRYŪJI in Nara, which he dedicated in 623 for the repose of the souls of Prince Shōtoku and the prince's wife and mother. This masterpiece, in the style of the Chinese Northern Wei dynasty (386–535), is representative of the Tori style: lips upturned at the corners in an enigmatic, archaic smile, flat, rectilinear layers of pleats in the garment, and wide-open almond-shaped eyes.

kurayashiki

Business offices established in the Edo period (1600–1868) by the shogunate, *daimyō*, vassals *(hatamoto)*, domainal officials, and temples in major transport and market centers such as Ōsaka, Edo, Tsuruga, Ōtsu, and Nagasaki to sell tax rice (KURAMAI) and other products produced in their domains. Tax rice was the main commodity traded, accounting for about three-fourths of all rice traded in Ōsaka, the largest market. Other important products included sugar, indigo, paper, and *tatami* covers.

The number of *kurayashiki* increased as domains became less self-sufficient and needed to convert more goods to cash. In the late 17th century there were 90 *kurayashiki* in Ōsaka. By the mid-19th century there were 124. These trading activities were first conducted at daimyō residences in major cities, with leading merchants handling the transactions. Later, domain officials were appointed to supervise the activities of the *kurayashiki*. The senior official *(myōdai)* represented the *kurayashiki* and oversaw transactions. His deputies, the *kuramoto*, were frequently townsmen and supervised the arrival and departure of goods from the warehouse. Agents called *kakeya* handled accounts. (Both these functions were sometimes fulfilled by the same person.) Lesser clerks and accountants were generally townsmen. Those domains not having *kurayashiki* sometimes appointed *kuramoto* and lesser clerks to transact business for them.　　Philip BROWN

Kurayoshi

City in central Tottori Prefecture, western Honshū. It was the seat of the provincial capital and provincial temple (KOKUBUNJI) from the 8th century on. A castle town of the Yamana family in the 14th century, it later became known for its *kasuri* (cotton ikat cloth) and rice-threshing machines. Textile, machinery, and food industries flourish. Pop: 52,271.

Kurayoshi Plain

(Kurayoshi Heiya). Alluvial plain located in central Tottori Prefecture, western Honshū. Bordering the Sea of Japan, this fertile grain-producing area also grows pears in the highlands in the east and grapes in the sandy soil by the sea. Numerous mounded tombs *(kofun)* dot the plain, which also has several hot springs. The major city is KURAYOSHI. Area: 50 sq km (19 sq mi).

Kure

City in southwestern Hiroshima Prefecture, western Honshū, on Hiroshima Bay. With an excellent natural harbor, Kure was an important naval base until the end of World War II. Shipbuilding, steel, and pulp industries have been set up on the site of the old naval facilities. Norosan, a mountain with a magnificent view of the Inland Sea, and ONDO STRAIT are popular with visitors. Pop: 234,550.

Kureha Chemical Industry Co, Ltd

(Kureha Kagaku Kōgyō). General chemical firm producing and selling synthetic resin, organic and inorganic chemicals, agricultural chemicals, insecticides, medicines, and carbon products. Founded in 1944, it engaged in high-level utilization of chlorine, later expanding to include petrochemicals, and in 1977 initiated production of pharmaceuticals. The basis of the firm's growth has been the development of technology, an area in which it continues to be strong. It established Kurehalon Industry in the Netherlands for the fabrication of food-packaging materials. In the future, the firm plans to emphasize research and development of fine chemicals. Sales for the fiscal year ending March 1982 totaled ¥103.8 billion (US $431.2 million) and capitalization was ¥9.9 billion (US $41.1 million). Corporate headquarters are in Tōkyō.

Kure Ken (1883–1940)

Internist. Born in Kyōto Prefecture. Graduate of Tōkyō University. Professor at Kyūshū and Tōkyō universities. Kure, known for his studies on the autonomic nervous system, discovered and determined the nature of the efferent (or centrifugal) spinal parasympathetic system in the spinal posterior root. He also confirmed that the nervous system exerts control over the tension and nutrition of voluntary muscles and added to knowledge of progressive muscular dystrophy. He received the Japan Academy Prize in 1939. Kure's publications include *Jiritsu shinkeikei* (1934, The Autonomic Nervous System) and a widely used textbook on internal medicine, *Naikasho* (1931), which he coauthored with Sakamoto Tsuneo (1888–1972).　　NAGATOYA Yōji

Kurihama

District in the southeastern part of the city of Yokosuka, Kanagawa Prefecture, central Honshū. An industrial district facing the port of Kurihama, it has several thermoelectric power plants and factories for processing seafood products. Commodore PERRY landed here in 1853, an event commemorated every year on 14 July by the Black Ship Festival (Kurofune Matsuri).

Kurikaradani, Battle of

(Kurikaradani no Tatakai). Battle in 1183 between Minamoto and Taira forces (see TAIRA-MINAMOTO WAR) at Kurikara Pass in the Tonamiyama Mountains between Etchū and Kaga provinces (now Toyama Prefecture and part of Ishikawa Prefecture, respectively); also called the Battle of Tonamiyama. MINAMOTO NO YOSHINAKA was marching from the north-central provinces against the Taira regime in Kyōto; an army under Taira no Koremori (1157–84) was dispatched to intercept him. They met at Tonamiyama on 2 June (Juei 2.5.11). According to the military chronicle GEMPEI SEISUIKI, Yoshinaka mounted a surprise attack that night; driving a herd of oxen with torches tied to their horns, he terrified and overwhelmed the numerically superior Taira forces. Now unimpeded, Yoshinaka entered Kyōto on 16 August (Juei 2.7.28).

Kurikara Pass

(Kurikara Tōge). Located on the border of Toyama and Ishikawa prefectures, central Honshū. The highway Hokurikudō ran through the pass in ancient times. The surrounding regions are known as old battlefields of the wars between the Minamoto and Taira families. Kurikara Fudōson, a temple dedicated to the god of fire, is located

Kurobe Dam

Lake Kurobe and Kurobe Dam photographed from the east with the surrounding Hida Mountains visible in the background.

here, and the pass also serves as a hiking course. Altitude: 277 m (909 ft).

Kurikomayama

Also known as Sukawadake. Stratovolcano situated at the junction of the borders of Akita, Iwate, and Miyagi prefectures, northern Honshū. Northwest of the summit is the central cone, Tsurugiyama. Alpine flora abound. Sukawa Hot Spring is located on the northwest slopes. Kurikomayama is part of Kurikoma Quasi-National Park. Height: 1,628 m (5,340 ft).

Kuril Current → Oyashio

Kuril Islands

(Chishima Rettō). Group of islands extending from south of the Kamchatka Peninsula, northeastern Siberia, to Hokkaidō. They form the boundary between the Sea of Okhotsk to the northwest and the Pacific Ocean to the southwest. The group is made up of more than 30 large and small islands including, from northeast to southwest, Shumushu (Shumshu), Araito (Alaid), Paramushiru (Paramushir), Onekotan, Harimukotan, Shashikotan, Matsua (Matua), Rashuke, Ketoi, Shinshiru (Shimshir), Uruppu (Urup), ETOROFU (Iturup), KUNASHIRI (Kunashir), SHIKOTAN, and the HABOMAI ISLANDS. Of volcanic origin, these islands include many active volcanoes and hot springs. The highest peak is Araitosan on Araito, with an elevation of 2,239 m (7,344 ft). The climate is wet; the winters are cold with much snow, and the summers are cool and foggy. Abundant mineral deposits include sulfur, iron, copper, and gold ores. Surrounded by rich fishing grounds for salmon and codfish, the islands also have active forestry, hunting, and trapping industries; grains and vegetables are cultivated in the southern islands. The Kuril Islands are currently under occupation by the Soviet Union. See also TERRITORY OF JAPAN.

Kurimoto Iron Works, Ltd

(Kurimoto Tekkōjo). Manufacturer of cast iron pipes, industrial machinery, castings, and valves; also engaged in construction of floodgates and bridges. It is Japan's second leading producer of iron castings behind KUBOTA, LTD. Founded in 1909, it assumed its present organization in 1934 and began to manufacture machinery and castings in addition to cast iron pipes; in 1939, it initiated production of valves. The company has been successful in developing an export market. Future plans call for expansion into the field of nonferrous metal products. Sales for the fiscal year ending March 1982 totaled ¥97.5 billion (US $405 million), of which sales of cast iron pipes constituted 37 percent. In the same year capitalization stood at ¥4.3 billion (US $17.9 million). Corporate headquarters are in Ōsaka.

Kurimoto Joun (1822–1897)

Shogunate official of the latter part of the Edo period; later active as a journalist. Real name Kurimoto Kon; also known as Kurimoto

Hōan. Born in Edo (now Tōkyō). After teaching at the Shōheikō, the shogunate school for Confucian studies, he was named naval commissioner (gunkan bugyō) and commissioner of foreign affairs (gaikoku bugyō) in 1865. In 1867 he attended the Paris Exposition as a member of a delegation headed by Tokugawa Akitake, younger brother of the shōgun TOKUGAWA YOSHINOBU. While there, however, the shogunate fell, and he returned to Japan in 1868. Kurimoto took up farming for a while after his return, and then in 1872 joined Japan's first daily Japanese-language newspaper, the YOKOHAMA MAINICHI SHIMBUN. In 1873 he was invited to become chief editor of the YŪBIN HŌCHI SHIMBUN. Kurimoto was especially well known for his finely styled essays, a collection of which was published posthumously titled Hōan ikō (1900).　HARUHARA Akihiko

Kurishima Sumiko (1902–　)

Movie actress. After starring at age 19 in the enormously popular Gubijinsō (1921, Red Poppy) directed by Henry Kotani, Kurishima topped the list of stars under exclusive contract to Shōchiku Kinema Co (see SHŌCHIKU CO, LTD). Ikeda Yoshinobu, her husband and a director at Shōchiku, provided her with many roles in his melodramatic works aimed at popular audiences: Hototogisu (1922, Nightingale), Sendō kouta (1923, Boatman's Song), Shinju fujin (1927, Madam Pearl), and Onna no isshō (1928, A Woman's Life), among others. After retiring from acting, Kurishima became head of the Mizuki school of traditional Japanese dancing.　ITASAKA Tsuyoshi

Kuriyagawa Hakuson (1880–1923)

Scholar of English literature and literary critic. Real name Kuriyagawa Tatsuo. Born in Kyōto; graduate of Tōkyō University. Professor at Kyōto University. He lectured on 19th-century Western literary trends, but later turned from literary to social concerns, criticizing from a Western ethical viewpoint Japanese ideas of human nature and love. Among his writings are Kindai bungaku jukkō (1912, Ten Aspects of Modern Literature), Zōge no tō o dete (1920, Leaving the Ivory Tower), and Kindai no ren'aikan (1921, Modern Views of Love).　ASAI Kiyoshi

Kuriyama Sempō (1671–1706)

Confucian scholar and historian of the MITO SCHOOL. Born in Yodo, near Kyōto. Real name Kuriyama Gen. A precocious student of the Kyōto scholar Kuwana Shōun (1670–1706), a disciple of YAMAZAKI ANSAI, at the age of 18 he wrote the history Hōken taiki, an account of events from the HŌGEN DISTURBANCE of 1156 to the appointment of MINAMOTO NO YORITOMO as shōgun in 1192. In 1697 TOKUGAWA MITSUKUNI, the scholar-daimyō of the Mito domain (now part of Ibaraki Prefecture), invited Sempō to become head of the domain's research facility, SHŌKŌKAN, in Edo (now Tōkyō), where he assisted in the compilation of the DAI NIHON SHI, the monumental history of Japan from earliest times to the days of Emperor Go-Komatsu (r 1382–1412).

Kurobe

City in northwestern Toyama Prefecture, central Honshū; on the lower reaches of the river Kurobegawa. Formerly a market town and fishing port, the city is now a commercial and industrial center with lead refining and lumber plants, as well as a large factory belonging to Yoshida Kōgyō, the zipper manufacturer. Rice and watermelon are grown on the outskirts. Pop: 35,443.

Kurobe Dam

Electric power-generating dam located on the upper reaches of the river KUROBEGAWA, southeastern Toyama Prefecture, central Honshū. Commonly called Kurobe Daiyon Damu or Kuroyon Damu. Completed in 1963, it is an arch-type dome dam. The dam created the artificial Lake Kurobe (area: 3.5 sq km; 1.4 sq mi), a part of Chūbu Sangaku National Park. The Number 4 Kurobegawa Electric Power Plant is located about 10 km (6 mi) below the dam and has a maximum output of 335,000 kilowatts. Height: 186 m (610 ft); length of embankment: 492 m (1,614 ft); storage capacity: 149 million cu m (5,260 million cu ft).

Kurobegawa

River in eastern Toyama Prefecture, central Honshū, originating in the central Hida Mountains and flowing north to empty into the Sea of Japan. It is a swift river, and the lower reaches below Kurobeko, a large man-made lake, form gorges with steep overhanging cliffs. The KUROBE DAM and a number of electric power plants are located along the river. Some of the gorges, designated Scenic Natural Monuments, have more than a million visitors annually. Length: 85 km (53 mi).

Kurobe Kyōkoku

Gorge on the upper and middle reaches of the river Kurobegawa, eastern Toyama Prefecture, central Honshū. One of Japan's deepest gorges and part of Chūbu Sangaku National Park. Surrounded by rugged mountains with scenic spots, including granite rock formations, towering cliffs, waterfalls, and rapids. Numerous hot spring resorts located near the gorge include Kuronagi, Unazuki, and Babadani. The Kurobe Railway Line extends to Keyakidaira, part way to the gorge.

Kuroda Hisao (1899–)

Politician. A native of Okayama Prefecture and a graduate of Tōkyō University, where he was a member of the socialist study group SHINJINKAI. He worked for the FARMERS' MOVEMENT, becoming an executive member of the National Farmers' Association (Zenkoku Nōmin Kumiai) in 1923. In 1948 he helped form the Labor-Farmer Party (RŌDŌSHA NŌMINTŌ) and served as its chairman. After the party's merger with the JAPAN SOCIALIST PARTY in 1957, he aligned himself with its extreme left faction. Except for the war years and his imprisonment in connection with the POPULAR FRONT INCIDENT in 1937, he served in the House of Representatives from 1936 to 1972. *HARADA Katsumasa*

Kuroda Kiyotaka (1840–1900)

Politician and elder statesman of the Meiji period (1868–1912); prime minister from 1888 to 1889. Born in Kagoshima, the castle town of the Satsuma domain (now Kagoshima Prefecture), Kuroda was an early student of Western gunnery techniques in Edo (now Tōkyō). Before the Meiji Restoration of 1868 he worked for union between Satsuma and Chōshū loyalists. His first appointment in the new Meiji government was as deputy director of the Hokkaidō Colonization Office (Kaitakushi). In that capacity he recommended that the government develop Hokkaidō rather than the more distant island of Sakhalin. This proposal influenced Japan's early negotiations with Russia, which resulted in the Treaty of ST. PETERSBURG (1875), whereby Japan obtained the Kuril Islands and Russia Sakhalin. In 1874 Kuroda became director of the colonization office and concurrently a *sangi* (councillor) in the central government. In the same year he reorganized the colonist-militia (TONDENHEI) system of the latter part of the Edo period (1600–1868) to develop Hokkaidō agriculture, defend Japan's northern borders, and employ former *samurai* now deprived of their stipends. Later that year Kuroda was promoted to lieutenant general in the imperial army, and in 1877 he served in the force that subdued the SATSUMA REBELLION.

Kuroda was dispatched as an envoy to Korea in 1875 following a Korean attack at Kanghwa on a Japanese gunboat sent as part of a Japanese attempt to open diplomatic relations with Korea. The following year the Treaty of KANGHWA was concluded, whereby Korea opened the port of Pusan and two other ports and granted Japan consular jurisdiction in Korea.

In 1881 Kuroda was approached by a Satsuma merchant, GODAI TOMOATSU, with an offer of ¥380,000 for purchase of Hokkaidō properties on which the government had expended ¥10 million since 1872. Since the 10-year appropriation for Hokkaidō development was about to expire, Kuroda supported the scheme. When this arrangement was leaked to the press by the popular politician ŌKUMA SHIGENOBU, it became a scandal. Kuroda later agreed to cancel the scheme if Ōkuma were dismissed from the government (see HOKKAIDŌ COLONIZATION OFFICE SCANDAL OF 1881; POLITICAL CRISIS OF 1881).

In 1887 Kuroda became minister of agriculture and commerce in the first ITŌ HIROBUMI cabinet, and in 1888 Kuroda himself became prime minister. The most troublesome problem facing his cabinet was revision of the Unequal Treaties, an issue that several other politicians had failed to resolve (see UNEQUAL TREATIES, REVISION OF). Ōkuma Shigenobu, now foreign minister, drafted a treaty, but when it was leaked to the press, a controversy erupted over some of its terms. Kuroda secured for Ōkuma's draft the official support of Navy Minister SAIGŌ TSUGUMICHI, Army Minister ŌYAMA IWAO, and Finance Minister MATSUKATA MASAYOSHI. Although these ministers actually opposed the draft, they, unlike the Chōshū men in the cabinet, could not openly voice their opposition to Kuroda, their superior and fellow native of Satsuma. Kuroda attempted to win the support of others in the government; but the split within his cabinet was irreparable, and it was forced to resign when a would-be assassin attacked Ōkuma, who lost a leg as a result and temporarily retired from politics.

In 1892 Kuroda became minister of communications in the second Itō cabinet and in 1895 president of the Privy Council. Throughout his career Kuroda favored a government "transcendentally" above political parties and was a member of the GENRŌ, the exclusive elite of elder statesmen.

📖 ——Kuroda Kiyotaka, *Kan'yū nikki* (1887). Roger F. Hackett, *Yamagata Aritomo in the Rise of Modern Japan* (1971). Masakazu Iwata, *Ōkubo Toshimichi: The Bismarck of Japan* (1964). Joyce C. Lebra, *Ōkuma Shigenobu: Statesman of Meiji Japan* (1973).

Joyce C. LEBRA

Kuroda Kiyoteru → Kuroda Seiki

Kuroda Nagamasa (1568–1623)

Daimyō of the Azuchi–Momoyama period (1568–1600) and early part of the Edo period (1600–1868); son of the CHRISTIAN DAIMYŌ Dom Simeão KURODA YOSHITAKA and himself baptized Damião. When his father, a provincial baron of Harima (now part of Hyōgo Prefecture), adhered to the hegemon ODA NOBUNAGA in 1577, Nagamasa was sent as hostage to Nobunaga's general in the region, the future national unifier TOYOTOMI HIDEYOSHI. He served Hideyoshi in the Battle of SHIZUGATAKE (1583) against SHIBATA KATSUIE and was also active, with his father, in Hideyoshi's conquest of Kyūshū four years later. The Kuroda were rewarded by Hideyoshi, and Nagamasa became a major daimyō upon Yoshitaka's retirement in 1589, inheriting the 180,000-*koku* (see KOKUDAKA) domain of Nakatsu in Buzen (now Ōita Prefecture). Nagamasa participated in Hideyoshi's INVASIONS OF KOREA IN 1592 AND 1597; after Hideyoshi's death, however, on account of his hostility to the self-appointed defender of Toyotomi interests and leader of an anti-Tokugawa party, ISHIDA MITSUNARI, Nagamasa drew close to the future shōgun TOKUGAWA IEYASU. At the climactic Battle of SEKIGAHARA in 1600, Nagamasa was instrumental in persuading KOBAYAKAWA HIDEAKI to defect to Ieyasu's side, thus ensuring the defeat of Mitsunari and his allies. Ieyasu recognized his services by enfeoffing him with a 523,100-*koku* domain at Fukuoka. At first Nagamasa supported the Christian mission in his new fief, but he gradually abandoned the faith. His last exploit was participation in Ieyasu's Ōsaka Campaign of 1614–15 (see ŌSAKA CASTLE, SIEGES OF), in which Hideyoshi's heritage was destroyed. *George ELISON*

Kuroda Seiki (1866–1924)

Also known as Kuroda Kiyoteru. Western-style painter who introduced impressionism to Japan. Born in what is now Kagoshima Prefecture and adopted by his uncle, Viscount Kuroda Kiyotsuna (1830–1917). In 1884 he went to Paris to study law, and there he met the art dealer Hayashi Tadamasa (1851–1906) and the art students YAMAMOTO HŌSUI and Fuji Masazō (1853–1916). His early love of art was rekindled, and for two years he studied both law and painting. But when he finally received permission from his family, he devoted himself wholeheartedly to painting, under the direction of Raphael Collin. His artistry was recognized and he was admitted to several prestigious French fine-arts societies. He returned to Japan in 1893, on the crest of his Paris successes, eager to launch Meiji Western painting in a whole new direction. When he joined the Meiji Fine Arts Society (Meiji Bijutsukai), the younger members immediately sensed his leadership and the conservative factions saw him as a rival. With a fellow student of Collin's, Kume Keiichirō (1866–1934), he opened the Tenshin Dōjō, a studio patterned on the French system. In 1896 he and his followers left the Meiji Fine Arts Society to form an independent association of Western-style painters called the White Horse Society (HAKUBAKAI). An invitation to

Kuroda Seiki

Detail of a painting entitled *Maiko (Apprentice Geisha)*. Oil on canvas. 1893. Entire work 80.5 × 65.0 cm. Tōkyō National Museum.

join the faculty of the Tōkyō Bijutsu Gakkō (now Tōkyō University of Fine Arts and Music) signified an important victory for the advocates of Western-style painting; by the turn of the century, Kuroda was the undisputed leader of progressive Western-style painters. His painting *By the Lake* (1897), perhaps his best-known work, dates from this period. In 1900–1901, he served in Paris as a representative of the Japanese Ministry of Education and exhibited at the Paris international exposition. He enjoyed such honors as an appointment in 1907 to a judgeship of the BUNTEN, the annual Ministry of Education exhibitions; a 1910 appointment as an artist for the imperial household (*teishitsu gigeiin*); and election in 1919 to the Imperial Fine Arts Academy (Teikoku Bijutsuin), of which he became president in 1922. In 1920 he was elected to the House of Peers. Through his bequest the Institute for Art Research (now TŌKYŌ NATIONAL RESEARCH INSTITUTE OF CULTURAL PROPERTIES) was established in Tōkyō in 1930.

Kuroda Yoshitaka (1546–1604)

Also known as Kuroda Josui or Kodera Kambyōe; Christian name, Simeão. *Daimyō* of the Azuchi-Momoyama period (1568–1600); son of Kodera Noritaka (d 1585), the lord of Gochaku Castle in what is now the city of Himeji. The Kodera (originally called Kuroda, a name they later resumed) were prominent among those provincial barons of Harima (now part of Hyōgo Prefecture) who supported the hegemon ODA NOBUNAGA in the campaign he waged from 1577 in the Chūgoku region against the powerful MŌRI FAMILY, serving under his general TOYOTOMI HIDEYOSHI. Yoshitaka, whose counsel Hideyoshi valued highly, remained in his service after Nobunaga's violent death and distinguished himself in several of his campaigns of unification, notably the conquest of Shikoku in 1585; late in 1586 he led an advance contingent of Hideyoshi's invasion forces into Kyūshū and, at the victorious conclusion of that campaign the next year, was awarded a 120,000-*koku* domain in Buzen Province (now divided between Fukuoka and Ōita prefectures). Although Yoshitaka formally retired from affairs in 1589, taking the name Josui and passing on an augmented domain to his son KURODA NAGAMASA, he took an active part in Hideyoshi's ODAWARA CAMPAIGN of 1590 and the INVASIONS OF KOREA IN 1592 AND 1597. In the great conflict of the year 1600 he took the side of the victor and future shōgun TOKUGAWA IEYASU and along with KATŌ KIYOMASA was responsible for securing northern Kyūshū against Ieyasu's opponents, such as Ōtomo Yoshimune (1559–1605), whom Yoshitaka defeated in a swift campaign.

Yoshitaka was converted to Christianity in 1585 through the efforts of TAKAYAMA UKON, KONISHI YUKINAGA, and the new convert GAMŌ UJISATO, three of the most notable CHRISTIAN DAIMYŌ; he himself showed an uncommon missionary zeal and was also helpful to his Jesuit mentors in diplomatic affairs. The Jesuits themselves attributed the positive attitude Ieyasu took toward Christianity after the Battle of SEKIGAHARA (where the Christian Konishi was one of his principal opponents) to Yoshitaka's intercession. He was buried in the Jesuit church in Hakata. *George* ELISON

Kurōdo-dokoro

(Bureau of Archivists, or Chamberlains' Office). An extrastatutory office (RYŌGE NO KAN) established by Emperor SAGA in 810 after the so-called KUSUKO INCIDENT; Saga required secrecy and security, and he staffed this private office—separate from the formal bureaucracy—with loyal men to handle his most important documents. The office later became permanent, its duties expanding to include the transmission of imperial edicts, the conduct of palace ceremonies, and even the supervision of the emperor's food and clothing. Because they were in close attendance upon the emperor, Kurōdo-dokoro officials came to exercise great political influence, and appointment as a chamberlain (*kurōdo*) was regarded as a *sine qua non* for bureaucratic success. Control of these appointments is thought to have been one important basis of the power of the FUJIWARA FAMILY. By the end of the 10th century, retired emperors (see INSEI) as well as the Fujiwara and other great families had established their own private offices modeled on the Kurōdo-dokoro (see MANDO-KORO). *G. Cameron* HURST III

kurofune

("black ships"). Term used to refer to all Western ships that visited Japan from the 16th century to the end of the Edo period (1600–1868) and also to Western-style ships and warships built in Japan during this time. These ships were called *kurofune* because they were painted black, unlike the ships from China and Southeast Asia.

Kurohimeyama

Stratovolcano in the Fuji Volcanic Zone, northern Nagano Prefecture, central Honshū. It is covered by primeval forests abounding in beech trees and black pines. Kagami Pond is a deep crater lake on the mountain, famous for its clear waters. Popular with skiers in winter, the mountain is a major peak in JŌSHIN'ETSU KŌGEN NATIONAL PARK. Height: 2,053 m (6,734 ft).

kurohon → kusazōshi

kuroi kiri

(literally, "black mist"). In its broader meaning the term refers to wide-scale corruption in government. More specifically, it refers to a series of scandals that occurred in 1966 involving LIBERAL DEMOCRATIC PARTY (LDP) politicians and government officials. Although the phrase was popularized by journalists, it was probably first coined by MATSUMOTO SEICHŌ, the author of *Nihon no kuroi kiri* (1962, The Black Mist over Japan).

The scandal first erupted in the spring of 1965, when 17 LDP members of the Tōkyō Metropolitan Assembly were indicted for having given or received bribes in the contest for the post of assembly speaker. But this incident was only the prelude, for a succession of disclosures followed in 1966. At first, newspapers were reticent in reporting the scandals, especially when a prominent politician was involved. The press, however, became quite aggressive after the arrest in August 1966 of Tanaka Shōji, LDP chairman of the Audit Committee of the House of Representatives. Tanaka was charged with blackmail, fraud, tax evasion, and extortion; he subsequently resigned from the House in disgrace.

The Tanaka case touched off a series of exposés. The socialists saw an excellent opportunity to discredit the government of Prime Minister SATŌ EISAKU; they began the attack with the help of information passed on by newspaper reporters. Transportation Minister Arafune Seijūrō (1907–80), Defense Agency Director-General Kambayashiyama Eikichi (b 1903), and Agriculture Minister Matsuno Raizō (b 1917) were accused of malfeasance and abuse of the privileges of office. Both Arafune and Matsuno were forced to resign their cabinet posts. Other LDP politicians were accused of accepting money and giving preferential treatment to certain importers. The year ended with the resignation of House Speaker Yamaguchi Kikuichirō (b 1897) because of his close association with a bankrupt company.

The reputation of the LDP was badly tarnished, and the party lost several legislative seats in local and national elections. In the 1965 House of Councillors election, the LDP lost four seats. A much worse defeat occurred in the July 1965 election for the Tōkyō Metropolitan Assembly: the LDP won only 38 seats in the 120-member body, a sharp decline from its previous majority of 69, and lost control of the assembly for the first time.

However, the impact of the scandals on the general election of 29 January 1967 was mixed. The LDP's share of the total vote declined by almost 6 percent, and for the first time the party failed to win a majority of the popular vote. Nevertheless, several conservative candidates from rural constituencies who were involved in the scandals were reelected. Rural voters were quite willing to overlook misconduct in office if their representatives had served them well. Arafune, Kambayashiyama, Matsuno, and Yamaguchi were returned to office; indeed, Arafune and Kambayashiyama received the highest number of votes in their districts. In contrast, in the fourth district of Niigata Prefecture, the successor of Tanaka Shōji was defeated.

Scandals have periodically erupted in Japanese politics, but the "black mist" scandals were significant in their magnitude. They occurred during a period of spectacular economic growth, however, and their repercussions were muted by a growing complacency on the part of the Japanese, who had begun to enjoy affluence. The "black mist" scandals may have damaged the credibility of the government and the ruling LDP and led to disillusionment and cynicism, but they did not change the nature of conservative rule in Japan.

📖——Gendai Seiji Mondai Kenkyūkai, ed, *Jimintō gigoku shi* (1973). Yomiuri Shimbun Sha Shakaibu, ed, *Gigoku* (1976).

Minoru YANAGIHASHI

Kuroi Senji (1932–   )

Novelist. Real name Osabe Shunjirō. Born in Tōkyō. Graduate of Tōkyō University. Kuroi began to write while working for an automobile manufacturing company, and first gained recognition with the publication of his short story "Jikan" (1969). A primary theme of his work is the white-collar worker's alienation from his true self in highly industrialized contemporary society and his vain struggle to regain it. His principal works include *Mekanizumu No. 1* (1958) and *Hashiru kazoku* (1971).

Kuroishi

City in central Aomori Prefecture, northern Honshū. A castle town during the Edo period (1600–1868), it is known for its rice, apples, and complex of hot springs. It is also a gateway to Lake Towada. Pop: 40,719.

Kuroiso

City in northern Tochigi Prefecture, central Honshū. It is a gateway to the Nasu Hot Spring resort and the Nikkō National Park. Principal activities are rice cultivation and dairy farming. Pop: 46,573.

Kuroita Katsumi (1874–1946)

Historian and one of the founders of the discipline of DIPLOMATICS in Japan. Born in Nagasaki Prefecture, after graduation from Tōkyō University he joined the staff of *Tōkyō Keizai zasshi,* a liberal economic journal edited by TAGUCHI UKICHI. With Taguchi, he contributed to the publication of several landmark historical works, including the re-edition of GUNSHO RUIJŪ, a collection of important classical writings, and KOKUSHI TAIKEI, a voluminous compilation of all books and documents related to premodern Japanese history. He later worked as a professor at Tōkyō University and as an editor-compiler for the Ministry of Education and dedicated himself to the preservation of historical sites and art treasures. He was also a pioneer in the ESPERANTO movement in Japan.

Kuroiwa Jūgo (1924–   )

Novelist. Born in Ōsaka. Graduate of Dōshisha University. His military service during World War II and subsequent battle with polio are the major influences on his literature, which portrays the ambition and vanity of human egoism in modern society. He was awarded the Naoki Prize (see LITERARY PRIZES) for *Haitoku no mesu* (1960). Among his other works are *Hadaka no haitokusha* (1965), *Maboroshi e no shissō* (1975) and *Kuroi yuki* (1978).

Asai Kiyoshi

Kuroiwa Ruikō (1862–1920)

Journalist, critic, translator, novelist. His real name was Kuroiwa Shūroku, but he published under various pen names. Born in what is now Kōchi Prefecture, he was well versed in Chinese and English before he entered Keiō University in Tōkyō. He soon became involved in political activities and withdrew from school. After publishing a book on politics, he became editor of the newspaper *Dōmei kaishin shimbun* in 1883; when the newpaper went bankrupt, Kuroiwa moved from one publisher to another. In 1892 he launched *Yorozu chōhō,* a newspaper that earned its popularity through serializations of Western novels and sensational reportage on social issues. He was always concerned with the problems of the times, but his inconsistent political stance contributed to the downfall of the *Yorozu chōhō.* His interests extended to numerous other areas as well, and he associated with many educators, religious leaders, and writers and widely influenced the general public. Representative works: *Gankutsuō* (1901–02), an adaptation of Alexandre Dumas's *Le Comte de Monte Cristo,* and *Aa mujō* (1902–03), an adaptation of Victor Hugo's *Les Misérables.*

James R. MORITA

Kurokawa Kishō (1934–   )

Architect and urban planner. Born in Aichi Prefecture. After graduation from Kyōto University in 1957, he studied at Tōkyō University under TANGE KENZŌ. In 1960 Kurokawa joined architectural critic Kawazoe Noboru (b 1926), architect KIKUTAKE KIYONORI, and others in organizing the Metabolist group, which sought to express the dynamic, cyclical quality of urban growth. In 1962 he started his own firm and in 1969 established a social engineering and urban planning research institute. His buildings include Andersen Memorial Hall (1965) and the Takara Group Pavilion, both for Ōsaka EXPO '70, the Nakagin Capsule Tower Building (1971), and the Sony Tower Building in Ōsaka (1976).

WATANABE Hiroshi

Kurokawa Toshio (1897–   )

Internist. Born in Hokkaidō. Graduated from and later president of Tōhoku University. Kurokawa is noted for his contributions in diagnosing diseases of the digestive organs, involving, for example, the x-ray examination of the digestive tract and cytological confirmation of gastric cancer. The author of *Shōkakan no rentogen shindan* (1936, Roentgenological Diagnosis of the Digestive Tract) and *I oyobi jūnishichō kaiyō no shindan* (1942, Diagnosis of Gastric and Doudenal Ulcers), he received the Order of Culture in 1968.

ACHIWA Gorō

kuromoji

(Japanese spicebush). *Lindera* or *Benzoin umbellatum.* Deciduous shrub of the laurel family (Lauraceae); it is indigenous to Japan and grows wild in Shikoku, Kyūshū, and western Honshū to a height of about 2–3 meters (7–10 ft). Its bark bears distinctive black spots resembling Chinese characters, giving rise to the name *kuromoji* (literally, "black character"). The branches give off a pleasant aroma when broken. The leaves are alternate and narrowly elliptical. In spring it bears small yellow or yellowish green flowers before or accompanying the appearance of the leaves; the flowers are borne on umbels and cluster at leaf nodes. *Kuromoji* is dioecious, with male flowers slightly bigger and more numerous than female flowers. After flowering it bears globular fruits, which ripen into black berries, usually in October. Oil extracted from the leaves is used to make perfume and soap, and the wood to make toothpicks. It was introduced to the West by the Swedish botanist C. P. THUNBERG in his *Flora Japonica* (1784).

MATSUDA Osamu

Kurosawa Akira

Kurosawa on location for *Kagemusha* in 1979.

Kuropatkin, Aleksei Nikolaevich (1845–1925)

Commander-in-chief of the Russian armed forces in the Far East during the RUSSO-JAPANESE WAR of 1904–05. A graduate of the Pavlovsk Military School (1866) and of the General Staff Academy (1874), Kuropatkin saw active military service in the Central Asian Campaign of 1876, the Russo-Turkish War of 1877–78, and the Akhal Tekhu Expedition of 1880–81. He distinguished himself repeatedly by his bravery and was wounded four times. From 1883 to 1890 he was on the General Staff as general in charge of strategic questions. He served as minister of war from 1898 until the spring of 1904, when he was appointed commander-in-chief of the Manchurian Army of Operations. Unable to rout the Japanese forces, Kuropatkin was replaced as commander-in-chief following the Battle of MUKDEN. He stayed on as commander of the First Army and after the war superintended the demobilization of the Russian troops in Manchuria. Like most of his countrymen Kuropatkin underestimated the strength and resolution of the Japanese. The indecision and lack of coordination which characterized his campaigns were not entirely his fault, however. They were due in part to the nature of the joint command, Kuropatkin being subordinate most of the time to Viceroy Admiral Evgenii Ivanovich Alekseev, who was in another part of Manchuria and had a different view on how the war should be pursued.

During World War I Kuropatkin served as commander of the northern front and then as governor-general of Turkestan. Dismissed from service following the overthrow of the tsarist government in March 1917, Kuropatkin spent his last years teaching in a middle school and in an agricultural school he founded.

▬▬▬General Kuropatkin, *The Russian Army and the Japanese War*, tr Captain A. B. Lindsay, ed Major E. D. Swinton, 2 vols (1909). Reginald Hargreaves, *Red Sun Rising: The Siege of Port Arthur* (1962). *Sovetskaia istoricheskaia entsiklopediia*, vol 8 (1965). John Albert White, *The Diplomacy of the Russo-Japanese War* (1964).

George Alexander LENSEN

Kurosawa Akira (1910–)

Film director. One of the few Japanese directors to achieve international fame (the others would be MIZOGUCHI KENJI and OZU YASUJIRŌ). Born in Tōkyō. After graduating from middle school in 1927 Kurosawa decided to become a painter. A number of his paintings were exhibited and he became known as an illustrator. This talent was to serve him well in his later career. The preproduction work of most of his films contains masses of drawings and paintings which help him to visualize the intended cinematic result. Eventually he realized that he could not make a living as an artist and cast about for a new profession. In 1936 he happened to see an advertisement that the P. C. L. Studios wanted people to try out for assistant directorships. He did and was taken on. Fortunately, he became attached to the group of YAMAMOTO KAJIRŌ, a director to whom Kurosawa gives full credit for both educating and forming him. With him he made a number of pictures, including *Uma* (1941, Horses). Yamamoto has remembered the Kurosawa of those days as a man who was "completely engrossed in separating what is real from what is false." He had this quality as a painter, said Yamamoto, and he certainly kept it as a director. When the opportunity came to direct his first film he was ready for it.

The picture was *Sugata Sanshirō* (1943, shown abroad as Sanshiro Sugata), a film so popular that it was followed in 1945 by a sequel. Though this was a wartime picture, Kurosawa's concern for "truth" led him to ignore most of the objectives of the national-policy pictures of the period (he was to an extent forced to make up for this in the chauvinism of the sequel), and it was severely attacked by the official government and military board in charge of passing film scripts. It was, indeed, only through the diplomacy of Ozu Yasujirō that the film was allowed to be made at all.

Kurosawa's concern for what is real and what is false is visible even in this debut picture, as is his adamant refusal to compromise his own standards or those of his film. In this picture, and in most of his others, the true/false dichotomy took the form of reality/illusion. Usually we are shown first the illusion and then, later, the reality. In *Sanshirō*, the young man is convinced that he is a *jūdō* champion. And so he is, physically. Spiritually, he is still a child, and the film is about his becoming mature, realizing that he knows nothing, then learning eventually to become a real *jūdō* champion.

One can move through the canon of the Kurosawa films noting this dichotomous structure. In *Tora no o o fumu otokotachi* (1945, The Men Who Tread on the Tiger's Tail) the illusion is the elaborate paraphernalia of the *kabuki* play, *Kanjinchō*, upon which the film is based, with its heroics and its inflated emotions. Kurosawa's single addition is a cowardly, worried, and very human porter. He is the reality—he is us. In the best of his early pictures, *Waga seishun ni kui nashi* (1946, No Regrets for Our Youth), the heroine is a typical young Japanese girl living a life filled with illusion. The war teaches her reality and we witness her often-difficult education. Again, in his first big postwar hit, *Yoidore tenshi* (1948, Drunken Angel), the braggart life of the Tōkyō gangster (MIFUNE TOSHIRŌ, in his first appearance in a Kurosawa film) is illusion; his illness (tuberculosis) and the efforts of the doctor (SHIMURA TAKASHI, also to become a favorite Kurosawa star) represent postwar Japanese reality. RASHŌMON (1950), Kurosawa's first international hit, is, of course, a seminal examination, on many levels, of the nature of illusion and reality. It is not that the bandit, the lord, and the lady are lying; it is that they believe in an illusion they have created. The entire basis of reality is questioned in this picture, and the question is deliberately left unanswered.

A like confrontation of illusion and reality occurs in IKIRU (1952, To Live), where an illusion of the hero is recreated during his wake (but we already know the truth). In *Shichinin no samurai* (1954, SEVEN SAMURAI) as well, the big battle between *samurai* and bandits is not the final reality of the picture. This reality is plainly stated in the final dialogue of the picture, when everything that went before is questioned as one samurai says to another, "They, the farmers, they are the real winners."

In later pictures the illusion/reality dichotomy becomes even more apparent. *Warui yatsu hodo yoku nemuru* (1960, The Bad Sleep Well) opens with an enormous Japanese wedding, one of the many "fronts" of official Japan. The rest of the picture is devoted to the hideous reality behind this placid and completely illusionary appearance. In both *Yōjimbō* (1961) and *Tsubaki Sanjūrō* (1962, shown abroad as Sanjuro) much humor is derived from the hopeful venality of the townsfolk on the one hand and the idealistic boy samurai on the other, as contrasted to the complete reality of the hero. In *Tengoku to jigoku* (1963, shown abroad as High and Low), illusion and reality exist in an even more complicated relationship. The good but victimized shoe merchant whose chauffeur's son is kidnapped has been living in illusion. Life is not the way he has thought. At the same time the police hold a full rehearsal for the capturing of the culprit and that too is illusion because reality (that of the kidnapper) turns out to be quite different. In *Akahige* (1965,

Red Beard), the young doctor hero (very like Sanshirō) thinks that he knows everything. But this is an illusion. During the course of the film he learns that the reality of being a doctor is far different. In the script that Kurosawa wrote for *Tora, Tora, Tora* (never filmed because Twentieth-Century Fox took away the directorship and gave it to Richard Fleischer), there is a beautiful example of the illusion/reality syndrome. In Kagoshima the military goes through a complete (and perfect) rehearsal for the Pearl Harbor attack. This is later contrasted with the real attack, which is far, far different. In *Kagemusha* (1980), this steady theme is explicit. A great lord has died and a lowly man, who happens to resemble him precisely, is forced to play his part. The man knows nothing, of course, of court life, and even less of the civil war that makes such impersonation necessary. The reality in which he finds himself is obviously not his own and, like the porter in *The Men Who Tread on the Tiger's Tail*, he cannot but comment upon it by his very presence. Unlike the porter, however, he understands that his own identity is an illusion and attempts to create a new and lordly authenticity. This is a mistake.

There are, of course, other themes in the work of Kurosawa, but these, by comparison, seem to be minor. Sometimes the reality/illusion outcome is reversed. In *Subarashiki nichiyōbi* (1947, One Wonderful Sunday), the Schubert-filled fantasy of the young lovers erupts beneficially into their drab reality. In *Ikimono no kiroku* (1955, Record of a Living Being), the fantasy, not to say insanity, of the hero is seen as "wiser" than his reality. In *Dodesukaden* (1970) the illusion of the young boy who plays train is seen as somehow a higher wisdom. In *Derusu Uzāra* (1975, Dersu Uzala), the new reality (development in Siberia) is seen as a kind of illusion by the old hunter whose old reality has now really become an illusion. And in other films—*Shizukanaru kettō* (1949, The Quiet Duel), *Norainu* (1949, Stray Dog), *Shūbun* (1950, Scandal), *Hakuchi* (1951, The Idiot), *Kumonosujō* (1957, shown abroad as The Throne of Blood), *Donzoko* (1957, The Lower Depths), and *Kakushi toride no san'akunin* (1958, shown abroad as The Hidden Fortress)—the major theme, illusion versus reality, though present is not the true motivation of the picture.

Nonetheless, this major theme is so ubiquitous in Kurosawa's films that it can truly be said of him (as, indeed, it is said of a number of other directors, Japanese or not) that he has made only one film and that he keeps remaking it. This major theme—the nature of reality—means that his pictures must also be as realistic as possible. This has undoubtedly led to his reputation as a director who is both difficult and rewarding to work with. Many are the stories of whole sets torn down because they did not look "real enough." And many are the stories of actors and actresses forced again and again to emulate and recreate the reality that Kurosawa wants and needs. "That is fine," he once told an actress after a rehearsal for a tearful scene, "but now I want real tears."

Yet staff and cast are in agreement as to what the experience of working with Kurosawa has taught them. As Yamamoto has noted, he is a director who knows what he wants and will not compromise. Consequently he imbues those with whom he is working with an enthusiasm for the "truth" which is rare indeed in filmmaking. Though he himself may have some doubts about his life (for example, his suicide attempt in the 1960s), he has none about his work. His somewhat optimistic and certainly humanistic hopes may interfere (*One Wonderful Sunday* and *Dodesukaden*) with the sternness of his vision of reality, but it is usually the truthfulness of Kurosawa that triumphs. This quality has strongly appealed to moviegoers in the West and particularly in America, where he seems entirely free of the spirit of compromise and accommodation that so often intrudes itself into contemporary cinema. It is indeed just this quality that makes him a great film director. He is one of the few who can tell the real from the false, and this he shows. *Donald Richie*

Kuroshima Denji (1898–1943)

Novelist. Born in Kagawa Prefecture. Studied at Waseda University until he was drafted to participate in Japan's Siberian Intervention (1919). He became ill and was discharged in 1921. His experience in the army provided an important basis for his antiwar fiction, such as "Sori" (1927) and "Uzumakeru karasu no mure" (1928), both short stories written after his return to Japan. As a contributor to the magazine *Bungei sensen* and active participant in the PROLETARIAN LITERATURE MOVEMENT of the late 1920s and early 1930s, he also wrote a number of stories about poor farmers in poor regions such as his own home area. His diary during his stay in Siberia was

published posthumously in 1955 under the title *Guntai nikki*. Another of his works is *Busō seru shigai* (1930), a novel.

Kuroshio

(Black Stream). Also known as the Japan Current. The largest ocean current in the seas off Japan. A warm current, originating from the area east of the Philippines, the Kuroshio flows northward between Taiwan and the island of Ishigakijima into the East China Sea. After passing along the Ryūkyū Islands, it splits into two currents just south of Kyūshū. The main current proceeds between Yakushima and Amami Ōshima islands, flowing northeastward along Japan's Pacific coast. It turns east off northeastern Honshū, where it meets the southbound current known as OYASHIO. The branch current, known as the TSUSHIMA CURRENT, flows west of Kyūshū and enters the Sea of Japan through the Tsushima Strait. The Kuroshio exerts a varied influence on the climate of Japan: it is responsible for Japan's muggy summers and for the heavy winter snowfalls in the part of Honshū that faces the Sea of Japan. At the same time, it provides for one of the world's richest fishing grounds off the SANRIKU COAST of northeastern Honshū where it meets the cold Oyashio.

Kurozumikyō

A new Shintō-oriented religious sect founded by Kurozumi Munetada (1780–1850) in the latter part of the Edo period (1600–1868), with headquarters located in the city of Okayama. It originated in 1814 when Kurozumi, a Shintō priest, experienced a divine union with the sun goddess AMATERASU ŌMIKAMI, in which he received a "direct bestowal of the Heavenly Decree." In his subsequent proselyting efforts he gained followers by healing people of their illnesses and by offering magical prayers and spells for people's welfare and good fortune, all of which he attributed to the workings of the sun goddess.

Kurozumikyō holds that Amaterasu Ōmikami is the deity of the creation of the universe and nurtures all things and that man partakes of that divinity. It emphasizes such virtues in daily life as sincerity, selflessness, hard work, and gratitude and affirms the established social order. It was formally organized as a body in 1846 with the writing of the *Osadamegaki*, a kind of Kurozumikyō credo put together by senior disciples. Its missionary activities were approved by the Okayama domain because its doctrine supported the feudal order and did not conflict with the established religions. By the Meiji Restoration (1868) its influence had spread among the warrior class and well-to-do commoners of the Chūgoku (southwest Honshū) and Kinki (west central Honshū) regions and to Kyūshū in the south and Tōkyō in the north. It developed as a religion centered upon the acquisition of worldly benefits, worship of the emperor, and semifeudal ethics. In 1876 it became independent of the Board of Shintō Affairs, becoming one of the SECT SHINTŌ groups, and in 1885 the Munetada Shrine was established in Okayama. However, from the latter part of the Meiji period (1868–1912) onward, it stagnated because of its inability to cope with modernization. Kurozumikyō is a regional religion centered in Okayama. It claimed about 218,000 followers in 1978. *Murakami Shigeyoshi*

Kurume

City in southern Fukuoka Prefecture, Kyūshū. A castle town of the Arima family during the Edo period (1600–1868), it was an army base until the end of World War II. It is known for its rubber goods industry, Kurume ikat cloth *(kasuri)*, and flower nurseries. Pop: 216,974.

Kurusu Saburō (1886–1954)

Diplomat; born in Kanagawa Prefecture. A graduate of Tōkyō Kōtō Shōgyō Gakkō (now Hitotsubashi University), he joined the Ministry of Foreign Affairs in 1909. After many diplomatic assignments in the United States, Europe, and elsewhere, he became ambassador to Germany in 1939 and helped negotiate the TRIPARTITE PACT of 1940. In 1941, on the eve of the Pacific War, he was sent as a special envoy to Washington DC, where he assisted Ambassador NOMURA KICHISABURŌ in striving to ease the growing tensions between Japan and the United States. He was returned to Japan, where his American wife and their daughters had remained, in an exchange of diplomats in 1942; their son died as a pilot fighting for Japan.

■——Kurusu Saburō, *Hōmatsu no sanjūgonen: Gaikō hishi* (1948).

kusaboke → quince, dwarf Japanese

Kusaka Genzui (1840–1864)

Samurai of the Chōshū domain (now Yamaguchi Prefecture) and a leading figure in the proimperial, antishogunate movement of the early 1860s. A disciple and brother-in-law of YOSHIDA SHŌIN, Kusaka was much influenced by his radical loyalist doctrines. In 1862, impatient with Chōshū's moderate political policy, which at the time sought cooperation between the Tokugawa shogunate and the imperial court (see MOVEMENT FOR UNION OF COURT AND SHOGUNATE), Kusaka decided to abandon his domain and join other imperial loyalists in plans to expel foreigners from Japan. Early in 1863 he and fellow activist TAKASUGI SHINSAKU set fire to the British legation at Shinagawa; returning to Chōshū, he participated in the bombardment of Western ships in the Shimonoseki Strait. He then went to Kyōto, but with the expulsion of activists by the forces of Satsuma (now Kagoshima Prefecture) and Aizu (now part of Fukushima Prefecture) in the COUP D'ETAT OF 30 SEPTEMBER 1863, Kusaka returned once more to Chōshū and helped to formulate its new antiforeign, antishogunate policy. In the summer of 1864 he joined a Chōshū expeditionary force in an attempt to retake the Imperial Palace (see HAMAGURI GOMON INCIDENT). His contingent was defeated by Satsuma and Aizu forces; Kusaka was wounded in the engagement and later committed suicide.

Kusama Naokata (1753–1831)

Also known as Kusama Isuke. Ōsaka merchant and writer. Employed by the great Ōsaka merchant house of the KŌNOIKE FAMILY from the time he was a young boy, he was adopted into a branch of that family and was later allowed to set up his own money-changing business. Kusama was an accomplished calligrapher and practitioner of the tea ceremony; after his retirement in 1810, he devoted himself to these pursuits and to writing. He is best known for his *Sanka zui* (Illustrated Encyclopedia of Coins), a history of Japanese coins and commodity prices from 1575 to his own time. Begun in 1792, the work took more than 30 years to complete and was not published until 1916. Kusama's other writings include *Chaki meibutsu zui* (Illustrated Encyclopedia of Treasured Tea Utensils), his notes, *Kusama Isuke hikki*, and *Shinden kaihatsu jiryaku* (A Brief Outline of Land Reclamation). Kusama is also remembered for the financial aid he extended to the blind scholar HANAWA HOKIICHI.

Kusano Shimpei (1903–   )

Poet. Born in Fukushima Prefecture. After attending Keiō High School in Tōkyō, he studied at Lingnan University in Guangzhou (Canton). He started to write poetry in the late 1920s, having been heavily influenced by the anarchist poetry movement. His anarchist verse is distinguished by its vigor and full use of colloquial speech patterns. Kusano is especially known for his series of poems describing human life and feelings through the eyes of a frog. These were collected in *Teihon kaeru* (1948), which won the first Yomiuri Literary Prize. Other collections of his poetry include *Daihyaku kaikyū* (1928) and *Fujisan* (1943).

kusarigama

A sickle-shaped weapon with a metal weight and chain attached to the neck of the handle; its use developed into a martial art *(bujutsu)* form in the Edo period (1600–1868) known as *kusarigamajutsu*. The shaft was made of hard wood and ranged in length from approximately 20 to 60 centimeters (8 to 24 in). The chain, on the end of which was a small weight, was 2 to 3 meters (6.5 to 10 ft) in length. Holding the sickle in one hand and the chain in the other, the weight was swung in a circular motion at the opponent's head or neck. The chain could be used to lasso the opponent or wrapped around his weapon so that he could be pulled into a position to be beheaded with the sickle. Various schools of *kusarigamajutsu* existed, like the Ōkusa, Tendō, and Ōgishi schools, and it remains a part of several schools of the MARTIAL ARTS.   TOMIKI Kenji

Kusatsu

City in southern Shiga Prefecture, central Honshū. The river Kusatsugawa runs through its center. Kusatsu prospered in the Edo period (1600–1868) as a POST-STATION TOWN at the junction of the highways Tōkaidō and Nakasendō. It has numerous knitted goods and electrical appliance factories. Fruits are grown in the hilly regions to the east. Pop: 77,008.

Kusatsu

Town in northwestern Gumma Prefecture, central Honshū, on the southeastern foothills of SHIRANESAN. Kusatsu has been known for its hot springs since the 12th century. A part of the Jōshin'etsu Kōgen National Park, it is the base for skiing and climbing in such mountain areas as SHIGA KŌGEN, Shiranesan, and ASAMAYAMA. Tourist attractions include the hot spring festival in early August. Pop: 9,341.

kusazōshi

A type of popular fiction of the Edo period (1600–1868), published in books known as *akahon*, *kurohon*, *aohon*, KIBYŌSHI, and GŌKAN, essentially being picture books with narrative and dialogue written in phonetic characters in the blank spaces of the full-page illustrations. The pictures were of central importance, and at first the artists who drew them composed the texts as well. *Kusazōshi* were produced in Edo (now Tōkyō) on cheap recycled paper in the form of slim booklets or fascicles, each containing five double pages (folios) measuring about 19 by 13 centimeters (7.5 by 5.1 in) and stitched together at the cut edges. They were usually printed with cheap, smelly ink; thus the name *kusazōshi* probably originally meant "smelly books"; however, the word is usually written with Chinese characters meaning "grass books."

Akahon (red books), so called because of their covers, first appeared in 1662 and derived their content from didactic children's folktales. They were mainly confined to juvenile literature and ghost stories, but when their popularity began to wane, their publishers sought a more sophisticated readership by including abridged plots of KABUKI and JŌRURI plays.

Kurohon (black books) were first published in 1744, almost concurrently with *aohon* (green books), which they closely resembled in content. In addition to plots adapted from popular dramas, they presented stories of folk heroes and great battles as well as miracle tales from Buddhist and Shintō literature. Although with the *aohon* of Kansuidō Jōa (active ca 1750–60) author and artist were separately acknowledged for the first time, it was still customary for artists to write the texts themselves. Prominent among these author-artists were OKUMURA MASANOBU (1686–1764), TORII KIYOMITSU I (1735–85), and Tomikawa Ginsetsu (active ca 1770–80), the last of whom alone produced more than 200 works. In his *Ryūgū Soga monogatari* (1771, Tale of the Soga Brothers and the Dragon Palace), Ginsetsu follows the plot of a traditional historical narrative but places the characters in a totally fanciful setting, a device much used by later *kusazōshi* writers.

Kibyōshi (yellow covers), which first appeared in the 1770s, normally ran to two or three fascicles. Specifically intended for a sophisticated adult readership, they treated themes drawn from contemporary social life, especially the ways of the licensed quarter, in an urbane and often satirical manner. The political implications of this satire disturbed shogunal authorities, and following the KANSEI REFORMS of 1787–93 *kibyōshi* authors were restricted to more acceptable subjects such as righteous vengeance and virtue rewarded.

Partly through the influence of the larger YOMIHON (called "reading books," to distinguish them from *ehon* or picture books), a then current genre intended for a more literary readership, *kusazōshi* showed a gradual shift toward greater depth of characterization and intricacy of plot. This trend was facilitated by their increasing length, as multivolume stories became common. In 1804 the term *gōkan* (assembled fascicles) was first applied to these more complex works, and they soon became extremely popular. *Gōkan*, with elaborate multicolor covers by such masters of UKIYO-E printmaking as UTAGAWA TOYOKUNI (1769–1825), had as many as six fascicles, bound into a single volume and sold as a set. They remained popular well into the Meiji period (1868–1912) but eventually lost their readers to novels serialized in the newly introduced daily newspapers.

Although *kibyōshi* and *gōkan* took their physical format (the text appearing within the illustrations) from earlier *kusazōshi*, their content was wider in range and they are usually considered part of the larger genre GESAKU (the general term for popular fiction ca 1750–1868).

While *kusazōshi* are not generally regarded as works of high literary value, they evolved in close harmony with the changing tastes of Edo townsmen (CHŌNIN) and are a valuable resource for the study of the urban culture of their period. They also exerted an influence on some later authors such as IZUMI KYŌKA.

David DUTCHER

Kusha school

A school of Buddhist studies; one of the six schools of NARA BUDDHISM. The Kusha school was based upon the *Abhidharmakośa* (J: *Abidaruma kusha ron;* shortened to *Kusharon*), attributed to the Indian thinker Vasubandhu (4th century), and similar scriptures. It was introduced, along with the HOSSŌ SECT, from China by the monk DŌSHŌ and others in the latter half of the 7th century. As a systematic exposition of Buddhist doctrine on being, the *Kusha ron* has been widely studied by Buddhists of all denominations. Although it was regarded as a division of Buddhist studies at the outset, no institutional school or sect formed around it.

TSUCHIDA Tomoaki

Kushida Tamizō (1885–1934)

Marxian economist. One of the founders of academic Marxism in Japan. Born in Fukushima Prefecture, the son of a middle-class rural landholding family, he majored in economics at Kyōto University under the pioneer Japanese Marxist KAWAKAMI HAJIME, who influenced him greatly. Hoping to pursue a career in journalism, Kushida enrolled in the graduate school of Tōkyō University and in 1917 joined the staff of the newspaper *Ōsaka asahi shimbun.* There he met ŌYAMA IKUO and HASEGAWA NYOZEKAN, two of the leading liberal journalists of their day, and contributed to *Warera* (We), the journal they founded in 1919. After serving as head of the Faculty of Law of Dōshisha University in Kyōto (1918–20), Kushida returned to Tōkyō to teach economics at the university, but he soon resigned in protest over the forced resignation of MORITO TATSUO (see also MORITO INCIDENT) and joined the newly established ŌHARA INSTITUTE FOR SOCIAL RESEARCH, a private organization. He was the editor of the institute's journal in its early years and a leading member for the rest of his life.

Kushida's major research on Marxist economics began after his return from a trip to Germany (1920–22). He developed his Marxist theoretical interpretations by criticizing leading economists of the 1920s such as KOIZUMI SHINZŌ and especially his own mentor, Kawakami Hajime. His debates with them, famous in the history of Japanese economic thought, centered on the interpretation of Marxist theories of historical materialism, value, and rent.

Kushida remained aloof from the socialist revolutionary movement of the 1920s, devoting himself to research. After 1930 he turned increasingly to Japan's agrarian problems, especially relations between tenant farmers and landlords. He came to emphasize the "modern," capitalistic features of Japan's economy, as did the RŌNŌHA (Labor-Farmer faction), the school of Marxist historical analysis he helped found. A theoretician who grounded his research in concrete empirical studies, Kushida is regarded by Japanese scholars today as responsible for developing high standards of scholarship in Japanese Marxist economic research. His writings are collected in *Kushida Tamizō zenshū,* 5 vols (Kaizōsha, 1935).

Gail Lee BERNSTEIN

Kushikino

City in Kagoshima Prefecture, Kyūshū. A gold-producing area since the Edo period (1600–1868), it is still the leading producer of gold in Japan. It is also one of the largest fishing ports in the prefecture. Local products include *kamaboko* (boiled fish paste), ham, and bacon. Pop: 30,747.

Kushima

City in southern Miyazaki Prefecture, Kyūshū, on Shibushi Bay. It is mainly a farming area, producing rice, sweet potatoes, cucumbers, and other vegetables. The coast of the city is part of the Nichinan Coast Quasi-National Park. The cape TOIMISAKI and the island of KŌJIMA are popular. Pop: 29,420.

Kushimoto

Town in southern Wakayama Prefecture, central Honshū. Principal industries are fishing and tourism. Excursion ships ply between Ku-

shimoto and the island of Ōshima. Kushimoto's coast is part of the Yoshino–Kumano National Park; scenic attractions include the cape Shionomisaki and Hashikuiiwa, an interesting rock formation in the sea. Pop: 18,849.

Kushiro

City in southeastern Hokkaidō, at the mouth of the river Kushirogawa, on the Pacific Ocean. It was settled by fishermen from northeastern Honshū early in the Meiji period (1868–1912). Besides being the administrative and commercial center of southeastern Hokkaidō, it is the main base for north sea fishing in Japan, with a large catch of salmon, cod, and mackerel. The paper, seafood processing, metallurgy, and lumber industries are also important. The Kushiro Coal Mine is situated in the eastern part of the city. Pop: 214,694.

Kushirogawa

River in eastern Hokkaidō, originating in Lake Kutcharo and flowing through the Kushiro Plain into the Pacific Ocean. The upper reaches are a part of Akan National Park. Land along the lower reaches is low and swampy. The port of Kushiro is located at the river's mouth. Length: 129 km (80 mi); area of drainage basin: 2,510 sq km (969 sq mi).

Kusuko Incident

(Kusuko no Hen). An attempted usurpation of 810. Pleading illness, Emperor Heizei (774–824; r 806–809) abdicated in favor of his younger brother Emperor SAGA. Fujiwara no Kusuko, the daughter of the powerful court official Fujiwara no Tanetsugu (737–785) of the Shikike branch of the Fujiwara family and the favorite of Heizei, feared that her branch of the family would lose influence at the court. With her brother Nakanari, she persuaded Heizei to reclaim the throne. Heizei secretly assembled a military force for that purpose, but the plot was discovered. Kusuko poisoned herself, her brother was killed, and Heizei took Buddhist orders. After the incident Saga established an extrastatutory office, the KURŌDO-DOKORO (Bureau of Archivists, or Chamberlains' Office), at the court to handle confidential documents. FUJIWARA NO FUYUTSUGU was appointed as its head, and the Hokke branch of the family, which he represented, outstripped the Shikike in power and prestige. KITAMURA Bunji

Kusumi Morikage (ca 1620–ca 1690)

KANŌ SCHOOL painter; best known for his genre painting of rural life, particularly farming. Born in Kaga (now part of Ishikawa Prefecture). He studied painting with KANŌ TAN'YŪ at the Kajibashi atelier in Edo (now Tōkyō), married one of Tan'yū's nieces, and assisted in such important commissioned painting projects as the TŌSHŌGŪ in Nikkō, an honor that should have secured his position in the Edo Kanō school. However, it is generally believed that, for reasons unknown, he was dismissed from the Kajibashi atelier. According to one account, in the mid-1670s he was summoned to the city of Kanazawa by the head of the Kaga domain to make designs for KUTANI WARE potters. A few years later it seems that he went to Kyōto, where he spent the rest of his life.

While Morikage broached a broad range of subjects—landscapes, flowers and birds, figures, and Buddhist themes—he is best remembered for his vivid genre paintings executed in a fluid ink style with restrained color. His most famous work of this type is *A Peasant Family beneath a Hanging Gourd Trellis* (*Nōryōzu*). He also painted a number of screens depicting *Agriculture in the Four Seasons* (*Shiki kōsaku zu*), a didactic theme expressing the Confucian ideal of a prosperous agricultural state as favored by the Tokugawa shogunate. Morikage's screens *Horseracing at the Kamo Festival* (*Kamo no kurabeuma zu*) and *Tea-leaf Picking at Uji* (*Uji chatsumi zu*) are also characteristic of his genre style, embodying strong interests in landscape painting and the activities of the common folk. Another group of works, chiefly landscapes and bird-and-flower paintings, are in a monochrome ink style rooted in the 15th-century Japanese *suibokuga* (see INK PAINTING) tradition. Although dependent on landscape models in the Southern Song (Sung) style via 15th- and 16th-century Japanese masters like SESSHŪ TŌYŌ, SESSON SHŪKEI, and KANŌ MOTONOBU, Morikage's paintings are imbued with a fresh interpretation not found in contemporary Kanō school monochrome paintings.

📖——Kobayashi Tadashi and Sakakibara Satoru, *Morikage, Itchō,* vol 16 of *Nihon bijutsu kaiga zenshū* (Shūeisha, 1978).

Catherine KAPUTA

kusunoki → camphor tree

Kusunoki Masashige (?-1336)

Warrior chieftain from Kawachi Province (now part of Ōsaka Prefecture) who fought and died as a supporter of the ill-fated KEMMU RESTORATION (1333–36) of Emperor GO-DAIGO. In later centuries Masashige was elevated in folk mythology to the position of supreme paragon of imperial loyalty. He was portrayed in primary school textbooks before World War II as the finest of all models for Japanese youth as they prepared for lives of service to throne and country.

Little is known of Masashige's origins and background. Even our knowledge of his brief career of glory and heroic death is derived largely from passages in the TAIHEIKI—a chronicle covering the decades of civil strife and warfare from about 1318 (the year of Go-Daigo's accession to the throne) until 1367—that seem to be more literarily fanciful than historically convincing. The *Taiheiki,* for example, introduces Masashige to the stage of history in a dream that Go-Daigo had after he had been forced to flee Kyōto in 1331 for secretly plotting to overthrow the Kamakura shogunate. Go-Daigo interpreted his dream as a sign from heaven that he would be victorious over the warrior "barbarians" from the east and would soon become the true and direct ruler of the country. He summoned Masashige, who assured him that by means of bold and skillful stratagems the armies of Kamakura would be destroyed. The stalwart warrior also promised the emperor that even though battles might be lost, the loyalist cause would prevail so long as he, Masashige, lived.

Shortly after his meeting with Masashige, Go-Daigo was captured by officials of the shogunate who forced him to abdicate the throne in favor of a member of a rival branch of the imperial family and exiled him to the Oki Islands in the Sea of Japan (see GENKŌ INCIDENT). During the nearly two years of Go-Daigo's exile, his cause was kept alive in the central provinces around Kyōto mainly through the guerrilla operations of his son Prince MORINAGA and Kusunoki Masashige. It was at this time that Masashige established his reputation as a brilliant military tactician. Constantly outnumbered and often short of supplies, he nevertheless held the shogunate forces at bay, and eventually it was the shogunate's inability to reduce by siege Masashige's position at Chihaya in Kawachi Province that led directly to its overthrow.

In the first month of 1333, with Masashige still holding on at Chihaya, the shogunate dispatched an army from Kamakura under the command of ASHIKAGA TAKAUJI. Entering the central provinces, Takauji changed allegiance and proclaimed his support for Go-Daigo's loyalist movement. Under attack by forces of the Ashikaga and others, the shogunate quickly collapsed, and the Kemmu Restoration became a reality. For his services in bringing about the restoration, Masashige was appointed governor *(kokushi)* and military governor *(shugo)* of Kawachi Province and military governor of Izumi Province (now part of Ōsaka Prefecture).

Go-Daigo's Kemmu Restoration was a highly impractical, reactionary attempt to turn the historical clock back some 500 years to a time when it was believed that the emperors had ruled directly. Before long it deteriorated into a competition between Ashikaga Takauji and NITTA YOSHISADA for the position of new military leader of the land. In 1335 Takauji was driven into revolt against the restoration government. After gathering forces in Kyūshū and receiving an edict from the rival branch of the imperial family that legitimized his actions, Takauji returned to the central provinces in 1336 with the intent of capturing Kyōto. The decisive battle was fought in July 1336 (Engen 1.5) at the river Minatogawa, near what is now Kōbe, between the Ashikaga and loyalist forces that included Masashige and Nitta Yoshisada (see MINATOGAWA, BATTLE OF). The *Taiheiki* account of this battle tells us that Masashige knew before it began that victory was impossible and that he faced certain death. And indeed, after many hours of ferocious battling in a sweltering heat, Masashige and his brother withdrew from the battle and committed suicide.

📖——Ivan Morris, *The Nobility of Failure* (1975). Uemura Seiji, *Kusunoki Masashige* (1962). H. Paul Varley, *Imperial Restoration in Medieval Japan* (1971). *H. Paul* VARLEY

Kutani ware

(kutani-yaki). Porcelain ware. A variety of porcelains both for everyday and TEA CEREMONY use made in Kaga Province (now part of Ishikawa Prefecture) from 1655 to 1704 and again from 1807 to the present. The Old Kutani kiln (1655–1704), operated by Gotō Saijirō (d 1704) at Kutani for the Maeda *daimyō,* is best known for its boldly designed tableware in dark, restrained overglaze enamels, mostly dishes and bowls but also lidded containers, *sake* bottles, and ewers. Their bodies are grayish and coarse-grained. The white glazes vary from dull white to a shiny, even white with a bluish tinge; the underglaze blue decoration, when present, varies from pale indigo to sooty, dark blue. Their color schemes, derived from Chinese three-color ware, known in Japanese as *kōchi,* and from its Kyōto versions, emphasize green and yellow; green Kutani has preponderantly green designs supplemented by yellow, purple, or dark blue. The colorful, vigorously brushed designs draw on late Ming (1368–1644) and early Qing (Ch'ing; 1644–1912) dynasty porcelains, KANŌ SCHOOL and TOSA SCHOOL paintings, and textiles. On the bases there are often inscriptions reading *fuku* (good fortune). Recent excavations at Kutani have yielded remnants of other kinds of porcelain as well, and the full range of Kutani production has not yet been determined.

In the 19th century the Old Kutani style was revived at a number of kilns, most notably in Kutani at the Yoshidaya kiln (1823–31), founded by Toyoda Den'emon (d 1827). The name Kutani has also been applied to the red and gold pieces so popular in the West, and, in order to produce them, kilns, some of them still operative, arose throughout Kaga Province during the last years of the Edo (1600–1868) through the Meiji (1868–1912) periods. Red Kutani was first made at the Minzan (1818–44; founded by Takeda Shūhei, d 1844) and Ono (founded 1819) kilns. It was later made in a more meticulous, richly decorated manner, introduced by Iidaya Hachirōemon (d 1849) at the Miyamotoya kiln (founded in 1835), and was brought to a peak of technical excellence by the Kyōto potter Eiraku Wazen XII (1823–96) at the Eiraku kiln (founded in the 1860s). An important later Kutani potter was Kutani Shōzō (1816–83), who developed an eclectic, colorful, and intricate style, introduced a number of technical innovations, and was an influential teacher.

Frederick BAEKELAND

Kutcharo, Lake

(Kutcharoko). Also known as Lake Kussharo. Crater lake in eastern Hokkaidō. Located within the Kutcharo caldera and part of Akan National Park. An island called Nakajima, a composite volcano, is situated in the center of the lake. The water is acid and fish are practically nonexistent. Popular tourist attraction. Area: 79.7 sq km (30.8 sq mi); circumference: 57 km (35 mi); depth: 117.5 m (385.4 ft); altitude: 121 m (397 ft).

kutōten → punctuation marks

Kutsuki Masatsuna (1750–1802)

Daimyō of the Fukuchiyama domain (now part of Kyōto Prefecture) and scholar of WESTERN LEARNING; also known as Kuchiki Masatsuna. As both the lord of a domain and a student of Western knowledge, he was exceptional for his time, cultivating the friendship of scholars like SUGITA GEMPAKU and ŌTSUKI GENTAKU as well as Izaak TITSINGH, the overseer of the Dutch trading post in Nagasaki. Kutsuki was particularly drawn to the study of geography; with the help of a former official interpreter (Oranda *tsūji*), he translated a Dutch version of a geographical treatise by the German scholar Johann Hübner (1668–1731) and published it as *Taisei yochi zusetsu* (1789, Illustrated Account of the Western World). He was also interested in collecting old coins and wrote several books on the subject.

Kuttara, Lake

(Kuttarako). In southwestern Hokkaidō. Located to the east of Noboribetsu Hot Spring, this lake was created when the volcano Kuttaradake erupted, forming a round-shaped caldera which filled with water. Ezo salamander and the fish known as *himemasu (Oncorhynchus nerka* var. *adonis)* make this lake their habitat. Area: 4.3 sq km (1.6 sq mi); circumference: 9 km (6 mi); depth: 148 m (485 ft); transparency: 28.3 m (92.8 ft); altitude: 258 m (846 ft).

kuwa

(hoes). The use of *kuwa* or hoes in Japan goes back to the Yayoi period (ca 300 BC–ca AD 300), although it was not until the Kofun period (ca 300–710) that it became widespread. Different types of hoe have gradually developed in different regions, so that there are distinct local names for each; there is also a wide variety distinguished according to function, appearance, and design. Some examples are the *itaguwa,* for furrowing and plowing fields; the small *karaguwa,* with a thick blade for clearing land; the three-pronged *bitchūguwa* for rice cultivation; and the *kusakezuri kuwa* for weeding.　　　　　　　　　　　　　　　　　　NOGUCHI Takenori

Kuwabara Takeo (1904–)

Critic; scholar of French literature. Born in Fukui Prefecture, son of the historian Kuwabara Jitsuzō (1870–1931). Graduate of Kyōto University. A student and translator of Stendhal and Alain, Kuwabara emerged after World War II as a leading liberal, writing extensive criticism on traditional Japanese culture. He is also known as an alpinist. Kuwabara's main works include "Daini geijutsu: Gendai haiku ni tsuite" (1946), a controversial criticism of HAIKU as a modern art form, and *Nakae Chōmin no kenkyū* (1966), a critical biography of NAKAE CHŌMIN.

Kuwada Yoshinari (1882–)

Cytologist. Born in Ōsaka. A graduate of Tōkyō University, he later taught at Kyōto University. Kuwada conducted research concerning the structure of the chromosome and contributed to development in this area. He received the Order of Culture in 1962. His works include *Kakubunretsu no shinka* (1954).　　　SUZUKI Zenji

Kuwaki Gen'yoku (1874–1946)

Philosopher. Born in Tōkyō. A graduate of Tōkyō University, he was influenced early on by neo-Kantian philosophy. In 1907 he studied in Germany and was particularly influenced by the philosophy of critical realism. Finding the study of Kant meaningful in discovering the a priori basis of culture, Kuwaki sought to define the basis of Japan's modernization. As a professor at Tōkyō University from 1914 to 1935 and through his articles in the *Tetsugaku zasshi* (Journal of Philosophy), he worked for the spread of "culturalism," a movement based on German idealist philosophy. Kuwaki also traveled frequently to Europe and the United States and worked to introduce Japanese philosophical studies to the West. His writings include *Tetsugaku gairon* (1900, Outline of Philosophy) and *Kanto to gendai no tetsugaku* (1917, Kant and Contemporary Philosophy). See also MODERN PHILOSOPHY; NISHIDA KITARŌ.

　　　　　　　　　　　　　　　　　　TAKAHASHI Ken'ichi

Kuwana

City in northern Mie Prefecture, central Honshū, 25 km (15 mi) southwest of Nagoya. Kuwana prospered in the Edo period (1600–1868) as a castle town of the Matsudaira family, a post-station town on the highway Tōkaidō, and a river port on the river Ibigawa. It is an industrial and residential suburb of Nagoya, with steel and machine industries. Pop: 86,606.

Kūya (903–972)

Also known as Kōya. Along with GYŌGI (668–749), one of the prototypes of the HIJIRI, charismatic itinerant Buddhist monks who carried out missionary and social welfare work independently of the religious and political establishments. Kūya is best known for his popularization of PURE LAND BUDDHISM via group chanting, to the accompaniment of bells, drums, and ecstatic dancing, of the NEMBUTSU, an invocation of the name of the Buddha AMIDA, which had originally been a solitary contemplative practice of monks and some noblemen.

Kūya's origins are unclear, though by traditional accounts he was a scion of the imperial family. In his twenties, having already made a tour of holy sites in various provinces and assisted in temple repair, the construction of roads, bridges, and wells, the cremation of abandoned corpses, and the dissemination of the *nembutsu,* he privately undertook religious vows at the provincial temple (KOKU-BUNJI) in Owari Province (now part of Aichi Prefecture), adopting

Kūya

This detail of a statue of Kūya made by Kōshō several centuries after the priest's death shows him invoking the name of the Buddha Amida (represented by the small figures issuing from his mouth) to the accompaniment of a small gong. Colors on wood. Height 117.6 cm. Early 13th century. Rokuharamitsuji, Kyōto.

the Buddhist name Kūya. Thereafter he spent some years in the study of the Buddhist sutras at the temple Mineaidera in Harima Province (now part of Hyōgo Prefecture) and underwent a period of ascetic discipline and devotion to the bodhisattva KANNON of Yushima (now Ishima) in Awa (now Tokushima Prefecture) on Shikoku. Following a period of evangelization in the far northeastern provinces of Mutsu (now Fukushima, Miyagi, Morioka and Aomori prefectures) and Dewa (now Akita and Yamagata prefectures), he returned to Kyōto in 938 and took up the role of a mendicant monk, chanting the *nembutsu* and distributing the alms he received among the poor and sick. He came to be known as Ichi no Shōnin (or Ichi no Hijiri), "Saint of the Marketplace," and his popular following grew. In 948 he ascended Mt. Hiei (HIEIZAN) and for the first time underwent formal ordination as a Buddhist monk, receiving the appellation Kōshō. In an appeal to the Buddhist deities to grant relief from an epidemic which raged through the capital in 951, Kūya constructed an image of the Eleven-headed Kannon (still housed at Saikōji, later renamed ROKUHARAMITSUJI, founded by Kūya in 963) and undertook a vow to copy the *Daihannyaharamitta kyō* (Skt: *Mahāprajñā-pāramitā-sūtra*) in 600 chapters. He is said to have predicted the time of his own death and to have passed away at Saikōji, facing west and chanting the *nembutsu.* The image of Kūya housed in this temple, which depicts miniature Amida Buddhas *(edabutsu)* issuing from his mouth, is famous. Other conventional attributes associated with Kūya are the deerskin clothing and antler-surmounted staff (according to legend fashioned from the remains of a deer, Kūya's companion in solitude, slain by a hunter) and the conch shell (HORAGAI) he blew during his missionary expeditions. ——Hori Ichirō, *Kōya* (1963).

　　　　　　　　　　　　　　　　　　Kyōko Motomochi NAKAMURA

Kuze Hirochika (1819–1864)

Daimyō of the Sekiyado domain (now part of Chiba Prefecture) and senior councillor *(rōjū)* of the Tokugawa shogunate. Born in Edo (now Tōkyō). Kuze became senior councillor in 1852, but in 1858 he was removed from office for openly criticizing the great elder *(tairō)* II NAOSUKE's suppression of political dissent (ANSEI PURGE). Reappointed senior councillor after Ii's assassination in 1860, Kuze and ANDŌ NOBUMASA worked to strengthen the shogunate, together promoting a policy of cooperation between the imperial and military governments (see MOVEMENT FOR UNION OF COURT AND SHOGUNATE). They arranged the marriage of Emperor KŌMEI's sister Prin-

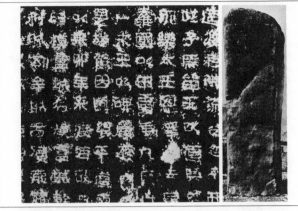

Kwanggaet'o monument

Shown are a detail of the inscription on the stone monument and a full-length view of one of its four sides. The text, which begins on the side shown, continues on the other three.

cess KAZU to the shōgun TOKUGAWA IEMOCHI and initiated several military and economic reforms. In 1862 Kuze sent a mission to Europe to seek postponement of the opening of additional treaty ports as provided in the ANSEI COMMERCIAL TREATIES; the resulting London Protocol extended the deadline to 1868. But this did not appease the imperial court nor the antiforeign and antishogunate extremists; Andō was attacked by assassins in February 1862 and forced to resign, and Kuze was dismissed in June and placed under house arrest for having been "disrespectful" to the court and "subservient" to the West.

kuzu

(kudzu vine). *Pueraria thunbergiana.* A perennial herbaceous climbing vine of the pea family (Leguminosae). Large and strong, it grows wild in fields and mountains all over Japan. It is one of the seven flowers of autumn *(aki no nanakusa).* The vines are covered with brown hairs and may reach 10 meters (33 ft) in length. The stems are woody at the base. The leaves are large, alternate, and ternately compound; the leaflets are nearly round. The leaves are thick and green above, but their undersides are pale and covered with white hairs. In autumn, flower stalks 15–18 centimeters (6–7 in) in height grow from the leaf axils, and bear reddish purple butterfly-shaped flowers in raceme clusters.

Starch from pounded roots has long been used by the Japanese as a food; root fibers were also used to make cloth for work clothes. In Chinese pharmacological practice, dried *kuzu* root is employed in preparing a medicine for colds. The leaves make excellent livestock feed and are used for that purpose in the United States as well as Japan. MATSUDA Osamu

Kuzuryūgawa

River in eastern Fukui Prefecture, central Honshū, originating in the mountains between Fukui and Gifu prefectures and flowing through the Fukui Plain into the Sea of Japan. The upper reaches have been dammed to create a huge reservoir. Length: 116 km (72 mi); area of drainage basin: 2,930 sq km (1,131 sq mi).

Kwanggaet'o monument

(J: Kōkaido Ō *ryō hi* or Kōtai Ō *hi*). A stone tablet, a little over 6 meters (20 ft) high, erected in AD 414 to commemorate the deeds of King Kwanggaet'o (J: Kōkaidō Ō or Kōtai Ō), ruler of the Korean kingdom of KOGURYŎ from 391 to 413. Located on the Manchurian (Chinese) side of the Yalu River, in Ji'an (Chi-an) County, Jilin (Kirin) Province, it was unearthed in 1882. Its text, in about 1,800 elegantly carved Chinese characters, celebrates the king's wars of conquest in Manchuria and the Korean peninsula as well as his campaigns against the Japanese-dominated state of KAYA in the south. It is an important source of information on early Korean history and Korean-Japanese relations. The monument came to public notice

during the Korean War, when Syngman RHEE (Yi Sŭng-man), president of the Republic of Korea, argued with the support of some South Korean historians that United Nations forces could legitimately engage Chinese and North Korean troops north of the Yalu because the monument proved that southern Manchuria was historically Korean territory. C. Kenneth QUINONES

Kwangju Student Resistance Movement

A nationwide explosion of violent, anti-Japanese sentiment that swept Korea during the winter of 1929–30. It began when Japanese male students ridiculed Korean female students at the Naju train station located just west of Kwangju, capital of South Chŏlla Province in southwestern Korea. On 3 November 1929 some 600 Japanese and Korean middle and high school students clashed in the streets of Kwangju. Harsh treatment by Japanese police, especially of Korean girls, combined with support from the patriotic Korean group SIN'GANHOE led to a bloody, five-month demonstration against Japanese prejudice and rule in which more than 54,000 students at 194 schools participated. The thoroughness and brutality of police suppression made it the last outburst for independence to come from within Korea until liberation from Japanese rule in 1945. See also KOREA AND JAPAN: Japanese colonial control of Korea. C. Kenneth QUINONES

Kwantung Army → Guandong (Kwantung) Army

Kwantung Territory → Guandong (Kwantung) Territory

kyahan

Leggings traditionally worn for outdoor work or when traveling to protect the legs from cold. They are still used by farmers and others who must work long hours outdoors. In ancient times they were called *habaki* and were made of the stems and leaves of cattails, reeds, bulrush, straw, and other plants. Leggings made from cotton, hemp, silk, and other cloth materials were worn from the Muromachi period (1333–1568) and came to be known as *kyahan.* There are three different types of *kyahan. Ōtsukyahan* are fan-shaped pieces of cloth strapped to the leg with cord. *Edokyahan* are cloth pieces fit to the calf, cut to size, and secured with cord and clasps. *Tsutsukyahan* are cylindrically shaped pieces of single cloth that are slipped snugly onto the lower leg. MIYAMOTO Mizuo

kyaku and shiki → Engi Shiki

Kyōbushō

(Ministry of Religion). Government ministry of the Meiji period (1868–1912), established in April 1872 to replace the Jingishō (Ministry of Shintō Religion). In an effort to revive Shintō, the Meiji government had founded the Jingikan (Office of Shintō Worship) and the Senkyōkai (Board of Missionaries) in 1868, immediately after the MEIJI RESTORATION. In 1871 the Jingikan was replaced by the Jingishō, and following a proposal from the Seiin (Central Chamber), the highest administrative board of the Grand Council of State (DAJŌKAN), the Jingishō was in turn replaced by the Kyōbushō. The new ministry abandoned the previous exclusive emphasis on Shintō affairs and took charge of Buddhist temples as well as Shintō shrines, the ordination of Shintō and Buddhist priests, and the care of the imperial tombs; it also absorbed the Senkyōshi. The Kyōbushō was abolished in 1877 when the government decided to liberalize its religious policy, and its administrative duties were assumed by the Home Ministry (Naimushō).

Kyōdai Jiken → Kyōto University Incident

Kyōdō Insatsu sōgi → Kyōdō Printing Company strike

Kyōdo kenkyū

(Local Studies; literally, "native place studies," i.e., studies on local traditions). The first journal in Japan devoted exclusively to FOLK-

LORE STUDIES; founded in 1913 by the noted folklorist YANAGITA KUNIO and Takaki Toshio (1876–1922), originally a scholar of German. In its inaugural issue Takaki stated that scholars should carry out basic research on every aspect of traditional Japanese life, following the German concept of *Volkskunde,* or folk studies. In addition to articles and essays, the journal published reports from various parts of Japan on folklore research materials and sources. Among its contributors were such leading folklore scholars as ORIKUCHI SHINOBU, MINAKATA KUMAKUSU, and KINDAICHI KYŌSUKE. Although it ceased publication in 1917, it was revived in 1931 by Okamura Chiaki (1884–1941) and was continued until 1934.

Ōtō Tokihiko

Kyōdō News Service

(Kyōdō Tsūshinsha). One of Japan's largest cooperative news agencies whose membership is composed of the 63 most influential national and local newspapers and Nippon Hōsō Kyōkai (NHK; Japan Broadcasting Corporation), Japan's public broadcasting company. Kyōdō News Service began operation in 1945 when the news agency DŌMEI TSŪSHINSHA disbanded after World War II. Over the years it has become one of the world's major wire services and now has contracts with 26 international agencies for the exchange of news including the Associated Press, United Press International, Reuters, Deutsche Presse Agentur, and Tass. The agency daily offers approximately 12,000 lines of domestic and foreign news, 5,000 lines of feature story material, stock market reports, and 1,000 wirephotos to the nation's newspapers and broadcasting stations. The Kyōdō also operates some 28 foreign bureaus, deploys special correspondents, and has over 100 participating and associate news media providing services to national and foreign subscribers.　　　*Arai Naoyuki*

Kyōdō Oil Co, Ltd

(Kyōdō Sekiyu). Company engaged in the sale and transportation of petroleum products. Kyōdō Oil Co was formed in 1965 when the marketing divisions of three independent oil companies (NIPPON MINING CO, LTD, Asia Oil, and Tōa Sekiyu) were integrated under the guidance and support of the Japanese government. Subsequently, FUJI OIL CO, LTD, became the fourth member of the Kyōdō Oil group in 1966, followed by Kashima Oil in 1967. Group refineries are run by Asia Kyōseki Co, formed jointly by Asia Oil and Kyōdō Oil in 1970; and by Tōa Kyōseki Co, set up by Tōa Sekiyu, Kyōdō Oil, and ARABIAN OIL CO, LTD, in 1973.

In response to the growing need for crude oil, Kyōdō Crude Oil of Japan, Ltd, was incorporated in 1970 to help promote and stabilize the group's crude oil procurement and tanker-chartering operations. Together with group member companies, Kyōdō Oil has worked actively to expand capacities in all fields of oil operations in order to keep up with Japan's rapidly increasing energy consumption. As a result, it now ranks among the top three oil companies in the nation. Total sales for the fiscal year ending March 1982 were ¥2.8 trillion (US $11.6 billion); capitalization stood at ¥18 billion (US $74.8 million) in the same year. Corporate headquarters are located in Tōkyō.

Kyōdō Printing Company strike

(Kyōdō Insatsu *sōgi*). Major labor dispute in 1926 between the Kyōdō Printing Company in Tōkyō and its employees. The company's announcement on 8 January of a reduction of working hours triggered a massive strike by workers, many of whom belonged to the Kantō Publishing Industry Labor Union (Kantō Shuppan Rōdō Kumiai). In retaliation, the company dismissed all 2,142 striking union members, retaining about 300 nonmembers to man the factory. Under the direction of the union's parent organization, the Japan Labor Union Council (Nihon Rōdō Kumiai Hyōgikai), the workers decided on a long-term strike. The dispute, marked by some 1,500 cases of arrest or detention by military police, ended in defeat for the union when the exhausted strikers submitted on 18 March to dismissal in return for severance pay averaging ¥100. Despite the union's failure, the development of sophisticated strike tactics marked a turning point in the history of the Japanese labor movement. The strike was the subject of the novel *Taiyō no nai machi* (1929, City without Sun) by the proletarian writer TOKUNAGA SUNAO.

Kyōdō Shiryō Co, Ltd

Manufacturer and vendor of poultry and swine feeds; engaged also in the sale of livestock. Founded in 1946. An independent firm

unaffiliated with any group of trading companies, it is the second leading Japanese manufacturer of feeds behind NIHON NŌSAN KŌGYŌ. The firm imports feed grain, soybean tailings, fish meal, raw molasses, and other materials from the United States, Brazil, and Australia, and processes them at five modern factories located throughout Japan. The firm is attempting to diversify in order to establish itself as a comprehensive manufacturer of livestock-related products. Sales for the fiscal year ending March 1982 totaled ¥129.9 billion (US $539.6 million), of which feed sales constituted 57 percent. In the same year capitalization stood at ¥4.2 billion (US $17.4 million). Corporate headquarters are in Yokohama.

Kyōfūkai

(WCTU; Nihon Kirisutokyō Fujin Kyōfūkai or, from 1923, Fujin Kyōfūkai; Woman's Christian Temperance Union of Japan). Women's social reform organization. Inspired by the visit of the American WCTU campaigner Mary Leavitt (1830–1912), YAJIMA KAJIKO and some 50 other Japanese women started the Tōkyō Kirisutokyō Fujin Kyōfūkai in 1886. Reorganized on a national scale in 1893, the Kyōfūkai became Japan's largest women's organization in the 1890s. Among its prominent early members were Ushioda Chiseko (1843–1903), Sakurai Chikako (1855–1928), Hayashi Utako (1864–1946), Tsuneko Gauntlett (1873–1953), Moriya Azuma (1884–1975), and SASAKI TOYOJU. The group campaigned against alcohol, tobacco, and legalized prostitution, including the practice of sending Japanese prostitutes abroad (see KARAYUKI SAN). In 1894 it established in Tōkyō the Jiaikan, a settlement to rehabilitate prostitutes and other women in trouble. In 1901–02 the group also called attention to the pollution victims in the ASHIO COPPER MINE INCIDENT. The Kyōfūkai's official magazine *Fujin shimpō* (Women's News) has helped to publicize such causes ever since. The group was headed 1962–71 by the feminist and reformer KUBUSHIRO OCHIMI. Since World War II, it has continued campaigns against prostitution and for world peace, with a membership of several thousand.

kyōgen

A form of comic drama which evolved, as did NŌ, in the earlier tradition of SARUGAKU (or *sangaku*), flourished from the middle of the 14th century, and is still performed today. Most specifically, the comic plays that exist as independent pieces and are traditionally performed between two separate Nō plays. The relationship between *kyōgen* and Nō is one of complementary development, but Nō in the largest sense includes *kyōgen*.

The word *kyōgen* is also used to refer to comic roles within a single Nō play, of which the most common are those known as *aikyōgen* (intermission *kyōgen*). It eventually came to mean simply "play" or "theatrical performance," as in "*kabuki kyōgen*"(kabuki plays). This article deals with both the comic roles within Nō plays and the independent comic plays. When used without qualification, the word *kyōgen* will refer to the latter.

The Name and Its Variants —— Originally *kyōgen* was an ordinary Chinese word meaning "deviant, wrong-headed words" or "jocular, amusing words," and these are the usual meanings when it occurs in early Japanese works from the 8th century onwards. The use of the word to mean a particular type of dramatic performance dates from about the middle of the 14th century; and in the next century diaries sometimes mention "*kyōgen nō*" (*kyōgen* plays) to distinguish the comic plays from the serious ones known as "*sarugaku nō,*" "*dengaku nō,*" and so forth.

At the same time, the comic plays were also sometimes called *okashi* (entertainments, comedies) in the writings of ZEAMI (1363–1443), one of the two greatest figures in the history of Nō. Then, in the Edo period (1600–1868), the general use of the word *kyōgen* to mean simply "play" gave rise to the term "Nō *kyōgen*," when it was necessary to distinguish the old comedies from the newer forms of drama such as KABUKI.

History —— Traditionally, *kyōgen* is said to have its origin in comic dances described as having been performed in the Age of the Gods, but historically its roots certainly go back to the 8th century. At that time one of the many cultural imports from Tang (T'ang; 618–907) China was an entertainment called in Japanese *sangaku* ("scattered," i.e., miscellaneous, "entertainments"), which contained such items as acrobatics, juggling, magic, and comic imitations. At first it came under the patronage of the court, where it was performed as a diver-

Kyōgen———Fuku no Kami

A scene from *Fuku no kami* (The God of Good Fortune). The god, at left, has an elaborate costume and mask reminiscent of the Nō drama. Performers: Yamamoto Tōjirō (the god), Takai Noriyasu and Nakajima Noboru (pilgrims).

sion at ceremonies and other gatherings, but its popularity gradually spread and, as time went on, it assumed an increasingly Japanese character. This was typified by a change in the name to *sarugaku*, usually written with the characters for "monkey music," which was itself sometimes further corrupted to the very Japanese form *sarugō*. Although items such as acrobatics and juggling survived in *sarugaku* and DENGAKU for some five centuries, the comic-imitation element became more and more important. The titles of some comic pieces recorded in the middle of the 11th century by Fujiwara no Akihira in his *Shin sarugaku ki* (Record of the New Sarugaku) indicate very clearly the same kind of humorous material that is found in later *kyōgen* plays: *Fukuō hijiri no kesa motome* (The Holy Man Fukuō Searches for His Stole); *Myōkō Ni no mutsuki-goi* (The Nun Myōkō Asks for Baby's Swaddling Clothes); *Azumaudo no ui kyō-nobori* (The First Visit to the Capital by a Man from the East); and *Kyōwarambe no sorazare* (The Tricks of a Lad from the Capital).

Throughout its history, *sarugaku* was given as an entertainment at many shrines and temples, particularly those in the provinces around Kyōto and Nara and, as a result, it came into close contact with religious rituals and ceremonies and with other forms of entertainment given on the same occasions. It was thus strongly influenced by, for example, the musical chanting of Buddhist scriptures, by the esoteric rituals and other activities carried out by a special type of priest known as *jushi* or *shushi* (spell master), and by the serious and didactic plays called ENNEN. It seems likely that the professional *sarugaku* players were gradually called upon to take over the performance of some of these other entertainments because, between the 10th and 14th centuries, *sarugaku* came to have two main and distinct elements: on the one hand, the original *kyōgen*-type comic pieces and, on the other, serious plays based on music and dance—i.e., Nō plays—developed from the Buddhist temple entertainments.

In spite of its temple connections, *sarugaku* remained until at least the end of the 14th century primarily a popular entertainment, dependent on its appeal to audiences of common people in country towns and villages, who gathered to watch performances by touring groups of players. These groups were called *za* (guilds), and each of them contained all the players, musicians, and so forth needed for full performances of Nō and *kyōgen*. By the early 14th century, however, a clear distinction was being made between the performers of Nō and the *kyōgen* players, with the serious and literary Nō plays as the overwhelmingly dominant element in *sarugaku* performances. Most of what is known about *sarugaku* at this time comes from Zeami who, in 1400, began an invaluable series of writings on the art of Nō. He was greatly concerned to elevate the literary and aesthetic standards of Nō performances, to conform to the tastes of his patrons among the military rulers. His references to such things as his reluctance to take *kyōgen* players to perform with him before the nobility because of the embarrassment they sometimes caused by their largely impromptu dialogue are a good indication of the continued existence of the element of earthy humor in *kyōgen* that was suggested by some of the titles of the 11th-century comic *sarugaku* pieces.

The patronage of *sarugaku* by the most powerful groups in the land began in 1374, when the supreme military ruler ASHIKAGA YOSHIMITSU saw a performance for the first time. This was given by the Kanzeza, and from then on Yoshimitsu gave his protection to KAN'AMI, the head of the group, and in particular to his son Zeami. His example led others of his kind to become the patrons of other *sarugaku* groups, especially the other three which, with the Kanzeza, made up the four main *sarugaku* groups of the province of Yamato (now Nara Prefecture).

The patronage of these groups by the richest and most powerful families in Japan continued right up until the Meiji Restoration in 1868 and had far-reaching effects on the development of Nō and *kyōgen*. During the 16th century, for example, it was largely instrumental in causing the earlier comprehensive *za* to lose much of their cohesion and to be fragmented into different schools for each type of player and musician within the *za*, when patrons adopted various skilled performers as their favorites and came to treat them and their followers as part of their retinue. As a result, the first independent *kyōgen* school, the Ōkura, was established in the latter part of the century, and around the turn of the century it was followed by the emergence of two others, the Sagi and Izumi schools. The policy of the authorities in the Tokugawa shogunate (1603–1867) consolidated this process through its concern to organize all facets of society into rigid hierarchical structures, and each head of the now separate specialist schools, with the official recognition of the authorities and the patronage of one or another of the great lords, enjoyed almost unlimited power within his own school.

The minor groups of *kyōgen* players from other, less fortunate types of entertainment were either absorbed into these three main schools, or went off into the new world of kabuki; and by the second quarter of the 17th century *kyōgen* consisted, in effect, of the official schools alone. The Ōkura and Sagi schools were henceforth direct retainers of the Tokugawa ruling family, while the Izumi school was under the patronage of the Tokugawa family of the province of Owari (now part of Aichi Prefecture) and the Maeda clan of the province of Kaga (now part of Ishikawa Prefecture), and also took part in performances at the imperial court in Kyōto. As an integral part of Nō, which became an official and ceremonial entertainment under the Tokugawa, *kyōgen* thus went through two-and-a-half centuries of calm and protected existence, until the Meiji Restoration of 1868.

At a stroke, this event caused the disappearance of the rich patrons of Nō and *kyōgen* and, with it, seemingly the end of their long history. A number of *kyōgen* family groups which had been based in the fiefs of lords in different parts of the country tried to maintain their livelihood by joining up with related groups in Kyōto or Tōkyō; but by the early 1880s the Sagi school had broken up when most of its players went off into other forms of entertainment, and the main house of the Ōkura school had been disbanded. In 1916 the same thing happened to the main house of the Izumi school, and for more than 20 years after that there was no school-head active in the world of *kyōgen*. It was only through the activities of strong and now largely independent families—the Miyake group within the Izumi school, and the Shigeyama group within the Ōkura school—that *kyōgen* was kept alive, until the two head families were able to reestablish themselves.

Since then the two schools have continued to perform, in spite of a second critical period because of World War II. Most performances are within Nō programs, but rising interest since the war in *kyōgen* as a popular drama form, and the interest stimulated in Japan by successful tours to Europe and America have led to occasional performances of *kyōgen* plays alone, a practice which has occurred from time to time since at least the late 16th century. The main function of *kyōgen* remains, however, as a traditional and integral element in Nō performances.

Schools and Players———Having been the leaders of small groups within the old Nō *za*, the heads of the *kyōgen* schools never had the authority and dominance enjoyed by the heads of the Nō schools, and their position was further weakened by the situation that developed after the Meiji Restoration. Thus although the organization into schools (*ryū*) is recognized on a formal basis, the main unit in *kyōgen* is the extended family group, and *kyōgen* performances are at present based on the three main centers in the following way:

Tōkyō area: A Nomura group and the Miyake group (both of the Izumi school); the Ōkura and Yamamoto groups (both of the Ōkura school)

Kyōto–Ōsaka area: Two Shigeyama groups and the Zenchiku group (all of the Ōkura school)

Nagoya: The Kyōgen Kyōdō Sha (Kyōgen Joint Society) and a Nomura group (both of the Izumi school)

It is usual for only a single group to perform on any particular occasion, whether it be as part of a full Nō performance or in a wholly *kyōgen* program. Like the Nō actors, all professional *kyōgen* players are men, and since they are few in number, at least compared with those in the main-actor *(shite)* schools of Nō, their services are in steady demand. The income from stage performances is supplemented by the teaching of amateurs, who learn *kyōgen* as a pastime, in the same way as the larger numbers who take up Nō singing and dancing.

Kyōgen Roles within Nō Plays——There are no clear dividing lines to be drawn between the functions of *kyōgen* players within Nō plays. At one end of the spectrum are roles that involve performing together with Nō actors and that are an inseparable part of the Nō play itself. Somewhere in the middle are Nō in which *kyōgen* players have a tenuous involvement in the action of the play but, in fact, present what is virtually a separate scene in the course of the play. At the other extreme is the most common role of all, which consists of a lone *kyōgen* player, not directly concerned with the action of the play, who holds the empty stage during the interval in a two-act Nō to tell the audience the story of the play.

The most notable *kyōgen* roles at the first extreme are those in the ceremonial piece called *Okina* (Old Man). This is a set of songs, chants, and dances which has its roots in ancient folk beliefs, and is still found in a variety of forms in local festivals and ceremonies in many parts of the country. In a developed and polished form, it holds a unique place in Nō as an auspicious, ceremonial piece performed only on very special occasions of celebration or commemoration, and so strong is its sacred character even now that only performers who are free of any ritual defilement take part in it, and even they undergo ceremonies of purification before the performance. Within Nō itself *Okina* has had different forms and different roles at various times in its history, and even today there are differences between schools and in the choice of the form of presentation available to each school according to the particular circumstances of the occasion; but the main roles in the piece are now Okina, Sambasō, and Senzai. Of these, Okina and Sambasō are of more or less the same importance in the piece as a whole, but whereas Okina is played by a Nō actor, the role of Sambasō is taken by a *kyōgen* player who, in the latter part of the piece, performs a dance which parodies that of Okina himself, as a supplication for a good harvest and prosperity. Moreover, although in the Kanze and Hōshō schools of Nō, the *kyōgen* player who brings the Okina mask on to the stage has no other function, in the Komparu, Kongō, and Kita schools he also takes the role of Senzai. Finally, while the type of *Okina* given nowadays is usually that known as the "Fourth-day Style" in the numerous categories set up during the Edo period, in a certain especially congratulatory type of *Okina* performance a number of colorfully dressed *kyōgen* players have roles known as *furyū*, in which they give a lively performance as an invocation of long life and happiness.

Although *Okina* is clearly a unique case, there are plenty of examples of *kyōgen* roles having a more or less direct connection with the action of ordinary Nō plays. One such is *Dōjōji:* in this the angry spirit of a woman spurned assumes the form of a dancer and manages to bring the new bell of Dōjōji (a Buddhist temple) crashing down, and two *kyōgen* players in the roles of temple attendants have a scene in which, when they recover sufficiently from their alarm and shock at what has happened, they rush off to report to the priests.

The *kyōgen* player in *Funa Benkei* (Benkei in the Boat) appears as a boatman in both acts of the play, and together with Benkei, played by the *waki* (secondary actor), he bears the responsibility of providing a strong link between the two unusually disparate halves of the play.

In this play he also acts as an *aikyōgen* (intermission *kyōgen*), the most common function of *kyōgen* performers within the Nō plays generally. This consists typically of a single *kyōgen* player occupying the stage during the interval of a two-act Nō play and telling the story on which it centers in what was the ordinary colloquial language of the late 16th century. There are two reasons for this being done. First, in the early centuries of the development of Nō when

Kyōgen——Bōshibari

Nomura Mansaku as Tarō Kaja trying to drink *sake* from a flat bowl while tied to a pole in *Bōshibari* (Tied to a Pole). The use of realistic stage properties and lively movement is common in *kyōgen*.

mainly uneducated audiences watched the plays, the texts must have been very difficult for them to understand because of their complicated poetic language, its literary and classical allusions, and their distortion through being sung, often by actors wearing masks; and it was therefore necessary for them to be told the story of the play in everyday spoken language which they could readily understand. Also, then as now, it was necessary to separate the halves of a two-act play by an interval long enough for the *shite* (the main actor) to make a complete change of costume, and a linking *aikyōgen* did this in addition to providing some continuity of mood and content between the two parts. All two-act Nō plays have such *kyōgen* accounts available for their intervals, and the player concerned usually appears as an ordinary villager or local god of the place in which the action of the play is set.

Independent Plays——The two current schools of *kyōgen* have between them about 260 *honkyōgen* (main, i.e., independent, *kyōgen*) in their repertoires, roughly the same number as the plays available in the five schools of Nō. Also like Nō, almost all of these come from collections of plays compiled in the Edo period on the orders of the authorities. The *kyōgen* are made up of about 180 in the Ōkura school (which has discarded another 20 in modern times), and 254 in the Izumi school, 174 of them being common to both schools.

Traditionally, an independent *kyōgen* was given between each pair of Nō plays in a full program of five Nō—and some of them are parodies of particular Nō plays—but nowadays, when there are only two or three Nō in an ordinary program, only one *kyōgen* is usually given.

There are one or two plays no longer performed, such as *Nasu no Yoichi,* which have only one role and, at the other extreme, the current repertoires have some like *Tōzumō* (Chinese Wrestling) in which an odd number of players up to nine or so may appear. Most *kyōgen* plays, however, use two or three players, who are referred to either as the *shite* or *omo* (for the main actor) and *ado* (for the secondary actor); or, more commonly, by the names of their roles in the particular play, since *kyōgen* does not put emphasis on the one main role to the same extent as Nō.

Classification and Content——The number of roles in *kyōgen* plays provides one of several possible ways of classifying them. Other groupings are based, for example, on the general content of the plays (their auspicious, celebratory character; "country-

Kyōgen —— Setsubun

The *oni* (devil) with the wife in *Setsubun* (The Eve of Spring). The *oni*, as a supernatural being, wears a mask and wig. Note also the white head-dress used to indicate women. Performed by Izumi Motohide *(oni)* and Nomura Matasaburō (wife).

bumpkin'' humor; situations arising from confusion among the many homophones in Japanese; the escapades of rascally servants; etc); on a grading decided according to the degree of difficulty involved in learning to perform each play; or the preponderance in a play of one or another of the three possible constituents of speech, song, and dance. The most general and, for most purposes, the most useful classification, however, is according to the dominant role or main characteristic of the play; and the following arrangement is based on this criterion. It gives the general characteristics of each type and, at the end of the entry, the total number of plays in the two schools within each group.

1. First-group Plays: Like the first-group Nō plays, these convey an atmosphere of felicitation. The main roles are gods, rich men, or farmers, and the humor is of a quiet, gentle kind. For example, in *Fuku no kami* (The God of Good Fortune), the god appears before two pilgrims, tells them that happiness is to be found in an honest and contented way of life, and dances and sings for them. (35 plays.)

2. *Daimyō* (Feudal Lord) Plays: The main character in these plays is a lord who, though haughty and overbearing, is basically stupid and dull-witted and, as a result, always comes off worse at the hands of his subordinates. In *Futari* (or *Ninin*) *daimyō* (The Two Lords), for example, the main characters set off for the capital together and, neither of them having a retainer in attendance, they press a passerby into their service and force him to carry their swords. Much aggrieved at this treatment, he thereupon uses their own swords to force them to take off their top-robes and then do such foolish things as pretend to be fighting-cocks and dogs, before he finally runs off with their swords and robes. (16 plays.)

3. Tarō Kaja, or *shōmyō* ("small landowner"), Plays: The most important role in these plays is Tarō Kaja, a lord's retainer who is often something of a drunkard and a coward, but is always sharp enough to get the better of his master. In *Bōshibari* (Tied to a Pole), for example, he and his fellow servant regularly get drunk on their master's wine when he goes out, and on one such occasion, therefore, he tricks them into having their hands tied, one to a pole across the shoulders and the other behind his back. In spite of this, however, they cleverly manage to help each other to drink the wine, and he returns to find them in their usual state. (45 plays.)

4. *Muko* (Bridegroom, Son-in-law) Plays: These center on a young, newly married man and his embarrassing incidents with his wife's family, which arise typically from his naiveté and weakness of character. Thus, in *Kuchimane muko* (The Mimicking Bridegroom), the young man is so worried about what to say and do at his first formal meeting with his future father-in-law that a friend tells him to imitate exactly all the words and actions of his host. He does this so faithfully that Tarō Kaja, the servant of the house, begins to laugh at him. This rudeness to his guest finally leads the master to beat him, and the bridegroom, following his instructions to the letter, does the same, much to the bewilderment of poor Tarō Kaja. (19 plays.)

5. *Oni* (Devil) Plays: Devils are usually thought of as frightening and dangerous, but in these plays they are shown to be as weak and vulnerable as humans. *Setsubun* (The Eve of Spring), for example, is the story of a devil who, tired after a long journey, seeks shelter in the house of a woman whose husband is away on a pilgrimage. He becomes disconcerted and upset at her coldness to him when he makes timorous advances to her, and she realizes that he is not to be feared. She then tricks him out of his magic hat and coat, and drives him out of the house by throwing handfuls of beans at his eyes, the traditional way to drive out devils on that night of the year. (9 plays.)

6. *Yamabushi* (mountain ascetic) Plays: The ascetic priests known as *yamabushi* were credited, like the devils mentioned above, with fearsome mystical powers, but these plays show them to be as foolish and human as anyone else. In *Kani yamabushi* (The Crab and the Mountain Priest), such a priest is bragging to his disciple about his powers as they travel along, when they reach a place called Crab Marsh and are both frightened by a weird creature which emerges to confront them. Learning that it is the spirit of the crab, the priest sends his disciple to deal with it—but he is caught by the ear and the priest's prayers only serve to make the crab spirit pinch it more firmly. The *yamabushi* is then caught too, and when they are both eventually thrown to the ground, they continue their journey with the priest much humbled. (9 plays.)

7. *Shukke* (Buddhist priest) Plays: Priests in *kyōgen* are usually mercilessly exposed as being worldly, ignorant, and self-seeking. In *Fuse nai kyō* (A Sermon With No Donation), for example, a priest who makes his usual monthly visit to a parishioner for a sermon and prayers but is not then given the expected donation, goes back there time and time again on various pretexts to try to jog the parishioner's memory. When he finally hides his priest's sash in the front fold of his robe and returns once more, pretending that he has lost it, the parishioner at last remembers his donation and presses the priest to take it. He, however, makes such a great show of refusing it, in case he should be thought to have returned merely for the money, that the man tries to put the money in the fold of his robe—only to find the sash hidden there all the time. (24 plays.)

8. *Zatō* (blind men) Plays: A number of plays depict men who are blind or suffer from some other such disability, and they either make cruel fun of their handicaps or treat them with subtlety and pathos. *Tsukimi zatō* (The Moon-viewing Blind Man), for example, shows a man who goes moon-viewing on the night of the full autumn moon but, being blind, finds his pleasure in it by listening to the sounds of the insects. Another person who has also come to view the moon talks with him, they exchange poems and drink together, and then part the best of friends. The second man then decides to tease the blind one, however, and after bumping into him and finally throwing him to the ground, runs off without revealing who he is. The blind man then retrieves his cane and makes his way home, wondering to himself how one person can be so pleasant and another so unkind. (8 plays.)

9. *Mai* (Dance, i.e., Nō-type) Plays: A number of *kyōgen* are closely based on particular Nō plays, or at least follow the Nō style in their composition, so that they are in effect a kind of simple Nō play. *Tsūen*, perhaps the best-known of these, is the story of a priest who comes across an empty teahouse and asks a villager about it. He tells him that it used to belong to a priest called Tsūen and, since that day happens to be the anniversary of his death, asks the priest to pray for his soul. When he does so, the ghost of Tsūen appears, tells his story, dances for the priest, and then serves him tea. There are many similarities, including parts of the text, with the Nō play *Yorimasa*, and the structure of the *kyōgen*, with its sequence of traveling priest, villager, and ghost of the main character exactly parallels the standard Nō play arrangement of *waki* (secondary role), *maeshite* (1st-act main role), and *nochijite* (2nd-act main role). (7 plays.)

10. Miscellaneous Plays: It is possible to establish still smaller groups of plays, but *kyōgen* which do not fit into any of the above

types are usually grouped together as "miscellaneous plays." A few newly written *kyōgen,* such as *Hikoichi-banashi* and *Susugigawa,* are sometimes included in this group. (62 plays.)

Song, Music, and Dance——Although *kyōgen,* like Nō plays, can contain singing and dancing as well as spoken parts, the balance of these elements is altogether different. The three plays *Kobuuri* (The Seaweed Seller), *Natorigawa* (The Name-stealing River), and *Yobigoe* (The Calling Voice) have as their main feature a great variety of popular songs and music of the 16th and 17th centuries, quite apart from the *kouta* ("small song") which is the standard type of song in *kyōgen;* but even they are like all the other *kyōgen* plays in not using singing for the main parts of the basic text in the fashion of Nō, but only for songs that happen to arise in the action of the play. The same is true of dances in *kyōgen;* they too are the exception rather than the rule and, when they do occur, have some basis in the situation of the play.

In 1660, two years before his death, the 13th head of the Ōkura school, Ōkura Toraakira, wrote a work entitled *Warambegusa,* the first to deal wholly with *kyōgen.* In this, he claims that a priest from Mt. Hiei called Gen'e Hōin (d 1350) was the first author of this type of play and gives the titles of nearly 60 of his compositions; and he credits another 78 plays to two men who both lived around 1500, Komparu Shirojirō, the founder of the Ōkura school, and Uji Yatarō, another *kyōgen* player. There is, however, no corroboration of this, and it seems unlikely that they were authors of *kyōgen* in any real sense.

Throughout their history, *kyōgen* have been essentially plays to be performed rather than read, and there is every indication that, until about the middle of the 17th century, performances of the plays depended on an oral tradition which allowed the players considerable freedom for impromptu dialogue. This is borne out by the earliest extant collection of *kyōgen,* the *Tenshō kyōgen-bon (Kyōgen Texts of the Tenshō Era)* of 1578, for this is no more than a collection of simple *kyōgen* stories or plots and cannot be identified with any particular school or tradition.

Ōkura Toraakira was the first to record the texts of *kyōgen* plays exactly as they were heard in performance: in 1638 he began to write out the texts of 203 plays, and in his postscript dated 1642 he explains that he was concerned to provide standard texts which would no longer be at the mercy of an ever changing oral tradition. There were still changes, however, even within his own school, for the transcription of 165 texts in 1792 by the 19th head, Ōkura Torahiro, show many minor differences. The head of the Izumi school also recorded the texts of more than 200 plays at about the same time as Toraakira, but the oldest extant written texts of the Sagi school are the 120 or so recorded ca 1700 by Sagi Den'emon Yasunori (1675–1724).

These were all official texts of the *kyōgen* schools and, as such, were jealously guarded as secret writings, which could be disclosed even to professional players of other schools only in the most exceptional circumstances and with solemn safeguards.

Meanwhile, however, a publisher in Edo (now Tōkyō) had produced in 1660 the first of four volumes of a work called *Kyōgen ki* (Records of Kyōgen) which were the earliest generally available collections of *kyōgen* texts. The volumes contained 200 texts in all, but, although the publication was very popular, the texts are not identifiable with any particular school and seem to be very uneven versions derived from a number of sources. It was not until the Meiji period (1868–1912) and after that the official texts of the professional schools were published.

Kyōgen texts were thus treated very differently from those of Nō. They did not have the same literary value and were therefore not sought after to be read for the beauty of their language. Rather, they were the working scripts of professional entertainers who felt obliged to try to keep them from others who might use them as the basis of their own, inferior performances.

Stage Properties——*Kyōgen* are performed on Nō stages and use as few large stage properties as Nō plays themselves. Some *kyōgen* use the same properties as are found in Nō—*Naruko* (The Birdscarers), for example, uses the same simple framework to represent a thatched hut as the Nō *Ōhara gokō* (The Imperial Visit to Ōhara)— and there are others, such as cane sticks with tufts of hair or cloth tied on the ends to represent a horse or ox, which are peculiar to *kyōgen.* Small properties too are sometimes mere symbols of the real thing: the fan in particular can be used as in Nō to represent a wine bottle or a dozen other handheld objects. There is, however, a great range of small objects used in *kyōgen* which are very realistic and provide good material for social study. These include many

Kyōgen——Fuse nai kyō

A scene from *Fuse nai kyō* (A Sermon With No Donation). The priest (right; played by Shigeyama Sengorō) prays while his parishioner (left; Shigeyama Sensaku) listens. In the background can be seen the pine tree that decorates the bare Nō stage.

agricultural tools, weapons, dishes, containers, kitchen utensils, and so forth.

Costume——*Kyōgen* costume is markedly different from the rich and lavish brocades so characteristic of Nō in that, although in total it contains many varied types, it is mainly based on the simple realistic dress of the ordinary people of medieval Japan. The costume of *kyōgen* is typified by the dress of its two stock characters: the servant Tarō Kaja wears a bold-check under-robe, a wide-shouldered sleeveless top-robe *(kataginu),* and wide trousers, while his master dresses in a bold-striped under-robe, *kataginu,* long wide trousers the legs of which trail behind him along the ground, and a sword. Like all *kyōgen* players, they also wear the unique mark of their profession—yellow socks *(tabi)* instead of the otherwise universal white ones.

Masks——The most typical *kyōgen* are those that do not use masks, even when the character represented is an ordinary woman. (Her distinguishing item of dress in *kyōgen* is a long length of white cloth wound round the head and fixed so that the ends trail down the chest from over each ear.) There is nevertheless a range of some 20 types of mask available for portraying special characters. These are usually divided into three main groups: masks for gods, spirits, and other supernatural beings; masks for human beings; and masks for animals (e.g., monkey, badger, fox). Certain of them were adapted from Nō masks and, at the other extreme, some of the animal masks are used with imitation animal skins so that the player's body is completely covered and he is made to look as much like the particular animal as possible.

General Characteristics——After the rise of Nō, the history and development of *kyōgen* became inextricably bound up with that serious, literary and poetic, aesthetic type of drama, which is based on song and dance. *Kyōgen* complements and contrasts with Nō perfectly, because it is the opposite of Nō in almost every respect.

It is straightforward and spoken, takes ordinary people and their real world as its material and, instead of idealizing characters like the Nō, it seizes on their weaknesses and portrays these ruthlessly but, usually, with subtlety and compassion. Thus, its priests are unprincipled, ignorant, and grasping; its women domineering and treacherous; its servants cowardly, stupid, and dishonest; its lords vain and slow-witted; and its demons weak and pitiable.

It is also, and above everything else, humorous. Its humor comes basically from concentrating on aspects of its characters that are far removed from those normally presented to the outside world, but they are looked on with tolerance and good humor as all part of our imperfect world, in which it must be accepted that not everything is what it seems or should ideally be.

Kyōgen has always been overshadowed by Nō, which consciously strove to reach the highest levels of aesthetic development, and it is easy to underrate its importance and value, and the difficulty of its performance. If its players do not need to have quite the same degree of slow precision as the main actors in Nō, and do not perform in the same kind of tense and solemn atmosphere, they do instead have to have a wider range of talent, for their performances

Kyōgen———Tsukimi zatō

The blind man with his cane listening to the sound of insects near the beginning of *Tsukimi zatō* (The Moon-viewing Blind Man). The performer is Shigeyama Sensaku.

will include at times singing and dancing similar to those in Nō, and they must always have in addition the indefinable qualities needed for an effective comic performance.

Kyōgen as a whole is important for a number of reasons: for its remarkable survival as a live drama form after a history which shows it to be centuries older even than the ancient art of Nō; for the insights it provides into many aspects of life in medieval Japan; for the linguistic value of its texts; for the variety of popular songs and musical styles which it preserves; for its use as a rich source of material and comic inspiration by many later forms of literature and drama, especially kabuki; and, most of all, as a body of plays with settings and characters that are uniquely Japanese but with a humor and humanity that are universal.

■——Andō Tsunejirō, *Kyōgen sōran* (1973). André Beaujard, *Le Théatre Comique des Japonais* (1937). Araki Yoshio, *Kyōgen* (1956). *Engeki hyakka dai jiten* (Heibonsha, 1960). Furukawa Hisashi, *Kyōgen no kenkyū* (1948). Furukawa Hisashi, *Kyōgen no sekai* (1960). Ikeda Hiroshi and Kitagawa Tadahiko, ed, *Kyōgen: 'Okashi' no keifu* in *Nihon no koten geinō*, vol 4 (Heibonsha, 1970). Yoshinobu Inoura, *A History of Japanese Theater*, vol 1, *Noh and Kyōgen* (1971). Japanese National Commission for UNESCO, *Theatre in Japan* (1963). Don Kenny, *A Guide to Kyōgen* (1968). Kitagawa Tadahiko, *Kyōgen hyakuban* (1964). Koyama Hiroshi, ed, *Kyōgenshū* in *Nihon koten bungaku taikei*, vols 42 and 43 (Iwanami Shoten, 1960). Matsuda Tamotsu, *Nō kyōgen nyūmon* (1976). Shio Sakanishi, *Japanese Folk-plays: The Ink-smeared Lady and Other Kyōgen* (1960). Yokomichi Mario and Masuda Shōzō, *Nō to kyōgen* (1959).

P. G. O'NEILL

Kyōgoku family

Warrior family active from the Kamakura (1185–1333) through the Edo (1600–1868) periods; an offshoot of the Sasaki family of the Uda Genji branch of the MINAMOTO FAMILY. Founded by Sasaki Nobutsuna's (1180–1242) fourth son, Ujinobu, who was appointed military governor (SHUGO) of the northern half of Ōmi Province (now Shiga Prefecture) by the Kamakura shogunate. Ujinobu took the name Kyōgoku from his place of residence in Kyōto; his brother Yasutsuna, who took the name Rokkaku, was appointed shugo of the southern half of Ōmi (see ROKKAKU FAMILY). Ujinobu's great-grandson Takauji (1306–73) was made shugo of five provinces by ASHIKAGA TAKAUJI as reward for his services at the time of the

founding of the Muromachi shogunate (1338–1573), notably the compilation of its basic code, the KEMMU SHIKIMOKU. The Kyōgoku prospered for several generations, becoming one of the four families who held in rotation the post of administrative director (shoshi) of the Board of Retainers (SAMURAI-DOKORO). After the ŌNIN WAR (1467–77) the family fell into decline and lost most of their domains. In the Azuchi–Momoyama period (1568–1600) Kyōgoku Takatsugu (1563–1609) served the national unifiers ODA NOBUNAGA and TOYOTOMI HIDEYOSHI, and the family's fortunes revived. The Kyōgoku sided with TOKUGAWA IEYASU in the Battle of SEKIGAHARA (1600), and during the Edo period they served as *daimyō* of several domains in succession.

This Kyōgoku family should not be confused with the courtier family that produced such outstanding poets as KYŌGOKU TAMEKANE.

Kyōgoku Tamekane (1254–1332)

Poet and courtier. A member of the Mikohidari branch of the Fujiwara family, Tamekane belonged by inheritance to the liberal Kyōgoku, one of the rival poetic branches of the Fujiwara family which was descended from FUJIWARA NO SADAIE, or Fujiwara no Teika, through Teika's son and heir FUJIWARA NO TAMEIE (1198–1275). He began his formal study of poetry under his grandfather Tameie's supervision at about the age of 15, and began to follow at the same time the usual upward path of court ranks and offices. The court at the time had come to be sharply divided into two political factions supporting rival claimants to the throne: the senior or Jimyōin line descended from Emperor Go-Fukakusa (r 1246–60) and the junior or Daikakuji line descended from Emperor Kameyama (r 1260–74). An uneasy truce had been worked out by which sovereigns were chosen alternately between the two lines, the line in power at the time favoring its own courtiers and supporters in the distribution of ranks, offices, and honors. Thus Tamekane became visibly active in public affairs upon the accession in 1287 of Emperor Fushimi of the senior line supported by the Kyōgoku house. He had been passed over for promotion during the reign of the previous emperor, but had worked behind the scenes, gradually establishing his position as both political and poetic leader (despite his family's relatively low position in the ranks of the nobility) of the Jimyōin party. The new emperor Fushimi had been devoted to poetry from a young age, and he showed particular favor to Tamekane, encouraging him in both poetic and political endeavors. Tamekane's faction was also supported by the Reizei family, descended from REIZEI TAMESUKE (1263–1328), Tameie's son by his second wife, the lady known as ABUTSU NI, and allied with the Kyōgoku house by shared opposition to the Nijō line descended from Tameie's eldest son and chief heir Nijō Tameuji (1222–86). Under Fushimi's protection, Tamekane rose rapidly at court during the 1290s, receiving the senior second rank in 1295. At the same time he proved an active if not subtle politician, working to strengthen the power of the Jimyōin line, and he also participated in a great many poetry gatherings and contests sponsored by Fushimi and high courtiers close to him, including Tamekane himself. Both poetic and political activities brought him into conflict with NIJŌ TAMEYO (1250?–1338), son of Tameuji. A poetry contest or other occasion in which both participated with their supporters was sure to lead to disagreement, recriminations, and an exacerbation of the hostility between the two sides. Thus a dispute between Tamekane and Tameyo in 1293 over plans for an imperial anthology of Japanese poetry led two years later to a Nijō polemic against Tamekane entitled *Nomori no kagami* (Mirror of the Watchman of the Fields).

Tamekane played a dangerous game of politics along with his vigorous defense of his side's poetic interests, and in 1298 he was sent into exile on the island of Sado for trying to undercut the shogunate's policy of alternating sovereigns between the two rival lines. He was pardoned and recalled in 1303, and this was an occasion for numerous poetic events celebrating his return to the capital. In 1311 Tamekane was commanded by the now abdicated emperor Fushimi to compile the 14th imperial anthology—a commission which Tamekane and his supporters had eagerly awaited. No sooner did the Nijō side get wind of the former sovereign's intention than Tameyo lodged a protest alleging that Tamekane's "criminal record" and "illegitimacy" disqualified him for such an honor. Tamekane rejoined to the effect that Tameyo was mentally incompetent, Tameyo replied with another broadside, and so on, until 11 such exchanges had taken place. Tamekane gave his anthology the unconventional name of GYOKUYŌ WAKASHŪ (*Gyokuyōshū*; Collection of Jeweled

Leaves), a title recalling the KIN'YŌ WAKASHŪ (Collection of Golden Leaves) compiled by another radical poet, MINAMOTO NO TOSHI-YORI (1055?–1129), some 200 years before. As the two preceding anthologies had been compiled by representatives of the conservative Nijō line, this imperial commission afforded Tamekane and his party a rare opportunity to publish their poetry, and at the same time to humiliate their political and literary opponents by including few of their poems, and those few chosen carefully from among their least distinguished work.

Briefly stated, the poetic styles developed and practiced by the Kyōgoku–Reizei poets were innovative in stressing imagism and description in their nature poetry and nonimagism and psychological realism in their poetry on human affairs, particularly love. They found precedents for these concerns in some older Japanese poetry, in the example of Chinese poetry of the Song (Sung) dynasty, and in the search for truth of Zen Buddhists and Chinese Neo-Confucian philosophers; but their emphasis was new and their techniques sufficiently radical to cause a storm of criticism from their conservative Nijō adversaries. Tamekane was himself a major poet and innovator in the new styles, showing in his poetry an indifference to the traditional niceties of elegant poetic diction and a cavalier skirting of such poetic "sicknesses" *(yamai)* as the repetition of the same word in a poem, ending successive lines with the same vowel, and the like. Knowing that the *Gyokuyō wakashū* would outrage the Nijō faction and that they would endeavor to prevent a recurrence, he made the most of his opportunity by packing the collection with his own poems and those of his patrons. The resulting anthology with its 2,796 poems is the largest of all 21 imperial collections, exceeding its immediate predecessor by more than a thousand poems.

His ambition of more than 20 years satisfied, Tamekane took holy orders, but he failed to comport himself with a priestly sobriety, and in 1315 joined his supporters in a celebration at Nara, including a kickball meet, numerous poetic events, and ostentatious prayers that the Jimyōin line of emperors might reign in unbroken succession. The splendor of the celebration incurred the displeasure of Saionji Sanekane, the court's go-between in relations with the shogunate, who felt that his policy of alternating emperors from the two lines was under attack, and in 1316 at the age of 66 Tamekane was exiled again, this time to the province of Tosa (now Kōchi Prefecture) in Shikoku. Once more he was pardoned and returned to the mainland, but his last years are obscure. He left no children, and although he had a number of disciples and foster children, the Kyōgoku line as such died out with him.

Tamekane's poetics are set forth in his treatise known as "Lord Tamekane's Poetic Notes" *(Tamekane kyō waka shō)*. Although he is thought to have written a great many poems (his ambition is said to have been to compose at least 10,000 poems before his death), only a relatively small number survive, represented by the 132 poems preserved in various imperial anthologies.

📖——Robert H. Brower and Earl Miner, *Japanese Court Poetry* (1961).
Robert H. BROWER

Kyōgyōshinshō

(full title: *Ken jōdo shinjitsu kyōgyōshō monrui*; A Collection of Passages Revealing the True Teaching, Practice, and Attainment of the Pure Land). The major work of SHINRAN (1173–1263), the founder of the JŌDO SHIN SECT of Buddhism. The text is a compilation of extensive quotations from the scriptures, commentaries, and exegetical works of the Pure Land masters of India, China, Korea, and Japan woven together into a coherent and systematic exposition of his basic thought.

The *Kyōgyōshinshō* consists of six chapters structured on the most significant of the 48 vows fulfilled by the Buddha AMIDA. Chapter 1 reveals the Larger *Sukhāvatī-vyūha* as the "True Teaching" among the Mahāyāna sutras, for expounding the Primal Vow of Amida, which affirms the enlightenment of all sentient beings. Chapter 2, on "True Practice," elaborates upon the name of Amida (see NEMBUTSU) and encourages its recitation as the highest religious act, being the manifestation of the working of Amida in everyday life, as found in the 17th vow. Chapter 3, on "True Faith," expresses the intention of the 18th vow and demonstrates the working of Amida in releasing beings from blind passion and self-concern to an openness to the world. Chapter 4, entitled "True Attainment," discusses the ultimate goal of the Buddhist life as *nirvāna*, based upon the 11th vow, and as self-giving for the sake of suffering humanity, based upon the 22nd vow. Chapter 5, on the "True Land and True Buddha," shows their content as being inconceivable light and im-

measurable life, metaphors for wisdom and compassion, as evidenced in the 12th and 13th vows. Chapter 6 criticizes false and incomplete teachings under the title, "Provisional Land and Provisional Buddha," in contrast to the previous chapters which set forth that which is true, real, and authentic. Here Shinran's critical spirit is directed against the teachings of the 19th and 20th vows, placing them within Amida's salvific design. The contrast between the first five chapters and the final chapter is said to highlight the significance of Shinran's religious thought.

Some controversy exists concerning the precise dating of the text, the earliest suggested being the year 1224, although textual evidence shows that Shinran continually revised and added to it until his death.

📖——Shinran, *The Kyōgyōshinshō: The Collection of Passages Expounding the True Teaching, Living, Faith, and Realizing of the Pure Land,* tr D.T. Suzuki (1973), contains the first four chapters. Shinran, *Kyōgyōshinshō*, tr Kōshō Yamamoto (1958), gives a complete translation.
Taitetsu UNNO

Kyōha Shintō → Sect Shintō

Kyōha Shintō Rengōkai → Sect Shintō, Association of

Kyōhō Famine

The first of three major famines during the Edo period (1600–1868); it occurred in southwestern Japan in 1732 (Kyōhō 17) as a result of a severe locust plague and an unseasonably cold and wet summer. The harvest decreased by 4 million *koku* of rice (1 *koku* = about 180 liters or 5 US bushels; see KOKUDAKA), and prices, which had been unusually depressed, soared out of control. Stricken farmers flocked to the cities to seek relief, further adding to the misery of urban residents, and early in 1733 a large riot (UCHIKOWASHI) broke out in the shogunal capital of Edo (now Tōkyō). The Tokugawa shogunate organized relief efforts, sending officials to various domains to direct emergency measures, controlling the distribution and storage of rice, emptying its own grain reserves, and granting loans and tax remissions to the most severely afflicted areas. It issued directives prohibiting rice hoarding, limiting *sake* production, and exhorting wealthy individuals and religious institutions to provide food for the starving. It also distributed insecticides (mainly whale oil) and encouraged the recitation of prayers against the locusts. Although no deaths were reported in the shogunate's own territories, some 67,000 people were affected by the famine. In the domains, a total of 1,990,000 were affected, and more than 12,000 died of starvation. Relief finally came with the bumper crops of 1734 and 1735. See also TEMMEI FAMINE; TEMPŌ FAMINE.

Kyōhō Reforms

(Kyōhō no Kaikaku). A series of reforms and retrenchments carried out by the Tokugawa shogunate during the Kyōhō era (1716–35) and the following decade under the direction of the eighth shōgun, TOKUGAWA YOSHIMUNE. The Kyōhō Reforms have traditionally been regarded as the most successful of the three great retrenchments of the Edo period (1600–1868), and as the model for the KANSEI REFORMS of the 1780s and 1790s and the TEMPŌ REFORMS of the 1840s. More recent scholarship has tended to deemphasize the importance of the reforms as a model for later eras in favor of a stress on their significance as the culmination of social, political, and economic trends dating from the beginning of the rule of the fifth shōgun, TOKUGAWA TSUNAYOSHI, in the 1680s, and as the foundation of developments occurring during the subsequent Tanuma period of the 1760s to 1780s.

The immediate intent of the reforms was to resolve the financial crisis facing the shogunate and the *samurai* class as a result of the increasing dislocation between the theoretical socioeconomic base of samurai political power and the socioeconomic structure as it had actually evolved in the hundred years since the founding of the shogunate. The reforms sought both to increase the financial resources available to the shogunate and, through curbing of expenditures and stabilization of prices, to make it possible for the shogunate and samurai class to live within their means.

Although the reforms were oriented to basically economic issues, they had important political repercussions. These included the further enhancement and institutionalization of the personal authority of the shōgun as head of the shogunate bureaucracy, the expansion and development of bureaucratic offices, particularly those under the aegis of the commissioners of finance (KANJŌ BUGYŌ), and closer control of the intendants (DAIKAN) responsible for local governance of shogunate territories (TENRYŌ). The inauguration of the first wave of major reforms in 1721 was immediately followed by revival of the post of senior councillor with special responsibility for financial affairs (kattegakari rōjū); during the course of the reform the line of authority descending from shōgun through kattegakari rōjū to the offices under the jurisdiction of the kanjō bugyō became the central decision-making apparatus of the shogunate, continuing the trend toward reduction of the collegial authority of the senior councillors (RŌJŪ) begun under Tsunayoshi. In line with this increased importance of the kanjō bugyō, there was a significant expansion in the number of officials employed within the Finance Commission, a more specific division of responsibilities among those officials, and greater weight given to ability and technical financial expertise in promotion to the highest-ranking posts within the commission. Such merit promotions were facilitated by the institution in 1723 of a system of supplementary stipends (TASHIDAKA) whereby those shogunate retainers whose hereditary stipends were below the level established for a certain office (e.g., 3,000 koku [see KOKUDAKA] in the case of the kanjō bugyō) could be granted a supplementary amount to bring their stipend up to the established level for the duration of their appointment. In the area of local administration there was further effort, inspired by the desire to increase the amount of tax rice forwarded to Edo (now Tōkyō), to transform the daikan from tax farmers into obedient bureaucratic servants of the shogunate. Although in preceding reigns punitive measures had been the principal means to this end, the reform saw such measures underwritten by changes in the methods of tax levying, tax accounting, and covering of office costs.

The economic reforms of the Kyōhō era ranged from efforts to curb expenditures (through retrenchment, moral revitalization of the samurai class, and the promulgation of detailed sumptuary regulations) to positive efforts to increase the tax yield. The latter included such measures as encouraging the opening of new fields and the development of supplementary crops and a shift in the method of tax assessment from one based on yearly estimation of the size of the crop standing in the fields (KEMI) to one based on a fixed average annual yield (JŌMEN). The reforms also sought to come to terms with the burgeoning urban commercial economy which was the single largest cause of samurai economic problems. Yoshimune continued the policy of restoration and stabilization of the currency begun in the previous reign after two decades of massive debasements. He also sought to stabilize commodity prices and to control more closely the urban commercial class, particularly the stratum of wholesale dealers (TOIYA) which was playing an increasingly prominent role within that class. To this end the shogunate reversed its earlier policy and positively encouraged the formation of licensed guilds (KABUNAKAMA) among wholesale merchants.

These various economic measures point to a number of contradictions lying at the heart of the reform. On the one hand the reforms sought to restore the agricultural economic base on which samurai political power rested, but such methods as the encouragement of the opening of new lands and the development of supplementary crops served, in effect, to encourage further penetration of the peasant economy by urban merchant capital. In the 1740s this situation was acknowledged, after a period of vacillation, by relaxation of the restrictions against forfeiture and sale of agricultural land. Likewise, the other side of the effort to regulate the wholesale dealers through adoption of a guild system was recognition of the place they had come to occupy in Tokugawa commercial life and of the shogunate's inability to contain their growth within the framework of the early Tokugawa system of a small number of privileged merchants with a special relationship to the shogunate (GOYŌ SHŌNIN).

The extent of these contradictions became increasingly clear in the course of the reform. The reform has been periodized in a variety of ways. Following the periodization utilized by Tsuji Tatsuya (b 1926), the initial stage of the reform, lasting from 1716 to 1722, concentrated on retrenchment through curbing of expenditures and restoration of the currency. Such measures failed to solve the financial crisis, however, and in 1721–22 the shogunate was unable to pay its retainers' stipends in full. Under such pressures, in 1722 the reform entered a more active phase which lasted until 1735. To meet its immediate financial needs the shogunate levied a series of

forced loans on the daimyō in return for which it relaxed the SANKIN KŌTAI regulations, which required the daimyō to spend approximately half their time in Edo (now Tōkyō). Parallel to this emergency measure, the shogunate also instituted measures such as the shift to the jōmen system of tax levy designed to increase its absolute tax yield. In response to such measures the tax income of the shogunate rose steadily, enabling it to abolish the forced loans and restore the sankin kōtai regulations in 1731. Thereafter, however, the shogunate's tax income again declined in the face of peasant protests and demands for tax relief. Equally critical, the reduction in the amount of currency in circulation that accompanied restoration of the currency, together with an imbalance in the economic relations between the shogunate and daimyō domains mediated through the Ōsaka rice market, led to economic stagnation and depression. The depression was characterized by a fall in the price of rice, both in absolute terms and relative to other commodities, that had a pernicious effect on samurai finances and resisted a variety of shogunate efforts to check it.

These problems were surmounted only by the fundamental shift in direction that marked the third stage of the reform. In this stage, lasting from 1735 to 1745, the shogunate again adopted an expansionary financial policy, reverting to the debasement of gold and silver and accompanying it with a large-scale minting of copper coins. Simultaneously the shogunate resumed a hard-line policy on increasing the tax yield, balanced (as was signaled by relaxation of the restrictions on forfeiture and sale of land) by greater tolerance of the penetration of the countryside by urban merchant capital and by reduced emphasis on preserving the small peasant as the backbone of the shogunate's agricultural base. These trends laid the ground for the commercial development and close shogunate-merchant ties characteristic of the ensuing Tanuma period. To the extent that the Kyōhō Reforms succeeded in resolving the financial problems faced by the shogunate, their success may be attributed more to the adaptation to changing socioeconomic circumstances seen most fully in the third stage of the reform than to the stance of resistance and retrenchment essayed during the earlier stages.

■——Ōishi Shinzaburō, "Kyōhō kaikaku," in Iwanami kōza: Nihon rekishi, vol 11 (Iwanami Shoten, 1963). Tsuji Tatsuya, Kyōhō kaikaku no kenkyū (1963). Kate NAKAI

Kyōiku Chokugo → Imperial Rescript on Education

kyōiku kanji

(literally, "education kanji"). Popular name for the Chinese characters (KANJI) that Japanese students are expected to have learned to read and write by the end of elementary school. In 1946, 1,850 characters out of the existing thousands were designated by the government as sufficient for general use in all sectors of Japanese society. These were named TŌYŌ KANJI (Chinese characters for daily use). Of these, 881 were designated in 1948 as the most essential characters, which are supposed to be learned within the six years of elementary school. In 1968, 115 more tōyō kanji were added to the elementary school list, increasing the so-called kyōiku kanji to 996. Then in 1981 the tōyō kanji were increased to 1,945 characters, and the name changed to JŌYŌ KANJI (Chinese characters for common use). However, the number of kyōiku kanji remained 996, with the remaining jōyō kanji to be learned by the ninth grade.

INOUE Shōbi

Kyōikurei → Education Order of 1879

kyōka

(literally, "mad verse"). A 31-syllable poem like the WAKA, depending heavily on the KAKEKOTOBA (pivot word) and engo (related word) techniques of that form but given to vocabulary and content foreign in character to and often derisive of the waka.

The kyōka developed, tradition holds, from the humorous poems of the MAN'YŌSHŪ, an 8th-century anthology of Japanese verse, but it did not have a name of its own until the Kamakura period (1185–1333), with the appearance of Kyōka sakehyakushu (100 Poems about Sake) by the priest Gyōgetsubō (1265–1328).

The form still did not begin to come into its own until early in the Edo period (1600–1868), when it was half-heartedly taken up by certain haikai (comic verse) poets (see RENGA AND HAIKAI). Thereafter it developed first in Kyōto, then Ōsaka, then Edo (now Tōkyō), changing its style and broadening its appeal as it moved.

In Kyōto it was developed by the *haikai* poet MATSUNAGA TEITOKU on models provided by his teacher HOSOKAWA YŪSAI. Teitoku published only one thin volume of *kyōka*, however, entitled *Teitoku kyōka hyakushu* (1636). A disciple of a disciple of Teitoku, Seihakudō Gyōfū, carried on the tradition with three collections of *kyōka*, published between 1666 and 1678.

NAGATA TEIRYŪ, a disciple of Teitoku's disciple Hōzōbō Shinkai (1626–88), became the first poet to make a living by writing *kyōka* and in the process established the Ōsaka, specifically "Naniwa," variation. At least one of his efforts was received in the imperial court with considerable interest. His anthology *Kyōka iezuto* (1729, Souvenirs) established its fame and the future of the form.

The Edo, or Temmei, style (so called after the period 1781–89) was developed by the disciples of the *waka* poet Uchiyama Gatei (1723–88), principally two young *samurai*, KARAGOROMO KISSHŪ and ŌTA NAMPO (also known as Yomo no Akara and Shokusanjin) who started a *kyōka* group in Kisshū's home in 1769. They were joined by, among others, the townsmen Ōne Futoki, Moto no Mokuami (1737–1811), and Mokuami's wife Chie no Naishi. The Edo *kyōka* thus began with the broad class involvement which would eventually take its language and its content as far from the patrician *waka* as it was possible to go.

Though the Kyōto and Naniwa *kyōka* were primarily polite, though humorous, variations on the *waka*, the Temmei style—which actually began a decade before the era it is named for—combined politeness and crudity. Thus Karagoromo could compose one poem about how his day's Edo compared with the city of Nara of the *waka*, but he wrote another un-*waka*-like poem about how the plum blossoms on that spring morning make him think of the fragrance of the mountain goddess's body as she awakes. He also wrote another poem combining the names of three places famous for cherry blossoms in a context which is primarily concerned with the question of who has the advantage in a hypothetical game of GO (a comparison with the riddle "If Mississippi gave Missouri her New Jersey, what would Delaware?" is not frivolous here).

Ōta Nampo, who disassociated himself from *kyōka* when it became politically unpopular, showed a variation of themes similar to Kisshū's. He was able to move from a poem about how even a mean house with torn *shōji* might display in front the traditional *kadomatsu* decoration of bamboo and pine for the celebration of the New Year, to another poem punning on the song little girls sing as they play battledore and shuttlecock, to another poem filled with classical allusions that finally comes out as a garrulous prostitute's report that an abbot has fallen from his horse. All exhibit the marked *kyōka* propensity for urbane treatment of nature in the established literary tradition combined with reverence for the common people and their folkways.

The excitement created by the Edo *kyōka* reached throughout Japanese society and brought its practitioners adulation and prestige. *Kyōka* poets were sought out by UKIYO-E artists, who published many of their works on special, small-edition prints called SURIMONO. Groups of *kyōka* poets, calling themselves the "so-and-so" *ren* or "so-and-so" *gawa*, combined to publish prints and picture books (*kyōka ehon*) and to present *kyōka* poetry contests whenever the opportunity arose.

The appeal to poets and readers of all classes, however, proved too unsettling for a state that had always preferred clear separation among classes, and before the Temmei era was over, the repressions named for the next era, namely the KANSEI REFORMS (roughly 1787–93), made themselves felt, with *kyōka* an important object of suppression. The form survived, but it never regained the popularity it once knew. A certain vogue of the *kyōka* continued through the 1820s, as the teachers who had won their laurels in the 1770s and 1780s aged, but it never again reached the heights it knew between 1770 and 1786.

📖 ——Hamada Giichirō, "Kyōka," in *Kōza Nihon bungaku*, vol 8 (Sanseidō, 1969). Hamada Giichirō, Suzuki Katsutada, and Mizuno Minoru, *Kibyōshi, senryū, kyōka*, vol 46 of *Nihon koten bungaku zenshū* (Shōgakukan, 1971). Donald Keene, *World Within Walls* (1976). Miyazaki Kenzō and Nose Asaji, *Nihon bungaku gaishi* (1951). Edward Putzar, *Japanese Literature: A Historical Outline* (1973). Sugimoto Nagashige and Hamada Giichirō, *Senryū, kyōka shū*, vol 57 of *Nihon koten bungaku taikei* (Iwanami Shoten, 1958).

Alfred H. MARKS

kyōkaku

General term for gangsters during the Edo period (1600–1868). The common Japanese usage of the term, meaning "righteous" or "valiant" *(kyō)* and "outsider" *(kaku)*, dates from the 19th century. The early-17th-century equivalent was *kabukimono* or *otokodate*. The *kyōkaku* organization was much like that of the modern YAKUZA, composed of a head and his followers (OYABUN–KOBUN) and known as a gang (KUMI). Major *kyōkaku* groups in Edo (now Tōkyō) included those in the service of the shōgun's bannermen (HATAMOTO YAKKO) and unattached town groups (MACHI YAKKO). The Kantō and Tōkaidō regions in particular produced many famous *kyōkaku*. There were also numerous *kyōkaku* groups in provincial towns, and these *kyōkaku* were primarily gamblers. Some *kyōkaku* have become legendary heroes through glorification in KABUKI plays, modern KŌDAN and NANIWA-BUSHI, and films. Among the best known were the *machi yakko* Banzuiin Chōbei (1622–57) and Shimizu no Jirochō (1820–93) from the port of Shimizu. *Yoshiyuki* NAKAI

Kyōkasho Gigoku → Textbook Scandal of 1902–1903

Kyokutei Bakin → Bakin

Kyokutō Hōsō

(JOTF). An AM radio station with headquarters in the city of Naha serving all of Okinawa Prefecture. It originally began broadcasting in Japanese in 1957 as an affiliate of the Far East Broadcasting Company (FEBC), and was licensed by the Ryūkyū government. With the return to Japan of Okinawa in 1972, Kyokutō Hōsō became a Japanese firm and commenced its broadcast activities under the rules and regulations of the RADIO LAW (Dempa Hō). It incorporated in 1978. Kyokutō Hōsō's programming format is mainly music. It is affiliated with the FM Tōkyō radio station network. *Sudō Haruo*

Kyokuyō Co, Ltd

Firm engaged in enterprises related to the fishing industry, including processing, frozen-food packaging, export, and domestic sales. Founded in 1937, Kyokuyō originally operated factory ships in the Antarctic whaling fisheries. Today it operates ordinary trawlers and, jointly with foreign firms, shrimp trawlers; it engages in crabbing and net fishing and runs factory ships in cooperation with other companies in the industry for salmon and sea trout fishing. The firm is working to develop new fishing grounds and commercialization of certain varieties of fish. Sales for the fiscal year ending October 1981 totaled ¥188.9 billion (US $816.4 million), of which export and domestic sale of commercial products constituted 66 percent, fishing operations 13 percent, processing 12 percent, and ocean transport 9 percent. In the same year capitalization stood at ¥5.6 billion (US $24.2 million). Corporate headquarters are in Tōkyō.

Kyō Machiko (1924–)

Film actress. Real name Yano Motoko. Her glamour and starring roles in such award-winning films as KUROSAWA AKIRA's RASHŌMON (1950), MIZOGUCHI KENJI's *Ugetsu monogatari* (1953, Ugetsu), and KINUGASA TEINOSUKE's *Jigokumon* (1953, Gate of Hell) made her a leading performer in Japanese motion pictures for almost two decades and brought her international recognition.

Born in Ōsaka, she joined the Ōsaka Shōchiku Girl's Opera in 1936. She was recruited by Daiei Motion Picture Co (see DAIEI CO, LTD) in 1949, and her first featured role was in *Saigo ni warau otoko* (1949, He Who Laughs Last). From the outset of her motion picture career she was publicized by Daiei studios as something of a sex symbol. Recognition of Kyō's talent came from a much acclaimed performance as the bride in *Rashōmon*, Kurosawa's elaborately woven tale of rape and murder. Her other outstanding pictures include NARUSE MIKIO's *Ani imōto* (1953, Older Brother, Younger Sister), ICHIKAWA KON's *Kagi* (1959, The Key; shown abroad as *Odd Obsession*), and YOSHIMURA KŌZABURŌ's *Onna no kunshō* (1961, Women's Prize). She is known to Western audiences for her appearance in Daniel Mann's *Teahouse of the August Moon* (1956).

ITASAKA Tsuyoshi

kyoryūchi

Restricted areas for foreign residence and commerce established by the Japanese government after the ANSEI COMMERCIAL TREATIES of 1858 opened Japan to trade with Western nations. The *kyoryūchi* were self-governing units and the only places in the country where foreigners were allowed to live and move about freely. Entrance by Japanese and exit by foreigners were strictly controlled. The Dutch settlement on the island of DEJIMA at Nagasaki, which had been the only port open to foreign commerce during Japan's long period of NATIONAL SECLUSION, served as a model for the *kyoryūchi*. The first of these settlements was built in Yokohama in 1859; it was soon followed by others in Nagasaki, Kōbe, Ōsaka, and Edo (now Tōkyō). With the revision of the Ansei Treaties in 1899 (see UNEQUAL TREATIES, REVISION OF), restrictions on foreigners' residence, travel, and commercial activities within Japan were lifted, and the *kyoryūchi* were abolished. See also NAICHI ZAKKYO.

Kyōsai → Kawanabe Gyōsai

kyōsei shikkō

(execution of judgment). Judicial proceeding to enforce obligations embodied in a judgment or other document given executory force under the law, such as notarial deed, record of settlement, record of conciliation, and also to foreclose contractual or other liens, such as a mortgage, for the benefit of a lien creditor. This proceeding is now regulated by the Civil Judgment Execution Law (Minji Shikkō Hō) of 1979, effective 1 October 1980. There are different kinds of execution of judgment: (1) Execution to enforce monetary obligations begins with the attachment of the debtor's property on application by the creditor, followed by raising proceeds from such property and payment to the creditor up to the amount of debt. Certain properties, such as daily necessities and a certain percentage of wages, are exempted from attachment. Where several creditors have concurrently initiated execution on the same property, proceeds are distributed pro rata among them. The district court is in charge of execution on immovables and intangibles, including any debt owed by a third person to the debtor. Attachment of immovables is done by the registry of immovables by order of the court. The court then either sells the property at a public auction or appoints an administrator who raises the rent of the property. To attach a debt the court serves an attachment order on the person owing the debt to the debtor. The attached debt is then either turned over to the creditor in place of payment or collected by the creditor. A bailiff is in charge of the execution on movables, which he attaches by taking into his actual or constructive custody and sells at public auction. (2) Execution to enforce an obligation to deliver a certain object is carried out by a bailiff, who takes actual possession of the object, movable or immovable, and delivers it to the obligee. (3) Execution to enforce an obligation to do or to refrain from doing a certain act takes either one of the following forms: where the nature of obligation allows, the court may authorize a third person to perform the obligation and collect the costs from the obligor; any other enforceable obligations are enforced by assessing the obligor a fixed daily penalty equivalent to damages incurred by the obligee until the obligation is performed. (4) Lien foreclosure proceeding follows a pattern similar to the first execution of judgment described above.

TANIGUCHI Yasuhei

kyōshi and kyōbun

Kyōshi (literally, "wild Chinese-style poetry") was poetry written entirely in Chinese characters from about 1770 to 1800, the poets often observing to a high degree the formal rules governing the composition of poetry in Chinese, but deliberately disregarding accepted standards of decorum in language and subject matter. *Kyōshi* poets purposely used language not usually considered to be poetic in the service of similarly "unpoetic" subjects, with results that were often, but not necessarily, humorous. *Kyōbun* (literally, "wild prose") was Chinese prose written in a mock-serious classical style, in which language and themes are treated in much the same way as in *kyōshi*, with similar results.

The sudden flowering of *kyōshi* as a poetic genre during the Temmei era (1781–88), and its rapid decline into almost total desuetude thereafter, suggests that something about the genre was particularly responsive to its times, a notion reinforced by the often-noted rapid growth in the same period of longer-lived comic verse like *senryū* (see ZAPPAI AND SENRYŪ) and KYŌKA as well as fictional forms like KOKKEIBON and SHAREBON. These literary forms were normally regarded as "frivolous" by the standards of the strict Confucian orthodoxy espoused by Tokugawa statesmen, but during the regime of TANUMA OKITSUGU (ca 1767–86) the usual restraints on such genres were not enforced with the severity that they were before and after. The result was that literary forms tended to veer sharply from their usual sober courses in the direction of frivolity, only to be brought up sharply again by the effects of the KANSEI REFORMS of 1787–93 under the regime of MATSUDAIRA SADANOBU.

In the light of these facts, it is clear that the brief duration of *kyōshi* was due in no small measure to its very form. *Kanshi* (any poetry written in Chinese) was the quintessential cultural embellishment of the ruling class; its practice according to accepted norms demonstrated commitment to shared cultural values and to the philosophy that shaped the lives of upper-class *samurai*. A lack of technical ability in *kanshi* was excusable; but the deliberate attempt by *kyōshi* poets to vulgarize *kanshi* by rejecting its stylized and elevated language and themes was tantamount to undermining the prevailing value system, and so could not be tolerated for long.

Poets——The poets who wrote *kyōshi* were primarily members of the lesser samurai class—few others had the sort of education necessary to compose verse in Chinese, or the cultural tradition that required its use. By 1800, however, it had been taken up by relatively uneducated samurai as well as by members of the CHŌNIN (townsman) class with pretensions to upper-class culture. The frequent and justifiable complaints by educated writers that the *kyōshi* of these later poets did not make sense either in Japanese or in Chinese attest to the degradation of the genre at the hands of a social class that no longer possessed either the means or the motives of the lesser samurai to mock the *kanshi* tradition and turn it to other ends.

The best *kyōshi* poet of the Edo region, if not of all Japan, was undoubtedly Ōta Tan (1749–1823), more familiar for his fame in *kyōka* under the names of ŌTA NAMPO, Shokusanjin, Neboke Sensei, and Yomo no Akara, among others. He published *kyōshi* from the age of 18 in such collections as *Neboke sensei bunshū* (Literary Works of Master Groggy), *Danna sanjin geishashū*, and *Tōshisen shōchi* (The Humor that Pervades the "Selected Tang Poems"), the last a parody of the Ming-period Chinese classic *Tang shi xuan* (*T'ang shih hsüan*) by Li Yü-lin and of its Japanese commentaries. Nampo's *kyōbun* appeared in collections with titles such as *Yomo no aka* (Bilge All Around) and *Yomo no tomegasu* (Dregs All Around), which punned on his pen name Yomo no Akara.

The other outstanding figure in *kyōshi*, representing the Kansai region around Kyōto, was Hatanaka Tanomo (1752–1801), alias Metsubōkai, Taiheikan Shujin, and other names, but best known under the pen name Dōmyaku Sensei. His first collection of *kyōshi*, entitled *Taihei gafu* (Yuefu Poems on the Great Peace) was published two years after Nampo's. The two poets became acquainted at the start of their literary careers, and the poetic correspondence between them over nearly 20 years was published in 1790 as *Nitaika fūga* (Elegant Compositions by Two Masters). One of Tanomo's most remarkable works is his *kyōshi* account of the 1771 religious pilgrimage *(okagemairi)* to the Ise Shrine, published in that year under the title *Seta no karahashi* (The Chinese Bridge on the Seta Road).

Themes and Techniques——*Kyōshi* represents a special development at the end of the long tradition of *kanshi* poetry, and it is equally unique in the history of humor, or *haikai* ("nonseriousness"), in Japanese poetry. The flourishing of the *kyō* or "wild" literary genres, principally *kyōka*, followed by *kyōshi* and *kyōbun*, parallels the earlier development of the *hai* genres of HAIKU and HAIBUN. What appears to be common to both of these movements, each a literary response to a particular social and cultural milieu, is the use of new language and themes, hitherto thought unsuited to the poetic tradition, that had the effect of pushing that tradition onto new ground. Before the inevitable conservative reaction set in and the mainstream reasserted itself, the tradition had been moved in a perceptibly new direction.

The term *kyōshi* actually subsumes two distinct modes represented in the native poetry by the genres of *kyōka* and *senryū*. *Kyōka* appears to concern itself more often with the use of parody, punning, and dazzling displays of wit; *senryū*, on the other hand, is occupied with the human condition and with satire on the human comedy in all its manifestations. This distinction is emphasized because *kyōshi* has often been characterized in Japanese criticism as a superficial genre that relies on superficial effects, and so is often dismissed as a kind of macaronic verse—which, indeed, it had become by the beginning of the 19th century. *Kyōshi* does not appear to have depended on puns any more than *kyōka*; in each case it is the ability of the poet that determines the quality of the verse.

A contemporary Edo-period critic recognized three separate roles played in *kyōshi* by language alone: a complex sort of punning that arises from the interplay of oral and written aspects of the Chinese and Japanese languages; the use of vernacular idiom that permitted the use of words never used before in poetry; and the lavish incorporation of words used as sound effects, all of these hallmarks also of Edo GESAKU fiction. The same critic also enumerated three types of treatment of subject matter: topical interest; boasting of one's own region; and, broadest of all, satire on the human comedy. Most poems involve the use of two or more of these "elements" in combination.

In form, *kyōshi* spans the range of *kanshi* poetry, that is, of Chinese poetry in general. With a poetic line of either five or seven words, *kyōshi* could be as short as four lines or as long as more than one hundred—a fact that says a great deal about the possibilities for thematic development in light of the extreme brevity of the Japanese verse forms. The best poets were able to observe the exacting rules of such Chinese forms as "ruled verse" (*lüshi* or *lü-shih*), even in the difficult, long "extended ruled" (*p'ai-lü* or *pailü*) form. The freer Chinese "old style" (*gushi* or *ku-shih*) or "folk-song style" (*yuefu* or *yüeh-fu*) modes were often used as they were in China, in the service of longer poems of greater social or personal import. Finally, the poets treated every possible subject, from fleas to cities to the lives of members of the lower social orders—subjects that otherwise rarely appeared in poetry before modern times.

▄ ——Ebara Taizō, "Kyōshi gaisetsu," in Ebara Taizō, *Edo bungei ronkō* (1937). Hamada Giichirō, *Ōta Nampo* (1963). Nakamura Yukihiko, "Kyōshi kyōbun," in *Kinsei bungaku minkambon sōsho,* vol 3 (Yōtokusha, 1949). Noguchi Takehiko, *Edo bungaku no shi to shinjitsu* (1971). David Pollack, "Kyōshi: Japanese 'Wild Poetry,'" *Journal of Asian Studies* 38.2 (1979). Tamabayashi Akira, *Shokusanjin no kenkyū* (1944). Yamagishi Tokuhei, "Mojirishi oyobi kyōshi ni kansuru shōsho," in Yamagishi Tokuhei, *Nihon kambungaku kenkyū* (1972). Yamagishi Tokuhei, ed, *Gozan bungaku shū, Edo kanshi shū,* in *Nihon koten bungaku taikei,* vol 89 (Iwanami Shoten, 1967). David POLLACK

kyōtaku

(public deposit). Deposits of money or materials made by a party (obligor) to a joint and several obligation (RENTAI SAIMU) with a public deposit office *(kyōtakusho)* located in the district where the obligation is to be performed in order to obtain release from said obligatory duty. The public deposit system may be utilized for both monetary and nonmonetary obligations, but in actual practice it is most frequently used for the former. Under this system, an obligor may place a deposit with a public deposit office when the obligee has refused to accept payment, cannot accept payment because his whereabouts are unknown, or some other such reason, or when the obligor, through no fault of his own, cannot confirm the identity of the obligee. By the act of deposit, the obligor discharges his obligatory duty with respect to the obligee, and the obligee acquires an obligatory right against the public deposit office to receive the funds or materials of the deposit. SASAKI Kinzō

Kyōto

City in southern KYŌTO PREFECTURE, central Honshū, in the northern part of the Kyōto fault basin. The ancient capital of Japan and home of the imperial court from 794 to 1868, Kyōto is today the seat of the prefectural government. Rich in historical sites and relics, the city attracted an estimated 37 million visitors in 1979. Kyōto is renowned for its fine textiles and traditional products and is also a thriving industrial center.

Natural features. The low Tamba Mountains surround the city to the north, east, and west. Two peaks, HIEIZAN and Atagoyama, both under 1,000 meters high, dominate the northeast and northwest of the city. The rivers Kamogawa and Katsuragawa flow through the center and western districts of the city to join the Yodogawa in the south before draining into Ōsaka Bay. Kyōto's landlocked location accounts for its unusually cold winters and hot summers: the average highest temperature in summer is 32.9° C (91.2°F), and the annual

Kyōto——Kiyomizudera

Located in the Higashiyama district, Kiyomizudera was originally founded in the 8th century by the monk Enchin. Today the temple, situated on a high hill, is known for its panoramic view of Kyōto. Shown is the main hall; built out over a cliff, it was completed in 1633. National Treasure.

Kyōto——Nijō Castle

Nijō Castle was completed in the early 17th century as the shogunal residence in Kyōto. Shown here is the Ninomaru Palace viewed from the south. A series of spacious rooms, this palace typifies the *shoin-zukuri* style of medieval architecture. National Treasure.

average temperature 14.8° C (58.6°F). Annual precipitation is 1,600 mm, with more rain falling in the summer months.

History. Although archaeological sites dating from the Jōmon (ca 10,000 BC–ca 300 BC) and Yayoi (ca 300 BC–ca AD 300) periods have been found in and around Kyōto, the Kyōto fault basin was first settled in the 6th century by the HATA FAMILY, immigrants from Korea. Members of the family were skilled in silkworm culture and silk weaving and amassed great wealth through their commerce in silk goods. In 603 KŌRYŪJI, the family temple of the Hata, was constructed at Uzumasa in the western part of the basin. The northern part was also developed early on as the residence of such powerful families as the Kamo, Izumo, and Ono. However, it was not until 794 that Kyōto or HEIANKYŌ, as it was then called, became the capital. The plan of the new city, like that of Heijōkyō in Nara, was patterned after the Tang (T'ang) dynasty (618–907) capital of

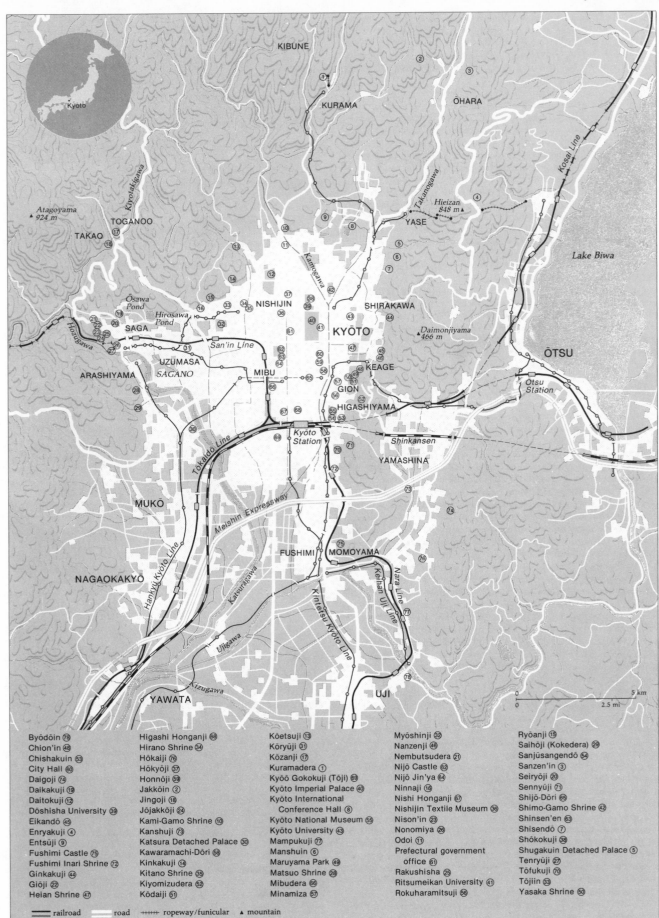

Byōdōin 78
Chion'in 48
Chishakuin 53
City Hall 60
Daigoji 74
Daikakuji 19
Daitokuji 12
Dōshisha University 39
Eikandō 45
Enryakuji 4
Entsūji 9
Fushimi Castle 75
Fushimi Inari Shrine 72
Ginkakuji 44
Giōji 22
Heian Shrine 47

Higashi Honganji 68
Hirano Shrine 34
Hōkaiji 76
Hōkyōji 37
Honnōji 59
Jakkōin 2
Jingoji 18
Jōjakkōji 24
Kami-Gamo Shrine 10
Kanshuji 73
Katsura Detached Palace 30
Kawaramachi-Dōri 58
Kinkakuji 14
Kitano Shrine 35
Kiyomizudera 52
Kōdaiji 51

Kōetsuji 13
Kōryūji 31
Kōzanji 17
Kuramadera 1
Kyōō Gokokuji (Tōji) 69
Kyōto Imperial Palace 40
Kyōto International
　Conference Hall 8
Kyōto National Museum 55
Kyōto University 43
Mampukuji 77
Manshuin 6
Maruyama Park 49
Matsuo Shrine 28
Mibudera 66
Minamiza 57

Myōshinji 32
Nanzenji 46
Nembutsudera 21
Nijō Castle 62
Nijō Jin'ya 64
Ninnaji 16
Nishi Honganji 67
Nishijin Textile Museum 56
Nison'in 23
Nonomiya 26
Odoi 11
Prefectural government
　office 61
Rakushisha 25
Ritsumeikan University 41
Rokuharamitsuji 56

Ryōanji 15
Saihōji (Kokedera) 29
Sanjūsangendō 54
Sanzen'in 3
Seiryōji 20
Sennyūji 71
Shijō-Dōri 65
Shimo-Gamo Shrine 42
Shinsen'en 63
Shisendō 7
Shōkokuji 38
Shugakuin Detached Palace 5
Tenryūji 27
Tōfukuji 70
Tōjiin 33
Yasaka Shrine 50

━━━ railroad　━━━ road　+++++ ropeway/funicular　▲ mountain

Chang'an (Ch'ang-an; modern Xi'an or Sian). Its rectangular shape measured 4.5 kilometers (2.8 mi) east to west and 5.2 kilometers (3.2 mi) north to south. The city gradually expanded eastward across the Kamogawa, and the Heian-period (794–1185) residences of the powerful FUJIWARA FAMILY and TAIRA FAMILY were constructed in Shirakawa and Rokuhara in central Kyōto.

Kyōto was temporarily eclipsed as the center of national power during the Kamakura period (1185–1333), when the warrior chieftain MINAMOTO NO YORITOMO gained political ascendancy and established a military government (shogunate) in Kamakura. In the Muromachi period (1333–1568), a shogunate was established in Kyōto for the first time, and the city regained its former status as the nation's political center. It was during this period that many major temples were built, including TENRYŪJI, NANZENJI, KINKAKUJI, and GINKAKUJI. (Because of the undue influence of religious institutions in Nara, the building of temples within the boundaries of Heiankyō had long been forbidden. The building of temples in Kyōto began only after the spread of new Buddhist sects during the Kamakura period.) During the ŌNIN WAR (1467–77), which signaled the end of the Muromachi shogunate, a large part of the city was destroyed.

After a century of civil war, TOYOTOMI HIDEYOSHI succeeded in unifying the country. In 1590 he embarked on an ambitious building program that included the lavishly decorated Jurakudai mansion and FUSHIMI CASTLE along the Yodogawa.

During the Edo period (1600–1868), the Tokugawa shogunate was firmly established in Edo (now Tōkyō) and the political focus of the country again shifted away from Kyōto. However, the ROKU-HARA TANDAI, who had been stationed in Kyōto as a shogunal representative since the transfer of political authority to Kamakura, continued to be appointed, and in 1603 the shogunate completed NIJŌ CASTLE in Kyōto to serve as a temporary shogunal residence. In the years of peace during the Edo period, Kyōto prospered once again as an artistic, economic, and religious center. Particularly notable were fabrics such as NISHIJIN-ORI and *yūzen-zome* (see YŪ-ZEN), pottery (see KYŌTO CERAMICS), lacquer ware, doll making, and fan making. Many merchants from the dry-goods dealers guild (KA-BUNAKAMA) lent money to the feudal lords or to the shogunate.

Kyōto received a great blow when the capital was transferred to Tōkyō after the Meiji Restoration (1868). To compensate for this the city embarked on a rapid program of modernization: the BIWAKO CANAL linking Kyōto to Lake Biwa was completed in 1890; the first hydroelectric plant in the country was constructed at Keage in the northeastern section of the city; and the first streetcars in Japan began operation in Kyōto in 1895.

Kyōto today. Lacking a harbor and surrounding open land, Kyōto was slow in developing modern industries, but today, as part of the HANSHIN INDUSTRIAL ZONE, it has numerous electric, machinery, and chemical plants. Its traditional industries continue to flourish. Fushimi is known for its superior *sake*. The city is also an educational center, with some 39 universities and private institutes of higher learning, including Kyōto and Dōshisha universities. As of 1980, Kyoto had 34 museums, including the KYŌTO NATIONAL MUSEUM, which was established in 1889. The Kyōto International Conference Hall was completed in 1966.

Transportation. Kyōto is served by the Tōkaidō Trunk Line and the SHINKANSEN of the Japanese National Railways. Kyōto is also the starting point of the San'in Trunk Line, the Kosei Line, and the Nara Line. Private railway lines connect Kyōto with Ōsaka as well as with Nara and Kōbe. The Meishin Expressway runs through the southern part of the city, connecting Kyōto with Nagoya and Kōbe.

Culture and tourism. Kyōto possesses a total of 202 National Treasures (20 percent of the country's total) and 1,596 Important Cultural Assets (15 percent). In addition to this outstanding collection, the city itself is a veritable historical storehouse. The Kyōto Imperial Palace and the Nijō Castle are both remarkable examples of Japanese architecture. The KATSURA DETACHED PALACE with its lovely pond and teahouses, and the SHUGAKUIN DETACHED PALACE, famed for its fine garden, draw visitors from afar. Located close to Kyōto Station are two temples of the Jōdo Shin sect, NISHI HON-GANJI and HIGASHI HONGANJI, both imposing examples of Buddhist architecture, as well as TŌJI, noted for its five-tiered pagoda.

East of the Kamogawa are KIYOMIZUDERA, with its wooden platform built out over a deep gorge; the YASAKA SHRINE, where the annual GION FESTIVAL is held in July; and HEIAN SHRINE, where the annual JIDAI FESTIVAL is held in October. Other noted temples

Kyōto —— Kyōto Imperial Palace

The Shishinden, main ceremonial hall of the palace. Although it is an Edo-period construction, the hall preserves a Heian-period architectural format and style. It is open to public view every spring and autumn.

Kyōto —— Gion Festival

Held in July to honor the deity of Yasaka Shrine, the Gion Festival features a parade of two types of elaborate floats. Shown is one of the giant (24 m) wheeled floats called *hoko* (spear). Topped by a tall pole, it carries musicians and children dressed up as historical or legendary figures.

include CHION'IN; Ginkakuji, built in 1482 and famed for its garden; and Nanzenji, situated in a pine grove east of Heian Shrine. In the north of the city are the KAMO SHRINES, where the AOI FESTIVAL is held in May each year. To the northwest are the Zen temple DAITO-KUJI, with its priceless art objects; KINKAKUJI, with its three-story golden pavilion; NINNAJI, renowned for its cherry blossoms; and KŌRYŪJI. The natural beauty of the Hozukyō gorge, the Sagano district, and the hills of Takao also attracts visitors.

In addition to the three festivals mentioned above, the Miyako Odori, or Cherry Dance, and Mibu Kyōgen pantomine farces, both held in April, and the bonfire on Daimonjiyama (see DAIMONJI OKURIBI) during the Bon Festival in August are noteworthy. Kyōto is the national center for the tea ceremony and flower arrangement and is the birthplace of NŌ, KYŌGEN, KABUKI, and other traditional performing arts.

Area: 610.6 sq km (235.7 sq mi); pop: 1,472,993.　　　*Oda Takeo*

Kyōto Basin

(Kyōto Bonchi). Southern Kyōto Prefecture, central Honshū. One of several fault basins in the central Kinki (Kyōto–Nara–Ōsaka) region, it consists of the flood plains of the rivers Katsuragawa, Uji-gawa, and Kizugawa (all of which flow into the Yodogawa). At the basin's north end lies the city of Kyōto. Rice is cultivated on the lowlands in the south, where numerous industrial plants are also found. Ogura Pond, formerly the lowest point in the basin, has been reclaimed. Area: approximately 270 sq km (104 sq mi).

Kyōto ceramics

(kyō-yaki). The ceramics produced in and around the city of Kyōto, with the exception of RAKU WARE. Sometimes called *kiyomizu-yaki*, after the kilns in the Kiyomizu area of Kyōto. However, the term *kiyomizu-yaki* came into use only after porcelain came to be a major Kyōto product in the later part of the Edo period (1600–1868); these Edo-period Kiyomizu wares are sometimes referred to as *koki-yomizu-yaki* (Old Kiyomizu ware). Since Kyōto was the center of court and culture for about a thousand years until the Meiji Restoration of 1868, its ceramics carry associations of elegance and refinement. Though embracing a wide range of products, Kyōto ceramics generally display a high standard of technical proficiency and decoration, including overglaze enamel work, first on pottery and later on porcelain.

Three-colored lead-glazed wares seem to have been made in Kyōto in the 8th century, and monochrome green wares from the 9th to the 11th centuries. The next ware known to have been produced there is Oshikōji ware in the late 16th century. Little is known about it, but it is said to have been influenced by the Chinese three-color ware which was then in vogue, known in Japanese as Kōchi ware. Oshikōji ware was probably colored and fired at low temperatures. In some respects it can be seen to be the forerunner of the low-fired Raku pottery developed by CHŌJIRŌ, who worked under the guidance of the tea master SEN NO RIKYŪ in the late 16th century. However, the Raku tradition stands apart in terms of aesthetic taste and ideas of craftsmanship.

The first Kyōto kilns were apparently located in the Awataguchi district in the eastern foothills, near clay sources, and were probably established toward the end of the 16th century. At this time Chinese iron-glazed wares and Korean pottery were greatly valued for use in the TEA CEREMONY, and early Kyōto potters, many recruited from Seto and Shigaraki, sometimes using clays from those centers, developed corresponding styles (see SETO WARE; SHIGARAKI WARE). Kilns were built in the 1630s and 1640s at Yasaka, Otowa, and Kiyomizu, all in the eastern foothills and close to clay sources. More kilns were built farther north, for example, at Mizoro. In addition to these so-called commercial kilns, other kilns were established to make wares for the personal use of the imperial family or powerful warrior families. Emperor GO-MIZUNOO sponsored a kiln at the SHUGAKUIN DETACHED PALACE, and Emperor Gosai (1637–85), one at Nogami. The commercial kilns were usually affiliated with a temple, or, in some cases, with a family, partly because of the strict control of land use in Kyōto. The Awataguchi kilns were built on land belonging to the temple Shōren'in, for example, and the Yasaka, Otowa, and Kiyomizu kilns were attached to the temple Seikanji. Initially, these wares were unmarked and were all very similar in style; early wares can often be identified only on the basis of the inscriptions written on the boxes in which they have been handed down. Potters began to use stamps and seals from about the mid-17th century.

Though there are many undecorated early *kyō-yaki* pieces made after Chinese, Korean, Seto, or Shigaraki styles, Kyōto potters soon became interested in decoration, first using underglaze iron-oxide and cobalt. The most characteristic *kyō-yaki* is probably overglaze enameled ware. The claim that NONOMURA NINSEI introduced enameling techniques to Kyōto potters is now discredited, although his famous enameled jars and bowls must have stimulated other potters to innovate.

The throwing or shaping process of *kyō-yaki*, like its decoration, is characterized by remarkable technical proficiency. Kyōto potters became very imaginative in their approach to shapes, and some even applied techniques from wood or lacquerwork to ceramics. Kyōto potters were as skilled at slab-building, reticulation, carving, and sprigging as they were precise at throwing, and they frequently used glazes in a special way. Some typical *kyō-yaki* is covered in a thick glaze of one color, often dark blue or green, with additional decoration in a restricted area. The decorative motif is often built up in thick layers of enamel, giving a three-dimensional effect very different from the enamel work of the KUTANI WARE or ARITA WARE porcelain kilns. Brown and gold were also used, red less frequently.

The history of Kyōto ware after Ninsei is punctuated with the names of famous individual potters. Ogata KENZAN (1663–1743), who may have been a pupil of Ninsei's, is sometimes said to have been responsible for turning pottery from a craft into an art. Ken-

zan's forte was low-temperature ware decorated in overglaze enamels, and he is famous for the boldness and casualness of his decoration, in contrast to the more meticulous work of Ninsei. Reflecting the later change in taste, OKUDA EISEN (1753–1811) is credited with the introduction of porcelain manufacture to Kyōto, especially in the late Ming-dynasty (1368–1644) style. One of his pupils was AOKI MOKUBEI (1767–1833), a painter and calligrapher as well as a potter. Another of Eisen's pupils, NIN'AMI DŌHACHI (1783–1855), is famous for his wide variety of imitations. EIRAKU HOZEN (1795–1854) produced pieces in many styles; he was also influenced by Kōchi work and made many imitations, especially of Ninsei's pieces.

It is usually admitted that by the end of the Edo period much of the creative energy of Kyōto ware had gone. The present century has seen a number of individual *kyō-yaki* potters of note, however, including Kiyomizu Rokubei (1875–1951). The contemporary industry is generally flourishing, though oil, gas, or electric kilns have almost entirely replaced the old wood-burning kilns. This has partly been forced by city ordinances concerning pollution. Because of lack of space and these city ordinances, much of the industry has moved from the Higashiyama area to Kiyomizu-yaki Danchi in Yamashina, Kyōto, on the road to Ōtsu.

■——Satō Masahiko, *Kyoto Ceramics*, tr Anne Ono Towle and Usher P. Coolidge (1973).   *David* HALE

Kyōto Daigaku Jimbun Kagaku Kenkyūjo → Kyōto University Research Institute for Humanistic Studies

Kyōto Gozan → Gozan

Kyōto National Museum

(Kyōto Kokuritsu Hakubutsukan). Located in Higashiyama Ward, Kyōto. First opened in 1897 as the Imperial Kyōto Museum (Teikoku Kyōto Hakubutsukan), it was originally built to house and display art treasures owned by temples and shrines and items donated by the Imperial Household Ministry, all of which are now on more or less permanent loan. Besides housing a large collection of items on loan from private collectors, it has built up its own extensive collection of ancient Japanese and Chinese art and archaeology. The museum's collection is divided into three parts: fine arts, which includes sculpture, painting, and calligraphy; handicrafts, which includes pottery, fabrics, lacquer ware, and metalwork; and archaeology, which includes objects of archaeological and historical interest. The fine arts division has especially impressive holdings, containing more than 230 items that have been classified as National Treasures (Kokuhō) or Important Cultural Properties (Jūyō Bunkazai). These include superb specimens of Japanese and Chinese calligraphy and painting. Its collection of rare ancient Chinese and Japanese sutras is among the finest the world over. In its especially valuable Japanese art collection are such well-known items as an 11th-century *senzui byōbu* (landscape screen), a 12th-century *Gakizōshi* (Scroll of Hungry Ghosts), and SESSHŪ TŌYŌ's famous painting *Amanohashidate*.   *FUJIKAWA Kinji*

Kyōto Prefecture

(Kyōto Fu). Located in central Honshū, bounded by Fukui, Shiga, and Mie prefectures on the east, Nara Prefecture on the south, and Hyōgo and Ōsaka prefectures on the west. It faces the Sea of Japan to the north. This prefecture is divided roughly into two parts, north and south, by the TAMBA MOUNTAINS. The southern part, formerly called Yamashiro Province, is centered on the KYŌTO BASIN, and the northern part, formerly called Tamba and Tango provinces, is composed of the TANGO MOUNTAINS. The southern part flourished after the capital was moved in 794 to HEIANKYŌ, as Kyōto was then known. The southern part of the prefecture, of which the center is Kyōto, is part of the TŌKAIDŌ MEGALOPOLIS and is undergoing continuous urbanization. The center of the northern part is the port city of MAIZURU on the Sea of Japan.

Geography and Climate——Kyōto Basin, located in the southern part of the prefecture, is a graben basin. The mountains surrounding the basin are horst mountains and generally low. Mt. Hiei (HIEIZAN) located northeast of Kyōto, is only 848 meters (2,781 ft) high. The mountains of Tango and Tamba in the northern part of the

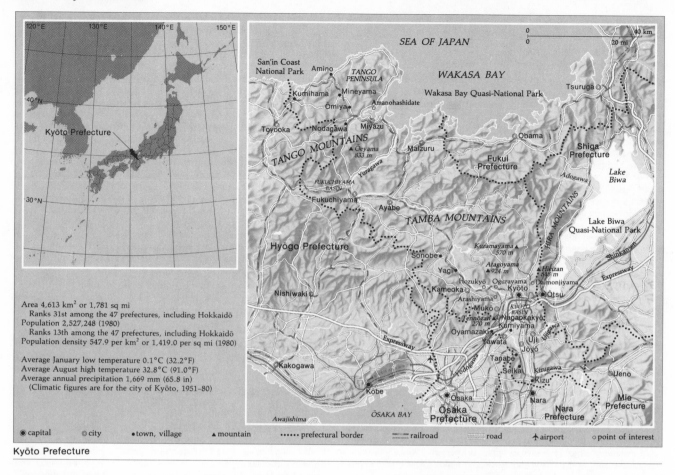

● capital	◎ city	● town, village	▲ mountain

●●●●● prefectural border   ══ railroad   ═══ road   ✈ airport   ○ point of interest

Area 4,613 km² or 1,781 sq mi
  Ranks 31st among the 47 prefectures, including Hokkaidō
Population 2,527,248 (1980)
  Ranks 13th among the 47 prefectures, including Hokkaidō
Population density 547.9 per km² or 1,419.0 per sq mi (1980)

Average January low temperature 0.1°C (32.2°F)
Average August high temperature 32.8°C (91.0°F)
Average annual precipitation 1,669 mm (65.8 in)
  (Climatic figures are for the city of Kyōto, 1951–80)

Kyōto Prefecture

prefecture are also not high; part of the Tango Mountains forms the Tango Peninsula and juts out into the Sea of Japan. WAKASA BAY to the east forms a heavily indented coast with a number of good natural harbors. The principal rivers of the prefecture are the UJIGAWA, the KATSURAGAWA, and the KAMOGAWA, all in the southern part of the prefecture and all of which flow into the YODOGAWA. The only notable river in the northern part is the YURAGAWA. The temperature tends to run to extremes in the Kyōto Basin. Because of the Tsushima Current the coastal regions on the Sea of Japan are warmer in the winter. Precipitation is heavier in the north.

History —— Remains from the Jōmon (ca 10,000 BC–ca 300 BC) and Yayoi (ca 300 BC–ca AD 300) periods have been discovered in the prefecture. After the third century, the Kyōto Basin was settled by the HATA FAMILY and other naturalized immigrants (KIKAJIN) from Korea and China. Under the ancient provincial system (see KOKU-GUN SYSTEM), Kyōto Prefecture was known as Yamashiro, Tamba, and Tango provinces. The prefectural system was established in 1871, and the boundaries of the prefecture were fixed in 1876.

Industries —— Commerce, traditional industries, and tourism are the main industries. Representative products include NISHIJIN-ORI and YŪZEN silks, Kiyomizu ware (see KYŌTO CERAMICS), lacquer wares, fans, dolls, and other crafts. The manufacture of these traditional wares is concentrated in the city of Kyōto. The northern part of the prefecture is renowned for its Tango *chirimen* silk and Fushimi *sake*. Modern industries include machinery, metal, and synthetic fiber industries. The southern part of the prefecture, an extension of the HANSHIN INDUSTRIAL ZONE, has highly developed industries. Farming is centered on rice cultivation, but vegetables are produced in the suburban districts surrounding Kyōto. Tea is grown on the highlands surrounding the Kyōto Basin, centering on the city of UJI. Cryptomeria and cypress grow from north of the city of Kyōto to the southern part of the Tamba Mountains. Fish such as yellowtail, mackerel, and sardine are caught off the coast of the Sea of Japan.

Tourism and Culture —— As the capital region for over a thousand years, Kyōto Prefecture has many historical sites. Each year more than 35 million people visit the city of Kyōto, whose attractions include the Imperial Palace, NIJŌ CASTLE, HEIAN SHRINE, and temples such as HONGANJI, KIYOMIZUDERA, NINNAJI, DAITOKUJI,

KINKAKUJI, GINKAKUJI, KŌRYŪJI, and SAIHŌJI. The temple BYŌ-DŌIN in Uji, the Hozukyō gorge on the upper reaches of the river HOZUGAWA between Kameoka and ARASHIYAMA, and such places as Ōhara, Kurama, Sagano, and Takao on the outskirts of Kyōto are also well known. On the Sea of Japan coastline are AMANOHASHI-DATE and other scenic spots that belong to Wakasa Bay Quasi-National Park and SAN'IN COAST NATIONAL PARK. Area: 4,613 sq km (1,781 sq mi); pop: 2,527,248; capital: Kyōto. Other major cities include Uji, Maizuru, Jōyō, and NAGAOKAKYŌ. See also KYŌTO.

Kyōto shoshidai

(Kyōto deputy). Originally a deputy *(dai)* to the head *(shoshi)* of the Board of Retainers (SAMURAI-DOKORO) of the Muromachi shogunate (1338–1573) after the Ōnin War (1467–77). Later the hegemons ODA NOBUNAGA and TOYOTOMI HIDEYOSHI appointed *shoshidai* to govern the populace of Kyōto. During the first half-century of the Tokugawa shogunate (1603–1867) the post was held in succession by three influential shogunal vassals—Okudaira Nobumasa (1556–1615), ITAKURA KATSUSHIGE, and the latter's son Shigemune (1586–1656)—who governed the city and developed a body of administrative guidelines that were used by their successors. The Kyōto deputies oversaw the affairs of the imperial court and the many temples in the city and were responsible for the administration of justice in the adjacent provinces. They also supervised the city commissioners (MACHI BUGYŌ) of Kyōto, Fushimi, and Nara, and together with the keeper of Ōsaka Castle they were charged with surveillance of the *daimyō* of western Japan. After Shigemune's retirement in 1654, 58 men served in the post; because of its political importance, they were usually middle-ranking FUDAI daimyō of proven ability who were later promoted to senior councillors (RŌJŪ).   *Conrad* TOTMAN

Kyōto shugoshoku

(military commissioner for Kyōto). A post established in September 1862 by the Tokugawa shogunate (1603–1867) to counteract the growing SONNŌ JŌI (Revere the Emperor, Expel the Barbarians) movement that was centered in Kyōto. The new commissioner, who outranked the long-established Kyōto deputy (KYŌTO SHOSHIDAI), assumed full police powers in the Kyōto and Ōsaka areas. Except during the brief tenure of MATSUDAIRA YOSHINAGA, the post of Kyōto *shugoshoku* was held by MATSUDAIRA KATAMORI from its inception until the overthrow of the shogunate in 1867–68. The office should not be confused with that of military governor of Kyōto (Kyōto *shugo*), established in 1185 by the Kamakura shogunate to oversee Kamakura vassals stationed in Kyōto and to act as liaison between the imperial court and the shogunate. This latter office was replaced in 1221 by that of Rokuhara deputy (ROKUHARA TANDAI).

Kyōto University

(Kyōto Daigaku). A national, coeducational university located in Sakyō Ward, Kyōto. The second national university in Japan, it was founded in 1897 as Kyōto Imperial University, and renamed Kyōto University in 1949. Since its inception it has been known for its tradition of academic freedom. It maintains faculties of letters, education, law, economics, science, medicine, pharmacology, engineering, and agriculture, and has the following research institutes: Research Institute for Fundamental Physics, Research Institute for Mathematical Sciences, Research Reactor Institute, Primate Research Institute, Institute for Chemical Research, Research Institute for Humanistic Studies, Chest Diseases Research Institute, Institute of Atomic Energy, Wood Research Institute, Research Institute for Food Science, Disaster Prevention Research Institute, Institute for Virus Research, Institute of Economic Research. Enrollment in 1980 was 11,323.

Kyōto University Incident

(Kyōdai Jiken; abbreviation of Kyōto Daigaku Jiken). A term used to refer to a number of incidents concerning "defense of university autonomy and academic freedom" at Kyōto University. The first, that of 1913, gained for the faculty autonomy in the hiring and firing of faculty as opposed to arbitrary actions of the university president at the behest of the Ministry of Education. Also known as the Sawayanagi Incident, from the name of the president against whom the faculty protested, this is the only Kyōto University incident that ended in greater freedom. That of 1924–26, otherwise known as the Gakuren Incident, witnessed the first use of the new antisubversive PEACE PRESERVATION LAW OF 1925 (Chian Iji Hō) by the government. The victims were militant students. That of 1933, also known as the Takikawa Incident, signaled the spread of thought control to cover moderate liberals. The incidents of 1949, 1951, and 1955 occurred in the atmosphere of the RED PURGE and the "reverse course" (see OCCUPATION), when many feared the revival of prewar thought control. The two best known of these Kyōto University incidents are the Gakuren and the Takikawa.

Gakuren Incident——A predawn police raid opened the Gakuren Incident on 1 December 1925. It netted 33 members, from Kyōto, Dōshisha, and other universities, of the Gakusei Shakai Kagaku Rengōkai (Student Social Science Federation), known by its abbreviation, Gakuren. They were detained for interrogation while their dormitory or off-campus rooms were searched for evidence. Equating communist sympathizers with "traitors" and "disturbers of the peace," the police had decided to destroy the Gakuren. At its second congress earlier that year, the Gakuren had labeled itself as "one wing of the proletarian movement with Marxism–Leninism as its guiding principle." This meant in practice that it supported the Nihon Rōdō Hyōgikai (Council of Japanese Labor Unions), the most militant section of the small organized labor movement. The announced reason for the arrests was suspected violation of the PUBLICATION LAW OF 1893, but the police had hoped from the beginning to prosecute under the still untested Peace Preservation Law. The evidence, however, did not support charges even under the Publication Law. Massive student protests sprang up, the faculty condemned the arrests, and the press took courage and roundly criticized the police. As a result, the students were released within a week, and only minor charges were pressed.

Nevertheless, on orders from higher authorities, the police began a second roundup on 15 January 1926, which continued sporadically through 22 April, detaining a total of 38 people, half of whom had been arrested in the previous offensive. All press comment this time was banned by the police. The students were confined until indicted in September; they were then released on bail or recognizance. By the following April, all were convicted of violation of the Peace Preservation Law and given sentences ranging from 8 to 12 months.

Appeals were not completed until 12 December 1929, when convictions were upheld for all but a few. This incident initiated the attempt of the government and university authorities to eliminate the militant student movement.

Takikawa Incident——The Takikawa Incident occurred in 1933, when civil liberties had been further eroded. This time the objective was liberal professors. Kyōto University law professor TAKIKAWA YUKITOKI and several Tōkyō University faculty had been accused in a right-wing brochure of favoring leftist students while serving as members of the entrance examination committee for Justice Ministry officials. The charge was aired in the Diet by RIKKEN SEIYŪKAI politicians. As a result, Education Minister HATOYAMA ICHIRŌ had Takikawa dismissed from the examination committee in March 1933 and had two of his widely used textbooks on criminal law banned. Kyōto University President Konishi Shigenao (1875–1948), with faculty support, resisted ministry pressures to force Takikawa to resign. Hatoyama then persuaded the cabinet to recommend Takikawa's resignation. This undisguised violation of academic autonomy provoked a burst of protest from both faculty and students, even at other imperial universities. Many of Takikawa's colleagues in the law faculty offered to resign in protest.

This incident temporarily revived the radical student movement and attracted many moderates. The campaign soon became nationwide among students and intellectuals; antifascist and peace groups formed and joined the protest. Despite the crisis atmosphere, Hatoyama forced President Konishi to resign. A passive successor approved the dismissal of Takikawa and the resignation of several others. Lacking a popular base, the movement tapered off in the fall, revealing the chasm between the isolated intellectuals and the masses at the time. An autobiographical novel by NOMA HIROSHI entitled *Waga tō wa soko ni tatsu* (1962, My Tower Stands There) contains a description of the Takikawa Incident.

The postwar Kyōdai incidents have carried on the prewar tradition. Although Takikawa was restored to his faculty post in 1946 and even made university president in 1953, the limits of his prewar type of "liberalism" were revealed in his attempts to contain postwar radical student activities. And, as part of the "reverse course" and return of prewar politicians to power, Hatoyama became prime minister (1954–55).

■——Richard H. Mitchell, *Thought Control in Prewar Japan* (1976). Shihōshō, ed, "Taishō jūgonen Kyōto o chūshin to suru gakusei jiken chōsa kiroku," 21 vols (mimeo), summarized in Shihōshō Keijikyoku, ed, *Shisō kenkyū shiryō: Gakusei chian iji hō ihan jiken kōgai*, vol 7 (1928). Takikawa Yukitoki, "Kyōdai jiken no shinsō: Tennōsei no na no moto ni," *(Tokushū) Bungei shunjū: Tennō hakusho* (October 1956). George Oakley TOTTEN III

Kyōto University Research Institute for Humanistic Studies

(Kyōto Daigaku Jimbun Kagaku Kenkyūjo). Established in 1939, incorporating in 1949 the Institute of Oriental Culture (est 1929) and the private Research Institute of Western Culture (est 1946). It is composed of a Documentation Center for Oriental Studies and 16 research sections grouped under three departments focusing on the West, Japan, and the rest of Asia. The 29-member staff conducts research in the humanities, emphasizing interdisciplinary projects that often entail overseas stays lasting from three to five years and that encourage foreign scholarly participation. Journals published include: *Tōhō gakuhō, Jimbun gakuhō,* and *Zimbvn* (an English journal for scholars abroad); library resources: 320,000 volumes.

Gina Lee BARNES

Kyōwa Bank, Ltd

(Kyōwa Ginkō). One of Japan's major banks. Independent from any industrial group, it is a medium-sized city bank with over 230 offices throughout the country. Business is concentrated on transactions with individuals and small enterprises. Formerly the Savings Bank of Japan, Ltd, formed in 1945 by a merger of nine savings banks, it assumed its present name in 1948 after shifting to commercial banking. Kyōwa's international banking network has been consolidated through branches in London, New York and Los Angeles; nine representative offices, including one in Chicago; and three overseas subsidiaries, including the Kyōwa Bank of California. At the end of March 1982 total assets were ¥7.5 trillion (US $31.2 billion), deposits ¥5.9 trillion (US $24.5 billion), the annual operating profit was ¥24 billion (US $99.7 million), and capitalization stood at ¥52.5 billion (US $218.1 million). Corporate headquarters are located in Tōkyō.

Kyōwa Hakkō Kōgyō Co, Ltd

Diversified manufacturer of pharmaceuticals, chemicals, alcohol, alcoholic beverages, food, and food additives. Established in 1949, the company is well known for its development in 1956 of a fermentation process for the production of amino acids. The process utilizes control of the fermentation culture to affect the metabolic action of microorganisms, and it has won several prizes, including an award from the Japan Academy. One of the largest makers of alcohol in the world, Kyōwa Hakkō engages in research on the potential use of alcohol as an alternative energy source. Among the company's products, pharmaceuticals have recorded the highest annual revenue growth in recent years. The company has eight subsidiaries and representative offices overseas, including two in the United States. In 1981, total sales were ¥206 billion (US $940.9 million), distributed as follows: pharmaceuticals 35 percent, chemicals 31 percent, food and food additives 22 percent, alcohol and alcoholic beverages 12 percent. Fermented products accounted for 70 percent of the total sales. The company was capitalized at ¥13.6 billion (US $62.1 million) in 1981. The head office is in Tōkyō.

Kyōwakai → Concordia Society

kyōyujo

(literally, "place of instruction"). Educational facilities for commoners during the middle years of the Edo period (1600–1868). In many cases, they were established together with GŌGAKU. Such facilities were founded in various parts of the country by domainal authorities during the Kansei era (1789–1801) and about 50 were in operation during the Bunka and Bunsei era (1804–30); they were dissolved at the time of the Meiji Restoration (1868). Two or three times a month the kyōyujo offered simple lectures on the conduct of one's everyday life and on the Confucian classics. In addition, when the occasion required, instruction was offered in farming methods and penmanship, and housekeeping for women. It was also common for the Confucian scholars attached to the school to travel from village to village to lecture during the farmers' slack season. See also EDUCATION: Edo-period education.　　　　Etō Kyōji

kyū → moxa treatment

Kyūchū Bō Jūdai Jiken

(literally, "Grave Incident in the Imperial Palace"). A dispute over the betrothal of Crown Prince HIROHITO; lasting from 1919 to 1921, it mainly involved politicians from the former domains of Satsuma (now Kagoshima Prefecture) and Chōshū (now Yamaguchi Prefecture). In June 1919 the imperial court officially announced its choice of a fiancée for the crown prince: Princess Nagako, daughter of Prince Kuni no Miya Kunihiko and grand-daughter of Shimazu Tadayoshi (1840–97), the last daimyō of Satsuma. YAMAGATA ARITOMO, the leader of the Chōshū political clique, opposed the match, asserting that the Shimazu family had long been known for color blindness. Prince Kuni no Miya enlisted the support of right-wing nationalists such as SUGIURA SHIGETAKE and TŌYAMA MITSURU. In February 1921 the Imperial Household Ministry and the Home Ministry jointly declared that the betrothal was final. Yamagata's protégé Nakamura Yūjirō (1852–1928) took full responsibility for the incident and resigned from his position as imperial household minister. The incident was symptomatic of the continuing rivalry between the Satsuma and Chōshū cliques (see HAMBATSU) and represented the only serious political defeat that Yamagata ever suffered. Prince Hirohito and Princess Nagako were married in 1924.

kyūdō

Japanese archery; literally, "the Way of the bow." Kyūjutsu, the technique of the bow, was the term more commonly used until well into the 19th century. Under the influence of Chinese culture from the 6th century, Japanese archery was divided into military archery and civil archery. Military archery was primarily mounted archery,

and civil archery shooting in the standing position, with emphasis on form and etiquette. There is evidence of a tradition of Japanese equestrian archery dating back to the 3rd century AD. With the influx of Chinese institutions and learning in the late 6th century, Chinese civil archery and its etiquette left an indelible influence on Japanese archery.

The civil wars of the 12th and 13th centuries renewed an emphasis on mounted archery training. The rules of archery became systematized and schools began to proliferate. Those of the Ashikaga family were compiled by Ogasawara Sadamune (1292–1347), and the Ogasawara family continued to provide masters of mounted archery and protocol until the end of the feudal period. Heki Danjō Masatsugu (d 1502) founded the Heki school of archery and Honda Toshizane (1836–1917) established the Honda school. While there were many more schools, these three dominate modern kyūdō.

The bow is 2 meters 21 centimeters (7 ft 3 in) in length and of laminated construction, with alternating strips of wood and bamboo. It is faced front and back with bamboo and the sides are faced with wood. It is an eccentric bow: that is, two-thirds of its length is above the grip and one-third below. The bowstring is of twisted hemp coated with resin and reinforced at the nocking point with fine hemp fibers coated with glue. The arrows are of reed bamboo made in sets of four with blunt metal caps at the tips and matching fletching. The bowstring and arrow are drawn with a yugake (usually a three-fingered glove with the thumb reinforced with plastic but formerly with water buffalo horn) with a deep groove to hold the bowstring near the base of the thumb.

After due ceremony the archer advances with deliberate steps to the shooting line and shoots at a target 36 centimeters (14 in) in diameter set in the azuchi (a bank of sand which is roofed over, 28 meters [92 ft] away). There are usually five targets. Two arrows are shot at a time and the archer retires. In tournaments normally 20 arrows are shot. Of all the martial arts, kyūdō puts the most emphasis on form, and certain schools are very strongly influenced by Zen.

Benjamin H. HAZARD

Kyūji

Also known as Kuji. An ancient collection of myths and legends; it is said to have been completed in the first half of the 6th century but is no longer extant. Kyūji, along with the TEIKI, an imperial genealogy, is believed to have formed the basis for the writing of the KOJIKI (712) and NIHON SHOKI (720), Japan's oldest chronicles. There are slightly different interpretations, however, about the process. TSUDA SŌKICHI contended that the Teiki was an imperial genealogy and the Kyūji, a collection of simple legends and stories without any political or institutional records. He also claimed that they were first edited during Emperor KIMMEI's reign, further edited during SUIKO's reign, and then used as the basis for the Nihon shoki and Kojiki in Emperor TEMMU's time. Whether the Kyūji was a written record or an oral tradition and to what extent the records of prominent lineages were incorporated are other points of scholarly debate.　　　　KITAMURA Bunji

Kyūshū Electric Power Co, Inc

(Kyūshū Denryoku). One of the nine Japanese electric companies, this firm supplies electricity to the seven prefectures of Kyūshū. It was founded in 1951 to meet the large demand for electric power from the industrial district of northern Kyūshū. The composition of the firm's generating facilities is thermoelectric 71 percent, hydroelectric 18 percent, and nuclear and geothermal 11 percent. In the fiscal year ending March 1982 the firm sold 39.2 billion kilowatt-hours of power and total revenue was ¥979 billion (US $4.1 billion). In the same year capitalization stood at ¥220.9 billion (US $917.7 million). The head office is in Fukuoka.

Kyūshū Matsushita Electric Co, Ltd

(Kyūshū Matsushita Denki). Manufacturer and vendor of electric, electronic, and communications equipment. It is a member of the Matsushita group of companies, serving mainly as the Kyūshū manufacturing division of MATSUSHITA ELECTRIC INDUSTRIAL CO, LTD. Founded in 1955, the firm has six factories which contribute to the development of local economies in Kyūshū. It produces portable televisions, radios, pumps, high-precision motors, and other products. Sales for the fiscal year ending November 1981 totaled ¥85.3

billion (US $381.2 million), of which 47 percent was derived from the export market. In the same year capitalization stood at ¥4.5 billion (US $20.1 million). The head office is in Fukuoka.

Kyūshū Mountains

(Kyūshū Sanchi). Mountain range running northeast to southwest through central Kyūshū, dividing the island in two. The highest peak is Sobosan (1,757 m; 5,763 ft). Precipitation is heavy except during winter. It is the source of the rivers Ōnogawa, Kumagawa, and Mimikawa. The Kami Shiiba Dam, located on the Mimikawa, is Japan's first arch-type dam and a hydroelectric power source for Kyūshū. There are vast virgin forests of hemlock-spruce, fir, and beech. The village of Gokanoshō, located near the central area of the mountains, is said to have been settled by survivors of the TAIRA FAMILY after its defeat in the TAIRA-MINAMOTO WAR of the 12th century.

Kyūshū region

(Kyūshū chihō). Region consisting of Kyūshū, the third largest and southernmost of the four major islands of Japan, and numerous surrounding islands. The island of Kyūshū comprises Fukuoka, Nagasaki, Ōita, Kumamoto, Miyazaki, Saga, and Kagoshima prefectures. Okinawa Prefecture is included in the term "Kyūshū" when the latter is considered as a wide-area administrative unit. It is separated from HONSHŪ by the Kammon Strait, and a tunnel under the strait now links them. Geographically divided into north, central, and south Kyūshū, the region has a mountainous interior with numerous coastal plains, volcanoes, and hot springs. The climate is subtropical with heavy precipitation.

Rice, tea, tobacco, sweet potatoes, and citrus fruit (especially mandarin oranges) are the major crops, and stock farming, hog raising, and fishery also flourish. Coal is mined, but its production is rapidly decreasing. Heavy and chemical industry is concentrated in northern Kyūshū, especially around the city of KITA KYŪSHŪ. The major industrial products are iron, steel, chemicals, and metals.

The region, particularly northern Kyūshū, was the first in Japan to be touched by continental culture. Consequently, industry and culture developed early. The major cities are Kita Kyūshū and FUKUOKA, the former an industrial center and the latter a center of administration, economics, commerce, traffic, and culture. Six national parks, Unzen–Amakusa, Kirishima–Yaku, Saikai, Aso, Inland Sea, and Iriomote, as well as 10 quasi-national parks, including the Amami Islands, Iki–Tsushima, and Okinawa Coast, are located here. There are also numerous historical relics. Area: 43,065 sq km (16,623 sq mi); pop: 14,071,412.

Kyūshū University

(Kyūshū Daigaku). A national, coeducational university in the city of Fukuoka. Founded in 1910 as Kyūshū Imperial University. It maintains faculties of letters, education, law, economics, science, medicine, dentistry, pharmacology, engineering, and agriculture. Research institutes include the following: the Research Institute of Balneotherapeutics, the Research Institute of Applied Mechanics, the Research Institute of Industry and Labor, and the Research Institute of Industrial Science. Enrollment was 9,425 in 1980.

Japanese Union Organizations and Membership			
	Number of unions	Union membership (in thousands)	Percentage of wage and salary employees organized
1925	457	254	5.6
1930	712	354	7.5
1935	991	409	6.9
1940	49	9	0.1
1945	509	381	—
1950	29,144	5,774	45.8
1955	32,012	6,166	34.7
1960	41,561	7,516	31.7
1965	52,879	10,070	35.0
1970	60,954	11,481	34.7
1975	69,333	12,473	34.5
1978	70,868	12,233	32.2
1979	71,780	12,174	31.4
1980	72,693	12,241	30.8

SOURCE: For 1925–75: Nakajima Hideo, "Senzen sengo no rōshi kankei shihyō no suii," *Rōdō tōkei chōsa geppō* (January 1977). For 1978–80: Prime Minister's Office, Statistics Bureau, *Japan Statistical Yearbook* (annual): 1982.

labor

Organized labor in Japan traces its beginnings to the late 19th century, the time when industrialization first took hold and an industrial working class started to emerge. However, many years were to elapse before unions became firmly established, and not until after 1945 did Japan have a durable labor movement of widespread proportions. Today, organized labor in Japan boasts the second largest membership in the noncommunist world (see Table 1).

Among the economic, political, and social conditions which shape labor movements in industrialized nations, changes in the labor market over the long run appear to play a key role. Whatever the goals and ideologies labor organizations profess, their structure, strategy, and action seem to reflect the evolving structure of labor markets. The history of organized labor in Japan offers no exception in this respect, so it is well to begin with an examination of LABOR MARKET development from the time Japanese industrialization commenced in the late 19th century.

Emergence of an Industrial Labor Force—— At the time of the MEIJI RESTORATION (1868) the Japanese economy was primarily nonindustrial, with as much as 80 percent of the working population engaged in farming and fishing. Despite concerted efforts, largely under government leadership, to achieve rapid industrialization (see INDUSTRIAL REVOLUTION IN JAPAN), it was not until the end of World War I that a majority of the Japanese labor force pursued gainful employment outside of agriculture. Full commitment of most workers to industrial wage labor as their lifetime occupation emerged slowly over several decades. Deterrents to industrial work were insecurity of income, competitiveness and alienation of urban life, and reluctance to leave traditionally tight-knit farm families and well-ordered rural villages despite low living standards. Even by 1918, most workers in the industrial sectors were still not wage and salary earners hired directly by companies and organizations to work under the direction of supervisors and managers. Rather they were either self-employed or unpaid family workers often engaged in handicraft trades. Many were still very close to their agrarian

origins, as exemplified by the large number of migrants, or DEKA-SEGI, who moved back and forth between farm and factory. Thus, an important characteristic of the industrial labor force throughout much of the pre–World War II era was its "half-peasant, half-worker" status. Given these labor market conditions, organization of labor unions remained limited, short-lived, and divided in goals and structure.

Even as recently as the early 1930s, a majority of Japanese wage earners was female, mainly young girls brought from rural areas to work in textile mills and other light manufacturing industries for a relatively few years. Only when Japan began concentrated efforts to build up such heavy industries as steel, machinery, and chemical manufacturing, following the Manchurian Incident of 1931, did male employees begin to outnumber females. Not until after the post–World War II reconstruction and entry into the period of remarkably high economic growth in the 1950s and 1960s did Japan emerge as a society primarily of wage and salary earners—fully a century after the United Kingdom had reached this stage and a half-century after the United States. Only the present generation in Japan has fully experienced this conversion. In 1950, barely one-third of the labor force was wage and salary employees; by 1975 the proportion exceeded two-thirds.

Dualistic Labor Markets—— As in other newly developing countries attempting rapid industrialization, Japan's economic structure long remained dualistic. Alongside one another emerged a huge mass of small, technologically backward, family-centered shops, work places, and farms, and a relative handful of large-scale, in some instances mammoth, organizations and enterprises with the most advanced technologies and processes. Both sectors grew apace over the decades, with the large-scale sector controlled or dominated by the ZAIBATSU (financial and industrial combines), the military establishment, or the central government. While a considerable degree of coordination grew up between the two sectors through large firms subcontracting production to small ones, the eventual result for industrial workers was also the emergence of "dual" labor markets, in which employees in large-scale firms received wages and benefits notably greater than those in the small-scale sector.

Wage differentiation among workers by size of employing firm became clear-cut after World War I. Until that time, such WAGE DIFFERENTIALS were almost nonexistent, since workers in industry tended to be highly mobile, moving from employer to employer, regardless of firm size, in search of the best-paying jobs. Their mobility tended to equalize wages by level of skill among firms, large and small. At the same time, labor markets tended to be unstable, if not chaotic, and were only slowly systematized for allocating workers among industrial enterprises. Such slow development is thought to have been due fundamentally to rapid population growth in agricultural areas from the 1870s to the 1920s, resulting in surplus labor which could not be productively employed on the near-subsistence family farms and which as a result often sought work on an ad hoc basis in the rising industrial and commercial sectors. There were few conscious efforts to equip potential industrial workers with appropriate skills through preemployment and on-the-job training even though Japan had achieved universal elementary education, developed several high-quality universities, and launched secondary-level technical schools by the early 1900s. As a result, the new industries continually suffered from shortages of skilled workers, especially during the economic boom of World War I. For a period of decades, many employers, believing that all they needed were timid, unskilled laborers, sought out those workers who would work most cheaply, often under abysmal conditions. The cotton TEXTILE INDUSTRY was among the most notorious examples in recruiting low-paid young girls from rural areas. See also ECONOMIC HISTORY: early modern economy.

The Early Patron-Client System—— As commonly occurs in emerging economies in which open labor markets are not rationally organized and elaborated, personalized relationships, such as patron-client groupings, served to match supplies of and demand for workers in the new industries of Japan. Despite abolition by the early Meiji leaders of long-established craft guilds as part of the effort to wipe away feudal practices of the Edo period, there quickly emerged tight-knit, personalized clusters of patrons (oyakata), or labor "bosses," and their followers (kokata: see OYABUN-KOBUN). As entities, these groups each possessed various degrees of traditional and modern skills utilizable in the new industrial undertakings and offered their services collectively to employers under the leadership of the oyakata. Many oyakata acquired technical knowledge, skill training, and practical work experience during the early industrializing efforts in government owned and operated mills, factories, shipyards, and arsenals, which were set up as "models" for private entrepreneurs to emulate, and of which most were indeed turned over to private owners in the 1870s and 1880s. A typical oyakata not only provided a work force to an employer, but also managed and supervised his kokata in the work performed.

Typically, under the leadership of oyakata, these entities would move from one work site to another, offering services to the highest bidder. Kokata might break away on their own or, as new oyakata, establish still other patron-client groups, usually in close relationship to the original oyakata—a practice reminiscent of the traditional custom of establishing a main house and branch houses among extended families and commercial shops. For several decades managements of most new industrial enterprises took little direct responsibility for recruiting, selecting, and training wage employees, or even for assigning them to specific jobs or tasks. Indeed, the labor "boss" institution remained well-entrenched in parts of Japanese industry such as construction and shipbuilding, down to the end of World War II, when it was legally abolished as an undemocratic practice under the reforms of the Allied Occupation.

Spread of "Closed" Employment Systems in Large Firms

As Japan's industrialization progressed, especially with the booms associated with the Sino-Japanese War (1894–95), the Russo-Japanese War (1904–05), and World War I (1914–18), it became clear to the increasingly professional managers, engineers, and technical personnel of the expanding zaibatsu enterprises, most of whom were now graduates of the elite universities and high level secondary schools, that oyakata and their followers actually possessed insufficient skills and discipline to cope efficiently with rapidly, almost continuously changing technologies, processes, and organizations. High turnover rates among workers taking advantage of rising wage opportunities, especially during the boom of World War I, dramatized the need for stabilizing work forces within the large companies. Establishment of such "closed," or internal, employment systems came into sharp conflict with the "open" and fluid labor markets that had previously characterized Japan's industrial sectors. The changeover entailed prolonged competition between professional management and oyakata over control of workers in the large-scale firms. Some of the early labor unions in fact were oyakata-kokata groupings rather than democratic organizations of workers.

The closed systems did not appear overnight, but took several decades to evolve. In the early 1900s major companies began to launch their own internal skill-training programs, taking their cue from the then newly established government-operated YAWATA IRON AND STEEL WORKS. The rapidly expanding iron and steel, shipbuilding, machinery, and related modern industries at that time could not wait for graduates to come out of the vocational tracks then being developed in the public schools. Ill-equipped in any event for instruction in specific manual skills, these schools were better suited for turning out potential employees for clerical and white-collar occupations. However, these enterprise schools and programs grew slowly in the face of major reliance on established patron-client groups. Only in the 1920s did large firm managements on a wide scale recruit, train, and promote employees directly and exclusively by themselves.

Concerted efforts by major enterprises in the 1920s to develop their own exclusive internal employment systems basically reflected rapid expansion in factory size, introduction of new technologies and processes, and adoption of "scientific management" techniques as means of meeting intensifying international competition. Thus, despite a sharp economic depression following World War I that left in its wake plentiful supplies of unskilled labor, the big enterprises now became even more bent on eliminating inefficiencies and holding down labor costs by directly controlling their own work forces. Once such closed systems were firmly established, companies could retain workers on a long-term basis. This development was to lead

to the practice of "lifetime," or career-long, employment in the large-scale organizations, which continues to the present.

Still another factor that underlay management's promotion of closed employment systems was the rise of labor unrest in Japan during the 1920s, initially dramatized by the RICE RIOTS OF 1918. During World War I, labor unionism spread rapidly after the founding of the moderate Yūaikai (Friendship Society) in 1912 (see below). The movement took an increasingly radical turn as the impact of the Russian Revolution reached Japan. No doubt alarmed by the threat of unionization, and fearful of interference with plans to reduce labor costs, managements of large Japanese enterprises were determined to eliminate "outside" influences by strengthening internal work force controls. Throughout the 1920s and 1930s, most big companies fiercely resisted unionization. The employers' federation successfully defeated attempts by the government, despite Japan's membership in the new International Labor Organization (ILO), to adopt legislation supporting the right of labor to organize and bargain collectively.

To justify their position, managements claimed that employer PATERNALISM was more suitable for Japanese industry. The use of paternalism by management in Japan, it should be noted, paralleled a similar trend in the United States at that time. Managements, of course, stressed principles of traditional Japanese family relationships, drawn from social and political organization of the feudal period, with their features of tight superior-subordinate hierarchy, intense worker loyalty, and reciprocal obligations between employer and employee within the enterprise (see CORPORATE CULTURE; COMPANY WELFARE SYSTEM). In this ideological context, large firm managements also developed elaborate personnel administration, giving special attention to selection, training, promotion, and welfare of those who would become shain, or permanent members of the company. At first, management concentrated attention primarily on white-collar employees, but skilled blue-collar workers were gradually included as well.

The concept of permanent attachment of blue-collar workers to a firm received major impetus only as Japan increasingly turned to militarism in the 1930s and began to adopt labor controls on a nationwide basis. However, with the great expansion of heavy industry in the 1930s, large firms, constantly facing a shortage of skilled and reliable labor, had to lure away "mid-career" workers from small- and medium-scale companies with some promise of long-term employment and increased wages, although they were difficult to fit into the established work groups within these companies.

As the closed employment systems formed, management often brought the old-time oyakata into the organization on a permanent basis, giving them high pay and status and to an extent relying on them to build and train tight-knit work groups within the company. In this way, features of the long-standing patron-client relationships became built into the new internal employment systems. During the 1920s and 1930s a number of major firms also fostered formal worker representation and participation schemes within the company, which for the most part were management-controlled or dominated. See also EMPLOYMENT SYSTEM, MODERN.

Nenkō Wages and Benefits

As part of the closed systems with their feature of permanent employment, large companies increasingly began to adopt pay, benefit, and promotion schemes based primarily on the employee's initial level of school education, age, and length of service within the company rather than on individual skill, productiveness, or merit. Known as nenkō, these schemes meant that companies would hire prospective permanent employees, usually males only, directly upon school graduation, subject them to intensive testing and a probationary period, and give them moral indoctrination as well as skill training within the company. Under nenkō, starting pay rates for young recruits were very low, but as length of service increased they rose regularly each year and were supplemented with a variety of money and nonmoney benefits covering various living needs. Thus, a new recruit selected to become a shain was assured of continuing employment and income security until retirement, which was usually set at the early age of 55 with liberal severance, or retirement, benefits. Even though the long-time shain might do the same work as the young recruit, his wage, usually paid on a monthly basis, would be several times higher. Exit from the company at age 55 of course cleared out the high wage workers and made way for the next generation of young school graduates brought in at the bottom of the wage scale. To ensure adaptability in the fast-changing technologies and processes, continual training within, and specific to, the firm was essential.

It was the *nenkō* system as well as prospects for continued employment which chiefly underpinned management efforts to achieve close identification of the employee with the company on a permanent basis. A major outcome was that the permanent employees of large companies not only received considerably higher wages and benefits than in the small- and medium-size firm sector, but also could not transfer their skills and experience from one large company to another.

It should not be assumed, however, that career-long employment systems with their *nenkō* wage and promotion features became prevalent throughout Japan. They were confined almost entirely to the modern large-scale organizations. With the emergence of a dualistic economy, SMALL AND MEDIUM ENTERPRISES still accounted for most of industrial employment. These firms continued to rely mainly on family members, external labor markets, and outside patron-client arrangements for obtaining supplies of workers and for setting wage rates and conditions of work usually considerably below those of the large companies. Also, to serve as buffers for the permanent employees, when economic conditions worsened, the big firms themselves utilized sizable numbers of temporary and casual workers or subcontracted operations to small, dependent enterprises. See also WAGE SYSTEM; SENIORITY SYSTEM.

Pre–World War II Labor Movement —— The history of labor unionism before World War II is important mainly for its ideological influence on organized labor after Japan's surrender in 1945. Although not totally outlawed, organized labor faced severe government repression and employer resistance throughout the period. The movement, as a result, developed with radical and moderate wings, which have carried over to the present. At its height in the early 1930s, the prewar labor movement never embraced more than about 8 percent of the wage and salary earners. With the advent of World War II, the independent union movement ceased to exist and was replaced by a government-sponsored labor front for the duration of the war.

As in most other industrializing nations, Japan experienced sporadic worker protests against employer exploitation and debased working conditions as early as the 1870s. The first continuing unions emerged among relatively skilled workers such as printers, iron workers, and streetcar operators in the late 1890s. Under the leadership of TAKANO FUSATARŌ and KATAYAMA SEN, who had had personal experience with the American Federation of Labor, the Rōdō Kumiai Kiseikai (Society for Formation of Labor Unions) was established in 1897 (see SHOKKŌ GIYŪKAI). As Japan's first national labor organization, it sought, following the American example, to develop "business" unionism based on collective bargaining by skilled craft groups. However, these early unions were mutual benefit associations set up for providing unemployment and illness insurance rather than organizations for collective bargaining and strike action. Moderate in their outlook and demands, they proved to be short-lived, collapsing from financial difficulties and severe employer opposition. They all but disappeared after passage of the oppressive PUBLIC ORDER AND POLICE LAW OF 1900. What few worker organizations lingered on took the form of "study groups," often clandestine and usually interested in fostering socialism or anarchism as a possible ideological base for a future Japanese labor movement. These groups, led by intellectuals rather than workers, were constantly hounded by the police authorities, culminating in the conviction and execution of several anarchist leaders in 1911 on charges of allegedly plotting to assassinate the emperor (see HIGH TREASON INCIDENT OF 1910; ANARCHISM). Several severe spontaneous strikes, however, occurred, particularly during the depression following the Russo-Japanese war among miners who protested against extremely poor working conditions (see ASHIO COPPER MINE LABOR DISPUTE; BESSHI COPPER MINE LABOR DISPUTES).

First National Labor Federations: Yūaikai and Sōdōmei —— Japan's first lasting national labor federation was the YŪAIKAI. It was founded in 1912 under the leadership of SUZUKI BUNJI, a Tōkyō University graduate, and, following the model of the American Federation of Labor, took an exceedingly moderate posture in order to gain acceptance or toleration by employers and government. Advocating self-help and "business" unionism, the Yūaikai achieved notable success in extending unionization during the boom conditions of World War I—so much so that more aggressive elements began to enter the new unions by 1919 and succeeded in changing the name of the national organization to SŌDŌMEI (Japan Federation of Labor). Sōdōmei engaged in increasingly active organizing campaigns especially as economic depression struck and unemployment became severe in Japan in the early 1920s. The first parade on May

Day, an event still celebrated today, was held in Tōkyō in 1920.

Japanese labor unity did not last long. Sharp ideological competition arose within organized labor immediately following World War I. It reflected the rivalries that had emerged in the Western world. Socialists, anarchists, communists, and nonpolitical "business" unionists were pitted against one another, resulting in a series of splits and reformations throughout the 1920s and 1930s. Their ideological differences revolved around the threat of violence versus parliamentary action. The anarchists were virtually destroyed with the police execution of their chief leader ŌSUGI SAKAE following the TŌKYŌ EARTHQUAKE OF 1923. The communists were driven underground or jailed, and their repression was at its height after passage of the PEACE PRESERVATION LAW OF 1925. Permitted to continue its existence, the moderate wing of Sōdōmei shunned any appearance of political radicalism.

Despite repression, labor disputes with employers steadily increased, unions established close ties with new left-wing political parties, and some beginnings of collective bargaining emerged. The moderate seamen's union, for example, which became the largest and longest-lasting labor organization in pre–World War II Japan, reached collective bargaining agreements with management. During the relatively liberal 1920s, the government gave some recognition to the labor movement by granting union representation in the ILO, permitting the existence of nonrevolutionary socialist parties, enacting universal male suffrage in 1925, and encouraging peaceful settlement of labor-management disputes through a new law in the same year to generate tripartite conciliation and mediation efforts. However, without an explicit legal right to organize, the union movement could successfully penetrate only a few of the big enterprises with their large concentrations of workers in closed employment systems and company-controlled worker organizations, although it did make more headway among small- and medium-size firms. Moreover, with the frequent splitting of the movement, by the 1930s the more conservative labor leadership, some with labor-boss backgrounds, held sway over those unions tolerated by the government as legitimate.

Sampō: Wartime Labor Front —— The militarists gained direct state control over labor with the establishment of Sampō (Sangyō Hōkoku Kai or Industrial Patriotic Association) in the late 1930s. With the formation of Sampō, an independent labor movement, however moderate, could not be tolerated for long. By 1941, the unions had dissolved or gone underground. Like similar "labor fronts" in Nazi Germany and Fascist Italy, Sampō's functions included allocating workers on a priority basis to the industries deemed most essential for military purposes. In organizing the Sampō movement, not only were all labor unions abolished, but each company set up its own internal councils from top to bottom devoted to improving productivity and expanding production for the war effort under supervision of the government. These organizations heavily emphasized traditional loyalty, family-centeredness, and ultranationalism. Frozen within an enterprise, labor was, in effect, forbidden to move about in the labor market from employer to employer.

No doubt the Sampō movement strengthened the closed employment systems by closely identifying the worker with his employing firm, and by reducing status distinctions within companies between white- and blue-collar employees. Within the enterprise, management tended to treat all workers alike, extending the *nenkō* system to everyone, and otherwise fortifying their common employment status in the company. There is reason to believe that because of the tight unity they created among workers at the enterprise level, the Sampō organizations at the company level provided an important base for rapid unionization after 1945.

Allied Occupation Labor Reforms —— Immediately after the surrender of Japan in 1945, labor reform became an important part of the wholesale democratization of the Japanese economic, political, and social structure under the Allied OCCUPATION. Guaranteed FUNDAMENTAL LABOR RIGHTS for virtually all workers, including the RIGHT TO ORGANIZE LABOR UNIONS of their own choosing, COLLECTIVE BARGAINING RIGHT, and the right to conduct concerted activities, such as the RIGHT TO STRIKE, were among the earliest decrees issued by the Supreme Commander for the Allied Powers (SCAP) in the fall of 1945. The decrees were implemented by LABOR LAWS that went into effect the following spring. Failure by employers to accept these rights would result in charges and penalties for committing UNFAIR LABOR PRACTICES. In 1946 the principles, drawn primarily from the 1935 Wagner Act of the United States, were embodied in the Labor Union Law (Rōdō Kumiai Hō), and supplemented by the Labor Relations Adjustment Law (Rōdō Kankei Chōsei Hō). The latter set up tripartite employer, worker, and public member LABOR RELATIONS COMMISSIONS at the national and prefectural levels to assist in the settlement of labor disputes through conciliation, mediation, and arbitration (see LABOR DISPUTE RESOLUTION PROCEDURES); to determine whether unions were truly bona fide and democratic; and to decide upon unfair labor practice charges against employers. Equally important for underpinning the new labor rights and protections was adoption in spring 1947 of the Labor Standards Law (Rōdō Kijun Hō), which set legal minimums for conditions and terms of work. These standards, as advanced in principle as those found anywhere in the world at that time, were in compliance with many of the conventions formulated by the ILO. The Labor Standards Law was soon followed by still other labor protective legislation dealing with such matters as unemployment insurance, WORKERS' COMPENSATION, and old age SOCIAL SECURITY PROGRAMS. The new national constitution of 3 May 1947 further explicitly included all these rights and guarantees, and for the first time in Japanese history a MINISTRY OF LABOR was established to administer most of the new labor legislation. See also LABOR REFORMS OF 1945–1947; EMPLOYMENT SECURITY LAW OF 1947.

The Growth of Unionism (1945–1950)

It must be stressed that by the end of World War II economic and social conditions in Japan were abysmal. The major cities were in ruins; to a large extent industrial plants were destroyed; untold numbers, soon to be swollen by large-scale repatriation from overseas, were unemployed; food supplies were extremely short. There was widespread fear of mass starvation, as most Japanese could eke out only a bare existence at best. One of SCAP's immediate objectives was to avoid a major social and economic disaster while at the same time preserving order; promoting democratization; and purging the wartime military, industrial, and political leadership. With near chaos gripping Japan's economy in the months following the surrender, it proved difficult to renew production even in the most essential industries such as coal mining and foodstuffs. Because of enormous uncertainty and confusion, worsened by galloping price inflation, industrial recovery remained paralyzed for months (see ECONOMIC HISTORY: Occupation-period economy). Unsure of the direction in which SCAP would allow Japan's economy to go, and under threat of purge, industrial managers made few concerted efforts to restore even the most essential production, despite urgent SCAP and government directives. The number of instances of workers themselves taking direct control of plants and factories grew. These actions, which were at first permitted by SCAP as a means of supplying needed goods, were later declared illegal invasions of private property rights.

In these circumstances, it is not surprising that Japanese workers responded dramatically to SCAP's initial strong encouragement for organizing LABOR UNIONS. Unionization grew rapidly, rising from a membership of zero in August 1945 to more than three million a year later. Never in the history of any industrial nation had labor unions spread so rapidly. Notably, in contrast to the prewar period, most of these organizations formed quickly in the large-scale industrial and government entities. Typically, a union with its own constitution embraced all the employees in a given plant, company, or government agency and included both blue-collar and white-collar workers, often reaching well up into management ranks themselves. A few unions formed on an occupational or industrial basis, cutting across enterprises. Under SCAP pressure, in most instances employers put up little resistance to such unionization, and probably many of the new unions were simply transformations of the previous company-level Sampō units, which SCAP had abolished as part of the industrial and labor reforms. Yet, it may be said that, by and large, these unions were spontaneous attempts by workers to exercise their newly received rights and to protect their employment and income within the closed enterprise systems in the context of a highly unstable and chaotic economy. The formation of unions on an enterprise-by-enterprise basis fundamentally reflected the fact that employment security lay in becoming permanently attached to a large-scale firm. Thus, there was little drive at the grass-roots level to form strong unions on a "horizontal" basis across companies. As there had been little use of external labor markets among the large firms, in the prostrated postwar economy prospects for labor market mobility became even more dim.

It cannot be emphasized enough that this drive for security was the most fundamental reason for the spread of unionism at the enterprise level, which has come to characterize the basic structure of Japan's postwar labor movement. In this context, far less important were notions of loyalty or devotion to the employing firm, or other sociopsychological or cultural forces that have been posited as peculiarly strong or unique traits in Japanese labor relations.

Reemergence of Rival Labor Federations

Almost immediately after the surrender in 1945, efforts began to weld the rapidly growing unions at the enterprise level into nationwide organizations. Under SCAP orders, prewar labor leaders, most with left-wing connections, were released from jail and almost instantly went to work to establish a unified, national labor center. Their goal, however, was not realized, and to the present the Japanese labor movement has not achieved unity. Several reasons account for this failure. The most important was that beginning in 1946 the national labor leadership, in a repeat of the prewar experience, divided once again over issues of ideology and organizational structure. The chief rivalry sprang up between the communists and socialists.

Within a few months after the surrender, two competing major national labor federations had emerged: Sōdōmei, revived and led by moderate right-wing socialists and "business" unionists, and SAMBETSU KAIGI (Congress of Industrial Labor Unions of Japan), dominated by communists and left-wing socialists. At the same time a large number of the new unions, embracing as much as half of the total union membership, did not affiliate with either of these national bodies. Fearing that they would be torn apart by ideological and political divisions, they remained neutral, interested only in promoting unionism at the enterprise level, even though usually loosely confederated on an industrial basis. Although they expressed a common hope of eventually achieving industry-by-industry or industrial unionism as the basis for labor solidarity, enterprise-level unions were generally reluctant to transfer power to suprabodies, which, as outsiders to the closed employment systems, were seen as less effective for carrying out negotiations with management over issues particular to each enterprise. Their attention was almost exclusively riveted on employment security and advancement within the enterprise itself.

Restraints on Unionism after 1947

The rapid growth of unionization reached a peak by 1949 of almost seven million members (above 50 percent of all wage and salary earners) in about 35,000 basic plant- or enterprise-level unions throughout the private and public sectors of the economy. However, the organized labor movement began to experience a series of setbacks as early as 1947. Especially in pursuit of demands for wage increases to keep ahead of the rampant inflation and for enterprise democratization, both public and private sector unions had engaged in an increasing number of strikes and other direct actions, some involving violence, throughout 1945 and 1946. This spreading labor unrest culminated in a joint call by the national labor centers for a general strike to be conducted on 1 February 1947. Its aim was not only to achieve economic improvement but also to topple the conservative party in power and to install a left-wing government. Believing that such action would constitute a challenge to the authority of SCAP itself as well as its efforts to preserve order, the MacArthur headquarters after some vacillation prohibited the general strike on the very evening before it was scheduled to occur. See GENERAL STRIKE OF 1947.

SCAP's reaction was to modify labor union rights. Through a series of memoranda to the government, not only did SCAP in effect prohibit general strikes, but also forbade any walkouts by public sector employees. New legislation, adopted in the following three years, specifically excluded government workers from the full rights granted under the Labor Union Law and Labor Relations Adjustment Law. Unions in publicly owned enterprises, such as the national railways and postal service, were still permitted to organize at the enterprise level and engage in collective bargaining limited to wages and working conditions, but were denied the right to strike. Civil servants in government agencies and departments were deprived of all these rights, except for the privilege of forming personnel associations solely within their own agencies to present requests for improvement and engage in consultation with management. Parallel enactments were applied to local government levels by the early 1950s. Since about one-third of the labor organizations were made up of unions in the public sector, the new laws had the effect of separating organized labor into two distinct divisions. Still other amendments to the Trade Union Law and Labor Relations Adjustment Law in the late 1940s aimed at curbing union political activities, forbidding the use of violence, strengthening internal union democracy, prohibiting management personnel from joining employee unions, and increasing the role of the public members of the labor relations commissions in determining union autonomy and employer unfair labor practices.

Labor——Table 2

	Number of employees per establishment	Wage and salary employees (in thousands)	Percentage of employees unionized
Unionization by Size and Type of Establishment, 1974			
Private sector	1–29	11,244	3.4
	30–99	5,356	9.0
	100–499	5,284	31.5
	500 & over	9,281	63.6
	Total	31,165	28.0
Public sector		4,350	76.8

SOURCE: Ministry of Labor, *Yearbook of Labor Statistics* (annual): 1974. Rōdōshō (Ministry of Labor), *Rōdō hakusho* (annual): 1976.

SCAP now no longer strongly encouraged unionism as a means for democratization but turned increasingly to policies of rebuilding the Japanese industrial economy in order to make Japan an ally in the cold war. It favored the conservative government led by Prime Minister YOSHIDA SHIGERU, restoring the prestige and prerogatives of big business management, and taking firm measures for achieving economic stabilization, especially through the DODGE LINE in 1949. Largely as a result of these reversals and SCAP policies to retrench the economy, by 1949 labor organizations came to a near halt. Membership fell off to less than six million, and for the next several years grew at a comparatively slow pace. Not until 1958 did it once again reach the 1949 peak. However, with the reconstruction and expansion of the economy by that time, the proportion of wage and salary earners who were unionized had dropped to about one-third. In the meantime, the labor movement underwent a major restructuring.

Labor Movement Reorganization and Splits: Sōhyō and Dōmei

Reorganization came in the form of a new national labor center, SŌHYŌ (General Council of Trade Unions of Japan), which was established in 1950 and still remains the largest national union federation, with 4.6 million members, more than 37 percent of the 12.5 million unionists in the mid-1970s. Sōhyō initially was the product of union attempts to rid themselves of both radical left-wing leadership and right-wing labor bossism and to establish collective bargaining on an industry-wide basis. Both Sambetsu and Sōdōmei dissolved in the process of forming Sōhyō, although Sōhyō at its outset succeeded in bringing together only about half of organized labor. Further, Sōhyō announced its intention to affiliate with the newly formed International Confederation of Free Trade Unions (ICFTU), which in 1949 had been organized as a cold war counterweight to the communist-dominated World Federation of Trade Unions (WFTU). For these aims, SCAP gave Sōhyō its blessings.

Sōhyō, however, rapidly veered toward the Left. Almost immediately after its founding, Sōhyō objected to United Nations military action in the Korean conflict and to the possible involvement of Japan despite its "peace" constitution. Also, it opposed the proposal for a separate United States–Japan peace treaty. Proclaiming a role of "positive" neutrality for Japan, Sōhyō condemned any type of Japanese rearmament, allied itself primarily with the Marxist left-wing socialists, and permitted communist activity within its ranks. Thus, it quickly became fully involved in political activism despite initial resolves to concentrate on industrial action. It did not join the ICFTU as a body.

As a result, a number of major unions, embracing about one-third of organized labor and favoring a neutral position in Japanese politics, never joined Sōhyō. In 1954 an important bloc of unions, chiefly in the private sector and originally Sōdōmei affiliates, withdrew from Sōhyō to form a rival national center, eventually called DŌMEI (Japanese Confederation of Labor). This became Japan's second largest national labor center, which by the mid-1970s had more than 2.2 million members, or 18 percent of all organized workers, almost all in the private sector. Dōmei has closely supported the moderate DEMOCRATIC SOCIALIST PARTY, which, after an uneasy alliance, formally split off from the JAPAN SOCIALIST PARTY in 1960. Dōmei is affiliated with the ICFTU.

Still other union groups formed separate national bodies. In 1956 a group of unions in the private sector, which wanted to remain neutral in the conflict between Sōhyō and Dōmei, founded a loose organization called CHŪRITSU RŌREN (Federation of Independent Unions). This group today accounts for about 1.4 million, or 10.9 percent, of the Japanese union members. Also, a tiny federation, SHINSAMBETSU (National Federation of Industrial Labor Organizations), devoted to the ideal of pure industrial unionism and opposed to communism, but with less than 70,000 members, has existed since the demise of Sambetsu. In 1979 Chūritsu Rōren and Shinsambetsu announced their merger. As a result of these divisions, Sōhyō's membership is heavily dominated by public sector workers. Some 4.7 million union members, 37.4 percent of the total, were unaffiliated with national centers in the mid-1970s.

Structure and Function of Japanese Unionism——A notable feature of Japanese unionism is that its membership is found mainly in the larger-scale private enterprises and in government units. While today there are about 70,000 basic unions with their own individual constitutions, the majority of the membership is in large establishments, with 500 employees or more each. Close to two-thirds of such establishments have unions, almost all of which have been formed on an enterprise basis. There has been relatively little union penetration of the small- and medium-sized firm sector. Some 31.5 percent of workers in private companies with 100 to 499 employees are organized; 9 percent of those in firms with 30–99 employees are in unions; and a mere 3.4 percent of workers in firms with less than 30 employees are organized (see Table 2). Unionism tends to be well established in such industries as finance, insurance, real estate, transportation and communication, and government service, all of which have 60 to 80 percent of their employees in unions. Average percentages are found in mining and manufacturing. Far below average are agriculture, construction, wholesaling, retailing, and personal services, in which small enterprises abound.

Moreover, despite the existence of three major national labor centers and more than 100 industry-wide union federations, there is little doubt that enterprise-based unions wield the most significant collective bargaining power within the organized labor movement. They tend to retain most of the financial resources for themselves, engage in direct negotiations with management, and carry on day-to-day workshop activities with little assistance from upper union bodies. National organizations are essentially excluded from participating in formal negotiations with employers and serve primarily as informational, educational, and research centers, coordinators of bargaining strategy among the enterprise unions, and organizers of political campaigns and actions. This does not mean that collective bargaining in Japan is less vigorous than in other countries, but only that it tends to focus primarily on issues of immediate concern within the given enterprise rather than whole industries or the economy in general. Typically the membership of an enterprise-based union embraces all the permanent employees of the firm or agency. There are few concerted efforts to organize the unorganized among the temporary workers or in the smaller firms, primarily because enterprise unions are heavily preoccupied with their own internal affairs and because the cost of organizing small mobile groups is high.

Almost all unions in the private sector have formal collective bargaining agreements with management. Although not explicitly stated in these agreements, a principal accomplishment of the enterprise-level unions has, in fact, been to ensure employment security and equal treatment of permanent employees within the enterprise, regardless of their status as blue- or white-collar workers. Indeed, formal agreements hardly mention layoff procedures, essentially on the assumption that discharges of permanent workers will not take place, and a large majority of these agreements stipulate that permanent workers must join the union in recognition of their permanent status. Employers do not dare to risk the wrath of the close-knit enterprise-level unions by resorting to arbitrary layoffs or dismissals without close consultation with the unions. Lengthy strikes, for example in the coal mines in the late 1950s and early 1960s, have resulted from such action (see MIIKE STRIKE; DISMISSAL OF AN EMPLOYEE). On the other hand, assured of permanent employment and equal treatment for its members, enterprise-level unions have tended to cooperate formally and informally with management in expanding and adjusting production, introducing technological changes, and utilizing employees in a highly flexible fashion. In a sense, the enterprise-level unions have been a means for worker participation in management. In many collective bargaining agreements unions have joined in establishing labor-management consultation committees; these committees are involved in such matters as improving safety and health conditions, arranging personnel transfers, increasing productivity, and settling worker complaints outside of the GRIEVANCE PROCEDURE. The enterprise-level union, moreover, has been particularly supportive of the *nenkō* wage, promotion, and benefit system; in the absence of meaningful external labor market wage rates and of job classification within the firm, the system is seen as the primary means of ensuring equitable treatment of the permanent employees over their careers within a given enterprise. A highly democratic institution with a wide variety of occupational groups as its members, the enterprise-level union typically focuses its collective bargaining demands upon common issues, particularly the raising of the wage level of all the workers rather than tampering with the wage and benefit structure that may favor one segment over another.

The Shuntō Wage Pattern——First launched in 1955 under the leadership of Sōhyō, SHUNTŌ (spring wage offensive) has the objective of obtaining general annual wage increases in key enterprises and industries, which then become the pattern throughout the industrial economy in both private and public sectors. As its name implies, *shuntō* takes place in the spring, when Japan's fiscal year for government and business begins (1 April), and when enterprises hire their annual crop of school graduates. In addition to the general wage demands (called "base-ups," since they involve an increase in base pay), *shuntō* raises other economic demands, such as starting wages for new recruits, minimum wages, and income tax cuts for employees. Political demands aimed at unseating the conservative government or at affecting government policy, including foreign affairs, are made as well. *Shuntō* generally spans four to six weeks and involves a series of coordinated walkouts lasting up to 36 hours. Nonetheless, final settlements are essentially made at the enterprise level, which allows for variations in outcome relating to business conditions facing each industry and firm. Over the years settlements have tended to become increasingly closer.

There is little doubt of the success of *shuntō*. Since 1955, the number of participants has steadily grown from about 800,000 to almost 10 million workers, covering more than three-fourths of the organized labor movement. Other bargaining, such as demands for the semiannual wage BONUS, usually given in July and December, also follow the *shuntō* pattern.

In a sense, *shuntō* has become a device for setting something like a national wage increase policy, with the expectation and result that almost all workers, organized or unorganized, will receive about the same proportional wage raise each year. The approach was especially effective in keeping wages throughout the economy abreast of the rapid economic growth from the late 1950s to early 1970s. With the slowdown of the Japanese economy following the OIL CRISIS OF 1973, the national labor centers have been attempting to convert the spring struggle into a "people's *shuntō*" by demanding improvements from the government in social welfare, tax cuts, and employment security, as well as wage increases. Essentially, *shuntō* has been a means for counterbalancing the decentralized system of collective bargaining at the enterprise level.

Particularly important for achieving wage bargaining coordination among major enterprise-level unions was the formation in the early 1960s of the International Metalworkers' Federation–Japan Council (IMF–JC), a grouping of the union federations in such major private-sector industries as steel, automotive, electrical, heavy machinery, and shipbuilding, affiliated with the worldwide IMF trade union secretariat and especially sensitive to rapidly changing foreign trade relationships. While not a national labor center such as Sōhyō or Dōmei, IMF–JC brings together unions with a combined membership of almost two million from all the major national organizations in the metal-working fields, and, at least for collective bargaining purposes, overcomes the deep rivalry which has plagued labor movement unification. As a result, IMF–JC coordination has become a key element in setting the pattern for *shuntō* and other collective bargaining. See also LABOR DISPUTES; STRIKES AND OTHER FORMS OF LABOR DISPUTE.

Employer Organization for Collective Bargaining——Employers, too, have been highly active in developing a coordinated collective bargaining strategy vis-à-vis the unions. Federations of employers for labor policy at the industrial level go back to the 1890s, and, as mentioned, a nationwide employer federation successfully defeated attempts to enact a trade union recognition law in the 1920s and 1930s. While SCAP at first did not favor employer organization after the surrender, by 1947 it allowed the formation of NIKKEIREN (Japan Federation of Employers' Associations), which became the spokesman for large-scale enterprise management with respect to labor relations. Other employer groups also emerged,

notably KEIDANREN (Federation of Economic Organizations), concerned with overall economic policy; Keizai Dōyū Kai (JAPAN COMMITTEE FOR ECONOMIC DEVELOPMENT), composed of influential individual executives rather than company affiliates; and federations such as the JAPAN CHAMBER OF COMMERCE AND INDUSTRY for small- and medium-size businesses. Nikkeiren's position has been to promote harmonious labor relations at the enterprise level and to oppose the influence of industry- or national-level unions in collective bargaining. However, Nikkeiren does not participate directly in any collective bargaining, but makes general policy pronouncements and offers bargaining guidelines. Its main function is to furnish information, research, and educational services along with such organizations as the JAPAN PRODUCTIVITY CENTER and the Ministry of Labor and other government agencies. It also serves as a pressure group for legislative and administrative purposes.

Government Role in Labor Relations——One of the most important elements in Japanese labor relations is the stance of the central government itself. This derives both from the government's role as a major employer and, of course, its crucial influence over the economy through fiscal, monetary, and administrative policy. As mentioned, public sector employees are highly unionized, with about 1.3 million members in PUBLIC CORPORATIONS and government enterprises and at least 2 million members at the local and prefectural levels. Most belong to unions affiliated with Sōhyō, so that close to two-thirds of Sōhyō's membership are government workers. The largest single national union in Japan is the Sōhyō affiliate JICHIRŌ, the federation of local public workers' unions, with more than 1.2 million members. Although denied the right to strike, these unions are among the most militant in Japan and at times resort to illegal dispute actions. See SUTŌ KEN SUTŌ.

The special laws enacted from 1948 to 1953 for unions and collective bargaining in government-owned enterprises and corporations established separate labor relations commissions to mediate and arbitrate disputes on a compulsory basis (see PUBLIC CORPORATIONS AND GOVERNMENT ENTERPRISES LABOR RELATIONS LAW). Subject to the strike and bargaining restrictions and the compulsory arbitration provision, the public employee labor unions have played an important role in the annual *shuntō* and other bargaining campaigns to achieve favorable settlement patterns, since the central public enterprise labor relations commission, followed by local government counterparts, tends to recommend awards in line with those achieved in the private sector, and these awards get incorporated into the government's budgets. Such a heavy element of public employee bargaining in turn feeds into the tendencies toward militant political action, particularly among the Sōhyō unions.

The Outlook for Labor-Management Relations——It has been clear from the time SCAP's policy turned from eliminating Japan's military capability to rebuilding Japan as a strong industrial ally in the cold war, that "production first" became the keystone of governmental policy, at least until the early 1970s. As a result, huge structural shifts in the economy and rapid technological change came at a dizzying pace. Almost overnight, for example, the government encouraged abandonment of coal mining, with its work force of close to 400,000, and the substitution of petroleum as the chief energy source for industrial and domestic use. The nonagricultural labor force expanded from about 25 million in 1955 to almost 45 million in 1975, large and small enterprises growing apace. In this upsurge, the proportion of white-collar workers of the labor force increased notably, as managerial, professional, technical, clerical, and service occupations expanded. At the same time, organized labor itself, recovering from the setback of the early 1950s, steadily rose in numbers and kept pace with the growing nonagricultural labor force (including white-collar workers) through the basic enterprise-level union structure. By the 1970s, with more than 12 million unionized workers, Japan could boast one of the largest organized labor movements among the market economies of the world (second after the United States), with a union organization rate well above the United States' and equal to that of many other economically advanced nations.

Although during these years wages and other work benefits increased commensurately with Japan's economic growth and reached or exceeded levels in some Western European countries, organized labor has been increasingly dissatisfied with the workers' share in the gross national product and with their quality of life. This attitude has been especially marked among young workers, who have been schooled in democratic theory and whose levels of formal education have risen notably. But there also has been considerable dissatisfaction among older workers, most of whom, while enjoying a

Labor disputes——Table 1

International Comparison of Labor Disputes

1. Disputes with work stoppages

	Japan	United States	United Kingdom	West Germany	France
1970	2,260	5,716	3,906	129	2,942
1975	3,391	5,031	2,282	201	3,888
1976	2,720	5,648	2,016	1,481	4,348
1977	1,712	5,506	2,703	81	3,302
1978	1,517	4,230	2,471	1,239	3,206
1979	1,153	4,827	2,080	40	3,104
1980	1,133	3,873	1,330	132	3,542

2. Workers involved (in millions)

	Japan	United States	United Kingdom	West Germany	France
1970	1.720	3.305	1.801	0.184	1.080
1975	2.732	1.746	0.809	0.036	1.827
1976	1.356	2.420	0.668	0.169	2.023
1977	0.692	2.040	1.166	0.034	1.920
1978	0.660	1.624	1.042	0.487	0.705
1979	0.450	1.727	4.608	0.077	0.967
1980	0.563	1.366	0.834	0.045	0.501

3. Man-days lost (in millions)

	Japan	United States	United Kingdom	West Germany	France
1970	3.915	66.414	10.980	0.093	1.742
1975	8.016	31.237	6.012	0.069	3.869
1976	3.254	37.860	3.284	0.534	5.011
1977	1.519	35.822	10.142	0.024	3.666
1978	1.358	36.922	9.405	4.281	2.200
1979	0.930	34.754	29.474	0.483	3.657
1980	1.001	33.389	11.964	0.128	1.674

SOURCE: Rōdōshō (Ministry of Labor), *Rōdō tōkei yōran* (annual): 1982. International Labor Organization, *Yearbook of Labor Statistics* (annual): 1981.

much longer lifespan than previous generations, face early RETIREMENT from the large firms, inadequate incomes, and postretirement job prospects only in the lower end of Japan's dualistic economy.

Grievances such as these underlay a growing number of union-management disputes and work stoppages throughout the 1960s and early 1970s. Indeed, it is a fallacy to depict Japanese industrial relations as unusually harmonious and peaceful. In some years the relative amount of work lost to strikes over labor conditions has equaled the level in France and, while far below the level of countries such as Italy or the United States, has significantly exceeded that of West Germany and the Scandinavian countries. However, one difference is that Japanese unions engage in relatively large numbers of short stoppages; although these average about two to three days each, through such practices as *shuntō*, they involve a large proportion of organized labor.

It is now apparent that the Japanese economy has reached the end of its rapid postwar growth period (see ECONOMIC HISTORY: contemporary economy). In jeopardy as a consequence is the closed-enterprise employment system, since this new phase of economic activity will probably require significant changes in Japan's occupational structure and increasing use of external labor markets. The result has been increasing demands, largely on the part of organized labor and opposition parties, for improved social welfare throughout the nation and a broadening of collective bargaining from its past limited focus on wage increases. There is also notable pressure for shifting negotiations to the industrial and national levels.

In essence, one may expect a further evolution of organized labor in Japan. The era since 1945 has seen the establishment of the basic institutions of the labor movement, which, while representing a degree of continuity with the past, set the stage for further dynamic changes in labor-management relations. In view of the remarkable transformations that have been occurring in Japan's economy and

From this perspective, the experience of Japanese labor parallels that of other industrialized market economies in moving toward wider and wider union participation in the decision-making processes which affect the lives of workers. See also FACTORY LAW OF 1911; MINIMUM WAGE LAW; ŌTA KAORU; IWAI AKIRA; TAKITA MINORU; DENKI RŌREN; JIDŌSHA SŌREN; KŌRŌKYŌ; NIKKYŌSO; ZENSEN; WOMEN IN THE LABOR FORCE.

——James C. Abegglen, *Management and Worker: The Japanese Solution* (1973). Iwao Ayusawa, *A History of Labor in Modern Japan* (1966). Robert E. Cole, *Japanese Blue Collar: The Changing Tradition* (1971). Alice H. Cook, *Japanese Trade Unionism* (1966). Ronald P. Dore, *British Factory–Japanese Factory: The Origins of National Diversity in Industrial Relations* (1973). Tadashi Hanami, *Labor Law and Industrial Relations in Japan* (1979). Hazama Hiroshi, *Nihon rōmu kanri shi kenkyū* (1964). *Nihon rōdō kyōkai zasshi* (monthly since April 1959). *Japan Labor Bulletin* (monthly since April 1962). Komatsu Ryūji, *Kigyōbetsu kumiai no seisei* (1971). Stephen S. Large, *The Yūaikai, 1912–1919: The Rise of Labor in Japan* (1972). Solomon B. Levine, *Industrial Relations in Postwar Japan* (1958). Robert M. Marsh and Hiroshi Mannari, *Modernization of the Japanese Factory* (1976). Ministry of Labor, *Rōdō hakusho* (Labor White Paper; annual). Rōdō Undō Shiryō Kankōkai, ed, *Nihon rōdō undō shiryō* (1959–), 10 vols plus supplement. Kazuo Ōkōchi, Bernard Karsh, and Solomon B. Levine, ed, *Workers and Employers in Japan: The Japanese Employment Relations System* (1973). Sumiya Mikio, *Gendai shihon shugi to rōdō kumiai* (1975). Kōji Taira, *Economic Development and the Labor Market in Japan* (1970). Tsuda Masumi, *Nenkōteki rōshi kankei ron* (1968).

Solomon B. LEVINE

labor dispute resolution procedures

Procedures for the resolution of LABOR DISPUTES in Japan are governed by the Labor Relations Adjustment Law of 1946 (Rōdō Kankei Chōsei Hō). The law provides three procedures for labor dispute resolution: conciliation (*assen*), mediation (*chōtei*), and arbitration (*chūsai*). (Note that *chōtei* means conciliation when used in civil proceedings; see CONCILIATION.)

Conciliation, the most informal of the three procedures, is conducted through conciliators designated by one of the nation's LABOR RELATIONS COMMISSIONS. Mediation, a more formal procedure, is performed by a mediation committee established by a labor relations commission, with representatives from labor, management, and the public. This committee is expected to present mediation proposals to the affected parties. Settlement proposals developed in either mediation or conciliation have no binding power over the parties to the dispute. Settlement can only come about through the voluntary compliance of the parties.

In contrast, the third type of dispute resolution procedure, arbitration, results in settlement decisions that are binding on the parties. Arbitration is performed by an arbitration committee, which is established by a labor relations commission and is composed of members of the public. Arbitration commences only with the consent of both parties. Compulsory arbitration is not practiced in Japan.

The Labor Relations Adjustment Law also provides for emergency reconciliation (*kinkyū chōsei*). Under these provisions, the prime minister is authorized to suspend a dispute for up to 50 days if there is danger that the strike will seriously damage the national interest or popular livelihood.

SUGENO Kazuo

labor disputes

Most Japanese labor disputes involve scheduled one- or two-day strikes during the annual spring labor offensive (SHUNTŌ). Although the level of strike activity in Japan is comparable to that of other industrialized nations, the short duration of the strikes and their predictability significantly reduce the economic impact of work stoppages. Strikes which occur during the wage negotiations are not a result of a rupture in the negotiation process, but are more a ceremonial means of hastening the process.

Labor disputes over issues other than wage negotiations often extend over a longer period of time and sometimes result in a lockout by the employer. Since the EMPLOYMENT SYSTEM and labor-management relations are based largely on the promise of guaranteed employment, the discharge of employees often results in bitter, prolonged disputes. Almost all of the major disputes in Japan have been of this kind (see, for example, the ASHIO COPPER MINE LABOR DISPUTE and the MIIKE STRIKE). LABOR DISPUTE RESOLUTION PRO-

Labor disputes——Table 2

Major Japanese Labor Disputes

Name	Date	Remarks
Amamiya silk mill	14–16 June 1886	Strike by women silk mill workers; the first strike by factory workers in Japan.
Ashio Copper Mine labor dispute[1]	4–7 February 1907	A dispute that turned violent; military forces called out.
Tōkyō Newspaper Printing Workers' Union	30 July–4 August 1919	Publication of 16 newspapers suspended for 4 days because of strike.
Yawata Iron and Steel Works	4 February–2 March 1920	25,000 workers strike, demanding shorter working hours and a 30 percent raise in wages.
Kawasaki and Mitsubishi shipyards	25 June–9 August 1921	Simultaneous strikes at two Kōbe shipyards; largest dispute prior to World War II.
Kyōdō Printing Company strike[1]	19 January–18 March 1926	Led by a Japan Communist Party–related national federation.
Nippon Gakki Co, Ltd	26 April–8 August 1926	Led by a Japan Communist Party–related national federation.
Noda Soy Sauce	16 September 1927–20 April 1928	The longest prewar strike.
Tōyō Muslin Kameido factory	24 September–21 November 1930	Strike over dismissals; clashes with police.
Kanegafuchi spinning mills	5 April–6 June 1930	Four mills strike over 40 percent reduction in wages.
Sino-Japanese War of 1937-1945; World War II [2]		
Yomiuri Shimbun Sha	23 October–11 December 1945; 13 June–16 October 1946	Successful strike for democratization of management through use of production control strategy; management reasserts control in 1946, causing second strike.
General Strike of 1947[1]	Scheduled for 1 February 1947	Planned general strike of all government and public workers; suspended by order of Allied Occupation forces.
Tōhō movie company	8 April–19 October 1948	Dispute over dismissals and the abolition of the management council; intervention by the Occupation authorities.
Tōshiba Corporation	10 February–16 November 1949	Strike over dismissals during industrial reorganization.
Electrical Workers' Union (Densan)	14 April–18 December 1952	Long dispute leads to September strike that halts production of electricity, resulting in the 1953 enactment of restrictions against strikes in electric and coal industries.
Japan Coal Miners' Union (Tanrō)	13 August–17 December 1952	Long dispute coordinated with Densan; strike begins in October, ended through use of the national emergency provision of the Labor Relations Adjustment Law.
Nissan Motor Co	25 May–21 September 1953	Dispute over management prerogatives and regulation of union activities.
Mitsui Mining Co, Ltd	7 August–27 November 1953	Strike by workers resulting in the rehiring of dismissed workers.
Japan Steel Works, Ltd, Muroran factory	17 June–26 December 1954	Strike over dismissals; the largest and last of struggles involving the whole community.
Japan Steel Industry Labor Union Federation	8 October–6 December 1957	One-round negotiation system established after a series of 11 indecisive strikes.
Ōji Paper Co, Ltd	18 July–9 December 1958	Strike protesting the introduction of 24-hour operations; a representative technological innovation dispute.
Mitsui Mining Co, Ltd, Miike Coal Mines (Miike strike[1])	25 January–1 November 1960	Strike over the dismissal of workplace activists; a representative workplace struggle.
Shin Nippon Chisso (now Chisso Corporation), Minamata factory	21 April 1962–22 January 1963	Strike against the introduction of a formula wage system; led to the establishment of a processing industry labor relations board.
Kōrōkyō (Council of Public Corporation and National Enterprise Workers' Unions)	26 November–13 December 1975	A series of strikes demanding restoration to public employees of the right to strike. (Suto Ken Suto)[1]

[1] See separate entries.

[2] Labor union activities were suppressed during the Sino-Japanese War of 1937-1945, and World War II. Most unions were dissolved and their members forced to join the patriotic *sampō* movement (see LABOR). In 1940 independent organized labor virtually ceased to exist, although a small number of small-scale disputes occurred between 1941 and 1945. Unions were restored by Allied Occupation authorities in the fall of 1945.

CEDURES are often utilized in such lengthy disputes. Many cases taken to these services are resolved before a final decision is handed down, indicating that negotiations continue even while official hearings are taking place.

Prolonged disputes often result in a split in the labor union and the formation, often with the assistance of the enterprise management, of a second union more sympathetic to the employer. This occurs primarily from the strikers' fear that further extension of the dispute will cause irreparable harm to the struck business and thus undermine their future employment security. This fear gives Japanese management a strong advantage in collective bargaining and serves to limit the length of strikes during wage negotiations. Another limiting factor is that unions do not generally accumulate large strike funds.

In complicated disputes, workers will sometimes occupy the work place and harass the management; where an enterprise is shut down because of bankruptcy, the union may take over the operation of the firm while demanding its reorganization. Plant occupation

and workers' control of production were particularly common tactics in the years immediately after World War II.

Labor's lack of success in the long strikes of the early postwar period is one of the reasons the Japanese do not look favorably on such disputes. Strikes were also illegal during the war, and there is still carryover of the wartime view that strikes disrupt the social order. The prosperity of most Japanese enterprises, especially after 1955, has made accommodation and cooperation between management and labor increasingly attractive. There is, in addition, a cultural tendency among the Japanese to avoid conflict whenever possible. Strikes are thus undertaken as formalities rather than as efforts to impose costs on the management. Tactics which might cause damage to the enterprise are carefully avoided so that work may resume quickly upon the resolution of a strike.

Although few in number, strikes for political purposes are often very significant. Strikes to put pressure on the Diet, such as the effort to amend the United States–Japan Security Treaty in 1960 and 1970, and strikes to win the right to strike for public employees

(SUTO KEN SUTO) are usually led by public-employee unions, which tend to be politically more radical. Especially during recent years, the schedule of *shuntō* strikes has included demonstrations for purely political demands, such as improvements in the social security system. See also LABOR; STRIKES AND OTHER FORMS OF LABOR DISPUTE; RIGHT TO STRIKE. ———— Kurita Ken

Labor-Farmer Party → Rōdō Nōmintō

labor laws

Since 1945 Japan has adopted a comprehensive legal framework dealing with labor conditions. This framework has been elaborated ever since the Allied OCCUPATION instituted far-reaching labor reforms soon after Japan's surrender. As in other countries, labor law covers the three major areas of labor relations, labor protection, and social security.

Prewar Labor Legislation——Prior to 1945 the development of labor law in Japan was exceedingly slow. By and large, the Meiji government left the regulation of employment conditions to employers. There were a few major exceptions, usually in response to international protests that Japan gained unfair advantage in world trade by permitting exploitation of "cheap" labor. Otherwise, a basic assumption, especially following the promulgation of the Meiji Constitution in 1889, was that under the benign rule of the emperor, benevolent paternalism of employers, and wide prevalence of an extended family system there was little need for government interference with rules of employment. Essentially, this was a concept of master-servant relations. Whatever cases might arise over terms of work could be disposed of primarily through the established code of civil law rather than specific labor legislation. The most important exception was the passage of the FACTORY LAW OF 1911 after more than 20 years of debate in which employers claimed that within the Japanese socioeconomic framework direct government regulation was superfluous. This law, which did not begin to take effect until 1916, stipulated minimum conditions for the employment of women and children in industrial plants, including such measures as limiting hours of work and prohibiting night shifts. It also regulated apprenticeships for young workers (see JUVENILE WORKERS, PROTECTIVE LEGISLATION FOR; WOMEN WORKERS, PROTECTIVE LEGISLATION FOR; APPRENTICE SYSTEM). Adult male workers were unaffected by this legislation, although in the 1890s, special legislation had been adopted to improve working conditions for miners.

A second major prewar development was the adoption in 1926 of the Labor Dispute Mediation Law (Rōdō Sōgi Chōtei Hō), which provided for tripartite government, employer, and worker commissions for settling strikes and other conflicts between management and employees in industry. This legislation emerged after Japan joined the International Labor Organization (ILO) when it was established in 1919 in affiliation with the League of Nations. At first, elements in the government proposed that there should be legislation granting recognition to labor unions and the right of workers to engage in collective bargaining, but a strong federation of employers successfully opposed such an enactment after a series of intense debates. The 1926 labor law was, in effect, a compromise. While the law did not forbid unions, it did not grant them legal rights of organization and recognition. Actually, the PUBLIC ORDER AND POLICE LAW OF 1900 (Chian Keisatsu Hō) and its replacement, the PEACE PRESERVATION LAW OF 1925 (Chian Iji Hō), although not specifically directed against labor, effectively curbed union activity through government surveillance. In any event, the question of labor union legitimacy was swept aside with the establishment of the government-controlled "labor front" or "Sampō" (Sangyō Hōkoku Kai) as part of the wartime mobilization in the late 1930s and, in turn, the dissolution of the few unions that remained.

The only other notable labor law in the prewar period was the establishment of retirement pension systems and health and work accident insurance plans for certain limited groups of employees, notably associations of government civil servants, seamen, and workers in individual large enterprises. These schemes were to become the bases for a significant expansion of social security legislation after 1945.

Labor Reforms during the Occupation——One of the first steps of the Supreme Commander of the Allied Powers (SCAP) was initiation of wholesale legal reforms regarding the status of workers. The aim of the reforms was to establish equal relations between employers and employees as a major means for achieving industrial democracy and to eliminate labor abuse and exploitation under the traditional master-servant concept of employment. In the fall of 1945, SCAP required the Japanese government to adopt the Labor Union Law (Rōdō Kumiai Hō) and in 1946, the Labor Relations Adjustment Law (Rōdō Kankei Chōsei Hō). Also by 1947 the government put into effect the Labor Standards Law (Rōdō Kijun Hō) as well as a host of other new laws providing a basis for security and regulation of minimum conditions of work. With subsequent revisions and additions, these laws have remained the basis of government labor policy to the present. They were reaffirmed within the context of the new CONSTITUTION promulgated in 1947 and, compared to the pre-World War II era, represent part of the "democratic revolution" since 1945.

In order to administer and develop this large new area of law and public policy, the government established the MINISTRY OF LABOR in 1947, although other ministries and agencies, notably the MINISTRY OF HEALTH AND WELFARE, are responsible for specialized labor legislation. The Ministry of Labor was a new concept, as labor matters in the prewar period had been handled largely by the HOME MINISTRY.

Labor Relations Law——The Labor Union Law, which went into effect in 1946, granted virtually all employees the right to organize independently, to engage in collective bargaining with employers on an equal footing, and to carry on collective actions, including strikes, against employers. Only firemen, police, and prison guards were excluded from this law. Another exception was that strikes in public utilities, such as gas and electricity, were prohibited for 30 days (later 10) after notification to the Ministry of Labor that a dispute existed. In general, the law followed closely provisions of the National Labor Relations Act (Wagner Act) passed in the United States in 1935 (see RIGHT TO ORGANIZE LABOR UNIONS; COLLECTIVE BARGAINING RIGHT).

The Labor Relations Adjustment Law, also put into effect in 1946, prohibited employer practices that would interfere with or obstruct the workers' exercise of these rights, following almost the exact wording of the Wagner Act. UNFAIR LABOR PRACTICES included employers' refusal to recognize unions or to engage in collective bargaining, discrimination against or discharge of workers for union activities, and interference in internal labor-union affairs. There were no parallel "unfair" practices stipulated for unions, such as those in the Taft-Hartley Labor Act (1947) of the United States, but the law did require unions to register with the government and to establish that they were bona fide democratic, independent, and collective bargaining organizations in order to gain protection. An organization established solely for political activities would not qualify as a union under the law.

To administer these laws, the law established tripartite (employer, union, and public or neutral members) commissions, one at the national level and one in each prefecture. The functions of the commissions are to assist in the settlement of labor-management disputes by offering conciliation *(assen)*, mediation *(chōtei)*, and arbitration *(chūsai)* services on a voluntary basis; to conduct hearings and render decisions with sanctions in unfair labor practice cases; and to certify unions as autonomous and democratic organizations. It should be noted that the commissions do not have exclusive jurisdiction regarding these matters, as appeals may also be made to the civil courts. See LABOR DISPUTES; LABOR DISPUTE RESOLUTION PROCEDURES.

Initially, the Labor Union Law and the Labor Relations Adjustment Law applied to all workers, whether in private or government employment. Since 1948, they have regulated labor relations only in the private sector and to a limited extent in local public enterprises. Following the threatened GENERAL STRIKE OF 1947, SCAP adopted the policy of treating the public sector under separate laws in order to assure continuity of government operations and services. In 1947 the National Civil Service Law (Kokka Kōmuin Hō) was enacted and the following year, after a series of administrative actions, the law was revised to deny the rights under the Labor Union Law to national government employees, although it did permit civil servants to form "associations" within their individual agencies for the purposes of petitioning and consulting with management regarding personnel matters. The NATIONAL PERSONNEL AUTHORITY (Jinjiin), which governs civil service employment, moreover, requires government agencies to follow equitable practices, and it requests the government to make general wage and benefit adjustments when civil-service pay levels lag behind those of comparable employees in the private sector. A parallel law, the Local Civil Service Law (Chihō Kōmuin Hō), was enacted in 1950 for local government civil servants with separate personnel authorities, but in practice they follow decisions made at the national level. In the mid-1970s, of nearly 3.6 million national and local civil service employees, including public school teachers, more than three-fourths were organized in "personnel associations" that were legally forbidden to bargain and conduct stoppages but in fact behaved much like labor unions in applying economic pressure and engaging in political action.

The second major change was the adoption in 1948 of the PUBLIC CORPORATIONS AND GOVERNMENT ENTERPRISES LABOR RELATIONS LAW (Kōkyō Kigyōtai Tō Rōdō Kankei Hō; revised in 1952) to regulate employment relations in government-owned industrial operations such as the railways, telephone and telegraph, postal service, tobacco and alcohol monopolies, forestry agency, printing bureau, and mint (see PUBLIC CORPORATIONS). In the early 1950s similar laws were enacted for labor relations in local-government-operated enterprises. These laws permitted employees in the government-owned companies limited rights to organize and engage in collective bargaining but denied them the right to strike or carry on other forms of dispute. They stipulated that a union organization not only must follow the requirements for private-sector unions but also must be confined to an appropriately designated unit, in essence the employees of a given enterprise, and that union leaders must be elected from the membership of that unit. Further, collective bargaining could not go beyond wages, hours, and narrowly defined working conditions.

Like the laws for the private sector, these laws utilized tripartite national and prefectural labor-relations commissions to conciliate, mediate, and arbitrate labor-management disputes and to hear charges of unfair labor practices in the public corporations and enterprises; but the public members carry much greater weight, and in cases of impasse, mediation and arbitration may be made compulsory, with the public members of the commission making final recommendations for settlement to the appropriate government agency for budgetary approval. Over the years the recommendations of the National Personnel Authority have become extremely important, especially in the annual nationwide wage-bargaining activity known as the spring labor offensive (SHUNTŌ). For the most part, the parties in the major public enterprises have been unable to reach agreement by themselves, so the compulsory procedures have gone into effect. In the process, the unions have often engaged in illegal stoppages, and leaders and participants have been subjected to various penalties, including discharge. See PUBLIC EMPLOYEES.

Subsequent Revisions of Labor Relations Laws —— While the above laws have remained almost wholly intact to the present, there have been several amendments of some significance. For example, in a revision of the Labor Union Law in 1949, management personnel with clear supervisory responsibility were forbidden to join unions, although this exclusion did not extend to foremen and other workshop supervisors. Also, a 1952 amendment to the Labor Relations Adjustment Law, reminiscent of the Taft-Hartley Labor Act, empowered the prime minister, after consultation with the CENTRAL LABOR RELATIONS COMMISSION (Chūō Rōdō Iinkai), to obtain a 50-day injunction against any strike which the government felt would seriously threaten national economic activities or the daily life of the nation. Although this provision has never been invoked, in 1953 the government adopted a special law, commonly known as Suto Kisei Hō, prohibiting wide-scale strikes in electric power and coal mining after prolonged stoppages in those industries in 1952.

By and large, it has been left to the labor relations commissions and to the court system, which was also reformed during the Occupation period, to adjudicate conflicts over the exercise of rights under the labor relations laws and to interpret the meaning of the laws. The commissions, with large professional staffs, give special attention to conciliating nascent disputes as well as settling unfair labor practice charges, often on an informal basis. Many such charges involve allegations of discharge from employment for engaging in union activities. When there are undue delays in achieving settlements through the labor relations commissions, the disputing parties frequently resort to the courts for final judgment.

The most notable change in the laws since the early 1950s was a 1965 amendment to the Public Corporations and Government Enterprises Labor Relations Law removing the stipulation that unions in such enterprises must select leaders solely from their respective membership bodies; that is, they were now free to choose whomever they wished, even from the "outside." This change followed a decade of dispute and wrangling, particularly in the Diet, including the filing by various public workers' unions, with the support of international labor bodies, of charges that the Japanese government was in

violation of the ILO Convention 87, even though Japan had not then ratified it. The convention provides for freedom of association and protection of the right to organize. First filed at the ILO headquarters in Geneva in 1957, the complaints arose from the discharge of government-employee union officers for instigating illegal dispute activities and, then, when the discharged leaders remained in their union positions, refusal by management to engage in further collective bargaining. After several years of debate, in 1965 the ILO dispatched a special investigating commission to Japan to study the situation on the spot and recommend revisions in the Japanese laws to bring them into line with Convention 87. This investigation, which placed the Japanese government in an embarrassing position before world opinion, led to speedy ratification of the convention and to a series of compromise amendments of the labor laws. Most important was legal recognition of the right of public-enterprise employee unions to designate officers as they wished, with the proviso that employees who served in union posts beyond a specified period would lose tenure in any government post they held. Still unresolved is the related controversy over granting even a limited right to strike to government employees, although a series of officially appointed commissions and study groups has continued to examine the issue.

Labor Protection Laws —— The Labor Standards Law of 1947 has been the basis of regulating minimum protection for workers in industry. As part of the Occupation labor reforms, it went far beyond the Factory Law of 1911 and in many respects brought Japan abreast of the standards stipulated in ILO conventions. The law is wide-ranging in that it not only deals with the establishment of such matters as minimum wages, maximum hours of work, rest and holidays, plant safety and health, apprentice training, employment of women and minors, and other working conditions, but it also provides a "bill of rights" for individual workers in their relations with employers. For the first time in Japan, this law set the eight-hour day and 48-hour week as the general standard, with the minimum requirement of time-and-a-quarter overtime payment (see WORK HOURS). An interesting provision of the law is the requirement that an employer may establish WORK REGULATIONS only after consultation with the workers or their representative and approval by the Ministry of Labor. The ministry maintains a sizable labor inspection section to enforce the Labor Standards Act. See LABOR STANDARDS INSPECTION OFFICES.

Over the years, the government has continuously elaborated the Labor Standards Law with a wide variety of special enactments in the numerous areas it covers. Among the most notable is the MINIMUM WAGE LAW (Saitei Chingin Hō) of 1959, which for the first time established a procedure for setting minimum-wage rates. While the 1959 law does not stipulate a universal wage, it provides for determination of minimum wage by region, industry, or occupation, mainly on the basis of agreements by employers with worker or union representatives. Such minimum wages must be approved by the Ministry of Labor. By the mid-1970s, a network of minimum-wage stipulations had emerged to cover virtually all industrial workers, although their actual effect in raising wage levels has been problematic.

Another important set of enactments has been a series of laws dealing with industrial training and manpower policy, beginning with the VOCATIONAL TRAINING LAW (Shokugyō Kunren Hō) of 1958, which underwent major strengthening and expansion in the late 1960s because of increasing labor shortages, especially of young workers. Under these laws, Japan has moved to enlarge both public and private facilities for training in needed industrial skills and for upgrading and diversifying skill training not only within particular enterprises but for flexible deployment across enterprises. These programs are still in the process of development but have become an important public-policy instrument for meeting skill needs as the structure of Japanese industry continues to undergo rapid change. There has also been special legislation for retraining and reemployment of workers displaced from declining industries such as coal mining, docks, and military bases, and of handicapped and older workers.

Social Security Legislation —— In prewar Japan, protection of workers against unemployment, hazards of work, and old-age destitution was extremely limited. Enormous expansion of such SOCIAL SECURITY LEGISLATION began in 1947, and by the late 1960s a comprehensive legal framework for social security was in place. Most important was the enactment of the EMPLOYMENT SECURITY LAW OF 1947 (Shokugyō Antei Hō), which set up a wide network of government-operated employment offices, soon followed by the Unem-

Labor market——Table 1

Industry	1872	1890	1910	1920	1930	1940	1950	1960	1965	1970	1975	1977
Industrial Distribution of Employment (in percentages)												
Agriculture	75.0	69.2	55.0	51.6	47.4	42.4	46.5	30.0	23.4	16.5	11.8	11.0
Fishing	3.2	2.4	2.3	2.0	1.9	1.7	1.9	1.6	1.3	0.8	0.8	0.8
Mining	—	0.4	1.5	1.6	1.1	1.8	1.7	1.2	0.7	0.4	0.3	0.4
Construction	1.0	1.7	2.7	2.7	3.3	3.0	4.3	6.1	7.1	7.7	9.0	9.3
Manufacturing	5.9	10.2	16.3	16.5	16.0	21.2	15.9	21.8	24.5	27.0	25.8	25.0
Trade	8.1	8.7	11.8	9.8	14.0	12.7	12.1	17.6	20.2	22.5	24.8	25.7
Transportation and communications	1.0	1.1	0.9	4.2	4.4	4.7	5.1	5.6	6.6	6.9	6.9	6.9
Public and other services	4.3	3.3	5.6	9.8	11.6	11.8	12.4	14.9	16.1	17.9	20.1	20.5
Others	1.6	1.7	2.1	1.9	0.2	0.7	—	—	—	—	—	—

NOTE: Data for 1872–1910 are estimates based on the 1920 census and projected backward. Note that similar table at INDUSTRIAL STRUCTURE has a different source, and figures differ slightly.
SOURCE: For 1872–1910: Hijikata Seibi, "Shokugyōbetsu jinkō no hensen o tsūjite mitaru shitsugyō mondai," *Shakai seisaku jihō* (September 1929). For 1920–40: Irene B. Taeuber, *The Population of Japan* (1958). For 1950–65: Japan Institute of Labor, *Japan Labor Statistics* (annual): 1970. For 1970–77: Prime Minister's Office, Statistics Bureau, *Japan Statistical Yearbook* (annual): 1980. The agricultural estimates for 1872, 1890, and 1910 are from James I. Nakamura, *Agricultural Production and the Economic Development of Japan, 1873–1922* (1966).

ployment Insurance Law (Shitsugyō Hoken Hō; now, Koyō Hoken Hō) and other measures for unemployment relief (see UNEMPLOYMENT). Also in 1947 came the passage of a comprehensive and mandatory compensation insurance law for industrial accidents and disease (see WORKERS' COMPENSATION).

Over the years, there has been continual improvement in the provisions of these acts with respect to coverage, amount of insurance contributions, benefit levels, and coordination with vocational training programs. As the growth of the economy slowed after the OIL CRISIS OF 1973, for example, the Japanese government developed innovative legislation, adopted in 1976 and 1977, to maintain employment within enterprises in designated depressed industries through employer and employee insurance contributions to a special fund. These premiums are utilized to maintain wages for a limited period and to provide retraining within enterprises of workers who would otherwise be laid off or discharged. As an alternative to the unemployment insurance scheme, it remains to be seen whether the program actually prevents declines in employment.

Comprehensive and adequate social security for the aged, ill, and disabled has had slower development, and today has become a major political issue in Japan. In 1950, after considerable study, the government began to draw up plans for a unified system of old-age pensions, public assistance, social welfare, and health. Legislation emerged on a piecemeal basis, however, beginning with a major revision in 1950 of the LIVELIHOOD PROTECTION LAW (Seikatsu Hogo Hō), which provided minimum subsistence for the poverty-stricken. Although MEDICAL AND HEALTH INSURANCE schemes for workers and the general population were started long before World War II, major improvements of the programs did not occur until the 1950s. However, a truly nationwide compulsory medical insurance system was finally instituted in 1961.

In the area of old-age pensions, government-administered pension insurance was first enacted in 1954 for workers, amending a wartime law, organized mainly on the basis of insurance societies within individual enterprises. In 1959, the government passed the National Pension Law (Kokumin Nenkin Hō), requiring all persons to contribute premiums who have no other coverage for retirement, disability, child support, and other welfare benefits. If an employee is qualified, pension payments begin at age 60, although workers in most enterprises must retire as early as 55. Retired workers, therefore, are forced to live on their savings or find other employment with much lower pay for up to five years. Workers who retire from large corporations, however, usually receive sizable retirement allowances.

In general, in both the old-age and health areas, a wide variety of programs has emerged over the years, largely because they are operated under government-set standards within separate enterprises or groups of firms. Under this system, however, major differences in benefits have existed between workers in large and small enterprises. By the mid-1970s, when the Japanese economy encountered a period of slower growth and the need to reallocate its labor force,

the threat of unemployment to older workers, especially those above 55 years of age, had become increasingly severe. These developments have generated strong pressures not only for improving employment opportunities for older workers but also for making old-age benefits more uniform and adequate. In all likelihood, there will be a notable expansion of the social security system as Japan turns increasingly toward improvement of its welfare policies. See also LABOR; LABOR UNIONS.

■——*Japan Labor Bulletin* (monthly since April 1962). *Nihon rōdō kyōkai zasshi* (monthly since April 1959). Ōkōchi Kazuo, Bernard Karsh, and Solomon B. Levine, eds, *Workers and Employers in Japan: The Japanese Employment Relations System* (1973). Shirai Taishirō, Hanami Tadashi, and Kōshiro Kazuyoshi, *Rōdō kumiai tokuhon* (1977).   Solomon B. LEVINE

labor market

The market in which the supply of and demand for labor operate to determine wages and the conditions and extent of employment. In the long run, the market reflects changes in industrial structure and thus affects occupational and industrial distributions of employment. The functioning of the market is influenced by many factors, including a nation's system of employment, the education of the work force, the retirement patterns, the extent of female labor, and the level and growth of population.

In the past century, the labor market in Japan has undergone dramatic change, reflecting the impact of industrial revolution, the Great Depression, two world wars, and the rapid economic growth of the post–World War II years. The labor force has grown and changed, as reflected in Tables 1 and 2, which present the industrial and occupational distribution of Japanese employment.

The dominant change has been the shift away from agriculture. In 1872 3 out of every 4 Japanese workers were employed in agriculture. By 1920 this had declined to 1 of every 2 workers, and to 1 in 4 by 1965. The decline continued until, in 1977, only slightly more than 1 in every 10 Japanese workers was employed in agriculture and forestry. During the 70 years prior to 1940, the movement out of agriculture was slow but steady, about 0.5 percent every year. From 1950 to 1970 the rate was three times as swift, 1.5 percent per year. See also AGRICULTURE: agricultural modernization.

The movement out of agriculture has been associated with a variety of other changes, including the transition from SELF-EMPLOYMENT to wage employment, from rural to urban living, and from agricultural to modern industrial and commercial skills. Table 3 indicates the proportion of individuals who work for others in return for wages; for themselves in a self-employed capacity; and as family workers in a family enterprise. As recently as 1950, fewer than 40 percent of the gainfully employed were classed as employees. Since then, two related changes have been taking place. The number of family workers has declined by half, and the number of employees has grown by a factor of almost three. As a consequence,

Labor market——Table 2

Occupational Distribution of Employment
(in percentages)

Occupation	1930	1940	1950	1955	1960	1965	1970	1975	1977
Professional and technical workers	2.5	4.0	4.3	4.6	5.0	5.1	5.8	7.0	7.3
Managerial workers	0.2	0.6	1.7	1.8	1.7	2.4	2.6	3.9	4.0
Clerical and related workers	4.7	7.3	8.6	9.0	11.2	13.5	14.8	15.7	15.9
Sales personnel	13.3	9.1	8.2	11.1	12.1	11.8	13.0	14.1	14.6
Fishermen, loggers, and farmers	49.4	44.0	47.7	40.0	32.7	25.4	17.3	12.6	11.7
Mine workers	0.8	1.1	1.2	0.7	0.7	0.4	0.2	0.2	0.2
Transportation and communications workers	1.5	1.5	1.4	1.7	2.4	4.1	4.6	4.5	4.5
Craft and production workers, laborers	19.8	25.3	22.0	25.4	28.1	30.2	33.9	33.0	33.0
Service workers	7.6	5.8	4.5	4.8	6.1	6.9	7.6	8.8	8.7
Others	0.2	1.2	0.1	—	—	—	—	—	—

NOTE: Similar table at OCCUPATIONAL STRUCTURE has different source, and figures differ slightly.
SOURCE: For 1930–50: Adapted from *Kokusei chōsa ni yoru shokugyō jinkō no saikōsei*, Census Research Series 70 (1965). For 1955–77: Prime Minister's Office, Statistics Bureau, *Japan Statistical Yearbook* (annual): 1966 and 1978.

Labor market——Table 3

Employment Status of the Gainfully Employed
(in millions)

	Total	Self-employed	Family workers	Employees	Employees as percentage of total employed
1940	32.2	8.5	10.3	13.5	41.9%
1950	35.6	9.3	12.2	14.0	39.3%
1955	39.2	9.4	11.9	18.0	45.8%
1960	43.7	9.6	10.5	23.5	53.8%
1965	47.6	9.3	9.3	28.9	60.7%
1970	52.2	10.2	8.5	33.5	64.2%
1975	52.2	9.4	6.3	36.5	69.8%
1976	52.7	9.3	6.2	37.1	70.4%

SOURCE: For 1940–70: Japan Institute of Labor, *Japan Labor Statistics* (annual): 1974. For 1975 and 1976: Ministry of Labor, *Yearbook of Labor Statistics* (annual): 1975 and 1976.

by 1977, 70.5 percent of those who worked were employees. See also OCCUPATIONAL STRUCTURE; INDUSTRIAL STRUCTURE.

In 1920, when 53.6 percent of the gainfully employed were in agriculture, forestry, and fishing, only 18 percent of the population lived in urban areas, with 8.3 percent living in cities of half a million or more. Over the next 55 years, 1920–75, the POPULATION doubled from 55.9 to 111.9 million, and there was extensive URBANIZATION. In 1975 almost three-quarters of the population lived in urban areas, with almost one-quarter (24.7 percent) residing in cities with populations of half a million or more.

In the early years of growth, movements out of agriculture typically are absorbed by dramatic increases in the manufacturing work force. In Japan, the proportion employed in manufacturing almost tripled between 1872 and 1910. This was followed by 20 years of relative stagnation in manufacturing and trade; during this time, services and transportation absorbed the out-migration from agriculture. From 1950 to 1970 employment in manufacturing expanded again. Peak relative employment occurred in 1972, after which Japan apparently entered into the third, or postindustrial, stage of growth, in which employment in the tertiary (service) sector grows relative to the primary and secondary sectors.

The industrial and occupational patterns of the Japanese labor force displayed in Tables 1 and 2 represent the economy as a whole. Table 4 repeats the 1977 data for men and women separately. Surprisingly, it shows a higher percentage of women than men engaged in professional and technical employment as well as in fishing and agriculture. The former is a relatively new phenomenon, for as recently as 1970 the male professional figure (5.7 percent) exceeded that for women (5.3 percent). These figures must be interpreted

carefully, for the 1977 data from the employment status survey indicate that male professionals have higher levels of education than do woman professionals. Almost 70 percent of the male professionals have had some college education or are graduates. The comparable figure for women is only slightly over 50 percent. Among all workers the proportion of college-educated is about twice as high for men (17.9 percent) as for women (9.4 percent). Since women make up about 40 percent of the work force, this means that in 1977 there were about three college-educated male workers to every such woman in the labor force.

The relatively large proportion of women in agriculture, evident in both the industrial and the occupational breakdowns of Table 4, reflects the small scale of much of Japanese agriculture and a pattern of male employment away from the family farm, where the agricultural responsibilities are left to the female members of the household. The relatively large proportion of women in service industries, clerical and related occupations, balanced by insignificant representation in the construction, transportation, and communications industries, is not surprising. These percentages are similar to world patterns, and reflect the less than equal employment opportunities available to women.

Labor Force Participation—— The concept of labor force participation, according to which an individual is either in the labor force or not, is a modern one. It is limited in its applicability to an earlier and largely agricultural world where the line between household activities and economically productive activities was ill defined. During periods of transplanting and harvesting rice, every member of the household was in the labor force. Even today, for many members of the labor force, there is a complex interplay between employment and other duties.

Occupational and Industrial Distribution by Sex, 1977
(in percentages)

	Proportion of employed males	Proportion of employed females
Occupational distribution		
Professional and technical workers	6.6	8.4
Managerial workers	6.1	0.5
Clerical and related workers	12.2	22.0
Sales personnel	14.6	14.5
Fishermen, loggers, and farmers	9.6	15.1
Mine workers	0.3	0.0
Transportation and communications workers	6.7	0.8
Craft and production workers	34.4	22.8
Laborers	3.0	2.9
Service workers	6.2	12.7
Industrial distribution		
Agriculture	8.7	14.8
Fishing	1.1	0.4
Mining	0.5	0.05
Construction	13.1	3.2
Manufacturing	25.4	24.6
Trade	22.6	30.7
Transportation and communications	9.9	2.2
Public and other services	18.5	23.8
Total number employed	33.1 million	20.3 million

NOTE: Figures do not total to 100 percent because the total number of workers employed includes workers who did not report their occupations.
SOURCE: Prime Minister's Office, Statistics Bureau, *Japan Statistical Yearbook* (annual): 1978.

Labor Force Participation Rates
(in percentage of total in each category)

Male

Age	1955	1965	1970	1975	1977
15–19	53.7	36.3	31.4	20.4	18.2
20–24	87.4	85.8	80.7	76.1	72.3
25–29	95.9	96.8	97.1	96.3	96.4
30–34	97.5	97.0	97.8	98.1	97.9
35–39	97.5	97.1	97.8	97.9	97.8
40–54	97.1[1]	96.3	96.9	96.8	96.8
55–59	93.3[1]	90.0	91.2	92.2	91.1
60–64	65.9[1]	82.8	81.5	79.8	78.2
65+	65.9[1]	56.3	49.4	44.4	42.4
Overall	85.9	81.7	81.8	81.3	80.5

Female

Age	1955	1965	1970	1975	1977
15–19	50.1	35.8	33.6	21.9	19.9
20–24	68.2	70.2	70.6	65.9	67.9
25–29	51.8	49.0	45.5	42.5	45.8
30–34	51.3	51.1	48.2	43.9	46.3
35–39	51.6	59.6	57.5	54.0	55.5
40–54	53.8	60.2	61.8	59.8	61.1
55–59	45.7	49.8	48.7	49.0	50.3
60–64	38.4	39.8	39.1	38.0	38.0
65+	20.6	21.4	17.9	15.2	15.4
Overall	50.6	50.6	49.9	45.8	46.7

[1] In 1955 the age categories were 40–49; 50–59, and 60 and older.
SOURCE: For males, 1955: Japan Institute of Labor, *Japan Labor Statistics* (annual): 1974. Remainder of male figures: Prime Minister's Office, Statistics Bureau, *Japan Statistical Yearbook* (annual): 1978. For females: K. Ōkōchi et al, *Workers and Employers in Japan* (1974).

Accepting this modern—and at times artificial distinction—it is usual to define the potential labor force as all those over the age of 15, and to analyze the labor force participation rates—the proportion employed or looking for work—of various population groups. Such rates are sometimes determined through complete population enumerations such as the decennial census, but most are estimates based upon sophisticated sampling techniques. In 1976 one such survey contacted 33,000 households which included 76,000 individuals 15 years of age and older.

Table 5 contains the labor force participation rates for men and women by broad age groups in selected years between 1955 and 1977. In general, both men and women entered the labor force upon the completion of their formal education. Consequently, changes in the number of years of required education and in individual proclivities for additional education have had major impacts upon the labor force participation rates for young people and, to a lesser extent, upon the labor force as a whole.

Table 5 indicates that for men the period of greatest change was 1955–65, while for women it was between 1970 and 1975. Among both groups there were significant declines in participation among those of ages 15–19. The 1955 rates were approximately 2.5 and 3.0 times as high as those in 1977 for women and men, respectively. Similarly, women and men over the age of 65 experienced 25 and 35 percent declines in participation. Between the ages of 25 and 60 or 65 there was little change, though there were exceptions and some major differences. The nearly 20 percent decline in male participation in the age range 20–24 was not found among women. There was also a modest decline in female participation at ages 25–34, while those 35–59 had increased their participation since 1955.

The decreased labor force participation among the young reflects profound changes in Japanese educational practices. In 1958 only 50 percent of Japan's middle school graduates went on to high school. The other 50 percent entered the work force, though a few were in employer-supported combination programs of work and education. Indeed, the middle school graduate was the backbone of blue-collar employment, and there were many questions raised in government publications and the mass media about whether that role could be taken over by high school graduates. By 1969, 75 percent of all middle school graduates were going on for additional education, and

in 1975, 90 percent were continuing. A similar change was taking place for high school graduates, but not as dramatically, until 1970. Between 1963 and 1970 the proportion of high school students entering college was approximately 22 percent. Then, between 1970 and 1975, there was a dramatic increase to the point where 33 percent were continuing. The fact that male, but not female, labor force participation in the 20–24-year age group has declined probably indicates a greater impact of college and postgraduate attendance.

Women and the Labor Force——All of the factors associated with probabilities of labor force participation for males apply equally to females. In addition there is exit from the labor force because of marriage or childbirth. Consequently, for women there are special patterns, a few of which are illustrated in Table 6. The data reflect the complex interplay of employment opportunities and marital status which affects women's labor force participation not only in Japan but also in other countries. Unmarried and formerly married women, except during the educational years, have the highest participation rates. The pattern of working until marriage and/or childbirth, with a return to employment later in life, may be seen in the growth in the participation rate from 32.7 percent at ages 25–29 to 56.8 percent at ages 40–54. The opportunities evident in being in a household which has its own business can be seen in the significantly higher employment rates for women in such households, though the importance of family enterprises as a source of employment is declining. See also WOMEN IN THE LABOR FORCE.

Retired Workers——Exit from the labor force may be for either voluntary or involuntary reasons. Over most of one's life, it is the latter which predominates. Usually these are short- to long-term disabilities associated with illness and accident. At older ages, voluntary withdrawal from the labor force in the form of retirement begins to play an increased role. Unlike the United States, where retirement ages and withdrawal from the labor force have tended to occur at the same age, formal retirement and actual withdrawal from

Labor market——Table 6

					Age				
	Overall	15–19	20–24	25–29	30–34	35–39	40–54	55–64	65+
1975									
Household headed by employed male	36.9	15.3	59.9	32.1	36.9	36.9	48.2	30.5	9.7
Household headed by self-employed male	54.2	15.5	71.0	59.9	68.1	68.1	73.2	51.8	18.9
Single women	62.9	66.3	78.8	84.6	83.8	83.8	76.3	55.0	17.9
1977									
Never married	53.4	18.5	77.7	80.4	83.2	78.3	77.4	59.8	30.5
Married	44.9	29.2	39.3	32.7	42.0	50.7	56.8	39.7	18.7
Divorced or widowed	33.2	36.4	77.0	77.6	82.5	75.4	74.3	43.5	10.5

Female Labor-Force Participation, 1975 and 1977
(in percentage of total in each category)

SOURCE: For 1975: Japan Institute of Labor, *Japan Labor Bulletin* 15 (January 1976). For 1977: Japan Institute of Labor, *Monthly Report on Labor* (March 1977).

the labor force do not coincide in Japan. For many years larger firms had a mandatory retirement age, usually 55. In the period of rapid economic growth and apparent labor shortages beginning in the mid-1960s and continuing into the 1970s, firms were raising formal retirement ages. Many retired Japanese workers are immediately reemployed by their employers, though at lower wages and with no assurance of how long the reemployment will last. See also RETIREMENT; OLD AGE AND RETIREMENT.

A survey of retired steel workers by their union, Tekkō Rōren (Japanese Federation of Iron and Steel Workers' Union), indicated that 64.8 percent of those past the usual retirement age of 55 were employed, 75.9 percent of those age 56–59, and 55 percent of those age 60–64. Among those who were not working, 21 percent were ill or disabled, and only 12.3 percent did not need to seek employment. Reemployment after the age of formal retirement and the adequacy of retirement funds will become even more important in the future as Japan's labor force grows older. In 1955, 12.2 percent of the population over 15 years of age was 60 or older. By 1975 the percentage had risen to 15.5, and by the turn of the century, it is expected to rise to 23.9 percent. Indeed, there will be almost as many people over 60 years of age as under 15 years of age—a rather dramatic turnaround since 1955, when there were four times as many children as old people.

Unemployed Workers——In every country the various shocks and shifts in the demand for labor result in certain workers' acting as buffers and absorbing the impact. Change can mean both new opportunities in an expanding economy and economic loss when the economy experiences contraction. Changes in the number of people classed as unemployed clearly reflect changing job opportunities. The impact of economic change may also be seen in the proportion of the population in the labor force. As employment conditions worsen, some individuals will drop out of the labor force, while others, who in better times would have entered the labor force, will remain outside. Since the demand for labor is a demand for labor hours, one also would expect that the number of unanticipated or overtime hours would rise or fall with shifts in the economy. In addition to these expected patterns, easily demonstrated by the experience of the United States, the pattern of career-long employment among the larger firms has given rise to some particularly Japanese approaches to the need to provide elasticity in the labor force.

One system has been the extensive use of subcontractors, firms which operate in lower-wage markets and do not offer the security of long-term employment. In addition to contract employees there are temporary employees. While temporary employees are supposedly hired for short-term jobs, some remain as temporary employees for long periods of continuous employment. At times compulsory transfers to other firms or early retirement plans are put in effect. See EMPLOYMENT, FORMS OF.

In 1976, 17.7 percent of those gainfully employed were self-employed, and an additional 11.7 percent were family workers. Both of these categories are ideal cushions to absorb downward

changes in economic opportunities. An example from an earlier period illustrates the point. In the 1920s manufacturing employment grew by only 7 percent, and was unable to absorb the new workers from population growth and movements out of agriculture. As a consequence, service and trade employment involving less than full utilization of a worker's potential grew. For example, employment as fish dealers, tea dealers, and grocers increased by about 50 percent.

Earlier discussions of workers strongly affected by changing economic conditions would have referred to the DEKASEGI phenomenon, in which individuals moved out of agriculture into nonagricultural employment either seasonally or in times of ample economic opportunities, but would flow back into the agricultural labor force when economic opportunities in the overall economy decreased. Some such workers exist today, but their number has been greatly reduced.

Lastly, there is the willingness of large firms to absorb temporarily a labor surplus among their work forces rather than lay off or discharge extra employees. All of these aspects have meant that the number of totally unemployed workers has not been the best estimate of the state of labor demand. One must look at a variety of measures, including the ratio of job openings to applicants at PUBLIC EMPLOYMENT SECURITY OFFICES. Changes in these principal measures of the state of labor demand are shown in Table 7.

The data reflect that the period 1974–75 was not a good one for the Japanese economy. The growth in real national income, which had averaged 9.6 percent for the preceding five years, averaged 0.5 percent for those two years, and in 1974 it was a negative 1.3 percent. The unemployment rate jumped from 1.3 to 1.9, an increase of close to 50 percent. The labor force participation rate declined from 64.6 in 1973 to 63.0 in 1975, an amount equivalent to the decline over the preceding nine years, while the ratio of job offer to applicant dropped from 1.8 to 0.6. In addition, the government paid subsidies for 3.4 million workers who were temporarily idle but not listed as unemployed between January 1975 and October 1976. Clearly, then, the unemployment rate gives an indication of the direction of economic change, and even the degree of change, but it provides only a hint of the absolute loss of potential output, since so many workers whose potential is not being utilized are in a category of quasi-employment and for statistical purposes considered employed. See also UNEMPLOYMENT.

Job Tenure——Two idealized aspects of Japan's labor economy stand out. One is *nenkō joretsu*, the SENIORITY SYSTEM, and the second is *shūshin koyō*, career-long employment (see EMPLOYMENT SYSTEM, MODERN). Career-long employment has as its idealized relationship the mutual responsibility between the worker and the company, sometimes referred to as "management familism" or PATERNALISM. In this idealized form a worker is hired upon graduation from school or college and spends an entire working life with the initial employer. The seniority system operates in conjunction with career-long employment, providing regular wage increases throughout an employee's career. While forming the basis for many

Labor market —— Table 7

			Indicators of Labor Market Conditions			
	Unemployment rate	Unemployment compensation rate[1] (%)	Ratio of job offers to applicants[2]	Labor force participation rate (%)	No. of unemployed (000)	Growth in real national income (%)
1955	2.5	5.6	0.3	70.8	1,050	9.1
1956	2.3	5.9	0.3	70.5	980	8.0
1957	1.9	3.3	0.4	70.7	820	8.0
1958	2.1	4.3	0.3	69.7	900	5.4
1959	1.7	3.6	0.4	69.0	980	9.2
1960	1.7	2.9	0.6	69.2	750	14.1
1961	1.3	2.7	0.7	69.1	660	15.6
1962	1.3	3.0	0.7	68.3	590	6.4
1963	1.1	3.5	0.7	67.1	590	10.6
1964	1.1	3.5	0.8	66.1	540	14.3
1965	1.2	3.2	0.6	65.7	570	4.6
1966	1.1	3.0	0.7	65.8	540	9.8
1967	1.3	2.8	1.0	65.9	630	12.9
1968	1.2	2.6	1.1	65.9	590	13.4
1969	1.1	2.4	1.3	65.5	570	10.7
1970	1.2	2.3	1.4	65.4	590	10.9
1971	1.2	2.5	1.1	65.0	640	7.4
1972	1.4	2.6	1.2	64.4	730	9.1
1973	1.3	2.3	1.8	64.6	670	9.8
1974	1.4	2.4	1.2	63.6	740	−1.3
1975	1.9	2.4	0.6	63.0	1,000	2.4
1976	2.0	2.7	0.6	63.0	1,080	—
1977	2.0	2.6	0.6	63.2	1,100	—

[1] The number receiving unemployment compensation divided by the number covered.
[2] Excludes newly graduated students.
SOURCE: Japan Institute of Labor, *Japan Labor Statistics* (annual): 1967 and 1974. Japan Institute of Labor, *Japan Labor Bulletin* 17 (November 1978).

aspects of the employer-employee relationship, this system applies primarily to male workers employed by the government and large corporations. Perhaps 33 to 40 percent of all employees work under such an employment policy. The origins of career-long employment and its current pattern reflect a complex interaction between Japan's cultural and economic history. The rise of the enterprise union (which includes both blue- and white-collar workers in a single organization) in the post–World War II years resulted in the extension of career-long employment and the age-based wage system to all regular workers; before the war they had applied only to administrative, professional, and selected skilled workers.

The extent of career-long employment is subject to debate. Some scholars point out that blue-collar workers identify less strongly with their employers than do white-collar workers, and others cite high turnover rates among employees of certain large enterprises. A recent study of a major electric company and a shipyard determined that 24 and 61.4 percent, respectively, of the blue-collar employees had worked for companies other than their current employer. Yet 84 and 89 percent, respectively, expected to continue to work for these firms until their retirement, suggesting the complexity of knowing the exact extent of career-long employment. The practical impact of the Japanese pattern is that job mobility is lower in Japan than in countries like the United States. Workers in both countries change jobs less often as they grow older, but in America, at all ages there is significantly more job shifting among workers. Mobility increased somewhat during the boom years in Japan.

Thus this century the number of people in the Japanese labor force has more than doubled. The labor force has been transformed from one based on traditional agriculture to one serving the needs of a modern urbanized nation. It has passed from one supporting an economy centered in primary production, through industrialization, to a postindustrial service orientation. The rest of the century holds more change, the most obvious of which will be the increased age of the average worker.

■ —— Robert E. Cole, *Japanese Blue Collar: The Changing Tradition* (1971). Robert E. Cole and Ken'ichi Tominaga, "Japan's Changing Occupational Structure and its Significance" in Hugh Patrick and Larry Meissner, ed, *Japanese Industrialization and its Social Consequences* (1976). Ronald P. Dore, *British Factory–Japanese Factory:*

The Origins of National Diversity in Industrial Relations (1973). Robert Evans, Jr., *The Labor Economics of Japan and the United States* (1971). Walter Galenson and Konnosuke Odaka, "The Japanese Labor Market" in Hugh Patrick and Henry Rosovsky, ed, *Asia's New Giant: How the Japanese Economy Works* (1976). *Japan Labor Bulletin* (monthly). Solomon B. Levine, "Labor Markets and Collective Bargaining in Japan" in William W. Lockwood, ed, *The State and Economic Enterprise in Japan* (1965). Robert M. March and Hiroshi Mannari, *Modernization of the Japanese Factory* (1976). Ministry of Labor, *Yearbook of Labor Statistics* (annual). Prime Minister's Office Statistics Bureau, *Japan Statistical Yearbook* (annual). Kazuo Ōkōchi, Bernard Karsh, and Solomon B. Levine, ed, *Workers and Employers in Japan: The Japanese Employment Relations System* (1973). Kōji Taira, *Economic Development and the Labor Market in Japan* (1970). *Robert Evans, Jr.*

labor reforms of 1945–1947

The establishment of the basic legal framework for the organization of labor unions and the conduct of collective bargaining undertaken by the Japanese government under the direction of SCAP (the headquarters of the Allied Occupation of Japan) during the first years of the American OCCUPATION. The Occupation authorities considered the development of an organized labor movement, along with the LAND REFORMS OF 1946 and the EDUCATIONAL REFORMS OF 1947, one of the primary means of preventing the resurgence of militarism in post–World War II Japan, and steps were taken in 1945 to encourage the formation of unions. This was followed by the establishment of a system of dispute resolution and the setting of labor standards. Militant labor union activity was met with restrictions, and limits on labor's rights, particularly in the public sector, were also enacted during the early years of the Occupation.

The fundamental legislation enacted during this period, commonly referred to as the "Three Labor Laws" (Rōdō Sampō), was the following: the Labor Union Law (Rōdō Kumiai Hō, 1945), the Labor Relations Adjustment Law (Rōdō Kankei Chōsei Hō, 1946), and the Labor Standards Law (Rōdō Kijun Hō, 1947). For the first time, Japanese workers were given the legal right to organize unions, to bargain with their employers, and to strike. The FACTORY LAW OF

1911 had established minimal restrictions on working conditions, and a dispute resolution law had been established in 1926, but the labor movement had made little progress in prewar Japan and had been virtually outlawed during the war (see LABOR).

SCAP directed the government to encourage the formation of labor unions in October 1945, and in December the Labor Union Law was enacted. Modeled after the American Wagner Act (National Labor Relations Act, 1935), the law extended the right to organize, bargain, and strike to all workers except prison guards, firefighters, and police officers; protected workers from discharge because of union activities; established LABOR RELATIONS COMMISSIONS composed of labor, management, and public representatives to apply and enforce the law; and required the registration of labor organizations. The growth of the organized labor movement that followed enactment of this law is unparalleled anywhere in the world. By January 1946, there were 900,000 workers organized into nearly 1,200 unions; the numbers had swelled to 4.8 million workers in 17,000 unions by the end of the year, and to 6.7 million workers in 33,900 unions by mid-1948.

The newly formed labor movement was politically active in the context of the poverty and food shortages of the early postwar years, and large demonstrations were mounted on the first postwar May Day in 1946 and later that same month in the SHOKURYŌ MĒDĒ (Food May Day). Strikes were common, some including plant occupations and production control (seisan kanri). Particularly militant was the SAMBETSU KAIGI (Industrial Labor Unions of Japan), a federation that was especially strong among public employees and largely controlled by the Japan Communist Party. SCAP considered these developments threatening and issued a number of warnings against militant activity. These were followed by the enactment of the Labor Relations Adjustment Law in September 1946. In addition to establishing a system of conciliation, mediation, and arbitration of labor disputes, the new law banned strikes by public employees and ordered the arbitration of disputes of public utility workers during a mandatory 30-day cooling-off period; the government was given the power to designate any important industry a "public utility" along with the railroads, communications system, public schools, and other public enterprises.

The labor movement, especially Sambetsu, considered this new law a restriction of its newly acquired rights and responded with demonstrations, culminating in a plan for a general strike on 1 February 1947 (see GENERAL STRIKE OF 1947). The strike was to have involved about four million workers, many in the public sector, and would have raised economic and political demands, including a demand for the repeal of the Labor Relations Adjustment Law. At the last minute, however, the strike was banned by Douglas MACARTHUR, the head of the Occupation. The strike ban sent shock waves through the labor movement and signaled the limits of the new rights of labor. The ban on the general strike is often considered the point at which the thrust of Occupation policy turned from reform to the reconstruction of Japan as an anticommunist ally of the United States in the Pacific—the so-called "reverse course."

Further restrictions on the labor rights of public employees were enacted in 1948, when the National Personnel Law (Kokka Kōmuin Hō) was revised to prohibit central government employees from organizing labor unions, bargaining, and striking. These workers were allowed to form associations that could petition the government for improvements in wages and working conditions, but they were denied full union rights. Also in 1948 the Public Corporation Labor Relations Law (later named the PUBLIC CORPORATIONS AND GOVERNMENT ENTERPRISES LABOR RELATIONS LAW or Kōkyō Kigyōtai Tō Rōdō Kankei Hō) was enacted to regulate employment relations in the public railways, communications systems, government monopolies, and other public operations. Workers in these industries were granted collective bargaining rights over a limited number of issues, but the prohibition of their right to strike was maintained.

Other laws enacted during this period include the Labor Standards Law of 1947, which set the maximum work day at 8 hours and the maximum work week at 48 hours, regulated the working conditions of women and minors, and established the principle of equal pay for equal work; the EMPLOYMENT SECURITY LAW of 1947; the Unemployment Compensation Law (1947); and the Workers' Accident Compensation Law (1947). Further efforts to depoliticize the labor movement included the revision of the Labor Union Law in 1948 (in order to democratize the leadership and curb direct political action) |and a series of purges (see RED PURGE) that eliminated much of the communist leadership of the movement and accelerated the demise of Sambetsu. In short, the Occupation-period labor re-

forms established both the minimum rights of workers and the political limits of the labor union movement in postwar Japan. See also LABOR LAWS.

labor relations commissions

(rōdō iinkai). Administrative boards with responsibility to resolve LABOR DISPUTES, remedy UNFAIR LABOR PRACTICES, and oversee the affairs of LABOR UNIONS. These boards are composed of representatives of labor, management, and the public. Members serve for two years and select a chairperson from among the public representatives.

The commissions are authorized to investigate unfair labor practices and provide remedies for them; screen the qualifications of labor unions and determine the jurisdiction of COLLECTIVE LABOR AGREEMENTS; and regulate the procedures for dispute resolution. Regional labor relations commissions (chihō rōdō iinkai) have jurisdiction over all nonmaritime employees in the private sector, employees of local government-operated enterprises, and nonclerical local government employees. One such commission operates within each prefecture and has jurisdiction over matters occurring within the prefecture. The CENTRAL LABOR RELATIONS COMMISSION (Chūō Rōdō Iinkai), which is an agency of the central government as an external bureau of the MINISTRY OF LABOR, has authority over labor disputes of a national scale and serves as an administrative court of second hearing for appeals of decisions of the local commissions. It also has authority to promulgate regulations pertaining to commission procedures. Local and central labor relations commissions for seafarers (chihō, chūō sen'in rōdō iinkai) have jurisdiction over maritime workers and employers. The local commissions operate wherever there is a Shipping Bureau of the MINISTRY OF TRANSPORT, and they have jurisdiction over cases occurring in those localities. The central commission is an external bureau of the Ministry of Transport and serves as an administrative court of second hearing in appeals from the local commissions on unfair labor practice cases. The Public Corporations and National Enterprise Labor Relations Commission (Kōkyō Kigyōtai Tō Rōdō Iinkai) is an external bureau of the Ministry of Labor and has jurisdiction over nonclerical employees of the national government and all employees of PUBLIC CORPORATIONS. It has a local mediation commission as a subordinate organization. See also LABOR LAWS.   KATŌ Shunpei

labor standards inspection offices

(rōdō kijun kantokusho). Local offices of the MINISTRY OF LABOR charged with enforcement of the Labor Standards Law, the Labor Safety Law, the MINIMUM WAGE LAW, and the Workers' Accident Compensation Law (see LABOR LAWS; WORKERS' COMPENSATION). There are about 350 such offices, including one in each prefecture and major city. The inspection offices are under the authority of the Labor Standards Bureau of the Ministry of Labor and the prefectural labor standards offices and are staffed by superintendents, labor standards inspectors, and other employees.

The inspectors are employees of the national government who supervise the enforcement and expose violations of the above laws. They have the authority to investigate labor conditions and safety standards in all industries, request the submission of account records and documents, question employers and workers, and act as judicial police officers to expose and provide remedies for violations of the law. Superintendents work under the direction of the head of the prefectural labor standards offices and are authorized to investigate industries; question workers and employers; approve exceptions to laws concerning work hours, rest time, and child labor; authorize dismissals without notice; and investigate, mediate, and award accident compensation.   KATŌ Shunpei

Labor Standards Law → labor laws

Labor Union Law → labor laws

labor unions

The first labor unions in Japan were organized among skilled workers (metalworkers, printers, and locomotive engineers) in the 1890s. From that time until the end of World War II, Japanese labor went through a number of cycles of organization and repression. All la-

Labor unions

Labor Federations and Their Member Federations and Unions, June 1981

Abbreviated name	Full name	Number of members
Sōhyō	Nihon Rōdō Kumiai Sō Hyōgikai (General Council of Trade Unions of Japan)	4,568,826
Jichirō	Zen Nihon Jichi Dantai Rōdō Kumiai (All Japan Prefectural and Municipal Workers' Union)	1,273,261
Nikkyōso	Nihon Kyōshokuin Kumiai (Japan Teachers' Union)	677,300
Dentsū Rōren	Denki Tsūshin Jōhō Sangyō Rōdō Kumiai Rengō (Federation of Telecommunications, Electronic Information, and Allied Workers)	331,987
Kokurō	Kokutetsu Rōdō Kumiai (National Railway Workers' Union)	245,405
Tekkō Rōren	Nihon Tekkō Sangyō Rōdō Kumiai Rengōkai (Japanese Federation of Iron and Steel Workers' Unions)	223,213
Shitetsu Sōren	Nihon Shitetsu Rōdō Kumiai Sō Rengōkai (General Federation of Private Railway Workers' Unions of Japan)	203,631
Zentei	Zen Teishin Rōdō Kumiai (Japan Postal Workers' Union)	186,107
Zenkoku Kinzoku	Zenkoku Kinzoku Rōdō Kumiai (National Trade Union of Metal and Engineering Workers)	163,336
Gōka Rōren	Gōsei Kagaku Sangyō Rōdō Kumiai Rengō (Japanese Federation of Synthetic Chemical Workers' Unions)	125,292
Irōkyō	Nihon Iryō Rōdō Kumiai Kyōgikai (Japan Council of Medical Workers' Unions)	135,632
Zenkoku Ippan	Zenkoku Ippan Rōdō Kumiai (National Union of General Workers)	121,535
Dōmei	Zen Nihon Rōdō Sōdōmei (Japanese Confederation of Labor)	2,181,903
Zensen	Zensen Dōmei (Japan Federation of Textile Industry Workers' Unions)	468,948
Zenkin Dōmei	Zenkoku Kinzoku Sangyō Rōdō Kumiai Dōmei (National Federation of Metal Industry Trade Unions)	300,586
Jidōsha Rōren	Nihon Jidōsha Sangyō Rōdō Kumiai Rengōkai (Japan Federation of Automobile Workers' Unions)	213,125
Zōsen Jūki Rōren	Zenkoku Zōsen Jūkikai Rōdō Kumiai Rengōkai (National Federation of Shipbuilding and Heavy Machinery Workers' Unions)	178,699
Kaiin	Zen Nihon Kaiin Kumiai (All Japan Seamen's Union)	142,733
Denryoku Rōren	Zenkoku Denryoku Rōdō Kumiai Rengōkai (Federation of Electric Workers' Unions of Japan)	136,704
Ippan Dōmei	Zenkoku Ippan Rōdō Kumiai Dōmei (National Federation of General Workers' Unions)	110,938
Shinsambetsu	Zenkoku Sangyōbetsu Rōdō Kumiai Rengō (National Federation of Industrial Labor Organizations)	63,997
Chūritsu Rōren	Chūritsu Rōdō Kumiai Renraku Kaigi (Federation of Independent Unions)	1,391,346
Denki Rōren	Zen Nihon Denki Kiki Rōdō Kumiai Rengōkai (All Japan Federation of Electric Machine Workers' Unions)	552,709
Seiho Rōren	Zenkoku Seimei Hoken Rōdō Kumiai Rengōkai (National Federation of Life Insurance Workers' Unions)	334,407
Zenken Sōren	Zenkoku Kensetsu Rōdō Kumiai Sōrengō (National Federation of Construction Workers' Unions)	289,250
Independent unions		
Jidōsha Sōren	Zen Nihon Jidōsha Sangyō Rōdō Kumiai Sōrengōkai (Japan Confederation of Automobile Workers' Unions)	615,672
Shiginren	Shichū Ginkō Jūgyōin Kumiai Rengōkai (Federation of City Bank Employees' Unions)	174,135
Un'yu Rōren	Zen Nihon Un'yu Sangyō Rōdō Kumiai Rengōkai (Council of All Japan Transport Workers' Unions)	130,516
Affiliates of international organizations		
IMF–JC	Zen Nihon Kinzoku Sangyō Rōdō Kumiai Kyōgikai (International Metalworkers' Federation–Japan Council)	1,917,492
ICEF–JAF	Nihon Kagaku Enerugī Rōdō Kumiai Kyōgikai (International Federation of Chemical, Energy and General Workers' Unions–Japanese Affiliates Federation)	666,382

SOURCE: Rōdōshō (Ministry of Labor), *Nihon no rōdō kumiai no genjō* (annual): 1982.

bor unions were disbanded by the government during World War II. See LABOR.

During the postwar Allied OCCUPATION, the FUNDAMENTAL LABOR RIGHTS were guaranteed by the constitution, and the rights of workers to organize, bargain collectively, and strike were guaranteed for the first time. Organization of labor unions proceeded at an explosive rate, and, by 1949, 55.8 percent of Japan's workers had been organized. The organization rate declined from this peak and stood at about one-third of the work force at the end of the 1970s.

Almost all Japanese labor unions are organized at the level of the enterprise, and include in their membership all white- and blue-collar workers and certain low-level managerial personnel. Enterprise unions maintain independence in decision making, officer selection, and finances; membership is limited to regular employees of the enterprise. Immediate and automatic induction into the union upon hiring is standard practice. Loss of membership is likewise automatic upon termination of employment or promotion above a certain level in the management hierarchy, usually the level of section head (kachō).

Union dues are usually deducted from workers' salaries and amount to an average of 1.3 percent of monthly pay, although the rate in large enterprises may be as high as 2 percent. Officers, elected from among union members, are employees in almost every case. They return to employee status when their term of office is finished. Care is taken that officers suffer no financial disadvantage from their position, and their compensation is increased in line with the increase in employee compensation. In smaller businesses, offi-

cers conduct union affairs in their spare time and receive only moderate compensation.

As a result of internal dissension or during the course of a dispute, enterprise unions occasionally split. In most such cases, new unions called "secondary unions" are formed through the cooperative efforts of management and the dissident faction of the original union. The "primary union," though discriminated against by management and representing a diminishing minority of the employees, often continues to exist side by side with its rival for many years. There is no law requiring exclusive representation by one union, as there is in the United States.

Where large enterprises operate numerous branch facilities, a union will be organized at each branch. These branch unions then form an enterprise-wide federation with other branch unions. Single-enterprise unions and federations of branch unions in one industry or a number of related industries are organized into industrywide federations. Unions in such public enterprises as the Japanese National Railways and the postal service or such recognized monopolies as the Nippon Telegraph and Telephone Public Corporation are customarily treated as industry federations, although they are technically single enterprises.

Industry-wide federations in turn combine to form national labor federations, or labor centers, as they are sometimes called. In the early 1980s there were four such centers, each with its own political leaning and approach to labor movement strategy. SŌHYŌ (General Council of Trade Unions of Japan) is the largest, with a high concentration of membership in the public sector. It is closely aligned with the JAPAN SOCIALIST PARTY. DŌMEI (Japanese Confederation of Labor) is more moderate and is linked with the DEMOCRATIC SOCIALIST PARTY. The third center, CHŪRITSU RŌREN (Federation of Independent Unions), is much smaller and generally cooperates with Sōhyō in collective bargaining strategy. A fourth center, SHINSAMBETSU, (National Federation of Industrial Labor Organizations), takes a neutral political stance.

The IMF–JC (International Metalworkers' Federation–Japan Council) became active in the mid-1960s as an umbrella organization of industrial unions in various national federations, but it does not yet represent an independent policy-making center. Repeated attempts to create a single national organization over the years have not borne fruit. Roughly 25 percent of single-enterprise unions are entirely independent, belonging to neither industry nor national federations.

On the international level, Dōmei is affiliated as a body with the International Confederation of Free Trade Unions (ICFTU). Various industry-wide federations are also affiliated with the ICFTU or with its international industry secretariats, while other federations are affiliated with appropriate industrial divisions of the World Federation of Trade Unions (WFTU).

Collective bargaining is generally conducted directly between the enterprise union and the enterprise, with little involvement by the industry and national federations. SHUNTŌ, the annual spring wage offensive, has been utilized since 1955 to place the unified power of the labor movement behind these enterprise-level negotiations, usually through a pattern-setting industry. The pattern setter is usually a prospering industry where the unions' bargaining power is great. In addition to nationwide strikes and demonstrations in support of wage demands, shuntō also raises political demands. There is a strong tendency for the pattern-setting industry to be followed by the major industries in Japan, although the pattern has no binding power. Methods of wage payment and issues concerning working conditions are decided through negotiations at the enterprise level. Among small businesses there is a tendency to reach piecemeal agreements in the absence of formal labor pacts. Differences in working conditions among enterprises arise as a consequence.

In addition to laws guaranteeing labor's fundamental rights, there is a general law concerning the chartering and internal organization of labor unions. The rights of PUBLIC EMPLOYEES are restricted by national and local civil service laws and by the PUBLIC CORPORATIONS AND GOVERNMENT ENTERPRISES LABOR RELATIONS LAW (Kōkyō Kigyōtai Tō Rōdō Kankei Hō); all public employees are prohibited from striking, while some classes of public employees are further restricted from collective bargaining or organizing labor unions. The activities of labor unions are protected from unfair employer practices by the Labor Relations Adjustment Law (Rōdō Kankei Chōsei Hō), which established LABOR RELATIONS COMMISSIONS to adjudicate charges of unfair practice and to oversee LABOR DISPUTE RESOLUTION PROCEDURES. These provisions also established emergency government powers to declare a temporary end to labor disputes in certain circumstances. See also DENKI RŌREN; JICHIRŌ; JIDŌSHA SŌREN; KŌRŌKYŌ; ZENSEN; NIKKYŌSO.　　　Kurita Ken

lacquer tree

(urushi). Rhus verniciflua. A deciduous tree of the sumac family (Anacardiaceae), cultivated as a source of lacquer since ancient times. Indigenous to China, India, and Tibet, it reaches more than 10 meters (36 ft) in height and 30–50 centimeters (12–20 in) in diameter. The bark of young trees is grayish white and that of older ones is dark gray. The branches are thick and grow from the main trunk in a regular pattern. The compound leaves consist of leaflets arranged like a feather (imparipinnate) and cluster alternately at the ends of branches. Trees bear either male or female flower clusters in panicles at the leaf axils. The many small yellowish green blossoms flower in May and June. The fruit is a spheroid drupe, which ripens to a yellowish brown color in October and November. The tree is suited to cool, sunny places with a deep layer of moist, fertile soil. It is planted along streams and rivers, in ravines, on ridges between rice fields and around houses throughout Japan, and also grows wild in various places. Similar species found in Japan include tsutaurushi (R. ambigua), nurude (R. javanica), hazenoki (R. succedanea), yamahaze (R. sylvestris) and yamaurushi (R. trichocarpa). Like the poison ivy (R. toxicodendron) of North America, the sap of these trees contains an oily toxic irritant, urushiol.

The lacquer sap is usually gathered when the tree is 10 years old and its trunk is at least 10 centimeters (4 in) in diameter. The sap

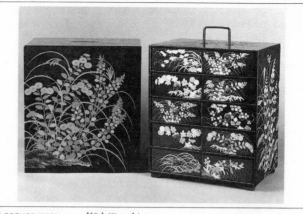

Lacquer ware —— Kōdaiji maki-e

Portable cabinet for poem booklets with matching case; once part of the household furnishings of Toyotomi Hideyoshi and his wife Kita no Mandokoro. The design of autumn flowers and plants is in the hira (flat) maki-e technique, with gold flakes sprinkled over a black lacquer ground. 38.8 × 33.0 cm, depth 23.5 cm. Late 16th century. Kōdaiji, Kyōto.

oozes naturally out of the tree from mid-June through late October; the best quality is obtained from mid-July through early September. Japanese methods of gathering the sap differ from those in China, Korea, and Indochina. The most common Japanese method, called koroshikaki, entails the peeling of strips of the outer bark from the tree trunk at four-day intervals starting in mid-June. After each stripping, about 25 horizontal incisions are made into the wood with a sickle (kakigama) to facilitate collection of the sap. Once the sap is out, the tree is cut down.

Lacquer is made by removing water and impurities from the raw sap in a refinement process, after which dehydrating agents and dye are added. It is used to coat Buddhist altar fittings and household furnishings, and to make lacquer ware. The wood of the lacquer tree is used in construction work as well as in the making of various tools and GETA (clogs); wax is extracted from the fruits.

Lacquer has been used in China since very ancient times. The date of its introduction into Japan is unknown, but lacquer ware has been found in archaeological digs of Final (Latest) Jōmon period (ca 1000 BC–ca 300 BC) sites and urushi is mentioned in the KOJIKI (completed in AD 712). Lacquer has been an important product throughout Japanese history, and the tree has been counted among the four valuable trees (shiboku), along with mulberry, tea, and paper mulberry or kōzo (Broussonetia kazinoki).

The annual production of raw lacquer totaled about 800 metric tons (880 short tons) in 1877, but has decreased to about 5 metric tons (5.5 short tons) in recent years. Imports of lacquer from China, which totaled about 1,000 metric tons (1,100 short tons) per year in the mid-1930s, now stand at about 400 metric tons (about 440 short tons) per year. Although lacquer was produced all over the country in the Meiji period (1868–1912), production is currently limited to Aomori, Iwate, Yamagata, Ibaraki, Aichi, Nara, Kyōto, and Okayama prefectures.　　　Hayashi Yasaka

lacquer ware

(shikki). Containers, utensils, furniture, and other useful objects employing lacquer as a protective varnish and often as a decorative medium as well. Lacquer ware has been manufactured in many regions of East and Southeast Asia. In Japan, lacquer ware has reached an outstanding level of technical and artistic quality, incorporating a rich variety of shapes and decorative techniques in useful objects, and it ranks among the most distinctive achievements of traditional Japanese crafts.

Lacquer (urushi) is prepared by evaporation and filtration of sap collected by cutting through the bark of the LACQUER TREE (J: urushi no ki; Rhus verniciflua). Raw lacquer is a viscous emulsion with toxic properties, but under proper conditions it hardens permanently by oxidation to form a lustrous, durable film that is remarkably inert and impervious to moisture. One of the most durable natural adhesives and varnishes known in the premodern world, lacquer appears to have been recognized as a useful substance in China and Japan by the second millennium BC.

Lacquer penetrates and seals porous surfaces, rapidly taking on an amber to deep brown color and a glossy sheen as it hardens. An application of lacquer increases the durability and utility of materials such as wood, the most common material for the construction of lacquer ware. Basketry, woven textiles, bamboo, pottery, metal, paper, and leather have also been used in the making of lacquer ware. An excellent adhesive, lacquer can be used for structural reinforcement of joints of wooden ware, for joining dissimilar materials, and even for mending cracks and fractures in ceramics, a uniquely Japanese technique.

The decorative appeal of lacquer can be enhanced by numerous methods. The simplest is the addition of certain pigments, chemically compatible with raw lacquer, to produce opaque colors. Red and black lacquer occur in some of the earliest extant fragments of Chinese and Japanese lacquer, and these remain the most common colors throughout the history of lacquer manufacture in East Asia. Yellow, green, and brown occur in Japanese lacquer prior to the Meiji period (1868–1912). Within the past century, blue, violet, and white lacquer have been successfully produced through the incorporation of pigments unknown to premodern lacquerers.

Hardened lacquer is amenable to polishing with abrasives to achieve a brilliant, mirrorlike finish. If the lacquer veneer is sufficiently thick—the result of numerous separate applications of thin layers of lacquer—it can be carved, incised, or inlaid with metals, mother-of-pearl, and other materials.

Outstanding among Japanese decorative techniques is MAKI-E, literally, "sprinkled-picture." This term encompasses a variety of techniques employing gold or silver powder or particles sprinkled on areas defined by liquid lacquer. The gold or silver adheres permanently to the lacquer as it hardens, forming rich and luxurious decoration. Maki-e first appeared in lacquer datable to the 8th century AD, and subsequently became the dominant decorative technique in the highest-quality Japanese lacquer ware.

History——Archaeological excavations of Jōmon-period (ca 10,000 BC–ca 300 BC) sites have yielded numerous remains of lacquered objects made of wood, woven bamboo, or pottery. These artifacts confirm the use of lacquer in neolithic Japan, possibly as early as the second millennium BC. Both red and black lacquer appear, sometimes in combination. The decorative potential of the medium is expressed in simple meander patterns painted in red and black lacquer in a style related to the decoration of JŌMON POTTERY.

According to the fragmentary evidence, there were few significant innovations in the making of lacquer ware prior to the introduction of Buddhism in the mid-6th century AD, when many new techniques of fabrication and decoration were introduced from China and Korea. The requirements of newly established Buddhist temples for furniture, shrines, and icons resulted in a vastly increased demand for lacquer. That lacquer had economic importance is indicated by the legal requirement in the TAIHŌ CODE (701) that each household plant lacquer trees and remit a certain amount of lacquer as tax.

Lacquer ware of the Nara period (710–794) reveals a rich variety of materials and techniques, many of which probably originated on the Asian continent. Wood, molded leather, and hemp cloth soaked in lacquer were used to form lacquer objects, though the latter two materials were not extensively used in later periods. Lacquer ware preserved in Buddhist temples and in the mid-8th century SHŌSŌIN imperial repository employs many decorative techniques, including MOTHER-OF-PEARL INLAY (raden), inlay of sheet silver and gold (heidatsu or hyōmon), and lacquer painting (URUSHI-E) using colored lacquer or lacquer mixed with powdered silver and gold. Dry lacquer (kanshitsu), a technique of Chinese origin utilizing hemp cloth soaked in liquid lacquer, was used for construction of Buddhist sculpture. Kanshitsu as a technique for sculpture disappeared after the Nara period, but is still used occasionally by lacquerers for constructing objects with shapes difficult to execute in less flexible materials. The most significant new technique to appear in lacquer ware of the Nara period was maki-e; Nara-period designs in maki-e employ coarse gold powder sprinkled over simple, linear designs drawn in lacquer.

Maki-e was the dominant decorative technique of lacquer ware from the subsequent Heian period (794–1185). Both silver and gold powders were used in combination on most Heian lacquer ware, and the potential of maki-e to achieve techniques analogous to painting was fully realized. Powders were sprinkled sparsely to create a glittering background, densely and irregularly to form cloud-like designs, and over linear patterns for details and stylized floral arabesques. In a few examples datable to the late Heian period inlay

of mother-of-pearl is used. Heian-period lacquer ware parallels contemporary trends in Japanese art and literature toward the evolution of uniquely Japanese themes and modes of expression reflective of the tastes of the aristocratic patrons of the arts.

Maki-e of the Kamakura period (1185–1333) shows sleek, precisely defined designs, often incorporating the togidashi maki-e technique in which the areas sprinkled with gold or silver are burnished after hardening of the lacquer to create a softly metallic finish. Gold and silver leaf and inlaid mother-of-pearl are frequently combined with maki-e in the decoration of Kamakura-period lacquer ware. In general the designs show precision and regularity. Many are based on literary and poetic sources.

Maki-e of the Kamakura and Muromachi (1333–1568) periods have many designs based upon Japanese WAKA poetry. The poem-picture (UTA-E), combining some written characters with pictorial elements, appears in many Muromachi-period maki-e designs. Takamaki-e, a technique in which areas of the design are brought into relief by building up with priming materials and lacquer, is a prominent feature of Muromachi-period maki-e.

Concurrently, other types of lacquer ware, such as NEGORO-NURI and KAMAKURA-BORI, both influenced by Chinese lacquer ware, were produced for use in Buddhist temples. Both depend upon the aesthetic appeal of unembellished black and red lacquer. Kamakura-bori, still made today, is one of the few types of Japanese lacquer ware to have been inspired by Chinese carved lacquer. Technically simpler than a true carved lacquer, kamakura-bori has the carving executed directly on the wooden object prior to lacquering rather than into a thick veneer of lacquer.

The Azuchi-Momoyama period (1568–1600) was an age of innovation in all the Japanese arts, including lacquer ware. KŌDAIJI MAKI-E, characterized by simplified, bold patterns often based on the theme of flowering autumn grasses (akikusa), typifies the Momoyama style in lacquer ware. In the same period, Japanese lacquerers produced numerous items specifically for European use. Most of these were decorated with maki-e in combination with mother-of-pearl inlay. Usually referred to as namban lacquer ware, many of these objects were exported during the earliest phase of Japanese trade with Europe. There they were greatly admired and inspired new trends in European decorative arts.

The surviving lacquer ware of the Edo period (1600–1868) suggests by its range of themes, styles, and quality a significant broadening of usage, especially among the prosperous merchant class. The vast range of themes in Edo lacquer ware decoration, from references to classical Japanese and Chinese literature and painting to themes from popular legend and customs, reflects the expansion of both privately sponsored and commercial production of lacquer ware. The names and lineages of some families that specialized in the production of lacquer ware are helpful in interpreting the complex history of the many surviving examples of lacquer ware from this period.

Edo-period lacquerers drew their inspiration from many sources, including designs by professional painters or from illustrated books which could be interpreted in maki-e. The close interaction between lacquer decoration and painting is especially evident in the lacquer ware associated with the so-called RIMPA style.

There were numerous technical innovations in lacquer ware during the Edo period. Powdered, colored lacquers and charcoal were incorporated into maki-e decoration, which had formerly been limited to silver and gold. Ogawa Haritsu (Ritsuō; 1663–1747) is credited with having invented many new techniques. He seems to have been especially fascinated with the use of lacquer to imitate other materials, such as metalwork and even molded sticks of Chinese ink.

In the Meiji period, the industry was stimulated by a renewed domestic and foreign demand for lacquer ware. The manufacture of lacquer ware requires many separate steps and is not generally amenable to rapid mass-production; however, large workshops were organized in which many processes could be carried on simultaneously, resulting in the production of quantities of lacquer ware. Much of this was for use within Japan, particularly for food service, but it also became important in trade with Europe and America.

Japanese lacquer ware still maintains a high standard of quality. Japan's most skillful lacquer artists produce works of great originality and beauty, incorporating a vast repertoire of techniques reflecting the local heritage of many lacquer-producing regions.

In recent decades, the cost of producing lacquer and lacquer ware has risen so steeply that substitute materials have virtually replaced the simple lacquered bowls and utensils that were once in common use, and owning true lacquer ware has once again become a luxury. Yet the flourishing of lacquer workshops in many regions of Japan and the accomplishments of individual lacquerers who have achieved international recognition for their art attest to the contemporary vitality of lacquer ware as one of Japan's foremost craft traditions.

🔖 ——Sawaguchi Goichi, *Nihon shikkō no kenkyū* (2nd ed, 1966). Beatrix von Ragué, *A History of Japanese Lacquerwork,* tr Annie R. de Wassermann (1976). Ann Yonemura, *Japanese Lacquer* (1979).

Ann YONEMURA

Ladybird Incident

An international incident that occurred early in the SINO-JAPANESE WAR OF 1937–1945 when the Japanese were advancing on Nanjing (Nanking). On 12 December 1937 the British gunboat *Ladybird* and several commercial vessels cruising the Yangzi (Yangtze) River near Wuhu, Anhui (Anhwei) Province, were fired upon by the Japanese army. Casualties included one dead and several injured. On the same day, the British gunboats *Cricket, Scarab,* and *Bee* and the American gunboat *Panay* (see PANAY INCIDENT) were attacked by Japanese naval planes further down the Yangzi, near Nanjing. The following day the Japanese foreign minister, HIROTA KŌKI, personally delivered an official apology to Robert L. Craigie, the British ambassador in Japan, and YOSHIDA SHIGERU, the Japanese ambassador to Great Britain, also expressed his regrets to the British government. In a further attempt to avert an international crisis, on 14 December the Japanese government issued an official apology, promising to make financial reparations for the incident and to punish those responsible. It was accepted by the British government. The truth about the incident did not come out until after World War II, when HASHIMOTO KINGORŌ testified at the WAR CRIMES TRIALS that General Yanagawa Heisuke (1879–1945), chief commander of the 10th Army in China, had ordered that all non-Japanese boats on the Yangzi moving toward Nanjing be sunk, regardless of nationality.

Lady Chatterley's Lover case

A landmark Supreme Court decision on obscenity, 1957. The publisher Koyama Kyūjirō and the translator Itō Sei (novelist and D. H. Lawrence specialist) were charged in 1950 under the obscenity provisions of the Criminal Code (art. 175) for translating, publishing, and distributing *Lady Chatterley's Lover.* Courtroom and mass media debate attending the trials was generally critical of both the indictments and the general distribution of the unexpurgated translation. In an unusual procedure, the Tōkyō District Court, at the request of both defense and prosecution, heard the divided opinion of 24 witnesses (professors of medicine, literary critics, psychiatrists, high school principals) as to the charge of obscenity of the book. Appeals from convictions were ultimately quashed by the Supreme Court (G. B. 13 March 1957; 11 Keishū [no. 3] 997 [1957]), which held that the 12 passages at issue infected Lawrence's entire work with obscenity. The court defined obscenity as follows: "In order for a writing to be obscene, it is required that it wantonly arouse and stimulate sexual desire, offend the normal sense of shame, and run counter to proper concepts of sexual morality." Neither the book's admitted literary value, nor the author's serious intent in analyzing sex, nor the sincerity of the accused could offset the work's abuse of freedom of expression, as judicially determined in accord with the "public welfare" principle of articles 12 and 13 of the constitution and "prevailing social ideas, which are the norms of sound men of good sense." The court added that if the moral sense of the great majority regarding obscene writings should become dull, the courts should exercise a "clinical role" to correct this situation— a turn of thought commonly attacked by legal scholars and litterateurs ever since. The *Chatterley* decision remains, along with the DE SADE CASE, the most influential obscenity holding under the 1947 constitution.

🔖 ——"Obscenity and Freedom of Expression (The *Lady Chatterley's Lover* Decision)," tr in John M. Maki, *Court and Constitution in Japan: Selected Supreme Court Decisions, 1948–1960* (1964).

Lawrence W. BEER

laity

In Shintō lay believers are called *ujiko;* in Buddhism they are called DANKA. The *ujiko* are parishioners of a community shrine enshrining the local deity (UJIGAMI); they are considered parishioners by the shrine authorities by virtue of their residence in the community under the *ujigami's* protection. The *ujiko* system developed gradually throughout Japanese history, but by the Edo period (1600–1868), all families of a certain geographical area were considered the *ujiko* of the local shrine. The system was institutionalized by the Meiji (1868–1912) government as a means of keeping a census of the population, but this was abolished after World War II.

In the Buddhist tradition, those who support a particular temple (*dannadera*) are called *dan'otsu, danna,* or *danka.* This system of patronization began in the Kamakura period (1185–1333) with the rise of the popularly oriented Pure Land sect (JŌDO SECT), ZEN, and the NICHIREN SECT and was institutionalized by the Tokugawa shogunate (1603–1867) into a system whereby all families were required to be affiliated with a certain temple. Thus in Japan, it is not unusual for a single individual to be an *ujiko* of a shrine and a *danka* of a temple at the same time. From around the Meiji Restoration of 1868, there have been active lay Buddhist movements, some of which have been organized into new religious organizations such as the REIYŪKAI and RISSHŌ KŌSEIKAI. See also SŌKA GAKKAI.

Fujita Tomio

landlordism

(*jinushisei*). The land tenure system whereby tenants tilled a landlord's fields and paid him a heavy annual rent. Having first appeared in the 18th century, it flourished in the Meiji period (1868–1912) and lasted until the LAND REFORMS OF 1946. From 1927 to the present, Japanese scholars engaged in the Japanese Marxist debate on Japanese capitalism (NIHON SHIHON SHUGI RONSŌ) have argued over whether the historical character of this type of landlordism was basically feudal or modern. Since World War II another major Japanese interpretation has contended that, as in Europe, such landlordism constituted a semifeudal system of property ownership that appears in the early period of absolutist rule, itself the closing stage of feudal society.

Origins —— Because of increasing agricultural productivity combined with the fixed levels of domanial land taxes under the Tokugawa shogunate's BAKUHAN SYSTEM, some 18th-century peasant landholders (HOMBYAKUSHŌ) came to enjoy agricultural surpluses. They consequently began to raise cotton, tobacco, rapeseed, and other commercial crops. Some of these *hombyakushō* went on to become landlords by acquiring agricultural land from less successful peasants, who became their tenant farmers. The resulting landlord-tenant relationship appears to have developed from these village landlords' accumulation of commerical and usury capital. Tenancy appeared first, and most extensively, in the vicinity of Ōsaka and Kyōto, the region where commercial farming had started. Landlords normally acquired property when it was pawned and then left unredeemed by its original owner, who ended up as its tenant in a relationship known as *shitchi kosaku*. In addition, some commercial capitalists became landlords by reclaiming unused land for cultivation by tenants.

Development —— Landlord-tenant relationships became increasingly common throughout Japan during the Meiji period. Determined to encourage the development of capitalism, the Meiji government based its industrialization program on tax revenues from private landownership. The abolition of daimyo domains (see PREFECTURAL SYSTEM, ESTABLISHMENT OF), an important reform of the MEIJI RESTORATION, had deprived former *daimyō* of their land possessions. Between 1871 and 1883 the Land Tax Reform (see LAND TAX REFORM OF 1873–1881) hastened the spread of landlordism by legally recognizing the "ownership of private land."

Nonetheless, most peasants found it difficult to acquire their own land since Meiji taxes were not reduced from their high Tokugawa levels. Furthermore, the deflation brought on by the MATSUKATA FISCAL POLICY of 1881–1885 affected peasant households so severely that by 1887 some 39.4 percent of agricultural land was worked by tenant farmers, and 67 percent of all peasant families were tenants or tenant-owners; by 1902 the former figure had risen to 44.5 percent. Since tenants on average paid half of their rice crop as rent, they were soon forced to send their wives and daughters to work in textile mills as cotton weavers or silk spinners, usually for subsistence wages. See INDUSTRIAL REVOLUTION IN JAPAN.

In 1890 the government designated 3.65 million *chō* (1 *chō*=about 1 hectare or 2.5 acres) of land as imperial land, and at the same time it conferred on the PEERAGE rights whereby they acquired extensive tracts of land in Hokkaidō. Giant financial com-

Land problem

	Japan	West Germany	United Kingdom	United States
		International Comparison of Land Area, Population, and Economic Activity		
Total area (1,000 sq km)	377.7 (1980)	248.6 (1975)	244.1 (1977)	9,371.8 (1974)
Inhabitable area (1,000 sq km)	80.5 (1980)	159.4 (1975)	156.4 (1977)	4,581.4 (1974)
Population per sq km of inhabitable land	1,452 (1980)	386 (1979)	357 (1979)	55 (1979)
1980 GNP per sq km of inhabitable land (US $ million)	$12.9	$5.2	$3.3	$0.6
1979 energy consumption per sq km of inhabitable land (coal equivalent tons)	5,360	2,310	1,830	550
Average 1979 land price (US $ per sq meter)	$204	$38	$16	$13

NOTE: Definitions of "inhabitable land" vary slightly among countries listed, but in general include total land area minus the area occupied by forests, wasteland (deserts, tundra, etc), and lakes, rivers, and other bodies of water.
SOURCE: Kokudochō (National Land Agency), *Kokudo riyō hakusho* (annual): 1982.

bines (ZAIBATSU) also bought up much land, thereby becoming big landlords with important political ties.

The spread of landlordism throughout the countryside was reflected in the composition of both houses of the Imperial Diet. To the lower house were elected the small and middle landlords and to the upper house the large landlords, who paid a higher proportion of the taxes. These landlords were the beneficiaries and supporters of the "emperor system" of Japan from the Meiji period through World War II.

Japanese scholars have disagreed over when this landlord system became fully entrenched. One group dates it from 1890, when the political measures were taken, the other from the early 1900s, when industrial capitalism became established in Japan.

Decline——Tenant farmer disputes began to occur in the late 1890s. During the Taishō period (1912–26), especially after the RICE RIOTS OF 1918 and the Russian Revolution, many peasants fell under the influence of the urban labor movement and formed their own tenant unions, such as the Japan Peasant Union (Nihon Nōmin Kumiai, 1922). Large-scale disputes broke out when tenants demanded lower rents and tenant rights.

By the 1920s, however, landlordism was no longer so powerful. The economic boom during World War I had greatly stimulated urban industrialization and had thus initiated the gradual demise of landlordism's hold over the rural economy. The number of large landlords with over 50 *chō* reached its peak in 1919, as did tenanted land's share of the total arable land in the following year.

Under the prewar capitalist system, in which the imperial family was the largest landowner and the *zaibatsu* families were also major landholders, opposition to the land tenure system represented a radical attack on the state. Tenant disputes consequently were suppressed. Yet, when the SHŌWA DEPRESSION and the development of Japan's wartime economy made it evident that landlordism impeded agricultural production, wartime agricultural laws, such as the Tenant Rent Control Ordinance (Kosakuryō Tōsei Rei), were passed. These reforms weakened landlordism and helped pave the way for its abolition in the land reforms after World War II.

■——Araki Moriaki, "Jinushisei no tenkai," in *Iwanami kōza: Nihon rekishi*, vol 16 (Iwanami Shoten, 1962). Furushima Toshio, ed, *Nihon jinushisei shi kenkyū* (1958). Kurihara Hakuju, *Nihon nōgyō no kiso kōzō* (1943). Nakamura Masanori, *Kindai Nihon jinushisei shi kenkyū* (1979). Yamada Moritarō, *Nihon shihon shugi bunseki* (1934). KATŌ Kōzaburō

land problem

Land utilization in Japan is highly intensive because of the extremely mountainous terrain. This heavy utilization has resulted in a number of serious social problems, including dense urbanization and high land prices. Of the total land area of 377,708 square kilometers (145,800 sq mi), 66.9 percent is uninhabitable mountains and forests. Farmland constitutes 14.9 percent of the archipelago; urban areas 3.7 percent; roads 2.8 percent; rivers, lakes, and canals 3 percent; and others 8.8 percent. Of the urban land area, 77.1 percent is residential, 10.7 percent industrial, and 12.1 percent commercial.

An international comparison of land area, population, and economic activity is presented in the accompanying table. The extreme density of population in Japan is apparent from the data. Gross national product (GNP) per square kilometer gives an indication of the effective demand for land: the data show dramatically the high concentration of economic activity in a small land area.

There have been two major problems with regard to land since the end of World War II: the rapid URBANIZATION and the rapid rise in land prices resulting from urbanization and the high rate of economic growth. The comparative land price figures given in the table give some idea of how serious is the problem of land prices. The denser the population, the higher the price of land. For example, the average land price per square meter in Kōbe, in the industrial Kinki region of central Japan, was ¥77,900 (US $263) in 1976. The comparably populated city of Munich in West Germany had an average land price of ¥49,600 (US $167). The much less-populated city of Kumamoto, in Kyūshū, had an average land price of ¥16,000 (US $54), compared with the level in the similar West German city of Karlsruhe of ¥15,200 (US $51).

In comparison to the United States and West Germany, Japan has experienced a more rapid rise in the price of land. Using 1970 as an index (100) year, land prices in residential areas rose to 188.4 by 1976 in Japan, compared to 147.7 and 158.8 in the United States and West Germany, respectively. Comparable figures for the United Kingdom, however, are higher: there, the land price index peaked at 294.2 in 1973 and in 1976 stood at 203.4.

It is of interest to note the high correlation between growth in the urban land price index and current GNP. Japanese government figures show that when there is a sharp rise in the current GNP, there is a corresponding rise, to a somewhat amplified extent, in the price of land. When GNP contracts, there is a similar amplified downward movement in the land price.

The rapid climb in urban land prices in Japan accompanied the decades of rapid economic growth that began in the mid-1950s. Price increases have also correlated with the improvement of TRANSPORTATION services in urban and suburban areas, as well as with the improvement of residential amenities.

Large regional differentials in land prices are another characteristic of Japanese land problems. At the beginning of 1979, land prices were highest in Tōkyō, averaging ¥86,300 (US $394) per square meter, followed by ¥82,200 (US $375) in the Ōsaka area; in Nagoya, the average was substantially lower, ¥39,300 (US $179). The northern parts of Japan had the lowest land prices, averaging ¥23,600 (US $108) in Hokkaidō, for instance.

The high prices and rents for urban dwellings have not been generally accompanied by improvements in the quality of housing. According to a housing demand census conducted by the Ministry of Construction in 1973, nearly 40 percent of urban residents were dissatisfied with the quality of their homes. Most of these people lived in wooden apartment houses, 65.5 percent of which had only one room, 56.4 percent of which had shared toilet facilities, and 91.3 percent of which had no bathrooms. These wooden structures were in disrepair, had poor ventilation, and no fire safety equipment. Most were built in the decade after 1955 and by the early 1970s were in poor condition. A large percentage of the inhabitants of such dwellings, however, felt little hope that they would ever find better housing (see also HOUSING PROBLEMS). Landowners, however, received unprecedented capital gains from the sale of land during this period. The contrast between the windfall profits on land sales and the discouraging prospects for aspiring homeowners has the potential to cause lasting morale problems among the working class.

Other problems have accompanied urbanization, including the sprawling growth of suburbs. Often the provision of public services lags behind this growth: poor sanitation land water supply have resulted in epidemics of dysentery in some cases. Another associated problem has been the increasing difficulty of obtaining land for public purposes such as the building of roads, railways, parks, schools, and hospitals. Even where sellers can be found, the price of land is often beyond the budget of local municipalities.

NAKAUCHI Tsuneo

land reclamation

(tochi zōsei). Land reclamation in Japan covers a wide range of activities, including the conversion of wasteland into fertile fields and the transformation of shallow coastal waters into industrial land. Land reclamation and land development thus play a key role in urban development, industrial development, and agricultural policy.

At the time of the Manor Regulation Edict of 902 there were 1.08 million hectares (about 2.67 million acres) under cultivation in Japan, including paddy fields. This amount remained virtually unchanged until the beginning of the Edo period (1600–1868) when it began to increase gradually, reaching 4 million hectares (about 9.88 million acres) in 1846. After 1900 the area under cultivation increased rapidly, and approximately 5.7 million hectares (14.08 million acres) were under cultivation in the early 1980s. The increase of land under cultivation is almost directly proportionate to the population increase.

The most outstanding land reclamation project before the Meiji period was the reclaiming of a vast land mass out of Edo Bay (now Tōkyō Bay) for the construction of EDO (now Tōkyō) at the beginning of the 17th century. After 1900 land development programs underwent marked changes. In the first decades of the 20th century there was a great deal of new construction of industrial cities. In order to disperse factories, vast areas of land were purchased in rural areas and turned into factory sites at the same time that land readjustment programs were carried out.

Paddy fields for rice, Japan's main crop, have long depended on irrigation and land improvement projects. Drainage reclamation was conducted extensively during and after the Meiji period to increase farmland, including conversions of tidelands, lakes, or ponds into paddy fields by building embankments around them and drying them out. The largest and most ambitious of such projects was the drainage reclamation of KOJIMA BAY in Okayama Prefecture. Approximately 1,300 hectares (3,200 acres) of farmland were reclaimed from the bay by 1912 in a private enterprise led by Fujita Denzaburō (1841–1912). A total of 2,568 hectares (6,343 acres) was reclaimed in the second major reclamation of Kojima Bay, which was conducted by the Ministry of Agriculture and Forestry from 1949 to 1963.

In the period after World War II, priorities were placed on stepped-up production of food and hydroelectric power generation with the aim of rapidly rehabilitating the land laid waste by the war. Construction of multipurpose DAMS and reclamation of farmland was carried out in various places. Reconstruction and modernization of war-damaged major cities were carried out by the government. During the period of economic growth after 1950, dredge reclamation of vast coastal areas and utilization of interior land secured land for industry. At the same time, large-scale new suburban housing areas were developed to accommodate growing populations in major urban centers. Urban renewal programs were also conducted in large cities to relocate factories and make new use of the vacated land.

Increases in national income owe much to the promotion of secondary industries. Land reclamation for industries, especially in such key sectors as the heavy and chemical industries, has been particularly important in Japan. In order to secure land for such industries in the coastal areas, the shoaling beaches of bays were dredged. One reason for the selection of coastal areas as industrial land is that, in heavy and chemical industries, a new industrial system has been introduced where various plants are connected with one another by means of pipelines in order to lower transportation costs (see INDUSTRIAL COMPLEXES). Large flat areas of land have been indispensable, and such land has been reclaimed through dredging of coastal areas. A second reason is the necessity of industrial ports capable of handling large ships, as Japanese industries depend heavily on imported oil and other raw materials and on foreign markets as outlets for their products.

📖 ——Suzuki Masatsugu et al, Tochi zōsei (1970). Watanabe Yoshirō et al, Tochi kaihatsu (1977). WATANABE Yoshirō

land reforms of 1946

The effort to redistribute land holdings was one of the most successful reform measures of the post–World War II Allied OCCUPATION

Land reclamation——Kōbe Port Island

Completed in 1981 and composed entirely of land reclaimed from the sea, Kōbe Port Island in the port of Kōbe took 15 years to create. It is used for both residential and commercial purposes. The city of Kōbe can be seen in the distance, as well as another reclamation project in progress.

of Japan. A curious mixture of Jeffersonian idealism and carefully planned, hard-nosed bureaucratic politics, the reform aimed at establishing an American-style democracy through the creation of a broad class of independent yeoman farmers. Popular with the many Japanese who were troubled by the problems of the tenant farmer prior to the war, land reform was implemented with relatively little opposition. It brought substantial changes to the countryside but was dependent for its ultimate success upon industrial policy and other seemingly unrelated factors.

At the end of World War II, close to 50 percent of Japan's 72 million people still lived in largely rural surroundings. About 36 percent of some 5.9 million farm families owned 90 percent or more of their land, while 20 percent owned 50–90 percent, 17 percent owned 10–50 percent, and a distressingly large 27 percent owned less than 10 percent. Holdings varied by region, but averaged less than 1 chō (1 hectare or 2.47 acres), most of which was normally divided into inefficiently scattered plots. Tenants paid rents in kind that averaged as much as 60 percent of the crop; many were bound by strong communal rights to paternalistic landlords, but they had few contractual rights and little incentive to undertake technological innovations. Since landlords were also worried by the rise of tenant disputes, a fall in the relative price of rice, and wartime measures designed to boost rice production by granting bonuses directly to cultivators, they too reluctantly concluded that some form of land legislation would be necessary (see TENANT FARMER DISPUTES; LANDLORDISM).

Most Americans agreed, although some "old Japan hands" in the State Department worried, as they did in the matter of ZAIBATSU DISSOLUTION, that too radical a restructuring of the traditional order might lead to social chaos, and they succeeded in keeping land reform out of the initial directives sent to the Supreme Commander for the Allied Forces (SCAP), General Douglas MACARTHUR. Other officials such as agricultural specialist Wolf Ladejinsky and particularly State Department official Robert Feary stressed that elimination of tenant farming was essential to the destruction of MILITARISM; this argument was pressed with particular force once Feary was transferred to Japan. By 9 December 1945, SCAP had issued a public pronouncement listing the kinds of reform measures needed and calling for a formal response by the Japanese government by 15 March 1946. SCAP's statement had the apparently unintended effect of ending debate on a Japanese-sponsored land reform bill submitted to the Diet four days earlier. This bill was formally passed on 28 December 1945, but it failed to gain SCAP approval not only because it permitted resident landlords to hold on to amounts of rented land of up to 5 chō (5 hectares or 12.35 acres) but also because provisions for determining landlord titles and transferring ownership of lands to tenants seemed far too open to abuse.

A 30 April 1946 proposal by the Russian delegate General Derevyanko to the third session of the ALLIED COUNCIL FOR JAPAN then led, in a rather rare example of international cooperation, to discussions between Japanese, SCAP bureaucrats, and William MacMahon BALL of Australia, the British Commonwealth representative.

Fully aware from this public debate that there was considerable pressure for nationalization or collectivization rather than merely compensated land purchases and reform, the Japanese government, now under the leadership of Prime Minister YOSHIDA SHIGERU, incorporated the main features of Ball's proposals into its own bill, which passed the Diet over the last flutters of landlord opposition on 21 October 1946.

This second land reform bill permitted the government to buy all the land of absentee landlords, as well as all land which might be cultivated but was not. Landlords resident in villages were permitted to lease small amounts of land, ranging from 0.5 chō (0.5 hectares or 1.2 acres) in Ōsaka Prefecture to an average of 1 chō on the islands of Honshū, Kyūshū, and Shikoku, and an average of 4 chō (4 hectares or 9.9 acres) in Hokkaidō. Such landlords were now forced to grant their tenants substantial contractual rights, to limit their rents to money payments, never more than 25 percent of annual crop values, and to limit the total size of their cultivated and rented land to amounts ranging from 1.8 chō (1.8 hectares or 4.45 acres) in Hiroshima to an average of 12 chō (12 hectares or 29.6 acres) on Hokkaidō. (The average for the three islands of Honshū, Shikoku, and Kyūshū as a whole was 3 chō [3 hectares or 7.41 acres].) Excess land was to be purchased by the state under a complicated price formula based upon 1945 production costs and yields and sold to the tenants for a slightly lower rate on 30-year mortgages bearing 3.2 percent interest.

Enforcement of these complicated regulations was to be on three levels. At the village level, local land commissions determined what lands should be sold to whom and set the purchase price. Each committee consisted of 5 tenants, 3 landlords, and 2 owner-cultivators, elected by their various constituencies, with an optional three additional "learned and experienced" members appointed by the group. Each of Japan's prefectures also had a prefectural land commission of 10 tenants, 6 landlords, and 4 owner-cultivators elected by local commission delegates, plus 5–10 expert members appointed by prefectural authorities. This group set standards for the prefecture (slight variations for total landownership were allowed), heard cases upon appeal, and even ordered new commission elections at the local level. Nationally, a central land commission consisting of 8 tenants, 8 landlords, 2 representatives of national farm organizations, and 5 expert members, all appointed by the minister of agriculture, advised on national policy. All told, some 36,000 paid officials, 115,000 partially paid committee members, and 250,000 hamlet-level volunteers participated in the difficult process of implementation.

Aided in part by a 4 February 1948 SCAP statement which stressed that land reform had become "one of the foremost objectives of the Japanese people as well as the Allied Occupation," land transfers significantly altered economic relationships within rural Japan. The percentage of paddy land owned by the cultivator increased from 55.7 in 1947 to 88.9 in 1949, while the percentage of dry fields increased from 66.5 to 91.2. The percentage of farm families owning more than 90 percent of their lands rose from 36 in 1947 to 62 in 1950 and the percentage of those owning 50–90 percent of their cultivated land rose from 20 to 26. The percentage of tenant farmers owning only 10–50 percent of their land, on the other hand, dropped from 17 in 1947 to 7 in 1950, while the percentage of those families owning less than 10 percent of their land fell most sharply from 27 to 5. These marked changes represented a considerable victory for advocates of a strict land reform program.

The steep inflation that took place during the late 1940s also helped make land reform effective by reducing the actual purchasing power of the 30-year mortgages by 1950 to an estimated 5 percent of annual crop yields. This rapid decline in the nominal value of the mortgages consequently allowed tenants to pay back their obligations with plenty of cash to spare. Landlord objections that the plummeting prices deprived them of their constitutional property rights were rejected by the Japanese Supreme Court in 1953, but the ruling Liberal Democratic Party in 1965 did pass, for obvious political reasons, a ¥145.6 billion (US $404.4 million) measure designed technically to reward landlords for their cooperation rather than concede underpayment. Inflation created new opportunities for social mobility in the countryside, in other words, by taking valuable land from the landlords at exceedingly low prices and all but wiping out debts owed by the poorer former tenants. This helped produce a greater sense of harmony in the villages and a tradition of bloc voting for conservative candidates, a fact which, if it did not exactly fit SCAP's image of the independent yeoman farmer, did at least contribute to making the villages a source of support for private enterprise and market capitalism.

Economically the results were somewhat more controversial. The enthusiasm of the new owner-cultivators and the increased harmony of the villages led to increased uses of advanced technology, a fact which, when combined with the tremendous demand for foodstuffs in a half-starved nation, led to an immediate improvement in the status of a rural population that remained throughout the postwar period at slightly over 5 million families. Critics noted that land reform failed to consolidate widely scattered plots, and they claimed that restrictions on total landownership (some of which were slightly revised in the 1960s) prevented the natural growth of more efficient commercial farm factories. By the 1970s the percentage (as opposed to the number) of farm families had dropped from close to 50 at the close of the war to about 12, and the percentage of farm income, now roughly equal to urban incomes, that came from nonfarm sources was as high as 50. This suggests that industrialism contributed as much as land reform to the postwar prosperity of the farming population.

The land reform of the Allied Occupation of Japan, in sum, was one of the most ambitious and most consistently applied reform policies of the entire period. Popular both because they addressed long-standing social problems and because they benefited far more people than they harmed, the reforms were effectively implemented without violence and carefully maintained throughout the postwar period. The reforms were radical in the sense that they greatly helped many tenant farmers, but they were moderate also both in the ways in which the legislation essentially transferred land titles rather than evict many families from the land and in the political effects of providing a solid base for conservative governments. Ultimately dependent upon industrial policy for their success, the land reform legislation and subsequent implementation stand, nonetheless, as a monument to the Occupation's democratic idealism. See also AGRICULTURE: farmland.

🐟——R. P. Dore, *Land Reform in Japan* (1959). Fukutake Tadashi, *Japanese Rural Society* (1967).   *Peter* FROST

landscape painting, traditional → sansuiga

Land Tax Reform of 1873–1881

(Chiso Kaisei). Thorough revision of the land tax system carried out by the government from 1873 to 1881. One of the most important reforms of the early part of the Meiji period (1868–1912), it was the basis for Japan's subsequent modernization.

The early Meiji government bore heavy financial burdens: it had to finance its developing civil and military administration, and it continued to pay hereditary stipends to *samurai* of the former Tokugawa shogunate (1603–1867). It relied initially on paper money and domestic and foreign loans to supplement ordinary land-tax revenues, but it found that such short-term measures were insufficient. To secure adequate tax revenues and to create a reliable budgetary system, a total reform of the national revenue system was necessary.

The need for some kind of tax reform was widely recognized from the outset. Under the so-called Unequal Treaties (see ANSEI COMMERCIAL TREATIES), which Japan had been forced to sign with foreign powers, protective tariffs were out of the question. Internal tax reform was the only alternative. An increase in internal revenues, including excise taxes and stamp taxes, however, depended on the growing prosperity of domestic commerce and industry, and signs were not encouraging. The only solution seemed to lie in a total reform of the land tax, that is, a nationwide standardization of the land-tax system based on land values and an equalization of its burden.

During the Edo period (1600–1868), lands had been bestowed by the Tokugawa shogunate as fiefs (*chigyō*) upon *daimyō*, who collected dues or taxes in kind from farmers in exchange for the right of land use. The concept of landownership, however, was not exclusive but ambiguous and overlapping. Farmers were allowed to hold lands as long as they paid taxes. Furthermore, in many cases, rich farmers and merchants, who financed reclamation projects or acted as moneylenders, also claimed a share in the produce of the soil. In 1723 the shogunate permitted lands on which mortgages were unpaid to be transferred to creditors, giving them a legal claim on land.

The appearance, during the period, of rich farmers and merchant "landlords" between the daimyō and active cultivators demonstrates that there was a surplus even after feudal taxes and the cultivators' income were taken out. The surplus derived from improvements in agricultural technology and commercial cropping, combined with virtually unchanging tax assessments. But not all farmers benefited equally. "Landlords" tended to hold lightly taxed lands, while poor farmers often held heavily taxed lands. This inequality gives a partial explanation why, in spite of a constant tax burden on the national level, farmers increasingly protested against heavy taxation from the last years of the Tokugawa shogunate up to 1871. Other inequalities derived from differences among domains and from exemptions given by the Tokugawa rulers to certain urban areas, temples, and shrines. Having overthrown the shogunate, the Meiji government saw that it would have to clarify the confusion in Tokugawa landholding customs by establishing single ownership and tax liability for a given piece of land. Once the inequalities were removed, the new government could collect the same amount of taxes justly and without difficulty. Fixed money taxes based on land values would provide a solid financial base.

Ideas for tax reform appeared soon after the Meiji Restoration. They included a proposal for cash payment coupled with a nationwide land survey and a plan for recognizing private ownership of land to enable tax assessment based on market value. The second idea was especially appealing to the new government, for it would enable it to reassess the tax without undertaking a nationwide land survey that might cause peasant unrest. The idea was not feasible, however, since the market value would necessarily reflect the existing inequitable tax assessment, and, furthermore, its nationwide application was almost impossible. MUTSU MUNEMITSU recommended using productivity as the basis for computing land value, but this too was rejected since it would inevitably involve the government in assessment.

Reforms —— On 28 July 1873 the government issued the Land Tax Reform Law. Assuming that levying an amount equal to the total annual tax revenue of the Edo period would not overburden the public, once uniformity and equity were realized, the government decided on a tax rate of 3 percent of the land value for land tax and 1 percent of land value for local surtax, that is, 34 percent of the total annual yield. Evaluation of land was left to the landowners, who were instructed to follow the "Examples for Investigation" of the Land Tax Reform Law and submit a figure for approval. According to the "Examples," the yield of 1 tan (roughly 0.10 hectare or 0.25 acre) of land was calculated first in terms of a cash equivalent. From this gross amount, the cost of seeds and fertilizer (15 percent of the value of gross output), the land tax (3 percent of the land value), and the local surtax (one-third of the land tax) were deducted, and the remainder was divided by a fixed rate (6 to 7 percent for owner-cultivated land and 4 to 5 percent for tenant land). For land held by owner-cultivators, the entire yield was directly computed in terms of cash. For land held by tenants, the rent paid in kind (68 percent of the entire yield) was the basis for the calculation. The prices of crops were generally established at prevailing local rates. The farmers' evaluations were accepted if they were less than 10 percent below official calculations. Thus, the amount of tax levied was established on the basis of a predetermined budget, rather than vice versa.

Rational as the law might have seemed, its actual application required amendments. Article 8 added to the Land Tax Reform Law (12 May 1874) established that the land value determined at the time of the reform would be the official value for tax assessment, irrespective of subsequent changes in market values. The government ordered the initial values frozen for five years.

To overcome delays in valuation, the government also resorted to more high-handed methods. A proviso to article 7 (7 October 1875) threatened to apply the old crop-yield inspection method to lands for which landowners submitted unacceptable values. Since the area of many of these landholdings had been enlarged by the new land surveys, the old method would have meant heavier burdens. This method proved impractical, and the so-called Proclamation 68 was issued (12 May 1876), stipulating that disputed land values should follow those of neighboring lands for which official values had already been fixed.

A Land Tax Reform Agency was established to implement the reform. Land grading was to be put into practice from the prefectural level on down to individual plots of land. Based on productivity and geographical convenience, grading would be decided by the concerned personnel at each level. To help expedite matters, the model village method was widely adopted in the later projects. The grading system contributed greatly to balancing different areas and speeding up the reform as well as providing an apparatus through which the estimated land values could be apportioned. Local impositions were estimated by the agency, taking into account averages of former taxes, results of local inspections, and projections of population and food consumption. The estimates were not firm but were adjusted as the projects advanced, though the range of adjustment was small.

Most of the projects were completed in eight years, a short period considering the magnitude of the tasks and the conditions of the time. The Meiji government had succeeded in realizing its goals: to collect a fixed money tax based on land value from newly certified owners; to assess equitable tax liabilities on all private land; and to assure regular tax revenues, the annual amount equal to the yearly aggregate sum of taxes collected during the Edo period. In order to attain these goals local customs and practices had been disregarded. Toward the end of 1876 rural uprisings increased, and these, coupled with rebellions by former samurai in several regions, persuaded the government to make compromises. On 4 January 1877 the government reduced the 3-percent land tax and 1-percent local surtax to 2.5 percent and 0.5 percent respectively.

In absolute terms, however, it did not lighten the tax burden on the farmers. In fact, the burden was heavier if we consider that rice prices under the deflationary MATSUKATA FISCAL POLICY (1881–85) were not at all advantageous to small farmers. Nevertheless, farmers' incomes did increase because of the spread of commercial crops, more efficient agricultural techniques, and new by-employments, making the burden of fixed taxes a relatively smaller portion of total income.

Results —— What did the Land Tax Reform achieve? First, taxes were equalized, but landholdings were not. Holders of small plots still did not have enough to live on after taxes. Second, since under the new system taxes were fixed in cash, farmers had to borrow money at high rates of interest in bad years or when the price of rice was extremely low. This forced small landowners to sell their rice as soon as it was harvested, when the market price was lowest; rich landowners could afford to wait for the price to rise. Third, although poor farmers made gains from the inflation after 1878 and taxes became a declining portion of income as the price of a koku (1 koku = 180 liters or 5 US bushels) of rice rose from ¥6.22 (1878) to ¥10.20 (1880), yet during the deflationary period of the early 1880s the price dropped from ¥11.40 (1881) to ¥5.74 (1886), reversing the earlier trend. Many were unable to pay their taxes, and lands were confiscated in lieu of tax payments. Together with an increase in debt and mortgage foreclosures, this resulted in a noticeable rise in tenancy, a trend that continued until the early 1920s. The fixed money tax was not solely responsible for this trend; economic conditions were so harsh during the 1880s, for example, that many small landowners were forced into tenancy. Since the Land Tax Reform allowed free transaction of land and did not modify the existing tenancy system where rent was still paid in kind, land purchase became a convenient means to profit. From the beginning, when ownership was generally settled in favor of the old claimant, the reform paved the way legally for an expanding landlord system.

The Land Tax Reform was successful in providing the national government with a solid financial base. Until 1887 more than 60 percent of the nation's revenue derived from land taxes. The reform also supplied the institutional means to divert the wealth of the rich farmers from agriculture into other sectors of the economy. Land could be mortgaged as private property, furnishing valuable capital for industrial enterprises. The Land Tax Reform thus provided the financial and institutional basis for the initial stages of Japan's transition into a modern nation.

Yongdeok KIM

Lansing–Ishii Agreement

(Ishii–Ranshingu Kyōtei). The name commonly given to the diplomatic notes exchanged on 2 November 1917 in which Japan and the United States enunciated the principles that were to guide their conduct in dealings with a China torn by war and revolution. In the published texts, ISHII KIKUJIRŌ, the distinguished career diplomat who led a special mission to the United States, and Secretary of State Robert LANSING affirmed the intent of their two nations to uphold a basic principle of the OPEN DOOR POLICY—to respect China's independence and its territorial and administrative integrity. The American government also professed to recognize that "territorial propinquity creates special relations between countries and consequently . . . that Japan has special interests in China, especially the part to which her possessions are contiguous." Finally, in a secret protocol that was attached to the public notes, the two governments agreed not to take "advantage of the present [World War I] conditions to seek special rights or privileges in China which would abridge the rights of the subjects or citizens of other friendly states."

These products of some two months of high-level talks were presented to the world as evidence of an understanding that laid to rest an increasingly troublesome Japanese-American rivalry over China. The hard fact, however, was that the notes were filled with ambiguities and therefore offered no far-reaching solutions. In April 1923, following still another definition of international conduct in the NINE-POWER TREATY (signed in Washington, 6 February 1922), Japan and the United States agreed to annul the Lansing–Ishii Agreement.

The Lansing–Ishii negotiations were unquestionably important as a temporary measure, helping to maintain harmony among members of the coalition at war with the Central Powers. Since the 1890s Japanese-American amity had been threatened by the collision of expansionist ambitions: Japanese immigrants had moved eastward to Hawaii and California, where they encountered racial discrimination; both nations had vied for insular empires in the Pacific basin; and finally, in China, where an ancient order was disintegrating and the search for a new nationalism had begun, Japanese and Americans had been at cross-purposes as they pursued policies that promised to influence China's future. The clash in China became particularly intense from 1914 onward, when the outbreak of World War I removed virtually all European opposition to Japanese expansion into China and left the United States as the only power that might check the Japanese. These new circumstances in fact had increased tensions as American officials interpreted Japan's seizure of German holdings in Shandong (see SHANDONG [SHANTUNG] QUESTION) and its TWENTY-ONE DEMANDS on China as evidence that the Japanese were determined to capitalize on an opportunity to reduce China to puppet status. On their side, the Japanese were alarmed by America's quick recognition of the newly established Chinese republic in 1913, its aid to the government of Yuan Shikai (Yüan Shih-k'ai) during the Twenty-One Demands crisis, and its efforts to spur American investment in China. These suggested to the Japanese an American determination to capture China's emerging nationalism and to direct it against Japan. Thus, when the United States entered World War I in 1917, both nations were ensnarled in recriminatory exchanges that imperiled their partnership against the Central Powers. In the short run, the Lansing–Ishii Agreement, which, by being worded so as to conceal differences and by being presented as an "agreement," had the effect of easing tensions and enabling the two governments to continue the war.

Historians, however, have generally agreed that the Lansing–Ishii Agreement was a landmark in Japanese and American relations, one that stood above wartime expedients. For a time, during the years between World Wars I and II, the agreement seemed important because it spoke to the continuing Japanese and American duel over China. Did the American recognition that Japan had "special interests in China" encourage Japanese expansionists? Or, alternatively, did Japan's pledges to uphold the Open Door policy and to forswear opportunities that were presented by war to advance in China weaken the legality of its expansionist claims? In general, American historians emphasized the importance of the pledges extracted from Japan, saying that, although the United States might have been unable to devise any immediate measures to check Japanese expansionism, the reiteration of the Open Door pledges denied Japan's empire builders international approval of their actions in China. Thinking along these lines prompted American, but not Japanese, historians to applaud the Wilson administration for its achievements.

In recent years, especially since the full diplomatic archives began to open in the 1950s, the histories of American-Japanese relations have tended to be more critical of the Lansing–Ishii Agreement. The once confidential records indicated that within Japan and the United States there were to be found important economic and political forces working toward a solution of difficulties between the two nations. Moreover, as these records made clear, both Ishii and Lansing were personally committed to capitalizing on these forces by striking a bargain wherein the United States would have conceded Japan's claims to exclusive privileges in Manchuria in return for Japanese pledges to treat the remainder of China as an area where no new special privileges would be sought. Lansing also would have had Japan forswear further complaints against American treatment of Japanese residing in the United States. Here was a possible compromise that provided Chinese nationalism with some safeguards against new foreign encroachment, one that promised to ease racial tensions, and one that held potential for ending increasingly dangerous rivalries. When possibilities for a settlement were weighed against the ambiguities embodied in the notes that were actually exchanged, historians were more inclined than they once had been to question the wisdom of two nations' having settled for the limited accomplishments of the Lansing–Ishii Agreement. Perhaps the bargain that Ishii and Lansing wished to strike would have failed to alter the course of East Asia's international relations. Yet, it was said, none of the interested parties would have suffered from the attempt. Viewed in this way, the Lansing–Ishii Agreement was a monument to a missed opportunity.

■————Burton F. Beers, *Vain Endeavor: Robert Lansing's Attempts to End the American-Japanese Rivalry* (1962). Roy W. Curry, *Woodrow Wilson and Far Eastern Policy, 1913–1921* (1957).

Burton F. BEERS

Lansing, Robert (1864–1928)

A noted American specialist in international law, Lansing was appointed by President Woodrow Wilson to the Department of State as counselor (legal adviser) in 1914 and as secretary of state in 1915. The president envisioned Lansing's functioning in these positions mostly as a legal technician, a man who could put diplomatic notes in order. Lansing, however, became an influential policy adviser. In an era of American-Japanese tensions, he was to be a key figure in the search for more amicable relations. The LANSING–ISHII AGREEMENT, the highly publicized negotiations of 1917 through which Japan and the United States professed to have resolved their differences, is probably the episode in East Asian affairs that has been most closely associated with his name.

Lansing's public stance on questions relating to American-Japanese relations frequently differed from the one that he took within the privacy of the Wilson administration's policy debates. Like another key presidential adviser, Edward M. House, Lansing believed that Japan was rapidly emerging as the leading power in East Asia and that the United States would be well advised to come to terms with that country. In pursuing this idea, Lansing clashed with the president, who had become a champion of Chinese nationalism. Lansing was determined, however, that Japan's growing influence should be directed toward economic expansion rather than toward militarism and territorial empire. To this end he secretly advocated during his first years in the Department of State a compromise settlement wherein the United States would recognize Japan's claims to a special position in Manchuria in return for explicit Japanese pledges to respect the territorial and administrative integrity of the remainder of China and to accede to American treatment of Japanese residing in the United States. Later, having become convinced that Japan's military was gaining undue influence in the conduct of Japanese foreign policy and that this influence was behind efforts to enlarge Japan's empire, Lansing became an unyielding opponent of Japan's imperial designs. At the Paris Peace Conference (1919) he urged Wilson to risk Japan's withdrawal from the proceedings rather than accede to its demands that its prior acquisition of German privileges in Shandong (Shantung) be formally recognized. Lansing's shifting strategies were intended to strengthen those Japanese who advocated international cooperation and to embarrass Japanese militarists, whom he identified as the chief proponents of empire-building. But in taking both of these stands, Lansing found himself at cross-purposes with Wilson. Wilson first rejected Lansing's proposed bargain, because Lansing suggested it at a time when it seemed to threaten the president's plan to help China. He later rejected Lansing's plea for a firm stand on the SHANDONG (SHANTUNG) QUESTION, because it would rob the League of Nations of Japanese support. Thus, Lansing lost key battles to change the direction of Japanese-American relations. His efforts to effect a change, however, continue to attract the attention of historians. Between 1914 and 1919, American policy toward Japan was indecisive, mixing conciliatory gestures with threats. Historians have found in the policy disputes of the president and the secretary a key explanation of the zigzags in American policy. Moreover, historians have employed the differing approaches of Lansing and Wilson in their assessments of American policy. They have asked which approach—Lansing's or Wilson's—would have best served the cause of peace in East Asia.

Burton F. BEERS

lanterns

(*tōrō*). The lantern, originating from an Indian prototype, was introduced to Japan along with Buddhism in the 6th century. The most distinctive form of Japanese lantern is the *ishi-dōrō*, or stone lantern, which is used widely on the grounds of temples and shrines and as a garden ornament. It is said that the oldest stone lantern in Japan was erected in AD 594 at a Buddhist temple built for Prince SHŌTOKU. Large numbers of such stone lanterns can be seen in the sacred precincts of Buddhist and Shintō sanctuaries. The most famous of these are the 2,000 *ishi-dōrō* lining the approaches of the KASUGA SHRINE in Nara, which are lighted twice a year, in February and in the middle of August. The secular use of such lanterns dates from the Azuchi-Momoyama period (1568–1600), when masters of the TEA CEREMONY began to use them to ornament tea gardens.

Ishi-dōrō are usually made of granite or syenite. They come in many different sizes and shapes, with different types named after the place where they are located or the individual who designed them. The usual height of these lanterns is 2 meters (6.5 ft), but smaller ones may be used to light footpaths or for decoration. Garden lanterns are intended to blend with their setting and are located near trees or shrubs; they are often placed near a lake or river so that they may cast a reflection on the water. Stone lanterns should have an aged appearance; weathered examples with lichen or green moss growing on them are particularly admired and much sought after. There are at least three main types: tall, slender ones with a hexagonal lamp chamber and a rounded, hexagonal roof tilted at the eaves; short, broad ones with mushroom tops, often resting on four legs; and some, consisting of a number of separate sections, resembling a small pagoda. All have a hollowed-out upper section to contain a candle or lamp that is lighted on special occasions.

Bronze or iron *tōrō* are also widespread. The most famous of these is the octagonal bronze lantern in front of the main hall of the temple TŌDAIJI in Nara. It dates from the Nara period (710–794), is 4 meters (13 ft) high, and is decorated with beautiful, pierced metal carvings in low relief. Hanging lanterns, which are usually made of bronze, are called *tsuri-dōrō*; there are some one thousand hanging-metal lanterns on the precincts of the Kasuga Shrine.

Smaller standing lanterns, usually made of iron, are known as *andon*. *Andon* became popular during the Edo period (1600–1868) for interior illumination, especially within the home. They usually rest on four legs and have cut-out designs decorating their sides; the finest are much admired today and are eagerly collected by folk arts connoisseurs.

Andon come in many different shapes and sizes and serve a decorative as well as utilitarian function. Some *andon* are made of paper with a rigid wooden frame and open top. These usually contained lamps burning rapeseed oil or candles; the modern version is often wired for electricity. One of their most attractive features is the oil plate (*aburazara*) designed to catch the dripping oil; these are often decorated with beautiful pictorial designs and are highly valued today.

The *bombori* is a portable lantern, though some are used as permanent fixtures in the home; it has a pole attached horizontally at the base of the lamp by which it can be carried. The distinctive feature of the *bombori* is its hexagonal shade, often made of a delicate structure of wood or metal backed with paper or glass.

The paper lanterns used outside of the house are known as *chōchin*. They are suspended from the eaves of a building, often a house or restaurant, or are carried in processions to light the way at night. Their frame is a collapsible structure of bamboo strips formed into a spiral shape with a tough paper covering. A candle is placed inside. *Chōchin* come in a variety of shapes and colors and are often decorated with crests, inscriptions, or names of restaurants or inns. Plain white was avoided because of the association with Buddhist funerals. One especially prized local specialty is the Gifu *chōchin*, made with very fine paper delicately painted with flowers and grasses.

📖 ——Edward Morse, *Japanese Houses and Their Surroundings* (1886).

Hugo MÜNSTERBERG

LARA

(Licensed Agencies for Relief in Asia). A group of American private charitable and religious agencies that contributed food, clothing, medical supplies, and other relief items to Japan and other Asian nations after World War II. LARA was organized in 1946, after permission had been granted by SCAP (Supreme Commander for the Allied Powers), to help alleviate Japan's critical shortage of food and other necessities. By 1950 it had contributed to Japan 9,486 metric tons (10,456 short tons) of supplies worth $6.5 million.

Richard B. FINN

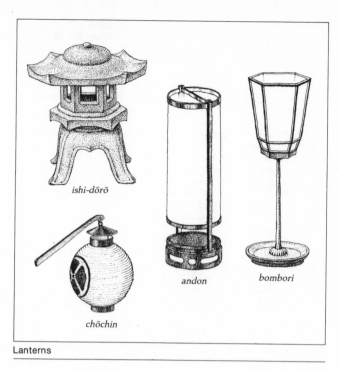

Lanterns

larch, Japanese

(*karamatsu*). *Larix leptolepis*. A deciduous tree of the family Pinaceae which grows wild in volcanic regions of central Japan, especially at the foot of Mt. Fuji (Fujisan), and is also planted widely. The tree sometimes attains a height of 30 meters (98 ft) and has a conical crown. The needles are bright green, 3 centimeters (1 in) long, and grow in clusters of 20 to 30 on short branches. Unlike the needles of most other conifers, they turn a brilliant yellow color and are shed in late autumn. It is prized for logs because of its straight trunk. The wood is hard and straight but is easy to split and resists water well and thus is often used in construction, and for tools and pulp. The bark serves as the source of a dye and the resin as material for turpentine.

In the United States it is prized as an ornamental tree, and a short subspecies (*L. leptolepis* var. *minor*) has been developed. Another subspecies with golden-variegated leaves (*L. leptolepis* var. *murrayana*) was developed in Germany.

MATSUDA Osamu

larks

(*hibari*). In Japanese, *hibari* is the general name for small birds of the family Alaudidae. It is also used specifically for the skylark (*Alauda arvensis*). This bird is about 17 centimeters (7 in) in length, colored golden brown with vertical black stripes on the breast and back. It has a small crest and long-clawed hind toes. The bird resides in meadows and fields throughout Japan north from Kyūshū, but those living in the northernmost areas or regions of deep snow migrate to warmer areas in the autumn. Its nest is built on the ground among grasses; the male declares his territorial rights by singing while flying for long periods over his domain. Widely distributed through central Eurasia, the family Alaudidae also includes in Japan the *hamahibari* (shore lark or horned lark; *Eremophila alpestris*) and the *himekōtenshi* (short-toed lark; *Calandrella cinerea*).

TAKANO Shinji

The song of the lark has been loved and celebrated since ancient times in Japan. Larks were also prized as pets, and there was a type of amusement called *agehibari* in which tame larks were released and their owners watched to see how long they would sing in flight and which bird would return most quickly to its cage after descending.

SANEYOSHI Tatsuo

Later Three Years' War

(Gosannen no Eki). Military campaign in which MINAMOTO NO YOSHIIE subdued the fractious Kiyohara family of northeastern Japan between 1083 and 1087; only three of these years saw actual fighting. The Kiyohara were hereditary commanders in Dewa Province (now Akita and Yamagata prefectures) who had helped court forces to crush ABE NO SADATŌ in the EARLIER NINE YEARS' WAR (1051–62), thus becoming masters of Mutsu Province (now Aomori, Iwate, Miyagi, and Fukushima prefectures) as well. Armed conflict arose among branches of the family and by the 1080s was seriously disrupting the region. In 1083 Yoshiie became governor of Mutsu and commander of court forces in the northeast. Though not supported by the court, he intervened and ultimately put an end to the violence. The principal events of the war are dramatically depicted in a 14th-century scroll, *Gosannen kassen ekotoba,* preserved in the Tōkyō National Museum. Through this victory, Yoshiie created a strong Minamoto power base in eastern Japan.

G. Cameron HURST III

lathes → rokuro

Latin America and Japan

Many scholars hold that the Japanese and the indigenous peoples of the Americas share a prehistoric racial origin and perhaps had contact in ancient times; however, the first historical record of contact dates from the 16th century, when a number of trans-Pacific voyages occurred. Later, after the 1870s, large numbers of Japanese emigrated to Latin America, and in the 20th century Japanese investments and developmental assistance in the region have been significant.

Premodern Relations——The indigenous population of the American continent are believed by some to be descendants of paleolithic hunters who migrated from northeastern Asia across the Bering Strait, which was a land bridge in the glacial age at the end of the Pleistocene period. Clifford Evans has advanced the theory that pottery made during the middle of the Jōmon period (ca 10,000 BC–300 BC) in Japan found its way into Valdivian culture in Ecuador during the formative period of prehistory. Furuta Takehiko has conjectured that the Kokushikoku ("country of black-toothed people") mentioned in the chapter about Japan in the Chinese historical work WEI ZHI *(Wei chih),* compiled in the 3rd century, refers to a region on the Pacific seaboard of South America.

The first positive proof of contact between Japan and Latin America dates from the latter half of the 16th century when a sea route between Acapulco in Nueva España (Mexico) and the Philippines was established. When the Spanish founded the city of Manila in 1571, it was noted that there were approximately 20 Japanese living in the area. The number of Japanese increased rapidly in the following years and, according to research conducted by Iwao Seiichi, a NIHOMMACHI (Japanese town) with a population of 3,000 existed early in the 17th century. Thus, a large number of Japanese were exposed to products and information from Nueva España. In 1592, the national unifier TOYOTOMI HIDEYOSHI dispatched a merchant, HARADA MAGOSHICHIRŌ, to Manila to urge the Spanish colony to pay tribute; this marked the commencement of official negotiations between Japan and Spain.

TOKUGAWA IEYASU, the founder of the Tokugawa shogunate (1603–1867), also held negotiations several times with the governor of Manila and the viceroy of Nueva España, expressing his hope that Spanish galleons would stop at Japanese ports in the Kantō region. It was in 1608 that the first Spanish ship cast anchor in the port of Uraga. Ieyasu hoped to establish trade with Nueva España and to import mining technology. In 1609 the vessel carrying Rodrigo VIVERO DE VELASCO, the governor ad interim of Manila, was shipwrecked on its way to Acapulco, and Vivero landed at Iwada, Kazusa Province (now part of Chiba Prefecture). He was treated kindly by Ieyasu, who provided a 120-ton sailing ship on which the governor continued his voyage in 1610. Aboard the ship were more than 20 Japanese, including Tanaka Katsusuke, a merchant of Kyōto. When the *daimyō* DATE MASAMUNE dispatched HASEKURA TSUNENAGA to the Vatican in 1613, Tsunenaga's ship also carried some 140 Japanese to Acapulco. The same ship returned to Uraga carrying a Spanish mission, dispatched by Filipe III, to Ieyasu and his son Hidetada. When it sailed again for Acapulco in 1616, 200 Japanese, including the merchant Minakawa Yogorō, were on board. Historical evidence of Japanese settlements from the 16th and 17th centuries has been discovered in Mexico, Argentina, and Peru.

In 1624, with the adoption of the NATIONAL SECLUSION policy by the Tokugawa shogunate, relations between Japan and Spain, as well as other countries, were severed. Nonetheless, quite accurate information about various regions of the American continent was available during the Edo period (1600–1868) through such geographical studies as NISHIKAWA JOKEN's *Zōho kai tsūshō kō* (1709), ARAI HAKUSEKI's *Sairan igen* (1713), and YAMAMURA SAISUKE's *Teisei zōyaku sairan igen* (1802). There were also reports of Japanese drifting ashore in Latin America. Reports of the crew of the *Eiju maru* of Nishinomiya, Hyōgo, who were shipwrecked and landed in Mexico in 1841, were published upon their return as *Aboku shingo* and *Tōkō kibun.* These are considered the first written Japanese accounts of Latin America.

Relations Since 1868——A great number of independent nations had been established in Latin America by the time the Meiji government was formed in 1868. Of these, Peru was the first to have formal diplomatic ties with Japan. In July 1872, when the Peruvian ship *Maria Luz* on its way back from China docked in the port of Yokohama for repairs, two of the Chinese coolies who were being transported escaped. The Japanese government intervened and helped to negotiate the freeing of some 200 coolies on board (see MARIA LUZ INCIDENT). The Peruvian government dispatched Aurelio Garcia y Garcia to negotiate with the Japanese in the wake of the incident. Such negotiations led to a treaty of amity, commerce, and navigation, which was signed on 19 June 1873. A similar treaty was concluded with Mexico in 1887, which is remembered as the first "equal" treaty Japan signed. Japan later established diplomatic relations with Brazil (1895), Argentina (1898), Panama (1904), Chile (1906), and Colombia (1908). During the Sino-Japanese War of 1894–95, Japan purchased the battleship *Esmeralda* from Chile.

The most important aspect of relations between Japan and Latin America prior to World War II was that of Japanese emigration. The earliest emigrants went to Guatemala in 1893 and to Guadeloupe in 1896, but both ventures proved failures. The first Japanese emigration to Mexico began in 1897 when a contingent went to the state of Chiapas. Emigration to Peru began in 1899 through the efforts of Tanaka Teikichi, and some of the emigrants moved on to Brazil and Bolivia. Mass emigration to Brazil started in 1908. The number of Japanese who emigrated to Latin America from the early Meiji period until 1945 totaled approximately 244,000, of which 189,000 (about 77 percent) went to Brazil and 33,000 (about 13 percent) to Peru.

Practically all of the countries of Latin America sided with the Allies during World War II, although actual battles between them and Japan did not occur. When the SAN FRANCISCO PEACE TREATY came into effect in 1952, diplomatic ties were restored and Japanese emigration resumed. More than 80,000 Japanese emigrated to Latin America between then and 1980, more than 80 percent of whom went to Brazil. Other countries to which a large number of Japanese emigrants went after the war were Paraguay, the Dominican Republic, Bolivia, and Argentina; emigration to some countries, Peru, for example, became difficult because of strict entry limitations. By 1980, there were approximately 750,000 Japanese and people of Japanese ancestry living in Latin America.

Economic Relations——Economic relations between Japan and Latin America have flourished since 1945. Before the war, North America dominated trade with Latin America, with Japan accounting for a mere 1 percent of the region's total trade. However, since the war, paralleling the expansion of the Japanese economy, this figure has increased to between 3 and 7 percent. The Latin American share of Japanese trade in the 1970s was 3 to 5 percent of imports and 6 to 9 percent of exports. These figures are not high but are expected to rise with growing Japanese demand for raw materials. Particularly in regard to primary products, for example, oil from Mexico and other countries, Japan anticipates heavy reliance on Latin America. Direct Japanese capital investments in Latin America between 1951 and 1978 totaled $4.3 billion. By region, 28.6 percent of Japan's total overseas investments were in Asia, 25.2 in North America, and 16.3 in Latin America. Japanese economic development aid is small compared with investments by private enterprises, in part because the level of economic development in Latin America is higher than that in Asia and Africa. However, of total Japanese aid between 1960 and 1978, 27.9 percent went to Southeast Asia and 26.6 to Latin America.

Relations between Japan and Latin America are becoming closer, and the exchange of culture and technology is on the increase. The study of Japan has been initiated in Mexico, Brazil, Peru, and elsewhere, while Latin American studies have commenced in several universities and research institutes in Japan. The Japan Association for Latin American Studies was established in June 1980. See also SPAIN AND JAPAN; BRAZIL AND JAPAN; BRAZIL, JAPANESE IMMIGRANTS IN; PERU AND JAPAN; MEXICO AND JAPAN.

———Charles Boxer, *The Christian Century in Japan* (1967). Lothar Knauth, *Confrontacion Transpacifica* (1972).

MASUDA Yoshio

Laurel, José Paciano (1891–1959)

President of the Republic of the Philippines during the Japanese occupation and an influential politician in the post-World War II period. Born in Batangas, Luzon, on 9 March 1891. After studying law at Yale University, he served as secretary of the interior, senator, delegate to the Philippine Constitutional Convention of 1935, and associate justice of the Supreme Court of the Commonwealth Government. Practicing and teaching law intermittently, he formed connections with the local Japanese community, many of whom were his clients, in the years before World War II.

During the Japanese occupation (1942–45), Laurel was made president of an "independent" Republic of the Philippines, the existence of which he proclaimed on 14 October 1943. His cautious collaboration with the Japanese served substantially to relieve Filipino hardship. Laurel left the Philippines in March 1945 with his family and a few cabinet members to live in exile in Nara, Japan. He was arrested by the Allied authorities in September and subsequently confined as a war criminal in Sugamo prison. After his repatriation on 23 July 1946, he successfully defended himself against a charge of treason at the People's Court and in January 1948 was granted complete amnesty by President Manuel Roxas. Laurel ran in the 1949 presidential election, losing narrowly to President Quirino, but two years later was elected to the senate. He and other members of his family contributed much to Japanese-Philippine relations and were instrumental in helping to bring about such agreements as the reparations agreement and the Treaty of Amity, Commerce, and Navigation between the two countries. His second son, José S. Laurel, Jr, who was educated at a Japanese military academy, is a former ambassador to Japan. See also PHILIPPINES AND JAPAN.

YOSHIKAWA Yōko

Laures, Johannes (1891–1959)

German scholar and Jesuit missionary who wrote widely about the early Christian mission in 16th- and 17th-century Japan. Born at Fleringen in the Rhineland, he entered the Society of Jesus in 1913. After receiving his doctorate at Columbia University, he joined the staff of Jōchi Daigaku (Sophia University), Tōkyō, in 1928 and worked in Japan for the rest of his life. Laures wrote extensively about the early Japanese Christians, particularly TAKAYAMA UKON and HOSOKAWA GRACIA. He made a special study of the JESUIT MISSION PRESS, and his *Kirishitan Bunko: A Manual of Books and Documents on the Early Christian Mission in Japan* (1940; rev ed, 1941, 1957) remains the standard reference work on the subject.

Michael COOPER

Laurilignosa culture → shōyō jurin bunka

laver → nori

law → legal system

law, attitudes toward

There is a widespread belief that Japanese dislike litigation and prefer less formal means of dispute resolution. The belief is based on the low litigation rate in Japan and the persistence of traditional Japanese attitudes said to be antithetical to the processes of a modern legal system. Part of this interpretation of Japanese attitudes is the assumption that Japanese will begin to use litigation more frequently as traditional concepts of proper behavior erode and are replaced with modern values more similar to those of the West. This belief in what is often termed the "low legal consciousness" of the Japanese has been challenged in recent years, however, by conflicting interpretations of the causes for the relatively infrequent use of the courts and the correspondingly heavy dependence on nonjudicial modes of dispute resolution.

If one were to construct a hierarchy of Japanese means for dealing with social conflict, it is true that litigation would rank fairly low statistically. The use of mediation and CONCILIATION, both involving the relatively informal intervention by a third party into a dispute, is much more common and preferred by many Japanese to litigation. The Japanese have often been said to possess an aversion to open hostility and a corresponding desire for the preservation of social harmony which would be perceived as shattered by the spectacle of a public trial. The concept of harmony and the importance of submission to social superiors in Confucian philosophy is cited as both evidence and cause for these attitudes, as are the economic and social patterns of the traditional Japanese village, with its basis in the cooperative spirit necessary for wet rice cultivation.

Although the low litigation rates are generally attributed to relatively immutable cultural factors, this interpretation is not universally accepted. Conscious government policies to discourage litigation have worked to reinforce these traditions and may be the real cause for the prevalence of informal means of dispute resolution. These policies include maintaining the number of lawyers and judges at an extremely low level, so that litigation is both expensive and time consuming, while simultaneously establishing administrative alternatives to litigation, such as the laws passed in the 1970s providing for the administrative compensation of pollution victims and for institutionalized, publicly funded mediation and conciliation of pollution disputes, which tend to direct potential litigants away from the courts.

Whether to attribute the predominance of extrajudicial, informal means of dispute resolution in Japan to unique cultural factors or to institutional factors, consciously adopted by a government politically wary of an expansion of private litigation, is perhaps a false dichotomy. Presumably the two forces complement each other, and as long as the government maintains the objective barriers to litigation, the traditional perspective will be strengthened. What remains to be seen, however, is whether the government will be universally successful. Although litigation rates in general show no significant increase in recent years, there has been an increase in politically sensitive litigation, particularly in the environmental and consumer fields, that may indicate a new inclination, at least within certain social groups, to use litigation despite the considerable obstacles. These cases, however, have not as yet been shown to be evidence of a general shift in Japanese attitudes toward law. See also DISPUTE RESOLUTION SYSTEMS OTHER THAN LITIGATION; JUDICIAL SYSTEM; LAWYERS; LEGAL EDUCATION.

———John O. Haley, "The Myth of the Reluctant Litigant," *Journal of Japanese Studies* 4.2 (1978). Dan F. Henderson, *Conciliation and Japanese Law: Tokugawa and Modern* (1965). Kawashima Takeyoshi, *Nipponjin no hōishiki* (1967).

Frank K. UPHAM

Law concerning the Control of Important Industries

(Jūyō Sangyō Tōsei Hō, or more correctly, Jūyō Sangyō no Tōsei ni Kansuru Hō). Enforced by the HAMAGUCHI OSACHI cabinet in 1931, this law legitimized government control over private cartels. Its aim was to encourage monopolization of important industries (more than 20 altogether, including the textile industry) in order to help the economy recover from the world economic crisis of the early 1930s (see SHŌWA DEPRESSION). It placed restrictions on cartel activities that might "threaten economic activity as a whole and general public welfare," but at the same time it imposed on noncartel enterprises the obligation to abide by cartel agreements. It paved the way for the growth of cartels with state sanction, close cooperation between big business and government, and eventual state control of the economy. Revised and strengthened in 1936, it was voided in 1941 with the full-scale mobilization of the economy for World War II.

law examination

(shihō shiken). A national examination under the direction of the Shihōshiken Kanri Iinkai (Law Examination Control Committee) of the Ministry of Justice, designed to select those with legal knowledge and ability to apply legal principles appropriate to service as judge, public prosecutor, or practicing lawyer. The *shihō shiken* is open to university graduates, university students credited with general education subjects at a university, and all other persons who wish to take it. The test consists of a first and a second examination. Applicants in the first and second categories above are exempt from the first examination, but those in the third category must pass it before they may apply for the second examination. The first examination covers one foreign language and general education subjects; the level of the test is equivalent to that of the general education curriculum at a university. The second examination is comprised of a multiple-choice test, an essay examination, and an oral test. It is necessary to pass the first test before taking the second; on passing the latter, one is qualified to appear for the oral test which may be attempted twice. The second examination centers on legal subjects like constitutional law, civil law, criminal law, commercial law, civil or criminal procedure law, labor law, and criminology. For the essay and oral tests an additional subject must be selected from among cognate disciplines like economics, psychology, and social policy.

In 1979 there were 28,622 applicants for the second examination, of which 4,167 (14 percent) passed the multiple-choice test, 534 (12 percent) the essay test, and 503 (94 percent of the latter group) the final examination. The final success rate was only 1.7 percent, and the median age of the successful candidates 27.9 years (the youngest was 20 and the oldest 60), much higher than the usual graduation age of 22 to 23 in university law departments. This age disparity is partly a result of the organization of law departments, which are designed to give students only a basic knowledge of law appropriate to careers as generalist government officials, business executives, etc., but not as members of the legal profession. In fact, many law graduates never attempt the examination or, having once failed, choose not to try again. To fill the gap between law department curricula and bar examination content, preparatory study groups affiliated with law departments and private preparatory schools have been established. Under such circumstances, the two-year period of special study at the LEGAL TRAINING AND RESEARCH INSTITUTE (Shihō Kenshūjo) of the Supreme Court that is required of all successful examination candidates is indispensable to preparation for a professional legal career.   *NAGASHIMA Atsushi*

law of evidence

(shōkohō). In Japan, as in most modern nations, it is a fundamental legal principle in the conduct of trials that findings of fact must be based on evidence (principle of trial by evidence). In a criminal trial, the existence and scope of the right to impose punishment is based on findings of the fact constituting the offense, which findings are in turn based on evidence. Such evidence must be both admissible and taken in accordance with the procedures prescribed by law. The evaluation of the probative force of the evidence is left to the free determination of the judge, who is the finder of fact (the principle of free evaluation of evidence). The only exception to this principle is in the case of a defendant's CONFESSION, where there may be no finding of guilt unless there is corroborative evidence. In this case, the principle of evidence required by law (as a prerequisite to the finding of a certain fact) applies. As a general rule, the burden of proving guilt rests unilaterally on the public prosecutor.

The most important of the rules of evidence are the restrictions on admissibility. With regard to testimonial proof, there are such restrictions as the following. (1) There is recognized a right to refuse to testify on grounds of self-incrimination or because testimony would incriminate certain relatives, as well as a right on the part of a doctor, lawyer, or the like to refuse to testify with regard to confidences relating to their professional duties. Therefore, testimony obtained in violation of these rights is not admissible. (2) Involuntary confessions are not admissible. (3) Hearsay evidence is, as a general rule, inadmissible. The rules relating to confessions and hearsay have been imported from the Anglo-American legal system, but liberal exceptions not seen in England or America are recognized in Japan, especially with regard to the hearsay rule.

With regard to nontestimonial proof, there is a right to refuse to allow seizure of evidence on the grounds that it contains official or business secrets, and evidence obtained in violation of this right is not admissible. With regard to certain other items of evidence, case law recognizes the rule of exclusion of illegally obtained evidence where there has been a major violation of law in the gathering of such evidence, and such exclusion is deemed necessary in order to restrain future violations.

In civil cases, too, findings are made as a rule on the basis of evidence. However, because there are no strict limitations on admissibility, as in the case of a criminal trial, and because of the principle of the adversary system, there is no need for substantiation if there is no dispute between parties, as where one of the parties confesses. The principle of free evaluation by the judge obtains; this decision is not based on a judgment of the evidence alone but on an evaluation of the total thrust of the parties' arguments. The burden of coming forward with proof rests on the party asserting the facts necessary to establish the cause of action and thus may be distributed among the parties. In addition, the system of legal presumptions is allowed to operate. See also CRIMINAL PROCEDURE; CIVIL PROCEDURE, CODE OF.   *TAMIYA Hiroshi*

lawyers

(bengoshi). The largest and only private branch of the legal profession. Compared to judges and prosecutors, Japanese lawyers have long had a reputation for independence and separation from government. Although earlier suffering from a lack of tradition and social prestige, lawyers since 1945 have benefited from postwar legal and political reforms and from the exclusivity of the profession and have generally become highly respected and prosperous.

Although there were to some extent functional equivalents of judge and prosecutor in the Edo period (1600–1868), the concept of the private attorney was almost entirely without precedent. Moreover, the government of the Meiji period (1868–1912) was not eager to foster a group of legal specialists outside the official bureaucracy. Representation of parties to civil litigation was recognized in 1872. However, it was not until 1880 that *daigennin* (advocates), the forerunner of the present *bengoshi,* were allowed to participate in criminal defense. In contrast to active governmental efforts to develop a core of competent judges and prosecutors, little was done to improve or ensure the quality of the private bar until 1893, when for the first time the Attorneys Law (Bengoshi Hō) required a demonstration of legal knowledge for qualification as an attorney. Despite this requirement and the later Attorneys Law of 1933, the recruitment and training of lawyers remained distinct from that of the other branches of the profession, and their legal competence, social position, and role in the judicial system were generally considered inferior to those of judges and prosecutors. It was not mere bureaucratic oversight that led to this situation. Rather, it arose because *daigennin* were identified with liberal politics and also because Japan's need for private attorneys was not considered great, particularly under the Constitution of 1889.

This situation was drastically altered by post–World War II reforms. Recruitment and training were consolidated for all three branches, and private practice has now become the first choice of career for most graduates of the LEGAL TRAINING AND RESEARCH INSTITUTE. As is the case with judges and public prosecutors, lawyers must pass the national LAW EXAMINATION and attend a two-year course at the Legal Training and Research Institute. The Attorneys Law of 1949 and the 1947 constitution have guaranteed both the autonomy of the bar and the fundamental position of civil rights and the rule of law in the Japanese polity. Private attorneys have in turn become effective advocates of those values. Nonetheless, the role of the legal profession in Japanese society remains small, at least in comparison with American society, and there are relatively few attorneys involved in elective politics and legislative or administrative lobbying.

One reason for this limited role is the small number of attorneys in Japan. In 1977 there were 11,035 lawyers, including 361 women, a per capita ratio that is less than 10 percent that of the United States. Exacerbating the situation is their concentration in Tōkyō and Ōsaka, where 60 percent of all practicing attorneys are registered, so that while there is one lawyer for every 2,200 inhabitants of Tōkyō, there is only one lawyer for over 40,000 residents of several rural prefectures. This dearth of attorneys has affected the pattern of their professional activities. Although the situation may be changing somewhat in large cities, most Japanese lawyers concentrate on litigation, with relatively little time spent on counseling, either of individuals or commercial enterprises. Most are sole practitioners or members of firms with two to four attorneys. Large firms are rare, even in Tōkyō. Perhaps partially because of these conditions, many legal functions are performed by nonlawyers in Japan. All large corporations have legal departments staffed by nonlawyer graduates of university law faculties, which provide the bulk of legal drafting and counseling, although the retention of outside counsel is also common. There are also several quasi-legal professions with limited competence in certain fields, including the drafting of legal and administrative documents *(shihō shoshi* and *gyōsei shoshi)* and patent *(benrishi)* and tax *(keirishi)* matters.

Although there is not necessarily a cause and effect relationship, the scarcity of lawyers is also a factor in the low rate of litigation in

Japan, a phenomenon which the Japanese government is not eager to change. Since the organized bar is also ambivalent toward a significant increase in the number of lawyers, ostensibly for fear of lowered standards and competence but perhaps also because of economic considerations, the situation is unlikely to change much in the near future. See also LAW, ATTITUDES TOWARD.

📖 ——Takaaki Hattori, "The Legal Profession in Japan," in Arthur von Mehren, ed, *Law in Japan* (1963). Kenzō Ōtsubo, *Japan Federation of Bar Associations* (1978). Frank K. UPHAM

Laxman, Adam Erikovich (1766–1796?)

Russian army lieutenant who headed the Russian expedition of 1792–93 to Japan. Organized by his father, the noted Finnish naturalist, Eric Laxman, the mission was dispatched by the empress Catherine the Great under the pretext of returning Japanese castaways but actually to collect information about Japan and to explore the possibility of establishing commercial relations between the two countries. In spite of Japan's seclusion policy (see NATIONAL SECLUSION), Adam Laxman and his companions were hospitably received at Nemuro, Hokkaidō, where they spent the winter. In July 1793 they sailed to Hakodate and from there proceeded overland to Matsumae to confer with Ishikawa Shōgen and Murakami Daigaku, who had been sent there by the Tokugawa shogunate to forestall a threatened visit by the Russians to the capital.

The Japanese officials accepted the castaways and formally exchanged gifts with the Russians, but they returned Laxman's credentials and the letters he had transmitted and refused to discuss the question of trade. Asserting that such matters must be negotiated in Nagasaki, the only port open to foreigners, they handed Laxman a permit allowing one Russian vessel to enter Nagasaki harbor. Laxman did not make use of the permit but took it back to Russia.

The death of Eric Laxman and of Catherine the Great, as well as of the enterprising merchant Grogorii Ivanovich Shelikhov, who was equipping a commercial expedition to Japan, postponed the testing of the Nagasaki permit. Not until 1804 did another Russian, Shelikhov's aristocratic son-in-law, Nikolai Petrovich REZANOV, enter Nagasaki in another futile attempt to open the country.

📖 ——George Alexander Lensen, *The Russian Push toward Japan: Russo-Japanese Relations, 1697–1875* (1959). Takano Akira, *Nihon to Roshia* (1971). George Alexander LENSEN

lay Buddhist movement

Lay men and women played important roles in the early Buddhist community in India. Although MONASTICISM was normative in southern (Hīnayāna, Theravāda) Buddhism, both monastic and lay paths were accepted in the Mahāyāna tradition of East Asia.

In Japan the establishment of Buddhism as the state religion owes much to Prince SHŌTOKU, the lay Buddhist par excellence. His views on Buddhism were greatly influenced by the soteriological universalism of the LOTUS SUTRA as well as by the teaching of the Indian lay Buddhist sage Vimalakīrti, and Buddha's discourse with Queen Srīmālā (see SANGYŌ GISHO). During the 7th and 8th centuries Japanese Buddhism came under strict government control as is illustrated by the Regulations for Monks and Nuns (Sōniryō). But this did not curtail the popularity of the unorthodox shamanistic Buddhists called UBASOKU (Skt: *upāsaka*), who combined pre-Buddhist indigenous folk piety with simple faith in Buddha. The resultant path of the holy man (J: HIJIRI) strongly influenced subsequent lay Buddhist movements.

From the late 10th century, belief in the imminence of the millennium, the Period of the Latter Day of Buddha's Law (J: *mappō*; see ESCHATOLOGY), stimulated the growth of devotional confraternities, which included clergy and laity, outside of temples and monasteries. Although initially rejecting the clergy-laity distinction, some new Buddhist groups of the 13th century later developed into hierarchical ecclesiastical institutions. Even though established Buddhism again came under the rigid control of the Tokugawa shogunate (1603–1867), simple faith in Buddhism survived in numerous lay devotional associations (KŌ).

In the modern period the government imposed STATE SHINTŌ above Buddhism and other religions. But with its disestablishment and the new policy of FREEDOM OF RELIGIOUS FAITH as guaranteed by the new constitution of 1947, vigorous lay activity reappeared in such lay Buddhist movements as REIYŪKAI, SŌKA GAKKAI (affiliated with the Nichiren Shō sect [Nichiren Shōshū]), RISSHŌ KŌSEIKAI and others. See also NEW RELIGIONS; RELIGION AND SOCIETY.

Joseph M. KITAGAWA

Lay, Horatio Nelson (1833–1898)

British government employee in China who was commissioned by the Meiji-period (1868–1912) government to raise its first foreign loan, aimed at financing the construction of Japan's first railways. Born in London, Lay went to China in 1849 as a translator and became commissioner of the Chinese Imperial Maritime Customs in 1859. In 1869 he went to Japan with an offer to supply the Japanese government with funds for railway and telegraph construction. Through the good offices of the British minister to Japan, Sir Harry S. PARKES, Lay entered negotiations concerning a railway loan with progressive members of the government who had been persuaded by Parkes to embark on railway construction and to import the necessary capital from abroad. By December 1869 government leaders had concluded an agreement with Lay by which they commissioned him to raise a loan of £1 million, to purchase materials, and to hire engineers in England. Having led the government to believe that he would raise the money privately among his acquaintances, Lay proceeded to float Japanese national bonds on the London stock exchange, publicly pledging Japan's customs and railway receipts as security and arranging the interest on the bonds so as to leave himself a large profit. The Japanese government responded to Lay's action and the resulting public uproar by canceling his commission and appointing the British Oriental Bank Corporation to replace him as its agent.

📖 ——Grace Fox, *Britain and Japan, 1858–1883* (1969). Tanaka Tokihiko, *Meiji ishin no seikyoku to tetsudō kensetsu* (1963). Steven J. ERICSON

Leach, Bernard Howell (1887–1979)

English potter and author who introduced Japanese aesthetic standards to the West and was one of the major guiding influences in modern studio pottery. Born in Hong Kong and educated in England, he lived in Japan from 1909 to 1920. During those 11 years Leach came in contact with members of the SHIRAKABA SCHOOL, a literary group, and became close to TOMIMOTO KENKICHI, YANAGI MUNEYOSHI (Sōetsu), and HAMADA SHŌJI. In 1920 he and Hamada founded The Leach Pottery in St. Ives, Cornwall. He returned to Japan in 1934–35 and made numerous subsequent visits. Leach was the first to build a climbing kiln in the West; his work centered around reduction-fired stoneware, with glazes ranging from celadon to *temmoku*; he also worked in porcelain with underglaze cobalt. Leach reached a wide audience through his books, particularly *A Potter's Book* (1940), in which he introduced the techniques of East Asian kilns and glazes and established a philosophy and a standard for studio pottery in the West. His aesthetic ideas and craft principles paralleled those of Hamada Shōji and Yanagi Muneyoshi, the major proponents of the *mingei* (see FOLK CRAFTS) or folk-craft concept in Japan.

📖 ——Other works by Leach include: *Beyond East and West* (1978). *Drawings, Verses and Belief* (1977). *The Potter's Challenge* (1976). *Hamada, Potter* (1975). *A Potter's Work* (1967). *Kenzan and His Tradition* (1966). *A Potter in Japan* (1960).

lead-glazed wares → ceramics

League for Establishing a National Assembly

(Kokkai Kisei Dōmei). National political organization formed in 1880 to petition for the establishment of a national assembly; the immediate predecessor of the JIYŪTŌ (Liberal Party), Japan's first political party. On 15 March 1880, 114 delegates from 24 prefectures met in Ōsaka for the fourth national convention of the AIKOKUSHA (Society of Patriots), an organization founded by ITAGAKI TAISUKE to promote the FREEDOM AND PEOPLE'S RIGHTS MOVEMENT. On 17 March the delegates voted to dissolve the Aikokusha and form the League for Establishing a National Assembly to initiate a petition campaign for a representative assembly. It opened headquarters in Tōkyō and divided the country into 12 districts for the purpose of political agitation. By mid-April the league had gathered 96,900 signatures, and league leaders KŌNO HIRONAKA and KATAOKA KENKICHI formally presented a petition to the government. Although it was rejected, league members continued their campaign, and by November they had collected around 130,000 signatures. At the convention in December it was resolved to form a nationwide political party. The following year, within days of the government's promise to establish a parliamentary system by 1890 (see POLITICAL CRISIS OF 1881), the Jiyūtō was formed, with Itagaki as president.

League of Blood Incident

(Ketsumeidan Jiken). Assassinations of INOUE JUNNOSUKE, former finance minister and a leader of the Rikken Minseitō (Constitutional Democratic Party), and DAN TAKUMA, director-general of the Mitsui holding company, by the civilian terrorist organization Ketsumeidan (League of Blood) on 9 February and 5 March 1932. The arrest of the two assassins led to the discovery of the group, which had been formed by the ultranationalist INOUE NISSHŌ. Under the slogan *ichinin issatsu* ("one person, one death"), the group had drawn up a list of more than 20 important figures in political and financial circles as prospective targets. Inoue and the two assassins were sentenced to life imprisonment; the 11 remaining members were given sentences ranging from 3 to 15 years. Most of the terrorists were youths from farming villages that were suffering acutely from the economic depression of the time. The incident was closely related to the MAY 15TH INCIDENT of the same year, in which navy officers (similarly influenced by Inoue) murdered Prime Minister INUKAI TSUYOSHI.

League of Nations and Japan

The League of Nations was an international organization established to settle international disputes, promote international cooperation, and maintain international peace in the aftermath of World War I. Japan was a charter member of the league and an active participant in its activities during the 1920s. However, in the 1930s Japan came to disagree with the actions of the League of Nations on its involvement in China and withdrew in 1933.

The League of Nations was the embodiment of the concepts and movements concerning peace that had developed in various countries as a result of self-examination regarding World War I. It was established on 10 January 1920, based on the League Covenant stated in part 1 of the Treaty of Versailles and in the other peace treaties that marked the official end of World War I. Initially, the league comprised only a Secretariat; the League Council, its central organization, commenced activities one week later; and the League Assembly, the general meeting, was convened in November of that year. The Permanent Court of International Justice and the International Labor Organization (ILO) were formed later as related but autonomous organizations. In the league itself, the number of permanent and temporary specialized committees gradually increased.

At the time of the formation of the league, Japan lacked experience with international organizations and therefore adopted a rather passive role in the discussion concerning the League Covenant. However, as one of the principal Allied and Associated Powers, Japan was a founding member of the league and had permanent membership in the council. Japan possessed the right, granted to great powers, to attend all council meetings, to act as a member of the executive board of the assembly, and to take part in each of the specialized committee meetings and international conferences. In addition, Japan was empowered to dispatch a judge to the Permanent Court of International Justice, was designated one of the eight great industrial nations in the International Labor Organization, and became a member of the ILO council.

NITOBE INAZŌ, who assumed the post of under-secretary-general of the league and director-general of its international bureau, assisted the secretary-general and endeavored, through lectures in various European cities and contributions to newspapers and magazines, to propagate and popularize the activities of the league. ISHII KIKUJIRŌ and Matsui Keishirō (1868–1946) played an active role in council meetings and in the assembly; Ishii in particular, as president of the council and at times its reporter, settled territorial disputes concerning the Aaland (Ahvenanmaa) Islands, Upper Silesia, and the island of Corfu. Japanese delegates were able to cope impartially with purely European affairs in which Japan had little interest, but in Japan, general interest in the league was slight since most of its affairs were concerned with the West.

The League of Nations changed a great deal in the years that followed, reflecting a relaxation in the European political situation. Having solidified its various organizations, the league gradually extended its area of activity beyond Europe and changed its reputation of being an organization limited to the settlement of postwar matters or of being too Europocentric. With the admission of Germany in 1926, a change in the executive board of the Secretariat took place. Sugimura Yōtarō (1884–1939) succeeded Nitobe as under-secretary-

general and also took up the position of director of political affairs, another important post. Sugimura was involved with political matters such as the disputes in Upper Silesia, Transylvania, and Gran Chaco. Adachi Mineichirō (1869–1934), the delegate to the assembly meeting, settled questions as a member of the council. Because of his broad knowledge of international law, he attended a variety of international meetings and, in 1930, succeeded Oda Yorozu (1868–1945) as a judge in the Court of International Justice.

During this time, the Sino-Japanese problem, about which Japan was highly sensitive, became an issue in Geneva. Although China's appeal to the league over the Jinan (Tsinan) Incident of May 1928 (in which Japanese troops shelled and occupied the city of Jinan in Shandong [Shantung] Province during the Nationalist government's Northern Expedition) was successfully turned aside by Japan, the league began to provide China with technological aid in various fields from the beginning of the 1930s. The MANCHURIAN INCIDENT, which occurred in September 1931, finally forced the league to examine the Japanese occupation of Chinese territory. Despite strong opposition from YOSHIZAWA KENKICHI, a council member, the council decided to dispatch the LYTTON COMMISSION to make an on-the-spot investigation. The SHANGHAI INCIDENT, a Sino-Japanese military skirmish, and the establishment of the puppet state of MANCHUKUO by the Japanese military aroused further criticism from league members. Japanese representatives SATŌ NAOTAKE and Nagaoka Harukazu (1877–1949) had great difficulty defending Japanese policies. The findings of the commission were drawn up and submitted to the assembly, which issued a report criticizing both parties to the dispute but in effect naming Japan as the aggressor. The Japanese delegation, headed by MATSUOKA YŌSUKE, cast a negative vote on the adoption of the report and walked out. Japan notified the league of its withdrawal on 27 March 1933.

Although Japan notified the league of its withdrawal, according to the covenant, its membership did not expire until March 1935. Japan announced that it would cooperate with the league on peace programs but would refrain from the league's political activities. Germany withdrew from the league in October 1933, followed by Italy in 1937, and the Soviet Union was admitted in September 1934.

When the second Sino-Japanese War broke out in July 1937, China appealed to the league and the issue of Japanese aggression once again was formally addressed. The council invited Japan, now an outsider, to participate in the discussions, but Japan refused. The council applied sanctions against Japan but, since the implementation of sanctions was left to the discretion of member nations, they were ineffective. Soon afterward Japan, claiming that national dignity did not permit it to continue its relationship with various specialized agencies, notified the league of its decision to break off all ties on 2 November 1938. World War II broke out in September 1939, and when the Soviet Union declared war against Finland, the league expelled the Soviet Union. But the League of Nations had by now proven itself incapable of preventing war; it ceased activities during World War II and on 18 April 1946 it was replaced by the United Nations. See also UNITED NATIONS AND JAPAN; INTERNATIONAL RELATIONS.

■ ——Satō Naotake, ed, *Kokusai remmei ni okeru Nihon*, in *Nihon gaikō shi*, vol 14 (1972). Unno Yoshirō, *Kokusai remmei to Nihon*, in *Kindai Nihon gaikō shi sōsho*, vol 6 (Hara Shobō, 1972).

Unno Yoshirō

League of the Divine Wind → Jimpūren Rebellion

learned societies

(gakkai). Along with the introduction of European learning and the establishment of universities in the Meiji period (1868–1912), learned societies were formed in the various academic disciplines. Those in the field of the natural sciences were established early on: the Japan Mathematical Society (1877), the Japan Physics Society (1877), the Japan Chemical Society (1878), and the Japan Zoological Society (1879). The growth of learned societies was particularly active in the second and third decades of the 20th century. In the fields of the social sciences and humanities, however, an individual academic society usually represented at most a single university or research group, and it was not until after World War II that societies in these fields became national.

With the rapid development of scholarship in Japan in recent years, there has been a tendency for specialist fields to further subdivide into smaller specialties, resulting in an ever greater need for interdisciplinary research among the various areas of specialization. To meet this need for communication and cooperation, federations have been formed. In the field of the natural sciences, from early on there had been confederations such as the Japan Federation of Engineering Societies (1879) and the Japanese Association of Medical Sciences (1902).

The majority of Japanese learned societies are informal groups rather than registered legal corporations. As a result, it is difficult to determine the exact number. According to a survey by the SCIENCE COUNCIL OF JAPAN, however, in 1980 there were 1,003 national academic societies in Japan (humanities 271, social sciences 93, natural sciences 639). In addition, there were 390 college-based or research-facility-based academic groups. Japanese learned societies use the Science Council of Japan as their line of communication with societies abroad. WATANABE Tadashi

leased house rights

(shakuyaken). The rights of a tenant, based on a building lease contract, to use the leased building either for habitation as a dwelling or for business purposes such as a shop or factory in the manner set forth in the contract. These rights are protected by the Leased House Law (Shakuya Hō), enacted in 1921. The law provides the following rights. (1) A tenant may, if he is using the building, claim leased house rights against any new owner to whom the building is assigned or any hypothecator on the building. (2) If, upon expiration of the term of the lease set forth in the lease contract, the tenant wishes to continue to rent the building, the landlord may not refuse to renew the contract except when he has a "justifiable reason" for doing so. A justifiable reason is said to exist if the landlord needs the building more than the tenant does, but there are few actual precedents for this. (3) If the lease contract does not set forth the term of the lease, the contract may be canceled at any time upon three months advance notice by the tenant or six months advance notice by the landlord. Cancellation by the landlord is not recognized, however, unless he has a justifiable reason. The contract may be canceled if the tenant commits an act which violates the trust of the landlord, such as being several months in arrears on the rent. (4) If the rent is set forth in the contract but there is an increase in commodity prices or taxes, the landlord may unilaterally raise the rent. However, courts are empowered to determine whether the size of such an increase is legally justified. (5) Provisions of the lease contract which are less advantageous to the tenant than the provisions of this law are invalid. KAI Michitarō

leased land rights

(shakuchiken). The rights of a renter to use the land of another and own a building on it in return for paying rent. These rights are protected by the Leased Land Law (Shakuchi Hō), enacted in 1921. The Japanese right of leased land is similar to the leasehold right in Anglo-American law. The Japanese Civil Code provides for two types of leased land right: superficies and lease. Under Japanese law, land and the structures on it are legally distinct, so that land leases in which one rents the land of another but owns the buildings on it are frequently used.

Under the principles of the Civil Code, a leased land right must be recorded in order for the renter to assert this right against a third party who might claim a right to the land. The Buildings Protection Law (Tatemono Hogo Hō) of 1909 provides that after the holder of a leased land right has recorded ownership of the buildings on the rented land, he may claim a right to the land itself against the claims of a third party.

The Leased Land Law provides for the protection of land lease rights as follows. (1) The term of the leased land right must, if stipulated by contract, be at least 20 years. When the term of the land lease right is not stipulated by contract, it is 30 years in the case of a wooden structure and 60 years in the case of a steel-frame or other structure of similar durability. (2) If there is a building on the land after the term of the leased land right has expired, the holder of the leased land right may demand that it be renewed, and the owner of the land may not refuse to do so except for a "justifiable reason." A justifiable reason is established by determining whether the landowner needs the land more than the land leaseholder. When a justifiable reason is recognized and the leased land right is removed, the holder of the leased land right may compel the landowner to buy the structures which stand on the land. (3) If the holder of a leased land right assigns a building on the land to a third party, he must also

simultaneously assign the leased land right. If the leased land right is a superficies, the holder of the superficies need not obtain the landowner's consent to do so, but if it is a lease, the landowner's consent is necessary. KAI Michitarō

leeches

(hiru). In Japanese, hiru is the common name for segmented worms of phylum Annelida, class Hirudinea. The chisuibiru (Hirudo nipponica), similar to the medicinal leech (Hirudo medicinalis) of Europe, lives in ponds and swamps throughout Japan and was once used in the medical treatment of boils. The umabiru (Whitmania pigra) is the largest leech in Japan, but it does not suck blood. The umibiru (genus Pontobdella) lives in the sea and attaches itself to fish; the kaibiru (Hemiclepsis kasmiana) is parasitic on freshwater bivalves. The land leech yamabiru (Haemadipsa zeylanica japonica) lives in mountainous areas of southern Japan and is a source of annoyance to hikers in summer.

The leech appears early in Japanese mythology. In the accounts given in the ancient chronicles KOJIKI (712) and NIHON SHOKI (720) a mistake in the order of the rituals at the marriage of the deities IZANAGI AND IZANAMI leads to the birth of a hiruko ("leech baby"), who is put into a boat woven of reeds and abandoned. A description of leeches appears in the Honzō wamyō (918), the oldest Japanese book of natural history. HABE Tadashige and SAITŌ Shōji

Lee Hwe-song (1935–)

(also spelled Yi Hoe-sŏng; J: Ri Kaisei). Author; one of the first of second-generation Koreans in Japan to win literary acclaim for Korean fiction written in Japanese. He was born on Sakhalin, relocated with his family to a refugee camp in Kyūshū in 1947, and attended high school in Sapporo. He worked his way through Waseda University, and received a degree in Russian literature in 1961. Lee's early works tended toward short but complex semiautobiographical accounts, punctuated with symbolism drawn from Korea's cultural tradition and structured along the lines of traditional Korean oral narrative (p'ansori). Among these, the most highly regarded are the 1972 Akutagawa Prize–winning "Kinuta o utsu onna" (tr "The Woman Who Ironed Clothes" in David McCann, ed, Black Crane: An Anthology of Korean Literature, 1977) and Warera seishun no tojō nite (1973). In 1979 he completed a six-volume novel, Mihatenu yume, in which he articulates his utopian vision and analyzes revolutionary dreams. C. Kenneth QUINONES

legal education

The undergraduate discipline leading to a bachelor's degree in the study of law but not leading directly to entry into the legal profession. Every major university in Japan has a faculty of law (hōgakubu) that often includes courses of study in economics or political science. The students of the law faculty are generally third and fourth year undergraduates who have completed an initial year and a half to two years of general cultural education.

Since only a very small number of law graduates enter the legal profession per se, the course of study at law faculties is intended to provide a broad general knowledge of law useful to those students who will enter government service or become company employees. The curricular emphasis is on an understanding of the Six Codes (Roppō), the CONSTITUTION, the CIVIL CODE, the Code of CIVIL PROCEDURE, the Penal Code, the Code of CRIMINAL PROCEDURE, and the COMMERCIAL CODE, with the most stress being put on an understanding of their theoretical bases and a knowledge of their contents. As with the European patterns of legal education on which it is modeled, the Japanese system has been criticized for its bias toward memorization and acceptance, rather than evaluation and criticism. Classes are usually large lectures with little, if any, give-and-take between faculty and students, although small group seminars and classes are also offered within the limits of a generally restrictive budget. The content of the education is fairly detached from the practical application of law to society, perhaps in part because only a very few law professors are also trained legal professionals.

Because of very restricted entry into the legal profession, few law graduates become lawyers, judges, or prosecutors. Instead they use their legal education as public officials, members of corporate legal departments, or in one of the several quasi-legal professions that supplement the small number of private lawyers in Japan. See also LAW EXAMINATION; LAWYERS; LEGAL TRAINING AND RESEARCH INSTITUTE.   *Frank K. UPHAM*

legal scholarship

During the first decade following the Meiji Restoration of 1868 French law and scholarship strongly influenced Japanese law. Progressivism and the natural law philosophy prevailed in Japan. From the 1880s legal scholarship turned more toward German sources, when a constitution based on German models was adopted. The German preference for abstract conceptualism and formalistic logical analysis of legal concepts without substantial reference to social implications had both merits and demerits. Legal certainty *(Rechtssicherheit)* was the main achievement of this newly acquired modern system of law which was based on a universalistic point of view. Under the banner of universalism Japanese legal scholarship endeavored for a long time to do away with feudalistic status discrimination inherited from the past, though with little success.

Legal scholarship from the 1860s until about 1926 favored modernization to attain civil liberties and equality. However, residues of the old inequities based on feudalistic status consciousness remained. Under the Meiji Constitution (1889) certain privileges and instances of discrimination continued in political and civil relationships. A deep and persistent antagonism between those for and against the traditional system continued through all stages of development of law and legal scholarship. The call for social justice from the late 19th century, however, was reflected in both legal scholarship and legislation, especially after World War I. With the help of such imported legal concepts as "general welfare" from the US constitution and *Gerechtigkeit* from the Weimar constitution, modern legal scholarship in Japan has promoted social equality by adapting Western scholarship to Japan's needs.

In constitutional law, MINOBE TATSUKICHI, with his theory of the emperor as an organ of the state (TENNŌ KIKAN SETSU), interpreted the Meiji Constitution to strengthen the power of the elective Diet to the widest possible extent. His opponent, UESUGI SHINKICHI, denied the validity of this legal theory and argued in favor of the mythical history of Japan and its "national polity" (KOKUTAI), supporting the quasi-absolutist theory of the power of the emperor as stipulated in article 1 of the Meiji Constitution.

In criminal law there was antagonism between the old school (objectivist theory) and the new school (subjectivist theory). MAKINO EIICHI advocated the subjectivist view that penalties are intended for the correction of criminals so that they can be accepted back into society. He relied on the German doctrine of *Freirechtsschule* and similar French concepts. The old school insisted that the Penal Code was a Magna Charta for criminals, as advocated at the time of the French Revolution. A representative scholar of the old school, TAKIKAWA YUKITOKI, believed that only after fundamental social change might a new subjectivistic criminal system become acceptable, but until that time the criminal law must require criminals to pay objectively determined penalties for similarly determined crimes.

There was also a new school in the field of civil law. In judging a case, interpretations of abstract legal regulations were thought to be less important than analyses of the social relationships involved. Such analysis of social relationships should lead to concrete, appropriate, and rational solutions compatible with positive laws. This pragmatic approach to legal questions was applied by SUEHIRO IZUTARŌ, who studied law in the United States during World War I. In the 1920s he organized a case study group, the Mimpō Hanrei Kenkyūkai (Civil Case Study Group), based on this point of view.

There was also a school that advocated a "Japanese philosophy of law" *(Nihon hōri)*. This was supported by nationalists and disappeared from scholarship with the collapse of the empire in 1945. In addition, there were the followers of Hans Kelsen (1881–1973), who advocated a theory of pure law, free from politics. Kelsen's thought was suppressed by the power of the ultranationalists. Yokota Kisaburō (b 1896), Kiyomiya Shirō (b 1898), and Miyazawa Toshiyoshi (1899–1976), well-known Japanese Kelsenists, attempted passive resistance against the militaristic regime. Other leading scholars are Tanaka Kōtarō (1890–1974) and Suzuki Takeo (b 1905) in commercial law, Wagatsuma Sakae (1897–1973) and Suekawa Hiroshi (1892–1977) in civil law, and Tanaka Jirō (1906–82) and Yanase Yoshimoto (b 1905) in administrative law. Through their efforts legal scholarship survived the war with its identity and integrity intact.

Post–World War II legal scholarship has become more influenced by sociological methods. One social science-oriented group, for example, advocates the prediction of court judgments by determinate factors. Other groups prefer analyzing court activities from the standpoint of class struggle rather than abstract legal concepts.

Until the end of World War II there were no nationwide academic associations of legal science. At present there are 22 academic organizations of law registered with the Science Council of Japan. Some are small and highly specialized, and others focus on broad areas of law such as public law (the Nihon Kōhō Gakkai) and private law (the Nihon Shihō Gakkai). All of these learned societies as well as a great many university faculties of law (altogether 60 national, public, and private universities have faculties of law) publish scholarly journals, making for diverse and highly developed legal scholarship in modern Japan.

━━Lawrence Beer and Hidenori Tomatsu, *A Guide to the Study of Japanese Law* (1978). Rex Coleman and J. O. Haley, *An Index to Japanese Law: A Bibliography of Western Language Materials, 1967–1973* in *Law in Japan, An Annual, Special Issue* (1975). Hōritsu Jihō, *Sōkan gojusshūnen kinen: Shōwa no hō to hōgaku* (1979). Hōmu Toshokan, *Hōritsu kankei zasshi kiji sakuin* (from 1952). Japanese American Society for Legal Studies, *Law in Japan: An Annual* (from 1968). Kawashima Takeyoshi, ed, *Hōshakaigaku kōza*, 10 vols (Iwanami Shoten, 1972–73). Kobayashi Naoki and Mizumoto Hiroshi, ed, *Kindai Nihon no hōshisō: Kindaihō hyakunen no ayumi ni manabu* (1976). Arthur von Mehren, ed, *Law in Japan: The Legal Order in a Changing Society* (1963). Murakami Jun'ichi, *Einführung in die Grundlagen des japanishen Rechts* (1974). Nihon Hōshakai Gakkai, *Sōritsu sanjūnen kinen: Nihon no hōshakaigaku* (1979). Nihon Hyōronsha, ed, *Nihon no hōgaku: Kaiko to tembō* (1950). Noda Yoshiyuki, *Introduction to Japanese Law* (1976). Saikō Saibansho Toshokan, *Hōbun hōritsu zasshi kiji sakuin* (from 1958). Saikō Saibansho Toshokan, *Hōritsu tosho mokuroku, washo no bu* (from 1951). Science Council of Japan, *The Japan Science Review: Law and Politics* (1950–62). Science Council of Japan, *The Japan Annual of Law and Politics* (from 1952). Tanaka Hideo, assisted by M. D. H. Smith, *The Japanese Legal System* (1976).

UKAI Nobushige

legal system

history of Japanese law
law in contemporary Japan

HISTORY OF JAPANESE LAW

Since laws, defined broadly as rules of conduct made obligatory by social sanctions, are present in every society, the history of Japanese law can be said to begin with Japan's earliest form of society. The few extant records of this society, contained in Chinese accounts dating from AD 239, give some indication of ancient customs and community norms. But legal historians are interested primarily in changes in codified, formal law made by societies that articulate a concept of rules and have distinct government bodies empowered to apply those rules to societal interaction.

The surviving legal codes allow a division of the history of Japanese law into five major stages, beginning with the late-7th-century establishment of a centralized government organized according to a Chinese-style legal code (see RITSURYŌ SYSTEM). Primarily an administrative regulator, this body of law was concerned with state operations under a theoretically supreme EMPEROR and a centralized, hereditary bureaucracy subordinate to him. Its framework served as the theoretical basis for the delegation of political authority until the issuance of the first modern constitution in 1889. Nonetheless, its administrative apparatus and substance fell into disuse, and its administrative sections were used by de facto powerholders to legitimize their rule. Thus, the second period of Japanese legal history can be dated from the 9th to the late 15th centuries, 500 years during which political organization was characterized by the gradual decentralization of jurisdiction and reliance upon local legal procedures.

The third stage of legal history developed between the late 15th century and 1868, during which time an absolutist military government grafted new forms of law onto the roots of the *ritsuryō* system's delegation of authority. The fourth stage of legal development lasted from 1868 to 1945. Japan implemented governmental reform and economic modernization with the aid of Western concepts of an absolute monarchy. The application then of the radically new principle of the separation of legislative and judicial, if not also executive, powers provided a useful precedent for the constitutional and judicial reforms instituted in Japan's fifth stage of legal development, from 1945 to the present.

I. LAW AND THE EARLY STATE (600–800)

The Ritsuryō Period ——— In 604 a 17-article "constitution" was issued by the Japanese government. Although it may not, as some claim, have been written by Prince SHŌTOKU, the general character of these Chinese-inspired injunctions embodied his vision of political centralization, a plan that entailed integration of the chieftains of previously independent UJI (clans) into an aristocracy that would function as an imperial bureaucracy subordinate to the emperor. Actual codification of law began with the TAIHŌ CODE (Taihō Ritsuryō) of 701 and the YŌRŌ CODE of 718 (promulgated 757). The Yōrō Code, parts of which survive, contained approximately 1,500 articles in 10 chapters that comprehensively regulated the central administration of the growing national government. As the name *ritsuryō* implies, these articles were either criminal law provisions *(ritsu)* or administrative statutes *(ryō)*. Administrative statutes were classified under 30 headings, such as *denryō* (land allotment), *koryō* (household registration), *buyakuryō* (labor tax), *gumbōryō* (military conscription), and *shokuinryō* (bureaucracy). This last section set forth a hierarchy of ranks and positions, as well as duties, for the courtier elite.

Supplements and revisions to the criminal laws and administrative statutes, called *kyaku* and *shiki,* were issued until circa 927. The major *kyaku* and *shiki* compilations, collectively called the Sandai Kyakushiki, are the Kōnin Kyakushiki (820), Jōgan Kyakushiki (869, 871), and the Engi Kyakushiki (Engi Kyaku, 907; Engi Shiki, 927; see ENGI SHIKI).

Principles of criminal law. The Japanese criminal code, like its Chinese model, was intended to correct and edify the criminal by application of punishments appropriate to his crime. Crimes of both intent and neglect were punishable, but punishment was mitigated under certain conditions, such as age or illness. Since the ruling class, by reason of its education in the Confucian classics, was regarded as morally superior to all other classes, it held the power to determine what constituted a crime. Therefore, early Chinese and Japanese legal systems never had an equivalent of the Western concept of "no crime, no punishment, without legal provision." The seriousness of a crime was determined by the degree to which it had upset the Confucian moral order, which was embodied in the legal code. The formal provisions of criminal law underwent very little revision, but its administration did change considerably. For example, the death sentence, perhaps because of Buddhist influence, was not imposed after about 820. More significantly, the decentralization of authority encouraged the application of native norms for criminal procedures; one non-*ritsuryō* technique, trial by ordeal, was employed by local land adminstrators until the early modern period.

The judicial function. The *ritsuryō* government was not divided into judiciary and executive branches. Rather, administrative officers generally held judicial authority over their subordinates. Records for judicial investigations were transmitted from a capital official to the Ministry of Punishments (Gyōbushō) or from a regional district official to the provincial level and thence to the capital, where from the Ministry of Punishments they passed to the Grand Council of State (Dajōkan), then to the Ministry of Central Imperial Affairs (Nakatsukasashō), and finally to the emperor. This process followed the Chinese pattern, with little differentiation between civil and criminal cases. The court procedure adhered to an inquisitorial, as opposed to an adversary, system. Some important civil cases were handled under procedural rules for criminal cases because their urgency required an immediate hearing. All decisions at all levels had to cite the determining provision of the *ritsuryō kyakushiki,* regardless of how vague that provision might be. A party in disagreement with the court's decision could appeal, but only after obtaining from the original court a document authorizing the appeal. Civil litigation procedure included provisions for the issuance of summons to the defendant, penalties for the instigation of false suits, and nonappearance.

Throughout the Heian period (794–1185) many statutory offices gradually lost their authorized duties and powers to the increasingly numerous extrastatutory offices (RYŌGE NO KAN). For example, the police force (KEBIISHI) was originally only a Kyōto municipal office with police and judicial functions, but gradually it expanded its jurisdiction by dispatching its constables *(Kebiishi tsuibushi)* to provinces and districts and its sheriffs *(sō tsuibushi)* to SHŌEN (private landed estates), where they supplanted central government officials who had previously exercised police power.

Land law. Under *ritsuryō* law the state owned most land. It distributed all cultivated rice land, with the exception of officials' "salary land" *(shikiden),* equally to the peasantry and granted the use of forest lands to their communities. Residential land, however, was not "nationalized," and its sale was unrestricted. Such sales could be made in perpetuity once the parties drew up contracts (KŌKEN) and petitioned local officials, usually at the district level, for authorization.

Regulations concerning transfer of property soon became significantly different from their Tang (T'ang) dynasty (618–907) Chinese models. The Chinese household regulations prescribed equal inheritance among sons, but the Japanese very early amended their laws to allow for unequal division, providing a greater share for the succeeding family head, and for female inheritance (see PRIMOGENITURE). In fact, female inheritance was practiced by courtier and *samurai* families alike until the 15th century, even though it was in the interests of the medieval military governments to encourage a patrilineal family organization.

The Nara-period (710–794) government, in order to encourage private reclamation of uncultivated lands, issued edicts authorizing exemptions from taxation, in 723 for three generations (SANZE ISSHIN NO HŌ) and in 743 for perpetuity (KONDEN EISEI SHIZAI HŌ). Religious institutions, high-ranking aristocratic households, and other landholding enterprises exempt from taxes because of their special status were thereby able to develop huge landed estates. Eventually, commendation of land and tax-exemption grants to these powerful landlords resulted in a shift of control over the land from the central government to estate *(shōen)* proprietors.

Development of Ritsuryō Law ——— *Commentaries.* Two commentaries made by jurists and legal scholars during the 12th and 13th centuries, the *Hossō shiyō shō* and *Saiban shiyō shō,* indicate that adjustments were necessary to reconcile the *ritsuryō* code with Japanese conditions in matters of criminal law, inheritance, landownership, and financial transactions. For instance, in criminal proceedings these jurists increasingly refrained from citing the criminal code, referring instead to Japanese custom and collections of precedent made by provincial police agencies; police and judicial functions were thereby decentralized. Furthermore, inheritance was discussed in only one *ritsuryō* statute but received detailed treatment in these two commentaries in cases arising from the discrepancy between Japanese practice and Chinese law. Third, the jurists, in great contrast to the code, made no mention of family and marriage subjects, suggesting their declining significance as legal issues to legal authorities.

New regulations. New regulations of *ritsuryō*-based law, generically called *shinsei,* were issued intermittently by the imperial government from the 10th through the 13th centuries. Unlike the *kyaku* and *shiki,* these did not merely revise the code. Rather they effected institutional innovations in government, particularly in its administration and internal affairs. The earliest *shinsei* dates from 947, and many were issued throughout the Kamakura period (1185–1333), the best-known in 1191, 1231, and 1273.

II. THE SHŌEN PERIOD: DECENTRALIZED JURISDICTIONS (800–1500)

The Tang Chinese legal system upon which *ritsuryō* law was modeled rested in part on two principles that were ignored in Japanese law and practice. First, qualification for office in Tang China was usually demonstrated in a competitive academic examination. Second, the amount of land a Tang subject could hold was limited by law. However, in Japan, the imported legal framework was used to strengthen a system of hereditary political offices and to permit ownership of land reclaimed at the state's urging. State power over the land assumed more and more the function of a tax-collecting institution, delegating administrative authority over the land to managers of *shōen.* Since the state also granted other kinds of authority over the land to many other levels of social organization, the political system began to function in terms of private rights over productive land and its residents, which the legal system had theoretically denied. By the middle of the 9th century, decentralization of government had reached the point where peasants had no direct contact with the state legal apparatus and were governed instead by the proprietors of *shōen.* These new jurisdictions were not illegal; they were merely inconsistent with the ideals of *ritsuryō* law.

Shōen Law—— After *shōen* proprietors, either court aristocrats or religious institutions, acquired land management rights, they appointed managers to administer their *shōen* independent of state control. Furthermore, upon receipt from the state of exemptions from tax payment and the intrusion of provincial government police (FUYU AND FUNYŪ), the proprietors effectively barred government officials from their *shōen*. Consequently, the legal process there was detached from the confines of *ritsuryō* statutes, and a type of law called *honjohō* (*shōen* office law) grew up to define the mutual obligations of cultivators, managers, and the proprietor. *Shōen* law varied considerably from place to place, but one commonly shared feature was that *shōen* court procedure began to show elements of an adversary, as opposed to an inquisitorial, system. This change was an early manifestation of the noninquisitorial adjudication technique already used to advantage by early military governments to win over independent military men involved in property disputes. The actual making of *shōen* law included documents of confirmation of rights, commendation of *shiki* (appointments), bylaws, etc. Uncodified norms recognizing precedent developed over generations in local communities and came to be the core of "private" land law.

During the *shōen* period, the principal objects of litigation were *shiki,* that is, various kinds and levels of claims and obligations pertaining to land tenure, such as proprietorial *shiki,* managerial *shiki,* police *shiki,* and cultivator *shiki.* Each type of *shiki* carried specific administrative authority or economic benefits, for example, rent collection rights or the right of usufruct. *Shiki* differed from modern landownership rights in being property rights to a part of the agricultural enterprise. Furthermore, it differed in two basic ways from the landholding pattern under the laws of both the *ritsuryō* state and the post-1500 state. First, an individual could concurrently hold different *shiki* to a single or several *shōen,* and, second, *shiki* were attached to private, as opposed to public, landholdings. Thus, the *shōen* and *shiki* systems are considered to characterize the medieval period (13th–16th centuries) of legal history.

Military Law—— Exercise of political authority by military leaders (*buke*) was legitimized by legal procedures stemming from the *ritsuryō* code. After the KAMAKURA SHOGUNATE (1192–1333) acquired the right to exercise nationwide control over all police and military agents, it set up a Board of Inquiry (MONCHŪJO) to make and apply rules for the resolution of land disputes among its own retainers. This military judiciary gradually assumed jurisdiction over all parties with proprietorial and managerial *shiki,* since the shogunate alone proved effective in enforcing judicial decisions.

In 1232 the Kamakura shogunate issued a legal code, the GOSEIBAI SHIKIMOKU (also called the Jōei Shikimoku), which institutionalized and rationalized shogunate organization after the death of the charismatic leaders of the founding period. In essence, this new military code was meant to handle conflicts over private property, problems the old *ritsuryō* code had no reason to treat. Regulations were issued by the Council of State (HYŌJŌSHŪ) in its review of opinions of the three High Courts' (HIKITSUKE) handling of cases regarding real estate, other property, and criminal actions. Supplementary to the Goseibai Shikimoku, these regulations (Jōei Shikimoku Tsuikahō), issued in a piecemeal fashion and later compiled in a 750-article compendium, reflected the widening range of military jurisdiction in local economic and criminal matters. However, scholars have found that the Hyōjōshū relied increasingly on precedent rather than on statute and allowed at times the use of an adversary system in civil law cases, both features of English common law as well.

The legal system of the Goseibai Shikimoku and its supplementary regulations endured until the end of the medieval period. In 1336 the 17-article KEMMU SHIKIMOKU was issued by ASHIKAGA TAKAUJI, the founder of the MUROMACHI SHOGUNATE (1338–1573). It consisted mainly of moral injunctions that demonstrated the shogunate's political philosophy rather than constituted its legal code. The same was true of the shogunate's Kemmu Irai Tsuikahō (Kemmu Supplementary Provisions) issued after 1338.

Both the Kamakura and Muromachi shogunate legal systems issued regulations mainly concerned with the affairs of their own samurai retainers, men who grew increasingly powerful in local government because of their military ties. Especially from the late Muromachi period, after the ŌNIN WAR (1467–77), these military men performed an even wider range of civilian administrative functions. Samurai control of all civilian affairs and direct application of military law to all nonmilitary sectors, including religious communities, farmers, artisans, and merchants, brought Japan in the 16th century to an absolutist form of government that lasted through the three succeeding centuries.

III. ABSOLUTIST GOVERNMENT UNDER MILITARY LAW
(CA 1500–1868)

Codes of the Warring States Period (1467–1568)—— During the Warring States (Sengoku) period SENGOKU DAIMYŌ (territorial warlords) issued legal codes (BUNKOKUHŌ) to govern the areas they had seized, often as rebellious local strongmen or as military governors (SHUGO) of the Muromachi shogunate. These codes regulated the property dealings, marriage relations, and alliances of a daimyō's retainers. They taxed merchants, artisans, and the agricultural population, circumscribing the power of the landlords to charge rent and administer judicial and police affairs. They also prescribed litigation procedures and all forms for financial transactions as well as detailed security and military measures such as the erection of toll barriers, roads, postal stations, and other public works. As is evident from such concerns, these legal codes were intended to regulate tightly the social and economic activities of all the inhabitants within a daimyō's territory. The comprehensive character of these codes thus significantly distinguished them from earlier shogunate law with its almost exclusive concern with the affairs of its military retainers.

This expansion of legal interests arose from the disappearance of the personal lines of authority that had once linked such social and economic groups as the family, extended family, *shōen* organization, religious community, and warrior band (BUSHIDAN). By the 16th century it was only in the class division between retainer and nonretainer that these personal ties still survived. Thus, with his seizure of the military governor's police authority, the judicial authority of the *ritsuryō*-period civil governor (KOKUSHI), and numerous tax-collection rights within *shōen,* each Sengoku daimyō could impose his will on the entire population within the area he alone ruled. The predominant basis of jurisdiction and military rule became territorial, and when the Sengoku daimyō eventually yielded to Tokugawa rule, this principle of territorial jurisdiction was adopted by the new shogunate for the entire nation.

Foundation of the Tokugawa Shogunate—— There were three major stages of legal development during the Edo period (1600–1868). The first and most successful stage saw the establishment of political regulations for the state's transition to the relatively centralized BAKUHAN SYSTEM. The new government's first body of national law, the BUKE SHOHATTO (1615), consisted of abstract principles to guide daimyō in the independent administration of their domains (HAN). But the major provisions of its second body of law, issued in 1635, were far more specific and restrictive. Daimyō were required to spend alternate years in residence at the shogunal capital of Edo (now Tōkyō), leaving their families as hostages when they returned to the domain (see SANKIN KŌTAI). They also had to notify the shogunate before arranging a marriage of any family member. The construction of new castles or large ships was prohibited, and all samurai had to study both military arts and Confucian moral teachings.

The shogunate then extended its legal control to less disruptive social groups. The KINCHŪ NARABI NI KUGE SHOHATTO regulated the imperial court and Kyōto aristocracy descended from the *ritsuryō*-period elite and barred the emperor from taking part in political activity. Temples and shrines, the only remaining groups with the potential for seizing political power, were controlled by a series of regulations collectively known as the Shoshū Jiin Hatto and the Shosha Negi Kannushi Hatto.

The second stage of Tokugawa legal development (ca 1640–1853) saw the Confucian refinement and rationalization of the shogunate's political control. Shogunate jurists, influenced by studies of Ming-dynasty (1368–1644) Chinese statutes, created new *ritsuryō*-type provisions, the best known of which is the KUJIKATA OSADAMEGAKI, issued in 1742. Part 1, with 81 articles, covered administrative regulations as had the *ryō* of Heian-period law. Part 2 was a 103-article penal code like the *ritsu* provisions. The code was meant to guide judicial officials in making decisions, and its contents were not made public. Certain domains promulgated law based on this code or on the Ming code itself. In addition, shogunate proclamations to the general public were issued and collected (see OFUREGAKI SHŪSEI) after 1744.

After 1742, despite the shogunate's issuance of laws to maintain its original polity, many of the conflicts that arose from growing commercialization and social change remained unresolved. Social legislation became more repressive. But, since judges were free to foster conciliation and make decisions in keeping with commercial demands, the area of private law was not completely stagnant.

In the final stage of Tokugawa legal development, 1853–67, the shogunate lost control over the economy and then collapsed. After the entrance into Edo Bay of Commodore Matthew PERRY in 1853, the shogunate was faced with foreign aggression as well as economic instability and domainal independence. Insurgents joined to crush its regime and establish the Meiji government in 1868.

IV. INSTITUTIONALIZATION OF ABSOLUTIST MONARCHY (1868–1945)

Since the first reorganization of government at the time of the MEIJI RESTORATION in 1868, the Japanese have repeatedly revised their legal system. During the 1870s jurists still depended on Chinese models of law, but during the 1880s they abandoned them in favor of Western legal systems in order to persuade the Western powers to revise the so-called Unequal Treaties (see UNEQUAL TREATIES, REVISION OF). As with the importation of Chinese law in the 7th century, Japanese lawmakers tended to search for a "closed system" in French, English, American, and German law. They rejected English law with its liberal common-law tradition as a model for the Meiji codes, for Japan's legal heritage consisted of codified law based on the Chinese legal framework and Japanese authoritarian practices. Instead, they initially showed preference for French law and, after a period of intense translation of five Napoleonic codes, invited Gustave Emile BOISSONADE DE FONTARABIE, a French scholar of criminal law, to assist in drafting a new penal code.

By the time the Penal Code was issued in 1880 (see CRIMINAL LAW), Japanese leaders had begun to shift their attention to German models. Sharing with Tokugawa law the conception of law as a system imposed by an absolute monarch, and not as the embodiment of justice, German law provided a model of a "constitutional state" *(Rechtsstaatprinzip)*, which the Japanese authorities adapted in a severely restricted manner.

Public Law——From the first, public law remained the most conservative part of the new legal system. In the 1870s the government declared that it was dedicated to developing a legal system based upon the separation of powers and the guarantee of human rights. When actually promulgated, however, the 1889 CONSTITUTION did not guarantee even rule by law. Its drafters described it as a gift of the emperor to the people, with the legislature, cabinet, and judiciary all under his authority. When the emperor delegated this authority to government officials, they were beholden not to the constitution but to him. In fact, since the constitution did not explicitly subordinate military and civil administration to law, authoritarian groups in the army and cabinet used their imperially delegated powers to thwart the process of liberalization evident in Japan after World War I. Indeed, the legislature, anxious to restrict civil rights, passed the PEACE PRESERVATION LAW OF 1925, which stipulated punishment for anyone who organized, participated in an organization, or induced participation in action against the private property system or the state polity (KOKUTAI).

The Meiji oligarchs who drafted the 1889 constitution were far less concerned with establishing a rule of law than with achieving military and economic modernization. Through the constitution they definitely did create a sovereign state organization capable of handling the aggressive Western powers, but law was little more than a tool for implementing the reforms they desired.

V. DEVELOPMENT OF A RULE OF LAW (1945 TO THE PRESENT)

The constitution of 1947 superseded the 1889 constitution with revisions of those features that had seriously hampered the development of a rule of law. First, it finally established the principle of the division of power by abolishing the ADMINISTRATIVE COURT. Second, it formally introduced the American system of JUDICIAL REVIEW by granting the courts supreme judicial power. The growing strength of judicial review, in addition to a strong consciousness of judicial independence nurtured since the Meiji period (1868–1912), indicates that the public law field is a fertile ground for the growth of rights consciousness. Third, the new constitution provided for extensive protection of civil liberties. This reform entailed the complete revision of the Code of CRIMINAL PROCEDURE, and the enactment of new laws protecting workers' rights, such as the Labor Standards Law, Labor Union Law and Labor Relations Adjustment Law (see LABOR LAWS).

In the area of public law, the most radical feature of the current constitution is article 9, on the RENUNCIATION OF WAR, which states that "The Japanese people forever renounce war as a sovereign right

of the nation . . . The right of belligerency of the state will not be recognized." The clause that "land, sea, and air forces . . . will never be maintained" has placed Japan in a unique position during the postwar period and poses a problem for defining sovereignty in international law.

Private Law——Legal practices concerning private transactions and litigation have a different tradition from public law. Although judicial consideration of private law, or civil litigation, was considered a privilege rather than a right even in the Edo period, the premodern Japanese judiciary differed greatly from the Chinese in its making of laws and use of conciliation for disputes in private law. Judicial decisions mentioning conciliation and its legal ramifications date from the Kamakura period, having been fostered by the strongly communal nature of Japanese society. In the early Meiji period also, litigation and formal judicial decisions were found not to work in many social settings, and in 1876 the government recognized informal resolution methods by reinstating conciliation. In 1922 mediation was recognized for the resolution of land and house lease disputes, pecuniary debts, and domestic relations. Even today, the wide discrepancy between the judicial system and actual social behavior has prompted some to denounce traditional methods of resolution, arguing that these methods are apt to undermine justice if the parties are socially or economically unequal. Increasingly in present-day Japan disputants seek resolution by litigation, hoping to obtain judgments made in accordance with universal standards.

One problem with the present CIVIL CODE, still basically the 1898 civil code, is the ever-widening gap between legal needs and legal codification. For example, although provisions for contracts are numerous and elaborate, very few are actually taken up in court cases. On the other hand, there are only a few articles covering torts. Attorneys must represent clients, such as industrial pollution victims, by means of only one tort provision. Case law has developed since Meiji times, but it is not the principal source of law as it is in the Anglo-American tradition.

Anglo-American influence was most strongly felt in the post-World War II era. The OCCUPATION government, under American direction, paid strict attention to regulating economic and political organizations that it believed had contributed to national militarization in the 1930s. To dissolve permanently the huge business combines known as ZAIBATSU, the ANTIMONOPOLY LAW and the Fair Trade Commission were instituted and are two of the most significant legal reforms outside constitutional law. The American influence in business-related fields can also be seen in the partial revision of company law, which emphasizes the protection of shareholders and the fiduciary duties of management, and in the newly enacted CORPORATE REORGANIZATION LAW.

Some Japanese laymen and lawyers, recognizing that their present legal system is the product of an eclectic selection of foreign law, believe that its principles differ little from those of the parent legal systems. Why then, they ask, is it relevant to study Japanese legal history? Japan's present legal system is an intricately woven fabric of codes, whose design has been often modified in the past century. Its warp of traditional political concepts and woof of social and economic change are producing a continually new blend of law. Legal techniques are tried, discussed, and analyzed at length by jurists. The jury system, for example, has been tried (1923) and discarded (1943) as inappropriate. On the other hand, other principles like judicial review (1946) have been slowly nurtured and appear likely to survive.

From the early Meiji period Japanese jurists have concentrated on studies of Western laws that served as models for Japan's legal development. Largely ignored was the history and philosophy of Western law, which was as basic to modern Western political theory as Neo-Confucian thought was to the government of Qing (Ch'ing; 1644–1912) dynasty China or Tokugawa Japan. Through recent studies of Japanese legal history, we are discovering elements in the premodern legal systems (the judicial decision-making process, informal conflict resolution, group consensus, etc.) that continue to affect social behavior. Some critics, including conservative government officials, occasionally cite the "excesses of individualism," the high cost of voluminous litigation, and the failure of social norms in Western societies when they stress the values of traditional Japanese social mores.

These criticisms have merit in terms of Japan's need for a balance between social conservatism and economic modernization. The legal community, however, has so far shown a high respect for the law as an instrument of justice. The period of borrowing law to implement social reform is now drawing to an end. There is no doubt that the overall operation of the Japanese legal system and its realization of a rule of law will be aided by greater study of those unique historical and sociological factors that have deeply influenced the adoption and administration of a largely imported system of law in Japan. *Carole A. RYAVEC*

LAW IN CONTEMPORARY JAPAN

The law in Japan provides, along with the ethical imperatives of society, the framework of general and specific rules within which citizens carry on social, political, and economic life and settle disputes in a reasonably predictable manner. Some characteristics of four principal legal elements are fused in Japan's distinctive legal system: modern Japanese law, civil law, common law, and customary law. As in every democratic nation, law and society influence and occasionally ignore each other in complicated ways.

Four Sources of Law——In its civil law aspects Japan, like many other countries, operates under very comprehensive codes, called the Six Codes (Roppō). Of these, the CONSTITUTION is the primary document governing legal and political relationships; and in fact, the democratic principles of this "supreme law" have formed the basis for continuing fundamental modifications of society, law, and government since it came into effect in May 1947. The constitution establishes popular sovereignty, an emperor symbolic of the nation, human rights, a strong bicameral legislature (the Diet), a counterbalancing judiciary, and a unique prohibition on war and normal armament (art. 9). The five other codes are quasi-constitutional in nature—the CIVIL CODE, the Code of CIVIL PROCEDURE, the Penal Code, the Code of CRIMINAL PROCEDURE, and the COMMERCIAL CODE—and add to the constitutional foundations the outlines of various parts of the legal structure, which are in turn filled in with detail by statutes, cabinet orders, local ordinances, and various types of administrative regulations.

Japan has been a civil law country since the late 19th century, while it began to become a quasi-common law nation, emphasizing more the importance of judicial holdings as a form of law, under the post-1945 Anglo-American influence of the Occupation period. Although Japan's judges began to enjoy independence in deciding cases in the late 19th century, the courts were limited under the Constitution of 1889 (Meiji Constitution) in the kinds of cases they could decide and were not administratively independent. Today "the whole judicial power is vested in a Supreme Court," 8 high courts, 50 district courts, 50 family courts, and 575 summary courts. All courts are administered by the Supreme Court, separate from the executive and legislative organs of government. Their power of judicial review extends to judging the validity of all laws and official acts, but it has been used sparingly, in part because of civil law theories of judicial deference to the democratically elected Diet's laws.

In deciding how to deal with a legal problem, a Japanese judge, legal scholar, or lawyer today may see if useful hints for solution can be found in the laws and judicial decisions of other civil law and common law countries, in particular, West Germany and the United States; but two Japanese elements in the legal system will more likely guide the legal professional in his understanding of the issues: modern Japanese legal practice, especially but not only since 1946, and customary law.

A great body of Japanese statutes and other official rules has been accumulated, refined, and annually added to for decades, and judges have authoritatively settled hundreds of thousands of disputes in light of these laws and the constitution; but, as in all legal systems perhaps, customary law interflows with written law and often affects, either by design or implicitly, the way statutory law is understood and applied. A few examples will illustrate the Japanese way of fusing civil law, common law, and customary law in daily life.

Law and Custom——Japanese family law respects related custom, but law and custom now differ from those of predemocratic modern times, when the father and the eldest son of a house enjoyed precedence over others. Now, for instance, when the father of a family dies, the widow is accorded special rights of inheritance and all the children have a right to claim equal shares under the Civil Code. However, the special place of the eldest son is still recognized by custom, principally by giving him the primary responsibility for settling the affairs of the deceased on behalf of the family but not according him special privilege over the inheritance. Judges uphold the constitutional and legal equality of surviving children when settling inheritance law disputes.

A mixture of ethics, customary law, and written law also serves the general preference in Japan for using a go-between when making the often elaborate arrangements for MARRIAGE (the NAKŌDO custom), when developing new business agreements, or when pursuing settlement of a political, personal, or business dispute in the presence of a third party. Formal law protects the equal rights of men and women to decide who they will marry without parental or other coercion, in contrast to prewar practice. Nevertheless, most young Japanese like to use a mutually respected third party, usually their senior, to assist them or their families with introductions and preparations for the wedding and future interfamily harmony. For example, a young eligible may be introduced to quite a few prospective spouses before he or she decides upon a suitable partner. In many contexts where the Japanese tend to use go-betweens the principal parties remain independent decision makers in the final analysis.

Disputes and Their Settlement——Like other peoples, the Japanese like to avoid going to court to settle their arguments, and the legal system is perhaps particularly well organized to facilitate out-of-court problem resolution. Under special law and procedures, disputes are very often resolved by compromise on one or both sides in the presence of an empathetic and conciliating third party who puts a seal of approval on the newly attained, at least formal, harmony. The third party's task is not so much to authoritatively arbitrate a dispute and impose a solution as to draw the opposing sides closer together on the issues in as civil an atmosphere as possible. Such a mediator may be a friend or relative or one or more people with some official status, such as a conciliation commissioner, a family court counselor, a judge, or a policeman. Lay civil liberty commissioners play a major role in dealing with human rights problems in over 10,000 towns and neighborhoods. Japan has too few judges, and they often cannot provide speedy settlement of legal problems, civil or criminal; but various modes of adjustment and conciliation of differences between parties somewhat alleviate the problem and supplement the litigation proceedings of courts. See DISPUTE RESOLUTION SYSTEMS OTHER THAN LITIGATION; LAW, ATTITUDES TOWARD.

Perceptions and Uses of Law——The preference for conciliation does not mean Japanese people are less prone to argument or litigation than other peoples or that disputants usually settle for less than they would receive if they asserted their rights in court. However, most Japanese seem more comfortable in a group context, as is created by mediation, than in a situation in which they must face an adversary, a superior, an official, or the public alone. Many Japanese adults, especially white-collar workers, tend to belong to tightly knit, rather closed in-groups—occupational groups, for example, such as a company, government office, or university department. Though legal rights inhere in individual legal persons, the sense of legal right in such contexts, as well as of competition, seems to live strongest not in individuals as such, but in the group owed loyalty in its relations with other groups. Each company or ministry, or student organization, for example, might be likened to a quasi-feudal domain which is closed to and at times in democratic competition with "outsiders," especially those engaged in the same type of productive activity.

A substantial number of Japan's officials, cultural leaders, and business leaders majored in law as undergraduates at university faculties of law, and they refer to the written law on a regular basis in conducting their affairs. Members of the local and national higher civil service tend to be legalistic in their approach to problems. In foreign economic relations, some observers of Japan's bureaucracy at work have suggested that customary practices of ADMINISTRATIVE GUIDANCE, protective of the interests of the "feudal domain" against outsiders, both domestic and foreign, have been more important than published forms of written law. But in general, Japan follows common international law practices in its trade relations.

Well-used copies of the Six Codes and of a wide array of pertinent laws and regulations will be found not only in law offices and judicial chambers but also in the offices of thousands of Japan's private organizations, government units, mass media companies, schools, and scholars. In addition, many companies have their own codes, which may best be classified as customary law. Company rules embody the traditions, values, goals, and regulated practices within the company, add to a sense of quasi-familial pride and solidarity, govern internal and external relations, and express and promote company loyalty. Other essentially private "legal systems" blend with formal law; for example, the Railroad Benefit Association's regulation of the sales of obscene magazines in railroad stations interacts with other industry systems and local youth protection ordinances.

The Legal Profession and the Public——Virtually all judges, prosecutors, and lawyers have been trained since 1947 in the same post-graduate education program at the Supreme Court's LEGAL TRAINING AND RESEARCH INSTITUTE in Tōkyō, entrance to which is only by severely competitive national law examinations. Law and legal professionals touch the lives of other citizens in many ways outside courts and offices.

General and specialized law books and law journals in great abundance are regularly advertised in national newspapers with a daily circulation surpassing 50 million. Synopses of the law in special interest areas and popularized treatments of the law and famous cases appear in books, magazines, and newspapers for the general reader and for the householder concerned about consumer rights or the intricacies of real estate and tax law. In addition, both legislative disputes and major judicial decisions receive substantial coverage in the mass media. Roundtable discussions of legal problems by legal scholars and other private or public specialists in an issue area are carried on radio, television, and the print media. Legal scholars act as guest commentators for national and local media. Japanese thus have ready access to information and concern about law and legal problems on a regular basis.

Criminal Justice——Japan's system of criminal justice is effective and only rarely severe. The crime rate is very low, and Japan is a physically safe country in which to live. What happens when a crime is committed? Many offenders surrender to the authorities, and most confess their wrongdoing; but a coerced confession is not accepted as evidence in court. The courts are clear on that point. Even if a prosecutor has sufficient evidence to virtually assure a conviction, he is likely to refrain from indictment about 40 percent of the time for criminological reasons. If he does not feel sure of a conviction, a prosecutor very rarely goes to trial.

Most cases are decided in summary courts (minor crimes) or district courts; the conviction rate is around 99 percent. Although the death penalty is imposed on the average a few times each year for particularly heinous crimes, penalties are usually small fines. Only a small percentage of those convicted are sentenced to prison for even a short time, and about two-thirds of these sentences are suspended. Compassion for offenders, particularly if they obey the customary laws of repentence and apology, characterizes Japanese law in many civil and criminal problem areas. Just as a convicted criminal receives a lesser and often suspended sentence if repentent, so a magazine that has defamed a person may well be required to pay a smaller amount in damages if it has published a retraction and apology. The Supreme Court has held that judicial orders to apologize do not clearly violate constitutional freedom of conscience. See CRIME.

A Few Legal Tensions——Although the Supreme Court has the right of final say in any given case, both that court and other courts may rule contrary to prior doctrine in other cases. Moreover, sometimes customs or politics substantially affect the way the intent of a Supreme Court judgment is carried out in practice. For example, in the 1970s: the Supreme Court dismissed a case on grounds of unconstitutional delay of justice, but other cases remained very slow of resolution without serious attention to that factor by courts; the highest tribunal struck down the heavier penalties imposed by code law for murder of an ascendant than for other homicide (1973 Partricide Decision) as contrary to constitutional guarantees of equal procedural justice before the law, but the Diet has not taken clear action to modify the law accordingly; similarly, the Diet has not taken adequate remedial action after the Supreme Court in 1976 ruled unconstitutional the degree of malapportionment of Diet seats existing in 1972; the Supreme Court upheld a company's right to dismiss a worker who had not been candid about his political activities during student days, but mediation led to the full reinstatement of the employee with back pay.

As in all rule-of-law systems, the task of law in Japan is to provide generally operative guidelines and procedures for making and implementing formal agreements and for approximating justice in a civilized settlement of disputes and criminal cases. In pursuing these ends, the legal system of Japan nudges society toward perceptions and practices ever more in keeping with the principles in the constitution of Japan while respecting its rich legal heritage.

■——Lawrence W. Beer and Hidenori Tomatsu, *A Guide to the Study of Japanese Law,* Occasional Papers/Reprint Series in Contemporary Asian Studies (1978). *Hanrei jihō* (Nihon Hyōronsha), case reporter, thrice monthly. Dan Fenno Henderson, *Conciliation*

and Japanese Law: Tokugawa and Modern, 2 vols (1965). *Hōritsu jihō* (Nihon Hyōronsha), monthly general journal. *Hōsō jihō* (Hōsōkai), authoritative legal statistics and analyses. Hiroshi Itoh and Lawrence W. Beer, *The Constitutional Case Law of Japan: Selected Supreme Court Decisions, 1961–70* (1978). *Jurisuto* (Yūhikaku), authoritative general legal journal. *Law in Japan: An Annual* (Nichibei Hōgakkai). John M. Maki, *Court and Constitution in Japan: Selected Supreme Court Decisions, 1948–60* (1964). Hideo Tanaka, assisted by Malcolm D. H. Smith, ed, *The Japanese Legal System: Introductory Cases and Materials* (1976). Arthur T. Von Mehren, ed, *Law in Japan: The Legal Order in a Changing Society* (1963).

Lawrence W. BEER

Legal Training and Research Institute

(Shihō Kenshūjo). A national educational institution charged with sole responsibility for providing professional legal training to those pursuing careers in law; it was established by law in 1947 in Tōkyō as an agency of the Supreme Court. Its major functions are, first, to provide legal apprentices with comprehensive professional training in the practice of civil and criminal jurisprudence and, second, to offer judges continuing advanced legal education.

Aspirants wishing to enter the legal profession in Japan must, with few exceptions, meet three requirements: (1) successfully pass parts one and two (part one is waived for certain qualified candidates) of the national LAW EXAMINATION *(shihō shiken)*; (2) complete two years of training at the Legal Training and Research Institute; and (3) pass the final qualifying law examination. A law degree from a university is not a formal requirement for sitting for the national law examination. As a matter of practice, however, the majority of applicants are graduates of university law departments. The Japanese legal system consists of three branches: namely, the judiciary, the procuracy, and the bar. The three qualifications listed above are required of all candidates for any of these three branches.

Faculty members are selected from among experienced judges, public prosecutors, and practicing lawyers. The former two groups serve on a full-time basis, while the latter group serves on a part-time basis. Each year about 500 applicants successfully pass the national law examination; almost all of them are admitted to the institute as legal apprentices called *shihō shūshūsei*.

The institute's two-year training program is divided into three terms. The first 4 months are a general training period, the purpose of which is to provide an introduction to the practical skills and techniques of the legal profession. The curriculum is composed of five courses: civil trial, criminal trial, public prosecution, civil practice, and criminal practice. Exercises in legal draftsmanship constitute an important part of the learning process. Apprentices are supplied with copies of actual trial records and are required to draft judgments for the trial courses, indictments for the prosecution course, and pleadings for the practice courses. Following this initial introduction is a 16-month field-training term, which is subdivided into four 4-month rotations in the civil and criminal sections of district courts, district prosecutors' offices, and offices of practicing lawyers respectively. During this term, apprentices are expected to develop their legal skills and cultivate their legal thinking by actual work experience. After field training apprentices again gather at the institute for 4 months of final training to consolidate the learning from their field experiences and to correct discrepancies inevitably resulting from uneven field experiences.

Upon successful completion of the two-year training program and the final examination, apprentices may either be appointed assistant judges or public prosecutors or may register as practicing lawyers. In recent years, the tendency among the institute's approximately 500 graduates has been for about 70 to become assistant judges, about 50 public prosecutors, about 370 practicing lawyers, and the remainder law professors and others. As of April 1979 the institute's graduates accounted for approximately 77 percent of the entire Japanese legal profession.

The institute has also been given the responsibility for providing advanced judicial training and research by way of continuing legal education. Since in the Japanese judicial system most assistant judges begin their judicial careers immediately after graduation from the institute, advanced training is essential in preparing them to assume their responsibilities on the bench. During their 10 years of tenure, all assistant judges have a chance to complete various advanced training programs.

The Legal Training and Research Institute is credited with having significantly raised the educational standards of the legal profession in Japan from its pre–World War II level and made the standards of the three branches uniform. It has made a great contribution to the achievement of the idea that the legal profession is one integrated profession aiming at the same objective of promoting justice and good judicial administration. See also LEGAL EDUCATION.

■ ——Jirō Matsuda, "The Japanese Legal Training and Research Institute," *The American Journal of Comparative Law* 7.3 (1958). Supreme Court of Japan, ed, *The Legal Training and Research Institute of Japan* (1977).   *MUTŌ Shunkō*

Le Gendre, Charles William (1830–1899)

American general and diplomat; as an adviser to the Japanese Ministry of Foreign Affairs from 1872 to 1875, he played an important role in organizing the TAIWAN EXPEDITION OF 1874, a Japanese punitive attack on that island. After serving as a commander in the American Civil War, in 1866 Le Gendre was appointed US consul at the Chinese treaty port of Xiamen (Amoy). While there he led a punitive expedition against Taiwan aborigines who had massacred the crew of a shipwrecked American vessel. On his way home in 1872, Le Gendre stopped in Japan and on the recommendation of American minister Charles de Long was hired by Foreign Minister SOEJIMA TANEOMI as an adviser. The Japanese government was at that time considering its own expedition to Taiwan to avenge the murder of shipwrecked Ryūkyū islanders in 1871. Le Gendre twice accompanied Soejima to Beijing (Peking) to seek redress from the Chinese government (Taiwan being under Chinese sovereignty), but without success. Then, in defiance of his own government's declaration of neutrality in the matter, he helped to organize the expedition, procuring ships and training soldiers. For these activities he was confined briefly at the US consulate, but the Japanese government showed its appreciation by awarding him—the first foreigner so honored—the Order of the Rising Sun in 1875. He remained in Japan until 1890, working in a private capacity for the political party leader ŌKUMA SHIGENOBU, and then worked for the Korean government until his death. Le Gendre was the author of *Progressive Japan: A Study of the Political and Social Needs of the Empire* (1878).

leisure-time activities

The Early Historical Period: Courtly Pastimes—— With the establishment of the RITSURYŌ SYSTEM of government at the end of the 7th century, noblemen of the imperial court constituted the principal leisure class of the time. Particularly during the Heian period (794–1185), the courtly pursuit of leisure thrived. Favorite pastimes in the imperial court included poetry composition, music, indoor games, sports, and seasonal excursions of various kinds.

Among the most popular of the indoor games were GO, SUGO-ROKU, SHŌGI, and *tagi*, all board games, and *tōko*, a game in which players attempt to throw arrows into a jar. Most of these games originated in China. However, one type of indoor game, *mono-awase*, was developed in Japan and became very popular. *Mono-awase* is a general term used to refer to a game in which the competitors bring certain objects and line them up opposite each other for judgment; *mono-awase* may also refer to a game in which skills are similarly matched. There are numerous variations of *mono-awase*, each with a different theme; among them are *kusa-awase* (plant matching), *kiku-awase* (chrysanthemum matching), *hana-awase* (flower matching), and *ōgi-awase* (fan matching). The most sophisticated of the *mono-awase* was the UTA-AWASE (poem matching), in which the participants competed in composing *tanka* (31-syllable poems) on a given subject.

Outdoor sports included KEMARI (kickball) and *takagari* (FALCONRY). Excursions and picnicking in the countryside had a wide range of forms varying with the seasons: *yukimi* (SNOW VIEWING) in the winter, *wakanatsumi* (herb picking) and HANAMI (cherry-blossom viewing) in the spring, and *momijigari* (foliage gathering) in the autumn.

Medieval Period: Warrior Pastimes—— During the Kamakura (1185–1333) and Muromachi (1333–1568) periods, the warriors who replaced the noblemen as the rulers of the country became the principal leisure class. Their favorite pastimes were active outdoor sports, the most popular of which were three mounted archery sports: YABUSAME, which used three wooden targets; KASAGAKE, which employed a single sedge hat for a target; and INUOUMONO, or dog shooting. SUMŌ wrestling, which had existed as a sport in the imperial court, was also encouraged and gained a great deal of popularity.

The more elegant courtly pastimes of poetry and music were also taken up by the higher ranks of warriors and popularized. It was during the Kamakura period that *renga* (linked verse) developed from WAKA (court poetry). *Renga* parties, in which the participants composed linked verse according to set conventions and patterns, became common. The warrior class adopted the traditional pastime of excursions as well, combining it with falconry and banquets to create a new form of outdoor entertainment. Indoor pastimes were increased with the growing popularity of tea, introduced from China by Zen monks in the early Kamakura period; it was during the Muromachi period, however, that the intricate practices of the TEA CEREMONY were established. Board games continued to be very popular throughout the medieval period.

Major diversions for the peasants of the premodern period were farming ceremonies and village festivals related to folk religion. Pilgrimages to ISE SHRINE, KŌYASAN, and other temples and shrines were also important sources of enjoyment for the rural population, but few peasants were able to make more than one or two such trips in a lifetime.

The Early Modern Period: The Leisurely Pursuits of the Townspeople—— During the Azuchi-Momoyama (1568–1600) and Edo (1600–1868) periods, the merchant classes, or CHŌNIN, who gained a great deal of economic power, became the core of the new leisure class. They adopted both courtly and warrior pastimes, the richest merchants indulging in any extravagance that money could buy.

The growth of the cities brought about the development of entertainment quarters, most typically Shijō Kawaramachi in Kyōto and Namba Shimmachi in Ōsaka, where theaters of various types and other entertainment facilities were clustered. These reflected every level of taste, from sophisticated drama such as KABUKI and JŌRURI (puppet plays), to more popular art forms such as RAKUGO and *kō-shaku*, which were forms of storytelling. Street entertainment, such as acrobatics and feats of strength, became increasingly popular in these areas. It was at this time that *sumō* wrestling became a professional spectator sport. During the Edo period licensed prostitution quarters developed, and with them a unique culture of the demimonde. YOSHIWARA in Edo (now Tōkyō) and Shimabara in Kyōto were two typical examples of such licensed quarters.

Indoor games such as *shōgi* and *go* became widespread among the common people. Various kinds of card games, including *uta karuta* (see HYAKUNIN ISSHU), IROHA KARUTA, *unsun karuta*, and HANAFUDA, also gained popularity (see PLAYING CARDS). Playing the SHAMISEN (a three-stringed instrument), singing KOUTA (short ballads), and traditional dancing also became cultural pastimes for ordinary people. *Haikai* poetry replaced *renga*, which had become extremely complex and had declined in popularity (see RENGA AND HAIKAI). *Haikai* composition parties were often held, even among the common people. Very often people would enjoy leisure activities together in public places such as public baths and barber shops, which performed an increasingly vital function during the Edo period as general social centers for the less wealthy.

Introduction of Western Leisure Activities—— During the Meiji (1868–1912) and Taishō (1912–26) periods, many Western pastimes, such as card games, billiards, and ballroom dancing, were imported. A more significant development was the introduction of Western sports, such as TENNIS, BASEBALL, TRACK AND FIELD EVENTS, TABLE TENNIS, soccer, rugby, basketball, VOLLEYBALL, and boating. Many of these sports became part of school curricula, and thus took root in Japan. Mountaineering and ocean bathing also gained popularity.

Western theater was imported and developed indigenously as a modern Japanese dramatic art form known as SHINGEKI or new theater. Operas and musical reviews were also imported and adapted to suit Japanese tastes. From the middle part of the Taishō period onwards, two uniquely Japanese popular musical theater companies evolved out of Western musical drama, the Asakusa Opera and the TAKARAZUKA KAGEKIDAN. At the same time, many traditional forms of entertainment, such as *rakugo*, MANZAI, NANIWA-BUSHI, and KŌDAN all remained popular among the common people (see YOSE).

Motion pictures (see FILM, JAPANESE), introduced into Japan for the first time in 1896, quickly gained acceptance, and by the Taishō period they were the main source of entertainment for the masses. At the same time, there was a conspicuous development of newspapers and mass-oriented magazines. In 1925 the first radio broadcasts were made, and gradually most people's leisure activities came to involve the mass media (see BROADCASTING).

From the late Taishō to the early Shōwa (1926–) periods, urban entertainment districts burgeoned with cafes, shows, movies, and ballrooms. After the MANCHURIAN INCIDENT (1931), the social atmosphere was increasingly influenced by militarism and nationalistic right-wing politics, and such lively diversions were gradually suppressed.

Leisurely Pursuits since World War II —— During the difficult days that immediately followed World War II, the radio was an important source of entertainment. Songs, *rakugo, manzai,* and radio dramas helped many people to forget the hardships they were daily facing. Partly encouraged by the Occupation forces, various sports were revived, although such martial arts as JŪDŌ and KENDŌ were forbidden for some time. Among the revived sports, baseball was the most popular. As early as 1946, four major baseball events had been revived: the Tōkyō "Big Six" university tournament, the inter-high school tournaments, inter-city nonprofessional tournaments, and professional games. Baseball fever spread quickly among young children, who held impromptu sandlot games wherever there was enough space.

From the early 1950s, sports on which gambling was allowed, such as horse racing and bicycle racing, became very popular, as did PACHINKO, a type of pinball machine. MAH-JONGG, which had been popular in the early Shōwa period, was also revived. However, it was only from the 1960s onwards that leisure pursuits were taken up on a large scale. It was during this time of high economic growth that the English word "leisure," rendered as *rejā,* entered the Japanese vocabulary. Phrases such as *rejā jidai* (age of leisure) and *rejā būmu* (leisure boom) became common.

The Growth of the Leisure Industry —— Working hours in Japan have always tended to be longer than in Western countries, but they have decreased slightly, especially since the adoption of the five-day workweek by some companies. With the rise in income levels, there has been a wider distribution of durable household appliances, such as washing machines, vacuum cleaners, refrigerators, and rice cookers, which in turn has brought about more free time for women (see STANDARD OF LIVING). In a 1975 Japan Broadcasting Corporation (NHK) survey, the free time for the average person on a weekday increased from 5 hours in 1960, to 6 hours and 24 minutes in 1975. Increases in income and free time have provided a rewarding market for the leisure industry: from 1960 on there has been rapid growth in various leisure-related industries and a vast increase in the amounts of money spent by individual families for various leisure activities. According to a report made by the Prime Minister's Office, the annual expenditure of the average family on leisure activities increased by three and a half times between 1965 and 1975. The ratio of leisure expenditures also increased from 18 percent to 22 percent of total expenditures.

Mass Leisure —— With more leisure time available and with the growth of the leisure industry, the range of activities has diversified in recent years. A large amount of people's spare time continues to be occupied by the mass media, especially television. The average Japanese watches more than three hours of television on weekdays, and as much as four hours on Sundays. First introduced to Japan in 1953, television had completely outstripped radio by around 1961, both in number of sets and in popularity. It has also driven the movies from their former place of prominence, becoming the principal source of entertainment for the masses. Movies reached a height of popularity during the last few years of the 1950s, when an estimated 100 million people attended films annually. Since then, with the growth of television, film attendance has dwindled: during 1978 and 1979 it was at only 20 or 25 percent of the peak figures. Professional baseball and *sumō* would not have developed into the immensely popular spectator sports they are now without the assistance and influence of television. The links between the mass media and leisure time are also reflected in the printed media, as can be seen in the boom in sales of WEEKLY MAGAZINES, COMIC MAGAZINES, and cheap paperbacks since the mid-1960s.

Not only passive pastimes, such as watching television, but also more active diversions, such as sports and travel, have become increasingly popular. The most popular participation sports in Japan include baseball, softball, volleyball, table tennis, swimming, and more recently golf, skiing, and tennis. Tourism has become very popular, and many Japanese have begun to travel abroad: according to Ministry of Justice reports, 660,000 people went abroad in 1970, and that figure had increased to 3.5 million by 1978 (see TRAVEL). The countries Japanese tourists visited the most were, in order of popularity: the United States (including Hawaii and Guam), Taiwan, Hong Kong, South Korea, Great Britain, and Canada.

Board games such as *go, shōgi,* and Mah-Jongg have remained popular, while gambling, whether in the form of *pachinko* or betting

sports such as horse, bicycle, and speedboat racing, has not lost its appeal. Night life also continues to be an important source of relaxation, with major entertainment districts existing in all cities. Interest in traditional Japanese crafts and rituals, such as FLOWER ARRANGEMENT *(ikebana)* and the TEA CEREMONY, is as strong as ever, particularly among young women. More recently, there seems to have been a basic change in people's attitudes toward work and play. The view of leisure as subordinate to work or as a means of refreshing physical energies for work has become obsolete, especially among the young, whose thinking is moving away from the traditional work-centered ethic.

■ —— Ronald P. Dore, *City Life in Japan* (1958). Hidetoshi Katō, *Japanese Popular Culture* (1959). David W. Plath, *The After Hours: Modern Japan and the Search for Enjoyment* (1969). INOUE Shun

Lelang (Lolang)

(J: Rakurō; Kor: Nangnang). A Former (206 BC–AD 8) and Later (25–220) Han-dynasty Chinese colony established in the northwestern region of the Korean peninsula, in the area surrounding what is now the city of P'yŏngyang, by Emperor Wu-ti (Wudi) in 108 BC. Lelang facilitated the sinicization of ancient Korean tribal society, setting the stage for the rise of the three Korean kingdoms of KOGURYŎ, PAEKCHE, and SILLA after Han China fell prey to nomadic invasions in the 3rd century. The colony submitted to forces of Koguryŏ in AD 313. Extensive excavation and preservation of Lelang-period artifacts and tombs—a prime source of knowledge of Han Chinese culture—was initiated by Japanese scholars between 1910 and 1940 and is continued today by scholars of the Democratic People's Republic of China. According to the Chinese chronicle WEI ZHI *(Wei chih),* HIMIKO, the female ruler of Yamatai, sent tribute to Lelang. C. Kenneth QUINONES

Lenin and Japan

Vladimir Il'ich Lenin (1870–1924), the founder of the modern Soviet state and a major contributor to the theory of communism, studied the history of Japan in depth. His statements about Japan are to be found in his various works, speeches, papers, interviews, and in the materials preserved in his study-apartment in the Kremlin. They contain a concise yet profound economic and political description of Japan at various stages of its development, starting at the end of the 1860s and the beginning of the 1870s.

In "An Attempt at the Summary of the Data of World History after 1870" Lenin saw the Meiji Restoration of 1868, which had ushered in Japan's capitalist era, as revolutionary in character. He noted that of all the countries of Asia it had been in Japan that the conditions for the widest and most rapid growth of capitalism had been created, and that in its rate of industrial development Japan had overtaken many capitalist states. Lenin's greatest contribution was to identify the military-feudal nature of Japanese imperialism, which, according to his analysis, had the following characteristics: the preservation of feudal remnants in the economy and political structure; the retention of the monarchy and a certain independence of the imperial bureaucracy and the military cliques (GUMBATSU); the aggressiveness and frequency of war in Japan's foreign policy at all stages of development; the relatively rapid transition to a policy of oppressing other nations and enslaving colonies, facilitated by the proximity of Japan to the countries of East and Southeast Asia; and the financial weakness and lack of independence of Japan, which limited the ability of its rulers to finance a major war and forced them to seek financially powerful allies.

Lenin also pointed out that the primary sphere of Japan's military aggression was China, in particular Manchuria, and Korea, and that in the course of this aggression the contradictions between the imperialist powers in the Far East and the Pacific Ocean were drastically sharpened, leading to military conflicts. He devoted much attention to analyzing the causes of Japan's victory over tsarist Russia in 1904–05 (see RUSSO-JAPANESE WAR), the contradictions inherent in Japanese-American relations and the inevitability of war between Japan and the United States, the reasons for the Japanese intervention in the Soviet Far East, and the historical role of the buffer FAR EASTERN REPUBLIC, founded at his own initiative to ensure victory over the occupiers.

Lenin was well acquainted with the development of the socialist movement in Japan. In the autumn of 1918 the Dutch socialist S. J. Rutgers brought with him a resolution concerning the solidarity of the Japanese socialists with their Russian comrades. In the early

1920s he had a number of meetings with prominent figures in the Japanese socialist movement, notably with KATAYAMA SEN (three times), Taguchi Unzō, and Yoshida Hajime. Of great significance in the characterization of Lenin as a statesman and political leader are his conversations with the Japanese journalists Fuse Katsuji of the *Ōsaka mainichi* and *Tōkyō nichinichi* newspapers and Nakahira Ryō of the *Ōsaka asahi,* which took place in June 1920. Upon his return to Japan, Fuse published a book entitled *Rōnō Rokoku yori* (1922, From Worker-Peasant Russia), which contained chapters on "An Interview with Lenin" and "The Leader of the Bolsheviks." Another correspondent, Ōba Kakō, published a book entitled *Rēnin to Roshia kakumei* (1923, Lenin and the Russian Revolution).

The publication of Lenin's writings in Japan dates back to the period of the Russo-Japanese War. The antimilitarist weekly newspaper of the Japanese socialists, HEIMIN SHIMBUN, on 24 April 1904 published an abridged translation from the German leaflet of the Central Committee of the Russian Social Democratic Labor Party under the title "To the Russian Proletariat," written by Lenin. On 7 July 1904 the editor of *Heimin shimbun* addressed a letter to Lenin in Geneva, informing him that socialist literature had been sent to Russian prisoners of war in Japan.

Most of the translations of Lenin's works appeared in Japan after the October Revolution in Russia. In October 1917 the journal *Shinshakai* (New Society) published a translation by the Japanese socialist SAKAI TOSHIHIKO of Lenin's essay "About the Tasks of the Russian Social Democratic Labor Party in the Russian Revolution." A number of translations of Lenin's works were printed by Japanese revolutionary emigrants in the United States, including those in the newspaper *Heimin,* published in San Francisco by Katayama Sen. Subsequently, various publishers began to disseminate translations of Lenin's writings in Japan. Separate works of Lenin were issued periodically and many were also included in collections, notably *The State and Revolution, Imperialism as the Highest Stage of Capitalism,* and *Materialism and Empiriocriticism.*

Between 1921 and 1937, 292 separate editions of the works of Lenin were published in Japan; between 1945 and 1967, 134 separate editions and 32 collections of his writings appeared. In 1969, a 45-volume translation of the complete works of Lenin was completed, the first such effort among the capitalist countries of the world. In recent years a number of biographies of Lenin have been published in Japan in translation from Russian.

——D. I. Gol'dberg, *V. I. Lenin i Iaponiia* (1970). This book and *Bibliografiia Iaponii* (1960) list the writings of Lenin on Japan as well as other works on the subject in the Russian language. Japanese translations of Lenin's writings as well as related Japanese studies will be found in *Nisso kankei tosho sōran* (1968).

David I. GOLDBERG

Lerch, Theodor von (1869–1945)

Austrian officer who introduced skiing in Japan. He was posted to Japan in 1910 as a military attaché at the Austrian embassy and in the following year he taught skiing to members of the Takada 58th Infantry Regiment stationed in Niigata Prefecture. Afterward he moved to Hokkaidō, where he taught skiing to the Asahikawa army division. He returned to Austria in 1912.

TAKEDA Fumio

lese majesty

(fukeizai). A crime against the dignity of the emperor or a member of the imperial family. Lese majesty was recognized under the Meiji Constitution of 1889 but is not included in the 1947 constitution. The Meiji Constitution states (art. 3) that the emperor "is sacred and inviolable." In his official commentary on that article Itō Hirobumi, the principal drafter of the 1889 constitution, wrote: "Not only shall there be no irreverence for the Emperor's person, but he shall not be made a topic of derogatory comment nor one of discussion."

On the basis of that constitutional provision, the old PENAL CODE provided (art. 74) that anyone found guilty of lese majesty toward the emperor, the grand empress dowager, the empress dowager, the empress, the crown prince, the imperial grandson, a Shintō shrine, or an imperial mausoleum would be punished by imprisonment of from three months to five years. The same crime against any other member of the imperial family was punishable by a prison term of from two months to four years. The GREAT COURT OF CASSATION (Daishin'in, also referred to as the Great Court of Judicature) had jurisdiction over the crime of lese majesty. The old Penal Code further provided the death penalty for anyone found guilty of inflict-

ing or intending to inflict bodily harm on members of the imperial family. See HIGH TREASON INCIDENT OF 1910.

The 1947 constitution establishes the principles of equality under the law and of nondiscrimination for any reason, thus eliminating the special status of the emperor and the imperial family under the old order. Consequently, the current Penal Code, as revised under the 1947 constitution, does not contain the crime of lese majesty. However, it recognizes the crime of defamation and provides that the emperor, the empress, the grand empress dowager, the empress dowager, and the crown prince may lodge complaints of defamation in the courts through the prime minister. No such complaint has ever been filed, although there have been several incidents of publications which have allegedly impaired the dignity of the emperor or the imperial family.

John M. MAKI

Leyte Gulf, Battle of

(Reite Oki Kaisen; also known in Japan as Firipin Oki Kaisen or Battle off the Philippines; not to be confused with the Battle of the PHILIPPINE SEA). Also known as the Battle of the Philippine Islands. Largest naval engagement in the Pacific in World War II; fought near the Philippine Islands from 23–26 October 1944. The Combined Fleet of the Imperial Japanese Navy was divided into three groups, with the final objective of attacking the American landing craft assembled in Leyte Gulf for the invasion of Leyte Island. The southern force, under Vice Admiral Nishimura Shōji, was intercepted by American forces in the Battle of Surigao Strait. The central force, under Vice Admiral Kurita Takeo, was able to advance as far as Samar before being turned back. Vice Admiral Ozawa Jisaburō's northern force, which comprised the bulk of Japan's remaining aircraft carriers, was chosen as the bait to draw the American forces northward. The Japanese lost ships, including the MUSASHI, and hundreds of aircraft, leaving the Combined Fleet incapable of any further large-scale naval operations. See also WORLD WAR II.

ICHIKI Toshio

liability for negligence

(kashitsu sekinin). A legal term which refers to the principle that no liability is incurred without negligence. The principle of liability for negligence is clearly set forth in article 709 of the Civil Code: "A person who by willful intent or negligence infringes the rights of another shall be responsible for indemnifying the injury which is thereby incurred."

All other types of tort liability (except the liability of the owners of structures as set forth in article 717) are also forms of negligence liability in which the burden of proof concerning negligence shifts to the offending party. In contrast to this, liability without fault is imposed on businesses for injury to human life or health resulting from air or water pollution. In mining cases, the holder of the mining concession is also subject to liability without fault. The principle of liability for negligence is modified in the case of fires, however. The person who causes a fire is not liable unless it is the result of willful intent or gross negligence. This is because Japanese houses were traditionally constructed of wood and paper, so that fires spread quickly and the person who caused the fire also suffered the misfortune of having his own buildings destroyed.

The criterion for judging negligence is "whether there has been a violation of the obligation to exercise the care which is demanded of an ordinary person in social life." Enterprises, however, are obligated to exercise a high degree of caution. For example, in a series of lawsuits involving damages caused by chemicals, medicines, food products, and pollution, the courts, imposing a duty on enterprises to foresee such consequences, recognized their responsibility to compensate for damages. Thus, the liability of enterprises, although subject to the principle of negligence liability, virtually amounts to liability without fault.

NOMURA Yoshihiro

liability without fault

(mukashitsu sekinin). Liability to compensate for damages where there was no intent or neglect involved in the damages; also called absolute liability and liability for effects, as compared to liability for negligence. Liability without fault is recognized in the field of contract law, but the problem is for the most part in the domain of tort law.

With regard to torts, the Japanese CIVIL CODE takes negligence as its standard. However, the development of industry has resulted in a situation where many enterprises make large profits from types of business that create unavoidable dangers to society, and it is no longer considered adequate to base liability solely on a negligence standard. As a result, a number of theories recognizing liability without fault have been advocated. The responsibility for compensation theory, for example, holds that the party receiving benefits from a profitable activity is liable for damages arising therefrom. The hazard liability theory holds that the party that creates a danger to society is liable for any damages arising therefrom. The Civil Code recognized product liability on the basis of the hazard liability theory. Based on the compensation liability theory, the code recognized an employer's liability where the requirements of negligence and intention had been substantially lowered. With these provisions as precedent, it has been possible to establish an expanded liability for corporations, for example, through an expanded definition of product, a broader interpretation of the concept of defects, or a stricter interpretation of the standards of supervision by an employer. The same effect can be achieved through a wider recognition of foreknowledge and a reversal of the burden of proof. For example, in the case of a victim of the side effects of a drug, if some kind of relation of cause and effect is established, then it is possible to presume the negligence of the manufacturer and to place the burden of proof of absolute liability on the manufacturer.

However, with the increasing number of problems caused by industry, such as mining pollution, water pollution, and air pollution, and in the case of traffic accidents, it has been difficult to impose a fair share of the liability on everyone concerned. It has thus been necessary to provide a solution by legislation. Damage compensation systems were already established for industrial accidents, but new systems were necessary to administer external liabilities; examples are the compensation systems for damage caused by mines and nuclear energy plants. When strong protests developed against pollution in the latter half of the 1960s, absolute liability laws were enacted in rapid succession. Examples are laws to prevent air and water pollution. There is also the AUTOMOBILE LIABILITY SECURITY LAW which does not formally establish liability without fault, but is so structured that the proof by the defendant of his absence of fault is not easily established.

This legislation substantially improved the legal position of victims, but a system of providing compensation was also needed. Thus, for example, the Automobile Liability Security Law provides insurance payments (equivalent to compensation payments) to the victim based on compulsory insurance. In addition, a law for the compensation of pollution victims established a system whereby compensation payments are made by a special corporation created with corporate funds. A system for the compensation of victims of the side effects of medicines was established in 1979 on substantially the same basis. It is likely that liability-without-fault legislation will continue to spread, with increased attention to product liability legislation for food products, automobiles, and other products. However, with the proliferation of this kind of legislation and social security laws, their relationships will become difficult to understand, and quite contrary to intentions, compensation could become more difficult to obtain. With more complete dependence on insurance systems, there is also the concern that corporations will be freed from guilt for the problems they cause, so some consideration must be given to the enactment of criminal penalties. To provide effective compensation, it is desirable that the recognition of victims be provided quickly and with neutrality, and it may be necessary to establish a government organ for the purpose of reviewing compensation claims. See also PRODUCT LIABILITY. — ENDŌ Hiroshi

Liang Qichao (Liang Ch'i-ch'ao) (1873–1929)

(J: Ryō Keichō). The most influential Chinese intellectual leader of the first decade of the 20th century. An advocate of reform and constitutionalism, Liang Qichao was impressed by Japan's transformation following its opening to the West and introduced his countrymen to Western philosophy and history, which he had discovered through Japanese translations while a political refugee in Japan.

As the leading disciple of KANG YOUWEI (K'ang Yu-wei), the reform leader of the latter part of the Qing (Ch'ing) dynasty (1644–1911), Liang was active in the movement that culminated in the Hundred Days' Reform of 1898. In this Liang saw himself and other reformers as following the example of patriotic *samurai* from Satsuma (now Kagoshima Prefecture) and Chōshū (now Yamaguchi Prefecture), the domains that had led the MEIJI RESTORATION (1868) in Japan.

Following the failure of the Hundred Days' Reform, Liang, with the help of the Japanese legation in Tianjin (Tientsin), escaped to Tōkyō, where he was befriended by the politician INUKAI TSUYOSHI and other Japanese supporters of the Chinese reform movement. It was during his years in Japan that Liang exerted his greatest influence as a publicist, publishing a series of journals, including the important *Xinmin congbao (Hsin-min ts'ung-pao;* New People's Miscellany; 1902–07), in Yokohama. Echoing FUKUZAWA YUKICHI, the early advocate of Western thought in Japan, whose work he had read, Liang emphasized the importance of individualism in building up the nation in a world that he saw as determined by the principles of Social Darwinism. The brilliance of style as much as the quantity of Liang's articles on Western ideas accounted for much of their impact. Although his political stance fluctuated, Liang continued to support Kang Youwei's constitutional monarchy movement against the revolutionary, anti-Manchu movement of SUN YAT-SEN and the Tōkyō-based revolutionary United League (Tongmeng Hui; T'ung-meng Hui).

After the fall of the Qing dynasty in 1912, Liang returned to China. Now reconciled to the revolution, Liang engaged in politics. He continued to write and in 1915 tried to rouse public opinion against Japan's TWENTY-ONE DEMANDS. He encouraged his former student CAI E (Ts'ai O) in Cai's successful opposition to the monarchical ambitions of YUAN SHIKAI (Yüan Shih-k'ai). In 1917 Liang, then minister of finance in the cabinet of DUAN QIRUI (Tuan Ch'i-jui), retired from politics, disillusioned with Duan's flirtation with Japan. See NISHIHARA LOANS.

Hao Chang, *Liang Ch'i-ch'ao and Intellectual Transition in China, 1890–1907* (1971). Philip C. Huang, *Liang Ch'i-ch'ao and Modern Chinese Liberalism* (1972). Joseph R. Levenson, *Liang Ch'i-ch'ao and the Mind of Modern China* (1953).

Liao Chengzhi (Liao Ch'eng-chih) (1908–   )

(J: Ryō Shōshi). Chinese communist official active in Sino-Japanese relations. Born in Tōkyō, the son of Liao Zhongkai (Liao Chung-k'ai; 1878–1925), a revolutionary associate of SUN YAT-SEN then in exile in Japan, Chengzhi studied at Waseda University from 1925 to 1928. He negotiated the repatriation of Japanese nationals from China in 1953. In 1962 Liao and Takasaki Tatsunosuke (1885–1964), a prominent Japanese Diet member, signed an agreement that increased Sino-Japanese trade and established informal trade missions between the two countries. See also CHINA AND JAPAN: China and Japan after 1912. — Robert ENTENMANN

Libel Law of 1875

(Zambōritsu). Law enacted on 28 June 1875 to control the press and limit freedom of expression. It provided varying penalties for publicly misrepresenting or defaming a person in writing, print, or drawing. Along with the PRESS ORDINANCE OF 1875 issued the same day, and the final version of the PUBLICATION ORDINANCE OF 1869 issued later that year, it was used by the Meiji government to stifle public political discussion stimulated by the growth of the FREEDOM AND PEOPLE'S RIGHTS MOVEMENT.

Liberal Democratic Party

(LDP; Jiyū Minshutō). Political party. Japan's ruling party since its establishment in November 1955 through the merger of the LIBERAL PARTY (Jiyūtō) and the Japan Democratic Party (see NIHON MINSHUTŌ). The Liberal and Democratic parties had developed from two post–World War II parties, the Japan Liberal Party (Nihon Jiyūtō) and the Japan Progressive Party (Nihon Shimpotō), both founded in November 1945 by conservative Diet members formerly affiliated with the prewar parties RIKKEN SEIYŪKAI and RIKKEN MINSEITŌ. As their predecessors had dominated party politics in prewar Japan, the Liberals and Democrats had dominated party politics in postwar Japan, except during the short tenure of a coalition government led by a Socialist prime minister in 1947–48.

The LDP has enjoyed wide support among farmers, businessmen, professionals, upper- and middle-level civil servants, and non-unionized workers. Until the late 1960s the party won every Diet election and the majority of local elections with substantial margins. Its policy of rapid economic growth achieved impressive results in a generally favorable international and domestic environment. During the 1970s, however, the LDP's popularity at the polls declined steadily until, towards the end of the decade, many observers began to predict its imminent fall from the position of absolute majority in both houses of the Diet and the inevitable arrival of an era of coalition governments. In June 1980 the party managed to reverse the trend and disprove the dire predictions by making substantial gains in simultaneously called elections in both the House of Representatives and the House of Councillors. Dominance of Japan's parliamentary politics by the LDP is likely to continue at least until the middle of the 1980s, if not indefinitely.

Ideology and Policies——The LDP is a conservative party in the sense that the majority of its leaders uphold such traditional political and civic values as patriotism, deference to authority, respect for the institution of the family, and belief in law and order. Even in such basic ideological commitments, however, the party is by no means monolithic. On particular policy issues opinion in the party has almost always been divided. In most cases consensus is achieved by compromise. As a result, highly eclectic and often contradictory positions have been propounded as official party lines.

While the LDP has advocated individual initiative, free enterprise, and the sanctity of private property, it has also supported government-sponsored medical insurance, old-age pension, and social welfare programs; it has defended the right of management to profits but also the right of labor to a minimum wage and improved working conditions; it has called for academic freedom and liberal education but also for government control of school textbooks and teachers. The party has supported United Nations–centered diplomacy, while also promoting special ties with the industrialized West and with the nations of Asia; it has called for development of a substantial independent self-defense capability but within the framework of mutual defense arrangements with the United States; and it has espoused free trade but also attainment of self-sufficiency in staple agricultural products.

On issues not easily amenable to compromise, divisions of opinion within the LDP have been often intense and well-publicized. The original LDP platform called for review and voluntary revision of the postwar CONSTITUTION. The plank was somewhat watered down in 1975 by the insertion of a qualifying phrase, "with the consent of the people," but has remained otherwise intact on paper. Since the late 1950s, however, this has been a dead letter invoked periodically by a small but vocal minority for rhetorical purposes but consistently ignored by the leadership. On the issue of relations with the People's Republic of China (PRC), opinion was once divided even more sharply and visibly. After early 1965 the opposing views were represented by two rival groups in the party, the pro-Taipei Asian Problems Study Group (Ajia Mondai Kenkyūkai), and the pro-Beijing (Peking), Asian-African Problems Study Group (Ajia Afurika Mondai Kenkyūkai). Even after diplomatic relations were established with the PRC in 1972, the two groups continued to fight over such issues as the conclusion of a civil aviation agreement and the peace treaty with the mainland government.

The LDP has thus embraced diverse ideological and policy interests and positions. The diversity has given the party the benefit of breadth and versatility; it has also caused disunity and immobilism in the decision-making process, which in turn has inhibited initiative and innovation in coping with the increasingly complex and intractable issues of public policy.

Organization and Leadership——The LDP inherited its basic organizational principles and structure, as well as the majority of its original members, from the Liberal and Democratic parties and, through them, from the prewar Rikken Seiyūkai and Rikken Minseitō (see POLITICAL PARTIES). The party's local organizations are weak and dominated by members of the Diet and local assemblies. The national headquarters is controlled exclusively by Diet members.

The president (sōsai) is the top party official and serves concurrently and almost automatically as the prime minister of each LDP cabinet. The president is assisted by a secretary-general (kanjichō) who directs the management of the party secretariat, including the bureaus of budget and personnel. The most important among the standing committees of the party are the Executive Council (Sōmukai) and the Political Affairs Research Committee (Seimu Chōsakai). The Executive Council consisted originally of 40, and since 1964 of 30, LDP Diet members and functions as a substitute for the annual party conference which is formally the highest decision-making body. The Political Affairs Research Committee consists of a number of standing and ad hoc committees, each concerned with policy and budgetary problems in a particular issue area. Along with the secretary-general, the chairmen of the two councils constitute a triumvirate that acts as the ultimate arbiter of disputes between the party and various groups outside the party, such as government

agencies and private interest groups, as well as among groups within the party. The LDP headquarters has several other standing committees: Diet Policy, National Organization, Finance, Public Relations, and Discipline. The conferences of party-affiliated members of the House of Representatives and the House of Councillors are convened either separately or jointly on an ad hoc basis as needs arise.

Factions——Because of the extensive powers and prerogatives vested in his office as the leader of the party and the government, the election of an LDP president is the focal point of competition and maneuver among rival groups within the party. Before 1973 a president was elected to a renewable two-year term during a party conference by LDP members of the Diet and representatives of prefectural branches. Each Diet member and prefectural delegation had one vote to cast. Between 1973 and 1977 the term of office was three years, but the vote remained restricted to the same two types of delegates to the party conference.

Under this system LDP presidential elections have bred intense competition among candidates and their factional followers. Since even the largest faction did not control more than about one quarter of the voting delegates, competing alliances of several factions were formed in support of rival candidates. Following each presidential election, the winning coalition became the "mainstream" and the losing bloc the "antimainstream." The competition and campaigning continued into periods between elections and became a constant preoccupation of both the incumbent office holders and their opponents.

In the perennial quest for votes represented by the numerical strength of one's factional following, each candidate invested his efforts and funds in the retention of the loyalty of members of his own faction and in the recruitment of new members, mainly at the time of a Diet election. During the late 1950s and through the 1960s, a half dozen major factions with up to about 100 parliamentarian affiliates, and as many minor groups with a few to a few dozen affiliates, fought, bargained, and compromised with one another for control of high party and government posts. In the process, large amounts of money routinely changed hands among candidates and their supporters.

"Money Politics"——Funds expended in the never-ending electioneering activities of rival LDP factions were supplied mainly by conservative businessmen associated with particular faction leaders. A successful candidate for LDP president was virtually synonymous with the leader of a large faction or coalition of factions with access to the wealthiest and most generous businessmen. Intimate personal relationships developed between influential LDP politicians and corporate executives.

Funds were needed by the LDP as a whole, too, in order to finance periodic Diet election campaigns, parliamentary activities of members, and even the regular maintenance of party offices and their staffs. These funds as well were raised mainly from corporate sources through the medium of a donor consortium called, originally, the Economic Reconstruction Round Table (Keizai Saiken Kondankai). This group was formed in January 1955 at the instigation of the leaders of KEIDANREN, a powerful business federation. Reorganized and renamed Kokumin Kyōkai (not to be confused with the two prewar organizations of the same name) in July 1961, the group supplied over 90 percent of the LDP's officially reported annual incomes in the late 1960s and 1970s. The bulk of the money was expended to support LDP candidates in Diet elections, to pay the wages and benefits of the party office staff and, occasionally, to bribe opposition members during Diet debates on controversial bills. The generous contributions of the consortium, however, did not prevent faction leaders and other Diet members from soliciting additional donations from individual businessmen and firms. All these funds made available by the business community contributed to the rise of "money politics," which seriously damaged the LDP's public image and electoral performance in the 1970s.

Party Reform——The public image of the LDP as a party dominated by a few hundred conservative Diet members, internally fragmented by factionalism and beholden to big business interests, has long impeded the party's efforts to build strong grassroots organizations and recruit members. The nominal membership figures did rise to about a quarter million by the mid-1960s and a half million by the mid-1970s. These figures, however, were grossly inflated, the bulk of the "members" being those who were affiliated with the campaign organizations (kōenkai) of individual Diet members and whose membership dues were frequently paid, directly or indirectly, by the politicians.

With a view to correcting the situation and improving the party's public image, the LDP leadership has undertaken time and again to purge the factions and "modernize" the party structure. But the changes have always been merely temporary. In 1977, for example, all the factions were declared disbanded, apparently prompted by the passage (in 1975) of a revised and stricter Political Fund Control Law and the repercussion of the 1976 LOCKHEED SCANDAL. Barely a few months later, the old factions were all back in business, if anything, more vigorous and competitive than before the purge.

In 1977 the rules governing the election of the LDP president were also amended. According to the new rules, any LDP Diet member recommended by 20 or more fellow Diet members can become a candidate; all bona fide party members can vote in prefectural party primaries to elect two candidates per prefecture; the votes cast for each candidate are then converted into points at the ratio of one point to 1,000 votes; the two candidates with the highest numbers of points nationwide compete in the second and final election where only LDP Diet members have the vote; and, finally, the winner in the second election becomes president of the party. The change resulted in an immediate quadrupling of LDP membership to about 1.7 million, although the increase was due largely to a mechanical reclassification and renaming of members of LDP politicians' personal supporters. The first election held under the new rules in November 1978 led to the surprise election of ŌHIRA MASAYOSHI as LDP president and prime minister.

LDP as Government——During the quarter century since its founding, the LDP has been in power without interruption. By the summer of 1980, 10 LDP presidents had served as prime ministers of Japan. Some stayed in power for a long time and left their distinctive marks on the history of postwar Japanese politics and society; others held power only briefly and did not influence the course of events, whether domestic or international, to any significant extent.

The first LDP prime minister was HATOYAMA ICHIRŌ whose election to the office of prime minister preceded the birth of the LDP by nearly a year. During his two-year tenure, Hatoyama formed three cabinets and undertook several important and controversial legislative and administrative actions. Notable among them in the field of domestic policy were the creation of the Commission on the Constitution, implicitly designed to pave the way for a major revision of the postwar Japanese constitution, and the amendment of the Board of Education Law that abolished the election of members of local boards of education and made them appointive. For these and similar actions, the Hatoyama cabinets were accused by their political critics of deliberately reversing the postwar program of disarmament and democratization. In foreign policy, on the other hand, Hatoyama took an initiative, much against the opinion of many of his fellow conservative politicians, in reestablishing diplomatic relations with the Soviet Union, as well as initiating a reappraisal of the first of the UNITED STATES–JAPAN SECURITY TREATIES, which had been concluded in 1951, simultaneously with the Peace Treaty.

Hatoyama's successor, ISHIBASHI TANZAN, had no time to initiate, not to mention implement, any significant policy action before he fell ill and resigned his office only two months after he was elected LDP president and prime minister.

The LDP was at the zenith of its power and stability during the 1960s when three presidents of the party led progressively more durable governments. The first of these, KISHI NOBUSUKE, stayed in power for 40 months; the second, IKEDA HAYATO, served 51 months, then resigned due to illness; and the third, SATŌ EISAKU, lasted for 92 months. Satō's has been so far the longest uninterrupted prime ministerial tenure in Japanese history.

The prime ministers of the 1960s and their cabinets each left an impressive, though highly controversial, record of achievements, both in domestic and foreign policy. Kishi's cabinet strengthened government control of school education by legislating a national teacher evaluation program. It failed, however, to have the Diet pass legislation to expand police powers. In foreign policy, legal restrictions on foreign trade and foreign investments in Japan were gradually reduced under Kishi's rule. More important, the 1951 United States–Japan Security Treaty was replaced by a new treaty, despite fierce opposition from within as well as without the LDP.

Kishi's successor, Ikeda Hayato, was understandably wary of controversial political and diplomatic issues and chose to concentrate on economic matters. He is known for the widely publicized "high-growth" and "income-doubling" plans which have been credited for a substantial share of Japan's postwar "economic miracle." It was also during Ikeda's tenure as prime minister that Japan signed, but

did not immediately ratify, the Nuclear Non-Proliferation Treaty and officially joined the Organization for Economic Cooperation and Development (OECD).

Ikeda's successor and Kishi's younger brother, Satō, had to deal with a series of crises during his long tenure: a crisis involving universities, an environmental crisis, a foreign trade crisis, and an exchange-rate crisis. In response to these crises, Satō and his cabinets acted on a crowded legislative and administrative agenda, resulting in major changes in the legal relationship between government and universities, the enactment of new laws and the creation of institutions for pollution control and protection of environment, the conclusion of a voluntary restraint agreement with the United States on Japanese textile exports, and revaluations and floating of the yen. Satō, however, achieved his most notable success in dealing with the OKINAWA reversion issue. At the outset of his tenure he promised to get the United States to return the administration of the islands to Japan; toward the end of his tenure he fulfilled the promise.

By contrast with their predecessors of the 1960s, the LDP prime ministers of the 1970s and their cabinets were progressively short-lived. TANAKA KAKUEI's cabinet lasted 28 months; MIKI TAKEO's 24 months; FUKUDA TAKEO's 23 months; and Ōhira Masayoshi's only 18 months. Tanaka was first confronted by an oil crisis, then by what threatened to become runaway inflation. He and his cabinet were at least partially successful in dealing with both. Meanwhile, diplomatic relations with the People's Republic of China were restored under Tanaka's personal leadership, and without his direct involvement, an agreement was reached with the Republic of Korea on the joint development of the potentially oil-rich continental shelf lying between the two countries. Tanaka's ambitious and well-publicized plan to "remodel the Japanese archipelago" (NIHON RETTŌ KAIZŌ RON), however, fizzled, and his tenure ended ignominiously amidst charges of his involvement in the Lockheed Scandal.

Miki's cabinet accomplished little, apart from the signing of a symbolically important treaty with Australia. Domestically, the cabinet was embroiled in a dispute over its proper role in the investigation of the Lockheed Scandal and prosecution of the culprits; internationally, it became involved in a dispute with the Soviet Union over the treatment of a MiG 25 fighter plane that was flown to Japan by a Soviet pilot seeking political asylum in the United States.

Fukuda's record of accomplishments is somewhat more substantial. During his tenure, a pair of important marine laws were enacted, and a peace treaty as well as a long-term trade agreement with the People's Republic of China were concluded. In both instances, however, Fukuda's decisions were prompted by foreign governments' actions, rather than by his or his cabinet's own policy. His tenure came to an unexpected end in 1978 when he was defeated by a rival candidate, Ōhira, in the first party primaries held under the new rules of party presidential elections.

Ōhira's service as an LDP prime minister has been so far the shortest save Ishibashi's. His cabinet helped consolidate economic and political relations with the People's Republic of China and repair those with the industrial powers of North America and Western Europe. Ōhira bravely called for tax increases in order to begin to reduce the mounting government debts, but he was not only forced to renounce the plan under pressure from fellow LDP politicians, but he even lost a no-confidence motion in the House of Representatives as a result of a factional revolt among LDP Diet members. The LDP won the general elections that followed, but Ōhira died in the summer of 1980, less than two weeks before the elections were held.

Ōhira was succeeded by Suzuki Zenkō, who resigned in the fall of 1982. His successor, Nakasone Yasuhiro, faced an uncertain future clouded by the perennial intraparty factional strife and threatened by a number of controversial domestic and foreign policy issues.

◼——Haruhiro Fukui, *Party in Power: The Japanese Liberal Democrats and Policy-Making* (1970). Gendai Seiji Mondai Kenkyūkai, ed, *Shiawasena Jimintō* (1974). Jiyū Minshutō, ed, *Jiyū Minshutō nijūnen no ayumi* (1975). Tanaka Zen'ichirō, "Hoshu seiji no shihai katei," in *Kokka gakkai zasshi* (December 1973; February 1974; August 1974). Nathaniel B. Thayer, *How the Conservatives Rule Japan* (1969). Watanabe Tsuneo, *Habatsu: Nihon hoshutō no bunseki* (1964).   Haruhiro FUKUI

liberalism

(jiyū shugi). Movement or set of beliefs generally supporting individual freedom. The concept, which was introduced from the West

in the latter half of the 19th century, has followed its own course of development in relation to the history of modern Japan.

NAKAMURA MASANAO's 1872 translation of J. S. Mill's *On Liberty* was one of the earliest attempts to understand the idea of liberalism. The impact of the Meiji Restoration and the decision of government leaders to modernize Japan were motivating factors behind his translation and other similar efforts. Social upheavals were bound to accompany the modernization process, and Japanese liberalism, like other new concepts, was subject to the particular pressures of the times.

Japanese liberalism before 1945 must be understood within the context of the Japanese national polity (KOKUTAI), in particular, the Meiji Constitution (see CONSTITUTION) that placed the emperor at the pinnacle of power. This "sacred and inviolable" emperor was regarded as the embodiment of traditional values, and in his name every form of civil liberty, including freedom of thought and speech, was put under the constraints of the state. The constitution was also based on the assumption that the state is more important than the individual. To be true to the original spirit of liberalism under such conditions required great tenacity and commitment. Thus, many intellectuals tended to use abstruse language in dealing with a nonorthodox, potentially subversive notion like liberalism.

It is also important to note that Japanese capitalism in the late 1800s was in an underdeveloped stage and very dependent on the government. Japanese capitalism grew rapidly under the aegis of the government, which sought "a rich country and a strong military" *(fukoku kyōhei)*. Given this close tie between the state and business interests, there was little reason, as was common in Western Europe, for capitalists to support liberalists, like TAGUCHI UKICHI, who argued for free trade without government interference.

Imperialism was a potent force throughout the world at that time, and Japan too pursued an expansionist policy on the Asian continent. Issues such as freedom in trade or industry ceased to engage the interest of most Japanese thinkers. Moreover, in the wake of the rapid development of capitalism, serious social dislocations had taken place, and labor leaders and socialist thinkers began to attack capitalism and to demand social reforms. They also criticized liberalism as an ideology that had supported, or at least tolerated, capitalism. Marxist intellectuals, in particular, especially after the Russian Revolution of 1917, leveled criticism against Japanese liberalism, pointing out its historical limitations.

To understand Japanese liberalism, it is also necessary to see what was implied by *jiyū*, the Japanese term. This word had originally been introduced through Chinese Buddhist writings, in which it meant "as one pleases" or "the heart at peace." When FUKUZAWA YUKICHI, the leading advocate of Westernization, published his SEIYŌ JIJŌ (1866–70, Conditions of the West), he used *jiyū* to translate the English word "liberty" or "freedom." But to forestall any misunderstanding, he also included a footnote that a suitable word did not yet exist. Nevertheless, the original connotation of *jiyū* as the unrestricted fulfillment of one's individual desires persisted, and like another Western idea—individualism *(kojin shugi)*—tended to be viewed negatively.

Historically, then, in Japan liberalism had to fight for its existence; it never developed as a system of thought that could contend with other systems, nor was it internalized as a norm for action. The few who enlisted in its cause were leaders of the FREEDOM AND PEOPLE'S RIGHTS MOVEMENT in the early 1880s like UEKI EMORI, NAKAE CHŌMIN, and TANAKA SHŌZŌ, who opposed the new authoritarian government, and academics like MINOBE TATSUKICHI, KAWAI EIJIRŌ, and YOSHINO SAKUZŌ in the 1920s and 1930s, who in their writings stressed the supremacy of rule by law and freedom of speech. In addition, a small number of intellectuals, including Kawai Eijirō and HANI GORŌ, struggled against the rising tide of fascism and militarism during World War II. Their examples were crucial to new developments in Japanese liberalism in the postwar years.

——Ishida Takeshi, *Nihon kindai shisō shi ni okeru hō to seiji* (1976). J. Victor Koshmann, ed, *Authority and the Individual in Japan: Citizen Protest in Historical Perspective* (1978). Shisō no Kagaku Kenkyūkai, ed, *Kyōdō kenkyū: Tenkō* (1978). Tada Michitarō, ed, *Jiyū shugi,* in *Gendai Nihon shisō taikei,* vol 18 (Chikuma Shobō, 1965). YAMARYŌ Kenji

Liberal Party

(Jiyūtō). Political party formed on 1 March 1950. Not to be confused with the JIYŪTŌ, the party formed in 1881. Its principal forerunner was the Minshu Jiyūtō (Democratic Liberal Party; March 1948–March 1950), which was formed through a merger of the Nihon Jiyūtō, founded by HATOYAMA ICHIRŌ in November 1945, with dissidents from the MINSHUTŌ. In an effort to increase Diet representation, this party joined forces with remnants of the newly dissolved Minshutō in 1950, forming the Liberal Party.

The Liberal Party was in power until December 1954. The main forces in the party were its president, YOSHIDA SHIGERU, who formed three Liberal Party cabinets; Hirokawa Kōzen (1902–67), a veteran party politician; and IKEDA HAYATO and SATŌ EISAKU, both former bureaucrats. With the return to the political scene in 1951 of Hatoyama, who had been barred from public office under the Occupation purge, a power struggle rocked the Liberal Party. Hatoyama gathered together elements within the party opposed to Yoshida and seceded from the party in March 1953. This rupture was temporarily healed with the return of Hatoyama to the Liberal Party fold in November of the same year.

However, the Yoshida cabinet faced a new crisis the following year when a series of scandals involving government officials broke out (see SHIPBUILDING SCANDAL OF 1954). Hatoyama's anti-Yoshida faction then joined forces with the Kaishintō (Reform Party; in existence from February 1952 to November 1954) and other parties to form the NIHON MINSHUTŌ in November 1954. As a result, the number of Liberal Party seats in the Diet sharply declined, and the Yoshida cabinet was forced to resign on 7 December 1954. Yoshida resigned as president of the Liberal Party, and the next cabinet was formed by Hatoyama, president of the Nihon Minshutō. On 15 November 1955 the Liberal Party and the Nihon Minshutō merged to form the LIBERAL DEMOCRATIC PARTY (Jiyū Minshutō). See also POLITICAL PARTIES. HARADA Katsumasa